DICTIONARIES OF THE PRINTERS AND BOOKSELLERS WHO WERE AT WORK IN ENGLAND, SCOTLAND AND IRELAND 1557-1775

BY

H. R. PLOMER,
H. G. ALDIS, G. H. BUSHNELL, E. R. McC. DIX,
A. E. ESDAILE, R. B. McKERROW,

AND OTHERS.

Reprinted in Compact Form in one volume

THE BIBLIOGRAPHICAL SOCIETY
1977

Unrevised reprint of the Original Volumes:
1557-1640: First printed 1910;
1641-1667: First printed 1907;
1668-1725: First printed 1922;
1726-1775: First printed 1932.

Reprinted by Grove Press Ltd., Ilkley, Yorkshire.
1977

A DICTIONARY OF PRINTERS AND BOOKSELLERS IN ENGLAND, SCOTLAND AND IRELAND, AND OF FOREIGN PRINTERS OF ENGLISH BOOKS 1557—1640.

BY

H. G. ALDIS; ROBERT BOWES; E. R. McC. DIX; E. GORDON DUFF; STRICKLAND GIBSON; G. J. GRAY; R. B. McKERROW; FALCONER MADAN, AND H. R. PLOMER.

GENERAL EDITOR: R. B. McKERROW.

THE BIBLIOGRAPHICAL SOCIETY
1968

PREFACE.

THE present volume is intended to contain the names of all printers, booksellers, binders and other persons connected with the book trade who are known to have worked in Great Britain and Ireland, or to have dealt in English books on the Continent during the years 1557–1640, and thus to fill the gap between Mr. E. Gordon Duff's *Century of the English Book Trade, 1457–1557*, and Mr. H. R. Plomer's *Dictionary of Booksellers, Printers, etc., 1641–67*. It does not, however, contain notices of all these persons, for a number of men, who were in business during our period, overlap into the periods dealt with by Mr. Duff and Mr. Plomer, and they have consequently been already included in the *Century* or *Dictionary*. As almost all of those into whose hands the present volume is likely to come will possess these two other books, it was felt to be undesirable to repeat here information which was already to be found in them. As a rule, therefore, when a man has been dealt with by Mr. Duff or Mr. Plomer a cross reference alone is given. Now and then, however, a few particulars are added concerning the work done within our period.

The notices are the work of several writers. By far the greater part of the book is from the pen of Mr. H. R. Plomer, who undertook the London printers and stationers. The Scottish articles are by Mr. H. G. Aldis, who has also dealt with the Scottish period in the lives of the English printers J. Norton and R. Waldegrave. For the accounts of the Irish printers, etc., I am indebted to Mr. E. R. McC. Dix.

Mr. F. Madan and Mr. Strickland Gibson have very kindly revised the notices of the Oxford printers and stationers, and Mr. R. Bowes and Mr. G. J. Gray have done the same for those of the Cambridge men. Most of the notices of these were written by Mr. Gray.

Foreign printers of English books have been dealt with, very imperfectly, I fear, by myself. For information about these men, one is necessarily dependent upon the bibliographical work done abroad, which varies enormously in value and completeness in the different countries. I have also added the indices and a very brief introduction.

We have to thank Mr. E. Gordon Duff for kindly looking through the proofs of the book, and adding a number of particulars from the Registers of the Chester Stationers' Company, and several new names. The proofs have also been read, to their great advantage, by Mr. A. W. Pollard.

Lastly we are indebted to Mr. R. L. Steele for some important notes on the wills of London printers and booksellers from the Registers of the Dean and Chapter of St. Paul's.

R. B. McK.

INTRODUCTION.

THE excellent account of the English Book-Trade from 1557 to 1625 which has recently been given by Mr. H. G. Aldis in the fourth volume of the *Cambridge History of English Literature* seems to render it superfluous to attempt here any general survey of the period which the present work covers, or any comparison of the state of the book-trade during it with that of earlier or later times. There is, however, one aspect of the matter which deserves special attention, namely, the attitude of the government towards printing and publishing, and the various attempts made to establish an effective censorship. In the latter half of the sixteenth century, more perhaps than at any other time, the restraints laid upon the press had a powerful influence upon the condition of the book-trade in general. It might indeed even be maintained that the censorship was the main if not the sole cause of the decline which the trade shows, both as regards the class of men engaged in it and the quality of work produced, from what it had been during the first century after the introduction of printing. It seems therefore necessary to pass briefly in review the legislation by which it was principally affected.

In his *Century of the English Book Trade* Mr. Duff has given an account of the relations of the government and the trade up to the time of the incorporation of the Stationers' Company. Most of the earlier enactments dealt mainly with foreign printers and bookbinders, and were intended for the protection of the native artificer, but at least as early as 1538 began the long series of injunctions, decrees, and proclamations which were aimed at the suppression of literature obnoxious to the government of the day. There are earlier proclamations and orders against particular books or classes of books, but the proclamation of 1538[1] seems to be the first attempt to establish a regular censorship and to require that all works dealing with certain subjects should be examined and approved before being printed. Other ordinances and proclamations of a similar character, though of course aimed at writings of a different tendency appeared in the reigns of Edward VI and Mary, but the importance of these as measures of censorship is quite overshadowed by the incorporation of the Stationers' Company in 1557.

The granting of a charter to the Stationers, though ostensibly intended to benefit the book-trade, was undoubtedly dictated in the main by the wish more effectively to control it. Not only did the restriction of printing, and consequently of the teaching of the art, to a definite and comparatively small number of men, all of whom would be more or less well known to each other, render the establishment of secret presses much more difficult, but by making the corporation as a whole responsible for the doings of its members, the government assured to itself the co-operation of those who had the most intimate knowledge of the trade in the detection of illicit work. It is easy to see how much more efficient such a man as John Wolf, himself a past dealer in contraband literature, would be in the discovery of secret presses, than the bishops, justices, sheriffs and bailiffs, whose duty it had been under earlier enactments.

The charter of the Company was confirmed by Elizabeth on November 10th, 1559, and in the same year was issued the first of her ordinances against heretical and seditious literature. This is contained in the *Injunctions given by the Queen's Majesty, Anno domini 1559*, of which it forms the 51st section. The more important part of it runs as follows :

"51. *Item* because there is a great abuse in the printers of bokes, which for couetousnes cheifly regard not what they print, so thei may haue gaine, whereby arriseth great dysorder by publicatyon of vnfrutefull, vayne

(1.) Printed in Strype's *Cranmer*, Apx. no. viii.

and infamous bokes and papers : The Quenes maiestie straytly chargethe and commaundeth, that no manner of person shall print any manner of boke or paper, of what sort, nature, or in what language soeuer it be, excepte the same be first licenced by her maiestie by expresse wordes in writynge, or by . vi . of her priuy counsel, or be perused and licensed by the archbysshops of Cantorbury and yorke, the bishop of London, the chauncelours of both vnyuersities, the bishop beyng ordinary, and the Archdeacon also of the place where any suche shalbe printed, or by two of them, wherof the ordinary of the place to be alwaies one. And that the names of such as shal allowe the same, to be added in thende of euery such worke, for a testymonye of the allowaunce therof. And bycause many pampheletes, playes and balletes, be often times printed, wherein regard wold be had, that nothinge therin should be either heretical, sedicious, or vnsemely for Christian eares : Her maiestie likewise commaundeth, that no manner of person, shall enterprise to print any such, except the same be to him lycenced by suche her maiesties commyssioners, or . iii . of them, as be appoynted in the citye of London to here, and determine diuers causes ecclesiasticall, tending to the execution of certayne statutes, made the last parliament for vnyformitye of order in religion. And yf any shall sell or vtter, any manner of bokes or papers, beynge not licensed as is abouesaid : That the same party shalbe punyshed by order of the sayde commyssyoners, as to the qualitie of the faulte shalbe thought mete."[1]

It was not, however, new books alone which came under the control of the official censors, for authority is given to the same commissioners to prohibit any book dealing with religious policy or government which has already been printed, whether in England or abroad, an exception, however, being made in favour of profane authors and works in any language which have heretofore been commonly received and allowed in universities or schools. The direction of this injunction by her Majesty to "al manner her subiectes, and specially the wardens and company of Stationers" is

(1.) Arber, *Transcript*, i. xxxviii.

worth notice as showing the intention of the government to compel the assistance of the Company in carrying it out.

One of the provisions of this injunction is rather puzzling, namely that which requires that the names of the licensers of a work shall be added at the end "for a testymonye of the allowance therof." One would naturally take this to mean that the names of the licensers were to be *printed* at the end of the books licensed by them. So far, however, as I can discover, the names of the licensers do not appear in any work printed in England before the seventeenth century, and we must therefore suppose either that this provision was allowed to lapse by common consent, or that it was merely intended that the names should be added in the manuscript. The most that we find is an occasional notice on a title-page that a book has been allowed according to Her Majesty's injunctions. John Day, who had especial reasons for keeping in favour with the authorities, frequently placed such a notice in his publications and we sometimes find it in those of Reyner Wolfe. The majority of printers, however, seem to have troubled little about the matter, though there does not seem to be any reason for supposing that the licensing provisions were generally ignored, as has sometimes been stated. The absence, at this date, of reference to the official licensers in the Company's records cannot, I think, be taken as a proof that the books had not been passed by them before entry.

The next move on the part of the authorities, the Star Chamber Decree of 1566, seems to have been connected with the controversy about Ecclesiastical Vestments. Some time before June of that year there appeared a small pamphlet entitled *A brief discourse against the outward apparel of the popish Church*, as well as some five other tracts on the same subject, which are similar in type and general appearance and presumably came from the same press. One of these has the imprint "Printed at Emden," and the whole group has consequently been attributed to that place, but a letter of June 6th, 1566, from John Abel to Henry Bullinger seems to make it certain that these works were

printed in England.[1] The *Brief Discourse* attracted much attention and seems to have been deemed worthy of an official reply, while the printers of it are said to have been thrown into prison. It is highly probable that this affair was the cause of the more stringent legislation which followed.

The decree, which is dated June 29th, 1566, imposes heavy penalties, both by fine and imprisonment, upon all who print or deal in books "against the forme and meaning of anie ordinance, prohibition, or commandement, conteined, or to be conteined in anie of the Statutes or Lawes of this Realme, or in anie Iniunctions, Letters patents, or ordinances, passed or set foorth, or to be passed or set foorth by the Queenes most excellent Maiesties grant, commission, or authoritie,"[2] and reaffirms very explicitly the right of the Wardens of the Stationers' Company to search for and seize all such books. The importance of it, however, lay in its last clause, whereby all printers, booksellers, binders, and in fact all persons connected with the book-trade were required to enter into recognizances of reasonable sums of money that they would obey all the ordinances and assist the Wardens of the Company in causing others to obey them.

If these regulations had been systematically observed they would surely have made secret printing exceedingly difficult, if not impossible, but there seems to be no evidence that much attention was paid to them. So far, at any rate, as puritan works are concerned, it is difficult to believe that any great effort was ever made by the Company to bring the dealers in them to book. The explanation probably is that then and throughout the whole period there was in the Company—as there certainly was among Londoners in general—a strong party which was secretly, if not openly, in sympathy with the movement.

The decree of 1566 seems to have satisfied the authorities for twenty years, though in the meantime several proclamations were issued dealing with particular books or groups of books. The first, in March, 156$\frac{8}{9}$, was

(1.) *Zurich Letters* (Parker Society), ii. 119. (2.) Arber, i. 322.

directed against the importation of any works of a seditious nature from abroad and forbade all persons to deal in them, keep them, or read them.[1] Two others on the same subject are dated respectively July 1st and November 14th, 1570.[2] On June 11th, 1573, a proclamation was signed against the anonymous *Admonition to the Parliament*,[3] and on September 28th of the same year one condemning certain books which had been published against two members of the Privy Council.[4] Both in this proclamation and in a later one dated March 26th, 1576, against "certaine infamous Libels full of malice and falshood,"[5] the description of the works referred to is so vague that it is now difficult to identify them. Lastly, on June 30th, 1583, a proclamation condemned the books of Robert Browne the Anabaptist and his follower Robert Harrison.[6]

The next important step taken by the government was probably one of the consequences of the elevation of John Whitgift to the primacy in 1583. Whitgift's attempt to secure absolute uniformity in the observances of the Church made it necessary for him to strengthen the hands of the government in every possible way, and there can be little doubt that the extremely rigorous Star Chamber decree of June 23rd, 1586, was merely the continuation of his general policy.

The chief requirements of this decree were as follows :

(1) Every printer was to deliver a note of the number of his presses.

(2) No printing to be allowed anywhere save in London and the suburbs, with the exception of one press at Cambridge and one at Oxford.

(3) Presses might not be set up in obscure or secret places, and the Wardens of the Company were to have access to them at any time.

(4) The penalty for keeping a secret press was that it and the type used at it should be destroyed and the printer imprisoned for a year and disabled for ever from working save as a journeyman.

(1.) Arber, i. 430. (2.) Arber, i. 452-3. (3.) Arber, i. 464.
(4.) Arber, i. 461-2. (5.) Arber, i. 474.
(6.) Arber, i. 502. The proclamation has *Richard* Harrison, presumably in error.

(5) No new presses were to be set up until the number of existing ones was diminished, and then the Archbishop of Canterbury and the Bishop of London were to decide who should be allowed to have one.

(6) No books to be printed unless allowed according to the Queen's injunctions, and perused by the Archbishop of Canterbury and the Bishop of London, but the Queen's printer was exempted from this rule, as also those privileged to print law books. These last were to be read by certain of the justices. For contravention of this regulation the same penalty was imposed as for keeping a secret press except that the imprisonment was only for six months and the offender does not seem to have been allowed to print even as a journeyman afterwards. A lesser penalty is also decreed against those who bind or sell unlicensed books.

(7) The wardens of the Company are allowed to search for secret presses and seize any found.

(8) The apprentices that might be taken are limited to three, two, or one, according to the master's rank in the Company, save in the case of the Queen's printer who may have six.[1]

This decree of the Star Chamber was certainly the most important of the period and it seems to have served the purpose even of so rigid a disciplinarian as Whitgift for many years. It was in fact to a great extent effective in suppressing unlicensed printing in England, for after the seizure of the Marprelate Press in 1589, we hear little of secret printing for some years, though no doubt the importation of books printed abroad continued in defiance of all attempts to put a stop to it.

During the reign of James I the book-trade does not seem to have been treated with anything like the same severity, but with the accession of Charles I in 1625 a new series of attacks on the trade began, and in the twelve years which followed few printers seem to have escaped fine

(1.) Arber, ii. 807-12.

or imprisonment.[1] The culmination of a long series of attacks by the government upon the trade was another Star Chamber decree, dated July 11th, 1637, even more severe than that of 1586. Besides reiterating most of the earlier regulations this decree laid down that two copies of every book were to be submitted to the licensers, whereof one was to be retained for future reference, an obvious precaution against the insertion of fresh matter in the printed copy. All dedications, epistles, etc., as well as the text of the works themselves, were to be licensed, and the licensers' names were to be printed in the works. Works on law were to be licensed by the Chief Justices, those on English History, Statecraft and the like by the principal Secretaries of State, those on Heraldry by the Earl Marshal, and all others by the Archbishop of Canterbury or the Bishop of London. All books must bear the name of the printer. Catalogues of books imported from abroad were to be sent to the Archbishop of Canterbury or the Bishop of London, and no consignment of such books was to be opened save in the presence of their representatives, and of the Wardens of the Stationers' Company. The importation of English books printed abroad was altogether forbidden. The number of master printers was limited to twenty, and a list of these is given. Each of them was to be bound in sureties of £300, some £1,500 of our money, for his good behaviour. The number of presses each might possess was strictly limited according to the printer's rank in the Company. None but persons who had served a regular apprenticeship might sell books. The decree also contains the first legislation concerning type-founders, four of whom were licensed, and all type-founding by other persons was forbidden.[2]

This decree of 1637 is the last which comes within our period. Severe as it seems, it was practically of no effect ; for in the years that followed, the government was concerned with more important matters than printing. For the dealings of the Long Parliament with the book-trade the reader may be referred to Mr. Plomer's *Dictionary*.

(1.) Plomer, *Short History of Printing*, p. 170 (2.) Arber, iv. 529-36.

The very numerous references to the Stationers' Company in the present volume make it desirable to say a few words about the constitution of the Company and the officials by whom it was governed.

At its incorporation on May 4th, 1557, it consisted, according to the charter, of a Master, two Wardens, and 94 freemen.[1] The number of members was not fixed and probably increased from year to year, but no statistics of the exact number at any subsequent date within our period are known to exist.

The Master and Wardens were elected annually by the freemen. The Master's office seems to some extent to have been a sinecure, though of course as head of the trade he would have had to take the chief part on all ceremonial occasions, and his help may sometimes have been required in settling matters with which the Wardens were unable to deal. These, the Upper and Under Warden, evidently had the actual management of the Company's ordinary affairs. They had control of the finances and prepared the annual statement of accounts : they appear to have been responsible for seeing that all books were properly licensed before entry in the Registers ; and all disciplinary measures, all searches for secret presses, and the like, were in their hands.

The governing body of the Company, the Court of Assistants, consisted at first of some eight or ten of the senior members of the Livery, but their number was gradually increased until in 1645 it was as many as 28.[2] They appear not to have been elected by the general body of freemen, but to have co-opted additional members at their own pleasure. They acted as judges in disputes between members of the Company, and its general policy was presumably in their control. They also were empowered to punish offending members. It was, for example, the Court of Assistants that decided that the press and type used by Waldegrave in printing *Diotrephes* in 1588 should be destroyed in accordance with the Star

(1.) The list given in the charter appears, however, to be incomplete. *See* Duff, *Century*, p. xxix.
(2.) Arber, i. xliv.

Chamber Decree of two years before ; but it is not quite clear to what extent they had discretion in the matter of fines and other punishments and to what extent they merely carried out the orders of the licensing authorities.

The freemen of the Company were of two grades, the Livery and the Yeomanry. The Livery consisted of the senior or more wealthy members of the Company, and seems to have numbered only about a sixth of the whole. From 1510 to 1596 only sixty-three persons are recorded to have been admitted to the Livery, which, allowing for deaths, would make the probable number at any one date not more than twenty or thirty.[1] In 1619 they numbered forty-nine. It was the liverymen alone who had the right of voting for the Lord Mayor, Sheriffs, and other officers of the City. The remainder of the freemen made up the Yeomanry of the Company.

There was also a small class of persons known as "Brothers." These seem generally to have been alien book-merchants such as Richard Schilders, Salamon Kirtner and Arnold Birckman. There is some doubt as to what rights they had. Mr. Duff thinks that they could take apprentices,[2] but Mr. Arber states that they could only do this on behalf of freemen of the Company.[3] It is clear from what happened to Schilders when he was found printing a book for Hans Stell that the privileges attaching to the rank of "Brother" were not great.

Besides the Master and Wardens there were a few other officials who should be mentioned. The most important was perhaps the Beadle, whose duty it was to act as a kind of secretary, summoning meetings, and occasionally transcribing records. He also supervised repairs of the hall when necessary,[4] and perhaps acted as general caretaker or steward of the Company's property.

There were also two Renters, or Renter-Wardens, appointed annually from among the liverymen, who had charge of the petty cash of the

(1.) Arber, i. xliii. (2.) Duff, *Century*, p. xxviii.
(3.) Arber, i. xl. (4.) Arber, i. xliii.

Company, and whose duty it was to collect rents and other sums due. Lastly, there was a scribe or clerk who kept the Registers.

Membership of the Company was obtainable in several ways :

(1). Sons of freemen of the Company, born after their fathers had become free, had a right to claim freedom "by patrimony" on attaining the age of twenty-four years.

(2). Persons who had served an apprenticeship of at least seven years to a freeman of the Company, and who were at least twenty-four years of age, could be made freemen by the presentation of their master.

(3). Certain persons who had not been apprenticed in the usual way and had no right to freedom "by patrimony" were admitted "by redemption." This generally meant the payment of greatly increased fees.

(4). Occasionally a freeman of another Company was allowed to be transferred to the Stationers.

Lastly, it is well to remember that though a printer, unless specially privileged by the Sovereign, was bound to be a member of the Stationers' Company, this was not necessary in the case of a bookseller or bookbinder. It was probably more convenient for a man whose chief business lay in book-dealing to belong to the Stationers, but at all times there seem to have been men engaged in the trade who were members of other Companies. In some cases they may have had other businesses, while sometimes family reasons or other considerations may have prevented them from being transferred. On the other hand, many members of the Stationers' Company had apparently nothing to do with the book-trade at all.

LIST OF SOME BOOKS AND ARTICLES REFERRED TO BY ABBREVIATED TITLES.

Aldis (H. G.). A List of Books Printed in Scotland before 1700. Edinburgh Bibliographical Society, 1904. [Aldis, *Scottish Books.*]

Arber (E.). A transcript of the Registers of the Company of Stationers of London, 1554-1640. 5 vols. London, 1875-94. [Arber.]

Bannatyne Miscellany. Bannatyne Club. Vols. 19, 52, 105. Edinburgh, 1827-55.

Bibliographica. 3 vols. London, 1895-97.

British Museum. Catalogue of Books in the Library of the British Museum printed in England, Scotland, and Ireland, and of Books in English printed abroad, to the year 1640. London, 1884. [B.M., *with page.*]

Bowes (R.). A Catalogue of Books printed at or relating to . . . Cambridge. Cambridge, 1894.

Bowes (R.). Biographical Notes on the [Cambridge] University Printers. Cambridge Antiquarian Society Communications. Vol. V. Cambridge, 1886. [Bowes, *University Printers.*]

Clark (A.). Register of the University of Oxford, Vol. ii. (1571-1622). Oxford Historical Society. Oxford, 1887-9. [Vol. i. was edited by C. W. Boase.] [Clark, *Register.*]

Dickson (R.) and Edmond (J. P.). Annals of Scottish Printing. From the introduction of the art in 1507 to the beginning of the seventeenth century. Cambridge, 1890 [89]. [Dickson and Edmond.]

Dictionary of National Biography. London, 1884-1900. [*D.N.B.*]

Duff (E. G.). A Century of the English Book Trade. Short Notices of all Printers, Stationers, Bookbinders . . . from . . . 1457 to the Incorporation of the Company of Stationers in 1557. Bibliographical Society, London, 1905. [Duff, *Century.*]

Duthillœul (H.-R.). Bibliographie Douaisienne. Nouvelle édition considérablement augmentée, Douai, 1842. [Duthillœul.]

Edinburgh Bibliographical Society. Papers. 1896, ff. Edinburgh. [*E.B.S. Papers.*]

Foster (J. E.). Churchwardens' Accounts of St. Mary the Great, Cambridge, from 1504 to 1635. Cambridge Antiquarian Society Publications, no. xxxv (octavo series), 1905.

Frère (E.). Manuel du bibliographe normand, ou Dictionnaire bibliographique et historique . . . des ouvrages relatifs à la Normandie, &c. 2 vols. Rouen, 1858-60. [Frère, *Manuel.*]

Gibson (S.). Abstracts from the Wills and Testamentary Documents of Binders, Printers, and Stationers of Oxford, from 1493 to 1638. Bibliographical Society. London, 1907. [Gibson, *Oxford Wills.*]

Gibson (S.). Early Oxford Bindings. Bibliographical Society. Oxford, 1903. [Gibson, *Oxford Bindings.*]

Gillow (J.). A Literary and Biographical History, or Bibliographical Dictionary of the English Catholics. London, 1885-1902.

Gray (G. J.). The earlier Cambridge Stationers and Bookbinders and the first Cambridge Printer. Bibliographical Society. Oxford, 1904. [Gray, *Cambridge Stationers.*]

Gray (G. J.). The Shops at the West End of Great St. Mary's Church, Cambridge. Cambridge Antiquarian Society Proceedings and Communications, Vol. XIII (New Ser., vol. vii). Cambridge, 1909.

Hazlitt (W. C.). Handbook to the Popular, Poetical, and Dramatic Literature of Great Britain, from the Invention of Printing to the Restoration. London, 1867. [Hazlitt, H., *with page number.*]

Hazlitt (W. C.). Collections and Notes. 6 vols. 1876-1903. [Hazlitt.]

[References as follows :—I = 1st Series, 1876 : II = 2nd Series, 1882 : III = 3rd Series, 1887 : IV = Supplements to 3rd Series, 1889 : V = Second Supplement to 3rd Series, 1892 : VI = Appendix to Gray's *Index*, 1893 : VII = 4th Series, 1903.]

Herbert (W.). Typographical Antiquities. 3 vols. 1785-90. [Herbert.]

Ledeboer (A. M.). Alfabetische lijst der Boekdrukkers, Boekverkoopers en Uitgevers in Noord-Nederland. Utrecht, 1876. [Ledeboer, *A.L.*]

Ledeboer (A. M.). De Boekdrukkers, boekverkoopers en uitgevers in Noord-Nederland sedert de uitvinding van de boekdrukkunst tot den aanvang der negentiende eeuw. Deventer, 1872. [Ledeboer, *Boekdrukkers.*]

[Lee (J.).] Memorial for the Bible Societies in Scotland : . . . with an Appendix consisting of many original papers. Edinburgh, 1824. [Lee, App.]

[Lee (J.).] Additional Memorial for the Bible Societies. Edinburgh, 1826. [Lee, *Add. Mem.*]

Madan (F.). The Early Oxford Press. A bibliography of printing and publishing at Oxford, "1468"-1640. Oxford, 1895. [Madan, *Oxford Press.*]

Miscellany of the Maitland Club, consisting of original papers and other documents illustrative of the history and literature of Scotland. Maitland Club. 4 vols. Glasgow, 1834-47. [*Maitland Club Miscellany.*]

Montjardin (X. de Theux de). Bibliographie Liégeoise, Deuxième édition, augmentée. Bruges, 1885.

Olthoff (F.). De Boekdrukkers, boekverkoopers, en uitgevers in Antwerpen, sedert de uitvinding der boekdrukkunst tot op onze dagen. Antwerpen, 1891. [Olthoff.]

Plomer (H. R.). Abstracts from the Wills of English Printers and Stationers, from 1492 to 1630. Bibliographical Society, 1903. [Plomer, *Wills.*]

Plomer (H. R.). A Dictionary of the Booksellers and Printers who were at work in England, Scotland and Ireland from 1641 to 1667. Bibliographical Society. London, 1907. [Plomer, *Dictionary.*]

Renouard (P.). Imprimeurs parisiens, libraires, fondeurs de caractères . . . jusqu'à la fin du XVIe siècle. Paris, 1898. [Renouard.]

Sayle (C.). Early English Printed Books in the University Library, Cambridge, 1475–1640. Cambridge, 1900–7. [Sayle, *with page or number.*]

Scottish Antiquary. Edinburgh, 1890–1903.

[A continuation of *Northern Notes and Queries.* Edinburgh, 1888[6]–90.]

Worman (E. J.). Alien Members of the Book-Trade during the Tudor Period. Bibliographical Society. London, 1906. [Worman, *Alien Members.*]

OTHER ABBREVIATIONS.

B.M.	British Museum.
P.C.	Privy Council.
P.C.C.	Prerogative Court of Canterbury.
P.R.O.	Public Record Office.

A DICTIONARY OF PRINTERS AND BOOKSELLERS IN ENGLAND, SCOTLAND, AND IRELAND, AND OF FOREIGN PRINTERS OF ENGLISH BOOKS 1557—1640.

ADAMS (ELIZABETH), bookseller in London, 1620–38; The Bell in St. Paul's Churchyard. Widow of Thomas Adams. First book entry May 12th, 1620 [Arber, iii. 674]. On May 6th, 1625, she assigned her remaining copyrights to Andrew Hebb [Arber, iv. 139–40]. From this entry it would appear that she held a share in Hakluyt's *Voyages*, Camden's *Britannia*, the old *Calendar of Shepherds*, as well as many classical and theological works. In 1638 William Juxon, Bishop of London, demised to her two messuages with three shops in the great churchyard of St. Paul's Cathedral, on the north side adjoining the Charnel House, one being known as the Parrot and Angel and the other as the King's Head [*Hist. MSS. Comm., 9th Report, App.* p. 52a]. She made her will on July 3rd, 1638, and desired to be buried in St. Faith's, and mentions that she was born in the parish of St. Dunstan's in the West [Dean and Chapter of St. Paul's, Book E, fol. 130].

ADAMS (FRANK), bookseller in London, 1581–1601; The Aqua Vitae Still in Distaff Lane near Old Fish Street (and the Old Exchange). Apprentice to Michael Lobley, for nine years from June 24th, 1559 [Arber, i. 117]. Took up his freedom on March 7th, 1568 [Arber, i. 366]. Adams is chiefly remembered as the publisher of a series of memorandum-books, or as he termed them, "Writing-Tables," consisting of blank slips of vellum, to which he added various printed tables, such as a calendar for

24 years, a list of the gold coins and their equivalents. Frank Adams was one of the most prominent agitators against the monopolists in 1582, and suffered imprisonment in consequence. Afterwards, in 1584, he was made one of the assigns of Richard Day's patent [Arber, i. 144, 498; ii. 790–793]. He died before April 6th, 1601, and was succeeded in his business by Robert Triplet [Arber, v. 202].

ADAMS (JOHN), (?) stationer in London, 1598–9. Son of Thomas Adams of Wallington, co. Herts. On July 6th, 1590, he was apprenticed to Henry Wall, citizen and stationer of London, for eight years, and is found taking an apprentice on May 7th, 1599 [Arber, ii. 170, 235].

ADAMS (JOHN), bookseller, bookbinder and printer in Oxford, 1604–37. On March 13th, 16$\frac{09}{10}$, a house in St. Mary's parish was leased to John Adams, stationer [Oxford Univ. Archives, box A, No. 23]. He was a bookbinder from about 1610 to 1637. On July 29th in the latter year a house just North of the Schools Quadrangle was described as "lately" in the tenure of John Adams, bookbinder [Univ. Reg. R. 24, fol. 149]. In the same year an edition of Scheibler's *Metaphysica* was printed for him by William Turner. [Madan, *Oxford Press*, pp. 276, 308, 312; Gibson, *Oxford Bindings*, 13, 38, 39, 48, 51–5, 59.]

ADAMS (RICHARD), bookseller in London, 1559–79. Was apparently one of Richard Kele's apprentices, as he was presented for his freedom some time between July 10th, 1558, and July 10th, 1559, by John Wetherall, one of Richard Kele's executors [Arber, i. 98]. In the same year Richard Adams was fined for printing Thomas Brice's *Compendious register in metre* without license [Arber, i. 101]. The last entry under his name in the Registers occurs on June 26th, 1579 [Arber, ii. 354]. His address is unknown.

ADAMS (THOMAS), bookseller in London, 1591–1620; (?) The White Lion in St. Paul's Churchyard, 1591–1604; (2) The Bell, St. Paul's Churchyard. Son of Thomas Adams of Nyensavage, co. Salop, yeoman. Apprentice first to Oliver Wilkes and afterwards to George Bishop [Arber, ii. 115, 119]. Took up his freedom in the Company of Stationers on October 15th, 1590. On October 12th, 1591, Robert Walley assigned over to him the copyrights in seventeen books and various ballads, all which were to be printed for him by John Charlewood [Arber, ii. 596].

Thomas Adams at the outset of his career was associated with John Oxenbridge. Together they published Barnaby Rich's *Adventures of Brusanus, Prince of Hungaria*, 1592 [Arber, ii. 622], and *Greene's Newes both from Heaven and Hell*, perhaps by the same author [Arber, ii. 626]. In 1611 Adams became junior warden of the Stationers' Company, and in the same year acquired the copyrights of the late George Bishop, who had died before January 28th. These were fifty-nine in number and included shares in Hakluyt's *Voyages*, Camden's *Britannia*, Chaucer's *Works*, Holinshed's and Stow's *Chronicles* and many Greek and Latin classics. As Bishop in his will referred to Adams as his "kinsman," he was probably a relative by marriage. Thomas Adams was the publisher of several music books, *e.g.*, some of Dowland's Books of Songs and Thomas Ravenscroft's *Deuteromelia*. Thomas Adams was Warden of the Company in 1611, 1614 and 1617, but never rose to the position of Master. He died between March 2nd and May 4th, 1620. In his will mention is made of his three daughters, but no son is named. He bequeathed £100 to the Company of Stationers and a bason and ewer to the Bishop of London. William Leake and George Swinhowe were nominated overseers and William Aspley and Andrew Hebb were among the witnesses [P.C.C., 37, Soame].

ADDERTON (WILLIAM), *see* Plomer, *Dictionary*.

AELST, *see* Janssen van Aelst, or d'Aelst.

AGGAS (EDWARD), bookseller in London, 1576–1616; (1) The Red Dragon, West End of St. Paul's, 1576–1602; (2) The Oaken Tree [or the Green Oak] in Long Lane, 1603. Son of Robert Agas or Aggas of Stokenaylonde, co. Suffolk, yeoman, apprenticed at Easter, 1564, for nine years to Humphrey Toy [Arber, i. 229]. First book entry July 1st, 1577 [Arber, ii. 314]. He was probably related to Ralph Aggas (or Agas). Amongst his publications were several translations from the French, some signed E. A. being probably his own work. He employed John Windet, John Wolf, Thomas Orwin, Thomas Dawson, and Thomas Gardiner amongst others to print for him. In many of his books a block of a wyvern resting upon a crown is seen. This was probably used as an ornament and not as a device. Edward Aggas died before January 21st, 162$\frac{4}{5}$, on which day his will was proved in the Prerogative Court of Canterbury. In it he mentions a son Samuel and his three children. It would appear from the Registers that he had another son named Elmore, who was apprenticed to Gregory Seton on November 7th, 1603. As nothing more is heard of him and there is no reference to him in the will, the probability is that he pre-deceased his father. [*D.N.B.*; Arber, ii. 274; P.C.C., 9, Clark.]

AINSWORTH alias ENSOR (MARTIN), stationer in London, 1587–96. Son of Richard Ensor of Exeter. Apprenticed on April 11th, 1580, for eight years to Thomas Ainsworth, alias Ensor, stationer, possibly a brother, by whom he was made free on July 3rd, 1587 [Arber, ii. 96]. In 1596 he is found taking an apprentice [Arber, ii. 213].

AINSWORTH alias ENSOR (THOMAS), stationer in London, 1577–1604. Admitted freeman by redemption on July 6th, 1570 [Arber, i. 420], and the same year contributed twelve pence towards the enlargement of the hall [Arber, i. 428]. He is found taking apprentices from July, 1577, to 1604 [Arber, ii. 79, 128, 700, 736], and in August of the latter year he was fined for using "undecent language" [Arber, ii. 839]. He does not appear to have published books and his address has not been found.

ALBYN or ALBINE (SAMUEL), bookseller in London, 1621–8; Near the Six Clerks' Office, Chancery Lane. Son of Hugh Albyn or Albine of Wanstrowe, Somerset. Apprentice to Richard Serger for nine years from Christmas, 1601 [Arber, ii. 261]. Took up his freedom December 10th, 1610 [Arber, iii. 683]. In 1621 Albyn published the third edition of a poem entitled, *The Passion of a discontented mind*, erroneously attributed to Nicholas Breton [B.M. 1076. i. 20]. He is mentioned in a list of second hand booksellers who, in 1628, were ordered to submit catalogues of their books to the Archbishop of Canterbury [*Dom. S. Papers, Chas. I*, Vol. 117. (9)]. He appears to have succeeded to the business formerly kept by John Bailey [*q.v.*].

ALCHORNE (THOMAS), bookseller in London, 1627–39; The Green Dragon, St. Paul's Churchyard. First book entry March 10th, 1627 [Arber, iv. 174]. In 1631 he issued Ben Jonson's play of the *New Inn.* In 1636 Thomas Knight assigned over to him his copyrights in fifteen works [Arber, iv. 357], but these were reassigned by Alchorne to Knight on March 23rd, 1639 [Arber, iv. 461].

ALDAY, *see* Allde.

ALDEE, *see* Allde.

ALDRED (ROBERT), bookseller in London, 1620; Southwark, near the Market Place. Took up his freedom in the Company of Stationers, November 6th, 1620 [Arber, iii. 685]. He published an edition of *Reynard the Fox*, printed by Edward Allde, 1620 [Hazlitt, H. 501].

ALEN, *see* Allen.

ALLAM (JOHN), bookseller and bookbinder in Oxford, 1617–38. Reprimanded for setting up as a bookseller without the Vice-Chancellor's leave [Clark, *Register*, ii. 1. 321]. Admitted on June 11th, 1617, at the age of twenty-one [*ibid.*, p. 404]. He is found binding books for the Bodleian from 1613 to 1618 [Gibson, *Oxford Bindings*, p. 49]. There was another John Allam, stationer, who was admitted on March 24th, 16$^{09}_{10}$, at the age of thirty [Gibson, *Oxford Wills*, p. 41].

ALLAM (THOMAS), bookseller in Oxford, 1636–9. His imprint is found on a copy of Nathanael Carpenter's *Philosophia Libera*, Oxford, 1636. [Madan, *Early Oxford Press*, 189, 307.]

ALLDE (EDWARD), printer in London, 1584–1628; (1) The Long Shop in the Poultry; (2) The Gilded Cup in Fore Street, Cripplegate; (3) Aldersgate, over against the Pump, 1597; (4) Upon Lambert Hill, near Old Fish-street, 1604; (5) Near Christ-Church, 1615. Son of John Alde or Alday, printer. Made free of the Company of Stationers "by patronage" on February 15th, 1584, and carried on the business at the Long Shop in the Poultry, for some years after the retirement of his father. But about 1589 he set up another press at the Gilded Cup in Fore Street, Cripplegate, and became largely a trade printer, being employed by most of the publishers of that time. His first book entry occurs in the Registers on August 1st, 1586 [Arber, ii. 450]. His earlier work consisted chiefly of ballads, but in later days he is found printing the works of Thomas Churchyard, Samuel Daniel, Thomas Dekker, Christopher Marlowe, John Taylor the water poet, and many other noted writers. In character his printing differed little from that of his father, but his later books were printed throughout in Roman letter and he favoured quarto rather than smaller sizes. In 1597 the Company of Stationers seized his press and letters, which had been used in printing a Popish Confession, and forbade him to print; but the

Archbishop of Canterbury afterwards authorized the Company to allow him to resume his trade. He was again in trouble in 1599 and with several others was mentioned in an order of the Master and Wardens against printing certain books that had been condemned and ordered to be burnt [Arber, iii. 677, 678]. The date of his death is uncertain but he is believed to have died in 1628. His widow Elizabeth Allde continued to carry on the printing business for some years. [*Bibliographica*, vol. ii. pp. 61–80.]

ALLDE (ELIZABETH), bookseller in London, 1628–40; (?) The Gilded Cup in Fore Street, Cripplegate. Widow of Edward Allde (1584–1628). She had been previously married to Ralph Joyner, by whom she had a son, Ralph, who is believed to have carried on Edward Allde's printing business for some years. One of her daughters married Richard Oulton, stationer, and on April 22nd, 1640, Elizabeth Allde made over to him all her copyrights. [Arber, iii. 687, 700, 701; iv. 507.]

ALLDE or ALDAY (JOHN), *see* Duff, *Century.*

ALLDE (MARGARET), bookseller in London, 1584–1603; The Long Shop in the Poultry, under St. Mildred's Church. Widow of John Allde. After her husband's death she carried on the business with her son Edward until 1589, when he moved to premises in Cripplegate. Margaret Allde then continued the business in the Poultry alone, and is found taking apprentices from 1593 to 1600. In 1602 she put the latest over to Robert Ryder, to serve out the remainder of his time [Arber, ii. 263], but she entered two ballads on May 18th, 1603. Soon afterwards she appears to have sold the business to Henry Rockett.

ALLEN (BENJAMIN), *see* Plomer, *Dictionary.*

ALLEN (GEORGE), stationer in London, 1562–1600. A prominent member of the Stationers' Company, though no book bearing his name has been found. He took up his freedom on April 16th, 1562 [Arber, i. 187], and is found entering apprentices from 1565 [Arber, i. 256 *et seq.*]. He was Renter of the Company for the year ending July 10th, 1589 [Arber, i. 531], and Warden of the Company for the year ending July, 1592 [Arber, i. 553]. In 1586 he was appointed one of the searchers with H. Conway and Master Middleton. The last heard of him is in 1600 [Arber, ii. 247].

ALLEN (JOHN), bookseller in Leicester, 1639. Leonard Lichfield, the Oxford printer, printed for him G. Foxley's *Groanes of the spirit*, 1639. [Madan, *Early Oxford Press*, 313.]

ALLOT (MARY), bookseller in London, 1635–7; The Black Bear in St. Paul's Churchyard. Widow of Robert Allot. She appears to have carried on the business until 1637, when she transferred her copyrights to R. Legatt and Andrew Crooke [Arber, iv. 387]. Her name is found in the imprint to a work entitled *The Countryman's Instructor*, 1636 [B.M. 779. b. 9. (3)].

ALLOT (ROBERT), bookseller in London, 1625–35; (1) The Greyhound, St. Paul's Churchyard, 1626; (2) The Black Bear, St. Paul's Churchyard. Born at Criggleston in the West Riding of Yorkshire. There is no record of his apprenticeship, but he took up his freedom in the Company of Stationers on November 7th, 1625 [Arber, iii. 686]. In January, 162$^{5}_{6}$, he purchased from Margaret Hodgetts for £45, the copyrights in four works, one of them being George Sandys' *Travels*, and in September of the same year the much more extensive rights of John Budge, numbering some forty-one copies, mostly theological. He was also the publisher of many plays, and had a share in the second folio of Shakespeare's works, published in 1632. In that year an action was brought against him in the Court of Chancery by Rowland Vaughan respecting the printing, binding, and selling of *The Practice of Piety* in the Welsh language. Five hundred copies of the work were printed and Vaughan agreed to pay Allot £50 for them, but he alleged that the books were not delivered in the time specified, and that the bulk of them were spoiled by wet on their arrival in Wales. Allot admitted that the books were not delivered in time, owing to the Welsh language being so hard and unusual a language to set for the press. He further said that five copies were expensively bound for presentation. [Chancery Proceedings, Chas. I, V. 3–53]. Robert Allot died in 1635. His will was dated October 18th, and proved on November 10th in that year. His only child was a daughter Mary. He mentioned an uncle, Robert Allot, a Doctor in Physic. Christopher Meredith and Richard Thrale, stationers, were his brothers-in-law, the former having married his sister Elizabeth, and the latter his sister Dorothy. To his servant Andrew Crooke he left a bequest of twenty pounds on condition that he remained in the service of Mary Allot his wife for a further term of three years. He left the Company of Stationers a sum of £10 for a dinner and a further sum of £10 for the poor of the Company. Amongst the witnesses were Edward Pigeon, Philemon Stephens and Richard Thrale, all stationers. [P.C.C., 114, Sadler.] Two years after his death his widow transferred all her remaining copyrights to R. Legatt and Andrew Crooke [Arber, iv. 387]. Unless he took up his freedom in the Company of Stationers very late in life, which was the exception rather than the rule, it does not appear possible that this Robert Allot had anything to do with *England's Parnassus*. The compiler of that work was probably his uncle.

ALLOT (THOMAS), bookseller in London, 1636–9, and at Dublin, ?1639–43; London: The Greyhound in St. Paul's Churchyard. Took up his freedom on April 4th, 1636 [Arber, iii. 687]. In 1639 in company with John Crooke he issued Beaumont and Fletcher's tragedy *The Bloody Brother*. He was in partnership with John Crooke, Richard Serger, and Edmund Crooke, stationer, of Dublin, and is mentioned by the last named in his will, proved in Dublin in 1638 or 1639. He was dead by June, 1643, when administration of his goods was granted to Ferdinando Blaker of Dublin, gent., his next-of-kin [information from E. R. McC. Dix].

ALSOP (BERNARD), *see* Plomer, *Dictionary*.

ALSOP (NICHOLAS), *see* Plomer, *Dictionary*.

ANDERSON (GEORGE), printer at Edinburgh, *see* Plomer, *Dictionary*.

ANDERSON (JOHN), printer in Scotland, 1611. Mr. John Johnston, second master in St. Mary's College, St. Andrews, who died October 20th, 1611, bequeathed "to John Anderson printer, *Tremellius Bible*, in octavo." Anderson was probably a journeyman, but where and for whom he worked cannot be guessed at, as there was no press in St. Andrews at that time. [*Maitland Club Miscellany*, i. 343.]

ANDREWES (THOMAS), bookseller and bookbinder in London, 1624. Described as a "bookbinder" in John Gee's *Foot out of the Snare*, 1624, in a list of those who "disperse print binde or sell Popish bookes about London."

ANDREWES (THOMAS), bookseller in London, 1621–37; In Smithfield. Took up his freedom June 4th, 1621 [Arber, iii. 685]. On April 26th, 1637, he entered in the Registers a book called *Meditations* [Arber, iv. 382]. The work, by J. Henshaw, Bishop of Peterborough, was printed for him "by R. B." in the same year [Hazlitt, I. 209].

ANTONY called VELPIUS (WIDOW OF HUBERT), printer or bookseller at Brussels, 1633. She issued Pierre Matthieu's *History of St. Elizabeth* [B.M., p. 1081; Hazlitt, I. 285].

APPLAY or APPLOWE (RICHARD), *see* Duff, *Century*.

ARBUTHNET (ALEXANDER), printer in Edinburgh, 1576–85; The Kirk of Field. He was partner of Thomas Bassandyne in the printing of the folio *Bible* of 1576–9, and seems to have obtained his introduction to printing in connection with that undertaking. In the course of the work differences arose between the two partners, which led to an appeal to the Privy Council, and, in January, 157$^{6}_{7}$, Bassandyne was ordered to deliver up to Arbuthnet the printing house and the *Bible* so far as printed. Bassandyne died in 1577, and the printing of the *Bible* was completed by Arbuthnet alone. Only five other works, including the first edition of Buchanan's *Rerum Scoticarum historia* (1582), are known to have issued from his press before it ceased work in 1584. On April 1st, 1579, Arbuthnet received a gift under the Privy Seal of the exclusive privilege of printing the psalm book in prose and metre with the prayers and catechisms in both English and Latin for the space of seven years, and on August 24th of the same year he was appointed king's printer for life with additions to his monopoly. His device, a copy of that of Richard Jugge, bears in the centre a pelican in her piety with the motto "Pro lege rege et grege," and the architectural framework carries his name, initials and arms; of this device he had two sizes. Arbuthnet, who dwelt at the Kirk of Field, died September 1st, 1585, being survived by his wife, Agnes Pennycuike, and five children. His inventory, printed in the *Bannatyne Miscellany*, ii. 207, mentions no books. Some of his initial letters passed into the hands of Waldegrave and then Finlason, the latter of whom also used the smaller device and other ornaments. [Dickson and Edmond, 312; *D.N.B.*; Aldis, *Scottish Books*, 108; Lee, App. vi, vii.]

ARCHER (FRANCIS), draper and stationer, 1600–16. Originally a member of the Drapers' Company. Transferred to the Stationers on June 3rd, 1600 [Arber, ii. 725]. He kept as his apprentice William Fisher who was indentured to Thomas Gubbin, and Archer paid 2s. 6d. as a fine to the Company when he made Fisher free in 1604 [Arber, ii. 279]. In April, 1616, George Potter, stationer, assigned over to him his copyright in Philip de Mornay's *Trueness of Christian Religion* [Arber, iii. 586], but in the same year Archer parted with it to George Purslowe. Nothing more is known about him.

ARCHER (HUMFREY), bookseller and bookbinder in Oxford, 1577–88. Admitted a bookseller on April 24th, 1577 [Clark, *Register*, ii. 1. 321]. Administration of his effects was granted on February 13th, 158$^{7}_{8}$ [Gibson, *Oxford Wills*, pp. 16, 17].

ARCHER (THOMAS), bookseller in London, 1603–34; (1) The little shop by the Royal Exchange; (2) The long shop under St. Mildred's Church, 1604 [Hazlitt, H. 417]; (3) In Pope's Head Palace, near the Royal Exchange, 1607; (4) Over against the sign of the Horse-shoe, in Pope's Head Alley, 1625. Apprentice to Cuthbert Burby, who made him free of the Company on January 15th, 1603, and at the same time paid a fine of ten shillings for having kept him unpresented during the whole of his apprenticeship. First book entry February 4th, 1603. Dealer in plays, jest-books and other popular literature. In 1622 he was associated with Nicholas Bourne. On February 10th, 163$^{0}_{1}$, he assigned certain copies to Hugh Perry, after which nothing further is known of him.

ARDELEY, *see* Yardley (R.)

ARISONE (ANDREW), printer in Edinburgh, 1600. He was witness at the baptism in Edinburgh of Margaret, daughter of Patrick Johnstoun, bookbinder, on August 17th, 1600. Possibly the same as Andro Aysoun. [Aldis, *Scottish Books*, 108; *Scottish Antiquary*, v. 90.]

ARNOLD (JOHN), bookseller in London, 1569–81; The North Door of St. Paul's Church. Admitted a freeman of the Company of Stationers on February 3rd, 1568. First entry in the Registers 1568–9 [Arber, i. 387]. He chiefly published ballad literature. He was fined for keeping open his shop on St. Andrew's day. The last heard of him is in 1581, when he transferred a book to J. Charlewood [Arber, ii. 387].

ARONDELL, *see* Arundell.

ARUNDELL, or ARONDELL (WILLIAM), bookseller in London, 1614–17; The Angel in St. Paul's Churchyard. Published a number of pamphlets on French affairs in 1617; also a *Survey of the East Indies* from the travels of Monsieur de Monsart and Sir Thomas Roe.

ASH, (FRANCIS), *see* Plomer, *Dictionary*.

ASH (HENRY), *see* Esch.

ASKELL (LEONARD), printer in London, 1560–3. One of three apprentices presented by Thomas Marshe on October 14th, 1556 [Arber, i. 41]. On October 4th, 1557, he paid 3s. 4d. for the breakfast on the occasion of his admission to the freedom of the Company [Arber, i. 69]. In 1562 he was printing broadsides. One of these entitled *A description of a monstrous child*, is in the Huth collection. In the following year he issued a work on the plague for Thomas Purfoot. His address is unknown.

ASPLEY (WILLIAM), bookseller in London, 1598–1640; (1) The Tiger's Head in St. Paul's Churchyard; (2) The Parrot in St. Paul's Churchyard. Son of William Aspley, of Raiston in the County of Cumberland, clerk. Apprenticed to George Bishop, stationer of London, for nine years from February 5th, 1588: admitted a freeman of the Company on April 11th, 1597; first book entry October 5th, 1598. Joint publisher with Andrew Wise of the first editions of Shakespeare's *Much Ado about nothing* and *2 Henry IV*, and, with William Jaggard and others, of the First Folio. He was also the publisher of George Chapman's *Eastward Hoe*, Dekker's *Westward Hoe*, and other plays. William Aspley was Master of the Company of Stationers in 1640, but died during his year of office, August 18th, 1640. [Arber, v. lxiv, lxxxii; *D.N.B.*]

ASPLIN (THOMAS), stationer, 1567–72. Son of William Asplyn of London, cooper. Apprenticed on March 25th, 1567, for eight years, to John Day, stationer of London. During his apprenticeship he appears to have left his master, and was caught in 1572 printing Thomas Cartwright's *Second Admonition to the Parliament*. He was taken back to service by John Day, but attempted to murder him and his wife. Asplin was then imprisoned and no more is heard of him. [Arber, i. 327, 466.]

ASSIGNS OF JOHN BATTERSBY, RICHARD DAY, FRANCIS FLOWER, WILLIAM SERES, senr. and junr., *see* the names of the assignors.

ASTLEY (HUGH), bookseller in London, 1588–1609; St. Magnus Corner (Thames Street, near London Bridge). Son of Roger Astley, of Maxtocke, co. Warwick, yeoman. Apprentice to William Seres for seven years from July 25th, 1576 [Arber, ii. 65]. In 1588 appeared a poem entitled *A Godly Exhortation, whereby Englande maye knowe, What sinfull abhomination there nowe dooth flowe*, which bore the imprint, "At London, Printed by Edward Allde, and are to be solde at Saint Magnus Corner by Hugh Astley Anno 1588." At that time however Astley would appear to have been a "draper," and it was not until June 3rd, 1600, that he was admitted to the freedom of the Company of Stationers "by translation" from the Company of Drapers [Arber, ii. 725]. His first book entry is found under date August 11th, 1600 [Arber, iii. 168], and on November 3rd he entered eight copies, five of which he had attempted to enter in 1596, when for some reason, probably the discovery that he was not a stationer, the entry was cancelled by the authority of the Court of Assistants. Hugh Astley dealt largely in nautical books, and amongst his most notable publications was Martin Cortes' *Art of Navigation* translated by Richard Eden, first published by Richard Watkins in 1561. This was transferred to Astley by Watkins' assigns and published by him in 1596. In the same year he also published an edition of Robert Norman's *New Attractive*, a work on the Magnet: and in 1605 the *Safegard of Saylers, or Great Rutter*, translated out of Dutch. On June 16th, 1609, his copies were transferred to Thomas Man, junr. [Arber, iii. 412].

ASTON (JOHN), *see* Plomer, *Dictionary*.

ATFEND (ABRAHAM), bookseller in Norwich, 1640. Mr. Sayle records a copy of Giles Fletcher's *Christ's Victory* as having this name in the imprint [Sayle, pp. 1292, 1307].

ATKINS (JOHN), mentioned as a journeyman bookbinder in the Chester Stationers' Registers in the year 1592.

ATKINSON (JOHN), stationer of London, 1587–98. Son of Richard Atkinson of Adwick on the Street in the County of York, yeoman. Apprenticed to Gabriel Cawood, stationer of London, for ten years from Midsummer, 1587; admitted to the freedom of the Company on April 4th, 1597. He began taking apprentices April 3rd, 1598. [Arber, ii. 146, 225, 251, 718.]

ATKINSON (TROYLUS), bookseller at Cambridge, 1626–35; in St. Mary's Parish. Paid church rate in St. Mary's Parish from 1626 to 1635 [Foster's *Churchwardens' Accounts*]. Dr. Peile "On Four MS. Books of Accounts kept by Jos. Mead, B.D., of Christ's College, 1614–33" [Camb. Ant. Soc. *Communications*, Vol. xiii, p. 253–4] . . . "The sick man was removed to 'Raper's' or 'G. Pindar's'—college servants, I suspect, of some sort, as 'Troylus' certainly was, though he is dignified with the title 'Mr. Atkinson' when he receives rent for rooms in the Brazen George, the old Inn where Post-Office Place now is, unstatutably used by the College to accomodate the overflowing number of pupils in those days." His will, dated 1675, is at Peterborough.

ATKYNS, *see* Atkins.

AUBRI (DANIEL), printer at Hanau, 1607, and (?) at Frankfurt, 1620–9. In 1607 he printed Hugh Broughton's *Daniel* [B.M., p. 199] with initial letters used from 1622 by E. Raban at Aberdeen [*Bibl. Soc. Trans.*, vii. 46; Sayle, p. 1495.] He may presumably be identified with the Daniel Aubry who printed at Frankfurt from 1620 to 1629 [Heitz, *Frankfurter Druckerzeichen*, x–xi, nr. 102–4], but there seems no evidence. At Hanau his device was Wechel's Pegasus. He was probably an heir of John Aubri, one of the successors of Andrew Wechel; *see* Marni (Claude).

AUROY (PIERRE), printer at Douai from 1596 to his death in or before 1628, from which year until 1640 his widow carried on his establishment, using his imprint [Duthillœul, pp. 144, 228–9]. In 1631 she printed for J. Heigham *A Hive of Sacred Honeycombs*, from the writings of St. Bernard, by Anthony Batt [B.M., p. 133].

AUSTEN (ROBERT), *see* Plomer, *Dictionary*.

AVERY (RICHARD), (?) bookseller in London, 1624; In Wood Street. Mentioned in John Gee's *Foot out of the Snare*, 1624, as a dealer in Popish books. He was probably a descendant of George Avery, who took up his freedom as a stationer in 1592 [Arber, ii. 711].

AWDELEY (JOHN), *see* Duff, *Century*.

AWSTEN (ROBERT), *see* Austen.

AYSOUN (ANDRO), printer in Edinburgh, 1593–? 1600. In 1593 Catherine Norwell, wife of Robert Smyth, printer in Edinburgh, left by her will "to Andro Aysoun prentar, thrie merkis." Aysoun may have been one of Smyth's workmen, and was possibly the same as Andrew Arisone. [*Bannatyne Miscell.*, ii. 221; Aldis, *Scottish Books*, 108.]

BACHE (JOHN), bookseller in London, 1604–14; Pope's Head Passage. Took up his freedom in the Company of Stationers March 6th, 1607 [Arber, iii. 683]. Amongst his publications was Samuel Rowlands' *Knave of Hearts*, 1613, and Henry Brereton's *Newes of the present Miseries of Rushia*, 1614.

BADGER (GEORGE), *see* Plomer, *Dictionary*.

BADGER (RICHARD), *see* Plomer, *Dictionary*.

BADGER (THOMAS), *see* Plomer, *Dictionary*.

BAGFET (JOSEPH), bookseller in London, 1611–34. Son of John Bagfet of Guildford in Surrey, chandler. Apprenticed to Thomas Man, stationer of London, for seven years from September 4th, 1598 [Arber, ii. 230]: took up his freedom May 27th, 1611 [Arber, iii. 68.] In 1613 he was joint publisher with Nathaniel Butter, of *Sir Antony Sherley his Relation of his Travels into Persia* [B.M. 790. c. 28]. He died early in 1635, his will being proved in the court of the Dean and Chapter of St. Paul's on January 22nd, 163$\frac{4}{5}$. He left all his real and personal estate to his wife Mary. [Dean and Chapter of St. Paul's, Book B, fol. 27.]

BAHERE (ROBERT), printer in London, 1562–99. Mentioned in Kirk's *Returne of Aliens* as a "typographus." Mr. Worman thinks him to be identical with the Robert Bahere, feltmaker, of Southwark, who apprenticed his son Isaack to John Hunsworth, stationer, on October 28th, 1581. [Arber, ii. 108; Worman, *Alien Members*, pp. 1–2.]

BAILEY (——), (?) bookseller in London, 1624; Holborn. Mentioned in John Gee's *Foot out of the Snare*, 1624, as a dealer in popish books.

BAILEY, BALEY, BAYLY, or BAILY (JOHN), bookseller in London, 1600–10; (1) The Little North door of St. Paul's Church, 1600–3; (2) At the door of the Office of the Six Clerks in Chancery Lane, 1603–10. There would appear to have been two if not three men of this name trading as booksellers between 1600 and 1610. The only entry of an apprenticeship is that recorded on August 24th, 1592, when John Baylye, son of John Baylye of Whetstone, Middlesex, was apprenticed to Joseph Hunt, stationer of London, for eight years from that date [Arber, ii. 182]. This term would have expired in 1600, and we find two men of this name made free during that year. The earliest was on June 25th, when one John Baylie was admitted by translation from the Company of Drapers [Arber, ii. 726], while the other was presented by John Newberry on September 1st [Arber, ii. 727]. There was also a John Bayly to whom John Wight, draper and bookseller, who died in the latter half of 1589, left a bequest of unbound books to the value of forty shillings [Plomer, *Wills*, p. 29]. Whether any of these men was identical with Joseph Hunt's apprentice it is not possible to say. On September 8th, 1600, a John Baylie entered in the Registers *Acolastus his after-witte*, a poem by Samuel Nicholson [Arber, iii. 172], the imprint to which ran "At London. Imprinted for John Baylie, and are to be sold at his Shop, neere the little North-doore of Paules Church. 1600." Between 1602 and perhaps 1610 he had a second shop "at the doore of the office of the Six Clerks in Chancery Lane," from which in 1602 he issued an edition of (?) Southwell's *Passion of a Discontented Mind*, while in 1603 Thomas Creed printed for him a laudatory poem on the reign of Queen Elizabeth and the accession of James I, entitled *Eliza'es Memoriall, King Iames his arrivall, and Romes Downefall*, which was issued from St. Paul's Churchyard. John Bailey was also the publisher of Francis Davison's *Poetical Rhapsody*, 1602, but in 1603 he transferred his rights in this to Roger Jackson [Arber, iii. 242]. About this time there is also an entry in the Registers by "John Bayley ye younger" [Arber, iii. 206]. In 1610 a John Baily is found associated with William Barley in the publication of pamphlets relating to public affairs in France, *The Apologie of George Brisset* [B.M. 3901. e. 7], and *The Terrible . . . death of Francis Ravilliack* [B.M. C. 33. g. 25], but in neither instance is the publisher's address given.

BAILEY, BAYLEY or BAILY (THOMAS), *see* Plomer, *Dictionary*.

BAILY, *see* Bailey.

BAKER (GEORGE), bookseller in London, 1627–31; Near Charing Cross, at the sign of the White Lion. Took up his freedom June 8th, 1627 [Arber,

iii. 686]. In 1631 he published George Simotta's *Theater of the Planetary Houres* [B.M. 1141. a. 23. (4)] and Aurelian Townsend's *Tempe Restored* [Hazlitt, I. 425].

BAKER (MICHAEL), bookseller in London, 1610–11; St. Paul's Churchyard, at the sign of the Greyhound. Son of Philip Baker of Cliston, co. Bedford, yeoman. Apprentice to Robert Dexter for nine years from Michaelmas, 1598. On June 28th, 1602, he was put over to George Potter to serve out the rest of his time. Robert Dexter died between October 24th and December 26th, 1603 [Plomer, *Wills*, p. 37]. Michael Baker took up his freedom on June 16th, 1606 [Arber, iii. 683]. On October 1st, 1610, he received from William Welby all the latter's rights in seventeen works. Most of these were theological, but amongst them was a work entitled *Good Speed to Virginia*, which Welby had printed in the previous year, and *Virginia Newes*.

BALL (ROGER), bookseller in London, 1634–6; (1) The Golden Anchor, Strand, near Temple Bar, 1636; (2) The Golden Anchor, next the Nag's Head Tavern in the Strand, without Temple Bar [Sayle, p. 1149]. Took up his freedom September 1st, 1634 [Arber, iii. 687]. He published during the year 1636, the comedy of *Sir Gyles Goosecappe, knight*, William Sampson's play *The Vow Breaker or, The Faire Maide of Clifton*, Sir T. Salusbury's *History of Joseph* [Hazlitt, H. 532], and T. Cogan's *Haven of Health* [Hazlitt, IV. 127].

BALLARD (HENRY), printer in London, 1597–1608; The Bear [in the Strand] over against St. Clement [Danes] Church, without Temple Bar [Arber, v. 197]. On August 25th, 1586, Richard Tottell presented Henry Ballard to the freedom of the Company of Stationers, from which it may be assumed that Ballard was one of Tottell's apprentices. Sir John Lambe surmised that he succeeded to the business of Valentine Simmes in 1604, but he gives no authority for the suggestion [Arber, iii. 703], and Simmes was in business long after this date. In 1597, Ballard is found printing heraldic books for Richard Tottell. Then nothing more is heard of him until 1604, when he enters his first apprentice on September 3rd [Arber, ii. 283]. During 1608 he is found printing several books, notably Sir John Davies' *Nosce Teipsum* and the play of the *Merry Devil of Edmonton*. His place of business is not given in the imprints of these later books.

BALLARD (RICHARD), bookseller in London, 1579–85; at St. Magnus Corner (Thames Street, near London Bridge). The first notice that we have of this bookseller is the imprint to the 1579 edition of Anthony Munday's *Mirrour of Mutabilitie*, which he published from the above house, previously in the occupation of William Pickering. Ballard also dealt in nautical books. His last book entry in the Registers was on March 30th, 1585 [Arber, ii. 440], and on December 6th in the same year Henry Carre was licensed to retain in his service John Proctor late apprentice to Richard Ballard, deceased [Arber, ii. 137]. Ballard was succeeded at his address by Hugh Astley.

BAMFORD (HENRY), printer in London, 1571–86. Son of Edmond Bamford of Rochdale, Lancashire. Apprentice to John Cawood, stationer of London, for eight years from Christmas, 1562 [Arber, i. 196]. Took up his freedom on January 11th, 1571 [Arber, i. 447]. On January 30th, 1577, he received license to publish *A briefe Treatise of the Anatomy of mans bodye*, and on March 4th of the same year he took over several copyrights from William Hoskins, but a twelvemonth later assigned them to Richard Jones. Later he joined John Wolfe and his fellow agitators in their protest against the monopolists, and in 1583 was reported as one of the disorderly persons who printed privileged copies, being then described as a "compositor." He also gave a bond for £20 not to print privileged copies, and this bond appears annually in the statement of the Wardens down to the year 1586 [Arber, i. 501; ii. 19, 308, 309, 325]. The position of his printing house is unknown.

BANKWORTH (RICHARD), draper and bookseller in London, 1594–1612; The Sun in St. Paul's Churchyard. Originally a member of the Company of Drapers, Richard Bankworth set up as a bookseller and stationer in the year 1594. On March 26th in that year, Thomas Barnes was apprenticed to Henry Conway, stationer of London, for eight years, but the following memorandum was added to the entry in the Registers:—"Memorandum it is ordered that Richard Bankworth Draper, using the trade of a stationer shall have the service of this apprentice and teache him his occupation, and discharge master Conneway of all charges concernyng the same apprentice. And the same apprentice not to be accompted for any of master Conwaies apprentices which he may kepe by the ordonances" [Arber, ii. 190].

Bankworth was frequently fined during the next few years for printing other men's copies, and was one of those who in 1598 combined to issue a pirated edition of Sir Philip Sidney's *Arcadia*, printed by Robert Waldegrave in Edinburgh [*Library*, March, 1900, p. 195 *et seq.*]. In spite of his irregularities, Bankworth was admitted to the freedom of the Company of Stationers on June 3rd, 1600, and was chosen an assistant of the Company on May 18th, 1612 [Arber, ii. 874; v. lxxxiii]. Amongst his publications was George Peele's tragedy *The Battell of Alcazar*, 1594, 4to, and he held a share in Camden's *Britannia*.

BARBAR (CHRISTOPHER), bookseller and bookbinder in Oxford, 1614–17. Was binder for the Bodleian in 1613–14 [Gibson, *Oxford Bindings*, 39, 49, 51, 55, 59]. On May 23rd, 1617, in company with several other persons, he was reprimanded for setting up as a bookseller without the Vice-chancellor's leave [Clark, *Register*, ii. 1. 321].

BARBER (HENRY), (?) bookseller in London, 1624; Holborn. Mentioned in John Gee's *Foot out of the Snare*, 1624, as a dealer in popish books, having been "once imprisoned upon this occasion." He was perhaps related to Joseph Barber, 1653–8 (*see* Plomer, *Dictionary*).

BARKER or BARKAR (CHRISTOPHER), draper, bookseller and printer in London, 1569–99; (1) The Grasshopper in St. Paul's Churchyard; (2) The Tiger's Head in St. Paul's Churchyard; (3) The Tiger's Head in Paternoster Row; (4) Bacon House, near Foster Lane, Cheapside; (5) Northumberland House, Aldersgate Street. Christopher Barker is believed, on somewhat doubtful authority, to have been related to Christopher Barker, Garter king of arms, and to have been the son of Edward Barker. He was born about the year 1529, and was originally a member of the Drapers' Company, but in middle age turned his attention to the printing and publishing of books. Unfortunately practically all the records of the Company of Stationers for the years 1571–6, the period when he first makes his appearance, are missing, and we have no knowledge as to which of the stationers he was apprenticed to. The first heard of him is in 1569, when he entered in the Registers of the Company, *serten prayers of my Lady Tyrwhett* [Arber, i. 398]. At this time he is believed to have been a bookseller only, living at the sign of the Grasshopper in St. Paul's Churchyard, but so few and so rare are books bearing his imprint at this

date that it is unsafe to speak definitely on this point. A singular entry occurs in the Company's accounts for the year 1571–2: "To Christopher Barker for 111 loades and 6 foot of timber. xliis." [Arber, i. 455]. Now, one of Christopher Barker's earliest devices was that of a woodman splitting the bark off a tree, a punning device on his name, but in the light of this entry it might also mean something more. On December 23rd, 1573, in company with Garret Dewes, John Harrison the Eldest, William Norton, John Wight, and Richard Watkins, he became one of the assigns of Francis Flower, who a few days previously had secured the patent of Queen's Printer in Latin, Greek and Hebrew in succession to Reginald Wolfe. It is generally asserted that Christopher Barker began to print in the year 1576; but there is some reason for believing that he was at work as a printer at the time he took over Francis Flower's patent, even if not earlier. One of the first books which undoubtedly came from his press was an octavo edition of the Genevan *New Testament* which bears the date 1575 on the titlepage, and has the imprint "Imprinted at London, by Christopher Barkar dwelling in Powles Churchyard at the signe of the Tyger's head 1576." The titlepage of this was in a border familiar to all students of Barker's work, that having the royal arms at the top, the "tiger's" head and the coat of arms on either side and two shields at the bottom. These shields are generally found blank, but in this book one is occupied by the arms of the Stationers' Company and the other has what appear to be three triple crowns, with the letters C. B. At this time Barker was evidently very closely associated with the family of Sir Francis Walsingham. Time will perhaps reveal what that association was, but proof of it is abundant. In the first place the Tiger's Head which he adopted as his device was the crest of the Walsingham family. The Walsingham coat of arms is found in many of his books and in his initial letters and border pieces. Again many of the early productions of his press were dedicated either by him or at his instance to members of the Walsingham family. In 1577 Barker obtained from Sir Thomas Wilkes the residue of his patent as Queen's Printer and from that time became one of the most powerful and important members of the Company of Stationers, into the Livery of which he was taken on June 25th, 1578 [Arber, ii. 865]. By this patent he obtained the sole printing of the *Bible*, the *Book of Common Prayer*, the *Statutes of the Realm* and all *Proclamations*. As showing how recklessly these monopolies were granted, it may be said that the Queen had in the first year of her reign granted to Richard Tottell a license to "imprint all manners of books concerning the common laws of this realme" *for his lifetime*, under which patent he had been printing the statutes of the realm, until Christopher Barker claimed the right under his new patent as Queen's Printer. In 1578 he issued a printed circular to the Companies of London offering them copies of his large *Bible* on advantageous terms [Arber, ii. 748]. In 1582 there was much unrest amongst the printers owing to the growth of the printing monopolies, and Christopher Barker drew up a long and valuable report on the whole subject, which is printed at length by Mr. Arber in the first volume of his *Transcript*, pp. 111, 114–16, 144, 246. He was Warden of the Company at that time and again in the year 1585–6. In 1583 he was returned as having five presses [Arber, i. 248]. Christopher Barker died at his house at Datchet, near Windsor, on November 29th, 1599, aged 70. In 1588 he had nominated as his deputies George Bishop and Ralph Newbery. He left a son Robert Barker who succeeded him in the Royal printing house.

BARKER (CHRISTOPHER), DEPUTIES OF, 1588–99. In 1588 Christopher Barker nominated as his deputies George Bishop and Ralph Newbery, and in 1594 they were joined by Robert Barker, the printer's eldest son.

BARKER (ROBERT), *see* Plomer, *Dictionary*.

BARLEY (WILLIAM), draper, bookseller and printer in London, 1591–1614; (1) Newgate Market; (2) Gratious [Gracechurch] Street over against Leadenhall; (3) Little St. Helens. The earliest notice of this somewhat remarkable man is an entry in the account of the Wardens of the Stationers' Company for the year 1591, recording his committal to prison for contempt [Arber, i. 555]. He was probably in business as a bookseller and dealer in ballads before this date, and the entry perhaps refers to some privileged book that Barley had sold or published without license. From some information supplied by himself in June, 1598, in a deposition, we learn that he was born about 1565, and that on two previous occasions he had been before the Court of High Commission, once for selling a twopenny book relating to Her Majesty's progress, and again for selling a ballad concerning the safe return of the Earl of Essex from Cadiz. Both these sales took place at Cowdry in Sussex. There is no record of

William Barley's transfer from the Drapers' to the Stationers' Company, but he appears to have joined the ranks of those who opposed the monopolists. His chief claim to notice lies in the fact that he was one of the early publishers of music. In 1593 he brought out a book of *Citterne Lessons*. Again in 1596 we find him issuing a *Pathway to Musicke* and the *New Book of Tabelture*. In 1598 he was joined with Thomas East and others as one of the assigns of Thomas Morley the musician, who on September 28th was granted a license for twenty-one years to print song books of all kinds and music paper. Morley was then living in Little St. Helens, Bishopsgate Street, and he would appear to have supplied a press which was worked by Barley at that address. In addition to being the assign of Morley, William Barley also printed Allison's *Psalms of David in metre*, 1599, and Thomas Weelkes' *Music*, 1608. His last book entry occurs in the Registers on February 18th, 1613, and in the same year he assigned his musical copyrights to M. L. (? Mathew Lownes), J. B. (? John Baylie), and T. S. (? Thomas Snodham). He died before November 12th, 1614, when his widow Mary assigned over all her rights to John Beale. [Arber, iii. 516, 557.]

BARLEY (WILLIAM), stationer at Oxford, 1603. Became a privileged stationer of the University of Oxford in 1603 at the age of thirty-five. He may be identical with the London stationer of the same name [*q.v.*].

BARLOW (TIMOTHY), bookseller in London, 1616–25; The Bull-head, St. Paul's Churchyard. Took up his freedom June 19th, 1615 [Arber, iii. 684]. In 1617 he published an edition of the play called *The Famous Victories of Henry the Fifth*, 4to, which had furnished Shakespeare with material for his plays of *Henry IV* and *Henry V*. The last heard of him is in 1625, when he assigned over several copies to John Beale.

BARLOW (WILLIAM), ? bookseller in London. Admitted to the freedom of the Stationers' Company April 15th, 1583. On April 14th, 1606, William White entered a ballad on the execution of traitors at Worcester, which was to be printed by him for Will. Barlow. Barlow's address has not been found [Arber, ii. 688].

BARNES (JOHN), bookseller in London, 1600–21; (1) Fleet Street at the sign of the Great Turk's Head; (2) Without Newgate by St. Sepulchre's Church,

at the sign of Paris, 1605; (3) The Cardinal's Hat, without Newgate, 1614; (4) Hosier Lane, near Smithfield, 1616 (perhaps the same as No. 2). Son of Joseph Barnes, the University Printer at Oxford. Apprenticed on September 3rd, 1594, to Richard Watkins for seven years [Arber, ii. 195]. On August 6th, 1599, he was transferred to John Wolfe, owing to the death of his first master [Arber, ii. 238]. Barnes was admitted a freeman of the Company of Stationers on the last day of September, 1601 [Arber, ii. 730]. His first book entry, a volume of Essays by Robert Johnson, occurs on October 9th in the same year [Arber, iii. 192]. In 1602 he was allowed to publish Rider's *Dictionary*, but only on condition that it was printed in London and not elsewhere [Arber, iii. 223], but within a month he assigned his right in it to Cuthbert Burby. There is no entry by or for him of any copy between February 23rd, 1603, and June 27th, 1612, and meanwhile he parted with the only two copyrights he possessed. But, unless there is a misprint in the date, his father printed for him in 1605 an edition of John Davies of Hereford's *Microcosmus*, which shows that he had moved into Holborn. He was still there in 1612, when the address appears in an edition of Travers' *Supplication to the Privy Council*. By his father's will proved on January 17th, 1619, he received a legacy of £20 [Gibson, *Oxford Wills*, p. 26] and several copyrights, but these he appears to have assigned over to others almost immediately. The last book entry under his name occurs in the Registers on February 26th, 162$\frac{0}{1}$, when he entered *Merry Jests concerning Popes, Monks and Friars*, and assigned it over to John Wright [Arber, iv. 49]. Another John Barnes took up his freedom as a stationer on June 4th, 1638 [Arber, iii. 688].

BARNES (JOHN), bookbinder in Oxford, 1626–74. Son of Roger Barnes, bookbinder, and nephew of Joseph Barnes, printer. [Gibson, *Oxford Bindings*, pp. 13, 41, 50, 58; *Oxford Wills*, p. 41; Madan, *Early Oxford Press*, p. 277.]

BARNES (JOSEPH), printer to the University, and bookseller in Oxford, 1573–1618; St. Mary's Parish. Admitted a bookseller on September 8th, 1573 [Clark, *Register*, ii. 1. 321]. In 1574 he was occupying two tenements in High Street between Grape Lane (Grove Street) and Schidyard Street (Oriel Street) [*Oriel leases*]. Joseph Barnes was licensed to sell wine from October, 1575, to October, 1596. On August 15th, 1584, the University

lent him £100 with which to start a press, and he was also in that year appointed printer to the University. He lived and printed in a house at the West end of St. Mary's, now St. Mary's Entry [see *Letters from the Bodleian*, ii. 428]. He remained printer to the University until 1617, his press being actively employed during the whole of that time, no less than three hundred books being traced to it. Joseph Barnes died on December 6th, 1618, aged 72, and was buried in St. Mary's. By his will proved on January 17th, 161$\frac{8}{9}$, he left bequests of money to the University Library and also to those of Brasenose and Magdalen [Gibson, *Oxford Wills*, pp. 26–7]. He left a son John, who carried on the business of a bookseller in London between 1600 and 1621. This John Barnes must not be confused with John the son of Roger Barnes, bookbinder of Oxford.

BARNES (RICHARD), bookseller in London, 1631–2. Took up his freedom in the Company of Stationers on February 7th, 1631 [Arber, iii. 686]. He was the publisher of Nicholas Goodman's *Holland's Leaguer* in 1632 [Arber, iv. 270], a copy of which is in the Grenville Library. His address has not been found.

BARNES (ROGER), bookseller in London, 1610–17; (1) In Chancery Lane over against the Rolls; (2) St. Dunstan's Churchyard under the Dial. Son of Ralph Barnes, cordwainer of London. Apprenticed on November 1st, 1601, to John Smethwick for eight years, and took up his freedom December 4th, 1609 [Arber, ii. 258; iii. 683]. Amongst his publications were Silas Jourdan's *Discovery of the Barmudas*, 1610, 4to, Christopher Marlowe's *Troublesome raigne and lamentable death of Edward the Second*, 1612, 4to, and John Stephen's *Satyricall Essayes*, 1615. On April 17th, 1617, he assigned his rights in Marlowe's *Edward II* to Henry Bell [Arber, iii. 607].

BARNES (ROGER), bookseller and bookbinder in Oxford, 1613–31. Brother of Joseph Barnes, University printer. Admitted a bookseller on May 16th, 1617 [Clark, *Register*, ii. 1. 321]. He was also a bookbinder and bound some books for the Bodleian in 1613. He was one of the most skilful of Oxford binders. He and Ralph Beckford, the apprentice of John Barnes, seem to have been the last binders to use the old-fashioned roll. Roger Barnes lived in All Saints' parish. His will was proved on November 30th, 1631. He was not a rich man, as the whole of his effects were valued at a sum under twelve pounds. He left the residue of his goods to his son John, whom he appointed executor, and who must not be confused with John Barnes the bookseller, the son of Joseph Barnes. [Gibson, *Oxford Wills*, pp. 29–30; *Oxford Bindings*, pp. 13, 34, 36, 38, 49–54, 56, 58, 59.]

BARRENGER or BARRINGER (WILLIAM), bookseller in London, 1600–22; near the Great North Door of St. Paul's. Son of Thomas Barrenger of Steventon, co. Bedford, yeoman. Apprentice to Clement Knight, stationer of London, for eight years from Midsummer, 1600 [Arber, ii. 245]. Took up his freedom January 8th, 160$\frac{7}{8}$ [Arber, iii. 683]. Early in 1609, in partnership with Bartholomew Sutton, he published Barnaby Rich's *Short Survey of the Realm of Ireland* [Arber, iii. 403], and amongst his other publications were Thomas Heywood's dramatic history *The Golden Age*, 1611, 4to, and Robert Daborn's tragedy, *A Christian turn'd Turke*, 1612, 4to. The last book entry under his name occurs on September 23rd, 1622 [Arber, iv. 81].

BARRETT (HANNAH), bookseller in London, 1624–6; The King's Head in St. Paul's Churchyard (? R. Whitaker's address). Widow of William Barrett. Associated with Richard Whitaker in the publication of an edition of Francis Bacon's *Essays*, 1625, and other works [Arber, iv. 137]. Her name is not found after April 3rd, 1626, when she assigned over the remainder of her copyrights to John Parker, who appears to have set up in William Barrett's old house, The Three Pigeons [Arber, iv. 157].

BARRETT (WILLIAM), bookseller in London, 1607–24; (1) In St. Paul's Churchyard, at the sign of the Green Dragon, 1608; (2) In St. Paul's Churchyard, at the sign of the Three Pigeons, 1614. Son of Thomas Barrett of Loweth, co. Lincoln, yeoman. Apprenticed to Bonham Norton, stationer of London, for eight years from Christmas, 1597. For receiving this apprentice without presenting him, Bonham Norton was fined 1s. 6d. [Arber, ii. 226, 828.] William Barret took up his freedom on January 31st, 1605 [Arber, iii. 683], and soon afterwards set up in St. Paul's Churchyard. He appears to have been a man of some capital, and during the next seventeen years was associated in the publication of some interesting literature, such as Francis Bacon's *Historie of the raigne of King Henry the Seventh*, 1622, folio, and his *Historia Naturalis*. He shared with

Edward Blount the publication of Coryat's *Crudities*, 1610, the translation of Don Quixote that appeared in 1611, and the second edition of John Florio's translation of Montaigne's *Essayes*, 1613. He was also the publisher of many interesting and notable books of travel. Thus in 1608 he published in a quarto pamphlet of thirty pages a translation from the Dutch of a voyage made by Admiral Cornelis Matelief into the East Indies in May, 1605. In 1610 he entered in the Registers *A True Declaration of the estate of the colony in Virginia* [Arber, iii. 448]. In 1615 he published in folio George Sandys' *Relation of a Journey begun An. Dom. 1610*, which contained descriptions of the Turkish Empire, of Egypt, Palestine and Italy. On February 16th, 1617, William Leake assigned over to William Barrett nineteen copies, including amongst them *Venus and Adonis* and John Lyly's *Euphues* [Arber, iii. 603]. The bulk of these however Barrett made over to John Parker three years later. The last book entry to him is on January 23rd, 162$\frac{3}{4}$, when he entered a "*Life*" of Mary Queen of Scots. He died before November 8th, 1624, when his widow transferred some of his copies to John Parker [Arber, iv. 128]. At one time or another William Barrett was associated with W. Aspley, John Bill, Ed. Blount and Richard Whitaker, and amongst those who printed for him were William Stansby and John Haviland.

BARTELEY, *see* Bartlett.

BARTLETT (JOHN), *see* Plomer, *Dictionary*.

BARTLETT (WILLIAM), bookseller in London, 1578–87. Publisher of ballads and other ephemeral literature [Arber, ii. 334, 464]. On January 21st, 158$\frac{2}{3}$, in company with Ric. Jones, he was committed to prison for printing a "thinge" *of the fall of the galleries at Paris Garden*, without licence [Arber, ii. 853]. His address is unknown.

BASSANDYNE (THOMAS), printer, bookseller, and bookbinder in Edinburgh, 1564–77; The Nether Bow. He is best known by the folio *Bible*, called after his name, which in 1574–5 he undertook, with Alexander Arbuthnet, to print. This *Bible*, the first printed in Scotland, was not completed until after Bassandyne's death, and the titlepage, dated 1579, bears Arbuthnet's name alone, but the *New Testament* title carries Bassandyne's name as printer, and the date 1576. Bassandyne is said have learned his trade abroad and to have worked in Paris and Leyden before commencing

business in Edinburgh. In March, 1564, the confiscated types of John Scot were delivered to Bassandyne by order of the Town Council of Edinburgh, but they were apparently in Scot's hands again by 1567. In 1568 he was ordered to call in copies of *The Fall of the Romane Kirk* and a psalm book, which, it was stated, he had printed without licence; but it seems probable that Bassandyne did not print for himself before 1571–2, and that these books were produced for him by Scot. For a device he adopted Jean Crespin's anchor, with the initials T. B. Only six separate works, including the *Bible*, are known with his imprint, and they bear dates between 1572 and 1578; but as a bookseller he evidently held a large stock, for his inventory [*Bannatyne Miscell.*, ii. 191] enumerates as many as 350 different works. His place of business was in the Nether Bow, on the south side of the gate. Salomon Kerknett [*q.v.*], a compositor, was in his employ, and Robert Lekpreuik, the printer, received from him a half-yearly pension and a legacy. Bassandyne died October 18th, 1577, being survived by his wife Catharine Norwell, who afterwards married Robert Smyth [*q.v.*]. *See also* Arbuthnet (Alexander). [Dickson and Edmond, 273; *D.N.B.*; Aldis, *Scottish Books*, 108; *E.B.S. Papers*, Vol. I, Nos. 15, 17, 22.]

BASSE (ROBERT), bookseller in London, 1615–16; Under St. Botolph's Church. Only known by an edition of Dekker's *Honest Whore*, printed for him by Nicholas Okes in 1615.

BASSOCK or BASSOKE (CLEMENT), stationer at Canterbury, 1571–6. Mentioned in the Subsidy Roll of 13th Elizabeth, as living in the ward of Burgate. His goods were assessed at £14. He is mentioned again in the 1st series of *Canterbury Marriage Licences*, edited by J. M. Cowper, as bondsman to John Yonge of Cranbrooke, on May 11th, 1576. His name does not occur in the Registers of the Stationers' Company.

BASSON (THOMAS), bookseller at Leyden, 1585–1613; "opte breede-straet by de Blauwe steen." In 1586 he sold Whetstone's *Honourable reputation of a soldier* in Dutch and English. He was also the publisher of the Dutch translations of Greene's *Quip for an Upstart Courtier*, 1601 (? second ed.), and of Scot's *Discovery of Witchcraft*, 1609, of which a second edition was issued by his son G. Basson in 1637. He is said to have been an Englishman [Ledeboer, *A.L.*, p. 10].

BATE (HUMPHREY), bookseller in London, 1586–9. Is believed to be identical with the Humphrey Bate who was made free of the Company of Stationers by Master Harrison the Warden, on October 8th, 1579 [Arber, ii. 681]. He was previously a member of the Clothworkers' Company [Arber, ii. 96]. His first book entry occurs on November 10th, 1586 [Arber, ii. 459], his last on September 8th, 1587; but he is found taking apprentices till May 10th, 1589 [Arber, ii. 157].

BATTERSBY (JOHN), patentee, 1597–1619. By letters patent dated April 6th, 1597, John Battersby was appointed Queen's Printer in Latin, Greek and Hebrew for life, in succession to Francis Flower, and was to receive the annual fee of 26s. 8d. At the accession of King James I, although John Battersby was still living, John Norton petitioned the king to be allowed to exercise the office, alleging that Battersby's patent was void in law, and no doubt backing up his petition with a substantial sum of money, obtained a patent on precisely similar terms to that already granted to Battersby, on May 12th [*Patent Roll*, 1 Jas. I, Pt. 2]. This led to extensive litigation and eventually Battersby sold the office to Thomas Adams and Cuthbert Burby, who were secret agents for John Norton, for a sum of £700, of which Norton found £200. It is difficult to understand what actually was Battersby's position after this, as his imprint is found on the fourth edition of John Stockwood's *Disputatiuncularum grammaticalium libellus*, printed in 1619 [B.M., 827. a. 27]. In the documents connected with the law suit, Battersby is described as "a merchant of Plymouth." [*Exchequer K. R. Bills and Answers, London and Midd.*, 1018.]

BATTERSBY (JOHN), Assigns of, 1597–1605. The names of those whom Battersby chose to print for him under his patent have not been ascertained before 1605, when we learn from a law suit that he assigned over his interests for a sum of £700 to Thomas Adams and Cuthbert Burby [*Exchequer K. R. London and Midd.*, 1018].

BAUDOIS (ROBERT DE), bookseller and engraver at Amsterdam, 1608—after 1648. In 1608 an edition of Jakob de Geyn's *Maniement d'Armes*, which is mostly in English, was printed at the Hague with the notice "On les vend aussi a Amsterdam chez Henri Laurens." In some copies a slip is pasted over the letterpress of the title, stating that "They are to bye at Amsterdam by Robert de Baudois" [Sayle, pp. 1429, 1496].

BAUDRY (GUILLAUME), printer at Paris, 1640. He printed in this year J. Fisher's *Treatise of prayer and of the fruits of prayer* [Sayle, p. 1388].

BAYLEY, BAYLY, *see* Bailey.

BAYNES (ROBERT), (?) bookseller in London, 1613; Parish of St. Giles without Cripplegate, Redcross Street. The will of this stationer dated October 1st, 1613, was proved in the Court of the Dean and Chapter of St. Paul's (Book D, fol. 93), on November 12th, 1613. He left everything to his wife Joan Baynes. The will mentions a son Robert, and a brother William, the latter a glover.

BEALE (JOHN), *see* Plomer, *Dictionary*.

BEARKES (RANDALL), bookseller in London, 1602; The White Unicorn in Pope's Head Alley. In Mr. Arber's *Transcript* there appears to be much confusion as to the identity of this bookseller. From an entry in Vol. ii, p. 229, it would appear that he was the son of Randall Bearkes of Apedell Hall, co. Stafford, yeoman, and was apprentice to Ralph Howell, stationer of London, for eight years from September 29th, 1598. This would mean that his time was not up until 1606, but on April 20th, 1602, there is an entry of the admission of a Randall Barker, "by redemption and according to a grant of the Lord Mayor sett down for his freedom xxs." [Arber, ii. 731]. Then we find a Randall Barkes taking an apprentice on June 28th, 1602 [Arber, ii. 264], and a Randall Berkes entering two books in 1602. One of these was Nicholas Breton's *Soul's Harmony*, in the imprint to which his name is spelt Bearkes.

BEAU CHESNE (JEAN DE), (?) printer in London, 1567–1618. An alien of French extraction, who came over to England about 1565, and settled in Blackfriars as a schoolmaster. In 1570 Thomas Vautrollier printed for him *A Booke containing Divers sortes of hands*. In 1594 his name appeared in the imprint of Thomas Timme's *Book containing the true portraiture of the . . . Kings of England* [Hazlitt, H. 124, 608]. This was a series of engraved plates; but it is highly doubtful if Beau Chesne was the printer.

BECKET (JAMES), *see* Plomer, *Dictionary*.

BECKET (LEONARD), bookseller in London, 1608–32; In the Temple, near to the Church. Son of William Beckett of Weddesfield, parish of Wolverhampton, co. Stafford, carpenter. Apprentice to John Hodget, stationer

of London, for eight years from July 25th, 1598 [Arber, ii. 231]. Took up his freedom July 2nd, 1605 [Arber, iii. 683]. His first book entry in the Registers occurs on May 29th, 1609 [Arber, iii. 410], and his last on December 1st, 1623 [Arber, iv. 108]. Mr. Sayle records a copy of W. Crashaw's *Querela* (*Manuale*) as published by him in 1632 [*Early Printed Books*, p. 795]. The date of his death is unknown, but in 1636 his widow had married Nicholas Vavasour, to whom all Leonard Becket's copyrights were transferred on May 18th in that year [Arber, iv. 363].

BECKFORD (RALPH), bookbinder in Oxford, 1630–66; St. Mary's Parish. Son of Ralph Beckford, husbandman, of Long Witnam [Wittenham], co. Berks; was apprentice to John Barnes, bookbinder [Clark, *Register*, ii. 1. 343]. During 1646–7 he bound books for the University [Wood's *Life and Times*, iv. pp. 199, 200, 209, 211]. He was binder to the Bodleian in 1650–2—1660–1. He died in 1666 [Gibson, *Oxford Bindings*, 13, 38, 41, 50; *Oxford Wills*, 41; *Notable Bodleian Bindings*, 9, 10].

BEE (CORNELIUS), *see* Plomer, *Dictionary*.

BEESTON (HUGH), bookseller in London, 1633–4; Near the Castle in Cornhill. Took up his freedom December 5th, 1631 [Arber, iii. 687]. Publisher of John Ford's plays, *The Broken Heart*, 1633, *Love's Sacrifice*, 1633, *The Chronicle Historie of Perkin Warbeck*, 1634.

BELE (SAMPSON), bookbinder in Oxford, 1624–5. *See* Gibson, *Oxford Bindings*, p. 50.

BELL (HENRY), bookseller in London, 1606–38; (1) Near the Cross Keys, Holborn Hill, 1608; (2) Without Bishopsgate, 1616–18; (3) The Sun in Bethlem, 1620; (4) At the Lame Hospital Gate in Smithfield, 1622; (5) In Eliot's Court, Old Bailey, 1631. Son of Francis Bell of Barney Castle, co. York, yeoman. Apprentice to Abel Jeffes, stationer of London, for eight years from Christmas, 1594. On June 6th, 1597, he was transferred to Master Robinson for the remainder of his term; but was presented for his freedom by Richard Bradock on January 18th, 1602 [Arber, ii. 199, 217, 231]. This is explained by the fact that Bradock had married the widow of Robert Robinson, and this presentation fixes the date of Robinson's death as after 1597 and before 1602 [Arber, iii. 702]. Henry Bell

is first found taking apprentices in 1604. He appears to have been in partnership with Moses Bell, possibly a brother, their first joint entry occurring on March 29th, 1606 [Arber, iii. 317]; but he also appears to have published largely on his own account. Copyrights were transferred to him by Elizabeth Cliffe, Roger Barnes, and Ralph Blower. Henry and Moses Bell transferred their copyrights to John Haviland and John Wright on September 4th, 1638 [Arber, iv. 434]. Nothing more is heard of Henry Bell, who presumably died about this time. He used as a device a punning allusion to his name, "Hen, Rye and Bell."

BELL (MOSES), *see* Plomer, *Dictionary*.

BELLAMY (JOHN), *see* Plomer, *Dictionary*.

BELLERUS, or BEELAERT (BALTHAZAR), printer at Douai, 1590–? —; At the Golden Compass. He was born in 1564, the son of John Bellerus, printer at Antwerp, and may have printed there before his removal to Douai. Books bearing his imprint appeared at Douai in an unbroken series from 1590 to 1684, and we must suppose them to have been the work of two or perhaps three printers of the same name. One of these in 1630 printed *Certain Instructions and Motives profitable to increase Christian Faith*, by R. C. [Duthillœul, p. 124], and in 1632 *The Testament of William Bell . . .* by Francis Bell [Hazlitt, II. 45]. [Olthoff, p. 6.]

BELLERUS, or BEELAERT (JOANNES), bookseller at Antwerp, ? 1553–1595, and (?) at Douai, 1575. At Antwerp his address was "In de Cammerstraete, In den Salm"; from 1559, in the same street "In den Valck"; and, in 1564, "In den gulden Arent." He was born at Luik in 1526, became a citizen of Antwerp in 1553, and was admitted to the St-Lucasgild as "vrijmeester boekverkooper" in 1559. In 1575 the *Notable Discourse who are the right Ministers* of Jean d'Albin de Valsergues, called de Seres, was printed at Douai "Per Iohannem Bellerum" [Hazlitt, VII. 208; B.M. p. 27], but nothing seems to be known of his having an establishment there, and he does not appear in Duthillœul's *Bibl. Douaisienne*. He died in 1595. A bookseller of the same name was associated with S. Fierabent at Frankfurt in 1572 [*cf.* Heitz, *Frankfurter Druckerzeichen*, p. x, No. 51]. [Olthoff, pp. 5–6.]

BENSON (JOHN), *see* Plomer, *Dictionary*.

BENSON (PETER), bookseller in Exeter, 1569–83; Parish of St. Keriam. Apprentice to Luke Harrison, stationer of London, for nine years, and admitted to the freedom of the Company of Stationers on February 18th, 1568 [Arber, i. 99, 366]. Between 1568 and 1570 he published the *Injunctions* of the Bishop of Meath (Hugh Brady), and a *Preservative against the Pestilence* [Arber, i. 388, 412]. On one occasion he was fined for keeping his shop open on St. Andrew's Day. From his will, dated June 3rd, 1583, we learn that he was then living in Exeter. He died before August 2nd in that year and was buried in the parish church of St. George in that city. He left a widow Agnes, and a son Peter. [P.C.C., 40, Rowe.] In the Subsidy Roll for Exeter of 18th Eliz. [*i.e.*, 1575–6] he is returned amongst the inhabitants of the parish of St. Keriam, his goods being valued at £3 [P.R.O. *Lay Subsidy Roll*, $\frac{100}{380}$].

BESONGE (JACQUES), printer at Rouen, 1626; dwelling within the Court of the Palace. In this year his imprint and address appear in *The Articles which were Propounded to the Jesuits* [B.M. 4629. bb. 12, and Sayle, p. 899, no. 4188], but Mr. Sayle attributes this work to B. Alsop and T. Fawcet on the ground of an initial letter. The book certainly has the appearance of English printing.

BEST (RICHARD), *see* Plomer, *Dictionary*.

BEWLEY (W.), (?) bookseller, 1595, *see* Herbert, p. 1728.

BILL (JOHN), King's Printer and bookseller in London, 1604–30; Northumberland House, St. Martin's Lane, Aldersgate Street, and Hunsdon House, Blackfriars. Son of Walter Bill of Wenlock, co. Shropshire. Probably through the influence of the Nortons, also natives of Shropshire, he was sent to London and apprenticed to John Norton, the printer, from the Feast of St. James the Apostle [*i.e.*, July 25th], 1592, and took up his freedom in 1601. As John Norton was Sir Thomas Bodley's stationer, it was presumably on Norton's suggestion that John Bill was selected by the founder of the Bodleian to travel abroad and buy books for the library on commission. At the same time it speaks highly for his own ability that at the outset of his career he should have been chosen as the best man for such an undertaking. It is uncertain at exactly what period he was abroad, but it was probably between 1596 and 1602 or 1603. In one of his letters Sir Thomas Bodley writes as follows: "You need make no doubt, but Jo.

Bill hath gotten everywhere, what the place would afford, for his commission was large, his leisure very good, and his payment sure at home." In another he speaks of Bill as having visited the chief cities in Italy, and as having bought books to the value of upwards of four hundred pounds [*Reliq. Bodl.*, p. 66 *et seq.*]. After his return home he set up as a bookseller in London, where among his customers was Isaac Casaubon [Pattison's *Casaubon*, 1875, pp. 406, 433–4]. He had a close and intimate friendship with both John Norton and Bonham Norton; in fact there is very little doubt that he managed the printing business of the former during the later years of his life. There is no doubt also that these three men, John Norton, Bonham Norton and John Bill, advanced the money necessary to enable Robert Barker, the King's Printer, to carry through what is known as the Authorized version of the Bible, and in return for this help some sort of compact was entered into between the parties, by which John Bill and Bonham Norton became shareholders in the King's Printing House. A bitter family quarrel subsequently broke out between Bonham Norton and Robert Barker, and as a result, Robert Barker brought an action in the Court of Chancery against both John Bill and Bonham Norton, which was the forerunner of a long and costly series of law suits. By a decree of May 7th, 1619, the Court decided that John Bill was a bona-fide purchaser of his share and was entitled to enjoy it. Consequently he continued to be King's Printer for the remainder of his life. The imprints may be arranged as follows: (1) Robert Barker alone down to July, 1617; (2) Bonham Norton and John Bill from July, 1617, to May 7th, 1619; (3) Robert Barker and John Bill from May 8th, 1619, to January, $162\frac{0}{1}$; (4) Bonham Norton and John Bill from January, $162\frac{0}{1}$, to October 21st, 1629; (5) Robert Barker and John Bill from October 20th, 1629, till John Bill's death on May 5th, 1630. Further evidence that John Bill was carrying on the business of a bookseller at this time is found in the *Hist. MSS. Comm., 6th Report*, where amongst the Manuscripts of the Duke of Northumberland is a list of fifty-three books, mostly foreign works, purchased from John Bill. He also became an extensive publisher of books from 1604 onwards. John Bill regularly visited Frankfort Book Fair and amongst the Domestic State Papers is an interesting letter from him, to Dr. Widemann of Augsburg, dated June 22nd, 1619, relating to some books that Widemann had offered to King James, and which John Bill desired should be sent to the next

Frankfort Fair for his inspection [*Library*, March, 1900, p. 175]. For some years John Bill issued an edition of the Frankfort catalogue for circulation in England, and all the issues from 1622 to 1626 contained a special appendix of *Books Printed in English* [*ibid.*]. John Bill made his will on April 24th, 1630, and died shortly afterwards. He bequeathed a sum of £15 to the poor of his native place, and a sum of £10 to pensioners of the Company of Stationers, as well as two pieces of plate valued at £20, and a sum of £5 for a dinner to the Livery on the day of his burial. To Bonham Norton and Robert Barker he left £5 apiece, and to his wife Jane Bill an annuity of £300 to be paid out of the profits of his share in the King's Printing House, and all those his parts of the houses in Blackfriars and St. Andrew's in the Wardrobe. He left three sons, John, Charles, and Henry, the first of whom succeeded to his father's share in the King's Printing House. John Bill nominated as his executors the Rev. John Mountford, William Austin, and Martin Lucas, gent. [Plomer, *Wills*, pp. 51–54].

BILLINGSLEY (RICHARD), bookbinder in Oxford, 1620–4. Bound books for the Bodleian between these dates [Gibson, *Oxford Bindings*, 13, 37, 49, 51, 59].

BILLINGSLEY (ROBERT), bookseller and bookbinder in Oxford, 1601–6. Admitted a bookseller of the University in 1601 [Clark, *Register*, ii. 1. 398, 342]. Administration of his effects with an inventory was exhibited on November 17th, 1606. His widow Anne afterwards married Nicholas Smith [Gibson, *Oxford Wills*, p. 20].

BING (ISAAC), bookseller in London, 1572–1604; ? Christchurch, Newgate Street. Son of Thomas Byng, late of Canterbury, yeoman. Apprenticed to Henry Denham, stationer of London, for seven years from Christmas, 1565 [Arber, i. 287]. The date at which he took up his freedom is unrecorded, but he was received into the Livery of the Company of Stationers during the year ending on July 10th, 1582. He served as Warden in the years 1594–5, 1595–6, and 1598–9, and was Master of the Company in 1603–4, but died during his year of office [Arber, i. 571, 577; ii. 722, 735]. The only book on which his name has been found as publisher is Anthony Fletcher's *Similes*, published without date, but about the year 1595. By his will, which was proved in the Court of the Dean

and Chapter of St. Paul's on March 5th, $160\frac{3}{4}$, he left the residue of his estate to his wife Alice, who had previously been the wife of two other stationers, Richard Waterson and Francis Coldock [Dean and Chapter of St. Paul's, Book C, fol. 197; Plomer, *Wills*, pp. 37–9].

BIRCH (PHILIP), bookseller in London, 1618–23; (1) At the Guildhall, 1618; (2) The Bible, near Guildhall-gate, 1619. Chiefly a publisher of ballads and broadsides. His first book entry occurs in the Registers on June 10th, 1619 [Arber, iii. 650]. He also held a share with Anne Helme and Thomas Langley in Samuel Rowlands' *Paire of Spy Knaves*, 1619, and Gervase Markham's *Art of Fowling*, 1620 [Arber, iii. 660, 674]. On February 7th, 1623, he assigned his copyrights to Robert Bird [Arber, iv. 91].

BIRCKMAN (ARNOLD), printer at Cologne. From 1561 to 1568, books in English appeared with this imprint, namely, J. Hollybush's translation of Braunschweig's *Homish Apothecary*, 1561, The Second Part of W. Turner's *Herbal*, 1562, and *The First and Second Parts* of the same, 1568. The imprint may mean that they are the work of the heirs of the Arnold Birckman who died in 1542, or that they are from the press of a later person of the same name. The history of the whole family is confused [*see* Duff, *Century*; Heitz and Zaretzky, *Die Kölner Büchermarken*, xxii, and Worman, *Alien Members*]. The "Brickmans" are mentioned as trading in books in England in 1579 [*Acts of the Privy Council, New Ser.*, xi. 144], and from the *Returns of Aliens* cited by Worman it appears that the firm had an agent or a shop in London until 1582 at least.

BIRD (JOHN), printer, 1601. Arrested in that year on his way to Ireland and described as "practized in the printing and publishing of certaine seditious bookes" [*Acts of the Privy Council, New Ser.*, xxxii. 85].

BIRD (ROBERT), bookseller in London, 1621–38; The Bible, St. Lawrence Lane, Cheapside. Took up his freedom in the Company of Stationers on June 22nd, 1621 [Arber, iii. 685]. Dealt chiefly in theological literature. On February 7th, 1623, Philip Birch assigned over to him his copyrights. The last heard of him is on August 3rd, 1638, when he made an assignment of his rights in *The English Farrier* to John Beale [Arber, iv. 427]. He died in April, 1641.

BISHOP (EDWARD), bookseller in London, 1604–10; The Brazen Serpent, St. Paul's Churchyard. Son of Edward Bishop of Neend Savage, co. Salop, yeoman. Apprentice to his kinsman, George Bishop, stationer of London, for nine years from Midsummer, 1591 [Arber, ii. 174]. Dealt chiefly in theological books, but was associated with Cuthbert Burby in publishing a work called *The English Schoolmaster* [Arber, iii. 285], and shared with Thomas Adams a third part in Camden's *Britannia*, 1610 [Arber, iii. 435]. In 1612 he published the ninth edition of Mathew Virel's *Treatise concerning the principal grounds of the Christian Religion* [B.M. 3559. a. 30]. Cuthbert Burby left him a legacy of five pounds, and appointed him one of the overseers of his will, and he was also mentioned in the will of George Bishop [Plomer, *Wills*, pp. 41, 43].

BISHOP (GEORGE), bookseller and printer in London, 1562–1611; The Bell, St. Paul's Churchyard. George Bishop, whose birthplace is unknown, but who is believed to have been a native of Shropshire, was one of Robert Toye's apprentices and was presented on October 13th, 1556, but he had probably served some years of his term before the entry was made, as he took up his freedom on April 16th, 1562 [Arber, i. 39, 187]. He began taking apprentices in 1566, although his first book entry does not occur before the year 1569–70. At this time he appears to have been in partnership with Lucas Harrison. Bishop married Mary, the eldest daughter of John Cawood. He rose to the highest positions in the Company of Stationers, being Warden in the years 1577–8 and 1583–4, and Master of the Company for no fewer than five terms, viz., in 1589–90, 1592–3, 1599–1600, 1602–3, and 1607–8. He was also elected an alderman of the City of London. In 1588, in company with Ralph Newberry, he was appointed by Christopher Barker one of his deputies. He issued a large number of books and held shares in such ventures as Holinshed's *Chronicles* and Hakluyt's *Voyages*. Bishop died early in January, $161\frac{0}{1}$, his will being proved on the 28th of that month. From this we learn that his only son John had died whilst a student at Christ Church College, Oxford. Bishop left a bequest of sixty pounds a year to three scholars in divinity of that college. He also left a sum of money to be lent to young men free of the Company and ten pounds a year to preachers at Paul's Cross; and his premises in St. Paul's Churchyard to his cousin, Thomas Adams, stationer, who succeeded to the business. To William

Apsley, a former apprentice, he bequeathed five pounds and a release from all debts, while to two other apprentices, Joseph Browne and William Arundell, he left respectively five pounds and forty shillings. The overseers of his will were John Highlord, John Norton and Thomas Adams. His widow transferred the copyrights to Thomas Adams on March 14th, 1611 [Arber, iii. 453; Plomer, *Wills*, pp. 43, 44]. She died in August or September, 1613, and desired to be buried beside her husband in the church of St. Faith. She left the residue of her estate to Gabriel Cawood, her godson, the son of her brother Gabriel, and appointed William Aspley his guardian and overseer of her will [P.C.C., 78, Capell].

BISHOP (RICHARD), *see* Plomer, *Dictionary*.

BLACKMAN (WILLIAM), bookseller in London, 1596–8; Near the Great North Door of St. Paul's Church. Son of William Blackman, late of Ensam or Eynsham, co. Oxford, yeoman. Apprenticed to Thomas Chard, stationer of London, for seven years from July 14th, 1589. Made free of the Company July 24th, 1596 [Arber, ii. 160, 717]. On January 29th, 1597, he entered in the Registers *A tragical discourse of Africa and Mensola*, a copy of which is described by Hazlitt [H. 234], and the last heard of him is on March 6th, 1598, when he entered a book intituled *The Counsellour* [Arber, iii. 105].

BLACKMORE (EDWARD), *see* Plomer, *Dictionary*.

BLACKWALL (GEORGE), bookseller in London, 1623–36; (?) Cateaton Street over against Guildhall Gate. Son of William Blackwall, stationer (1586–1618). Took up his freedom July 22nd, 1623. Between 1626 and 1636 he entered several works in the Registers, some of which had belonged to his father, but no book bearing his name in the imprint has been found [Arber, iv. 159, 349, 361].

BLACKWALL (WILLIAM), bookseller in London, 1586–1618; Cateaton Street, over against Guildhall Gate. Son of George Blackwall of Lytton, co. Derby, husbandman. Apprenticed to Thomas Turnor, stationer of London, for eight years from June 24th, 1578, and admitted a freeman on September 5th, 1586 [Arber, ii. 89, 698]. William Blackwall dealt largely in ballad literature and was fined on several occasions for selling ballads without license and for keeping apprentices not presented.

Amongst his other publications may be noticed one of the old romances, *The Pleasant Historie of Blaunchardine*, which he entered on May 20th, 1595 [Arber, ii. 298]. Hazlitt states that only one imperfect copy of this is known to exist, and that is in the public library at Hamburg. Blackwall also published a play called *The Warres of Cyrus King of Persia*, 1594, two copies of which are in the British Museum. He was also associated with George Shaw and George Vincent in the publication of popular literature such as, *Two Notorious Murders*, 1595, 4to, and *Strange Fearful and true newes which happened at Carlstadt in . . . Croatia*, 1605, 4to. The last entry to him in the Registers is *Newes from Spain*, entered on March 1st, $161\frac{7}{8}$ [Arber, iii. 620]. He left a son George, who succeeded to the business. In the will of Thomas Bright, stationer, proved in the Court of the Dean and Chapter of St. Paul's on October 31st, 1588, occurs this entry: "Due unto William Blakewell one new Bible, paying 4sh. To receive of him 15d. for binding two books."

BLACKWELL (GEORGE), (?) bookseller in London, 1591. Son of Henry Blackwell, of Mansfield in Sherwood, co. Notts, saddler. Apprenticed to Benjamin Segar, stationer of London, for eight years from August 24th, 1582. Made free of the Company of Stationers May 3rd, 1591 [Arber, ii. 114, 709]. There was also a George Blackwall [*q.v.*], and the subsequent entries given by Mr. Arber relate to him and not to this man.

BLADEN (WILLIAM), *see* Plomer, *Dictionary*.

BLAEU, or BLAEUW (WILLIAM JANSZOON), printer at Amsterdam, ?1612–38; Upon the Water, by the Old Bridge, at the sign of the Golden Sun-dial. Blaeu, the well-known geographer, was born at Amsterdam in 1571. In or before 1612 he established a press and produced a number of works on navigation and geography, among which were at least two in English. The first of these, *The Light of Navigation*, 1612, bears in the imprint the name William Johnson [B.M. p. 233], as does another edition of the same work issued in 1622 [Hazlitt, IV. 55]. In 1625 he published *The Sea Mirror containing . . . the art of navigation*, translated from the Dutch by Richard Hynmers [B.M.], of which there was a second edition in 1635 [Hazlitt, IV. 10–11]: in the imprint of this work he used the name Blaeuw. After his death in 1638, the press was carried on by his son John, who seems to have produced nothing in English. [*Nouv. Biog. Générale.*]

BLAGEART or BLANGEART (MISTRESS), printer at Paris, 1636–7. This person, who may possibly have been a daughter of Heureux Blancvillain and the wife of Jérome Blageart, bookseller "reçu en 1619" [Renouard, p. 32], printed in 1636 a translation of the *De Imitatione Christi* by F.B. [B.M. p. 757; Hazlitt, IV. 42], and in 1637 Saint Francis de Sales' *Introduction to a Devout Life*, the imprint of which has "Mistrise Blangeart" [B.M. p. 653; Sayle, p. 1388]. Mr. Sayle also attributes to her Sir T. Matthew's translation of the *Confessions* of St. Augustine "Printed at Paris" in 1638, which has the same initials and ornaments [B.M. p. 62; Sayle, u.s.]. She perhaps continued to print until 1653, when there appeared a translation of the Sermons of Thomas à Kempis *Of the Incarnation and Passion*, "Printed at Paris By Mrs Blageart" [Hazlitt, VII. 159].

BLAIKLOCK (LAWRENCE), *see* Plomer, *Dictionary*.

BLAINCHER (WILLIAM), (?) bookseller in London, 1613; In Fleet Lane at the sign of the Printer's Press. Only known from the imprint to a quarto entitled *Of the Most auspicious Marriage Betwixt . . . Frederick Count Palatine of Rheine . . . and . . . the Ladie Elizabeth . . . sole daughter to . . . James King of great Brittaine, &c.*, 1613 [B.M. 1070. l. 10. (3)].

BLEWET, *see* Bluett (Henry).

BLOND (JOHN LE), (?) bookbinder in London, 1564–6. A person of this name was admitted a Brother of the Stationers' Company on November 21st, 1564, paying 2s. 6d. as a fee. Again in 1566 the Wardens' accounts record the payment by John Blond of 4d. for his order when he was "hyred with Lesyng for a quarter of a yere." [Arber, i. 279, 318.] It seems probable that he was some relation to Nicholas Blond, but nothing further appears to be known about him.

BLOND (MANASSES), bookbinder in London, 1595–7. Son of Nicholas Blond or Le Blond, bookbinder. Apprenticed to Richard Watkins in 1577; but allowed to serve his father for six years [Arber, ii. 72]. In 1595 Manasses Blond had to get Isaac Sheppard bound to Isaac Bing because he himself was not free of the Company [Arber, i. 200]. In the Registers of the Company under date April 18th, 1597, is the following entry: "Thomas Ensor, William Houghton, Richard Mabell, John

Oswalde. These fowre have yeilded their free consents for the admission of Manasses Bloome as a brother in thart of bookebyndinge, and are content that he should have his freedom."

BLOND (NICHOLAS), *see* Duff, *Century*—Le Blonde.

BLOOM (JACOB), *see* Plomer, *Dictionary*.

BLORE, *see* Blower.

BLOUNT (EDWARD), bookseller in London, 1594–1632; (1) Over against the Great North Door of St. Paul's; (2) The Black Bear, St. Paul's Churchyard. Son of Ralph Blount, merchant tailor of London. Born in London in 1564. Apprentice to William Ponsonby for ten years from June 24th, 1578, and admitted to the freedom of the Company of Stationers on June 25th, 1588. First book entry May 25th, 1594. Blount became one of the most enterprising of the booksellers of his day. He was a friend of Christopher Marlowe, and published several of his books. In 1603 he published the first edition of Florio's translation of Montaigne's *Essays*. In 1608 when he moved to the Black Bear he was joined by William Barrett, and amongst their notable undertakings was the second edition of the same work. Blount was also an extensive publisher of dramatic literature and in conjunction with Isaac Jaggard, William Jaggard, John Smethwicke and William Aspley issued the First Folio of Shakespeare's works in 1623. Toby Cooke, stationer, at his death left Blount a bequest of £20, and he was witness or executor to the wills of several other stationers. The last book entry by him in the Registers was on January 17th, $163\frac{1}{2}$, and from a law suit in the Court of Requests it appears that he died in October, 1632. On October 3rd, 1636, his widow assigned the remainder of his copyrights to Andrew Crooke. ["An Elizabethan Bookseller" by Sidney Lee, in *Bibliographica*, vol. i., pp. 474–98.]

BLOWER or BLORE (RALPH), printer in London, 1595–1618; Near the Middle Temple Gate, Fleet Street. Son of William Blowre of Worthen, co. Salop, husbandman. Apprentice to Richard Tottell for seven years from October 1st, 1587, and took up his freedom on October 3rd, 1594 [Arber, ii. 152, 715]. He would appear to have been originally a bookseller, but in 1600 he printed for Isaac Jaggard a pamphlet of six leaves concerning Sir Anthony Shirley's *Voiage*. On May 9th, 1615, he was returned as having one press [Arber, iii. 699]. His last entry in the Registers was on March 14th, 161$\frac{7}{8}$, and on June 22nd, 1626, his widow made over to William Jones her estate in his copyrights [Arber, iv. 161].

BLUETT, or BLEWET (HENRY), bookseller and bookbinder in Oxford, 1606–33. Admitted tavern-keeper June 18th, 1606 [Clark, *Register*, ii. 1. 327], and bookseller in December, 1610, in Saint Mary's parish. He bound books for the Bodleian from 1617 to 1633. He married Elizabeth Devonshire on February 27th, 160$\frac{5}{6}$ [St. Mary's *Register*]. His will was proved on January 3rd, 163$\frac{3}{4}$. He left no son; the residue of his goods he left to his wife Elizabeth. An inventory of his goods, consisting chiefly of his binding implements and the lease of his house, amounted to £72 10s. 4d. [Gibson, *Oxford Wills*, p. 31].

BLUNDEN (HUMPHREY), *see* Plomer, *Dictionary*.

BODELEIGH (JOHN), patentee for Bibles, 1561; *see* Arber, ii. 63.

BOGARD (JEAN), printer at Louvain, 1564–7, and at Douai, 1574–? 1626. At Louvain, at the Golden Bible, he printed in 1564 Harding's *Answer to Jewel's Challenge*, in 1566 J. Martiall's *Reply to Calfhill*, and in 1567 S. Hosius' *Of the express word of God* [Herbert, pp. 1608, 1619, 1621]. In 1566 he also printed Sir T. More's *Latina Opera*. Duthillœul enumerates 156 books printed by him at Douai, where he used the same sign as at Louvain, but nothing in English. He, however, printed Latin works by R. Buchanan, J. Cheyne, and E. Rishton. Duthillœul describes him as printing until 1634, but as the last dated work in his list is 1626, and we find a Pierre Bogard printing at the same sign in 1628 [W. Drury's *Dramatica Poemata*], this may be an error. The fact that one of his books [Duth., 177] was reprinted by B. Bellerus in 1629 and 1630 also suggests that he was not in business at these dates [Duthillœul, pp. 16–66, 403–4, 457–8].

BOGARD (MARTIN), printer in Douai, 1630–5; At the sign of Paris, or "aux Parisiens." He used the monogram of the Jesuits. In 1630 he printed *The Reply of the Cardinal of Perron to the King of Great Britain* [B.M. p. 455; Hazlitt, VII. 119], and in 1635 Luke Wadding's *History of St. Clare*, and A. Montague's translation of Bonaventura's *Life of St. Francis* [Hazlitt, IV. 11]. [Duthillœul, pp. 220–1, 410.]

BOLER (ANNE), bookseller in London, 1635–7; The Marigold in St. Paul's Churchyard. Widow of James Boler. On September 7th, 1638, the Company of Stationers entered as trustees for James Boler and Thomas Boler, the copyrights of James Boler and Anne his wife deceased [Arber, iv. 436]. With one or two exceptions these are all theological works.

BOLER (JAMES), bookseller in London, 1626–35; (1) The Flower de Luce, St. Paul's Churchyard; (2) The Marigold, St. Paul's Churchyard. Took up his freedom in the Stationers' Company on March 1st, 161$\frac{2}{3}$ [Arber, iii. 684]. At the time of making his first book entry on September 13th, 1626, he appears to have been associated with Robert Milborne. On June 1st, 1629, the widow of Cantrell Legge of Cambridge assigned over to him all her copyrights consisting wholly of works of divinity [Arber, iv. 212]. His last book entry occurs on July 31st, 1635, and he died before the end of the year: his widow Anne carried on the business for a short time [Arber, iv. 351, 435].

BOLLIFANT, alias CARPENTER (EDMUND), printer in London, 1584–1602; Eliot's Court, Little Old Bailey. Apprentice to Henry Denham, printer, and made free by him on April 10th, 1583, being entered in the Registers as "Bollifant alias Carpinter" [Arber, ii. 688]. He then appears to have joined the syndicate who were running the printing house in Eliot's Court, viz., John Jackson, draper, Ninian Newton and Arnold Hatfield. In consequence of an act of piracy by Joseph Barnes of Oxford, Jackson and Bollifant retaliated by printing, in 1586, Bishop Bilson's *True Difference between Christian Subjection and Unchristian Rebellion*, which was Barnes' copyright. For this their printing house was entered, their tools taken away and Edmund Bollifant was committed to prison [*Dom. S.P. Eliz.*, vol. 185. 73; Arber, ii. 794]. Again in 1595 an entry in the accounts of the Company records the seizure of a forme and certain sheets of a "Cato," which was [? R.] Robinson's copyright. For this offence Bollifant was fined 20s. and committed to prison [Arber, i. 578, 581; ii. 824]. Jackson and Newton appear to have died or dropped out of the concern before 1596, after which date the names of Bollifant and Hatfield are found alone. Bollifant died before May 3rd, 1602, when his apprentice was transferred to Richard Bradocke. His place in the firm was taken by Melchisidec Bradwood.

BOLT (SAMUEL), bookbinder in Oxford, 1631–42. Mentioned in the will of Hugh Jones, printer, who bequeathed a sum of three pounds to "Judith the daughter of Samuel Bolt bookbinder in Oxon," and to Samuel Bolt himself a copy of Byfield's "Treatises" [Gibson, *Oxford Wills*, pp. 33–5].

BOLTON, or BOULTON (RICHARD), bookseller in London, 1612–15. Took up his freedom on January 20th, 161$\frac{1}{2}$ [Arber, iii. 683]. Entered a sermon in the Registers on February 12th, 161$\frac{4}{5}$ [Arber, iii. 563]. He was perhaps a son of Robert Bolton (1598–1610).

BOLTON, or BOULTON (ROBERT), bookseller in London, 1598–1610; (1) In Smithfield, near Long Lane End, 1598; (2) Chancery Lane End, near Holborn, 1604. Son of Humfrey Bolton of Dubridge, co. Derby, husbandman. Apprentice to Thomas Dawson, stationer, for eight years from July 25th, 1576 [Arber, ii. 67]. Took up his freedom August 17th, 1584 [Arber, ii. 692]. His first book entry in the Registers does not occur before April 11th, 1598, and was qualified with the condition that he was not to print the book until he got better authority [Arber, iii. 110]. As his next entry is not until five years later [Arber, iii. 265], and no book has been found with his name earlier than 1604, it may be assumed that his first attempt as a publisher was not successful. Amongst his publications was John Reynolds' *Dolarnys Primrose; or the first part of the Passionate Hermit*, 1606. His last entry in the Registers occurs on November 24th, 1610, when in company with William White he entered John Jackson's *The soule is immortall.*

BONHAM (WILLIAM), *see* Duff, *Century*.

BONION (RICHARD), bookseller in London, 1607–11; (1) The Spread Eagle near the great North Door of St. Paul's Church, 1607–10; (2) The Red Lion upon London Bridge, 1609; (3) At his shop in St. Paul's Churchyard, at the sign of the Floure de Luce and Crown, 1611. Son of Richard Bonyon, late of Hayes, co. Middlesex. Apprenticed to Richard Watkins for eight years from Christmas, 1598. Watkins dying in the following year, Bonyon's indentures were cancelled and he transferred his services to Simon Waterson, for eight years and a half, from Midsummer, 1599 [Arber, ii. 232, 239]. He took up his freedom on August 6th, 1607 [Arber, iii. 683]. Bonion's chief claim to remembrance is that in company

with H. Walley he was the publisher of the first quarto of Shakespeare's *Troilus and Cressida* in 1609. The last entry under his name in the Registers is on February 19th, 161$\frac{0}{1}$ [Arber, iii. 453].

BONNER, *see* Bover.

BOSCARD (CHARLES), printer at Douai, 1596–1610, and at St. Omer, 1610–19. He was a son of Jacques Boscard; in 1592 he established a press at the "Missel d'or, rue des Ecoles, vis-à-vis le Public." He used the device of Loys de Winde: *Opera et numine*. At Douai he printed R. White's *Historiae Britanniae*, books vi.–xi., 1598–1607. At St. Omer, where he used the sign "au nom de Iesus," he printed in 1614 *Edward Gennings Priest his life and death* [Herbert, p. 1717, and B.M.]. After his death in 1619 his widow continued to print, at the same sign, until 1652. [Duthillœul, pp. 158–63, 407.]

BOSTOCK (ROBERT), *see* Plomer, *Dictionary*.

BOULENGER (JEAN), printer at Rouen, 1630. In that year he printed Nicholas Smith's *Modest Discussion of some points taught by Doctor Kellison* [Hazlitt, I. 391].

BOULENGER (PAUL), (?) printer in London, 1615; In the Blackfriars. His only known work is the following: *The picture of the unfortunate gentleman, Sir Gervis Elvies, Knight, late Leifenant of his Majesties Tower of London. Printed at London in the Black-Friers by Paul Boulenger*, 1615 [Lemon, *Cat. of Broadsides of Soc. of Antiquaries*, pp. 45–6]. A sheet with cut and verses below. The imprint is perhaps fictitious. "Elvies" is usually written "Helwys."

BOULTER (JOHN), printer of Catholic books, ? 1600. Servant to John Danter [Arber, ii. 265, 734]. He assisted William Wrench in printing Catholic books, for which he was arrested, but a pardon was obtained for him by Richard Bancroft. [*Library*, April, 1907, pp. 174–5.]

BOULTON, *see* Bolton.

BOURNE (JOANE), (?) printer in London, 1593–6. Widow of Robert Bourne. On June 11th, 1593, Robert Weekes' apprentice was transferred to her to serve the remainder of his time [Arber, ii. 186]. On August

27th, 1596, she consented that a book called *A shorte summe of the whole catechism* should remain to Thomas Gosson and William Blackwall [Arber, ii. 603].

BOURNE (NICHOLAS), *see* Plomer, *Dictionary*.

BOURNE (ROBERT), printer in London, 1586–93. In the year 1586, Robert Bourne shared the ownership of a printing press with Henry Jefferson and Laurence Tuck. This press was seized by the Company and defaced for printing Grammars contrary to the Decree of the Star Chamber, and the parties were disabled from ever keeping a printing press of their own, or from printing otherwise than as journeymen [Records of the Company of Stationers]. In relation to this seizure there is an entry in the Warden's accounts for the year ending July 10th, 1587, showing that Bourne was paid 20s. "for his printinge stuffe defaced, which was missing" [Arber, i. 520]. In spite of his suspension, Bourne was printing in 1592, when in company with John Porter he printed W. Perkins' *Exposition of the Lord's Prayer*, and in Peterborough Minster library there was formerly a pamphlet entitled *Tell-Trothes New-yeares Gift* which had the imprint "London, Imprinted by Robert Bourne, 1593." His address has not been found. It may have been that of John Porter.

BOURNE or BORNE (THOMAS), bookseller in London; In Bethlehem, 1628. Took up his freedom on January 15th, $162\frac{2}{3}$ [Arber, iii. 685]. Mentioned in a list of second-hand booksellers who, in 1628, were ordered to submit a catalogue of their books to the Archbishop of Canterbury [*Dom. S. Papers, Chas. I*, vol. 117 (9)].

BOUWENSZOON (JAN), *see* Jacobszoon.

BOVER, BOVIER, or BONNER (FRANCIS), bookseller in London, 1583–1618; Blackfriars. In the *Returns of Aliens*, edited by Messrs. Kirk for the Huguenot Society 1900, Part ii. 356, this bookseller is described as a bachelor, born in Savoy. He is mentioned as executor in the will of Thomas Vautrollier, 1587 [Plomer, *Wills*, p. 27], and in the will of Ascanius de Renialme in 1600, as his "brother in law," and is further mentioned in that will as having sold to Renialme the house adjoining that in which he dwelt in the Blackfriars [Plomer, *Wills*, pp. 35, 36]. In 1618 he was returned as a Frenchman who confessed himself under the sovereignty of

King James [*Returns of Aliens*, iii. 204]. In 1584 he published the second edition of Jewel's *Apologia Ecclesiae Anglicanae*, 8vo, and in 1589 *Francisci Vietaei Opera Mathematica*, fol., of which there is a copy in the Bodleian.

BOVIER, *see* Bover.

BOWEN (JOHN), bookseller in London, 1586–90; (?) St. John's Street, Clerkenwell. Son of William Bowen, of Hereford, capper. Apprentice to Thomas Dawson for seven years from September 29th, 1578: took up his freedom on January 31st, $158\frac{5}{6}$ [Arber, ii. 87, 696]. On October 17th, 1588, he entered in the Registers a *Catechism* by Patrick Galloway, used in the families of Scottish noblemen then resident in Newcastle [Arber, ii. 503]. Herbert (p. 1168) in his notice of Edward Aggas mentions this work as printed for him and John Bowen, and it was presumably on the strength of this entry that Mr. Arber placed it in his *Bibliographical Summary* (vol. v, p. 148). Watt had apparently seen a copy of this catechism. In 1590 Bowen was associated with John Morris and issued the Rev. Edward Harris's *Sermon preached at Hitchen* in 1587. Their joint address was then St. John's Street, Clerkenwell. Both men disappear after this date.

BOWES (RALPH), patentee of Playing Cards, 1578–? 1600. On June 4th, 1578 [20 Eliz.], a patent was granted to Ralph Bowes and Thomas Bedingfield, for twelve years, in consideration of an annual payment of one hundred marks, to import all sorts of playing cards [Pat. Roll, 20 Eliz., 7th Part]. This patent was surrendered in 1588, and a new patent granted to Ralph Bowes and his assigns for a further period of twelve years on the same terms, not only to import but also to print playing cards [Pat. Roll, 30 Eliz., 12th Part]. On September 23rd in the same year he was admitted a freeman of the Stationers' Company by "redemption" [Arber, ii. 703], and on October 18th he was allowed by the Company the "mouldes belonginge to the olde fourme of plaieinge cardes commonlie called the Frenche carde, etc." [Arber, ii. 503, 512, 572].

BOWMAN (FRANCIS), *see* Plomer, *Dictionary*.

BOYCE or BOYSE (DANIEL), bookbinder at Cambridge, 1616–30; St. Mary's Parish. Stepson to Jarmin Warde [J. W. Clark's *Riot at the Great Gate of Trinity College*, 1610–11, Camb. Ant. Soc., 1906, p. xxv].

In the University Accounts for 1616–17 is "Item to Daniell Boyse for binding the booke given to his Maiestie, xxiiij^{s}" [J. W. Clark]. He paid Church rate in St. Mary's Parish from 1616 to 1630 [Foster's *Churchwardens' Accounts*]. His name appears in a list of privileged persons in the University of Cambridge, 1624 [Bowes, *University Printers*, p. 336]. He is also mentioned as a bookbinder in *Vox Piscis, or the Book-fish*, 1627 (p. 10).

BOYCE or BOYSE (REYNOLDE), bookseller (?) in Cambridge, 1568. Son of William Boyse, of Darlyngton, co. Northampton; was apprenticed to John Cuthbert, the Cambridge bookseller, from September 29th, 1568, for eight years [Gray, *Cambridge Stationers*, p. 71; Arber, i. 374].

BOYLE (RICHARD), bookseller in London, 1584–1615. Son of Thomas Boile, of Hereford, capper, apprenticed to Thomas Woodcock, stationer of London, for eight years from Michaelmas, 1576, and took up his freedom in the Company of Stationers on September 15th, 1584 [Arber, ii. 68, 692]. Herbert, p. 1279, says that he published in 1588 S. Bredwell's *Rasing of the foundations of Brownisme*, and dwelt at the Rose in St. Paul's Churchyard. The same authority states that in the Tanner Manuscripts at Oxford there is a statement that Boyle was a puritan. There is a reference to "Boyle's shop at the Rose," in Martin Marprelate's *Just Censure of Martin Junior*, July, 1589, sig. A3^{v}, from which it is to be gathered that he sold puritan works. Mr. Sayle, in his *Early Printed Books at Cambridge*, p. 1234, gives an edition of Thomas's *Dictionary* as published by Boyle about 1588. The last book entry under Boyle's name occurs on February 7th, $161\frac{4}{5}$ [Arber, iii. 562], but it was not until the last day of June, 1625, that his widow, Ellen Boyle, transferred her late husband's copyrights to Nicholas Bourne [Arber, iv. 143].

BRADOCK (RICHARD), printer in London, 1581–1615; Aldermanbury, a little above the Conduit. Bound apprentice to John Filkyn, or Filken, and served his time with Henry Middleton. Took up his freedom on October 14th, 1577 [Arber, ii. 675], and was admitted to the Livery on July 1st, 1598 [Arber, ii. 872]. In 1600 he printed a book of prayers called *The Godlie Garden*, and a dispute arising with the Company over it he promised not to issue any copies until it was settled. In the following September,

another book of prayers called *The Pensive Mans Practice*, which Bradocke had promised Mathew Lownes not to print, was found on the press at his premises and he was ordered to bring into the Hall the six leaves already finished [Herbert, p. 1298]. According to Sir John Lambe, Richard Bradocke married the widow of Robert Robinson [Arber, iii. 702]. The last heard of him is on July 9th, 1615, when he assigned over to John Wright and Edward Wright his rights in a book called *The Booke of Fortune* [Arber, iii. 570].

BRADSHAW (HENRY), printer in London, 1559–61. Some copies of Fabyan's *Chronicle*, 1559, are stated to be "Imprinted at London by Henry Bradsha" [*Offer Catalogue*, No. 2405], and his name also occurs in some copies of the *Chaucer* of 1561. Bradshaw seems to have been connected with Kingston, the printer of these two books, and like him was a member of the Grocers' Company.

BRADSHAW (THOMAS), stationer at Cambridge, 1573–1610. He appears in a list of "persons privileged by the University," *circa* 1592–4 [Bowes, *University Printers*, p. 336]. He built two shops at the West end of Great St. Mary's Church on a lease granted 1585 [G. J. Gray's *Shops at west end of Great St. Mary's Church*], for which he paid 5s. yearly during 1587 and 1588. He was elected an overseer of the "heyghe wayes" in 1581, and gave 20s. towards the repairing or building of the steeple, 1573 [Foster's *Churchwardens' Accounts*]. He died in 1610 in the parish of St. Sepulchre's, and by his will dated July 22nd and proved August 20th, he left his house to his wife, and amongst other bequests left £60 to each of his four sons [Gray, *Cambridge Stationers*].

BRADWOOD (MELCHISIDEC), printer in London and Eton, 1584–1618; (1) Eliot's Court, Old Bailey; (2) Eton. This printer was one of John Day's apprentices, and was presented for his freedom by Day's widow on August 15th, 1584 [Arber, ii. 692]. Bradwood succeeded to the place of Edmund Bollifant in the printing house in Eliot's Court in 1602, and in that year the booksellers George Bishop, William Ponsonby, Simon Waterson, John Norton, and George Adams were joint publishers of an edition of the works of Plutarch [*i.e.*, P. Holland's translation of the *Moralia*], and they agreed to give the printing of it to Arnold Hatfield and M. Bradwood [Arber, iii. 211]. Amongst other notable books that came from this press during Bradwood's connection with it were a splendid edition of Ortelius' *Theatre of the Whole world*, printed for John Norton and John Bill in 1606, an edition of Montaigne's *Essays* in folio, printed in 1613, and the various dictionaries and vocabularies compiled by John Minshew. Bradwood was also the printer of Sir Henry Savile's edition of the works of Chrysostom, usually ascribed to John Norton. The work in eight folio volumes was printed in Greek type obtained from abroad, but an examination of the volumes suggests that Bradwood took down to Eton, presses, workmen and all the supplementary types, initials and ornaments. John Norton was the publisher of the work. Bradwood remained in Eton till his death and was the printer of other Greek works. He died between the 6th and the 30th June, 1618, and by his will left to his wife all his stock in the Company of Stationers [P.C.C., 63, Meade]. Arnold Hatfield had apparently pre-deceased him and the business in Eliot's Court passed to Edward Griffin.

BRAECKVELT or BRAKVELT (PAULUS), printer at Antwerp, 1579–85; In Huydevettersstraet (Tanners Street), In den gulden Bybel, 1583–5. Received into the St. Lucasgild in 1579. In 1583 he printed T. Deloney's *Proclamation and edict of the Archbishop and Prince Elector of Cologne* (Lambeth). [Olthoff, p. 13.]

BRAMRIDGE (JOHN), bookseller in London, 1621–3; near Strand Bridge. Took up his freedom January 15th, 1621 [Arber, iii. 685]. Entered on April 4th, 1623, Ralph Jennings' *Description of Heaven* [Arber, iv. 94].

BREUGHEL (C. GERRITS VAN), printer "in the Netherlands," 1632. In that year he printed G. Wither's version of the *Psalms* [B.M. p. 189]. Perhaps identical with the Cornelis van Breughel who printed a book for Hendrick Laurentsz at Amsterdam in 1633 or 1636, *see* Ledeboer, *A. L.*, p. 26.

BREWER (? HUGH), printer in London, ? 1608–? 1623; St. Martin's in the Vintry. Only known from the following passages in the will of Alice Startute, widow, dated September 22nd, 1623 (P.C.C., 123, Swann):—"Item I give to the goodwife Brewer, the wife of goodman Brewer of the parish of St. Martine in the Vintrey . . . printer, my old paragon gowne

laced with coullored fringed lace . . . Item, I give to the aforesaid goodman Brewer printer, five poundes sterling to be paid to him, within one monethe next after my decease." The only stationer of this name recorded in the Registers is Hugh Brewer, the son of William Brewer, of Harrold, in the County of Bedford, who was apprenticed to Ralph Blore, or Blower, on July 7th, 1600, for eight years. He took up his freedom on October 3rd, 1608. [Arber, ii. 246; iii. 683.]

BREWSTER (EDWARD), *see* Plomer, *Dictionary*.

BRICKMAN, *see* Birckman (Arnold).

BRIGHT (THOMAS), bookseller and bookbinder in London, 1583–8. Son of Francis Bright, mercer, of London. Apprenticed to John Bishop, stationer of London, for seven years from March 25th, 1576. He took up his freedom on March 26th, 1583, and on October 17th, 1586, he took an apprentice. [Arber, ii. 73, 687, 143.] This is all the registers have to tell us about this interesting stationer, who was both a bookseller and a bookbinder, and evidently had extensive dealings with his neighbours. He died some time between September 10th and October 31st, 1588, and his will was proved in the court of the Dean and Chapter of St. Paul's (Book B., f. 315). The following passages occur in it: "Nicholas Smythe owes me for a great Bible 12^{s}." "Due unto William Blakewell one new bible payinge 4^{s}." "To receive of him for binding two books 15^{d}." "To receive of Mr. Kidson draper 32^{s}. 6^{d}." "I owe unto Mr. [Richard] Watkynnes stationer 30^{s}." "To my landlord Mr. Edward Ryder for one quarters rent 15^{s}." "For the housinge of books for Mr. Poonsonber [? Ponsonby] one whole year." "My boy Morris [*i.e.*, Morris Pettefer, his apprentice] to be turned over to serve his yeares with some honest man."

BRINCKLEY (STEPHEN), printer in England, 1580–1, and at Rouen, 1583–(?). In 1580 or 1581 he, with other Catholics, under the direction of Parsons and Campion, set up a secret press at a house called Greenstreet at East Ham in Essex, but it does not appear what they printed there. After a short time the press was removed to Henley Park, where certain books including Parsons' account of John Nichols, the informer, were printed, but the press is said to have been soon taken back to Greenstreet. Later it was transferred to Stonor Park, near Henley, where Brinckley printed Campion's *Decem Rationes*. In July, 1581, the place was raided

and Brinckley captured and sent to the Tower. He was discharged thence in 1583 and went to Rouen, where he joined George Flinton [*q.v.*] and Parsons, who had a press there. The date of his death is unknown. [Gillow, *Dict. of Catholics*; *Bibliographica*, ii. 161–5; *Acts of the P.C., New Ser.*, xiii. 264; Sayle, p. 1743.]

BRISCOE (THOMAS), bookseller in London, 1626–38. Took up his freedom in the Company of Stationers on September 28th, 1626 [Arber, iii. 686]. His only book entry appears in the Registers on November 8th, 1638 [Arber, iv. 443]. His address has not been found.

BROME, *see* Broome.

BROOKE (THOMAS), printer in Cambridge, ? 1608–29. Thomas Brooke was M.A. of Clare College and Esquire Bedell. His name first appears as a printer in 1608 in company with that of Cantrell Legge, in Perkin's *Godly . . . exposition of Christs Sermon on the Mount* [Sayle, p. 1257]. On June 2nd, 1614, there was a Grace for granting him a new patent as printer to the University, as he had lost the old one. He probably resigned in 1624. He died in 1629. [Bowes, *University Printers*, 298.]

BROOKES (WILLIAM), bookseller in London, 1636–40; at his shop in Holborn, in Turnstile Lane, 1639. On May 16th, 1636, John Spenser assigned over to William Brookes the copyright of a book called *An Introduction to a devout life* [Arber, iv. 362]. The last book entry under his name occurs on May 19th, 1640 [Arber, iv. 511.] His address is found on the imprint of some copies of J. P. Camus' *Admirable Events*, 1639.

BROOME (JOAN), bookseller in London, 1591–1601; The Great Bible, Great North Door of St. Paul's Church. Widow of William Broome. On October 4th, 1591, she entered in the Register three comedies played by the Children of Paul's, called *Endymion*, *Galathea*, and *Midas*, all from the pen of John Lyly. The last entry under her name is found on June 16th, 1601 [Arber, iii. 185]. She died soon afterwards, her copyrights being transferred to George Potter on August 25th in the same year [Arber, iii. 191].

BROOME (WILLIAM), bookseller in London, 1577–91. There is no entry of his apprenticeship or freedom in the Registers of the Company of Stationers, those events probably being recorded in the missing volume which covers from 1571–6. He is found taking an apprentice on December

6th, 1585, but his first book entry occurs in the Registers on July 1st, 1577 [Arber, ii. 314]. In 1582 he is found holding a share with Thomas Chard, Henry Denham, and Andrew Maunsell, in *The Commonplaces of Peter Martyr* [Arber, ii. 411]. In 1585 he was associated with Thomas Man in publishing Seneca's *Tragedies* [Arber, ii. 444]. He was dead by October 4th, 1591, as on that date "Mistress Broome" described as "Wydowe late wife of William Brome" is found entering books [Arber, ii. 596].

BROWN (JAMES), bookbinder in Edinburgh, 1598. He witnessed the baptism in Edinburgh of a son of "John Owene, glasinwright" [*i.e.*, glazier], on December 8th, 1598 [*Scottish Antiquary*, v. 90].

BROWN (JOHN), printer in Edinburgh, 1593. In 1593 Catharine Norwell, wife of Robert Smyth, printer in Edinburgh, left by her will "to John Broun, prentar, v merkis" Brown may have been one of Smyth's workmen. [*Bannatyne Miscell.* ii. 221; Aldis, *Scottish Books*, 109].

BROWNE (CHARLES), stationer in Lincolnshire, 1571. Mentioned in a list of stationers living in the country, who paid "scot & lott" to the Company in London in 1571 [Arber, v. lii].

BROWNE (G), bookseller in London, 1601. His name appears in a list of those who were fined on March 3rd, 160^{0}_{1}, for buying copies of a book called *Humours letting blood* [*i.e.*, S. Rowlands' *Letting of Humours Blood*] [Arber, ii. 832]. Nothing more is known of him.

BROWNE (JOHN), senior, bookseller and bookbinder in London, 1598–1622; (1) The Bible, Fleet Street; (2) The "Shugerloafe," against the Whitefriars, Fleet Street; (3) St. Dunstan's Churchyard, Fleet Street; (4) Little Britain. Son of John Browne of Reading, Berks, mercer. Apprentice to Ralph Newbery, stationer, for nine years from Michaelmas, 1586 [Arber, ii. 142]. Took up his freedom on August 5th, 1594 [Arber, ii. 714]. First book entry in the Registers in April, 1598 [Arber, iii. 112]. Dealt in all kinds of literature, cookery books, jest books, works on husbandry and household management, masques, plays, and music. Amongst the most notable of his publications were John Davies of Hereford's *Witt's Pilgrimage*, 1605, Thomas Ford's *Musick of sundry kinds*, 1607, Nicholas Breton's *Poste with a Packet of Madde Letters*, 1609, the anonymous *No whippinge nor trippinge but a kind friendly snippinge*, 1601, John Murrell's *Book of Cookery*, 1614, and *Ladies Practice*, 1617. He also held a share in Drayton's *Polyolbion*. He is also probably identical with the John Browne of Little Britain, who published the various Dictionaries compiled by John Minsheu, on the titlepages of which he is also referred to as a "bookbinder," but, as there was another John Browne in London in 1617, it is difficult to say which is referred to. His will was proved on October 10th, 1622. He left two sons, Thomas and Samuel [P.C.C., 92, Saville]. In February of the following year, his widow, Alice Browne, transferred the remainder of his copyrights to John Marriott [Arber, iv. 92].

BROWNE (JOHN), junior, bookseller and (?) bookbinder in London, 1612–28; Little Britain. Admitted freeman of the Company of Stationers on July 2nd, 1605 [Arber, ii. 739]. His first book entry, a pamphlet concerning the burning of some witches abroad, was made on September 26th, 1612. He perhaps published John Minsheu's Dictionaries in 1617 [*see* John Browne, senior]. He was no doubt identical with the John Browne mentioned in John Gee's *Foot out of the Snare*, 1624, as a disperser of popish books, and also with the bookseller of that name who is mentioned in 1628 in a list of those who were ordered to submit catalogues of their books to the Archbishop of Canterbury [*Dom. S. Papers, Chas. I*, Vol. 117 (9)].

BROWNE (JOSEPH), bookseller in London, 1611–21. Son of Gregory Browne, citizen and goldsmith of London. Apprentice to George Bishop for nine years from March 5th, 1604 [Arber, ii. 275]. Made free of the Company, April 1st, 1611, and made his first entry in the Registers on December 6th, 1611, and his last on May 18th, 1621 [Arber, iii. 472, 683]. His address has not been found.

BROWNE (NATHANIEL), bookseller in London, 1617–31. Took up his freedom in the Company of Stationers on October 6th, 1617 [Arber, iii. 684]. He dealt in ballads and other ephemeral literature. His address has not been found.

BROWNE (NICHOLAS), bookseller in London, 1608–9. Took up his freedom March 26th, 1608 [Arber, iii. 683]. Associated with George Potter in the publication of a pamphlet entitled: *Articles, Of A Treatie of Truce. Made and concluded in the Towne and Citie of Antwerp, the 9. of April 1609*, etc. [B.M. 1193. l. 46 (2)].

BROWNE (ROBERT), bookbinder in Cambridge, 1645–71. In a list of Wills and Inventories in the Cambridge University Registry occurs twice the name of Robert Browne bookbinder, apparently between 1645 and 1671 [Letter to G. J. Gray from the Rev. Dr. Stokes].

BROWNE (SAMUEL), *see* Plomer, *Dictionary*.

BROWNE (THOMAS), (?) bookbinder in Cambridge, 1621–? 1636; West End of St. Mary's Church. In 1636 complaint was made to Archbishop Laud that the western windows of St. Mary's Church were "half blinded up with a Cobler's and a bookbinder's shop." Thomas Browne was then occupying one of these shops, but whether or not he was a bookbinder is not clear. The other shop was occupied by John Hearne, who was not a bookbinder [G. J. Gray, *Shops at the West end of Great St. Mary's Church*]. He paid Church rate from 1621 to 1622 [Foster's *Churchwardens' Accounts*].

BRUDENELL (THOMAS), *see* Plomer, *Dictionary*.

BRUMEN (THOMAS), bookseller and printer at Paris, 1559–88; "in clauso Brunello, sub signo Olivae," 1573, or "sub Olivae signo, ex adverso ædis D. Hilarii, rue du Mont-St.-Hilaire" [Renouard]. He was born in 1532, son of William Brumen, marchand de vins, was a libraire juré, and carried on business from 1559 to his death in 1588. In 1573 appeared "apud" him James Tyrie's *Refutation of an Answer made be Schir John Knox*, and in 1582 Luis de Granada's *Of Prayer and Meditation*, translated by R. Hopkins, "Imprinted at Paris by Thomas Brumeau [*sic*], at the signe of the Olyue." [Renouard, p. 50.]

BRUMEREAU (JACQUES), bookseller at Avignon, 1601. In that year there appeared "apud" him William Chisholme's *Examen confessionis fidei Caluinianæ*, which contains the English text of the confession of the Scotch Kirk [Sayle, p. 1468].

BRUNEAU or BRUNEY (ROBERTUS) printer at Antwerp, 1602–8. Received into the St. Lucasgild in 1602 [Olthoff, p. 14]. In 1605 he printed Verstegan's *Restitution of decayed Intelligence in Antiquities*, for sale in London by Norton and Bill.

BRYSON (JAMES), printer in Edinburgh, *see* Plomer, *Dictionary*.

BRYSON (ROBERT), printer in Edinburgh, *see* Plomer, *Dictionary*.

BUCK (FRANCIS), printer at Cambridge, 1630–2. Brother of Thomas Buck. He was appointed printer to the University by Grace of October 27th, 1630, and resigned July 21st, 1632. He is not known to have printed anything. [Bowes, *Univ. Printers*, 304.] He was dead when his brother Thomas made his will in 1667.

BUCK (JOHN), printer and bookbinder at Cambridge, 1625–68. *See* Plomer, *Dictionary*.

BUCK (THOMAS), printer and bookbinder at Cambridge, 1625–70. *See* Plomer, *Dictionary*.

BUCKE (GEORGE), bookseller in London, 1560–7. Took up his freedom in the Company of Stationers on September 13th, 1560, and began taking apprentices in 1563, about which time he entered in the Registers *The History of L. Aretinus* [Arber, i. 197, 210]. He also published a translation of the *Troades* of Seneca.

BUDGE (JOHN), bookseller in London, 1606–25; (1) The Great South Door of St. Paul's and Britain's Burse, 1609–15; (2) The Green Dragon, St. Paul's Churchyard, 1621–3; (3) The Windmill, Britain's Burse, 1625. Took up his freedom in the Company of Stationers on January 21st, 160$\frac{8}{9}$ [Arber, iii. 683]. Dealt chiefly in theological literature. He died during the plague year, 1625, and his will was proved on December 30th. He left no son. He bequeathed a sum of £10 to the Company to buy two silver bowls; Thomas Walkeley, Hugh Perry and Richard Horseman were his apprentices. Budge also left a sum of thirty shillings each to Edmond Weaver and Ralph Mabb, stationers. The will refers to his "late master" Clement Knight, while amongst the witnesses to the document were Humphrey Robinson and Henry Featherstone. [P.C.C., 139, Clarke.] His copyrights passed to R. Allot [Arber, iv. 168].

BULKLEY (JOSEPH), bookseller at Canterbury, 1622. In the British Museum is a copy of a sermon preached in Canterbury Cathedral by the Rev. Thomas Jackson, with the imprint "London, printed by John Haviland for Joseph Bulkley and are to be sold at his shop in Canterbury, 1622." This provincial bookseller had two sons, Thomas and Stephen, both apprenticed to stationers. The second was afterwards the Royalist printer at Newcastle [*see* Plomer, *Dictionary*].

BULLOCK (   ), (?) bookseller in London, 1624; Fetter Lane. Described as mistress "Bullock" in John Gee's *Foot out of the Snare*, where she is mentioned as a dealer in popish books. She may have been the widow of Peter Bullock, the bookbinder [*q.v.*].

BULLOCK (PETER), bookbinder, 1601. Executed on April 19th of that year for selling popish books. [*Library*, April, 1907, p. 169.] He may have been the Peter Bullock, son of Robert Bullock of Darley, co. Derby, who was apprenticed to G. Cawood for ten years from June 24th, 1591 [Arber, ii. 175], and took up his freedom on September 4th, 1598 [Arber, ii. 722]. There was an earlier man of the same name who took up his freedom in 1569 [Arber, i. 171, 419].

BULMER (   ), ? bookseller in London, 1624; Holborn. Mentioned in John Gee's *Foot out of the Snare*, 1624, as a dealer in popish books.

BURBY (CUTHBERT), bookseller in London, 1592–1607; (1) The Poultry, by St. Mildred's Church, 1592; (2) Cornhill, near the Royal Exchange, 1601–7; (3) The Swan, St. Paul's Churchyard, 1602–7. Son of Edmund Burbie of Ersley, co. Bedford, husbandman. Apprentice to William Wright for eight years from Christmas, 1583. Took up his freedom on January 13th, 1592, and was admitted to the Livery on July 1st, 1598 [Arber, ii. 710, 872]. His first book entry, the *Axiochus* of Plato, was made on May 1st, 1592. He dealt in general literature, and amongst the books entered by him was *The Trimming of Thomas Nash*, 1597, the imprint of which bore the name "Philip Scarlet," which has been regarded as a pseudonym. Cuthbert Burby died between August 29th and September 16th, 1607. By his will he desired to be buried in the parish church of St. Mildred in the Poultry. He left a sum of money to be lent to poor young booksellers, and left his stock and the lease of his premises in Cornhill to his apprentice Nicholas Bourne, in consideration of his true and faithful service. He also left bequests to the stationers Thomas Adams, Edward Bishop and Edmund Weaver, whom he appointed overseers. Cuthbert Burby had two sons, Cuthbert and Edward, and his daughter Elizabeth was married to Thomas Snodham, stationer. [P.C.C., 76, Hudlestone.] His widow appears to have carried on the business for a couple of years.

BURBY (ELIZABETH), bookseller in London, 1607–9; (1) Cornhill, near the Royal Exchange; (2) The Swan, St. Paul's Churchyard. Widow of Cuthbert Burby. She appears to have carried on the business until Nicholas Bourne was in a position to take it over. On October 16th, 1609, she assigned over thirty-eight copies to William Welby, and the remainder to Nicholas Bourne [Arber, iii. 420, 421].

BURDON (JOHN), bookseller in Edinburgh, 1622–? 1641; beside the Trone. The colophon of David Browne's *The New Invention, intituled, Calligraphia*, printed at St. Andrew's by Edward Raban, in 1622, states that the book is "to be solde in Edinburgh, by John Burdon, at his Shoppe, beside the Trone, on the South side of the Streete." The will of a John Burdon, merchant, burgess of Edinburgh, was registered February 1st, 1641. [Aldis, *Scottish Books*, 110.]

BURNET, alias CORNYSHE (GILBERT), parchment seller in Oxford, 1567. Admitted a parchment seller April 3rd, 1567 [Clark, *Register*, ii. 1. 326].

BURRE (WALTER), bookseller in London, 1597–1622; (1) The Flower-de-Luce, St. Paul's Churchyard, 1597–1601; (2) The Flower-de-luce and Crown, 1601; (3) The Crane, St. Paul's Churchyard, 1604. Son of a yeoman of South Mimms, co. Herts. Apprentice to Richard Watkins, stationer of London, for nine years from June 24th, 1587, and became a freeman of the Company on June 25th, 1596 [Arber, ii. 148, 716.] His first book entry occurs in the Registers on September 2nd, 1597 [Arber, iii. 90]. He was the publisher of Thomas Middleton's *A Mad World, My Masters*, 1608, and several of Ben Jonson's plays. His last entry in the Registers was made on December 11th, 1621, and his death took place during the next twelve months, as on December 13th, 1622, his widow transferred her rights in Sir W. Ralegh's *History of the World* to Matthew Lownes and George Latham. She held the remainder until 1630, when she transferred them to John Spencer [Arber, iv. 87].

BURRELL (JAMES), (?) printer in London, 1559; Without the North Gate of St. Paul's, in the corner house of Paternoster Row, opening into Cheapside. Only known from the colophon to a book entitled, *A godly and wholsome preservative against desperation*, 1559 [Herbert, p. 875]. He may have been a relative of John Borrell, the stationer, who was an apprentice with Thomas Raynaldes in 1541 [Duff, *Century*, p. 16].

BURTON (FRANCIS), bookseller in London, 1603–17; (1) The White Lion, St. Paul's Churchyard, 1603; (2) The Green Dragon, St. Paul's Churchyard, 1614. Son of William Burton of Onebury, co. Salop, yeoman. Apprentice to Thomas Adams, stationer of London, for eight years from Michaelmas, 1594. Took up his freedom on November 8th, 1602 [Arber, ii. 199, 734]. His first book entry occurs in the Registers on June 23rd, 1603 [Arber, iii. 239], and his last on June 3rd, 1616 [Arber, iii. 589]. Dealer in miscellaneous literature and publisher of some curious pamphlets on passing events, such as *A true relacon of the late commotion in Herefordshire occasioned by the buriall of one Alice Wellington a recusant in a Towne called Allen's Moor nere Hereford uppon Whytsun Tuesday last paste* [*i e.*, May 21st, 1605] [Arber, iii. 296]. *A reporte of a fearfull Thunder and lightninge, &c., which happened at Olveston in the countie of Gloucester* was licensed to him on January 13th, 160$^{5}_{6}$ [Arber, iii. 309].

BURTON (JOHN), bookseller at Wells, 1634. Some copies of John Blaxton's *English Usurer*, 1634, have the imprint "Printed by Iohn Norton, and are to be sold by Iohn Burton, in Wells" [Hazlitt, II. 51]. This book was also to be sold by John Long in Dorchester, and Francis Bowman in Oxford.

BURTON (SIMON), bookseller in London, 1636–41. He took up his freedom on May 2nd, 1636 [Arber, iii. 687], and on August 2nd, 1637, entered J. Rueff's *Expert Midwife* [Arber, iv. 391], printed for him in the same year by E. G. *See* Plomer, *Dictionary*.

BURWELL (HUGH), stationer in Cambridge, ? 1593–? 1601; Great St. Mary's Parish. In the years 1593 and 1594, Hugh Burwell, stationer, gave sums of 4s. and 6s. 8d. towards the building of the steeple of St. Mary's Church, and in 1601, he was elected churchwarden [Foster's *Churchwardens' Accounts*]. His name appears in a list of "privileged persons" in the University, *circa* 1592–4 [Bowes, *Univ. Printers*, 336].

BUSBY (JOHN), senior, bookseller in London, 1590–1619; St. Dunstan's Churchyard. Son of William Busby, cordwainer of London. Apprentice to Oliver Wilkes for nine years from Michaelmas, 1576, but allowed to serve his time with Andrew Maunsell, draper, exercising the art of a stationer [Arber, ii. 71]. Admitted a freeman of the Company on

November 8th, 1585 [Arber, ii. 695]. He appears to have been for some time in partnership with Arthur Johnson, and is chiefly remembered as the procurer of Shakespeare's *Merry Wives* and as having had a share in *Henry V.* and apparently in *King Lear* [Arber, iii. 366]. The last heard of him in the Registers is on September 27th, 1619, when he assigned over his copyright in Thomas Dekker's *O per se O* to Augustine Matthewes [Arber, iii. 657].

BUSBY (JOHN), junr., bookseller in London, 1607–31. Took up his freedom in the Company of Stationers on June 15th, 1607, on the same day as John Helme, with whom he appears to have begun business, his first book entry, on August 27th, 1607, being in their joint names [Arber, iii. 358, 683]. Amongst his publications was J. Melton's *Six fold Politician*, entered on December 15th, 1608 [Arber, iii. 398], and John Mason's *Tragedy of the Turke*, 1609. He also held shares in Ben Jonson's *Epicoene or The Silent Woman*, and Drayton's *Polyolbion*. The last heard of him is in 1631, when he transferred his interest in Mason's tragedy to Francis Falkner [Arber, iv. 257].

BUSH (EDWIN), (?) bookbinder in London, 1611–34. Son of Thomas Bushe of Cottdrell, co. Hertford, clerk. Apprentice to Robert Barker for eight years from March 25th, 1602: took up his freedom March 1st, 161$^{0}_{1}$ [Arber, ii. 261; iii. 683]. Only two book entries occur under his name, and as these copies were transferred to Francis Constable under a bill of sale, it may be gathered that he was in a small way of business [Arber, iv. 308, 327].

BUSHEL or BUSSHELL (THOMAS), bookseller in London, 1599–1617; The North Door of St. Paul's. Son of Robert Bushell of Norwich, tailor. Apprentice to Nicholas Ling, stationer of London, for eight years from February 1st, 159$^{0}_{1}$ [Arber, ii. 173]. Admitted to the freedom February 3rd, 159$^{8}_{9}$ [Arber, ii. 723]. His last book entry occurs on December 13th, 1617 [Arber, iii. 617].

BUTLER (THOMAS), bookseller in Oxford, ? 1619–28. John Lichfield printed a sermon by J. Wall for T. Butler, who may be the same as a certain Butter or Butler who was a stationer at Oxford in 1619.

BUTLER (WILLIAM), senior, bookseller in London, 1614–25. Took up his freedom September 4th, 1615, but had made his first entry in the Registers on October 23rd, 1614 [Arber, iii. 684, 555]. He probably died of the plague in 1625, as on July 4th, 1626, his widow transferred all his copyrights to William Stansby [Arber, iv. 162]. His address has not been found.

BUTLER (WILLIAM), junior, bookseller in London, 1615–19. Possibly son of the preceding. Made his first entry in the Registers in company with Nathaniel Butter, on September 8th, 1615 [Arber, iii. 572]. Dealt chiefly in theological works, but published one or two news-books. His last entry occurs on September 17th, 1619. His address has not been found.

BUTTER (NATHANIEL), *see* Plomer, *Dictionary*.

BUTTER (THOMAS), bookseller in London, 1576–90; Near St. Austin's Gate, St. Paul's Churchyard. Son of Robert Butter late of Ludlow, Shropshire. Apprentice to William Norton, stationer of London, for ten years, from August 24th, 1564 [Arber, i. 251]. His first book entry occurs in the Registers on November 13th, 1579 [Arber, ii. 362]. Thomas Butter was one of the band of stationers who in October, 1582, appealed to Lord Burghley against the monopolists. He was also one of the assigns of Richard Day. He died before July 9th, 1590. His widow Joan afterwards married John Newbery. She entered works in the Register in 1590 and 1594, but her name is not known to appear in any imprint. Thomas Butter left a son Nathaniel Butter, who was also a stationer.

BYNNEMAN (HENRY), printer in London, 1566–83; (1) The Black Boy, Paternoster Row, 1566; (2) The Mermaid, Paternoster Row, 1567; (3) The Mermaid, Knightrider Street, 1567–80; (4) The Three Wells, North West Door of St. Paul's Cathedral, 1572; (5) Thames Street, Near Baynard's Castle, 1580–3. Henry Bynneman is first heard of in 1559, when, on June 24th, he apprenticed himself for eight years to Richard Harrison, stationer of London, and printer, who carried on business in White Cross Street, Cripplegate. Richard Harrison died in 1563, and Bynneman's movements between that date and August 15th, 1566, when he took up his freedom as a stationer, are unknown. The first book bearing his name was Robert Crowley's *Apologie, or Defence of Predestination*, 4to., October, 1566; some copies of the work have Henry Denham's name as printer. So largely did his business increase that in 1572 he had a bookseller's shop or shed in St. Paul's Churchyard, known as The Three Wells, in addition to his printing house. At the death of Reginald Wolfe, in 1573, Henry Bynneman secured a large part of the stock of letters and devices in his office and struck out a new line for himself. In 1574 he issued four books in folio, two being different editions of Calvin's *Sermons on Job*, and the others Walsingham's *Historia Brevis* and Whitgift's *Defence of the Aunswer to the Admonition*, and all of them were excellently printed. He had a special woodcut border cut for his folio titlepages, modelled on that used by Reginald Wolfe in the *Historia Major* in 1571, and embodying his device of the mermaid. From this time until his death in 1583 he turned out some very artistic books. In these he substituted one or other of Wolfe's devices for that of the mermaid, and frequently placed on the titlepages of his books the coats of arms of his patron, Sir Christopher Hatton, or one or other of the Court nobility. His greatest work during the latter part of his life was the printing of Holinshed's *Chronicle* for Reginald Wolfe's executors. About 1579 or 1580 Henry Bynneman moved into premises in Thames Street, and served as constable to the parish of St. Bennet, Paul's Wharf. In 1580 he was involved in serious trouble for printing a libellous letter sent from one member of Parliament to another, but this was the only occasion in which he offended the authorities. About this time he was working in partnership with Henry Denham, whom, with Ralph Newbery, he appointed his deputy. In the year of his death, 1583, he was returned as possessing three presses, but he died before the end of the year, and on January 8th, 158$\frac{3}{4}$, Ralph Newbery and Henry Denham delivered to the Company certain copies that had belonged to "Henry Bynneman deceased." He left a widow who afterwards married a Mr. Sled [Herbert, p. 1288], and several children, one of whom, Christopher Bynneman, was in 1600 apprenticed for seven years to Thomas Dawson. The business was taken over by a syndicate composed of Ninian Newton, Arnold Hatfield and Edmond Bollifant, three of Henry Denham's apprentices, with whom was joined John Jackson, a draper. [*Library*, July, 1908.]

BYRDE (WILLIAM), Assign of, see East (T.).

CADMAN (THOMAS), bookseller in London, 1584–9; The Bible, Great North Door of St. Paul's. Took up his freedom on June 16th, 1560 [Arber, i. 123]. Cadman appears to have been one of the most active of

the band of stationers who defied the Masters and Wardens of the Company and resisted the decrees of the Star Chamber. He was one of those who sold John Day's *A B C*. He was fined for selling Powell's edition of *Nostradamus* and was constantly in trouble for disorderly conduct and quarrelling with other stationers. Amongst Cadman's publications were Lyly's *Campaspe*, 1584, and Greene's *Spanish Masquerado*, 1589.

CALY (ROBERT), *see* Duff, *Century*.

CANIN (ABRAHAM), printer at Dort. In 1601 he printed an edition of *The CL psalmes of David in prose and meter* "at the expenses of the aires of Henrie Charteris, and Andrew Hart in Edinburgh" [Aldis, *Scottish Books*, no. 346].

CANIN or CAEN (ISAAC), printer at Dort, 1597–1621. His earliest work in English seems to be *The French Chirurgerye* by J. Guillemeau, translated by A.M., the titlepage of which is dated 1597, the colophon 1598. In 1599 he produced a translation, also by A.M., of O. Gaebelkhover's *Book of Physic*, in the imprint of which he is called "Isaack Caen." In 1601 he printed the *Psalms of David in Metre* [Sayle, p. 1466], and the *New Testament*, translated by Beza, and Englished by L.T., both at the expense of the heirs of H. Charteris and A. Hart in Edinburgh [Hazlitt, IV. 103]. These books appear to have been printed at the instigation of Bonham and John Norton, who had arranged with Hart to send out English printers to do the work [*Acts of the Privy Council, New Ser.*, xxxii. 14].

CANTER (RICHARD) (?) bookseller in London, 1603; Pope's Head Alley. Hazlitt, III. 93, has the following entry: *A Perticular and true Narration of that great and gratious Deliuerance, that it pleased God of late to vouchsafe vnto the Cittie of Geneva, namely vpon the xij of December last in the yeere 1602. At London, Printed for George Potter and Richard Canter, dwelling in the Pope's Head Alley neare the Exchange, 1603.* No stationer of this name is found in the Registers.

CARMARDEN (RICHARD), 1562–6. Cranmer's *Bible* was reprinted at Rouen in 1562 [Herbert, p. 1606] and 1566 at this person's expense. The edition of 1566 was printed by C. Hamillon, whose imprint appears in some copies at the end of the prologue [B.M., p. 150].

CARPENTER (EDMUND), *see* Bollifant (E.).

CARRE (HENRY), bookseller in London, 1578–1604; (1) St. Paul's Churchyard, over against the Blazing Star, 1578–93; (2) The Three Conies, Old Exchange, 1581; (3) The Cat and Fiddle, Old Exchange, 1583–93. Son of John Carre of Berwick, draper. Apprentice to Henry Kyrham, stationer, for seven years from Michaelmas, 1569 [Arber, i. 397]. His first entry in the Registers appears in 1578, and he dealt almost wholly in ballad literature. The last book entry under his name occurs in 1604. Carre was another of those against whom Richard Day brought an action in the Court of Star Chamber for the infringement of John Day's patents [Arber, ii. 790 *et seq.*].

CARTER (WILLIAM), printer in London, ? 1580–4. Son of Robert Carter, draper, of London. Apprentice to John Cawood, printer, from February 2nd, 156$\frac{2}{3}$, for ten years [Arber, i. 196]. William Carter was a Roman Catholic, and worked secret presses in various places, being several times imprisoned [Arber, ii. 749]. On December 30th, 1579, Aylmer, bishop of London, wrote to Burghley that he had found in Carter's house copies of a very dangerous book called the *Innocency of the Scottish Queen*. Finally on January 10th, 158$\frac{3}{4}$, Carter was condemned on a charge of high treason for printing a work called *A Treatise of Schisme*, and was hanged at Tyburn on the following day. [Stow's *Annals*, ed. 1600, pp. 1176–7; Gillow's *Dict. of Catholics*; *D.N.B.*]

CARTWRIGHT (RICHARD), *see* Plomer, *Dictionary*.

CARTWRIGHT (SAMUEL), *see* Plomer, *Dictionary*.

CASSON or CAUSON (EDMUND), bookseller at Norwich, 1617–23; In the Market Place at the sign of the Bible. Son of Thomas Casson of London. Apprentice to William Firebrand, stationer, for eight years from June 24th, 1600 [Arber, iii. 255]. In 1623 he was in business as a bookseller at Norwich, two books being found with his name in that year, (1) *Norfolke Furies, and their foyle, under Kett, their accursed captaine. With a Description of the famous City of Norwich etc. . . . Englished by Rich. Woods . . . out of the Latine copie of A. Nevill*, 1623 [B.M., C. 33. g. 11], and (2) *Jentaculum Judicum* by S. Garey, 1623 [Sayle, p. 1307].

CASTLETON (THOMAS), printer in London, 1610; Without Cripplegate. Son of Andrew Castleton of London, preacher, apprentice to Ralph Howell for ten years from August 2nd, 1602, and took up his freedom on March 30th, 1610 [Arber, ii. 265; iii. 683]. In 1610 he entered in the Registers a book called *More Fools Yet*, of which there is a copy in the Bodleian Library [Arber, iii. 435].

CATHKIN (EDWARD), bookseller and bookbinder in Edinburgh, 1585–1601. He fled to England in 1585, with his brother James [*q.v.*], to escape the consequences of taking part in religious disturbances, and in 1596–7 they were again in trouble on the same account. It is probable that, like his brother, he was at first a skinner; but by 1592 he had become a bookseller, for his name appears as one of the seven complainers who in that year appealed to the Edinburgh Town Council against John Norton of London, who was infringing their privileges by retailing books within the burgh. His wife, Jonet Hart, may have been a sister of Andro Hart [*q.v.*], with whom he was closely concerned in business matters. When Norton gave up his Edinburgh business (*circa* 1596), Cathkin and Hart bought his stock of books and took over the debts. His name has not been found in the imprint of any book; but the list of debtors in his inventory [*Bannatyne Miscellany*, ii. 229] shows him to have had an extensive business connection, and the £96 15s. 3d., which he owed to John Norton of London, may have been either a residue of the above named transaction, or, more probably, on account of books supplied from England. He died March 9th, 1601. [Aldis, *Scottish Books*, 110; Calderwood's *History of the Kirk of Scotland*; Lee, *Add. Mem.*, App. lxxi.]

CATHKIN (JAMES), bookseller in Edinburgh, 1601–31. He was at first "a worker of mariken leather" and afterwards took up bookselling, perhaps on the death of his elder brother Edward [*q.v.*] in 1601. In 1593 he was stated to be then 34 years of age, and he seems to have been related by marriage to Richard Lawson [*q.v.*]. Previous to 1614 he had been, for a time, in partnership with Andro Hart in printing. Cathkin's penchant for getting into trouble in connection with the religious dissensions of the time pursued him in later years, and in February, 1619, he and Lawson were summoned before the High Commission for not coming to the Kirk on Christmas Day, for opening of their booths and walking before them in time of sermon, and dissuading others from going to the Kirk. In the following June he was arrested in London—where he had just arrived from Scotland—on suspicion of being concerned in the publication of Calderwood's *Perth Assemblie*, which had recently been issued anonymously. His account of his examination by the King and imprisonment in the Gatehouse has been printed in the *Bannatyne Miscellany* [i. 199]. During his absence his shop in Edinburgh was searched, but no copies of the obnoxious tract were discovered. At the time of his death, September 30th, 1631, he had in stock some 4,400 books, more than half being works in divinity, including a Syriac *New Testament* in folio, two little Hebrew *Bibles*, and ten Greek *New Testaments*. Among his creditors were the London stationers, Robert Allot and Godfrey Emondson, and "Robert Crumby, servand, keiper of his buith." He was survived by his wife, Jonet Mayne [*q.v.*], who continued the business for some years. [Aldis, *Scottish Books*, 111; Calderwood's *History of the Kirk of Scotland*; *Bannatyne Miscellany*, i. 199, ii. 249; *Reg. P.C. Scot.* x, xi, xii.]

CAVEY *alias* STUFFOLDE (CHRISTOPHER), bookbinder in Oxford, 1536–78 [*See* Duff, *Century*]. From 1549 to 1568 he was living in High Street just west of Schidyard Street, now Oriel Street. Robert Cavey was also living there in 1586.

CAUSON, *see* Casson.

CAVEY *alias* STUFFOLDE (ROBERT), bookseller, bookbinder, and Clerk of the University of Oxford, 1573–94; High Street. Probably the son of Christopher Cavey. Admitted a bookseller on September 8th, 1573 [Clark, *Register*, ii. 1. 321]. In the Vice-Chancellor's Computus from $157\frac{6}{7}$ to 1594 there are entries of payments to him as "clericus Universitatis" and bellringer. In these he is sometimes referred to as Robert Stuffolde *alias* Cavey. His will was dated December 6th, 1593, and the inventory of his effects was taken on March 20th, $159\frac{3}{4}$, so that he died sometime between these two dates. He left no son, the whole of his estate going to his wife Jane. All his tools for binding were left to his nephew and servant Edward Miles. The witnesses included Dominique Pinart and Nicholas Smith, both bookbinders [Gibson, *Oxford Wills*, pp. 17, 18]. In 1586 Robert Cavey was living in High Street just west of Schidyard Street, now Oriel Street.

CAWOOD (GABRIEL), bookseller in London, 1576–1602; Holy Ghost, St. Paul's Churchyard. Second son of John Cawood, printer. Came on the Livery of the Stationers' Company, July 30th, 1578, and served in the office of Renter in 1586, as Under Warden in 1589 and 1590, Upper Warden in 1593–4, and Master in 1597 and 1599. His first book entry was made on December 10th, 1576, and his last on June 26th, 1598 [Arber, ii. 306, iii. 120]. Amongst his copyrights were John Lyly's *Euphues*, printed for him by Thomas East in 1579, 1580 and 1581, and Thomas Watson's *Hekatompathia*, printed for him by John Wolf in 1582. Gabriel Cawood died before July 2nd, 1602, when his copyrights were transferred to W. Leake, senior [Arber, iii. 210].

CAWOOD (JOHN), *see* Duff, *Century*.

CERTAINE (WILLIAM), bookseller in London, 1635–8. Took up his freedom, August 4th, 1635 [Arber, iii. 687]. On March 30th, 1638, in company with Lawrence Chapman, he entered a book entitled *A liberall maintenance due to Ministers* by John Meen [Arber, iv. 414].

CHAMBERS (GEORGE), bookseller in Oxford, 1590. Appointed a privileged bookseller in 1590, at the age of twenty-seven [Clark, *Register*, ii. 1. 396].

CHAMBERS (JOHN), bookseller in Oxford, 1617. On May 23rd, 1617, he was reprimanded, with several others, for setting up as a bookseller, without the Vice Chancellor's leave [Clark, *Register*, ii. 1. 321].

CHAMBERS (RICHARD), (?) bookseller in London, 1618. Took up his freedom in the Company of Stationers on March 6th, 1618 [Arber, iii. 684]. Nothing more is known of him.

CHAPMAN (LAWRENCE), *see* Plomer, *Dictionary*.

CHARD or CHARE (THOMAS), bookseller in London, 1577–1618; (1) The Helmet, St. Paul's Churchyard; (2) Bishopsgate Churchyard. This stationer, whose name was as often written Chare as Chard, is entered as the son of Thomas Chare of Dartforth, Kent, apprentice to Humphrey Toye for ten years from Christmas, 1565 [Arber, i. 289], and appears to have succeeded to the business on Toye's death in 1577. His first book entry was made on November 3rd, 1578 [Arber, ii. 340]. Amongst his publications was an edition of Jewell's *Apologia* in the Welsh tongue, and

also a *Prymer* in Welsh. Most of his publications were theological. Chard was a troublesome member of the Company of Stationers and was frequently fined for disobeying its orders [Arber, ii. 852, 860, 861]. On January 22nd, 1613, he transferred his copyrights in Bishop Babington's works to Edmund Weaver, and on March 10th, $161\frac{7}{8}$, he and Weaver once more transferred their rights in those books to George Eld and Miles Flesher [Arber, iii. 622]. He died about 1622, when his widow Anne Chard assigned over her copyrights to J. Beale and T. Dewe. The majority of Chard's books were issued without any indication of his place of business. For a lawsuit in which he was concerned in 1588, see the *Library*, January, 1909, pp. 102–3.

CHARLEWOOD (ALICE), printer in London, 1593. Widow of John Charlewood. She printed *An Homily* of U. Regius, and E. Dering's *Godly Prayers* in 1593, and Peele's *Honour of the Garter*, n.d. She afterwards married James Roberts.

CHARLEWOOD (JOHN), *see* Duff, *Century*.

CHARLTON or CHORLTON (GEOFFREY), bookseller in London, 1603–14; The North door of St. Paul's. Apprentice to Thomas Wight, draper. Admitted to the freedom of the Company of Stationers March 7th, 1603 [Arber, ii. 734]. Made his first book entry on March 21st, $160\frac{3}{4}$. Amongst his publications was T. M's *Black Book*, 1604, and Barnaby Rich's *Roome for a gentleman*, 1609. The last entry under his name is found on August 25th, 1613.

CHARTERIS (HENRY), bookseller and printer in Edinburgh, 1568–99; In the High Street, "on the north syde of the gait, abone the Throne" (weigh house). Books were printed for him by John Scot, 1568–71, Robert Lekpreuik, 1570–1, Thomas Vautrollier, 1577–8, and John Ross, 1574–80. On the death of Ross, in 1580, Charteris acquired his plant and commenced printing on his own account. His device represents two figures emblematical of Justice and Religion, with the initials H. C. in the foreground. He issued at least five editions of the works of Sir David Lindsay; that of 1568, to which he wrote a long preface, was printed by Scot, and is the first edition known to have been printed in Scotland, and is also the earliest of the forty books which bear Charteris's name. Charteris, who was one of the most notable of the sixteenth century Edinburgh stationers

and a burgess of considerable standing in the city, died August 29th, 1599. His inventory, printed in the *Bannatyne Miscellany*, ii. 223, contains the name of Richard Watkins, stationer in London, among the debtors. His eldest son, Henry, afterwards became Principal of Edinburgh University, and another son, Robert, succeeded to the business. [Dickson and Edmond, 348; Aldis, *Scottish Books*, 111; *D.N.B.*; *Bannatyne Miscell.*, ii. 223; *E.B.S. Papers*, vol. i, no. 15.]

CHARTERIS (HEIRS OF HENRY), booksellers in Edinburgh, 1601. In 1601 Isaac Canin of Dort [*q.v.*] printed a *Bible* and the *Psalms in Meter*, both in octavo, "at the expenses of the aires of Henrie Charteris, and Andrew Hart, in Edinburgh;" and in the same year an edition of *The CL psalmes of David in prose and meter*, bearing a similar imprint, was printed at Dort by Abraham Canin. As Robert Charteris, Henry Charteris's successor, was already printing in his own name, it is not clear exactly who was concerned in these three publications [Aldis, *Scottish Books*, 111].

CHARTERIS (ROBERT), printer in Edinburgh, 1599–1610; "At the west side of Auld Provosts closehead on the North side of the Gate, ane lytill above the Salt-trone," 1603. He succeeded in 1599 to the business of his father, Henry Charteris, whose device he continued to use. On December 8th, 1603, he was appointed King's printer, probably in succession to Waldegrave who had returned to London. His address is given in an advertisement at the end of a copy of his *Priests of Peblis*, 1603. From the list of his publications it would appear that, like his father, he especially favoured the vernacular literature, and this feature is also noticeable in the inventory of his stock taken on the death of his wife, Margaret Wallace, in February, 1603. In 1604 he sought an English market for some of his superfluous stock, and the Lindsay's *Satyre of the Thrie Estates* and Colvill's *Palinod* of that date are to be sold in London by Nathaniel Butter and Walter Burre respectively. Charteris seems not to have prospered in business, for he was denounced rebel and put to the horn for debt in August, 1609, and soon after this he disappears from view, probably having fled the country. Andro Hart, the bookseller, who appears to have succeeded him, commenced to print in 1610, and in 1612 Thomas Finlason was appointed king's printer in his stead. [Dickson and Edmond, 490; Aldis, *Scottish Books*, 111; *Bannatyne Miscell.* ii. 235; Lee, 55 and App. xiv; *Reg. P.C. Scot.* ix.]

CHARTERIS (HEIRS OF ROBERT). Peter Smart's *Vanitie & Downefall of Superstitious Popish Ceremonies*, 1628, bears the imprint "Printed at Edenborough in Scotland, 1628. By the Heyres of Robert Charteris." But the book was not printed in Scotland. [Aldis, *Scottish Books*, 111.]

CHETTLE (HENRY), printer, stationer and dramatic author, 1584–91. Son of Robert Chettle of London, dyer. Apprenticed to Thomas East, printer, for eight years from September 29th, 1577 [Arber, ii. 81]. Took up his freedom on October 6th, 1584 [Arber, ii. 693]. In the year ending July 10th, 1588, Chettle was paid six shillings for going to Cambridge on the Company's business [Arber, i. 528], and on September 17th, 1591, he entered in the Register a work called *The bayting of Diogenes* [Arber, ii. 595]. At this time he was in partnership with William Hoskins and together they printed for Nicholas Ling and John Busby a sermon of the Rev. Henry Smith's, *The Affinitie of the Faithful*, 1591 [B.M. 4474. b. 68]. As nothing further is heard of Chettle in the Registers, it may be assumed that soon after this date he gave up printing and publishing and devoted himself to authorship. In 1592 he wrote the prose tract *Kind-heart's Dream*, and *Piers Plainnes*, 1595, is also supposed to be his, but he devoted himself chiefly to play-writing. In a letter to Thomas Nashe written in or after 1593 and printed in Nashe's *Have with you to Saffron-Walden*, sig. V2[v], he uses expressions which suggest that, at that time, he had still some connection with his old trade.

CHORLTON, *see* CHARLTON.

CHRISTIAENS or CHRISTIAN (W.), printer at Leyden, 1631–43 [Ledeboer, *A.L.*]. In 1634 he printed W. H.'s *True Picture of Prince Henry* [B.M. p. 755], and in 1643 *The Power of the Laws of a Kingdom over the Will of a Misled King* [Hazlitt, I. 79].

CHRISTIAN (RICHARD), (?) bookseller in London, 1591. Son of John Christian of Ely, Cambridgeshire. Apprentice to Richard Jones for eight years from June 24th, 1583 [Arber, ii. 117]. Took up his freedom in the Company of Stationers on June 25th, 1590. On April 2nd, 1591, he entered a ballad, but beyond that nothing is known of him and his address has not been found.

CHRISTIE (GEORGE), chapman, 1599–1604. In November, 1604, George Christie owed the sum of £242 1s. 8d. (Scots) to Andro Hart, the Edinburgh bookseller, and the George Christie who is named among the debtors in the inventories of the two Edinburgh stationers, Henry Charteris (1599) and Edward Cathkin (1600), was probably the same person. [*Bannatyne Miscell.* ii. 226, 230, 239.]

CHURCH (FRANCIS), (?) bookseller in London, 1634. Took up his freedom March 26th, 1634 [Arber, iii. 687]. Nothing more is known of him.

CHURTON (OLIVER), bookseller and bookbinder in London, 1616–25; Parish of St. Antholins. Took up his freedom in the Company of Stationers on September 17th, 1616 [Arber, iii. 684]. From his will, dated July 19th, 1625, it appears that he came of a numerous family in Launceston in Cornwall. From the following passage it appears that he was a bookbinder: "Item, I give to Walter Oake the use of my presse and past bordes and plates for one whole year, and at the end thereof to paye the value of the one halfe which they shalbe praysed at his first enjoying them. Soe he is to have the other halfe of those presses past bordes and plates as my free gift" [P.C.C., 106, Clarke].

CLAESSONIUS or CLAESZOON (CORNELIS), printer at Amsterdam, 1582–1609. In 1602 he printed for Andro Hart of Edinburgh J. Jonston's *Inscriptiones historicae Regum Scoticorum* [Aldis, *Scottish Books*, p. 11]. [Ledeboer, *A.L.*, pp. 34–5.]

CLARKE (   ), bookseller in Ludlow, 1633. Referred to as one of those to whom copies of William Prynne's *Histrio-Mastix* was sent for sale in 1633 [*Privy Council Register*, March 7th, $163\frac{3}{4}$, Printed in *Documents relating to W. Prynne* (Camden Society, 1877), New Series, xviii, p. 60. See also *N. & Q.* 10th Ser. V, p. 183].

CLARKE (JOHN), bookseller in London, 1608. Took up his freedom January 18th, $160\frac{7}{8}$ [Arber, iii. 683]. Nothing more is known of him.

CLARKE (JOHN), senior, *see* Plomer, *Dictionary*.

CLARKE (JOHN), junior, *see* Plomer, *Dictionary*.

CLARKE or CLERKE (MARTIN), bookseller in London, 1606–11; St. Paul's Churchyard, Ad novam Librariorum Officinam. Took up his freedom in the Company of Stationers on November 11th, 1605 [Arber, iii. 683]. Dealt chiefly in theological literature. His first book entry was on February 18th, $160\frac{5}{6}$, and his last in 1611 [Arber, iii. 315, 474].

CLARKE or CLERKE (ROBERT), bookseller in London, 1616; The Lodge, in Chancery Lane, over against Lincoln's Inn. Son of John Clarke of the parish of Saint Giles in the Fields, clerk. Apprentice to William Spink, for eight years from Michaelmas, 1597 [Arber, ii. 220]. Took up his freedom on January 22nd, $160\frac{4}{5}$ [Arber, ii. 738]. On June 3rd, 1616, he entered in the Registers Captain John Smith's *Description of New England* [Arber, iii. 588].

CLARKE (SAMPSON), bookseller in London, 1583–98; (1) By the Guildhall, 1583; (2) Behind the Royal Exchange, 1589–91. This stationer was made free of the Company on March 26th, 1583, by George Buck and William Broome [Arber, ii. 687]. His first book entry was made on November 4th, 1583, and related to Thomas Lodge's *Tryed experiences of worldlie abuses* (*i.e.*, *An Alarm against Usurers*) [Arber, ii. 428]. He also dealt in ballads. Sampson Clarke was one of the defendants in the suit brought in 1585 by the assigns of Richard Day against certain stationers for unlawfully printing and selling *The A B C and Litell Catechisme* [Arber, ii. 791, 792]. He was admitted to the livery on July 1st, 1598 [Arber, ii. 873]. Amongst his publications in 1591 was the play entitled *The First and Second Part of the troublesome Raigne of King John of England*, which a later publisher ascribed to Shakespeare.

CLARKE or CLERKE (THOMAS), (?) bookseller in London, ? 1584. Son of Thomas Clarke or Clerke of Erith, Kent, yeoman. Apprenticed to Richard Greene, stationer, for eight years from June 24th, 1576. There was another Thomas Clerk, son of John Clerk of Wigdon in Cumberland, who took up his freedom on February 4th, $1\frac{599}{600}$ [Arber, ii. 725], and the Thomas Clerk referred to in the subsequent entries of books between 1604 and 1607 are believed to refer to the Cumberland man and not to the Kentish one, who never appears to have taken up his freedom.

CLARKE or CLERKE (THOMAS), bookseller in London, 1600–7; The Angel in St. Paul's Churchyard, 1607. Son of John Clerk of Wigdon in Cumberland, yeoman. Apprentice to William Norton, stationer of London, for eight years from February 2nd, $159\frac{1}{2}$ [Arber, ii. 179]. Made a freeman of the Company on February 4th, $1\frac{599}{600}$ [Arber, ii. 725]. His first book entry occurs on April 24th, 1604 [Arber, iii. 259], and his last on June 22nd, 1607 [Arber, iii. 354]. He appears to have dealt chiefly in theological books.

CLERKE, *see* Clarke.

CLIFTON (FULKE), *see* Plomer, *Dictionary*.

CLOETING (JAN ANDRIESZ), printer at Delft, 1626–32 [Sayle] or 1594–1632 [Ledeboer, *A.L.*, p. 36]. He printed *The firm Alliance and Agreement made between the King of Swethland aud the Duke of Statin and Pomerland*, 1631, a translation from the Dutch [Sayle, p. 1451].

CLOPPENBURG (EVERT, or EVERHARD), printer at Amsterdam, 1638–44. In 1640 was printed *The intentions of the army of the Kingdom of Scotland*, without printer's name or place, but having the device of Jan Evertz Cloppenburg, printer at Amsterdam, 1589–1636 [Sayle, p. 1428]. He had at this date been succeeded by Evert Cloppenburg, who may be the printer of this book, or the device may have passed to someone else. [Ledeboer, *A.L.*, p. 37; *De Boekdrukkers*, p. 23.]

CLUTTERBUCK (RICHARD), *see* Plomer, *Dictionary*.

CLYFTON (NICHOLAS), bookseller in Oxford, 1570–9. Admitted a bookseller June 28th, 1570 [Clark, *Register*, i. 321]. A complete inventory of his stock is printed by Mr. Gibson in his *Oxford Wills*, pp. 11–16. He probably died early in January, 1579, the inventory being taken on the 19th of that month. He left his goods to his wife Alice and his two daughters.

CNOBBAERT or KNOBBAERT (JAN), printer at Antwerp, 1614–35; (1) In de Koeperstraet, In den witten Helm, 1621; (2) Bij het Professie huys der Societeyt Jesu, In St-Peeter, 1622. Born 1590. In 1614 he printed John Robinson's *Of Religious Communion* [Sayle, p. 1371]. He was at work as late as 1635, and died in 1637. [Olthoff, p. 18.]

COCKS, *see* COX.

COCKYN (HENRY), bookseller in London, 1576–8; The Elephant, Fleet Street. Son of Henry Cocken of West Ham, Essex, yeoman. Apprentice to George Buck, stationer, for eight years from February 2nd, $156\frac{4}{5}$. His first book entry appears on December 10th, 1576 [Arber, ii. 306]. The only work known bearing his name in the imprint is John Bishop's *Beautiful Blossomes gathered . . . from the best trees of all kyndes*, 1577, afterwards reissued as *A Garden of Recreation*, 1578. He appears to have succeeded Henry Wykes at the above address.

COLBY, *see* Coleby.

COLDOCK (FRANCIS), bookseller in London, 1561–1603; (1) Lombard Street, over against the Cardinal's Hat; (2) The Green Dragon, St. Paul's Churchyard. Apprentice with William Bonham, stationer, and took up his freedom on December 2nd, 1557 [Arber, i. 70]. His first book entry in the Registers occurs during the year ending July 8th, 1561, and in the following year he and Thomas Hacket, his neighbour at the sign of the Pope's Head in Lombard Street, were fined by the Company for giving each other "unseemly words." Francis Coldock was received into the Livery on June 29th, 1570 [Arber, i. 421], and afterwards became an important member of the Company and one of the largest dealers in books in London. He appears to have moved about this time into other premises in St. Paul's Churchyard, known by the sign of the Green Dragon, which he rented of Reginald Wolfe, and his lease was confirmed to him by Johane Wolfe in her will [Plomer, *Wills*, p. 22]. In the year 1575–6 Francis Coldock and Thomas Hacket were acting as renters for the Company, and in Easter term, 1576, he brought an action in the King's Bench against John Hearn, or Herne, stationer and bookseller of Taunton, for the recovery of a debt of £88, doubtless for books supplied [*Coram Rege Roll*, Easter, 19 Eliz. m. 38]. In the years 1580–1 and 1581–2 he served as Junior Warden, in 1587–8–9 as Senior Warden, and he was Master of the Company in the years 1591–2 and 1595–6. Francis Coldocke married Alice, the daughter of Simon Burton of the Parish of St. Andrew Undershaft and the widow of Richard Waterson, stationer, but whether she was his first wife is unknown. He died between September 3rd, 1602, and February 1st, $160\frac{2}{3}$, when his will was proved. He left no son, but his daughter Joan was married to William Ponsonby the bookseller [Plomer, *Wills*, p. 37]. His widow afterwards married Isaac Bing.

COLE (GEORGE), stationer of London, 1602–37. An important member of the Company of Stationers. From a Chancery suit relating to the Latin Stock of the Company, we learn that he became a freeman by marriage with a stationer's widow. We are not told who the stationer's widow was. Cole was admitted on May 17th, 1602, by redemption [Arber, ii. 732], and received into the Livery on July 2nd, 1603 [Arber, ii. 874]. He served the offices of Renter and Warden, and was Master of the Company in the years 1627–8, 1628–9, 1631–2, and 1632–3 [Arber, iv. 183, 201, 257, 281]. In the course of the suit referred to he admitted that he had never traded in the buying or selling or printing of books; but for the greater part of his life he was a professor of the civil law and a proctor in the Court of Arches for upwards of 30 years [*Chancery Proceedings, Chas. I*, S. 124–5]. He was a shareholder of the first rank in the Latin Stock, and was one of the first six stock-keepers appointed. The only other record of his dealing in books is an assignment on November 6th, 1628, by Humphrey Lownes of his rights in twenty-one works to George Cole and George Latham; but on December 6th, 1630, they re-assigned them to Robert Young [Arber, iv. 205, 245]. The date of George Cole's death is unknown.

COLE (PETER), *see* Plomer, *Dictionary*.

COLEBY or COLBY (JOHN), bookseller in London, 1636–9; (1) The Unicorn, near to Fleet Bridge, 1637; (2) The Holy Lamb, on Ludgate Hill, 1638; (3) Under the King's Head Tavern, at Chancery-lane end in Fleet Street, 1639. Publisher of Dr. Jenison's *Newcastle's Call*, a reflexion upon the plague in that city in 1636; Sir William Berkeley's *Lost Lady, A Tragy Comedy*, 1638, and River's *Heroinae*, 1639.

COLES or COULES (FRANCIS), *see* Plomer, *Dictionary*.

COLIN or COLIJN (MICHIEL), bookseller or printer at Amsterdam, 1608–36. In 1624 an unknown printer reprinted *An Oration . . . wherein the right . . . of the Netherlandish war against Philip . . . is . . . demonstrated* "According to the printed Copie at Amsterdam, by Michael Collyne Stationer, dwelling upon the Water at the corner of the old Bridge street, Anno 1608" [Sayle, pp. 1557, 1429], but it is not clear whether Colin's edition was in English or Dutch.

COLLINS (JOHN), bookseller (?) in London, 1600. He was executed on April 19th, 1601, for selling popish books [*Library*, April, 1907, 169, 175; Gillow, *Dict. of Catholics*, i. 544].

COLLINS (RICHARD), *see* Plomer, *Dictionary*.

COLMAN (NICHOLAS), bookseller at Norwich, 1586; St. Andrews Churchyard. Son of Henry Colman of Harrington in the co. of Northampton. Apprentice to Arthur Pepwell for eight years from March 25th, 1565 [Arber, i. 258]; afterwards set over to Augustin Laughton. Made free on July 7th, 1579 [Arber, ii. 680]. On December 13th, 1586, he entered a ballad entitled *The lamentation of Beccles a market towne in Suffolk on Saint Andrew's Day last past being burnt with fire to the number of lxxx houses and losse of xx^{m} li* [i.e., £20,000] [Arber, ii. 461]. It was printed for him in the same year by R. Robinson [Hazlitt, I. 405–6].

COLWELL (THOMAS), printer in London, 1561–75; (1) St. Bride's Churchyard over against the North Door of the Church, 1562–3; (2) St. John the Evangelist, beside Charing Cross; (3) St. John the Evangelist, Fleet Street, beneath the Conduit. Apprentice with William Powell [Arber, i. 40]. Took up his freedom August 30th, 1560 [Arber, i. 159]. His first entry in the Registers was a ballad entitled *The Woman of Canyne*, which was entered before July 24th, 1562 [Arber, i. 177]. He succeeded Robert Wyer at the sign of St. John the Evangelist beside Charing Cross, and used his blocks and ornaments.

COMBES (JOHN), (?) bookseller in London, ? 1604–? 16. This stationer was admitted to the freedom of the Company on April 27th, 1604 [Arber, ii. 737], and in the same year he is found taking an apprentice [Arber, ii. 281]. In 1605, Combes was one of those who became suitors to the Company for Master Wright's privilege [Arber, iii. 698]. His name also occurs amongst those who held shares in the Latin stock; but no book has been found with his name as publisher, and his address is unknown.

CONINCX (ARNOUT), printer at Antwerp, 1579–1608; (1) In de Cammerstraet, In den rooden Leeuw, rechtover het Kerckhofstraetken, 1582; (2) In de Cammerstraet, In den witten Hond. Admitted into the St. Lucasgild

in 1579. He printed several works for English Catholics, including *Primers* in 1599 and 1604 [Sayle, p. 1368], R. Broughton's *Apological Epistle* in 1601, and R. Chambers' translation of P. Numan's *Miracles wrought at Mont-aigu*, 1606. [Olthoff, p. 20.]

CONSTABLE (FRANCIS), *see* Plomer, *Dictionary*.

CONWAY or CONNEWAY (HENRY), (?) bookseller in London, 1560–98; The Broad Axe without Aldgate. Apprentice to Richard Richardson, and made free of the Company of Stationers on April 8th, 1560. He does not appear to have been a publisher, but he became an important member of the Company, serving the offices of Warden in the years 1585–6, 1587–8, 1591–2 and 1592–3 [Arber, i. 41, 122 *et passim*]. He died in 1598, without male issue, and by his will proved on August 1st, 1598, he bequeathed his house in Aldgate, known by the sign of the Broad Axe, to his wife Mary [P.C.C., 72, Lewyn].

CONYNGTON (PAUL), bookseller in London, 1577–8; The Black Bear in Chancery Lane. Apprentice to William Seres for ten years from June 24th, 1562: admitted to the Livery of the Company in the year ending June 10th, 1589 [Arber, i. 174, 531]. Began taking apprentices in 1577 [Arber, ii. 75]. First book entry December 13th of that year [Arber, ii. 322]. The only book known bearing his name is *Wharton's Dream*, 1578 [B.M., C. 21. c. 71].

COOKE (HENRY), (?) bookseller in London, 1602–24. Son of William Cooke, stationer, who died in February, $159\frac{7}{8}$. Apprentice to his father on October 3rd, 1597 [Arber, ii. 220], and admitted a freeman "per patrimonium" on June 28th, 1602. In 1605 his name appears in a list of suitors for Master Wright's privilege [Arber, iii. 698]. Henry Cooke was elected Junior Warden in the year 1624. In the will of Anne Hooper widow, probably the widow of Humphrey Hooper, stationer, proved on December 7th, 1621, occurs this passage: "Item, I give and bequeath unto little Henry Cooke sonne of Henry Cooke stationer the somme of ffortie shillings" [P.C.C., 101, Dale]. No book has been found bearing his name in the imprint, and his address is unknown.

COOKE (MATTHEW), bookseller in London, 1606–7; The Tiger's Head, St. Paul's Churchyard. Son of Toby Cooke, stationer of London. Apprentice to Edward Blount for nine years from Christmas, 1595 [Arber, ii. 209]. Took up his freedom November 11th, 1605 [Arber, iii. 683]. On January 17th, 160$\frac{5}{6}$, in partnership with Samuel Macham, he entered the pseudo-Chaucerian *Ploughman's Tale* [Arber, iii. 310]. He died before July 9th, 1607, when his share in the copyright of this and other works appears to have become wholly vested in the hands of Samuel Macham. His widow married Lawrence Lisle [Arber, iii. 585]. She is mentioned in the will of Margery Cooke, widow of Toby Cooke [Dean and Chapter of St. Paul's, Book C., f. 239].

COOKE (TOBY), bookseller in London, 1577–99; The Tiger's Head in St. Paul's Churchyard. Son of James Cooke of London, yeoman. Apprentice to John Harrison for twelve years from Christmas, 1564; took up his freedom on January 14th, 157$\frac{6}{7}$ [Arber, i. 254; ii. 673]. Cooke made his first book entry in the Registers on September 11th, 1578 [Arber, ii. 337]. He dealt chiefly in theological literature. In January, 159$\frac{7}{8}$, he was chosen Beadle to the Company of Stationers in the room of John Wolfe, but a year later he appointed John Hardy as his deputy. In May, 1598, he assigned most of his copyrights to Richard Field and Felix Kingston [Arber, iii. 114]. Toby Cooke died some time in 1599, leaving a widow, Margery Cooke, and two sons, Mathew and Thomas. Margery Cooke made her will on June 8th, 1608, and died before July 9th. She left a bequest to Joane Lisle, the widow of her son Mathew; to Edward Blount stationer a sum of 20s for a ring; and appointed Lawrence Lisle stationer and her son Thomas her executors [Dean and Chapter of St. Paul's, Book C., f. 239].

COOKE (WILLIAM), stationer in London, 1561–98; St. Dunstan's in the West. *See* Duff, *Century*. From his will which was proved on February 8th, 159$\frac{7}{8}$, we learn that he was born at Langford in Bedfordshire. He bequeathed his lands in that county to his sons William and Henry, both of whom were stationers, and left the residue to his widow Anne Cooke. There is some reason to believe that she afterwards married Humphrey Hooper, stationer. She died in 1621 and left a bequest to one of the children of Henry Cooke, and a sum of money to the Livery of the Company of Stationers on condition that they were present at her funeral [P.C.C., 101, Dale].

COPE (DAMIAN), bookseller in Oxford, 1609. Admitted a privileged stationer in 1609, aged 28 [Clark, *Register*, ii. 1. 401].

COPLAND (WILLIAM), *see* Duff, *Century*.

CORNE (HUGH), bookseller in London, 1578–80. The son of John Corne of Ruton, co. Shropshire. Apprentice to Thomas Chapman, stationer of London, for eight years from Christmas, 1568 [Arber, i. 375]. Made free of the Company January 20th, 1578 [Arber, ii. 675]. First book entry May 31st, 1580 [Arber, ii. 371]. His address has not been found. He died before April 8th, 1583, when his apprentice, Henry Heath, was transferred to Timothy Rider [Arber, ii. 116].

CORNISHE (GILBERT), *see* Burnet.

CORNISHE (WILLIAM), bookseller in London, 1601. Only known from an entry in the Registers on March 4th, 160$\frac{0}{1}$, recording the names of those who were fined for selling the book entitled *humours lettinge blood in the vayne* (*i.e.*, Rowlands' *Letting of Humours Blood*) [Arber, ii. 832].

COSTE (NICHOLAS DE LA), *see* De La Coste.

COSTERDEN (MATTHEW), (?) bookseller in London, 1600–40. Son of Thomas Costerdyne, of London, mercer, apprentice to Richard Hollins, stationer, for nine years from December 21st, 1590, but on Hollins' death he was transferred to Francis Godlif. He took up his freedom on August 20th, 1599. [Arber, ii. 172, 213, 724.] He was the publisher of three editions of Ephraim Pagitt's *Christianographie* [Arber, iv. 330, 356]. His address has not been found.

COTES (RICHARD), *see* Plomer, *Dictionary*.

COTES (THOMAS), *see* Plomer, *Dictionary*.

COTTON (ABRAHAM), bookseller in London, 1582–5. Son of John Cotton of London, barber. Apprentice to Henry Kyrkham, stationer of London, for seven years from Christmas, 1568. The only book entry under his name in the Registers is on February 20th, 158$\frac{4}{5}$, when he entered a ballad entitled *A Warning to Witches* [Arber, ii. 440]. On November 26th, 1582, there is an entry in the accounts "gyven to Abraham Cotton, x[s]," but whether it was a payment of account or a benevolence is not clear [Arber, ii. 886].

COTTON (CLEMENT), Assigns of, 1631–40. On September 8th, 1629, Clement Cotton received a grant under the Privy Seal for the sole printing for 21 years of a *Concordance to the Holy Bible*, made by the Rev. John Downame [*State Papers, Dom., Charles I*, Vol. 149]. He assigned the printing to Nicholas Bourne for a sum of money. The Council however forbade the binding of the *Concordance* with the *Bible* and Cotton was obliged to petition Archbishop Laud that anyone might buy the *Bible* with or without the *Concordance* [*State Papers, Dom., Charles I*, Vol. 162. 53, 54].

COTTON (WILLIAM), bookseller in London, 1602–9; The Long Shop adjoining Ludgate. Son of William Cotton of Burnison, co. Derby, husbandman. Apprentice to William Leake, stationer, for eight years from March 26th, 1594: took up his freedom on April 19th, 1602 [Arber, ii. 191, 731]. On September 3rd, 1604, he was fined 10s. for arresting a freeman contrary to the custom of the Company [Arber, ii. 839, 840]. On August 11th, 1602, he entered *the lyfe and deathe of the Lord Cromwell, as yt was lately acted by the Lord Chamberleyn his servantes*, of which the only copy now known is in the Bodleian. On May 21st, 1604, he secured from the widow of Thomas Hayes, Heliodorus' *Ethiopian History*, originally the copyright of Francis Coldocke, and the first part of the *Flowers* of Luis de Granada [Arber, iii. 262]. The Heliodorus was in 1619 wrongfully claimed by Lawrence Hayes as having been his father's copyright [Arber, iii. 651]. The last book entry under Cotton's name occurs on June 2nd, 1609, and he was dead before the 27th of the following November, when his widow transferred one of his copyrights to Clement Knight [Arber, iii, 411, 424], but the bulk of his copies appear to have been in the hands of the Company and were by them assigned to William Barret on February 16th, 161$\frac{6}{7}$.

COULES, *see* Coles.

COURANT (NICOLAS), printer at Rouen, 1621–(?) 1633; "in the streete of the poterne neere to the Pallace," c. 1621. He printed without date *The angel-guardian's clock* by Hieremias Drexelius (assigned to 1621 in B.M. Cat.), and in 1630 or 1631 the *Defence of N. Smith* by A.B. [B.M. 701. a. 5. (3.)—the date 1631 is altered in MS. to 1630], and *An Apology of the Holy See Apostolic's Proceeding* by "Daniel of Jesus Reader of Diuinity" *i.e.*, John Floyd [Hazlitt, I. 481]. He died in or before 1633.

COURANT (WIDOW OF NICOLAS), printer at Rouen, 1633. In this year she printed the *Progeny of Catholics and Protestants* [B.M., p. 346], assigned to Laurence Anderton, alias Scroop [Sayle, p. 1404; *D.N.B.*, i. 397].

COUSTURIER (JEAN), bookseller at Rouen, ? 1609– (?), and printer at Rouen, 1633–8; "at the Escuyere streit at the seigne of the Read hare," ? 1609: device—the fountain. There was an Abraham Cousturier or Le Cousturier, bookseller, at Rouen from 1582 to 1628, and he apparently had a brother also called Abraham [Frère, *Manuel*, 297], but his or their publications seem to have consisted chiefly of *facetiae*, and Jean may have been of another family. The earliest work in English printed for him appears to have been Benedict Canfield's *Rule of Perfection* [Sayle, p. 1402], n.d., but attributed to 1609 [*D.N.B.*, art. Canfield]. There is also an edition of the *Gospel of Nichodemus*, by J. Warren, bearing his name but no place or date: assigned, with a query, to 1620 in B.M. Cat., p. 1149. His dated books seem to begin in 1633, when he printed four, a Rheims *New Testament*, Camden's *Institutio Graecae grammatices* [Sayle, p. 1402], the *Parthenia Sacra* of H. A. [*i.e.*, Henry Hawkins], and a translation of the *Imitatio Christi* [B.M., p. 757]. In 1634 he issued Nicolas Caussin's *Holy Court*, translated by Sir T. Hawkins, tomes i–iii, in folio with pictures [B.M., p. 348], and two other books; in 1635 a Douai *Bible*; in 1636 A. de Villegas' *Lives of Saints*, "all newly corrected and adorned with many brasen pictures"; in 1638 N. Caussin's *Holy Court fourth tome*, translated, as the others were, by Sir T. Hawkins [Sayle, p. 1403]. It seems not improbable that the undated books mentioned above either were issued by another Jean Cousturier, or are really later than the dates assigned to them, being perhaps reprints of earlier editions.

COWPER (JOHN), *see* Plomer, *Dictionary*.

COWPER (JOHN), bookseller in Edinburgh, 1582. He was servant to Thomas Vautrollier and seems to have been in charge of the latter's bookselling business in Edinburgh. On April 4th, 1582, he appeared before the Town Council on a charge of having retailed and bound books within the burgh, he being an unfreeman [Dickson and Edmond, 350].

COX or COCKS (JOHN), (?) bookseller in London, 1586–93. Admitted to the freedom of the Company of Stationers on October 4th, 1586 [Arber, ii. 698]. On August 30th, 1589, he entered *A lamentable songe, brieflie shewinge the miserable end of one John Randon* [Arber, ii. 529]. He was dead before March 5th, $159\frac{2}{3}$, when his apprentice, Stephen Cox, was put over to Thomas Gosson.

COX (REUBEN), bookseller in London, 1628; In Bethlehem. Took up his freedom December 1st, 1628 [Arber, iii. 686]. Mentioned in a list of second-hand booksellers who were directed in 1628 to bring in a catalogue of their books [*Dom. S. Papers, Chas. I*, Vol. 117 (9)].

CRAMOISY (SEBASTIEN I and II), booksellers and printers at Paris, 1589–1669. The elder Sebastien was "libraire" in 1589, "libraire-juré" in 1610, "en la grand' ruë Sainct Jacques, à l'enseigne des Cigongnes." The younger appears to have been born in 1585; he became director of the Imprimerie Royale in 1640. The *Nouv. Biog. Générale* appears to consider all the books issued from 1609 onwards with the imprint of Cramoisy as the work of the younger man, but the two may have been for a time in partnership. The younger died in 1669. The only English works which they issued seem to have been *The principal points of the faith of the catholic church* by Cardinal Richelieu, translated by M.C., *i.e.*, Thomas Carre alias Miles Pinkney, in 1635 [Sayle, p. 1387], and *A Declaration of the Principal Points of Christian Doctrine, set forth by the English Priests dwelling in Tournay College*, 1647 [Hazlitt, III. 42; VII. 384]. [Renouard, p. 86; *Nouv. Biog. Générale.*]

CREEDE (THOMAS), printer in London, 1593–1617; (1) The Catherine Wheel in Thames Street, 1593–1600; (2) The Eagle and Child in the Old Exchange, 1600–17. Thomas Creede's birthplace is unknown. The first heard of him is in 1578 when he was made a freeman of the Company of Stationers by the printer Thomas East [Arber, ii. 679]. He appears to have remained a journeyman until 1593, when he opened a printing office at the Catherine Wheel in Thames Street, and made his first entry in the Registers. His office was stocked with a varied assortment of letter and his workmanship was superior to that of many of his contemporaries. He was employed by the great Elizabethan publisher William Ponsonby, and not only did he print several of Shakespeare's plays, but much of the best

literature of the time passed through his press, as well as numerous ballads, broadsides, etc. In 1594 he printed *The First Part of the Contention betwixt the two famous houses of York and Lancaster* and *The true Tragedie of Richard the third*, and in 1598 *The famous Victories of Henry V*th. The first of these was the old play upon which Shakespeare founded *The Second Part of King Henry VI*, while the *Famous Victories of Henry V* was used by him in his *First and Second parts of Henry IV* and *Henry V.* Creed was also the printer and publisher of the pseudo-Shakespearian play *The Lamentable Tragedy of Locrine* in 1595. His first genuine Shakespeare quarto was the second edition of *Richard III*, printed for Andrew Wise in 1598. This was followed in the next year by the second quarto of *Romeo and Juliet*, which he printed for Cuthbert Burby, and in 1600 he put to press for Thomas Millington and John Busby *The chronicle history of Henry the fift.* During 1602 the first quarto of *The Merry Wives of Windsor*, the second quarto of *Henry V*, and the third quarto of *Richard III* all came from his press. In 1616 Creed took into partnership Bernard Alsop, who in the following year succeeded to the business on the retirement or death of Creed. Creed used as a device a figure of Truth crowned but stript and being beaten with a scourge held by a hand issuing from the clouds. [*Library*, April, 1906, pp. 155–7.]

CRESPIN (JEAN), printer at Geneva, 1551–72. A native of Arras. In early life "avocat au parlement de Paris," on becoming a Protestant he retired to Geneva. He aided Robert Constantin in his *Lexicon graeco-latinum.* Geneva, 1562, and wrote a number of religious works including *Le Livre des Martyrs*, 1554, of which, and of a Latin translation of the same, there are numerous editions. From 1556 to 1569 he published at least nine works in English, including an edition of the Geneva *Bible* in 1568–70 [B.M. p. 151]. Mr. Sayle attributes to his press John Knox's *First Blast against the Regiment of Women*, 1558, which is without printer's name, and A. Gilby's *Admonition to England and Scotland* appended to Knox's *Appellation* published in the same year, is also stated to have been printed by him [Herbert, p. 1599]. If this is the case perhaps two or three other tracts by Knox printed during his residence at Geneva may be Crespin's work. His devices were an anchor and serpent, with or without I.C., or "'Intrate per arctam viam', and Y," the latter in 1556. [Sayle, pp. 1421–2; *Nouv. Biog. Générale*; Heitz, *Genfer Buchdrucker*, no. 43–53.]

CRIPPS (HENRY), *see* Plomer, *Dictionary.*

CROKE (WILLIAM), stationer of London, 1563. This stationer was one of the witnesses to the will of John Dixon of the parish of St. Gregory, London, proved on September 4th, 1563. [Dean and Chapter of St. Paul's, Book B, fo. 35.]

CROKER (HENRY), stationer in Winchester, 1571. Mentioned in a list of stationers living in the country who paid "scott and lott" to the Company in London in 1571 [Arber, v. lii].

CROMBIE or CRUMBY (ROBERT), bookseller in Edinburgh, *see* Plomer, *Dictionary.*

CROOKE (ANDREW), *see* Plomer, *Dictionary.*

CROOKE (EDMOND), stationer in Dublin, 1638. Only known from his will which was proved in Dublin in 1638. In this he refers to his brother John Crooke, probably John Crooke afterwards King's Printer in Dublin, and speaks of having a sum of three hundred pounds in the hands of his partners John Crooke, Thomas Allot and Richard Serger. To John Moore, his servant, he bequeaths a sum of forty shillings, and to his apprentice Robert Fletcher forty shillings, and the residue of his goods he bequeaths to his wife Elizabeth. He also leaves a bequest to the poor of the town of Kingston Blunt in the parish of Aston Rowant, co. Oxford, possibly his birthplace [*Wills in Prerogative Court, Dublin*].

CROOKE (JOHN), *see* Plomer, *Dictionary.*

CROSLEY (JOHN), *see* Plomer, *Dictionary.*

CROSLEY (JOHN), bookseller in London and Oxford, 1597–1612; High Street, Oxford, 1607–11. Admitted a bookseller of the University of Oxford on March 16th, $159\frac{8}{9}$ [Clark, *Register*, ii. 1. 321]. By his will which was proved on February 12th, $161\frac{2}{3}$, he left bequests to his sons John and Henry, and the residue of his estate to his wife Elizabeth. The inventory of his effects amounted to £526 17s. 8d. [Gibson, *Oxford Wills*, pp. 24–6.] From 1607 to 1611 he was living in High Street, just west of Schidyard Street (Oriel Street) [*Oriel Leases*].

CROUCH (CHRISTOPHER), bookbinder in Oxford, 1623. He bound books for the Bodleian Library in that year [Gibson, *Oxford Bindings*, pp. 49, 51, 60].

CROUCH (JOHN), *see* Plomer, *Dictionary.*

CRUMPE (JAMES), *see* Plomer, *Dictionary.*

CURTEYNE (HENRY), *see* Plomer, *Dictionary.*

CUTHBERT (JOHN), stationer in Cambridge, 1566–97; Parish of Great St. Mary's, 1568–83. Was admitted to the freedom of the Company of Stationers on April 29th, 1566 [Arber, i. 318], and seems to have lived at Cambridge from that date or soon after, until his death. In 1568 the churchwardens of St. Mary's "received of Mr. Cuthberte stationer for all the books at ye time being which were in number 13, small and great. xs. vjd." In 1571 he was mentioned as one of several members of the Company of Stationers "abidinge in the Countrie." In 1583 Cuthbert was living in, or paid rent for, the small house at the west end of Great St. Mary's Church, which was afterwards pulled down, when he moved to another part of the parish [Gray, *Shops at West end of Great St. Mary's Church*]. He died in 1597.

CUTTIER (PHILLIPPE), *see* Duff, *Century.*

DAINTY (THOMAS), *see* Plomer, *Dictionary.*

DALDERNE (JOHN), bookseller in London, 1589. Son of Roger Dalderne of London, hackneyman. Apprentice to Toby Cooke for nine years from Christmas, 1579: took up his freedom January 9th, $158\frac{7}{8}$, and made his first book entry on June 23rd, 1589 [Arber, ii. 95, 701, 524]. Herbert [p. 1357] mentions six books published by him. His address has not been found.

DANIEL (ROGER), *see* Plomer, *Dictionary.*

DANTER (JOHN), printer in London, 1589–99; (1) Duck Lane, near Smithfield, 1591; (2) Hosier Lane, near Holborn Conduit, 1592. Son of John Danter of Eynsham, co. Oxford, weaver. Apprentice to John Day, printer, for nine years from March, 1582, but in 1588 he was transferred to Robert Robinson [Arber, ii. 114, 151]. During his apprenticeship he was found assisting in working a secret press at which Richard Day's patents the *Grammar* and *Accidence* were printed in large numbers. In consequence the Wardens of the Company of Stationers disabled him from ever becoming a master printer. This sentence was however remitted a year or two later, and after taking up his freedom on the last day of September, 1589, he was allowed to share a printing business with William Hoskins and Henry Chettle. The partnership only lasted a short time, and towards the end of 1591 John Danter set up for himself at Duck Lane, near Smithfield. On February 6th, 159$\frac{3}{4}$, he entered in the Registers *A booke intituled, a Noble Roman Historye of Tytus Andronicus.* This was the first quarto of Shakespeare's play, and no copy of it was known to exist until 1905, when a Swedish gentleman discovered a copy amongst his books. The imprint runs, "London, Printed by Iohn Danter, and are to be sold by Edward White & Thomas Millington, at the little North doore of Paules at the signe of the Gunne. 1594." In 1596 his press was seized for printing a Roman Catholic book of devotion called *Jesus Psalter* [Arber, i. 580; Herbert, p. 1270]. In the same year he also printed for Thomas Nashe, the satirist, who was apparently then living with him, *Have with you to Saffron-Walden* [*see* sig. S1. of that work]. In 1597 Danter printed the first (pirated) quarto of Shakespeare's *Romeo and Juliet.* Like all his work, it was very badly printed. He was shortly afterwards in trouble again for printing privileged books and was dead before the end of 1599. [Arber, iii. 153; *Library*, April, 1906, pp. 149–66.]

DARE (GAUTIER), printer in London, 1560–2; Blackfriars. A Gualterus Derry, probably identical with this alien printer, was made Brother of the Stationers' Company on January 15th, 15$\frac{59}{60}$ [Arber, i. 126]. He was a native of Rouen, and is described in Kirk's *Returns of Aliens* as "typographus" [Worman, *Alien Members*, p. 14].

DAVIES (RICHARD), printer, 1601. Arrested in that year on his way to Ireland, and described as "practized in the printing and publishing of certaine seditious bookes" [*Acts of the Privy Council, New Ser.*, xxxii. 85].

DAVIES (WILLIAM), bookseller, bookbinder and publisher in Oxford, 1603–51. Admitted a bookseller in 161$\frac{6}{7}$ [Clark, *Register*, ii. 1. 342–4].

He is found binding books for the Bodleian Library in the years 1620–2. He published books from 1622 to 1640. [Madan, *Oxford Press*, pp. 298, 311–13; Gibson, *Oxford Bindings*, pp. 48, 49, 51, 60.]

DAWLMAN (ROBERT), *see* Plomer, *Dictionary*.

DAVIS (JAMES), bookseller in London, 1628; Barbican. Mentioned in a list of second-hand booksellers who, in 1628, were ordered to send a catalogue of their books to the Archbishop of Canterbury [*Dom. S. Papers, Chas. I*, Vol. 117 (9)].

DAWSON (EPHRAIM), bookseller in London, 1609–36; Fleet Street, at the sign of the Rainbow neere the Inner Temple gate. Son of Thomas Dawson of the city of Coventry, mercer. Apprentice to Matthew Selman, stationer of London, for seven years from February 3rd, 160$\frac{0}{1}$: took up his freedom March 7th, 160$\frac{7}{8}$ [Arber, ii. 252; iii. 683]. He became partner with Thomas Downe or Downes. They began entering books on June 19th, 1609. Dawson's last book entry was made on March 14th, 163$\frac{2}{3}$, but he continued publishing as late as the year 1636.

DAWSON (JOHN), senior, printer in London, 1613–34; ? The Three Cranes in the Vintry. Son of Simon Dawson, of Manningtree, co. Essex, yeoman. Apprentice to Thomas Dawson the elder for seven years from January 31st, 160$\frac{1}{2}$: took up his freedom, February 6th, 160$\frac{8}{9}$ [Arber, ii. 260; iii. 683]. Made his first book entry in the Registers on January 12th, 1613. On January 23rd, 162$\frac{0}{1}$, he petitioned Archbishop Abbot that he might be admitted a master printer, as a vacancy had occurred owing to the death of his uncle Thomas Dawson, senior [Arber, iii. 689]. This petition was granted. The last book entry under his name is found on January 22nd, 163$\frac{3}{4}$ [Arber, iv. 313], but the date of his death is uncertain. *See* Dawson (Mary).

DAWSON (JOHN), junior, *see* Plomer, *Dictionary*.

DAWSON (MARY), printer in London, 1635–6; The Three Cranes in the Vintry. Widow of John Dawson, senior. For a short time after the death of her husband she carried on the printing house and several books bear her initials, M.D., in the imprint, but she eventually married a minister and left the business to be carried on by her son, John Dawson, junior.

DAWSON (THOMAS), senior, printer in London, 1568–1620; The Three Cranes in the Vintry. Thomas Dawson was apprenticed to Richard Jugge, printer, for eight years from the year 1559, and took up his freedom on February 18th, 156$\frac{7}{8}$ [Arber, i. 120, 366]. At the outset of his career he appears to have been in partnership with Thomas Gardiner, their first book entry appearing on November 2nd, 1576. Thomas Dawson was, however, chiefly a trade printer and his business appears to have been a large one. In 1578 Richard Schilders, the alien printer, was compelled to transfer a book he was then printing for Hans Stell to Thomas Dawson, and to work for him for wages until it was complete. The book is believed to have been *The Bee Hive of the Romish Church*, 1579 [Arber, ii. 882]. In the return made to the Bishop of London in May, 1583, he is entered as having three presses. He rose from Renter of the Company in 1591–2 to the Mastership in the years 1609 and 1615 [Arber, v. lxiii]. He died in the year 1620, and was succeeded in the business by his nephew, John Dawson.

DAWSON (THOMAS), junior, stationer of London, 1597–1600. Only known from various entries relating to his apprentices [Arber, ii. 222, 240, 249, 720].

DAY (JOHN), *see* Duff, *Century*.

DAY (RICHARD), printer and divine, 1578–84; The Long Shop at the West End of St. Paul's. Eldest son of John Day, the printer, by his first wife. Born on December 21st, 1552. He was educated at Eton [Harwood, *Alumni Eton.*, 1797, p. 184], and afterwards was sent to King's College, Cambridge, where he matriculated in November, 1571, was admitted a fellow August 24th, 1574, and proceeded B.A. in 1575. Meanwhile his mother had died and his father had married a second time, and in a Chancery suit which he brought against his step-mother, he declared that it was through her influence that he was compelled to give up his fellowship and to become a proof-reader in his father's printing office. Richard Day was admitted to the Livery of the Stationers' Company in 1577–8 [Arber, i. 477], and he was joined with his father in the patent for printing the Metrical *Psalms* and the *A B C and Little Catechism.* In 1578 he brought out *A Booke of Christian prayers, collected out of the Auncient Writers*, commonly known as "Queen Elizabeth's Prayer Book." It is noted for the beauty of its woodcut borders and illustrations. It was

printed by his father who is said to have compiled the first edition of 1569. He appears at this time to have had a shop of his own at the West End of St. Paul's known as the Long Shop; but his relations with his father seem to have been very strained, a fact which he attributed to his stepmother's influence, and after his father's death in 1584 she refused to give him any portion of his father's goods, hence the Chancery suit. The documents, unfortunately, are in a very mutilated and dirty condition, and very little can be made out from them. Richard Day subsequently took orders and was appointed to the vicarage of Reigate, in Surrey, on May 29th, 1583, but he only held the appointment a few months. His subsequent career and the date of his death are unknown. [*D.N.B.*; Chan. Proc. Eliz. Dd. 8 (53).]

DAY (RICHARD) Assigns of, 1585–1603. In 1584 Richard Day, who had succeeded to the patent granted to his father John Day and himself, for printing *The Psalmes of David in metre, the A B C and Little Catechism*, assigned his interest in these works to Edward White, William Wright, Thomas Butter, John Wolfe and Francis Adams. The works were, however, pirated extensively and in 1585 Richard Day was obliged to bring an action in the Star Chamber on behalf of his assigns, against those infringing his patent [Arber, ii. 790–3].

DEANE (JOHN), bookseller in London, 1601–19; Temple Bar. Son of William Deane of Somerford, co. Chester, yeoman. Apprentice to Humphrey Lownes for eight years from August 1st, 1594 [Arber, ii. 195]. Admitted to the freedom of the Company on August 3rd, 1601 [Arber, ii. 730]. In 1603 he was fined eight shillings for dealing in the second edition of the *Basilicon Doron* [Arber, ii. 837]. Deane was associated with John Browne, bookseller of Fleet Street, and they published much popular and interesting literature. His last book entry was made on September 18th, 1619 [Arber, iii. 657].

DE BEAU CHESNE (JEAN DE), *see* Beau Chesne.

DE BRUGES or DEBURGES (ISAAC), *see* Duff, *Century*.

DE HORSE, or DE HORST (JOHN), printer in London, 1580–3; Blackfriars, 1583. A feltmaker by trade and a French refugee. He came to England and took out letters of denization on October 29th, 1550. On

November 7th, 1580, he was admitted a "brother" by the Company of Stationers on payment of 10s. [Arber, ii. 683], and on July 4th, 1581, he paid 10s. for the entry of some books, the titles of which were not given [Arber, ii. 396]. In the Return of Aliens made in 1582–3 De Horse was reported to be "a free denizen, and useth selling of pictures and making of brushes" [Worman, *Alien Members of the book-trade*, pp. 32, 33], and in 1583 he was returned as having one press [Arber, i. 248]. Henry Johnson, alias De Horst, mentioned as a stationer of London in 1576 was perhaps a son [Arber, ii. 68].

DEISE (ANTHONY), printer in London, 1571. In Kirk's *Returns of Aliens* [Part 1. 412] under this date is entered "Anthony Deise printer, born in Antwerp, servant to Reynolde Wolfe, in England 1½ years, in the said Ward 1 year." In the *Ecclesiae Londino-Batavae Archivum* [ed. Hessels, Vol. 1] occurs a Latin letter [No. 144] from Abr. Ortelius at Antwerp to Jacob Colius, his nephew, at London, dated January 9th, 1586, in which he says, "There is here the widow of Anthony Diesthius, who would be glad to know through you how her brother Gabriel Gayot fares among you . . . [Worman, *Alien Members*, p. 15.]

DE LA COSTE (NICOLAS), printer at Paris, 1631; At the Mount of Saint Hilary, at the Crown of Britany. In 1631 he printed the *Meditations, Soliloquia, and Manual*, of St. Augustine [Sayle, p. 1387].

DENHAM (HENRY), printer in London, 1560–89; (1) White Cross Street, Cripplegate; (2) The Star, Paternoster Row; (3) The Star, Aldersgate Street. Henry Denham was one of Richard Tottell's apprentices and took up his freedom in the Company of Stationers on August 30th, 1560. In 1564 he was in possession of a printing house of his own in White Cross Street, Cripplegate, believed to have been the premises previously occupied by Richard Harrison. He made his first entry in the Registers, a sermon, during the year ending July 22nd, 1564 [Arber, i. 237]. In 1565 he moved to the sign of the Star in Paternoster Row and from this time onwards his press was a busy one. He was furnished with a large and varied assortment of letter, his blacks being noticeable for their clearness and beauty, while his nonpareil and other small sizes are remarkable for their regularity. Denham also had a varied stock of initial letters,

ornaments and borders, many of which were extremely good. Noticeable amongst his woodcut initials were those known as the A S series and attributed to Anton Sylvius an Antwerp engraver. Many of his smaller initials are noticeable for their grace. Perhaps the finest of his woodcut borders are those used in the *Monument of Matrones*, a collection of private prayers edited by Thomas Bentley of Gray's Inn and printed in 1582. About the year 1574 Henry Denham acquired the patent of William Seres for printing the Psalter, the Primer for little children and all books of private prayer in Latin and English. As Denham is said to have taken "seven young men free of the Company of Stationers" to help him, it is evident that there must have been a large output under this patent. In addition to the *Monument of Matrones* before alluded to, he printed Thomas Roger's edition of the *Imitatio Christi* in 1580, Abraham Fleming's *Footpath of Felicitie* in 1581, and the same author's *Monomachie of Motives or a Battell between vertues and vices*. In 1583, Henry Denham with Ralph Newbery was appointed one of Henry Bynneman's executors and shortly afterwards started the Eliot's Court Printing House in the Old Bailey which was run by a syndicate of printers, three of whom, Ninian Newton, Arnold Hatfield and Edmund Bollifant had been in his service as apprentices. There is also reason to believe that Denham was one of the assigns of Christopher Barker. The extent of his business is shown by the fact that in 1583 he was returned as having four presses. In 1586–7 and again in 1588–9 he served the office of Junior Warden of the Company but he never reached the Mastership. The last entry under his name occurs in the Registers on December 3rd, 1589, after which nothing more is heard of him. Henry Denham used two devices, the earlier a simple star and the later a star surrounded by a heavy frame in which the arms of the City of London and the Company of Stationers were incorporated. These marks passed to Richard Yardley and Peter Short who succeeded to the business. [*Library*, July, 1909, pp. 241–50.]

DEPUTIES OF CHRISTOPHER BARKER, *see* Barker (C.), Deputies of.

DERRY, *see* Dare.

DESSERANS (JOHN), bookseller in London, 1566–76. A native of France, who took out letters of denization in this country on April 26th, 1566. In the returns of aliens made in 1576 he was described as servant to

Robert Cambier, St. Anne's, Blackfriars. Christopher Plantin got Desserans and Vautrollier to take up an agency for him in London in 1567, but the arrangement only lasted for about a year. [M. Rooses, *Christophe Plantin*, p. 258; Worman, *Alien Members*, p. 16.] John de Sheron, servant to Thomas Hacket in 1564, may be the same man.

DEVALL (ROBERT), stationer of London, 1561–2. A stationer of this name was admitted a Brother of the Company on December 6th, 1561 [Arber, i. 186]. In the list of the French Church in 1562 a Du Val is mentioned in St. Bartholomews, Farringdon Ward Without. He may have been a relative of the Thomas Devyll, or Devell, of an earlier date [*see* Duff, *Century*].

DEW (THOMAS), bookseller in London, 1621–5; St. Dunstan's Churchyard. Took up his freedom March 5th, $162\frac{0}{1}$, and made his first book entry in the Registers on June 9th, 1621 [Arber, iii. 685; iv. 55]. On September 2nd in the same year John Trundle assigned to him the copyrights in two plays, *A Faire Quarrell* and *Greene's Tu Quoque* [Arber, iv. 58]. Dew shared with John Marriot and John Grismand the second part of Drayton's *Polyolbion*, entered on March 6th, $162\frac{1}{2}$ [Arber, iv. 65]. He made a nuncupative will on March 13th, $162\frac{4}{5}$, which was proved on April 1st, 1625 [P.C.C., 43, Clarke]. His copyrights passed to John Helme.

D'EWES or DEWES (GARRAT), bookseller and printer in London, 1560–91; St. Paul's Churchyard at the sign of the Swan. Garrat Dewes or D'Ewes, was the eldest son of Adrian D'Ewes, an immigrant from Holland. He was apprenticed to Andrew Hester and was made a freeman of the Company of Stationers on October 4th, 1557 [Arber, i. 70]. In 1568 he was taken into the Livery and served the office of Renter in 1572 and 1573, and that of Under Warden in 1581–2. Dewes married Grace Hinde of Cambridgeshire, a Dutchwoman, who died in 1583 and was buried in St. Faith's [Herbert, p. 941]. Soon after her death he retired to his estate at Upminster in Essex. He died on April 12th, 1591, leaving a son Paul who was the father of Sir Simon D'Ewes [Inq. P.M., 34 Eliz.]. He was buried at Gaines in Essex. Garret Dewes' earliest publication was a broadside recording the birth of a monstrous pig at Hampstead near London, which was printed for him by A. Lacy in 1562 and is reprinted in Huth's *Ancient Ballads and Broadsides*, p. 163 [Arber, i. 202]. In 1567

he entered the *Prognostication of Master Buckmaster* [Arber, i. 328]. He was a disorderly member of the Company, being frequently fined for such offences as keeping his shop open on Holy days and not attending the court: during the wardenship of Richard Jugge and John Day he was more heavily fined for printing "The Boke of Rogues" (*i.e.*, probably Harman's *Caveat for Cursetors*). In 1573 Garret Dewes was one of those who bought the patent of Francis Flower for printing grammars, and for whom a very original border was cut embodying all their devices. That of Garret Dewes represents the interior of a house showing two dice-players throwing a "deuce." In 1580 he was engaged in a lawsuit with Richard Ramsey, his mother's second husband, respecting some property left by his father [Court of Requests, $\frac{134}{47}$]. Sir John Lambe in his notes upon the London printing houses said that Thomas Dawson bought the business of Garret Dewes in 1590 [Arber, iii. 702]. It is singular that though he was the son of an alien there appears to be no mention of him in Messrs. Kirk's *Returns of Aliens*.

DEXTER (ROBERT), bookseller in London, 1590–1603; The Brazen Serpent, St. Paul's Churchyard. Son of Robert Dexter of Ipswich, sailor. Apprentice to Francis Coldock for nine years from Michaelmas, 1580, and made a freeman on June 25th, 1589 [Arber, ii. 102, 705]. Robert Dexter made his first entry in the Registers on January 20th, $15\frac{89}{90}$ [Arber, ii. 538]. He is believed to have succeeded Andrew Maunsell, the bookseller, at the Brazen Serpent, which was formerly the printing house of Reginald Wolfe. On November 2nd, 1590, he entered fourteen works [Arber, ii. 566], one of them being Thomas Johnson's *Pathway to Reading*. This book had also been licensed to Richard Jones; but on complaint made by Dexter, the Court of Assistants cancelled the entry to Jones and ordered him to deliver up the remainder of the books in his hands, about three hundred, Dexter to pay him 6s. 8d. a reame for them, and to give him the printing of any future edition [Herbert, p. 1047]. Dexter continued to publish extensively during his lifetime. He used as a device a right hand pointing with the forefinger to a star. He made his will on October 24th, 1603, and it was proved on December 26th, 1603. Amongst his bequests were the following:—"To Mistress Bing sometime my mistress I give fortye shillings to make her a ring." "To Peter Colldock and Isabell his sister fortye shillinges a piece." To the Company he left the sum of twenty pounds to be lent out to poor young men freemen of the Company for three years at a time, and he desired that his books should be sold by Mr. Bishop, Mr. Man, Mr. Bing and Mr. Ponsonby, and the money so made to go to the payment of his debts and legacies. [Plomer, *Wills*, pp. 37, 38.]

DICK (GILBERT), bookseller in Edinburgh, (?) 1603–19. In 1618 and 1619 he was granted a monopoly of printing and selling the Book of Common Prayer and the two Catechisms approved by the General Assembly at Aberdeen in 1616, but no book bearing Dick's name is known. A Gilbert Dick, merchant, burgess of Edinburgh, is mentioned in *Reg. P.C. Scot.* vi. 806 (1603) and ix. 291 (1611); and the will of Alison Forman, relict of Gilbert Dik, merchant, burgess of Edinburgh, was registered November 13th, 1645. [Aldis, *Scottish Books*, 112; *Reg. P.C. Scot.* xi. 30, 626, 643; xii. 77; Lee, App. xix, xx; Lee, *Add. Mem.* 72–3.]

DICKENSON (WILLIAM), bookseller in London, 1563–85. Took up his freedom December 3rd, 1565 [Arber, i. 318]. On January 14th, 158$\frac{4}{5}$, he entered a ballad [Arber, ii. 439].

DIEST or DIELYN (GILLIS I and II VAN), printers at Antwerp, 1533–67 and 1565–73. The elder was received as "vrijmeester printer" into the St. Lucasgild in 1533, and the younger in 1573. In the years 1563–5 were published at least ten English Catholic books with the imprint of Aegidius Diest including N. Winzet's *Book of Fourscore three Questions*, 1563 [Herbert, p. 1608], two works of J. Rastell, Lewis Evans' *Admonition unto the Ministers of England*, 1565 [Hazlitt, II. 209], and translations by R. Shacklock from Osorio da Fonseca and Cardinal Hosius. Mr. Sayle assigns most of these—all that are at Cambridge—to Gillis II, but the dates seem to fit better with Gillis I. [Olthoff, p. 25.]

DIGHT (EDWARD), *see* Dight (John).

DIGHT (JOHN), bookbinder at Exeter, *c.* 1635. In the Bodleian is a curious volume of complicated geometrical designs made by a deaf and dumb man John Dight, eldest son of Edward Dight, citizen, bookseller and bookbinder of Exeter. The son was also a bookbinder "who proved so ingenious at it that he excelled most men therein." A biography by a nephew is prefixed and from it John Dight's birth may be put down to about 1600–15.

DIGHT (WALTER), printer in London, 1590–1627; (1) The Falcon in Shoe Lane, St. Bride's parish; (2) The Harp in Shoe Lane [*Broadsides of the Soc. of Antiquaries*, no. 106]. Son of John Dight of Dunyate, co. Somerset. Apprentice to Henry Midleton for seven years from Christmas, 1581: admitted to the freedom of the Company on January 7th, 158$\frac{8}{9}$ [Arber, ii. 109, 703]. Admitted into the Livery June 30th, 1604 [Arber, ii. 875]. He made his first entry in the Registers July 12th, 1598, and his last on November 6th, 1615 [Arber, iii. 575]. His will was dated October 8th, 1618, and proved January 18th, 161$\frac{8}{9}$. In it he bequeathed all his "quiar bookes" to his nephew Edward Dight, and gave his two apprentices Richard and Lawrence the first refusal of his printing house, presses and other things [P.C.C., 6, Parker].

DISHER (SAMUEL), stationer at Cambridge, 1616–24. Paid Churchrate of xij[d] in Great St. Mary's parish, 1616 [Foster's *Churchwardens' Accounts*], and is amongst the "privileged persons" in the University, 1624 [Bowes, *Univ. Printers*, 336].

DISLE or DISLEY (HENRY), draper and bookseller in London, 1576–80; St. Paul's Churchyard, at the South West Door of St. Paul's Church. Son of John Disle of London, draper. Apprentice to William Jones for thirteen years from Midsummer, 1563 [Arber, i. 198]. Henry Disle was the publisher of a collection of verse called *The Paradise of Dainty Devices*. His last book entry appears on January 26th, 15$\frac{79}{80}$ [Arber, ii. 364].

DOOMS (JOSSE, JOOS, or JODOCUS), printer at Ghent, 1620–36; rue de la Monnaie, du côté de la place de Ste. Pharaïlde; at the sign of the press. In English he printed Hermann Hugo's *Siege of Breda*, n.d., c. 1628 [Sayle, p. 1501], *The Rule of St. Benedict*, n.d., and *Statutes for the observation of the holy rule of St. Benedict* (3 parts), 1632, presumably issued with the *Rule*. [Vanderhagen, *Bibl. Gantoise*, ii. 99–105; vi. 74–8.]

DORPE or DORPIUS (JAN CLAESZ VAN, or JOANNES NICOLAI F.), printer at Leyden, 1596–1648; at the sign of the Golden Sun. In 1616 he printed the third edition of *The Revelation of St. John, with an analysis, &c.*, by T. Brightman [Sayle, p. 1461; Ledeboer, *A.L.*, p. 48].

DOUCE (   ), widow, (?) bookseller in London, 1624. Mentioned in John Gee's *Foot out of the snare*, 1624, as a "famous" dealer in popish books. Her address is not given.

DOWCE or DOWSE (THOMAS), *see* Plomer, *Dictionary*.

DOWNES (BARTHOLOMEW), stationer of London, 1618–36. The career of this stationer is somewhat puzzling. On March 23rd, 161$\frac{7}{8}$, under a Privy Seal, Bartholomew Downes in company with two other London printers, Felix Kingston and Matthew Lownes, was appointed King's Printer in Ireland. About the same time he also took a share in what was known as the Latin Stock, for which he paid £25, but in the proceedings that followed upon the winding up of that venture, his brother Thomas Downes declared that Bartholomew was "only a workeman employed in binding of bookes and not using any other trade." He appears however to have had a share in the publication of several news-sheets between 1621 and 1623, being associated with Wm. Ley, Wm. Sheffard and Nath. Butter. [Arber, iv. 61, 78–80, 89; *Library*, July, 1907.]

DOWNES (THOMAS), *see* Plomer, *Dictionary*.

DOWSING (JOHN), bookseller in London, 1611–19. Took up his freedom on October 29th, 1611 [Arber, iii. 683]. On May 1st, 1619, he entered Henry Short's *Epitome of Love* [Arber, iii. 647]. Nothing more is known of him and his address has not been found.

DOWSYE (ROBERT), bookseller in London, 1566–97. Apprentice to Alexander Lacye for seven years from 1559 [Arber, i. 145], but was transferred to Thomas Marsh before July 22nd, 1563. He took up his freedom in the Company of Stationers on August 15th, 1566. On October 31st, 1597, he entered a ballad on the visit of the Queen to Parliament in the preceding week [Arber, iii. 94].

DRAWATER (JOHN), bookseller in London, 1593–7; (1) The Swan, in Paternoster Row (before August 26th, 1595); (2) Canon Lane near St. Paul's, at the sign of the Unicorn (after August 26th, 1595). Son of Anthony Drawater of Fotheringham, co. Northampton, miller. Apprentice to Richard Jones, stationer, for eight years from January 6th, 158$\frac{0}{1}$: took

up his freedom June 25th, 1593 [Arber, ii. 103, 712]. On January 23rd, 159$\frac{4}{5}$, he entered *A discourse of the usage of the Englishe fugityves by the Spaniardes*, but transferred the copyright to William Ponsonby on September 26th, 1597 [Arber, ii. 670; iii. 91].

DUCKETT (JAMES), bookseller (?) in London, 1600. Executed on April 19th, 1601, for selling popish books. [*Library*, April, 1907, pp. 169, 175; Gillow, *Dict. of Catholics*, ii. 133–5.]

DUFFIELD (THOMAS), bookseller in London, 1569–87. Apprentice to Henry Sutton for eight years from September 29th, 1561: admitted to the freedom on October 17th, 1569 [Arber, i. 169, 420]. He appears to have been a poor member, as in the year ending July 10th, 1586, the Wardens' accounts record a sum of 10s. as given to Thomas Duffielde [Arber, i. 515]. The only entry under his name is a ballad licensed to him on November 20th, 1587 [Arber, ii. 480].

DUNCON (CHARLES), *see* Plomer, *Dictionary*.

DUNSCOMBE (ROBERT), *see* Plomer, *Dictionary*.

DUNSTALL (JOHN), (?) bookseller in London, 1615–20. Son of John Dunstall of Lambeth, Surrey, yeoman. Apprentice to Christopher Wilson for seven years from April 7th, 1605 [Arber, ii. 291]. Took up his freedom December 4th, 1615 [Arber, iii. 684]. In partnership with William Jones he entered on April 3rd, 1620, Edward Gunter's *Canon Triangulorum* [Arber, iii. 672].

DURAND (ZACHARY), printer at Geneva, 1561. In this year he printed *The Form of Prayers . . . at Geneva, Four score and seven Psalms*, and *The Catechism* [St. Paul's Cath. Lib., *see* Hazlitt, VII. 434].

DUXSELL (THOMAS), *see* Duff, *Century*.

DYER (THOMAS), bookseller in Oxford, 1617–19. Apprentice to William Spire [Clark, *Register*, ii. 1. 343, 404; Gibson, *Oxford Wills*, p. 32].

DYOS (NICHOLAS), printer in London, 1582–7; The Talbot, a little above Holborn Conduit (Roger Ward's house). Apprentice to Roger Ward, printer, and admitted a freeman of the Company of Stationers on May

6th, 1587 [Arber, ii. 699]. During his apprenticeship he was employed in printing the *A B C and Little Catechisme*, and in the subsequent proceedings brought by John Day for the infringement of his copyright, admitted having done so. He was at that time eighteen years of age. What became of him afterwards is not known [Arber, ii. 753–69].

EAST (THOMAS), printer in London, 1567–1609; (1) Fleet Street, near to Saint Dunstan's Church, 1567–70; (2) Bread Street at the nether end, 1568; (3) At London Wall, by the sign of the Ship, 1571–7; (4) Thames Street, between St. Paul's Wharf and Baynard's Castle, 1577–88; (5) The Black Horse, Aldersgate Street, 1588–1609. This printer, who was a Buckinghamshire man, took up his freedom in the Company of Stationers on December 6th, 1565: there is no record as to his apprenticeship. He would appear to have set up in business with Henry Middleton in Fleet Street, over against or near to St. Dunstan's Church. In the following year however, East had a press of his own in Bread Street, and in 1571 he and Middleton removed to the Ship in London Wall. This partnership continued until 1572, during which time they printed several medical and theological books. In 1577 East took as an apprentice Henry Chettle, who afterwards became a dramatist, and about this time he moved into premises in Thames Street, where he printed the *Euphues* of John Lyly and an edition of Sir Thomas Malory's *Morte d'Arthur*. It is however as a printer of music that Thomas East is best remembered. William Byrd, organist of the Chapel Royal, had been granted in 1575 a license to print and sell music and to rule, print, and sell music paper, and this license he assigned to Thomas East, who on November 6th, 1587, entered Byrd's *Psalmes, Son ts and songs of sadnes and pitie*. East also printed the musical publications of John Dowland, Thomas Morley and Thomas Weelkes. On June 17th, 1609, Mistress East transferred the copyrights of Thomas East's books to Thomas Snodham, alias East, so that we may presume that the printer had died shortly before. The adoption of the alias by Snodham was probably a trade advertisement to show that he was the successor to the business. Most of East's musical copyrights were assigned to John Brown, Matthew Lownes and Thomas Snodham. Lucretia East, the widow, was living at Cudworth, co. Warwick, in 1627, when she made her will in which she mentioned her "stock" of £160 in

the Company of Stationers, and left bequests to Simon Waterson and Richard Badger; she nominated Edmund Weaver her executor. [*Library*, July, 1901; P.C.C., 61, Ridley.]

EDGAR (ELEAZAR), bookseller in London, 1600–13; (1) The Bull's Head, (?) St. Paul's Churchyard; (2) The Windmill, St. Paul's Churchyard, 1609; (3) The Jonas, (?) St. Paul's Churchyard, 1612 [Sayle, p. 685]. Son of Mark Edgar of Carlisle. Apprentice to Ralph Jackson for eight years from September 1st, 1589; took up his freedom June 25th, 1597 [Arber, ii. 163, 718]. Made his first book entry on January 3rd, 1$\frac{599}{600}$ [Arber, iii. 153]. Edgar dealt chiefly in theological literature. His copyrights were assigned to John Hodgetts on April 19th, 1613 [Arber, iii. 520–1]. Amongst his publications was Joseph Hall's *Characters of Vertues and Vices*, 1608.

EDMONDS (DENIS), *see* Edwards (Dionise).

EDMONDS (WALTER), *see* Plomer, *Dictionary*.

EDMONDS (WILLIAM), bookseller in London, 1568–97; St. Botolph without Aldgate. Apprentice to John Awdely for seven years from November 1st, 1561. Took up his freedom on November 18th, 1568. Made his first entry in the Registers, a ballad, during the year ending July 22nd, 1571, and his last on September 24th, 1576. [Arber, i. 168, 390; ii. 302]. His will, dated August 18th, 1597, was proved in the Archdeaconry of London by his widow Margaret on September 23rd, 1597. He left a son Ralph.

EDMONDSON (GODFREY), *see* Plomer, *Dictionary*.

EDMUNDES, *see* Edmonds.

EDWARDS (DIONISE), stationer in Oxford, 1608–22. Admitted stationer to the University, April 18th, 1608 [Clark, *Register*, ii. 1. 262, where his name appears as Denis Edmonds]. Edwards was appointed one of the valuers of the stock of Nicholas Smith, Joseph Barnes and Francis Peerse [Gibson, *Oxford Wills*, pp. 21–3, 27, 28].

EDWARDS (GEORGE), senior, bookseller in London, 1616–40; In the Old Bailey, in Green Arbour, at the sign of the Angel. Son of Richard Edwards of Sybbert, co. Oxford, yeoman. Apprenticed to Manasses

Blond, stationer of London, for eight years from Michaelmas, 1600, and took up his freedom in the Company on November 7th, 1608 [Arber, ii. 247, iii. 683]. George Edwards made his first entry in the Registers on December 19th, 1616, when Ralph Mabb assigned over to him the copyrights in six books [Arber, iii. 599]. He appears to have been in partnership with Jacob Bloome, as in a subsequent assignment made on June 4th, 1621, they are stated to be jointly concerned in the copyrights [Arber, iv. 54]. Edwards dealt chiefly in theological books.

EDWARDS (GEORGE), junior, (?) bookseller in London, 1624. Under date June 1st, 1624, there is an entry in the Registers to "George Edwards, Junior," of some of the Rev. Henry Smith's sermons [Arber, iv. 118]. This may have been a son of George Edwards, senior, in partnership with his father. There was another George Edwards who took up his freedom in the Company on December 1st, 1634 [Arber, iii. 687].

EGLESFIELD (FRANCIS), *see* Plomer, *Dictionary*.

ELD or ELDE (GEORGE), printer in London, 1604–24; The Printer's Press, Fleet Lane, 1615. Son of John Elde of Scrapton, co. Derby, carpenter. Apprentice to Robert Bolton for eight years from Christmas, 1592; took up his freedom on January 13th, 1$\frac{599}{600}$ [Arber, ii. 185, 725]. Sir John Lambe in his notes upon the master printers stated that George Eld married the widow of Richard Reade who had previously been the wife of Gabriel Simpson, and so succeeded to the business. On May 9th, 1615, Eld was returned as having two presses [Arber, iii. 699]. A large number of books came from his press, amongst them Stow's *Annales*, Camden's *Remains* and Bolton's *Elements of armorie*. George Eld died of the plague in 1624 and was succeeded by Miles Flesher or Fletcher [Arber, iii. 689].

ELFE, ELSE or (?) ELLIS (WILLIAM), bookseller in London, 1628; Holborn Conduit. Mentioned in a list of second-hand booksellers who in 1628 were ordered to submit catalogues of their books to the Archbishop of Canterbury [*Dom. S. Papers, Chas. I*, Vol. 117 (9)].

ELLIS, *see also* Elfe.

ELLIS (THOMAS), bookseller in London, 1629; The Christopher in St. Paul's Churchyard. A stationer of this name took up his freedom on June 26th, 1615 [Arber, iii. 684]. He may be identical with the publisher of the broadside entitled *Man's Creation, Adam's Fall and Christ's Redemption*, which was issued from the above address in 1629 [Hazlitt, I. 113].

ELSE, *see* Elfe.

ELY (FERDINAND), bookseller in London, 1626–8; Little Britain. Mentioned in a list of second-hand booksellers who in 1628 were ordered to submit catalogues of their books to the Archbishop of Canterbury. Bernard Alsop the printer confessed to having purchased from him the manuscript of Sir Robert Cotton's *Short View of the Long life and reign of Henry the Third*, in 1626. [*Dom. S. Papers, Chas. I*, Vol. 117 (9).]

ELZEVIER (BONAVENTURA AND ABRAHAM), booksellers and printers at Leyden, 1621–52. Bonaventura, born in 1583, was concerned in the publication of two books in 1608–10, but apparently not regularly established in business until 1617, when he joined his eldest brother Matthew, who died in 1622. In 1621 he admitted to partnership his nephew Abraham, born 1592, and they continued to publish together until 1652 in which year both died. From 1625 onwards they also printed. They did little work in English but in 1633 printed a Greek *New Testament* for sale in London by R. Whittaker [Willems, no. 397], and in 1636 the *Mare Clausum* of J. Selden, which contains some English [Sayle, p. 1462; Willems, no. 449]. Neither of these works bears the printers' name. [A. Willems, *Les Elzevier.*]

EMERSON, *see* Edmondson.

EMERY (JASPAR), *see* Plomer, *Dictionary*.

EMSLEY or EMILIE (DENNIS), bookseller in London, 1564–71. Apprentice to "Master Wally" and presented on October 9th, 1555 [Arber, i. 38]. Made a freeman on March 27th, 1564 [Arber, i. 240], and began taking apprentices at Christmas, 1566. In the year ending July 22nd, 1569, he entered a book entitled *An Introduction of Christians* [Arber, i. 378]. The last heard of him is in the year 1570–1, when he was fined for going to the Hall in his cloak [Arber, i. 445]. Hazlitt [III. 291] records a work entitled *An Answere in action to a Portingale Pearle, called a Pearle for a Prince* . . . . Imprinted at London in Fleet-streete, by William How for Dionis Emilie, 8vo. (copy at C.C.C. Cambridge).

ENDERBY (SAMUEL), *see* Plomer, *Dictionary*.

ENGLAND (NICHOLAS), *see* Duff, *Century*.

ENSOR *see* Ainsworth.

ESCH or ESSAEUS (HENDRICK VAN), printer at Dort, 1630–59. He was presumably the "Henry Ash" who printed John Paget's *Meditations of Death*. [Ledeboer, *A.L.*, 54.]

EVANS (HERMAN), *see* Duff, *Century*.

EWLAM (RICHARD), stationer at Cambridge, *c.* 1624. His name occurs in a list of "Privileged persons in the University," 1624 [Bowes, *Univ. Printers*, 336].

EXELL or EXOLL (EMANUEL), bookseller in London, 1594–1631. Son of Robert Exhole, merchant taylor of London. Apprentice to George Allen for eight years from March 25th, 1587 [Arber, ii. 145]. Admitted a freeman on February 4th, 1594 [Arber, ii. 713]. Renter of the Company in 1631 [Arber, iii. 693]. Mentioned in a list of stationers who held shares in the Latin stock [*Library*, January, 1909, p. 105].

FAIRBEARD (GEORGE), bookseller in London, 1618–29; The George, Pope's Head Alley, near the Royal Exchange. Took up his freedom May 6th, 1617 [Arber, iii. 684]. First book entry in partnership with Richard Fleming on April 13th, 1618 [Arber, iii. 624]. He dealt in prints and engravings as well as books [Arber, iii. 673]. He made his last entry in the Registers on May 25th, 1622 [Arber, iv. 69].

FAIRBEARD or FAIRBERNE (JOHN), *see* Duff, *Century*.

FAULKNER (FRANCIS), *see* Plomer, *Dictionary*.

FAWCET (THOMAS), *see* Plomer, *Dictionary*.

FAWNE (LUKE), *see* Plomer, *Dictionary*.

FEIRABENDIUS (SIGISMUND), bookseller at Frankfurt am Main, ? 1560–89. He was born *c.* 1527, as appears from his portrait (*see* P. Heitz's *Frankfurter Druckerzeichen*, fig. 1). He published T. Harriot's *Brief and true report of Virginia*, 1590, printed by John Wechel.

FENRICUS (M), (?) bookseller in London, 1627; Next to the Greyhound Tavern in the Blackfriars. T. Newman's translation of Terence's *Andria* and *Eunuchus*, 1627, were to be sold at his house. Nothing further seems to be known of him.

FERBRAND or FIREBRAND (WILLIAM), bookseller in London, 1598–1609; At his shop in Lothbury, at the hither end of Colman Street. First book entry May 3rd, 1598 [Arber, iii. 114]. Dr. Arber [v. xci.] gives the covering dates of this bookseller as 1588–1609, but I cannot trace his authority and conclude that the first date is a misprint for 1598. Ferbrand was the publisher of some of Rowlands' and Dekker's writings and a humorous work called *Quips upon Questions*, 1600. During the latter part of his life he was associated with John Budge. His last book entry occurs on the last day of October, 1608, and he died shortly afterwards, as on July 4th, 1609, his widow, Helen Ferbrand, transferred her interest in certain copies to John Budge, and the remainder to Thomas Archer on October 12th in the same year [Arber, iii. 393, 414, 419].

FERRIE (JOHN), bookbinder in (?) Edinburgh, 1609. He is mentioned in November, 1609, in the Register of the Privy Council of Scotland, viii. 373. His wife was Beatrix Weir. He lived probably in Edinburgh. [Aldis, *Scottish Books*, 112.]

FETHERSTONE (HENRY), *see* Plomer, *Dictionary*.

FIELD (NATHANIEL), bookseller in London, 1611–28. Son of John Field of London, clerk, apprenticed to Ralph Jackson, stationer, for eight years from Michaelmas, 1596, and took up his freedom on June 3rd, 1611 [Arber, ii. 215; iii. 683]. He thus served seven years beyond his term. Field's first book entry does not occur until 1624, and his last was on December 19th, 1627 [Arber, iv. 133, 191]. He dealt chiefly in theological literature, amongst which is found two sermons preached at Court by Theophilus Field, Bishop of Landaff. The bishop is stated in the

Dictionary of National Biography to have been the brother of Nathaniel Field, the actor and dramatist, who may be identical with this stationer. His place of business has not been found.

FIELD (RICHARD), printer in London, 1579–1624; (1) Blackfriars; (2) The Splayed Eagle, Great Wood Street, *c.* 1600. Son of Henry Field, tanner, of Stratford upon Avon, whose goods and chattels John Shakespeare, the poet's father, with two others was employed to value on August 25th, 1592. In 1579 Richard Field left Stratford and, coming to London, apprenticed himself to George Bishop for seven years. He was at once transferred for the first six years to Thomas Vautrollier, the Huguenot printer in Blackfriars [Arber, ii. 93]. Thomas Vautrollier died before March 4th, $158\frac{6}{7}$, and Richard Field who had taken up his freedom on February 6th, married his master's widow within a twelvemonth and thus succeeded to one of the best businesses in London. His first book entry is found in the Registers under December 24th, 1588. On April 18th, 1593, Field entered in the Registers "a booke intituled Venus & Adonis," the first of William Shakespeare's books that passed through the press. On May 9th, 1594, Field also printed for John Harrison the elder, Shakespeare's *Lucrece* and a second edition of *Venus and Adonis*. This was followed in 1596 by a third edition of the same work, in octavo. About 1600 Field removed from Blackfriars to the parish of St. Michael in Wood Street, at the sign of the Splayed Eagle. In 1615 he was returned as having two presses. He became a prominent member of the Stationers' Company, of which he was elected Master in 1619 and 1622. Field died in the autumn of the year 1624. By his will which was proved on December 14th in that year, he desired that he might be buried in the church of St. Michael, Wood Street. His property he divided into three parts, one of which he left to his wife, who is called Jane in the will. This was probably a second or third wife, and not the Jacqueline, or Jaklin, the widow of Thomas Vautrollier. He bequeathed The Splayed Eagle to his son Richard, and other property in Wood Street to another son Samuel. Small bequests were also left to Manasses and James Vautrollier, two of the sons of Thomas Vautrollier. The only other member of his family mentioned in the will was a sister Margaret, and there is no mention of Stratford upon Avon. Field's business eventually passed into the hands of George Miller, one of his apprentices. [P.C.C., 107, Byrde.] Field's

principal device was the "Anchora Spei" that had previously been used by Thomas Vautrollier. There were several sizes of it. He also used most of the borders and tail pieces as well as the types that had belonged to Vautrollier. On the whole his work as a printer was creditable, though it did not approach in excellence that of Vautrollier. It is in his brief connection with Shakespeare that its chief interest lies.

FINCH (ROBERT), (?) bookseller in London, 1595. Son of Nicholas Finch of Redbourn, co. Herts., husbandman. Apprentice to Thomas Woodcock, stationer, for nine years from Christmas, 1586 [Arber, ii. 145]. Admitted a freeman on March 3rd, $159\frac{4}{5}$, on the death of his master, and took over his fellow apprentice Thomas Wydowes [Arber, ii. 715, 205]. The only book entry under his name occurs on September 22nd, 1595 [Arber, iii. 48]. Nothing more is heard of him.

FINLASON (THOMAS), printer in Edinburgh, 1597–1628. Son of James Finlason, bailie and treasurer of Dundee. He was a burgess of that town in 1593, but by 1597 had removed to Edinburgh, and became a merchant burgess of that city. In 1602 he turned his attention to printing, and began by purchasing the privileges, stock, and plant of Robert Smyth [*q.v.*]. This was followed, in 1604, by the purchase of Waldegrave's patent from his widow, and two years later he bought up the licence formerly held by James Gibson, bookbinder, for printing the Bible and certain other books. Having thus acquired practically all the existing Scottish patents, he obtained, on June 16th, 1606, a gift under the Privy Seal of Scotland confirming to him all these privileges with sundry additions; and in 1612 he was appointed king's printer in succession to Robert Charteris. He seems to have commenced actual printing with the acquisition of Waldegrave's materials in 1604, and many of the ornaments formerly used by Waldegrave and other Scottish printers are to be found in his books. He made frequent use of Arbuthnet's small device, modified by the excision of Arbuthnet's name, initials, and arms, and the insertion of his own initials. His type and ornaments were acquired later on by Robert Young, and from him passed to George Anderson and then to Robert Bryson. The books which issued from Finlason's press consisted to a large extent of official and legal publications, and are as a whole by no means so interesting from a literary point of view as the productions of his more famous contemporary Andro Hart, nor are they so numerous. Among the more notable books are the two editions of Skene's *Regiam majestatem*, 1609, and *The Muses Welcome to the high and mightie prince James*, 1618, a collection of the loyal effusions called forth by the King's visit to Scotland in 1617. Upon this latter, Finlason seems to have expended the whole battery of typographical ornament contained in his printing house. Finlason died between September 27th and December 3rd, 1628, and was succeeded by his second son Walter. His inventory has not been found. [Aldis, *Scottish Books*, 112; *E.B.S. Papers*, vol. i., no. 20; *Reg. P.C. Scot.*, v–xi.; Lee, App., xv., xvi.; Wedderburn (Scot. Hist. Soc., 28), p. xxv.]

FINLASON (HEIRS OF THOMAS), printers in Edinburgh, 1628–30. An edition of the *Flyting of Montgomery and Poiwart*, 1629, and some half-dozen proclamations and acts of parliament printed 1628–30 bear the imprint of the Heirs of Thomas Finlason [*q.v.*].

FINLASON (WALTER), printer in Edinburgh, was the second son of Thomas Finlason [*q.v.*]. On January 17th, 1628–9, he was appointed printer of acts of parliament, proclamations, etc., in succession to his father. Nothing is known bearing his imprint, but apparently he worked under the style of Heirs of Thomas Finlason [*q.v.*]. He was succeeded by Robert Young. [Aldis, *Scottish Books*, 113; *E.B.S. Papers*, vol. i., no. 20; Lee, App., xxii.]

FIREBRAND, *see* Ferbrand.

FISHER (BENJAMIN), bookseller in London, 1621–37; The Talbot, Aldersgate Street. Took up his freedom July 15th, 1622 [Arber, iii. 685]. First book entry, a theological work, on July 16th, 1622 [Arber, iv. 75]. On April 30th, 1623, he took over from John White several of the writings of Hugh Broughton [Arber, iv. 95]. Amongst his publications were Abraham Darcye's *True Historie of Q. Elizabeth's reign*, 1624, Capt. John Smith's *Accidence or pathwaye to experience necessarye for all young sea men*, 1626, Thomas May's *History of the reign of K. Henry II*, 1632, and Heywood and Brome's play of *The late Lancashire Witches*, 1634. On August 12th, 1635, he acquired a very large number of copyrights that had belonged to Thomas Man, Paul Man and Jonah Man. The entries fill

nearly two pages of the Register [Arber, iv. 345]. These he assigned to Robert Young under a mortgage on March 27th, 1637. In 1628 he was mentioned in a list of dealers in second hand books who were required to send a catalogue to the Archbishop of Canterbury [*Dom. S. Papers, Chas. I*, vol. 117, (9)].

FISHER (THOMAS), draper and bookseller in London, 1600–2; The White Hart, Fleet Street. Translated from the Company of Drapers and admitted a freeman of the Stationers on June 3rd, 1600 [Arber, ii. 725]. On October 8th, 1600, he entered Shakespeare's *A Mydsommers nightes Dreame* [Arber, iii. 174], and on October 24th, 1601, with Mathew Lownes, Marston's *Antonio & Mellida* [Arber, iii. 193]. Nothing more is known of him. He used the device of a kingfisher.

FISHER (WILLIAM), bookseller in London, 1604–? 1622. Son of John Fisher of Bryneton, co. Northampton, yeoman. Apprentice to Thomas Gubbyn, stationer of London, for nine years from June 8th, 1595; admitted a freeman on June 4th, 1604 [Arber, ii. 205, 737]. On July 23rd, 1622, a William Fisher entered *The Spanish English Rose* by Michael Du Val [Arber, iv. 76], but there is no evidence that he was identical with the stationer who took up his freedom in 1604.

FITZER (WILLIAM), *see* Stolzenberger (J. N.).

FLASKET (JOHN), draper and bookseller in London, 1594–1613; (1) The North door of St. Paul's; (2) The Black Bear, St. Paul's Churchyard. Transferred from the Drapers' Company and admitted a freeman of the Company of Stationers on June 3rd, 1600 [Arber, ii. 725]. He is stated to have had a shop or shed at the Great North door of St. Paul's at the commencement of 1594, and upon the death of Thomas Woodcock who lived at the sign of the Black Bear in St. Paul's Churchyard, he and Paul Linley succeeded to the business. Amongst their customers was the Duke of Northumberland [see *Hist. MSS. Comm. Rept.* 6, App., p. 226]. Linley died in 1600, and the copyrights were then transferred to Flasket [Arber, iii. 164–5]. The last heard of him is on December 20th, 1613, when in company with E. Weaver he assigned two books to Richard More [Arber, iii. 538].

FLEMING (HUGH), (?) bookseller or printer in London, 1563–4. Only known from an entry in the Registers during the year ending July 22nd, 1564, *A preservative for the plage with also a medycene for the same* [Arber, i. 231].

FLEMING (RICHARD), bookseller in London, 1616–9; (1) At the great South Door of St. Paul's on the right hand going up the steps, 1617; (2) The Three Flower-de-Luces, in St. Paul's Alley, near St. Gregory's Church, 1619. He was made free of the Stationers' Company on December 2nd, 1616 [Arber, iii. 684]. His first entry in the Registers was made on January 21st, 161$\frac{6}{7}$, and his last on July 29th, 1619 [Arber, iii. 601, 654]. His publications seem all to have been theological.

FLESHER (MILES), *see* Plomer, *Dictionary*.

FLINTON (GEORGE), printer at Rouen, 1581–*c.* 1584. He was the first printer at the Catholic press established at Rouen by Parsons, and printed several of Parsons's works there, including the *Christian Directory* generally called the *Book of Resolution*. Later, in 1583 or 1584. he was printing there together with S. Brinckley [*q.v.*]. Flinton died soon after this date. [Gillow, *Dict. of Catholics*; Sayle, p. 1743.]

FLOWER (FRANCIS), Assigns of, 1573–96. Francis Flower, who received a grant in the year 1573 to print books in Latin, Greek and Hebrew, and grammars, on December 26th in the same year appointed Christopher Barker, John Wyghte, William Norton, John Harrison, Garret Dewes and Richard Watkins, to be his assigns [Arber, ii. 795]. They had a special block made embodying their several devices. This patent gave rise to much dissatisfaction amongst the poorer printers, who, headed by John Wolf [*q.v.*], secretly printed thousands of copies of these privileged books and refused to desist.

FOGNY (JEAN DE), printer at Rheims, 1561–93. In 1582 he printed the first edition of the Rhemish *New Testament* [B.M., p. 210], and Gregory Martin's *Discovery of the manifold corruptions of the Holy Scriptures*: in 1583 *A report of the apprehension of John Nichols at Rouen* [B.M., p. 1148].

FOOKES or FOWKES (THOMAS), stationer of London, 1585–94; Fleet Street. Only known from his will dated September 25th, 1600, and proved on October 15th in the same year. It gives no details as to his business. He may be identical with the Thomas Fowkes, stationer of London, who was taking apprentices between 1585 and 1594. [Arber, ii. 132, 147, 188, 722; P.C.C., 59, Wallopp.]

FORREST (EDWARD), bookseller in Oxford. *See* Plomer, *Dictionary*.

FOSBROOKE (NATHANIEL), bookseller in London, 1605–29; (1) The West door of St. Paul's, the corner shop, near to the Bishop of London's gate, 1611 [Sayle, p. 761]; (2) Upper end of the Old Bailey, among the Sadlers, 1614 [Sayle, p. 761]; (3) Pope's Head Alley, near Lombard Street, 1629. Entered in the Registers as Nathaniel Fosborough, son of Ralph Fosborough of Cranford, Northampton, clerk. Apprentice to Henry Carre, stationer, for eight years from July 25th, 1597, and admitted a freeman on April 5th, 1605 [Arber, ii. 219, 738]. His last book entry occurs in the Registers on January 21st, 1613 [Arber, iii. 512], but he was publishing in 1629 [Hazlitt, II. 205].

FOSTER (ANTHONY), bookseller at York, 1580–1607. Many books were purchased from him during these years by the Chapter. He dwelt within the precincts of the Cathedral. [Davies, *Memoir of the York Press*, p. 34.]

FOSTER (JOHN), bookseller at York, ?–1616. Probably son and successor of Anthony Foster. An inventory of his stock, made at his death in 1616, contains some three thousand books. It is printed in full by Davies. [*Memoir of the York Press*, pp. 34–5, 342–71.]

FOWLER (JOHN), printer at Antwerp, Louvain, and Douai, 1566–79; In de Cammerstraet, naby de Erfgen. Steelsius, Antwerp, 1576 [Olthoff]. He was born at Bristol, 1537, educated at Winchester School and New College, Oxford, where he became a fellow. He took the degree of M.A. in 1560, and in the same year or shortly after left England for religious reasons. In 1565 he was received as printer at Louvain [Olthoff, p. 33], where, early in 1566 he printed Saunders' *Supper of our Lord* [Sayle, p. 1445], and Pointz' *Testimonies for the Real Presence* [Herbert, p. 1620]. Later in 1566 he apparently had a press at Antwerp and printed there works by Rastell, Frarin and Harding [Herbert, pp. 1616–9]. From 1567 to 1572 he printed some eighteen works at Louvain in English by Rastell, Sanders, Harding and others. In 1570 he obtained permission to establish himself at Antwerp and seems to have removed thither in 1572 [Sayle, p. 1366]. At Antwerp he printed Sir T. More's *Dialogue of Comfort*, 1573, R. Bristow's *Brief Treatise*, 1574 [Herbert, p. 1635], and a *Jesus Psalter*, 1575 [B.M., p. 874]. In or before 1578 he seems to have left Antwerp, for in this year he printed G. Martin's *Treatise of Schism* at Douai, the only book which he is known to have printed there. He died February 13th, 157$\frac{8}{9}$ (or, according to Olthoff, in 1582). [*D.N.B.*; Gillow, *Dict. of Catholics*; Olthoff, p. 33.]

FOWLER (——), Mistress, (?) bookseller in London, 1624; Fetter Lane. Mentioned in John Gee's *Foot out of the snare*, 1624, as "one that trades much to St. Omers" [*i.e.*, in popish books]. She may have been the widow of a stationer.

FOXON (ROBERT), bookseller in Oxford, 1590–1. Admitted a bookseller November 27th, 1590 [Clark, *Register*, ii. 1. 321]. An inventory of his goods was taken on March 7th, 159$\frac{0}{1}$ [Gibson, *Oxford Wills*, 17].

FRANCIS or FRANCOIS (HERCULES), bookseller in London, 1576–1603; Parish of St. Benet Finck, Broadstreet Ward. Born in Warmenhuyse in Holland. The Cambridge University Library has a copy of Beza's *Psalms*, 8vo, of which the imprint runs: Londini, typis Thomae Vautrollerij & impensis Herculis Francisci 1580 [Sayle, no. 1539]. His will, dated October 14th, 1603, was proved on April 21st, 1604. He left the residue of his estate to his wife Mathurin. [P.C.C., 34, Harte; Worman, *Alien Members of the Book Trade*, p. 23.]

FRANCKTON, "FRANKE," FRANKETON, FRANKTON, FRANCTON or FRANTON (JOHN), printer at Dublin, 1600–?1618. First appears as printer in Dublin in 1600, in which year he printed two Proclamations for the Government. He lived in Dublin for many years, where he married Margery Laghlin, a freewoman of that city. Through her and at the instance of Archbishop Jones, Chancellor of Ireland, he obtained the City freedom. He had three or four children, some of whom obtained the freedom also. He was appointed State Printer in 1604 and

became Sheriff in 1612. His press turned out some excellent work and volumes of note and importance, *i.e.*, *The New Testament* and the *Book of Common Prayer* in Irish, 1602 and 1608, Sir John Davis' *Le Primer Report*, etc., 1615, etc., and also numerous Proclamations for the Government. There is no record of his death. He sold his Patent rights as State Printer to the London Stationers' Company, whose representatives came over in 1618 or 1619 to Dublin. The earliest form of Franckton's name, "Franke," suggests his foreign origin. His ability to use Irish type suggests his having learned to do so from William Kearney, his immediate predecessor as printer in Dublin, and as the latter practised his art in England and "foreign parts" for many years, it is not improbable that he met "Franke" abroad and brought him over with him to Dublin.

FRANKLIN (MICHAEL), bookseller in London, 1617–24. Took up his freedom in the Company of Stationers, September 26th, 1617 [Arber, iii. 684]. Mentioned in John Gee's *Foot out of the Snare*, 1624, as a "disperser" of popish books.

FREMORSHAM (ANDREAS), bookseller in London, 1561–86; St. Faiths, Farringdon Within. A Dutchman, Factor for Arnold Birckman in England, and said to have been in the ward for ten years in 1571 [Worman, *Alien Members*, p. 23]. His correct name was Vrimurs or Vrimursanus. For a law-suit in which he was concerned on account of some books bought from him by Dr. John Dee, *see* the *Library*, January, 1909, p. 102.

FRENCH (PETER), bookseller in London, 1555–84. This stationer is first mentioned in the Registers in a list of those paying fines for being late in their attendance at the Hall on July 6th, 1555. He also contributed to Bridewell and other charities [Arber, i. 44, 47]. French appears to have dealt in ballads and almanacks. The last entry under his name is on March 15th, 15$\frac{79}{80}$ [Arber, ii. 366]. He made his will on June 25th, 1584, and it was proved on December 19th in the same year. He was twice married, but left no son [*Dean and Chapter of St. Paul's*, Book B. fol. 277].

FRERE (DANIEL), *see* Plomer, *Dictionary*.

FRETHEN (THOMAS), (?) bookseller in London, 1581; The Royal Exchange, at the sign of the Half Rose and Half Sun, next to the North Door. Frank Adams' *Writing Tables*, 1581, is said to bear the above imprint [Hazlitt, III. 244].

FROSCHAUER (CHRISTOPHER I.), *see* Duff, *Century*.

FROSCHAUER (CHRISTOPHER II.), printer at Zurich, *c.* 1552–86. Nephew of the elder Christopher, printed with his uncle from *c.* 1552–64, and alone from 1564. Mr. Sayle attributes to him four books printed without place or printer's name in 1574–5 [Sayle, pp. 1414–15]. He seems to have acted as agent between the English Reformers and their friends at Zurich, especially on the occasion of his visits to Frankfurt fair, where he would meet English merchants [*Zurich Letters* (Parker Soc.), i. 224; ii. 180, 243, 294, 305].

FUSSELL (NICHOLAS), *see* Plomer, *Dictionary*.

FYFIELD (ALEXANDER), *see* Plomer, *Dictionary*.

GARBRAND (AMBROSE), bookseller in London, 1610–16; The Windmill in St. Paul's Churchyard. Son of Richard Garbrand of Oxford, bookseller. Apprentice to Cuthbert Burby for eight years from February 2nd, 160$\frac{2}{3}$: took up his freedom February 5th, 16$\frac{09}{10}$ [Arber, ii. 270; iii. 683]. On June 15th, 1610, William Welby assigned over to him two theological books [Arber, iii. 437]. Garbrand was in partnership with Eleazar Edgar at the above address. His last entry was on October 16th, 1616, when he assigned over one of his copyrights to Master Adams [Arber, iii. 596].

GARBRAND alias HARKES (JOHN), bookseller in Oxford, 1609–17. Born in 1585. Grandson of Garbrand Herks [*q.v.*] or Herks Garbrand. Scholar of Winchester College, Oxford, in 1596. Fellow of New College, Oxford, from 1606 to 1608. B.A., 1603–4: M.A., 1608. Licensed to sell wine [Clark, *Register*, ii. 1. 323]. Died before September 29th, 1617. His widow Martha married Christopher Rogers, Principal of New Inn Hall. [Kirby, *Winchester Scholars*, p. 157; *D.N.B.*]

GARBRAND or HARKS (RICHARD), bookseller in Oxford, 1574–1628; in St. Mary's parish. Son of Garbrand Herkes or Herks Garbrand. Admitted a bookseller on December 5th, 1573 [Clark, *Register*, ii. 1. 321]. Churchwarden of St. Mary's in 1569. Died in 1602.

GARDENER (LAWRENCE), stationer of London, 1578–89. Took up his freedom in the Company of Stationers on June 25th, 1578 [Arber, i. 677]. He is found taking apprentices between November 6th, 1581, and March 3rd, 1589 [Arber, ii. 108, 156]. He was perhaps a relative of Leonard Gardener. There is no evidence that he published books nor has his place of business been found.

GARDENER (LEONARD), bookseller in London, 1562–3. Took up his freedom in the Company of Stationers on January 21st, 15$\frac{62}{63}$ [Arber, i. 121]. During the year ending July 22nd, 1563, he entered a ballad called *An epetaph of the deathe of ye lorde Gray* [Arber, i. 205]. His address is unknown.

GARDENER (THOMAS), printer in London, 1576–7; (?) The Three Cranes in the Vintry. Son of John Gardener of Ipswich, Suffolk, tanner. Apprentice to Henry Wekes from June 24th, 1568, for seven years [Arber, i. 372]. Began taking apprentices of his own in January, 1577 [Arber, ii. 72]. Joined Thomas Dawson the printer, their only book entry occurring on November 2nd, 1576 [Arber, ii. 304]. Thomas Gardiner is not heard of after 1577. He had a son Thomas who was admitted to the freedom "per patrimonium" on March 26th, 1599 [Arber, ii. 723].

GARRET (WILLIAM), *see* Plomer, *Dictionary*.

GAYOT, *see* Guyeth.

GELLIBRAND (SAMUEL), *see* Plomer, *Dictionary*.

GELLIBRAND (THOMAS), (?) bookseller in London, 1597; Dwelling in St. Mary Axe. Mr. Arber [v. 188] states that Thomas Gellibrand was publishing at the above address in 1597, but does not give his authority, nor does he mention the work or works published.

GEMINI (THOMAS), *see* Duff, *Century*.

GETHING (RICHARD), writing-master in London, 1616–?1652; The Hand and Golden Pen, Fetter Lane. In 1616 he published at this address *A Coppie booke of the vsuall hands written* [Hazlitt, VII. 160]. [*D.N.B.*]

GIBBS (GEORGE), bookseller in London, 1613–33; The Flower de Luce, St. Paul's Churchyard. Son of George Gibbes of Southwark, Surrey, saddler. Apprentice to Thomas Hayes, stationer of London, for eight years from Christmas, 1600 [Arber, ii. 252]. On April 7th, 1605, he was put over to

William Cotton [Arber, ii. 290]. Gibbs took up his freedom in the Company of Stationers on January 18th, 160$\frac{7}{8}$, and his first book entry in the Registers was made on December 20th, 1613 [Arber, iii. 683, 538]. He dealt in literature of a miscellaneous character and was associated with Henry Holland in several publications. The last entry under his name is found on May 10th, 1633 [Arber, iv. 294].

GIBSON (JOHN), bookbinder in Edinburgh, 1580–1600. In 1580 he joined Lekpreuik in a complaint to the Town Council against Robert Woodhouse for retailing books within the burgh, and in 1582 he was party to a similar proceeding against Vautrollier. He acquired the printing rights of Gilbert Masterton [*q.v.*], and these privileges were extended by royal grants made to him in 1589 and 1590. In July, 1591, he was appointed bookbinder to the King. He does not appear to have himself engaged in printing, but in July, 1599, he obtained a licence for a psalm book which he had "causit imprent within Middilburgh." He died on December 26th, 1600, and his printing privileges were purchased from his son James by Thomas Finlason in 1606. His widow, Katherine Boyd, survived until July, 1622. For his inventory *see Bannatyne Miscell.*, ii. 222. [Aldis, *Scottish Books*, 113; Dickson and Edmond, 206, 349; *E.B.S. Papers*, vol. i. no. 12; Lee, 48; *Notes and Queries*, 3rd Ser., iv, 408.]

GIBSON (THOMAS), (?) printer and bookbinder in Bury St. Edmunds, Suffolk, 1582. Only known from a passage in Strype's *Annals of the Reformation*, vol. iii. pt. i., p. 177. Referring to certain words painted on the Queen's Arms in Bury Church in 1582, Strype says that Lord Burghley ordered certain persons to be called up for examination, one of them being "Thomas Gybson, bookebinder of Bury." Strype further says in reference to Gibson, "this man had printed Browne's books," referring presumably to Robert Browne, the founder of the sect of Brownists. No reference to this incident, nor any mention of Thomas Gibson is to be found in the Burghley papers printed by the Historical Manuscripts Commissioners, nor in the State Papers, and the name does not appear in the Registers of the Stationers' Company. "The badde practise of . . . the Booke-binder, and his accomplishes [*i.e.*, accomplices] at Bury" is mentioned in *An Almond for a Parrot* [1590], sig. C2, where the "newe Posie" added to the Queen's arms is given, but Gibson's name does not appear.

GIBSON (THOMAS), bookseller in Edinburgh, 1592. He was one of the seven booksellers who, in February, 1592, complained to the Town Council against John Norton of London for retailing books within the burgh [Lee, App. lxxi.].

GILBERT (THOMAS), bookseller in London, 1588–90; Fleet Street, near to the Castle. Associated with Thomas Newman in publishing Everard Digby's *Dissuasion from taking awaye the lyvinges and goodes of the Churche*, March 2nd, 15$\frac{89}{90}$ [Arber, ii. 540].

GILMAN (ANTHONY), bookseller in London, 1601–25. Son of Richard Gilman of Blechingley, Surrey, gent. Apprentice to Robert Walley, stationer of London, for eight years from November 1st, 1587: took up his freedom in the Company on May 15th, 1601, being admitted into the Livery in 1603 [Arber, ii. 149, 728, 874]. In 1618 Gilman was elected junior Warden, and held the office of senior Warden in the years 1622 and 1625. In 1616 he took a share or shares in the Latin Stock. His only book entry, made on November 9th, 1620, was Robert Newton's *Countesse of Montgomeries Eusebia* [Arber, iv. 42]. His address has not been found.

GLADWIN (RICHARD), bookseller in London, 1628; Holborn Conduit. Mentioned in a list of second-hand booksellers who in 1628 were ordered to submit catalogues of their books to the Archbishop of Canterbury [*Dom. S. Papers, Chas. I*, vol. 117 (9)].

GLOVER (JEROME), bookseller in London, 1559-68. Made free of the Company of Stationers by Robert Holder in the year ending July 10th, 1559. In 1563 his name occurs in a list of those who were fined for selling *Nostradamus* and in 1567–8 he entered Valentine Lee's *Survaynge of landes* [Arber, i. 217, 355].

GODHED or GODETT (GILES), *see* Duff, *Century*.

GODLIF or GODLEY (FRANCIS), stationer and bookbinder in London, 1562–96; At the West end of St. Paul's. The earliest reference to this bookseller in the Registers is the entry to him of a ballad called *A Description of a monstrous child*, during the year ending July 24th, 1562. It was printed for him by Leonard Askell, and is reprinted in Mr. Huth's *Ancient Ballads and Broadsides*, p. 299, ed. 1867 [Arber, i. 181]. Godlif or Godley was admitted a freeman of the Company of Stationers on January 20th, 156$\frac{1}{2}$.

In the following year he married, and an entry in the Wardens' accounts includes a sum of five shillings for the hire of the Hall on that occasion [Arber, i. 186, 218]. In the year ending July 22nd, 1565, he was fined for binding primers "unjustly and contrary to orders." In 1566–7 he appears to have been working as a bookbinder in Chester, and his name ("Godlof") is mentioned in the Registers of the Chester Stationers' Company. Later on he brought an action against the Company to uphold his right to bind books in vellum, and in the year ending July 9th, 1577, the Company paid him 40s. to "surcease his sute" [Arber, i. 475]. In 1582 he is found borrowing £3 13s. 4d. from the Company. He repaid it the following year; but shortly afterwards a larger loan was granted to him which was not repaid until 1591 [Arber, i. 494, 497].

GODWIN (JOSEPH), bookseller in Oxford, 1617–73, *see* Plomer, *Dictionary*, and Gibson, *Oxford Wills*, 45.

GODWIN (PAUL), (?) bookseller (?) in London, 1638. On March 7th, 163$\frac{7}{8}$, a stationer of this name entered a book called *Histoire de Larrons or the history of theeues* [Arber, iv. 410].

GOLDING (PER.), (?) bookseller in London, 1608. *An Epitome of Froissart*, translated from the Latin of Sleidan by P. Golding, was printed for him by T. Purfoot in this year. He does not seem to be otherwise known.

GORE (JOHN), bookseller at Oxford, *see* Duff, *Century*. In 1568 he was living in High Street, at corner of Grope Lane (Grove Street) [*Oriel leases*].

GOSSON (ALICE), bookseller in London, 1600–1 and 1622; Pannier Alley. Widow of Thomas Gosson [*q.v.*]. Nothing seems to be heard of her between 1601, when her son Henry was made a freeman, and 1622, when R. Tisdale's *Lawyer's Philosophy* appeared with the imprint "printed for I.T. and H.G. and are to bee sold at the Widdow Gossons in Pannier Alley." This was one of Henry Gosson's addresses, but as nothing of his is found bearing it later than 1622, it seems likely that he handed over his shop there to his mother in this year.

GOSSON (HENRY), bookseller in London, 1601–40; (1) The Sun, Paternoster Row, 1603–9; (2) London Bridge, near to the Gate, 1608–40; (3) Catherine Wheel Alley, 1613; (4) Pannier Alley, ? 1615–22. One of the sons of Thomas Gosson, admitted a freeman of the Company of Stationers, "per

patrimonium" and presented by his mother Alice Gosson, widow, on August 3rd, 1601 [Arber, ii. 730]. He entered his first book on May 18th, 1603 [Arber, iii. 36]. Dealt extensively in popular literature such as ballads, broadsides, newsbooks, romances and jest books. His last entry occurs on July 26th, 1640 [Arber, iv. 516]. From *The Last Terrible Tempestious Winds*, 1613, sig. C2ᵛ, it appears that at that date he dwelt in Catherine Wheel Alley, but this address does not appear on his publications.

GOSSON (THOMAS), bookseller in London, 1579–1600; (1) The Goshawk in the Sun in St. Paul's Churchyard, next the Gate; the corner shop to Cheapside; (2) In Paternoster Row [? at the Sun] next to the Castle tavern; (3) At his shop adjoining London Bridge Gate, 1595–1600. Admitted to the freedom of the Company on February 4th, 157$\frac{6}{7}$, by Thomas Purfoote [Arber, ii. 673]. He made his first entry in the Registers on March 24th, 1579, and dealt largely in ballads, plays and miscellaneous literature. Thomas Gosson was one of those who sold the pirated copies of John Day's *Psalmes* and the *A B C and Little Catechisme* [Arber, ii. 791], for which he was fined 20s. on October 11th, 1596 [Arber, ii. 826]. Thomas Gosson made his last entry in the Registers on November 6th, 1598, and died sometime between that date and September 1st, 1600 [Arber, v. 199]. After his death his widow Alice [*q.v.*] appears to have carried on the business until her son Henry was made a freeman on August 3rd, 1601.

GOURLAW (ROBERT), bookbinder in Edinburgh, 1585. Died September 6th, 1585. His will is printed in the *Bannatyne Miscellany* [ii. 209], and the list of his books in the inventory occupies six pages. Among his creditors at the time of his death were Thomas Vautrollier, Henry Charteris and Robert Smyth. His wife, Isabel Haldin, survived him. [Aldis, *Scottish Books*, 113].

GOWER (CHRISTOPHER), (?) bookseller in London, 1585–7. Son of George Gower or Gowre of York, merchant. Apprentice to Richard Grene for eight years from September 8th, 1566 [Arber, i. 324]. He was the compiler as well as the printer of a work on handwriting [Arber, ii. 465].

GRAFTON (RICHARD), *see* Duff, *Century*.

GRAPHEUS (RICHARDUS), *see* Duff (E.), *Century*, p. 60—Joannes Graphaeus.

GREEN (BENJAMIN), (?) bookseller in London, 1632. Associated with Moses Bell in issuing a broadside entitled *A yearely Continuacion of the Lord Maiours and Sherriffs of London* [Arber, iv. 287]. He may be the same as the Benjamin Greene who took up his freedom on June 9th, 1628 [Arber, iii. 686].

GREENE (CHARLES), *see* Plomer, *Dictionary*.

GREENE (FRANCIS), bookseller in Cambridge, 1628–35; Parish of Great St. Mary's. Possibly son of Leonard Greene. He paid the Church rate in the parish of Great St. Mary's from 1628 to 1635. He published the second edition of Giles Fletcher's *Christs Victory* in 1632 and various editions of George Herbert's *Temple* until 1634.

GREENE (JOANE), bookseller in Cambridge and (?) London, 1631–7. Widow of Leonard Greene. She was certainly living in Cambridge for two years after her husband's death, as she paid the church rate in the parish of Gt. St. Mary's until 1632 [Gray's *Shops at West End of Great St. Mary's*]. Her name appears on the 1631 edition of J. Preston's *Sermons* and again on the 1634 edition, but no address is given in either. On September 15th, 1637, she assigned over to Anne Boler, the widow of James Boler, all her interest in several publications [Arber, iv. 393], after which no more is heard of her.

GREENE (JOHN), (?) bookseller in London, ? 1630–? 1634. A stationer of this name is given as taking up his freedom in the Company on June 17th, 1624 [Arber, iii. 685]. But the references to John Greene in the 1640 catalogue of English Books at the British Museum, upon the authority of which Mr. Arber makes the statement that he was publishing between 1630 and 1634, are misleading. The J. Greene whose name appears in the imprint of Dr. Preston's *Sermons* in 1634 was *Joane* Greene, the widow of Leonard Greene of Cambridge, for whom the first edition of the work was published in 1630, while James Shirley's *Gratefull Servant* was published in 1630 by John *Grove* of Furnivall's Inn Gate.

GREENE (LEONARD), printer and bookseller in Cambridge, 1606–30; Parish of Great St. Mary's. Admitted a freeman of the Company of Stationers on April 14th, 1606, and made his first entry in the Register in company with John Porter on May 13th, 1606 [Arber, iii. 683, 321]. In 1607 he paid 3s. 4d. church rate, and from 1612 to 1630 he was assessed at 4s. annually. From 1612 to 1617 he paid rent for his shop at the south side of the steeple of St. Mary's church, Cambridge (figured in Loggan's *Cantabrigia Depicta*), and for the shop on the north side occupied by W. Williams, a bookbinder [*q.v.*]. By a Grace of October 31st, 1622, he was appointed one of the printers to the University, and on December 16th, 1625, there is a second Grace for sealing a patent to him in conjunction with Thomas and John Buck. The last entry under his name in the Stationers' Registers occurs on January 22nd, $16\frac{29}{30}$. Leonard Greene was associated with other Cambridge and London stationers, such as Cantrell Legge, Thomas Pavier and James Boler, and like most of the University stationers he had an agent in London, his edition of Giles Fletcher's *Reward of the Faithfull*, 1623, being "to be sold at the sign of the Talbot in Paternoster Row." He died some time in 1630 and was buried at Cambridge. His widow Joane continued to live in the same house for two years after his death. [Bowes' *University Printers*, 298–300; Gray's *Shops at West End of Gt. St. Mary's*; Foster's *Churchwardens' Accounts*.]

GREENE (RICHARD), (?) bookseller in London, 1556–1612; (?) St. Dunstan's in the West. There were two men of this name, Richard Grene, senior [*see* Duff, *Century*] and Richard Greene, junior, who was made a freeman February 3rd, $158\frac{3}{4}$ [Arber, ii. 690]. The will of a Richard Green, stationer of St. Dunstan's in the West, was proved on May 9th, 1612, in the Court of the Dean and Chapter of St. Paul's. He left a bequest to his son George and a sum of forty shillings to the Company of Stationers.

GRIFFIN (ANNE), *see* Plomer, *Dictionary*.

GRIFFIN (EDWARD), senior, printer in London, 1613–21; Dwelling in the Little Old Bayley near the sign of the King's Head. Son of Robert Griffin of Rydland, co. Flint, yeoman. Apprentice to Henry Conneway, citizen and stationer of London, for eight years from Michaelmas, 1589. He is found taking apprentices on his own account on October 3rd, 1597 [Arber, ii. 220]. A second Edward Griffen, Griffin, or Gryffyn, the son of John Griffen of Llandunes, co. Denbigh, was apprenticed to Arnold Hatfield for seven years from February 2nd, $160\frac{3}{4}$ [Arber, ii. 276], took up his freedom

February 18th, $161\frac{0}{1}$ [Arber, iii. 683], and entered his first book on November 2nd, 1613 [Arber, iii. 534]. On the death of Melchisidec Bradwood in 1618 he secured the business of the Eliot's Court Press. His last book entry occurs on December 14th, 1620 [Arber, iv. 44], and his death took place before June 7th, 1621, when his widow in conjunction with John Haviland took over the business [Arber, iv. 55].

GRIFFIN (EDWARD), junior, *see* Plomer, *Dictionary*.

GRIFFITH (WILLIAM), *see* Duff, *Century*.

GRISMAND or GRISMOND (JOHN), bookseller, printer and typefounder in London, 1618–38; The Gun, near the Little North door of St. Paul's, 1618; (2) The Gun, St. Paul's Alley, 1621; (3) The Gun, Ivy Lane, 1627–36. Took up his freedom in the Company of Stationers on December 2nd, 1616 [Arber, iii. 684]. Between 1618 and 1622 he was associated in the publication of books with John Marriott. He also printed and sold ballads, and his name occurs in a list of those to whom 128 ballads were entered on December 14th, 1624 [Arber, iv. 131]. As his name does not appear in the list of authorised printers in 1615, it is possible that he did not set up a press of his own until after his appointment as a recognised typefounder, under the Star Chamber decree of 1637 [Arber, iv. 535]. The last book entry under his name occurs on November 5th, 1635 [Arber, iv. 350]. John Grismand died before December 31st, 1638, when his will was proved in the Prerogative Court of Canterbury, being dated January 5th, 1636. He was twice married, but left no heir, and his property passed by will to his second wife Mary. Amongst the stationers to whom he left bequests were Richard Cotes, Nathaniel Man, Edwin Bush, and Philip Nevill, and he nominated Thomas Downes and John Parker overseers [P.C.C., 169, Lee]. He was succeeded by John Grismand II, believed to have been his nephew. *See* Plomer, *Dictionary*.

GROVE (FRANCIS), *see* Plomer, *Dictionary*.

GROVE (JOHN), bookseller in London, 1620–37; Furnivall's Inn Gate. Took up his freedom in the Company of Stationers on January 17th, $16\frac{19}{20}$ [Arber, iii. 685]. He was probably a relative of Francis Grove. He dealt in law-books, plays and sermons. Amongst the plays that bear his name may be mentioned *Holland's Leaguer* by Shakerly Marmion, *The Wedding* by James Shirley, *The tragedy of Hoffman*, and *The Grateful Servant*. These he transferred on September 25th, 1637, to William Leake [Arber, iv. 394].

GROYTER (AMELL DE), typefounder in London, 1583. In the Returns of Aliens in 1583 occurs this entry:—Groyter, Amell de, Criplegate Without, Dutchman, letter maker for printers [Kirk's *Returns of Aliens*, Part ii. 317]. An Aimé de Gruyter made some founts for Christopher Plantin in 1589 [M. Rooses, *Christophe Plantin*, p. 239; Worman, *Alien Members*, p. 26].

GUBBIN or GUBBINS (THOMAS), bookseller in London, 1587–1629; (1) The Griffin, Paternoster Row, over against the Black Raven; (2) In St. Paul's Churchyard. This stationer was apprentice to John Walley of the Hart's Horn in Foster Lane, by whom he was made free on January 31st, $158\frac{8}{9}$ [Arber, ii. 696]. In his first publication, entered in the Registers on September 18th, 1587, he was associated with Thomas Newman, and he is also found in partnership with John Busby, Thomas Man and John Porter. With Newman he shared the publication of Robert Greene's *Farewell to Folly* in 1591. Thomas Gubbin married Johane, the eldest daughter of John Harrison the eldest, by whom he had two sons, Francis and Charles, and a daughter Hester, mentioned in the will of John Harrison [Plomer, *Wills*, pp. 48, 49]. In 1603 Gubbin was admitted a freeman of York. His last book entry occurs on May 15th, 1614 [Arber, iii. 546]. His will dated August 15th, 1625, and proved on December 21st, 1629, is in the Prerogative Court of Canterbury [P.C.C., 106, Ridley]. The above addresses are recorded by Mr. Arber in his *Bibliographical Summary*, but the majority of Gubbins' books have no address. A person of the name of Gubbins is mentioned in 1624 in John Gee's *Foot out of the snare* as a disperser of popish books.

GUILLICKE, *see* Gulke (A. van).

GULKE, GUILLICKE, HILLOKE or VAUKYLL (ARNOLD VAN), bookseller in London, 1568. John Stell and Arnold Vaukyll, both "born in Andwerpe and stacyoners, Doutchmen," were committed to the Counter in the Poultry, by the Lord Mayor, for causing to be printed by John Allde a book of 8 pp. in French on the tyranny of the Duke of Alva, dated September 18th, 1568. Mr. E. J. Worman in his *Alien members of the*

Book Trade, considers the last named to be identical with Arnald van Gulke and also with Arnold Hilloke of Limestreet Ward, bookbinder, mentioned in part i., p. 410, of Messrs. Kirk's *Returns of Aliens*. An Aert van Guylick is mentioned in the list of those persecuted for religion who frequented the various London churches in 1568 [Worman, p. 31]. About the same time John Stell and Arnolde van Gulke entered in the Registers an "almanacke in Duche" [Arber, i. 383].

GURNEY (ROBERT), (?) bookseller in London, 1636. Only known from an entry in the Registers on July 19th, 1636, of a broadside by Martin Parker [Arber, iv. 367].

GUYETT or GAYOT (GABRIEL), typefounder in London, 1576–88; Criplegate Without. A Dutchman, resident in John Day's house in St. Anne's Aldersgate in 1576, and probably employed by him to cut letters. He came of a famous family of letter founders and was brother to the widow of Anthony Deise [*q.v.*]. [Worman, *Alien Members*, p. 26.]

GUYOT (CHRISTOPHER), printer at Leyden, 1598–1603. In 1603 he printed John Johnston's *Heroes ex omni Historia Scotica lectissimi* for Andro Hart, bookseller in Edinburgh [Hazlitt, I. 239]. [Ledeboer, *A.L.* p. 69.]

GWILLIM (JOHN), bookseller in London, 1615; Britain's Burse. Only known from an entry in the Registers on May 4th, 1615, of Nicholas Breton's *Caracters morall and divine* [Arber, iii. 567], which was printed for him by E. Griffin.

H. (J.), printer at Amsterdam, 1597–1611. Mr. Sayle queries whether he is Jodocus Hondius or Joos de Hondt [*q.v.*]. He printed W. Bradshaw's *Short Treatise of the Cross in Baptism*, 1604 [Sayle, p. 1428].

HACKET (THOMAS), *see* Duff, *Century*.

HACKFORTH (ROBERT), (?) bookseller in London, 1565–70. Apprentice with Thomas Marshe, by whom he was presented on October 14th, 1556. Made free of the Company of Stationers on December 3rd, 1565 [Arber, i. 41, 317]. He was dead before July 22nd, 1570, and was buried by the Company, which suggests that he was a poor man. He dealt chiefly in ballads [Arber, i. 315, 421].

HAESTENS (HENDRIK VAN), printer at Leyden, 1596–1629. In 1610 he printed *The Divine beginning of Christ's Visible Church* by Henry Jacob, in the imprint of which he is called "Henry Hastings" [Sayle, p. 1462]. This has as device a female [? Minerva] with "Acad. Lugd." above.

HAGEN (FRANCIS VAN), bookbinder in (?) Edinburgh, 1604. In 1604 he is named among the debtors in the inventory of Jonet Mitchelhill, wife of Andro Hart, printer in Edinburgh. As no place is mentioned it is probable that he was living in Edinburgh. [Aldis, *Scottish Books*, 113; *Bannatyne Miscell.* ii. 240.]

HALL (HENRY), printer at Oxford, 1637–?1679, *see* Plomer, *Dictionary*, and Gibson, *Oxford Wills*, 45.

HALL (ROWLAND), *see* Duff, *Century*.

HALL (WILLIAM), printer in London, 1598–1614. Son of William Hall of Lillisfield, co. Salop, clerk. Apprentice to John Allde for seven years from January 28th, 1577, and admitted to the freedom of the Company on February 3rd, $158\frac{3}{4}$ [Arber, ii. 73, 690]. His first work appears to have been an edition of *The Summe of the Conference betweene J. Rainolds and J. Hart*, 1598, 4to. On November 28th, 1608, he was allowed by the Company to print an edition of Justin in Latin [Arber, iii. 396]. In 1609 W. Hall and Thomas Haviland secured some of the copyrights for printing commercial papers from Richard Braddock. Sir J. Lambe in his notes says that they bought the business which had belonged to Robert Robinson [Arber, iii. 702]. In 1612 Hall was associated with John Beale, who eventually succeeded him and to whom his copyrights were transferred on April 7th, 1614 [Arber, iii. 544]. His place of business is unknown.

HALLEY (EDMUND), bookseller in London, 1562–5; The Eagle in Lombard Street near unto the Stocks Market. The first notice of Edmund Halley is the entry recording his freedom on February 26th, $15\frac{59}{60}$ [Arber, i. 122]. Some time between July 22nd, 1561, and July 24th, 1562, he entered a ballad *Against filthy writing and such like delighting* which was printed for him by John Allde and is reprinted by Mr. Collier in *Old Ballads* (Percy Soc.), 1840, p. 50. Hall also dealt in almanacs and was fined in 1563 for selling "Nostradamus" [Arber, i. 218]. The last entry under his name is found in the year ending July 22nd, 1566.

HAMILLON (CARDIN), printer at Rouen, 1566–? 1614. A person of this name printed an edition of Cranmer's *Bible* at the cost of Richard Carmarden in 1566, and from 1609 to 1614 we find six small English books bearing the same name in the imprint. The first of these is B. Canfield's *Rule of Perfection*, and the last St. Francis de Sales' *Introduction to a Devout Life*. It seems natural to suppose these later works to have been produced by a successor of the printer of the *Bible*. One or both was presumably related to the Richard Hamillon who printed at Rouen between 1541 and 1559; *see* Duff, *Century*. In the later books two devices are used (1) I H S (Sit nomen domini benedictum), (2) I H S (Nomen domini laudabile) 33 mm. [Sayle, p. 1400].

HAMMANDE or HAMONDE (HENRY), stationer in Salisbury, 1571–6. In a return of stationers living in the country, who paid "scott & lott" to the Company in 1571, occurs the name of "Henry Hamonde in Salisbury" [Arber, v. lii]. In the Subsidy Roll for that city, dated September 10th, 1571, in the ward of New Street is the entry: "Henrye Hammond in goods . . . iij[li] . . . v[s]." and again in that of 18 Eliz., 1575–6, it is repeated [Lay Subsidy $\frac{198}{283}$. $\frac{198}{294}$]. Again in the Wardens' Accounts for the year ending July 15th, 1590, is the entry: "Item, gyven by consent of a courte towarde the proceadinge of Master Hamonde's sonne of Salisburye who procedethe master of Artes at Oxon, at this commencement . . . . x[li.]" [Arber, i. 539]. John Waley of the Hart's Horn in Foster Lane, at his death in 1586, left a bequest "To my poor scholler Thomas Hamond in Oxford five poundes a yere for foure yeres after the date hereof" and also bequests to "Henry Hammondes children, Henry, Robert and Lionell." Stationers of this name are found in Salisbury till late in the seventeenth century.

HAMMON (JOHN), bookseller in London, 1614–30. Took up his freedom September 7th, 1612 [Arber, iii. 683]. His first book entry occurs on March 4th, $161\frac{3}{4}$ [Arber, iii. 542]. On December 16th, 1630, he assigned over his copyrights to John Beale [Arber, iv. 246]. One of these was John Taylor's *Booke of Martyrs*, 1617, a diminutive volume measuring 1½ in. by 1 in. A copy is recorded by Hazlitt [H. 595]. In 1616 a thumb-book entitled *Verbum Sempiternum* was printed by J. Beale for "John Hammam," presumably the same man [Hazlitt, VII. 377].

HAMMOND (WALTER), (?) bookseller (?) at Salisbury, 1632–40. This bookseller made his first entry in the Registers on March 24th, $163\frac{1}{2}$ [Arber, iv. 275]. He appears to have dealt chiefly in works of divinity. His last entry occurs on January 4th, $163\frac{7}{8}$ [Arber, iv. 403]. Amongst his publications was a sermon preached in Salisbury Cathedral at the Lent Assizes in 1636 by the Rev. Thomas Drant, and called *The Royall Guest* [B.M. 114. c. 31]. It seems probable that he was a successor to Henry Hammande or Hamonde of Salisbury.

HAMONDE, *see* Hammande.

HAMNER (WILLIAM), printer, 1590. Found with printing materials in a cave in "the Parke" in Shropshire and arrested, but escaped [*Acts of the Privy Council*, *New Ser.*, xix. 454].

HANCOCK (RALPH), bookseller in London, 1580–95; Over against St. Giles' Church, without Cripplegate. This stationer was apparently one of Thomas Man's apprentices, but there seems to be some confusion both as to his apprenticeship and the date upon which he was admitted to the freedom of the Company. On November 25th, 1580, he paid 2s. 6d. "for that he was not orderly presented" [Arber, ii. 852]. And he is found taking apprentices himself on March 6th in the following year. But his first book entry in the Registers does not appear until February 24th, $159\frac{2}{3}$ [Arber, ii. 627]. Peele's *Old Wives' Tale* was printed in 1595 by Danter for sale by him and John Hardy at the address given above. This seems to be the only book now known upon which his name appears.

"HANSE," a printer at Dort, 1590. In this year he printed certain Puritan books by Greenwood, Barrow and others [Sayle, pp. 1465–6; see *Egerton Papers*, ed. J. P. Collier, Camden Soc. 1840, p. 172]. Persons called Arthur Byllett and Robert Stookes were concerned in the affair, but probably merely as agents for the transmission of the books. It does not seem possible to identify him.

HARDESTY (JOHN), *see* Plomer, *Dictionary*.

HARDING (BRIAN), bookseller in Colchester, Essex, 1624. The will of this bookseller was proved on October 8th, 1624. He left the residue of his goods including his stock of books to his "kinsman" Robert Harding [P.C.C., 90, Byrde].

HARDY (JOHN), bookseller in London, 1594–1609; The Tiger's Head, St. Paul's Churchyard. Son of Christopher Hardy of Barnet, Middlesex, yeoman. Apprentice to Toby Cooke for eight years from Lady-Day, 1587, and made free on August 5th, 1594. In 1596 he was fined "for printinge a booke of Mr. Burtons without aucthoritie and entrance x sh." and was forbidden to sell the book until it was duly licensed. Imprisonment was also threatened, but was "stayed till another tyme." He succeeded Toby Cooke as Beadle of the Company of Stationers in January, $1\frac{599}{600}$. His last book entry occurs in the Registers on February 13th, $160\frac{8}{9}$ [Arber, iii. 401].

HARFORD (RAPHAEL), *see* Plomer, *Dictionary*.

HARISON, *see* HARRISON.

HARKES (GARBRAND), bookseller in Oxford, 1539–*c.* 1570. *See* Duff, *Century*. He lived in Bulkeley Hall, in the parish of St. Mary the Virgin [Wood, *Annals*, s.a. 1556].

HARKES (RICHARD), *see* Garbrand.

HARPER (RICHARD), *see* Plomer, *Dictionary*.

HARPER (THOMAS), *see* Plomer, *Dictionary*.

HARPER (WILLIAM), bookseller in London, 1614; (?) Little Britain. Son of William Harper of Woolsaston, co. Salop, clerk, and brother of Richard and Thomas Harper. Apprentice to John Bill for eight years from July 25th, 1604 [Arber, ii. 281]. Took up his freedom July 4th, 1612 [Arber, iii. 683]. Appears to have joined his brother Thomas, with whom he entered a book on July 1st, 1614 [Arber, iii. 549], and another on August 1st [Arber, iii. 551]. Nothing more is heard of him.

HARRIGAT (JOHN), bookseller in London, 1624–35; The Holy Lamb in Paternoster Row. Took up his freedom October 7th, 1622 [Arber, iii. 685]. Made his first book entry in the Registers on March 27th, 1624 [Arber, iv. 114], and his last on April 8th, 1635 [Arber, iv. 336]. His address is found in the imprint to the Rev. Richard Reek's sermon called *Faith & good workes united*, 1630 [B.M. 4473. aa. 30].

HARRIS (ANDREW), bookseller in London, 1595–8; The Pope's Head near the Exchange. Son of Thomas Harris, stationer of London [*see* Duff, *Century*, p. 67]. Apprentice to Thomas Hacket for eight years from Whitsuntide, June 4th, 1587. Made free of the Company February 25th, $159\frac{4}{5}$. On April 14th, 1598, he entered *The second parte of Hero and Leander, by Henry "Polone"* (*i.e.*, Petowe) [Hazlitt, H. 454; Arber, iii. 111].

HARRIS (ANTHONY), bookseller in London, *c.* 1577. He is mentioned as one of those that "do lyve by bookeselling being free of other Companies" in the Complaint of the printers against privileges, *c.* 1577 [Arber, i. 111]. Nothing else seems to be known of him.

HARRIS (JOHN), printer of Catholic books, 1581. Arrested at the time of the raid at Stonor Park; *cf.* Brinckley (S.) [*Acts of the Privy Council, New Ser.*, xiii. 177].

HARRIS (W), bookseller in London, 1640; Coleman Street, at the sign of the White Hind. This stationer's name occurs in the imprint to Dr. Alex. Reid's translation from Fabricius, *Lithotomia Vesicae*, 1640 [B.M. 1189. d. 7].

HARRISON (ANTHONY), bookseller in Cambridge, 1573–1625; In St. Michael's parish. This stationer was possibly one of the sons of Anthonie Harrison of Cambridge, gent., whose son Oliver was apprenticed to Felix Norton, stationer of London, on December 25th, 1600 [Arber, ii. 251]. Anthony Harrison, junior, was christened in St. Michael's Church, Cambridge, on March 12th, 1573. In June, 1603, St. John's College leased to him a tenement in St. Michael's parish for forty years at a yearly rental of 11s. [Baker's *History of St. John's College*, i. 453]. His name appears in a list of privileged persons in the University in 1624 [Bowes' *University Printers*, 336]. He died in January, 1625, and was buried in St. Michael's Church on the 31st of that month [Venn's *St. Michael's Register*].

HARRISON (JOHN I), the eldest, *see* Duff, *Century*.

HARRISON (JOHN II), the younger, bookseller in London, 1579–1617; The Golden Anchor in Paternoster Row. Believed to have been half brother to John Harrison the eldest, to whom he was apprenticed for eight years from Christmas, 1561 [Arber, i. 171]. He became free of the Company on October 17th, 1569 [Arber, i. 419], and was taken into the Livery in 1584–5 [Arber, i. 508]. John Harrison the younger's first book entry in the Registers was made on June 15th, 1579 [Arber, ii. 353]. He was constantly breaking the rules and orders of the Company and was fined on

several occasions for infringing other men's copyrights [Arber, ii. 828, 829, 854]. His most notable achievement in this direction was the part he played in the publication of Waldegrave's pirated edition of Sidney's *Arcadia* in 1599. One of the witnesses declared that John Harrison the younger had brought some of the pirated copies from Edinburgh "by sea." Harrison afterwards confessed to having had five pounds' worth of the stock, and this was probably below the mark [*Library*, March, 1900, p. 199]. John Harrison junior was elected Junior Warden of the Company in July, 1612 [Arber, iii. 491]. He died in 1618, his will being proved on August 10th in that year. He left four sons, John, Philip, Josias and Benjamin, the three first being all freemen of the Stationers' Company [Plomer, *Wills*, p. 50].

HARRISON (JOHN III), the youngest, bookseller in London, 1600–4; The White Greyhound, St. Paul's Churchyard. Son of John Harrison the elder and nephew of John Harrison the younger. He was admitted a freeman of the Company of Stationers "per patrimonium" on July 9th, 1599 [Arber, ii. 724]. John Harrison the youngest succeeded T. Judson as a master printer on February 4th, 1600 [Herbert, p. 1297]. He died before February 2nd, 1604, when his apprentices were transferred to his father [Arber, ii. 275, 289].

HARRISON (JOHN IV), the youngest (2), bookseller in London, 1603–39; At his shop in Paternoster Row, at the sign of the Unicorn, 1632. Son of John Harrison the younger (1579–1617), and referred to as John Harrison the youngest after the death of his cousin, the son of John Harrison the eldest, in 1604. Took up his freedom "per patrimonium" on June 25th, 1600 [Arber, ii. 726]. Appears to have made his first book entry on February 18th, $160\frac{0}{1}$, but the officials of the Company were evidently somewhat puzzled how to distinguish the various John Harrisons, of whom there were no less than four in business in London at this time. I have followed Mr. Arber's method of distinguishing them. This John Harrison was Senior Warden of the Company in the year 1636–7 and Master in the year 1638–9, after which nothing more is heard of him, but he may be identical with the John Harrison who was living at the Lamb or Holy Lamb, St. Paul's Churchyard, between 1641 and 1653 [Plomer, *Dictionary*, p. 92].

HARRISON (JOSEPH), bookseller in London; The Greyhound in Paternoster Row, 1608. Son of John Harrison the eldest, and admitted a freeman "per patrimonium" on February 6th, $160\frac{3}{4}$ [Arber, ii. 736]. On May 4th, 1608, he entered in the Registers Richard Myddleton's *Epigramms and Satyres*. [Arber, iii. 377; Hazlitt, H. 392.]

HARRISON (JOSIAS), bookseller in London, 1615–19; The Golden Anchor, Paternoster Row. Son of John Harrison the younger (1579–1617) and admitted to the freedom of the Company "per patrimonium" on June 25th, 1605 [Arber, ii. 738]. His first book entry, Fletcher's *Cupid's Revenge*, was made on April 24th, 1615 [Arber, iii. 566], but this and his other copyrights he parted with in April, 1619, after which nothing more is heard of him.

HARRISON (LUCAS or LUKE), *see* Duff, *Century*.

HARRISON (PHILIP), bookseller in London, 1603–8; At the Exchange. Son of John Harrison the younger (1579–1617), and admitted to the freedom of the Company "per patrimonium" on June 27th, 1603 [Arber, ii. 735], and in August of the same year he entered an apprentice [Arber, ii. 273]. On March 5th, $160\frac{7}{8}$, he entered a book relating to the East Indies [Arber, iii. 370; *see* Hazlitt, III. 235]. Another Philip Harrison, perhaps son of the above, took up his freedom in the Company on July 4th, 1631 [Arber, iii. 686].

HARRISON (RICHARD), *see* Duff, *Century*.

HARROWER (JAMES), bookseller in Edinburgh, ?1600. "In vol. 67 [of the Commissary Records of Edinburgh], May 10, 1654, is registered the Testament Dative of James Harrower, bookseller, burges of Edinburgh, 'quha deceist in the moneth of Fe. I[m] vj[c] zeirs'; and in vol. 68, August 4, 1654, that of Jeonet Patersone, his relict spous, 'quha deceist in the moneth of December, 1651 zeirs.'" [*Bannatyne Miscell.*, ii. 274.]

HART (ANDRO), bookseller, bookbinder and printer in Edinburgh, 1587–1621; High Street, on the north side of the Gate, a little beneath the Cross. He was in business as a bookseller at least as early as 1587, for in a successful petition presented to the Scottish Privy Council in February, 1589, by him and John Norton (of London) to be allowed to import books free of custom, it is stated that they "had two years ago enterprisit the hamebringing of volumes and buikis furth of Almane and Germanie." When Norton gave up his Edinburgh business about 1596, Hart and Edward Cathkin [*q.v.*] bought up his stock. Together with the two Cathkins and others, Hart was arrested and imprisoned in connection with the tumult in Edinburgh on December 17th, 1596. In 1601 books were printed for him and the Heirs of H. Charteris by Abraham and Isaac Canin [*q.v.*] of Dort; and for him alone by C. Claessonius [*q.v.*] at Amsterdam in 1602, and C. Guyot [*q.v.*] at Leyden in the following year. On the cessation of R. Charteris's press in 1610 Hart commenced printing on his own account; the first book known to have issued from his press being a folio *Bible* dated 1610, the second *Bible* printed in Scotland, and celebrated for its correctness. Hart was the most important Scottish stationer of the first half of the seventeenth century, and the distinctively literary character of his productions is a remarkable feature of his press, which continued actively at work until his death. For a device he used a head between cornucopiæ with the initials A.H., also a headpiece with heart monogram; and many of his titlepages show considerable taste. About 1613 James Cathkin [*q.v.*] was for a time in partnership with him, though to what extent is uncertain. In Sparke's *Scintilla*, 1641 [*see* Arber, iv. 35] it is related that the King's printers in London came to an agreement with Hart, and afterwards with his son John, to supply them with London *Bibles* at a cheap rate, so that they should not print any in Scotland. Bonham and John Norton seem also to have employed Andro Hart in 1601 to send out English printers to Dort and to arrange for the printing there of Bibles, etc., to the prejudice of Robert Barker [*Acts of the Privy Council, New Ser.*, xxxii. 14–15]. The books so printed were presumably those bearing the names of Abraham and Isaac Canin. Alexander Wattir [*q.v.*], a bookbinder, was in Hart's employ. Hart's first wife, Jonet Mitchelhill, died November 5th, 1604, and of three sons only one, Samuel [*q.v.*], survived her. By his second wife, Jonet Kene [*see* Hart, Heirs of Andro], he had seven children, John [*q.v.*], Andrew, James, Margaret, Jonet, Elizabeth, and Rachel. He died in December, 1621, and was succeeded by his Heirs [*q.v.*]. The inventory of his goods at the time of his death, and also that taken on the death of his first wife, are printed in the *Bannatyne Miscellany*, ii. 237, 241. [*E.B.S. Papers*, vol. i. no. 12; Aldis, *Scottish Books*, 114; *D.N.B.*; *Reg. P.C. Scot.*, iv, v, x, xi; Lee, App. xi; Calderwood's *History of the Kirk of Scotland*, v. 520, 535; vii. 382.]

HART (HEIRS OF ANDRO), printers in Edinburgh, 1621–39. After Hart's death in 1621 the business was continued by his widow and children till 1639, when the press was taken over by James Bryson, and probably the bookselling business was disposed of to John Threipland at the same time. Charteris's device is used in A. Ramsay's *Poemata sacra*, 1633. Widow Hart (Jonet Kene) seems to have taken a prominent part in the business, and she opposed the passing of Robert Young's appointment as King's printer for Scotland in 1632. She died May 3rd, 1642. The contents of her inventory [*Bannatyne Miscellany*, ii. 257] suggest that she had retired from business, and the chief debtor is John Threipland, who was due 3,400 marks "conforme to his band." The Edinburgh University Theses of 1631 bears the imprint "Excudebat Vidua Hart." *See also* Hart (John) and Hart (Samuel). [*E.B.S. Papers*, vol. i., no. 12; Aldis, *Scottish Books*, 114; *Spottiswoode Miscellany*, i. 298.]

HART (JOHN), printer in Edinburgh, 1630–? 1639. He was the eldest son of Andro Hart [*q.v.*] by his second wife. He was one of the partners in the business of the Heirs of Andro Hart, but two books (Drummond's *Flowres of Sion*, 1630, and Bayly's *Practice of Piety*, 1631) bear his name alone. His agreement with the King's printer in London concerning the Bible trade is referred to above, under Andro Hart. He died about 1639. [*E.B.S. Papers*, vol. i., no. 12; Aldis, *Scottish Books*, 114.]

HART (MICHAEL), bookseller in London, 1593. Son of John Hart of Exeter, co. Devon, shoemaker. Apprentice to John Windet, stationer of London, for eight years from Michaelmas, 1585, and immediately turned over to Andrew Maunsell, bookseller, who was a member of the Drapers' Company to serve out his time [Arber, ii. 136]. Hart took up his freedom on October 5th, 1592, a year before his term was out, when the clerk records that Hart had been "turned over to Robert Dexter and served his yeares out with him" [Arber, ii. 711]. The explanation is that Dexter succeeded Maunsell at the Brazen Serpent in St. Paul's Churchyard about the year 1590 [Arber, ii. 566]. Hart was associated with Toby Cooke in the publication of George Gifford's *Dialogue concerning Witches & Witchcraftes*

in 1593 [Hazlitt, H. 248.] This is the only book that has been traced bearing his imprint. His address has not been found. He may possibly be the "one *Mighell* (somtimes *Dexters* man in *Powles Church-yard*, though now he dwels at *Exceter*)" mentioned by Nashe in *Have with You to Saffron-Walden*, 1596, sig. O1[v]. If so, he probably had a bookselling business at Exeter.

HART (SAMUEL), bookseller in Edinburgh, 1599–1643 (?). He was the eldest son of Andro Hart [*q.v.*], and was baptised on January 7th, 1599. No books are known bearing his name, but there is extant an account for books sold to him by Robert Allot of London in 1635, and he probably took an active share in the management of the business carried on by his father's Heirs. He died about 1643. [*E.B.S. Papers*, vol. i., no. 12; Aldis, *Scottish Books*, 114; *Scottish Antiquary*, v. 90.]

HART (WIDOW), *see* Hart (Heirs of Andro).

HARVEY (JOHN), printer of Catholic books, 1581. Arrested at the time of the raid at Stonor Park; *see* Brinckley (S.) [*Acts of the Privy Council, New Ser.*, xiii. 177].

HARVEY (RICHARD), *see* Duff, *Century*.

HASLOP or HASSELLUP (HENRY), printer in London, 1586–91; (?) The Bible in St. Paul's Churchyard. Son of John Hasselup of Barwyck in Elmet in the county of York, miller. Apprenticed to William How, stationer of London, for eight years from November 1st, 1577; but at some time not recorded he must have been transferred to Roger Ward the printer, by whom he was made a freeman on August 25th, 1586 [Arber, ii. 82, 698]. He was also mentioned as Ward's apprentice in the Star Chamber case of J. Day *v.* R. Ward and W. Holmes [Arber, ii. 768]. In 1586 he printed *Certaine English verses*, by L. L., the titlepage of which bears a device of a pheasant and the letters R. W. [*i.e.*, Roger Ward]. In the following year he obtained the manuscript of an account of Sir Francis Drake's expedition to Spain. This he gave to William How to print for him and it was published by Edward White at the Gun in St. Paul's Churchyard, Haslop apparently editing it [B.M., G. 6512. (1)]. The last heard of him is on April 9th, 1591, when he assigned to William Wright a ballad only entered to him on March 31st [Arber, ii. 577, 578].

HASTENIUS (HENRICUS), printer at Louvain, 1628. He printed the *Siege of Breda* by Gerat Barry, the title of which is dated 1627, the colophon 1628 [Sayle, p. 1446; B.M., p. 109]. As device he used a winged tortoise with the words "Cunctando Propero" and a monogram of the letters H.V.L., which also appears in some of his ornaments. In the colophon to the above work he is described as "Vrbis & Academiae Typographus."

HASTINGS (HENRY), *see* Haestens.

HATFIELD (ARNOLD), printer in London, 1584–1612; Eliot's Court Printing Office, Old Bailey. Arnold Hatfield was made a freeman of the Company of Stationers by Henry Denham the printer on January 16th, 158¾. Early in 1584 he is found in partnership with Ninian Newton, Edmund Bollifant and John Jackson. This syndicate purchased the types, ornaments and initial letters of Henry Bynneman, and set up in Eliot's Court, Old Bailey. There would seem to have been an agreement between the partners that they should only put their names in the imprints of such books as they themselves actually printed. The result is that the names of all the partners never appear on any one book. Hatfield and Newton printed the first book issued by the press in 1584, Edmund Bunny's edition of Robert Parsons' *Booke of Christian Exercise*, and also editions of Cæsar's *Commentarii* and of Juvenal and Persius, both in 1585. [Herbert, p. 1211]. In 1596 Arnold Hatfield printed *The Historie of Philip Comines*, in folio, for John Norton. In 1598 in partnership with Edmund Bollifant he printed for Bonham and John Norton, R. Greneway's translation of the *Annals* of Tacitus. On the death of Bollifant in 1602, Hatfield was joined by Melchisidec Bradwood and issued for several London stationers Philemon Holland's translation of Plutarch's *Moralia*, 1603. They were also the printers of the splendid edition of the *Theatrum Orbis Terrarum* of Abraham Ortelius, published by John Norton and John Bill in 1606. Arnold Hatfield is believed to have died in 1612. He sometimes used a device of the Caduceus, but it was only one of several devices used by the members of this firm. His wife, whom he married in 1582, was named Winifred Howles.

HAVILAND (JOHN), printer in London, 1613–38; (1) In the Old Bailey in Eliot's Court, 1627; (2) In the Old Bailey over against the Sessions House, 1634. Son of John Haviland, clerk, and nephew of Thomas

Haviland (1582–1611). John Haviland took up his freedom on June 25th, 1613, and on June 7th, 1621, in company with the widow of Edward Griffin he entered several copies, some of which at any rate had previously belonged to Edward Griffin, and before him to the syndicate which ran the Eliot's Court Printing House. This was apparently the foundation of John Haviland's business. About the year 1628 John Haviland began to enter books in his own name alone, although Mistress Griffin was still living. In 1636 Sir John Lambe in his notes stated that John Haviland, Robert Young and Miles Flesher, or Fletcher, had acquired not only Mistress Griffin's business, but also those of William Stansby and Widow Purslow [Arber, iii. 701]. In 1637 Haviland was one of the twenty master printers appointed under the Star Chamber Decree. On September 4th, 1638, he appears to have entered into partnership with John Wright senior, and at the same time they acquired the copyrights of John Parker and Henry and Moses Bell [Arber, iv. 431–4].

HAVILAND (THOMAS), printer in London, (?) 1582–1619; A little above the conduit, Aldermanbury. Admitted to the freedom of the Company of Stationers on August 7th, 1582 [Arber, ii. 687]. Is believed to have succeeded to the business of Richard Bradock [Arber, ii. 701, 702]. Thomas Haviland was probably a bookbinder as well as printer, as in 1601, when he took Simon Farwell as an apprentice, it was expressly stipulated by the Company that he was not to be brought up to the Stationers' or printers' trade, but only to that "other trade" that Haviland "nowe useth in his shop" [Arber, ii. 252]. The first entry under Haviland's name in the Registers is found on April 3rd, 1609, when with William Hall he received licence to print sheriffs' warrants, recognizances for alehouses and other documents of that nature, which had previously belonged to Richard Bradock. He printed also, between 1609 and 1611, several theological works, but in no case does he give his address in the imprint [Arber, iii. 404]. His will was proved on November 24th, 1619, and he left his business to his nephew John Haviland, son of his brother John Haviland, clerk [Commissary of London, Vol. 23, fol. 333–5].

HAWKINS (RICHARD), bookseller in London, 1613–36; In Chancery Lane near Sergeant's Inn. Son of John Hawkins of Abbey Milton, co. Dorset, yeoman. Apprentice to Edmond Mattes, stationer of London, for eight

years from October 1st, 1604 [Arber, ii. 284]. Took up his freedom November 18th, 1611 [Arber, iii. 683]. Publisher of plays and miscellaneous literature. His first entry, *The tragedy of Mariam*, was made on December 17th, 1612 [Arber, iii. 508]. In 1628 his name occurs in a list of dealers in second-hand books, who were to send a catalogue to the Archbishop of Canterbury [*Dom. S. P., Chas. I*, Vol. 117 (9)]. His last entry was on December 6th, 1633 [Arber, iv. 309]. On June 5th and 6th, 1637, his widow Ursula Hawkins transferred to Richard Mead, Christopher Meredith and W. Leake all his copyrights [Arber, iv. 385, 420]. Richard Hawkins published several plays, such as the *Maid's Tragedy* of Beaumont and Fletcher, in 1630, and *A King and No King* by the same authors in 1631.

HAWLTON or HAULTAIN (JEROME), typefounder in London, 1574–86. A Frenchman, who took out letters of denization in England on November 30th, 1574 [Worman, *Alien Members*, p. 28]: in the return for 1583 he was described as "letter caster for printers." In a return of the presses and printers in London made to the Master and Wardens of the Company of Stationers in 1586 and printed in Mr. C. R. Rivington's *Records of the Stationers' Company* occurs this entry, "Heirom Hawlton, 1 press" [Arber, v. lii]. This was evidently a proof press, and Mr. Worman was mistaken in thinking that he ever published anything. He appears to have left England about 1586, and to have gone to La Rochelle [Worman, *Alien Members*, p. 29].

HAYES (LAWRENCE), bookseller in London, 1617–37. Son of Thomas Hayes, whose copyright in Shakespeare's *Merchant of Venice* was transferred to him on July 8th, 1619 [Arber, iii. 651]. He took up his freedom November 7th, 1614 [Arber, iii. 684], and made his first book entry on April 29th, 1617 [Arber, iii. 608]. His last book entry is on June 3rd, 1630 [Arber, iv. 236], but he published another edition of the *Merchant of Venice* in 1637.

HAYES or HAIES (THOMAS), bookseller in London, 1600–3; The Green Dragon, St. Paul's Churchyard. Thomas Hayes was first apprenticed to John Sheppard, but on January 8th, 1580, was by order of the Company of Stationers turned over to William Lownes to serve out the remainder of his time and was made a freeman on the last day of March, 1584 [Arber, ii.

94, 691]. He was admitted into the Livery on July 3rd, 1602, and took his first apprentice on March 2nd, 160$\frac{0}{1}$. His first book entry was a verse miscellany entitled *Englands Parnassus*, the copyright of which he shared with Nicholas Ling and Cuthbert Burby [Arber, iii. 173]. On October 28th, 1600, he entered *the booke of the Merchant of Venyce* [Arber, iii. 175]. His last book entry was made on September 6th, 1602, and his death took place before February 6th, 160$\frac{3}{4}$, when his widow assigned some of his copyrights to Humphrey Lownes [Arber, iii. 251]. She assigned some others to William Cotton on May 21st, 1604 [Arber, iii. 262]. The copyright of the *Merchant of Venice* passed to his son Lawrence Hayes.

HEARN or HERNE (JOHN), stationer and bookseller of Taunton, 1576. In this year Fraunces Coldock [*q.v.*] brought an action against him for the recovery of a debt of £88. He does not seem to be otherwise known.

HEARNE or HERNE (RICHARD), *see* Plomer, *Dictionary*.

HEBB (ANDREW), *see* Plomer, *Dictionary*.

HEIGHAM (JOHN), printer at Douai, 1609–22; bookseller at St. Omer, 1622–? 1639, and printer there, 1631. An Englishman, probably of an Essex family. About 1585 he was imprisoned in Bridewell on account of religion. Later he went to Spain and became a lay brother in the Society of Jesus. The first book bearing his imprint at Douai seems to be Luis de Granada's *Memorial of a Christian Life*, translated by R. Hopkins, 1612 [Duthillœul, p. 197; Hazlitt, VII. 101], but Sayle attributes to him books in 1609 and 1610 [Sayle, p. 1482]. From 1612 to 1622 he printed at Douai at least seven English books. In or about 1622 he seems to have gone to St. Omer, where he perhaps opened a bookseller's shop, for from this year until 1626 we find some eight books printed *for* him at that place. In 1631 we find a single work, a *Primer in English*, printed *by* him: there were two issues with the same date [Sayle, p. 1480]. After the closing of his press at Douai two books were printed there for him, namely the *Life of the reverend Fa. Angel of Joyeuse*, 1623, and the *Hive of Sacred Honeycombs* of St. Bernard, 1631. He appears to have been living at St. Omer in 1639. He was the author of a number of devotional works, including translations from French, Italian and Spanish. [Gillow, *Dict. of Catholics*; *D.N.B.*; Duthillœul, pp. 197, 409.]

HELIE, *see* Ely (F.).

HELLEN or HELLENIUS (HANS), printer at Middelburg, 1618–58; At the Gallery on the Market Place. He printed two sermons by John Wing entitled *The Crown Conjugal, or the Spouse Royal*, 1620 [Sayle, p. 1459].

HELME (ANNE), bookseller in London, 1617–27; St. Dunstan's Churchyard. Widow of John Helme. She carried on the business until 1627, when she assigned over all her late husband's copyrights to William Washington [Arber, iv. 190].

HELME (JOHN), bookseller in London, 1607–16; St. Dunstan's Churchyard. Son of John Helme of Little Saint Bartholomew's, West Smithfield, tailor. Apprentice to Nicholas Ling, stationer, for nine years from February 2nd, 159$\frac{8}{9}$ [Arber, ii. 233]. Took up his freedom June 15th, 1607 [Arber, iii. 683]. Made his first book entry in the Registers in company with John Busby, junr., on August 27th, 1607 [Arber, iii. 358]. Amongst his publications were George Chapman's play *The Revenge of Bussy D'Amboise*, 1613, the pseudo-Shakesperian play, *The first and second part of the troublesome Raigne of King John of England*, 1611, Selden's *Titles of Honour*, 1614, and he also held a share in Drayton's *Polyolbion*, 1613. Helme's last book entry was made in the Registers on May 12th, 1616 [Arber, iii. 588]. He was succeeded by his widow Anne Helme.

HENSON (FRANCIS), bookseller and bookbinder in London, 1581–1604; Blackfriars. There is no record in the Registers stating to whom this stationer was apprenticed or when he took up his freedom in the Company. The first heard of him is in 1581, when he took an apprentice [Arber, ii. 107]. In 1596 the sum of £4 12s. was paid to him by the Duke of Northumberland for binding books [*Hist. MSS. Comm., 6th Report*, App. p. 226]. In 1600 Ascanius de Renialme the Venetian bookseller in St. Anne's, Blackfriars, bequeathed to certain of his "welbeloved friends and neighbours," amongst whom he mentions Francis Henson, a ring each [Plomer, *Wills*, p. 35]. In 1601 Henson published Anthony Munday's translation of J. Teixeira's account of the voyage of Dom Sebastian, King of Portugal, to Africa [B.M. 1195. a. 1. (8)]. The last heard of him is on December 4th, 1604, when he was fined a shilling for not appearing at Stationers' Hall on the quarter day [Arber, ii. 840].

HERBERT (JOHN), (?) bookseller (?) in London, 1598. Son of John Harbert or Herbert of the city of Durham, tailor, apprentice to Paul Conyngton, stationer, for nine years from November 1st, 1588 [Arber, ii. 153]. Admitted to the freedom on October 29th, 1597 [Arber, ii. 719]. Herbert began taking apprentices on September 4th, 1598 [Arber, ii. 229]. On November 13th in the same year he entered a book called *Ilys or three severall boxes of sportinge familiars* [Arber, iii. 131]. No copy of this seems to be known. Nothing further is known of this stationer and his address has not been found.

HERFORD (WILLIAM), *see* Duff, *Century*.

HERKES, *see* Garbrand.

HERKES, *see* Harkes.

HESTER (ANDREW), *see* Duff, *Century*.

HEWE (JOHN), bookbinder in London, 1571; Blackfriars. In Kirk's *Returns of Aliens* [Part ii. p. 15] he is described as "French bookbinder, came 9 years past, and Suzan his wife came about 12 years past to see the country. They sojourn within Noell Gobert (jerkin maker.) French Church." A John Hue, perhaps the same man, is also described as servant to Lewis Senior, bookbinder, about this time [Worman, *Alien Members*, p. 60].

HEYNS (ZACHARIAS), bookseller and printer at Amsterdam, 1595–? 1616, and at Zwolle, 1606–29. He printed at Amsterdam in 1605 H. Broughton's *Reply upon Th. Winton for Heads of his Divinity*, and *The Family of David*. [Ledeboer, *A.L.*, 77.]

HIGENBOTHAM, *see* Higginbottam.

HIGGINBOTTAM or HIGENBOTHAM (RICHARD), bookseller in London, 1615–35; The Cardinal's Hat, without Newgate. Took up his freedom in the Company of Stationers on April 3rd, 1615 [Arber, iii. 684]. On September 3rd in the same year Thomas Bushell assigned over to him his rights in a book entitled *The uncasing of Machavill* [Arber, iii. 572]. Higginbotham was the publisher of the third edition of B. Holyday's translation of the *Satires* of Persius, 1635.

HIGLEY (HUGH), (?) bookseller in London, 1598–1625. The first heard of this stationer is the entry in the Registers of his transfer as an apprentice to Adam Mytton, on February 9th, 159$\frac{7}{8}$, upon the death of his first master, Richard Webber [Arber, ii. 209]. He was made a freeman of the Company on April 24th, 1598 [Arber, iii. 720]. His will was dated November 22nd, 1625, and proved on December 7th in the same year. It mentions his wife Judith, a son George and a daughter Margaret, and appoints as overseers Thomas Heron and John Beawly [P.C.C., 134, Clarke]. No book bearing Higley's name in the imprint has been found.

HILL (ANTHONY), printer in London, 1586–8. Mr. Arber in his Bibliographical Summary [v. 142] doubts if Anthony Hill was a stationer, but in the Records of the Company there is a note which distinctly speaks of him as a printer in London. In 1586 the Company of Stationers ordered that for transgressing the decree of the Star Chamber he should not keep any printing house as a master, but work as a journeyman for wages. This order was made as a punishment for the share Anthony Hill took in printing Richard Day's privileged copy of the *Psalms in Meter*. In the Bill of Complaint presented in the Star Chamber by Richard Day and his assigns, Anthony Hill is called a *stationer* and he and Humfrey Franck were accused of printing 4,000 copies of the book [Arber, ii. 791]. But the point is settled by reference to Mr. Arber's first volume of the Transcript [p. 292] where we find this entry: "Anthony hyll the sonne of John hyll of bosburye in the County of haryforde yeoman hath put hym self apprentes to Rycharde Jugge . . . from the feaste of penticoste . . . 1566 [for] vij yeres." The entry of his freedom was no doubt in the lost Register, 1571–6. His first book entry is on August 1st, 1586, and his last on December 16th, 1588, but no copies of the books then entered are known to exist [Arber, ii. 450, 511].

HILL (FRANCIS), bookseller in London, 1628; Little Britain. Mentioned in a list of dealers in second hand books who were required to send a catalogue to the Archbishop of Canterbury [*Dom. S. Papers, Chas. I*, Vol. 117 (9)]. He died September 9th, 1644.

HILL (JOHN), bookseller in London, 1588–90; (1) The Three Pigeons in Paternoster Row; (2) The Golden Eagle and the Child in Paternoster Row, 1590. John Hill was admitted a freeman of the Stationers' Company

on August 8th, 1586 [Arber, ii. 698]. On June 24th, 1588, he is found taking an apprentice: on November 21st in the same year he entered as his copyright a sermon preached by the Revd. Adam Hill at St. Paul's Cross, and on April 27th, 1590, another book of divinity is entered to him [Arber, ii. 507, 545].

HILL (NICHOLAS), *see* Duff, *Century*.

HILLOKE, *see* Gulke (A. van).

HILLS (WILLIAM), bookseller in London, 1636–9; Little Britain at the White Horse. Joint publisher with Daniel Pakeman of Edward Dacre's translation of the *Discourses* of Macchiavelli in 1636, and of the same author's *The Prince*, in 1639 [B.M. 9040. aa. 10; Arber, iv. 357, 468].

HINDE (JOHN), bookseller in London, 1561–83; The Golden Hind in St. Paul's Churchyard. John Hinde was admitted to the freedom of the Company of Stationers on February 26th, 15$\frac{59}{60}$ [Arber, i. 122], and commenced to take apprentices in 1561 [Arber, i. 170]. In 1561–2 he was fined 2s. 6d. for reviling Nicholas Cleston with "unsemely words" [Arber, i. 185], and again in 1562–3 a like amount for quarrelling with Thomas Cadman [Arber, i. 217]. He was again fined in 1564–5 for keeping his shop open upon a saint's day [Arber, i. 275], and for stitching books. On February 28th, 157$\frac{8}{9}$, he entered two ballads [Arber, ii. 349]. John Hinde's most important publication was Sir Humphrey Gilbert's, *A true Reporte of the late discoveries . . .* 1583. The "Golden Hinde" was the name of one of Drake's ships, and it has been suggested that the bookseller adopted it as his sign.

HIPPON (JOHN), (?) bookseller in London, 1602–3: Apprentice to Mathew Law, by whom he was presented for his freedom on July 1st, 1602 [Arber, ii. 732]. In 1603 Thomas Creede printed for him a book called *A casting up of accounts of certain errors* . . . . by W. T. [B.M. 698. d. 20. (2.)].

HODGES (GEORGE), bookseller in London, 1621–32; Little Britain. Took up his freedom May 7th, 1621 [Arber, iii. 685], and on June 4th in the same year George Edwards and James Bloome assigned over to him their rights in eight works, chiefly theological [Arber, iv. 54]. The last entry under his name is an assignment to Richard Allot made on January 11th,

163$\frac{1}{2}$ [Arber, iv. 269]. Mentioned in a list of second-hand booksellers who in 1628 were ordered to submit a catalogue of their books to the Archbishop of Canterbury [*Dom. S. Papers., Chas. I*, Vol. 117. (9)].

HODGETS (JOHN), bookseller in London, 1601–25; The Flower de Luce in Fleet Street, near Fetter Lane end. Son of Richard Hodgetts of Sedgeley, co. Stafford, blacksmith. Apprentice to William Norton, stationer of London, for nine years from Christmas, 1584 [Arber, ii. 130]. Took up his freedom on December 22nd, 1593 [Arber, ii. 713]. He then appears to have been lent a sum of money under the bequest of William Norton for the benefit of young freemen of the Company, as in the Wardens' accounts of the year 1595–6 a note is made of the transaction [Arber, i. 581]. He took his first apprentice on June 25th, 1596, but discharged him on December 5th, 1598, when he took another [Arber, ii. 211, 231]. Hodgetts dealt largely in plays, amongst those which he published being John Day's *Ile of Guls*, 1606, Dekker's *Honest Whore*, 1604, Dekker and Webster's *Westward Hoe*, 1607, Thomas Heywood's *A Woman kilde with kindnesse*, 1607, and John Marston's *The Dutch Courtezan*, 1605. The last book entry under his name occurs on August 12th, 1624, and he was dead before December 19th, 1625. His widow Margaret assigned over some of his copyrights to Robert Allott on January 25th, 162$\frac{5}{6}$, for a sum of £45 [Arber, iv. 148].

HODGKINS or HOSKINS (JOHN), printer of Marprelate tracts, 1589. He is described as a "saltpeterman" [Arber, *Intro. Sketch to Martin Marprelate Controv.*, p. 177], and nothing is known of his connection with the printing trade. He was hired by John Penry in April, 1589, to take the place of Waldegrave, who had up to that time been working for the Martinists, but becoming alarmed had left them. He engaged V. Symmes and A. Tomlyn as assistants and together they printed several books until the seizure of the press at Manchester in August. Hodgkins was tortured [*cf. Brit. Bibl.*, ii. 129, note], and condemned to death, but his fate is unknown [Arber, *Intro. Sketch*, pp. 134–6, etc.; Pierce, *Hist. Intro. to Marprelate Tracts*]. Mr. Arber thinks he may be identical with John Hodgets [Arber, ii. 816], but there is no evidence.

HODGKINSON (RICHARD), printer in London. *See* Plomer, *Dictionary*.

HODGKINSON (THOMAS), stationer in London, 1588–96; Parish of St. Gregory. Son of Evan Hodgkinson of Preston in Andernes, co. Lancashire, yeoman. Apprentice to Thomas Purfoot, stationer of London, for seven years from November 30th, 1580. Took up his freedom January 9th, $158\frac{7}{8}$ [Arber, ii. 102, 701]. He died before October 8th, 1596, when his will was proved. He left a son Gabriel and a daughter Joane [P.C.C., 73, Drake].

HOGES, *see* Hodges (G.)

HOLLAND (COMPTON), bookseller in London, 1618–21; over against the Exchange. He was perhaps a brother of Henry Holland [*q.v.*] whose *Basiliologia* was to be sold by him at the above address. In 1621 he published John Taylor's *Brief Remembrance of all the English Monarchs* [Hazlitt, VII. 445]. Nothing else seems to be known of him.

HOLLAND (HENRY), bookseller in London, 1609–47; The Holy Bush, Ivy Lane. Son of Dr. Philemon Holland of Coventry, where he was born on September 29th, 1583. On March 25th, 1599, he became apprentice to John Norton, stationer of London, for ten years, and took up his freedom on December 5th, 1608 [Arber, ii. 237; iii. 683]. In company with John Wright, Henry Holland made his first book entry in the Registers on February 4th, $160\frac{8}{9}$ [Arber, iii. 401]. In 1614 he compiled and published with M. Law a work entitled *Monumenta Sepulchraria Sancti Pauli*, but he is best known as the compiler of two books notable for their illustrations, the first, *Baziliωlogia, a book of kings, beeing the true and lively effigies of all our English Kings from the Conquest until this present* . . . 1618, folio. Perfect copies of this work contain thirty-one portraits, besides the titlepage. It was printed for H. Holland and to be sold by Compton Holland [*q.v.*]. The second and more important of the two was entitled *Herωologia Anglica*, and was printed in 1620 at the expense of Chrispin de Passe and Jan Jansson, bookseller at Arnheim. This, like its predecessor, was a collection of portraits of eminent Englishmen with letterpress by Holland. In this there are sixty-five portraits and two engravings of monuments. In 1626 Henry Holland published at Cambridge the posthumous works of his brother Abraham, under the title of *Hollandi Posthuma*. He also helped his father Philemon Holland with his later publications. Henry Holland's last book entry occurs in the Registers on May 14th, 1633 [Arber, iv. 296]. Details of

his later life are furnished by a broadsheet issued in 1647 appealing for alms on his behalf. From this it appears that he rented a house in the parish of St. Mary le Bow, and in 1643 served in the Life Guards of Basil Fielding [B.M., 669. f. 11. (34)]. He is believed to have been still alive in 1649. [*D.N.B.*]

HOLLINS (RICHARD), bookseller in London, 1581–4. Apprentice to Oliver Wilkes. Took up his freedom March 28th, 1580 [Arber, ii. 682]. On October 9th, 1581, he entered what was perhaps a ballad concerning the fire at East Dereham in Norfolk [Arber, ii. 402], and on February 1st, $158\frac{1}{2}$, in company with William Towreolde, a similar publication referring to the fire at Nantwich in Cheshire [Arber, ii. 430]. His address has not been found.

HOLME or HOLMES (WILLIAM), senior, (?) bookseller in London, 1571. Son of Roger Holmes of Hayles, co. Salop, gent. Apprenticed to John Hinde, stationer of London, for seven years from February 2nd, $156\frac{3}{4}$ [Arber, i. 227]. The entry of his freedom which would have been about 1571 was probably made in the lost Register 1571–6. The references given by Mr. Arber to the Star Chamber case of John Day *v.* Roger Ward and William Holmes, refer to William Holmes, junior, and not William Holmes, senior. No books have been found with his name in the imprint.

HOLME or HOLMES (WILLIAM), junior, (?) bookseller in London, 1580–2; (1) Great North Door of St. Paul's; (2) The Lamb, Ludgate Hill. Son of Richard Holme of Tranmere, co. Chester. This stationer was one of John Harrison the elder's apprentices and was admitted a freeman of the Company of Stationers on July 22nd, 1580 [Arber, ii. 683]. It is clearly this stationer and not William Holmes, senior, who was one of the defendants in the Star Chamber case of Day *v.* Roger Ward and William Holmes, for William Holmes in his defence says, "forasmuche this Defendant beinge a yonge man lately come owt of his yeares, etc.," which could not apply to William Holmes, senior, who was made free certainly not later than 1572 [Arber, ii. 755]. Roger Ward admitted having sold 500 copies of the *A B C* to Holmes and the latter pleaded that he received them as a set-off to a debt of £10 14s. What his punishment was we are not told, but nothing more is heard of him. Another stationer William Holme, 1589–1615, has been confused with him.

HOLME or HULME (WILLIAM), bookseller in London and Chester, 1589–1615. Son of Thomas Holme of Chester. This stationer has been confused with William Holmes, junior. Both were apprentices of John Harrison the elder, but William Holmes, junior, was made free on July 22nd, 1580, whereas William Holme was not out of his time until June 25th, 1589. As the average term of apprenticeship was seven or nine years, William Holme probably took out his indentures in 1580 or 1582. Further he is always referred to in the Registers as William Holme and not Holme*s* [Arber, ii. 705]. He was the publisher of many of Thomas Churchyard's writings. He subsequently returned to Chester and took up his freedom in the Chester Stationers' Company in 1591, and he is found later taking apprentices there.

HOLOST (HU.), printer at Bruges, 1576. In this year he printed *A brief directory how to say the Rosary*, by I. M. [B.M. p. 1040].

HONDT or HONDIUS (HENDRICK), bookseller, engraver, and printer at Amsterdam, 1629– after 1658; (1) At the Atlas, 1629; (2) A l'enseigne du Chien vigilant, sur le Dam, 1632. According to the *Nouv. Biog. Générale* he was a son of Joos Hondt and brother of an elder Hendrick Hondt (1573–1610). He was born at London in 1580, and died at Amsterdam *c.* 1650. He was chiefly an engraver and executed a number of portraits and views. Jacques Prempart's *Historical Relation of the siege of Busse*, 1603, was printed for him by J. F. Stam in 1630, and editions of the *Atlas* of Gerard Mercator and Joos Hondt, printed by him and "John Johnson," have English titles bearing his imprint pasted over the original Latin. A map of the Fen country has the imprint "Amstelodami, Sumptibus Henrici Hondii, 1632" [Sayle, pp. 1430–2].

HONDT or HONDIUS (JOOS DE), (?) printer at Amsterdam; *see* H. (J.). He was a well-known engraver, and is also described as a skilled typefounder. He was born in 1546, lived some time in London, where he engraved a number of portraits and maps, and about 1594 settled down in Amsterdam, where he died in 1611. [*D.N.B.*; *Nouv. Biog. Générale*; Ledeboer, *A.L.*, pp. 79–80.]

HOOD (GEORGE), stationer in Dublin, 1638. He was admitted to the franchise of the City of Dublin in July, 1638, but nothing further is known about him.

HOOD (HENRY), *see* Plomer, *Dictionary*.

HOOKE (HENRY), bookseller in London, 1583–1605. Apprentice to Richard Tottell, by whom he was presented for his freedom on May 30th, 1583 [Arber, ii. 688]. The only book known to have been published by him is a sermon, entered in the Registers on October 28th, 1590 [Arber, ii. 566]. On January 15th, 1593, the Company of Stationers ordered him to pay two shillings and sixpence for keeping an apprentice unpresented, and to "put the said apprentis from him because he is not capable of him." Mr. Arber construes this to mean that Hooke was not a master, but only a journeyman stationer; but he is found taking apprentices regularly from 1591 to 1600 [Arber, ii. 172 *et seq.*]. In 1603, on April 12th, in company with Simon Stafford he entered King James's *Lepanto or heroicall song* [Arber, iii. 232]. He was dead before January 21st, $160\frac{5}{6}$, when his apprentice, Brian Grenell, was transferred to Gregory Seton [Arber, ii. 288]. His address has not been found.

HOOPER (HUMPHREY), bookseller in London, 1596–1613; The Black Bear in Chancery Lane. Apprentice to Richard Tottell for ten years from November 1st, 1561 [Arber, i. 172]. Admitted into the Livery of the Company in 1591–2 [Arber, i. 553]. He took his first apprentice on April 27th, 1590. He became Warden of the Company in 1604 [Arber, ii. 875]. His first book entry was on March 1st, 1596 [Arber, iii. 60], and his last on May 20th, 1613 [Arber, iii. 523]. Believed to have married Anne the widow of William Cooke, stationer, whose will was proved in 1621 [P.C.C., 101, Dale]. Humphrey Hooper was the publisher of the first edition of Francis Bacon's *Essays* in 1597.

HOPE (WILLIAM), *see* Plomer, *Dictionary*.

HOPKINSON (JOHN), bookseller in London, 1628; In Little Britain. Mentioned in a list of second-hand booksellers who, in 1628, were required to furnish the Archbishop of Canterbury with a catalogue of their books [*Dom. S. Papers*, *Chas. I*, Vol. 117 (9)].

HOPKINSON (JONATHAN), bookseller in London, 1628; Without Aldgate. Mentioned in a list of second-hand booksellers who, in 1628, were required to furnish the Archbishop of Canterbury with a catalogue of their books [*Dom. S. Papers*, *Chas. I*, Vol. 117 (9)]. He died August 31st, 1647.

HORSEMAN (RICHARD), bookseller in London, 1639; In the Strand, near unto York House. Only known from the imprint to the second edition of G. Chapman's *Ovid's Banquet of Sence*, 1639 [B.M. 1068. g. 27]. He was perhaps father to Thomas Horseman, bookseller, 1664–5 [*see* Plomer, *Dictionary*].

HOSKINS (JOHN), *see* Hodgkins.

HOSKINS (WILLIAM), printer and bookseller in London, 1575–? 1600; (1) Fetter Lane; (2) At his shop joining to the Middle Temple Gate within Temple Bar. Apprentice to Richard Tottell, printer, for ten years from Michaelmas, 1560: admitted a freeman of the Company of Stationers on May 15th, 1571 [Arber, i. 146, 447]. In 1575 he published Ulpian Fulwell's *Flower of Fame*, but whether he was then a printer is not clear. On September 3rd, 1582, Hoskins was committed to prison for three days and fined 10s. for keeping an apprentice for seven years without the knowledge of the Company [Arber, ii. 583]. In 1591 he is found in partnership with Henry Chettle and John Danter in a printing business in Fetter Lane and his name with Chettle's appears on the imprint to a sermon of the Rev. Henry Smith's called *The Affinitie of the Faithful*; but the partnership was dissolved in the following year. During the latter part of his life he published several books on music, in company with Peter Short [Arber, iii. 72, 81]. He was dead before 1604 [Arber, ii. 735].

HOUDOIN (HENRI), *see* Poulain (James).

HOVIUS (GUILLAUME), bookseller and printer at Liège, 1612–27. In 1623 he printed *The second manifesto of Marcus Antonius De Dominis, Archbishop of Spalatro, wherein . . . he publicly repenteth*, etc. [Sayle, p. 1448]. Hovius died in or before 1630, when his heirs are found printing [De Theux de Montjardin, *Bibl. Liégeoise*, ed. 2, col. 56, 92, 99].

HOWCOTT or HOWCKOT (ROBERT), stationer in London, 1607–31; Creed Lane, Parish of St. Gregory, near St. Paul's Churchyard. Son of William Howckot of Coventry, gent. Apprentice to Richard Cross, stationer of London, for seven years from September 30th, 1602 [Arber, ii. 266]. Took up his freedom November 6th, 1609 [Arber, iii. 683]. By his will dated November 10th, 1631, he left to his wife Elizabeth his tenement

in the street called the Great Butcherie in Coventry and all his "stuff" in his dwelling house in Creed Lane [Dean and Chapter of St. Paul's, Book D, f. 405].

HOWE (WILLIAM), *see* Duff, *Century*.

HOWELL alias MATHEWS (RALPH), bookseller in London, 1600–3; The White Horse, near the Great North Door of St. Paul's Church. Admitted to the freedom of the Company of Stationers by Mistress Penny on April 24th, 1598 [Arber, ii. 720]. His first book entry occurs on April 26th, 1600 [Arber, iii. 160], and his last on March 19th, 160$\frac{2}{3}$ [Arber, iii. 229].

HOWES (ROBERT), bookseller in London, 1620. Took up his freedom in the Company of Stationers on April 20th, 1618 [Arber, iii. 684]. On June 9th, 1620, he entered *The writeing schoolmaster* by John Davies of Hereford [Arber, iii. 675].

HUBY (FRANÇOIS II), printer at Paris, 1602–10. He was a son of François Huby I, who traded as a bookseller from 1555 to 1598. In 1610 P. Pelletier's *Lamentable discourse upon the Assassination of Henry the Fourth* was printed by him for Ed. Blunt and W. Barret. His device was a unicorn pursuing an old man with the motto "Eripiam eum et glorificabo eum" [Renouard, p. 187].

HUDSON (RICHARD), bookseller in London, 1565–88; The Woolpack in Hosier Lane. Richard Hudson was one of the apprentices of Thomas Berthelet, was presented on October 15th, 1556 [Arber, i. 41], and was made a freeman of the Company on October 4th, 1557 [Arber, i. 70]. In 1559 he was fined 6d. for non-appearance at the Hall on quarter day [Arber, i. 94]. His first entry, a ballad, occurs in the Registers in the year ending July 22nd, 1566 [Arber, i. 293]. Richard Hudson's last entry was on August 27th, 1588 [Arber, ii. 497]. Another Richard Hudson, probably son of the above, was admitted a freeman on July 7th, 1600, "per patrimonium."

HUGGINS (THOMAS), stationer in Oxford, 1609–36; St. Mary's parish [Clark, *Register*, ii. 1. 343–4, 401]. Publisher, 1625–36 [Madan, *Oxford Press*, pp. 299, 311–13]

HULME, *see* Holme.

HULSIUS (WIDOW OF), *see* Mommart (Widow of Jean).

HUMBLE (GEORGE), bookseller, printseller and patentee in London, 1611–32; (1) The White Horse, Pope's Head Alley, 1610–27; (2) In Pope's Head Palace, 1627. On April 29th, 1608, privilege was granted to George Humble to print John Speed's *Theater of the Empire of Great Britayne with cartes and maps* [*Calendar of Dom. S. Papers, Jas. I*, 1603–10, p. 425]. He was also the publisher of others of Speed's works. Probably a son of Thomas Humble, 1566–81.

HUMBLE (THOMAS), bookseller in London, 1566–81; The George in Lombard Street. Apprentice with Edward Sutton; presented October 14th, 1556 [Arber, i. 41]. Took up his freedom on September 3rd, 1563 [Arber, i. 240]. In the year 1564–5 he was fined for "stitching" books contrary to the orders of the house. Thomas Humble entered during the year ending July 22nd, 1566, *A brefe Requeste or Declaration presented unto Madame the Duchese of Parme* [Arber, i. 311] and *An admonytion . . . to the Rulers . . . of Brabant* [Arber, i. 315]. His last book entry occurs on March 1st, 158$\frac{0}{1}$ [Arber, ii. 390].

HUMPHREYS (DAVID), stationer of Chester, *see* Humphreys (Thomas).

HUMPHREYS (THOMAS), notary public and stationer of Chester, 1621–48. In the Register of the Chester Stationers' Company there is a record of the admission of his son David as apprentice in 1621. This David was made free of the Company in 1635–6. David's son Thomas was apprenticed to his grandfather in 1648 and made free in 1655–6.

HUNSCOTT (JOSEPH), *see* Plomer, *Dictionary*.

HUNSFORTH or HUNSWORTH (JOHN), (?) bookseller in London, 1577–1604. John Hunsworth is found taking apprentices and making them freemen between 1577 and 1589. He was dead before 1604 [Arber, ii. 739]. John Hunsforth, who may be the same, entered a book in the Registers in the year 15$\frac{69}{70}$ [Arber, i. 409].

HUNT (CHRISTOPHER), bookseller in Exeter, 1593–1606. Son of Walter Hunt of Blandford, Dorset. Apprentice to Thomas Man, stationer of London, for eight years from Christmas, 1584 [Arber, ii. 130]. Admitted a freeman of the Company on October 2nd, 1592 [Arber, ii. 711], and made his first book entry on January 26th, 159$\frac{3}{4}$ [Arber, ii. 644]. On February 1st, 159$\frac{3}{4}$, he was fined £4 for selling pirated copies of the

Psalms [Arber, ii. 821]. His last book entry was made on May 26th, 1606 [Arber, iii. 322]. Amongst his publications was R. C.'s translation of Tasso's *Gerusalemme Liberata*, 1594.

HUNT (JOSEPH), bookseller in London, 1594–1613; Bedlam [*i.e.*, Bethlehem Hospital] near Moore-field Gate, 1613. Son of Richard Hunt of London, baker, apprentice to Robert Gosson, stationer of London, for the unusually long period of 11 years, from Christmas, 1578, and took up his freedom on October 19th, 1587, so that nearly two years of his apprenticeship was remitted [Arber, ii. 89, 701]. Amongst his publications was Thomas Dekker's *Strange Horse-Race*, 1613.

HUNT (MATTHEW), publisher in Oxford, 1639–40. [Madan, *Oxford Press*, pp. 278, 310, 313.]

HUNTER (JOHN), draper and bookseller in London, 1576–82; The Bridge [? in Holborn]. Born in 1549. Dealt chiefly in ballads [Arber, ii. 301, 348]. Was implicated with Roger Ward and others in the publication of John Day's *A B C*, etc. In his deposition he described himself as "of the bridge." He confessed to having bought eleven double reams of the book from Ward [Arber, ii. 753, *et seq.*].

HURLOCK (GEORGE), *see* Plomer, *Dictionary*.

HURLOCK (JOSEPH), bookseller in London, 1631–4. Took up his freedom July 3rd, 1626 [Arber, iii. 686]. On August 1st, 1631, Elizabeth Tapp, the widow of John Tapp, assigned to him her rights in fourteen copies, including Martin Cortes' *Art of Navigation*, and other nautical books [Arber, iv. 258, 259]. He was dead before January 16th, 163$\frac{3}{4}$, when Elizabeth Hurlock transferred the same copies to George Hurlock, apparently her son. No books bearing Joseph Hurlock's name in the imprints are known [Arber, iv. 312], nor has his address been found.

HURY (PIERRE I), sworn bookseller and printer at Paris, 1585–97; Au Mont S. Hylaire, à la Court d'Albret. In 1588 he printed *Ane Cathechisme or schort Instruction of Christian Religion*, translated from the Latin of P. Canisius [B.M. p. 326]. His device was "un enfant suspendu à la branche d'un palmier qui se redresse en l'enlevant," with the motto *Sursum tendit* [Renouard, p. 188].

HUTTON (GEORGE), *see* Plomer, *Dictionary*.

HUTTON (RICHARD), (?) patentee, 1583. The work of Gulielmus Morelius entitled *Verborum Latinorum cum Graecis Anglicisque conjunctorum, locupletissimi Commentarii*, 1583, has the imprint "In ædibus H. Bynneman, per assignationem Richardi Huttoni." Nothing seems to be known of him.

INCE (PETER), stationer in Chester, 1626–48. His name first appears in the Registers of the Chester Stationers' Company in 1626, when Daniel Vychau, son of Daniel Vychau, was bound apprentice to him. He was a staunch admirer of William Prynne and visited him in prison after the publication of the *Histriomastix*, 1630. Bishop Bridgeman in his letters frequently refers to Ince as the great disseminator of Puritanical books, and went so far as to have his premises raided "but all the birds were flown ere the nest was searched." Ince appears to have been a man of good family and position, for in 1627 he presented some volumes to the Bodleian with his quartered arms stamped upon the bindings.

INGLAND, *see* England.

INGRAM (WILLIAM), senior, bookbinder in Oxford, 1626–83. Son of Peter Ingram. Apprenticed to Roger Barnes and John his son, bookbinders of Oxford [Clark, *Register*, ii. 1. 343]. He was buried in 1683. His son William Ingram was baptized in 1649. They seem both to have been Bodleian binders. [Gibson, *Oxford Bindings*, p. 50; *Oxford Wills*, p. 46.]

IRELAND (ROGER), *see* Duff, *Century*.

ISAAC (GODFREY), (?) bookseller in London, 1581. His name occurs in the imprint of John Nicholls' *Pilgrimage*, printed by T. Dawson for Thomas Butter and him in 1581. He does not seem to be otherwise known.

ISAM (JOHN), bookseller in London, 1619. Took up his freedom April 28th, 1615 [Arber, iii. 684]. Entered in the Registers on December 13th, 1619, a book called *London's Cry* by Master Goodcole [Arber, iii. 661].

ISLIP (ADAM), printer in London, 1591–1640. On October 7th, 1578, Adam Islip who was originally bound to Hugh Jackson, stationer of London, was set over to Thomas Purfoote for the remainder of his term of apprenticeship [Arber, ii. 87]. During this time he was concerned

with Roger Ward and others in printing John Day's *A B C*, etc., without license. Ward admitted that Adam Islip had furnished him with some of the type from Thomas Purfoote's printing house, without his master's knowledge [Arber, ii. 765, 769]. There is no record of any punishment having followed this offence, and Islip was admitted a freeman of the Company on June 8th, 1585 [Arber, ii. 694]. His first book entry occurs on September 16th, 1591 [Arber, ii. 595]. In 1595 Islip took into partnership for a while William Moring, and about 1606 he sold his printing house for £140 to Robert Raworth and John Monger, but they were deprived for printing *Venus and Adonis* without license, and John Haviland was upon petition admitted in Raworth's room. Adam Islip, however, immediately set up another printing house, and in 1615 was returned as having two presses [Arber, iii. 699, 700–4]. He died between September 4th and 25th, 1639, his will being proved in the Prerogative Court of Canterbury on the latter date. By it he bequeathed to his kinsman Kenelm Islip all his copies after his wife's death, and to Richard Hearne all his printing presses, letters and implements used for printing, as well as a sum of one hundred pounds [P.C.C., 151, Harvey].

JACKMAN (JOHN), (?) bookseller in London, 1631. Took up his freedom in the Company of Stationers on September 1st, 1628 [Arber, iii. 686]. On May 16th, 1631, he entered in the Registers Thomas Dekker's *The Wonder of a Kingdome*, a comedy, and *The noble Spanish Souldier*, a tragedy, also attributed in the Registers to Dekker, but believed to be by S. Rowley [Arber, iv. 253].

JACKSON (HILDEBRANT), printer at The Hague, 1622. In 1622 he printed a *Proclamation prohibiting all Jesuits, Priests, Monks .... to come into the United Netherland Provinces* [B.M. p. 1142].

JACKSON (HUGH), printer and bookseller in London, 1576–1616; St. John the Evangelist in Fleet Street a little beneath the Conduit. Successor to Thomas Colwell. Apprentice to William Powell for ten years from 1562 [Arber, i. 174]. He married Thomas Colwell's widow [Arber, ii. 676], and began taking apprentices in 1577. His first book entry occurs on October 22nd, 1576 [Arber, ii. 303]. Hugh Jackson was dead before July 22nd, 1616, when his copies were transferred to Master [Roger ?] Jackson [Arber, iii. 593]. He used Robert Wyer's device No. 2.

JACKSON (JEREMY), (?) bookseller in London, 1624; Near Moor Fields. Mentioned in John Gee's *Foot out of the snare*, 1624, as a dealer in popish books.

JACKSON (JOHN), Grocer and printer in London, 1584–96; Eliot's Court, Old Bailey. John Jackson was one of the partners in the Eliot's Court printing house, the others being Ninian Newton, Arnold Hatfield and Edmund Bollifant. He was a member of the Grocers' Company, but there is no evidence to show where he learnt the art of printing. Jackson is first mentioned in the Registers on May 21st, 1586, when an apprentice named Richard Browne, who was bound to Richard Collins, stationer, was transferred to John Jackson to be taught printing. The partners were only allowed two apprentices, one of whom was already bound to Arnold Hatfield. Amongst the books in which Jackson's name appears alone in the imprint was a Latin version of the *Book of Common Prayer*, printed by him for the assigns of Francis Flower in 1594, and William Wyrley's *True use of Armorie*, which he printed for Gabriel Cawood. He is found printing until 1596.

JACKSON (JOHN), bookseller in London, 1634–40. *See* Plomer, *Dictionary*.

JACKSON (RALPH), bookseller in London, 1588–1601; The White Swan in St. Paul's Churchyard. Son of Thomas Jackson of the city of Coventry, draper. Apprentice to Garret D'Ewes for ten years from 1580 [Arber, ii. 100]. Admitted to the freedom of the Company on October 17th, 1588 [Arber, ii. 703]. Jackson's publications were almost entirely theological, and he shared some of them with Robert Dexter and William Young. He was one of the witnesses to the will of William Norton. Ralph Jackson died some time in 1601; by his will, which was proved on August 25th, 1601, he left his property between his widow Martha and his children Nathaniel and Joane [P.C.C., 25, Woodhall]. On April 27th, 1602, his copyrights were transferred to Cuthbert Burby [Arber, iii. 205].

JACKSON (RICHARD), bookseller in London, 1565–6. Apprentice with Harry Hammande. The term is not stated, but the indentures were taken out on April 18th, 1558 [Arber, i. 74], and he took up his freedom on September 26th, 1565 [Arber, i. 317]. He is probably the same as the Richard Jackson who entered three ballads during the year ending July 22nd, 1566 [Arber, i. 314]. There was another Richard Jackson, apprentice

to Richard Tottell, who was admitted a freeman on March 26th, 1583 [Arber, ii. 687], and a third Richard Jackson took up his freedom as a stationer on May 6th, 1613 [Arber, iii. 684].

JACKSON (ROBERT), bookseller in London, 1607. Son of Robert Jackson, cordwainer of London. Apprentice to Ralph Jackson, who was perhaps a kinsman, for eight years from Michaelmas, 1599 [Arber, ii. 243], and upon Ralph Jackson's death transferred to Cuthbert Burby [Arber, ii. 260]. Took up his freedom April 13th, 1607 [Arber, iii. 683]. He is only known from two entries in the Registers in May, 1607, one of them being a play called *The Woman Hater*, by Beaumont and Fletcher [Arber, iii. 349]. His address has not been found.

JACKSON (ROGER), bookseller in London, 1601–25; In Fleet Street over against the Conduit, or Near the Great Conduit in Fleet Street, or (?) The White Hart, Fleet St. [Arber, v. 204]. Son of Martin Jackson of Burnholme, co. York, yeoman. Apprentice to Ralph Newbery, stationer, for eight years from June 24th, 1591 [Arber, ii. 175]. Admitted a freeman of the Company August 20th, 1599 [Arber, ii. 724]. His first publication seems to have been a little work on dreams which bears the date 1601. In 1602 in partnership with John North he entered *Greene's Ghost Haunting Conycatchers*, and from that time until his death in 1625 he issued many notable and interesting books, including the 1624 edition of Shakespeare's *Lucrece*. On January 16th, $162\frac{5}{6}$, his widow transferred her rights in his copies to Francis Williams. The list fills a page of the Registers [Arber, iv. 149, 150].

JACKSON (SIMON), bookseller in Oxford, 1618. Only known from the imprint to Samuel Smith's *Aditus ad Logicam*, 1618 [Madan, *Oxford Press*, pp. 110, 278, 297, 311–12].

JACKSON (WILLIAM), stationer and bookbinder in Cambridge, ? 1593–5. On January 3rd, 1595, St. John's College leased to Wm. Jackson of Cambridge, stationer or bookbinder, a tenement in Great St. Mary's (at the corner of Pump Lane) "heretofore in the tenure of Rob. Joplin" for twenty years [Baker's *History of St. John's Coll.*, i. 440]. A "William Jaxson" gave 10d. towards the building of the steeple of Great St. Mary's Church in 1593 [Foster's *Churchwardens' Accounts*, 243].

JACOBSZOON or JACOBSZ (JAN PAEDTS), *see* Paedts.

JACQUES (JOHN), *see* Jaques.

JAEY (H.), bookseller at Mechlin, 1613–22. In 1611 *The Lyfe of the Mother Theresa* was printed at Antwerp for him. In the imprint he is called "Henrie Iaye" [Hazlitt, VII. 379–80]. In 1613 he issued a work called *Practice of Meditating with Profit* [Hazlitt, VII. 50], and in 1622 the *Spiritual Exercises* of A. de Molina.

JAGGARD (ELIZABETH), bookseller in London, 1625. Widow of John Jaggard. She is found entering a book in partnership with Robert Milbourne in January, $162\frac{4}{5}$, but she transferred her copyrights to J. Smethwick on February 24th, $162\frac{5}{6}$ [Arber, iv. 134, 151].

JAGGARD (ISAAC), printer in London, 1613–27; Barbican. Son of William Jaggard. Took up his freedom in the Company of Stationers on June 23rd, 1613 [Arber, iii. 684]. He succeeded his father in the printing business in Barbican and was the printer of the First Folio of Shakespeare's works. He died between February 5th and March 23rd, $162\frac{6}{7}$, his copyrights being assigned by his widow Dorothy Jaggard to Thomas and Richard Cotes, who succeeded to the business in June, 1627 [Arber, iv. 182]. Isaac Jaggard's will was proved in the Archdeaconry of London [Register 6]. He left no children.

JAGGARD (JANE), *see* Jaggard (William).

JAGGARD (JOHN), bookseller in London, 1593–1623; The Hand and Star in Fleet Street, between the two Temple Gates. Son of John Jaggar or Jaggard, citizen and barber-surgeon of London, and brother of William Jaggard. Apprentice to Richard Tottell for seven years from September 29th, 1584 [Arber, ii. 129]. Admitted a freeman of the Company of Stationers on August 7th, 1593 [Arber, ii. 711], and made his first entry in the Registers on the 22nd of the following March [Arber, ii. 646]. John Jaggard was admitted into the livery of the Company on July 3rd, 1602 [Arber, ii. 874], and he served the office of Under Warden in 1619–20. The last book entry under his name is on July 24th, 1622, and as he is not mentioned in the will of William Jaggard, who died in 1623, it seems possible that he predeceased him. His widow Elizabeth is found entering a book in company with Robert Milbourne on January 12th, $162\frac{4}{5}$. John Jaggard published several books of travel, an edition of Bacon's *Essays*, and an early topographical work, Richard Carew's *Survey of Cornwall*, 1602.

JAGGARD (WILLIAM), printer and bookseller in London, 1594–1623; (1) St. Dunstan's Churchyard, Fleet Street, 1594–1608; (2) The Half Eagle and Key, Barbican, 1608–23. Son of John Jaggard, citizen and barber surgeon of London, brother of John Jaggard (1593–1623), and father of Isaac Jaggard (1613–27). William Jaggard was apprenticed to Henry Denham for eight years from Michaelmas, 1584, and was admitted to the freedom of the Company on December 6th, 1591 [Arber, ii. 126, 710]. He began business as a publisher in a small way, in premises in St. Dunstan's Churchyard, his first venture, according to the Register, being a medical work called the *Booke of secretes of Albertus Magnus*, entered on March 4th, $159\frac{4}{5}$ [Arber, ii. 672]; but he quickly turned to more profitable work, and emulated and surpassed the methods of his contemporaries in the art of book production. In 1599 he collected a number of poems by various authors, and published them under the collective title of *The Passionate Pilgrime, by W. Shakespeare*, but there was little of Shakespeare's work in the volume, which however contained several of Thomas Heywood's poems, abstracted from *Troia Britanica*, a work of Heywood's that Jaggard had published. About the year 1608 William Jaggard bought the old established printing business of James Roberts in the Barbican, and became printer to the City of London. William Jaggard was a friend of Augustine Vincent, the herald. Vincent had written a very slashing examination of his brother herald Ralph Brooke's *Catalogue of Kings*, which he entitled *A Discovery of Errors*. While the *Discovery* was in the press Brooke published a second edition of his work in the preface of which he threw the blame for most of the errors of the first edition upon William Jaggard, who had printed it. Jaggard, therefore, added to the *Discovery* a prefatory letter replying to Brooke's strictures. From this letter it would appear that he had then (1622) become blind. But the work with which William Jaggard's name will always be connected is the First Folio of Shakespeare's *Works*. In 1899 Mr. Sidney Lee discovered a copy of the First Folio bearing the inscription on the titlepage "Ex dono Willi. Jaggard Typographi, a° 1623," and presented by him to his friend Augustine Vincent. This throws an interesting light on the date of printing of the book. The copy was entered in the Registers by Isaac Jaggard and Edward Blount on November 8th, 1623, and William Jaggard was dead and his will proved by November 17th. From the fact that his

name does not appear in the Registration of the book, we may infer that he was either already dead or on his death bed on November 8th, and this presentation copy suggests that the work was in print, if not actually published, some time before the date of registration. [Sidney Lee, *Life of Shakespeare*, Fifth ed., 1905.] By his will we learn that William Jaggard left two sons Isaac and Thomas, the latter a student at the University. He left a piece of plate to the Company of Stationers and appointed his wife Jane his executrix, Thomas Pavier, stationer, being one of the overseers [Archdeaconry of London]. His widow died two years later, her will being proved on November 22nd, 1625 [Archdeaconry of London, Register 6, fol. 217].

JAMES (JACQUES). The *Dialogi ab Eusebio Philadelpho*, 1574, bears the imprint "Edimburgi, ex typographia Iacobi Iamaei." This name and place are repeated in a French translation issued in the same year under the title of *Le Réveille-Matin des François*, and in a German translation published in 1593. All three imprints are fictitious, the books being of Continental origin [Dickson and Edmond, 512; Aldis, *Scottish books*, 115].

JAMES (YARATH), bookseller in London, 1581–91; Newgate Market, over against Christ Church Gate. Mr. Arber has included this name, but prints it in different type, as that of one who was not a stationer. But he was clearly a bookseller, and not only published several ballads, but was concerned with others in the piracy of John Day's *A B C*, etc., and was included in the action brought by Richard Day to uphold his father's patent [Arber, ii. 791, 792]. Again in 1590–1 several copies of the *Harmony of the Church* [i.e., *An Harmony of the Confessions of the faith of the Christian and Reformed Churches* (B.M. p. 375)] which had been seized at his shop, were returned to him on a payment of £2 [Arber, i. 543, 545, 550].

JANSS (ASHUERUS), printer at Gorcum (Gorinchem), 1624. He printed Thomas Scott's *Second Part of Vox Populi*, 1624 [Sayle, p. 1499].

JANSSEN VAN AELST or D'AELST (ANDRIES), printer at Zutphen, 1603–25. His only work in English seems to be in Jakob de Geyn's

Maniement D'armes . . . The Exercise of Arms [1619], printed in French, German, Dutch, and English [Sayle, p. 1499; Ledeboer, *A.L.*, p. 88 (*but see also under* "Aelst," p. 3, where different dates are given)].

JANSSON (JAN I), bookseller at Arnhem, 1604–34. In 1614 he published Crispin de Passe's *Hortus Floridus*, with an English preface, and *c.* 1620 Henry Holland's *Herwologia Anglica*. The expense of the latter was shared by Crispin de Passe. [Sayle, p. 1497.]

JANSSON (JAN II), printer and bookseller at Amsterdam, 1613–44. The third son of Jan Jansson, bookseller of Arnhem [*q.v.*]. He was associated in 1633 with Hendrick Hondt, or Hondius, in printing an edition of Mercator's *Atlas*, on the English cancel-slips for the title of which he is called "John Johnson" [Sayle, p. 1431]. *The Art of Fortification* translated from the French of Samuel Marolais by H. Hexham was printed for him in 1638. The imprint of this, which is stuck over the words "chez Jan Janssen" on the title originally engraved for the French edition, has "M. John Johnson," the M. presumably standing for Master.

JAQUES (JOHN), *see* Duff, *Century*, p. 80. This stationer is probably the one referred to in a list of those who had gone into the country in 1571 as John Jacques, Somersetshire [Arber, v. lii].

JASCUY (SAMUEL), of Paris, 1558. Two editions of Sir David Lindsay's *Ane Dialog and other Poems*, one in quarto and one in octavo, are found, both dated 1558 and purporting to be printed "at the command and expenses of Maister Samuel Jascuy, In Paris." It has been supposed that the name Jascuy is fictitious and that the books were printed at Rouen by a successor of Jehan Petit. *See* D. Laing's edition of Lindsay, iii. 265–70, for description and facsimiles.

JAYE (HENRY), *see* Jaey.

JEFFERSON (HENRY), printer in London, 1586. Apprentice to Roger Ward and admitted a freeman of the Company of Stationers on April 3rd, 1587 [Arber, ii. 699]. In 1586 he had a printing press in company with Robert Bourne and Lawrence Tuck, which was seized by the Company of Stationers and defaced for printing *Grammars* contrary to the Decree of the Star Chamber, and the parties were disabled from ever keeping a printing house on their own account, or from printing otherwise than as journeymen [Records of the Company of Stationers; Arber, ii. 760, 768, 800–4].

JEFFES (ABEL), printer in London, 1584–99; (1) The Bell in Fore Street without Cripplegate, near unto Grub Street, 1584–8; (2) The Bell in Philip Lane [London Wall], 1589–90; (3) St. Paul's Churchyard at the Great North Door of St. Paul's Church, 1591; (4) (?) Blackfriars, near Puddle Wharf, 1594–9. Abell Jeffes was one of Henry Bynneman's apprentices and took up his freedom in the Company of Stationers on February 26th, 1579–80 [Arber, ii. 682]. His first book entry occurs on August 28th, 1584 [Arber, ii. 435], and in the same year he printed for William Bathe *An Introduction to the true Art of Music* [Arber, v. 134]. During the year 1587 his press was busy, amongst the books which he printed being an edition of the Works of George Gascoigne, a translation from Boccacio, *A disport of divers noble personages*, Thomas Lupton's *Siuqila* and George Turberville's *Tragical Tales.* Again in 1592 he is found printing the writings of Robert Greene, Thomas Kyd, Thomas Lodge and Thomas Nashe. On December 3rd, 1595, his press and letters were seized for printing *The most strange prophecie of Doctor Cipriano* "and diverse other lewde ballades and thinges very offensive," and for this and resisting the searchers he was committed to prison until he made submission. His presses were not returned to him, but he continued as a bookseller probably at the shop or shed in St. Paul's Churchyard until August 13th, 1599, when he assigned over his rights in certain copies to William White [Arber, iii. 146]. Abell Jeffes appears to have been in poor circumstances, as the Company lent him various small sums of money on different occasions and gave his wife five shillings when her house was visited by the plague [Arber, i. 560–3, 566]. Jeffes used as a device a bell within an oval border and the motto, "Praise the Lord with Harpe and song," and the letters A.I. beneath.

JENCKES or JENKES (ROWLAND), bookseller and bookbinder in Oxford, 1572–7. Was accused of sedition before the Convocation held May 1st, 1577, and condemned at the assizes held at Oxford in that year, to have his ears nailed to the pillory. He married Alice Ford. He afterwards went abroad and is said to have died there [Wood, *City of Oxford*, iii. p. 210; Gillow, *Dictionary of Catholics*, iii. 614; Gibson, *Oxford Bindings*, p. 47].

JENNINGS (MILES), (?) bookseller in London, 1577–85; The Bible in St. Paul's Churchyard. Mr. Arber in his *Transcript* does not recognise Miles Jennings as a stationer, but on April 6th, 1579, the Company gave him licence to publish *The historie of Gerillion*, which he stated he had bought of John Jugge, *Ye discourse of husbandrie*, assigned to him by Andrew Maunsell, and George Whetstone's *Discourses of my Lord keper deceased.* He also published *A Booke of Military discipline* in 1581. In 1586 he was succeeded by Thomas Cadman and Henry Haslop [Arber, v. 141].

JENNINGS ( ), bookseller in Ludlow, 1633. Mentioned in a list of those in whose shops copies of William Prynne's *Histrio-Mastix* had been found [*Documents relating to W. Prynne* (Camden Soc.), p. 60].

JOBERT (PIERRE), bookseller in Paris, 1584–5, rue de la Harpe, "près Sainct Cosme et sur le quai des Augustins." In 1585 *An Oration or Funeral Sermon at Rome at the Burial of Gregory XIII* was printed for him. [Renouard, p. 194; Herbert, p. 1666.]

JOHNSON (ARTHUR), bookseller in London and Dublin, 1602–30; London, The Flower de Luce and Crown, St. Paul's Churchyard, 1602–21. Son of Thomas Johnson of Parkhall in the county of Derby, husbandman, served two years with William Yong or Young, draper, who carried on the trade of a bookseller, and was by him put over to Robert Dexter, stationer, to whom he was apprenticed for a further term of seven years from Midsummer, 1594 [Arber, ii. 193]. Admitted a freeman of the Company of Stationers on July 3rd, 1601 [Arber, ii. 729]. Arthur Johnson was an extensive publisher and dealer in all kinds of literature. He published several plays including a (pirated) edition of Shakespeare's *Merry Wives of Windsor* the copyright of which was assigned to him by John Busby. His last book entry occurs on February 12th, $162\frac{0}{1}$. In June, 1624, he began to assign his copyrights to others, the last of such assignments being on January 29th, $16\frac{29}{30}$. Meanwhile he appears to have gone over to Ireland and set up as a stationer in Dublin, where he died, his will being proved on February 9th, $163\frac{0}{1}$. This makes no mention of his trade beyond instructions to his executors to pay certain debts that he owed to Benjamin Fisher of London, stationer, and a bequest of one pound to William Bladen of Dublin, stationer [Wills in Prerogative Court, Dublin (information supplied by E. R. McC. Dix)].

JOHNSON (HENRY), stationer in London, 1588; Charterhouse Lane. Only known from his will proved in the Commissary Court of London on March 4th, $158\frac{7}{8}$. His widow Joane married Thomas Tyus or Tias, stationer [*q.v.*] [Com. of London, 1588, fol. 133, verso].

JOHNSON (JOHN or M. J.), printer and bookseller at Amsterdam, 1633 and 1638, *see* Jan Jansson II.

JOHNSON (THOMAS), bookseller in London, 1630; Britain's Burse. A set of plates of Beasts, Birds, etc., entitled *Animalium quadrupedum, Avium . . . . Veræ delinationes*, has the imprint "Ar to be sould by Thomas Johnson in Brittaynes Burse 1630" [B.M., p. 42]. A copy of what appears to be the same work in the Cambridge Univ. Lib. was to be sold by Roger Daniel [Sayle, p. 1070]. Nothing seems to be known of Thomas Johnson.

JOHNSON (W.), printer at Amsterdam, 1612–22, *see* Blaeu (W. Janszoon).

JOHNSON (WILLIAM), bookseller and bookbinder in Oxford, 1616–*c.* 1645. Apprentice to Edward Miles, bookbinder of Oxford. On May 23rd, 1617, in company with several others, he was reprimanded for setting up as a bookseller without leave of the Vice-Chancellor. [Clark, *Register*, ii. 1. 321, 404; Gibson, *Oxford Bindings*, pp. 49, 51, 60; *Oxford Wills*, 33, 47; Griffith's *Wills*, p. 35.]

JOHNSTON (JAMES), bookseller in (?) St. Andrews, ? 1599–1611. By his will, dated July 30th, 1611, Mr. John Johnston, second master in St. Mary's College, St. Andrews, left "to James Johnstoun buiksellar, and his barnes, tuantie lib." As no place is mentioned it is probable that this bookseller carried on business in St. Andrews. A James Johnestoun is named among the debtors in the inventory of Henry Charteris [*q.v.*] who died in 1599 [*Maitland Club Miscellany*, i. 339].

JOHNSTON (PATRICK), bookbinder in Edinburgh, 1600. His daughter Margaret was baptised August 17th, 1600; witness, Andr. Arisone, printer [*Scottish Antiquary*, v. 90].

JONES (HUGH), printer in Oxford, ?–1637; St. Mary's Parish. A "Hugh Joanes of Anglesea" was admitted a privileged person of the University December 11th, 1585 [Clark, *Register*, ii. 1. 394]. He was probably the

person apprenticed to Arnold Hatfield in 1595 [Arber, ii. 201] and made free of the Stationers' Company in 1602 [Arber, ii. 731]. His will was proved October 14th, 1637. [Gibson, *Oxford Wills*, 33–5.]

JONES or JOANES (JOHN), stationer in Cambridge, 1592–1624. Mentioned in a list of persons priviledged of the University *circa* 1592–4 and again in 1624 [Bowes, *Univ. Printers*, 336].

JONES (LAMBERT), bookseller in London, 1628. Mentioned in a list of second-hand booksellers who, in 1628, were ordered to submit catalogues of their books to the Archbishop of Canterbury [*Dom. S. Papers, Chas. I*, vol. 117 (9)].

JONES (RICHARD), printer and bookseller in London, 1564–1602. (1) The Little Shop adjoining to the North-west Door of St. Paul's Church; (2) The Spread Eagle in the upper end of Fleet Lane; (3) Under the Lottery House; (4) At his shop joyning to the South-west Door of St. Paul's Church, 1571; (5) At the West end of St. Paul's Church, between the Brazen Pillar and Lollards' Tower; (6) Dwelling over against St. Sepulchre's Church without Newgate, 1576–80; (7) At the Rose and Crown, over against the Falcon, near unto Holborn Bridge without Newgate, 1581–1602. There is no record as to what stationer Richard Jones, or Johnes, served his apprenticeship with. He was admitted into the brotherhood of the Company of Stationers on August 7th, 1564 [Arber, i. p. 278]. On one or two occasions he was fined for offences such as stitching books and printing and publishing privileged books; but on the whole he appears to have been an orderly member. Throughout the thirty-eight years of his business life he dealt largely in ballads, and he also printed and published much other curious literature, most of it of a popular character. He was for a time in partnership with William Hill, and Sir John Lambe in his notes on the printers stated that they sold the business in 1598 to William White [Arber, iii. 702]. Mr. Arber in the Index to his *Transcripts* gives the latest date at which Jones was in business as 1602, but the Registers record an entry to Richard Jones, of two ballads on March 19th, $161\frac{0}{1}$ [Arber, iii. 456]. This is perhaps a mistake of the clerk's in the Christian name as nothing known to have been printed or published by this Jones is found after 1602.

JONES (THOMAS), bookseller in London, 1600–37; (1) near Holborn Conduit, 1600 [Sayle, p. 686]; (2) The Black Raven near St. Clements Church, 1622; (3) Strand, near York House, 1637. Son of Richard Jones, printer. Admitted a freeman "by patrimony" August 16th, 1596. His first book entry is found in the Registers on May 8th, 1617 [Arber, iii. 608]. He dealt chiefly in theological literature, but issued a few plays. On August 24th, 1633, he assigned his copyrights to Augustine Mathews [Arber, iv. 307], but his name is found in books as late as 1637.

JONES (WILLIAM), bookseller in London, 1562–74; (1) The New Long Shop at the West Door of St. Paul's Church; (2) At the South-west Door of St. Paul's Church, joining unto Lollards' Tower [? the shop of R. Jones]. Probably a relative of Richard Jones. Was apprentice to Robert Toye and admitted to the freedom of the Company on March 11th, 1558 [Arber, i. 71]. He was constantly being fined for breaking the rules and orders of the Company, amongst other things "for selling a communion book of King Edwards time" in 1559, for which he was ordered to pay 20d. William Jones's first book entry was William Painter's *Citie of Civilitie* in the year 1562–3; and his last was made in the year ending July 22nd, 1566 [Arber, i. 204, 301]. His will was dated May 28th, 1574, and proved on June 2nd in the same year. He left no son, his property being divided between his wife Margaret and his daughter Amy [P.C.C., 24, Martyn].

JONES (WILLIAM), bookseller in London, 1589–1618; The Gun near Holborn Conduit. Son of Simon Jones of Tiffield, Northamptonshire, yeoman. Apprentice to John Judson for nine years from Michaelmas, 1578, and admitted to the freedom of the Company on October 19th, 1587 [Arber, ii. 87, 701]. Jones's first book entry occurs in the Registers on August 13th, 1589, and his last on June 28th, 1618 [Arber, iii. 618]. He died before September 17th in that year, when his widow Sarah assigned over her rights in two copies to John Wright [Arber, iii. 632].

JONES (WILLIAM), printer in London, 1601–26; Ship Alley, Redcross Street, Cripplegate. Son of William Jones of Northampton, clothworker. Apprentice to John Windet, stationer of London, for nine years from Midsummer, 1587, and admitted to the freedom of the Company on July 5th, 1596 [Arber, ii. 148, 716]. Down to 1618 it is not possible to distinguish between the books entered to this printer and the bookseller of

the same name. Jones the printer was somewhat of a puritan. In 1604 he laid information against Richard Bancroft, Bishop of London, for harbouring seminary priests and permitting the publication of Roman Catholic books. The document contains much interesting information relating to printers and booksellers, a good deal of which is borne out by the records of those times. King James however ignored the charges and kept Jones a prisoner for some months. Amongst those for whom he printed was Michael Sparke the bookseller. About 1627 he took into partnership Thomas Paine. The date of his death is unknown, but Michael Sparke in his will, made in 1653, left a bequest to Constance Jones who is believed to have been the widow of William Jones the printer. Another William Jones took up his freedom June 4th, 1621 [Arber, iii. 685]. He may have been a son of the printer but it is impossible to distinguish between them. [*Library*, April, 1907, pp. 164–76.]

JOSLIN (SAMUEL), stationer in London, 1614–? 1620. Took up his freedom in the Company of Stationers, October 14th, 1614 [Arber, iii. 684]. He held a share in the Latin Stock [*Chancery Proceedings, Chas. I*, 121/53].

JUDSON (JOHN), *see* Duff, *Century*.

JUDSON (THOMAS), printer in London, 1584–99. He was a son of John Judson (*see* Duff, *Century*), and was made free of the Stationers' Company by patrimony on January 16th, 158$^{0}_{1}$ [Arber, ii. 683]. In 1584, in partnership with John Windet, he printed Greene's *Arbasto* and R. G's *Godly Exhortation to Vertuous Parents* [Hazlitt, I. 176]. After this date nothing is heard of him until 1599, when he printed *A Brief Description of the Whole World*, and Thomas Hill's *School of Skill*. In the same year he was named among those printers especially forbidden to print epigrams, satires, etc. [Arber, iii. 678].

JUGGE (JOANE), bookseller in London, 1577–88; Dwelling near Christ Church, Newgate Street, Parish of St. Faith. Widow of Richard Jugge, printer. She continued to carry on the business in partnership with her son John. In 1579 they printed an edition of Richard Eden's translation of Martin Cortes' *Art of Navigation*, and an undated translation from P. M. Vermigli, *A briefe treatise, concerning the use & abuse of dauncing* [B.M., G. 19991 (3)]. From her will, dated June 13th, 1588, and proved

on September 2nd, it appears that she had two sons living, Richard and John, and five daughters married, one of whom, Katherine, was the wife of Richard Watkins [P.C.C., 56, Rutland].

JUGGE (JOHN), *see* Jugge (Joane).

JUGGE (RICHARD), *see* Duff, *Century*.

KEARNEY, KEARNY, CARNEY, KERNEY or KERNY (WILLIAM), printer in London and Dublin, ? 1573–97; London, Addling Street, 1590–2; Dublin, Trinity College, ? 1593–5. A relative of John Kearney. Mentioned in a letter (August, 1587) from the English Privy Council to the Lord Deputy and Council of Ireland, as having during fourteen years in England and foreign parts become a master of the Art of Printing, etc., and recommended by them to print the *New Testament* in Irish. The first notice of him in the Registers is the entry of a theological book on July 20th, 1590 [Arber, ii. 555]. In October, 1591, he was permitted by warrant to pass into Ireland with presses, etc., and to print Irish Bibles, but he was apparently still in London in September, 1592, as in that month certain books were seized at his premises and carried to Stationers' Hall [Arber, i. 560]. He probably went to Ireland in the following year. In 1593 (?) an appeal was formulated for funds to print the Irish *Bible*. The setting up of the *New Testament* in Irish type was begun by Kearney and in 1595 was in process, but probably very slowly, as in 1597 (calculating by the Address to the Reader prefixed to the *New Testament*) only the first two Gospels and six chapters of the third had so far been printed off. The printing was commenced in Trinity College, then first opened, but Kearney early disagreed with his employers there or became dissatisfied and left them and the College and took employment under the Irish Government in 1595, in which year he printed a Proclamation in English against the Earl of Tyrone, in Christ Church Cathedral. In March, 159$^{6}_{7}$, he was offered a re-engagement by the College authorities on certain terms. Whether he accepted them is not known, nor is there any further information about him. In a State Paper relating to him (in 1593?) he is described as having had twenty years' experience in printing.

KEERBERGHEN or KEERBERGIUS (JAN VAN, PEETERSZ), printer and bookseller at Antwerp, 1586–1616; (1) Op onser liever vrouwen Kerckhof, Int huys van Neeringhe, 1591; (2) In de rechte Cammerstraete, in de gulde Sonne, 1594. He was born in 1565 and received into the St. Lucas-gild in 1586. His only English work seems to have been a *Rosary of our Lady* in 1600 [B.M. p. 1071]. He was alive in 1616. [Olthoff, p. 54.]

KEERBERGHEN or KEERBERGIUS (PEETER VAN), printer at Antwerp, 1557–? 1569; (1) Op onse L. V. Kerckhof, Int gulden Cruys, 1563; (2) Op onser Vrouwen Kerckhof, In de gulde Sonne, 1567. He was received into the St. Lucas-gild in 1557. In 1567 he printed J. Weddington's *Instruction how to keep Merchants' Books* [Herbert, p. 1624]. He apparently died in 1569. [Olthoff, p. 54.]

KELLAM (LAURENCE), printer at Louvain, 1598–? 1604, and at Douai ? 1603–1614; (his widow, 1614–61). Kellam appears to have been a German. He is first heard of as printing an edition of R. Parsons's *Christian Directory* at Louvain in 1598. In the two following years he printed, at the same place, Luis de Granada's *Spiritual Doctrine* [Herbert, p. 1740] and John Hamilton's *Facile Treatise dedicat to Iames the Saxt*. According to Duthillœul, p. 408, he may have been at Valenciennes in 1602; but in 1604 George Doulye's (*i.e.*, W. Warford's) *Brief instruction concerning Christian Religion* [B.M. p. 492] appeared as printed by him at Louvain. In the previous year, however, he had commenced business at Douai in the rue Saint Jacques, at the sign of the Pascal Lamb, and printed Matthew Kellison's *Survey of the New Religion*, 1603. From this date until 1614 he printed there at least eight works in English, the most important being the Douai *Bible (Old Testament)* of 1609–10. He died in 1614, and the business was carried on by his widow until 1661. She generally used her husband's imprint, but her edition of Villegas' *Lives of the Saints*, translated into English, 1614, has "By the Widow of Laurence Kellam" [Hazlitt, VII. 394]. From 1622 to 1639 she printed at least seven English works, but they are of small size and little importance. [Duthillœul, pp. 163–86, 407–8.]

KELLAM (THOMAS), printer at Douai, 1618. A book by Thomas Worthington, the *Anchor of Christian Doctrine*, 1618, was "Printed at Doway by Thomas Kellam" [Sayle, p. 1488], but nothing further seems to be known of him. He is not mentioned by Duthillœul.

KEM or KEMBE (ANDREW), *see* Plomer, *Dictionary*.

KEMP (LEONARD), stationer in London, 1596–1616. Son of James Kemp of Roxham, co. Norfolk, yeoman. Apprentice to George Allen, stationer of London, for eight years from Midsummer, 1589, and took up his freedom June 26th, 1596 [Arber, ii. 157, 716]. Mentioned in a list of stationers holding shares in the Latin Stock in 1616. His address has not been found.

KENE (JONET), printer in Edinburgh. Widow of Andro Hart [*q.v.*].

KERKNETT (SALOMON), compositor in Edinburgh, 1576. Was in the employ of Thomas Bassandyne of Edinburgh, who brought him from Magdeburg to work upon the folio *Bible*. In January, $157\frac{6}{7}$, he brought an action against Bassandyne for non-payment of wages. He is possibly identical with Solomon Kirkner or Kirtner [*q.v.*]. [Dickson and Edmond, 286; *Reg. P.C. Scot.*, ii. 582.]

KEVALL (STEPHEN), stationer of London, 1535–71, *see* Duff, *Century*.

KID (JOHN), bookseller in London, 1591–2. This bookseller was one of Richard Jugge's apprentices and was made a freeman of the Company of Stationers by Joan Jugge on February 18th, $158\frac{3}{4}$ [Arber, ii. 691]. His first book entry occurs on May 12th, 1591 [Arber, ii. 582]. John Kid dealt in ballads and popular literature. He was dead before March 5th, $159\frac{2}{3}$, when a sum of money was lent to his widow by the Company [Arber, i. 562, 565]. His address has not been found. Another John Kid, perhaps son of the above, was admitted to the freedom of the Company on July 4th, 1612 [Arber, iii. 683].

KING (JOHN), *see* Duff, *Century*.

KINGSTON (FELIX), *see* Plomer, *Dictionary*.

KINGSTON (JOHN), printer in London, 1553–*c.* 1584 [Duff, *Century*]. By a Grace of February 8th, 1576–7, he was appointed printer to the University of Cambridge, and on July 18th, 1577, Lord Burghley wrote to the Vice-Chancellor on the subject of Kingston's appointment, and disapproved of printing *Psalters*, *Prayer Books*, etc., as interfering with the Queen's grants to Seres, Jugge, Day, and others, and Kingston seems never to have printed at Cambridge. [Bowes, *Univ. Printers*, 291.]

KIRKHAM (HENRY), bookseller in London, 1570–93; The Black Boy at the Middle North Door of St. Paul's Church. Henry Kirkham was presented as an apprentice by William Martin for seven years from March 25th, 1561 [Arber, i. 148]. There is no entry of his admission to the freedom of the Company. He appears to have dealt principally in ballad literature. He died before March 5th, $159\frac{2}{3}$, leaving a son William [Arber, ii. 712].

KIRKHAM (WILLIAM), bookseller in London, 1593–8; The Black Boy, Little North Door of St. Paul's Church. Son of Henry Kirkham. Admitted a freeman "per patrimonium" after his father's death, on March 5th, $159\frac{2}{3}$, on the presentation of his mother [Arber, ii. 712], but a month previously he had entered a book in company with Thomas Orwin. The last book entry under his name occurs on January 27th, $159\frac{7}{8}$.

KIRKNER or KIRTNER (SOLOMON), stationer of London, 1577. On August 4th, 1577, the following entry was made in the Registers of the Stationers' Company: "Memorandum that Solomon kyrkner is admitted brother of this Company the daie abouesaid. For whiche his admission it is ordered that he shall paie Tenne shillinges by Twelve pence a weeke vntill it be payde and master Bynneman muste staie the same xij^{d} weekelie out of his wages . . . . . xs." [Arber, ii. 675]. The sequel to the above order is found in the *Returns of Aliens*, ii. 308, where under the date 1582–3 is entered: "Kirtner, Salomon, admitted Brother of the Stationers' Company and shold have payd therefore to the same Co. to the use of the poore thereof xs by xij^{d} a weeke, but he hath payd no parte thereof. And it is reported he departed this land and wente over the sea five yeres agoe and is not yet returned" [Worman, *Alien Members*, p. 35].

KIRTON (JOSHUA), *see* Plomer, *Dictionary*.

KITSON (ABRAHAM), bookseller in London, 1581–94; The Sun, St. Paul's Churchyard. Apparently successor of Anthony Kitson. In 1581 T. Hill's *Natural and Artificial Conclusions* was printed for him by J. Kingston. He was amongst those who were complained against for infringing the printing privileges in 1583 [Arber, ii. 779]. From 1584 he seems to have acted as London agent for books printed at Cambridge by John Legate [*cf.* Sayle, pp. 412, 1630].

KITSON (ALEXANDER), stationer at Worcester, 1571. Mentioned in a list of stationers who in 1571 were living in the country [Arber, v. lii]. In a Subsidy Roll of the 14th Eliz. (1572) for the city of Worcester, in the High Ward, is found the entry "Alexander Kydson in goodes . . . vj^{li} . . . vj^{s}."

KITSON (ANTHONY), *see* Duff, *Century*.

KNIGHT (CLEMENT), Draper and bookseller in London, 1594–1629; The Holy Lamb, St. Paul's Churchyard. Clement Knight was originally a draper and the first heard of him is an entry in the Registers on February 25th, 1594, when he was fined for selling three psalm books [Arber, ii. 822]. With several other members of the Drapers' Company he was transferred to the Stationers on June 3rd, 1600 [Arber, ii. 725], and was admitted into the Livery on June 30th, 1604 [Arber, ii. 875]. Clement Knight became an important member of the Stationers' Company, being elected Junior Warden in 1621, and Senior Warden in 1626 and 1627. He held shares in the Latin Stock, but appears to have dealt almost wholly in theological literature. On October 12th, 1629, he assigned over his rights in fifteen copies to Thomas Knight, probably his son [Arber, iv. 220].

KNIGHT (PHILIP), bookseller in London, 1615–17; At his shop in Chancery Lane over against the Rolls. Took up his freedom September 4th, 1615. Probably a son of Clement Knight. His first book entry occurs on November 6th, 1615 [Arber, iii. 575, 684]. He held the copyright of Greene's *Groatsworth of Wit*, and two plays, *The Maides Metamorphosis* and *The Weakest goeth to the Wall*, but transferred the first to Henry Bell and the two plays to Richard Hawkins.

KNIGHT (THOMAS), *see* Plomer, *Dictionary*.

KNOX (WILLIAM), bookbinder in Edinburgh, 1640. He was the second son of William Knox, minister of Cockpen, and a descendant of William Knox, elder brother of the reformer. The Henry Knox who was a bookseller in Edinburgh in 1696 was probably the youngest of his three sons. [Aldis, *Scottish Books*, 115; Hew Scott's *Fasti*, i. 272; ii. 545].

KYDDE, *see* Kid.

LACY (ALEXANDER), *see* Duff, *Century*.

LACY ( ), puritan printer, 1572. He was arrested on a charge of assisting in the secret printing of Cartwright's *Reply to An Answer of D. Whitgift* in 1572 or 1573 [*Bibliographica*, ii. 159]. Nothing else seems to be known about him.

LAET or LATIUS (HANS or JAN), printer at Antwerp, ? 1546–after 1566; (1) Op die Lombaerde veste teghen over den Yshont, 1546–49; (2) In de Cammerstraet, In den Salm, 1552–3; (3) In de Cammerstraet, In de Meulen, 1554–7; and (4) In de Rape, 1557–64; (5) Op de Lombaerde veste, In den Zayer, 1566 to his death. He was born at Stabroek *c.* 1525, and was printing at least as early as 1549. He was received into the St. Lucas-gild in 1553 as 'Jan van Stabroeck.' His work in English seems to have been limited to the years 1564–6, when he printed nine books in the language, including works by J. Martiall, W. Allen, T. Harding, and T. Dorman, and Stapleton's translation of Bede's *History of the Church of England*, 1565. After Laet's death his widow carried on the business, but seems to have printed nothing in English. [Olthoff, p. 58.]

LAMBERT (THOMAS), *see* Plomer, *Dictionary*.

LANG (PAUL), printer at Hamburg, 1620. In this year he printed a religious treatise by William Loe, entitled *The merchant reall* [Sayle, p. 1500].

LANGFORD (BERNARD), bookseller in London, 1637–9; (1) The "Bybell" on Holborn Bridge, 1638; (2) The Blue Bible on Holborn Bridge, 1639. This stationer took up his freedom on February 6th, 1637 [Arber, iii. 688]. He dealt in miscellaneous literature, amongst his publications being a curious work on thieves and beggars called *The sonne of the rogue, or the politick theefe*, 1638 [B.M. 12330. a. 31]. The last book entry under his name occurs on October 17th, 1638 [Arber, iv. 440], but in 1639 he published a work called *The Converted Courtezan*.

LANGHAM (EDWARD), bookseller in Banbury, Oxfordshire, ? 1623–? 1641. Edward Langham took up his freedom in the Company of Stationers on June 4th, 1621 [Arber, iii. 685]. On June 24th, 1628, George Edwards, the London bookseller, assigned over to Langham his rights in William Whately's sermon entitled *Sinne no more* which had been preached in the parish church of Banbury on the occasion of a devastating fire in the town

[Arber, iv. 199]. A later edition of 1630 has the following imprint: "London, printed for George Edwards, and are to be sold by Edward Langham of Banbury" [B.M. 694. c. 9. (12)]. In a subsidy roll for Banbury of 17 Charles I [*i.e.*, 1641–2] is the following entry which doubtless refers to this bookseller: "Edward Langham . . . . . . iiij^{s} . . . . . vj^{d}" [P.R.O., Lay Subsidy $\frac{164}{493}$].

LANGLEY (THOMAS), bookseller in London, 1615–35; Over against the Saracen's Head without Newgate. Took up his freedom in the Company of Stationers on November 7th, 1614 [Arber, iii. 684]. Publisher of plays, sermons and ephemeral literature. The last entry under his name occurs on June 1st, 1635 [Arber, iv. 340]. Langley was one of those who held a share or shares in the Latin Stock.

LANGTON (RICHARD), (?) bookseller in London, 1581; In Swithin's Lane. Only known from the imprint to Bertrand de Logne's *Treatise of the Church*, 1581 [Herbert, p. 1349].

LANT (RICHARD), *see* Duff, *Century*.

LANT (——), bookseller in Lichfield. In the will of William Camden, the antiquary, proved on November 10th, 1623, occurs the following passage: "Item. To Lant the younger, bookseller in Litchfield fyve pounds" [P.C.C., 111, Swann].

LAPPAGDE (T.), bookseller at Rotterdam, 1640. In this year William Bridge's *True Soldier's Convoy* [B.M., p. 270] was printed for him.

LASH (WILLIAM), bookseller in London, 1628–34. Took up his freedom October 6th, 1628 [Arber, iii. 686]. On July 7th, 1634, he entered in the Registers, Francis Lenton's *The Inns of Court Anagramatist* [Arber, iv. 322]. His address has not been found.

LATHAM (GEORGE), *see* Plomer, *Dictionary*.

LAUDER (WILLIAM), bookbinder in Perth, 1591. Mentioned in November, 1591, in the Register of the Privy Council of Scotland, iv. 693.

LAUGHTON (AUGUSTINE), bookseller in London, 1567–90; (1) The Grasshopper, St. Paul's Churchyard, 1570–5; (2) Maiden Lane, near Wood Street, 1580–90. Took up his freedom in the Company of Stationers on

September 29th, 1564 [Arber, i. 278]. Began taking apprentices in July, 1567 [Arber, i. 352]. During the year ending July 22nd, 1571, he entered Fullwood's *Enemy of Idleness*, a work on letter writing, the copyright of which had previously belonged to Leonard Maylard [Arber, i. 440]. He also entered two books or pamphlets relating to affairs in France, the last entry under his name occurring on March 13th, 15$\frac{89}{90}$ [Arber, ii. 540].

LAURENSZ (HENDRICK), printer and bookseller at Amsterdam, 1608–48. An edition of Jakob de Geyn's *Maniement d'Armes*, which is mostly in English, was printed in 1608 at the Hague for him, but, in some copies at least, there is a cancel slip bearing the name of Robert de Baudois [*q.v.*]. In 1612 he printed John Fowler's *Shield of defense against the arrows of schism* [Sayle, p. 1429].

LAW or LAWE (MARTIN), (?) bookseller in London, 1601. This name occurs in a list of those who were fined on March 4th, 160$\frac{0}{1}$, for selling *Humours lettinge blood in the vayne* (*i.e.*, the *Letting of Humours Blood in the Head Vein*, by S. Rowlands) [Arber, ii. 832]. As nothing more seems to be known about him the entry may have been a clerical error for Matthew Lawe.

LAW or LAWE (MATTHEW), draper and bookseller in London, 1595–1629; (1) St. Paul's Churchyard, near Watling Street, 1601; (2) The Fox, near St. Augustine's Gate, St. Paul's Churchyard. Originally a member of the Drapers' Company, Matthew Lawe published in 1595 a volume of sonnets [Arber, v. 180]. On June 3rd, 1600, he was transferred from the Drapers' to the Stationers' Company [Arber, ii. 725]. He appears to have been an unruly member, as he was several times fined for disobedience, for keeping his shop open on Sundays and for selling pirated editions of books [Arber, ii. 835, 836, 840]. On June 23rd, 1603, he took over from Andrew Wise the following Shakesperian plays, *Richard the Second*, *Richard the third*, and *the First Part of Henry the Fourth* [Arber, iii. 239]. He was also the publisher of Henry Petowe's poems on the death of Elizabeth and the coronation of James I, and he held shares in the Latin Stock of the Company. The last entry under Matthew Lawe's name occurs in the Registers on July 2nd, 1624 [Arber, iv. 120]. His will was proved on November 26th, 1629. He left everything to his wife Joyce, who was a

widow at the time he married her, with instructions that she was to deliver "unto myne and her owne children Mathewe Lawe and Alice Norton" such portions of his small estate as she thought good. Joyce was the name of the widow of John Norton, the bookseller, who died in 1612, but there is no mention of any daughter Alice in his will. [Plomer, *Wills*, p. 45–7; Dean and Chapter of St. Paul's, Book D, fol. 371.]

LAW (THOMAS), bookseller in London, 1584–9; (?) West End of St. Paul's. Apprentice to William Seres the elder, and afterwards transferred to Henry Kirkham; took up his freedom on February 18th, 158$\frac{3}{4}$ [Arber, ii. 691]. Was associated with Thomas Nelson in the publication of sermons. On July 16th, 1589, he entered a pamphlet entitled *The execucon of three notorious witches at Chelmisford Sizes last* [Arber, ii. 525].

LAWSON (RICHARD), bookseller in Edinburgh, 1608–22. His name, with that of Andro Hart, appears on the titlepage of Stephanus's *A world of wonders*, Edin., 1608 (a re-issue, with new titlepage, of the London edition of 1607); and in 1610 Thomas Finlason printed for him a quarto edition of Lindsay's *Squyer William Meldrum*. Like James Cathkin [*q.v.*], to whom he was apparently related by marriage, he was probably a skinner by trade before he took up bookselling. In 1620 he was ordered by the King to be banished to Aberdeen for his share in the religious disturbances of the time, but the sentence was not put into execution. He died in September, 1622. Among the creditors mentioned in his inventory [*Bannatyne Miscell.*, iii. 199] are James Cathkin, and John Bill in London. His wife, Agnes Mayne, survived until August, 1651 [Aldis, *Scottish Books*, 115; *Reg. P.C. Scot.*, x, xii; *Bannatyne Miscell.*, ii. 244, 267; Calderwood's *Hist. of the Kirk of Scot.* vii.].

LEA, *see* LEE.

LEA (HENRY), bookseller in London, 1599–1612. On August 13th, 1599, this stationer presented an apprentice [Arber, ii. 238], and on December 7th, 1612, he entered a ballad on the death of Henry, Prince of Wales [Arber, iii. 506].

LEAKE (WILLIAM), senior, bookseller in London, 1592–1633; (1) The Crane in St. Paul's Churchyard, 1593; (2) The White Greyhound in St. Paul's Churchyard, 1596; (3) The Holy Ghost, St. Paul's Churchyard,

1602–18. This stationer was one of Francis Coldock's apprentices and was admitted to the freedom of the Company on October 6th, 1584 [Arber, ii. 693], and into the Livery on July 1st, 1598 [Arber, ii. 873]. William Leake's first book entry is found on February 17th, 159$\frac{1}{2}$, but that he was in business as a bookseller very much earlier than this is shown by the entry of a fine for keeping open his shop on holydays on October 24th, 1586 [Arber, ii. 859]. In 1592 he is found at the Crane in St. Paul's Churchyard, previously in the occupation of Richard Oliffe or Olive. In 1596 John Harrison the elder assigned to William Leake his rights in Shakespeare's *Venus and Adonis*, and Leake was the publisher of the 1602 edition. At the same time he appears to have moved from the Crane into Harrison's premises, the White Greyhound. In 1602 he obtained the copyrights of Gabriel Cawood, which included Southwell's *St. Peter's Complaint*, John Lyly's *Euphues*, Thomas Watson's *Hekatompathia or Century of Love*, and an edition of Boethius [Arber, iii. 210]. Leake served the office of Junior Warden in the years 1604 and 1606, and of Upper Warden in 1610 and 1614. He held shares in the Latin and Irish Stocks of the Company, and his share in the Irish Stock was the subject of a law suit in the Court of Chancery in 1653 [*Library*, July, 1907, p. 295]. On February 16th, 161$\frac{6}{7}$, William Leake assigned over practically all his copyrights to William Barret [Arber, iii. 603]. In July, 1618, he was elected Master of the Company, and after serving his year of office, he retired from business and settled in the county of Hereford. He died on April 3rd, 1633. William Leake was married four times and William Leake, junior, was his eldest son [Chan. Proc., Mitford, 53, 57]. On July 1st, 1635, his widow transferred to her son William Leake, junior, her rights in six copies that had previously belonged to his father.

LEAKE (WILLIAM), junior, *see* Plomer, *Dictionary*.

LEE, LEY, or LEA (RICHARD), bookseller in London, 1615–16. On November 26th, 1615, Richard Lea entered in the Registers a book called *The fall of man* by Godfrey Goodman [Arber, iii. 578]. Nothing more is known about him.

LEE, LEY, or LEA (WILLIAM), senior, *see* Plomer, *Dictionary*.

LEE, LEY, or LEA (WILLIAM), junior, *see* Plomer, *Dictionary*.

LE CHANDELIER (PIERRE), printer at Caen, 1598. In this year he printed "from the copie printed at London" W. Perin's *Spiritual exercises and ghostly meditations* [Herbert, p. 1736]. Some copies seem to have as a supplement Colet's *Order of a good Christian man's life* [Hazlitt, IV. 80], or there may have been two editions.

LEETE (ROBERT), printer at Cambridge, 1622–63; Gt. St. Mary's Parish. A stationer of this name took up his freedom in the Company of Stationers on August 6th, 1622 [Arber, iii. 685]. He paid church rate in Great St. Mary's parish, Cambridge, between 1627 and 1632 [Foster's *Churchwardens' Accounts*]. On August 28th, 1640, he entered in the Register Drexelius' *Forerunner of Eternity, or Messinger of Death*, etc. [Arber, iv. 519]. His will, dated 1663, is amongst the Cambridge Wills at Peterborough.

LEGATT or LEGATE (JOHN), printer in Cambridge and London, 1586–1620; Cambridge: West end of Great St. Mary's Church, and Regent Walk [Gray's *Shops at West end of Great St. Mary's*]. London: (1) Trinity Lane, between Old Fish Street and Bow Lane, 1609; (2) Great Wood Street, 1620. John Legatt was, it is believed, a native of Hornchurch in Essex. From an Indenture enrolled on the Close Roll of the 33rd Eliz. (*i.e.*, 1590–1) Bartholomew Legatt and William Legatt, both described as of Sutton in the parish of Hornchurch, sold lands in Essex to John Legatt, citizen and stationer of London. John Legatt was apprenticed to Christopher Barker, the Queen's printer, by whom he was presented for his freedom on April 11th, 1586 [Arber, ii. 696]. He was appointed printer to the University of Cambridge by Grace of November 2nd, 1588, in succession to Thomas Thomas, and on February 4th, 1588–9, he married Alice Speirs, by whom he had at least 12 children. He appears to have lived in a house at the West end of Great St. Mary's Church previously occupied by Thomas Bradshaw, whilst his printing was done in a house in the Regents' Walk a few yards away. He was the first who used (from 1603 onward) the device with the words *Alma Mater Cantabrigia* and the motto *Hinc lucem et pocula sacra.* Towards the close of the sixteenth century there was a good deal of ill-feeling between the Cambridge stationers and the Company of Stationers in London, and in 1598 John Legatt joined several of the smaller London booksellers in issuing a pirated

edition of Sidney's *Arcadia* which had been printed in Edinburgh by Robert Waldegrave. From evidence given by one of his servants it appeared that Legatt had sold 20 copies to Cuthbert Burby and Richard Bankworth, both London booksellers, and sold others in his shop at Cambridge [*Library*, April, 1900, pp. 195 *et seq.*]. In 1606 his former apprentice Cantrell Legge was also appointed University printer, and in 1609 Legatt moved to London, but still called himself "Printer to the University" and continued to use the Cambridge device. His right to this title is confirmed by an entry in an MS. account of the University written by John Scott in 1617, where his name appears, with those of Cantrell Legge and Thomas Brooke, as one of the three University printers [Bowes, *Univ. Printers*, p. 294]. In 1612 John Legatt is described as living in Trinity Lane, London, and in 1615 he is returned as having two presses [Arber, iii. 699]. He died before August 21st, 1620 [Arber, iv. 45].

LEGATT (JOHN), the younger, printer at Cambridge and London, 1620–58, *see* Plomer, *Dictionary*. He married Agatha the daughter of Robert Barker, the King's printer.

LEGGE (CANTRELL), printer at Cambridge, 1606–*c.* 1629. Son of Edward Legge of Bircham, Norfolk. He was apprenticed to John Legatt in 1589, and in 1599 was admitted freeman of the Stationers' Company. He was appointed printer to the University by Grace of June 5th, 1606. Besides the books which he printed at Cambridge he issued a number of works in partnership with London stationers. In the years 1620–4 he had a quarrel with the Stationers' Company concerning the printing of Lily's *Grammar*, the *Psalms*, and Almanacs, to which the Company denied his right. Cantrell Legge is believed to have died in 1626, for no books are found with his imprint after 1625. He paid church rate in Gt. St. Mary's parish up to Easter, 1625, but Mrs. Legge paid for 1626 and afterwards [G. J. Gray]. On June 1st, 1629, his widow transferred her interest in sixteen of his books to James Boler [Arber, *Transcript*, iv. 212]. [Bowes, *Univ. Printers*, 296–8].

LEIGH (JOHN), bookseller in London, 1602–3. Son of Nicholas Leigh of Asheton Moore, co. Cumberland, yeoman; apprentice to John Asheton, stationer, for seven years from October 2nd, 1587 [Arber, ii. 148]. Took

up his freedom on October 29th, 1594 [Arber, ii. 714]. On July 1st, 1602, he entered in the Registers *An Introduction to wrytinge* [Arber, iii. 209], and in 1603 *An Easye plaine waye to learne to read*, but this latter work was crossed out as it was found that the copyright belonged to others [Arber, iii. 225]. Nothing more is known of him.

LEKPREUIK (ROBERT), printer and bookbinder, printed at Edinburgh from 1561–71; at Stirling in 1571; at St. Andrews in 1572–3; and again in Edinburgh from 1573–82. In 1574 he was imprisoned for printing without licence John Davidson's *Dialog . . . betuix a Clerk and ane Courteour*, and nothing further is known to have issued from his press till 1581. In the earlier years of his career he received encouragement and patronage from the leaders of the reformed church, and in January, 1567–8, he was appointed king's printer. He had in his possession some of the printing materials formerly used by John Davidson and John Scot, and he printed two or three books for Henry Charteris. Ninety-one issues from his press are known, the majority of them being theological or political publications on the side of the reformers, including a number of broadside ballads by Robert Sempill. The Scottish statutes of 1556, known as the "Black Acts," and the first printed Gaelic book, *Foirm na nurrnuidheadh*, 1567 (a translation of the *Book of Common Order*), are among the more notable of his productions. In his latter years Lekpreuik seems to have fallen upon evil days, and from Bassandyne's inventory (1577) we learn that he was in receipt of an annual pension of ten marks from Bassandyne, who also left him a legacy of twenty pounds. His house in Edinburgh was at the Netherbow [Dickson and Edmond, 198; *D.N.B.*; Aldis, *Scottish Books*, 116; Lee, *App.* ii. iii.].

LE MOYNE DE MORGUES alias MORGAN (JACQUES), (?) bookseller in London, 1586–7; Farringdon Ward Within. A French engraver who came to England for religious reasons. His name appears in the *Returns of Aliens* for 1582–4 [Worman, *Alien Members*, pp. 36–7]. He published a series of plates of beasts, birds, flowers, etc., entitled *La Clef des Champs*, the imprint of which runs: "Imprimé aux Blackefriers, pour Jacques le Moyne, dit de Morgues Paintre." This was entered in the Registers on July 31st, 1587, to "James le Moyn alias Morgan" [Arber, ii. 474]. Nothing more seems to be known of him.

LEWES (WILLIAM), bookseller in London, 1559–66; (1) Over against the Plough in Cow Lane; (2) Dwelling in Cow Lane above Holborn Conduit, over against the sign of the Plough. This stationer was presented for his freedom by Richard Harvey in the year ending July 10th, 1559, and in the same year he paid 6d. towards a benevolence for the muster [Arber, i. 97, 105]. In 1566 he entered *The monstrous chylde which was borne in Buckenham shyre* [Arber, i. 310], and he published other broadsides of a similar character [Hazlitt, H. 66].

LEWTY (RICHARD), stationer in London, 1637–40. Took up his freedom in the Company of Stationers on October 2nd, 1637 [Arber, iii. 688]. He married Christian, the daughter of Richard Bathurst of Bromley, who had been living for two years at the house of Thomas Purfoot, junior. Thomas Purfoot shortly before his death in 1640 assigned his copyrights to R. Lewty, who in the Register is wrongly described as his son-in-law. There is no evidence that Lewty ever published any of these books, but a few days after receiving them he transferred one, William Crashaw's *Decimarum et oblationum tabula*, to Andrew Cooke, after which nothing more is heard of him [Arber, iv. 510, 511].

LEY, *see* LEE.

LICHFIELD (JOHN), printer in Oxford, 1605–35. Appointed printer to the University with William Wrench on February 12th, 161⁶⁄₇. Created Inferior Bedel March 31st, 1617. Resigned his offices January 7th, 163⁴⁄₅. John Lichfield's name is also found in the imprints of Oxford books in company with that of James Short. [Clark, *Register*, ii. 1. 259, 327; Madan, *Oxford Press*, 171, 191, 276, 297, 311.]

LICHFIELD (LEONARD), printer in Oxford, *see* Plomer, *Dictionary*.

LIGHTFOOT (BENJAMIN), bookseller in London, 1612–13; At the upper end of Gray's Inn Lane, in Holborn. Son of Richard Lightfoote of St. Albans, co. Herts. clerk. Apprentice for nine years to William Cotton, stationer of London, from Christmas, 1604. Took up his freedom in the Company on January 20th, 1612 [Arber, ii. 287; iii. 683]. Benjamin Lightfoot entered two books during the year 1613 [Arber, iii. 523, 534], and he was also the publisher of Thomas Heywood's *Silver Age*, 1613.

LIGNANTE (PETER), bookseller and bookbinder in London, 1568–71; St. Olave's, Cripplegate. Mentioned in the Return of Aliens in 1571, as a Frenchman who had lived in London for three years [Worman, *Alien Members*, p. 37].

LING (NICHOLAS), bookseller in London, 1580–1607; (1) The Mermaid in St. Paul's Churchyard 1580–3; (2) West Door of St. Paul's Church, 1584–92; (3) North-west Door of St. Paul's Church, 1593–6; (4) At the [Little] West Door of St. Paul's Church, 1597; (5) In St. Dunstan's Churchyard in Fleet Street, 1600–7. Son of John Lyng of Norwich, parchment maker, apprentice to Henry Bynneman for eight years from Michaelmas, 1570, and took up his freedom in the Company on January 19th, 1578/9 [Arber, ii. 679]. His first book entry in the Registers was made in company with John Charlewood on June 1st, 1582 [Arber, ii. 413], but between August 3rd, 1584, and October 6th, 1590, he entered nothing. But after that date he appears as joint publisher with John Busby, Thomas Millington, Cuthbert Burby and Robert Allot, in such works as Thomas Nashe's *Lenten Stuffe*, 1599, and R. Allot's *England's Parnassus*, 1600. In 1597 Nicholas Ling edited a collection of prose quotations called *Politeuphuia, Wits Commonwealth*, for which he wrote a dedication and preface to the reader. On November 19th, 1607, Nicholas Ling's copies were transferred to John Smethwicke, and his death may be presumed to have taken place between this time and 1610, when sentence on his will was pronounced by the probate court. He left no son. [P.C.C., 58, Wingfield.] Nicholas Ling used as his device a ling and honeysuckle, with the letters N. L., usually found on the titlepages of his publications.

LINLEY (PAUL), bookseller in London, 1586–1600; The Black Bear, St. Paul's Churchyard. Son of William Lynley of Lillingston Darell, co. Bucks. Apprentice for ten years to William Ponsonby from August 6th, 1576 [Arber, ii. 66]. Took up his freedom May 16th, 1586 [Arber, ii. 696]. Nothing more is heard of him until 1595, when with John Flaskett he succeeded to the business of Thomas Woodcock, at the Black Bear in St. Paul's Churchyard, Woodcock's copyrights being transferred to him in the following February [Arber, iii. 48]. Linley and Flaskett apparently had a good connection, as amongst their customers was the Duke of

Northumberland, who in 1596 bought books of them to the value of £21 [*Hist. MSS. Comm., 6th Report*, Appendix, p. 226, etc.]. Linley died between March 17th and April 14th, 1600. By his will he directed that all his goods and chattells which he jointly possessed with John Flaskett should be divided into four parts, one part being left to his mother and another part to Gabriel Cawood and Edward Blunt or Blount, stationers [Dean and Chapter of St. Paul's, Book C, f. 92]. His copyrights were transferred to John Flaskett on June 26th, 1600 [Arber, ii. 164, 165].

LISLE (LAURENCE), bookseller in London, 1607–26; The Tiger's Head, St. Paul's Churchyard. Son of William Lyle of Paddington, co. Middlesex, yeoman. Apprentice to Paul Linley for seven years from November 20th, 1599, but on the death of his master in the following year he was turned over to John Flasket. He took up his freedom January 19th, 1606/7 [Arber, ii. 241; iii. 683]. On July 28th, 1626, he assigned over to Robert Swaine his interest in Sir Thomas Overbury's *Wife*.

LLEWELLIN (WILLIAM), (?) bookseller in London, 1638. A stationer of this name took up his freedom November 13th, 1637 [Arber, iii. 688], and in the following year Richard Dey's *Theatre of Nature* and *Artificiall Table of Morall Philosophy* were entered to him [Arber, iv. 412]. His address has not been found.

LOBLEY (MICHAEL), *see* Duff, *Century*.

LOBLEY or LOBLE (WILLIAM), bookseller and bookbinder in London, 1557–83. Apprenticed to Michael Lobley [*see* Duff, *Century*], by whom he was made free on August 11th, 1557 [Arber, i. 73]. He was fined for selling *Nostradamus* in 1562–3 [Arber, i. 216]. In 1565–6 he entered in the Registers "muskelus vpon the lj psalme by master coxe" [Arber, i. 302], but the book does not seem to have been printed. This was his only entry and his name is not known to occur in any imprint. He took part in some disputes that arose in 1577, apparently about the employment of foreign bookbinders, but submitted himself to the Company in January, 1577/8 [Arber, i. 478, ii. 880]. He was on the side of John Wolf in the attack upon the printing privileges in 1582 [Arber, i. 144], and in one of the documents concerning this he is called a bookbinder [ii. 779].

LOE or LOO (GOVAERT-HENRIK VAN DER), printer and bookseller at Antwerp, (?) 1573–8; In de Cammerstraet, In den Swerten Arent, 1573–5. He was admitted to the St. Lucas-gild in 1575. In 1578 he printed H. Lyte's translation of Dodoens' *Herbal* for sale by G. D'Ewes in London. This appears to be his only work in English. He was succeeded in the business by his widow. [Olthoff, p. 64.]

LOFTUS or LOFTIS (GEORGE), bookseller in London, 1602–15; (1) At the Golden Ball in Pope's Head Alley, 1602–4; (2) In Pope's Head Alley, near the Exchange, 1605 (? the same as no. 1); (3) Under St. Sepulchre's Church, 1612; (4) In Bishopsgate Street, near the Angel, 1615. He is first heard of in 1602 when S. Rowlands' *'Tis Merry when Gossips Meet* was printed for him by W.W., and last in 1615, when the same author's *Melancholy Knight* was printed for him by R.B. Between these dates he published several other works of Rowlands, in two cases in partnership with W. Ferbrand. T. Andrewe's *Unmasking of a Female Machiavel*, 1604, was also printed for him, and he shared in the publication of *Pimlyco, or Runne Red-Cap* in 1609 [Hazlitt, VII. 302]. His name occurs once in the Stationers' Register in 1601 [Arber, iii. 194], but the meaning of the entry is not apparent.

LONG (JOHN), bookseller in Dorchester, 1634. Some copies of the Rev. John Blaxton's *The English Usurer or Usury condemned* bear the imprint, "London, Printed by Iohn Norton and are to bee sold by Iohn Long in Dorchester, 1634." His name does not appear in the Stationers' Registers.

LOVET ( ), (?) bookseller in London, 1624; Holborn. Mentioned in John Gee's *Foot out of the snare*, 1624, as a dealer in popish books.

LOW (GEORGE), printer in London, ? 1612–14; Lothbury. He printed an edition of Byrd and Gibbon's *Parthenia*, without date but attributed to 1612 [Hazlitt, II. 463], and in 1614 a *Map of New England* [Lemon, *Broadsides of Soc. of Antiquaries*, p. 48]. He does not seem to be otherwise known.

LOWNES (HUMPHREY), bookseller and printer in London, 1587–1629; (1) West Door of St. Paul's Church, 1587; (2) The Star on Bread Street Hill, 1608. Son of Hugh Lownes of Rode in the parish of Astbury, co. Chester,

husbandman and fletcher, brother of Matthew Lownes and cousin of Thomas Lownes III. Humphrey Lownes was also without doubt related to William Lownes to whom he was apprenticed for seven years from Midsummer, 1580 [Arber, ii. 96]. He took up his freedom on June 26th, 1587, and made his first book entry in the Registers on March 22nd, 1591/2 [Arber, ii. 606, 699]. He was admitted into the Livery in July, 1598 [Arber, ii. 873], and was Master of the Company in the year 1620–1, and again in 1624–5. Humphrey Lownes in 1591 married a daughter of Thomas Man, stationer, the wedding being celebrated in Stationers' Hall [Arber, i. 545]. His wife died before 1604, when he married Em or Emma, the widow of Peter Short, printer, and succeeded to the business in Bread Street Hill. Humphrey Lownes held shares in the English, Latin and Irish Stocks of the Company of Stationers, and in 1615 he was allowed two presses. On November 6th, 1628, he assigned the bulk of his copyrights to George Cole and George Latham, the last named being a cousin. Amongst the copies mentioned in this list were Sidney's *Arcadia*, Spenser's *Faerie Queene*, Drayton's *Polyolbion*, Bacon's *Apothegmes*, and Ben Jonson's *Poetaster*. Humphrey Lownes made his will on November 7th, 1629, and it was proved on June 24th, 1630. From this it appears that his sons, Humphrey and John, predeceased him and also his second wife. He left the bulk of his estate to his daughter Anne Grantham. George Cole, George Latham, and Robert Young were among the witnesses. [P.C.C., 53, Scroope.] Robert Young was in partnership with Lownes at the time of the latter's death.

LOWNES (HUMPHREY), junior, bookseller in London, 1612–28. Son of Humphrey Lownes, senior. Took up his freedom July 7th, 1612 [Arber, iii. 683]. Made his first book entry September 8th, 1612 [Arber, iii. 495], and his last on January 3rd, 1623/4 [Arber, iv. 133]. Mentioned in the will of his uncle Matthew Lownes, who left a bequest of ten pounds to his children. He is last heard of in 1628, when he assigned some copies to G. Cole and G. Latham [Arber, iv. 205].

LOWNES (JOHN), (?) bookseller in London, 1610–25. Son of William Lownes; one of the witnesses to the will of Thomas Lownes III (1609); and mentioned in the will of Matthew Lownes (1625). He took up his freedom January 16th, 1610 [Arber, iii. 683].

LOWNES (MATTHEW), bookseller in London, 1591–1625; St. Dunstan's Churchyard in Fleet Street. Son of Hugh Lownes of Rode in the parish of Astbury, co. Chester, and brother of Humphrey Lownes. Apprentice to Nicholas Ling from Michaelmas, 1582. Took up his freedom on October 11th, 1591 [Arber, ii. 711]. Admitted to the Livery on July 3rd, 1602 [Arber, ii. 874]. The first book entry under his name occurs on April 15th, 1596 [Arber, iii. 63]. In 1597 he married Anne Halwood a native of Chester [*London Marriage Licenses*, c. 865]. Matthew Lownes died before October 3rd, 1625. He served the office of Senior Warden to the Company in the year 1620–1, when his brother Humphrey was Master, and again from July, 1624, to July, 1625, they filled the same offices. They would appear to have held shares in the same ventures. Matthew Lownes made his will on September 29th, 1625, and it was proved on October 3rd in the same year. He left three sons, Thomas, who succeeded to the business and to whom his copyrights were transferred on April 10th, 1627 [Arber, iv. 176], Robert, who was not a stationer, and Henry who was a grocer. One of his three daughters, Susan, married George Latham, stationer of London. His widow Anne died in the following April. [P.C.C., 117, Clark; 49, Hele.]

LOWNES (ROBERT), bookseller in London, 1611–15. Son of Robert Lownes of Winslow, co. Bucks., yeoman. Apprentice to Richard Bankworth for seven years from November 30th, 1604. Took up his freedom November 4th, 1611 [Arber, ii. 286; iii. 683]. On February 21st, 161$^{4}_{5}$, he entered a play called *The valiant Welchman*. He was perhaps father of Richard Lownes or Lowndes from whom the booksellers of this name of the eighteenth century were descended, and was in no way related to the Lownes of Cheshire.

LOWNES (THOMAS I), bookseller in London, 1598–? 1609. Son of Roger Lownes of Astbury in Cheshire, tailor, not to be confused with Thomas the son of William Lownes, nor with Thomas the son of Matthew. Perhaps identical with Thomas Lownes III, who died in 1609. Apprenticed to William Lownes for seven years from July 5th, 1591 [Arber, ii. 175]. Took up his freedom August 7th, 1598 [Arber, ii. 722].

LOWNES (THOMAS II), bookseller in London, 1605–9. Son of William Lownes, stationer. Admitted a freeman of the Company "per patrimonium" on January 22nd, 160$^{4}_{5}$ [Arber, ii. 738]. On October 4th in the same year in company with Clement Knight he was fined a shilling, but the nature of the offence is not stated [Arber, ii. 840]. He is mentioned in the will of Thomas Lownes III (1609), but he appears to have died soon afterwards.

LOWNES (THOMAS III), bookseller in London, 1609; St. Sepulchre's parish. In all probability a native of Astbury in Cheshire. His will, dated August 31st, 1609, and proved in the Commissary Court of London on October 6th, mentions his son George Lownes. The following items in it prove him to have been a bookseller. "Debts that are due to me. Imprimis Thomas Stocke owes me for a booke vj^{s}. Henry Rose xij^{d}. Item Thomas Lownes [Query the son of Humphrey] xviij^{s}. Thomas Lownes owes me vij^{s}. Item Francis Collmbine ij^{s} vj^{d}. Item Thomas Sanson iiij^{s}. Item Thomas Lucar pastboard maker ix^{s}. . . . Debts that I owe. Imprimis, I owe to my cosen Humphrie Lownes iij^{li}. . . . to my cosen Mathewe Lownes 25^{s}. Item to Ambrose Garbin x^{s}. Item to James Randoll. v^{s}. Item to Mr. Stokes v^{s}. . . . to William Smith box maker xl^{s}." Amongst the witnesses were Thomas Lownes and John Lownes (probably the two sons of William Lownes) [*Commissary of London*, vol. 21, fol. 174]. This Thomas may be identical with Thomas Lownes I.

LOWNES (THOMAS IV), bookseller in London, 1621–7. Son of Matthew Lownes, stationer. Took up his freedom June 22nd, 1621 [Arber, iii. 685]. Assigned his copyrights to his uncle Humphrey Lownes and Robert Young on May 30th, 1627 [Arber, iv. 180–1].

LOWNES (WILLIAM), bookseller in London, 1579–1605. This stationer was a member of the Lownes family of Astbury in Cheshire and was perhaps the uncle of Humphrey and Matthew Lownes; but what relation he was to Thomas I and III is uncertain. Owing to the loss of the Register covering the period from 1571 to 1576, there is no record of his apprenticeship, but he was admitted to the freedom on January 19th, 157$^{8}_{9}$, by Mistress Toy the widow of Humphrey Toy, who is believed to have come from Wales [Arber, ii. 679]. William Lownes began taking apprentices on March 30th, 1579 [Arber, ii. 90], both Humphrey Lownes and Thomas Lownes III, his kinsmen, serving their time with him. In 1590 he entered in the Registers a sermon preached by the Revd. Edward Suckling in Norwich Cathedral, but no copy of the book is known. The date of his death is unknown, but it took place before 1605, when his son Thomas II was admitted to the freedom of the Company "per patrimonium" by Mistress Lownes, widow of William Lownes [Arber, ii. 738]. He also had a son John, mentioned in the will of Matthew Lownes. His will has not been found, neither is the position of his premises known.

L'OYSELET (GEORGE), printer at Rouen, 1584–99. J. Leslie's *Treatise touching the right . . . of Mary Q. of Scotland*, 1584, without printer's name, is attributed to him [Sayle, p. 1401], but the first English work bearing his name seems to be Luis de Granada's *Memorial of a Christian Life*, 1586 [Sayle, p. 1401]. He printed another edition of the same in 1599 [Herbert, p. 1740; Sayle, u.s.].

LUGGER (WILLIAM), *see* Plomer, *Dictionary*.

LYON (JOHN), printer at Louvain, 1580, and at Douai, 1580–1. He printed T. Hide's *Consolatory Epistle to the afflicted Catholics*, 1580, at Louvain [Sayle, p. 1447], and a *Discourse why Catholics refuse to go to Church*, 1580 [B.M., p. 346], and a *Brief Censure upon two books in answer to Campion*, 1581 [Herbert, p. 1655], both at Douai. He is not mentioned by Duthillœul.

MABB (RALPH), bookseller in London, 1610–40, *see* Plomer, *Dictionary*.

MACHAM (JOYCE), (?) bookseller in London, 1615–26; St. Paul's Churchyard, at the sign of Time. Widow of Samuel Macham I. On November 6th, 1615, she in company with Master (? Arthur) Johnson, assigned her rights in Bishop Hall's works to Henry Fetherston [Arber, iii. 577]. In April, 1628, John Grismond assigned over to John Haviland his rights in certain copies which he had received from Mistress Macham, and it was expressly stipulated that Haviland was to reassign them to Samuel Macham the younger as soon as he took up his freedom as a stationer, and in the meantime was to allow him two shillings upon every ream printed of any of the said works [Arber, iv. 196].

MACHAM (SAMUEL I), bookseller in London, 1608–15: The Bull-Head, St. Paul's Churchyard. Son of Thomas Macham of Ashby de la Zouch in the county of Leicester; apprenticed to Simon Waterson, for ten years from Michaelmas, 1595 [Arber, ii. 206]. Took up his freedom July 2nd, 1605 [Arber, iii. 683]. His first book entry occurs in partnership with Mathew Cooke, an edition of the pseudo-Chaucerian *Ploughman's Tale* [Arber, iii. 310]. Mathew Cooke died in 1607. Samuel Macham appears to have dealt chiefly in theological works. By his will, which was dated July 5th, 1615, and proved on the 22nd of the same month, he left bequests to his son Samuel and a daughter Sara, and appointed his wife Joyce executrix. Humphrey Lownes was named as one of the overseers. [P.C.C., 67, Rudd.]

MACHAM (SAMUEL II), bookseller in London, 1631–7. Son of Samuel Macham I. Took up his freedom in the Company of Stationers on December 5th, 1631, and in the following January John Haviland assigned over to him the copyrights that had previously belonged to Samuel Macham I. The last heard of Samuel Macham II is on September 15th, 1637, when he assigned one of his copies to John Beale [Arber, iv. 393].

McKENZIE (ROBERT), chapman of (?) Edinburgh, 1604. He owed xls. to Andro Hart, the Edinburgh bookseller, in November, 1604 [*Bannatyne Miscell.* ii. 239].

MANN (JOANE), (?) bookseller in London, 1635. Widow of Thomas Man, junior. On August 12th, 1635, the whole of the copyrights of the Man family were assigned to her and Benjamin Fisher, who was in occupation of the premises in Paternoster Row previously belonging to Thomas Man, senior [Arber, iv. 344–5].

MAN (JONAS or JONAH), bookseller in London, 1607–26; (1) The Star, West Door of St. Paul's Church, (?) 1608; (2) The Talbot in Paternoster Row. Son of Thomas Man, senior. Took up his freedom November 2nd, 1607 [Arber, iii. 683], but a book was entered in his name in the Registers on February 2nd, 160$^{6}_{7}$ [Arber, iii. 338]. In partnership with his father. After his father's death he is found issuing a book in partnership with Benjamin Fisher, who held the premises at the Talbot in Paternoster Row, and to whom the whole of the copyrights of the Man family were subsequently transferred.

MAN (PAUL), bookseller in London, 1622–35; The Talbot in Paternoster Row. Son of T. Man, senior, with whom he was for some time in partnership. Took up his freedom June 30th, 1621 [Arber, iii. 685]. Made his first book entry on July 18th, 1622 [Arber, iv. 76]. On May 3rd,

1624, Thomas Man assigned over to his sons Paul and Jonas his rights in a number of copies, chiefly theological [Arber, iv. 117], and on August 12th, 1635, these and many other books belonging to Thomas, Paul and Jonas Man were assigned to Benjamin Fisher and widow Man (*i.e.*, Joane Man) [Arber, iv. 344–5].

MAN (SAMUEL), *see* Plomer, *Dictionary*.

MAN (THOMAS), senior, bookseller in London, 1576–1625; The Talbot in Paternoster Row. Son of John Man, of Westbury in Gloucestershire, butcher. Apprentice to John Harrison the elder, stationer of London, for eight years from Midsummer, 1567, and made free of the Company some time before July 17th, 1576 [Arber, i. 351]. He dealt almost wholly in theological books, and rapidly rose to be one of the largest capitalists in the trade, and at the same time one of the most important men in the Company of Stationers, of which he was elected Master in the years 1604, 1610, 1614 and 1616. He was twice married, and had a numerous family. Of his sons three, Thomas, Paul and Jonas or Jonah, were stationers and booksellers. One of his daughters, Anne, married Humphrey Lownes. Thomas Man's second wife was Anne Syms, widow of Randall Syms, to whom he was married on September 10th, 1605 [Chester, *London Marriage Licenses*, col. 881]. She had a daughter, Sara Syms, who appears to have gone to America. On May 3rd, 1624, Thomas Man, senior, assigned over the bulk of his copyrights to his sons, Paul and Jonas [Arber, iv. 117]. His will was proved on June 16th, 1625. He left his house and lands in Hammersmith to his son Paul, and also his house in Paternoster Row, then in the occupation of Benjamin Fisher, who seems to have carried on the business of the Mans after 1625, although no formal transfer of the copyrights to him seems to have been made until August 12th, 1635 [Arber, iv. 344–5]. His will is given in H. F. Waters' *Genealogical Gleanings*, 1901, pp. 1065–6.

MAN (THOMAS), junior, bookseller in London, 1604–10; The Talbot in Paternoster Row. Son of T. Man, senior. Admitted a freeman of the Stationers' Company "by patrimony" on February 6th, 160$\frac{3}{4}$ [Arber, ii. 736]. In partnership with his father and brothers. His last book entry occurs in the Registers on July 23rd, 1611 [Arber, iii. 441]. He is not

mentioned in his father's will, made in 1625, and he was possibly dead at that time. He left a widow Joane, to whom, with Benjamin Fisher, all the copyrights of the Man family were transferred in 1635.

MAN (WILLIAM), (?) bookseller in London, 1624. Mentioned in John Gee's *Foot out of the snare*, 1624, as a dealer in popish books. Described as "Master Fishers man": perhaps Benjamin Fisher is meant.

MANNENBY (LEIGHE), (?) printer in Edinburgh, 1578. This name appears in the imprint of *A Request presented to the King of Spayn . . . by the inhabitantes of the lovve countreyes*, which runs, "At Edinburgh, imprintit be Leighe Mannenby. Anno Domini. 1578." There is no letter w in the Roman fount in which the book is printed, and Greek types occur at the end. Nothing further is known of this printer, and the imprint is probably fictitious [Herbert, p. 1499; *E.B.S. Papers*, vol. i. no. 17; Aldis, *Scottish Books*, 117].

MANSELL, *see* MAUNSELL (ANDREW).

MANTELL (WALTER), bookseller in London, 1583–7. There is some confusion in the records of this stationer. On July 25th, 1569, a *John* Mantell son of *Walter* Mantell of Horton, in the county of Kent, was apprenticed to John Day for seven years. There is no entry of this *John's* admission to the freedom of the Company; but on January 21st, 158$\frac{2}{3}$, we find a *Walter* Mantell, of whose apprenticeship there is no record, made free by Francis Godliff. This was perhaps another case of two brothers apprenticed to the same trade. In the Wardens' accounts for the year ending July 10th, 1588, there occurs the entry, "Paid to Walter Mantell for bookes that had been seised the yeare before this . . . xs." These were possibly copies of the *A B C and Little Catechism* for which he and others were cited before the Star Chamber in Michaelmas Term, 1585 [Arber, ii. 790 *et seq.*], but see Arber, i. 524.

MARCANT (JOHN), printer or bookseller at York, 1579. A book exists entitled *Phaselus Catulli, et ad eam quotquot exstant parodiae* and having the imprint "Eboraci, apud Ionnem Marcantium, 1579," but nothing further seems to be known of any stationer or printer of the name [E. G. Duff, on "The Printers, etc., of York," in *Bibl. Soc. Trans.*, v. 105–6].

MARCHANT (EDWARD), bookseller in London, 1612–16; St. Paul's Churchyard . . . over against the Cross. Probably son of John Marchant, stationer of London, by whom he was made free of the Company on November 8th, 1585 [Arber, ii. 685]. He dealt chiefly in ballads and other ephemeral literature [Arber, iii. 493, 500, 565], and sold books for Joseph Hunt.

MARIUS (ADRIAN), bookseller in London, ?1600–14. In 1614 the Duke of Lenox and Sir Thomas Parry wrote to the Lord Mayor of London, soliciting admission to the freedom of the City for Adrian Marius, "a bookseller, born in England of French parents, who had lived in London many years" [Overall, *Index to the Remembrancia*, p. 160, no. III, 163, 166]. He may be identical with the Adrian Marvie mentioned in the will of Ascanius de Renialme [Plomer, *Wills*, p. 35; Worman, *Alien Members*, p. 39].

MARNI (CLAUDE), printer at Frankfurt am Main, 1581–after 1603. On the death of Andrew Wechel, printer at Frankfurt, in 1581, his business passed to Claude Marni and John Aubri, who printed together until Aubri's death *c.* 1602. In 1603 Camden's *Anglica, Normannica, Hibernica a veteribus scripta* was printed at Frankfurt "Impensis Claudij Marnij & hæredum Iohannis Aubrij." This contains Alfred's preface to his translation of Gregory's *Cura Pastoralis* in Anglo-Saxon, printed in Roman type with an interlinear rendering into English. On 3* 6ᵛ the printer apologizes for his lack of Anglo-Saxon characters. Marni died before 1613, when his heirs and Aubri's are found printing together at Frankfurt. He used as his device Wechel's Pegasus.

MARR (DAVID), chapman of (?) Edinburgh, 1604. He owed iiijli. xiiis. iiijd. (Scots) to Andro Hart, the Edinburgh bookseller, in November, 1604 [*Bannatyne Miscell.*, ii. 240].

MARRIOT (JOHN), *see* Plomer, *Dictionary*.

MARRIOT (RICHARD), *see* Plomer, *Dictionary*.

MARSH (EDWARD), stationer of London, 1591. Son of Thomas Marsh, 1554–87. Admitted a freeman on February 1st, 159$\frac{0}{1}$, but does not appear to have followed the trade of a stationer, as on June 23rd in the same year he transferred his rights in his father's copies to Thomas Orwin [Arber, ii. 586, 709]. This assignment did not include the grammar books, which by letters patent reverted to Henry Stringer [Arber, iii. 87].

MARSH (HENRY), printer in London, 1584–7. Probably a son of Thomas Marsh (1554–87). He was made free of the Stationers' Company by patronage on February 3rd, 158$\frac{3}{4}$ [Arber, ii. 690]. He printed Peele's *Arraignment of Paris* in 1584, T. Watson's *Amyntas* in 1585 and an edition of the *Mirror of Magistrates* in 1587. His name seems last to occur in 1589 when an edition of Ascham's *Toxophilus* was printed by Abel Jeffes "by the consent of H. Marsh."

MARSH (THOMAS), printer in London, *see* Duff, *Century*.

MARSH (THOMAS), stationer and bookbinder of York. Son of William Marsh of Marfleet, Yorkshire. He had a lease of lands at Marfleet belonging to St. John's College, Cambridge, in 1590 and 1597 [T. Baker's *Hist. of St. John's Coll.*, ed. Mayor, pp. 433, 443].

MARTEN (JOHN), bookseller in Lichfield, co. Stafford, ?1567–?1584. His son James Marten was apprentice to Robert Walley, stationer of London, for eight years from Michaelmas, 1576 [Arber, ii. 70]. In the subsidy roll for Lichfield for the 10th year of Elizabeth (*i.e.*, 1568–9), John M[ar]tyn was assessed for 20s. worth of land, for which he was taxed 16d. Again in the roll for the 27th of Elizabeth (1585–6), Johanne M[ar]tyn wid[ow] was assessed for the same land [Lay Subsidies, $\frac{178}{185}$ $\frac{256}{23}$].

MARTYNE (WILLIAM), *see* Duff, *Century*.

MASON (ANDRO), printer in Edinburgh, 1596. His son, Robert, was baptised October 30th, 1596 [*Scottish Antiquary*, iv. 174].

MASSEN (JAN), printer at "Lydden," ? *c.* 1625. An edition of Middleton's *Game at Chess* has an engraved title with the words "Ghedruckt in Lydden by Ian Massē" [B.M., p. 672]. Nothing seems to be known of any printer of the name.

MASTERTON (GILBERT), (?) bookseller in Edinbugh, 1587. On April 15th, 1587, he acquired from Mr. George Young, Archdeacon of St. Andrews, the printing privilege which the latter had received in 1585. Masterton is not known to have exercised this privilege, which he in turn transferred to John Gibson [*q.v.*]. David Laing's copy of *The CL Psalmes*, T. Vautrollier, London, 1587, had at the foot of the title, in manuscript imitation of Roman type, "To be sauld at Gilbert Mastertonis in Edinburgh." [Aldis, *Scottish Books*, 117; Dickson and Edmond, 385, 481; Lee, 48, App. xv.]

MATHER (JOHN), bookseller in London, 1575: Red Cross Street, adjoining St. Giles' Church, without Cripplegate. Son of Thruston Mather of Vigon in the county of Lancaster, yeoman. Apprentice to Henry Bynneman for seven years from Michaelmas, 1566 [Arber, i. 325]. In 1575 he was in partnership with David Moptid at the above address, and two books have been found with the joint imprint, Théodore de Bèze's *Brief declaration of the chief points of Christian Religion* and Anthony Gilby's *Brief Treatise of election and reprobation.* He died before April 30th, 1575. His will is amongst those of the Dean and Chapter of St. Paul's [Book B, f. 182].

MATHEWES (AUGUSTINE), printer in London, 1619–53; (1) In St. Bride's Lane in Fleet Street in the Parsonage House, 1620; (2) Cow Lane near Holborn Circus. Augustine Mathewes took up his freedom as a stationer on May 9th, 1615 [Arber, iii. 684]. The first book entry under his name is Thomas Dekker's *O per se O, or the belman of London*, assigned to him on September 27th, 1619, by John Busby [Arber, iii. 657], and printed by him in the parsonage house of St. Brides. In the following year Mathewes is found in partnership with John White, son of William White, in Cow Lane. From 1624 to 1626 he printed several books for John Norton. On October 24th, 1633, Thomas Jones assigned over to him a dozen copyrights including May's translation of Lucan, and the following plays: *The Tragedy of Nero*, Massinger's *Virgin Martyr*, Thomas May's *The Heire*, Beaumont and Fletcher's *Cupid's Revenge* and *The Scornful Lady.* Sir John Lambe in 1634 referred to Augustine Mathewes as "pauper," and added "Let them agree who shall be, they have now three presses," but to whom he was referring is unknown [Arber, iii. 704]. Mathewes was taken reprinting Dr. Cole's *Holy Table*, and was condemned to lose his press, which was made over to Marmaduke Parsons; but from an entry in the Stationers' Registers we know that Mathewes was still publishing or printing books as late as the year 1653.

MATHEWS (RALPH), *see* Howell.

MATHUSIUS (AUGUSTINUS), *see* Mathewes (A.).

MATTES (EDMUND), bookseller in London, 1597–1613; The Hand and Plough, Fleet Street. Son of Robert Mattes of Kingsey, co. Oxford, and brother and successor of William Mattes [*q.v.*]. He was apprenticed to W. Lownes for seven years from April 15th, 1583 [Arber, ii. 116], and made free of the Stationers' Company on April 30th, 1590 [Arber, ii. 707]. His first entry in the Registers, on November 7th, 1597, was a book which had shortly before been entered to his brother William [Arber, iii. 90, 96]. Among his publications were John Marston's *Metamorphosis of Pigmalion's Image*, 1598, and A. de Torquemada's *Spanish Mandevile of Miracles*, 1600. His last entry in the Registers was on June 5th, 1606 [Arber, iii. 323], and he is not known to have published anything after this year. He was however alive on October 11th, 1613, when he transferred the two works above mentioned, with J. C's *Alcilia*, formerly the property of W. Mattes, to Richard Hawkins [Arber, iii. 533].

MATTES (WILLIAM), bookseller in London, 1594–7; The Hand and Plough, Fleet Street. Son of Robert Mattes of Kingsey, co. Oxford, gent. He was apprenticed to Simon Waterson for nine years from November 1st, 1583 [Arber, ii. 121], and admitted to the freedom of the Stationers' Company on November 7th, 1592 [Arber, ii. 711]. His first entry in the Registers was *The Lamentation of Troy for the Death of Hector*, by I. O. on February 22nd, 159$^{3}_{4}$ [Arber, ii. 645; Hazlitt, H. 426]. His publications were few but interesting: they include I. T's *Old Fashioned Love*, 1594, J. C's *Alcilia* and V. Saviolo's *Practise*, 1595, and Lodge's *Devil Conjured*, 1596. His last entry was on September 24th, 1597, and he died before November 7th of the same year, when the book was re-entered by his brother Edmund who succeeded to the business [Arber, iii. 90, 96].

MAUNSELL (ANDREW), bookseller in London, 1576–1604; (1) The Parrot in St. Paul's Churchyard, 1576–83; (2) The Brazen Serpent, St. Paul's Churchyard, 1584–90; (3) In Lothbury, 1595–6; (4) The Royal Exchange. Andrew Maunsell was originally a member of the Drapers' Company, but is found as a stationer, publishing books and taking apprentices as early as 1576 [Arber, ii. 71]. His first book entries were made on the 11th of the following February [Arber, ii. 308]. He is chiefly remembered for his *Catalogue of English printed books*, published in 1595, which was the first of its kind issued in this country. This catalogue was divided into two

parts, the first dealing with works on Divinity and the second with those relating to the mathematical sciences, physic and surgery. On April 19th, 1596, the Company bestowed upon him a benevolence in money and books, for his pains in the compilation of this catalogue. Although his last book entry is found on April 3rd, 1587, Andrew Maunsell is mentioned as a citizen and stationer in 1604, when he presented his son Andrew as an apprentice [Arber, ii. 285].

MAUNSELL or MANSELL (ANDREW), junior, bookseller in London, 1614. Son of Andrew Maunsell the elder. Apprenticed to Edmond Weaver, stationer, but ordered to serve his time with Thomas Wight, draper, for nine years from September 29th, 1604 [Arber, ii. 285]. Took up his freedom on December 6th, 1613 [Arber, iii. 684]. On May 4th, 1614, he entered S. Rowlands' *A fooles bolt is soone shot* [Arber, iii. 545], which was published in the same year by G. Loftus. Nothing more is heard of him.

MAXEY (THOMAS), *see* Plomer, *Dictionary.*

MAY (——), (?) bookseller in London, 1624; Shoe Lane. Mentioned in John Gee's *Foot out of the snare*, 1624, as a "disperser" of popish books.

MAYLORD or MAYLARD (LEONARD), bookseller in London, 1564–8; The Cock in St. Paul's Church-yard. Took up his freedom in the Company of Stationers on July 18th, 1564 [Arber, i. 278]. His first book entry is found in the year ending July 22nd, 1567 [Arber, i. 336]. In the same year he published John Sandford's translation of the *Manuell of Epictetus* [Arber, i. 339], and in 1568 Henry Bynneman printed for him G. Turberville's *Plain Path to perfect Vertue*, a translation of the *De Quatuor Virtutibus* of D. Mancinus.

MAYNARD (JOHN), *see* Plomer, *Dictionary.*

MAYNE (JONET), bookseller, Edinburgh, 1631–9. She was the widow of James Cathkin [*q.v.*] and carried on her late husband's business from 1631 until her death on April 30th, 1639. Her inventory, printed in the *Bannatyne Miscellany*, ii. 253, enumerates among the debts, one to John Threipland, her servant, who afterwards set up business on his own account. [Aldis, *Scottish Books*, 117.]

MAYNMOUR (ROMAIN), *see* Duff, *Century.*

MEAD (ROBERT), *see* Plomer, *Dictionary.*

MEIGHEN (RICHARD), *see* Plomer, *Dictionary.*

MELVILL (DAVID), bookseller at Aberdeen, 1622–43. He was a friend of Edward Raban, the printer, who printed at least 26 books for him between 1622 and 1633. Melvill, who was buried on February 8th, 1643, was survived by a son, Robert [Edmond, *Aberdeen Printers*; Aldis, *Scottish Books*].

MENSE (CONRAD), printer at Basle, 1560. In January of this year he printed *David Gorge* [*i.e.*, Joriszoon], *borne in Holland*, . . . *of his Lyfe and Damnable Heresy* [Hazlitt, III. 99; a copy in B.M.]. Nothing seems to be known about him.

MERCATOR (REYNOLD), bookseller in London, 1567–76; Farringdon Within. Son of Gerard Mercator and born in Cleveland or Duysburg. Appointed factor to Arnold Birckman, and came to England about 1567. He appears to have returned to Holland about 1576 [Worman, *Alien Members*, p. 41].

MEREDITH (CHRISTOPHER), *see* Plomer, *Dictionary.*

MESTAIS (JEAN), printer at Paris, 1640. In this year he printed W. Rushworth's *Dialogues of William Richworth* [B.M., p. 1333; Sayle, p. 1388].

METEREN (EMANUEL VAN), (?) bookseller in London, ?–1612. Son of James Cornelij de Matgre [*see* Duff, *Century*]. He was a merchant of considerable importance [*see* Worman, *Alien Members*, pp. 41–4, and *Acts of the Privy Council*, February 15th, 159$^{9}_{0}$, and September 29th, 1600, where he is called "Demetrius"]. His connection with the book-trade is not absolutely certain, but he may have been an importer of foreign works or agent for foreign stationers. There are letters of his in MS. Cotton, Julius, C. iii.

MICHEL (M), printer at Rouen, 1615. In this year he printed *A short declaration of the lives and doctrines of the Protestants and Puritans* [B.M., p. 1265].

MICHELL (ROGER), bookseller in London, 1627–31; The Bull's Head, St. Paul's Churchyard. Roger Michell took up his freedom as a stationer on January 14th, 1627, and made his first book entry, in partnership with Michael Sparke, on August 20th in the same year [Arber, iii. 686; iv. 184]. Amongst his publications was a metrical life of King Edward the Second, written by Sir Francis Hubert, and R. Hayman's *Quodlibets, lately come over from New Britaniola, Old Newfoundland.* His last book entry was made on April 29th, 1631 [Arber, iv. 252].

MIDDLETON (HENRY), printer in London, 1567–87; (1) The Black Horse, Ivy Lane; (2) The Ship, in London Wall; (3) The Falcon in Fleet Street; (4) In St. Dunstan's Churchyard. Son of William Middleton, printer, 1541–7. Admitted to the freedom of the Stationers' Company in the year ending July 22nd, 1567 [Arber, i. 344]. Henry Middleton at once joined Thomas East or Este, the printer, and together they printed, before the end of the year 1567, an edition of Thomas Phaer's *Regiment of Life.* In 1571 East and Middleton moved to premises in London Wall, but in the following year the partnership was dissolved, Henry Middleton having bought William Griffith's printing and bookselling business at the Falcon in Fleet Street, with a shop in St. Dunstan's Churchyard. Many interesting books came from his press, among them being Gascoigne's *Glasse of Governement*, which he printed for Christopher Barker in 1575; Sir Humfrey Gilbert's *Discourse of a discoverie for a new passage to Cataia*, 1576; an edition of the *De Imitatione Christi*, translated and illustrated by the Rev. Thomas Rogers, 1587, William Lambarde's *Perambulation of Kent*, 1576, one of the earliest of English topographical books, and an edition of the works of Virgil in 1580. In 1583 Henry Middleton was working three presses. He was chosen Junior Warden of the Company in July, 1587, but died before completing his year of office, leaving a widow Jane who afterwards married Richard Ayres [*Commissary of London*, p. 104]. From some depositions taken in a suit brought in 1591 by a certain Richard Brown, against Henry Middleton's executors, to recover a sum of £30 for printing indentures for licenses to sell wines, we learn that Robert Robinson bought the printing material and certain books and letters patent from Middleton's widow for the sum of £200, and that Thomas Newman bought the shop in St. Dunstan's Churchyard and the books in it for £150 [*Library*, January, 1909, p. 103].

MIDDLETON (THOMAS), bookseller and bookbinder in Oxford, 1590–1604. Admitted a bookseller on November 27th, 1590. He died before March 28th, 1604 [Clark, *Register*, ii. 1. 321; *Oxford Univ. Archives*—

Wills]. Administration of his goods was granted to Alice Middleton, his daughter. In 1601 there are entries in the Magdalen accounts to him for binding [*Magd. Reg.*, III, p. 35; Gibson, *Oxford Wills*, p. 19].

MILANGES (S.), printer at Bordeaux, 1589. In this year he printed *A declaration of the King concerning the Observation of his Edict of the Union of his Catholic Subjects* [Maitland, *Index of English Books . . . . at Lambeth*, p. 42].

MILBOURNE (ROBERT), *see* Plomer, *Dictionary*.

MILES (EDWARD), bookseller and bookbinder in Oxford, and Clerk of the University, 1593–1638. Robert Cavey [*q.v.*] alias Stuffolde in his will dated December 6th, 1593, bequeathed to his "nephew and servant Edward Miles," all his tools belonging to his science or trade of bookbinding. Edward Miles with Dominique Pinart bound many of the books that were bought for the Bodleian Library, and he remained one of the chief Bodleian binders down to 1613. His name first occurs as a bookseller on November 15th, 1616. He died in March, 1638 [Clark, *Register*, ii. 1. 404; Gibson, *Oxford Bindings*, *passim*; *Oxford Wills*, xxiii. 17, 22, 32, 33].

MILLESON (JOHN), bookseller in Cambridge, 1627–70; Over against Great St. Mary's Church, 1642. He first paid church rate in the parish of Great St. Mary's in 1627 [Foster's *Churchwardens' Accounts*]. His will dated 1670 is at Peterborough. *See* Plomer, *Dictionary*.

MILLER (GEORGE), *see* Plomer, *Dictionary*.

MILLINGTON (JOAN), bookseller in London, 1604. Widow of Thomas Millington, 1593–1603. She appears to have carried on the business for a short time after his death, as in 1604 she published a pamphlet describing the passage of Anne of Denmark through the streets of London [Hazlitt, H. 9].

MILLINGTON (THOMAS), bookseller in London, 1593–1603; Under St. Peter's Church in Cornhill. Son of William Millington of Hampton Gaie, co. Oxon, husbandman. Apprentice to Henry Carre, stationer of London, for eight years from August 24th, 1583 [Arber, ii. 123]. Admitted to the freedom of the Company on November 8th, 1591 [Arber, ii. 710].

His first book entry was the first part of the *Contention of the two famous houses of York & Lancaster* on March 12th, 159¾ [Arber, ii. 646]. He was also the publisher of Chettle's *England's Mourning garment*, 1603. Millington is found in partnership at various times with John Busby, Nicholas Ling and Thomas Gosson, and issued ballads and other ephemeral literature. The last entry under his name is found on May 9th, 1603 [Arber, iii. 234].

MILWARD (HENRY), bookseller in Oxford, 1536–1605; Beef Hall. He is frequently mentioned as taking the inventories of the goods of deceased booksellers in Oxford. He resigned his position as University stationer on April 11th, 1597, and was succeeded by Lancelot Waistell. [Clark, *Register*, ii. 1. 262; Gibson, *Oxford Wills*, pp. 11, 16–18, 21.]

MOMMART (JEAN), printer at Brussels, 1597–1608. In 1608 he printed the *Histoire de Aurelio et Isabelle* by Juan de Flores, in four languages, Italian, Spanish, French and English [Sayle, p. 1495]. In some copies this is described as "chez Iean Mommart & Iean Reyne" [Hazlitt, I, 17].

MOMMART (WIDOW OF JEAN), printer at Brussels, 1612–34. In the latter year she printed Gerald Barry's *Military Discipline*. Mr. Sayle attributes to her a French work by Salomon De Caus printed for John Norton. The imprint of this is "A fancfort [*sic*] chez la vefue de Hulsius," but it has the device of Mommart on plate 16 verso [Sayle, p. 1496].

MOODY (HENRY), stationer at Cambridge, 1575–1637; Great St. Mary's parish. Probably the Henry Moody christened at St. Michael's Church, Cambridge, on May 1st, 1575 [Venn's *St. Michael's Registers*, p. 2]. He paid church rate in Great St. Mary's parish from 1620 and was several times churchwarden, auditor, elector, etc. [Foster's *Churchwardens' Accounts*]. His will dated 1637 is at Peterborough.

MOODY (THOMAS), bookseller in Cambridge, 1627–61; Over against Great St. Mary's Church. He lived next door to John Milleson [*q.v.*], and first paid church rate in the parish of Great St. Mary's in 1627 [Foster's *Churchwardens' Accounts*]. His will dated 1661 is at Peterborough.

MOORE (JOHN), Assigns of, *see* Plomer, *Dictionary*, — More.

MOORE (JOHN), stationer in Dublin, 1639–40; St. Bridgets Parish. Married Elizabeth Doyle in October, 1639. Admitted to the franchise of the city in April, 1640, in right of his wife. He was possibly the John Moore mentioned in the will of Edmond Crooke, stationer, as his "servant."

MOORE (RICHARD), bookseller in London, 1607–31; St. Dunstan's Churchyard. Son of Anthony Moore of Appleby, co. Westmoreland. Apprentice to Mathew Lownes for nine years and a quarter from Michaelmas, 1598, and took up his freedom on November 2nd, 1607 [Arber, ii. 230; iii. 683]. Amongst his publications were John Day's play, *Law Trickes*, 1608, Warner's *Albion's England*, 1612, John Bodenham's *England's Helicon*, 1614, and Gervase Markham's *Whole art of husbandry*, 1631. His last book entry was made on April 29th, 1631. Richard Moore was nominated in 1627, by the will of Edward Latymer, one of the trustees of Latymer school. His copyrights were assigned over to John Marriot on June 27th, 1634, by his widow [Arber, iv. 322].

MOPTID (DAVID), printer in London, ? 1573–87; Red Cross Street, adjoining St. Giles' Church, without Cripplegate. Son of Henry Moptid or Moptyd of London, ironmonger, and related by marriage to Thomas East, printer, to whom he was apprenticed for seven years from Michaelmas, 1566 [*Library*, July, 1901, p. 298]. He joined John Mather, and together they printed Théodore de Bèze's *Brief Declaration of the chief points of Christian Religion*, and Anthony Gilby's *Brief treatise of election and reprobation.* Neither of these bears a date. His will was proved on March 15th, $158\frac{6}{7}$ [Commissary of London, vol. 17, f. 63].

MORBERIUS (GAUTIER), printer and bookseller at Antwerp, (?)–1558, and at Liège, 1560–95. He was appointed imprimeur juré at Liège in 1558, but his first known book printed there dates from 1560. A work by Morgan Philips, *i.e.*, John Leslie, appeared in 1571, "Apud Gualterum Morberium," entitled *A Treatise concerning the defense of . . . Mary Queen of Scotland . . . with a Declaration as well of her Right, Title, and Interest to the Succession of the Crown of England: as that the Regiment of woman is conformable to the laws of God and Nature.* The three books of which this consists have separate signatures, and the second at least has a separate title. [Herbert, pp. 1627–8; B.M. p. 1230; de Theux de Montjardin, col. viii.]

MORDEN (THOMAS), stationer at Cambridge, 1624. Mentioned in a list of privileged persons in the University in that year [Bowes, *Univ. Printers*, 336].

MORE or MOORE (JOHN), Assigns of, *see* Plomer, *Dictionary*.

MOREL (CLAUDE), printer at Paris, 1579–1626; Rue Sainct Iaques, à l'enseigne de la Fontaine. He was son of Frédéric Morel I. He printed in 1614 W. Bishop's *Disproof of D. Abbot's Counterproof* [Sayle, p. 1386]. [Renouard, p. 276].

MORETUS (JEAN), printer at Antwerp, *see* Plantin (Jeanne).

MORGAN, *see* Le Moyne.

MORING (WILLIAM), (?) bookseller in London, 1594. Apprentice to Hugh Singleton. Admitted a freeman of the Company on February 1st, 159$^{0}_{1}$ [Arber, ii. 708]. He appears to have been partner with Adam Islip in 1594 [Arber, ii. 662].

MORRANT (JOHN), (?) bookseller in London, 1609. On May 2nd of this year he entered in the Registers *Catholic Traditions, or a Treatise of the Belief of the Christians of Asia, Europe, &c.*, translated from the French by L. Owen [Arber, iii. 407]. On August 7th, however, he assigned it to Henry Fetherstone [Arber, iii. 417], for whom it was printed by W. Stansby [Hazlitt, I. 473]. Nothing else seems to be known of him.

MORRIS (JOHN), (?) bookseller in London, 1580–90. Took up his freedom in the Company of Stationers on May 2nd, 1580 [Arber, ii. 682]. Only two entries occur under his name, the first on April 26th, 1587, when he paid sixpence for the right of printing John de L'Espine's *Treatise of Apostacy* [Arber, ii. 469], and the second on October 15th, 1590, when in company with John Bowen he entered a sermon preached at Hitchin by Edward Harris, M.A. [Arber, ii. 565]. His address has not been found.

MOSELEY (HUMPHREY), *see* Plomer, *Dictionary*.

MOUNTFORD (THOMAS), (?) bookseller in London, 1614. Clerk to the Company of Stationers. Took up his freedom March 8th, 161$^{3}_{4}$ [Arber, iii. 684]. On June 30th, 1614, he entered a book of *Epigrams* (? T. Freeman's *Rubbe, and a Great Cast*) [Arber, iii. 549].

MUNDEE or MUNDAY (RICHARD), printer in London, 1578; Dwelling at Temple Bar in Fleet Street. Admitted into the freedom of the Company January 14th, 157$^{6}_{7}$, by Thomas Marshe [Arber, ii. 673]. Associated with Roger Ward in printing Thomas Lupton's *All for money* in 1578 [Arber, v. 109].

MURIS, MEURIS or MEURS (AERT or ARNOLD), printer at The Hague, 1602–41. He printed *The Faithful and wise preventer or counsellor* [Sayle, p. 1497] and *Reasons that make the ban against the K. of Bohemia of no value* [B.M., p. 655], both in 1621. [Ledeboer, *A.L.*, p. 118.]

MUTTON (EDMUND), (?) bookseller in London, 1598–1603; In Paternoster Row, at the sign of the Huntsman. Son of Thomas Mutton of Rockby, Warwick, butcher. Apprentice to John Penny, stationer of London, for seven years from Christmas, 1589, and took up his freedom on October 16th, 1598 [Arber, ii. 167, 722]. On May 10th, 1603, he entered a book called *The description of a true visible christian* [Arber, iii. 233]. He was also the publisher of a broadside entitled *Weepe with Joy*, 1603, commemorating the death of Queen Elizabeth and the accession of King James. He probably fell a victim to the plague which raged in London in the autumn of 1603.

MYLLER (CONRAD), bookseller in London and Oxford, *see* Duff, *Century*, p. 106.

MYN or MYNNE (RICHARD), *see* Plomer, *Dictionary*.

NAFEILD (JEAN). Three editions of Adam Blackwood's *Martyre de la Royne d'Escosse*, dated respectively 1587, 1588, 1589, have the fictitious imprint "A Edimbourg chez Jean Nafeild." They were probably printed in Paris. [Aldis, *Scottish Books*, 118; *E.B.S. Papers*, ii. 50, 59.]

NAYLAND (SAMUEL), *see* Nealand.

NEALAND (SAMUEL), bookseller in London, 1618–32; (1) King Lane; (2) The Crown, Duck Lane. He is no doubt identical with Samuel Nayland, son of Edmond Nayland, of Lalam, Middlesex, yeoman, who was apprenticed for ten years to Edmund Weaver from May 1st, 1603, and took up his freedom on May 6th, 1613 [Arber, ii. 271; iii. 684]. On May 28th, 1618, he entered in the Registers *The relacon of the death of Achmat, last Emperour of the Turkes*, etc. [Arber, iii. 623]. In 1628 he

was mentioned in a return of those who dealt in "old libraryes" [*Dom. S. Papers, Charles I*, vol. 117 (9)]. His last entry in the Registers was Tycho Brahe's *Astronomical conjectur*, entered on December 10th, 1631, and published in the following year. He died in May, 1640.

NEALE or NEILE (ANDREW), printer at Old Ford, Middlesex, 1626. Took up his freedom in the Company of Stationers, September 6th, 1619 [Arber, iii. 685]. In 1626 in company with John Phillips, he erected a secret press at Old Ford, near Bow, in the county of Middlesex. This was discovered by the Company and ordered to be battered and the letters melted [Records of the Stationers' Company].

NELMAN (CORNELIUS), bookbinder in London, 1568–83; Castle Baynard Ward. Born in Holland. Took out letters of denization in this country on October 29th, 1571. Is said to have married an Englishwoman. He is last mentioned in the Return of Aliens for the year 1583. [Worman, *Alien Members*, pp. 48–9.]

NELSON (THOMAS), bookseller in London, 1580–92; (1) West End of St. Paul's Church; (2) Over against the Great South Door of St. Paul's Church; (3) Silver Street, near to the Red Cross. This stationer was apprentice to Garrard or Garret D'Ewes, by whom he was presented for his freedom on October 8th, 1580. He appears to have dealt largely in ballads. During the year ending July 10th, 1586, he was arrested by the officers of the Company, but what his offence was is not stated [Arber, i. 515]. The last entry under his name in the Registers was made on August 14th, 1592 [Arber, ii. 619]. In the will of Jarrett Anderson, proved in December, 1592, occurs this passage: "and my walkinge staffe to Thomas Nelson, stacioner" [P.C.C., 13, Neville].

NEVILL (PHILIP), *see* Plomer, *Dictionary*.

NEWBERY (JOAN), widow of John Newbery, *see* Newbery (John).

NEWBERY (JOHN), bookseller in London, 1594–1603; The Ball in St. Paul's Churchyard. Son of Robert Newbery of Laurence Waltham, Berks, yeoman; cousin of Ralph Newbery (1560–1607), of Fleet Street, to whom he was apprenticed for seven years, from March 26th, 1584 [Arber, ii.

122]. Admitted to the freedom of the Company on May 3rd, 1591 [Arber, ii. 709]. On the last day of September, 1594, Ralph Newbery assigned over to him the copyrights in several books, including the quarto and octavo editions of Stow's *Chronicle*. The last book entry under John Newbery's name occurs on February 23rd, 160$^{2}_{3}$ [Arber, iii. 228]. Ralph Newbery, by a codicil to his will dated August 14th, 1603, enjoined that John Newbery should have the shop he was then living in, and be cleared of debt on giving security; but John Newbery died shortly afterwards, as on March 9th, 160$^{3}_{4}$, his widow Joan is found entering a book. She took apprentices as late as March 11th, 160$^{4}_{5}$ [Arber, ii. 290; iii. 254].

NEWBERY (NATHANIEL), bookseller in London, 1616–34; Under St. Peter's, Cornhill, and Pope's Head Alley. Took up his freedom in the Company on January 5th, 161$^{5}_{6}$. His first book entry was made on August 21st, 1616, and his last on March 2nd, 163$^{0}_{1}$ [Arber, iii. 594, 684; iv. 249]. There is no evidence to show whether he was in any way related to either John or Ralph Newbery.

NEWBERY (RALPH), bookseller in London, 1560–1607; Fleet Street, a little above the Conduit. Ralph Newbery took up his freedom in the Company on January 21st, 15$^{59}_{60}$, and made his first book entry in the Registers before May 4th in the same year [Arber, i. 121, 127]. He became an influential member of the Company, serving the office of Junior Warden in the years 1583–4 and 1584–5, that of Senior Warden in the years 1589–90 and 1590–1. He was Master in the years 1598 and 1601. He was appointed one of the deputies of Christopher Barker, and was in partnership with Henry Denham as assign of Henry Bynneman, printer. Ralph Newbery died before April 24th, 1607, when his will was proved in the Prerogative Court of Canterbury. He owned property in Berks, as well as his house and shop in Fleet Street. His stock of books in Stationers' Hall he directed should be sold and one part of the proceeds given to the poor of the Company, and further that Roger Jackson and John Norcott his late apprentices should have his stock of books in his shop at Fleet Street; but they do not seem to have availed themselves of the offer [P.C.C., 30, Hudlestone].

NEWMAN (ABRAHAM), draper and bookseller of London, 1578. Abraham Newman was one of those for whom Roger Ward printed Day's *A B C and Little Catechism.* In his depositions he stated that he supplied Ward with ten reams of paper for ten reams of the said books [Arber, ii. 763 *et seq.*].

NEWMAN (THOMAS), bookseller in London, 1587–98; St. Dunstan's Churchyard, Fleet Street. Son of John Newman, clothworker of Newbury, Berks. Apprentice for eight years from Michaelmas, 1578, to Ralph Newbery, stationer of London [Arber, ii. 87]. Admitted to the freedom of the Company on August 25th, 1586 [Arber, ii. 698]. On October 12th in the same year Thomas Chauncy, an apprentice of Thomas Woodcock's, transferred himself to Thomas Newman for the remainder of his term [Arber, ii. 88]. He bought the shop previously occupied by Henry Middleton in St. Dunstan's Churchyard, and the books in it, for £150 [Court of Requests, Hunts Series, Bundle 37, No. 110]. He entered his first book, a translation from the Italian, in partnership with Thomas Gubbyn on September 18th, 1587 [Arber, ii. 475]; his last on June 30th, 1593, in company with John Winnington [Arber, ii. 633]. In 1591 he was in trouble for publishing Sir P. Sidney's *Astrophel and Stella* [Arber, i. 555].

NEWTON (NINIAN), printer in London, 1579–86; Eliot's Court, Old Bailey. Son of Thomas Newton, gent., of Upsall, co. York. Apprentice to William Seres for ten years from Michaelmas, 1569 [Arber, i. 396]. He was made free of the Company on October 8th, 1579, by Henry Denham, who had succeeded to Seres' business. As nothing more is heard of Newton until the foundation of the Eliot's Court printing house in 1584, he probably was working as a journeyman in Denham's office during the interval. In company with Arnold Hatfield he printed in 1584, for John Wight, Edmund Bunny's edition of Robert Parsons' *Booke of Christian Exercise.* In 1585 these same two printers produced editions of Cæsar's *Commentaries* and of the works of Horace in sexto decimo. In 1586 Ninian Newton's name is found in the imprint to a quarto edition of Rembert Dodoens' *Herball*, after which nothing more is heard of him.

NEWTON (THOMAS), bookseller in London, 1578–9. Son of Richard Newton of Loughborough, co. Leicester, yeoman. Apprentice to Richard Hudson for eight years from Midsummer, 1568 [Arber, i. 371]. Admitted to the freedom of the Company on June 17th, 1577 [Arber, ii. 674]. On August 3rd, 1579, he was ordered by the Company to give up all the copies in his possession of a work called *a briefe instruccon in manner of a cathecisme*, which Richard Jones had illegally printed [Arber, ii. 850].

NICHOLES (THOMAS), *see* Plomer, *Dictionary*.

NICHOLSON, *see* Nycholas.

NICHOLSON (JOHN), *see* Plomer, *Dictionary*.

NIXON alias **WAY** (ROBERT), bookseller and bookbinder in Oxford, 1602–26. A native of Wiltshire. Robert Nixon was apprenticed to Robert Billingsley, bookseller of Oxford, and became a privileged bookseller of the University on October 29th, 1602, at the age of twenty-four. He bound books for the Bodleian between 1620 and 1626. [Clark, *Register*, ii. 1. 321, 343, 399; Gibson, *Oxford Bindings*, pp. 48, 60.]

NOLCK or **NOLICK** (MAERTEN ABRAHAMS VAN DER), printer at Flushing, 1573–1623; At the sign of the Printing house, 1621. In this year he printed John Wing's *Abel's Offering* [Sayle, p. 1500] and in 1622 the same author's *The best merchandise . . . our traffic with God* [B.M., pp. 1612–13]. [Ledeboer, *A.L.*]

NORTH (JOHN), bookseller in London, 1601–2; The White Hart, over against the Great Conduit in Fleet Street. Son of Richard North of London, hosier. Apprentice for nine years from Michaelmas, 1592, to Ralph Newbery [Arber, ii. 183]. Admitted a freeman of the Company on October 6th, 1601 [Arber, ii. 730]. In partnership with Roger Jackson he issued *Greene's Ghost Haunting Coniecatchers* by S. Rowlands in 1602.

NORTON (BONHAM), printer and bookseller in London, 1594–1635; (1) Northumberland House, Aldersgate Street; (2) Hunsdon House, Blackfriars. Bonham Norton was the only son of William Norton, the bookseller, by his wife Joane, the daughter of William Bonham, bookseller, the friend and contemporary of John Rastell. The Nortons were a Shropshire family. Bonham Norton was born in 1565 and was apprenticed to his father. He was admitted a freeman of the Company "per patrimonium" on February 4th, 159¾ [Arber, ii. 713]. His father had died a few months before, leaving a large fortune in real and personal estate, which Bonham Norton inherited. Bonham Norton married Jane, the daughter of Sir Thomas

Owen of Condover. He was sheriff of Shropshire and became an alderman of London. He was also Master of the Company of Stationers in the years 1613, 1626 and 1629. In 1612 Bonham Norton, already a rich man, received a further legacy from John Norton, his cousin, also a Shropshire man, and a wealthy stationer, who is best remembered as the publisher of Sir Henry Savile's edition of *Chrysostom.* Bonham Norton's character was that of a hard, calculating and grasping man, who was continually in the law courts prosecuting his brother stationers. His name first appears in the Registers on May 7th, 1594, when he assigned over to Richard Field the copyright of the *History of Guicciardini*, Fenton's translation [Arber, ii. 648]. Between 1602 and 1613 there are no entries under his name in the Registers, but he was during that time in partnership with John Norton and John Bill in the trades of bookselling and printing. In 1601 Robert Barker, the King's printer, complained to the Privy Council that Bonham Norton and John Norton had induced Andro Hart [*q.v.*] to send printers over to Dort in Holland for the purpose of printing *Bibles* and other privileged books [*Acts of the Privy Council, New Ser.*, xxxii. 14–15]. In 1613 Bonham Norton became Master of the Company in the room of his cousin John Norton deceased. He at once began an action against certain stationers who had been partners with John Norton in a large stock of *Bibles* and service books, and claimed the money standing in John Norton's name on the ground that by the deed of partnership the share of any partner who died was to go to his administrators. The defendants denied this, and referred to the "hard measure" offered to them by Bonham Norton in "suits and other vexations." They refer to him as a man of great estate, who had no need to "again become a bookseller." [Exchequer Bills and Answers, Jas. I, Lond. and Midd., No. 1005.] About this time he also seems to have been on friendly terms with Robert Barker, the King's printer, to whom there is reason to believe he advanced the money for the printing of the so called "authorised version" of the *Bible* in 1611. At any rate both he and John Bill, another native of Shropshire, held some sort of share in the King's printing house at this time. In 1615 Bonham Norton's eldest daughter Sarah married Robert Barker's son Christopher. But in 1618 trouble began between Barker and Norton and led to a bitter and protracted series of law suits, to which is due the bewildering series of imprints of the King's printing office between 1617 and 1629. Decree was at length pronounced in favour of Robert Barker, whereupon Bonham Norton accused the Lord Keeper of receiving a bribe, and was thrown into prison and fined. He died in 1635, but whether he was still a prisoner is not known. His sons Roger and John Norton were also stationers. [*Library*, October, 1901, pp. 353–75.]

NORTON (FELIX), bookseller in London, 1600–3; The Parrot in St. Paul's Churchyard. Son of Mark Norton citizen and grocer of London, who married one of the daughters of J. Cawood. Apprentice to George Bishop for nine years from June 24th, 1591, and took up his freedom on July 7th, 1600 [Arber, ii. 174, 727]. He succeeded John Oxenbridge at the Parrot in St. Paul's Churchyard, this stationer's books being transferred to him on September 1st, 1600 [Arber, iii. 171]. He died in 1603, and was succeeded at the same address by W. Aspley.

NORTON (GEORGE), bookseller in London, 1610–23; Temple Bar. Son of Robert Norton of Helmdon, Northampton, yeoman. Apprentice to Thomas Man for seven years from September 6th, 1602: took up his freedom December 4th, 1609 [Arber, ii. 266; iii. 683]. Made his first entry in the Registers on July 4th, 1610 [Arber, iii. 440]. On November 23rd, 1623, he made over his rights in W. Browne's *Britannia's Pastorals* to John Haviland and Mistress Griffin.

NORTON (JOHN), senior, bookseller and (?) printer in London, Eton and Scotland, 1586–1612; London: St. Paul's Churchyard. Son of Richard Norton of Billingsley, Salop, and nephew of William Norton, stationer of London (1561–93), to whom he was apprenticed for eight years from January 8th, 157⅞ [Arber, ii. 82]. John Norton took up his freedom on July 18th, 1586 [Arber, ii. 698], and rapidly rose to the highest position in the Company, being admitted to the Livery on July 1st, 1598, and being Master in the years 1607, 1611 and 1612. John Norton began business as a bookseller in St. Paul's Churchyard, and was one of the largest capitalists in the trade, besides being the publisher of some of the most important books of the day. His shop was resorted to by the chief book collectors and literary men, and he made regular visits to the Frankfort Fair. He was for a time in partnership with his cousin Bonham Norton [*q.v.*], and John Bill. About 1587 he set up a bookselling business in Edinburgh, and in 1589 obtained, with Andro Hart, the privilege of importing books free of custom, with a further licence to the same effect in June, 1591 [*Reg. P.C. Scot.*, iv. 439; Lee, App. x]. From a passage in Calderwood's *History*, v. 77, it would appear that Norton was living in Edinburgh in 1590; and in February, 1592, he appeared in person before the Town Council to answer a charge preferred against him and his servant Edmond Wats, by seven Edinburgh booksellers, of having usurped the liberty of the burgh by retailing books in "ane oppin chalmer upoun the foregaitt," and they were ordered to desist from selling "in smallis" [Lee, *Add. Mem.* App. lxxi]. After the death of Wats, about 1596, Norton gave up his Edinburgh business, and sold the books and debts to Edward Cathkin and Andro Hart, booksellers there [Calderwood, v. 511]. It has generally been supposed that John Norton was a printer as well as a bookseller, and it is true that in 1603 he was appointed King's printer in Hebrew, Latin and Greek, but on examination the books that bear his imprint are found to have been printed for him by Melchisidec Bradwood and his partners at the Eliot's Court printing office in the Old Bailey. Evidence of this is shown in the splendid edition of Abraham Ortelius' *Theatrum Orbis Terrarum*, 1606, the titlepage of which states distinctly that it was printed "by John Norton, printer to the King's most excellent Majesty in Hebrew, Greeke and Latin," but the colophon of which runs, "London, Printed *for* John Norton and John Bill," and the internal evidence proves it to have been printed at the Eliot's Court Press. So too with Sir Henry Savile's edition of Chrysostom. Each volume bears the imprint "Excudebat Joannes Norton," but we know that Sir Henry Savile obtained the Greek type from Moret, the Antwerp printer, and an examination of the volumes proves that the rest of the type, initials, ornaments and devices were those of Melchisidec Bradwood, who took the necessary workmen down with him to Eton for the purpose of printing the work, which was published by John Norton. Norton died in November, 1612, during his third term of office as Master of the Company. By his will which was proved on January 12th, $161\frac{2}{3}$, he left a sum of £1,000 to the Company of Stationers to buy lands, the income from which was to be lent to poor young men of the Company. The money was laid out in the purchase of houses in Wood Street, which now produce a considerable rental and form part of the endowment of Stationers' School [Arber, v. lxiii]. John Norton left his lands in Shropshire to provide bequests to his nephew Leonard Norton,

son of his brother Richard, and to Lucy and Thomas Wight, the children of Thomas Wight, draper. He made his cousin Bonham Norton his executor [Plomer, *Wills*, pp. 45–7].

NORTON (JOHN), junior, *see* Plomer, *Dictionary*.

NORTON (JOYCE), (?) printer in London, 1632–7; The King's Arms, St. Paul's Churchyard. John Norton who died in 1612 left a widow Joyce, but it is not clear whether she is to be identified with the subject of this note. Joyce Norton was in partnership during the above period with Richard Whitaker. A Joyce Norton, widow, married Mathew Lawe [*q.v.*].

NORTON (ROGER), *see* Plomer, *Dictionary*.

NORTON (THOMAS), bookseller in London, 1616–18; The King's Head in St. Paul's Churchyard. Took up his freedom in the Company on July 1st, 1616 [Arber, iii. 684]. On November 29th in that year he entered Hitchcock's *Abstract of humane wisdome* [Arber, iii. 598].

NORTON (WILLIAM), *see* Duff, *Century*.

NYCHOLAS or NICHOLSON alias SEGER (BENJAMIN), stationer of Cambridge, 1573–95. Apprentice for eight years from June 24th, 1565, to William Seres, citizen and stationer of London [Arber, i. 285]. He is found taking apprentices from 1582 to 1595 [Arber, ii. 114 *et seq.*]. In the margin of two of these entries his name is given as "Benjamin Segar alias Nycolson." Mr. Weale in *Bookbindings*, p. xxxix, says he was the son of Segar Nicholson the Cambridge binder, but does not give his authority [Gray, *Cambridge Stationers*, 64].

OCKOULD (HENRY), bookseller in London, 1639–40; The Swan in Little Britain. Son of Richard Ockould. Took up his freedom July 19th, 1632 [Arber, iii. 687]. On October 8th, 1639, his father's copyrights were transferred to him [Arber, iv. 482]. Amongst his publications was Thomas Hayne's *Generall View of the Holy Scriptures*, 1640, which was printed for him by I. B[eale] and S[tephen] B[ulkeley].

OCKOULD (RICHARD), bookseller in London, 1596–1639; (?) Gray's Inn Gate [Sayle]. Was admitted a freeman of the Stationers' Company on December 12th, 1593, by the presentation of Thomas Scarlet, who at the same time was fined for keeping him for seven years unpresented [Arber, ii.

713, 864]. His first book entry was made in the Registers on November 29th, 1596. This was a sermon preached at Paul's Cross and was printed for him by the widow Orwin and was to be sold at the Bible in St. Paul's Churchyard, then in the occupation of the widow Broom. In 1605 he was in partnership with Henry Tomes, and entered the first part of Bacon's *Advancement of Learning* [Arber, iii. 299], which however only has Tomes' name in the imprint. Ockould had been admitted into the Livery on July 1st, 1598, and served the office of Under Warden in the year $161\frac{3}{4}$. He was one of the shareholders in the Latin stock. In 1629 he assigned his copyright in Bacon's *Advancement* to W. Washington [Arber, iv. 207], and the remainder of his copies were transferred to his son Henry on October 8th, 1639 [Arber, iv. 482].

OKES (JOHN), *see* Plomer, *Dictionary*.

OKES (NICHOLAS), printer in London, 1606–39; (1) Near Holborn Bridge, 1613; (2) In Foster Lane. Son of John Oakes, citizen and horner of London. Apprenticed to William King for eight years from March 25th, 1596 [Arber, ii. 209]. Admitted a freeman of the Company on December 5th, 1603 [Arber, ii. 735], and became a master printer on April 19th, 1606 [Arber, iii. 700]. According to Sir John Lambe's statement, Nicholas Okes succeeded to the business founded by Thomas Judson in 1586. In 1615 he had one press, but some years later he took into partnership John Norton, junior [*see* Plomer, *Dictionary*], and they then had two presses. In 1621 Nicholas Okes printed George Wither's *Motto*, for which he got into trouble. Witnesses stated that he printed two impressions of 3,000 copies and that some of the most important booksellers in London were selling them [*S. Papers Dom.*, *James I*, vol. cxxii, Nos. 12 *et seq.*]. About 1627 Nicholas Okes took his son John into partnership and they were both called before the Court of High Commission for printing Sir Robert Cotton's *Short View of the long life and reign of Henry the third.* In 1630 Nicholas Okes was assessed to pay a sum of £15 towards the repair of St. Paul's. Owing probably to his previous record, neither he nor his partners were included in the list of master printers under the Star Chamber decree of 1637. The last entry under his name in the Registers was made on May 16th, 1636 [Arber, iv. 632]. The date of his death is unknown. He used the device of an oak tree.

OLIFFE (ELIZABETH), *see* Oliffe (R.).

OLIFFE or OLIVE (RICHARD), bookseller in London, 1590–1603; (1) The Crane, St. Paul's Churchyard, 1590; (2) Long Lane. Son of Thomas Oliffe of Edgecote, Northampton, yeoman. Apprentice to John Perrin, stationer of London, for eight years from June 24th, 1580, and took up his freedom June 28th, 1588 [Arber, ii. 101, 702]. Richard Oliffe published amongst other things the play called *The weakest goeth to the wall*, 1600. On March 1st, $160\frac{1}{2}$, he was fined with many other stationers for selling S. Rowlands' *Letting of Humours blood* [Arber, ii. 833]. He probably fell a victim to the plague which raged in London in the latter part of the year 1603. By his will, which was proved on January 14th, $160\frac{3}{4}$, he left the residue of his estate to his wife Elizabeth, who after his death transferred some of her copyrights to John Helme and Philip Knight. [Comm. of London, 1603–7, fol. 7; Arber, iii. 537, 576.]

OLNEY (HENRY), bookseller in London, 1595–6; (1) The George, Near to Cheap Gate in St. Paul's Churchyard; (2) Near the Middle Temple gate. The identity of this stationer is difficult to establish. Mr. Arber [v. 257] thinks that he is the same as Henry Ovie, son of John Ovie, citizen and turner of London, who was apprentice to John Harrison, the elder, for ten years from Michaelmas, 1584 [Arber, ii. 129]. On April 12th, 1595, Henry Olney entered Sir Philip Sidney's *Apologie for Poetrie*, but the entry was void as the copyright was proved to belong to William Ponsonby to whom the edition printed may have been transferred [Arber, ii. 295]. In 1596 he published *Diella*, a volume of sonnets by R. L., Gentleman.

ORPHINSTRANGE (JOHN), (?) bookseller in London, 1606–30; Near Holborn Bridge. Son of John Orphinstrange of London, doctor of the civil law. Apprentice to George Bishop for twelve years from February 5th, $158\frac{7}{8}$, and took up his freedom on August 4th, 1595 [Arber, ii. 150, 715]. On November 20th, 1606, he entered in the Registers a book entitled *Conclusions upon dances, bothe of this age and of the olde*, and on April 23rd, 1630, Alex. Strange's *Short directions for the better understanding of the catechisme* [Arber, iii. 333; iv. 233].

ORWIN (JOAN), printer in London, 1593–7; Over against the Checker in Paternoster Row. The widow of Thomas Orwin, and previously the widow of John Kingston (1553–84) and George Robinson (1585–7). She continued in business until 1597, and printed books for Thomas Man, Nicholas Ling, Cuthbert Burby, Thomas Woodcock and several other booksellers. In 1597 she was succeeded by her son Felix Kingston.

ORWIN (THOMAS), printer in London, 1587–93; In Paternoster Row over against the Checker. He was an apprentice to Thomas Purfoote, by whom he was presented for his freedom on May 5th, 1581 [Arber, ii. 684]. He succeeded to the business of George Robinson, whose widow he married. In 1587–8 Orwin appears to have got into trouble with the Court of Star Chamber, and consequently the Company ordered him to leave off printing until he received the permission of that court; but on May 20th following a letter was received by the Company, signed by the Archbishop of Canterbury, the Bishop of London and others, in consequence of which Orwin was admitted a master printer. This incident was referred to by Martin Marprelate in his *Epistle*, where addressing the Archbishop of Canterbury he says, "Did not your grace of late erecte a new printer . . . one Thomas Orwine (who sometimes wrought popish bookes in corners: namely, Jesus Psalter, our Ladies Psalter, etc.) with condition he should print no such seditious bookes as Walde-grave hath done?" [*Epistle*, ed. Arber, p. 23]. According to Cooper in his *Admonition*, Orwin denied this accusation, but in 1591–2 his press was seized by the Company [Arber, i. 555]. He died before June 25th, 1593, being succeeded by his widow Joan Orwin. Orwin sometimes used the device of an urn marked with T.O., at others that of two hands clasping each other, and the motto, "By Wisdom peace by peace plenty." A third device was that of Mars standing with sword and shield.

OSWALD (JOHN), (?) bookseller in London, 1573–95. Son of John Oswold of Darfield in the county of York, carpenter. Apprentice to John Judson, from March 25th, 1565, for eight years, being out of his time in 1573. In February, 157$\frac{7}{8}$, he was fined two shillings for keeping two young men in work unpresented [Arber, ii. 845], and in the same year he entered a pamphlet having the title *A marvelous discourse of a cruell and lamentable acte donne by a luxurious French Capten at Bescorte in Fraunce.* In 1595 he borrowed £2 from the Company [Arber, i. 572].

OULTON (RICHARD), *see* Plomer, *Dictionary*.

OVEN (HENRY), printer in London, 1600–24. Amongst the *Domestic State Papers* (*Jas. I*, vol. viii., pp. 22, etc.) are two documents presented by William Jones, printer, of Red Cross Street, Cripplegate, to the Speaker of the House of Commons on May 15th, 1604. One of these consisted of information that had come to Jones's knowledge respecting the printing and dispersal of popish books. In it is this passage: "Henry Oven had often times been imprisoned for printing popish books and after a six weeks imprisonment set at libertie; and being imbouldned by his easie imprisonment fell to printing againe, and was taken and put into the Clinke and there had a presse and printed diverse popish bookes till at last he was espied, yet notwithstanding he was released from prison. Afterwards againe he fell to the same worke of printing and for the same was committed to the White Lyon, where he broke prison and fled to Staffordshire where he was printing till Wrench and Warren were descried by Sir Edward Lyttleton and afterwards he the said Henry Oven was taken by a gentleman as he was flying with his presse and letters as it is said into Ireland." [*Cf. Acts of the Privy Council, New Ser.*, xxxii. 85.] Henry Oven was still at work in 1624, as John Gee in his *Foote out of the snare* mentions him as one of those who did "disperse, print, binde or sell Popish Books about London," and describes him as "brother to that Oven who ript out his owne bowels in the Tower, being imprisoned for the Gunpowder treason." No stationer of this name is mentioned in the Registers of the Company.

OWEN (WILLIAM), bookseller in London, 1562–3; At the Little Shop at the North Door of St. Paul's. In this year he entered in the Registers "the newe ballett of Strangwysshe" [Arber, i. 203]. It was printed for him without date by Alexander Lacy as *A new balade of the worthy Seruice of late doen by Maister Strangwige in Fraunce* [Hazlitt, I. 38]. He may be identical with a William Owen who dwelt in Paternoster Row at the sign of the Cock, *c.* 1548 [Hazlitt, H. 631].

OVERTON (HENRY), *see* Plomer, *Dictionary*.

OXENBRIDGE (JOHN), bookseller in London, 1589–1600; The Parrot, St. Paul's Churchyard. Son of John Oxenbridge of Croydon, Surrey, baker. Apprentice to George Bishop for twelve years from All Saints, 1579. Admitted a freeman of the Company on November 3rd, 1589. On August 30th, 1591, George Bishop and R. Watkins assigned over to him

their rights in certain copies [Arber, ii. 594]. John Oxenbridge died before June 2nd, 1600 [Arber, iii. 171]. He used as a device a block showing an ox passing over a bridge with the letter N on its back.

OXLADE (FRANCIS), senior, bookseller in Oxford, 1621–*c.* 1666, *see* Plomer, *Dictionary*, and Gibson, *Oxford Wills*, p. 48.

PAEDTS, PAETS, PATES or PATIUS (JACOBSZOON, JAN JACOBSZOON, etc.), printer at Leyden, 1579–1629. In 1582 he printed Stanyhurst's translation of the first four books of the *Aeneid*, in the imprint of which his name appears as "John Pates," and in 1586 George Whetstone's *Honourable Reputation of a Soldier* in Dutch and English was printed by him and Jan Bowenszoon for sale by Thomas Basson. [Ledeboer, *A.L.*, p. 129.]

PAINE (THOMAS), *see* Plomer, *Dictionary*.

PAINTER (RICHARD), *see* Schilders.

PAKEMAN (DANIEL), *see* Plomer, *Dictionary*.

PARKE (FRANCIS), (?) bookseller in London, 1619; Lincoln's Inn Gate in Chancery Lane. Only known from the imprint to *Pasquil's Palinodia*, printed by T. Snodham and sold by F. Parke, London, 1619 [B.M., C. 39. e. 50].

PARKER (JOHN), *see* Plomer, *Dictionary*.

PARNELL (JOSIAS), bookseller in London, 1584–1625. He was admitted to the freedom of the Company on August 12th, 1584, on the presentation of Gabriel Cawood [Arber, ii. 692]. His first book entry occurs on February 25th, 159$\frac{4}{5}$ [Arber, ii. 672]. On August 6th, 1604, on the death of Gabriel Cawood, he took over Robert Ayre, one of Cawoods's apprentices [Arber, ii. 283]. The last entry under his name in the Registers appears on March 18th, 159$\frac{7}{8}$ [Arber, iii. 108]. His will was proved in 1625 [P.C.C., 103, Clarke].

PARSONS (MARMADUKE), printer in London, 1607–40; (?) Cow Lane, near Holborn Circus. Took up his freedom January 18th, 160$\frac{7}{8}$ [Arber, iii. 683]. In Sir John Lambe's notes, made about 1636, he is stated to have "kept Mathews printing house," presumably Augustine Mathews, who

in the same notes is described as "pauper" [Arber, iii. 704]. He was accordingly appointed one of the twenty master printers, by the Star Chamber decree of 1637. He was the printer of Thomas Dekker's *English Villanies seven severall times prest to Death*, 1638, and probably most of the works bearing the initials M.P. between 1625 and 1639. The position of his printing house is unknown, as is also the date of his death.

PARTRICH, *see* Partridge.

PARTRIDGE (JOHN), *see* Plomer, *Dictionary*.

PARTRIDGE or PARTRICH (MILES), bookseller in London, 1613–18; Near Saint Dunstan's Church in Fleet Street. Son of Thomas Partridge of Beison, co. Norfolk, gent. Apprentice to William Holme, stationer of London, for eight years from Christmas, 1604, and took up his freedom January 21st, 161$\frac{2}{3}$ [Arber, ii. 289; iii. 684]. First book entry February 10th, 1615. Amongst Miles Partridge's publications was Beaumont and Fletcher's *Scornful Ladie*, 1616, and G. Chapman's translation of Hesiod's *Opera et Dies* in 1618 [Arber, iii. 626]. He was perhaps the father of John Partridge [*see* Plomer, *Dictionary*].

PASSE, PASS or PAAS (CRISPIAN DE), engraver and (?) bookseller at Utrecht, 1615–20. A translation into English of the *Hortus Floridus* was printed for him in 1615, and he shared in the expense of Henry Holland's *Herwologia anglica* about 1620; *see* Roy (Salomon de) and Jansson (Jan I).

PATES (JOHN), printer at Leyden, *see* Paedts.

PAULEY or PAWLEY (SIMON), bookseller (?) in London, 1603. Son of Robert Pawlee of Atherbery, co. Oxon, husbandman. Apprentice to John Baetman, stationer of London, for eight years from May 19th, 1594 [Arber, ii. 198]. There is no entry of his freedom in the Registers, but about 1602 Michael Sparke was in his employ as an apprentice, and at a later date stated that his master dealt in popish books at Wyrley Hall in Staffordshire [*Library*, April, 1907, p.169; *Bibliographer*, New York, vol. i, p. 410].

PAVIER (THOMAS), draper and bookseller in London, 1600–25; (1) Entering into the Exchange, 1604–11; (2) The Cats and Parrot, near the Royal Exchange 1612; (3) In Ivy Lane, 1623. Apprentice to William Barley.

Transferred from the Drapers' to the Stationers' Company on June 3rd, 1600 [Arber, ii. 725], and admitted into the Livery on June 30th, 1604. Pavier's first book entry was made on August 4th, 1600, and a few days later a number of copyrights were assigned over to him by William White, Warden of the Company. Amongst them were Shakespeare's *History of Henry Vth with the Battle of Agencourt*; Kyd's *Spanish Tragedy*; George Peele's chronicle-play of *Edward I*; Lodge and Greene's *Looking Glasse for London*, and Breton's *Solemne Passion of the Soul's Love* [Arber, iii. 169]. On April 19th, 1602, Thomas Millington assigned over to him *The First and second parte of Henry the vj^t ij bookes*, and *A booke called Titus and Andronicus* [Arber, iii. 204]. Pavier also published in 1619 an edition of *Pericles*. In addition to these Shakesperian publications, Pavier was also a publisher of ballads, news-books, jest books and much other interesting literature. He was elected Junior Warden of the Company in 1622, and died, probably of the plague, in 1625, his will being proved on February 17th, 162^{5}_{6} [P.C.C., 19, Hele]. After his death his widow Mary transferred her interest in his copyrights to Edward Brewster and Robert Bird [Arber, iv. 164–6]. He used as a device the figure of a pavior.

PAXTON (EDMUND), *see* Plomer, *Dictionary*.

PAXTON (PETER), bookseller in London, 1627; The Angel in St. Paul's Churchyard. Took up his freedom March 26th, 1618 [Arber, iv. 31]. Otherwise only known from the imprint to the Rev. Isaac Bargrave's *Sermon Preached before King Charles March 27, 1627*, printed for him by John Legatt [B.M., 693. f. 1. (3)], and entered on March 28th, 1627 [Arber, iv. 175].

PEELE (STEPHEN), bookseller in London, 1570–93; Rood Lane. Apprentice to John Burtofte for nine years from Christmas, 1561 [Arber, i. 170]. In the year 1563–4 there is an entry of the apprenticeship of Stephen Pele, son of Stephen Pele of Attelburnell, co. Salop, husbandman, to Symonde Coston, stationer of London, for seven years from November 1st [Arber, i. 227], which probably means that John Burtofte had died in the interval. Peele took up his freedom on November 13th, 1570 [Arber, i. 446]. He dealt chiefly in ballads, his last entry being October 1st, 1593 [Arber, ii. 636].

PEERSE (ELIAS), bookseller and bookbinder in Oxford, 1614–39. He was a son of Francis Peerse, stationer and bookbinder, and succeeded to his father's business [Gibson, *Oxford Wills*, p. 28]. Bound books for the Bodleian between 1614 and 1617 [Gibson, *Oxford Bindings*, pp. 39, 49, 51, 60].

PEERSE (FRANCIS), bookseller and bookbinder in Oxford, 1590–1622. Admitted a bookseller on November 27th, 1590. Died in December, 1622 [Gibson, *Oxford Wills*, pp. 27–9, 39]. Left the residue of his estate to his son Elias, who succeeded him in the business [Gibson, *Oxford Bindings*, pp. 9, 35, 39, 48, 51, 52–4, 60].

PEMELL (STEPHEN), bookseller in London, 1633–5; London Bridge, near the Gate. There is no record of this stationer's apprenticeship or of his becoming a freeman of the Company of Stationers. His first book entry occurs on January 8th, 163^{2}_{3} [Arber, iv. 290]. In 1635 he published *An Essay on Drapery* by William Scott, in the imprint of which his address is given.

PEN or PENN (GEORGE), bookseller in London, 1582–(?)1584; and at Ipswich, Suffolk, 1584–9. Son of Thomas Penne of Hackesbury, Gloucestershire, weaver. Apprentice to John Day, printer of London, for seven years from the feast of All Saints, 1564. In 1582 John Kyngston printed for him a medical work by Leonardo Fioravanti entitled *A Compendium of the Rationall Secretes of . . . L. Phioravante*. In 1584 he had moved to Ipswich and there published a pamphlet entitled *News out of Germanie*, which bore the imprint "Imprinted for George Pen, dwelling at Ipswich" [Hazlitt, H. 226].

PENNY (JOHN), bookseller in London, 1588–91; The Greyhound in Paternoster Row. Son of John Pennie of Bebbington, Cheshire, yeoman. Apprentice to John Harrison, the elder, for eight years from Christmas, 1583, and made free of the Company on October 17th, 1588 [Arber, ii. 120, 703]. In 1591 he published a collection of poems by John Davies under the title of *O Utinam*, which was entered in the Registers under its running-title, *A Private Mans Potion for the health of England*. The printers were Richard Yardley and Peter Short [Arber, v. 165]. John Penny died before 1598, when his widow is found presenting an apprentice for his freedom [Arber, ii. 720].

PEPERMANS (JOHN), bookseller and printer at Brussels, 1624–8; At the sign of the Golden Bible. In 1624 he issued Francis Bel's *Rule of the Religious* [Hazlitt, VII. 27], and in 1628 *A short Relation of the Life of St. Elizabeth, Queen of Portugal*, by F. Paludanus [B.M., p. 1190].

PEPWELL (ARTHUR), *see* Duff, *Century*.

PERCEHAY (HENRY), stationer of London, 1604–29. This stationer was admitted a freeman of the Company on June 17th, 1604, and the entry has the additional note, "Item, Receaved of him accordinge to the ordonance for admitting of Redempconers, xxxs." [Arber, ii. 737]. Henry Percehay died between July 20th and December 22nd, 1629, his will being proved on the latter date. He was then living at Burnham Norton in Norfolk, and desired to be buried in the churchyard there. He left three sons, William, Stephen and Henry, and bequeathed a stock of £70 in the Stationers' Company to his widow [P.C.C., 107, Ridley].

PERCIVALL (GEORGE), bookseller in London, 1628; The Bible in Fleet Street, near the Conduit. Took up his freedom in the Company of Stationers November 6th, 1625 [Arber, iii. 686]. His name occurs in the imprint to an edition of the romance of *Paris and Vienna*, entered in the Registers on May 25th, 1628 [Arber, iv. 198].

PERRIN (JOHN), bookseller in London, 1580–92; The Angel in St. Paul's Churchyard. One of Francis Coldock's apprentices. Took up his freedom on January 18th, 15^{79}_{80} [Arber, ii. 681]. In 1585 he was one of the defendants in an action brought by Richard Day against several stationers for infringing his patent of the *Psalmes* and the *A B C and Little Catechism* [Arber, ii. 791–2]. His first book entry was made on April 28th, 1580 [Arber, ii. 369]. Amongst his publications were Thomas Churchyard's account of the taking of Mechlin [1580], and Humfrey Gifford's *Posy of Gilloflowers*, 1580. Perrin died before 1593, when his widow issued an edition of the Revd. Henry Smith's sermon *The trumpet of the soule* [B.M., 4452. c. (3)].

PERRY (HUGH), *see* Plomer, *Dictionary*.

PHILLIPS (JOHN), printer at Old Ford, Middlesex, 1615–26. Took up his freedom in the Company of Stationers December 4th, 1615 [Arber, iii. 684]. In 1626, in company with Andrew Neale or Neile, he set up a secret

press at Old Ford, near Bow, co. Middlesex. This was discovered by the Company and ordered to be battered and the letters melted [Records of the Stationers' Company].

PICKERING (RICHARD), bookseller in London, 1562–90. Apprentice with William Powell in 1556, and made a freeman of the Company during the year ending July 10th, 1559 [Arber, i. 41, 98]. Made his first entry in the Registers in the year ending July, 1563 [Arber, i. 200]. Dealt chiefly in ballads. His last entry occurs on August 5th, 1590 [Arber, ii. 557].

PICKERING (WILLIAM), *see* Duff, *Century*.

PINART (DOMINIQUE), bookseller and bookbinder of Oxford, 1574–1619. A native of France. Received letters of denization on June 15th, 1573 [Huguenot Society's *Denizations*]. Admitted brother of the Stationers' Company on September 18th, 1564 [Arber, i. 278]. He appears to have settled at Oxford, where he was admitted a bookseller on March 25th, 1574 [Clark, *Register*, ii. 1. 321]. He was also a bookbinder, and in 1583 was paid a sum of £2 3s. for binding a *Bible* in "velvet and gilte" [Wood's *Annals*, ii, p. 215]. He was a Bodleian binder, 1601–5 [Gibson, *Oxford Bindings, passim*]. In 1593 Pinart was appointed by Robert Cavey, alias Stuffolde, one of the executors to his will. Dominique Pinart was buried on March 24th, 1619. His administration bond was dated February 18th, 162^{7}_{8}, but there are no particulars as to the value of his estate [Gibson, *Oxford Wills*, pp. xix, xxiii, 18, 29, 39].

PINCHON (GÉRARD), printer at Douai, 1609–34; At the sign of "Coleyn" (or "Coline"), or "à la Colongne (la Colonne)" [Duthillœul, p. 409]. From 1629 to 1634 he printed at least five books in English; among them being M. Kellison's *Treatise of the Hierarchy of the Church, against Calvin*, 1629 [B.M., p. 907], a work which gave rise to much controversy with John Floyd and other Jesuits. For mark he used the monogram of the Jesuits with "in hoc nomine Jesus." [Duthillœul, pp. 195–7, 409; Sayle, pp. 1484–5]

PINDER (JONATHAN), stationer at Cambridge, 1604. His will, dated 1604, is with the Cambridge Wills at Peterborough [*Calendar of Cambridge Wills*].

PINDER (JONATHAN), stationer at Cambridge, 1621–35. Along with others in a list of "Privileged persons in the University," 1624 [Bowes, 336]. Paid church rate in St. Mary's Parish from 1621 to *c.* 1635 [Foster's *Churchwardens' Accounts*].

PINDLEY (JOHN), printer in London, 1612–13. Son of Thomas Pindley of Shredicote, co. Staffordshire, husbandman. Apprentice to John Wolf, stationer of London, for eight years from June 24th, 1600 [Arber, ii. 250]. Took up his freedom June 25th, 1607 [Arber, iii. 683]. In or about 1609 John Pindley and John Beale bought the printing house that had originally been Robert Robinson's and afterwards Thomas Haviland's. On April 27th, 1612, the widow of John Wolf transferred all her rights in her husband's copyrights to John Pindley [Arber, iii. 483]. Pindley died before November 2nd, 1613, when his widow transferred these copyrights to George Purslowe [Arber, iii. 535].

PIPER (JOHN), bookseller in London, 1618–24; St. Paul's Churchyard. Son of Ralph Piper of Curry Rivel, co. Somerset, yeoman. Apprentice to Simon Waterson, stationer of London, for nine years from Christmas, 1604: took up his freedom in the Company November 2nd, 1613 [Arber, ii. 286; iii. 684]. The first entry under his name in the Registers was on October 6th, 1618 [Arber, iii. 633], and the last on April 12th, 1621 [Arber, iv. 52]; but he was publishing in 1624, in which year he issued a work on horsemanship by William Browne entitled *Browne his fiftie yeares practice*.

PLANCHE (JOHN DE), bookbinder in London, 1567–71; St. Martin's Outwich. A native of France. Admitted Brother of the Stationers' Company on October 10th, 1567 [Arber, i. 365]. Took out letters of denization in May, 1570, and is mentioned as a bookbinder, dwelling in St. Martin's Outwich, and having three servants, in the return of aliens in 1571 [Worman, *Alien Members*, p. 51].

PLANTIN (CHRISTOPHER), printer at Leyden, 1582–5. In 1582 Christopher Plantin, being then at Antwerp, purchased the house of William Sylvius [*q.v.*] at Leyden, where he was appointed printer to the University in the following year. Early in 1584 he left Antwerp and retired to Leyden, where he remained until towards the end of 1585. He then returned to Antwerp, leaving F. Raphelengius [*q.v.*] in charge of the Leyden

business. According to Herbert, p. 1666, and Hazlitt, III. 200, *The Explanation of the . . . Right and title of Anthonie, King of Portugal*, published at Leyden in 1585, has Plantin's imprint; later books printed in the house have that of Raphelengius. Plantin does not seem to have published any works in English at his chief place of business in Antwerp. [Degeorge, *La Maison Plantin*, pp. 122–3.]

PLANTIN (WIDOW JEANNE), printer at Antwerp, 1591. After the death of Christoffel Plantin in 1589, his business at Antwerp was carried on by Jean Moretus or Moeretorf (b. 1543, d. 1610), the husband of his second daughter Martine. In certain books the name of Jeanne Plantin appears with that of Moretus in the imprint, as in *Icones stirpium seu plantarum*, 1591, which has a "Table oft suches names off Herbes vsed in Engelland" [Sayle, p. 1365]. She died in 1596. [Degeorge, *La Maison Plantin.*]

PLATER (RICHARD), printer at Amsterdam, 1626–7. His only known English work seems to be the *Fruitful Sermon* on 2 Cor. xiii. 5, of John Forbes, 1626 [Sayle, p. 1430].

PLUMPTON (RANDALL), (?) bookseller of London, 1569–72. Son of William Plumpton and Mary his wife, one of the sisters and co-heirs of Richard Lawley of Strensham, co. Worcester. Apprenticed for eight years to John Allde, stationer of London, from March 25th, 1562, and took up his freedom on October 17th, 1569 [Arber, i. 173, 420]. His name has been found in a deed dated 1572.

PONSONBY (WILLIAM), bookseller in London, 1571–1603; The Bishop's Head, St. Paul's Churchyard. William Ponsonby may be described as the most important publisher of the Elizabethan period. He was apprenticed to William Norton of the King's Head in St. Paul's Churchyard, for the somewhat unusual period of ten years from Christmas, 1560, and took up his freedom in the Company of Stationers on January 11th, 157$\frac{0}{1}$ [Arber, i. 148, 446]. His first book entry, John Alday's *Praise and Dispraise of Women*, was made on June 17th, 1577, although this book was not published until 1579 [Arber, ii. 313, 354]. On the 24th of the following June he took as an apprentice Edward Blount, who became equally famous as a publisher. Ponsonby's business for the first few years was confined to a few political and religious tracts; but in 1582 he published the first part

of Robert Greene's *Mamillia* and in 1584 the same author's *Gwydonius.* On August 23rd, 1588, Ponsonby secured a licence for the publication of Sidney's *Arcadia*, the first edition of which appeared in 1590. For the second edition, which appeared in 1593, Sidney's sister, the Countess of Pembroke, by arrangement with Ponsonby revised the whole; and to the third she added other pieces of Sidney's. This edition, a small folio, was on the London market before the end of the year 1598 and sold for nine shillings. In the following year several London booksellers, including John Harrison the younger, Paul Lynley, Richard Banckworth and John Flaskett entered into an arrangement with Robert Waldegrave the printer in Edinburgh, to print an edition of the work, which was sold throughout the country at six shillings a copy. Ponsonby at once took proceedings against them in the Star Chamber, all the copies were seized, and the authors of the piracy were compelled to reimburse Ponsonby for his loss [*Library*, March, 1900, pp. 195 *et seq.*]. Another author whose works were first published by Ponsonby was Edmund Spenser. No less than ten volumes of Spenser's work were issued by him. The first three books of the *Faerie Queene* appeared in 1590, a fitting companion to Sidney's *Arcadia.* In the next year Ponsonby gathered into a volume various unpublished pieces by Spenser and published them on his own responsibility under the title of *Complaints*, and he subsequently issued *The Tears of the Muses* and *Daphnaida*, both in 1591, *Amoretti* and *Colin Clout's come home again* in 1595, and in 1596 the fourth, fifth and sixth books of the *Faerie Queene*, as well as a collected edition of the six books and two other volumes, respectively called *Fowre Hymns* and *Prothalamion.* Ponsonby was elected Junior Warden of the Company for the year ending June 28th, 1599 [Arber, iii. 146]. His name appears for the last time in connection with a book on July 5th, 1602, when he and several other important stationers entered an edition of North's *Plutarch* [Arber, iii. 211]. Ponsonby married Joane, the daughter of Francis Coldock, and died, probably of the plague, at the end of 1603, without issue [Plomer, *Wills*, pp. 36, 39].

PONT (ZACHARY), (?) printer in Scotland, 1590–1619. On October 28th, 1590, Zachary Pont was granted a licence by the Privy Council of Scotland to be chief printer within the realm, but he is not known to have exercised the privilege [Lee, App. ix]. Pont, who was a son of Robert Pont,

the Scottish reformer, graduated M.A. at St. Andrew's about 1583, and in 1608 was appointed minister of Bower in Caithness; he married Elizabeth, daughter of John Knox, and died prior to January 29th, 1619. In 1601 a Mr. Zacharie Pont is named among the debtors in the inventory of Edward Cathkin [*q.v.*]. [Lee, App. ix; Hew Scott's *Fasti*, iii. 356; *Bannatyne Misc.* ii. 229.]

PORTER (EDMUND), stationer at Cambridge, 1615–33; Great St. Mary's. Took up his freedom in the Company of Stationers on February 10th, 161$\frac{4}{5}$ [Arber, iii. 684]. Lived in Great St. Mary's parish from 1616 to about 1633 [Foster's *Churchwardens' Accounts*]. His name occurs in a list of privileged persons in the University in 1624 [Bowes, *Univ. Printers*, 336].

PORTER (JOHN), bookseller in Cambridge, 1576 (?)–1608; Great St. Mary's. Was probably the John Porter of Haslingfielde, co. Cambridge, who was apprenticed for eight years to John Cuthbert, citizen and stationer of Cambridge, in 1568 [Arber, i. 375]. There is no record of his appointment as stationer to the University; but his name appears in a list of privileged persons of the University *circa* 1592–4 [Bowes, *Univ. Printers*, 336], and books were printed for him and Legatt in 1595, etc., and for him and Leonard Greene in 1607. He lived in the parish of Great St. Mary's certainly from 1589 [Foster's *Churchwardens' Accounts*], and in 1593 joined with John Legatt in prosecuting John Tidder for selling books in the Cambridge market [Bowes, *Univ. Printers*, 296]. He died in 1608 and his will is at Peterborough.

PORTER (JOHN), senior, bookseller in London, 1587–1607. Son of Thomas Porter of Haslyngfylde, co. Cambridge, yeoman, apprentice to John Cuthbert, stationer of London, for eight years from Christmas, 1568 [Arber, i. 375]. His first book entry was made on October 19th, 1587 [Arber, ii. 476]. He was associated with Thomas Gubbyn, Robert Bourne, Thomas Man, Ralph Jackson, Samuel Macham, Mathew Cooke and Leonard Green. His publications were chiefly theological.

PORTER (JOHN), junior, bookseller in London, 1634–6. Took up his freedom June 3rd, 1634 [Arber, iii. 687]. He was possibly a son of John Porter, senior. The only entry in the Registers under his name occurs on May 18th, 1636 [Arber, iv. 363].

POTTER (GEORGE), bookseller in London, 1599–1627; The Bible in St. Paul's Churchyard. Son of Edward Potter of Nyensavage, Salop, weaver. Apprentice to William Browne for eight years from Christmas, 1589 [Arber, ii. 168]. George Potter made his first book entry on April 11th, 1599 [Arber, iii. 142]. In 1601 he succeeded Widow Broome at the above address, and secured all her copyrights, which included several of the works of John Lyly, Robert Greene's *Pandosto* and Warner's *Albion's England.* The last entry in which his name occurs was an assignment, on April 8th, 1616, of one of his copies to F. Archer; but he appears to have been in business at the time of his death in 1627. His will was proved on April 17th in that year. He left no children, and appointed Edward Weaver and Thomas Archer, stationers, his executors [P.C.C., 32, Skynner].

POTTS (ROGER), bookseller in London, 1621–3. Took up his freedom June 4th, 1621 [Arber, iii. 685]: first book entry August 17th, 1621 [Arber, iv. 58]. In 1623 he published Henry Wilkinson's *Short Catechisme.*

POTTS [STEPHEN], bookseller in London, 1628. Mentioned in a list of second hand booksellers who, in 1628, were ordered to submit catalogues of their books to the Archbishop of Canterbury [*Dom. S. Papers, Chas. I,* vol. 117 (9)]. Possibly a relative of Roger Potts.

POULAIN (JACQUES), printer at Geneva, 1556–8; *see* Duff, *Century.* In 1558 in partnership with Antony Rebul he printed a *Letter to Mary of Scotland from J. Knox, now augmented* [Hazlitt, VII. 214; B.M., p. 916].

POWELL (THOMAS), printer in London, 1556–63, *see* Duff, *Century.*

POWELL (THOMAS), printer in London, 1622–41, *see* Plomer, *Dictionary.*

POWELL (WILLIAM), *see* Duff, *Century.*

PRENTIS (THOMAS), (?) bookseller in London, 1584–1604; (?) St. Giles without Cripplegate. Son of William Prentis, or Prentyce, of Romford, Essex, plasterer. Apprentice for seven years from April, 15th, 1577, to Peter Connewey, stationer of London [Arber, ii. 76]. Took up his freedom on June 13th, 1584 [Arber ii. 691]. On January 19th, 15$\frac{89}{90}$, he was fined sixpence for not appearing at the Hall on quarter day [Arber ii. 862]. His will was proved in the court of the Dean and Chapter of St. Paul's on January 16th, 160$\frac{4}{5}$. He left a bequest of £10 to the poor of St. Giles without Cripplegate, probably the parish in which he was resident. He also named a son Edward [Book C, f. 205], who took up his freedom on April 9th, 1621 [Arber, iii. 685].

PREVOSTEAU (ESTIENNE), bookseller and printer at Paris 1579–1610; (1) In aed. Johannis Bene Nati in Clauso Brunello, iuxta puteum Certenum, or In via Aurigarum e regione trium Crescentium (au Mont Sainct Hilaire, rue Chartière): (2) In Collegio trium Episcoporum, or Via D. Ioannis Lateranensis in collegio Cameracensis, 1597. In 1602 he printed John Colville's *Parænese or Admonition unto his countrymen* [B.M., p. 400]. He was heir and successor of Guillaume Morel, whose mark, Θ with two serpents and an angel (Silvestre, 164) he used. [Renouard, p. 307.]

PRIME (BENJAMIN), stationer at Cambridge, 1592–4. His name is in the list of privileged persons of the University, *c.* 1592–4 [Bowes, *Univ. Printers,* 336].

PROCTOR (JOHN), bookseller in London, 1589–90; Upon Holborn Bridge. This stationer was originally apprenticed to Richard Ballard, and upon Ballard's death was transferred to Henry Carre [Arber, ii. 137]. He was the publisher of Richard Robinson's *Golden Mirrour,* 1589, and some theological works.

PULLEN or PULLEYN (OCTAVIAN), *see* Plomer, *Dictionary.*

PURFOOT (THOMAS), senior, *see* Duff, *Century.*

PURFOOT (THOMAS), junior, printer in London, 1591–1640; (1) At the sign of the Lucrece within the new rents in Newgate Market; (2) Over against St. Sepulchre's Church without Newgate. Son of Thomas Purfoot, senior. Apprentice to Richard Collins for seven years from June, 1584. Took up his freedom on October 8th, 1590, and was admitted a master printer on December 6th, 1591 [Arber, ii. 708; iii. 700]. Was in partnership with his father until the latter's death in 1615, when the copyrights and business of the firm passed to him. In 1615 he had two presses, and was employed by most of the leading publishers. In 1629 he served as Junior Warden and in 1634 as Senior Warden of the Company. Thomas Purfoot was one of the twenty master printers appointed by the Star Chamber decree of 1638. The last entry under his name in the Registers occurs on February 1st, 163$\frac{8}{9}$ [Arber, iv. 454], and he was dead before May 8th, 1640, when his copyrights were assigned to Richard Lewty [Arber, iv. 510].

PURSET (CHRISTOPHER), bookseller in London, 1604–11. Son of Edmond Pursett of Holborn, tailor. Apprentice to Richard Jones for seven years from September 29th, 1590 [Arber, ii. 170]. Took up his freedom September 5th, 1597 [Arber, ii. 719]. First book entry May 1st, 1604 [Arber, iii. 260]. Publisher of Richard Braithwait's *Golden Fleece,* 1611, and John Ford's *Fame's Memoriall,* 1606. His last entry in the Registers was made on October 14th, 1611 [Arber, iii. 469].

PURSLOWE (GEORGE), printer and bookseller in London, 1614–32; Near the East end of Christ Church. [? Newgate Street.] Son of John Purslowe of the Forest of Oxtowe, Salop, yeoman. Apprentice to Richard Braddock, stationer of London, for seven years from January 18th, 160$\frac{1}{2}$, and became a freeman of the Company on January 30th, 1609 [Arber, ii. 259; iii. 683]. He made his first entry in the Register on October 29th, 1616 [Arber, iii. 597]. In 1629 or 1630 he bought the business of Simon Stafford [Arber, iii. 701]. The last entry under his name occurs on February 13th, 1632 [Arber, iv. 272]. George Purslowe was succeeded by his widow Elizabeth, who made over the business to John Haviland, Robert Young and Miles Flesher [Arber, iii. 700–4].

PURSLOWE (THOMAS), printer in London, 1637. He was one of the twenty master printers recognized in this year [Arber, iv. 532], but his name is not known to appear in any imprint.

PURSLOWE (ELIZABETH), *see* Plomer, *Dictionary.*

QUERCUBUS (N. DE), *see* Okes (Nicholas).

QUINQUÉ (ADRIAN), printer at Tournai, 1623. He printed in 1623 *The Image of Both Churches* by "P. D. M.," attributed to Matthew Pattenson. There are two editions [Sayle, p. 1501; B.M., p. 1043].

R., I., printer at Douai, *c.* 1610. To him are attributed a number of small works of which one alone seems to have an imprint, namely, *Certain Devout and Godly Petitions commonly called Jesus Psalter* "Printed at Doway by I. R. cum Priuilegio." It has a device with "Ecce agnus dei." Mr. Sayle suggests that the printer may have been John Floyd [Sayle, p. 1486–7].

RABAN (EDWARD), printer at Edinburgh, St. Andrews, and Aberdeen, 1620–50; Edinburgh, at the Cowgate Port, at the sign of A.B.C., 1620; St. Andrews, South Street, at the sign of A.B.C., 1620; Aberdeen, (1) The Town's Arms upon the Market Place; (2) Broadgate. He was, as he announces in one of his imprints, an Englishman, but of German descent, and was most probably connected with the family of Raben, printers of Frankfurt. In the address to *The Popes New Years Gifts,* 1622 [Advocates' Library], he calls himself "Anglo-Britannus Gente Germanus," and in *Rabans Resolution against Drunkenness* [1622], also in the Advocates' Library, he tells us that he was at one time in the service of a printer at Leyden [Information supplied by Mr. E. Gordon Duff]. He first appears as a master printer at Edinburgh, where he printed one book, Archibald Symson's *Christes Testament Unfolded* "at the Cowgate Port, at the signe of A B C," in 1620. In the same year he removed to St. Andrews, setting up his press at the same sign in the South Street, and was appointed printer to the University. In 1622 he again moved north, this time to Aberdeen, where he established himself at "The Townes Armes" upon the Market Place, and here he remained during the rest of his business career, though from 1643 he also had a shop in the Broad Gate. He was the first to introduce the art of printing into Aberdeen, and almost immediately after his arrival was appointed printer to the University and the Town. He adopted as a device a cut of the city arms, and made frequent use, as a tailpiece, of a well-known figure of a bear seated holding foliage in its fore paws. Upwards of 150 books are known to have issued from his press before 1650, in which year he was succeeded by James Brown. Many of these books between 1622 and 1633 were printed for David Melvill, the Aberdeen bookseller. In 1638, Raban printed a compilation of his own entitled *The Glorie of Man, consisting in the excellencie and perfection of woman . . . whereunto is annexed The duetie of husbands.* Raban was twice married; his first wife Jeanett Johnstoun died in January, 1627, and some time before April, 1637, he married his second wife Janet Ealhous or Ailhous. It is not known under what circumstances

Raban retired from business in 1650, but he survived until 1658, being buried on December 6th of that year. [Edmond, *Aberdeen Printers*; Aldis, *Scottish Books*.]

RABAT (ANTHONIUS), printer in Norwich, 1567. "There is an 'Anthenius Rabbat' given in the Dutch Church Register (in 1561) [I, 278], who may be the Rabat given in the list of Norwich printers in the Addenda to Mr. Allnutt's *English Provincial Presses* (*Bibliographica*, Part 12, p. 481). He went to Norwich in 1567." [Worman, *Alien Members*, p. 53.]

RAND (SAMUEL), *see* Plomer, *Dictionary*.

RANDALL or RANDOLL (WILLIAM), (?) bookseller in London, ? 1600–21; St. Giles without Cripplegate. Son of Christopher Randall of Kynningnall, co. York, smith. Apprentice to James Gonneld, stationer of London, for eight years from August 24th, 1564 [Arber, i. 251]. On December 6th, 1602, he took his son Benjamin as an apprentice [Arber, ii. 269], and on February 6th, 160$^{3}_{4}$, another son James was admitted to the freedom of the Company "per patrimonium." His will was proved on October 10th, 1621, in the court of the Dean and Chapter of St. Paul's [Book D, f. 195].

RAPHELENGIUS, RAPHELINGEN, or RAULENGHIEN (FRANCIS), printer at Leyden, 1585–97. He was born in 1539, and visited England, where he taught Greek at Cambridge some time before 1565. In that year he married Christopher Plantin's eldest daughter Margaret, and settled down at Antwerp, where for several years he worked for Plantin as editor and corrector of the press, being especially concerned with the polyglot *Bible* of 1569–73. In 1585, Plantin, who had bought the business of William Sylvius, printer at Leyden, sold it to Raphelengius, who was appointed Printer to the University of Leyden in the following year, and from that time carried on a flourishing business there, his imprint being usually "ex officina Plantiniana apud F. Raphelengium." In 1586 he printed Geoffrey Whitney's *Choice of Emblems*, in 1593 *The Key of the Holy Tongue*, by P. Martinius, and in 1597 a work by Bonaventura Vulcanius *De Literis et Lingua Getarum*, which, on pp. 73–80, has the Anglo-Saxon version of Gregory's *Cura Pastoralis* printed in Roman type, with interlinear translation into English. Raphelengius became professor of Hebrew in the University of Leyden in 1587, and died in 1597 [Degeorge, *La Maison Plantin*, pp. 122–3, 125; Cooper, *Ath. Cant.*, ii. 226; Jöcher].

RAWORTH (JOHN), *see* Plomer, *Dictionary*.

RAWORTH (ROBERT), *see* Plomer, *Dictionary*.

READ (RICHARD), printer in London, 1601–3; Fleet Lane. Apprentice to Richard Jugge, by whom he was presented for his freedom on January 18th, 15$^{79}_{80}$ [Arber, ii. 681]. In 1601 he married Frances the widow of Gabriel Simson, and so became a master printer [Arber, v. 201]. He had a son Richard who took up his freedom July 6th, 1619 [Arber, iii. 685].

REBUL (ANTONY), *see* Poulain (James).

REDBORNE (ROBERT), stationer in London and Oxford, 1556–71. Mentioned in a list of stationers who had removed into the country in 1571 [Arber, v. lii; Duff, *Century*, p. 131].

REDMER (RICHARD), bookseller in London, 1610–32; The Star at the West door of St. Paul's. Son of William Redmer, citizen and butcher of London. Apprentice to William Ponsonby for seven years from Christmas, 1602, and took up his freedom in the Company on January 16th, 16$^{10}_{11}$ [Arber, ii. 268; iii. 683]. He dealt in plays and miscellaneous literature. For a time he was in partnership with John Stepneth. Richard Redmer is mentioned in a list of second-hand booksellers who in 1628 were ordered to submit a catalogue of their books to the Archbishop of Canterbury [*Dom. S. Papers, Chas. I*, vol. 117 (9)]. He made his last entry in the Registers on September 30th, 1631, and was dead before August 13th, 1634, when his widow transferred all her interests to Richard Badger [Arber, iv. 261, 325].

REDMORE, *see* Redmer (R.).

RENIALME (ASCANIUS DE), bookseller in London, 1578–1600; Blackfriars. A native of Italy, who took out letters of denization on December 12th, 1578. He was admitted a Brother of the Company of Stationers on June 27th, 1580, and in 1586 Archbishop Whitgift granted him a license to import some few copies of popish books printed abroad, for the use of the learned. Ascanius appears to have had an extensive connection both in this country and on the Continent. From an allusion in Nashe's *Have with you to Saffron-Walden*, 1596, sig. T2, it might be inferred that he published a catalogue of his stock. He is several times referred to in the *Ecclesiae Londino Batavae Archivum*. His will dated February 29th, 1599 [*i.e.*, 1600], was proved in the Prerogative Court of Canterbury on March 10th in the same year. He left a piece of plate value five pounds to the Company of Stationers and rings to the following stationers, George Bishop, Bonham Norton and John Norton. James Rime, another bookseller in Blackfriars, was his stepson, and Francis Bonner or Bovier, who published between 1584–9, was his brother-in-law. In company with George Bishop he published Christopher Wurtzung's *Praxis medicinae universalis* in 1597. [Arber, ii. p. 682; iii. 84; Worman, *Alien Members of the book-trade*, pp. 53–4; Plomer, *Wills*, pp. 35–6].

RENIALME (HEIRS OF ASCANIUS DE), booksellers or printers at Frankfurt am Main, 1605. In this year they issued Joseph Hall's *Mundus Alter et Idem*, which contains a few words of English. The imprint is "Francofurti apud hæredes Ascanij de Rinialme" [Sayle, p. 1493].

RESPEAWE (DERICK VAN), printer at Middelburg, 1584. In this year he printed *The True Report of the Death of William of Nassau* by B. Serack [*i.e.*, B. Gérard] [Herbert, p. 1666; B.M., pp. 1178–9].

RESSLIN (JOHN WYRICH), printer at Stuttgart, 1616. In 1616 he printed G. R. Weckherlin's *Triumphal Shows at Stutgart* [B.M., p. 1576; Hazlitt, IV. 109], and in 1619 the same author's *Panegyric to the Lord Hay* [Hazlitt, H. 647].

REYNE (JEAN), printer or bookseller at Brussels, 1608, *see* Mommart (Jean).

REYNES (JOHN), (?) printer in London, 1569–70. In this year he had a license for printing "Theatram Dialectices" and a "cathechismus in laten" [Arber, i. 418]. He does not seem to have had any connection with the older John Reynes who died in 1544 [Duff, *Century*], and nothing is known about him.

REYNOLDS (JOHN), bookseller in London, 1637. Took up his freedom on June 1st, 1635 [Arber, iii. 687]. On June 19th, 1637, he entered in the Registers a broadside entitled *Great Britains Joyful sight* [Arber, iv. 386].

RHODES or RODES (JOHN), bookseller in London, 1628; Little Britain. Mentioned in a list of second-hand booksellers who, in 1628, were ordered to send in catalogues of their books to the Archbishop of Canterbury [*Dom. S. Papers, Chas. I*, vol. 117 (9)].

RHODES (MATTHEW), bookseller in London, 1622–33; Upper end of Old Bayley near Newgate. Became a freeman of the Company of Stationers on November 3rd, 1619, and made his first book entry on February 22nd, 1622 [Arber, iii. 685; iv. 65]. Amongst his publications were Thomas Brewer's *Weeping Lady*, 1625, and Llodowick Carlell's *Deserving Favourite*, 1629. His imprint is found in *The true tragedy of Herod and Antipater*, 1622, by Gervase Markham and William Sampson.

RICHARDSON (HARRY), chapman of (?) Edinburgh, 1580. Among the debts due to John Ross, the Edinburgh printer, at the time of his death in 1580, was 30s. 8d. owing by "Harry Ritchesoun, cramer" [*Bannatyne Miscellany*, ii. 206]. "Cramer" was the Scottish term for a pedlar, or a dealer in small wares who occupied a crame or booth. This debt was quite probably for popular literature supplied to Richardson, who, no doubt, included such matter in his pack when tramping the country, or exposed it for sale in his booth, which may have been one of those set up between the buttresses of St. Giles's church.

RICHARDSON (THOMAS), stationer at York, 1600. His son Thomas was apprenticed to Alice Gosson, the widow of Thomas Gosson, stationer of London, for seven years from October 6th, 1600 [Arber, ii. 249].

RIDDELL (WILLIAM), bookseller in London, 1552–60, *see* Duff, *Century*. On May 28th, 1560, William Riddell was appointed one of the administrators of the effects of John Frisden, musician [P.C.C. Admons., May, 1560].

RIDER (ROBERT), bookseller in London, 1601–38. An edition of the *Odes and Epodes* of Horace, translated by Henry Rider, M.A., in 1638, bears the imprint "London: Printed by John Haviland for Robert Rider Anno Dom: 1638." He may be identical with the Robert Rider, son of Thomas Ryder of Layton, co. Salop, husbandman, who was apprenticed to Edward Day for seven years from February 4th, 1594, and who took up his freedom on February 3rd, 160$^{0}_{1}$ [Arber, ii. 188, 728]. His address has not been found.

RIDER (TIMOTHY) (?) bookseller in London, 1579–86. Son of John Ryder of Weedon Beck, co. Northampton, husbandman. Apprenticed to Richard Lynnell for seven years from February 2nd, 156$\frac{3}{4}$ [Arber, i. 250]. Made free of the Company March 21st, 157$\frac{0}{1}$ [Arber, i. 447]. He became the Company's Beadle on March 25th, 1578 [Arber, i. 478]. On July 26th, 1582, the *Paradise of Dainty Devices*, formerly H. Disle's, was entered to him, and on April 6th, 1584, *The Widow's Treasure* [Arber, ii. 414, 430]. He does not seem to have published either work, and on April 11th, 1584, he transferred both to Edward White [Arber, ii. 431]. On December 12th, 1586, he entered a ballad "Howe make-bates abused a man and his wife" [Arber, ii. 461], but no copy seems to be known. Two undated productions by L. Ramsey were printed for him, a pamphlet entitled *The practise of the Devil*, and a sheet concerning the death of Sir Nicholas Bacon (in 1579), entitled *A Short Discourse of Man's Fatal End* [Hazlitt, H. 496]. As the former was to be sold by Henry Kirkham, it seems probable that Rider had no shop. He was alive in 1588 [Arber, ii. 702].

RIME, RYME or RYMER (JAMES), bookseller in London, 1599–1600; Blackfriars. Step-son of Ascanius de Renialme. Rime obtained a special license to print the works of Hieronymus Xanthius in Latin [Arber, v. lvii], an edition of which, dated 1605, is in the University Library, Cambridge. He is probably identical with the James Rymer who sold books to the Duke of Northumberland in 1599 [*Hist. MSS. Comm. Sixth Report, App.*, p. 226, etc.].

RITHERDON (AMBROSE), bookseller in London, 1630–2; The Bull Head, St. Paul's Churchyard. Took up his freedom February 6th, 1627 [Arber, iii. 686]. Made his first entry in the Registers on April 24th, 1630, and his last on June 16th, 1632 [Arber, iv. 234, 279]. Ritherdon's premises were next door to the Tiger's Head, occupied by Henry Seile. These premises were condemned in 1631 and Ritherdon was given notice to quit, and his death, which occurred shortly afterwards, was attributed by his widow to his inability to find other premises [*Library*, July, 1902, pp. 261–70].

ROBERTS (HENRY I), stationer of London, 1580–5. Presented an apprentice, Nicolas Dulon, for his freedom on July 22nd, 1580 [Arber, ii. 683]. Had a son, Henry Roberts II, who took up his freedom "per

patrimonium" on August 18th, 1595 [Arber, ii. 716]. One of these appears to be identical with Henry Roberts, the writer. [Hazlitt, H. 510–12; I. 360; *D.N.B.*].

ROBERTS (HENRY II), stationer in London, 1595–1613. Son of Henry Roberts I. On July 30th, 1606, he entered in the Registers *The Kinge of Denmarkes entertainement at Tilberie Hope by the Kinge, etc.*, which appears to have been compiled either by him or his father. Again on March 7th, 160$\frac{6}{7}$, he entered a picture of the *Ridinge of the Asse.* His last book entry occurs on February 14th, 161$\frac{2}{3}$, *Great Brytanes generall Joyes. Londons glorious triumphes, etc.*, with a ballad on the same subjects. [Arber, iii. 327, 343, 515.]

ROBERTS (JAMES), bookseller and printer in London, 1569–1615; (1) Love and Death, Fleet Street; (2) Adjoining the little Conduit in Cheapside; (3) Barbican. Admitted a freeman of the Company of Stationers on June 27th, 1564, James Roberts began as a publisher of ballads. On December 3rd, 1588, a patent was granted to him and to Richard Watkins of the exclusive privilege of printing all almanacs and prognostications [Pat. Roll, 31 Eliz. pt. 10]. In 1593 he married the widow of John Charlewood, generally known as the Earl of Arundell's man, who had been in business as a printer at the Half Eagle and Key in the Barbican since 1567, and who died early in that year. Charlewood's copyrights were numerous and the printing house was well furnished with type blocks and devices. James Roberts' chief claim to notice is as a printer of Shakespeare quartos. In 1600 he printed the first quarto of *Titus Andronicus*, and in 1604 the second quarto of Hamlet. As to the quartos of *A Midsummer Night's Dream* and *The Merchant of Venice* which bear his imprint and the date 1600, but which were probably printed in 1619, *see* the *Library*, April, 1908, p. 113, etc. In or about 1608, James Roberts sold the business to William Jaggard. [*Library*, April, 1906, pp. 160–1.]

ROBERTSON (DAVID), bookbinder in Edinburgh, 1633. In December of that year he brought a complaint before the Scottish Privy Council against Manasses Vautrollier, bookbinder, for having ensnared him into his service by threatening him with a "pretendit captioun sinistrouslie purchast be him agains the compleaner," and for having thereafter imprisoned him [*Reg. P.C. Scot.*, 2nd Ser., v. 174, 177, 182, 572, 580].

ROBINS (JOHN), stationer of London, 1606–25. Son of Thomas Robins of Long Buckly, co. Northampton, yeoman. Apprentice for seven years from June 24th, 1599, to John Adams, stationer of London, and took up his freedom June 25th, 1606 [Arber, ii. 235; iii. 683]. No book entries occur in the Registers under his name. His will dated January 10th, 162$\frac{5}{6}$, was proved in the Court of the Dean and Chapter of St. Paul's on March 10th, 162$\frac{5}{6}$. He left a widow Susan and a daughter Susan, and bequests to his brothers and sisters. One of the overseers was Emanuel Exall or Exoll, stationer of London. [Dean and Chapter of St. Paul's, Book D, f. 298.]

ROBINSON (GEORGE), printer and bookseller in London, 1585–7; (?) West door of St. Paul's Churchyard. Originally a member of the Company of Grocers. Transferred to the Stationers on March 1st, 158$\frac{5}{6}$ [Arber, ii. 693]. He married the widow of John Kingston (1553–84). In July, 1586, he is returned as having two presses [Arber, v. lii]. His first book entry is found on October 6th, 1586 [Arber, ii. 457], and the only other entry under his name is on November 28th in the same year. But in 1585 he issued Thomas Wilson's *Art of Rhetorique*, probably from Kingston's house at the West door of St. Paul's Churchyard [Arber, v. 139]. He died apparently in 1586, and his widow married as her third husband Thomas Orwin, to whom the copyright of the *Art of Rhetorique* and other copyrights of John Kingston's were transferred on May 7th, 1593 [Arber, ii. 630].

ROBINSON (HUMPHREY), *see* Plomer, *Dictionary*.

ROBINSON (JOHN), bookseller in London, 1615. Entered in the Registers on April 28th, 1615, the Rev. John Hull's sermon *A Miror of Majestie* [Arber, iii. 566]. No copy has been found, and his address is not known.

ROBINSON (ROBERT), printer in London, 1583–97; (1) Fetter Lane, Holborn; (2) St. Andrew's, Holborn. There is no record of this stationer's apprenticeship or freedom in the Registers of the Company. The earliest notice of him occurs in the proceedings taken in 1585 by Francis Flower and his assigns against T. Dunn and Robert Robinson for illegally printing the *Accidence*. In his answer Robinson said that he had been apprenticed to a printer for eight years, and had been working as a journeyman for a further term of five years, so that he must have been out of his time about 1580 [Arber, ii. 796–800]. His first book entry was made in the Registers

on September 22nd, 1586 [Arber, ii. 457], but Mr. Arber states that a book called the *Sum of Christianity* was printed by him in 1585 [Arber, v. 139]. In 1588 Robinson bought the printing stuff of Henry Middleton from his widow, including three printing presses with sundry sorts of letters and other necessaries, certain copies of books and Letters Patent, for the sum of £200 [*Library*, January, 1909, p. 103]. He was frequently fined for disorderly printing [Arber, ii. 821, 826, 860, 862]. The last book entry under his name occurs on May 11th, 1597 [Arber, iii. 84]. His widow afterwards married Richard Braddock [Arber, iii. 702].

ROBINSON (THOMAS), stationer of London, 1568–89. This is perhaps the Thomas Robynson who was presented as an apprentice by Mistress Toy on June 24th, 1559, for nine years [Arber, i. 118]. There is no record of his taking up his freedom, and no book entries are found in the Registers under his name; but the will of a Thomas Robinson, stationer, was proved in the Prerogative Court of Canterbury on October 1st, 1589. Bequests were left to Richard Watkins, George Bishop, James Roberts, and Augustine Lawton, all of whom were stationers, and the testator left the residue of his estate and a sum of £180 to Richard Watkins. He owned lands and tenements in Worcester [P.C.C., 73, Leicester].

ROBINSON (THOMAS), bookseller in Oxford, *see* Plomer, *Dictionary*.

ROCHEFORTH (HENRY), (?) bookseller in London, 1563–7. He had license in 1562–3 to print a work called *Certayne medecyne for the plage*, and again in 156$\frac{4}{5}$ for *An Almanacke and a pronosticacon* of his own making for the year 1565. This almanac was continued until 1567. Nothing more is known of him.

ROCKADON (EDWARD), stationer in Lincoln, 1571. Edward Rokedyn, one of Thomas Hackett's apprentices, was admitted a freeman of the Company of Stationers on September 25th, 1570 [Arber, i. 446]. He is mentioned in a list of stationers living in the country, who paid "scot and lott" to the Company in London in 1571, as living in Lincoln [Arber, v. lii].

ROCKET (HENRY), bookseller in London, 1602–11; The Long Shop in the Poultry. Son of John Rockett of Bury St. Edmunds, Suffolk, gentleman. Apprenticed to Andrew Wise, stationer of London, for eight years from Christmas, 1593, but on March 3rd, 159$\frac{4}{5}$, entered again for seven years to Cuthbert Burby, by whom he was presented for his freedom on January 31st, 1602 [Arber, ii. 190, 201, 731]. In the following March he entered in the Registers, *Spirituall essaies conteyninge diverse poeticall and divine passions and poems*, and on August 7th, 1611, *The renowned history of Fragoso and his three sons* [Arber, iii. 202, 462]. Amongst his other publications were Chettle's *Patient Grissill*, 1603, Heywood's *Fayre Maid of the Exchange*, 1607, and Middleton's *Tricke to catch the old one*, 1608. Henry Rockett died on September 22nd, 1611, and his widow Katherine sold the premises and stock valued at £150 to John Smyth, stationer, who bought on behalf of the Company. On April 9th, 1616, she transferred her late husband's copyrights to Nicholas Bourne. [Documents at the Public Record Office; *Bibliographica*, ii. 79; Arber, iii. 586.]

RODES, *see* Rhodes (J.).

ROEBUCK (SIMON), stationer at Cambridge, 1616–35; Gt. St. Mary's. In a list of Privileged persons of the University, 1624 [Bowes, 336]. Lived in Gt. St. Mary's Parish and paid church rate from 1616 to *c.* 1635 [Foster's *Churchwardens' Accounts*].

ROGERS, or AP-ROGERS (OWEN), *see* Duff, *Century*.

ROLTE (HENRY), stationer in Exeter, 1571. His name occurs in a return of stationers living in the county, who in 1571, were paying "skott and lott" to the Company in London [Arber, v. lii].

ROMAEN, ROMAN or ROOMAN (AEGIDIUS or GYLIS), printer at Haarlem, 1585–1606. In 1597 he printed John Payne's *Royal Exchange* [Herbert, p. 1733; copy at Bodleian Lib.]. [Ledeboer, *A.L.*, p. 144.]

ROPER (ABEL), *see* Plomer, *Dictionary*.

ROSS (JOHN), printer and bookbinder, Edinburgh, 1574–80. During the whole of this period he was printing for Henry Charteris, who succeeded him. He was also employed by Arbuthnet in connection with the printing of the *Bible* issued by the latter in 1579. His device, of which he had two sizes, was a figure of Truth in an oval border bearing the motto "Vincet tandem veritas"; this was afterwards used by H. Charteris, Waldegrave,

G. Anderson, and A. Anderson and his Heirs (1699). Ross died in July, 1580. His inventory is printed in the *Bannatyne Miscellany*, ii. [Dickson and Edmond, 327; Aldis, *Scottish Books*, 119.]

ROTHWELL (JOHN), senior, *see* Plomer, *Dictionary*.

ROTHWELL (JOHN), junior, *see* Plomer, *Dictionary*.

ROTTEFORDE (PAUL or POLL), typefounder in London, 1571; Green's Rents and the Wharf, Farringdon Without. Believed to be son of Henry Rocheforth. In the return of Aliens for the year 1571 he is described as "Douche, no denyzon, of occupation founder of lettres for printers, hathe bene in England xiiij yeares, and in this ward one year" [Worman, *Alien Members*, p. 56].

ROUNTHWAITE (RALPH), bookseller in London, 1618–28; Flower de Luce and Crown, St. Paul's Churchyard. Took up his freedom on March 27th, 1617 [Arber, iii. 684]. Made his first book entry on July 2nd, 1618 [Arber, iii. 628]. Amongst his publications were a few news-books relating to foreign affairs. On July 3rd, 1628, he assigned one of his copyrights to Robert Allot and John Legate [Arber, iv. 200].

ROWBOTHAM (JAMES), bookseller in London, 1559–80; (1) The Rose and Pomegranate, in Cheapside under Bow Church; (2) The Lute in Paternoster Row. In a list of those freemen not of the Stationers' Company who were hindered by privileges occurs the name of James Rowbothame [Arber, i. 111]. He was probably a draper or haberdasher. During the year 156$\frac{3}{4}$ he was fined 2s. 6d. for binding two hundred primers "in skabertes" against the rules of the Company [Arber, i. 239]. He sold almanacks, ballads, general literature and music.

ROY (SALOMON DE), printer at Utrecht, 1592–1637. In 1615 he printed "for Crispian de Passe" *A Garden of flowers*, an English translation of Passe's *Hortus Floridus* [Sayle, p. 1498; Ledeboer, *A.L.*, p. 147].

ROYSTON (JOHN), bookseller in London, 1611–12; The Bible at the great North Door of St. Paul's. In partnership with William Bladen. Together they entered on July 1st, 1611, *The foundation of Christian Religion*, which was printed for them by Tho. Purfoot and published in 1612. On January 7th, 161$\frac{1}{2}$, they entered *Newes out of Germany* [Arber, iii. 460, 474].

ROYSTON (RICHARD), *see* Plomer, *Dictionary*.

RUSSELL (EDWARD), (?) bookseller in London, 1566. During the year ending July 22nd, 1566, Edward Russell entered two ballads in the Registers [Arber, i. 305, 308]. An undated copy of one of these, called *Churchyards Farewell*, is in Mr. Christie-Miller's collection at Britwell.

RYMER, *see* Rime, Ryme or Rymer.

S. (M.), printer at Rotterdam, 1626. In this year a printer with these initials printed J. B.'s *Plain and true relation of the going forth of a Holland Fleet to the Coast of Brazil* [B.M., pp. 72–3]. Matthias Sebastiani, or Matthys Bastiaansz Wagens, seems to be the only printer at Rotterdam at this date whose initials correspond [Ledeboer, *A.L.*, pp. 155, 10].

SADLER (LAWRENCE), *see* Plomer, *Dictionary*.

SALISBURY or SALESBURY (THOMAS), bookseller in London, 1593–1604. Son of Pierce Salberye of the parish of Clokanock, Denbigh, husbandman. Apprentice to Oliver Wilkes, stationer of London, for seven years from October 9th, 1581. Thomas Salisbury took up his freedom on October 17th, 1588, and the first entry under his name in the Registers is found on March 17th. [Arber, ii. 107, 293, 703.] He dealt chiefly in Welsh books, and was publishing as late as 1604, although the last entry made by him in the Registers was on July 7th, 1601 [Arber, iii. 187]. He is presumably the Salisbury, "a bookbinder dwelling in Powles churchyard," who is referred to in the *Calendar of MSS. of the Marquis of Salisbury* (*Hist. MSS. Comm.*), vi. 288–9, in connection with a book of [Peter] Wentworth's (1596).

SAMPSON (JOHN), stationer at Cambridge, 1610, "paid to John Sampson bookes to write acts ordres & customes into xxvj^{s}" 1610 [Cooper's *Annals of Cambridge*, iii. 42].

SANDERS (JAMES), bookseller at Glasgow, 1625–42; At the Hie Kirk. First heard of in 1625 when he sold a copy of Barker's 1617 edition of the *Bible* to the Cathedral authorities. He also appears as a debtor in the inventory (1642) of James Bryson, the Edinburgh printer. [Wm. Stewart on Early Glasgow Printers in *Glasgow Herald*, April 18th, 1903; *Bannatyne Miscell.* ii. 261.] A "Jeames Sanders" took up his freedom in the Stationers' Company on July 3rd, 1626 [Arber, iii. 686], but it is doubtful whether he can be identified with the Glasgow bookseller.

SANDERSON (HENRY), (?) bookseller in London, 1560–7; St. Paul's Churchyard, at the sign of the Red Bowl. Only known from two entries in the Registers, the first in the year 1564–5, *A compendious forme of prayers* [Arber, i. 269], and the other in the year 1567–8, *An Almanacke and Pronostication of Phillippe Moore for xl. years* [Arber, i. 359]. Calvin's *Catechism*, 1560, was printed for him by John Kingston [Hazlitt, I. 71].

SAUNDERS (THOMAS), bookseller in London, 1612–13; At his shop in Holborn at the sign of the Mermaid. Son of John Saunders of Cheddar, Somerset, yeoman. Apprentice to Joane Newbery, widow of John Newbery, for seven years from March 11th, 160$\frac{4}{5}$ [Arber, ii. 290], and took up his freedom March 23rd, 161$\frac{1}{2}$ [Arber, iii. 683]. Only two book entries occur under his name in the Registers, the first on April 20th, 1612, and the second on May 22nd, 1613 [Arber, iii. 481, 524]. His address appears in a work of Gervase Markham's called *The second and last part of the First Book of the English Arcadia* [Hazlitt, I. 276].

SAYER (THOMAS), (?) bookseller in London, 1560; St. Dunstan's in the East. Only known from his will in the Prerogative Court of Canterbury [41, Mellershe] proved July 30th, 1560.

SCARLET (PETER), stationer at Cambridge, 1590–1640; Great St. Mary's. He lived in Great St. Mary's parish and paid church rate from 1590 to *c.* 1635, being Churchwarden several times and Auditor [Foster's *Churchwardens' Accounts*]. He appears in a list of Privileged persons in the University, 1624 [Bowes, 336]. His name is found on *Ramus' Dialecticae libri duo*, 1640.

SCARLET (PHILIP), bookseller at Cambridge, 1563–82; Gt. St. Mary's. Brother of John Scarlett (d. 1551, *see* Duff, *Century*). Lived in St. Mary's parish and paid church rate from 1568, when he was elected Churchwarden. St. John's College paid him 3s. for cornering, bossing, and chayninge *Anatomiam Vessalii*, in 1563–4 [Gray's *Cambridge Stationers*, 67]. His will, dated 1582, is at Peterborough.

SCARLET (PHILIP), (?) bookseller, 1597. *The Trimming of Thomas Nashe*, 1597, has the imprint "London, Printed for Philip Scarlet." As the book was entered to Cuthbert Burby it has been thought that this is a pseudonym.

SCARLET (PHILIP), bookseller at Cambridge, 1605–34; Gt. St. Mary's. He lived in Gt. St. Mary's parish, and paid church rate from 1612 to *c.* 1635. Service books were bought from him in 1605 [Foster's *Churchwardens' Accounts*]. He is in a list of Privileged persons in the University, 1624 [Bowes, 336]. His name appears on *Russell's famous pitcht battles of Lypsich and Lutzen*, 1634.

SCARLET (THOMAS), printer and bookseller in London, 1590–6. Son of William Scarlett of Wardon, co. Hereford, yeoman. Apprentice to Thomas East for eight years from March 25th, 1577, and took up his freedom in the Company of Stationers on October 12th, 1586 [Arber, ii. 75, 699]. Thomas Scarlet made his first book entry on August 17th, 1590 [Arber, ii. 558], but he appears to have been an unruly member of the Company. In 1591 he was directed to appear before the Archbishop of Canterbury, no doubt for some illegal printing [Arber, i. 548], and again in 1593 he was fined for keeping an apprentice seven years without binding him [Arber, ii. 864]. On August 9th, 1596, he surrendered some of his copyrights to Thomas Creede [Arber, iii. 68]. He must have died soon afterwards, as his widow surrendered her rights to Cuthbert Burby on September 6th, 1596. According to Sir J. Lambe, Ralph Blower and George Shaw bought the printing business of Henry [? Thomas] Scarlet [Arber, iii. 702].

SCARLET (WILLIAM), stationer at Cambridge, 1581–1617; Gt. St. Mary's. He is probably the William Scarlett to whom John Sheres bequeathed forty shillings by will in 1581 [Gray, *Cambridge Stationers*, p. 69]. His name appears in a list of privileged persons of the University *circa* 1592–1594 [Bowes, *Univ. Printers*, 336]. William Scarlet was servant (? apprentice) to John Legatt the younger, and it was he who on behalf of John Legatt and others went to Edinburgh and arranged with Robert Waldegrave to print the edition of Sidney's *Arcadia* which was put on the London market in 1599, in opposition to the edition published by William Ponsonby. In his depositions, Scarlet stated that he was then acting as butler and caterer to Trinity Hall in Cambridge [*Library*, April, 1900, pp. 195–205]. He lived in the parish of Gt. St. Mary's and in 1593 and 1611 contributed towards the steeple and bells of the church. He was churchwarden in 1610–11 [Foster's *Churchwardens' Accounts*]. On March 27th, 1609, St. John's College leased to him "the

Burbolte in St. Andrew's parish for 40 years at a rent of 53s. 4d." [Baker's *History of St. John's College*, i. 461]. His will, dated 1617, is at Peterborough [G. J. Gray].

SCARLETT, *see* Scarlet.

SCHELLEM (JOHN), (?) printer or bookseller at Utrecht, 1626. In this year appeared Thomas Scott's *Sir Walter Rawleigh's Ghost* [B.M., p. 1285; Sayle, p. 1498] with this name in the imprint; but no printer of the name seems to be recorded and it looks like a pseudonym ("schelm" = knave). Several of Scott's tracts have fantastic imprints.

SCHENCK (JOHANNES), (?) printer in Edinburgh, 1596. The imprint "Edimburgi imprimebat Iohannes Schenck" appears on an edition of *Officina theologica Danielis Hofmanni*, dated 1596. No such printer is known to have worked in Edinburgh, and the book was probably printed abroad. A copy of the title-page is in the B.M. [Ames's Collection of Title-pages, i. 582].

SCHILDERS (ABRAHAM), printer at Middelburg, 1620. He printed *A declaration of the causes for the which we Frederich have accepted of the crown of Bohemia* [Sayle, p. 1460; B.M., p. 243], with "Divvs Ivlivs Caesar Avgvstvs" on a coin as his device, and in the same year *The late good success and victory . . . of the King of Bohemia's forces . . . achieved near Horne in Austria* [Hazlitt, VII. 151]. He is not mentioned by Ledeboer. He was presumably related to Richard Schilders, but the only son of the latter now known was named Isaac.

SCHILDERS, SHELDERS, SKILDERS, alias PAINTER or PITTORE (RICHARD), printer in London, 1568–? 1579, and at Middelburg, 1580–1618: London, (1) St. Michael's Bassieshaw Ward; (2) St. Martin's Farringdon Without. A native of Enghien in Hennegau ["Engye in Hennego," *Returns of Aliens*, II. 36]. Admitted brother of the Stationers' Company May 3rd, 1568 [Arber, i. 366]. In the *Returns of Aliens* (1571) (ii. 36) it is said that he "came to England at Lent last was iiij yeres, and lyveth as servaunte by pryntinge with Thomas East stacyoner." In 1575 he printed a Dutch work, entitled *Den Spieghel des Houwelicks*. No place of printing is indicated on the title, but the book was probably printed in England. On November 24th, 1578, R. Skilders "Dutchman" had a press and type, and was a compositor, and was printing a book for

Hans Stell. He was stopped and made to transfer the book to Thomas Dawson, printer, for whom he worked for wages till it was complete. The book has been conjectured to be Philip van Marnix' *Bee Hive of the Romish Church* [Arber, ii. 882; v. iii]. Soon after this date he left England and settled down at Middelburg, where he opened the first press known to have been established in the town. His first book, printed in 1580, was in Dutch. In 1582 he printed Robert Browne's *Book which showeth the life of all true Christians*, 1582 [Sayle, p. 1452], in the imprint of which he used the name of "Painter." More than fifty works in English are attributed to his press, but in many of them, including apparently almost all of those published between 1602 and 1614, his name does not appear. An Italian *Historia de la morte de . . . Giovanna Graia*, 1607, has, however, the imprint "Stampato appresso Richardo Pittore" [Hazlitt, II. 694]. The books consist for the most part of works by D. Fenner, H. Broughton, H. Jacob, and other Puritan divines, but include an edition of John Wheeler's interesting *Treatise of Commerce*, 1601, a defence of the policy of the Merchant Adventurers' Company. The last which bear Schilders' imprint are dated 1616. In 1618, when he was about eighty years of age, he was presented with a pension. He is said to have died in 1634 at the age of ninety-six. [*Nieuwsblad von den Boekhandel*, no. 97, December 3rd, 1872; Worman, *Alien Members of the Book-trade*, 58–9; Sayle, pp. 1452–9; *Paper read by J. Dover Wilson before the Bibliographical Society*, October 17th, 1910.]

SEALE (WILLIAM), bookbinder in Oxford, 1628–39. Bodleian binder between 1628 and 1639. [Gibson, *Oxford Bindings*, p. 50; Macray's *Annals*, p. 77.] A Thomas Seale is mentioned in the will of Hugh Jones, printer of Oxford, as one of the apprentices to Mr. Turner, printer [Gibson, *Oxford Wills*, p. 34].

SEATON (GREGORY), *see* Seton.

SEGER, *see* Nycholas.

SEILE or SEYLE (HENRY), *see* Plomer, *Dictionary*.

SELDENSLACH or SELDESLACH (JACOB), printer at Antwerp, 1620–1; Op het Vleminex velt, In de Sevester. He was admitted to the St. Lucasgild in 1620–1, and in the latter year printed the third edition of the Rhemish *New Testament* [Sayle, p. 1371; B.M., p. 211]. [Olthoff, p. 91.]

SELMAN (MATTHEW), bookseller in London, 1594–1627; (1) In Fleet Street, next the Inner Temple Gate; (2) In Fleet Street, near Chancery Lane. Son of John Selman of Ken, co. Devon, smith. Apprentice to Thomas Newman, stationer of London, for seven years from September 1st, 1587, and took up his freedom in the Company on September 3rd, 1594 [Arber, ii. 153, 714]. Matthew Selman made his first entry in the Registers on October 13th, 1600 [Arber, iii. 174]. Amongst his publications was George Chapman's translation of *Petrarchs Seven Penitentiall Psalms*, 1612 [Hazlitt, H. 82]. In 1627 he was appointed by Edward Latymer, founder of the Latymer School, one of the first trustees of that institution [P.C.C., 15, Skynner].

SENIOR (LEWIS), bookbinder in London, 1562–78; Aldersgate Ward. A native of France. Admitted Brother of the Stationers' Company on January 14th, 156$\frac{2}{3}$ [Arber, i. 186]. In the Return of Aliens for the year 1571, he was described as a bookbinder and was stated to have been resident in this country twelve years. In the year 1578 an apprentice of James Gonneld's and another of George Bishop's were put over to Lewis Senior to learn the art of bookbinding [Arber, ii. 83, 86].

SERES (WILLIAM), senior, *see* Duff, *Century*.

SERES (WILLIAM), junior. Assigns of, 1578–1603. William Seres, junior, the son of William Seres, senior, was joined with his father in the patent for printing *The Psalter of David, the Primer for little children*, with *the Catechisme* and *Books of Private prayers*. He did not follow the trade of a stationer, although he was "clothed," in other words admitted to the Livery of the Company, on June 30th, 1578 [Arber, ii. 865]. He appointed as his assigns Henry Denham and Ralph Newbery [Arber, i. 111, 116].

SERGIER (RICHARD), senior, bookseller in London, 1579–1627. Son of T. Sergyr of Naton, Norfolk, yeoman. Apprentice to Lucas Harrison, stationer of London, for seven years from June 24th, 1571, and took up his freedom in the Company on October 2nd, 1578 [Arber, i. 434; ii. 679]. Richard Sergier made his first entry in the Registers on February 4th, 157$\frac{8}{9}$, and his last on January 8th, 160$\frac{7}{8}$ [Arber, ii. 346; iii. 372]. He dealt chiefly in theological books, and was associated with Edmund Weaver in the publication of some copies. His will was proved on August 18th, 1627. He left a son, Richard, and nominated Edmund Weaver one of his overseers. His address has not been found.

SERGIER (RICHARD), junior, bookseller in London, 1638. Son of Richard Sergier, senior. Took up his freedom in the Company of Stationers on March 1st, 163$^{6}_{7}$ [Arber, iii. 688]. Richard Sergier, junior, was the publisher of several plays. He issued some works in partnership with Andrew and John Crooke.

SERLE (RICHARD), (?) bookseller (?) in London, 1563–6; The Half Eagle and Key in Fleet Lane, Old Bailey. Richard Serle published several interesting books, notably a theological discourse translated from the Greek of Agapetus, by Thomas White, 1564 [Arber, i. 234]. He also published several ballads. He is not heard of after July 22nd, 1566 [Arber, i. 305].

SERMATELLI (BARTOLOMEO), printer at Florence, 1570–1604. The *Palestina* of Robert Chambers, 1600, is stated in the imprint to have been printed by him, but the device used is found in books printed in England and the imprint may be fictitious; *see* Sayle, p. 1533.

SETON (GREGORY), bookseller in London, 1577–1608; Under Aldersgate. Son of Nicholas Seton of Helmedon, Northampton, husbandman. Apprentice to John Judson, stationer of London, for eight years from Michaelmas, 1566, and chosen into the Livery of the Company on July 4th, 1590 [Arber, i. 323; ii. 871]. Gregory Seton made his first entry in the Registers on March 10th, 157$^{7}_{8}$ [Arber, ii. 325]. He dealt chiefly in theological literature and used as a device a play upon his name, a tun floating on the sea. Seton was elected Under Warden of the Company in 1601, and Upper Warden in 1607. He died between May 2nd and 12th, 1612, his will being dated and proved on these two dates. Seton appears to have been an intimate friend of the family of John Day, the printer, who for a time lived over Aldersgate. To the printer's son John, who took holy orders, he left his best *Bible* and he refers to Lionel Day, another son, as his kinsman [P.C.C., 43, Fenner].

SEVESTRE (PIERRE), printer or bookseller at Paris, 1583–1612; Rue d'Arras. He printed H. Ely's *Certain brief notes upon a brief apology* [1603]. His device was "INRI" and cross, with Cross of Lorraine. [Sayle, p. 1386; Renouard, p. 342.]

SHARLAKERS, *see* Shorleyker.

SHARPE (HENRY), bookseller or bookbinder in Northampton, 1579–89. A stationer of this name, the son of Richard Sharpe of Torcester, co. Northampton, yeoman, was apprenticed to Richard Lynell, stationer of London, for ten years from March 25th, 1566, but does not appear to have taken up his freedom in the Company of Stationers until thirteen years later, namely on June 15th, 1579. From the fact that he was a Northamptonshire man, it seems possible that he is identical with the Henry Sharpe, bookbinder of Northampton, who figures in the Martin Marprelate Controversy [Arber, *Introductory Sketch to M.M. Controv.*, pp. 94–104, 131, 174]. He may also be identical with the Henry Sharpe, bookseller of Banbury (1608–19).

SHARPE (HENRY), bookseller in Banbury, Oxfordshire, 1608–19. This bookseller may be identical with the Henry Sharpe who took up his freedom in the Company of Stationers on June 15th, 1579, and who made his first book entry in the Registers on September 15th, 1608 [Arber, ii. 680; iii. 389]. In the University Library at Cambridge is a copy of the Revd. William Whateley of Banbury's sermon, *Gods Husbandry, the First Part*, with the imprint, "London, Imprynted by Felix Kyngston for Henry Sharpe dwelling in Banburie, 1619." He was also joint publisher with Thomas Man and his sons of the works of the Rev. John Dod.

SHARPE (JOHN), stationer of London, 1583–1624. Son of John Sharpe of Sysonby, co. Leicester, husbandman. Apprentice for seven years to Richard Hudson, stationer of London, from December 17th, 1576. Took up his freedom on February 3rd, 1584 [Arber, ii. 72, 690]. A "John Sharpe, stationer," probably the same man, was a witness to the will of William Harrison, joiner, in 1624 [P.C.C., 86, Byrde].

SHAW (GEORGE), printer in London, 1595–8. Son of Thomas Shaw, cordwainer of London. Apprentice for eight years from November 25th, 1577, to Roger Ward, but turned over to Henry Denham on December 1st,

1579, and again to Henry Middleton on February 3rd, 158$^{3}_{4}$ [Arber, ii. 121]. George Shaw became a freeman on January 31st, 158$^{5}_{6}$, and made his first book entry in the Registers on July 17th, 1595 [Arber, ii. 696; iii. 45]. He appears to have dealt chiefly in ballads and ephemeral literature and was for some time associated with William Blackwall. The writings of William Vaughan, published in 1598, bear the imprint, "Apud Georgium Shaw typographum," but the position of his printing house is unknown.

SHAW or SHAWE (JAMES), bookseller in London, 1601–3; near Lud Gate. Son of Bartholomew Shawe of Westminster, cordwainer. Apprentice to William Ponsonby, stationer of London, for twelve years from Christmas, 1588, and made a freeman of the Company on January 19th, 160$^{0}_{1}$. James Shaw made his first entry in the Registers on November 25th, 1601, and his last on June 10th, 1603. [Arber, ii. 154, 727; iii. 196, 237.]

SHEARES (WILLIAM), *see* Plomer, *Dictionary*.

SHEFFARD (WILLIAM), bookseller in London, 1621–30; Pope's Head Alley, at the entering in out of Lombard Street. Became a freeman of the Company of Stationers on February 7th, 161$^{8}_{9}$. Sheffard made his first book entry in the Registers on June 13th, 1621, and his last on October 30th, 1627. He must have died before May 13th, 1630, when his copyrights were transferred to Henry Overton, whom his widow had married. [Arber, iii. 187, 235, 685].

SHELDERS, *see* Schilders (R.).

SHELDRAKE (JOHN), bookseller in London, 1590–4. Took up his freedom in the Company of Stationers on October 6th, 1584 [Arber, ii. 693], and made his first book entry on April 12th, 1591. In the previous year however Roger Ward printed for him Du Chesne's *Sclopotarie of J. Quercetanus* [B.M., 783 d. 8 (1)], and W. Vallans' *Tale of two Swannes* [Hazlitt, H. 624–5]. He made his last entry in the Registers on October 29th, 1594 [Arber, ii. 663]. His address is unknown.

SHEPHARD (HENRY), *see* Plomer, *Dictionary*.

SHEPPARD (JOHN), bookseller in London, 1574–80; The Brazen Serpent, St. Paul's Churchyard. Son of Richard Shepperd of Gresby, Chester, husbandman. Apprentice for eight years to Reginald Wolfe, stationer of

London, from March 25th, 1566 [Arber, i. 291]. John Sheppard was just out of his time when Reginald Wolfe died in 1574. His mistress, Joane Wolfe, died six months afterwards, and by her will directed that her executors should take over the shop, the presses and the stock of books in it, and if they decided to let the business, John Sheppard was to have the first refusal. Sheppard appears to have taken on the shop and some of the printing materials, the bulk of which, however, are found in the hands of Henry Bynneman, printer, after 1574. On February 25th, 157$^{6}_{7}$, Sheppard received license to print Timothy Kendall's *Flowers of Epigrammes*, and his name and address appear in the imprint. He was dead before January 8th, 15$^{79}_{80}$, when his apprentice John Hayes was transferred to William Lownes. John Sheppard left a son, Mark, who took up his freedom in the Company "per patrimonium" on April 20th, 1601. [Arber, ii. 94, 309, 691, 728; Plomer, *Wills*, p. 20; *Library*, July, 1908.]

SHEPPARD (WILLIAM), bookseller in London, 1561–3; St. Giles, Cripplegate. Apprentice with William Hill, by whom he was presented for his freedom during the year ending July 10th, 1559 [Arber, i. 99]. In the year ending July 24th, 1562, he entered a ballad entitled *Tom Longe ye Caryer* [Arber, i. 177], and shortly afterwards was fined for selling William Powell's edition of "Nostradamus" [Arber, i. 217]. Made his will on August 10th, 1563. It was proved September 10th, 1563. He desired to be buried in St. Giles, Cripplegate. He was apparently a poor man. [Dean and Chapter of St. Paul's, Book B, f. 33.]

SHERES (JOHN), stationer at Cambridge, ? 1571–81; Gt. St. Mary's. He may have been the son of Peter Sheres and have succeeded to his business in 1569. In 1571 he is mentioned as having left the town, but returned in 1577. He resided in Gt. St. Mary's parish, certainly from 1577 [Foster's *Churchwardens' Accounts*]. From his will, proved in 1581 by his widow, he appears to have been a wealthy man. [Gray, *Cambridge Stationers*, 69.]

SHORLEYKER (RICHARD), bookseller and ? printer in London, 1624–30; In Shoe Lane at the Falcon, 1624–30. Apprentice with Walter Dight. Took up his freedom November 3rd, 1619 [Arber, iii. 685]. On June 4th, 1627, he secured the copyrights in three books formerly his master's, namely W. Gedde's *Booke of Sundry Draughtes* [*i.e.*, drawings] *for Glasiers*,

Plasterers and Gardiners, *A Scholehouse for the Needle*, a book of patterns of which he had already printed an edition in 1624 [Hazlitt, III. 169], and Peacham's *Emblems* [*i.e.*, *Minerva Britanna*]. He also published a sheet of satirical verses with a woodcut, called *The Armes of the Tobackonists* in 1630. Richard Shorleyker was dead before November 12th in that year, as in a return made of such printers as were to contribute to the repair of St. Paul's, mention is made of "Widdow Sherleaker who lives by printing of pictures" [*Dom. S. Papers*, *Chas. I*, vol. 175. 45]. She apparently used her husband's imprint, for a book entitled *Here Followeth Certaine Patternes of Cutworkes* professes to be printed "by Richard Shorleyker" at the address given above in 1632 [Hazlitt, H. 447].

SHORT (E   ), printer in London, 1603–4; The Star on Bread Street Hill. Widow of Peter Short. Soon after her husband's death she married Humphrey Lownes. Her imprint is found in a few books. [*Peter Short, printer, and his marks*, by Silvanus P. Thompson, *Bibl. Soc. Trans.*, vol. iv, p. 103 *et seq.*]

SHORT (JAMES), printer and bookseller in Oxford, 1618–24. Admitted bookseller on January 19th, 161$\frac{7}{8}$. Associated with John Lichfield as Printer to the University, 1618–24. [Madan, *Oxford Press*, 277, 297, 312.]

SHORT (PETER), printer in London, 1589–1603; The Star on Bread Street Hill. Admitted a freeman of the Company of Stationers by "redemption" on March 1st, 158$\frac{8}{9}$ [Arber, ii. 705], and admitted into the livery of the Company on July 1st, 1598 [Arber, ii. 873]. He appears to have succeeded to the business of Henry Denham and was at first in partnership with Richard Yardley, their first entry in the Registers being made on July 5th, 1591 [Arber, ii. 588]. Yardley's name is not found after 1593. Peter Short had an extensive business, printing for William Ponsonby and other important booksellers. Amongst many noted books that came from his press were Shakespeare's *Henry IV, Part 1*, printed for Andrew Wise in 1598; Shakespeare's *Lucrece*, printed for John Harrison, the younger, in 1598; Francis Meres' *Palladis Tamia*, printed for Cuthbert Burby in 1598; Foxe's *Acts and Monumentes*, begun by Henry Denham and finished by Peter Short in 1596–7; Thomas Morley's *Playne and Easie Introduction to Musicke* in 1596, and Dr. William Gilbert's *De Magnete*, 1600. Peter Short used several marks or devices, notably the

Star and the Serpent, both of which he derived from Henry Denham. He died some time in 1603, being succeeded by his widow. [*Peter Short, Printer, and His Marks*, by Silvanus P. Thompson, in *Bibl. Soc. Trans.*, vol. iv, p. 103 *et seq.*]

SHORTER (SAMUEL), (?) bookseller in London, ? 1598; At the Great North Door of St. Paul's. A book by Thomas Hood, called *The making and use of . . . a Sector*, was printed by John Windet for sale by Shorter at the above address. The date appears on the title-page as that of composition, and the book was presumably printed in the same year. Nothing seems to be known of him.

SIMMES or SYMMES (VALENTINE), printer in London, 1585–?1622; (1) The White Swan in Addle or Addling Hill; (2) White Friars neere the Mulberry Tree, 1610. Son of Richard Symmes of Adderbury, co. Oxford, shereman. Apprentice for eight years from Christmas, 1576, to Henry Sutton, stationer of London [Arber, ii. 74]. Henry Sutton was a bookseller, and at his own desire Simmes was transferred to Henry Bynneman, a printer. Bynneman died in 1584, and in the following year Simmes was presented for his freedom by Joane the widow of Henry Sutton [Arber, ii. 694]. From the outset of his career he was constantly in trouble for printing books that were obnoxious to the authorities, or were the property of other men. Thus in 1589 he was arrested as one of the compositors of the Martin Marprelate press. In 1595 he was caught printing the "Grammar and Accidence" and his press was seized, his type melted and he was compelled to transfer his apprentice to James Roberts, being forbidden to take another until that one was out of his time. In 1599 he was named in a list of fourteen printers who were strictly forbidden to print satyres or epigrams, and was fined a shilling, perhaps in connection with the same matter. On another occasion he was caught printing a ballad against Sir Walter Raleigh, when it is said Bishop Bancroft warned the printer that he could have hanged him long before, if he had wished to do so. In 1622 he was prohibited by the order of the High Commissioners from working as a master printer and was allowed a pension of £4 a year by the Company of Stationers. Simmes' press is chiefly interesting as having given us several of Shakespeare's works. His press work was generally good but most of his type was second hand. In

the autumn of 1597 he printed for Andrew Wise the first quarto of *Richard the Second* and the first quarto of *Richard the Thirde*. In 1600 for Andrew Wise and William Aspley he produced the *Second part of Henrie the fourth* and the first quarto of *Much Ado about Nothing*, this last being one of the few Shakespeare play books that was decently printed. In 1604 he printed for Mathew Lawe the second edition of the *First Part of King Henry the Fourth*. In 1610 he would appear to have been at work in Whitefriars, as his name is found in the imprint of a small volume entitled *Syrophenissa or the Canaanitish Woman's conflicts*, of which the title-page is preserved in the Ames collection at the British Museum. In December, 1619, he assigned over to Edward Griffin several of his copyrights [Arber, iii. 661]. [*Bibliographer*, New York, May, 1903.]

SIMMONS (MATTHEW), *see* Plomer, *Dictionary*.

SIMOND (JOHN), bookbinder in London, 1568–71; Blackfriars. A native of France, described in the return of aliens for 1571 as a bookbinder and resident in England three years [Worman, *Alien Members*, p. 62].

SIMPSON or SYMPSON (BENJAMIN), typefounder. In 1597 he was ordered to enter into a bond of £40 not to cast any letters or characters, or to deliver them, without advertising the Master and Wardens of the Company of Stationers in writing, with the names of the parties for whom they were intended [Reed, *Letter Foundries*, 128]. Also mentioned in the Registers as having an apprentice in 1598 [Arber, ii. 224]. Nashe in *Have with You to Saffron-Walden*, 1596, sig. O1v, mentions "*Beniamin* the Founders father who dwels by *Fleete-bridge*," perhaps the same.

SIMSON (GABRIEL), printer in London, 1583–1600; The White Horse in Fleet Lane, over against Seacoal Lane. Admitted to the freedom of the Company of Stationers on the presentation of Mistress Jugge on April 10th, 1583. A fellow apprentice, William White, was presented on the same day, and the two joined partnership for a few years [Arber, ii. 688]. Gabriel Simson made his first entry, a ballad, in the Registers on May 1st, 1585 [Arber, ii. 440]. On August 18th, 1595, Simson and White were fined ten shillings for printing part of a book of Master Broughton's without authority; they were ordered to bring in the sheets they had printed and were threatened with imprisonment [Arber, ii. 824] They

were both mentioned in the list of printers who were especially warned in 1599 not to print any satires, epigrams, plays or histories [Arber, iii. 678]. Their partnership was dissolved in 1597 when William White set up for himself in Cow Lane, near Smithfield. Gabriel Simson died before August 11th, 1600 [Arber, ii. 247]. He left two sons, Gabriel and Daniel, and two daughters, who are referred to in the will of Henry Sivedall who died in 1624 [P.C.C., 90, Byrde]. His widow Frances afterwards married Richard Rede, or Read, printer, and later took as a third husband George Elde, printer.

SINGLETON (HUGH), *see* Duff, *Century*.

SKELTON (HENRY), bookseller in London, 1623–34; (1) A little within Aldgate; (2) In Little Britain. Took up his freedom May 3rd, 1620. His first book entry was made on January 16th, 162$\frac{3}{4}$ [Arber, iii. 685; iv. 89], and the last heard of him is on July 2nd, 1634, when he transferred one of his copyrights to Thomas Payne [Arber, iv. 322].

SKILDERS, *see* Schilders (R.).

SKOT (JOHN), printer in Edinburgh, *see* Duff, *Century*.

SLATER (THOMAS), *see* Plomer, *Dictionary*.

SMETHWICK (JOHN), bookseller in London, 1597–1640; (1) Fleet Street, near the Temple Gate; (2) Under the Dial in St. Dunstan's Churchyard, Fleet Street. Son of Richard Smythick, draper of London. Apprentice to Thomas Newman, stationer, for nine years from Christmas, 1589: took up his freedom on January 7th, 159$\frac{6}{7}$ [Arber, ii. 166, 717]. Smethwick's first entry in the Registers was made on October 6th, 1597 [Arber, iii. 92]. He was at first a somewhat unruly member of the Company, being fined on several occasions for selling privileged books [Arber, ii. 832, 837, 840], but he rapidly rose to the highest position, being successively Junior Warden in 1631, Senior Warden in 1635, and Master of the Company in 1639. In 1609 the copyrights of Nicholas Ling were transferred to him and these included the old *Taming of a Shrew* and Shakespeare's *Romeo and Juliet*, *Love's Labour Lost*, and *Hamlet*. Of *Hamlet* Smethwicke published three quartos, one in 1611, another in 1637, and one without date. Smethwick was for some time the partner of John Jaggard, and as might be expected, held a share in the First Folio of 1623, and also the Second Folio of

1632. He also held shares in the Latin Stock of the Company, and was associated with the publication of the most important books of the period. John Smethwick died in 1641. By his will which was proved on July 15th, 1641, he bequeathed his shop and all the books in it, as well as the residue of his estate to his son Francis [P.C.C., 87, Evelyn]. The bird bearing the word "wick" in its bill, which he used as a device, is presumably a smee or smew.

SMITH or SMYTHE (ANTHONY), *see* Duff, *Century*.

SMITH (FRANCIS), bookseller in London, 1633–6; near Holborn Conduit, at the sign of the Sun. Took up his freedom July 3rd, 1632 [Arber, iii. 687]. The first entry under his name occurs in the Registers on May 9th, 1633, when Mathew Rhodes assigned over to him Gervase Markham's tragedy *Herod and Antipater* [Arber, iv. 295], but he almost immediately passed it on to Thomas Lambert [*ib.* 301]. He received it back again on January 2nd, $163\frac{3}{4}$. Francis Smith dealt chiefly in ballads and ephemeral literature. The last entry under his name occurs on June 17th, 1636. It had reference to the plague which was then raging in the city, and to which the publisher probably fell a victim.

SMITH (JOHN), bookseller in London, 1604. Apprentice to Edward Aggas, and took up his freedom on October 29th, 1597 [Arber, ii. 221, 720]. The only entry under his name was made on September 6th, 1604 [Arber, iii. 270].

SMITH (NICOLAS), bookbinder in Oxford, 1593–1609. Became a privileged bookseller on July 17th, 1608 [Clark, *Register*, ii. 1. 401]. He married the widow of Robert Billingsley on July 3rd, 1608. He was buried on May 30th, 1609 [S. Mary's Register]. By his will he bequeathed the residue of his estate to his wife Agnes. His goods, consisting entirely of his binding materials, were valued at £34 17s. 2d. [Gibson, *Oxford Wills*, p. 22; *Oxford bindings*, pp. xix. 18, 20–3.]

SMITH (PETER), bookseller and printer in London, 1624. Mentioned in John Gee's *Foot out of the snare*, 1624, in a list of those who printed and sold popish books. "Peter Smith and his sonne. They both print and sell popish bookes, and are very audacious pernicious fellowes. Their

house was scarcht of late, and great store of Worthingtons bookes found there." Peter Smith's name is not found in the Registers of the Stationers' Company.

SMITH (RALPH), *see* Plomer, *Dictionary*.

SMITH (RICHARD), bookseller in London, 1567–95; At the corner shop at the North-West Door of St. Paul's Church. Richard Smith is mentioned in a list of stationers and printers hindered by privilege, as one of those who lived by bookselling but was not a stationer [Arber, i. 111]. His first entry in the Registers was made during the year ending July 22nd, 1567 [Arber, i. 337]. In 1592 he gave John Charlewood certain sermons to print for him. These were published anonymously but were traced to Lancelot Andrewes, afterwards Bishop of Winchester. Some trouble arose over them, and there are several entries in the accounts of the Company for the year ending July 15th, 1593, in connection with them [Arber, i. 561]. Richard Smith was the publisher of George Gascoigne's *Hundreth sundrie Flowres*, and the same writer's *Posies* and *Steele Glas*. He used as a device Time bringing Truth to light [Herbert, p. 1324].

SMITH (TOBY), bookseller in London, 1580–3; The Crane in St. Paul's Churchyard. Originally apprenticed to Lucas Harrison, at whose death he was transferred to Richard Sergier [Arber, ii. 88]. He was admitted to the freedom of the Company on March 26th, 1580 [Arber, ii. 682]. He made his first book entry on June 9th following [Arber, ii. 371], and his last on January 18th, $158\frac{2}{3}$ [Arber, ii. 417].

SMYTH (JOHN) chapman of Edinburgh, 1580. Among the debts due to John Ross, the Edinburgh printer, at the time of his death in 1580, was eight pounds owing by "Johne Smyth, cramer, at the kirk dur" [*Bannatyne Miscellany*, ii. 206]. This debt may have been for books or tracts supplied to Smyth, who was probably in a small way of business and doubtless included popular literature among the wares which he exposed for sale in one of the crames or booths which clustered round St. Giles's church.

SMYTH (ROBERT), printer and bookbinder in Edinburgh, 1592–1602; the Netherbow. He was, possibly, the Robert Smythe of Westbury in Wiltshire, who in February, $156\frac{7}{8}$, was apprenticed to Hugh Singleton, the London printer. He was one of seven Edinburgh booksellers who appealed to the

Town Council in February, 1592, against John Norton of London for retailing books within the burgh. At the time of the death of his first wife (1593) he owed £6 to "Richert Field, Inglischman," and £2 10s. od. to "Mr. Herculeis Franceis," both, no doubt, the London stationers. In 1599 he obtained a licence under the Privy Seal giving him the exclusive privilege of printing certain books for a period of twenty-five years. Only six books from his press are known, but several others mentioned in his inventory were probably printed by him. He married, firstly, Catharine Norwell († August 8th, 1593), the widow of Thomas Bassandyne [*q.v.*]; and, secondly, Jonet Gairden, who survived him. Smyth, who dwelt at the Netherbow, died May 1st, 1602. His inventories, taken at the time of the death of his first wife and after his own decease, are printed in the *Bannatyne Miscellany*, ii. 218, 233. He was succeeded by T. Finlason, who in October, 1602, purchased from his heirs the privileges, stock and plant. A. Aysoun and John Brown [*q.v.*] were probably journeymen in Smyth's employ. [Dickson and Edmond, 475; Aldis, *Scottish Books*, 120; *E. B. S. Papers*, vol. i, no. 15; Lee, App. xv, lxxi; *Scottish Antiquary*, iv. 174.]

SNAPE (HENRY), bookseller in the parish of As[t]bery, co. Chester, 1585. On February 7th, $158\frac{5}{6}$, Richard Snape, son of the above, was apprenticed to Edward Aggas, citizen and stationer of London, for ten years [Arber, ii. 138]. This Henry Snape may have been a relative of the Thomas Snape, stationer of London, who is found mentioned in the Subsidy Rolls of 1523 and 1544. [*Library*, July, 1908, p. 258.]

SNAPE (THOMAS), stationer of London, 1623–44; Parish of St. Nicholas Shambles, Farringdon Within, (?) Rose Alley. This stationer was entered in the Lay Subsidy Rolls of 1623 and 1644. In the first his goods were valued at £20 and in the second at £40. [*Library*, July, 1908, p. 258.]

SNODHAM (LEONARD), printer in London, 1614. Was associated with Ralph Blower in printing an impression of 1,500 copies of Thomas Ashe's Appendix to his *Promptuarie or repertorie generall of the Common Lawe of England* in 1614 [Arber, iii. 554].

SNODHAM (THOMAS), printer in London, 1603–25; St. Botolph without Aldersgate. Apprentice to Thomas East, printer of London. The date of East's death is unknown, but on June 17th, 1609, his widow assigned

over to Thomas Snodham, who took the name of East for trade purposes, her rights in twenty-four of his copies. These were works of general literature, but two years later he obtained a share, in company with Matthew Lownes and John Browne, in a large number of East's musical publications [Arber, iii. 413, 465]. The earliest entry under Thomas Snodham's name in the Registers is on May 14th, 1603 [Arber, iii. 234]. In 1615 he had two presses [*Ibid.*, p. 699]. In 1619 Snodham was sent into Ireland by the Company "to take the account." This was in connection with the "Irish Stock," which proved a failure and was eventually wound up. During his absence, the Court agreed that he might work two presses, and allowed his wife £4 per week if the work done amounted to so much. [Records of the Stationers' Company.] Thomas Snodham married Elizabeth, sister of Cuthbert Burby. He died probably of the plague in the autumn of 1625. His will was dated October 16th and proved on the 17th. He appointed his wife sole executrix, and Edmund Weaver and William Stansby, stationers, his executors [P.C.C., 109, Clarke]. His widow died a few months later, and her will was also proved in the Prerogative Court of Canterbury [P.C.C., 24, Hele].

SNOWDON (GEORGE), printer in London, 1606–8. Son of Robert Snowdon of Kirk Ledam, York. Apprentice to Robert Robinson, stationer of London, for seven years from April 27th, 1590, and became a freeman of the Company on May 11th, 1597 [Arber, ii. 168, 718]. In 1606 he was joined with a relative, Lionel Snowdon. Amongst the books they printed were William Covell's *Brief answer unto certaine reasons, etc.*, and William Bucanus' *Institutions of Christian Religion*. In 1608 they transferred their business to Nicholas Okes, and it was at this printing house that Nathaniel Butter's "Pide Bull" edition of Shakespeare's *King Lear* was printed in that year. [*Library*, April, 1906.]

SNOWDON (LIONEL), printer in London, 1606–8. Son of Cuthbert Snowdon of Eyseby, York. Apprentice to Robert Robinson, stationer of London, for seven years from February 7th, $159\frac{0}{1}$, and became a freeman on February 13th, $160\frac{3}{4}$ [Arber, ii. 215, 736]. He joined his kinsman George Snowdon [*q.v.*].

SOLEMPNE (A. DE), printer at Norwich, *see* Duff, *Century*.

SOMERSET (THOMAS), (?) printer or publisher, 1562. In June of that year he was imprisoned for "translating an oratyon out of Frenche, made by the Cardinall of Lorraine, and putting the same without authority in prynte" [*Acts of the Privy Council, New Series*, vii. 108]. No person of this name connected with the book-trade seems to be known.

SPARKE (MICHAEL), senior, *see* Plomer, *Dictionary*.

SPARKE (MICHAEL), junior, *see* Plomer, *Dictionary*.

SPARKE (WILLIAM), bookseller in Oxford, 1609. He was presumably the William Sparke, son of Richard Sparke of Eynsham, co. Oxford, who was apprenticed to John Barnet, stationer of London, for seven years from December 25th, 1601 [Arber, ii. 260], but the entry in the Registers was cancelled and a note added that he had gone to another trade. He became a privileged bookseller of the University of Oxford on January 27th, 160$\frac{8}{9}$, at the age of thirty [Clark, *Register*, ii. 1. 401].

SPEED (DANIEL), bookseller in London, 1616–20; The Blazing Star, St. Paul's Churchyard. Son of John Speed, the historian. Apprentice to Matthew Law, stationer, for nine years from June 24th, 1603, and became a freeman of the Company of Stationers on December 5th, 1614 [Arber, ii. 272; iii. 684]. Daniel Speed's first entry in the Register related to his father's book *The Clowd of Witnesses*, and was made on May 6th, 1616 [Arber, iii. 587], and the last entry under his name was made on November 8th, 1619 [Arber, iii. 659].

SPEIDELL (JOHN), professor of mathematics, 1616–28; In the Fields between Prince's Street and the Cockpit. Certain mathematical works printed for him by Edward Allde were to be sold at his house [Hazlitt, VII. 364–5].

SPENCER (JOHN), bookseller in London and Librarian of Sion College, 1617–80; London Bridge and Sion College. The son of Robert Spencer of Uttoxeter, co. Stafford, yeoman. Apprentice to Walter Burre for nine years from Candlemas day, 1617. Took up his freedom in the Company on March 1st, 162$\frac{4}{5}$ [Arber, iii. 685]. In the same year in partnership with John Bartlett, he issued a sermon preached before the House of Commons by the Rev. Isaac Bargrave, which was to be sold at Bartlett's shop, the Gilded Cup, in Cheapside. Later in the same year Spencer issued a chap book called *Love's Garland, or Posies for Rings*, which was to be sold at his shop "on London Bridge" [*Library*, February, 1903]. On July 3rd, 1630, Mistress Burre, the widow of Walter Burre, assigned over to John Spencer her rights in nine books formerly her husband's copies. These included the following notable works, Thomas Middleton's *A Mad World my Masters*, Ben Jonson's *Alchemist* and *Silent Woman*, John Taylor's *Odcombe's Complaint*, and G. Ruggles' *Ignoramus* [Arber, iv. 238]. On the foundation of Sion College, John Spencer, on the recommendation of the Rev. John Simpson, the founder of the library, was appointed Clerk to the College and sub-Librarian. Shortly afterwards he published a sermon preached by the Rev. Robert Willan on the death of Lord Bayning, Viscount Sudbury, and on the title-page he spoke of himself as "Hypo-Bibliothecary of Syon College." This sermon was printed about Midsummer, 1630. In 1635 he published an edition of Middleton's *Mad World* and in the same year the Oxford play entituled *Bellum Grammaticale*, to which he prefixed a Latin preface in the course of which he said that it was on sale next to the Gateway of Sion College. The last entry under his name in the Registers is on December 6th, 1638 [Arber, iv. 446]. He remained Library Keeper of Sion College until his death in 1680.

SPENCER (THOMAS), bookseller in London, 1635–6. Took up his freedom December 2nd, 1633 [Arber, iii. 687]. On April 15th, 1636, he entered in the Registers Sir Francis Kynaston's *Constitutions of the Musaeum Minervae* [Arber, iv. 360].

SPEWE (WILLIAM), *see* Spire (William).

SPILMAN (SIMON), *see* Duff, *Century*.

SPIRE (WILLIAM), senior, bookseller in Oxford, 1571–97. He was presented by Robert Redbourne as his apprentice on October 13th, 1556, and made free of the Stationers' Company on January 16th, 156$\frac{4}{5}$ [Arber, i. 40, 276]. On March 21st, 157$\frac{0}{1}$, he was admitted bookseller in the University of Oxford [Clark, *Register*, ii. 1. 321]. His will, dated November 9th, 1597, was proved on the 16th of the same month. [Gibson, *Oxford Wills*, 19.]

SPIRE (WILLIAM), junior, bookseller and bookbinder in Oxford, 1607–36; St. Mary's Parish. Son of William Spire (1571–97); admitted a privileged person of the University on January 30th, 160$\frac{6}{7}$ [Clark, *Register*, ii. 1. 400]. Made free of the Stationers' Company on July 31st, 1615 [Arber, iii. 684]. He bound books for the Bodleian between 1621 and 1629. He died in September, 1636, and was buried on the 13th of that month. Administration of his effects was granted to his widow Joan. The value of the books and things in his shop was £29 13s. 6d., but against this there were claims amounting to more than £45. [Gibson, *Oxford Bindings*, 48, 49, 51, 60; *Oxford Wills*, pp. 19, 24, 32, 39]. In 1621 he was living in High Street, near Schidyard Street (Oriel Street), in a tenement formerly occupied by Garbrand Herks.

SPOONER (HUGH), bookseller and bookbinder in London, 1573–86; The Cradle in Lombard Street. Son of Hugh Spoyner, or Sponer, of Sheffield, Yorks, yeoman. Apprentice to Thomas Humble for eight years from August 24th, 1565 [Arber, i. 286]. On September 25th, 1578, he entered in the Registers a work with the title *A Thousand notable thinges of sundrie sorts*, which was printed for him by John Charlewood [Arber, ii. 338]. Amongst the accounts of the Stationers' Company for the year ending July 10th, 1586, is the following entry:—"Item paid to Hughe Sponer for byndinge certen bookes prynted againste Master Tottells privylege—iijs. whiche shold be answered agayne by Master Tottell . . . iijs." [Arber, i. 515].

SPURRIER (JOHN), bookseller in London, 1615–26. Took up his freedom August 1st, 1615 [Arber, iii. 684]. Mention of him is made in the will of Joan Darby, proved on December 29th, 1626 [Dean and Chapter of St. Paul's, Book D, f. 312].

STAFFORD (JOHN), *see* Plomer, *Dictionary*.

STAFFORD (SIMON), draper and printer in London, 1596–1626; (1) Black Raven Alley, St. Peter's, Cornhill; (2) The Three Crowns in the Cloth Fair, 1606; (3) Addling Hill, neere Carter Lane, 1600; (4) Dwelling in Cloth-fair, near the Red Lion, 1607. Served his apprenticeship for ten years with Christopher Barker, the Queen's Printer, who was a member of the Drapers' Company. On the completion of his time he was made free of the Drapers' Company. On February 9th, 159$\frac{5}{6}$, he entered in the Registers of the Stationers' Company a work called *The Black Dog of Newgate's Lamentation* [Arber, iii. 58], but he does not appear to have had a press of his own until January 14th, 159$\frac{7}{8}$, when he took premises in Black Raven Alley and printed Nicholas Breton's *Solemne Passion of the Soules love*. In the following March it came to the ears of the Company of Stationers that Stafford had printed a large impression of the *Accidence*, a privileged book, and they thereupon seized his press and letters. An action in the Star Chamber followed, the result of which was that his press was redelivered to him by order of the Privy Council dated September 10th, 1598, and the Company gave notice that they were willing to admit Stafford to their freedom if he would transfer himself from the Drapers' Company, but he would not be allowed to act as a master printer until he did so. He was accordingly admitted a freeman of the Company of Stationers on May 7th, 1599 [Arber, ii. 723], and on October 20th he entered two sermons in the Registers and took his first apprentice on December 1st, 1600 [Arber, ii. 250; iii. 150]. His press was a very busy one. He printed large numbers of ballads and sermons, and amongst other things we find that he printed the anonymous *True Chronicle History of King Leir and his three daughters*, the copyright of which he transferred to John Wright on May 8th, 1605, with the stipulation that he was to have the printing of it. The later history of Stafford's press is involved in some obscurity. He is not mentioned in the list of printers of May 9th, 1615 [Arber, iii. 699], but he entered a book on June 24th, 1624 [Arber, iv. 119], and was apparently still printing in 1626 [Arber, iv. 161]. Sir John Lambe in his notes made in 1635 states in one place that George Purslowe succeeded Simon Stafford "about 5 yeeres since [*i.e.*, about 1630], and in another that Purslowe bought the business in 1614 [Arber, iii. 701, 703]. The first is probably the more correct statement.

STAFFORD (THOMAS), printer at Amsterdam, 1640. He printed a *Bible* (*Genevan Version, Tomson's Revision*) in 1640, according to the copy printed at Edinburgh by A. Hart in 1610 [B.M., p. 161].

STAM (JAN FREDERICKSZ), printer at Amsterdam, 1629–57; The Hope, by the South Church. In the years 1629–39 he printed about a dozen books or pamphlets in English, including the *Psalms* with arguments by A. Top, 1629, J. Prempart's *Historical Relation of the siege of Busse* [*i.e.* Hertogenbosch], for H. Hondius, three tracts of William Prynne, and other religious pamphlets. [Ledeboer, *A.L.*, 162; Sayle, pp. 1431–2.]

STANDISH (JOHN), bookseller in London, 1599–1608. Son of Henry Standish of Kingscliffe, Northampton, yeoman. Apprentice to William Cooke, citizen and stationer of London, for ten years from December 25th, 1576: took up his freedom January 16th, 158$\frac{6}{7}$ [Arber, ii. 75, 699]. On March 26th, 1604, he paid £10 in lieu of serving as Renter of the Company [Arber, ii. 837]. Standish was admitted into the Livery on July 1st, 1598 [Arber, ii. 873]. His first book entry occurs on April 14th, 1599, being Sir John Davies' *Nosce Teipsum*, and in the same year he published the *Hymns of Astrea* by the same writer. He served the office of Under Warden in 1607 and 1609. Standish died before January 20th, 1617, when his copyrights were transferred by his widow to Richard Hawkins [Arber, iii. 601]. His address has not been found.

STANSBY (WILLIAM), printer and bookseller in London, 1597–1639; Cross Keys at St. Paul's Wharf [Windet's shop]. Son of Richard Stansby of Exeter, cutler. Apprentice to John Windet, stationer of London, for seven years from Christmas, 1590 [Arber, ii. 173]. Admitted a freeman January 7th, 159$\frac{8}{7}$ [Arber, ii. 717], and appears to have been taken into partnership by his former master, at whose death about 1615, he succeeded to the business [Arber, iii. 701]. His first book entry occurs on April 28th, 1597 [Arber, iii. 83]. He entered nothing else until April 1st, 1611, after which date until 1635 the entries under his name are continuous. Stansby never appears to have held any office in the Company, but he is frequently mentioned in the wills of other stationers and was a man of considerable position in the trade. On February 23rd, 162$\frac{5}{6}$, the widow of Thomas Snodham transferred all her copyrights to William Stansby. These copies had previously belonged to Thomas East, and included all his music books. The transfer fills more than two pages of the Register. William Stansby died some time in 1638 or the beginning of 1639, and on March 4th, 163$\frac{8}{9}$, his widow assigned her copyrights to George Bishop [Arber, iv. 459].

STATIONERS (THE COMPANY OF), London. The Company of Stationers was not only a guild for the protection and welfare of its members, it was and still is a large trading concern. From the day of its incorporation it became from one cause and another the possessor of certain copyrights. Others it bought or obtained by Act of Parliament, and in this way created

the various "stocks" which were known as The Ballad Stock, The Bible Stock, the Irish Stock, the Latin Stock, and the English Stock. Two of these, the Latin Stock and the Irish Stock, proved failures, and after involving the shareholders in heavy losses, were abandoned. During the reign of Elizabeth the Company claimed the right of printing *Bibles*. The matter was referred to the High Commissioners, who gave Richard Jugge the sole right of printing the *Bible* in quarto and the *Testament* in decimo sexto; and the Company the right of printing all other *Bibles* and *Testaments*; but Richard Jugge might also print all these other *Bibles* and *Testaments* [C. R. Rivington, *Records of the Stationers Co.* (in Arber, v.), p. xlviii]. The English Stock took its beginning from the patent granted to the Company by King James I in 1603 for the printing of *Primers* and other books [P.R., 1 Jac. No. 1619. Part 13]. This grant was renewed in 1615. [As to the Latin and Irish Stocks, *see* the *Library*, July, 1907, pp. 286–97, and January, 1909, p. 105.]

STATIONERS (THE SOCIETY OF), printers at Dublin, 1618–? 1640. The members of the Stationers' Company who came over to Dublin in 1618 were Felix Kingston and Thomas Downes. The latter resided in Dublin and described himself as of that city "Stationer." The only agents or Factors of the Society here were Robert Young (probably), and William Bladen. The latter purchased the Patent Rights and Stock in or about 1640, *after* which date his name appears in imprints. There was a considerable output from the "Dublin" Press of the Society of Stationers, judging by the works bearing their local imprints. Usher in one of his published Letters states that the Stationers' Company had sent over and were setting up in Dublin a press and would shortly print one of his works. [E. R. McC. Dix, *Earliest Dublin Printers and The Company of Stationers in London*, in *Transactions* of the Bibliographical Society (1904).]

STEELE (   ), bookseller at Nantwich in Cheshire, 1633. Mentioned in a return of booksellers who sold William Prynne's *Histrio-Mastix* in 1633 [*Documents relating to W. Prynne*, Camden Soc., p. 60].

STELL (HANS or JOHN), (?) bookseller in London, 1569–85; Duke of Norfolk's Place by Cree Church. In 1568 this stationer and Arnold Vaukyll, both born in Antwerp, were committed to the Poultry Compter by

the Mayor, for causing a book to be printed on the tyranny of the Duke of Alva [Arber, ii. 745]. In 1578 the printing by Richard Schilders of a book for Stell was stopped on tbe ground that both were aliens [Worman, *Alien Members*, pp. 64, 65]. Stell was the publisher of P. van Marnix' *Beehive of the Romishe Church*, 1579–80.

STEMPE (JOHN), bookseller in London, 1628. Took up his freedom June 21st, 1627 [Arber, iii. 686]. In 1628 he published a sermon by John Davenant, Bishop of Salisbury. His address is unknown.

STEPHENS (PHILEMON), *see* Plomer, *Dictionary*.

STEPNEY or STEPNETH (JOHN), bookseller in London, 1609–12; The Crane at the West End of St. Paul's. Son of Frauncis Stepney of Hatfield, co. Hertford, yeoman. Apprentice to Gregory Seton for eight years from March 25th, 1595 [Arber, ii. 201]. He made his first book entry on December 14th, 1609 [Arber, iii. 425]. Published B. Jonson's *Alchemist*, 1612, C. Tourneur's *Atheist's Tragedy*, 1611, and *A true and sincere declaration of the purpose and ends of the Plantation begun in Virginia*, 1610, and entered, on May 15th, 1612, Ben Jonson's *Epigrams* [Arber, iii. 485].

STEPNEY (JOHN), stationer in Dublin, 1632. Admitted to the franchise of the city of Dublin in July, 1632.

STEVENSON (RICHARD), bookseller in London, 1633–40. Took up his freedom in the Company of Stationers on November 25th, 1633. Stevenson made his first entry in the Registers on March 20th, 1640, and his last on June 12th in the same year. [Arber, iii. 687; iv. 503, 512.]

STIRROPP (THOMAS), bookseller in London, 1576–1600; The George in St. Paul's Churchyard. Thomas Stirropp became a freeman of the Company of Stationers on January 16th, 156$\frac{0}{1}$, and was admitted to the Livery during the year ending July 10th, 1582 [Arber, i. 160, 493]. He was elected Under Warden of the Company for the years 1593 and 1594, and Senior Warden in the years 1596 and 1598. The first book entry under his name occurs on October 29th, 1576, and the last on November 6th, 1599 [Arber, ii. 304; iii. 150]. He died before April 7th, 1600, when his widow presented an apprentice for his freedom [Arber, ii. 725].

STOLZENBERGER (JOHN NICHOL:), printer at Frankfurt a. M., 1628. In this year he printed *Characters and Diversitie of Letters* by J. T. de Bry for William Fitzer [Sayle, p. 1494; B.M. p. 627].

STRINGER (HENRY), patentee, 1597. He was the Queen's footman. On January 25th, 1597, the reversion of Thomas Marshe's privilege for grammar books was granted to him for fourteen years [*State Papers, Dom., Eliz.*, vol. 262]. Together with Robert Dexter he entered these books in the Registers on July 4th of the same year [Arber, iii. 87].

STUCKEY (THOMAS), (?) bookseller in London, 1581–96. This stationer, who was the son of Richard Stuckey, is found taking apprentices from July 4th, 1581, to June 23rd, 1593 [Arber, ii. 105, 186]. No book has been found bearing his imprint. Thomas Stuckey died in the latter part of March, 1596, his will being proved in the Archdeaconry of London on April 1st, 1596. He left no children, but made a bequest of £20 to the Company of Stationers, to be lent out yearly to four young men who were freemen of the Company [Archdeaconry of London, Register 5. 45].

STUFFOLDE, *see* Cavey.

STUNSTALL (ADAM), bookseller in London, 1628. Named in a list of second-hand booksellers who in 1628 were ordered to submit a catalogue of their books to the Archbishop of Canterbury [*Dom. S. Papers, Chas. I*, vol. 117 (9)].

SUDBURY (JOHN), bookseller in London, 1610–15; (1) The White Horse, Pope's Head Alley, 1611; (2) Pope's Head Palace, 1615. He was partner with George Humble [*q.v.*] in John Speed's *Theatre of the Empire of Great Britaine*, 1611 (some maps dated 1610); also in some description of the separate counties dated 1615 [B.M. 796. a. 1]. Nothing seems to be known of him.

SUTTON (BARTHOLOMEW), bookseller in London, 1609; St. Paul's Churchyard. Son of Bartholomew Sutton, citizen and draper of London. Apprentice for eight years to Edward Whyte, stationer of London, from December 25th, 1601; took up his freedom on January 18th, 1608 [Arber, ii. 255; iii. 683]. Made his first book entry in partnership with William

Barrenger on March 3rd, 160$\frac{8}{9}$ [Arber, iii. 403]. Amongst his publications was Ben Jonson's *Case is alterd*, 1609, and Barnabe Rich's *Short survey of Ireland*, 1609.

SUTTON (EDWARD), *see* Duff, *Century*.

SUTTON (HENRY), *see* Duff, *Century*.

SUTTON (JOAN), bookseller in London, 1569–85; (?) The Cradle in Lombard Street. Widow of Edward Sutton, stationer. In 1569 she took as apprentice William Kynge [Arber, i. 397]. She afterwards married Dunstan Whapland, stationer [Arber, ii. 673].

SWAIN (ROBERT), senior, bookseller in London, 1621–32; The Bible, Britain's Burse. Took up his freedom in the Company of Stationers, September 1st, 1617 [Arber, iii. 684], and made his first entry in the Registers on September 18th, 1621, and his last on December 20th, 1629 [Arber, iv. 59, 224]. Robert Swain died before February 6th, 163$\frac{1}{2}$, when Martha Swain, presumably his widow, made over one of her copyrights to Richard Royston [Arber, iv. 271].

SWAIN (ROBERT), junior, *see* Plomer, *Dictionary*.

SWINHOWE (GEORGE), stationer of London, 1589–1637. Son of William Swynnowe, late of Wadworthe, co. York, gentleman. Apprentice to Christopher Barker, the Queen's printer, for seven years from June 3rd, 1582. This entry was not made until May 2nd, 1586, for which Barker was fined xxs. [Arber, ii. 139, 858]. Swinhowe was admitted a freeman of the Company on June 26th, 1589, and quickly rose to a high position, being admitted to the Livery on July 3rd, 1602, and serving as Under Warden in the years 1615–16 and again in 1617–18. He was Senior Warden in the years 1619–20 and again in 1621–2. He was three times Master of the Company, in the years 1623–4, 1625–6 and 1630–1. Although no books are found with his imprint or entered in the Registers under his name, he is known to have been associated in 1609 with John Norton, George Bishop and others, in the purchase of a large stock of *Bibles* and service books from Robert Barker, the King's printer [Exchequer, Bills and Answers, James I, London and Middlesex, No. 1005]. Swinhowe also held shares in the English and Latin stocks of the Company and in 1637, after the failure of the latter venture, he brought an action in the

Court of Chancery against his fellow shareholders in respect to money borrowed to finance the business. Some of the defendants in their answers declared that George Swinhowe and others converted the money so raised to their own uses. [*Library*, July, 1907.] His place of business is unknown.

SYLVIUS (WILLIAM), printer at Antwerp, 1561–79, and at Leyden, 1577–80; At Antwerp: (1) In de Cammerpoortbrugge, In den Gulden Engel; (2) in de Stentelstraete, In den Gulden Engel, 1572–9. He was born at 's Hertogenbosch, received into the St. Lucasgild in 1561, and became Royal Printer. By 1577 he had apparently opened a house at Leyden, and in this year was appointed printer to the University of that town. He seems however not to have resided there, at least until 1579. He was presumably dead in 1582 when his Leyden house was purchased by Plantin. At Antwerp he printed in 1565 Harding's *Answer to Jewel's Challenge* [Herbert, p. 1609; Sayle, p. 1367] and in 1566 T. Heskyns' *Parliament of Christ* [Herbert, p. 1617; Sayle, u.s.]. His device was an angel with book and scythe, with and without the motto "Scrutamini." [Ledeboer, *A.L.*, p. 157; Olthoff, pp. 97–8.]

SYM (JAMES), bookbinder in Perth, 1595. He was a burgess of Perth, and his will was registered on January 21st, 1595–6. [Commissariot of Edinburgh: Register of Testaments. *British Record Society*, 1897.]

SYMCOCK (THOMAS), patentee, 1619–29. Nothing whatever is known of the history of this patentee prior to 1618. In October of that year he applied for a patent for the sole printing of all things that were printed on one side only. When it is remembered that all the best paying work in the printing trade was already in the hands of a few privileged stationers, either by Royal appointment or special grants, and that the remainder had to be content with jobbing work, such as was included in the term "things printed on one side only," this attempt to rob them of the bulk of their trade was one of the most daring and merciless attempts to secure a monopoly of which the annals of the Stationers' Company furnish an instance. Unfortunately it was for a time successful. The letters patent were granted to Roger Wood and Thomas Symcock for thirty-one years at a rental of £10 per annum, but they were never entered on the patent roll. Nevertheless Symcock and his partner promptly acted on them. Symcock

bought a press and letters and appointed assigns, of whom no doubt Roger Wood was one, to work the patent. The Company of Stationers at once took steps to protect its poorer brethren, by petitioning the King for the withdrawal of the patent; but it was not until August, 1622, that the King directed a letter to the Lord Chief Justice of the King's Bench instructing him to peruse the patent, nor is there any evidence available, that anything was done at that time. [State Papers Domestic, Docquet.] In the fourth year of Charles I [*i.e.*, 1628] the patent was renewed and was at once made the subject of an action in the Court of Chancery in which the Company of Stationers were plaintiffs, and Thomas Symcock defendant. The Company also petitioned the King and moved Parliament in the matter. They succeeded in getting the King to appoint a committee to examine the whole question. This committee reported that the patent had been surreptitiously procured upon untrue suggestion, upon which the Court of Chancery on June 30th, 1629, decreed that the patent should be cancelled, but that Symcock should be recompensed for his expenses in buying a press and letters. [Chancery Proceedings, Charles I, S. 66/13; Chancery Decree Roll 295.] Symcock does not appear to have printed much under this patent.

SYMMES, *see* Simmes.

SYMPSON, *see* Simpson.

SYMSON (JOHN), bookseller and bookbinder in Edinburgh, 1592–1604. He was one of the seven booksellers of Edinburgh who, in February, 1592, complained against John Norton of London for retailing books within the burgh. "John Symsoun" is named among the debtors in E. Cathkin's inventory in 1601; and "Johne Symsoun, buikbinder," was a debtor to A. Hart in 1604. [Aldis, *Scottish* Books, 121; Lee, *Add Mem.*, 171; *Bannatyne Miscell.* ii. 231, 239.]

TAILER (W.), (?) bookseller in London, 1596. In this year Simon Harward's *Encheiridion Morale* was printed by Edmund Bollifant "Impensis W. Tailer." Nothing seems to be otherwise known of him.

TALLIS (THOMAS), patentee, 1575–85. A well-known musician. In 1575 together with William Byrd he was granted a monopoly of music-printing for twenty-one years. He however died in 1585, before half the term had expired. [*D.N.B.*; Herbert, p. 1643.]

TAPP (JOHN), bookseller in London, 1600–31; (1) On Tower Hill, near the Bulwark Gate; (2) Saint Magnus Corner, London Bridge. Originally a member of the Drapers' Company, John Tapp was transferred to the Company of Stationers on June 3rd, 1600 [Arber, ii. 725]. His first book entry in the Registers occurs on October 2nd, 1600 [Arber, iii. 173]. After carrying on business for some years on Tower Hill, he moved into Hugh Astley's premises at Saint Magnus Corner. He dealt largely in nautical books. His last book entry is found on March 17th, 162$\frac{3}{4}$ [Arber, iv. 114]. John Tapp died before August 1st, 1631, when his widow Eliz. Tapp transferred his copyrights to Joseph Hurlock [Arber, iv. 258].

TAUNTON (HENRY), bookseller in London, 1634–8; St. Dunstan's Churchyard, Fleet Street. Took up his freedom June 30th, 1631 [Arber, iii. 687]. His first book entry, a share in George Withers' *Emblems*, was made on March 10th, 163$\frac{3}{4}$, [Arber, iv. 314], and his last on April 8th, 1636 [Arber, iv. 359]. In 1638 he issued a second edition of John Preston's *Doctrine of the Saints Infirmities*.

TAYLOR (HENRY), bookseller or printer at Douai, 1624. In this year he issued Edward Kinsman's *Appendix of Saints lately canonized* [B.M., p. 913], in the preface of which he speaks of having "reprinted" the work. He is not given by Duthillœul, and nothing seems to be known of him.

TAYLOR (RICHARD), bookbinder in London, 1601–29. Son of John Taylor of Barnewell, co. Northampton, husbandman. Apprentice to Richard Tommes, stationer of London, and also a bookbinder, for nine years from Michaelmas, 1594 [Arber, ii. 192]. Admitted a freeman of the Company on October 11th, 1601 [Arber, ii. 730]. On October 4th, 1605, he was fined tenpence for an offence not stated [Arber, ii. 840]. In 1616 he was mentioned in a suit in Chancery as binding books for the booksellers Bonham Norton, John Norton and John Bill [Chan. Proc. Jas. I. B. 35. 10]. Richard Taylor died about May 28th, 1629.

TEAGE (JOHN), bookseller in London, 1620–3; In St. Paul's Churchyard, at the sign of the Ball, or the Golden Ball. Took up his freedom on September 27th, 1619 [Arber, iii. 685]. His first book entry occurs on June 12th, 1620 [Arber, iii. 675], and his last on July 10th, 1622 [Arber, iv. 74].

TÉLU (PIERRE), printer at Douai, 1618; At the sign of the nativity. In 1618 he printed *The safeguard from shipwreck* by I. P. [B.M., p. 1180; Sayle, p. 1488]. He died in or before 1622, when his widow is found printing. [Duthillœul, p. 213.]

THACKWELL ( ), printer in Wales, ? 1588. Only known from a passage in Martin Marprelate's *Epistle* [ed. Arber, p. 22]: "Knaue Thackwell the printer, which printed popishe and trayterous welshe bookes in wales . . . is at libertie to walke where he will, and permitted to make the most he could of his presse and letters: whereas Robert Waldegraue dares not shew his face . . . for printing of bookes which toucheth the bishops Myters." Martin's charge is referred to in Cooper's *Admonition* [ed. Arber, p. 34], and *Hay any Work for Cooper* [ed. Petheram, p. 65], but these give us no further information save that Thackwell was "knowen and liuing" in 1589.

THOMAS (JOHN), bookseller in London, 1582–7. The identity of this stationer is not quite clear. He could hardly have been the John Thomas, son of John Thomas of Southwark, smith, who was apprentice to Christopher Butler for ten years from May 26th, 1577, as he did not take up his freedom until his full time had expired on July 31st, 1587 [Arber, ii. 77, 701], whereas the John Thomas now under notice took his first apprentice, William Erle, on March 29th, 1582 [Arber, ii. 111], and was admitted into the Livery in 1585 [Arber, i. 508]. He died some time at the end of the year 1587 or the beginning of 1588, as his will was proved in the Court of the Dean and Chapter of St. Paul's on March 1st, $158\frac{7}{8}$. He left four sons, one of whom was named John. Ralph Newbery was his brother-in-law, and to William Erle, his apprentice, he left twenty shillings [Dean and Chapter of St. Paul's, Book B, fol. 310]. His widow afterwards married a man of the name of Hill [Arber, ii. 709].

THOMAS (JOHN), *see* Plomer, *Dictionary*.

THOMAS (THOMAS), printer in Cambridge, 1583–8; In the Regent Walk, opposite to the west door of Great St. Mary's Church. He was born in London, December 25th, 1553, educated at Eton and King's College, Cambridge (admitted scholar August 24th, 1571), where he became a fellow August 24th, 1574. He proceeded B.A. in 1575 and commenced M.A. in 1579. By a Grace of May 3rd, 1583, he was appointed Printer to the University, and at once began to print a work by W. Whitaker, regius professor of divinity. His press however was seized by the Stationers' Company, who refused to recognize the validity of his appointment. By the agency of Lord Burghley matters were arranged and from 1584 to 1588 Thomas printed at least 17 books, most of them Puritan in tone or associated with the Continental reformers such as an English translation (now apparently lost) of Travers' *Ecclesiastica Disciplina*, and one of the *Harmonia Confessionum Fidei*. He also printed an edition of the *Dialectica* of Pierre de la Ramée (Ramus) by (Sir) William Temple in 1584. He was a scholar of distinction and author of a Latin Dictionary which, first published in 1587, went through a very large number of editions. He died at Cambridge, August 9th, 1588. [R. Bowes, *Univ. Printers*, 292–4; *D.N.B.*; Mullinger, *Cambridge*, ii. 292–7; 320–1.]

THOMASON (GEORGE), *see* Plomer, *Dictionary*.

THORP (GILES), printer at Amsterdam, 1608–19. In 1608, 1609 and 1613 he printed three books by Henry Ainsworth, in 1612 Ainsworth's version of *The Psalms in Prose and Metre*, with musical notes [B.M., p. 177; Hazlitt, I. 5], and in 1619 John Harrison's *Messiah already come* [B.M., p. 774]. He is not given by Ledeboer.

THORPE or THROPPE (RICHARD), stationer and bookseller of Chester, 1635–(?), younger brother of Thomas Thorpe, was a son of Thomas Thorp an innkeeper of Barnet in Middlesex. He was apprenticed in 1596 to Robert Ensor for seven years, but is not mentioned again in the Registers. In 1635–6 he was admitted to the freedom of the city of Chester, and in the Chester Stationers' Company Registers for 1637 is the entry "Richard Throppe Stationer: and by extraordinary favour was admitted a brother upon ye 22 day of February 1637, and was never wth any of our Company but at London, and payd for his fine xvi^d." His two sons William and Richard succeeded him as stationers in Chester.

THORPE (THOMAS), bookseller in London, 1603–25. Son of Thomas Thorpe, or Throp, of Barnet, co. Middlesex, innholder. Apprentice to Richard Watkins, stationer of London, for nine years from Midsummer, 1584; and was made a freeman of the Company on February 4th, $159\frac{3}{4}$

[Arber, ii. 124, 713]. Thorpe's first book entry, made in partnership with William Aspley, was Marston's *Malcontent*, entered on July 5th, 1604 [Arber, iii. 268]. It was printed by Simmes for Aspley in the same year. He continued to publish plays for some time, and was also the publisher of Shakespeare's *Sonnets*, which he entered on May 20th, 1609 [Arber, iii. 410]. The last entry under his name is that of November 3rd, 1624, when he and Thomas Blount assigned over to Samuel Vicars their rights in Christopher Marlowe's *Hero and Leander* [Arber, iv. 126]. His address has not been found.

THRALE (RICHARD), *see* Plomer, *Dictionary*.

THREIPLAND (JOHN), bookseller in Edinburgh, *see* Plomer, *Dictionary*.

TIDDER (JOHN), *see* Porter (John), bookseller in Cambridge.

TIAS, *see* Tyas.

TILLETSON (WILLIAM), *see* Telotson.

TISDALE (JOHN), *see* Duff, *Century*.

TOBIE (GEORGE), (?) printer in London, 1594. Certain copies of R. Holland's *Holie Historie of Our Lord . . . Jesus Christs natiuitie, &c.*, 1594, are stated to be "Printed by George Tobie." The book appears however to have been printed by Richard Field, to whom it was licensed and whose name appears in the imprint of other copies [Hazlitt, I. 220]. Nothing seems to be known of Tobie.

TOLDERVEY (WILLIAM), bookseller in Oxford, 1617–18. Admitted bookseller to the University March 21st, $161\frac{7}{8}$ [Clark, *Register*, ii. 1. 321]. He committed suicide. His goods were valued at £62 9s. 8d. on June 14th, 1619 [Gibson, *Oxford Wills*, p. 51].

TOMBES, *see* Tomes or Tommes.

TOMES (HENRY), bookseller in London, 1598–1607; (1) The White Bear at St. Sepulchre's door; (2) Gray's Inn Gate. This stationer was in all probability father or brother of Richard Tommes, or Tomes, who gave his address as in St. Faith's parish. Henry Tomes is found taking an apprentice in February, $159\frac{7}{8}$, but he did not make any entry in the Registers until June 4th, 1604 [Arber, iii. 265]. His name does not occur in the Registers after November 12th in that year, but in 1607 he published George Wilson's *Commendation of Cockes and Cock-Fighting* [Hazlitt, H. 659].

TOMMES, TOMES or TOMBES (RICHARD), bookseller and bookbinder in London, 1593–1631; Parish of St. Faith. Son of John Tomes of Stretton upon Fosse, co. Warwick, mason. Apprentice for seven years from November 8th, 1585, to Thomas Stirroppe and took up his freedom on January 9th, $159\frac{2}{3}$ [Arber, ii. 136, 711]. Presented his first apprentice on June 3rd, 1594 [Arber, ii. 192]. The only other notices concerning him in the Registers are a note of a fine paid by him in 1601 for not presenting an apprentice, and another for quarrelling with a brother stationer, Thomas Ensor, in August, 1604 [Arber, ii. 833, 839]. In 1616 he is mentioned as binding books for John Norton, Bonham Norton and John Bill [Chan. Proc., Jas. I, B 35. 10]. By his will proved in the Court of the Dean and Chapter of St. Paul's on November 11th, 1631, he left to his widow Anne his house in the parish of St. Faith and a house and garden in Moorfields. To his son John a house at Stretton or Stratton upon Fosse in the county of Warwick and to his children John and Anne one-third of his goods and personal estate, which were valued at £127 17s. 2d. [Dean and Chapter of St. Paul's, Book D, fol. 406]. He was probably a relative of Henry Tommes, or Tomes.

TOTTELL (RICHARD), *see* Duff, *Century*.

TOWREOLDE (WILLIAM), bookseller in London, 1578–84; Adjoining to the little Conduit in Cheap. Son of Thomas Toworolde of Nantwich, Cheshire, husbandman. Apprentice to Richard Watkins, stationer of London, for eight years from March 25th, 1570: took up his freedom October 2nd, 1578 [Arber, i. 396; ii. 679]. Amongst his publications was a quarto pamphlet entitled *The true description of the burning of Nantwich*, 1584, which is the only publication entered to him in the Registers, but he also published Edmund Bicknoll's *Sword against swearing*, without date, but ascribed to 1580.

TOY (ELIZABETH), *see* Duff, *Century*.

TOY (HUMPHREY), bookseller in London, 1560–78; The Helmet, St. Paul's Churchyard. Son of Robert Toy, printer (1542–56): matriculated as a sizar of Queens' College, Cambridge, November, 1551 [Cooper, *Athen.*

Cantab. i. 4]. Humphrey took up his freedom in the Company of Stationers on March 11th, 155$\frac{7}{8}$, and made his first entry in the Registers on August 30th, 1560 [Arber, i. 71, 150]. He was admitted to the Livery on July 6th, 1561 [Arber, i. 161]. His father left him the reversion of the premises known by the sign of the Bell, after his mother's death. Meanwhile he set up in business at the sign of the Helmet. In 1564 Humphrey Toy brought an action in the Court of Chancery against Robert Leche, Chancellor of West Chester, to recover the balance of a sum of £50 6s. 8d., owed to him for copies of *The second tome of Homelyes with the boke of Articles* [Chan. Proc. Series II, Bundle 177, 93]. He married Margaret the daughter of James Revell, surveyor of works, who nominated Toy one of the overseers of his will [P.C.C., 20, Stevenson]. He served the office of Under Warden in the year 1571–2, and died on October 16th, 1577. [W. Barret, *History of Bristol*, edition 1789, p. 442.]

TOY (ROBERT), *see* Duff, *Century*.

TRESSELL (CHARLES), typefounder in London, 1566–83; St. Albans. Wood Street. In the return of aliens for the year 1571 he is thus described: "eldest son of Adrian Tressell schoolmaster, Dutch, a graver of letters for printers; they have dwelled in and about London five years" [Worman, *Alien Members*, p. 66].

TRIPLET (ROBERT), bookseller and bookbinder in London, 1604–24; Distaff Lane, sign of the Aqua Vite Still near Old Fish Street. Son of Richard Triplett of Hampton Gay, Oxford, husbandman. Apprentice to Thomas Middleton for seven years from June 24th, 1592, and admitted a freeman of the Company of Stationers on January 17th, 160$\frac{2}{3}$ [Arber, ii. 181, 734]. Robert Triplet was the compiler and publisher of small pocket books and writing tables containing much valuable information such as tables of weights and measures, values of coinage, etc. One of these is described at some length by Herbert [p. 1762], and copies of two of the writing tables, for the years 1604 and 1611, are preserved at the British Museum.

TRIPP (HENRY), (?) bookseller in London, 1599–1609. On June 26th, 1599, Henry Tripp was transferred from the Goldsmiths' to the Stationers' Company and was made a freeman [Arber, ii. 723]. On January 16th,

160$\frac{8}{9}$, he entered in the Registers Otho Casman's *Ethickes and Oeconomykes*, which he had translated [Arber, iii. 399]. He was possibly the son of the Rev. Henry Tripp.

TROGNESIUS (JOACHIM), printer and bookseller at Antwerp, 1587–1624; (1) Op onser liever vrouwen Kerckhof, In 't gulden Cruys, 1609; (2) Op 't klein Kerckhof en Merckmerdt. He was admitted to the St. Lucasgild in 1589. In 1587 he issued W. Allen's *Letter . . . concerning the yielding up of Daventry* [B.M., p. 34] and in 1593–6 three other works in English including W. Rainold's *Treatise concerning the Sacrament* [B.M., p. 1299]. He died in 1624. [Olthoff, p. 101; Herbert, pp. 1730–1.]

TROTS (FRANCIS), bookseller and bookbinder in London, 1583–5; Algate Ward. Described as a Fleming, and as both a bookseller and bookbinder in 1583 [Worman, *Alien Members*, p. 66].

TRUCK (   ), (?) bookseller in London, 1624; Southwark. Mentioned in John Gee's *Foot out of the Snare*, 1624, as a disperser of popish books. Described as "Mother Truck dwelling in Southwarke."

TRUNDELL, *see* Trundle.

TRUNDLE (JOHN), bookseller in London, 1603–26; In Barbican at the sign of Nobody, 1613. Son of John Trundle or Trundell of Barnet, Herts, yeoman. Apprentice for eight years to Ralph Hancock, stationer of London, from June 24th, 1589: took up his freedom on October 29th, 1597 [Arber, ii. 168, 270]. His first book entry is found on July 27th, 1603 [Arber, iii. 243]. Trundle dealt in ballads, news-books, plays and ephemeral literature. He was associated with Nicholas Ling in the publication of the first quarto of *Hamlet* in 1603. The last entry under his name is found on July 18th, 1626 [Arber, iv. 163]. On June 1st, 1629, Margaret Trundle, widow of John Trundle, assigned her copyrights to John Wright, senior, John Grismand and others. In 1636 a bookseller of this name had a shop in Paris and it is referred to in a letter from Sir Kenelm Digby to Edward, second Viscount Conway [see *Library*, April, 1904, pp. 158–72], but nothing is known of any other John Trundle.

TUCK (LAURENCE), printer in London, 1586. In 1586 Laurence Tuck shared a printing press with Robert Bourne and Henry Jefferson, which was seized by the Company of Stationers and defaced for printing

Grammers contrary to the decree of the Star Chamber, and the parties disabled from ever keeping a printing house of their own, or from printing otherwise than as journeymen [Records of the Company of Stationers].

TUCKER (JOHN), printer of Catholic books, 1581. Arrested at the time of the raid at Stonor Park; *see* Brinckley (S.) [*Acts of the Privy Council, New Ser.*, xiii. 177].

TURK (JOHN), *see* Duff, *Century*.

TURNER (THOMAS), bookseller in London, 1577–92; Guildhall Gate. Son of Richard Turner of Sheffield, Yorks, husbandman. Apprentice to Thomas Marshe, stationer of London, for eight years from November 1st, 1564 [Arber, i. 255]. Turner made his first entry in the Registers on July 8th, 1577 [Arber, ii. 316]. The last heard of him is on July 1st, 1592, when he presented one of his apprentices for freedom [Arber, ii. 710].

TURNER (WILLIAM), printer in Oxford, *see* Plomer, *Dictionary*.

TUTHILL (HENDRIK), bookseller at Rotterdam, 1638. In this year *The Book of Psalms in English Metre* was printed for him [Sayle, p. 1503]. His widow is found printing in 1649–50 [Ledeboer, p. 172].

TWYFORD (HENRY), *see* Plomer, *Dictionary*.

TYAS or TIAS (THOMAS), stationer in London, 1588–91. Son of Thomas Tyas of Heckleton, co. York, yeoman. Apprentice to Christopher Barker, stationer of London, for eight years from Christmas, 1580. He appears to have married Joane, the widow of Henry Johnson, stationer. His will was proved in the Commissary of London on April 14th, 1591. In it he mentions his two sons, Richard Johnson, alias Tias, and Charles Tias. The latter was probably the bookseller on London Bridge, 1656–64; *see* Plomer, *Dictionary*. [Com. of London, 1590, f. 332.]

TYLER (EVAN), printer in Edinburgh, *see* Plomer, *Dictionary*.

TYMME (WILLIAM), bookseller in London, 1601–15; Flower de luce and Crowne, Paternoster Row, near Cheapside. Son of John Tymme of Kemberton, Gloucester, yeoman. Apprentice to Humfrey Bate for eight years from Christmas, 1588: admitted a freeman of the Company of Stationers on March 26th, 1596 [Arber, ii. 157, 716]. His first book entry, Gerard de Malynes' *Historye of Saint George*, was made on May 13th, 1601

[Arber, iii. 184]. He is last heard of on April 28th, 1615, when in company with John Robinson he entered certain of Dr. Hull's sermons [Arber, iii. 566].

UDALL (   ), bookseller in London, 1624; Gunpowder Alley. Mentioned in John Gee's *Foot out of the Snare*, 1624, as a disperser of popish books. He may have been a relative of Lawrence Udall, who took up his freedom as a stationer on August 1st, 1636 [Arber, iii. 688].

UNCKELS (JOHANN KARL), bookseller at Frankfurt a. M., 1619. In this year *A book of Arms* in seven languages, including English, by Georgetta de Montenay was printed for him [Sayle, p. 1494].

UPHILL (ANTHONY), *see* Plomer, *Dictionary*.

UPTON (JAMES), bookseller in London, 1630. Took up his freedom December 7th, 1629 [Arber, iii. 686]. The only book entry under his name in the Registers is Baptist Goodall's *Triall of Travaile*, entered on February 4th, 16$\frac{29}{30}$ [Arber, iv. 227].

USHER (JOHN), (?) publisher at Dublin, 1571. His name appears on two works in Irish issued in this year: a broadside containing a poem on the Last Judgement, the imprint of which states that it was put into print by Mr. John Usher in Dublin above the Bridge [Hazlitt, VII. 300], and an *Alphabet and Catechism* described as printed at the cost of John Usher, Alderman. It is probable that he had no connection with the booktrade, and simply provided money for the printing of these works. [*See* an article by E. R. McC. Dix on William Kearney in *Proceedings of R. Irish Academy*, xxviii, section C, no. 8.]

VALENTIN (FLORENT), bookseller at Rouen, 1555–9. *See* Duff, *Century*; Herbert, p. 1589; Frère, *Manuel*, p. 587.

VAN METEREN, *see* Meteren.

VAUKYLL, *see* Gulke (A. van).

VAUTROLLIER (JAKLIN or JACQUELIN), printer in London, 1588; Blackfriars. Widow of Thomas Vautrollier. By an order of the Company of Stationers she was prohibited from printing any books whatsoever, her husband not being a printer at the time of his death, and because she was debarred by the decree of the Star Chamber. In 1588 however the Company allowed her to finish a leaf of the Greek Testament and also Luther's *Commentary upon Galatians*; but not to undertake anything more until she procured authority to print according to the decree of the Star Chamber [Records of the Stationers' Company]. Within a year of her first husband's death she married Richard Field his apprentice [Arber, iii. 702].

VAUTROLLIER (MANASSES), stationer and bookbinder, (?) London, Cambridge and Edinburgh, 1587–1634. Son of Thomas Vautrollier, printer, who at his death in 1587 bequeathed him the printing press and its appurtenances which he had brought back with him from Scotland [Plomer, *Wills*, p. 27]. In 1592–4 Manasses Vautrollier is found living at Cambridge as a privileged stationer of the University [Bowes, *Univ. Printers*, 336]. Again in 1633–4 he is met with as a bookbinder in Edinburgh, where a complaint is brought against him to the Privy Council for illegal caption [*Reg. P.C. Scot.*, 2nd Ser., v]. Richard Field who married the widow of Thomas Vautrollier, at his death in 1624 bequeathed Manasses Vautrollier a sum of forty shillings, and a release for debts [Plomer, *Wills*, pp. 50, 51]. [Worman, *Alien Members*, p. 68.]

VAUTROLLIER (THOMAS I), printer, bookseller and bookbinder in London and Edinburgh, 1562–87; London: Blackfriars. Thomas Vautrollier and his wife Jacqueline, or Jaklin, were Huguenot fugitives from France, who settled in England and took out letters of denization on March 9th, 1562 [Worman, *Alien Members*, pp. 67–8]. Vautrollier was admitted a brother of the Company of Stationers on October 2nd, 1564 [Arber, i. 279]. In 1567 he was joined with John Desserans as agent for Christopher Plantin. His first book entry in the Registers was made during the year ending July 22nd, 1570 [Arber, i. 417]. On April 18th, 1573, Vautrollier received letters patent permitting him to print Lodowick Lloyd's *Plutarch* [? *The Pilgrimage of Princes*], and on the 22nd of the same month another grant was made to him to print Aldus Manutius' Latin phrases and Sylva's *Cosmographia* for ten years. Further, on June 19th, 1574, letters patent were granted him to print certain Latin books including Beza's *Novum Testamentum* and the works of Ovid and Cicero for a period of ten years, and he was allowed six workmen, French or Dutch, for that period. [Arber, ii. 746, 886.] Referring to these patents, Christopher Barker in a report made in 1582, declared that Vautrollier "doth yet, neither great good nor great harme withal" [Arber, i. 144]. In 1579 Richard Field of Stratford on Avon was put over to Vautrollier for six years to learn the art of printing. Vautrollier was importing books into Scotland at least as early as April, 1580 [*see* Dickson and Edmond, p. 379], and in July of that year the General Assembly recommended that the question of granting him a license to print be considered [*ib.* 378], but no immediate action was taken in the matter, and it was not till 1584, when he fled to Scotland in order to avoid imprisonment for printing the writings of Giordano Bruno, that he set up a press in Edinburgh [Dickson and Edmond, p. 381]. He seems however to have kept his bookselling business there under the charge of his servant John Cowper, for on April 4th, 1582, a complaint was laid before the Town Council against Vautrollier and Cowper, for retailing books and binding them within the burgh, they being unfreemen [Dickson and Edmond, p. 349]. In answer to this charge Cowper appeared before the Council, and as Vautrollier did not appear it may be assumed that he was not in Edinburgh at that time. In a document supposed to belong to 1583, he was returned as having two presses in London [Arber, i. 248]. Vautrollier returned to London in 1586, and died in July, 1587, his will being dated the 10th and proved in the Court of the Commissary of London on the 22nd of that month. Vautrollier left four sons, Simeon, Manasses, Thomas and James. To his son Manasses he bequeathed the printing press which he had brought back from Scotland, "furnished with all her appurtenances, that is to saye, with fower chassis, and three Frisketts, two timpanes and a copper plate." The residue he left to his wife Jacqueline and his four children. This will settles once for all, that Vautrollier had no daughter and that Richard Field the apprentice married his widow, and thus secured a good business [Plomer, *Wills*, p. 27]. As a printer Thomas Vautrollier ranks above most of his contemporaries, both for the beauty of his types and the excellence of his press work. His device was an anchor held by a hand issuing from clouds, with two sprigs of laurel and the motto "Anchora Spei," the whole enclosed in an oval frame. It is found in various sizes and was afterwards used by his successor.

VAUTROLLIER (THOMAS II), bookseller in London, 1604–5. Son of Thomas Vautrollier, the Huguenot printer. Took up his freedom on May 7th, 1604 [Arber, ii. 737]. The only book known with his name is *Alberici Gentilis . . . Regales Disputationes tres*, which has the imprint "Londini Apud Thomam Vautrollerium MDCV."

VAVASOUR (NICHOLAS), *see* Plomer, *Dictionary*.

VEALE (ABRAHAM), *see* Duff, *Century*.

VELPIUS, *see* Antony.

VENGE (EDWARD), bookseller and printer in London, 1588–1605; (1) The Vine in Fleet Street; (2) Bishop's Hall, Stepney; (3) The Black Bull [? in Thames St.]. Son of Edward Venge of Reading, Berks, painter. Apprentice to Henry Carre, stationer of London, for nine years from Christmas, 1578: took up his freedom July 3rd, 1588 [Arber, ii. 703]. Edward Venge was one of the band of printers and booksellers who set themselves to oppose the privileged monopolists of the Company, and was frequently in trouble for printing other men's copies. In September, 1595, he was ordered to bring in to Stationers' Hall all the leaves that he had printed of the second impression of the *Catechism*, that is "The brief Catechisme with the A. B. C. Letany and other thinges inserted" and he gave a promise not to meddle with the printing, binding or stitching of the same in future [Arber, ii. 824], but on March 14th, 1596, there is an entry in the Registers of the Company showing that the searchers had discovered a press with "certayne pica and Romayne English and other letters," at a house called Bishop's Hall in the parish of Stepney, where Edward Venge and his complices had printed "the Primmer or book of private prayer." The press was ordered to be sawn in pieces and the letters melted [Stationers' Register B, fol. 462 verso: *Library*, July, 1903, pp. 236 *et seq.*]. The last entry in the Registers under his name is found on December 2nd, 1605 [Arber, iii. 306]. On March 15th, 1615/16, his widow transferred her rights in one of his copies to John Beale [Arber, iii. 584].

VENGE (WALTER), (?) bookseller in London, 1584–5; In Fleet Lane, over against the Maidenhead. Possibly another son of Edward Venge of Reading, and brother of Edward Venge [*q.v.*]. On the last day of September, 1584, he received licence to print Blagrave's *Mathematicall Jewel*, and on the 7th of the following January he entered a ballad [Arber, ii. 436, 439].

VERDON (ANDREW), stationer in Dublin, 1612. Admitted to the franchise of the city of Dublin in 1612.

VERNON (RICHARD), (?) bookseller in London, 1581; The Brazen Serpent in St. Paul's Churchyard. Apprentice to William Jones, but served out his time with Richard Day. Admitted a freeman of the Company on June 27th, 1580 [Arber, ii. 682]. In 1581 in partnership with T. Dawson he published a work called *The Jesuites Banner*.

VERSTEGEN, VERSTEGAN or ROWLANDS (RICHARD), printer at Antwerp, ? 1576–1603. He was born in London, entered at Christ Church, Oxford, 1565, but being a Catholic did not take a degree. Went to Antwerp soon after 1576, where he set up a printing press, printed many Catholic books [Gillow], and acted as agent for the transmission of books, letters, etc., to England. Some time between 1584 and 1588 he was imprisoned for a while at Paris. He afterwards returned to Antwerp, and in 1595 went to Spain, returning to Antwerp at the end of the year, where he is said to have died at the age of 87, about 1636. In 1603 there appeared as "Printed at Antwerp by Richard Vertegan" (*sic*), a work entitled *The First Part of the Resolution of Religion*, by R[ichard] B[roughton]. [Gillow, *Dict. of Catholics*; *D.N.B.*]

VERVLIET (DANIEL), printer and bookseller at Antwerp, 1564–after 1600; (1) Op de Lombaerde veste, In den Wolsack, 1565; (2) In de Cammerstraet, In de Schilt van Artoys, 1585. In 1600 he printed the second edition of the Rheims *New Testament*. His business was continued by his widow, who died in 1625. [Olthoff, p. 110.]

VESELER or VESELAER (JORIS or GEORGE), printer or bookseller at Amsterdam, 1618–28. In 1618 he issued John Paget's *Arrow against the separation of the Brownists* [B.M., p. 1187], and in 1621 *A Notable and wonderful sea-fight between two . . . Spanish ships and a small . . . English ship* [B.M., p. 1430]. [Ledeboer, *A.L.*, p. 179.]

VICARS (SAMUEL), (?) bookseller in London, 1624–5. Took up his freedom March 1st, 1619 [Arber, iii. 685]. On November 3rd, 1624, Edward Blount and Thomas Thorpe assigned over to him their interest in Christopher Marlowe's *Hero and Leander* [Arber, iv. 126]. Samuel Vicars died, probably of the plague, in 1625, when the copyright in the above book passed to the Company, and was by them transferred to Master Hawkins [Arber, iv. 147].

VINCENT (GEORGE), bookseller in London, 1595–1629; (1) The Hand in Hand in Wood Street, over against St. Michael's Church; (2) The Cross-Keys, St. Paul's Churchyard, 1627; (3) The Cross-Keys, St. Paul's Gate, 1629. Son of John Vincent of Pakington upon the Heath, co. Leicester, yeoman. Apprentice for eight years from Christmas, 1581, to Augustin Laughton, stationer of London: admitted to the freedom of the Company on June 25th, 1590 [Arber, ii. 112, 707]. George Vincent made his first entry in the Registers on October 15th, 1595 [Arber, iii. 50], but the earliest book found with his name on the imprint is a play entitled *A pleasant comedie, shewing the contention betweeen Liberalitie and Prodigalitie*, 1602, 4to [B.M., C. 34. b. 13]. He was the publisher of other plays, and some ballads and newsbooks, in which he was associated with William Blackwell. The last entry under George Vincent's name in the Registers was made on June 23rd, 1629 [Arber, iv. 214]. His widow Anne Vincent assigned her copyrights to Richard Thrale on April 28th, 1637.

VINCENT (JOHN), printer, 1601. Arrested in that year on his way to Ireland, and described as "practized in the printing and publishing of certaine seditious bookes" [*Acts of the Privy Council, New Ser.*, xxxii. 85].

VINCENTSZ or VINCENTEN (NICLAES), printer at Dort, 1612–32; Bij de Vis-merkt, In de Nieuwe-Drukkerij. In 1623 he printed, for George Waters, John Wodroephe's *The spared hours of a soldier in his travels.* [Ledeboer, *A.L.*, p. 179.]

VOLFEO (GIOVANNI), *see* Wolfe (John).

VOLMARE (WIDOW ANNE MARIE), printer at Würzburg, 1628. In this year she printed Alexander Baillie's *True Information of the unhallowed offspring . . . of our Scottish-Calvinian gospel* [Sayle, p. 1502].

VOORN (JACOBUS), printer at Leyden, 1591. In this year he printed a *Catalogue of all the chiefest rarities in the Public Theatre of the University of Leyden* [B.M., p. 343].

VUOLFIUS (REGINALDUS), *see* Wolfe (Reginald).

WAELPOTS or WAALPOT (JAN PIETERZ), printer at Delft, 1621–58. In 1633 he printed for N. Butter, London, and for sale at the house of Henry Hondius at the Hague, Henry Hexham's *Journal of the taking in of Venlo, Roermont, Strale, &c.*, in the imprint of which his name appears as Walpote. [Ledeboer, *A.L.*, p. 184; *Bockdrukkers*, p. 121.]

WAESBERGE (ISAAC VAN), bookseller or printer at Rotterdam, 1621–47. In 1636 he issued John Davenport's *Apologetical reply to a book called: An answer to the unjust complaint of W. B.* [Ledeboer, *A.L.*, pp. 186–7.]

WAESBERGHE (PIETER VAN), printer and bookseller at Rotterdam, 1622–60; Op't Stepgher, inde Swarte Klock. In 1639 he printed an English-Dutch dictionary, *Den grooten Vocabulaer Engels ende Duyts* (Sayle, pp. 1502–3). [Ledeboer, *A.L.*, p. 186.]

WAIE, *see* Nixon alias Waie (Robert).

WAISTELL or WAYSTAYLE (LANCELOT), stationer in Oxford, 1597–1608. Admitted a Stationer on April 11th, 1597. Resigned in 1608. He was dead before June 23rd in that year, when his will was proved. He left various bequests to Queen's College, Oxford, and the residue of his goods to his wife Lottice. [Gibson, *Oxford Wills*, pp. 20, 21.]

WALBANCK (MATTHEW), *see* Plomer, *Dictionary*.

WALDEGRAVE (ROBERT), printer in London, 1578–1589, (?) at Rochelle, 1589, and in Edinburgh, 1589–1603; London: (1) Without Temple Bar in the Strand, near unto Somerset House; (2) The Crane in St. Paul's Churchyard. Son of Richard Waldegrave, or Walgrave, of Blacklay in the county of Worcester, yeoman. Apprentice to William Griffith, stationer of London, for eight years from June 24th, 1568 [Arber, i. 372]. Robert Waldegrave made his first entry in the Registers on June 17th, 1578 [Arber, ii. 328]. From the outset of his career he appears to have attached himself to the Puritan party, and in 1581 we find him employed to print

John Knox's *Confession* and other Scottish books. In the year 1582–3 he gave the Company of Stationers a bond of £40 not to print anything of Seres' patent [Arber, i. 501]. When in 1583 the agitation was begun against the privileged printers, Robert Waldegrave joined the malcontents [Arber, ii. 784]. At that time he is returned as having two presses. In the following year [1583–4] he is found borrowing five pounds of the Company, which he repaid twelve months later, and in 1584 we find him printing for John Harrison, junior, who afterwards went to Edinburgh in connection with Waldegrave's pirated edition of the *Arcadia*. In that year a warrant of the High Commissioners was directed to the Wardens of the Company to seize Robert Waldegrave, his workmen and presses, with all unlicensed books [Records of the Company of Stationers]. This was no doubt in connection with the two following books printed in that year, *A brief declaration concerning the desires of all those faithfull ministers that do seek for the discipline and Reformation of the Church of England*, and a work in two parts, called respectively *A dialogue concerning the strife of our Church*, and *A declaration of some such monstrous abuses as our Bishops have not been ashamed to foster.* For this Waldegrave was thrown into the White Lyon prison in Southwark for six weeks, and again in 1585 he was imprisoned there for twenty weeks, for printing Puritan literature [*see Hay any worke for Cooper*, ed. Petheram, p. 68]. Again in 1588 the records of the Company state that a press with two pair of cases was seized from Robert Walgrave and ordered to be defaced, for printing John Udall's work entitled *The state of the Church of England laid open, etc.*, and the books to be burned. However, the printer and his wife appear to have had warning as they succeeded in carrying away a small portion of type. Waldegrave then managed to secure another press which he set up at (?) Kingston upon Thames, where he printed a second edition of the *Exhortation* of John Penry. From thence Waldegrave removed his press to Mrs. Crane's house at East Molesey, and there he printed the first of the famous Marprelate tracts, generally known as the *Epistle.* The hierarchy and the Company of Stationers raised a "hue and cry" all over the country, and fearing discovery it was decided to move the press again, and it was carried to Northamptonshire to Fawsley House, the residence of Sir Richard Knightley. There, the second of Martin's tracts, known as the *Epitome*, was printed, after which the press was removed to Coventry where the third Martinist

pamphlet, *Hay any work for Cooper*, was printed in March, 158$\frac{8}{9}$. By this time Waldegrave had had enough of the dangerous work. The close confinement was affecting his health, and some of his Puritan friends had expressed their strong dislike of Martin's methods. He therefore gave it up, and successfully evading his pursuers, is said to have reached Rochelle, and there to have printed two more Puritan tracts. Whether Waldegrave visited Rochelle or not, it would seem that he was at Edinburgh about the end of 1589, for on March 13th, 15$\frac{89}{90}$, he received a license from the Privy Council of Scotland to print the *Confession of Faith* [Dickson and Edmond, p. 407], and this appeared with his imprint in 1590. On October 9th, 1590, he was appointed King's printer [Lee, App. viii], and from this time until 1603 his press was actively at work, upwards of one hundred books having been noted with his Edinburgh imprint. Among these was a pirated edition of Sidney's *Arcadia* [*Library*, April, 1900, pp. 195–204]. For device he used the cut of a swan standing on a wreath within an oval frame bearing the motto "God is my helper"; he also used John Ross' devices and initial letters. His son Robert was baptised in Edinburgh on September 26th, 1596, one of the witnesses being the "Lord Ambassidour" [*Scottish Antiquary*, iv. 174]. On the accession of James to the English throne in 1603, Waldegrave returned to London, and on June 11th of that year a book was entered to him in the Stationers' Register. His Edinburgh printing materials passed into the hands of Thomas Finlason, who on March 31st, 1604, purchased from Widow Waldegrave her late husband's privilege for printing certain books. In the Public Record Office is a Proclamation of February 16th, 1604, concerning search for gold and silver mines, which bears the imprint of Widow Waldegrave, Edinburgh. [*D.N.B.*; Arber, *Introductory sketch to M.M. Controversy*, pp. 84–104, 124–5, 179–81; J. D. Wilson in the *Library*, October, 1907, pp. 337–59; *Works of Nashe*, ed. McKerrow, v. 184–90; Dickson and Edmond, *Annals*; Aldis, *Scottish Books*].

WALDKIRCH (CONRADUS), printer and publisher at Basle, 1582–1612. He became bürger of Basle in 1580, and in 1582 succeeded to the business of Peter Perna, his father-in-law. About 1592 he established himself at Schaffhausen for a while, but soon returned to Basle. In 1597 he printed Hugh Broughton's *Answer to the Lords of the Privy Council* [Lambeth]. He lived until at least 1612. [Heitz, *Basler Büchermarker*, p. xxxvi.]

WALKER (HEIRS OF JAMES), (?) printers at Rouen, 1601. In this year appeared *The copies of certain discourses which were extorted from divers* "Imprinted at Roane, by the heirs of Ia. Walker" [Sayle, p. 1638]. On the ground of the initial letters used Mr. Sayle however assigns the book to J. Windet, London. Nothing seems to be known of any printer of the name at Rouen.

WALKER (JOHN), bookseller in London, 1625. Two stationers of this name took up their freedom in the year 1619, one on March 1st and the other on October 4th. On September 28th, 1625, the will of John Walker "citizen and stationer" of London was proved in the Prerogative Court of Canterbury [P.C.C., 102, Clarke]. To Roger Norton he bequeathed a diamond ring "pauned unto mee for twentie powndes, by Mr. Christopher Barker." To Bonham Norton "five pounds in remembrance of his love and kindness towards mee," and stated that a certain Robert Floyd owed him seventeen shillings and sixpence for a *Caesar's Commentaries*.

WALKER (PETER), *see* Duff, *Century*.

WALKER (ROBERT), bookseller in London, 1597–9; (1) Near the Golden Lion in the Old Bailey; (2) The Talbot, in Paternoster Row. Son of the Revd. John Walker of Denham, Suffolk. Apprentice to Thomas Man, stationer of London, for eight years from September 29th, 1589. Robert Walker took up his freedom in the Company on October 29th, 1597, and made his first entry in the Registers on November 14th in the same year [Arber, ii. 167, 720; iii. 96]. He was associated with Toby Cooke in publishing some of the Rev. George Gifford's sermons, but they assigned their rights to Thomas Man in the following year, and nothing more is heard of Robert Walker [Arber, iii. 129, 148].

WALKLEY (THOMAS), *see* Plomer, *Dictionary*.

WALLER (   ), bookseller in Manchester, 1633. Mentioned in a list of booksellers in *Documents relating to William Prynne* (Camden Soc.), p. 60.

WALLEY (HENRY), *see* Plomer, *Dictionary*.

WALLEY (JOHN), *see* Duff, *Century*.

WALLEY (ROBERT), bookseller in London, 1576–91; St. Paul's Churchyard, 1580. Son of John Walley, stationer (1546–86). Became a freeman of the Company by patrimony. Admitted into the Livery in 1585 [Arber, i. 508]. Renter of the Company in 1591–2 [Arber, i. 553]. Took his first apprentice on November 8th, 1576 [Arber, ii. 70]. The first book entry under his name occurs on July 21st, 1577, when he was granted the reversion of *An abstract of all the penall statutes*, etc., after the deaths of Richard Tottell and Ralph Newbery [Arber, ii. 316], but previous to this he had published in 1576 George Whetstone's *Rocke of Regard*. In 1586 Robert Walley entered with John Charlewood W. Webbe's *Discourse of English Poetry* [Arber, ii. 456]. On February 26th, 159$\frac{7}{8}$, he entered all his father's copyrights, and on October 12th in the same year he transferred these and all his own copyrights to Thomas Adams, with a proviso that John Charlewood should have the printing of them [Arber, ii. 576, 596].

WALLYS (RICHARD), stationer in Canterbury, 1571. A stationer of this name was returned in 1571 as living at Canterbury [Arber, v. lii]. There was a Rychard Wallys, in Worgate or Worthgate ward, returned as "gent" in the subsidy roll for the city of Canterbury for 13th Eliz., and in the Prerogative Court of Canterbury is the will of Richard Wallis, senior, of Canterbury dated September 24th, 1601, who described himself as a notary and one of the procurator generals of the ecclesiastical court there, and desired to be buried in the church of St. Margaret. He does not appear to have practised his trade as a stationer in the city, nor is it clear whether he was the same with the Richard Wallys who in 1556 was admitted a bookseller in Oxford. [Duff, *Century*, p. 164; P.C.C., 13, Montague.]

WALPOTE (J. P.), *see* Waelpote.

WALTEM (THOMAS), (?) printer in Edinburgh, 1572. The French translation of George Buchanan's *Detectio (Histoire de Marie Royne d'Escosse)* has the fictitious colophon, "Acheué d'imprimer à Edimbourg, ville capitalle d'Escosse, le 13. de Feurier, 1572. par moy Thomas Vvaltem." It is believed to have been printed at Rochelle. [Dickson and Edmond, 252; *E.B.S. Papers*, ii. 27.]

WALTENELL (JOHN), stationer in London, 1576–83; St. Anne's, Blackfriars. Admitted Brother of the Stationers' Company February 1st, 15$\frac{79}{80}$ [Arber, ii. 681]. He is described as a Dutchman in the Returns

of Aliens. He left the country in 1583, owing the Company the balance of his fee for admission to the Brotherhood. [Worman, *Alien Members*, p. 70.]

WALTER (RICHARD), bookseller in London, 1607. Son of John Walter of Addlestrop, co. Gloucester, husbandman. Apprentice to William Tym, stationer of London, for eight years from March 25th, 1597, and became a freeman of the Company on June 25th, 1605 [Arber, ii. 219, 739]. On March 21st, 160$\frac{6}{7}$, John Barnes assigned over to him the copyright of two books, the *Essays* of Robert Johnson, and *Three Pastorall Elegies*, done by William Basse, but nothing is known with his name in the imprint.

WARD (PEREGRINE), stationer in London, 1615–24; St. Faith's parish. Took up his freedom in the Company of Stationers on May 9th, 1615 [Arber, iii. 684]. Died on January 3rd, 162$\frac{3}{4}$. He made a nuncupative will, bequeathing his goods and estate to his brother Gilbert Ward [Dean and Chapter of St. Paul's, Book D, fol. 228].

WARD (ROGER), printer in London, 1577–95; (1) The Talbot by Holborn Conduit, 1577–88; (2) Upon Lambert Hill near Old Fish Street, 1589; (3) Hammersmith (a secret press), 1590; (4) At the Purse, in the Little Old Bailey, 1590–2; (5) At the Castle, in Holborn, over against Ely House, 1593; (6) The Castle, in Salisbury Court, 1594–8; (7) In the Temple (a secret press), 1595. Son of Humphrey Ward of Ryton, Salop, husbandman. Apprentice to Thomas Marsh, stationer of London, for nine years from March 25th, 1566 [Arber, i. 291]. Roger Ward made his first entry in the Registers on July 8th, 1577 [Arber, ii. 316]. This printer is chiefly remembered as the most persistent and violent of those who agitated against the privileged printers. He is referred to as "a man without all government" and as "a most dangerous person." He succeeded John Wolf as the leader of the malcontents, and his boldest feat was the printing of ten thousand copies of the *A B C and Little Catechism*, for which John Day held the exclusive privilege. Ward obtained the paper from Abraham Newman and Thomas Man. He bribed one of Thomas Purfoot's apprentices to supply him with type from that printer's office, and he further employed a Frenchman living in Blackfriars to copy John Day's mark [Arber, ii. 753, etc.]. For this offence he was imprisoned in Ludgate. Again in 1585 he was committed to the Counter in Woodstreet for

disorderly printing, and his printing materials were seized [Arber, i. 510; ii. 39]. In the following year on October 17th the Wardens found him printing *Albion's England* of which they seized three heaps, and Lily's *Grammar* (Francis Flower's patent) in octavo, of which they seized the first leaf; formes were found ready set for printing Day's *Catechisme* and for prymers, psalters and other books, and upon that occasion they seized three presses [Herbert, p. 1190]. In 1590 Ward was discovered with a secret press on the Bankside in Southwark, where he printed *The Sermon of Repentance* and the *Grammar* in octavo. This press he removed to Hammersmith, where it was seized and defaced [Arber, i. 546]. In 1591 he pawned a press and letters with the Company, who lent him £12 10s. on them. Finally in 1595 he was discovered to have set up another secret press in the Temple, at which he was printing Primers. Meanwhile he was carrying on a legitimate business as a printer in various parts of London between 1577 and 1595. The date of his death is unknown, but in March, 1598, his widow presented an apprentice [Arber, ii. 224].

WARD (SAMUEL), bookseller in London, 1627–9; At his shop under St. Peter's Church in Cornhill at the sign of the Star. Samuel Ward took up his freedom in the Company of Stationers on October 14th, 1625 [Arber, iii. 686], and made his first book entry in the Register on April 1st, 1629 [Arber, iv. 210]. He had however published a theological work of William Bradshaw's in 1627 [B.M., 4327.a].

WARD (WILLIAM), stationer of London, 1628; dwelling on Lambeth Hill near Old Fish-Street. In this year a broadside containing the *Names of all the High Sheriffs*, etc., was printed for him [Lemon, *Broadsides of Soc. of Antiquaries*, p. 81]. He does not seem to be otherwise known.

WARREN (THOMAS), *see* Plomer, *Dictionary*, and the *Library*, April, 1907, pp. 170, 175.

WASE (RICHARD) bookseller in London, 1628; Little Britain. Mentioned in a list of second-hand booksellers who in 1628 were ordered to submit a catalogue of their books to the Archbishop of Canterbury [*Dom. S. Papers, Chas. I*, vol. 117 (9)]. He died February 22nd, 163$\frac{4}{5}$.

WASHINGTON (WILLIAM), bookseller in London, 1627–9; In St. Dunstan's churchyard. Took up his freedom in the Company of Stationers on September 3rd, 1627, and on December 3rd in the same year the copyrights of the "widow Helme" were transferred to him. The last entry under his name in the Registers occurs on January 15th, $162\frac{8}{9}$. [Arber, iii. 686; iv. 190, 207.]

WATERHOUSE (PHILIP), bookseller in London and Cambridge, 1629–32. Took up his freedom in the Company of Stationers on August 4th, 1628 [Arber, iii. 686]. Made his first entry in the Registers on January 15th, $16\frac{29}{30}$ [Arber, iv. 226]. In 1631 he published Thomas Heywood's *England's Elizabeth.* He afterwards moved to Cambridge where he published another edition of the same work in 1632.

WATERS (GEORGE, or JORIS), printer and bookseller at Dort, 1608–23. In 1610 he printed a corrected edition of John Rainolds' *Defence of the iudgment of the reformed churches*, and from this year to 1619 issued some half-dozen works in English, among them being the two poems of Patrick Gordon, *The Famous History of Robert the Bruce* [Hazlitt, VII. 164] and *The First Book of the Famous History of Penardo and Laissa*, both issued in 1615. In some of the English imprints his name appears as Walters. In 1623 John Wodroephe's *Spared hours of a soldier in his travels* was printed for him by N. Vincentz. [Ledeboer, *A.L.*, p. 189; Sayle, p. 1467.]

WATERS (PETER), stationer of Cambridge, 1581–2. In the *Remembrancia* of the City of London [vol. i. 198] is a letter (*c.* 1581) from Alexander Nowell and William Fulke to the Lord Mayor of London, asking that Peter Waters, a stationer of Cambridge, shall be admitted to the freedom of the City of London [Overall's *Index to the Remembrancia*, p. 150]. The same man was admitted a freeman of the Stationers' Company by redemption on July 31st, 1581, paying iiis. iiijd., and a further sum of a shilling at Michaelmas [Arber, ii. 685]. He may have been related in some way to Christopher Waters, cordwayner of Cambridge, whose son Christopher was apprenticed to Richard Field, stationer of London, in 1594 [Arber ii. 199].

WATERSON (JOHN), *see* Plomer, *Dictionary.*

WATERSON (SIMON), bookseller in London, 1584–1634; The Crown in St. Paul's Churchyard. He was a son of Richard Waterson [*see* Duff, *Century*], and was admitted to the freedom of the Stationers' Company on August 14th, 1583, by patrimony [Arber, ii. 690], and to the Livery in

1591–2 [Arber, i. 553]. His first entry in the Registers was on November 26th, 1584, and referred to Daniel's translation of the *Imprese* of Paolo Giovio, which was printed for him in the following year. From this time until 1635 he carried on an active business, his publications including, among others, many of Samuel Daniel's works and the *Epigrams* of John Owen. He also, from *c.* 1601, was the London agent for John Legatt of Cambridge, and, 1603–6, for Joseph Barnes of Oxford. His last entry in the Registers was on April 30th, 1633 [Arber, iv. 295], and on August 19th, 1635, his copies were transferred to his son John [*see* Plomer, *Dictionary*].

WATKINS (RICHARD), *see* Duff, *Century.*

WATSON (SIMON), bookseller at Cambridge, ? 1553–?60; Great St. Mary's. His name occurs in the accounts of St. Mary's Church, Cambridge, from 1554 to 1560, of which he was several times churchwarden, certain service books having been bought from him [Gray, *Cambridge Stationers*, 70].

WATTIR (ALEXANDER), bookbinder in Edinburgh, 1603. He was in the employ of Andro Hart, and died on August 30th, 1603 [*Bannatyne Miscell.* ii. 237].

WAYE (RICHARD), *see* Duff, *Century.*

WEAVER (EDMUND), bookseller in London, 1603–38; St. Paul's Churchyard. Edmund Weaver was originally a member of the Drapers' Company and was transferred to the Stationers on June 3rd, 1600. He made his first entry in the Registers on June 1st, 1603 [Arber, iii. 235]. Down to the year 1631 he carried on business in St. Paul's Churchyard at the great North Door of St. Paul's Church, in a row of shops that stood between that door and the church of St. Faith's. These shops were demolished by order of Archbishop Laud [*Library*, July, 1902, pp. 261–70]. Edmund Weaver became Master of the Company in 1637 [Arber, v. lxiv]. He was nominated overseer to the will of Cuthbert Burby (1592–1607). He died before December 19th, 1638, when his copyrights were transferred to his son Thomas [Arber, iv. 449].

WEAVER (THOMAS), bookseller in London, 1627–40. Son of Edmund Weaver. Took up his freedom in the Company of Stationers on June 4th, 1627, and made his only book entry in the Registers in partnership with

his father on April 19th, 1633. On December 19th, 1638, his father's copyrights were transferred to him, and on June 28th, 1639, he reassigned them to George Miller [Arber, iv. 471].

WEBB or WEBBE (WILLIAM), bookseller and bookbinder in Oxford, 1616–52. *See* Plomer, *Dictionary*, and Gibson, *Oxford Wills*, p. 52.

WEBBER or WEBSTER (RICHARD), printer in London, 1578–95. Son of William Webber of Tiverton, Devonshire, (?) weaver. Apprentice to William Griffith, stationer of London, for eight years from the feast of Pentecost, 1566 [Arber, i. 292]. Richard Webber made his first entry in the Registers on January 8th, $157\frac{7}{8}$, and his last on April 6th, 1579 [Arber, ii. 323, 351]. In 1585 he entered into bond with the Company that he and his apprentice should not supply more than one workman's place at a time in printing [Arber, i. 512]. At some time before 1593 his apprentice was transferred to Ralph Newbery [Arber, ii. 711]. He died before June 2nd, 1595, when his will was proved in the Prerogative Court of Canterbury. He left a widow and three daughters [P.C.C., 42, Scott]. The only book that has been found with Webber's imprint is the second part of the *Mirror for Magistrates,* which he printed in 1578. The presswork is evidently that of a beginner, and this may account for his omitting to state the position of his printing house.

WECHEL (JOHN), printer at Frankfurt am Main, 1587–99. In 1590 he printed T. Harriot's *Brief and true report of the new found land of Virginia* at the costs and charges of Th. de Bry [Herbert, p.1714; B.M., p. 285].

WELBY (WILLIAM), bookseller in London, 1604–18; (1) The Greyhound, St. Paul's Churchyard, 1605–9; (2) The Swan, St. Paul's Churchyard, 1612–14. William Welby was admitted a freeman of the Company of Stationers on March 26th, 1604; took his first apprentice on June 25th following, and made his first book entry in the Registers on October 11th in the same year [Arber, ii. 280, 736; iii. 272]. On October 16th, 1609, the widow of Cuthbert Burby assigned over to him her rights in thirty-eight copies which included Ben Jonson's *Every man in his humour,* and several other works of a lighter character [Arber, iii. 421]. Welby dealt largely in theological literature and also published many books relating to the English Colonies in the Bermudas, Guiana and Virginia. On March 2nd, $161\frac{7}{8}$, he assigned over all his copyrights to Thomas Snodham [Arber, iii. 621, 622].

WELLS (JOHN), bookseller in London, 1620; Fetter Lane and in The Temple. Only known from two translations from Ovid, published in 1620 [B.M., pp. 747, 1175].

WELLS (WILLIAM), *see* Plomer, *Dictionary.*

WESTALL (JOHN), bookseller and bookbinder in Oxford, 1609–43. Admitted a bookseller of the University on November 17th, 1609 [Clark, *Register*, ii. 1. 401]. Bound books for the Bodleian between 1613 and 1641, and published books between 1638 and 1640. He died in 1643 [Gibson, *Oxford Bindings*, p. 49; *Oxford Wills*, p. 39, 52; Madan, *Oxford Press*, p. 312].

WETHERED (WILLIAM), bookseller in London, 1638–45. Took up his freedom in the Company of Stationers on June 23rd, 1637 [Arber, iii. 688]. On September 1st, 1638, Andrew Crooke assigned over to him half his rights in certain books of divinity [Arber, iv. 430]. Wethered also entered on October 7th, 1639, and published in 1640, Francis Beaumont's *Poems.* He entered at the same time a poem by John Fletcher called a *Poem against stargaizers* [Arber, iv. 482]. He was still publishing in 1646. His address has not been found.

WHALEY ( ), bookseller in Northampton, 1633. Mentioned in a list of those who sold William Prynne's books [*Documents relating to William Prynne* (Camden Soc.), p. 60].

WHAPLANE (DUNSTAN), *see* Duff, *Century.*

WHITAKER (RICHARD), *see* Plomer, *Dictionary.*

WHITCHURCH (EDWARD), *see* Duff, *Century.*

WHITE (ANDREW), bookseller in London, 1584–92; At the Royal Exchange, over against the Conduit, in Cornhill. Son of John White of Bury St. Edmunds, Suffolk, mercer. Apprentice to Edward White his brother, for seven years from November 1st, 1576 [Arber, ii. 69]. Took up his freedom on August 15th, 1584 [Arber, ii. 692]. His first entry in the Registers was a pamphlet relating to a sea-fight, and was made on May 15th, 1591 [Arber, ii. 582], and his last on July 22nd in the same year [Arber, ii. 591].

WHITE (EDWARD), senior, bookseller in London, 1577–1612; The Gun, Little North Door of St. Paul's. Son of John White of Bury St. Edmunds, Suffolk, mercer. Apprentice to William Lobley, stationer of London, for seven years from September 29th, 1565 [Arber, i. 291]. Made his first entry in the Registers on January 21st, 157$\frac{6}{7}$ [Arber, ii. 307]. Admitted into the Livery of the Company on June 29th, 1588 [Arber, ii. 866]. Edward White dealt largely in ballads and on June 25th, 1600, was fined ten shillings for selling one called *The Wife of Bath* [Arber, ii. 831]. He died before January 12th, 161$\frac{2}{3}$, and his widow Sarah continued the business [Arber, iii. 511, 524].

WHITE (EDWARD), junior, bookseller in London, 1605–24. Son of Edward White, senior. Took up his freedom "per patrimonium" on February 22nd, 160$\frac{3}{4}$, and made his first book entry on September 13th, 1605 [Arber, iii. 300], and his last on July 10th, 1620 [Arber, iii. 676]. On June 29th, 1624, a Mistress White assigned her property in a number of copies to E. Allde [Arber, iv. 120].

WHITE (JOHN), printer in London, ? 1613–24; Cow Lane, near Holborn Conduit. Son of William White, printer (1597–1615). Took up his freedom on May 17th, 1614 [Arber, iii. 684], and was probably in partnership with his father. John White made his first entry in the Registers on September 8th, 1613 [Arber, iii. 532]. Between that date and 1623 he entered several ballads and devotional books. On September 6th, 1623, he assigned to Augustine Mathewes his rights in Abraham Fleming's *Conduit of Comfort*, and Sir John Lambe in his notes upon the printers, made in 1634, stated that Augustine Mathewes farmed his printing house of John White from the year 1624 [Arber, iii. 703]. In 1628 a bookseller of the same name is mentioned as living in Little Britain [*Dom. S. Papers, Charles I*, vol. 117. (9)].

WHITE (SARAH), *see* White (Edward), senior.

WHITE (WILLIAM), printer in London, 1597–1615; (1) The White Horse in Fleet Lane, over against Sea Coal Lane, 1588–96; (2) Cow Lane, near Holborn Conduit, over against the White Lion. William White was apparently one of Richard Jugge's apprentices, as he was presented for his freedom by Mistress Jugge on April 10th, 1583 [Arber, ii. 688]. He entered into partnership with Gabriel Simpson and their first book entry is

recorded on December 13th, 1588 [Arber, ii. 511]. The partnership was dissolved in 1597, when William White having purchased the business of Richard Jones and William Hill, moved to Cow Lane [Arber, iii. 702]. In 1598 White printed for Cuthbert Burby the first quarto of Shakespeare's *Love's Labour's Lost*, and in 1600 for Thomas Millington the second quarto of the *Third part of King Henry vj*. He also entered a large number of ballads and other ephemeral literature. The last entry under his name was made on September 5th, 1615 [Arber, iii. 572]. The date of his death is unknown, but he was succeeded by his son John White.

WHITING (EDMUND), bookseller in London, 1616–40. Took up his freedom in the Company of Stationers, August 3rd, 1616 [Arber, iii. 684]. On February 3rd, 16$\frac{39}{40}$, William Wilson assigned over to Edmund Whiting his rights in a broadside called *Come ye blessed, &c.* [Arber, iv. 497]. His address has not been found and nothing else is known of him.

WHITNEY (WALTER), printer in London, 1578–83. In 1578 a licence was granted to Walter Whitney to print *An epitaph upon the ladie Lomney* [Arber, ii. 335]. In 1583 he was returned as having one press [Arber, i. 248]. Mr. Arber concludes that he was not a member of the Company of Stationers.

WIGHT (JOHN), *see* Duff, *Century*.

WIGHT (THOMAS), draper and bookseller in London, 1580–1608; The Rose in St. Paul's Churchyard. Son of John Wight, draper and bookseller. In 1599 in company with Bonham Norton he obtained a patent for printing law books for thirty years, in succession to C. Yetsweirt [Patent Roll, 41 Eliz. Part 4]. On May 6th, 1605, ten copies were entered to Edmund Weaver, but with the proviso that Thomas Wight should be at liberty to dispose of them [Arber, iii. 288–9]. Though no books are entered by him in the Registers, there are several that bear his name in the imprint, particularly law books. In 1609 a commission was issued by the Prerogative Court of Canterbury to Jocosa Wight, widow of Thomas Wight, to administer the will of John Wight during the minority of her children [Plomer, *Wills*, p. 30].

WILDGOOSE (ANTHONY), printer in London, 1636–40. Took up his freedom in the Company of Stationers, November 7th, 1636 [Arber, iii. 688]. In 1640 he was plaintiff in an action in the Court of Requests against William White of Sunderland [Court of Requests, 15th Chas. I, Bundle 13].

WILDGOOSE (WILLIAM), bookseller and bookbinder in Oxford, 1617–26. Admitted a bookseller on June 10th, 1617 [Clark, *Register*, ii. 1. 321]. Reprimanded for setting up as a bookseller without the Vice Chancellor's leave [Clark, *id.* 321]. Mr. Gibson refers to another William Wildgoose "famulus priv. 1604 aet. 34" [Clark, *Register*, ii. 1. 399; Gibson, *Oxford Wills*, p. 52]. He was binder to the Bodleian Library from 1621 to 1626, and amongst the books bound by him was the first folio *Shakespeare* [Gibson, *Oxford Bindings*, pp. 40, 48, 51, 57, 58, 60; copy of First Folio in Bodleian Lib.]. In 1640 there was an Anthony Wildgoose working as a printer in London, who was perhaps a descendant from the above William [Court of Requests, 15 Chas. I].

WILFORDE (JAMES), printer in London, 1571–85; Aldersgate ward and Cripplegate ward. This printer seems to be distinct from the James Woelfaert noted by Mr. Duff in his *Century*. They both came from Holland, and both had wives named Catherine, but whereas Woelfaert is said to have been resident in England for fourteen years in 1571, Wilforde is said to have been here only one and a half years [Worman, *Alien Members*, p. 71].

WILKES (OLIVER), bookseller and bookbinder in London, 1564–88. Made free of the Company of Stationers on October 3rd, 1564, and admitted into the Livery in 1582 [Arber, i. 279, 493]. His only book entry occurs in the Registers on February 11th, 157$\frac{6}{7}$ [Arber, ii. 308]. Oliver Wilkes bound books as well as selling them; in 1582 he was paid five shillings for binding a *Bible* for the King's Bench, and again in 1588 a similar sum for binding a *Chronicle* for a pursuivant. He died before August 8th in that year, when his will, dated a fortnight earlier, was proved in the Prerogative Court of Canterbury. He desired to be buried in the church of St. Faith's under St. Paul's, and he left a sum of six and eightpence to the Company of Stationers [P.C.C., 53, Rutland].

WILKINS (TIMOTHY), printer at Oxford, 1640. [Madan, *Chart of Oxford Printing*, p. 29.] He may perhaps have been identical with the bookseller of the same name who was in business in London in 1641 [*see* Plomer, *Dictionary*].

WILLIAMS (FRANCIS), bookseller in London, 1626–30; The Globe, over against the Royal Exchange. He took up his freedom in the Company of Stationers on November 11th, 1625 [Arber, iii. 686], and on January 16th, 162$\frac{5}{6}$, a large number of copyrights were transferred to him by the widow of Roger Jackson [Arber, iv. 149]. His first entry in the Registers was made on May 17th, 1626 [Arber, iv. 160]. His publications, all of which seem to be dated 1626, included editions of *Scoggin's Jests*, Breton's *Fantastics*, Greene's *Arbasto*, and several other works, mostly of a popular character. He made his last entry in the Registers on March 1st, 162$\frac{7}{8}$, and on June 29th, 1630, he assigned most of his copies to Master Harrison [Arber, iv. 237].

WILLIAMS (JACOB), (?) printer in Edinburgh, ? 1635. An edition of Lewis Bayly's *Practice of Piety* bears the fictitious imprint "Printed at Edynburg by Iacob Williams. for the good of Great Britaine." It was possibly printed at Amsterdam about 1635 [Aldis, *Scottish Books*, 123].

WILLIAMS (JOHN), *see* Plomer, *Dictionary*.

WILLIAMS (WILLIAM), bookbinder in London, 1571; St. Faith's, Farringdon Within. Born in Antwerp, servant with William Norton, in England five years, in the said ward four [Worman, *Alien Members*, p. 49]. Mr. Worman thinks he may be identical with William Williamson [*q.v.*], who published at the White Horse in St. Paul's Churchyard in 1571, but as Williamson was apprenticed to Richard Jugge as early as 1562 this seems hardly probable.

WILLIAMS (WILLIAM), bookbinder at Cambridge, 1607–35; West end of Great St. Mary's Church. His name appears in the St. Mary's parish book as paying rent for the north shop at the West end of the church from 1607 to 1617, for most of the time jointly with Leonard Greene [*q.v.*], the printer, who occupied the south shop. He is found paying church rate as late as the year 1635, and occupied various parish posts such as that of churchwarden, etc. He was one of the privileged persons in the University in 1624. [Bowes, *Univ. Printers*, 336; Gray, *Shops at West end of Great St. Mary's Church.*]

WILLIAMSON (ANDRO), (?) bookseller in Edinburgh. An ordinance of the Town Council of Edinburgh, October 28th, 1580, advertises that copies of Bassandyne's *Bible* (1579) "ar to be sawld in the merchant buith of Andro Williamsoun on the north syde of this burgh, besyde the meill mercatt." [Dickson and Edmond, 315].

WILLIAMSON (WILLIAM), printer and bookseller in London, 1571–4; (1) The White Horse, St. Paul's Churchyard, 1571; (2) Dwelling in Distaff Lane, 1572; (3) In St. Paul's Churchyard, 1573–4; (4) At his shop adjoining St. Peter's Church in Cornhill. One of Richard Jugge's apprentices for nine years from February 2nd, $156\frac{1}{2}$ [Arber, i. 171]. Admitted a freeman of the Company on April 23rd, 1571 [Arber, i. 447]. There are no entries of separate copies under his name in the Registers, but on January 15th, $158\frac{1}{2}$, a large number of copies, including several plays, were assigned over to John Charlewood; but it is not clear which of them belonged to William Williamson [Arber, ii. 405–6]. He appears to have succeeded Andrew Hester at the White Horse in St. Paul's Churchyard and to have carried on both a printing and bookselling business between 1571 and 1574.

WILLIS (ROBERT), senior, (?) bookseller in London, 1617–22; At the house of Mistress Stubbes in the alley adjoining Ludgate on the outside of the Gate. Took up his freedom in the Company of Stationers on October 9th, 1617 [Arber, iii. 684]. Willis made his first book entry in the Registers on October 16th, 1617 [Arber, iii. 614]. He published for John Willis, bachelor of divinity and possibly a relative, *The schoolemaster to the arte of stenography*, in 1621. Robert Willis died before December 2nd, 1622, when the above work was transferred to Henry Seile [Arber, iv. 87].

WILLIS (ROBERT), junior, (?) bookseller in London, 1637. Took up his freedom July 4th, 1636. He may have been a son of Robert Willis, senior [Arber, iii. 687]. He made his first book entry in the Registers on March 11th, $163\frac{6}{7}$ [Arber, iv. 375], but a few months later he transferred his

rights in the book, Richard Norwood's *Fundamental problems in the practice of Navigation*, to George Hurlocke [Arber, iv. 386]. It seems doubtful whether he was in business at all.

WILLOUGHBYE (JOHN), (?) book importer, 1574. Arrested for importing "erroneous" books [*Acts of the Privy Council, New Ser.*, viii. 331 (*cf.* p. 118)].

WILMOT (JOHN), bookseller in Oxford, *see* Plomer, *Dictionary*.

WILNE (GEORGE), bookseller in London, 1638–9. Took up his freedom in the Company of Stationers, October 16th, 1637 [Arber, iii. 688]. On March 6th, $163\frac{7}{8}$, he entered in the Registers John Hodge's *Viaticum animae*, and again on August 10th, 1638, William Park's *The rose and the lilley* [Arber, iv. 410, 428]. The last named was a series of sermons preached at Ashby de la Zouch.

WILSON (CHRISTOPHER), bookseller and bookbinder in London, 1603–16. Son of Ralph Wilson of Barmeby Moor, co. Nottingham, joiner. Apprentice to Francis Henson, stationer of London, for seven years from February 2nd, 1565, and became a freeman of the Company on July 1st, 1602 [Arber, ii. 200, 733]. He made his only book entry, a (?) translation of the *Première Semaine* of Du Bartas, on July 2nd, 1603 [Arber, iii. 37]. In 1616 he is mentioned in a suit in Chancery as binding books for the booksellers Bonham Norton, John Norton and John Bill. [Chan. Proc., Jas. I, B. 35. 10.]

WILSON (JOHN), stationer in London, 1616. A stationer of this name is recorded in the Registers as entering a book on January 27th, $161\frac{5}{6}$ [Arber, iii. 582], but nothing further is known about him.

WILSON (JOHN), bookseller in Glasgow, 1634–5. An edition of *True Christian Love* by David Dickson was printed by John Wreittoun of Edinburgh with the following imprint: "Printed by I. W. for Iohn Wilson and are to be sould at his shop in Glasgow. 1634." This is the earliest known imprint in which Glasgow appears. In the following year Ninian Campbell's *Treatise upon death* was printed for Wilson by Robert Young. Nothing further is known of his career. [Aldis, *Scottish Books*, 124.]

WILSON (ROBERT), bookseller in London, 1610–? 1639; (1) Holborn; (2) Gray's Inn Gate; (3) Fleet Street or Chancery Lane. Son of Robert Wilson of Egginton, co. Derby, yeoman. Apprentice to John Smith, stationer of London, for nine years from June 24th, 1600, and took up his freedom in the Company on May 2nd, 1609 [Arber, ii. 248; iii. 683]. Robert Wilson made his first book entry in the Registers on November 9th, 1610, and ten days later John Bache assigned to him five copies [Arber, iii. 448, 449]. He published a few plays including L. Barrey's *Ram Alley* and Beaumont and Fletcher's *Scornful Ladie*, 1639. In 1628 his name is mentioned in a list of second-hand booksellers who were ordered to submit catalogues of their books to the Archbishop of Canterbury [*Dom. State Papers, Chas. I*, vol. 117 (9)]. His widow Anne appears to have carried on the business for a short time after his death [Arber, iv. 512].

WILSON (STEPHEN), bookseller and bookbinder in Oxford, 1590–1. Admitted bookseller on November 27th, 1590. Described as a bookbinder in 1591, when he took an apprentice. [Clark, *Register*, ii. 1. 321, 342.]

WILSON (WILLIAM), *see* Plomer, *Dictionary*.

WINDER or WINDSOR (GEORGE), bookseller in London, 1622–8; St. Dunstan's Churchyard. This stationer took up his freedom in the Company on July 1st, 1622, and made his first entry in the Registers on September 24th in the same year [Arber, iii. 685; iv. 81]. George Winder published chiefly theological books. On May 21st, 1628, he assigned two of his copyrights to Miles Flesher or Fletcher, after which nothing more is heard of him [Arber, iv. 197]. Richard Windsor in his will proved on February 19th, $162\frac{2}{3}$, mentions his "nephew" George Windsor, "citizen & stationer of London," who was probably identical with the subject of this notice [P.C.C., 11, Swann].

WINDET (JOHN), printer in London, 1584–1611; (1) The White Bear in Addling St. nigh Baynard's Castle; (2) The Cross Keys on St. Paul's Wharf, Thames St. On April 13th, 1579, John Allde, the printer, presented for his freedom an apprentice who is entered in the Registers as John Wyndyert, and who may be identical with John Windet [Arber, ii. 680]. If so, he served some years as a journeyman, as it was not until 1584 that he began to print on his own account. In that year he printed

Thomas Rogers' *English Creed*. In the same year he took over one of Henry Bynneman's apprentices, and appears to have set up in business at the White Bear in Addling Street. As several books are found in 1584 with the joint names of Windet and John Judson, and they are not found in partnership after that date, it is possible that he succeeded to the business. John Windet was on several occasions fined for taking apprentices without presenting them and for other trivial offences. But his business increased rapidly and in 1586 he had three presses [Arber, v. lii]. On July 4th in that year he was admitted to the Livery of the Company [Arber, ii. 866]. In the years 1593–4–5 he was renter of the Company [Arber, i. 565, 571], and in 1599 he served the office of Under Warden, but upon being elected to serve a second time in 1604 he agreed to pay £10 for exemption, and he never appears to have held any other office in the Company [Arber, ii. 838]. Between 1592 and 1603 John Windet's name is frequently found in the records of St. Bennet's, St. Paul's Wharf, either as constable of the parish or as serving on the wardmote inquest. In 1603 he succeeded John Wolf as official printer to the city of London. The last book entry under his name is found on May 14th, 1604; but he continued in business until 1611 when he assigned over his copyrights to William Stansby, who ultimately succeeded to the business [Arber, iii. 465–7].

WINDSOR (GEORGE), *see* Winder (G.).

WINNINGTON (ELIZABETH), *see* Winnington (John).

WINNINGTON (JOHN), bookseller in London, 1587–95; The Golden Tun near St. Dunstan's Church in Fleet Street. Son of Gilbert Winnington of Terne, co. Salop, carpenter. Apprentice to Richard Watkins, stationer of London, for eight years from August 24th, 1578, it being agreed that he should serve the whole of his term with Andrew Maunsell, draper, who was in business as a stationer [Arber, ii. 86]. John Winnington was admitted to the freedom of the Company on September 5th, 1586 [Arber, ii. 698]. The only entries under his name in the Registers occur on January 29th, $158\frac{7}{8}$, and June 30th, 1593 [Arber, ii. 483, 633]. He died some time in 1595 and on October 30th his widow Elizabeth Winnington transferred her rights in certain copies to John Busby [Arber, iii. 51].

WISE or WYTHES (ANDREW), bookseller in London, 1589-1603; The Angel in St. Paul's Churchyard. This stationer whose name is frequently written in the Registers as Wythes or Withes, was the son of Henry Wythes of Ollerton Mallyveres, co. York, yeoman, and was apprentice to Henry Smith, stationer of London, for eight years from March 25th, 1580, but on April 10th, 1581, was transferred to Thomas Bradshaw, by whom he was made free on May 26th, 1589 [Arber, ii. 96, 104, 705]. He appears to have taken over the business of John Perrin and in 1593 published Thomas Nashe's *Christ's tears over Jerusalem*, which having originally been entered to Alice Charlewood was printed for Wise by James Roberts. Andrew Wise is chiefly remembered as a publisher of Shakespeare's works. On August 29th, 1597, he entered *The tragedye of Richard the Second* [Arber, iii. 89], and on October 20th of the same year, *The tragedie of kinge Richard the Third with the death of the Duke of Clarence* [Arber, iii. 93]. On February 25th, 1598, Wise entered *The history of Henry the IVth*, and on August 23rd, 1600, *Henry IV, Part ii*, and the play *Much ado about Nothing* [Arber, iii. 105, 170]. Andrew Wise transferred his copyrights to Mathew Law on June 25th, 1603, and is not heard of again [Arber, iii. 239].

WOLF (ALICE), *see* Wolf (John).

WOLF or WOLFE (JOHN), printer in London, 1579-1601; (1) Distaff Lane, over against the Castle; (2) Over against the South Door of St. Pauls, or, at St. Paul's Chain, 1592. John Wolf was a member of an old Sussex family, and was a retainer of the family of Goring [Lower's *Hist. of Sussex*, vol. 1, p. 23; Cartwright's *Rape of Bramber*, vol. ii, pt. 2, p. 102]. He is spoken of originally as a member of the Fishmongers' Company, perhaps by "patrimony," but there is no evidence on the point. The first heard of him in connection with printing is on March 25th, 1562, when he began an apprenticeship of ten years with John Day [Arber, i. 172]. He was therefore rightly out of his time in 1572, after which he appears to have gone abroad and to have been for some time in Italy. In 1576 two *Rapresentazione* were printed in Florence "ad instanzia di Giovanni Vuolfio, Inglese." One of these is in the British Museum [C. $\frac{34}{30}$, h. 6.]. Professor Gerber in his articles in *Modern Language Notes*, vol. xxii, p. 131, suggests that Wolf worked for a time in the printing office of

the Giunti. Seeing that he afterwards used one of the devices of Gabriel Giolito, he was probably intimate with that office also. The next heard of him is in 1579, in which year he entered a Latin book in the Registers and was given a license for it, on the condition that he gave the printing to John Charlewood. Shortly afterwards he set up a press of his own and became one of the ringleaders of the agitation against the monopolies of the privileged printers. This began as early as the year 1581, when John Wolf, John Charlewood and Roger Ward joined with other members of the Company in printing and selling the most valuable books for which letters patent had been granted to other men. On June 19th, 1581, Wolf entered into recognisances before the Privy Council not to print the Latin Grammar that belonged to Francis Flower [*Acts of the Privy Council*, N.S., xiii. 88]. But he and his companions went on printing large numbers of privileged books such as John Day's *ABC and Little Catechisme*. When remonstrated with by Christopher Barker, the Queen's printer, Wolf retorted that the Queen had no right to grant privileges, and that just as Luther had reformed religion, so he, Wolf, would reform the government of the printing and bookselling trades. He was thrown into prison in 1582, but was released on the intervention of George Goring, who claimed John Wolf as his "man" [*i.e.*, his tenant or vassal]. Before the end of the year, however, Wolf was again a prisoner. In May, 1583, he was declared to have "iij presses and ij more since found in a secret vault" [Arber, i. 248], but a few months later he suddenly gave up the struggle, as on July 18th the Commissioners who were appointed to enquire into the whole matter reported that "Wolf hath acknowledged his error, and is releved with work." After this his promotion was rapid. In the following year in company with Francis Adams, he was appointed one of the assigns of Richard Day's patent. He was next appointed a searcher for the Company and actively hunted down his former associates. In 1587 he was appointed Beadle of the Company and had four presses at work. In 1593 he became printer to the City of London in succession to Hugh Singleton, and on July 1st, 1598, he was admitted to the livery of the Stationers' Company; but in 1600 he was again in trouble with the authorities for printing Hayward's *Life of King Henry IV* [*Library*, January, 1902, pp. 13-23]. Between 1580 and 1600 John Wolf printed numerous books in Italian, amongst others the writings of Petruccio Ubaldini, an Italian refugee who

seems to have acted as editor and reader for his press. Some of these Italian books of Wolf's were printed secretly and with fictitious imprints. John Wolf died during the year 1601, and several years afterwards his widow assigned over a large number of his copyrights to John Pindley; but his printing business and stock were transferred at his death to Adam Islip. John Wolf used several devices, none of which however can be said to have been his own. The best known is the fleur de lys, which is similar to the device of the Giunti of Florence. [The chief authorities for the above are, Arber's *Transcripts*; S. Bongi, *Annali di Gabriel Giolito de' Ferrari*, vol. ii, pp. 421, 422; *Modern Language Notes*, Baltimore, 1907, vol. xxii, Articles by Prof. A. Gerber, pp. 2–6, 129–135, 201–6.]

WOLFE (REYNER or REGINALD), *see* Duff, *Century*.

WOLLYE or WALLEY (JOHN), bookbinder in London, 1616. Mentioned in a suit in Chancery as binding books for the booksellers, Bonham Norton, John Norton and John Bill [Chan. Proc., Jas. 1, B 35. 10].

WOOD (GEORGE), printer in London, ? 1613–? 1624; (1) Stepney, 1621; (2) Grub Street, 1622. A stationer of this name took up his freedom in the Company on November 15th, 1613 [Arber, iii. 684]. Although no books are known with his imprint, and he entered nothing in the Registers, George Wood was one of the wandering and irregular printers who caused the officers of the Company so much trouble. The records of the Company for the year 1621 testify that a press and implements of George Wood of Stepney were seized and destroyed for printing Almanacks and Primers contrary to the decree of the Star Chamber. In the following year (1622) another press with materials set up by George Wood in Grub Street was seized and destroyed. About this press there was a good deal of correspondence. Wood petitioned the Archbishop of Canterbury for the return of his goods and the Company presented a counter petition stating the violent opposition and ill treatment they had received from George Wood's workmen, and praying that if the Company desist from punishing him, these workmen may be compelled to give bond for their future good behaviour. The Company expressed their willingness to compensate Wood for his materials and to do him any good offices. The Archbishop smoothed the matter over and suggested that George Wood should be allowed to work as a journeyman, and upon testimony of his good

behaviour, and sufficient security, he should be admitted a master printer upon any vacancy. Wood never reached that position, and the records testify that in 1624 more secret presses belonging to him were seized and destroyed. About this time Wood appears to have bought the printing materials that had belonged to Thomas Snodham, the successor of Thomas East, and to have had some dealings with Thomas Harper which became the subject of litigation in the Court of Requests and Star Chamber. [Records of the Stationers' Company; Arber, iii. 701–4.]

WOOD (JOHN), bookseller in Edinburgh, 1629–33; On the south side of the High Street, a little above the Cross. He is known only from the imprints of four books printed for him by the Heirs of T. Finlason, J. Wreittoun and Robert Young, between 1629 and 1633 [Aldis, *Scottish Books*, 124].

WOOD (ROBERT), bookbinder in (?) Edinburgh, 1585. Is named among the debtors in the inventory of Robert Gourlaw, bookbinder in Edinburgh, who died September 6th, 1585 [*Bannatyne Miscell.*, ii. 216].

WOOD (ROGER), patentee, 1619–29. Associated with Thomas Symcock [*q.v.*] in the patent for the sole printing of all things to be printed on one side only. The patent was cancelled by decree of the Court of Chancery in 1629.

WOOD (WILLIAM), bookseller in London, 1598–1602; West End or West Door of St. Paul's. Son of William Wood of Harfeild, Middlesex, yeoman. Apprentice to George Allen, stationer of London, for eight years from March 25th, 1589. On November 6th, 1598, he entered nine copies, including Gascoigne's *Works*, Markham's *Horsmanship*, Aesop's *Fables* in metre and H. Constable's *Diana*. The last reference to him in the Registers is on August 2nd, 1602, when two of the above nine copies were declared to belong to Edward White [Arber, iii. 131].

WOOD (   ), (?) bookseller in London, 1565–6. In this year a Master Wood entered in the Registers a sermon preached at Edinburgh by "Master Nokes" in August, 1565 [Arber, i. 309]. Nothing seems to be known of him.

WOODCOCK (ISABEL), *see* Woodcock (Thomas).

WOODCOCK (THOMAS), bookseller in London, 1570–94; The Black Bear, St. Paul's Churchyard. Apprentice to Francis Coldock, stationer of London, for nine years from Midsummer, 1561, and became a freeman of the Company on July 6th, 1570 [Arber, i. 446]. Thomas Woodcock made his first entry in the Registers on April 19th, 1577. In the following year he was imprisoned in Newgate for selling Cartwright's *Admonition to the Parliament*, and the Master and Wardens of the Company with William Seres and John Day petitioned Lord Burleigh for his release [Arber, i. 485]. He was admitted to the Livery on May 6th, 1582, served as renter in the years 1589 and 1590, and was chosen Under Warden in July, 1593, but did not complete his year of service, as he died on April 22nd, 1594. Thomas Woodcock married Isabel, one of the daughters of John Cawood, the Queen's printer, and had a son Simon who was apprenticed to John Flasket, stationer, for eight years on June 24th, 1600, and took up his freedom December 7th, 1607 [Arber, ii. 245; iii. 683]. On February 9th, 159$\frac{5}{6}$, Thomas Woodcock's books and copyrights were turned over to Paul Linley [Arber, iii. 58].

WOODHOUSE (ROBERT), bookseller and bookbinder in Edinburgh, ?1569–?1632. On September 28th, 1580, a complaint was laid before the Town Council of Edinburgh "that Robert Wodhous, Inglisman, being ane forane straynger and unfrieman, has this lang tym bygane usurpitt upoun him the privelege of ane frie burges be selling and bynding of all kynd of buiks within the fredome of this burgh;" and he was discharged from binding any books within the burgh. At some period after this, Woodhouse must have become a freeman of the city, for in 1592 he appears among the seven booksellers and burgesses who complained against John Norton for a similar offence. He may have been the "Roberte Wodhowse" of Humble in Staffordshire, who was apprenticed to William Wodhowse, stationer of London, on August 24th, 1569. The will of Robert Woodhous, bookbinder, burgess of Edinburgh, was registered February 21st, 1632; and, as wills were sometimes registered a considerable time after the date of death, this may quite well be the same man. [Aldis, *Scottish Books*, 124; Dickson and Edmond, 206; Lee, *Add. Mem.*, App. lxxi; Arber, i. 395].

WOODNET, *see* Woodnote.

WOODNOTE (ROBERT), bookseller in London, ?1602–23. This stationer, whose name occurs to a book entry in company with that of John Haviland, on February 1st, 162$\frac{2}{3}$ [Arber, iv. 90], is possibly identical with Robert Woodnet, son of Thomas Woodnet, citizen and merchant tailor of London, who was apprentice to Robert Barker for seven years from September 30th, 1594, and took up his freedom on January 18th, 160$\frac{1}{2}$ [Arber, ii. 196, 731].

WOODROFFE (RICHARD), bookseller in London, 1614–23; The Golden Key near the Great North Door, St. Paul's Churchyard. Took up his freedom in the Company of Stationers, August 1st, 1614 [Arber, iii. 684]. Made his first book entry in the Registers on August 10th, 1614 [Arber, iii. 552]. He dealt chiefly in theological books; but towards the end of the year 1622 he assigned most of his copyrights to Timothy Barlow [Arber, iv. 88, 89].

WOUW (WIDOW AND HEIRS OF HILLEBRANT JACOBS VAN), printers at the Hague, 1631. In this year they printed *Laws and Ordinances touching military discipline* [in the Netherlands] . . . *established the 13 of August, 1590* [B.M., p. 1142]. Ledeboer states that van Wouw printed 1588–1629, and his widow in 1630, and under another heading describes his widow and heirs as printing from 1626 to 1657. [Ledeboer, *A.L.*, 195, *De Boekdrukkers*, 179.]

WRAY (HENRY), stationer at Cambridge, 1617–28; Great St. Mary's. Resided in Great St. Mary's parish and paid church rate from 1617 [Foster's *Churchwardens' Accounts*]. He is in a list of privileged persons in the University, 1624 [Bowes, 336]. His will, dated 1628, is at Peterborough. His widow continued to live in the parish [Foster].

WREITTOUN (JOHN), printer in Edinburgh, (?) 1621–40. Hardly anything is known of the personal history of this printer, but he may have been the John Wreittoun who, with his brother Daniel, "sones to umquhile Allexander Wreittoun, minister at Kilmarnok" [? Kilwinning], were witnesses to Andro Hart's will on December 21st, 1621. Between 1624 and 1636 he produced upwards of sixty books. His name has not been found in any imprint after the latter year, but an edition of the *Protestation* made by the Covenanters at Edinburgh on July 4th, 1638, was printed in

his types. In 1634 he printed Dickson's *True Christian Love*, for John Wilson, the Glasgow bookseller; and his edition of *Venus and Adonis*, 1627, is notable as being the only work of Shakespeare printed in Scotland before the eighteenth century. The characteristic ornaments used in his books are a pelican in her piety, and the Scottish arms crowned. In his first imprint his "buith" is stated to be "at the Nether-Bowe," but in 1628 and 1635 he dates from "his shop a little beneath the Salt Trone;" probably these two addresses refer to one and the same place. Wreittoun died February 13th, 1640, and was survived by his wife, Margaret Kene, who was possibly a relative of A. Hart's second wife. His inventory is printed in the *Bannatyne Miscellany*. [Aldis, *Scottish Books*, 124; *Bann. Misc.*, ii. 249, 255; Hew Scott's *Fasti*, ii. 181.]

WRENCH (WILLIAM), printer in Oxford, 1617–18. Appointed printer to the University in company with John Lichfield in 1617. His career was a short one as he only held the office until January 19th, 161$\frac{7}{8}$. [Madan, *Oxford Press*, 276, 297, 311; *cf.* Arber, iii. 648.]

WRENCH (WILLIAM), (?) printer or bookseller in London, 1624. Mentioned by John Gee in his *Foot out of the snare*, 1624, as a dealer in or disperser of Popish books. There was a William Wrench, a printer, mentioned by William Jones in his information against Bishop Bancroft in 1640 [*Library*, April, 1907, pp. 165, 174]; there was a William Wrench, a printer, at Oxford in 1617; and there was a William Wrench, a bookbinder in London, about the same time, who is described in a Chancery suit of the year 1616 as binding books for the booksellers Bonham Norton, John Norton and John Bill. [Chan. Proc., Jas. I, B 35. 10.]

WRIGHT (ABIGAIL), *see* Wright (Cuthbert).

WRIGHT (CUTHBERT), bookseller in London, 1613–39. Son of Thomas Wright of Buckbrook, co. Northampton, yeoman. Apprentice to Felix Kingston, stationer of London, for eight years from June 24th, 1603 [Arber, ii. 272]. Took up his freedom on November 5th, 1610 [Arber, iii. 683]. Cuthbert Wright made his first entry in the Registers on August 11th, 1613 [Arber, iii. 531]. He appears to have been one of the partners in the Ballad Stock of the Company, as on December 14th, 1624, in

company with Thomas Pavier, John Wright, Edward Wright, John Grismond and Henry Gosson he entered 128 ballads [Arber, iv. 131–2], and again on June 1st, 1629, in partnership with other stationers, several books and ballads which had belonged to Margaret Trundle, widow of John Trundle [Arber, iv. 213]. Cuthbert Wright died before February 22nd, 163$\frac{8}{9}$, when some of his copies were transferred by his widow Abigail Wright to Andrew Kembe [Arber, iv. 456].

WRIGHT (EDWARD), *see* Plomer, *Dictionary*.

WRIGHT (GILBERT), bookseller in London, 1624; Little Britain. Only known from the following passage in the will of Henry Sivedall Esquire [P.C.C., 90, Byrde]: "Item I give and bequeath unto George Wright, Thomas Wright and John Wright, sons of Gilbert Wright bookeseller in litle Britten . . . twentie pounds a peece, . . . and I give to Katherine Wright their sister, twentie pounds."

WRIGHT (JOHN), senior, *see* Plomer, *Dictionary*.

WRIGHT (JOHN), junior, *see* Plomer, *Dictionary*.

WRIGHT (RICHARD), printer in Oxford, 1591 [Madan, *Oxford Press*, 229, 275, 295, 311; Arber, ii. 167]. In 1591 he received letters patent for life to print Tacitus' *History* in English [Patent Roll, 33 Eliz., part 17].

WRIGHT (THOMAS), typefounder and bookseller in London, 1627–39. Took up his freedom in the Company of Stationers May 27th, 1627 [Arber, iii. 686]. On February 1st, 163$\frac{8}{9}$, two copies were assigned over to him by Thomas Purfoot [Arber, iv. 454]. Thomas Wright was also a typefounder and was one of the four appointed under the Star Chamber decree of 1637 [Arber, iv. 535].

WRIGHT (WILLIAM), senior, bookseller in London, 1591–1603; (1) In the Poultry, the middle shop in the row, adjoining to St. Mildred's Church, 1579–90; (2) In St. Paul's Churchyard, near the French School. Son of Matthew Wright of London, carpenter. Apprentice to Anne Hester for ten years from August 24th, 1564 [Arber, i. 251]. William Wright made his first book entry in the Registers on July 22nd, 1579 [Arber, ii. 357].

He dealt largely in ballads, broadsides, news books and ephemeral literature. He was one of those who violently opposed the monopolies, and was imprisoned in the Counter for his share in issuing privileged books. He subsequently made his submission and with Edward White, John Wolf and others was nominated one of the assigns of the patent belonging to Richard Day [Arber, ii. 790–3]. One of William Wright's apprentices was Cuthbert Burby, who at his death in 1607 bequeathed to William Wright, "which was my master," the sum of eight pounds [Plomer, *Wills*, p. 41].

WRIGHT (WILLIAM), junior, bookseller in London, 1613; The Harrow on Snow Hill. On April 12th and 29th, 1613, he entered several copies in the Registers [Arber, iii. 519, 522].

WYER (NICHOLAS), *see* Duff, *Century*.

WYER (ROBERT), *see* Duff, *Century*.

WYKES or WEKES (HENRY), printer in London, 1557–69; The Oliphaunt, or Black Elephant, in Fleet Street. He was an apprentice of Thomas Berthelet, being presented on October 15th, 1556 [Arber, i. 41], but did not become free until August 15th, 1565 [Arber, i. 317]. His name is however found in books as early as 1557, in which year he printed an edition of *The Instruction of a Christian Woman*, by L. Vives. In 1564 he was fined for printing two books without licence [Arber, i. 274]. His first entry in the Registers was in 1565–6 [Arber, i. 308], referred to Adlington's translation of Apuleius, *The Golden Ass*, which he printed in 1566. His last entries in the Registers were in the year 1568–9 [Arber, i. 378, 381], and his last dated publications in 1569.

WYLCOCKS (RICHARD), bookseller in Oxford, 1617. Mentioned in 1617 [Clark, *Register*, ii. 1. 321 *bis*].

WYON (MARC), printer at Douai, 1609–30; At the Golden Phœnix. His only work in English seems to have been Edmond Stratford's *Disputation of the Church wherein the old religion is maintained*, 1629 [Sayle, p. 1485]. His device was a shield with M and W and a Phœnix; the motto *Do Flammae esse suum, Flamma dat esse meum*, or sometimes *Morieris revivisco*. [Duthillœul, pp. 189–95, 408–9.]

WYON (WIDOW OF MARC), printer at Douai, 1630–59. She printed at least nine works in English between 1630 and 1640, of which the most important was Richard Broughton's *Ecclesiastical History of Great Britain*, 1633. The other works include two editions, 1632 and 1640, of Stratford's *Disputation of the Church*, which had been published by her husband in 1629 [B.M., pp. 512, 605], and *The Rule of Penance of St. Francis*, 1644 [Hazlitt, VII. 252]. She used the same device as her husband [Duthillœul, pp. 221–8, 411].

YARDLEY (JANE), *see* Yardley (Richard).

YARDLEY (RICHARD), printer in London, 1589–97; The Star, on Bread Street Hill. Son of Thomas Yardelay of Morton, co. Warwick, gent. Apprentice to Richard Jugge, stationer of London, for seven years from March 25th, 1569 [Arber, i. 377]. In 1589 he joined Peter Short at the Star on Bread Street Hill, but he died before July 4th, 1597, when his widow presented an apprentice [Arber, ii. 218]. She presented several other apprentices for their freedom down to the year 1604, but it is not clear whether she was in business as a printer or bookseller.

YETSWEIRT (CHARLES), patentee for law books, 1594–5. On March 20th, 1594, Charles Yetsweirt, Clerk of the Signet, was granted a patent for thirty years to print law books in succession to Richard Tottell. He died on April 25th, 1595. His widow Jane Yetsweirt held the patent until 1597.

YETSWEIRT (JANE), *see* Yetsweirt (C.).

YOUNG (GEORGE), Archdeacon of St. Andrews, 1585. In 1585 a licence to print certain books was granted to him, but he is not known to have exercised this privilege, which, two years later, he assigned to Gilbert Masterton, an Edinburgh bookseller [Dickson and Edmond, 481; Lee, 48, and App. xv.].

YOUNG (MICHAEL), *see* Plomer, *Dictionary*.

YOUNG (ROBERT), printer in London and Oxford, *see* Plomer, *Dictionary*.

YOUNG (WILLIAM), draper and bookseller in London, 1589–1608; near the Great Door of St. Paul's. In company with Ralph Jackson, William Young published in 1589 *An order of catechysinge* by Richard Saintbarbe. In 1594 one of his apprentices was bound to Robert Dexter, in order that when his time was expired he might become a freeman of the Stationers' Company [Arber, ii. 193]. In 1600 William Young was transferred from the Drapers' to the Stationers' Company. On October 31st, 1608, he assigned his copies to Henry Fetherstone [Arber, iii. 393].

INDEX OF LONDON SIGNS.

INDEX OF LONDON SIGNS.

Men who traded at the same sign are placed approximately in chronological order, but in many cases the exact sequence has not been ascertained.

For the sake of completeness a number of signs certainly or possibly existing before 1641, with the names of persons trading at them, have been added from Mr. Plomer's *Dictionary of Booksellers, &c. 1641–1667*. The lists of those who traded at the older signs have also been supplemented from the same source. An asterisk is prefixed to the names thus added.

Certain shops appearing under different addresses may have been identical, *e.g.* those described as in St. Paul's Churchyard and as in Paternoster Row. In the absence of proof it is, however, safer to keep them separate.

Designations such as LONG SHOP, LITTLE SHOP, etc., were practically equivalent to signs and have therefore been treated as such.

INDEX OF LONDON SIGNS.

ANGEL, Duck Lane. **Thomas Slater.*

ANGEL, Ivy Lane. **Richard Royston.*

ANGEL, Lombard Street. **Roger Daniel.*

ANGEL, Pope's Head Alley. **Roger Daniel*; **John Sweeting.*

ANGEL, Old Bailey, in the Green Arbour. *George Edwards.*

ANGEL, St. Paul's Churchyard. *John Perrin*; *Andrew Wise*; *Thomas Clarke*; *William Arundell*; *Peter Paxton*; **Edward Blackmore.*

AQUA VITAE STILL, Distaff Lane, near Old Fish Street. *Frank Adams*; *Robert Triplet.*

AXE, Hosier Lane. **William Gaye.*

BALL, St. Paul's Churchyard. *John Newbery*; **John Parker*; *John Teage*; **Nicholas Fussell.*

BEAR, The Strand, over against St. Clement's Church, without Temple Bar. *Henry Ballard.*

BELL, St. Paul's Churchyard. *George Bishop*; *Thomas Adams*; *Elizabeth Adams*; **Andrew Hebb.*

BELL, Fore Street, without Cripplegate, near Grub Street. *Abel Jeffes.*

BELL, Philip Lane. *Abel Jeffes.*

BIBLE, Britain's Burse. *Robert Swain.*

BIBLE, Chancery Lane. (?) **Henry Shepheard.*

BIBLE, Duck Lane, near Smithfield. **Richard Cartwright.*

BIBLE, Fleet Bridge. **Edward Brewster.*

BIBLE, Fleet Street. *John Browne, sen.*; *George Percivall* (near the Conduit).

BIBLE, Giltspur Street, without Newgate. **William Gilbertson.*

BIBLE, or BLUE BIBLE, Holborn Bridge. *Bernard Langford.*

BIBLE, near Guildhall Gate. *Philip Birch.*

BIBLE, Pope's Head Alley. **Thomas Nicholls.*

BIBLE, or GILT BIBLE, Queen's Head Alley, Paternoster Row. **Ralph Harford.*

BIBLE, St. Lawrence Lane, Cheapside. *Robert Bird.*

BIBLE, St. Paul's Churchyard. *Miles Jennings*; (?) *Henry Haslop*; *Thomas Cadman* (Gt. N. Door); *John Royston* (Gt. N. Door); *George Potter*; **William Bladen* (Gt. N. Door); **Edward Brewster* (or near N. Door).

BIBLE, Tower Street. **Henry Shepheard.*

BIBLE AND HARP, Smithfield. **Richard Harper.*

BISHOP'S HEAD, St. Paul's Churchyard. *William Ponsonby*; **George Latham.*

BLACKAMORE'S HEAD, Great Wood Street, near Cheapside. **Simon West.*

BLACK BEAR, Chancery Lane. *Paul Conyngton*; *Humphrey Hooper.*

BLACK BEAR, St. Paul's Churchyard. *Thomas Woodcock*; *John Flasket*; *Paul Linley*; *Edward Blount*; *Robert Allot*; *Mary Allot.*

BLACK BOY, Little (or Middle) Door of St. Paul's. *Henry Kirkham*; *William Kirkham.*

BLACK BOY, Paternoster Row. *Henry Bynneman.*

BLACK BULL, (?) Thames Street. *Edward Venge.*

BLACK ELEPHANT, *see* OLIPHAUNT.

BLACK HORSE, Aldersgate Street. *Thomas East.*

BLACK HORSE, Ivy Lane. *Henry Middleton.*

BLACK RAVEN, near St. Clement's Church. *Thomas Jones.*

BLACK SPREAD EAGLE, St. Paul's Churchyard. **G. Calvert.*

BLAZING STAR, St. Paul's Churchyard. *Daniel Speed*; **Edward Blackmore.*

BLIND KNIGHT, Holborn. **William Luggar.*

BLUE BIBLE, Covent Garden. **Michael Young.*

BLUE BIBLE, Green Arbour Court, Old Bailey. **Michael Sparke, sen.*; **Michael Sparke, jun.*

BLUE BIBLE, *see also* BIBLE.

BRAZEN SERPENT, St. Paul's Churchyard. *John Sheppard*; *Richard Vernon*; *Andrew Maunsell*; *Robert Dexter*; *Edward Bishop*; **George Latham*; **Robert Dawlman.*

BROAD AXE, without Aldgate. *Henry Conway.*

BULL, or RED BULL, Little Britain. **Daniel Frere.*

BULL (or BULL'S) HEAD, St. Paul's Churchyard. *Eleazer Edgar*; *Samuel Macham I*; *Timothy Barlow*; *Roger Michell*; *Ambrose Ritherdon.*

BULL'S HEAD, Cateaton Street, Cheapside. **John Aston.*

CARDINAL'S HAT, without Newgate. *John Barnes*; *Richard Higginbotham.*

CASTLE, Cornhill. **Humphrey Blunden.*

CASTLE, Holborn. *Roger Ward.*

CASTLE, Salisbury Court. *Roger Ward.*

CAT AND FIDDLE, Old Exchange. *Henry Carre.*

CATHERINE WHEEL, Thames Street. *Thomas Creede.*

CATS AND PARROT, near the Exchange. *Thomas Pavier.*

CHRISTOPHER, St. Paul's Churchyard. *Thomas Ellis.*

CHURCH, Chancery Lane. **Thomas Gould.*

COCK, St. Paul's Churchyard. *Leonard Maylord.*

CRADLE, Lombard Street. (?) *Joan Sutton*; *Hugh Spooner*.

CRANE, St. Paul's Churchyard. *Toby Smith*; *Robert Waldegrave*; *Richard Oliffe*; *William Leake*; *Walter Burre*; *John Stepney* (west end of St. Paul's); (?) **Robert Mead*; **Christopher Meredith*; **Francis Constable*.

CROSS KEYS, St. Paul's Churchyard. *George Vincent*.

CROSS KEYS, St. Paul's Gate. *George Vincent*.

CROSS KEYS, St. Paul's Wharf. *John Windet*; *William Stansby*.

CROWN, Cheap Gate, (?) St. Paul's Churchyard. **John Waterson*.

CROWN, Cornhill. **John Sweeting*.

CROWN, Duck Lane. *Samuel Nealand*.

CROWN, Fleet Street, between the two Temple Gates. **William Leake*.

CROWN, near Ludgate. **Walter Edmonds*.

CROWN, Pope's Head Alley. **Benjamin Allen*.

CROWN, St. Paul's Churchyard (*cf.* Crown, Cheap Gate). *Simon Waterson*; **John Williams*.

DOLPHIN, Old Fish Street. **Bernard Alsop*.

EAGLE, Lombard Street, near the Stocks Market. *Edmund Halley*.

EAGLE AND CHILD, Britain's Burse. **Thomas Walkley*.

EAGLE AND CHILD, Old Bailey. *Thomas Creede*; **Bernard Alsop*.

EAGLE AND CHILD, St. Paul's Churchyard, near St. Austin's Gate. **Jasper Emery*.

ELEPHANT, Fleet Street (*see also* Oliphant). *Henry Cockyn*.

FALCON, Fleet Street. *Henry Middleton*.

FALCON, Shoe Lane, St. Bride's Parish. *Walter Dight*; *Richard Shorleyker*.

FLOWER DE LUCE, Fleet Street, near Fetter Lane end. *John Hodgets*.

FLOWER DE LUCE, St. Paul's Churchyard. *Walter Burre*; *George Gibbs*; *James Boler*.

FLOWER DE LUCE, *see also* WHITE FLOWER DE LUCE.

FLOWER DE LUCE AND CROWN, Paternoster Row. *William Tymme*.

FLOWER DE LUCE AND CROWN, St. Paul's Churchyard. *Walter Burre*; *Arthur Johnson*; *Richard Bonion*; *Ralph Rounthwaite*.

FLYING HORSE, near York House. **Thomas Walkley*.

FOUNTAIN, St. Paul's Churchyard. **Samuel Browne*.

FOX, St. Paul's Churchyard, near St. Augustine's Gate. *Matthew Lawe*.

GEORGE, Lombard Street. *Thomas Humble*.

GEORGE, Pope's Head Alley, near the Royal Exchange. *George Fairbeard*.

GEORGE, St. Paul's Churchyard. *Thomas Stirrup*; *Henry Olney* (near Cheap Gate).

GILDED CUP, Fore Street, Cripplegate. *Edward Allde*; *Elizabeth Allde*.

GILT BIBLE, *see* BIBLE.

GILT CUP, Goldsmiths' Row, Cheapside. **John Bartlet, sen.*

GLOBE, over against the Royal Exchange. *Francis Williams*.

GLOVE, Cornhill. **William Hope*.

GLOVE, near the Royal Exchange. **Peter Cole*.

GOAT, King Street, Westminster. **Francis Constable*.

GOLDEN ANCHOR, Paternoster Row. *John Harrison II*; *Josiah Harrison*.

GOLDEN ANCHOR, Strand, near Temple Bar (or Strand, next the Nag's Head, without Temple Bar). *Roger Ball*.

GOLDEN BALL, Little Britain. **Richard Clutterbuck*.

GOLDEN BALL, Pope's Head Alley. *George Loftus*.

GOLDEN BALL, St. Paul's Churchyard. *John Teage*.

GOLDEN BUCK, Fleet Street, near Sergeants' Inn. **William Lee*.

GOLDEN EAGLE AND CHILD, Paternoster Row. *John Hill*.

GOLDEN HIND, St. Paul's Churchyard. *John Hinde*.

GOLDEN KEY, St. Paul's Churchyard, near the Great North Door. *Richard Woodroffe*.

GOLDEN LION, Duck Lane. **Mathew Simmons*.

GOLDEN LION, Little Britain. **Laurence Sadler*.

GOLDEN TUN, Fleet Street, near St. Dunstan's Church. *John Winnington*.

GOSHAWK IN THE SUN, St. Paul's Churchyard, next the Gate, the corner shop to Cheapside. *Thomas Gosson*.

GRASSHOPPER, St. Paul's Churchyard. *Christopher Barker*; *Augustine Laughton*.

GREAT BIBLE, at the Great North Door of St. Paul's. *Joan Broome*.

GREAT TURK'S HEAD, Fleet Street. *John Barnes*.

GREEN DRAGON, St. Paul's Churchyard. *Francis Coldock*; *Thomas Hayes*; *William Barrett*; *Francis Burton*; *John Budge*; *Thomas Alchorne*; **Andrew Crooke*.

GREEN OAK, *see* OAKEN TREE.

GREYHOUND, Paternoster Row. *John Penny*; *Joseph Harrison* (*cf.* White Greyhound).

GREYHOUND, St. Paul's Churchyard. *William Welby*; *Michael Baker*; *Robert Allot*; *Thomas Allot*; **Ralph Mabb*; **Robert Milborne*; **John Crooke*; **Thomas Cowley*.

GRIFFIN, Paternoster Row, over against the Black Raven. *Thomas Gubbin*.

GUN, Ivy Lane. *John Grismand*; **Charles Green*.

GUN, near Holborn Conduit. *William Jones*.

GUN, near Little North Door of St. Paul's. *Edward White, sen.*; *John Grismand*.

GUN, St. Paul's Alley. *John Grismand*.

HALF BOWL in the Old Bailey. **Francis Coles*.

HALF EAGLE AND KEY, Barbican. *William Jaggard*.

HALF EAGLE AND KEY, Fleet Lane, Old Bailey. *Richard Serle*.

HALF ROSE AND HALF SUN, next the North Door of the Exchange. *Thomas Frethen*.

HAND AND BIBLE, Duck Lane. **Richard Cartwright*.

HAND AND GOLDEN PEN, Fetter Lane. *Richard Gething*.

HAND AND PLOUGH, Fleet Street. *William Mattes*; *Edmund Mattes*.

HAND AND STAR, Fleet Street, between the two Temple Gates. *John Jaggard*.

HAND IN HAND, Wood Street, over against St. Michael's Church. *George Vincent*.

HARP, Shoe Lane. *Walter Dight*.

HARROW, Snow Hill. *William Wright, jun.*

HART'S HORN, Foster Lane. **Henry Walley*.

HELMET, St. Paul's Churchyard. *Humphrey Toy*; *Thomas Chard*.

HOLY BUSH, Ivy Lane. *Henry Holland*.

HOLY GHOST, St. Paul's Churchyard. *Gabriel Cawood*; *William Leake*.

HOLY LAMB, Ludgate Hill. *John Coleby*.

HOLY LAMB, Paternoster Row. *John Harrigat*.

HOLY LAMB, St. Paul's Churchyard. *Clement Knight*; **Thomas Knight*.

HORSESHOE, near the Hospital Gate, Smithfield. *Thomas Lambert*.

HUNTSMAN, Paternoster Row. *Edmund Mutton*.

IRISH WAREHOUSE, Stationers' Hall. **Thomas Downes*.

ST. JOHN THE EVANGELIST, beside Charing Cross. *Thomas Colwell*.

ST. JOHN THE EVANGELIST, Fleet Street beneath the Conduit. *Thomas Colwell*; *Hugh Jackson*.

JONAS, (?) St. Paul's Churchyard. *Eleazar Edgar*.

KING'S ARMS, St. Paul's Churchyard. *Joyce Norton*; **Richard Whitaker*.

KING'S HEAD, Old Bailey. **John Wright, sen.*; **John Wright, jun.*

KING'S HEAD, St. Paul's Churchyard. *Thomas Norton*; (?) *Hannah Barrett*; **Robert Bostock.*

LAMB, Ludgate Hill. *William Holmes, jun.*

LAMB, New Fish Street Hill. **Fulke Clifton.*

LAMB, Old Bailey. **Francis Coles.*

LITTLE SHOP, at the North Door of St. Paul's. *William Owen.*

LITTLE SHOP, by the North-West Door of St. Paul's. *Richard Jones.*

LITTLE SHOP, by the Royal Exchange. *Thomas Archer.*

LODGE, Chancery Lane, over against Lincoln's Inn. *Robert Clarke.*

LONG SHOP, adjoining Ludgate. *William Cotton.*

LONG SHOP, at the West End of St. Paul's (*see also* New Long Shop). *Richard Day.*

LONG SHOP, in the Poultry, under St. Mildred's Church. *Edward Allde*; *Margaret Allde*; (?) *Thomas Archer*; *Henry Rocket.*

LOVE AND DEATH, Fleet Street. *John Roberts.*

LUCRECE, in the New Rents in Newgate Market. *Thomas Purfoot*; **Thomas Badger.*

LUTE, Paternoster Row. *James Rowbotham.*

MARIGOLD, St. Paul's Churchyard. *James Bowler*; *Anne Bowler*; **Francis Eglesfield.*

MERMAID, Holborn. *Thomas Saunders.*

MERMAID, Knightrider Street. *Henry Bynneman.*

MERMAID, Paternoster Row. *Henry Bynneman.*

MERMAID, St. Paul's Churchyard. *Nicholas Ling.*

NEW LONG SHOP, at the West Door of St. Paul's. *William Jones.*

NOBODY, Barbican. *John Trundle.*

NOVAM LIBRARIORUM OFFICINAM, AD, St. Paul's Churchyard. *Martin Clarke.*

OAKEN TREE, or GREEN OAK, Long Lane. *Edward Aggas.*

OLIPHAUNT, or BLACK ELEPHANT, Fleet Street. *Henry Wykes.*

PARIS, without Newgate, by St. Sepulchre's. *John Barnes.*

PARROT, St. Paul's Churchyard. *Andrew Maunsell*; *John Oxenbridge*; *Felix Norton*; *William Aspley*; **Luke Fawne.*

PIED BULL, St. Austin's Gate, St. Paul's Churchyard. **N. Butter.*

POPE'S HEAD, near the Exchange. *Andrew Harris.*

PRINCE'S ARMS, St. Paul's Churchyard. **Humphrey Moseley.*

PRINTER'S PRESS, Fleet Lane. *William Blaincher*; *George Eld.*

PURSE, Little Old Bailey. *Roger Ward.*

RAINBOW, Fleet Street, near the Inner Temple Gate. *Ephraim Dawson*; **Daniel Pakeman.*

RED BOWL, St. Paul's Churchyard. *Henry Sanderson.*

RED BULL, *see* BULL.

RED DRAGON, West End of St. Paul's. *Edward Aggas.*

RED LION, London Bridge. *Richard Bonion.*

ROSE, (?) *Richard Boyle.*

ROSE, St. Paul's Churchyard. *Thomas Wight*; **George Thomason*; **Octavian Pulleyn, sen.*

ROSE AND CROWN, over against the Falcon, near Holborn Bridge, without Newgate. *Richard Jones.*

ROSE AND CROWN, St. Paul's Churchyard. **George Thomason.*

ROSE AND POMEGRANATE, Cheapside, under Bow Church. *James Rowbotham.*

SHIP, London Wall. (?) *Thomas East* (*by* the Ship); *Henry Middleton.*

SHIP, St. Paul's Churchyard. **John Crooke.*

SPLAYED EAGLE, Great Wood Street. *Richard Field.*

SPREAD EAGLE, in the upper end of Fleet Lane. *Richard Jones.*

SPREAD EAGLE, near the Great North Door of St. Paul's. *Richard Bonion.*

STAR, Aldersgate Street. *Henry Denham.*

STAR, at the West Door (End) of St. Paul's. *Jonas Man*; *Richard Redmer*; **Edward Brewster.*

STAR, Bread Street Hill. *Richard Yardley*; *Peter Short*; *E. Short*; *Humphrey Lownes.*

STAR, Duck Lane. **T. Jackson.*

STAR, Paternoster Row. *H. Denham.*

STAR, under St. Peter's Church, Cornhill. *Samuel Ward.*

SUGARLOAF, Fleet Street, over against Whitefriars. *John Brown, sen.*; **Lawrence Blaiklock* (next Temple Bar).

SUN, Bethlem. *Henry Bell.*

SUN, near Holborn Conduit. *Francis Smith.*

SUN, Paternoster Row. *Henry Gosson*; (?) *Thomas Gosson.*

SUN, St. Paul's Churchyard. *Abraham Kitson*; *Richard Bankworth.*

SWAN, Little Britain. *Henry Ockould*; **Godfrey Emerson.*

SWAN, Paternoster Row. *John Drawater.*

SWAN, St. Paul's Churchyard. *Garrat D'Ewes*; *Cuthbert Burby*; *Elizabeth Burby*; *William Welby*; **Samuel Man*; **John Rothwell.*

TALBOT, Aldersgate Street. *Benjamin Fisher.*

TALBOT, a little above Holborn Conduit. *Nicholas Dyos.*

TALBOT, by Holborn Conduit. *Roger Ward.*

TALBOT, Paternoster Row. *Robert Walker*; *Thomas Man, sen.*; *Thomas Man, jun.*; *Jonas Man*; *Paul Man.*

THREE CONIES, Old Exchange. *Henry Carre.*

THREE CRANES, in the Vintry. *Thomas Dawson*; (?) *Thomas Gardiner*; (?) *John Dawson*; *Mary Dawson.*

THREE CROWNS, in the Cloth Fair. *Simon Stafford.*

THREE FLOWER DE LUCES, St. Paul's Alley, near St. Gregory's Church. *Richard Fleming.*

THREE FOXES, Long Lane. **William Wilson.*

THREE GOLDEN FALCONS, Duck Lane. **W. Adderton.*

THREE GOLDEN LIONS, Cornhill. **John Bellamy.*

THREE PIGEONS, Paternoster Row. *John Hill.*

THREE PIGEONS, St. Paul's Churchyard. *William Barrett*; **John Parker*; **Humphrey Robinson.*

THREE WELLS, North-West Door of St. Paul's. *Henry Bynneman.*

TIGER'S HEAD, Paternoster Row. *Christopher Barker.*

TIGER'S HEAD, St. Paul's Churchyard. *Christopher Barker*; *Toby Cooke*; *William Aspley*; *Matthew Cooke*; *John Hardy*; *Laurence Lisle*; **Henry Seile.*

TIME, St. Paul's Churchyard. *Joyce Macham.*

TURK'S HEAD, Fleet Street, next to the Mitre and Phœnix. **William Lee.*

TURK'S HEAD, Ivy Lane. **Joseph Blaiklock.*

TWO GREYHOUNDS, Cornhill. **John Bellamy.*

UNICORN, Cannon Lane, near St. Paul's. *John Drawater.*

UNICORN, Cornhill, near the Royal Exchange. **William Hope.*

UNICORN, near Fleet Bridge. *John Coleby*; **Robert Milborne.*

UNICORN, Paternoster Row. *John Harrison IV.*

VINE, Fleet Street. *Edward Venge.*

WHITE BEAR, Addling Street, near Baynard's Castle. *John Windet.*

WHITE BEAR, at St. Sepulchre's Door. *Henry Tomes.*

WHITE BEAR, Cornewell (*i.e.* Cornhill). **Thomas Jenner.*

WHITE BEAR, Foster Lane, over against Goldsmiths' Hall. **William Garrett.*

WHITE BEAR, near the Exchange. **Thomas Jenner.*

WHITE FLOWER DE LUCE, St. Dunstan's Churchyard, Fleet Street. **John Marriot.*

WHITE GREYHOUND, St. Paul's Churchyard. *William Leake*; *John Harrison III.*

WHITE HART, Fleet Street. *Thomas Fisher*; *John North* (over against the Great Conduit); (?) *Richard Jackson.*

WHITE HIND, Colman Street. *W. Harris.*

WHITE HIND, without Cripplegate. **Robert Wood.*

WHITE HORSE, Fleet Lane, over against Seacole Lane. *Gabriel Simpson*; *William White.*

WHITE HORSE, Little Britain. *William Hills.*

WHITE HORSE, near the Great North Door of St. Paul's. *Ralph Howell.*

WHITE HORSE, Pope's Head Alley. *George Humble*; *John Sudbury.*

WHITE HORSE, St. Paul's Churchyard. *William Williamson*; **Joshua Kirton.*

WHITE HORSE, without Newgate. **Henry Overton.*

WHITE LION, near Charing Cross. *George Baker.*

WHITE LION, St. Paul's Churchyard. (?) *Thomas Adams*; *Francis Burton*; **Francis Constable*; **Charles Green.*

WHITE SWAN, Addling Hill. *Valentine Simmes*; **Richard Badger.*

WHITE SWAN, St. Paul's Churchyard. *Ralph Jackson.*

WHITE UNICORN, Pope's Head Alley. *Randall Bearkes.*

WINDMILL, Britain's Burse. *John Budge.*

WINDMILL, St. Paul's Churchyard. *Eleazar Edgar*; *Ambrose Garbrand.*

WINDMILL, Snow Hill, near to St. Sepulchre's Church. **Francis Grove.*

WOOLPACK, Hosier Lane. *Richard Hudson.*

INDEX OF LONDON ADDRESSES.

INDEX OF LONDON ADDRESSES.

Names of Signs are printed as WHITE SWAN. For the printers or stationers who dwelt at them, *see* the Index of London Signs. Addresses are generally indexed under Streets or Lanes, when these are given.

INDEX OF LONDON ADDRESSES.

Addle, or Addling, Hill, WHITE SWAN: near Carter Lane, *S. Stafford.*

Addling Street, *W. Kearney*: nigh Baynard's Castle, WHITE BEAR.

Alban's, St., *see* Wood Street.

Aldermanbury, a little above the Conduit, *R. Bradock*; *T. Haviland.*

Aldersgate, opposite the Pump, *E. Allde*: Under, *G. Seton.*

Aldersgate Street, BLACK HORSE; STAR; TALBOT: Northumberland House, St. Martin's Lane, *C. Barker*; *J. Bill*; *B. Norton.*

Aldersgate Ward, *L. Senior*; *J. Wilford.*

Aldgate, A little within, *H. Skelton*: Without, *J. Hopkinson*; BROAD AXE.

Aldgate Ward, *F. Trots.*

Andrew's, St., *see* Holborn.

Augustine's (Austin's) Gate, *see* St. Paul's Churchyard.

Anne's, St., *see* Blackfriars.

Antholin's, Parish of St., *O. Churton.*

Bacon House, *see* Cheapside.

Bailey, *see* Little Old Bailey; Old Bailey.

Barbican, *J. Davis*; *I. Jaggard*; *J. Roberts*; HALF EAGLE AND KEY; NOBODY.

Baynard's Castle, *see* Castle Baynard; Addling Street; Thames Street.

Bedlem, or Bethlem, *T. Bourne*; *R. Cox*; SUN: near Moorfield Gate, *J. Hunt.*

Benet Fink, Parish of St., Broadstreet Ward, *H. Francis.*

Green's Rents and the Wharf, Farringdon Without, *P. Rotteford.*

Gregory's Church, St., *see* St. Paul's Alley.

Gregory's Parish, St., *T. Hodgkinson.*

Grub Street, *G. Wood*: *see* Fore Street.

Guildhall, *P. Birch*: By the, *S. Clarke.*

Guildhall Gate, *T. Turner*: Near, BIBLE: *see* Cateaton Street.

Gunpowder Alley, *Udall.*

Hammersmith, *R. Ward.*

Holborn, *Bailey*; *H. Barber*; *Bulmer*; *Lovet*; *R. Wilson*; BLIND KNIGHT; CASTLE; MERMAID: at upper end of Gray's Inn Lane, *B. Lightfoot*:- St. Andrew's, *R. Robinson*: *see* Turnstile Lane.

Holborn Bridge, (?) *J. Hunter*; BIBLE or BLUE BIBLE: Near, *N. Okes*; *J. Orphinstrange*: Near, over against the Falcon, ROSE AND CROWN: Upon, *J. Proctor.*

Holborn Conduit, *R. Gladwin*: A little above, TALBOT: By, TALBOT: Near, *W. Elfe* or *Ellis*; *T. Jones*; GUN; SUN: *see* Cow Lane; Hosier Lane.

Holborn Hill, near the Cross Keys, *H. Bell.*

Hosier Lane, AXE; WOOLPACK: near Holborn Conduit, *J. Danter*: near Smithfield, *J. Barnes.*

Hunsdon House, *see* Blackfriars.

Inner Temple Gate, *see* Fleet Street.

Ivy Lane, *T. Pavier*; ANGEL; BLACK HORSE; GUN; HOLY BUSH; TURK'S HEAD.

John's Street, St., Clerkenwell, *J. Bowen.*

King Lane, *S. Nealand.*

King Street, Westminster, GOAT.

Knightrider Street, MERMAID.

Lambert Hill, near Old Fish Street, *E. Allde*; *R. Ward*; *W. Ward.*

Lame Hospital, *see* Smithfield.

Lawrence Lane, St., Cheapside, BIBLE.

Leadenhall, *see* Gratious Street.

Lincoln's Inn, *see* Chancery Lane.

Little Britain, *J. Browne, sen.*; *J. Browne, jun.*; *F. Ely*; *W. Harper*; *F. Hill*; *C. Hodges*; *J. Hopkinson*; *J. Rhodes*; *H. Skelton*; *G. Wright*; BULL or RED BULL; GOLDEN BALL; GOLDEN LION; SWAN; WHITE HORSE.

Little Old Bailey, near the King's Head, *E. Griffin*; PURSE: *for* Eliot's Court *see* Old Bailey.

Little St. Helen's, *W. Barley.*

Lombard Street, ANGEL; CRADLE; GEORGE: near the Stocks Market, EAGLE: over against the Cardinal's Hat, *F. Coldock*: *see* Pope's Head Alley.

London Bridge, *J. Spencer*: near the Gate, *H. Gosson*; *T. Gosson*; *S. Pemell*; RED LION: *see* St. Magnus Corner.

London Wall, SHIP.

Long Lane, *R. Oliffe*; OAKEN TREE or GREEN OAK; THREE FOXES: *see* Smithfield.

Lothbury, *G. Low*; *A. Maunsell*: at hither end of Colman Street, *W. Ferbrand.*

Lottery House, Under the, *R. Jones.*

Ludgate, Adjoining, LONG SHOP: Near, *J. Shaw*; CROWN: The house of Mistress Stubbes in the alley adjoining, *R. Willis.*

Ludgate Hill, HOLY LAMB; LAMB.

Magnus Corner, St., by London Bridge, *H. Astley*; *R. Ballard*; *J. Tapp.*

Maiden Lane, near Wood Street, *A. Laughton.*

Martin's, St., in the Vintry, *H. Brewer.*

Martin's Lane, St., *see* Aldersgate Street.

Mary Axe, St., *T. Gellibrand.*

Michael's Church, St., *see* Wood Street.

Middle Temple Gate, *see* Fleet Street; Temple Bar.

Mildred's Church, St., *see* Poultry.

Moorfield Gate, *see* Bedlem.

Moor Fields, Near, *J. Jackson.*

New Fish Street Hill, LAMB.

Newgate, Without, CARDINAL'S HAT; PARIS; WHITE HORSE: over against the Saracen's Head, *T. Langley*: over against St. Sepulchre's Church, *R. Jones*; *T. Purfoot*: *see* Old Bailey.

Newgate Market, *W. Barley*: in the New Rents, LUCRECE: over against Christ Church Gate, *Y. James.*

Newgate Street, near Christ Church, St. Faith's Parish, *I. Bing*; *J. Jugge*: *see* Christ Church.

Nicholas Shambles, St., *see* Rose Alley.

Norfolk's Place, Duke of, by Cree Church, *H. Stell.*

Northumberland House, *see* Aldersgate Street.

Olave's, St., Cripplegate, *P. Lignante.*

Old Bailey, EAGLE AND CHILD; HALF BOWL; KING'S HEAD; LAMB: Eliot's Court (sometimes, more correctly, described as in Little Old Bailey), *H. Bell*; *E. Bollifant*; *M. Broadwood*; *A. Hatfield*; *J. Haviland*; *J. Jackson*; *N. Newton*: Green Arbour, ANGEL: Green Arbour Court, BLUE BIBLE: near the Golden Lion, *R. Walker*: over against the Sessions House, *J. Haviland*: Upper end of, among the saddlers, *N. Fosbrook*: Upper end of, near Newgate, *M. Rhodes*: *see* Little Old Bailey.

Old Exchange, CAT AND FIDDLE; THREE CONIES.

Old Fish Street, DOLPHIN: *see* Distaff Lane; Lambert Hill; Trinity Lane.

Pannier Alley, *A. Gosson*; *H. Gosson.*

Paternoster Row, BLACK BOY; GOLDEN ANCHOR; GOLDEN EAGLE AND CHILD; GREYHOUND; HOLY LAMB; HUNTSMAN; LUTE; MERMAID; STAR; SUN; SWAN; TALBOT; THREE PIGEONS; TIGER'S HEAD; UNICORN: near the Castle Tavern (? at the Sun), *T. Gosson*: near Cheapside, FLOWER DE LUCE AND CROWN; over against the Black Raven, GRIFFIN; over against the Checker, *J. Orwin*; *T. Orwin*: without the North Gate of St. Paul's, opening into Cheapside, J. Burrell.

Paul's, St., Great Door, Near, *W. Young.*

——, Great North Door, At or Near, *W. Barringer*; *W. Blackman*; *W. Holmes*; *A. Jeffes*; *S. Shorter*; GOLDEN KEY; GREAT BIBLE; SPREAD EAGLE: Over against, *E. Blount.*

——, Great South Door, *J. Budge*: on the right hand going up the steps, *R. Fleming*: Over against, *T. Nelson.*

——, Little (or Middle) Door, BLACK BOY.

——, Little North Door, *J. Bailey*: Near, GUN; WHITE HORSE.

——, Little West Door, *N. Ling*; LITTLE SHOP.

——, North Door, *J. Arnold*; *T. Bushel*; *G. Charlton*; *J. Flasket*; LITTLE SHOP: Over against, in St. Bride's Churchyard, *T. Colwell.*

——, North Gate of, *see* Paternoster Row.

——, North West Door, *N. Ling*; THREE WELLS: at the corner shop, *R. Smith.*

——, South Door, Over against, *J. Wolf.*

——, South-West Door, *H. Disle*, *R. Jones*, *W. Jones.*

——, West Door (or End), *F. Godlif*; *T. Law*; *N. Ling*; *H. Lownes*; *T. Nelson*; *G. Robinson*; *W. Wood*; LONG SHOP; NEW LONG SHOP; RED DRAGON; STAR; between the Brazen Pillar and

Lollards' Tower, *R. Jones*: corner shop near the Bishop of London's Gate, *N. Fosbrook.*

Paul's Alley, St., GUN: over against St. Gregory's Church, THREE FLOWER DE LUCES.

Paul's Chain, St., *J. Wolf.*

Paul's Churchyard, St., *T. Gubbins*; *J. Piper*; *B. Sutton*; *W. Telotson*; *R. Walley*; *E. Weaver*; *W. Williamson*; ANGEL; BALL (GOLDEN BALL); BELL; BIBLE; BISHOP'S HEAD; BLACK BEAR; BLACK SPREAD EAGLE; BLAZING STAR; BRAZEN SERPENT; BULL('S) HEAD; CHRISTOPHER; COCK; CRANE; CROSS KEYS; CROWN; FLOWER DE LUCE; FLOWER DE LUCE AND CROWN; FOUNTAIN; GEORGE; GOLDEN BALL; GOLDEN HIND; GRASSHOPPER; GREEN DRAGON; GREYHOUND; HELMET; HOLY GHOST; HOLY LAMB; JONAS; KING'S ARMS; KING'S HEAD; MARIGOLD; MERMAID; AD NOVAM LIBRARIORUM OFFICINAM; PARROT; PRINCE'S ARMS; RED BOWL; ROSE; ROSE AND CROWN; SHIP; SUN; SWAN; THREE PIGEONS; TIGER'S HEAD; TIME; WHITE GREYHOUND; WHITE HORSE; WHITE LION; WHITE SWAN: Cheap Gate, CROWN: near the French School, *W. Wright, sen.*: near the Gate, corner shop to Cheapside, GOSHAWK IN THE SUN: near St. Augustine's (Austin's) Gate, *T. Butter*; EAGLE AND CHILD; FOX; PIED BULL: near Watling Street, *M. Lawe*: over against the Blazing Star, *H. Carre*: over against the Cross, *E. Marchant*: *see also the various* Doors of St. Paul's *above*; Queen's Head Alley.

Paul's Gate, St., CROSS KEYS.

Paul's Wharf, St., CROSS KEYS: *see* Thames Street.

Peter's St., *see* Black Raven Alley; Cornhill.

Philip Lane, BELL.

Pope's Head Alley, *N. Newbery*; ANGEL; BIBLE; CROWN; GEORGE; GOLDEN BALL; WHITE HORSE; WHITE UNICORN: near the Exchange, *R. Canter*; *G. Loftus*: out of Lombard Street, *N. Fosbrook*; *W. Sheffard*; over against the Horseshoe, *T. Archer.*

Pope's Head Palace, *G. Humble*; *J. Sudbury*: near the Exchange, *T. Archer.*

Pope's Head Passage, *J. Bache.*

Poultry, by St. Mildred's Church, *C. Burby*: middle shop in the row adjoining to St. Mildred's Church, *W. Wright, sen.*: under St. Mildred's Church, LONG SHOP.

Puddle Wharf, *see* Blackfriars.

Queen's Head Alley, Paternoster Row, BIBLE or GILT BIBLE.

Red Cross Street, adjoining St. Giles' without Cripplegate, *J. Mather*; *J. Moptid*: parish of St. Giles without Cripplegate, *R. Baynes*: *see* Ship Alley.

Rood Lane, *S. Peele.*

Rose Alley, parish of St. Nicholas Shambles, Farringdon Within, *T. Snape.*

Royal Exchange, or Exchange, *P. Harrison*; *A. Maunsell*: 'Britain's Burse,' *J. Budge*; *J. Gwillim*; *T. Johnson*; BIBLE; EAGLE AND CHILD; WINDMILL: Behind the Royal Exchange, *S. Clarke*: By, BIBLE; LITTLE SHOP: Entering into, *T. Pavier*: Near, CATS AND PARROT; GLOVE; POPE'S HEAD: Next the North Door of, HALF ROSE AND HALF CROWN; WHITE BEAR: Over against, *C. Holland*; GLOBE: Over against the Conduit in Cornhill, *A. White*: *see* Old Exchange; *also* Cornhill; Pope's Head Alley; Pope's Head Palace.

Salisbury Court, CASTLE.

Seacoal Lane, *see* Fleet Street.

Sepulchre's Church, St., At door of, WHITE BEAR: Under, *G. Loftus*: *see* Newgate; Snow Hill.

Sepulchre's Parish, St., *T. Lownes III.*

Sergeant's Inn, *see* Chancery Lane; Fleet Street.

Sessions House, *see* Old Bailey.

Ship Alley, Redcross Street, Cripplegate, *W. Jones.*

Shoe Lane, *May*; FALCON; HARP.

Silver Street, near the Red Cross, *T. Nelson.*

Sion College, *J. Spencer.*

Six Clerks' Office, *see* Chancery Lane.

Smithfield, *T. Andrewes*: at the (Lame) Hospital Gate, *H. Bell*; HORSE-SHOE: near Long Lane End, *R. Bolton*; BIBLE AND HARP: *see* Duck Lane.

Snow Hill, HARROW: near St. Sepulchre's, WINDMILL.

Southwark, *Truck*: near the Market Place, *R. Aldred.*

Stationers' Hall, IRISH WAREHOUSE.

Stepney, *G. Wood*: *see* Bishop's Hall.

Stocks Market, *see* Lombard Street.

Strand, near York House, *T. Jones*; *R. Horseman*: without Temple Bar, *R. Waldegrave*; (next Nag's Head) GOLDEN ANCHOR: over against St. Clement's Church, BEAR.

Strand Bridge, Near, *J. Brambridge.*

Swithin's Lane, *R. Langton.*

Temple, The, *R. Ward*; *J. Wells*: near the Church, *L. Becket.*

Temple Bar, Fleet Street, *J. Dearne*; *R. Mundee*; *G. Norton*: Within, next Middle Temple Gate, *W. Hoskins*: *see* Strand.

Temple Gate, *see* Fleet Street.

Thames Street, (?) BLACK BULL; CATHERINE WHEEL: between St. Paul's Wharf and Baynard's Castle, *T. East*: near Baynard's Castle, *H. Bynneman.*

Tower Hill, near the Bulwark Gate, *J. Tapp.*

Tower Street, BIBLE.

Trinity Lane, between Old Fish Street and Bow Lane, *J. Legatt.*

Turnstile Lane, Holborn, *W. Brookes.*

Vintry, THREE CRANES: *see* St. Martin's.

Watling Street, *see* St. Paul's Churchyard.

Westminster, *see* King Street.

Wharf, The, *see* Green's Rents.

White Cross Street, Cripplegate, *H. Denham.*

White Friars, near the Mulberry Tree, *V. Simmes*: *see* Fleet Street.

Wood Street, *R. Avery*: parish of St. Alban's, *C. Tressell*: over against St. Michael's Church, HAND IN HAND: *see* Maiden Lane.

York House, Near, FLYING HORSE: *see* Strand.

INDEX OF PLACES OTHER THAN LONDON.

INDEX OF PLACES OTHER THAN LONDON.

The names of the printers, stationers, etc., at each place are arranged, as far as possible, in the order of the dates at which they begin business.

Names which appear to be fictitious are enclosed in square brackets.

For the sake of completeness a few names of persons who overlap the period 1557–1640 have been added from Mr. Duff's *Century of the English Book Trade*, and Mr. Plomer's *Dictionary, 1641–67.*

† is prefixed to those taken from Mr. Duff and * to those from Mr. Plomer.

INDEX OF PLACES OTHER THAN LONDON.

A.—England, Scotland, Ireland and Wales.

Aberdeen: D. Melvill, 1622–43; E. Raban, 1622–50.

Astbury, Cheshire: H. Snape, 1585.

Banbury, Oxfordshire: H. Sharpe, 1608–19; E. Langham, ? 1623–? 1641.

Bury St. Edmund's: T. Gibson, 1582.

Cambridge: † R. Noke, 1540–57; † P. Sheres, 1545–69; S. Watson, ? 1553–? 1564; † Baxter, 1557; Ph. Scarlet, sen., 1563–82; J. Cuthbert, 1566–97; R. Boyce, 1568; J. Sheres, ? 1571–81; B. Nycholas, *al.* Segar, 1573–95; T. Bradshaw, 1573–1610; A. Harrison, 1573–1625; H. Moody, 1575–1637; J. Porter, ? 1576–1608; P. Waters, 1581–2; W. Scarlet, 1581–1617; T. Thomas, 1583–8; J. Legatt, sen., 1586–1620; P. Scarlet, 1590–1640; B. Prime, 1592–4; M. Vautrollier, 1592–4; J. James, 1592–1624; W. Jackson, ? 1593–5; H. Burwell, ? 1593–? 1601; J. Pinder, sen., 1604; Ph. Scarlet, jun., 1605–34; C. Legge, 1606–*c.* 1629; L. Greene, 1606–30; W. Williamson, 1607–35; T. Brooke, ? 1608–29; J. Sampson, 1610; E. Porter, 1615–33; S. Disher, 1616–24; D. Boyce, 1616–30; S. Roebuck, 1616–35; H. Wray, 1617–28; * J. Legatt, jun., 1620–58; J. Pinder, jun., 1621–35; T. Browne, 1621–? 1636; R. Leete, 1622–63; T. Morden, 1624; R. Ewlam, *c.* 1624; * J. Buck, 1625–61; * T. Buck, 1625–70; T. Atkinson, 1626–35; T. Moody, 1627–61; J. Milleson, 1627–70; F. Greene, 1628–35; F. Buck, 1630–2; J. Greene, 1631–7; * W. Graves, ? 1631–65; P. Waterhouse, 1632; * R. Daniel, 1632–50; * R. Ireland, 1634–52; R. Browne, 1645–71.

Canterbury: R. Wallys, 1571; C. Bassock, 1571–6; J. Bulkley, 1622.

Chester: W. Holme, 1591; J. Atkins, 1592; T. Humphreys, 1621–48; D. Humphreys, 1635–(?); R. Thorpe, 1635–(?); P. Ince, (?)–1648.

Colchester: B. Harding, 1624.

Dorchester: J. Long, 1634.

Dublin: (?) J. Usher, 1571; W. Kearney, 1593–5; J. Franckton, 1600–? 1618; A. Verdon, 1612; Soc. of Stationers, 1618–? 1640; A. Johnson, 1629–30; J. Stepney, 1632; E. Crooke, 1638; G. Hood, 1638; J. Moore, 1639–40.

Edinburgh: † J. Skot, 1539–71; R. Lekpreuik, 1561–71, 1573–82; T. Bassandyne, 1564–77; H. Charteris, 1568–99; R. Woodhouse, ? 1569–? 1632; T. Waltem, 1572; [J. Jacques, 1574]; J. Ross, 1574–80; S. Kerknett, 1576; A. Arburthnet, 1576–85; L. Mannenby, 1578; (?) H. Richardson, 1580; J. Smyth, 1580; A. Williamson, 1580; J. Gibson, 1580–1600; J. Cowper, 1582; T. Vautrollier, 1584–6; R. Gourlaw, 1585; (?) R. Wood, 1585; E. Cathkin, 1585–1601; (?) G. Masterton, 1587; [J. Nafield, 1587–9]; A. Hart, 1587–1621; J. Norton, sen., 1589–96; R. Waldegrave, 1589–1603; T. Gibson, 1592; R. Smyth, 1592–1602; J. Symson, 1592–1604; J. Brown, 1593; A. Aysoun, 1593–? 1600; A. Mason, 1596; (?) J. Schenck, 1596; T. Finlason, 1597–1628; J. Brown, 1598; R. Charteris, 1599–1609; S. Hart, 1599–? 1643; A. Arisone, 1600; J. Harrower, ? 1600; P. Johnston, 1600; Heirs of H. Charteris, 1601; J. Cathkin, 1601–31; A. Wattir, 1603; G. Dick, ? 1603–19; (?) F. van Hagen, 1604; (?) McKenzie, 1604; (?) D. Marr, 1604; K. Lawson, 1608–22; J. Ferrie, 1609; E. Raban, 1620; Heirs of A. Hart, 1621–39; J. Kene, 1621–39; J. Wreittoun, ? 1621–40; J. Burdon, 1622–? 1641; Heirs of R. Charteris, 1628; Heirs of T. Finlason (? Walter Finlason), 1628–30; J. Wood, 1629–33; J. Hart, 1630–? 1639; J. Mayne, 1631–9; * R. Crombie, 1631–45; D. Robertson, 1633; M. Vautrollier, 1633–4; * E. Tyler, ? 1633–50; [J. Williams, 1635]; * G. Anderson, 1637–8; * R. Bryson, 1637–45; * J. Bryson, 1638–42; * J. Threipland, 1639–45; W. Knox, 1640: *see also* Scotland.

ETON : J. Norton, sen., 1610 ; M. Bradwood, 1610–18.

EXETER : P. Benson, 1569–83 ; H. Rolte, 1571 ; C. Hunt, 1593–1606 ; (?) M. Hart, 1596 ; E. Dight, *c.* 1600 ; J. Dight, *c.* 1635 ; * T. Hunt, 1640–8.

GLASGOW : J. Sanders, 1625–42 ; J. Wilson, 1634–5 ; * G. Anderson, 1638–47.

HAMMERSMITH (*secret press*) : R. Ward, 1590.

IPSWICH : G. Penn, 1584–9.

LEICESTER : J. Allen, 1635–7.

LINCOLN : E. Rockadon, 1571.

LINCOLNSHIRE : C. Browne, 1571.

LICHFIELD : J. Marten, ? 1567–84 ; Lant, 1623.

LUDLOW : Clarke, 1633 ; Jennings, 1633.

MANCHESTER : Waller, 1633.

NANTWICH, Cheshire : Steele, 1633.

NORTHAMPTON : H. Sharpe, 1579–89 ; Whaley, 1633.

NORWICH : A. Rabat, 1567 ; N. Colman, 1586 ; E. Casson, or Causon, 1617–23 ; A. Atfend, 1640.

OLD FORD, Middlesex (*secret press*) : A. Neale, 1626 ; J. Phillips, 1626.

OXFORD : C. Cavey, *al.* Stuffolde, 1536–78 ; H. Milward, 1536–1605 ; † H. Evans, 1538–63 ; G. Harkes, 1539–*c.* 1570 ; R. Redborne, 1556–71 ; † P. Cuttier, 1558 ; G. Burnet, *al.* Cornyshe, 1567 ; J. Gore, 1568–74 ; N. Clyfton, 1570–9 ; W. Spire, sen., 1571–97 ; J. Jenckes, 1572–7 ; R. Cavey, *al.* Stuffolde, 1573–94 ; J. Barnes, 1573–1618 ; R. Garbrand, *al.* Harkes, 1574–1628 ; D. Pinart, 1576–1619 ; H. Archer, 1577–88 ; H. Jones, ? 1585–1637 ; G. Chambers, 1590 ; R. Foxon, 1590–1 ; S. Wilson, 1590–1 ; T. Middleton, 1590–1604 ; F. Peerse, 1590–1622 ; R. Wright, 1591 ; N. Smith, 1593–1609 ; E. Miles, 1593–1638 ; L. Waistell, 1597–1608 ; J. Crossley, 1597–1612 ; R. Billingsley, 1601–6 ; R. Nixon, *al.* Way, 1602–26 ;

W. Bailey, 1603 ; W. Davies, 1603–51 ; J. Adams, 1604–37 ; J. Lichfield, 1605–35 ; H. Bluett, 1606–33 ; L. Lisle, 1607–26 ; W. Spire, jun., 1607–36 ; D. Edwards, 1608–22 ; D. Cope, 1609 ; W. Sparke, 1609 ; J. Garbrand, *al.* Harkes, 1609–17 ; T. Huggins, 1609–36 ; J. Westall, 1609–43 ; R. Barnes, 1613–31 ; C. Barbar, 1614–17 ; E. Peerse, 1614–39 ; W. Johnson, 1616–*c.* 1645 ; * W. Webb, 1616–52 ; J. Chambers, 1617 ; R. Wylcocks, 1617 ; W. Toldervey, 1617–18 ; W. Wrench, 1617–18 ; T. Dyer, 1617–19 ; W. Wildgoose, 1617–26 ; J. Allam, 1617–38 ; * J. Godwin, 1617–73 ; S. Jackson, 1618 ; J. Short, 1618–24 ; T. Butler, ? 1619–28 ; R. Billingsley, 1620–4 ; * H. Cripps, 1620–40 ; * F. Oxlade, 1621–*c.* 1666 ; C. Crouch, 1623 ; S. Bele, 1624–5 ; * W. Turner, 1624–43 ; * H. Curteyn, 1625–51 ; * E. Forrest, 1625–82 ; J. Barnes, 1626–74 ; W. Ingram, 1626–83 ; W. Seale, 1628–39 ; R. Beckford, 1630–66 ; S. Bolt, 1631–42 ; * F. Bowman, 1634–47 ; * L. Lichfield, 1635–57 ; T. Allam, 1636–9 ; * J. Wilmot, 1637–65 ; * H. Hall, 1637–79 ; M. Hunt, 1639–40 ; T. Wilkins, 1640 ; * T. Robinson, 1640–63.

PERTH : W. Lauder, 1591 ; J. Sym, 1595.

ST. ANDREWS : R. Lekpreuik, 1572 ; (?) G. Young, 1585 ; (?) J. Jackson, ? 1599–1611 ; E. Raban, 1620.

SALISBURY : H. Hammande, 1571–6 ; (?) W. Hammond, 1632–40.

SCOTLAND (town unknown) : (?) G. Young, 1585 ; Z. Pont, 1590–1619 ; G. Christie, 1599–1604 ; J. Anderson, 1611.

SOMERSETSHIRE : J. Jaques, 1571.

STEPNEY : E. Venge, 1596 ; G. Wood, 1621.

STIRLING : R. Lekpreuik, 1571.

TAUNTON : J. Hearn, 1576.

WALES (town unknown) : Thackwell, ? 1588.

WELLS : J. Burton, 1634.

WESTMINSTER : * F. Constable, 1640 ; *see* London Signs, GOAT.

WINCHESTER : H. Croker, 1571.

WORCESTER : A. Kitson, 1571 ; * F. Ash, ? 1644–51.

YORK : † T. Wraith, 1556–(?) ; † J. Gowthwaite, 1556–68 ; J. Marcant, 1579 ; A. Foster, 1580–1607 ; T. Marsh, 1590–7 ; T. Richardson, 1600 ; J. Foster, (?)–1616.

B.—FOREIGN.

[*The names of those who worked in more than one town are given under each, but where no English work is known to have been produced at a particular place the name under that heading is put within round brackets. In such cases the date is that during which the person is supposed to have carried on business in the town in question; in others it refers merely to the period during which he was connected with the English book-trade.*]

AMSTERDAM : C. Claessonius or Claeszoon, 1602 ; J. H., 1604 ; Z. Heyns, 1605 ; R. de Baudois, 1608 ; M. Colin, 1608 ; H. Laurensz, 1608–12 ; G. Thorp, 1608–19 ; W. J. Blaeu, 1612–25 ; J. Veseler, 1618–21 ; R. Plater, 1626 ; J. F. Stam, 1629–30 ; H. Hondt, 1630–2 ; (?) C. G. van Breughel, 1632 ; J. Jansson II, 1633–8 ; T. Stafford, 1640.

ANTWERP : (J. Bellerus, 1553–95) ; (G. Morberius, (?) –1558) ; G. van Diest or Dielin I & II, 1563–5 ; H. Laet, 1564–6 ; W. Sylvius, 1565–6 ; J. Fowler, 1566–75 ; P. van Keerberghen, 1567 ; G.-H. van der Loe, 1578 ; P. Braeckvelt, 1583 ; J. Trognesius, 1587–96 ; Widow Plantin, 1591 ; A. Conincx, 1599–1606 ; J. van Keerberghen, 1600 ; D. Vervliet, 1600 ; R. Verstegen, 1603 ; R. Bruneau or Bruney, 1605 ; J. Cnobbaert, 1614 ; J. Seldenslach, 1621.

ARNHEM : J. Jansson I, 1614–20.

AVIGNON : J. Brumereau, 1601.

BASLE : C. Mense, 1560 ; C. Waldkirch, 1597.

BORDEAUX : S. Milanges, 1589.

BRUSSELS : J. Mommart, 1608 ; J. Pepermans, 1624–8 ; Widow of H. Antony, 1633 ; Widow of J. Mommart, 1634.

BRUGES : H. Holost, 1576.

CAEN : P. le Chandelier, 1598.

COLOGNE : A. Birckman, 1561–8.

DELFT : J. A. Cloeting, 1631 ; J. P. Waelpots, 1633.

DORT : "Hanse," 1590 ; I. Canin, 1597–1601 ; A. Canin, 1601 ; G. Waters, 1610–23 ; N. Vincentsz, 1623 ; M. Wyon, 1626 ; Widow of M. Wyon, 1630–40 ; H. van Esch, 1639.

DOUAI : (J. Bogard, 1574–? 1626) ; J. Bellerus, 1575 ; J. Fowler, 1578 ; J. Lyon, 1580–1 ; C. Boscard, 1598–1607 ; L. Kellam, ? 1603–14 ; I. R., *c.* 1610 ; J. Heigham, 1612–22 ; T. Kellam, 1618 ; Widow of L. Kellam, 1622–39 ; H. Taylor, 1624 ; G. Pinchon, 1629–34 ; B. Bellerus, 1630–2 ; M. Bogard, 1630–5 ; P. Auroi, 1631.

FLORENCE : † L. Torrentini, 1553 ; (?) B. Sermatelli, 1600.

FLUSHING : M. A. van der Nolck, 1621–2.

FRANKFURT AM MAIN : S. Feirabendius, 1589 ; J. Wechel, 1590 ; C. Marni, 1603 ; Heirs of A. de Renialme, 1605 ; J. K. Unckels, 1619 ; (D. Aubri, 1620–9) ; J. N. Stolzenburger, 1628.

GENEVA : J. Crespin, 1556–69 ; † C. Badius, 1557 ; J. Poulain, 1556–8 ; † R. Hall, ? 1557–60 ; A. Rebul, 1558 ; Z. Durand, 1561.

GHENT : J. Dooms, *c.* 1628–32.

GORCUM (Gorinchem) : A. Janss, 1624.

HAARLEM : A. Romaen, 1597.

HAGUE, THE : A. Muris, 1621 ; H. Jackson, 1622 ; Widow and Heirs of H. J. van Wouw, 1631.

HAMBURG : P. Lang, 1620.

HANAU : D. Aubri, 1607.

LEYDEN : (W. Sylvius, 1577–80) ; J. Paedts, 1582–6 ; C. Plantin, 1585 ; T. Basson, 1586 ; F. Raphelengius, 1586–97 ; I. Voorn, 1591 ;

C. Guyot, 1603; H. van Haestens, 1610; J. C. van Dorpe, 1616; B. & A. Elzevier, 1633–6; W. Christiaens, 1634–43.

LIÈGE: G. Morberius; 1571; G. Hovius, 1623.

LOUVAIN: J. Bogard, 1564–7; J. Fowler, 1566; J. Lyon, 1580; L. Kellam, 1598–? 1604; H. Hastenius, 1627–8.

"LYDDEN": J. Massen, *c.* 1625.

LYONS: †J. de Tournes, 1553.

MECHLIN: H. Jaey, 1611–13.

MIDDELBURG: R. Schilders, 1582–1616; D. van Respeawe, 1584; H. Hellen, 1620; A. Schilders, 1620.

NETHERLANDS, THE: C. G. van Breughel, 1632.

PARIS: †G. Merlin, 1555–7; †J. Le Blanc, 1556–7; [S. Jascuy, 1558]; T. Brumen, 1573–82; P. Jobert, 1585; P. Hury I, 1588; E. Prevosteau, 1602; P. Sevestre, 1603; F. Huby II, 1610; C. Morel, 1614; N. de La Coste, 1631; S. Cramoisy I & II, 1635–47; Mistress Blageart, 1636–? 1653; G. Baudry, 1640; J. Mestais, 1640.

RHEIMS: J. de Fogny, 1582–3.

ROCHELLE: (?) R. Waldegrave, 1589.

ROTTERDAM: M.S., 1626; I. van Waesberge, 1636; H. Tuthill, 1638; P. van Waesberghe, 1639; T. Lappagde, 1640.

ROUEN: †N. Le Roux, 1533–57; †R. Hamillon, 1555–7; †R. Valentin, 1555–7; F. Valentin, 1555–9; R. Carmarden, 1562–6; C. Hamillon, 1566–? 1614; G. Flinton, 1581–*c.* 1584; (S. Brinkley, 1583–(?)); G. L'Oyselet, 1584–99; (?) Heirs of J. Walker, 1601; J. Cousturier, 1609–38; M. Michel, 1615; N. Courant, 1621–30; J. Besonge, 1626; J. Boulenger, 1630; Heirs of N. Courant, 1633.

ST. OMER: C. Boscard, 1614; J. Heigham, 1622–31.

STUTTGART: J. W. Resslin, 1616.

TOURNAI: A. Quinqué, 1623.

UTRECHT: S. de Roy, 1615; C. de Passe, 1615–20; (?) J. Schellem, 1626.

WÜRZBURG: Widow A. M. Volmare, 1628.

ZURICH: †C. Froschauer I, 1535–55; C. Froschauer II, 1574–5.

ZUTPHEN: J. van Aelst, 1619.

A DICTIONARY OF THE BOOKSELLERS AND PRINTERS WHO WERE AT WORK IN ENGLAND, SCOTLAND AND IRELAND FROM 1641 TO 1667.

BY

HENRY R. PLOMER.

THE BIBLIOGRAPHICAL SOCIETY
1968

PREFACE.

THE object of this work is to bring together the information available respecting the men and women who printed and sold books during the twenty-seven years from 1641 to 1667. It is an attempt to fill the gap between the Stationers' Registers and the Term Catalogues so ably edited by Mr. Edward Arber. The information consists of imprints showing the various places in which such booksellers and printers carried on their business, such biographical details as could be gleaned from various printed and manuscript sources, and an indication of the character of the trade carried on by each bookseller. As a further help to the bibliographer, I have included a notice of all publishers' lists that I have met with. It was my original intention to have given an indication of the work of each printing house, but I soon found that this was impossible. Such printing houses as those of the Fletchers, Roycroft, or Warren are in themselves a study, and any attempt to generalize was worse than useless.

The chief sources of information have been: (1) The Thomason Tracts; (2) the Bagford and Ames Collections of Title-pages; (3) Hazlitt's Collections and Notes through the medium of Mr. G. J. Gray's invaluable Index; (4) the Registers and Apprenticeship Books of the Company of Stationers; (5) the State Papers and other documents at the Public Record Office; (6) the Reports of the Historical Manuscripts Commission; (7) Wills in the Prerogative Court of Canterbury at Somerset House.

I have made no attempt to distinguish between booksellers and publishers. There is no evidence to show that any of the men mentioned in this dictionary, with the single exception of John Ogilby—who has been included for the excellence of his work—were publishers in the sense in which we understand the term now. Every publisher is a bookseller in so far that he sells the books he publishes, but some publishers, Longmans and Methuen for example, are not booksellers in the sense of selling all kinds of books. On the other hand, Hatchards, of Piccadilly, and others that could be named, are not only retail booksellers in a large way of business, but they are also publishers. Such I conceive Herringman and Moseley are to be considered. Others again, such as Cornelius Bee and Samuel Thompson, visited the chief marts abroad, and bought largely on commission, and though they held shares in all the most important literary ventures of their day, and their names appear in the imprints, they are to be considered rather as retail booksellers than publishers.

I have not inserted any initials in this book. In the first place it must be remembered that during this period, when the censorship of the press was severe, printers and booksellers often contented themselves with placing their initials in the imprints, and almost every name that figures in this volume might have been duplicated amongst the initials, thus swelling the volume to an inordinate size, without any corresponding advantage to the student. Identification of such initials as, say, "T. B.," which may apply to half a dozen different men, must be largely guesswork, unless based on a special study of the work in which they occur.

There are no doubt many shortcomings in this book. Names may have been omitted that ought to be here, and the information is in many cases meagre. But I trust the reader will accept it as "spade" work in a field which has hitherto been almost totally neglected, and as a foundation upon which in time to come another builder will erect a more lasting edifice.

In conclusion, my thanks are tendered to a host of friends for kindly help: to Mr. A. W. Pollard for bringing the work under the notice of the Bibliographical Society, and to the Council of the Society for undertaking its publication; to Mr. G. K. Fortescue, Keeper of the Printed Books in the British Museum, for permission to see the proofs of the catalogue of the Thomason Tracts; to Mr. F. C. Rivington for allowing me access to the Registers of the Stationers' Company; to Mr. G. J. Gray, of Cambridge, Mr. F. Madan, of Oxford, Mr. Robert Steele and Mr. R. A. Peddie, for many notes and suggestions; and lastly, to Mr. E. R. McC. Dix, of Dublin, for much valuable information respecting the booksellers and printers of Ireland. For those of Scotland, I am wholly indebted to Mr. H. G. Aldis's notes, published in his *List of Books printed in Scotland*, issued by the Edinburgh Bibliographical Society in 1905.

H. R. PLOMER.

44, CROWNHILL ROAD,

WILLESDEN, N.W.

INTRODUCTION.

WHEN, on the 3rd November, 1640, the Long Parliament met, it found the book-trade suffering from an acute attack of censorship. Ever since the days of Elizabeth there had been two great impediments to the expansion of that trade. One of these was the Government, which objected to criticism and sought safety by bribing the press and strangling the free circulation of books. The other was the Company of Stationers, which desired to keep the trade in the hands of its privileged members and objected to any increase in the number of presses, or of booksellers, because the greater the number the smaller the profits of the monopolists. The duty of meeting a legitimate demand weighed little with men who cared for nothing save their own interests, and naturally, the Company seeking its privileges from the Government, was at all times the willing instrument of that Government. The result was that the book-trade was cramped, printing was bad—there being no encouragement to the printer to produce artistic work—and the most saleable books, such as school books, bibles, and service books, were printed at secret presses.

All these evils had, during the previous ten years, been intensified by Archbishop Laud and his brother bishops, who attempted to stem the growing onset of Puritanism, with the pillory, branding iron, and prison cell. Sir John Lambe had carefully winnowed the London printing houses, and Laud and his friends hoped that by the Star Chamber Decree of 1637, which gave to the Stationers' Company increased powers

of search, they had effectually muzzled the press. As vainly did Mrs. Partington with her mop try to keep out the sea. Had the state of England been normal, there would have been no need for the decree of 1637, and conversely, the public mind being in a highly excitable state, the decree of 1637 was overwhelmed and swept aside by the events which immediately succeeded it. Almost the very first act of the Long Parliament[1] was to appoint a Committee for Religion, which called before it booksellers and printers who had been interfered with by "my lord of Canterbury," thrown into prison, and otherwise grievously maltreated, and great was the punishment they exacted in return. So too there were Committees of printing, which listened to the woes of Michael Sparke and recommended that he should be repaid the sum wrung from him by the Star Chamber. Meanwhile, with religion at fever heat, and public events moving with a rapidity hitherto unknown, the cry was for "News!" and "More News!" Thus the Star Chamber decree that there were to be no more than twenty printers was speedily disregarded.

So for the next three years printers and booksellers alike were left unmolested, and grew and multiplied prodigiously. News-sheets poured from the press in ever increasing numbers, and were hawked broadcast through the city and suburbs of London, and pens of all kinds "walked," to use the quaint expression of the period, fast and furiously in the political and religious controversies that were rending the country, to the entire exclusion of all other forms of literature.

Then came a change. The Parliament began to find itself criticised, as even the most popular of Parliaments is bound to make some enemies, and it liked the process as little as the King and the bishops had done. It looked about for weapons to defend itself and found two, the old rusty censorship and the pen. Half ashamed to go back to the methods it had so vigorously denounced, the Long Parliament adopted the censorship very mildly at first, while freely engaging writers such as Milton to meet the onslaught of its foes with the pen. The first

Ordinance against the book-trade was that of the 9th March, $164\frac{3}{4}$, which gave the Committee of Examinations power to appoint searchers for presses employed in printing scandalous and lying pamphlets. They were instructed to demolish and take away such presses, their materials and the printers' nuts and spindles, and to bring the printers, or their workmen, before the committee. They were also given power to commit to prison alike the printers, the vendors, and any persons who should refuse to allow their premises to be searched, and anyone so committed was not to be released until all the charges incurred in the seizure had been paid. The following stationers were appointed to act as searchers under the foregoing order, Felix Kyngston, Samuel Man, George Miller, John Bellamy, William Lee, junior, John Partridge, Christopher Meredith, Robert Dawlman, Matthew Walbancke, Richard Cotes, Joseph Hunscott, and John Raworth. Felix Kyngston was one of the oldest members of the Company, having taken up his freedom as far back as 1597. Samuel Man was warden of the Company, and the remainder were probably chosen for their known Presbyterian tendencies. At the same time, the Common Council of the City of London passed an act for the apprehending of all vagrant persons, men, women and children, who should be found hawking or crying pamphlets or books about the streets of the City.

Barely three months later, on the 14th June, Parliament sets out another Ordinance against the book trade. This begins with a preamble in which it is admitted that the previous Order had had little or no effect, and that in spite of it, *very many, as well stationers and printers, as others of sundry other professions not free of the Stationers' Company, have taken upon them to set up sundry private Printing Presses in corners, and to print, vend, publish, and disperse Books, Pamphlets, and Papers, in such multitudes, that no industry could be sufficient to discover or bring to punishment, all the several abounding delinquents*, and then proceeds to try and perform the feat which it has just declared impossible. The sundry other professions here alluded to were chiefly drapers and haberdashers, but no doubt Parliament had in its mind at that moment, Henry Walker (*q.v.*),

who from being an ironmonger, had turned tub-thumper, pamphleteer, and bookseller. This Ordinance further stated that several persons, stationers themselves and members of the Company, out of revenge against those appointed to carry out the orders of Parliament, had taken the liberty to print the most profitable vendible copies of books, belonging to those privileged members. It then proceeded to enact (1) That no order of either House of Parliament, should be printed by anyone, except by order of one or both Houses; (2) That no book, pamphlet, or paper, should be printed, bound, stitched, or put to sale, without the licence of the person appointed by Parliament to licence it and without being entered in the Registers of the Company; (3) That no book which was the property of the Company should be printed without their consent, or that of the owner of the copyright; (4) Nor should any such books formerly printed in England, be imported from abroad. The Company, the Serjeant of the House of Commons, Justices of the Peace, and Constables were given the right of search.

Incidentally, this ordinance affords an insight into the condition of the Company, which is amply borne out by the Registers of that period. The Company was at war within itself, and the men who entered in the Registers were those who, for the time being, were uppermost in its councils, and these took care that their opponents should not have the right of registration. Neutral men, such as Humphrey Moseley, who appears to have entered whatever and whenever he wished, were not meddled with; but the small number of men whose names are found in these Registers between 1641–1650, is the strongest possible evidence that they were not open to all impartially. Indeed, the fact is further emphasized by the action which Roger Norton brought against the Company, for striking out of the Register certain grammatical books, which were his copyright. Roger Norton was a Royalist, and the prevailing party in the Company at that time were Roundheads. Thus the entries in the Registers for those years, interesting and valuable as they must always be, represent only a fractional part of the output of the press.

Another Ordinance of the year 1643 must not be passed over, as it shows that amongst the much despised Roundheads, there were some in authority who sympathized with the book lover. It was the outcome of the wholesale sequestration of Royalist property that was then taking place, and let us hope that it had the effect of preventing the dispersal of many a valued library of books. This Ordinance, which was dated the 18th November, 1643, directed that books, evidences, records, and writings, sequestered or taken by distress, were not to be sold, but that an account of such books, etc., was to be rendered to Algernon, Earl of Northumberland, Theophilus, Earl of Lincoln, William, Lord Viscount Say and Seale, John Selden, Francis Rous, Sir Simonds D'Ewes, Samuel Browne, Edward Prideaux, Gilbert Millington, Roger Hill, and Walter Young, or any two of them. Nor is there wanting other evidence that Milton and his literary friends were exerting themselves to preserve what was worth preserving, as witness the order made in 1645 for printing the *Codex Alexandrinus*, a project that unfortunately came to nothing, and also Milton's own pamphlet on the Liberty of the Press. But in this the great thinker was at least two centuries ahead of his time. The din of battle was too loud and his voice was drowned. Yet for the next four years there was a lull in the persecution of the book-trade, and it was not until the 28th September, 1647, that any further attempt was made to regulate "the press." The Ordinance then issued by Parliament closely resembled those that had preceded it, but it went a step further, by fixing the penalties that were to be inflicted upon offenders. The author of the offending pamphlet or book was to be fined forty shillings, or imprisoned for a term not exceeding forty days, the printer was to be fined twenty shillings or twenty days, besides having his press and implements destroyed, the bookseller or stationer issuing the offending publication was liable to a fine of ten shillings or ten days' imprisonment, and the hawker or pedlar was to forfeit all his stock and be whipped as a common rogue.

Still the cry went up News! More News! and still the warring sectaries, mountebank astrologers, and frenzied politicians flooded the country

with pamphlets and, as if the gates of passion had not been opened wide enough, the unfortunate Charles was sent to his doom on Tuesday, the 30th January, $164\frac{8}{9}$. Sober men of all parties were shocked at the deed, and hastened to dissociate themselves from it, while the Royalist press became ten times more bitter than before. The Roundheads were split into two camps, and the Independents, who had now gained the ascendency, were assailed on all sides. Once again the old weapon of repression was brought from the armoury, and on the 20th September, 1649, Parliament passed the most drastic Act against the book-trade that had been known since the Star Chamber decree of 1637. In the preamble attention was called to the "assumed boldness" of the weekly pamphleteers, who, it was stated, "took upon them to publish, and at pleasure to censure the Proceedings of Parliament and Army, and other affairs of State," and to the licentiousness of printing which, in this country and in foreign parts, "hath been" and "ought to be" restrained.

This Act closely followed the model set before it in the Star Chamber decree of 1637, to such a pass had the reformers come. The first clause enacted that no persons were to write, print, or sell scandalous or libellous books under a penalty of ten pounds or forty days' imprisonment for the author, five pounds or twenty days for the printer, two pounds or ten days for the bookseller or stationer. The buyer of any book or pamphlet declared to be seditious was immediately to hand it over to the Lord Mayor, or to some Justice of the Peace of the County, under a penalty of one pound. No news-sheet was to be printed or sold without license, all such licenses to be obtained from the Clerk of the Parliament or the Secretary of the Army. No seditious books or pamphlets were to be sent either by post or carrier under a penalty of forty shillings for every copy found. For the better discovery of malignant (read Royalist) booksellers, magistrates were entrusted with full powers for searching any packs or packages which they might suspect of containing books or pamphlets of a seditious character. The clauses relating to printing contain a surprise. Printing was restricted to the City of London and the two universities,

"Provided, That this clause shall not be construed to extend to the Printing Press now used in the City of York, nor to the printing press now used in Finsbury for the printing of *Bibles and Psalms.*" This last was the press set up by William Bentley for printing the edition of the Bible authorised by the Assembly of Divines, which the Stationers' Company had so much resented that, in 1646, they passed a resolution: *no journeyman printer of this company who shall work at the printing house in Finsbury, ever to have any pension or gift whatsoever from the Company.* The Act further decreed that every printer should enter into bond in £300 to be of good behaviour, and no printer was to set up a press or to import any press or letters without first acquainting the Company of his intention.

Such were the conditions under which the book-trade was carried on from the time of the meeting of the Long Parliament until Oliver Cromwell became Lord Protector, and when it is remembered that the whole of that period was one of warfare and political unrest, the wretched character of the work produced is not to be wondered at. By far the largest part of the output of the press consisted of political and theological pamphlets, amongst which the writings of John Milton and James Howell shine out like stars in the night. Dramatic literature there was none, and the only poetry worth speaking of was the collection of Sir John Suckling's verse in 1646, and Herrick's *Hesperides* in 1647–8.

The art of printing in England at this period sank to its lowest point. Practically all the presses in London were busy turning out news-sheets as fast as they could print them, and any old type and blocks that could be secured for love or money were used to print them with. The largest printing house in London during this period was that of Miles Flesher and his partners in Little Britain. They also held the King's printing house by virtue of a mortgage executed by Robert Barker. The little good work done was mainly done by them. The press of Felix Kyngston was also a busy one, and his best work was creditable. Richard Cotes was also one of the largest printers of this time, while much of the hack work was

turned out by Bernard Alsop, Andrew Coe, and Thomas Brudenell. William Dugard, the head-master of Merchant Taylors' School, set up a press about this time, which will be noticed later on, and William Bentley's press at Finsbury turned out some well printed Bibles in miniature founts.

A marked improvement took place in the book-trade after 1650. The fury of partisan passions had spent itself. The Civil War was practically at an end, and men began to return to their old pursuits and their books. In 1652 the first announcement of the proposed Polyglot Bible was issued. The first volume appeared in September, 1654, the second in 1655, the third in 1656, and the last three in 1657. The printer was Thomas Roycroft of Bartholomew Close, and the type was supplied by the four recognized type founders, the double pica and italic used in the Dedication being that cut by John Day in the sixteenth century. The editor was Brian Walton, Bishop of Chester, and the work received every encouragement from Oliver Cromwell. This undertaking raised Roycroft's printing house to a leading position amongst the London printing houses, and John Ogilby's splendid reprints of the classical authors also came from this press. In 1653, Izaak Walton gave to the world his *Complete Angler.* In 1655 appeared the first volume of Sir William Dugdale's *Monasticon Anglicanum*, and in the same year William Dugard printed a folio edition of Sir Philip Sidney's *Arcadia.* But perhaps the best evidence of the revival of the book-trade is found in the two lists of books published by Humphrey Moseley with Brome's *Five New Plays*, in 1653, and Sir Aston Cokain's *Dianea* in 1654. The first of these contains one hundred and thirty five items, and the second, one hundred and eighty. Another important publisher of this time was Thomas Whitaker. On the 7th March, 165$\frac{2}{3}$, the whole of his copyrights were transferred by his widow and Alexander Brome, whom she had married, to Humphrey Moseley, Richard Thrale, Joshua Kirton, and Samuel Thompson. They fill upwards of four pages of the Stationers' Register, and, in addition to such classics as Tacitus, Aristotle, and Plutarch, included Bacon's Essays, Thos. Jones'

Catalogue of Manuscripts at Oxford and Cambridge, Camden's Britannia, Selden's Titles of Honour, Bede's Rerum Anglicarum Scriptores, besides the chief theological treatises and many school books. Henry Herringman's entries in the Registers also became more numerous year by year.

With the outbreak of the Civil War all the official printing, such as Acts and Orders of Parliament, Proclamations and the like, was farmed out by the Parliament and the Council of State to those of their supporters who made the best offer. Their number was large, and it is difficult to understand how the appointments were made. We find Joseph Hunscot, Edward Husbands, and John Wright, senior, successively printing for the Parliament. In 1653, Giles Calvert, Henry Hills, and Thomas Brewster were "printers" to the Council of State, Henry Hills and John Field were styled printers to the Parliament of England, while William Dugard and Henry Hills were printers to his Highness the Lord Protector. Later on we meet with Thos. Collins and Abel Roper as printers to the Council of State. Again, in 1660, John Macocke and John Streator were appointed printers to the Parliament, while John Macocke and Francis Tyton were also printers to the House of Lords. The most interesting of these appointments is that of Giles Calvert. The son of a Somersetshire clergyman, he espoused the cause of the Quakers, and became their first publisher. No evidence can be found that leads us to suppose that he joined their ranks, but the correspondence preserved at Devonshire House shows that he was in sympathy with them. He boldly placed his imprint on their writings, and this at a time when the writers and the printers were thrown into prison for their share in the publications. This appointment of Giles Calvert as one of the official "printers," shows clearly that he stood well with Cromwell and those in power, and accounts for his being able to publish Quaker writings as boldly as he did. Several of the men mentioned above were not "printers" by trade, they gave out the work to others, and shared the profits.

During the continuance of the Commonwealth, both printers and booksellers would seem to have had a quiet time. It had to be something

extremely virulent to rouse the anger of the Government. One noticeable feature of the time was the great reduction that took place in the number of news-sheets. Many, of course, died of inanition, but there is no doubt that the clause of the Act of 1649, which compelled all news-sheets to be licensed by the Clerk of the Parliament, had a salutary effect. The *Intelligencer* and the *Newes* became the two official papers and were the forerunners of the Oxford and London Gazettes.

With the Restoration the book-trade found itself once more under the heel of the oppressor. Monk's victory was marked by the publication of books and pamphlets, attacking the monarchy in the most violent manner. The old animosities were once more raked up, and the Government determined, if possible, to put a stop to this, and were ably seconded by the Company of Stationers for purely personal reasons. Early in 1660 the Company had passed the following resolution: "The table remarking the great want of a law to restrain the exorbitances of printing and to secure property in copies; and being informed that the Parliament before their adjournment had appointed a committee for that purpose, of which, Mr. Prynne is chairman, and a bill having been presented to him, but nothing therein done, Mr. Warden Crooke is earnestly desired to solicit the business with Mr. Prynne or otherwise as occasion may offer."

Meanwhile, certain of the printers, amongst whom were Roycroft, Hodgkinson, and other important men, were advocating severance from the Company, and the formation of a distinct Company of Printers. The reasons they put forward were that the old Company had become mainly a Company of Booksellers, and was grown so large that none could be Master or Warden until he was well advanced in life, and therefore unable to keep a vigilant eye on the trade.

The Government adopted two methods of dealing with the book-trade. They appointed an Official Surveyor of the Press, and they passed an Act for preventing the frequent abuses in printing, etc., known as 14 Charles II, cap. 33. The person chosen as Surveyor of the Press was Sir Roger

L'Estrange, whose only recommendation to the post was that he was an adherent of the Royal party and had suffered for his loyalty. He knew nothing about printing or bookselling, but he was a sycophant and time-server, and carried out his duties with unnecessary cruelty. The Warrant creating Sir R. L'Estrange Surveyor of the Press is here given as it appears in the State Papers :—

CHARLES R.

WHEREAS in contempt of our laws and authority many treasonous, seditious, and unlicenc'd Pamphlets, Libells, and Papers, are dayly printed vented and dispersed by the obstinate and implacable Enemies of Our Royall person and Government, for redresse and remedy hereof, Our Will and Pleasure is that you prepare a Grant for our Royall signature for the erecting and constituting of an Office for the surveying of the Imprimery, and Printing Presses, and for the preventing of the inconveniences aforesd. And it is Our Will and Pleasure that you prepare a grant for Our Royall signature of ye said Office unto Roger L'Estrange, Esq[r], of whose Loyalty and abilities Wee are well assured, and him to authorize and appoint to bee Our Surveyor of all the Imprimery and Printed Pictures and allsoe of all Books and Papers whatsoever hereafter to bee imprinted or reprinted, except Books concerning the Common-Laws of this Realme or Books of History concerning the State of this Realme or any other Books concerning Affairs of State, or concerning Heraldry Titles of Honor and Armes, or the Office of Earl Marshall, or Books of Divinity Phisick Philosophy Arts and Sciences and such other books and Papers as are granted by Our Letters Patents to Our proper and peculiar Printers and usually claimed and imprinted by them by virtue of the sd Letters Patents. To have and to hold the s[d] Office or Offices of Our s[d] Surveyor and Licencer for and during the terme of his naturall life to bee excersized by himselfe or his sufficient Deputie or Deputies which said Deputy or Deputies are from time to time to bee approved by the late Arch Bishop of Canterbury and Lord Bp of London or one of them and by Our Principall Secretaries of State or either of them with a sole Priviledge of

writing, printing, and publishing all Narratives or relacons not exceeding two sheets of Paper and all Advertisements, Mercuries, Diurnals and Books of Publick Intelligence; and likewise of Printing or appointing to bee printed All Ballads, Maps, Charts, Portraictures and Pictures not formerly printed and all Breifs and Collections, Bills of Ladeing, Play-Bills, and Quacksalvers Bills, of Custom and Excise Bills, Post Office Bills, Auditors Bills, Ticquets and all formes or Blanks of Bonds, Bills, Indentures and Warrants, with power to search for and seize all unlicensed Books and Papers and all seditious, treasonable, schismaticall and scandalous Books and Papers and to seize and apprehend all and every the offenders therein and to bring them before one of our Principall Secretaries or the next Justice of Peace, to bee proceeded against according to law, together with all other Priviledges and Powers necessary, or conducting to our Service in ye Premisses, For which this shall bee your warrant, Given at our Court at Whitehall the 15th day of August 1663, in the 15th year of our reigne.

By His Maj[ties] Command
Henry Bennet.

To Our Attorney or Sollicitor Generall.

Dom. S. Papers, Chas. II. Vol. 78. (96)

This document needs no comment. Nor is it necessary to say much about the Act of 1662, except that it was in a large measure a re-enactment of the Star Chamber decree of 1637, and the Act of 1649. York was again expressly mentioned as a place where printing might be carried on, and the printing house of John Streator was exempted from interference. Armed with ample power Sir Roger L'Estrange harassed the printers and booksellers without remorse. One of his unfortunate victims was Elizabeth Calvert, the wife of Giles Calvert, whom he imprisoned several times. Another, was John Twyn, a printer in Cloth Fair, who was tried for high treason and hanged at Tyburn for printing a pamphlet entitled *A Treatise of the execution of Justice*. That such men as Thomas Roycroft and James Fletcher should have acquiesced in a verdict which they must

have known condemned a fellow printer to death, for so trivial an offence, is the saddest part of the story. There is, however, abundant evidence that Sir Roger L'Estrange met with great opposition from the trade, and ultimately gave up his office in disgust.

Subjected to unfair competition and merciless restriction, it is not much to be wondered at that the stationers, whether printers or booksellers, did not bear a very high character for commercial probity, and that George Wither's sketch of the "Dishonest Stationer" in his *Schollars Purgatory* was applicable to only too many of them. On the other hand, we may hope he also drew his companion picture of the "Honest Stationer" from some of his acquaintance.

The closing years of the period under review were marked by two great disasters, the outbreak of plague in London, in the autumn of 1665, and the great fire of 1666. By the first, trade in the City was brought to a standstill and printers and stationers were reduced to idleness. By the second, the chief printing houses and booksellers' shops, with all their contents, were destroyed, and the ashes of books and manuscripts were carried by the wind as far as Eton and Windsor. Happily for us the Thomason Collection was out of reach of the flames.

ABBREVIATIONS.

App.	Appendix.
Arber	Transcript of the Registers of the Company of Stationers.
B.M.	British Museum.
Bibl. Lind.	Bibliotheca Lindesiana.
Bodl.	Bodleian.
Camb. Antiq. Soc. Comm.	Cambridge Antiquarian Society's Communications.
Chan. Proc.	Chancery Proceedings.
D.N.B.	Dictionary National Biography.
Dom. S. P.	Domestic State Papers.
Excheq. K. R.	Exchequer King's Remembrancer.
Edin. Bibl. Soc. Publ.	Edinburgh Bibliographical Society's Publications.
Harl.	Harleian Manuscript.
Haz.	Hazlitt.
Hist. MS. Comn.	Historical Manuscripts Commission.
Interr.	Interregnum.
Lutt. Coll.	Luttrell Collection.
P.C.C.	Prerogative Court of Canterbury.
P.R.O.	Public Record Office.
Rep.	Report.
Sayle	Early English Printed Books in the University Library, Cambridge.
Stat. Reg.	Stationers' Registers.
T.C.	Term Catalogues.

The Ames Collection of Title-pages is that at the British Museum catalogued under Title-pages (463 h. 4, 5).

The volumes of the Bagford Collection of Title-pages referred to in this work are Harl. MSS. 5915, 5919, 5921, 5923, 5927, 5928, 5929, 5932, 5936, 5949, 5963, 5965, 5967, 5973, 5990, now in the Printed Book Department.

A DICTIONARY OF THE BOOKSELLERS AND PRINTERS WHO WERE AT WORK IN ENGLAND, SCOTLAND AND IRELAND FROM 1641 TO 1667.

ADAMS (CHARLES), bookseller in London, (1) Marygold in Fleet Street; (2) Talbot, near St. Dunstan's Church, Fleet Street, 1654–62. Amongst his publications was an edition of the *Cynegeticon* of Gratius Faliscus, edited by Christopher Wase, 1654.

ADAMS (JOHN), bookseller in Oxford, 1610–71 (?). A stationer of this name leased a tenement in St. Mary's parish in 1610, and in 1637 a house to the North of the Schools Quadrangle was described as "lately" in the tenure of John Adams, bookbinder. [Madan, *Early Oxford Press*, p. 276.] His name is found on E. Brerewood's *Tractatus . . . . logici*, 1659.

ADAMSON (HUGH), bookseller (?) in London (?), 1643. Only known by the imprint to a pamphlet entitled *Sea-coale, Char-coale and Small Coale . . . . London: Printed for Hugh Adamson Ian. 27. Anno Dom. 1643.* His address has not been found.

ADDERTON (WILLIAM), bookseller in London; Three Golden Falcons in Duck Lane, 1628–71. Took up his freedom on June 30th, 1628. [Arber, iii. 686.] Made his first entry in the registers May 29th, 1629. Chiefly a publisher of theological literature. His name occurs for the last time in the Term Catalogue for Trinity, 1671. [Arber, *Term Catalogues*, vol. i. p. 78.]

ALLEN (BENJAMIN), bookseller and printer in London; The Crown, Pope's Head Alley, 1631–46. Took up his freedom on January 12th, 1631. [Arber, iii. 686.] He was the publisher of much of the political and

theological literature of the period, including some New England Tracts on Church and Church government. Henry Archer's *Personall Reign of Christ* bears the imprint "Printed and sold by Benjamin Allen." There are many references to him in Hazlitt's Collections. His will, dated May 5th, 1646, was very short and mentioned no names, but legacies were left to his wife and to a son and daughter. This will was proved on May 15th in the same year by his widow, Hannah Allen. [P.C.C. 57 Twisse.]

ALLEN (HANNAH), bookseller and printer in London; The Crown, in Pope's Head Alley, 1647–50. The widow of Benjamin Allen. The last entry by her in the Registers was on September 2nd, 1650. She dealt chiefly in theological literature. She afterwards married Livewell Chapman, *q.v.* [Stationers' Registers, Liber E, fol. 249.]

ALLEN (JOHN), bookseller in London, (1) Rising Sun in the New Buildings in Pauls Church Yard, between the two North Doors; (2) Little Britain. 1656–67. Amongst his early publications were some astrological tracts; but in 1659 he wrote and published two pamphlets against the practice of judicial astrology. The second of these, entitled *Judicial Astrologers totally routed*, contains on the last leaf a list of 14 books sold by him. [B.M. 718 d. 31.] His name occurs in the Hearth Tax Roll, 1666, as living in Little Britain. [P.R.O. Lay Subsidy $\frac{252}{32}$.]

ALLEN (NATHANIEL), bookseller in London; Angel & Bible in Lumber [*i.e.*, Lombard] Street, 1642–43. Took up his freedom as a stationer on August 4th, 1634. [Arber, iii. 687.] His name is found on C. Herle's *Independency on Scriptures*, 1643.

ALLESTRY, ALLESTRYE, or ALLESTREE (JAMES), bookseller in London, (1) Bell in St. Paul's Churchyard, 1652–64; (2) Rose & Crown, St. Paul's Churchyard, 1664–66; (3) Rose & Crown, in Duck Lane, 1667–69; (4) Rose & Crown, St. Paul's Churchyard, 1669–70. Was a relative, perhaps brother, of Richard Allestry the divine (1619–81), and father of Jacob Allestry, poetical writer (1653–86). Details of his early life are wanting, and the first heard of him as a bookseller is in the year 1652, when he is found in business at the Bell in St. Paul's Churchyard, in partnership with John Martin. In 1660 they were joined by Thomas Dicas,

and at one time Timothy Garthwaite seems to have been associated with them. At this time James Allestry was one of the largest capitalists in the trade, and his shop was the resort of the wealthy and the learned. Amongst the State Papers is a series of interesting letters written by him to Edward, second Viscount Conway, on the subject of books. About 1660 he was appointed bookseller and publisher to the Royal Society, and either altered his sign or removed to other premises, known as the "Rose & Crown." As a publisher he was interested in the chief and most important ventures of the time, such as the Duchess of Newcastle's Plays and Poems, the second part of Butler's *Hudibras*, and Ray's *Catalogus Plantarum*. Allestree employed the best printers of the day, much of his work being done by Thomas Roycroft, the printer of Walton's Polyglott. In the Great Fire of 1666 his premises were destroyed, and he was almost ruined. During the rebuilding of St. Paul's Churchyard he moved into Duck Lane, and there, by the help of his kinsman, Dr. Richard Allestry, who gave him the publishing of some sermons, he made a new start, returning to the Churchyard and resuming business under the old sign about 1669; but he did not live long afterwards, his death taking place on November 3rd, 1670. Smyth, the Secondary of the Poultry Compter, to whom we owe so much valuable information respecting the London booksellers of his day, records in his *Obituary* (p. 89): "Die Jovis hora 8ª ante merid. obiit Jacob Allestry bibliopola in cœmiter D. Paul's, Lond. Sepult Lunæ 7 Novʳ. Fitz-Williams capellan. Episcop. Winton. concionem facit funeb."

ALSOP, or ALLSOPP (BERNARD), printer in London, (1) with T. Creed, at the sign of the Eagle & Child; (2) Garter Place, in Barbican, 1617; (3) By Saint Anne's Church neere Aldersgate, 1618; (4) The Dolphin, in Distaff Lane, Old Fish Street, 1621; (5) Grub Street, in Honey Suckle Court, neere to the Flying Horse, 1641; (6) Grub Street, neere the Upper Pump, 1650 (1602–50). A native of Derby. Was apprenticed to Humphrey Lympenny, stationer of London, for eight years from Christmas, 1601, but in 1603 he was transferred for the remainder of his term to William White. (Arber, ii. 259.) In 1616 he is found in partnership with Thomas Creed, a printer who had begun printing about 1580, and whose printing house was known by the sign of the Eagle & Child. Creed either retired from business or died in the following year, when Alsop

appears to have succeeded to his printing materials, but whether he moved into new premises or whether the first and second imprints given above refer to the same place is not clear. Nine years later he entered into partnership with Thomas Fawcett, or Forsett. In the year 1626 they were summoned before the High Commission for being concerned in printing Sir Robert Cotton's *Short View of the Long life and reign of Henry the Third.* Alsop admitted that he had purchased the manuscript of Ferdinand Ely, a secondhand bookseller in Little Britain. He and his partner only printed one sheet. They were also the printers of much of the dramatic literature of Beaumont and Fletcher, Decker, Greene, and other writers. Bernard Alsop was one of the twenty master printers allowed by the Act of 1637, but his partner was not mentioned. In 1641 he was sent for by the House of Commons for printing the Hertfordshire Petition. [Commons Journals, January 25th, 1641. *See* GREENSMITH, J.]. On the outbreak of the troubles with the King, Alsop and Fawcett printed several news-sheets, the best known being the *Weekly Accompt of certain Special & Remarkable Passages from Both Houses of Parliament*, which first appeared on August 3rd, 1643, and in the same year they were committed to the Fleet Prison for printing a pamphlet entitled *His Majesty's Propositions to Sir John Hotham and the Inhabitants of Hull.* They petitioned the House of Lords for their release, declaring that the pamphlet was printed by their servants during their absence. Beyond the imprisonment, which lasted for some months, no further punishment followed. [Lords' Journals, v. 214, 533.] Bernard Alsop was reputed by his contemporaries to have printed pamphlets on Scotch affairs, using Evan Tyler's imprint. Fawcett appears to have retired from the partnership about 1644. Nothing is known as to the date of Bernard Alsop's death, but in 1653 his widow, Elizabeth Alsop, is found carrying on the business. Creed's type and ornaments, when they came into Alsop's hands, had been in use many years and were getting into bad condition, but his successor used them during the whole of his life. Consequently his later books are very poor specimens of typography, and his news-sheets were printed in the roughest possible manner.

ALSOP, or ALLSOPP (ELIZABETH), printer in London; "At her house in Grub Street near the Upper Pump," 1653–56. Is believed to have been the widow of Bernard Alsop. The last book entry to her was on April 22nd, 1656.

ALSOP, or ALSOPP (THOMAS), bookseller in London; Two sugar loaves over against St. Antholin's Church, at the lower end of Watling Street, 1657. His name is found in the following book: *Poems by Hugh Crompton, The Son of Bacchus and Godson of Apollo. Being a fardle of Fancies, or a medley of musick, stewed in four ounces of the Oyl of Epigrames.* [Hazlitt, *Handbook*, p. 130.]

ANDERSON (ANDREW), printer at Edinburgh, 1653–57; at Glasgow, 1657–61; again at Edinburgh on the north side of the cross, 1661–76. Son of George Anderson. Succeeded heirs of G. Anderson in 1653. Removed to Glasgow about July, 1657, by invitation of the Town Council, who offered him one hundred marks per annum as a pension. He returned to Edinburgh in the summer of 1661, and in 1663 was appointed printer to the town and college on the death of G. Lithgow. In 1671 he was appointed King's Printer for forty-one years, and took several partners. Andrew Anderson died in June, 1676, being succeeded by his widow, Agnes, and his son, James. Most of his type and ornaments had been in use in the printing offices of Edinburgh for many years, and were in a very worn condition, his productions and those of his successors being among the poorest and most slovenly that came from the press of Scotland. Ninety-three issues have been traced to his press. [H. G. Aldis, *List of books printed in Scotland before 1700 .... with brief notes on the printers and stationers.* Edinburgh Bibliographical Society Publications, 1905.]

ANDERSON (GEORGE), printer at Edinburgh, "in King James his college, 1637–38; at Glasgow in Hutshisons Hospitall in the Trongate," 1638–47. Commenced printing in Edinburgh in 1637, having acquired a considerable part of the printing materials of Robert Young, *q.v.* In 1638 Anderson removed to Glasgow, taking a press with him. He worked chiefly for the General Assembly, but in 1644 he printed the Rev. John Row's Hebrew Grammar and Vocabulary, probably one of the earliest books in that language, printed in Scotland. George Anderson is believed to have died in 1648. He left a son, Andrew Anderson, who ultimately succeeded to the business. [H. G. Aldis, *List of books printed in Scotland before 1700.*]

ANDERSON (Heirs of GEORGE), printers in Glasgow, 1648, and in Edinburgh, 1649–53. On the death of George Anderson in 1647 the Town

Council of Glasgow agreed to continue his pension to his widow and children so long as they continued to carry on the business; but in 1649 they had removed to Edinburgh, and in 1653 were succeeded by Andrew Anderson. [H. G. Aldis, *List of books printed in Scotland before 1700.*]

ANDERSON (WILLIAM), bookseller in London, 1660. His name occurs on the following ballad: "*Admire not Noble Sir, that you should hear.*" [Bibl. Lind. Catal. of Eng. Ballads, No. 810.] His address has not been found.

ANDREWS (ELIZABETH), bookseller in London; White Lyon near Pye Corner, 1663–64. The widow of John Andrews, *q.v.*

ANDREWS (HENRY), bookseller (?) in London, 1642. His name is found in the imprint to an eight-page pamphlet published in 1642, entitled, *Newes from Black-Heath concerning the meeting of the Kentish Men*, etc., etc. .... *London, Printed for Henrie Andrews*, 1642, E. 144 (13). His address has not been found.

ANDREWS (JOHN), bookseller in London; White Lyon near Pye Corner 1654–63. Appears to have dealt chiefly in the ephemeral literature of his time, such as ballads, broadsides, and all kinds of pamphlets. His will was proved on March 12th, $166\frac{2}{3}$: by this he divided the residue of his goods, books, quires, etc., between his wife Elizabeth and his three children, Elizabeth, Mary, and John. [P.C.C. 35 Laud.]

ARCHER (EDWARD), bookseller in London; Adam and Eve in Little Britaine, 1656. Publisher of plays, of which he issued a catalogue in 1656, "more exactly Printed then ever before." This list he added to a comedy called the *Old Law*, the joint production of Massinger, Middleton, and Rowley. He may have been a descendant of the Thomas Archer, bookseller, who flourished between 1603 and 1634. [W. W. Greg, *List of Masques, etc.*, App. II.]

ARDING (WILLIAM), (?) bookseller in London, (?) 1642. This name occurs in the imprint to a pamphlet entitled *Propositions for Peace* [E. 152 (1).] The printing is so bad that it might very possibly be a mis-reading

of Harding, as there are one or two stationers of that name noted in the Registers of the Company of Stationers [Arber, ii. 238; iii. 687]. Again it might be the name of a Lincoln bookseller, as portions of the tract refer to that place.

ARMSTRONG (WILLIAM), (?) bookseller in Cambridge, 1647. A pamphlet entitled *Animadversions upon a declaration of the proceedings against the xi. members*, bears the imprint, Cambridge, Printed for Will. Armstrong. Anno. Dom. 1647. [E. 398 (4).]

ASH (FRANCIS), bookseller and bookbinder of the City of Worcester, 1644–51. The earliest mention of this bookseller is an entry in the Register of Apprenticeships, 1605–60, at Stationers' Hall, where, under date of December 7th, 1646, it is recorded that Francis Rea, the son of Ann Rea, of Churchill, co. Worcester, had put himself apprentice to Francis Ash for seven years, the indenture bearing date January 6th, 1644. Francis Ash is said to have been a Papist, and to have done a large trade in Popish books and pictures in the West of England. In a pamphlet entitled *A second beacon fired by Scintilla* written by a London bookseller, Michael Sparke, Sen., *q.v.*, are some interesting particulars relating to Francis Ash, in which it is stated that he was largely employed in obtaining "pictures" for the English Bible, and that he went to France, and there commissioned Hollar to engrave them. In the *Historical Catalogue of the British and Foreign Bible Society*, the Edinburgh editions of the Bible of 1633 are noted as containing these pictures in the New Testament. *See* Nos. 367, 368. Clement Barksdale's *Nympha Libethris*, 1651, 8°., has this imprint, "*London, Printed for F. A. at Worcester,*" and in stanzas 56 and 67 the author refers to Ash's skill as a bookbinder. Ash is believed to have died either during, or soon after the siege of Worcester (September, 1651).

ASSIGNS OF JOHN BILL, *see* BILL (JOHN), Assigns of.

ASSIGNS OF JOHN MORE, *see* MORE (J.), Assigns of.

ASTON (JOHN), bookseller in London; Cat-eaten-streete (Cheapside, renamed in 1845 Gresham Street), at the signe of the Bul's Head, 1637–42. Took up his freedom February 6th, 1637 [Arber, iii. 688], in which

year he published Thomas Heywood's *True Description of His Majesties Royall Ship Built this Year 1637 at Woollwitch in Kent.* 4to.; and a satire on women called *A Curtaine Lecture*, 1637. 12°. In 1641 he was imprisoned for a short time for printing the *Preamble with the protestation made by the whole House of Commons, 3 May, 1641.* [B.M. 669, f. 3 (2), Commons Journals.]

ATKINSON (HENRY), bookseller in London; Staple Inn Gate in Holborn, 1642–59. Took up his freedom October 3rd, 1631 [Arber, iii. 686]. Amongst his publications was Richard Kilburne's *Brief survey of the County of Kent*, 1657.

ATKYNS (RICHARD), patentee of law books, 1639–77. The printing of books of common law was created a monopoly by letters patent, granted by King Edward VI to Richard Tottel, and renewed to him by Queen Elizabeth (January 12th, 1 Eliz.). After his death, *i.e.*, on March 20th, $159\frac{3}{4}$, it was granted to C. Yetsweirt for thirty years. He only enjoyed it for a short time, and at his death, in 1598, the reversion was granted to Thomas Wight and Bonham Norton, for the remainder of the term. They, however, surrendered it in consideration of a new grant which was made on March 10th, $159\frac{8}{9}$, for thirty years [Patent Rolls, 41 Eliz., 4th part]. That patent expired on March 10th, 1628. It was no doubt put up to the highest bidder, and was next granted by James I (January 19th, 15 James I) to John More, Esquire, for forty years. A few months afterwards More assigned his printing rights to Miles Fletcher, *q.v.*, and his partners, John Haviland and Robert Young, for an annuity of £60 and a third of the profits. John More died August 17th, 1638, leaving this annuity, etc., to his daughter Martha, then the wife of Richard Atkyns, who thus became patentee by right of his wife. Miles Fletcher attempted to evade paying this legacy, and in 1639 purchased the stock and premises of Charles More, son of John More, for a sum of £930, and subsequently sold his rights to the Company of Stationers. But Atkyns and his wife brought an action against Fletcher and the Company in the Court of Chancery. The outbreak of the Civil War stopped the case, but at the Restoration they recommenced proceedings, and were successful, Miles Fletcher being held to have bought of Charles More wrongfully, and being compelled to pay up all arrears up to 1643, and since the Restoration, to Richard Atkyns and his wife. [P.R.O. Chan. Proc. Before 1715. Reynardson, Bund. 31, 126.] At one time Henry Twyford and John Streator, *q.v.*, were two of the assigns of R. Atkyns, whose name does not appear in any law book before 1677. Richard Atkyns is chiefly remembered as the author of a work entitled *The Origin and Growth of Printing*, 1664, in which he put forward the theory that the art of printing was introduced into England and begun at Oxford by a certain Frederick Corsellis in 1468, and that the *Exposicio sancti Jeronimi* was printed by him. This story has long since been proved to be unfounded, and the date in the *Exposicio* has been proved to the satisfaction of all bibliographers to be a misprint for 1478. Atkyns subsequently fell into distress, partly, it is believed, by the vagaries and extravagances of his wife, and was committed to the Marshalsea for debt. He died without issue on September 14th, 1677, and was buried in the church of St. George the Martyr, Southwark. [D.N.B.]

AUSTIN (JOHN), bookseller in London, 1642. His name occurs on the following broadside: *A List of the names of such persons who are thought fit for their accommodation, and the furtherance of the service in Ireland, to be entertained as reformadoes.* [Bibl. Lind. *Catalogue of English Broadsides*, No. 29.] His address has not been found. He may be identical with John Aston.

AUSTIN, or AUSTEN (ROBERT), printer in London, (1) Old Bailey, 1643; (2) Addlehill, Thames Street, 1649–50. 1642–56. Took up his freedom November 7th, 1636. [Arber, iii. 688.] He is chiefly worthy of notice as the printer of George Wither's *Campo-Musæ*, 1643, and the same author's *Vox Pacifica* in 1645. In 1643, in company with Andrew Coe, he printed some numbers of a news-sheet entitled *A Perfect Diurnal of the Passages in Parliament.* There was another publication bearing a very similar title, *A Perfect Diurnall of some Passages in Parliament*, of which Francis Coles and Lawrence Blacklock were the publishers. Both claimed precedency, but the Stationers' Company apparently refused to recognise the *Perfect Diurnal* of Austin and Coe, as no entry of it is found in the registers, whereas that of Coles and Blacklock was regularly entered and continued to run for several years. Austin was also interested in other news-sheets. On November 3rd, 1643, he started *Informator Rusticus, or The Country Intelligencer*, which does not seem to have got beyond its first

issue. In the following January he began another, entitled *Occurrences of certain speciall and remarkable passages in Parliament and the affaires of the Kingdome*, which was still in existence in 1646.

BADDELEY (RICHARD), bookseller in London; Within the Middle Temple Gate, 1650–53. Was probably a native of Durham, as on October 29th, 1650, he took as an apprentice Richard Baddeley, son of Richard Baddeley of that city. [Stationers' Company Register of Apprenticeships, 1603–66.] He published a *Letter to a Gentleman in the Country*, 1653, attributed to John Milton. [Masson's *Life of Milton*, vol. 4, p. 520.]

BADGER (GEORGE), bookseller in London; In St. Dunstan's Churchyard at his shop turning up to Cliffords Inne, 1641; (2) St. Dunstan's Churchyard, Fleet Street, 1641–51. Was probably a relation of Richard Badger and Thomas Badger. His widow married Theodore Crowley. [Stationers' Registers, Liber F, p. 160.] Both the addresses given above relate to the same house, which had previously been in the possession of H. Taunton, stationer.

BADGER (RICHARD), printer in London; (?) White Swan, at the foot of Addling Hill, near Baynard's Castle, 1602–42. According to the entry in the Registers of the Company of Stationers, Richard Badger was the son of John Badger, of Stratford-upon-Avon. [Arber, ii. 261.] The parish registers of the town do not confirm this, the only entries of a Richard Badger being Richard, son to George Badger, born September 14th, 1580, and another son of the same name, born August 17th, 1585. There is no mention in the Registers of any son born to a John Badger. [Stratford-on-Avon Parish Registers, Parish Register Society, 1897.] R. Badger came to London and was apprenticed to Peter Short, a printer, on March 25th, 1602, for eight years, and took up his freedom in April, 1610. He then joined George Miller, *q.v.*, another Stratford man, who had succeeded to the printing business of Richard Field, also a native of Stratford, and the printer of Shakespeare's *Venus and Adonis* and *Lucrece*. How long he remained with Miller is unknown, but Sir John Lambe states that about 1630 Richard Badger succeeded to the printing office formerly kept by Valentine Simmes. [Arber, iii. pp. 699–704.] Badger was admitted a master printer on June 12th, 1629, and in 1639 spoke of himself as

"printer to the Prince his Highness." He was also spoken of as printer to Archbishop Laud, for whom he is said to have printed "Bibles with superstitious pictures" [*True Informer*, No. 34, June 8th, 1644.] Timperley (p. 488) mentions a copy of Laud's speech at the trial of Bastwick as printed on vellum by Richard Badger. He had a good assortment of letter, and his workmanship was far above the average. Amongst his devices is found the "Anchora Spei," successively used by T. Vautrollier, R. Field, and George Miller. The date of his death is unknown, but he had a son, Thomas Badger, and he was also probably related to George Badger.

BADGER (THOMAS), printer in London; (?) Lucrece without Newgate, over against St. Sepulchre's Church (the printing house of the Purfoots), 1639–46. Son of Richard Badger. Printed as the assign of Thomas Purfoot the second, and on that printer's death in 1639 was elected a master printer in his place, and in all probability took over the old printing office as it stood. He was certainly in possession of the types, initial letters, and ornaments used by the Purfoots. Amongst the notable books that came from his press was James Howell's *Dodona's Grove*, 1640, and Sir H. Vere's *Elegies*, 1642. [*Domestic State Papers*, Charles I, vol. 446 (54); Arber, iii. 702.]

BAILEY, or BAILY (GEORGE), bookseller (?) in London, 1642. His name appears in the imprint to a broadside *To the Honourable the knights*, etc. [B.M., 669, f. 4 (49).] He may have been a relative of Thomas Bailey, the bookseller of Middle Row, Holborn, and perhaps carried on business with him.

BAILEY, BALEY, or BAILY (THOMAS), bookseller in London; (?) Middle Row, neer Staple Inn, Holborn, 1617–42. Published the *Earle of Essex his speech in the Artilrie garden, July 28th, 1642.* 4°. [E 200. (54).] Is probably identical with the bookseller in Middle Row, Holborn, who in 1634 had published a second edition of Samuel Rowland's *Night Raven.*

BAILY (T.), *see* Bailey (T.).

BAKER (JOHN), bookseller in London; Ship in St. Paul's Churchyard, 1653. Smyth in his *Obituary*, p. 36, has this entry: "Novem. 16, 1653, John Baker, bookseller, died." Shirley's masque of *Cupid and Death*, which was

presented before the Portuguese Ambassador upon March 26th, 1653, and apparently printed before the end of that year, has the imprint, "London: Printed according to the Authors own Copy, by T. W. for J. Crook and J. Baker, at the sign of the Ship in St. Paul's Church yard, 1653." There was another bookseller of this name.

BAKER (JOHN), bookseller in London, (1) Peacock in St. Paul's Churchyard, 1659–66; (2) Peacock in Little Britain, 1667–70; (3) Three Pigeons, St. Paul's Churchyard, 1670–84. The Register of Apprenticeships at Stationers' Hall records a John Baker, son of Michael Baker, stationer, as bound to George Thomason on September 6th, 1647. He was out of his time in 1655. In 1659, in partnership with Edward Brewster, he published a Greek edition of *Hesiod* for the use of schools, which was printed for them by D. Maxwell. The title-page, printed in red and black, is preserved in the Ames Collection of title-pages in the British Museum, No. 2867.

BALDEN (RICHARD), bookseller (?) in London, 1642. His name occurs on the title-page of a pamphlet entitled *An Uprore at Portsmouth*, 1642. [Hazlitt, ii. 489.] His place of business is not indicated.

BALEY (T), *see* Bailey (T.).

BALLARD (WILLIAM), bookseller in Bristol; Bible in Corn Street, 1651–53. His name is found on Robert Purnell's *Way to Heaven discovered*, 1653. [E. 1489 (2).] He was a dealer in Welsh books. [Rowland's *Cambrian Bibliography*, p. 156.]

BANKS (THOMAS), bookseller in London, (1) Blackfriars, on the top of Bridewell Stairs; (2) In the Old Bailey, 1641; (3) At the sign of the Seal in Westminster Hall, 1641–49. Took up his freedom on June 26th, 1637. [Arber, iii. 688.] Dealt chiefly in theological and political tracts and broadsides. In 1647 and at other times he had a stall in Westminster Hall, distinguished by the sign of the "Seal," and he was associated with another stall-holder there, Mistress Breach, in the publication of the Rev. John Cotton's *Controversie concerning liberty of conscience*, 1649. [*Library*, N.S., October, 1905, pp. 382–3.]

BARBER (JOSEPH), bookseller in London; The Lamb, in the New Buildings, St. Paul's Churchyard, 1653-58. Was associated with Samuel Speed in the publication of Sir P. Temple's *Man's Master Piece*, 1658.

BARKER (CHRISTOPHER), the Third, printer, 1640-80, son of Christopher Barker the second, and grandson of Robert Barker, the King's Printer. In 1643 he was sequestered for carrying the printing presses to the City of York, and the inference is that he was also the printer of the documents that were printed subsequently at Nottingham, Shrewsbury, and Bristol. At the Restoration, Christopher Barker the third, and John Bill the second, were restored to their moiety of the King's Printing Office, but Barker immediately assigned his moiety over to Sawbridge, Hills, Kirton, Roycroft, and Mearne, for an annuity of £100 a year, and appears to have given up printing, although his name continued to appear in the imprints of books down to the expiration of the patent in 1680. [*Library*, October, 1901. *The King's Printing House under the Stuarts.*]

BARKER (ROBERT), King's printer, Northumberland House, Aldersgate Street, 1570-1645. The eldest son of Christopher Barker the first, printer to Queen Elizabeth. He was probably born at Sudely, near Datchet, co. Bucks, was made free of the Company of Stationers on June 25th, 1589, and held a partnership in the Royal Printing House until his father's death in 1599. He is said to have married Rachel, a daughter of William Day (afterwards Bishop of Winchester), by whom he had a large family. On the accession of James I, Robert Barker held the office of King's Printer by virtue of the reversionary patent granted to his father, and afterwards obtained the reversion for his eldest son Christopher the second, and a further reversion of thirty years to his second son, Robert, on the death of Christopher and himself. In 1605 and 1606 he was Master of the Company of Stationers. Robert Barker was the printer of what is known as the "Authorised" version of the Bible in 1611. It has been generally supposed that he bore the whole cost, but there is little doubt that he was financed throughout by Bonham Norton, John Norton, and John Bill, in return for a share in the profits of the office. The value of the office at that time is said to have been £30,000. In 1615 his son Christopher the second married Sarah, the eldest daughter of Bonham Norton. Soon afterwards they were in financial difficulties, and assigned their interest in the King's

Printing House to Bonham Norton and John Bill. In 1618 Robert Barker brought an action in the Court of Chancery to recover possession, stating that according to the agreements the assignments were only for one year. This Norton denied, and a series of law suits extending over many years followed. Down to the year 1616 the imprints bore Robert Barker's name only. In 1616 they bore the names of Robert Barker and John Bill, and after July, 1617, until May, 1619, they ran "Bonham Norton and John Bill." Barker was successful in his first suit, and a decree was pronounced in his favour, but John Bill was held to have been a bonâ fide purchaser, and accordingly the imprints were altered again to Robert Barker and John Bill. But in 1620 Norton ejected Barker from the office, and the imprints were again changed to Bonham Norton and John Bill, and they continued thus until October 20th, 1629, when a final decree was pronounced in favour of Robert Barker, and they became for the third time Robert Barker and John Bill. In the course of this dispute the statement was made that the King's Printing House was situated at Northumberland House, Aldersgate Street, and subsequently at Hunsdon House, Blackfriars. The death of John Bill in 1630 necessitated a further change in the imprints, which then became Robert Barker and the assigns of John Bill. In 1634 Robert Barker mortgaged his moiety of the office to Miles Fletcher and his partners, and in 1635 he was committed as a debtor to the King's Bench Prison, where he died in 1645. His will, if he made one, has not been found. Of the five sons borne him by his wife Rachel, Christopher the second and Robert the second were already dead. Of the rest, Mathew only is subsequently heard of. The King's Printing House, when it was in the hands of Christopher Barker, was rich in all forms of type, ornaments, initial letters, including the handsome pictorial initial letters once used by John Day, and many others previously in the office of H. Bynneman. As various editions of the Bible, Prayer Book and Statutes show, it turned out some very fine books. To this stock Robert Barker succeeded, but the beauty of his black letter printing was marred by careless workmanship. The Bible of 1611 is, of course, the chief glory of his press. It was printed, like all previous folio editions, in great primer black letter, and had an elaborate engraved title-page, the work of Cornelis Boel, and also an engraved map of Canaan, partly the work of John Speed. [*Library*, N.S., October, 1901. *King's Printing House under the Stuarts . . .*]

BARLEY (RICHARD), bookseller in Dover, 1654. Only known from the imprint to a pamphlet entitled, *An Antidote against Anabaptisme* . . . . By Jo. Reading, B.D. . . . London. Printed by Tho. Newcomb, for Simon York and Richard Barley, dwelling in Dover, 1654. 4°. [Ames Collection of Title-pages, No. 2,410.]

BARLOW (WILLIAM), bookseller in London; Without Aldersgate, 1658. His name occurs in the imprint to a work called *Fundamenta chymica*, by L. C. Philomedico Chemicus, 1658. 8°. Only known by the title-page preserved amongst the Bagford fragments. He may have been a descendant of Timothy Barlow, bookseller (1616-18).

BARTLET (JOHN), senior, bookseller in London, (1) Gilt Cup, Goldsmiths' Row, Cheapside, 1619-37; (2) Gilt Cup near St. Austines Gate, 1641; (3) In St. Faith's Parish, 1643-44; (4) In the new buildings on the South side of Pauls, neer St. Austine's-Gate, at the sign of the Gilt-Cup, 1655; (5) At the Golden Cup in Pauls Church Yard over against the Drapers, 1657; (6) Gilt-Cup in Westminster Hall, 1658. Took up his freedom in the Company of Stationers on July 26th, 1619, and set up in business at the Gilt Cup in Goldsmiths' Row, Cheapside, his chief publications being sermons and other theological works. He was one of the victims of Laud's persecution, being apprehended in December, 1637, and brought before Sir John Lambe on a charge of having given William Prynne's servant some of the writings of Dr. Bastwick and Mr. Burton to be copied. He was ordered by the Privy Council to shut up his shop, and as he did not obey the order quickly enough, he was imprisoned in the Compter in Wood Street for three months, until he had entered into bond of £100 not to use his trade in Cheapside, to quit his house within six months, and not to let it to anyone but a goldsmith under a penalty of £600. He was afterwards brought before the Privy Council on the Archbishop's warrant, and sent to the Fleet prison, where he remained six months. [*Domestic State Papers*, Charles I, vol. 374, 13, etc.; vol. 378, 86; vol. 501, 18; *Domestic State Papers*, 1643 (4).] He afterwards moved into St. Paul's Churchyard, where his imprint appears in four varieties, though probably all relating to the same house. He had a son, John, who held a stall in Westminster Hall under the same sign, but probably it belonged to the father also. John Bartlet the elder appears to have died between 1657 and 1660. [*Library*, N.S., October, 1905, pp. 384-5.]

BARTLET (JOHN), the Younger, bookseller in London, Westminster Hall, 1657. His name is found in the imprint to a broadside entitled *An Elegy on the death of the Rt. Hon. Robert Blake, Esq.*, 1657. [Lutt. Coll. I, 10.] Several other books have the Bartlets' Westminster Hall imprint between this date and 1660, and the stall was probably jointly held by father and son. [*Library*, N.S., October, 1905, pp. 384-5.]

BARWICK (HENRY), bookseller (?) in London, 164½. A pamphlet entitled *The Prince of Orange his Royall Entertainment to the Queen of England* . . . . [E. 138 (17)] bears the imprint "First imprinted at the Hague in Holland, and now Reprinted in London for Henrie Barwicke 1641."

BASSET (THOMAS), bookseller in London, (1) St. Dunstan's Churchyard, Fleet Street; (2) George, near St. Dunstan's Church, Fleet Street; (3) Westminster Hall, 1659-93. A dealer in law books, chiefly remembered for the Catalogue of Law Books which he published in 1673. Jacob Tonson was one of his apprentices. A list of 13 books published by him in 1659 follows the preface to *Hermaelogium, or An Essay at the rationality of the art of Speaking*, 1659. 8°.

BATEMAN (THOMAS), bookseller (?) in London, 1659. His name occurs in the imprint to a pamphlet entitled: *Letter from Maj. Genl. Massey to an Hon. Person in London*, 1659. 4°.

BATES (THOMAS), bookseller in London, (1) Maidenhead on Snow Hill, Holborn Conduit, 1645; (2) Old Bailey. 1640-47. May probably be identified with the person of that name whose address is given in a contemporary pamphlet as Bishop's Court, in the Old Bailey, and at whose house, in 1641, there was a dispute between Henry Walker the ironmonger and a Jesuit. He was the publisher of much popular literature, broadsides, ballads, and lampoons, as well as many political pamphlets. On December 13th, 1641, he, in company with John Wright, sen., published the *Diurnal or the Heads of all the Proceedings in Parliament.* Another news-sheet which they produced was *Mercurius Civicus*, probably the first illustrated newspaper, its front page having every week a portrait of some celebrity. It began on May 4th, 1643, and ended on December 10th, 1646, quite a long life for a news-sheet. Bates and Wright were also the publishers of *The True Informer*, and Bates was also associated with F. Coles, *q.v.*, in the issue of the *Diurnall Occurrences* in 1642. In connection with this he was imprisoned for a short time in the year 1642 for publishing false reports on the Army. [*Library*, N.S., April, 1905, pp. 184 *et seq.*; Commons Journals, June 8th, 1642.]

BATT (M.), bookseller in London, 1642. His name occurs on several political pamphlets such as the following: *True and exact relation of the Proceedings of His Majesty's Army in Cheshire, Shropshire, and Worcestershire.* [October 5th], 1642. [Hazlitt, iv. 19; E. 126 (43).]

BEAL (G.), (?) bookseller in London, (?) Old Bayley and neer Temple Bar, 1648. The following political pamphlets of the year 1648 have the imprint, London, Printed for G. Beal, and are to be sold in the Old Bayley, and neer Temple Bar (1) *A great and bloudy fight at Colchester* .... 1648. [E. 453 (18)]; (2) *Two petitions of the Lord Mayor* .... 1648. [E. 453 (45).]

BEALE (JOHN), printer in London; (?) Fetter Lane [the printing house of Robert Robinson], 1612–41. This printing house belonged from 1587–97 to Robert Robinson. After his death his widow married Richard Braddock, who continued the business till 1609, when it was bought by Thomas Haviland and William Hall. Two or three years later it was sold by Hall to John Beale, who took into partnership for a short time Thomas Brudenell. Sir John Lambe, from whose notes on the London printing houses this notice is compiled, says; "Master John Beale succeeded his partner Master William Hall about 15 yeares since (*i.e.*, 1620), never admitted (of great estate but a very contentious person) he tooke 50li to furnish ye pore with bread and doth not do it. He bought Hall [out] and took Thomas Brudenell to be his partner for £140, which Brudenell had much a doe to recover." [Arber, iii. 699–700.] Beale was a relation by marriage to Humphrey Robinson, *q.v.* [Excheq. K. R. Bills and Answers, Lond. and Midd., 34.] Towards the close of his life he was afflicted with blindness, but appears to have still carried on business with S. Buckly, *i.e.*, Stephen Bulkley, *q.v.*, afterwards the Royalist printer, at York and elsewhere, for their names appear together in the imprint to Lewis de Gand's *Sol Britannicus*, 1641, 8°. [B.M. 1137, a. 13]. John Beale

died on September 17th, 1643, and on March 16th, 164$\frac{8}{9}$, his copies were transferred to Humphrey Robinson. [Stationers' Registers, Liber F.] He printed some important works, including Speed's *Theatre*, 1611; Bacon's *Essays*, 1612 and 1639; Record's *Ground of Arts*, 1618; an edition of *Cicero*, 1628; and B. Jonson's *Bartholomew Fayre*, 1631.

BEAUMONT (ROBERT), bookseller in London; Little Britain, 1650. Was in partnership with Lawrence Sadler, *q.v.*, and their names are found in the imprint to a medical book entitled *De Rachitide sive morbo puerili*, by Francis Glisson, 1650. 8°. He was probably dead before 1660, when another edition of the book appeared with Sadler's name only.

BECKE (H.), bookseller in London; In the Old Bayley, 1643–48. His name occurs in the imprint to the following pamphlets: *Protestation of the Two and Twenty Divines for the setling of the Church*, 1643 [*i.e.*, March 10th, 164$\frac{2}{3}$, E. 92 (24)]; *A bad and Bloody Fight at Westminster*, 1648. [E. 443 (17)]; and *Sad newes out of Kent*, 1648. [E. 443 (41).]

BECKETT (JAMES), bookseller in London; Inner Temple Gate, Fleet Street, 1636–41. Took up his freedom August 1st, 1636 [Arber, iii. 688], and in the same year published T. Heywood's *Challenge for beautie*. His first registered publication was the same author's play of the *Royall King and the loyall subject*, 1637. [Arber, iv. 376.] He was also the publisher of J. Kirke's *Seven Champions of Christendome*, 1638; F. Lenton's *Great Britain's Beauties*, 1638; T. Middleton's *Mad World my masters*, 1640; L. Sharpe's *Noble Stranger*, 1640; J. Shirley's *Humorous Courtier*, as well as a romance called *Marianus* in 1641, after which no more is heard of him. Amongst his other publications were T. Decker's *English Villanies seven several times Prest*, 1638; H. Peacham's *Truth of our Times* and *Valley of Varietie*, both in 1638; R. Braithwaite's *Epitome of all the lives of the Kings of France*, 1639 [Hazlitt, i., p. 48], and John Taylor's *Woman's Sharpe Revenge*, 1640. Only three of his publications were entered in the Registers before 1640.

BEDELL (GABRIELL), bookseller in London; Middle Temple Gate, Fleet Street, 1646–68. Is first met with on November 7th, 1646, when, in partnership with Mercy Meighen, *q.v.*, the widow of Richard Meighen, he

made an entry in the Registers of the Company of nineteen books which had formerly belonged to R. Meighen. Twelve of these were plays. Later, however, they appear to have dealt principally in law books. In 1650 they took Thomas Collins, *q.v.*, as third partner. In 1654 Mercy Meighen died, and G. Bedell is found in partnership with R. Marriot, T. Garthwayte, and J. Crooke, but eventually he and T. Collins settled down together, and a list of 86 books, arranged under subjects, published by them in 1656 occurs at the end of T. Goffe's *Three excellent Tragedies*. Gabriell Bedell died on February 27th, 166$\frac{7}{8}$ "by taking a cup of poyson, as is reported." [Smyth's *Obituary*, p. 77; W. W. Greg, *List of English Plays*, p. 42.]

BEE (CORNELIUS), bookseller in London; Little Britain, 1636–7$\frac{1}{2}$. Was the son of Thomas Bee, citizen and haberdasher, of London, whose will was proved May 28th, 1621. [P.C.C. 33 Dale.] He appears to have been a man of some capital, and joined Laurence Sadler, *q.v.*, in 1637 in the publication of the *Atlas Major*. [*Domestic State Papers*, Charles I, vol. 371, 95.] He is frequently mentioned in the domestic correspondence of the Commonwealth period, and Doctor Worthington in his diary notes [vol. i., p. 185] that the library of John Hales was purchased by Cornelius Bee for £700. His great publication was the *Critici Sacri* in 9 vols. folio, 1660. He had thought of issuing a tenth volume, and he greatly resented the publication of Matthew Poole's *Synopsis* of the critical labours of biblical commentators. Lawsuits resulted, the result being given in favour of Poole. Bee thereupon abandoned his projected tenth volume. [*Domestic State Papers*, Charles II, vol. 244, 27; *Case betwixt Mr. Poole and Mr. C. Bee* (1677?). *Vindication of Mr. Poole's design* (1677?)]. Cornelius Bee lost between £6,000 and £10,000 by the great fire. He married a sister of Lancelot Toppyn, bookseller, *q.v.*, and his wife died in 1654. One of his daughters married James Fletcher or Flesher, son of Miles Fletcher or Flesher, and another married Nathaniel Hooke, bookseller, *q.v.* Cornelius Bee died on January 2nd, 167$\frac{1}{2}$, and was buried at Great St. Bartholomew. [Smyth, *Obituary*, p. 93.]

BEESLEY (WILLIAM), (?) bookseller in London; Charles Street, Covent Garden, near the Peates (?) 1641. His name occurs on the imprint to a pamphlet entitled *Beaten Oyle for the lamps of the Sanctuarie.* [E. 163 (14).]

BELL (HENRY), bookseller and printer (?) in London, 1660–61. There were two booksellers in London of this name during the seventeenth century. The earlier one is believed to have died about 1639 or 1640. The name of the second is found on the title-page of a work on the life and death of Charles I, called the *Royal Martyr*, published in 1660. [B. M. Gren, 3544.] He was also associated with Peter Lilliecrap, the printer, *q.v.*, in issuing a theological pamphlet called the *Female Duel*, by T. Toll, in 1661. [B.M., E. 1813 (2).] His address has not been found.

BELL (JANE), bookseller and printer in London; East end of Christchurch, 1650–59. Succeeded Moses Bell. Printer of popular literature such as *Amadis de Gaul* and *Reynard the Fox*. Hazlitt notes an edition of *Sir P. Sidney's Ourania* printed by her in 1655 with a curious list of books. [Hazlitt, i. 30.] Most of her type was old.

BELL (MOSES), bookseller and printer in London; neere Christ-Church [Newgate Street], 1628–48. Took up his freedom July 25th, 1624. [Arber, iii. 685.] Started as a bookseller with Henry Bell, possibly a brother, who died about 1639. He was also associated with Benj. Green, *q.v.*, in 1632. Henry and Moses Bell assigned over all their copies to John Haviland and John Wright, sen., on September 4th, 1638. [Arber, iv. 434.] After this, Moses Bell began printing on his own account. He died about 1649, and was succeeded by Jane Bell, *q.v.*, probably his widow.

BELLAMY, or BELLAMIE (JOHN), bookseller in London, (1) South entrance, Royal Exchange; (2) Two Greyhounds, Cornhill; (3) Three Golden Lyons, Cornhill. 1620–54. A noted publisher of Americana. A native of Oundle, in Northamptonshire. [Price, J. *The City Remonstrance Remonstrated.* 1646. E. 345 (18).] He served his apprenticeship with Nicholas Bourne, stationer, *q.v.*, and took up his freedom in February, 1620. For some time afterwards he continued to work for Bourne, and several books, including Richard Braithwaite's volume of verse entitled *Time's Curtaine Drawne*, bear Bellamy's name as publisher, but were sold at Bourne's shop. Some time during the year 1622 he set up for himself at the Two Greyhounds in Cornhill, and began to publish books relating to New England. The first was *A Sermon preached at Plymouth in New England Decr. 9th 1621. Together with a preface shewing the state of the contree, and condicon of the inhabitants*, which he entered on the Register on March 22nd, 162$\frac{1}{2}$, and published shortly afterwards. In the same year he also published Patrick Copland's *Virginia's God be thanked, a sermon of thanksgiving for the happie successe of the affayres in Virginia; A Brief Relation of the Discovery and Plantation of New England, and The Relation or Journal of the beginning and proceedings of the English Plantation settled at Plymouth in New England,* edited by G. Mourt. In 1623 he moved to his third address, and from there issued *Good Newes from New England .... Written by E. W.*, which bore the date 1624 on the title-page. In 1630 he published *The humble request of his Majesties loyal subiects the Governor & the Company late gone to New England, to the rest of their brethren in and of the Church of England,* and very shortly afterwards the Rev. J. Cotton's sermon, *Gods promise to his plantation.* Bellamy also published William Wood's *New Englands Prospect*, 1634, 1635, and 1639; Governor Winslow's *Hypocrisie Unmasked ....* 1646; Thomas Hooker's *Survey of the summe of Church Discipline*, 1648; John Cotton's *The Way of Congregational Churches Cleared*, 1648, and Thomas Sheppard's *Clear Sunshine of the Gospel*, 1648. John Bellamy took an active part in the political and religious controversies of the time. On the outbreak of the Civil War he took up arms for the Parliament and was given the rank of colonel. He also represented the Ward of Cornhill on the Common Council, and when the split took place between the Presbyterians and Independents he published *The humble Remonstrance and Petition of the Lord Mayor Aldermen & Commons of the City of London*, which was printed for him by Richard Cotes in 1646. This led him into a pamphlet war with the opposite party, and he wrote *A Vindication of the humble remonstrance*, and in answer to a further attack, *A Justification of the City Remonstrance and its Vindication.* [B.M. E. 350 (23).] In these pamphlets are some interesting biographical details concerning the publisher. Bellamy appears to have retired from business about 1650, and settled at Cotherstock, or Cotterstock, in his native county of Northamptonshire, where he died about January 20th, $165\frac{3}{4}$. By his will, which was dated January 14th, $165\frac{3}{4}$, he left the bulk of his property to his brothers and sisters and their children. Special mention was made of his house and two shops in St. Paul's Churchyard, London, one of which, the White Lion, was then in the occupation of Philemon Stephens, stationer, *q.v.*, and he bequeathed a certain number of books to form a standing library for the ministers of Cotherstock. The will was proved on February 7th, $165\frac{3}{4}$. [P.C.C. 92, Alchin.]

BELLINGER (JOHN), bookseller in London; Cliffords Inn Lane in Fleet Street, 1642–78. Son of William Bellinger, citizen and girdler of London; apprenticed on August 24th, 1642, to Humphrey Tuckey, *q.v.*, for eight years. [Stationers' Register of Apprenticeships.]

BENINGTON (EDWARD), bookseller (?) at Oxford, 1647. A pamphlet entitled: *A Gallant speech spoken by His Highness James Duke of York* [E. 399 (37)] has the imprint, "Printed at Oxford for Edward Benington, for the publike use of Great Brittain, Anno 1647." This appears to be one of the pamphlets printed by John Harris, *q.v.*, and to which he added names that cannot be identified as stationers. The Thomason copy of this pamphlet is apparently incomplete and mis-bound with a portion of another.

BENSON (JOHN), bookseller in London, (1) St. Dunstan's Churchyard, Fleet Street, 1641; (2) Chancery Lane. 1635–$6\frac{6}{7}$. Was chiefly a publisher of ballads and broadsides. In 1647 he was associated with John Saywell, *q.v.*, in the publication of Francis Quarles' *Hosanna, or Divine poems on the Passion of Christ*, which was entered on May 29th, 1647. [Stat. Reg., Liber F, p. 95.] In 1651 he began to issue music books in partnership with John Playford, *q.v.* He died on January 23rd, $166\frac{6}{7}$. [Smyth's *Obituary*, p. 73.]

BENTLEY (WILLIAM), printer in London; Finsbury, 1646–56. This printer is first heard of in 1646, when the Westminster Assembly of Divines proposed the issue of a new and cheap edition of the Bible. As no printer in London except Bentley would undertake the work, it was given to him, whereupon the Company of Stationers immediately issued an order that "no journeyman printer of the company who should work at the printing house in Finsbury should ever have any gift or pension whatsoever from the company." In the Act of 1649, and that of 1652, this printing house was specially mentioned as being exempt from their provisions, but, nevertheless, Bentley met with strong opposition from Hills and Field, who claimed the exclusive right of Bible printing as successors to Robert Barker and his assigns. In November, 1656, Bentley printed a broadside entitled *The Case of William Bentley printer at Finsbury .... touching his right to the printing of Bibles and Psalms* [B.M. 669, f. 20 (24)], in which he undertook

to furnish octavo Bibles with marginal notes better printed and corrected than any other edition at two shillings per volume as against the official price of 4*s.* 6*d.* He further stated that he had already finished five several editions. Two of these, dated 1646 and 1648, are amongst those in the collection of the British and Foreign Bible Society. In 1659 William Kilburne wrote a pamphlet entitled *Dangerous errors in several late printed Bibles*, which was printed at the Finsbury press, and was clearly written as a puff. *See* FIELD (JOHN).

BERRIMAN (THOMAS), bookseller (?) in London; Great St. Bartholomews, 1642. *Exceeding Joyfull Newes from the Earl of Bedford*, 1642 [E. 113 (17)] has the imprint, "London printed, for Thomas Berriman dwelling in Great St. Bartholomew, August 23, 1642."

BEST (JOHN), printer in London; Three Crowns, Giltspur Street, 1660–65. A printer of broadsides, ballads, and popular literature. In 1664 he printed for William Crook *The History of the Life and Martyrdom of St. George* .... by Thomas Lowick, gent.; Geo. Swinnock's *Christian-Man's-Calling*, 1663–65, and a broadside, *The King's Majestys Love to London* [*London's modest answer*]. [B.M. C. 20 f. 2 (60).]

BEST (RICHARD), bookseller in London; Gray's Inn, Holborn, 1640–53. Took up his freedom March 30th, 1640. [Arber, iii. 688.] He dealt chiefly in political pamphlets and law books, but amongst them is found Jo. Tatham's *Fancies Theatre*, 1640.

BIARD (JOHN), bookseller (?) in London, 1643. This name occurs in the imprint to a political squib, printed without date, but probably in 1643, *A Brief Dialogue between Zelotophit .... and Superstition .... London. Printed for John Biard.* [E. 140 (5).]

BILCLIFFE (JOSEPH), bookseller in London; Great Piazza, Covent Garden, 1661–63. Mentioned in "Mercurius Publicus" for April, 1661, as agent for certain "lozenges." He was also an agent for the receipt of letters for the Postmaster-General, but from a notice that appears in *Mercurius Publicus* of June 18th, 1663, he seems to have abused his trust.

BILL (JOHN), the First, Assigns of (1630–60). In his will, proved on May 12th, 1630, John Bill made especial mention of James Burrage, and desired him to continue the same employment in the printing office he then had. He also mentions a William Garrett. But there is no evidence that these were the assigns referred to. One of his executors was Martin Lucas, who, with Robert Barker, was fined £300 for leaving the word "not" out of the seventh commandment in the edition of the Bible printed in 1632, but Lucas was not a printer. In all probability the real printers and assigns were Miles Fletcher, John Haviland, and Robert Young, who controlled so many of the London printing houses at that time.

BILL (JOHN), the Second, printer in London; (?) Hunsdon House, Blackfriars, 1630–80 (?). The son of John Bill, the King's Printer, who died in 1630, and who by his will left all his estate and terme in his part of the King's Printing Office to his son. During the Commonwealth, Henry Hills, and John Field, *q.v.*, were appointed printers to the State, and it was said that John Bill the second and Christopher Barker the third, *q.v.*, sold to them the manuscript copy of the last translation of the Bible. On the Restoration, Christopher Barker the third and John Bill the second were restored to the position of King's Printers. John Bill the second continued to enjoy his share of the profits of the office during his lifetime, and his successors till the end of the Stuart period. [Plomer, *Wills*, p. 53; *Library*, N.S., October, 1901, pp. 353–75.]

BIRD (HENRY), bookseller (?) in London, 1641. His name is given as one of the "better sort of freemen" of the Stationers' Company, in a list of those who had paid their respective proportions of the poll tax on August 5th, 1641. [*Domestic State Papers*, Charles I, vol. 483, 11.]

BIRD (THEOPHILUS), bookseller in London, 1656. Associated with A. Penneycuicke in publishing Ford and Decker's masque, *The Sun's Darling*, 1656. His name appears at the end of the Epistle Dedicatory.

BISHOP (GEORGE), printer in London; (?) Warwick Court, Warwick Lane, 1641–44. In partnership with Robert White, *q.v.* Their work included the following news-sheets: *Certaine Informations from several parts of the kingdom*, 1643; *Kingdoms Weekly Intelligence*, 1643, and *Mercurius Britanicus.*

BISHOP (RICHARD), printer in London; St. Peter's Pauls Wharf, 1631–53. Took up his freedom March 29th, 1637, having in 1634 bought the business of William Stansby, printer, for £700. According to Sir John Lambe's Memoranda [Arber, iii. 700, etc.] this was originally John Day's business, being subsequently divided up between Peter Short and John Windet, Stansby having bought Windet's share.

BISSE (JOHN), bookseller in London; Bell in St. Paul's Churchyard, 1649–53. Only known through the entry in Smyth's *Obituary*, p. 35: "July 6. [1653] John Bisse, bookseller, died."

BLACKLOCK, *see* Blaiklock.

BLACKMORE (EDWARD), bookseller in London, (1) Blazing-Starre, St. Paul's Churchyard, 1620; (2) South door of Paul's Church; (3) Angel, St. Paul's Churchyard. 1618–58. Dealt chiefly in popular literature, such as Melton's *Astrologaster*, 1620, which contains his Blazing-Star address. He died September 8th, 1658. [Smyth's *Obituary*, p. 48.] The *Weekly Intelligencer* of November 25th, 1651, contains advertisements of two books issued by him.

BLADEN (WILLIAM), bookseller in London; Great North-doore of Pauls at the sign of the Bible, 1612–24; address unknown, 1640–42; printer in Dublin, 1630–63. First met with in 1612 as a bookseller in London in partnership with John Royston. In 1618 certain stationers of London formed themselves into a society "to trade in the city of Dublin by vending and selling of books and other commodities .... to be transported out of England thither, and there to be sold," the books stocked for this purpose being known as the Irish "stock." They appointed William Bladen their factor in Dublin. He was admitted to the Franchise of the city in January, $16\frac{30}{31}$, by special grace and on payment of a fine of £10 English money. In April, 1637, he was elected Sheriff for the following year. Meanwhile the trading venture of the London stationers had turned out a failure, and the partnership was dissolved in 1639, when William Bladen bought the stock for £2,600. His name first appears in imprints in 1641. In 1647 he filled the office of Lord Mayor of Dublin, and during the Commonwealth he acted as State Printer. His death took place in Dublin, in July, 1663, and he was buried on August 1st in St. Werburgh's Churchyard. Bladen's will was proved in the Prerogative

Court in August, 1663. His wife, "Elinor," was the principal beneficiary. He directed all his stock in his shop, printing house, and warehouse, both in Dublin and in London, together with his interest in his then dwelling-house and printing house, to be sold unto some person having served 7 years to a printer, stationer or bookseller. He mentions his "son, Dr. Thos. Bladen." Probably this was the editor of Clarke's *Praxis*. He also left a son of the same name, who is believed to have come to London and set up as a bookseller. [Information supplied by Mr. E. R. McC. Dix.; *Library*, July, 1907.]

BLAGRAVE (ROBERT), bookseller at Oxford, 1656–62. Son of John and Lydia Blagrave. His will was proved 1662. His imprint is found in Caius' *Suetonius Tranquilus*. [Information supplied by Mr. Madan.]

BLAGUE (JOHN), bookseller in London, (1) Pope's Head Alley, 1652; (2) Golden Ball in Cornhill, near the Poultry, 1652. 1642–52. John Blague, son of Benjamin Blague, barber-surgeon of London, apprenticed on October 30th, 1642, to John Burroughes for eight years. [Stationers' Registers, Apprenticeships.] Partner with Samuel Howes, *q.v.* They published jointly H. Whitfield's *Strength out of Weakness ....* 1652, and Phillip Barrough's *Method of Physick*, 1652.

BLAIKLOCK, or BLACKLOCK (JOSEPH), bookseller in London. Turk's Head, Ivy Lane, 1639–60. Took up his freedom April 29th, 1639. [Arber, iii. 688.] Chiefly a publisher of theological literature. He issued in 1651 an edition of the *Imitatio Christi* under the title of *The Christian's Pattern* [Harl. 5927, 501.] His name is found in the imprint to C. Ducket's *Sparks from the Golden Altar*, 1660.

BLAIKLOCK, BLAKELOCK, or BLACKLOCK (LAWRENCE), bookseller in London, (1) Sugar Loaf next [near] Temple Bar; (2) Middle-Temple-Gate. 1638–53. Took up his freedom March 5th, 1638. [Arber, iii. 688.] Amongst his publications were Fr. Beaumont's *Poems*, 1652; W. Bosworth's *Chaste and lost lovers*, 1651, and H. Mill's *Poems*, 1639. During the Civil War, in company with Fr. Coles, and Lawrence Chapman, he printed a news-sheet called the *Perfect Diurnall of some passages in Parliament*, 1643–49. The last heard of him is in 1653, when he issued a law book, Young, W., *A Vade Mecum, etc.*

BLAKELOCK, *see* Blaiklock.

BLOME (JACOB), bookseller in London; Knight Rider Street, 1619–61. Took up his freedom March 26th, 1618. [Arber, iii. 688.] Was originally in partnership with George Edwards, but on June 4th, 1621, they assigned over their copies to Geo. Hodges. [Arber, iv. 54.] In 1631 Blome obtained from Ralph Mabb the copyright of Guillim's *Display of Heraldry*, but he does not seem to have re-issued it until 1660.

BLUNDEN (HUMPHREY), bookseller in London; Castle in Cornhill, 1635–52. Took up his freedom June 15th, 1635. [Arber, iii. 688.] Before the Civil War he is found publishing plays and books of a popular character. In 1639 he issued Robert Davenport's comedy, *New Trick to cheat the Devill*; and in 1640 J. Johnson's *Academy of Love*. During the Civil War he issued a large number of political pamphlets, and was associated with John Partridge in the publication of many of the writings of William Lilly, the astrologer. But his chief claim to notice at that period was as editor of a news-sheet called *Speciall Passages and certain informations from several places*, the first number of which appeared on August 16th, 1642. It became popularly known as "Blunden's Passages" [*Mercurius Civicus*, June 8th, 1643.] Nothing more is heard of him after 1652.

BOAT (MARMADUKE), bookseller in London, 1642. Took up his freedom August 4th, 1640. [Arber, iii, 688.] Associated with Andrew Coe in publishing *Master Pyms Speech in Parliament* [March 17th], 1641. 4°. [B.M. E. 200 (37)], and *Master Hollis his Speech in Parliament*, March 21st, 1642. His address has not been found.

BODDINGTON (GEORGE), bookseller in London; In Chancery lain neer Serjants-Inn. 1648. His name is found on the imprint to James Beaumont's *Psyche or Loves Mysterie*, a poem printed in folio by John Dawson in 1648.

BODVELL or BODRELL (PETER), bookseller in London and Chester. 1664–70. Was apprenticed to Thomas Brewster, *q.v.*, and was one of the witnesses at his trial in February, 1664. [See *An Exact Narrative*, B.M. 1132, b. 57.] He is mentioned again in some Chancery proceedings brought by the Stationers' Company against certain Chester booksellers in the year 1699. John Minshull, one of the defendants, stated that he was

apprenticed to a London bookseller, Mr. Peter Bodrell or Bodvell, who was burnt out in the great fire of 1666, and then removed to Chester, where he died before John Minshull's term of apprenticeship was complete. [*Library*, 2nd Series, No. 16, pp. 373–83.] Peter Bodrell was associated with Edward Fowkes or Foulkes, *q.v.*, in publishing the Book of Common Prayer in the Welsh tongue in 1664. [Rowlands, *Cambrian Bibliography*, p. 191.] There is a memorial to a Peter Bodvell in St. Michael's Church, Chester (*see* Fenwick's *History of Chester*, 1896, p. 316).

BOLER (JAMES), bookseller in London; Marygold in Fleet Street, 1641–49. Son of James Boler, who died in 1634. [Arber, iv. 435.] Published a book on needlework called *The Needles Excellency*, 1640, and his imprint is found in a pamphlet entitled *Humble Advice .... of certaine ministers .... of Banbury .... Oxon and of Brackly .... Northampton.* 1649. 4°.

BOND (WILLIAM), bookseller (?) in London, 1641–2. Several political pamphlets issued in the years 1641 and 1642 have the imprint: "London, Printed for W. Bond," but his address is not given. He may possibly have been a relative of Charles or John Bond, stationers, of London. [Arber, iii. 685, 687; E. 131 (9); E. 181 (32).]

BOSTOCK (ROBERT), bookseller in London, (1) King's Head, St. Paul's Churchyard; (2) St. Faith's, Southwark, 1650. 1629–58. Took up his freedom December 5th, 1625 [Arber, iii. 686], and appears to have dealt chiefly in theological literature. During the Civil War he took an active part on behalf of the Parliament, and was appointed by the Committee of Sequestrations one of its Treasurers. At this time he was busily engaged in the publication of political pamphlets, one of the most noted of which is undoubtedly *The Kings Cabinet Opened*, consisting of the Royalist papers that were captured at the battle of Naseby. In 1645, and again in 1646, he was in trouble for publishing pamphlets relating to the disputes between England and Scotland. [*Domestic State Papers*, Charles I, vol. 510, 125; vol. 513, 30, 39; Hist. MS. Comm., 6th Report, App., pp. 111], and on June 5th, 1650, he was bound over in £500 not to print seditious pamphlets. [*Domestic State Papers*, 1650.] He died suddenly in the street at Banbury on December 11th, 1656 [Smyth, *Obituary*, p. 43], and his copyrights, fifty-four in number, were transferred to George Thomason. [Stationers' Company Registers, Liber F, p. 23.]

BOULTER (ROBERT), bookseller in London, (1) Turk's Head in Cornhill, 1666; (2) Turk's Head in Bishopsgate Street, near the Great James, 1667. Was one of the three publishers of the first edition of Milton's *Paradise Lost*, 1667. The first imprint given above is found on the title-page of one of the Rev. T. Doolittle's treatises on the great plague published in 1666, and the second in an edition of Sir Walter Raleigh's *Judicious and select Essays*, published by him in 1667.

BOURDEN, *see* Burden.

BOURKE (THOMAS), printer at Waterford and Kilkenny, Ireland, 1643–48. The authorised official printer of the Catholic Confederation. Sir J. T. Gilbert describes him as a "native printer." In 1643 he is found at Waterford, where he continued until 1645, when he appears to have moved to Kilkenny, where in that year was printed Henry Burkhead's *A tragedy of Cola's Furie, or Lirenda's Miserie*, of which there is a unique copy in the British Museum. The books that came from the Kilkenny press bore no printer's name, but Bourke's name is found on a broadside printed there entitled *Declaration by the Confederate Catholics' Council*, 1648. [*Library*, N.S., October, 1901. *Irish Provincial Printing*, by E. R. McC. Dix.]

BOURNE (NICHOLAS), bookseller in London; South entrance, Royal Exchange [Cornhill], 1601–57. Son of Henry Bourne, citizen and cordwainer of London, put himself apprentice to Cuthbert Burby, bookseller, for seven years from March 25th, 1601. Burby died between August 24th and September 16th, 1607, and by his will left Nicholas Bourne the offer of his stock on favourable terms and gave him the lease of the premises in Cornhill in consideration of his true and faithful service. Mistress Burby assigned over her late husband's copyrights to Nicholas Bourne on October 16th, 1609. These consisted mainly of theological works, and we have it on the evidence of John Bellamy, *q.v.*, one of his apprentices, that he would not allow them to sell play-books [see *A Justification of the City Remonstrance and its Vindication*, E. 350. (23).] Nicholas Bourne was Master of the Company in 1643 and again in 1651. He died in 1657. [Plomer, *Wills*, p. 42.] A list of 58 books, etc., printed for him occurs at the end of Robert Witbie's *Popular Errours*, 1651, 8°. [B.M. E. 1227.] It contains a few works relating to English trade and fishery rights.

BOURNE (THOMAS), bookseller in London; Bedlam [*i.e.*, Bethlehem Hospital], 1628–71. Took up his freedom January 15th, 1623. [Arber, iii. 685.] Smyth in his *Obituary*, p. 91, thus records the death of this bookseller "19 June 1671. Thomas Bourne bookseller at Bedlam (my old acquaintance) died hora 8 p[t] merid.; his corps carried from Lorimer's Hall to Bottol. Bishopsgate, Thurs., June 22, and there buried, with the service of the common prayer, though he died a recusant." The only book in which his name has been found is an edition of the *Articles of Visitation of the Bishop of Chichester*, in the year 1628. [B.M. 5155, c. 13.]

BOWDEN (WILLIAM), bookseller (?) in London, 1641. His name occurs in the imprints to several political pamphlets of the year 1641; but none of them give his address [E. 181 (1).]

BOWEN (PENYELL), bookseller (?) in London. Only known from the record of his death in Smyth's *Obituary*, p. 91. "Penyall Bowen, stationer, once apprentice to Octavian Pulleyn, sen., bookseller in St. Paul's Churchyard, dying of a veyne broken was buried at St. Butolph's without Aldersgate."

BOWLER (J.), *see* Boler (J.).

BOWMAN (FRANCIS), bookseller and printer (?) in Oxford and London, 1634–47. Published books in Oxford between 1634 and 1640. He is believed to have left Oxford about the year 1641. Several books are found printed in London in 1647 by *F. B.* These initials are found in G. Pretis' *Oranta the Cyprian Virgin*; Thomas Stanley's *Poems and Translations*, and also in Sir Robert Stapylton's *Musaeus or the loves of Hero and Leander*. The copyright of this last work belonged in the first place to Henry Hall, printer at Oxford, and was transferred by him on March 4th, 164$\frac{6}{7}$, to Humphrey Moseley. There is no other printer or bookseller in London at that date to whose name the initials apply, and the probability is that the printer of these books was Francis Bowman. [F. Madan, *Early Oxford Press*, pp. 278, 306, 313.]

BOWMAN (THOMAS), bookseller (?) of Oxford, 1664. Had a son, Thomas Bowman. Mentioned in a lease of property in Oxfordshire, dated 1664.

BOWTELL (STEPHEN), bookseller in London; Bible in Pope's Head Alley, 1643–64. Amongst his publications, which were chiefly of a political character, was a curious piece of Americana from the pen of Nathaniel Ward, under the pseudonym of Theodore de la Guard, entitled *The simple Cobbler of Aggawam in America* . . . . 1647. 4°.

BOYDELL (ROBERT), bookseller in London. In the Bulwarke neere the Tower, 1650–55. His name is found on the following work: Foster, N. *Briefe Relation of the late Horrid Rebellion*, 1650, and his death is recorded in Smyth's *Obituary*, p. 40, "March 16, 165$\frac{4}{5}$, Mr. Boyden, bookseller, by y[e] Tower died."

BRADFORD (NEHEMIAH), (?) bookseller in London, 1659. Only known from the imprint to a pamphlet entitled *Dialogue between Riches, etc.* London. Printed for Nehemiah Bradford, MDCLIX. [E. 999 (2).]

BRADLEY (DANIEL), (?) bookseller in London, 1642. His name is found on the imprints to several political tracts and broadsides of the year 1642. He may have been related to the George and John Bradley, stationers, who took up their freedom on December 1st, 1628, and September 15th, 1631. [Arber, iii. 686.]

BREACH ( ), Mrs., bookseller in London; Westminster Hall, "at the foot of the stone stairs going up to the Court of Requests," 1649–75. Was associated in 1649 with Thomas Banks, *q.v.*, who also kept a stall in the Hall, at the sign of the Seal, in publishing the Rev. John Cotton's *Controversie concerning libertie of conscience*, 1649. In 1675 she was in trouble for selling a pamphlet entitled *A Letter from a Person of Quality to his Friend in the Country*. One of the witnesses described Mrs. Breach as a fat woman. She must have been a familiar figure in the Hall throughout the Civil War, Commonwealth and the Restoration. [*Hist. MSS. Comm.*, 9th Report App. p. 66a; *Lords' Journals*, vol. xiii. 17; *Library*, N.S., No. 24, pp. 380–390.]

BREWSTER (A), bookseller in London; Three Bibles at the West end of St. Paul's, 1666–81. Appears to have succeeded Thomas Brewster, at this address.

BREWSTER (EDWARD), bookseller in London, (1) The Star, West end of Paul's, 1621–3; (2) The Great West Door of St. Paul's, 1624; (3) The Bible near the North door of Paul's, 1627–34; (4) Bible in Paul's Churchyard, 1635; (5) Bible on Fleet Bridge, 1640–47. Dealt exclusively in theological books. Treasurer of the English Stock of the Company of Stationers from 1639 to 1647. Under date October 7th, 1647, Smyth in his *Obituary*, p. 24, states "Mr. Brewster, stationer, buried." He left a son Edward.

BREWSTER (EDWARD), bookseller in London; Crane in St. Paul's Churchyard, 1654–99. Son of the preceding. Master of the Company of Stationers, 1689–92. [Arber, v. lxvi.] A list of books published by him in 1655 will be found in S. Birckbek's *Treatise of the four last things*. [E. 1460 (2).]

BREWSTER (THOMAS), bookseller in London, (1) Three Bibles under Mildred's Church in the Poultry, 1649; (2) Three Bibles in Paul's Churchyard, 1659. 1649–64. What relation, if any, this bookseller was to the two preceding has not been discovered. In company with Giles Calvert and Henry Hills he was appointed official printer to the Council of State on the accession of Cromwell, but he only held the appointment until the end of 1653, after which the name of Henry Hills is found alone or in conjunction with John Field, *q.v.* Thomas Brewster had as partner for a short time G. Moule, *q.v.* In 1654 he published an edition of the Bible in Welsh. [Ballinger, *Bible in Wales*, p. 10.] In 1664, in company with Simon Dover and Nathan Brooks, he was tried at the Old Bailey for having caused to be printed two pamphlets, the one entitled *The Speeches of some of the late King's Justices*; the other, *The Phœnix of the Solemn League and Covenant*. One of the witnesses against him was his servant, Peter Bodvell, *q.v.* Brewster was condemned to pay a fine of 100 marks and to stand in the pillory on two days. [*An Exact Narrative of the Tryal . . . . of John Twyn, etc.* 1664.] In a note in *The Newes* of April 28th, 1664, he is said to have died shortly afterwards. A list of books on sale by Thomas Brewster occurs at the end of Robert Purnell's *Little Cabinet*, 1657. [E. 1575.] It consists mainly of theological books and pamphlets against the Quakers.

BRIDGES, BRUGES, or BRUGIS (HENRY), printer in London; Sir John Oldcastle, Py-Corner, 1660–83. He is mentioned in a list of booksellers, printers, and stationers against whom search warrants were granted in 1664

[*Domestic State Papers*, Charles II, vol. 99, 165] and again as a printer in the survey of the press made on July 24th, 1668, but the number of his presses is not given. [Plomer, *Short History of English Printing*, pp. 224, 225.] In 1670 the Company of Stationers ordered that his press and materials should be defaced, and himself indicted for printing a Popish book entitled *Think well on't*. [Records of the Stationers' Company.] The name of Michael Brugis is found in the imprint to a political tract of the Commonwealth period.

BRIGGS (PHILIP), bookseller in London, (1) Dolphin, St. Paul's Churchyard, between the two north doores, 1655; (2) Mermaid Court near Amen Corner, Pater-Noster Row, 1671. 1655–72. His name is found on Edmond Ellis's *Dia Poemata*, 1655. Peter Lilliecrap, *q.v.*, printed several things for him. [Hazlitt, H. 183, ii. 585, iii. 30, ii. 260.]

BROAD (ALICE), printer at York; Stonegate over against the Star, 1660–67. Widow of Thomas Broad. Printed several books for Francis Mawbarn, *q.v.*

BROAD (THOMAS), printer at York, (1) At Mistris Rogers house on Stonegate, over againste the Starre, 1644; (2) In Stone-Gate over against the Starre, 1644; (3) Near Common-Hail Gate, 1649–60. On the occupation of the City of York by the Parliament's army, Thomas Broad was appointed printer in the place of Stephen Bulkey. His death took place about 1660, when he was succeeded by his widow, Alice Broad.

BROCAS (ABISHA), bookseller in Exeter, 1655–74. Mentioned in an advertisement of patent medicines in the "Newes" in 1663. Published the following books: Tickell (J.), *Sum and substance of religion*, a broadside, 1655 [816. m. 22 (28)]; Fullwood (F.), *General Assembly*, 1667.

BROCKLEBANK (RALPH), bookseller in York; In the Minster Yard, 1647. Only known from the imprint to a tract entitled *An Answer to the Poysonous Sedicious Paper of Mr. David Jenkins*, 1647, 4°, printed for him by Thomas Broad, of which there is a copy in the York Minster Library. [Davies, *Memoir of the York Press*, p. 79.] It was issued the same year in London by Robert Bostock.

BROME (HENRY), bookseller in London, (1) Hand, in Paul's Churchyard, 1657; (2) Gun, Ivy Lane, 1660–66; (3) Gun, St. Paul's Churchyard, or (4) Gun in Ludgate Street at the West End of Paul's, 1669; (5) Star, Little Britain, 1666–69. Publisher of broadsides, poems, plays, and general literature. According to the best authorities he was in no way related to Alexander or Richard Brome, the playwrights, though he published the works of both of them, and wrote a preface to Richard Brome's play *The Queens Exchange*. A list of 42 works published by him in 1664 will be found at the end of the *Songs and Poems* of Alex. Brome, which he published in that year. Another list for the year 1667 was issued with Sir P. Rycant's *Present State of the Ottoman Empire*, of which there is a unique copy—once belonging to Samuel Pepys—in Magdalene College, Cambridge. The date of his death is unknown, but he left a son, Henry, who succeeded him in business.

BROOKE (NATHANIEL), bookseller in London, (1) Angel, Cornhill; (2) At the Angel, in the second yard going into the Exchange from Bishopsgate Street. 1646–77. This bookseller must not be confused with Nathan Brooks, who was tried and convicted at the Old Bailey in 1664 for publishing seditious books. An extensive list of Nathaniel Brooke's publications will be found in Gray's Index to Hazlitt.

BROOKE (SAMUEL), bookseller in London, 1661. Hazlitt records the three following works as bearing this bookseller's name: *Catalogue of Peeres of the Realm*, 1661; Will. Ramsay, *Man's Dignity*, 1661; *Perfect List of the Knights*, 1661; none of which appear to be in the British Museum. [Hazlitt, ii. 86, 511; iii. 188.]

BROOKE (WILLIAM), bookseller in London; Black Swan Inne Yard in Holborn, 1661. Publisher of a curious romance entitled *The Princess Gloria or the Royal Romance*, 1661, the unsold copies of which were reissued in 1665 by Edward Man.

BROOKS (NATHAN) (?) bookseller in London; Bunhill near Moor Fields, next door to the Feathers, 1664. Must not be confused with Nathaniel Brooke, bookseller. He was perhaps the Nathan Brookes, son of Edward Brookes, of Onelip, co. Leicester, who was apprenticed to Randall Taylor for 8 years from March 25th, 1650. [Stationers' Register of Apprentice-

ships, 1605–66.] Nathan Brooks was tried and convicted with Thomas Brewster, and Simon Dover, in 1664, for publishing seditious books. In the indictment he is described as a "bookbinder" of Moorfields, but was found guilty of publishing the books. He was condemned to stand in the pillory at the Exchange and in Smithfield on two successive days, and to be confined during his Majesty's pleasure. [*An Exact Narrative of the Trial of J. Twyn* .... 1664.] His address appears in the *Domestic State Papers*, Charles II, vol. 113 (7).

BROUN (SAMUEL), *see* Browne (Samuel).

BROWN (JAMES), printer in Aberdeen, 1650–61; "Market Place at the Townes Armes." Son of William Brown, Minister of Innernochtie. Succeeded Raban, in 1650, occupying the same house, and was appointed printer to the Town and University. Died July, 1661. Succeeded by John Forbes. [H. G. Aldis, *List of books printed in Scotland before 1700*, p. 109.]

BROWN (P.), (?) bookseller in London, 1656. Is only known from the imprint to the first edition of the Rev. Henry Beesley's collection of sermons entitled, *Ψυχομαχία, or the Soules Conflict* .... 1656, of which the title-page is preserved in the Ames Collection, No. 2553. His place of business is not given.

BROWN, or BROUN (ROBERT), stationer in Edinburgh; The Sun, on the north side of the street, over against the Cross, 1649–85 (?). Probably the Robert Brown, "my prenteiss," to whom Robert Crombie, *q.v.*, in 1645 left his "best stand of cloaths." One of the six booksellers who in 1671 successfully appealed to the Privy Council against Anderson's attempted enforcement of his monopoly. His will was registered May 7th, 1685. [H. G. Aldis, *List of Books printed in Scotland before 1700*, Edin. Bibl. Soc. Publ., 1905, p. 109.] *See also* Swintoun (G.) and R. Brown.

BROWNE (JOHN), bookseller in London; Guilded Acorn in Paul's Churchyard, 1652–61 (?). According to Hazlitt (iii. 43) he was the publisher of the Rev. Samuel Clarke's *Martyrologie . . . of England*, 1652, folio; Hazlitt had apparently seen a copy of this work, as he gives the collation, but no copy of it appears to be in any of our national libraries. Browne was afterwards in partnership with William Miller.

BROWNE (SAMUEL), bookseller and printer in London and at the Hague. (1) Fountain, St. Paul's Churchyard, 1639; (2) St. Paul's Churchyard, at the sign of the White Lyon and Ball, 1641–43; (3) Hage. Samuel Browne English bookeseller dwelling in the Achter-Om at the signe of the English Printing Press, 1643–60; (4) At the sign of the Queen's Arms near the little north door of St. Paul's Church, 1661–65. (1638–65.) Took up his freedom June 3rd, 1633. [Arber, iii. 687], his first registered publication being an edition of Herodian's *History of Greece* in Greek and Latin, entered on February 3rd, 163 7/8. At the outbreak of the Civil War, having strong royalist sympathies, he left the country and settled at the Hague, where he printed and published much royalist literature, including an edition of the *Eikon Basilike* in 1649, Jeremy Taylor's *Martyrdom of King Charles*, 1649, and a broadside ballad entitled *Chipps of the Old Block*, in 1659. [Lutt. Collection, ii. 40.] Returning to England at the Restoration, he settled at the sign of the Queen's Arms in St. Paul's Churchyard, and in partnership with a Frenchman named John de l'Ecluse, *q.v.*, issued several French books. He died of the plague in the autumn of 1665, and Smyth, in his *Obituary*, p. 66, has the following notice of him: "Aug[t]. 1665, Mr. Brown, once a bookseller at y[e] Hague, who married the daughter of Mr. Nath. Hall of y[e] Exchequer, died at y[e] Pest House, ex peste, about this time."

BRUDENELL, or BRUDNELL (JOHN), printer in London; Maiden-Head-Alley, near Newgate, 1660–66. Appears to have succeeded Thomas Brudenell. He was ruined by the Fire of London. [Plomer, *Short History*, p. 225.]

BRUDENELL or BRUDNELL (THOMAS), printer in London; Newgate Market, 1621–60. Is first heard of as partner with John Beale, in 1621. [Arber, iii. 699–700.] He afterwards set up for himself as a printer in Newgate Market, taking as partner Robert White. A feature of their business was the printing of astrological works, this being one of the few houses in London that stocked astrological signs. They issued a duodecimo edition of the Bible in 1647, and appear to have had an extensive assortment of letter of varying merit, notably two founts of great primer roman and italic used in the latter half of Sprigges' *Anglia Rediviva*, which they printed in 1647. In 1651 Thomas Brudenell brought an action against the executors of John Partridge, a London bookseller, to recover a debt for printing various books, chiefly the writings of William Lilly, the titles, prices and quantities being set out at length. [*Library*, N.S., January, 1906.]

BRUGIS or BRUGES (HENRY), *see* Bridges (H.).

BRUISTER, *see* Brewster.

BRYSON (JAMES), printer in Edinburgh; a little above the Kirk Style at the signe of the Golden Angel, 1638–42. A bookseller who commenced printing in 1639 in succession to the heirs of A. Hart. He rented his house from Hart's widow. He was probably a relative of Robert Bryson, *q.v.* Died in April, 1642, his widow continued the bookselling business. Device: headpiece with I.B. in centre; and many of Hart's ornaments. Some of his ornaments were afterwards used by G. Lithgow and A. Anderson. [H. G. Aldis, *List of books printed in Scotland before 1700*, p. 110.] *See* also Bryson, R. and J.

BRYSON (ROBERT), printer in Edinburgh; at the signe of Jonah, 1637–45. A bookseller who commenced printing in 1640. Apparently had some connection with R. Young, *q.v.* His inventory discloses an extensive stock of books and the list of debtors includes several booksellers, among them "Mr. Cruik [Crooke] and Mr. Hope, buiksellars at Londone." Wife, Isobel Herring; children, Samuel, Isobel, Helen. Died 1645. Ornaments: tailpiece with monogram R.B. and several formerly in possession of Finlason and Young. [H. G. Aldis, *List of books printed in Scotland*, p. 110.]

BRYSON (Heirs of R.), booksellers in Edinburgh, 1646. Only known by the imprint of a book, No. 1241, in Mr. Aldis's *List of books printed in Scotland before 1700*.

BRYSON (R. and J.), printers in Edinburgh, 1641. Some official papers were printed (apparently by Robert Bryson) in their joint names in 1641, and at the end of that year, or in 1642, they petitioned unsuccessfully to have the recent appointment of Young and Tyler, *q.v.*, as King's Printers set aside in favour of themselves. [H. G. Aldis, *List of books printed in Scotland before 1700*, p. 110.]

BUCK (JOHN), printer and bookbinder at Cambridge, 1625–68. One of the Esquire Bedells, was appointed printer December 16th, 1625, and was in partnership first with his brother, T. Buck and Leonard Green, and afterwards with T. Buck and Roger Daniel. Although his name drops out of the imprints after 1635, he continued to have an interest in the printing office until 1668. [Camb. Antiq. Soc. Comm., vol. v, p. 304; Harl. MSS. 5929 (405).]

BUCK (THOMAS), printer and bookbinder at Cambridge, 1625–70. Was appointed by Grace, July 13th, 1625. He had several partners, including Leonard Greene, John Buck, Roger Daniel. From 1640 to 1650 his name disappears from the imprints of Cambridge printed books, but in 1651–2 he appears to have become once more printer to the University for a brief space. He is said to have resigned in 1653, but he continued to retain an interest in the office up to the time of his death in 1670. The bindery of the brothers J. and T. Buck is distinguished for the beauty of its stamps, and the skill shown in decorative treatment. Dr. Jebb, speaking of the remarkable bindings executed by the ladies of Little Gidding, says that "a Cambridge bookbinder's daughter that bound rarely" was engaged to teach them the art, and Mr. Cyril Davenport in an interesting article on the same subject shows the resemblance between the stamps used on Little Gidding books and those found on books bound by or for the Cambridge printers. He concludes that the "bookbinder's daughter" came either from the University printers themselves, or from some Cambridge bindery which they patronised. [*Bibliographica*, Vol. II, pp. 129 *et seq.*]

BUCKLEY (S.), *see* Bulkley (Stephen).

BUCKNELL (THOMAS), bookseller (?) in London; Golden Lion, Duck Lane, 1651–52. His name is found on Samuel Sheppard's *Epigrams: Theological, Philosophical and Romantick*, 1651.

BULKELEY, *see* Bulkley.

BULKLEY, BULKELEY, or BUCKLEY (STEPHEN), printer in London, York, Newcastle-on-Tyne, and Gateshead, 1639–80. One of the sons of Joseph Bulkley, bookseller, of Canterbury. He was apprenticed to a London printer, Adam Islip, for eight years from February 2nd (Candlemas Day), 163$^{0}_{1}$, and took up his freedom February 4th, 1639. Stephen

Bulkley then appears to have joined John Beale, *q.v.* Their initials are found in a book entitled *The Secretary in Fashion*, a translation by John Massinger, dated 1640. They also printed Lewis De Gand's *Sol Britannicus*, 1641, a pamphlet written in praise of King Charles, but in this instance Bulkley's name is printed Buckley, a mistake which also occurs in the spelling of the name in the Register of Apprenticeships at Stationers' Hall. In this same year, 1641, Stephen Bulkley printed for two London booksellers a book entitled *The Masse in Latin and English*, a translation by James Mountaine of Du Moulin's *Anatomie of the Masse*, of which three issues are known. Two political pamphlets have also been traced to Bulkley's London press, in consequence of which he was ordered to appear before the House of Commons as a delinquent, but fled to York, taking his press and letters with him. At York his first issue was Sir B. Rudyard's speech, which he printed on July 23rd, 1642. In 1646 he moved to Newcastle, where he remained till 1652; from thence he went to Gateshead, and it is said that during this time he was thrown into prison and plundered of his goods for his loyalty. He returned to Newcastle in 1659 and remained there till 1662, when he returned to York and set up his press in the parish of St. Michael le Belfrey. In 1666 he was in trouble for printing a book called *An Apology of the English Catholics*. In a letter to the Secretary of State written at this time, Bulkley is described as getting "but a poore livelyhood, a man well beloved amongst the ould cavaleers and an object of charity." He died in the month of February, 16$^{79}_{80}$, and was succeeded in his printing house by his son John. [Register of Apprenticeships, Stationers' Hall; Davies' *History of the York Press*; *Domestic State Papers*, Charles II, vol. 175, 28; *Library*, January, 1907.]

BULL (JOHN), bookseller in London; Grub Street, 1624–43. Is first heard of in 1624, when he published Sir Henry Wotton's *Elements of Architecture*. Nothing more is heard of him until after 1640, when he appears to have dealt chiefly in political pamphlets and broadsides. [Gray's *Index to Hazlitt*; Bibl. Lindes, *Catalogue of Broadsides*, 19, 26.]

BURDEN, or BOURDEN (W.), bookseller in London; Cannon Street, near London Stone, 1657. Issued Henry Bold's volume of verse called *Wit a sporting in a pleasant Grove of New Fancies .... 1657.* 8°. [B.M. 11630, a. 24], also an edition of Jo. Tatham's *Fancies Theatre* under the title of *The Mirrour of Fancies*, 1657. [Hazlitt, H. 592.]

BURDET (SAMUEL), bookseller (?) in London, 1660. Only known from the imprint to a broadside entitled *The Phanaticks Plot Discovered* [August 9th], 1660. [B.M. f. 25 (67).]

BURROUGHS (JOHN), bookseller in London, (1) Golden Dragon neare the Inner Temple-Gate; (2) Next door to the King's Head in Fleet-Street. 1641–52. Associated with John Franke. They were chiefly publishers of theological and political pamphlets. John Burroughs was clerk to the Company of Stationers in 1652. [Arber, v. lxxv.]

BURTON (RICHARD), bookseller in London. (1) Horseshoe West Smithfield; (2) Horseshoe at the hospitall gate in Smithfield. 1641–74. Took up his freedom November 2nd, 1640. [Arber, iii. 688.] Chiefly a publisher of ballads. [Bibl. Lind. *Catalogue of a collection of English Ballads*, 45, 786, 821, 997.]

BURTON (SIMON), bookseller in London; Next the Mitre taverne, within Algate, 1640–41. Only known from the imprint to Richard Crashawe's *Visions or Hel's Kingdome*, a translation from the *Visions of Quevado*. Hazlitt records [iii. 62] another translation from the same author, under the title of *Hell Reformed*, issued by the same publisher in 1641.

BUTLER (JAMES), bookseller (?) in London, 1644. Known only by a broadside entitled *Two Imcomparable Generalissimos*. [Hazlitt, H. 667.]

BUTLER (ROBERT), bookseller in London; Gray's Inn Gate, 1663. Only known from an advertisement in *Mercurius Publicus*, June 4th, 1663.

BUTLER (THOMAS), bookseller in London; Lincoln's Inn Fields near the Three Tuns by the Market Place, 1656–59. Published two books by William Blake, the author of *Silver Drops*, viz., *The Yellow Book*, 1656, and *Trial of the Ladies*, 1657.

BUTTER (NATHANIEL), bookseller in London, (1) Pyde Bull, St. Austins Gate, 1608; (2) Cursitors Alley, 1660. (1605–64). The son of Thomas Butter (1581–90). Admitted a freeman February 20th, 160$^{3}_{4}$. [Arber, ii. 736.] Entered his first publication in the registers December 4th, 1604. Two editions of *King Lear* bear his name and the date 1608, one without any address and the other with that of the Pyde Bull. That without address has the well-known "Heb Ddien, heb ddina ddim" device, the other the winged horse used by George Snowden and afterwards by Nicholas Okes, who took over the business of the Snowdens some time in the year 1608. In 1622, in conjunction with William Shefford, Butter published a sheet entitled *News from most parts of Christendom*, and from that time made journalism his chief business. In 1630 he began a series of half-yearly volumes of collected foreign news under titles such as the *Swedish Intelligencer*. Charles I granted to Butter and N. Bourne the right of publishing all matter of history or news, they paying the sum of ten pounds yearly to the repair of St. Paul's. On May 21st, 1639, Butter made over the copyrights of all plays in his possession to Miles Fletcher, or Flesher, devoting himself entirely to the issue of news-sheets. He is last heard of in the Registers on December 3rd, 1663, when he made over to Thomas Rookes, *q.v.*, his copyright in Dr. Halliday's *Sermons*. [Registers, Liber F, p. 274.] He died in the following February, and his death is thus recorded by Smyth in his *Obituary*: "22 Febry 166$\frac{3}{4}$. Nath: Butter an old stationer, died very poore." [D.N.B.; *Library*, N.S., No. 26, pp. 163–6; *Domestic State Papers*, 1638–9, p. 182.]

BYFIELD (ADONIRAM), bookseller in London, (1) Bible in Pope's Head Alley near Lombard Street, 1657; (2) Three Bibles in Cornhill next door to Pope's Head Alley, 1660 (1657–60). Son of the Puritan divine of this name. Apprenticed to Ralph Smith for seven years from May 7th, 1649. [Stationers' Register of Apprenticeships, 1605–66.] Amongst his publications was Samuel Morland's *History of the Evangelical Churches*, 1658. f°. [B.M.]

CADE (JOHN), bookseller in London, (1) Globe in Cornhill; (2) At the Royal Exchange. (1664–78). Nothing is known of the early publications of this bookseller, but in 1678 he is found selling Saxton's maps. [Arber, *Term Catalogues*, i. 304.]

CADWELL (J), printer in London, 1659–62. Son of Edward Cadwell of London, draper; apprenticed to Roger Norton, *q.v.*, for seven years from June 23rd, 1646. He was evidently in a small way of business, the only two books found with his imprint being an allegory called the *Voyage of the Wandring Knight*, 1661, printed in black letter, and *A Brief account of ancient Church-Government*, 1662, 4°., ascribed to Obadiah Walker. His type and ornaments were of the poorest. His address has not been found.

CALVERT (ELIZABETH), bookseller in London, (1) Black Spread Eagle, St. Paul's Churchyard, 1664–66; (2) Little Britain, 1666–67; (3) Black Spread Eagle, Barbican, 1667–73. The widow of Giles Calvert, *q.v.* During her husband's lifetime she was imprisoned for selling what was considered a treasonable book, and was in prison at the time of his death. After his death she continued to publish books that offended the authorities. In 1667 the Mayor of Bristol laid an information against her for sending books to certain Bristol booksellers about the Fire of London, and she was again arrested and imprisoned in the Gatehouse for some weeks. In the same year Samuel Mearne seized a private press of hers in Southwark, at which was printed a book entitled *Nehushtan*. After Sir Roger L'Estrange's retirement from the post of censor, she appears to have been left unmolested. The last year in which her name appears in the *Term Catalogues* is 1673. [*Domestic State Papers*, Charles II, vol. 43, 21; vol. 76, 29, 30; vol. 77, 49; vol. 209, 75; vol. 248, 88; Arber, *Term Catalogues*, vol. i.]

CALVERT (GEORGE), bookseller in London, (1) Half-Moon in Watling Street neare Paule's stump, 1650; (2) Half-Moon in the new buildings in Paul's Churchyard, 1655–66; 1675–82; (3) Bible in Jewen Street, 1667; (4) Golden Ball in Little Britain, 1669–74. 1648–82. Son of George Calvert, of Meere, in the county of Somerset, "clerk," and brother of Giles Calvert, *q.v.* Apprenticed to Joseph Hunscott, for eight years from Michaelmas, 1636. [Stationers' Register of Apprenticeships.] In conjunction with Thomas Pierrepoint, he issued in 1655 a folio edition of Sidney's *Arcadia*, and miscellaneous works. This edition was printed for him by W. Dugard. He published two other editions in 1662 and 1674, the first printed by Henry Lloyd, for W. Dugard, the second without printer's name. After the great fire he moved to the Bible in Jewin Street.

CALVERT (GILES), bookseller in London; Black-Spread-Eagle, St. Paul's Churchyard, 1639–64. Son of George Calvert, of Meere, in the county of Somerset, "clerk," and brother of George Calvert, *q.v.* He was first apprenticed to William Lugger, bookseller, for nine years from June 30th, 1628, but for some reason not stated his indentures were cancelled, and he

took out fresh indentures on June 11th, 163$\frac{1}{2}$, for the remainder of his term, seven years, with Joseph Hunscott. [Stationers' Register of Apprenticeships.] He took up his freedom on January 25th, 1639. [Arber, iii. 688.] He is chiefly noted as the publisher of the early Quaker literature, but so far as is at present known he was not openly of that society. On Cromwell's accession to power Giles Calvert, with Henry Hills and Thomas Brewster, was appointed official "printer" to the Council of State. This appointment shows that he was in favour with the Government, and explains how it was that he was able to publish Quaker books without restraint. On only one occasion, in 1656, does he appear to have been questioned, but nothing serious seems to have followed. [*State Papers*, 1656, p. 308.] In 1661 he was arrested and thrown into prison for publishing a pamphlet entitled *The Phœnix of the Solemn League and Covenant*, but he was released after a few weeks' confinement. He is believed to have died about April, 1664, and was succeeded in his business by his widow, Elizabeth Calvert.

CALVIN (JAMES), (?) bookseller in London, 1642. Only known from a pamphlet entitled *Prologue & epilogue to a comedie presented at the entertainment of the Prince his Highnesse, by the scholars of Trinity College, Cambridge, in March last.* 1641. By Francis Coles. [E. 144. (9).]

CAMPLESHON (LEONARD), bookseller in York, Stonegate, 1661. Alice Broad printed for him the *Good Husbands Jewel* . . . . The Fifth edition. [B.M. 779. b. 1.]

CARTWRIGHT (RICHARD), bookseller in London, (1) Bible in Duck Lane neere Smithfield; (2) Hand and Bible, Duck Lane. 1627–47. Took up his freedom June 15th, 1615, his first publication being a sermon preached by Matthew Brookes at Paul's Cross at Christmas, 1626, entitled the *House of God*. [B.M. 3932 f. 27.] He died on November 17th, 1647. [Smyth's *Obituary*, p. 25.] By his will he desired to be buried in the Church of Little St. Bartholomew. He mentions his brother Samuel Cartwright, and left the half of his stock to his wife and the other half to his son-in-law, Thomas Smith. One of his executors was Thomas Slater, *q.v.* The will was proved on April 11th, 1648. [P.C.C. 59, Essex.]

CARTWRIGHT (SAMUEL), bookseller in London, (1) Bible in Duck Lane; (2) Hand and Bible in Ducke Lane. 1623–50. Brother of Richard Cartwright, and evidently in business with him. Took up his freedom October 16th, 1622. [Arber, iii. 685.] Amongst his publications was an English edition of Mercator's *Atlas*, of which he held a half share with Michael Sparke. He died August 17th, 1650. [Smyth's *Obituary*, p. 29.]

CAVE (JOHN), ? bookseller in London, 1642. Only known from the imprint to the two following pamphlets, *Parliaments censure on Sir Richard Gurney*, 1642, and *True news from Portsmouth*, 1642.

CHANTLER (JAMES), bookseller in Newcastle, 1653–8. On November 10th, 1653, a daughter of James Chantler, "bookseller," was baptised at the Cathedral Church. On November 23rd (a fortnight later), Elizabeth, his wife, was buried there, and on June 6th, 1658, James Chantler, bookseller, himself was buried. There is no other record of him. (Information kindly supplied by Mr. Richard Welford).

CHAPMAN (LAURENCE), bookseller in London, (1) Upper end of Chancery Lane, next Holborn; (2) Against Staple Inn; (3) Next doore to ye Fountain Tavern in ye Strand neare the Savoy. 1620–55. Took up his freedom February 9th, 1618. [Arber, iii. 684.] During the Civil War he was associated with Lawrence Blaiklock and Francis Coles in the publication of the *Perfect Diurnal*, and also issued *The Scottish Dove*. Amongst his other publications may be noticed Inigo Jones's work on *Stone Henge*, 1655, folio.

CHAPMAN (LIVEWELL), bookseller in London, (1) Crown in Pope's Head Alley, 1651–61; (2) In Exchange Alley in Cornhill, 1665. Son of Edward Chapman, of London, scrivener. Apprenticed to Benjamin Allen November 6th, 1643, for seven years. Married, between 1650 and 1653, the widow of Benjamen Allen. [Stat. Reg., Liber E, f. 249.] In 1655 Chapman was apprehended for printing seditious pamphlets, and amongst the Thurloe State Papers [vol. 4, p. 379] is an interesting letter from Col. Barkstead, in which he says that Chapman "is the owner or at least a sharer in the private press, that hath and doth soe much mischiefe . . . ." He is said to have been the compiler of a notorious tract entitled *The Phoenix of the Solemn League & Covenant* in 1661, for the publication of which Thomas Brewster, Giles Calvert and others were punished. Amongst his other publications may be noticed an edition of Sir John Harrington's *Oceana*, published in 1655.

CHAPMAN ( ), Mrs., (?) bookseller in London, 1662. Perhaps the wife of Livewell Chapman, *q.v.* Mentioned in the *State Papers* [Charles II, vol. 67, 161], as having "managed" the printing of a pamphlet called *The Face of the Times*, written by Sir Harry Vane and printed with his *Epistle General* in 1662.

CHATFIELD (STEPHEN), bookseller in London, (1) In the middle of St. Dunstan's Churchyard in Fleet Street, 1654; (2) Under St. Dunstan's Church in Fleet Street, 1654. Only known from the imprint to the second edition of a book entitled *Festorum Metropolis* . . . by Allan Blayney, 1654. The first imprint is from the Bagford fragments [Harl. 5919 (294)], and belongs evidently to a different book or a different edition of the work noted.

CHETWIN, or CHETWIND (PHILIP), bookseller in London; Next to the Black Horse in Aldersgate, 1670 (1656–74). Married the widow of Robert Allot, 1626–36, and so became possessed of certain copyrights in various Shakespeare quartos. In 1663 he published the third folio, and followed it up with a re-issue in 1664, to which he added the seven spurious plays, no doubt with a view to increasing the sale. His address has not been found before 1670. [Arber, *Term Catalogue*, vol. i.]

CHIDLEY (SAMUEL), bookseller (?) in London; Bow Lane at the signe of the chequor, 1652. Only known from the imprint to a pamphlet entitled *A Cry against a crying Sinne*, 1652, 4°. [Hazlitt, *Handbook*, i. 112.]

CHILDE (THOMAS), printer in London; Dogwell Court, Whitefriars, 1660–66. In partnership with Leonard Parry, *q.v.* They carried on a small business, printing chiefly political tracts and broadsides. They were ruined by the Fire of London. [*Domestic State Papers*, Charles II, vol. 243, 126.]

CHISWELL (RICHARD), bookseller in London, (1) Two Angels and Crown, Little Britain; (2) Rose and Crown, St. Paul's Churchyard, 1666–1711. This eminent publisher was born in the parish of St. Botolph's, Aldersgate, on January 4th, 1639. The entry of his apprenticeship and the date of his taking up his freedom have not been found, but he was evidently in business as a bookseller before Lady Day, 1666, as his name is found in

the Hearth Tax returns for the parish of St. Botolph's for the half-year ending on that day. [P.R.O. Lay Subsidy $\frac{252}{32}$.] No book entry occurs in the Registers under his name before 1667, and the bulk of his work lies outside the period covered by this dictionary. He died in 1711, and was buried in St. Botolph's. [D.N.B.; Arber, *Term Catalogue, passim.*]

CHRISTOPHER (EDWARD), bookseller in London, 1642–43. Associated with Robert Wood, *q.v.*, in publishing political broadsides and tracts. His place of business has not been found.

CHURCHILL (WILLIAM), bookseller in Dorchester, 1659–88. His name is found on the following work:—Usher (J.), *Eighteen Sermons*, 1659. E. 1004. Later dates in *Term Catalogues*, vols. i and ii.

CLAPHAM (TH.), (?) bookseller in London (?) 1642. His name is found on the imprint to a pamphlet entitled *Newes from the City of Norwich*, 1642. [E. 114 (15).]

CLARKE (JOHN), bookseller in London, (1) Under St. Peter's Church in Cornhill; (2) Entring into Mercers' Chappell at the lower end of Cheapside; (3) Under Creechurch. 1620–69. Took up his freedom March 23rd, $16\frac{19}{20}$. [Arber, iii. 685.] Dealt almost entirely in theological literature. Smyth records his death in the *Obituary* (p. 82), 29th July, 1669; "Old John Clark, Bookseller under Creechurch (once in Cornhill), my old acquaintance, died this day, *plenus dierum et senii infirmitatum.*" A catalogue of 61 books, all theological, on sale by him in 1652 is given at the end of a work entitled *Sacred Principles Services and Soliloquies*, 1652.

CLARKE (JOHN), junr., bookseller in London; Lower end of Cheapside entring into Mercers' Chapel, 1651–90. Admitted a freeman September 1st, 1628. [Arber, iii. 685.] Son of the preceding.

CLARKE (ROBERT), bookseller in London; Rose in Ivy Lane, 1646–65. Took up his freedom December 2nd, 1639. [Arber, iii. 688.] Mentioned in the will of his brother Edmund Clarke, of St. Faith's parish [P.C.C. 152 Hyde], proved on December 9th, 1665, who bequeathed him and his wife Elizabeth the sum of 20s. a piece to buy them rings, and left bequests also to their children. Robert Clarke was the publisher of the *Genealogie of all Popish Monks*, 1646, 4°.

CLAVELL (ROBERT), bookseller in London, (1) Stags Head, near St. Gregory's Church in Paul's Churchyard; (2) Stag in Ivy Lane. 1658–1711. Son of Roger Clavell, late of the Isle of Purbeck, co. Dorset, gent., apprenticed to Richard Royston for seven years from March 11th, 1649, and took up his freedom on March 11th, 1656. He was Master of the Company of Stationers in the years 1698 and 1699. Robert Clavell, in partnership with John Starkey, founded and edited the periodical bibliography called *Mercurius Librarius*, which began in Michaelmas term, 1668, and was afterwards succeeded by the *Term Catalogues*. [Arber, *Term Catalogues*, i. viii.]

CLIFTON (FULKE), bookseller in London, (1) On New Fish-street Hill under St. Margaret's Church, 1620; (2) The Lamb, New Fish-street Hill, 1623–40; (3) Old Bailey, 1641–44. Took up his freedom March 29th, 1615. Chiefly a publisher of broadsides and political pamphlets, amongst which the following piece of Americana may be noticed: *A Proportion of Provisions needful for such as intend to plant themselves in New England.*

CLOWES (JOHN), printer in London; Over against the lower pump in Grub Street, 1647–60. One of the many small printers who set up in defiance of the authorities. His type was very bad, and his press-work most careless. In conjunction with Robert Ibbitson he printed several numbers of the news-sheet, *The Perfect Occurrences*, between 1647 and 1649.

CLUTTERBUCK (RICHARD), bookseller in London, (1) Little Britain, at the sign of the Golden Ball, 1637; (2) Gun, near St. Botolph's, Little Britain, 1641 (1633–48). Took up his freedom March 1st, $163\frac{2}{3}$ [Arber, iii. 687], dealt chiefly in popular literature such as Jo. Davenport's *Witches of Huntingdon*, 1646, 4°. [E. 343 (10)], and Jas. Oxenham's *True Relation of an apparition*, 1641, 4°. [E. 205. (6).] He died November 22nd, 1648. [Smyth's *Obituary*, p. 26.]

COATES, *see* Cotes (R.).

COE (ANDREW) the elder, printer in London, 1642–44. Took up his freedom February 6th, $163\frac{7}{8}$. [Arber, iii. 688.] Shared with R. Austin and John Clowes the printing of the *Perfect Diurnal of the Passages in Parliament* between 1642 and 1643. He was also the printer of many

political pamphlets, in which he was associated with Marmaduke Boat. His type, ornaments, and initials were old and worn, and his press-work bad. He died between April 12th and July 30th, 1644, and was succeeded by his son Andrew and his widow Jane. The position of his printing office has not been found.

COE (ANDREW), the younger, printer in London, 1644–67. The son of Andrew Coe. After his father's death, in 1644, carried on the business in partnership with his mother, Jane Coe, *q.v.* They continued to print the *Perfect Occurrences.*

COE (JANE), printer in London, 1644–47. Widow of Andrew Coe, senr. Carried on the business after his death with her son, Andrew Coe, junr.

COKE, *see* Cooke (William).

COLE (PETER), bookseller and printer in London, (1) Glove in Cornehill neere the Royal Exchange, 1637–42; (2) Glove and Lyon in Cornhil neare the Royal Exchange, 1643; (3) Printing Press in Cornhill near the Royal Exchange, 1643–65; (4) Living in Leaden-Hall, and at the sign of the Printing Press, 1660–65 (1637–65). Took up his freedom January 11th, $163\frac{7}{8}$, and was originally a bookseller, amongst his earliest publications being Captain John Underhill's *Newes from America*, 1638, 4°, printed for him by John Dawson, who did most of his printing at this time. Some time in 1643 Cole himself added printing to his bookselling business. It appears from the Records of the Stationers' Company that, as agent for the Company, he had seized a press and letters in Bell Alley, over against Finsbury, and he gave his word that they should not be used in a disorderly way, but in June of the same year an order was made by the Committee of Examinations "that the keys of the room where the printing presses and materials of Peter Cole now are shall be restored to him, he entering bond in 1000li not to remove the said presses or dispose of them without first acquainting this Committee and the Master and Wardens of the Company of Stationers and have their consent thereto. And that hereafter he do not presume to print with the said presses any book, pamphlet or paper not licensed according to the Ordinance of Parliament of the 14th of this present June." [*Domestic State Papers*, Charles I, vol. 498, 96.] A list of 30 books, chiefly theological, printed and sold by him in 1651, will be found in F. Glisson's *Treatise of the Ricketts*, at the end of the Preface. His death is thus recorded by Smyth in his *Obituary* (p. 70): "Decr. 4. 1665. Peter Cole, bookseller and printer in Cornhill, hanged himselfe in his warehouse in Leadenhall; reported to be distracted." His will was proved on December 22nd. By this he left the bulk of his property to his brother Edward's children, but made special bequests to Elizabeth Ridley, the youngest daughter of John Ridley, citizen and stationer of London, and to Samuel Thompson. [P.C.C. 153. Hyde.]

COLEMAN STREET PRESS, 1643 (?)—January 17th, 164$\frac{4}{5}$. On January 17th, 164$\frac{4}{5}$, a secret press was discovered in the house of Nicholas Tew, stationer, *q.v.*, at the above address, at which the following items were printed. (1) A slip of paper commencing *Alas pore Parliament, how art thou betrai'd?* written by some Independent against Ld. Gen. Essex and Ld. of Manchester, and scattered about the streets at night, December 9th, 1644. Identified by the officers of the Co. of Stationers, as printed in a letter similar to that used in other books which Tew confessed were printed at this press. (2) [*A copie of a Letter, Written by John Lilburne .... To Mr. William Prinne, Esq.*] Printed about January 15th, 164$\frac{4}{5}$. (3) *An Answer to nine arguments, Written by T. B. Written long since by ... John Lilburne, 1645, i.e.*, January 17th, 164$\frac{4}{5}$. In addition to the above, the undermentioned books are believed to have been printed at this press. (4) *Man's Mortalitie .... By R. O. Amsterdam.* Printed by John Canne, 1643. (5) *The Compassionate Samaritane* ... The second edition, 1644, *i.e.*, January 5th, 164$\frac{4}{5}$. [*Library*, N.S., October, 1904; *Secret Printing during the Civil War*, pp. 374–403.]

COLES (AMOS), printer in London; (?) Ivy Lane, 1649–51. In partnership with Thomas Mabb, *q.v.*

COLES, COULES, or COWLES (FRANCIS), bookseller in London, (1) In the Old Bailey; (2) At the halfe-bowle in the Old Bailey; (3) Lamb, in the Old Bailey; (4) Wine Street, near Hatton Garden. 1626–81. Took up his freedom July 1st, 1624. [Arber, iii. 685.] Chiefly celebrated as a publisher of ballads, in which he was associated with T. Bates, W. Gilbertson, T. Vere, and Jo. Wright. His ballads were invariably illustrated with curious woodcuts. He was also associated with Lawrence Blaiklock in

publishing the news-sheet called *The Perfect Diurnal.* It is likely that there was more than one publisher of this name and that the above imprints may refer to father and son.

COLLINGS (R.), *see* Collins (R.).

COLLINS (ARTHUR), bookseller (?) in London, 1641. Described as one of the "better sort of freemen" of the Company of Stationers, in a list of those who had paid their respective proportions of the poll-tax on August 5th, 1641. [*Domestic State Papers*, Charles I, vol. 483 (11).]

COLLINS (JAMES), bookseller in London, (1) King's Arms, Ludgate Street; (2) King's Arms in Ivy Lane, 1666; (3) King's Head, Westminster Hall, 1667–70 (1664–81). Dealer in all kinds of literature. A list of seven books printed for and sold by him at his shop in Westminster Hall in 1667 occupies the recto of the last leaf of J. Glanvill's *Some Considerations about Witchcraft.* In this list is mentioned *The Compleat Angler*, and Bishop Hall's works in three folio vols. [*Library*, N.S., No. 24; Arber, *Term Catalogues*, vol. i, *passim.*]

COLLINS (JOHN), bookseller in London; Neer the church in Little Britain, 1651–54. His name is found on Sir A. Weldon's *Court and character of King James*, 1651, and in John Turner's *Commemoration ..... of the .... Gunpowder Plot*, 1654. Smyth in his *Obituary* (p. 67), records his death:—"15 Septr., 1665. Collyns, bookseller agst ye church in Little Britain died *ex peste.*"

COLLINS (MATHEW), bookseller in London; Three Black Birds, Cannon Street, 1660–64. Only known from the imprints to two publications, the first a broadside, *The True Effigies of the German Giant*, 1660 [Bodleian]; and Daniel's *Copy Book*, 1664. [Hazlitt, H. 227, iii. 287.]

COLLINS (RICHARD), bookseller in London, 1630 (?)–48. His name is found on a political pamphlet entitled *A Declaration concerning the King .... 1648.* [E. 473 (17).] He may be identical with the Richard Collins, stationer, who took up his freedom January 30th, 1628. [Arber, iii. 686.]

COLLINS (THOMAS), bookseller in Northampton; Near All Hallows Church, 1651. His name is found on the imprint to a pamphlet entitled *A Patterne of Universall Knowledge .... Translated into English by Jeremy Collier.* [E. 1304 (1).]

COLLINS (THOMAS), bookseller in London; Middle-Temple-Gate in Fleet Street, 1650–67. In partnership with Gabriell Bedell between 1650 and 1655, when they issued several plays. In 1660, in conjunction with Abel Roper, he held the office of printer to the Council of State, and on April 24th a sum of £88 was paid to them for printing proclamations, etc. [*Calendar of State Papers*, 1659–60, p. 598.]

CONIERS (JOSHUA), bookseller in London, (1) Black Raven in the Long Walk, near Christchurch; (2) Black Raven, Duck Lane. 1662–88. His name, in company with that of Henry Marsh, is found on a book of anecdotes called *Fragmenta Aulica or Court and State Jests ....* by T. S. Gent. 1662. [B.M. 12316 a. 27.] At the end is an advertisement of a history of the Civil Wars, also published by him. After the fire Coniers appears to have moved to Duck Lane. In his reprint of the *Term Catalogues*, Mr. Arber has given his first name as "Joseph," instead of "Joshua."

CONSTABLE (FRANCIS), bookseller in London and Westminster, (1) White Lion, Paul's Churchyard, 1616–24; (2) In St. Paul's Church Yard at the sign of the Crane, 1631; (3) Under St. Martin's Church in Ludgate, 1637; (4) King Street [Westminster] at the sign of the Goat, 1640; (5) Westminster Hall, 1640. 1613–47. Took up his freedom July 2nd, 1614. [Arber, iii. 684.] His first registered publication was *Hymens Triumphes*, entered on January 13th, 161$\frac{4}{5}$. He published large numbers of plays, in which he was associated for some years with Humphrey Moseley. He died August 1st, 1647. [Smyth's *Obituary*, p. 24.] It is probable that he rented a stall in Westminster Hall very much earlier than 1640, the date given above, but that is the first appearance of the Hall in the imprint of any book. It occurs in the *Sparagus Garden*, a comedy by Richard Brome, published in that year. [*Library*, N.S., No. 24, p. 382; W. W. Greg, *List of English Plays and Masques.*]

CONSTABLE (RICHARD), (?) printer in London, Smithfield, 1649–50. Believed to have been brother or nephew of Francis Constable, *q.v.* He is mentioned amongst those who were bound over, in 1649, not to print seditious books. [*Calendar of State Papers*, 1649–50, pp. 522, 523.]

CONVERT (G.), *see* Calvert (Giles).

COOKE, or COOK (THOMAS), (?) bookseller in London, 1642. His name is found on a pamphlet entitled *Instructions from the House of Commons .... 1642.* [E. 111 (13).] A stationer of this name took up his freedom June 1st, 1635. [Arber, iii. 687.]

COOKE (WILLIAM), bookseller in London; Near Furnivall's Inn Gate in Holborn, 1632–41. A publisher chiefly of law books, but also shared with Andrew Crooke, the copyrights in several plays, including William Habington's *Queene of Arragon*, 1640, and several of those of James Shirley. He was also associated with M. Walbancke in the publication of Sir Henry Spelman's *De Sepultura*, 1641. The last heard of him is in 1641, when he issued Sir Ed. Coke's *The compleate Copy-Holder*, with a preface from his own pen.

COOPER, *see* also Cowper.

COOPER (THOMAS), journeyman bookseller, 1665. Only known from the following notice of his death in Smyth's *Obituary*, p. 67:—"Septem. 11. 1665. Tho. Cooper, journeyman bookseller to Mr. R. Royton [*i.e.*, Richard Royston], died *ex peste.*"

COSSINET (FRANCIS), bookseller in London, (1) Golden Anchor in Tower Street at Mincheon lane end; (2) Tower Street at the corner of Mincing Lane; (3) Anchor & Mariner in Tower Street. 1658–69. Dealt in seafaring books and Quaker literature. A list of seven books published by him in 1659 will be found at the end of the second edition of J. Heydon's *Advice to a Daughter*, which he published in that year. [B.M. 8415, a. 11.]

COTES (ELLEN), printer in London; Barbican, Aldersgate Street, 1653–70 (?). Widow of Richard Cotes, *q.v.* At the time of the Survey of the press made in 1668 she employed three presses, two apprentices and nine pressmen. [*Domestic State Papers*, Charles II, vol. 243, p. 181.]

COTES (NATHANIELL), (?) bookseller in London, 1660. Only known from the imprint to a pamphlet entitled *Mr. Pryne's Letters and Proposals* [August 17th], 1660. E. 1040 (4).

COTES (RICHARD), printer in London; Barbican, Aldersgate Street, 1635–52. In partnership with his brother, Thomas Cotes, until the death of the latter in 1642, when he succeeded to the business, and in the same year was appointed the official printer to the City of London. He died on January 13th, 165$\frac{2}{3}$. [Smyth's *Obituary*, p. 31.] His will was dated December 18th, 1652, and is an interesting document. He left a son, Andrew, under age, to whom he bequeathed a sum of money and his rights in Parkinson's *Herbal*. He also left bequests to Andrew Crooke, Michael Sparke, Anthony Dowse, and his apprentice, William Godbid. The residue he left to his wife, Ellen Cotes. One of his daughters was married to Thomas Williams, bookseller, of Little Britain. [P.C.C. 4 Bowyer.] His widow, Ellen, carried on the business for some years.

COTES (THOMAS), printer in London; Barbican, Aldersgate Street, 1620–41. Brother of Richard Cotes. Took up his freedom January 6th, 1606. He held the printing house originally established about 1560 by John Charlewood, printer to the Earl of Arundel, under the sign of the Half Eagle and Key. On the death of Charlewood in 1593, James Roberts married his widow and succeeded to the printing office and printed several Shakespeare quartos. About 1608 Roberts sold the business to William Jaggard, who eventually took his son Isaac Jaggard into partnership, and it was at this press that the first folio edition of Shakespeare was printed. On the death of Isaac Jaggard, his widow Dorothy assigned over the business and all the copyrights to Thomas and Richard Cotes, on June 19th, 1627. Thomas Cotes died in 1641. His will was dated June 22nd and proved on July 19th. He desired to be buried in the parish church of St. Giles, Cripplegate, of which he was the clerk. He had two sons, James and Thomas. His sister Jane was the wife of Robert Ibbitson, *q.v.*, and he mentioned a brother living in Yorkshire. His brother Richard Cotes was to have the printing house and all the implements on payment of £100. [Arber, iii. 700–704; iv. 182; *Library*, N.S., April, 1906, p. 149; P.C.C. 87, Evelyn.]

COTTON (GILES), (?) bookseller in London, 1648. His name is found in the imprint to a pamphlet entitled *His Majesties Declaration*, 1648. [E. 475 (4).]

COTTON (RICHARD), (?) bookseller in London, 1641. Only known from the imprint to the following pamphlet, *L. F. Lord Keeper His Speech Before the King's Majesty* .... which reads, "Printed and are to be sold by Richard Cotton, 1641." An R. Cotton was living near the King's Arms in Little Britain in 1660 and published *The Traytors Tragedy* [B.M., E. 1035. (6).] *See* also COTTON (Robert).

COTTON (ROBERT), bookseller (?) in London, 1641. Only known from the imprint to an official document, *Expresse commands from both Houses of Parliament*, which reads: London, Printed for Robert Cotton, 1641. This may be a misprint for Richard, *q.v.*, or *vice versa.*

COTTON (SAMUEL), (?) bookseller in London, 1652. Only known from the imprint to two political pamphlets: (1) *A declaration of the L. Admiral Vantrump* .... [June 25th], 1652 (E. 668, 14), and *A Letter sent from the Court of* .... *the King of France* .... [June 29th], 1652. [E. 668 (21).] His address is not given.

COTTRELL (JAMES), printer in London; Black & White Court, Old Bailey, 1649–70. Set up as a printer about 1649. During the Commonwealth he printed a good many pamphlets that offended the authorities. In 1664 he was arrested with others for illegally printing law books, *see* Fletcher (M.). At the time of the survey of the press made in July, 1668, he employed two presses, two compositors and no apprentices, so that we may infer that his business was not a large one. [Thurloe, *State Papers*, vol. 3, pp. 738–9; *Domestic State Papers*, Chas. II, vol. 243, p. 181.]

COULES (FRANCIS), *see* Coles (Fr.).

COURTNEY (JOHN), bookseller in Salisbury, 1650–64. His name occurs on the following: W. Creede, *Judahs purging* .... n.d., 4° [B.M. 694 k. 5. (6)]; George Ditton, *Symbolum Apostolicum* [a broadside], n.d. [B.M. 669 f. 14 (84)]; J. Priaulx, *Confirmation Confirmed*, 1662, 4°. [B.M. 226 g. 18 (5).]

COWLES (F.), *see* Coles (F.).

COWLEY (THOMAS), bookseller in London; Greyhound in St. Paul's Churchyard, 1640–70. Took up his freedom March 26th, 1640. [Arber, iii. 688.] His name is found on an edition of Peter du Moulin's *Anatomy of the Masse*, translated by James Mountaine, and printed by Stephen Bulkley in 1641 in London under the title of *The Masse in Latine and English with a Commentary.* Of this a copy is in the Bodleian, and the title-page only is preserved among the Ames Collection of title-pages in the British Museum. [No. 1678.] Thomas Cowley died in 1670, and left a legacy of £100 to the poor of the Stationers' Company. [Timperley, p. 546.]

COWPER (THOMAS), (?) bookseller in London, 1638–41. Only known from documents in the *State Papers*, in which he declared that he had imported large numbers of foreign bibles, prayer books and psalters, which were seized by the Stationers' Company and not returned to him. [*Domestic State Papers*, vol. 478 (54).] He may be identical with the Thomas Cooper, *q.v.*, described in 1665 as a journeyman bookseller to Richard Royston, whose death is recorded in Smyth's *Obituary*, p. 67.

CRAGGS (JAMES?), bookseller in London; Next door to the Harp and Ball near Charing Cross, c. 1667. Only known from a letter sent by Lodowick Lloyd to Robert Francis, in which an appointment is made at the above house. [*Domestic State Papers*, Charles II, vol. 244 (136).]

CRANFORD (JOSEPH), bookseller in London, (1) Phœnix St. Paul's Churchyard near the little north door, 1653; (2) King's Head, Paul's Churchyard, 1658; (3) Castle & Lion in St. Paul's Church Yard, 1659; (4) The Gun, in St. Paul's Church yard, 1661 (1653–64). Dealt chiefly in theological literature. There was another bookseller of the same name with a shop in Norwich in 1659.

CREAKE (THOMAS), bookseller in London, 1642–60. Took up his freedom September 3rd, 1638 [Arber, iii. 688.] Associated with Christopher Latham in the publication of political pamphlets. His address is unknown.

CRIPPS (HENRY), bookseller at Oxford and London, (1) Oxford, 1620–40; (2) London: The first shop in Pope's Head-Alley, next Lombard Street, 1650–61. Very little is known respecting this bookseller. He is found

publishing books at Oxford from 1620 to 1640, notably the first and second editions of Burton's *Anatomy of Melancholy*, 1621 and 1624, but between 1640 and 1650 he left Oxford and settled in London, where he joined Lodowick Lloyd, *q.v.*, in several ventures. His death took place about 1661, and he was succeeded by his widow, who continued the business for several years. [Madan's *Early Oxford Press*, pp. 278, etc.]

CRIPPS (MRS.), bookseller in London; First shop in Pope's-Head-Alley, 1661–64. Widow of Henry Cripps. The initials S.C. found in the imprint to C. Trenchfield's *Historical Contemplations*, 1664, may refer to her.

CROFT, or CROFTS (EDWARD), bookseller in London; Against St. Botolph's Church, Little Britain, 1666–67. His name occurs in the Hearth Tax Roll for the half-year ending Lady Day, 1666, as having premises in Little Britain. [P.R.O. Lay Subsidy, $\frac{252}{32}$.] His death is recorded in Smyth's *Obituary* (p. 77), under date December 29th, 166$\frac{7}{8}$: "Edw. Croft bookseller against St. Buttolph's Church in Little Brittain died hora 5 *ante merid.*: his relict, remarried since to Mr. Blagrave, an honest bookseller, who live happily in her house in Little Brittain."

CROFTS (ROBERT,) bookseller in London, (1) Crown in Chancery Lane next the Rowles; (2) Crown in Chancery Lane under Serjeants Inne, 1657–64. Dealt largely in plays and broadsides. [*See* Hazlitt, H. 163, H. 39, H. 79, iv. 160.]

CROMBIE (ROBERT), bookseller in Edinburgh, 1645. Probably the Robert Crumby, "servand, keeper of his buith," named in 1631 in the inventory of James Cathkin. Apprentice, Robert Brown, *q.v.* Died August or September, 1645. [H. G. Aldis, *List of books printed in Scotland before 1700*, p. 112.]

CROOKE (ANDREW), bookseller in London; Green Dragon in St. Paul's Churchyard, 1630–74. Took up his freedom March 26th, 1629. [Arber, iii. 686], and became one of the leading publishers of his day. He dealt largely in plays, in the publication of which he was associated with G. Bedell and W. Cooke, and he published the first authorised edition of Sir T. Browne's *Religio Medici.* A list of 17 plays by Beaumont and Fletcher sold by him is given at the end of the play *Wit without Money*, which he issued in 1661. He sometimes supplied books to Scottish booksellers. [*See* HILL (J.).] Andrew Crooke was master of the Stationers' Company in the year 1665–66. Smyth in his *Obituary*, p. 103, thus records his death: "Sep. 20. [1674.] Andrew Crooke bookseller, this evening died, being well the day before among his acquaintance in Little Britain, my old acquaintance." He left no will. Administration of his effects was granted to his widow on October 15th. [P.C.C., Admons.]

CROOKE (JOHN), bookseller in London, and King's Printer in Dublin, 1638–69, (1) Greyhound in St. Paul's Churchyard, 1638–39; (2) Ship in St. Paul's Churchyard, 1640–66; (3) Duck Lane, 1667–69; (4) Dublin, King's Printing Office, 1660–69. Brother of Andrew Crooke. He was associated with R. Sergier, J. Baker, and G. Bedell, and during this time issued several plays. In July, 1660, he was appointed Printer General in Ireland with a fee of £8 per annum and power to print all books and statutes, and he still retained his London business. Smyth in his *Obituary*, p. 80, thus records his death: "20th March 166$\frac{8}{9}$ Mr. John Crook bookseller in Duck Lane, brother to Andr. Crook, died this morning: buried at Botolphs Aldersgate, Mar, 23." He left no will, administration of his effects being granted to his widow Mary on April 20th. He was succeeded in the office of King's Printer in Ireland by Benj. Tooke, but in a book noted by Mr. E. R. McC. Dix in his *Books printed in Dublin*, under date 1671, the imprint runs: "Typis Regiis et impensis Mariæ Crooke." He left two sons, John and Andrew, both of whom were afterwards associated with the King's Printing House in Dublin. [Information supplied by Mr. E. R. McC. Dix; W. W. Greg, *List of English Plays & Masques*, Appendix 1, p. xxxvi.]

CROOKE (WILLIAM), bookseller in London; Three Bibles on Fleet Bridge, 1664–65. Published T. Lowick's *History of . . . St. George*, 1664. A list of seven books published by him is given at the end of *The Truth & Excellency of Christian Religion Demonstrated*, 1665, 4°.

CROSLEY (JOHN), bookseller at Oxford, 1664–1703. Was perhaps son or grandson of John Crosley, stationer in Oxford, who died February 12th, 16$\frac{12}{13}$. [Madan, *Early Oxford Press*, p. 276.] His imprint is found in M. Prideaux's *Easy & compendious Introduction, for reading all sorts of Histories*, 1664.

CROSSE (JOHN), English bookseller in Amsterdam; in the Calver Street, near the English Church, 1646. His imprint is found in John Featly's *Fountain of Tears*, 1646.

CROUCH (EDWARD), printer in London; Hosier Lane, Snow Hill, 1649–64. This printer is mentioned in the list of those bound over in 1649 not to print seditious pamphlets. [*Calendar of State Papers*, 1649-50, pp. 522, 523.] He was chiefly a printer of ephemeral literature such as the following broadside, *An elegy on the most execrable murther of Mr. Clun one of the comedeans of the Theator Royal*, 1664. [Lutt. Col. 1 (44).]

CROUCH, or CROWCH (JOHN), bookseller in London, 1635 (?)–1653. Two men of this name took up their freedoms in the Stationers' Company within a few years of each other, the earlier of the two on February 4th, 1635, and the other on December 2nd, 1639, but whether they were related is not known. The first was the publisher of several of Thomas Heywood's plays, and cannot be traced after 1640. The second was apparently in partnership with Thomas Wilson, *q.v.*, at the Sign of the 3 Foxes in Long Lane, and printed with him *Mercurius Democritus*, and also a pamphlet entitled *The Tyranny of the Dutch against the English*, in 1653. [Arber, iii. 687, 688.]

CRUMPE (JAMES), bookseller (?) and bookbinder in London; Little St. Bartholomews Well Yard, 1630–61. Took up his freedom on May 5th, 1628. He was the chief publisher of that voluminous writer Robert Younge, of Roxwell, in Essex.

CURTEYNE (ALICE), bookseller at Oxford, 1651. Widow of Henry Curteyn, *q.v.*

CURTEYNE (AMOS), bookseller in Oxford, 1665. His imprint is found in a little book of orthography called *The Vocal Organ . . . . Compiled by O. P. Master of Arts . . . .* Oxford. Printed by William Hall for Amos Curteyne, 1665. [B.M. G. 16589.]

CURTEYN (HENRY), bookseller at Oxford, 1625–51. The probate of his will is dated 1651. [Madan, *Early Oxford Press*, pp. 278, 299, etc.]

CUTLER (ROBERT), bookseller in London; Newgate Market near Butchers Hall, 1663–75. Gave a bond dated August 1st, 1663, that he would neither sell publish or dispose any unlawfull or unlicensed book. Henry Brome, *q.v.*, was one of the sureties. [*Domestic State Papers*, Charles II, vol. 78 (10).]

DAGNALL (STEPHEN), bookseller at Aylesbury, 165$\frac{0}{1}$. Only known from the imprint to *Severall proposalls for the general good of the Common-Wealth*, 165$\frac{0}{1}$. [E. 624. (7).]

DAINTY (THOMAS), bookseller in London; Parish of St. Michael in the Querne, 1623–52. Took up his freedom October 6th, 1623 [Arber, iii. 685], the earliest entry in the Register being on April 12th, 1639; but he published Martin Billingsley's *Coppie Book* in 1637. No other book is known to have been published by him, nor has any other book been found bearing his name, but there are many entries in the Stationers' Registers of this period showing that he had large dealings in books. For example, on November 3rd, 1647, he transferred fourteen copies under a bill of sale to the widow of Christopher Meredith, copies which had formerly belonged to Mr. Milborne deceased, presumably Robert Milbourne, or Milborne, *q.v.* These, with the exception of two, Jo. Clarke's *Dux Grammaticus* and Lord Carey's *Pacata Hiberniæ*, were all theological. Thomas Dainty died in 1652, and his will was proved in the P.C.C. on March 4th, 165$\frac{1}{2}$. [218, Bowyer.] A suit was afterwards commenced in the Court of Chancery against his estate, from which it would appear that towards the close of his life he gave up the trade of a bookseller for that of a coat-seller. [Chancery Proceedings. Mitford, 112, 81.]

DAKERS (ROBERT), printer in London; Angel Alley Aldersgate Street, 1666. Mentioned in the Hearth Tax Rolls for the six months ending Lady Day, 1666. [P.R.O. Subsidy Roll. $\frac{252}{32}$.]

DAKINS (JOHN), bookseller in London; Near the Vine Tavern in Holborn, 1650–65. Smyth, in his *Obituary* (p. 64), under date July 21st, 1665, records: "M. Daykyn bookseller, a recusant in High Holborn died there *ex peste*." This is probably the same with the above, whose name will be found on J. P. Camus' *Loving Enemie*, 1650, 12°. [E. 1336 (2).]

DALLAM (JOHN), bookseller in London; Shoe Makers Row, near Carter Lane, Blackfriars, 1641–48. Only known from the imprint to the following pamphlet, *The Humble representation of the Commissioners of the General Assembly*, 1648. [Harl. 5936. (409).]

DANCER (SAMUEL), bookseller in Dublin; Horse-shoe, Castle Street, 1662–68. The recognized publisher to the Irish Church Convocation, by which he was sent into England in February, 1666, to obtain the Royal assent to the adoption of the Book of Common Prayer approved by the Primate and Bishops of Ireland. A catalogue of books sold by him in 1663 is given at the end of Jeremy Taylor's *Discourse of Confirmation*. From this it appears that he dealt in statutes, proclamations, political pamphlets, and general literature. The date of his death appears to be unknown. [J. R. Garstin, *The Book of Common Prayer in Ireland*, 1871, pp. 10, 16; E. R. McC. Dix, *List of Books printed in Dublin*, part iii, 1651–75.]

DANIEL (JOHN), bookseller in London; Three Hearts in St. Paul's Churchyard, near the West-end, 1663. Only known from the imprint to a comedy called *Love a la Mode*, 1663, 4°. [B.M. 643. d. 38.]

DANIEL (ROGER), printer and bookseller in London and Cambridge. London, (1) Angell in Lumbard Street; (2) Angell in Pope's Head Alley, 1627-66; (3) In vico vulgo dicto Pater-noster Row, Aula vero Lovelliana, 1651; Cambridge: Augustyne Fryars, 1632–50. An edition of the *Whole Book of Psalms*, printed by the University printers in Cambridge in the year 1628, was to be sold "at London, by R. Daniell at the Angell in Lumbard Street." This seems to show that Roger Daniell was at work in London several years before he joined Thomas Buck as one of the University printers in that town. There is reason to believe that the shop with the sign of the Angel stood at the Lombard Street entrance to Pope's Head Alley, and that the first and second London addresses represent the same shop, and this is perhaps identical with "the first shop next Lombard Street," in Pope's Head Alley, afterward occupied by another University stationer, Henry Cripps, *q.v.* On July 24th, 1632, Roger Daniel was appointed one of the two printers to the University of Cambridge, and on August 21st of that year a formal deed of partnership was drawn up with Thomas Buck, *q.v.*, who, however, seems to have retired for a time from the business in 1640, as Roger Daniel's name alone figures in the imprints to Cambridge books from 1640 to 1650. In 1642 and 1643 he was in trouble with the House of Commons for printing certain things to which it took offence, and his patent as University printer was cancelled for neglect on June 1st, 1650, but he continued his business in London, and at the Restoration he petitioned to be reinstated as University printer, but without success. The last heard of him is in the year 1666. [R. Bowes, *Bibl. Notes on the University Printers .... in Cambridge*, Camb. Antiq. Soc. Com., vol. 5, pp. 283–362; Commons' *Journals*, ii. 733, 751, 900, 951; *Domestic State Papers*, Charles II.]

DARBY (CLEMENT), bookseller in London, 1659. Only known from the imprint to Richard Lovelace's *Lucaste*, printed for him by W. Godbid. His address has not been found.

DARBY (JOHN), printer in London; Bartholomew Close, 1662–67. A printer in a small way of business whom Sir R. L. Estrange threatened to prosecute for having set up contrary to the Act of 1662. John Darby was constantly in trouble with the authorities for printing satires, lampoons, and other unauthorised literature, of which it is enough to mention Andrew Marvell's *Rehearsal Transposed.* [*Calendars of Domestic State Papers*, 1663–67.]

DAVENPORT (RALPH), printer in London; St. Mary Magdalene, Old Fish Street, 1660–65. The following books came from his press: Burton (John), *History of Eriander*, 1661; Leigh (Edward), *Select & Choice observations concerning all the Roman & Greek Emperors*, 1663; Stevenson (M.), *Poems*, 1665. He died about September 17th, 1665, probably of the plague, having made a nuncupative will. [P.C.C. 27, Mico.]

DAVIES (JOHN), bookseller (?) in London, 1662. Only known from the imprint to the following pamphlet: *Strange and wonderfull visions and Predictions of William Juniper .... London: Printed for J. Davies and are to be sold by Simon Miller at the Star in St. Paul's Churchyard, 1662.*

DAVIES (THOMAS), bookseller in London, (1) Bible, over against the little North Door of St. Pauls Church, 1659; (2) Bible near North dore of St. Pauls, 1660; (3) Bible in St. Pauls Churchyard. 1656–60. Son of Humphrey Davies, of Cranbury, co. Warwick, gent., apprentice to William Holden for seven years from November 4th, 1641. Issued in partnership with Simon Miller and J. Crooke Parivale's *History of the Iron Age*, 1659, folio, a work notable for the portraits it contains. At the end is a list of ten books, chiefly theological, issued by him. He also dealt in school books. In 1660 Thedore Sadler, *q.v.*, joined him.

DAVIS (E   ), bookseller (?) in London, 1662. This name is found in the following book; Audley (Hugh), *The Way to be Rich ....* 1662.

DAVIS (JAMES), bookseller in London; Greyhound St. Paul's Churchyard, 1660–62. Published masques and plays on the subject of the Restoration. [Hazlitt, H. 513; I. 371.]

DAVIS (JAMES), bookseller in London; Little Britain, 1656. Only known from the entry in Smyth's *Obituary*, p. 43: "Augt 9th. [1656.] James bookseller in Little Britain, buried."

DAVIS (RICHARD), bookseller at Oxford; near Oriell College, 1646–88. A list of 25 books sold by this bookseller will be found on the last leaf of Zach. Bogan's *Meditations or the mirth of a Christian Life.* [1653.] This consists of classical, scientific and religious works, with one play, *The Amorous War.*

DAWES (GEORGE), bookseller in London; White Horse, over against Lincoln's Inn Gate in Chancery Lane, 1665–66. Dealer in law books.

DAWKES or DAWKS (THOMAS), bookseller in London, 1635–67. Took up his freedom October 5th, 1635. [Arber, iii. 687.] In 1642 Felix Kyngston printed for him Humfry Vincent's *Professours Hurt to Profession.* [Harl, 5927 (106).] A Thomas Dawkes "printer" is noted in Arber's *Term Catalogues* as printing at various addresses in London between 1679 and 1689. This may be the same man.

DAWLMAN (ROBERT), bookseller in London; Brazen Serpent in St. Paul's Churchyard, 1627–59. Dealt solely in theological literature. After 1635 Luke Fawne was apparently in partnership with him. He died in 1659, and his copies were assigned to John Grismond, *q.v.*

DAWSON (GERTRUDE), printer in London, (1) Aldersgate Street; (2) Living in Bartholomew Close the second door from the Half-Moon Tavern's Alley, that goes into Aldersgate-Street, 1657 (1649–61). Successor to John Dawson. She was in possession of most if not all of the latter's initial letters and ornaments, but seems to have had a new fount of l.c. roman cut for her. The second imprint given above is found in a book called *Seaman's Secrets*, printed in 1657, the title-page of which is found in the Ames collection of title-pages at the British Museum (No. 2646).

DAWSON (JOHN), printer in London, 1634–48. Son of John Dawson, printer, who died about 1634, when he succeeded to the business. He had a large and varied assortment of letter, and some pictorial initials that are not without merit, while his presswork, particularly in his folios, shows care. He had amongst his ornaments a variation of the Aldine device, to which he added the letters I.D. on either side of the anchor stock (*see* Harl. 5963/182). He is believed to have died in 1648, being succeeded by Gertrude Dawson. The situation of his printing house has not been found, but it was possibly in Bartholomew Close, from which Gertrude Dawson afterward printed.

DAYKYN (M), *see* Dakin (J.).

DEACON (H   ), bookseller in London, 1660. His imprint is found in the following pamphlet: *The Tryall and Condemnation of Col. D. Axtell ....* London. Printed for H. Deacon, 1660. [E. 1046 (8).]

DEAVER, *see* Dewer or Dever.

DE PIENNE, *see* Pienne (Peter de).

DERRICKE, *see* Gilbertson.

DEVER, *see* Dewer (J.).

DEWER, or DEVER (JOHN), printer in London; Smithfield, 1646–47. Took up his freedom September 4th, 1626. [Arber, iii. 686.] Is found in partnership with Robert Ibbitson, *q.v.* Together they printed for T. Jenner a play called *The Royall Exchange*, 1646. A John Deaver is mentioned in the Registers in 1666, possibly the same.

DEXTER (GREGORY), printer in London; Near Christchurch Newgate St., 1641–43. Took up his freedom December 18th, 1639. [Arber, iii. 688.] In partnership with R. Oulton, *q.v.* He printed amongst other things, *A True Relation of the late Fight betweene Sr William Wallers Forces and those sent from Oxford ....* 1643. [B.M.]

DICAS (THOMAS), bookseller in London, (1) Bell in St. Paul's Churchyard; (2) Hen & chickens, St. Paul's Churchyard. 1660–69. In 1660 he joined James Allestree, *q.v.*, and John Martin. Smyth's *Obituary*, p. 80, has this record of him: "6 Febry. [1669] Tho Dicas bookseller, died at midnight of a consumption, much indebted. He was partner in some books with Mr. Martin and Mr. Alestry." Letters of administration of his effects were taken out in April by Thomas Johnson, the principal creditor. [P.C.C. Admon. Act Book, 1669.]

DOBSON (EDWARD), bookseller in London; Without Newgate, 1643–4. Only known from the following reference to him in a contemporary news-sheet: "By letters from Northampton we are advertised that Edward Dobson, alias Codpeece-Ned, some time a bookseller without Newgate, an abusive malignant, who had printed many scandalous pamphlets against the Parliament, was taken with a crucifix about his neck, by that garrison March 12. There is a warrant sent to bring him to London." [*True Informer*, No. 26, March 16–23, 1643, p. 190.] He published a pamphlet entitled *The Declaration Vindication & Protestation of Edward Dobson, Citizen & Stationer of London .... Bristoll* [*London*] *Printed in the Yeere M.DC.XLIIII.* 4°. [E. 257 (36)], November 6th. From this we learn that he was imprisoned (1) for selling a book about the Earl of Essex, first printed in 1600; (2) For beating Nicholas Tew, stationer, after which he escaped to Oxford; (3) On a false charge of carrying a saw to the Irish Lords.

DOD (EDWARD), bookseller in London; Gun in Ivie Lane, 1646–57. In partnership with Nath. Ekins, *q.v.* They were the publishers of several of Sir Thomas Browne's writings. A list of 17 books on sale by them in 1657 occurs at the end of R. Bayfield's *Bulwarke of Truth*, published in that year. Amongst them is an edition of Lovelace's *Poems* and a work entitled *America*, by N. N. gent.

DOVER (J.), printer; St. Bartholomew's Close, 1664–65. This may have been the widow and probably the successor of Simon Dover. The imprint is found in a medical work by William Drage of Hitchin, entitled *A Physical Nosonomy*, which has a second title-page entitled *Daimonomageia A Small treatise of sicknesses & Diseases from Witchcraft*, 1665. [B.M. 776, g. 3.]

DOVER (SIMON), printer in London, 1660–64. Tried at the Old Bailey in February, 166$\frac{3}{4}$, with John Twyn, Thomas Brewster, and Nathan Brooks. Dover's crime was printing a pamphlet entitled *The Speeches of some of the late King's Justices*. He was condemned to pay a fine of 100 marks, to stand in the pillory on two successive days, and to remain a prisoner during the King's pleasure. He is believed to have died in April, 1664, shortly after his conviction. [*An exact Narrative of the Tryal .... of John Twyn....* 1664; *The Newes*, April 28th, 1664.]

DOWSE (ANTHONY), bookseller in London; Little Britain, 1641–72. Smyth in his *Obituary*, p. 95, says: "8th April [1672.] Mr. Anthony Dowse stationer in Little Britain, died this day before noone; buried at St. Butolph's Aldersgate ye 13th, Dr. Meriton preached at his funerall." He is also mentioned in the will of Richard Cotes. No books have been found with his name.

DOWNES (THOMAS), bookseller in London; Irish Warehouse Stationers Hall, 1609–58. Brother of Bartholomew Downes, bookbinder, who died in December, 1636. Appears to have had a share in the Irish Stock of the Company of Stationers. No books are found entered to him in the Registers after 1631, but in the University Library, Cambridge, there is a book dated 1635 bearing his address. He was Master of the Stationers' Company in 1642 and again in 1648. He died on February 19th, 165$\frac{7}{8}$, without issue [Smyth's *Obituary*, p. 46], and his will was proved on

March 9th. Bartholomew Downes also had a son Thomas, probably the Thomas Downes who took up his freedom December 5th, 1636. [Arber, iii. 688.] Another DOWNES, a printer, is mentioned in the *Domestic State Papers*, Charles II, vol. 67 (161) about the year 1664.

DOWSE (JOHN), bookseller in London; Great North Door of Pauls, 1664. Only known from an advertisement in the *Intelligencer* for that year.

DRADOUN (GEORGE), bookseller at St. Andrews, Scotland, 1654. Named as a debtor in the inventory of Andrew Wilson, *q.v.* [H. G. Aldis, *List of books printed in Scotland to 1700*, p. 112.]

DRENNANE (JOHN), bookseller at St. Andrews, Scotland, 1645. Named as a debtor in the inventory of Robert Bryson, *q.v.* [H. G. Aldis, *List of books printed in Scotland to 1700*, p. 112.]

DRING (PETER), bookseller in London, (1) The Sun in the Poultry, next door to the Rose Tavern, 1660–66; (2) Old Jewry, 1666. Amongst his publications was George Alsop's *Character of the Province of Maryland*, 1666, described by Sabin [Vol. i. 118] as one of the rarest of Americana. It contains on the last two leaves a list of 13 books printed for and sold by him. These included a romance called *Eliana* "by an English hand," one music book, two books on cookery, a jest book, and a commentary on Chaucer. On May 8th, 1666, he became surety for Thomas Johnson, printer, *q.v.* [*Domestic State Papers*, Charles II, vol. 155, 70.]

DRING (THOMAS), bookseller in London; George in Fleet Street, near St. Dunstan's Church, 1649–68. Dealt principally in law books, but was also the publisher of some plays. He died in 1668, his will being dated September 12th and proved on December 21st. He left small bequests to John Place, bookseller, *q.v.*, and Thomas Bassett, bookseller, *q.v.*, the residue to his son Thomas, and the premises in Fleet Street in trust for his younger son Joshua. Thomas Roycroft and John Bellinger were among the witnesses. [P.C.C. 154, Hene.]

DRIVER (THOMAS), bookseller in London; near the Bishop's Head in S. Paul's Churchyard, 1661. Only known from the imprint to Dr. Edward Sparke's *Scintillula Altaris*, 1661. [B.M. 4257 aaa. 42.]

DUDLEY (H.), (?) bookseller in London, 1461 [*i.e.*, 1641]. His name occurs on *A Discourse of divers petitions of high concernment and great consequence .... By John Spencer, Gentleman, 1641.* [E. 133 (1).]

DUGARD (WILLIAM), schoolmaster and printer in London; Merchant Taylors School; 1644–62. Born at the Hodges on the Lickhaynde in Shipley Yield, in the parish of Bromsgrove, in the County of Worcester, on January 9th, 1605; King's scholar at Worcester School, graduated M.A. at Sidney Sussex College, Cambridge, was successively usher of Oundle School in Northamptonshire, Master of the Free School in Stamford, co. Lincoln, Master of the Free School in Colchester, co. Essex, and in 1644 was appointed Master of the Merchant Taylors School in London. About this time he became a member of the Stationers' Company and set up a private printing press at the school. William Dugard's name first appears in the Registers of the Company on September 11th, 1648, when he entered a school book entitled *Rhetorice Elementa.* In 1649 he printed the first edition of the *Eikon Basilike*, and followed it with Salmasius' *Defensio Regia.* This roused the ire of the Council of State, which immediately ordered his arrest, seized his presses and implements, and wrote to the governors of the school directing them to dismiss him. The governors, however, contented themselves with desiring him to relinquish his press work. Sir James Harrington, author of *Oceana*, and John Milton interceded with the Council on his behalf, and persuaded him at the same time to give up the Royal cause. Upon this his presses were restored to him and he was appointed Printer to "His Highnes the Lord Protector." In addition to his official work, and also the writing, editing and printing of many school books, he printed John Milton's answer to Salmasius; an edition of Sir Philip Sidney's *Arcadia* and miscellaneous works, in 1655; a three volume quarto edition of Luther's *Table Talk*, and Selden's *Mare Clausum*, 1652. But he was again in trouble in 1651–2 for printing the *Catechesis Ecclesiarum.* This book and some others the Council of State ordered to be burnt. In 1661 W. Dugard was dismissed from his post at Merchant Taylors' School and set up a private school in White's Alley in Coleman Street. He died December 3rd, 1662. By his will he left £10 worth of his own books to Syon College and the rest of his property to his daughter Lydia. [P.C.C. 153, Laud.] From the numerous transfers noted in the Registers after his death, it is

evident that William Dugard had an interest in a large number of copyrights. His work as a printer will bear favourable comparison with the best of the period. His press was furnished with a good assortment of type, but how far he was his own compositor and pressman, and whether all the books bearing his name were really printed by him, are questions difficult to answer. [D.N.B.]

DUKESON (JAMES), (?) bookseller in London, 1660. Only known from the imprint to a broadside entitled *The Message of John Lambert Esq in answer to the Proclamation. London. Printed for James Dukeson, 1660.* [B.M. 190 g. 13 (145).]

DUNCAN, DUNKAN, or DUNCON (CHARLES), bookseller in London, 1636–46. Took up his freedom April 4th, 1636. [Arber, iii. 687.] First book entry March 8th, 163$\frac{9}{40}$. [Arber iv. 501.] His place of business is unknown.

DUNCOMB, *see* Dunscombe.

DUNCON, *see* Duncan.

DUNKAN, *see* Duncan.

DUNMORE (JOHN), bookseller in London, (1) Kings Arms Little Britain; (2) Three Bibles, Ludgate Street. 1665–67. In partnership with Octavian Pulleyn, junr., *q.v.* They printed a French Liturgy and other French literature.

DUNSCOMBE, or DUNCOMB (ROBERT), bookseller in London, (1) Lillipot Lane [Sayle, ii. 1156]; (2) Golden Falcon in Cateaton Street, over against St. Lawrence Church; (3) Duck Lane, 1666 (1638–66). Sayle, in vol. ii. 1156, gives under Robert Dunscombe a theological work printed in 1638. Hazlitt gives two political tracts as printed for Robert Dunscombe in 1642. [ii. 454, 455.] Addresses 2 and 3 are found in the Ames Collection of title-pages (Nos. 3257 and 3280).

DUNSTER (THOMAS), printer and bookseller in London; Red Lion in Grub Street, 1650. Assisted Bernard Alsop, *q.v.*, to print a pamphlet entitled *A Brief Narration of the Plotting, Beginning and carrying on of that Execrable Rebellion in Ireland. London: Printed by B. Alsop and T. Dunster, And are to be delivered at Bernard Alsop's house in Grub Street,* 1650. [March 19th, $16\frac{49}{50}$.] His imprint is also found again the same year in *The Fallacie of the great water drinker, discovered by Mr. Tho. Peedle and Mr. Thos. Corbie.* 1650. [Harl., 5921. 180, 181.]

ECCLESTON (CHRISTOPHER), bookseller in London; Middle shop under St. Dunstan's church in Fleet Street, 1662–64. His name is found on the two following books: *Sale's Epigrammatum. Being the choicest disticks of Martial's Fourteen Books of Epigrams*, 1663, 8°. [B.M. 833. c. 4.]; Howel (John), *Discourse concerning the precedency of kings*, 1664.

EDMONDS (WALTER), bookseller in London; Crown near Ludgate, 1638–41. Took up his freedom March 26th, 1635. [Arber, iii. 687.] Mentioned in a list of stationers, dated August 5th, 1641, as paying ten shillings as his proportion of the poll tax. [*Domestic State Papers*, Charles I, vol. 483. 11.]

EDWARDS (THOMAS), (?) bookseller in London, 1642. Only known from the imprint to a pamphlet entitled *The Scots resolution Concerning this present Expedition .... London: Printed for Tho. Edwards.* His address has not been found.

EELES (ROBERT), printer in London, 1646. Only known from certain papers in the House of Lords, in which it is stated that he was employed by a committee of the Lords to suppress seditious books, and had seized a press and letters, belonging to William Larner, which had been used in printing *London's Last Warning; A Remonstrance to the House of Commons; An Alarum to the House of Lords*, and all or most of Lilburne's books. He further obtained the arrest of Richard Overton, a notorious writer among the Independents. The Stationers' Company referred to him as "a common printer and seller of unlicensed books," and did their best to ruin him. [*Library*, October, 1904, pp. 390–91.]

EGLESFIELD (FRANCIS), bookseller in London; Marigold, St. Paul's Churchyard, 1637–67. Took up his freedom July 4th, 1636. [Arber, iii. 687.] Became one of the largest and most important publishers of theological literature. At the end of David Dickson's *Short Explanation of the Epistle of St. Paul to the Hebrews*, 1649, there is a list of 72 books published by him, mostly Divinity, but including Herrick's *Hesperides*. [A. W. Pollard, *Library*, October, 1901, p. 436.] This is one of the earliest book lists known, as they are seldom found before 1650. In 1660, in company with John Williams, he published an edition of the Book of Common Prayer, which was at once seized by the agents of Christopher Barker the third. Eglesfield and his partner excused themselves by saying that they did not know who was the King's printer. [*Domestic State Papers*, Charles II.] He received a bequest of a ring from Peter Parker, *q.v.*

EKINS (NATHANIEL), bookseller in London; Gun in St. Paul's Churchyard, 1641–60. Son of John Ekins, of Ringsted, co. Northampton, gent., apprentice to John Bellamy for eight years from July 7th, 1641. [Register of Apprentices, Stationers' Hall.] Partner with Edward Dod, *q.v.* In 1660 he was granted the office of licenser of Pedlars and Petty Chapmen. [*Domestic State Papers*, Charles II, vol. 25, 94.]

ELES (ROBERT), bookseller in London (?), 1651. Only known from the imprint to the following pamphlet: *True Speech delivered on the scaffold by James, Earl of Derby ....* 1651. His address has not been found. He may possibly be identical with Robert Eeles, *q.v.*

ELLIS (WILLIAM), printer in London; Thames Street, 1649–51. On June 3rd, 1650, a person of the name of Ellis was committed to Newgate for printing *Pragmaticus*. [*Domestic State Papers*, Interr., vol. 64, pp. 415–416.] He is further mentioned in that year as one of those giving security for good behaviour. [*Domestic State Papers*, 1649–50, pp. 522, 523.] The only thing traced to his press is a pamphlet in verse entitled *News from Newcastle*, 1651, a copy of which is in the Malone Collection in the Bodleian.

EMERSON (GODFREY), bookseller in London; The Swan Little Britain, 1637–46. Took up his freedom March 1st, 1613. [Arber, iii. 684.] He may be identical with the Godfrey Emonson or Edmondson who was publishing between 1623–37. His name occurs in the Churchwardens' Books of St. Botolph without Aldersgate as paying 26*s.* towards the restoration of the church in 1637. Amongst his later publications was a work on the subject of letter writing entitled *The Secretary in Fashion*, 1640, 4°., edited by John Massinger and printed, it is believed, by John Beale and Samuel Bulkley.

EMERY (JASPAR), bookseller in London; In Paul's Church-yard at the signe of the Eagle and Child, neare St. Austin's Gate, 1629–41. Took up his freedom March 26th, 1629 [Arber, iii. 686], and at once began to publish plays, amongst his first entries in the register being Thomas Drew's *Duchess of Suffolk*, which he entered on November 13th, 1629. He was also the publisher of Thomas Heywood's *Life of Merlin*, issued in 1641. [B.M. 292. f. 35.]

ENDERBY (SAMUEL), bookseller in London; Popes Head Alley, at the signe of the Starre, 1643–45. Son of Daniel Enderby of London, merchant tailor, apprentice to Nathaniel Newberry for eight years from March 5th, $163\frac{1}{2}$. Took up his freedom August 27th, 1638. Published a few political pamphlets.

EUSTER or EWSTER (THOMAS), bookseller in London; Gun in Ivy Lane, 1649. The publisher of Richard Lovelace's collection of verse entitled *Lucasta*, which was printed for him by Thomas Harper in 1649. William Dugard also printed for him the same year a little school manual entitled *The Plainest Directions for the true-writing of English .... By Richard Hodges ....* 1649. [E. 1377 (1).]

EVERSDEN (GEORGE), bookseller in London, (1) Over against the little North gate of S. Paul's Church, 1650; (2) Golden Ball, Aldersgate Street, 1652; (3) At the Mayden-head in St. Paul's Church Yard, 1656–65; (4) Adam & Eve, St. John's Lane, 1666–73. A list of 15 books published by him is given on the last leaf of J. Smith's *Mysterie of Rhetorique Unveil'd*, 1665. [B.M. 11805. b. 24.] With the exception of a medical work by Culpeper, and the *Life of Sir Thos. More*, these are all theological. This same list was reprinted without addition or alteration in the edition of the same work printed in 1673. The following are the references to his addresses in the order given: (1) Hoddesdon (J.), *Sion and Parnassus or Epigrams*, 1650; (2) T. More, *Vita & Exitus*, 1652; (3) Smith (J.), *Mysterie of Rhetorique unveil'd*, 1665; (4) Arber's *Term Catalogues*, vol. 1, p. 157.

EVERSDEN (HENRY), bookseller in London, (1) Gray-Hound in St. Paul's Churchyard; (2) Under the Crown Tavern in West Smithfield. 1657-67. A list of 17 books published by Henry Eversden and three forthcoming works, occurs on sigs. L. 7, 8 of Arminius' *Just Man's Defence*, 1657. [B.M. 4257, a. 10.] With one exception, Will. Elder's *Pearls of Eloquence*, all these are theological.

EWSTER, *see* Euster.

FAIRBEARD (SARAH), bookseller in London; At the North Doore of the Royal Exchange, 1646. Only known from the imprint to the following: *The State of a Christian* [a broadside]. [669, f. 10, 70.]

FALCONER, FAULKNER, or FALKNER (FRANCIS), bookseller in London, (1) Under St. Margaret's Church, New Fish Street, 1614; (2) Near St. Margarets Hill, Southwark, 1627 (1605–48). Son of Thomas Falconer or Falkener, late of Stanton Harcourt, co. Oxon, yeoman, apprentice to Andrew Wise for eight years from Midsummer, 1598. [Arber, ii. 229.] Took up his freedom July 2nd, 1605. [*Ibid*, iii. 683.] Entered *The Jests of George Peele* on December 14th, 1605. Amongst his other publications may be noted T. Brewer's *Merry Devil of Edmonton*, 1626, 1631; N. Breton's *Pasquil's Mad Cappe*, 1626; J. Mason's *Tragedy of Muleasses*, 1632; Robert Greene's *Dorastus & Fawnia*, 1648. [Sayle, vol. ii, p. 670.]

FALCONER (JOHN), bookseller at Glasgow, 1659–62. Named among the debtors in inventory of G. Lithgow, *q.v.* [H. G. Aldis, *List of books printed in Scotland before 1700*, p. 112.]

FALKNER, *see* Falconer.

FARNHAM (EDWARD), bookseller in London, (1) Neere the Exchange, 1657; (2) Pope's Head Alley neere Cornehill, 1657–60. In partnership with W. Hope, *q.v.*

FAULKNER, *see* Falconer.

FAWCETT or FORCET (THOMAS), printer in London, (1) Grub Street; (2) Heydon Court in old Fish Street neere the upper end of Lambert Hill. 1621–43. Took up his freedom May 7th, 1621 [Arber, iii. 685.) Partner with Bernard Alsop, *q.v.* In Sir J. Lambe's *Notes* [Arber, iii. 704], he is described as the abler man, better workman and better governor. The second address given above is from a title-page in the Bagford Collection entitled, *True Character of Mercurius Aulicus*, a work of which no copy has been traced.

FAWNE (LUKE), bookseller in London; Parrot in St. Pauls Churchyard, 1631–66. Took up his freedom March 26th, 1629. [Arber, iii. 687.] In partnership for some time with Robert Dawlman at the Brazen Serpent in St. Paul's Churchyard. Afterwards set up for himself at the sign of the Parrot. Dealt exclusively in works of divinity and was a strong supporter of the Presbyterian party. In 1652, in conjunction with five other booksellers, he published a pamphlet entitled *A Beacon set on fire or the humble information of certain booksellers stationers of London, to the Parliament & Commonwealth of England.* In this attention was directed to the Popish books that had been printed of late years, and to other books favoured by the Independents. The Independents replied with *The Beacons Quenched*, while Michael Sparke, *q.v.*, published on his own account *A Second Beacon fired by Scintilla.* These pamphlets were the object of much satire in the news-sheets of the time. Luke Fawne died without issue on March 20th, 166$^{5}_{6}$. [Smyth's *Obituary*, p. 71.] In his will he left a bequest to his apprentice, Brabazon Aylmer, and nominated John Macock, *q.v.*, one of his executors. [P.C.C. 23, Mico.]

FEATHERSTONE (HENRY), bookseller in London; St. Anne's Blackfriars, 1609–47. Son of Cuthbert Fetherston. Apprenticed to Bonham Norton, September 29th, 1598, for nine years. [Arber, ii. 230.] Warden of the Company of Stationers in 1635 and 1639. Master of the Company in 1641. He was the publisher of *Purchas his Pilgrimage*, 1612. Seems to have given up publishing in 1627. He died March 18th, 164$^{6}_{7}$. [Smyth's *Obituary*, p. 23.] George Thomason, *q.v.*, was one of the executors to his will. [P.C.C. 69, Essex.]

FELTON (JOHN), bookseller at Stafford, 1658. Only known from the imprint to the following work: *Iter Mediteranium. A True Accompt Given of the Proceedings of the Right Honourable Lord Glin, The Lord Chief Justice of England, and the Honourable Barron Hill one of the Barrons for the Exchequer, in their Summer Circuit in the Counties of Berks, Oxford, Gloucester, Monmouth, Hereford, Worcester, Salope and Stafford. Printed for the author John Lineall, and are to be sold by John Felton in Stafford,* 1658. 4°., 10 leaves. In verse. [Hazlitt, I, 258].

FENNER ( ), bookseller at Canterbury, 1663. Mentioned in an advertisement of patent medicines in *The Intelligencer & Newes* of that year.

FERRIS (SAMUEL), bookseller in London, (1) In Cannon Street under St. Swithin's Church; (2) Cannon Street near London Stone, 1662–63. Was the publisher of some of Archbishop Usher's sermons (*see* Ames' Collection of Title-pages, 3058) and an edition of P. Boaistuau's *Theatre of the World*, 1663.

FIELD (JOHN), printer in London and Cambridge. London: (1) Addle Hill, neer Baynard's Castle, 1644; (2) St. Andrews in the Wardrope, 1649; (3) Seven Stars Fleet Street, 1659. Cambridge: Silver Street, 1655–68 (1635–68). Took up his freedom February 4th, 1635. [Arber, iii. 687.] Appears to have been originally a bookseller only, as in 1644 the imprint, found in several tracts by Adam Steuart, reads "London, Printed *for* John Field, and are to be sold at his shop on Addle Hill" [B.M. E. 20 (7); E. 274 (14).] On January 25th, 1649, he was joined with Edward Husbands, *q.v.*, as printer to the Parliament. [*House of Commons Journals*, vol 6, p. 349.] He was also appointed printer to Oliver Cromwell. On October 12th, 1655, Field was appointed by Grace printer to the University of Cambridge, and about the same time it was ordered by Cromwell that the copyright of the Bible should be entered to him and Henry Hills, *q.v.*, in the Stationers' Registers. This was opposed by John Streator and other printers on the ground that it would lay them open under the Act of September 20th, 1649, to be sued for 6*s*. 8*d*. on every copy they possessed. [*Domestic State Papers*, 1656, vol. 126, 92.] Field printed many editions of the Bible, notably a quarto edition in 1648, a duodecimo edition in 1652, and a 32mo edition in 1653, all of which were noted for the number and variety of the misprints, the general badness of the printing, and their excessive price. In connection with this William Kilburne wrote a pamphlet entitled *Dangerous errors in several late printed Bibles . . . .* "Printed at Finsbury, 1659." This pamphlet was written not so much out of zeal for the purity of the Bible, as on behalf of those whose trade had been injured by the monopoly given to Field and Hills by Cromwell. Field was also fiercely attacked in another pamphlet entitled *The London Printers Lamentacon, or, the Press opprest, and overprest*, the chief paragraphs in which are reprinted by Mr. Arber in his *Transcript*, vol. iii. 27, 28. In 1655 Field built a new printing office in Silver Street, Cambridge, the University having for that purpose taken a lease of the ground from Queens' College for a term of years; and by several renewals

this continued to be the University Printing Office till about 1827, when the Pitt Press was commenced. It stood on the north side of Silver Street, on a portion of the site now occupied by the new Master's Lodge of St. Catherine's College. [Bowes, *Biographical Notes on the University Printers*, pp. 307, 308.] John Field died in 1668.

FIELDING (JACOB), (?) bookseller in London, 1652. His name is found on the imprint to a pamphlet entitled *A terrible and bloudy fight at Sea between the English and the Dutch.* 1652. This and its publisher are referred to in a paragraph in *Mercurius Democritus* for the week ending July 21st, 1652. He may have been a relative of William Fielding.

FIELDING (WILLIAM), (?) bookseller in London, 1642. His name occurs in the imprint to several political pamphlets in 1642. His address has not been found.

FIRBY (THOMAS), bookseller in London; near Grays Inn-Gate in Holbourn, 1657. Only known from the imprint to a pamphlet entitled *First Fruits and Tenths*, 1657.

FISHER ( ), barber & bookseller; Old Bailey. Smyth in his *Obituary*, p. 29, has the following entry:—"July 30, 1650. Mr. Fisher, barber and bookseller in Old Baily, died." In the same year the following imprint occurs on a pamphlet by A. Speed, *Privately Printed and sold Privatly at Mr. Fisher's house in King street.* [B.M. E. 599 (1).]

FISHER (WILLIAM), bookseller in London; Posterne Gate neer the Tower, 1657–63. Dealer in nautical books. In partnership for some time with William Lugger or Lugard, *q.v.* Fisher was also the publisher of Edward Cocker's *Art's Glory, or the Penman's Treasury*, 1659.

FLESHER, *see* Fletcher.

FLETCHER (HENRY), bookseller in London; Three Gilt Cups in Paul's Church Yard near the West End, 1656–61. Publisher of several of Sir John Harrington's works and miscellaneous literature.

FLETCHER (JAMES), printer in London; Little Britain, 1652–67. Son of Miles Fletcher. He married a daughter of Cornelius Bee the bookseller. In 1664 he, with his father, was proceeded against for illegally printing law

books. In the survey of the press made in July, 1668, he is returned as keeping five presses, thirteen workmen and two apprentices. He died in 1670. [Smyth's *Obituary*, p. 89; Plomer, *Short History*, pp. 224, 225.]

FLETCHER, or FLESHER (MILES), printer in London; Little Britain, 1611–64. Took up his freedom November 4th, 1611 [Arber, iii. 683], and in 1617 joined George Eld, who died in 1624. Fletcher then petitioned the Archbishop of Canterbury to be appointed a master printer in his place, and the request was granted. From this time his business prospered and he joined partnership with Robert Young, *q.v.*, and John Haviland. These three men were the largest capitalists in the trade for many years. They had a share in the King's Printing House, and they bought up the businesses of William Stansby, George Purslow and Edward Griffen. In 1629 John More assigned over to Miles Fletcher and his partners his patent for printing law books in return for a sum of £60 per annum and a third of the profits. In 1661 the Company of Stationers bought the remainder of the lease from Miles Fletcher and his son James for £200, but a lawsuit arose over this in 1664. [Chan. Proc. Reynardson, Bundle 31.] Miles Fletcher was Master of the Company of Stationers in the years 1652, 1653, 1662, and 1663. He was also a prominent man in the parish of St. Botolph without Aldersgate, serving as churchwarden with Richard Cotes, *q.v.*, in 1645, 1646, and 1647. He was assessed in the parish books in the sum of £1 14*s*. 8*d*. towards the restoration of the church, this being the largest sum paid by any stationer in Little Britain In March, 1637, Robert Young assigned over to him 80 works previously the copies of Benjamin Fisher. Miles Fletcher died November 13th, 1664. [Smyth's *Obituary*, p. 61.] By his will, which consisted of only a few lines, he left everything to his son James, no one else being mentioned. [P.C.C. 121, Bruce.] He made a gift of plate to the Company of Stationers. [Timperley, p. 543.]

FORBES (JOHN), the elder and the younger, booksellers and printers at Aberdeen; above the Meal Market, at the Sign of the Town's Armes, 1656–1704. Succeeded James Brown, *q.v.*, from whose widow they purchased his printing materials in 1661–2. Became printers to the Town and the University, and occupied the house formerly rented by Raban and by Brown. The elder Forbes died in November, 1675, and the business was continued by his son. [H. G. Aldis, *List of Books printed in Scotland before 1700*, p. 113; Edinburgh Bibliographical Society, 1905.]

FORCET, *see* Fawcet (T.).

FORREST (EDWARD), bookseller in Oxford, 1625–82. There may have been two men of this name during this period, probably father and son. In 1669 an Edward Forrest is found in partnership with John Forrest, *q.v.* William Hall printed for him: Cowell (Jo.), *Institutiones Juris Anglicani*, 1664. [Ames Collect. 3213. *See also* F. Madan, *Chart of Oxford Printing*, pp. 29, 31.]

FORREST (JOHN), bookseller in Oxford, 1660–69. In partnership with E. Forrest, *q.v.*, in 1669. [Arber, *Term Catalogues*, vol. i. p. 11; F. Madan, *Chart of Oxford Printing*, p. 30.]

FOSTER (MARK), bookseller in York, 1642. Stephen Bulkley, the York printer, printed three broadsides for this bookseller in July, 1642: (1) *Sir B. Rudyard's Worthy speech .... in the .... H. of Commons .... July 1642*, [B.M. 190. g.]; (2) *The petition of Sir F. Wortley to the king on behalf of the Commons of York.* [190 g. 12. (13)]; (3) *The petition of divers baronets of the County of Lincoln.* [190 g. 12. (68).]

FOSTER (RICHARD), bookseller in York; Minster Yard, 1659. His name is found on a pamphlet entitled *The Rendezvous of General Monck.* 1659. [E. 1005. (11).]

FOULKES, *see* Fowkes.

FOWKES, or FOULKES (EDWARD), (?) bookseller in London, 1664. Associated with Peter Bodvell, *q.v.*, in publishing the Book of Common Prayer in Welsh, printed for them by S. Dover in 1664. He may have been a descendant of Thomas or Nicholas Fowkes, mentioned in Arber's *Transcript*, ii. 132. His address has not been found. [Rowland's *Cambrian Bibl.*, p. 191.]

FOWLER (HENRY), bookseller (?) in London, 1642. Hazlitt mentions several political tracts printed for him, none of which has been traced. [Hazlitt, ii. 680; iii. 283, 290, 292.]

FOWLER (ROBERT), bookseller (?) in London, 1641–42. Took up his freedom January 15th, 1621. [Arber, iii. 685.] Only known from a broadside entitled *Some passages that happened the 9th March, between the Kings Majestie and the Committee of both Houses, when the Declaration was delivered. London printed for Robert Fowler.* 1641. [Hazlitt, ii. 94.]

FRANCK, *see* Frank.

FRANCKLING, *see* Franklin.

FRANK, or FRANCK (JOHN), bookseller in London; Next door to the King's Head Tavern, Fleet Street, 1641–42. Associated with Jo. Burroughes and Edward Husband in the publication of political broadsides.

FRANKLIN (J.), bookseller (?) in London, 1642. Only known from the imprint to a pamphlet entitled *Dialogue between a Brownist and a Schismatick*, 1642. [Hazlitt, iii. 65.]

FRANKLIN, or FRANCKLING (WILLIAM), bookseller in Norwich; In the Market-place, 1646–55. He was the publisher of a political pamphlet entitled *Vox Norwici; or, The City of Norwich*, 1646 [E. 358 (4)], and also of a sermon by John Carter, pastor of Great St. Peters, entitled *The Nail and the Wheel*, 1647, 4°. [B.M. 4473. aa. 9.]

FREEMAN (G.), bookseller (?) in London, 1666. Hazlitt, ii. 43, gives the following: *The Prophecie of Thomas Becket, Archbishop of Canterbury .... London, Printed for G. Freeman*, 1666. 4°.

FRERE (DANIEL), bookseller in London; Bull [or Red Bull] Little Britain, 1634–49. Took up his freedom July 7th, 1634. [Arber, iii. 687.] In 1637, under the name of Fryer, he was assessed in the Churchwardens' Accounts of St. Botolph's Without Aldersgate, 17s. 4d. towards the restoration of the church. Frere was a publisher of facetiæ. He died on May 16th, 1649. [Smyth's *Obituary*, p. 27.] His will was proved on May 24th, 1649. From this it appears that he had a son Henry. [P.C.C. 72. Fairfax.]

FUSSELL (NICHOLAS), bookseller in London; the Ball, Pauls Churchyard. 1627–50. Took up his freedom May 3rd, 1624. [Arber iii. 685.] In 1627 he married Judith, the daughter of Lawrence Camp, draper, the match being a

runaway one. A curious lawsuit resulted. [*Chan. Proc.*, Charles I, F. 34, 58.] At this time he was in partnership with Humphrey Moseley; the partnership was apparently dissolved in 1635. His subsequent address is unknown, that given above being recorded by Mr. Sayle in the Cambridge Catalogue (p. 1101). As a member of the Livery of the Company of Stationers he paid a sum of £3 to the poll tax on August 5th, 1641. [*Domestic State Papers*, Charles I, vol. 483 (11).]

FYFIELD, or FIFIELD (ALEXANDER), printer and typefounder in London, 1635–44. Took up his freedom July 20th, 1635. [Arber, iii. 687.] He was one of the four typefounders allowed by the Star Chamber Decree of 1637. Nothing is known of his foundry. Like other typefounders he also carried on the business of a printer, and was one of those who printed the "Directory" for public worship issued by the Assembly of Divines in 1644.

GALTON (GIFFORD), (?) bookseller in London; Kings Armes in the Poultrey, 1646. His name is found on the following political pamphlets: *The Burden of England, Scotland and Ireland; or, The Watchman's Alarum .... 1646.* [E. 351 (1)]; *Truth Vindicated from the unjust accusations of the Independent Society, in the City of Norwich .... By S. T.* .... 1646. [E. 351 (4).]

GAMAGE (NICHOLAS), bookseller in London, (1) On London Bridge neere the Gate, 1646; (2) Three Bibles on London Bridge, next the Gate, 1648. From a deed of assignment dated January 10th, 1645, it appears that Nicholas Gamage was the son of Thomas Gamage, of Walden, in Essex. He had a brother John and a sister Mary. The earliest book found with his name is *The World's Prospect ....* by John Emersone, 1646. [E. 1183 (2).] He also published Thomas Decker's *English Villanies* [Ninth Edition], 1648. This is probably the same house, afterwards occupied by C. Tyus and T. Passinger, *q.v.*

GAMMON (RICHARD), bookseller in London; Over against Excester [*i.e.*, Exeter] house in the Strand, 1661–62. His imprint has been found in the following books: Brett (Arthur), *Patientia Victrix; or the Book of Job in Lyrick Verse*, 1661; Hemings (W.), *Fatal contract, a French comedy*, 1661; Davenport (Robert), *King John and Matilda. A Tragedy*, 1662.

GARFIELD (JOHN), printer (?) & bookseller in London; The Rolling Press for Pictures, near the Royal Exchange in Cornhill, over against Pope's Head Alley, 1656–1659. On the title-page of George Thornley's *Daphnis and Chloe*, 1657. [B.M. E. 1652 (2)], is a plate of Garfield's press, labelled "The Printing Press for Pictures," showing three men at work, one employed with hands and feet in pulling the levers, one inking, and one removing the prints. The books sold by Garfield were printed for him by others.

GARRETT (WILLIAM), bookseller in London; Foster Lane, over against Goldsmiths' Hall, at the sign of the White Bear, 1622–74. Took up his freedom March 5th, 1621. [Arber, iii. 685.] Dealt largely in school books, but in March, 165⁸⁄₉, he took over from W. Humble, *q.v.*, all his copyrights in Speed's works. His address is given in a letter sent by T. Milbourne to the Secretary of State. [*Domestic State Papers*, Charles II, 182 (69).] He may have been the Mr. William Garrett described as "my loveinge freind" in the will of John Bill, the King's Printer, who died in 1630. [Plomer, *Wills*, p. 52.] He died between June 17th, 1674, and January 16th, 167⁴⁄₅.

GARTHWAITE (ROGER), (?) bookseller in London. His name occurs in the imprint to the following: *A Royal letter from the King of France to the King of England ....* First printed in Paris by Peter de Boys and now reprinted in London for Roger Garthwaite. [E. 137 (30).]

GARTHWAITE (TIMOTHY), bookseller in London, (1) George in Little Britain, 1650; (2) King's Head in St. Paul's Churchyard, 1664; (3) Golden Lion in St. Bartholomew's Hospital, 1668 (1650–69). Associated for a short time with J. Allestree, *q.v.* Dealt chiefly in theological literature. His death took place on November 18th, 1669. [Smyth's *Obituary*, p. 84.] His will was proved in the Prerogative Court of Canterbury on the 24th of the same month, by which he left the profits of his £80 share in the stock of the Company of Stationers to his wife Mary, who was the daughter of Geo. Latham, *q.v.* He left no son, and was succeeded in the business by his widow. [P.C.C. 140 Coke.] The inventory of his effects is printed in the *Bibliographical Register*. [Autumn, 1905, pp. 20–22.]

GARWAY (JOHN), bookseller in London; White-Lion near Py-Corner, 1660. Associated with John Andrews, *q.v.*, in the publication of John Reading's *Christmas Revived*, 1660.

GASCOIGNE (ROBERT), bookseller at Oxford, 1665. His name is found on Sir Balthazar Gerbier's *Subsidium Peregrinantibus*, 1665. [B.M. 1049, a. 25 (1).]

GAYE (WILLIAM), bookseller in London, (1) Hosier Lane, at the sign of the Axe; (2) Goldsmiths' Alley (21 June 1642). Publisher of political tracts. [Hazlitt, iii. 36, 310.]

GELLIBRAND (SAMUEL), bookseller in London, (1) The Brazen Serpent in Paul's Church Yard, 1643; (2) The Ball in St. Paul's Churchyard, 1650–66, 1669–75; (3) St. James Clerkenwell, 1666–68 (1637–75). Son of Henry Gellibrand, of London, Dr. of Physic, deceased, apprenticed to Henry Fetherstone, *q.v.*, from Midsummer, 1630. Took up his freedom June 26th, 1637. [Arber, iii. 688.] First book entry, July 18th, 1637. Became a well known bookseller, dealing chiefly in theological books, and was one of those who subscribed to Luke Fawne's *Beacon set on Fire*. There is an interesting reference to Samuel Gellibrand in the will of Walter Floyd, apparently a soldier, who died in 1645, and directed his executor to pay a sum of Five Pounds "to Mr. Samuel Gellibrand at the Brasen Serpent in St. Paul's Churchyard for Capt. Golledge." [P.C.C. 102, Rivers.] He is also mentioned in the marriage license of Henry Gellibrand in 1666, where his address was given as St. James' Clerkenwell. Samuel Gellibrand died between August 5th and November 10th, 1675. By his will it appears that he had three sons, John, Edward, and Henry, the latter pre-deceasing him. To his wife he left his stock of books bound and unbound, and also all his part in the English stock. One of the witnesses was Moses Pitt, who afterwards became a noted bookseller. [P.C.C. 110, Dycer.]

GIBBES, *see* Gibs.

GIBBS, *see* Gibs.

GIBS, GIBBES, or GIBBS (GEORGE), bookseller in London; Flower de Luce in Popes-Head-Alley, 1646. Only known from the imprint to L. Owen's *Unmasking of all Popish Monks*, 1646. [B.M. E. 339 (15).] Possibly a son of George Gibbs the elder, who was publishing at this address from 1613 to 1633. [Arber, v. 237; Sayle, 839.]

GIBS, GIBBES, or GIBBS (ROBERT), bookseller in London; Golden Ball in Chancery Lane, 1650–60. Dealt principally in political tracts. His name is found on *A Seasonable Exhortation of sundry Ministers*, 1660. [Ames' *Collection of Title-pages*, 2947.] Robert Gibs was perhaps another son of George Gibbs senior, noticed in the preceding entry.

GIBSON (ANTHONY), bookseller (?) in London, 1642. His name occurs in the imprint to a pamphlet entitled *Some wiser then some*, 1642. [E. 86 (30).]

GIBSON (JOHN), bookseller (?) in London, 1642. There were several stationers of the name of Gibson in London before 1640. [Arber, v. 237.] John Gibson is only known from the imprint to a pamphlet entitled *Humble remonstrance .... of many .... prisoners*, 1642. [Hazlitt, 1, 342.]

GILBERT (JOHN), (?) bookseller in London; neer Temple Bar, 1641–8. His name will be found on the following pamphlets: (1) *Foure Wonderfull, Bloudy, and Dangerous Plots discovered*, 1642. [E. 147 (1)]; (2) *Articles exhibited against the King*, 1648. [E. 536 (21).]

GILBERTSON, *alias* DERRICKE (WILLIAM), bookseller in London, (1) Bible in Giltspur Street, without Newgate; (2) Bible, near Newgate Street, 1640–1665. In partnership with Francis Coles, John Wright, and T. Vere, in the publication of ballads. In April, 1655, he acquired from Edward Wright a large number of copyrights of miscellaneous literature, amongst which may be noted *The Tragicall History of King Leire and his 3 daughters; A Play called The Shoomakers Holiday or the Gentle Craft; Scoggins Jests; The Crown Garland of Golden Roses, both parts.* [Stationers' Register, Liber E, pp. 339–42.] Gilbertson died between March 29th, 1665, and April 15th, 1665. His will was proved in the Prerogative Court. [P.C.C. 38, Hyde.] From this it appears that he was a native of Guildford, in Surrey, where he owned some property, and where he desired to be buried. He nominated Francis Coles, Thomas Vere, and Robert White his pall bearers. On April 18th, 1666, his copyrights were assigned to Robert White. [Register, Liber F, p. 314.]

GILES (J.), *see* Gyles (J.).

GLEN (JAMES), printer and bookseller, Edinburgh; In the Parliament Yard, 1656–87. A James Glen appears among the debtors in Lithgow's Inventory, 1662. Probably one of the booksellers who in 1671 acquired the printing-house of the Society of Stationers. A partner of A. Anderson in the privilege and appointment of King's printer, 1671. His name as printer, alone and in partnership, appears in books from 1667 to 1681. In 1687 he was ordered to be imprisoned for causing to be reprinted *The Rout of Romish Rites*. [H. G. Aldis, *List of Books printed in Scotland*, 1905, p. 113.]

GODBID (WILLIAM), printer in London; Over against the Anchor Inn in Little Britain, 1656–77. Apprenticed to Richard Cotes, who at his death left him a legacy of forty shillings. A notable feature of Godbid's work was the printing of music. In 1657 and 1659 he printed John Gamble's *Ayres and Dialogues*, in 1658 Henry Lawes' *Ayres and Dialogues*, and in 1669 the same author's *Treasury of Music*; in 1658, 1667, and 1669 John Hilton's collection of catches under the title of *Catch that Catch can*. Amongst his other work as a printer was Richard Lovelace's *Lucasta*, 1659, and Sir Aston Cokain's *Plays and Poems*. In the survey of the press made in July, 1668, he was returned as having three presses, five workmen, and two apprentices. [Plomer, *Short History*, p. 226.]

GODWIN, or GOODWIN (JOSEPH), printer and bookseller in Oxford, 1637–67. His imprint is found in the following work: *Christophori Scheibleri Antehac in academia Gissena professoris .... Metaphysica .... editio ultima*, 1637. [F. Madan, *Oxford Press*, pp. 201, 308.] He was also the publisher of the later edition of 1665.

GOLDING (E), (?) bookseller in London, 1647. Only known from the imprint to the following pamphlet: *A True and Full Relation of the late Sea-Fight .... London, Printed for E. Golding*, 1647 (May 10th). [E. 386 (12).] He may have been a relative of John or Percival Golding mentioned in Mr. Arber's *Transcript*, iii. 684; v. xcii. His address has not been found.

GOODMAN'S FIELDS PRESS, London, 1645. A secret press, supposed to have belonged to William Larner, the Independent bookseller, was seized by Joseph Hunscot, the searcher for the Stationers' Company, in a house

in Goodman's Fields, Whitechapel, some time between July and December, 1645. It is believed to have been the same press from which the Martin Mar-Priest tracts had appeared earlier in the year, and to have been hurriedly removed from Bishopsgate Street to avoid seizure. The following books are known to have been printed at it: (1) *The Copy of a Letter from Lieutenant Colonell John Lilburne, to a friend.* [August 9th, 1645.] 4°.; (2) *England's Birth-right justified against all Arbitrary Usurpation, etc.* [October 10th, 1645.] 4°. [*Library*, N.S., October, 1904, *Secret Printing during the Civil War*, pp. 374–403.]

GOODWIN, *see* Godwin.

GOULD (THOMAS), bookseller in London; The Church in Chancery Lane, 1635–59. Took up his freedom May 6th, 1633. [Arber, iii. 687.] His name is found on a broadside entitled *A Perfect List of the Lords* [Hazlitt, ii. 712], and other political pamphlets.

GRANTHAM (WILLIAM), bookseller in London, (1) Black Bear in St. Paul's Churchyard; (2) Bear in St. Paul's Church Yard, near the little North door. 1646–75. In partnership for a time with Nathaniel Webb, who, some time between 1655 and 1660, set up for himself at the King's Head in St. Paul's Churchyard. T. Gerey's *Meditations upon God*, 1658, contains after the "Contents" a four-page list of books sold by Grantham and Webb in 1658. It consists entirely of theological works, and was re-issued without alteration and without date two years later, at the end of a sermon by the same preacher called *A Mirrour for Anabaptists*. The last entry to Grantham in the *Term Catalogues* is Michaelmas, 1675.

GRAVES (WILLIAM), bookseller in Cambridge; Regent Walk, 1631(?)–65. His name is found on Richard Watson's *Sermon touching Schism*, 1642, *Liber Job Graeco carmine redditus per J. D. Editio altera ....* 1653. [Bowes' *Cambridge Books*, p. 28, No. 75; p. 34, No. 99.] A William Graves paid church rate from 1631 to $163\frac{4}{5}$ for Great St. Maries. [Foster's *Churchwardens' Accounts*.]

GRAY (JAMES), bookseller in Edinburgh; At the upper side of the Great Kirk Stile, 1647. Known only from the imprint to D. Dickson's *Brief Exposition of .... Matthew*. No. 1271 in Mr. Aldis's *List of Books Printed in Scotland*.

GREEN (BENJAMIN), bookseller in London; Three Leg Court in Fleet Street, over against the White Friars, 1632–46. Took up his freedom June 9th, 1628. [Arber, iii. 686.] In partnership with Moses Bell, *q.v.* On October 27th, 1632, they entered in the Registers a broadside called *A Yearly Continuation of the Lord Maiours and Sherriffs of London.* [Arber, iv. 287.] Benj. Green's name is found on another broadside beginning *To the Right Honourable Thomas Adams* .... [B.M. 669. f. 10, 74.]

GREEN (CHARLES), bookseller in London, (1) White Lion, St. Paul's Churchyard; (2) Gun in Ivy Lane. 1631–48. Took up his freedom June 30th, 1631. [Arber, iii. 686.] Publisher of plays and romances. On November 13th, 1633, he entered in the Stationers' Registers Thomas Morton's *New Englands Canaan.* This is a remarkable instance of the registration of copyright long before publication, as no copies of the book have been found with an earlier date than 1637, when it was printed at Amsterdam by Frederick Stam. Some copies are found with Greene's name, but without date, while internal evidence goes to prove that the book could not have been printed in 1633. [Publications of the Prince Society, Boston, Mass., 1883, edited by Ch. F. Adams, junr.] Charles Green was afterwards associated with Peter Whaley. He is probably the Charles Greene to whom Peter Parker, *q.v.*, left a bequest of a ring in 1648.

GREEN (GEORGE), senior, bookseller in London, 1621–42. Took up his freedom April 9th, 1621. [Arber, iii. 685.] There was also a George Green, junior, *q.v.* One of them was associated with John Jackson and F. Smith, in 1642, in publishing a broadside entitled *A Catalogue of sundry knights* .... [Hazlitt, ii. 359.] Their addresses have not been found.

GREEN (GEORGE), junior, bookseller in London, 1637–42. Took up his freedom February 6th, 1637. [Arber, iii. 688.] There was also a George Green, senior.

GREENE (THOMAS), bookseller in London, 1643. Only known from the imprint to a pamphlet entitled *A Chaleng sent from Prince Rupert and the Lord Grandison, to Sir William Belford .... London, Printed for Thomas Greene,* 1643. [B.M. 21 b. 10 (34).] A Thomas Greene, son of Robert Greene, of Brotherton, co. York, was apprenticed to William Jaggard on October 25th, 1602, for eight years. [Arber, ii. 267], but there is no record of his having taken up his freedom.

GREENSMITH (JOHN), bookseller in London, 1641–2. Took up his freedom January 19th, 1635. [Arber, iii. 687.] Chiefly a publisher of political pamphlets and broadsides. In 164$\frac{1}{2}$ he was examined before a Committee of the House of Commons in connection with the Hertfordshire Petition, and confessed that Martin Eldred, of Jesus College, Cambridge, and Thomas Harbert brought a copy of the petition to him and he paid them half-a-crown for it. He also confessed to having published various other pamphlets, *Good newes from Ireland, Bloudy Newes from Ireland,* and the *Cambridge petition,* which were composed by the same authors, and for each of which he gave the same sum. These pamphlets were printed by Bernard Alsop, *q.v.* [*House of Commons Journal,* January 25th, 164$\frac{1}{2}$.] Greensmith was sent to the Gatehouse for this offence. His address has not been found.

GRIFFIN (ANNE), printer in London; Old Bailey, St. Sepulchre's parish, 1634–43. Widow of Edward Griffin I, printer, 1613–21. She continued to carry on the business, and in 1638 her son, Edward Griffin II, was in partnership with her. Anne Griffin apppeared as a witness against Archbishop Laud in January, 164$\frac{2}{3}$, and is described in her depositions as a widow, forty-eight years of age. She deposed to reprinting, in 1637, Thomas Becon's *Displaying of the Popish Masse,* for which she was reprimanded by Laud, who threatened to put down her printing house. [*Domestic State Papers,* Charles I, vol. 500, No. 6.]

GRIFFIN (EDWARD) II, printer in London; Old Bailey, St. Sepulchre's parish, 1638–52. Son of Edward and Anne Griffin, 1613–38. Took up his freedom January 18th, 163$\frac{6}{7}$. This was an old-established printing house, originally founded in 1590 by John Jackson, Ninian Newton, Edmond Bollifant and Arnold Hatfield. Edward Griffin I began to print here in 1613. He died in 1621, and was succeeded by his widow Anne, who took John Haviland into partnership, and the press for some years was run by a syndicate consisting of John Haviland, Robert Young and Miles Flesher, who controlled several printing houses in London. [Arber, iii. 700–704.] On October 26th, 1638, Edward Griffin the second and his mother jointly entered in the register Dr. Sibbes' *Seven Sermons on Psalm 68* [Arber, iv. 442], and eventually Edward Griffin II succeeded to the business, which he continued to carry on until his death in 1652, when he in turn was succeeded by his widow Sarah Griffin.

GRIFFIN (SARAH), printer in London; Old Bailey St. Sepulchre's parish, 1653–73. Widow of Edward Griffin II, *q.v.* Succeeded to the business on the death of her husband in 1652. The last entry to her in the *Term Catalogues* is under date February 7th (Hilary), 1673. [Arber's *Term Catalogues,* vol. 1, 129.]

GRISMAND, *see* Grismond (J.).

GRISMOND (JOHN) II, printer in London; Ivy Lane, 1639 (?)–1666 (?). This was not the type founder mentioned in the Star Chamber Decree of 1637, for he died in 1638, his will being proved on the last day of December in that year. [P.C.C. 169, Lee.] He left no son. This John Grismond may have been the son of his brother, William Grismond, mentioned in the will. John Grismond II is first met with in the list of printers who were bound over in 1649 not to print seditious books. [*Calendar of State Papers,* 1649–50, pp. 522, 523.] In 1664, he was arrested at the instance of the Company of Stationers for illegally printing law books (*see* Fletcher, M.). The John Grismond who, in 1654, was entered as a scholar at Merchant Taylors' School, may have been a son of John Grismond II. [Reed, *Old English Letter Foundries,* 1887, p. 166, n.].

GROVE (FRANCIS), bookseller in London, (1) On Snow Hill, at the sign of the Windmill, neere vnto St. Sepulchre's Church, 1629; (2) Upper end of Snow Hill neere the Sarazen's Head, without Newgate, 1640. 1623–61. Took up his freedom June 30th, 1623. [Arber, iii. 685.] Dealt chiefly in ballads and the lighter literature of the period. The above addresses are taken from (1) R. Tarlton's *Newes out of Purgatory,* 1630, (2) *Pleasant history of Cawood the Rook,* 1640.

GROVE (JOHN), bookseller (?) in London; Betwixt St. Katharine's Stairs and the Mill, next door to the sign of the Ship, 1658. Only known from the imprint to a scarce pamphlet entitled *Wine, Ale, Beer and Tobacco,* 1658.

GUSTAVUS (CHARLES), bookseller in London, 1657–60. Chiefly a dealer in broadsides. His address has not been found. His name occurs on a broadside entitled *The Gang or the Nine Worthies and Champions.* [Lutt. Coll. II, 85.]

GUY (WILLIAM), bookseller in London, 1642. Only known from the imprint to the following pamphlet, *Votes and Declarations of both Houses of Parliament concerning the taking away .... the power of the Clergy .... Printed for Francis Leach and William Guy,* 1642. [Hazlitt, ii. 449.]

GYLES (JOHN), bookseller in London, (1) David's Inn, Holborn, 1642; (2) Furnivall's Inn, 1648 (1642–48). His name has been found on the following: (1) *The True Petition .... of the Kingdome of Scotland,* 1642. A broadside. [Bibl. Lind. Catal. of Broadsides, No. 28]; (2) *Works of .... Judge Jenkins,* 1648. [Harl, 5921 (341).]

HALES (THOMAS), bookseller in London, 1641. Took up his freedom June 5th, 1626. [Arber, iii. 686.] *To the Right Honourable the House of Peers .... the humble Petition of many thousands .... inhabiting within the cities of London and Westminster,* 1641. A broadside. [Lutt. Coll., 3, 66.] His address has not been found.

HALL (HENRY), printer at Oxford, 1642–79 (?). Apprentice to William Turner, *q.v.*, and upon the death of the latter, in 1643, purchased his "presses, letters, and utensils." Hall was elected printer to the University in Turner's place on November 21st, 1644. [Madan, *Chart of Oxford Printing,* p. 29.] He was the printer of the famous Oxford news-sheet, *Mercurius Aulicus.* In October, 1649, he was bound over in a sum of £300 not to print seditious or unlicensed books or pamphlets. [*Calendar of State Papers,* 1649–50, p. 524.] Hall married Dorothy Bowring not later than 1644, and had six children born between 1645 and 1653, in St. John the Baptist's parish, Oxford.

HALL (RICHARD), bookseller in London; Westminster Hall at the sign of the Golden Ball, 1661–62. Associated with Thomas Bassett, *q.v.*, in the publication of the *Life and Death of Thomas Cawton,* 1662. He was also the publisher of a tragedy called *Andronicus* in the previous year.

HALL (WILLIAM), bookseller in Colchester, 1663. *The Arithmetical Questions,* by John Duke or Le Duke, were advertised in the *Mercurius Publicus* of June 25th, 1663, to be sold by this bookseller. His name is also found on another book of local interest, John Le Duke's *Tables for the ready casting up of the price of Colchester Bays,* 1663.

HALL (WILLIAM), printer at Oxford, 1656–72. Briefly noticed by Mr. Madan in his *Chart of Oxford Printing*, p. 30. Probably related to Henry Hall, *q.v.* In 1662 he was University printer, with Henry Hall.

HAMMOND (JOHN), printer in London; Over against S. Andrews Church in Holborne, 1642–51. In partnership with M. Rhodes, *q.v.* Hammond was the printer of the news-sheet, *The Kingdoms weekly Post*, 1643, and a curious piece of Americana entitled *Of the Conversion of Five Thousand and Nine Hundred East Indians .... By means of M. Ro. Junius .... related by .... M. C. Sibellius .... Translated .... by H. Jessei .... with a Postscript of the Gospels good successe also amongst the West Indians in New England. London. Printed by John Hammond, and are to be sold at his house voer* [*i.e.* over] *against S. Andrewes Church in Holborne; and in Pope's-Head-Alley by H. Allen. 1650.* [E. 614 (6).]

HAMMOND (THOMAS), bookseller (?) in London, 1662. Only known from the imprint to the following, *Trade Revived, Or a way proposed to restore the .... trade of this our English Nation .... London, Printed by T. Leach for Tho. Hammond .... 1662.* [Hazlitt, ii. 287.]

HANCOCK (JOHN), bookseller in London, (1) Bible in Birchen Lane; (2) Pope's Head neer the Exchange; (3) In Cornhill at the entrance unto Pope's Head Alley. 1643–66. Took up his freedom October 1st, 1638. [Arber, iii. 688.] Dealt largely in political broadsides, but amongst his publications was an edition of Gildas' *Description of Great Britain*, 1652.

HANKEN (JER.), bookseller (?) in London, 1660. Only known from the imprint to the following pamphlet, *An exact accompt of the receipts and disbursements expended by the Committee of Safety*, 1660. [Hazlitt, ii. 107.]

HANSON (THOMAS), bookseller (?) in London, 1643. Only known from the imprint to the following, *The Humble Petition Of divers of the knights, gentry and other Inhabitants of the County of Berkes .... London. Printed for Thomas Hanson Anno Dom. 1643.* [B.M. C. 21, b. 10 (6).]

HARDESTY (JOHN), bookseller in London, (1) In the Strand, nigh Worcester House; (2) Black-Spread-Eagle in Duck Lane. 1646–48. Took up his freedom August 4th, 1634. [Arber, iii. 687.] Amongst his publications was Richard Boothby's *Brief discovery or description of the .... Island of Madagascar*, London, 1646. Smyth in his *Obituary* (p. 46), under date April 26th, 1658, records, "Thos. Hardesty, bookseller in Duck Lane, a poore man, willingly leaping out of his window into the street 3 stories high, broke his neck and so died." As Smyth sometimes made mistakes in the spelling of names, he was probably referring to John Hardesty.

HARDY (HENRY), bookseller (?) in London, 1660. Only known from the imprint to a broadside entitled *A serious manifesto and declaration of the Anabaptist and other Congregational Churches.* [Bibl. Lind. *Cat. of B.*, No. 84.]

HARE (ADAM), (?) printer in London; Red Cross Street, 1649–50. His name occurs in a list of printers and stationers who were bound over by the Council of State not to print seditious literature. [See *Calendar of State Papers*, 1649–50, p. 524.]

HARFORD (ELIZABETH), bookseller in London; Bible and States Arms, Little Britain, 1666. Probably the widow of Ralph Harford, *q.v.* She is mentioned in the Hearth Tax Roll for the half-year ending Lady Day, 1666, as a bookseller in Little Britain, and was assessed for four hearths. [P.R.O. Lay Subsidy $\frac{252}{32}$.]

HARFORD (RALPH), bookseller in London, (1) Queenes-head-alley in Paternoster Row at the guilt Bible; (2) The Bible in Queens Head Alley in Paternoster Row, 1641; (3) The Bible and States Arms, Little Britain, 1651 (1629–51). Took up his freedom January 14th, 1627. [Arber, iv. 30.] Publisher of sermons, political tracts and miscellaneous literature.

HARINGMAN (HENRY), *see* Herringman.

HARNOM (J.), (?) bookseller in London, 1642. His name is found on the following pamphlet, *Sad and fearfull newes from Beverley*, 1642. [B.M. E. 108 (8).]

HARPER (RICHARD), bookseller in London; Bible and Harp in Smithfield, 1633–52. Took up his freedom May 6th, 1633. [Arber, iii. 687.] First book entry May 22nd, 1633. [Arber, iv. 296.] Dealt chiefly in ballads, broadsides, political tracts and sermons.

HARPER (THOMAS), printer in London; Little Britain, 1614–56. The son of William Harper, of Woolraston, co. Salop, minister. Apprentice to Melchisedeck Bradwood, September 29th, 1604. [Arber, iii. 549.] Took up his freedom October 29th, 1611. First book entry July 14th, 1614, at which time he appears to have been in partnership with his brother William. [*Ibid.*] In 1634 he bought the printing business of George Wood and William Lee, which had previously belonged to Thomas Snodham, who in his turn had succeeded Thomas East or Este. Wood brought several actions against Harper in the Court of Requests and the Court of Chancery, in all of which he was non-suited. In 1639 Harper was in partnership with Richard Hodgkinson. [Sayle, 866.] During the early years of the Rebellion he was more than once in trouble for printing pamphlets against the Parliament. [*Commons Journals*, ii. 168.] He died March 22nd, 16$\frac{55}{56}$. [Smyth's *Obituary*, p. 41.] Many notable books came from his press, amongst them George Ruggle's *Ignoramus*, 1630; John Weever's *Ancient Funeral Monuments*, 1631; Camden's *Annales*, 1635, and Camden's *Remaines*, 1636. He also printed music for John Playford.

HARRIS (JOHN), printer and bookseller, London and Oxford, 1647–69. Mr. W. H. Allnutt in his papers on the English Provincial Presses, after noticing the presses of Newcastle and Gateshead, refers to a statement made by Lord Holles in his *Memoirs*, that the Parliamentary Army was in 1647 accompanied by a printing press. He also notices a statement made by Mr. C. H. Firth, who in 1891 edited the Clarke Papers for the Camden Society, to the effect that, "The printer of these pamphlets seems to have been a certain John Harris, who himself wrote several pamphlets under the name of Sirrahniho." [*Bibliographica*, vol. 2, pp. 292–3.] This seems to be confirmed by the two following imprints: (1) *Declaration of Master William Lenthall, Speaker of the House of Commons* .... Oxford, printed by J. Harris and H. Hills, living in Pennifarthing Street, 1647. [B.M. 103, a. 39.] (2) *The humble address of the agitators 14th Augt 1647.* London, for J. Harris, Printer to His Excellency Sir Thomas Fairfax. There was also a John Harris carrying on the trade of a bookseller at Addle Hill off Thames Street in 1649, who may have been the same person whose name is found on a pamphlet entitled *The Accuser sham'd* [E. 624 (2)], while Hazlitt in his Collections, and Notes (ii. p. 530), notices another book issued in 1669 by a John Harris, of which, however, no copy has been traced.

HARRISON ( ), Mrs., bookseller in London; Lamb, St. Paul's Churchyard, 1654. Widow of John Harrison, *q.v.*, 1641–53. Her name is mentioned in an advertisement of a lost horse in the *Perfect Account* of September 27th, 1654. [E. 812 (15).]

HARRISON (JOHN), bookseller in London; [Lamb or Holy Lamb (?)] St. Paul's Churchyard, 1641–53. Dealer in miscellaneous literature. Published amongst other things John Dennis's *Secrets of Angling*, 1652. [B.M. C. 31. d. 43.] Believed to have died before 1653.

HARRISON (JOHN), junr., bookseller in London; Holy Lamb East End of Pauls, 1654–56. Probably son of the preceding. His name is found on Robert Turner's *Microkosmus*, 1654.

HARRISON (MARTHA), bookseller in London; Lamb. East end of Paul's, 1649–57. Probably widow of John Harrison, *q.v.*, and mother of John Harrison, junr., *q.v.* On July 13th, 1649, a warrant was issued by the Council of State for the apprehension of Martha Harrison and Francis Heldersham, *q.v.*, for printing and publishing a seditious libel called *Pragmaticus.* [*Calendar of State Papers*, 1649–50, p. 541. *See also* Ellis, W.] A list of ten books published by her, including Mascal's *Government of Cattle*; Wentworth's *Miscellanea*; an edition of the fourth book of Cornelius Agrippa in English, as well as medical and astrological works, is given at the end of R. Turner's translation of L. Cambachius, *Sal, Lumen & Spiritus Mundi*, 1657. [B.M. 8630. a. 21.]

HARRISON (MILES), bookseller at Kendal in 1660. His name will be found on the following pamphlet: Brownsward (W.), *The Quaker Jesuit*, 1660. [E. 1013 (4).]

HARRISON (THOMAS), bookseller in London, 1643. Only known from the imprint to a pamphlet entitled *The Priviledges of Parliament .... London Printed for Thomas Harrison*, 1643. [B.M. 1093. b. 118.] His address has not been found.

HARROWER (JAMES), bookseller in Edinburgh, 1600 (?)–54. "In vol. 67, May 10, 1654, is registered the testament dative of James Harrower bookseller, burges of Edinburgh, 'quha deceist in the moneth of Fe. 1^{m} vj^{c}

[. . . ?] ziers'; and in vol. 68, August 4, 1654, that of Jeonet Patersone, his relict spous, 'quha deceist in the moneth of December. 1651. ziers.'" [Bann. Misc. ii. 274; H. G. Aldis, *List of Books*, p. 114.]

HARSELL (RICHARD), bookseller in Bristol, 1643. Mr. Allnutt, in his papers on the English Provincial Presses, referring to Bristol notes the following: *Disloyalty of language Questioned and Censured. Or, a sermon Preached . . . . by Rich. Towgood, B.D., one of His Majesties Chaplains, and Vicar of Saint Nicholas Church in Bristoll. Jan 17. 1642 . . . . Bristoll, Printed for Richard Harsell, and are to be sold by him in Bristoll.* 1643. Sm. 8°. A copy in Trin. Coll., Dublin. [*Bibliographica*, vol. ii. p. 287.] His name is found again on *Certain observations upon the New League & Covenant*, 1643. [B.M. 8142. bb. 6.]

HART (JONA), bookseller in London, 1664. Only known from the imprint to Velthusius' (Lambert) *Renati Des Cartes Meditationes . . . . Londini: Excudebat J. F. pro Jona Hart.* 1664. [Ames Collection, 3192.]

HART (SAMUEL), bookseller in Edinburgh, 1621–43. Son of Andro Hart, bookseller. Baptised January 7th, 1599. Died about 1643. [H. G. Aldis, *List of Books*, p. 114.]

HART (Widow), printer and bookseller at Edinburgh. (?) On the North side of the gate, a little beneath the Crosse, 1621–42. Jonet Kene, second wife of Andro Hart. Opposed the passing of Young's appointment as King's printer in 1632. Died May 3rd, 1642. [H. G. Aldis, *List of Books*, p. 114.]

HARWARD, or HAWARD (HUMPHREY), bookseller in London; George on Ludgate Hill over against Bell-Savage, 1647–8. Publisher of political pamphlets, notably a series issued in 1648 by the Dissenters, of which the following was the most important: *Reasons presented by the Dissenting Brethren against certain propositions concerning Presbyteriall Government . . . .* London, Printed by T. R. and E. M. for Humphrey Harward . . . . 1648, 4°.

HATFIELD (RICHARD), bookseller (?) in London, 1647. Only known from the imprint to the following pamphlet: *A Declaration from the Right Honourable, the Lord Major, Aldermen, and Commons of the City of London, Presented to His Excelleney* [sic] *Sir Thomas Fairfax . . . .* Imprinted at London for Richard Hatfield, 1647. [B.M. E. 401 (11).]

HAYWARD (HUMPHREY), *see* Harward.

HAYES (JOHN), printer in London; Little Wood Street, 1658–66. Possibly a descendant of Lawrence Hayes, who was publishing up to 1637. [Arber, v. 241.] He was one of the eleven printers who in 1660 or 1661 drew up a petition for the incorporation of printers into a body distinct from the Company of Stationers. [Plomer, *Short History*, p. 200.] In 1662 Sir R. L'Estrange seized several books at the office of this printer, a list of which is extant. John Hayes was ruined by the Great Fire of 1666. [*Ibid.*, 202 and 225.]

HAYWARD (BERNARD), (?) bookseller in Manchester, 1643. Only known from the imprint to a pamphlet entitled *Manchester's Joy for Derbie's overthrow . . . .* Printed for Bernard Hayward, 1643.

HEAD (RICHARD), author and bookseller; The Heart and Bible in Little Britain, 1666–7. Born in Ireland about 1637. His father is believed to have been John Head, B.A., New Inn Hall, 1628, who became a nobleman's chaplain and was killed in Ireland by the rebels in 1641. Richard and his mother, after many sufferings, reached England, and Winstanley says that after studying for a short time at Oxford at the same hall as that from which his father had graduated, Richard Head was apprenticed to a Latin bookseller in London, and that he afterwards married and set up for himself. He gives no dates, but makes these events occur before the publication of Head's first work, the play of *Hic et Ubique*, which was written in Ireland and printed in London in 1663, that is before he was twenty-two years of age. There is no confirmation of this story. The earliest date at which Richard Head's name is found in the imprint of a book is the year 1666, when he issued Saml. Hieron's *Fair Play on both sides.* 4°. [B.M. 1077, h. 71 (4).] In the same year Richard Head and Francis Kirkman jointly issued a book of jests entitled *Poor Robin's Jests*, of which a copy is noted by Hazlitt. In the Luttrell Collection is a broadside dated 1667 entitled *The Citizens Joy for the re-building of London*, which was also one of Head's publications. His career as a bookseller was a short one, as he was a great gambler and was ruined by losses at play. He is said to have been drowned in 1686 when crossing to the Isle of Wight. Head is chiefly remembered as the author of *The*

English Rogue, in which a thief's career is set forth. The work became popular, and Francis Kirkman issued several additions to it, until its author began to doubt whether he would ever make an end of pestering the world with them. [Head (R), *Proteus Redivivus: Epistle Dedicatory.*]

HEARNE, HERNE, or HERON (RICHARD), printer in London; neer Smith-Field, 1632–46. Probably one of Adam Islip's apprentices, for that printer at his death in 1639 left Richard Hearne his "printing presses, letters and implements used for printing," besides a sum of £100. [P.C.C. 151, Harvey.] Hearne had taken up his freedom February 6th, 1632, and his first book entry in the Registers of the Company was T. Heywood's *Pleasant Dialogues*, entered on August 29th, 1635. [Arber, iii. 687; iv. 347.]

HEATH (THOMAS), bookseller in London; Russell Street, neere the Piazza of the Covent Garden, 1651–54. Issued an edition of Sidney's *Arcadia*, 1651; Ed. Chamberlayne's *Rise & Fall of . . . . the Count Olivares*, 1652, and a few plays.

HEATHCOAT, or HEATHCOTE (NATHANIEL), bookseller in London; Gilded Acorn in St. Paul's Churchyard, 1656. Only known from the imprint to the following pamphlet: Stephens (Nath.), *Plain and easie calculation*, 1656. [Harl. 5965 (158).]

HEATHCOTE, *see* Heathcoat.

HEBB (ANDREW), bookseller in London; Bell in St. Paul's Churchyard, 1625–48. Took up his freedom June 22nd, 1621. [Arber, iii. 685.] On May 6th, 1625, all the copyrights and parts belonging to Thomas Adams were transferred to Andrew Hebb. Andrew Hebb died October 28th, 1648, "of a dropsie." [Smyth's *Obituary*, p. 26.]

HEDGES (ROBERT), *see* Hodges.

HELDER (THOMAS), bookseller in London; Angel in Little Britain, 1666–85. In 1667 he issued an edition of a very popular book of humour called *Wits Recreations*, or *Recreations for Ingenious Headpieces*, but he is chiefly remembered as one of the booksellers whose name appeared on the 1669 title-page of *Paradise Lost.* His name is first met with in the Hearth Tax Roll for the half-year ending Lady Day, 1666, where he is returned as having three hearths. [P.R.O. Lay Subsidy, $\frac{252}{32}$.]

HELDERSHAM (FRANCIS), bookseller (?) in London, 1649. Only known from a warrant granted by the Council of State on July 13th, 1649, to Serjeant Dendy to apprehend Francis Heldersham and Martha Harrison, for printing and publishing a seditious libel called *Pragmaticus.* The actual printing was done by William Ellis, *q.v.* [*Calendar of State Papers*, 1649–50, p. 541.]

HERNE, *see* Hearne (R.).

HERON, *see* Hearne (R.).

HERRICK, or HEYRICK (SAMUEL), bookseller in London; Gray's Inn Gate in Holborn, 1662–7. Mentioned in an advertisement in *Mercurius Publicus*, March 27th, 1662. His name occurs on John Dover's play, *The Roman Generall; or the Distressed Ladies . . . .* 1667. [B.M. 644, d. 80.]

HERRINGMAN (HENRY), bookseller in London; Blue Anchor in the Lower Walk of the New Exchange, 1653–93. Next to Humphrey Moseley, the most important bookseller in the period covered by this dictionary. He was the son of John Herringman, of Kessalton [*i.e.*, Carshalton], in Surrey, yeoman, and was apprenticed to Abell Roper, bookseller of Fleet Street, for eight years from August 1st, 1644. [Register of Apprenticeships, Stationers' Hall.] His first book entry, which curiously enough follows one by his great contemporary Moseley, was Sir Kenelm Digby's *Short Treatise of Adhearing to God, written by Albert the Great*, entered on September 19th, 1653, and he followed this on October 12th in the same year with Lord Broghall's *Parthenissa, a Romance.* At the time of Moseley's death in 1661, Herringman possessed copyrights of books by Sir Kenelm Digby and James Howell, and many of Sir R. Davenant's pre-Restoration operas. He was Dryden's publisher, and in 1663 acquired the copyright of Cowley's poems, and in the following year the copyright of Waller's poems, which he obtained no doubt by purchase from Moseley's widow. Herringman was also an extensive publisher of plays and all the lighter literature of the Commonwealth and Restoration periods. His shop was the chief literary lounging place in London, and is frequently referred to in Pepys' *Diary.* Herringman also held a share in the King's

Printing House, and in 1682 was defendant in a suit brought in the Court of Chancery by the trustees of Charles Bill, one of the children of John Bill II. [Chan. Proc., P.R.O., Mitford, 298, 69.] Mr. Arber, in his reprint of the *Term Catalogues* [vol. ii. p. 642] says that Herringman was apparently the first London wholesale publisher in the modern sense of the words. He turned over his retail business at the Blue Anchor to F. Saunders and J. Knight, and devoted himself to the production of the Fourth Folio Shakespeare, Chaucer's works, and other large publishing ventures. His last entry in the *Term Catalogues* was in Trinity, 1693, shortly after which he appears to have retired to his native place, Carshalton, in Surrey. Here he died on January 15th, 170$\frac{3}{4}$, and was buried in Carshalton Church, where a monument was erected to his memory. [Manning, *History of Surrey*, vol. ii. p. 516.] By his will, which was dated the day before his death, he left to his "kinsman" John Herringman all his copies and parts of copies when he attained the age of twenty-three, the profits meanwhile to go to his widow. To the Company of Stationers he left a sum of £20 to purchase a piece of plate. [P.C.C. 40, Ash.]

HEWER (THOMAS), bookseller in London; Old Bailey, 1638-53 (?) Took up his freedom October 1st, 1638. [Arber, iii. 688.] Associated with W. Moulton in 1642. His name is found on a pamphlet entitled *A subsidie granted to the King*, 1653. A "T. Hewer" is described as a printer in the imprint to Sylvanus Morgan's *Armilogia*, 1666. This may be the same as the above.

HEYRICK, *see* Herrick.

HICKMAN (JOHN), (?) bookseller in London, 1648. Took up his freedom April 1st, 1639. [Arber, iii. 688.] Published Borialis Guard's *Jovial Tinker*, 1648. [Hazlitt, i. 446.] His address has not been found.

HIERONS, or HIRONES (JEREMIAH), (?) bookseller in London; Bottle, Near the Great North Door of St. Pauls, 1656. Entered in the Registers on June 19th, 1656, a book or pamphlet entitled *The Unparaleled Thiefe, or an exact relation of the notable exploits Acted by that matchless Robber Richard Hanum.* [Stationers' Registers, Liber F, p. 473.]

HIGGINS (CHRISTOPHER), printer at Leith, 1652-54 (?), and Edinburgh; in Harts-Close over against the Trone-Church, 1655-60. Succeeded Evan Tyler, and printed for the Government. According to Watson, "Tyler made over his part of the forfeited gift [of King's printer] to some stationers at London, who sent down upon us Christopher Higgins and some English servants with him." This was about 1652, and the tracts printed at Leith in 1652-4 were probably printed by Higgins, but his name does not appear till 1655, when he was printing at Edinburgh. Though Higgins printed in his own name, Watson's statement is probably correct, and he was succeeded by a Society of Stationers in 1660, in which year he seems to have either died or retired. [H. G. Aldis, *List of Books*, p. 114.]

HILL (FRANCIS), bookseller in London; Little Britain, 1644. Only known from Smyth's entry as to his death on September 9th, 1644. [*Obituary*, p. 21.]

HILL (JOHN), bookseller at Edinburgh, 1652. Little is known of this bookseller beyond the date of his death, 1652. Amongst the items in his inventory was a debt to "Androw Crook, Inglischman." [H. G. Aldis, *List of Books*, p. 114.]

HILLS (HENRY), printer in Oxford and London. Oxford: Pennyfarthing Street, 1647. London: (1) sign of Sir John Oldcastle in Fleet yard next door to the Rose & Crown; (2) At the sign of Sir John Old-Castle in Py-Corner; (3) Over against St. Thomas's Hospitall in Southwark. 1641-88. Son of a rope-maker in Maidstone. Sent to London when very young and acted first as postillion to Harrison the regicide, who transferred him to John Lilburne, by whom he was apprenticed to Simmons & Payne, printers. In 1642 he ran away and joined the army, and was present at the battle of Edge Hill. In 1648 he was a Leveller and subsequently an Independent, and offered to print Cromwell's *Remonstrance*. He was subsequently made printer to the Rebel Army, *see* Harris (J.). In 1649, in company with Thomas Brewster and Giles Calvert, he was appointed "printer" to the Council of State. After 1653 he held the position alone. He was also appointed one of the "printers" to the Parliament in

conjunction with John Field, *q.v.*, a post he held until the Restoration. He was still living in 1684, when a broadside was issued entitled *A View of part of the many traiterous, disloyal, and turn-about actions of H. H. senior, sometimes printer to Cromwell, to the Commonwealth, to the Anabaptists Congregation, to Cromwells Army, Committee of Safety, etc.* [B.M. 816, m. 2 (60); Solly, E.; Henry Hills, the pirate printer; *Antiquary*, vol. ii. April, 1885, pp. 151-154.] Amongst his publications was *Ill-Newes from New England. By John Clark*, 1652.

HIRONES, *see* Hierons.

HODGES (ROBERT), bookseller in London, 1649. Only known from the imprint to W. Prynne's *Loyall vindication of the liberties of England*, 1649. He may have been a descendant of George Hodges, who was publishing between 1621 and 1632. [Arber, v. 242.]

HODGKINSON (RICHARD), printer in London; Thames Street, near Baynard's Castle, 1624-68. Took up his freedom April 8th, 1616. [Arber, iii. 684.] In Sir John Lambe's notes he is said to have been the son of a printer, possibly Thomas Hodgkinson, who is mentioned in the Registers between 1580 and 1597. Some time in 1635, Richard Hodgkinson was in trouble with the Star Chamber and his press and letters had been seized, but on the recommendation of the Commissioners they were restored to him. This, however, had not taken place at the time when Lambe made these notes. [Acts of the Court of High Commission, *Domestic State Papers*, Charles I, vol. 324, f. 307^{b}.] On March 21st, 1637, another entry in the State Papers shows that he had purchased type from Arthur Nicholls the type-founder, and some dispute as to payment resulted. [*Domestic State Papers*, Charles I, vol. 350, 53, 53 (1).] In the same year he was in trouble for printing Doctor John Cowell's *Interpreter*, but this did not prevent his being chosen as one of the twenty printers appointed under the Act. He was the printer of the first volume of Sir W. Dugdale's *Monasticon*, which, next to the Polyglott Bible, must be considered a "magnus opus" of the Commonwealth period. He was still a master printer in 1668, but as no return of his office is given with the rest, he would have appeared to have died or retired from business about that time.

HOLDEN (JOHN), bookseller in London, (1) Blue Anchor in the New Exchange; (2) The Anchor in the New Exchange. 1650-1. Apparently the predecessor of Henry Herringman at this address. Publisher of Abraham Cowley's *Guardian*, 1650, and Sir W. Davenant's *Gondibert*, 1651. A list of thirteen miscellaneous books sold by him in 1651 occupies one leaf following the dedicatory epistle to L. Lessius' *Sir W. Rawleighs Ghost.*

HOLEMAN (WILLIAM), bookseller (?) in London; near the Hermitage-stairs, next to the Black-Swan in Wapping, 1666. Only known from the imprint to a pamphlet entitled, Horne (Henry), *Perfect and Compleat Bel-man*, 1666. [Douce Coll.]

HOLMER (THOMAS), printer in London, 1641. In the *Commons Journals* (vol. ii., p. 160), under date May 27th, 1641, is an order that Thomas Holmer, who was committed to the Gatehouse for printing an Elegy upon the Earl of Strafford, which was considered to be scandalous, should be admitted to bail. No master printer of this name is known, and Holmer was probably a journeyman. There are two broadsides in the British Museum of this date with the imprint, *Printed in the year 1641*. The first, entitled *The Earl of Strafford his Ellegaick Poem as it was pen'd by his owne hand a little before his death*, and the second *Verses lately written by Thomas Earle of Strafford.* [C. 20, f. 2 (6) (7).] It was perhaps the first of these that was referred to in the order.

HOMER (T .), bookseller (?) in London, 1642. Associated with J. Jackson and G. Tomlinson. He was the publisher of numerous political pamphlets, and may be identical with the preceding. His address has not been found.

HOOD (HENRY), bookseller in London; St. Dunstan's Churchyard, 1636-54. Took up his freedom July 1st, 1635. [Arber, iii. 687.] Believed to have married the widow of Richard More or Moore, who carried on business at this address until his death in 1631. On May 12th, 1641, John More or Moore, the son of Richard, received from his mother the assignment of his father's copies, and the same day assigned them to Henry Hood. [Stationers' Registers, 1641.]

HOPE (WILLIAM), bookseller in London, (1) Glove in Cornhill, 1636; (2) Unicorn near the Royal Exchange in Cornhill, 1639–40; (3) the Blew Anchor at the back-side of the Roiall Exchange, 1657; (4) Blue Anchor Old Exchange; (5) Near the Exchange, 1657; At the Anchor over against St. Bartholomew's Church, near the Royal Exchange, 1665 (1634–65). Took up his freedom October 4th, 1630. First book entry April 14th, 1636. [Arber, iii. 686; iv. 360.] In partnership for a time with Edward Farnham. Bought books of Robert Bryson, of Edinburgh, *q.v.* A list of 31 books "printed or sold" by this bookseller in 1653 occurs on sig. 17 of *The Holy Lives of God's Prophets*, 1654 (1653). [B.M. E. 1493 (1).]

HOPKINSON (JONATHAN), bookseller in London; Without Aldgate, 1647. Only known from the entry in Smyth's *Obituary*, p. 24: "Aug 31. 1647 Jonathan Hopkinson, bookseller wthout Algate, died."

HORNE (ROBERT), bookseller in London, (1) Turk's Head near the Royal Exchange, 1661; (2) Angel, in Pope's Head Alley, 1664; (3) In the first court entering into Gresham College, next Bishopsgate, 1669; (4) At the South Entrance to the Royal Exchange, Cornhill. 1660–85. Amongst his publications was *A Brief Description of the Province of Carolina, on the coasts of Floreda .... Together with a most accurate map of the whole Province. London, Printed for Robert Horne, in the first Court of Gresham College, neer Bishopsgate-street. 1666.* [B.M. 10412, c. 16.]

HORNISH (JAMES), bookseller (?) in London, 1647–48. Publisher of political pamphlets. His address has not been found.

HORSEMAN (THOMAS), bookseller in London, (1) between York House & the New Exchange; (2) Three Kings in the Strand. 1664–5. Publisher of Sir W. Killigrew's *Three Plays*, 1665.

HORTEN (SAMUEL), (?) bookseller in London (?) 1641. His name is found on a pamphlet entitled, *A True Coppie of divers papers* .... [E. 180 (21).]

HORTON (GEORGE), bookseller in London, (1) Royal Exchange in Cornhill; (2) Near the three crowns in Barbican; (3) Figg-Tree-Court in Barbican; (4) Lower end of Red Cross Street over against St. Giles Church, neer Cripplegate. 1647–60. Publisher of political pamphlets and news-sheets.

HOWELL (JOHN), bookseller (?) in London, 1642. Only known from the imprint to a political pamphlet entitled *Delightful news for all loyal subjects*, 1642. 4 leaves. His address has not been found.

HOWES (SAMUEL), bookseller in London, (1) Popes Head Alley; (2) Golden Ball in Cornhill near the Poultry. 1644–54. Son of Robert Howes, stationer, apprenticed to his father January 21st, $164\frac{3}{4}$. [Stationers' Register of Apprenticeships.] Partner with John Blague, *q.v.* They published jointly H. Whitfield's *Strength out of Weakness*, 1652, and Phillip Barrough's *Method of Physick*, 1652.

HUCKLESCOTT (THOMAS), bookseller in London; George in Little Britain, 1653. Only known from the imprint to Sir William Denny's *Pellicanicidium, or the Christian Adviser against self murder* .... London, Printed for Thomas Hucklescott and are to be sold at the sign of the George, in Little Britain, 1653. [B.M. E. 1233.]

HUGHES (ROBERT), bookseller or printer in Dublin, 1648–51. Robert Hughes was admitted to the franchise of the City of Dublin in October, 1648, when he was described as a "stationer." In the same year he published a catalogue of the manuscripts in the library of James Ware, the imprint to which reads: "Dublinii. Excudebat Robertus Hughes. M.DC.XLVIII." In April, 1650, Hughes was appointed to collect the 'Keyadge' of Dublin city, and to account for it to the Mayor and Auditors at a commission of two shillings in the £, and in the January following, 1651, was jointly appointed with another person to collect the 'threepenny customs' at a commission of one shilling in the £. Each time his name is mentioned he is described as a 'stationer.' [Information supplied by E. R. McC. Dix.]

HUMBLE (WILLIAM), bookseller in London; The White Horse (?) in Pope's Head Alley, 1646–59. Probably a descendant of George Humble, who sold books at the White Horse in Pope's Head Alley. Publisher of John Speed's works, which he assigned over to William Garrett, *q.v.*, in March, $165\frac{8}{9}$.

HUNDGATE (JO), (?) bookseller in London (?), 1642. This name is found on political pamphlets in 1642. No address is given.

HUNSCOT (JOSEPH), bookseller in London; Stationers Hall, 1624–60. Son of John Hunscot, of Wardenton, co. Oxon. Apprentice to Thomas Ensor for eight years from March, 1604. [Arber, ii. 275.] Took up his freedom March 23rd, 1612. [Arber, iii. 683.] First book entry January 9th, 1624. Appointed Beadle to the Company of Stationers. Was for some time printer to the Long Parliament, in which he was succeeded by Edward Husband. Joseph Hunscot was very active in seeking out secret presses, and in 1645 he unearthed one such press at Goodman's Fields in the East end of London. In 1649 he was appointed to assist the Masters and Wardens of the Company in carrying out the Act of that year, and seized a press belonging to Edward and John Crouch and was allowed to retain it as a reward for his services. He was still living in 1660, when he appointed a deputy to carry the Company's banner on horseback at the entry of Charles II into the City, and was allowed 20*s.* for his fee. [Timperley, p. 529; *Library*, October, 1904, pp. 385 *et seq.*]

HUNT (JOHN), (?) bookseller in London (?), 1642. His name is found on a political pamphlet entitled *Most Joyful Newes by Sea and Land*, 1642. [E. 126 (11).] No address is given.

HUNT (THOMAS), bookseller in Exeter; St. Peter's Churchyard, 1640–48. Probably the son of Christopher Hunt, of Exeter, who was publishing between 1593 and 1606. His name is found on a broadside in verse entitled *Stand up to your belief.* [Lutt. Coll. ii. 209.] A contemporary news-sheet, *Mercurius Civicus*, for October 1st, 1645, states that a press had lately been brought to Exeter and that Thomas Fuller's *Good Thoughts in Bad Times* was printed at it for "malignant Hunt." Mr. Allnutt in his papers on English Provincial Presses notices some other books on sale by Thomas Hunt, notably Robert Herrick's *Hesperides*, 1648. [*Bibliographica*, vol. ii. p. 289.]

HUNT (WILLIAM), bookseller and printer in London; Pye-Corner, 1647–60. His name is first met with on the petition of the Clothiers and Weavers presented to the House of Commons in 1647. [B.M. 669, f. 11 (2).] In 1651 he added printing to his bookselling business, and jointly with Edward Griffin printed an edition of Amos Komenski's *Janua Linguarum Reserata* in 1652. His most important work was Randle Cotgrave's

French and English Dictionary, of which he printed two editions in folio, those of 1650 and 1660. In order to make the edition of 1660 as complete as possible he sent out interleaved copies of the previous edition to scholars inviting corrections and additions.

HUNTER (JOSEPH), (?) bookseller in London, 1648. His name is found on a political pamphlet entitled, *King's .... Declaration for Peace*, 1648. [E. 465 (3).] No address is given.

HUNTINGDON (THOMAS), bookseller in London; The Stars in Duck Lane, 1648–50. Publisher of school books and miscellaneous literature. In partnership with T. Slater, *q.v.*

HURLOCK (GEORGE), bookseller in London; neere St. Magnus Corner, Thames Street, 1634–46. Took up his freedom May 12th, 1624, and is believed to have succeeded to the business of John Tap. Dealt in works on navigation. In 1633 a fire destroyed a large number of houses on the north side of London Bridge, but apparently this house escaped. His name occurs in 1641 in a list of those stationers who had paid the poll tax. [*Domestic State Papers*, Charles I, vol. 483 (11).]

HUSBAND (EDWARD), printer (?) and bookseller in London; The Golden Dragon, near the Inner Temple, 1641–60. Took up his freedom March 3rd, 1634 [Arber, iii. 687], at which time he was certainly not a printer. He appears to have been one of several stationers to whom the Long Parliament farmed out its printing. In the *Calendar of Domestic State Papers*, Charles I, Addenda (March, 1625, to January, 1649), pp. 626–7, the statement is made that he was the publisher of the *Diurnal Occurrences of this great and happy Parliament*, 1641, and of a companion volume entitled *Speeches & Passages in this great and happy parliament*, 1641, but the imprints state that these works were printed for William Cooke, of Furnival's Inn. There is no mention of Husband either as printer or publisher, and the only foundation for the statement appears to be a MS. note bound in with the Burney copy of the *Diurnal*, which does not quote any authority for its assertion. As early as August 1st, 1642, the *Commons Journals* record an order made for payment to "Usbands & Francke of their account for printing divers parcels by order of this House," but this proves nothing more than that they were given the order, and Husband certainly gave the printing to others. In 1646 he published a *Collection of Orders, Ordinances and Declarations of Parliament .... from Mar 9th 1642 .... until December 1646*. Again in 1650 the Council of State ordered him to collect all the ordinances down to the Act for the trial of the King, examine them, and "have them printed," as well as all the Acts from the trial of the late King to that date. [*Calendar of State Papers, Domestic*, 1650, p. 157.] On May 5th, 1660, he was again selected, this time with T. Newcombe, as printer to the Council of State, but he disappears at the Restoration.

HUTCHINSON (WILLIAM), bookseller in Durham, 1655. Only known from the following: *Fourteen Queries and ten absurdities about the extent of Christ's Death .... London: Printed by Henry Hills for William Hutchinson bookseller in Durham, 1655.* [E. 1492 (4).]

HUTTON (GEORGE), bookseller in London; Turnstile in Holborn, 1636–41. Publisher of R. Braithwaite's *Lives of .... the Roman Emperors*, 1636, and Glapthorne's *Tragedy of Albertus Wallenstein*, 1639. [Hazlitt, H. 492; Sayle, p. 1150.]

HUTTON (HENRY), bookseller (?) in London, 1642. Only known from the imprint to a political tract entitled *A Wonderful & Strange Miracle or God's Just Vengeance against the Cavaliers .... London Printed for Henry Hutton*, 1642.

HYETT (NATHANIEL), bookseller at Winchcombe, Gloucestershire, 1653. Only known from the imprint to some copies of a pamphlet entitled *The Disputation at Winchcombe Nov. 9. MDCLIII ....* Oxford, printed by L. L. and are to be sold at Winchcombe by Nathaniel Hyett. [Hyett and Bazeley, *Bibliographer's Manual of Gloucestershire Literature*, 1896, p. 380.]

IBBITSON (ROBERT), printer in London, (1) Smithfield near the Queen's-Head-Tavern; (2) Near Hosier Lane; (3) Kings Head in the Old Bayley (?). 1646–61. Printed much of the literature of the Commonwealth period, and was joint printer with John Clowes and others of the news-sheet called *Perfect Occurrences* (1647–49). In 1653 his name was

put forward for the office of printer to the Council of State, but the appointment was given to Hills and Field. There are many references to him in the State Papers and Journals of Parliament. The third address given above is possibly that of M. Wright, *q.v.*

INMAN (MATTHEW), printer in London; Addle hill. Thames St., 1660–63 (?). Printed for James Crump and James Magnes. Dead before 1664, when he was succeeded by his widow.

INMAN ( ), widow, printer in London; Addlehill Thames Street, 1664. Succeeded her husband, Matthew Inman.

IRELAND (RICHARD), bookseller at Cambridge, 1634–52. His name appears in a list of the privileged persons in the University of Cambridge, *circa* 1624. [Bowes, *Cambridge University Printers*, p. 336.] Paid church rate in Great St. Maries from 162$\frac{4}{5}$ to 163$\frac{4}{5}$, and was churchwarden for the year 1635–6. Amongst his publications were two editions of Thos. Randolph's *Jealous Lover*, those of 1634 and 1640.

ISLIP (SUSAN), printer in London; (?) Smithfield, 1641–61. Widow of Adam Islip, who died in 1639, leaving his printing presses, etc., to Richard Hearne or Herne, *q.v.* Hearne appears to have died about 1646, when probably Susan Islip succeeded to the business.

JACKSON (EDWARD), bookseller in London, 1643. Took up his freedom December 20th, 1633. [Arber, iii. 687.] Dealt in political pamphlets.

JACKSON (JOHN), bookseller in London; Without Temple Bar, 1634–40. Took up his freedom December 20th, 1633. [Arber, iii. 687.] Associated with G. Green, T. Homer, and F. Smith, *q.v.*

JACKSON (T), bookseller in London; Starre in Duck Lane, 1623–48. Took up his freedom June 9th, 1623. [Arber, iii. 685.] Amongst his publications was Christian Ravius' *General Grammar for the Ebrew, Samaritan, Calde, Syriac, Arabic and Ethiopic tongues*, 1648. He was apparently succeeded by Thomas Huntingdon, *q.v.*, at this address.

JENKINS (THOMAS), bookseller in London; Next the Eagle and Child, Giltspur Street, 1656. Only known from the imprint to a pamphlet entitled *Englands Golden Legacy .... Written by Laurence Price. London ....* 1656.

JENNER (THOMAS), bookseller, printseller and engraver in London, (1) At the White beare in Cornewell [*i.e.*, Cornhill]; (2) At the White Beare neare the exchange; (3) South Entrance to the Royall Exchange. 1623–66. Dealer in all kinds of illustrated books and pamphlets, maps and prints. He was himself an engraver, amongst his work being portraits of Oliver Cromwell and Queen Christina of Sweden, an etching of a ship called "The Sovereign of the Seas," and presumably a set of plates for a work dealing with the twelve months.

JOHNSON (EDWARD), bookseller in London, 1642–3. Publisher of political pamphlets. [Hazlitt, *Handbook*, 526, 638.] His address has not been found.

JOHNSON (JAMES), bookseller in London, 1660 (?)–1663 (?). Publisher of political broadsides and pamphlets. His address has not been found.

JOHNSON (JOHN), bookseller in London, 1642–7. Publisher of political pamphlets. His address has not been found.

JOHNSON (MARMADUKE), bookseller and printer in London, 1660. Publisher of political pamphlets. Subsequently went to Cambridge, Massachusetts, as a printer, where he worked in the same building as Samuel Green. He died in 1675. [Plomer, *Short History*, p. 219.] He was the author of a work entitled *Ludgate what it is not, what it was*, which was entered in the Registers by Thomas Johnson, *q.v.* It was reprinted by Strype in his *Survey of London & Westminster*, 1755.

JOHNSON (SALOMON), bookseller in London, 1641. Only known from the imprint to a pamphlet entitled *The Generous usurer Mr. Nevell.* [Hazlitt, *Handbook*, 415.]

JOHNSON (THOMAS), printer in London, (1) Key or Golden Key, St. Paul's Churchyard, 1661–4; (2) White Cock, Rood Lane, Margaret Pattens (St. Dunstans in the East), 1660–6 (1642–77). In the survey taken in 1668 he is returned as having two presses and three workmen.

[Plomer, *Short History*, p. 226.] In April, 1666, he was imprisoned in Ludgate for printing a book that offended the censor, and was bound over in £500 to be of good behaviour. [*Domestic State Papers*, Charles II, 155, 70.] In 1659 he entered in the registers a work entitled *Ludgate what it is not, what it was, Or a full discovery and description of the nature and quality, orders and government of that Prison. By Mr. Johnson Typograph a late prisoner there.* [Stationers' Registers, Liber F, p. 156.] This was written by Marmaduke Johnson, printer. A list of books printed and sold by Thomas Johnson in 1658 occupies sigs. E e 5–8 in T. Polwhele's *Treatise of Self Denial*, 1658. [E 1733.] It consists of 36 works on various subjects, arranged in sizes, the titles being set out in full.

JOHNSON (W), bookseller in London, 1642. Publisher of political pamphlets. His address has not been found.

JONES ( ), bookseller at Worcester, 1663. Mentioned in an advertisement of patent medicines in *The Intelligencer* and *Newes* of that year.

JONES (JOHN), bookseller in London, (1) Near to the Pump in Little Britain; (2) Royal Exchange in Cornhill. 1658–65. Publisher of political pamphlets and broadsides. Died August 9th, 1665. [Smyth's *Obituary*, p. 64.]

JONES (RICHARD), bookseller in London; Jermins Yard, Aldersgate Street, 1666. Mentioned in the Hearth Tax Roll for the half-year ending Lady Day, 1666. [P.R.O. Lay Subsidy $\frac{252}{32}$.]

JORDAN (TOBIAS), bookseller in Gloucester, 1644–64. Sheriff of Gloucester in 1644 and Mayor in 1659. [Bibl. Glouc., pp. liii, clvi.] His name is found on a broadside entitled *A Perfect and most useful table to compute the year of our Lord*, 1656, which was to be sold in London at the shop of Master Michell in Westminster Hall. [B.M. 669, f. 20 (32).] On September 13th, 1664, a warrant was issued to certain Aldermen of Gloucester to search his house for seditious books and papers. [*Domestic State Papers*, Charles II, vol. 102, 51.]

JOYCE (GEORGE), bookseller in London; Westminster Hall, 1662. Advertisement of patent medicine in the *Kingdoms Intelligencer* for that year.

JUNIUS (JAMES), *see* Young (James).

KELS (R.), (?) bookseller in London, 1653. Only known from the imprint to a broadside entitled *Lillies Banquet, or the star gazer's feast. London: Printed for R. Kels*, 1653.

KEMBE (ANDREW), bookseller in London, (1) By St. Margaret's Hill in long Southwarke, 1636; (2) St. Margaret's Hill in Southwark, 1642; (3) St. Margarets Hill, near the Talbot in Southwark. 1635–64. Took up his freedom June 7th, 1631. [Arber, iii. 686.] Under the year 1653, May 17th, Smyth records the death of "Mr. Kemm bookseller in Duck Lane." [*Obituary*, p. 34.] No books with a Duck Lane imprint and bearing Andrew Kembe's name have been found, but if the entry relates to him then the above list of imprints must be revised, and those books dated after 1653 must be held to have been published by his successor, possibly a son. A list of eight books published by Andrew Kembe in 1664 is given at the end of *Palladine of England*, 1664. [B.M. 12450, d. 7.]

KEMM ( ), bookseller in London; Duck Lane, 1653. Smyth in his *Obituary*, p. 34, under date May 17th, 1653, has the following entry: "Mr. Kemm, bookseller in Duck Lane, died." This may refer to Andrew Kembe.

KENDAL (G.), bookseller (?) in London; near the Old Bayly, 1663. Only known from the imprint to a pamphlet entitled *Merry Newes from Epsom Wells*, 1663. [Hazlitt, iii. 242.]

KEYNTON (MATTHEW), bookseller in London; Fountain in St. Pauls Churchyard, 1656. Only known from the imprint to a pamphlet entitled: Stephens (Nath.) *Plain and Easie calculation*, 1659. [Harl. 5965 (158).]

KINGSTON, or KYNGSTON (FELIX), printer in London, (1) Over against the sign of the checker, Paternoster Row, 1603 [Sayle, p. 604]; (2) In Pater-Noster-Row, at the Signe of the Gilded Cock, 1644. 1597–1651. Son of John Kingston, printer, 1553–84. Originally a member of the Company of Grocers, from which he was transferred to the Company of Stationers and admitted a freeman June 25th, 1597. [Arber, ii. 718.] According to Sir John Lambe's notes he succeeded his father in 1615, in

which year he had two presses. [Arber, iii. 699.] In 1618, in company with Matthew Lownes and Bartholomew Downes, Felix Kingston was appointed by Privy Seal one of the King's Printers in Ireland. He also held a share in the Latin stock, in which he was one of the second rank, but only paid £35 out of the £50 due from him, and subsequently withdrew from the venture. [*Library*, July, 1907, p. 290 *et seq.*] Master of the Company of Stationers, 1635–6. One of the twenty printers appointed under the Act of 1637. Mr. Sayle states that he used five devices before 1640. At the time of his death he must have been one of the oldest printers in London. For a list of books printed by him the reader is referred to Gray's *Index to Hazlitt*, p. 425. In the will of John Reeve, of Teddington, co. Middlesex, husbandman, proved on December 24th, 1621, several bequests are made to a Felix Kingston and other persons of the name of Kingston, but there is no evidence that they refer to the printer. [P.C.C. 89 Savile.] The second imprint given above occurs in Richard Bernard's *Thesaurus Biblicus seu Promptuarium Sacrum*, 1644.

KIRBY (GEORGE), (?) bookseller in London, 1642. Only known from the imprint to a pamphlet entitled *Organs Funeral*, 1642.

KIRKMAN (FRANCIS), bookseller in London, (1) John Fletcher's Head, over against the Angel-Inn, on the back side of St. Clements, without Temple Bar, 1661–2; (2) Princes Arms, Chancery Lane, 1662, 1666–8 (?); (3) Under St. Ethelborough's Church in Bishopsgate Street, 1669; (4) Ship, Thames Street, over against the Custom House, 1671; (5) Over against the Robin Hood, Fenchurch Street, near Aldgate, 1674; (6) Next door to the Princes Arms, St. Paul's Churchyard, 1678. 1657–78. Francis Kirkman was the eldest son of Francis Kirkman, citizen and blacksmith of London. In the "Preface to the Reader," in the Second Part of the *English Rogue*, printed in 1668, he gives some interesting particulars of his life. He was first apprenticed to a scrivener, but in 1656 set up as a bookseller, but "having knaves to deal with" he abandoned bookselling and confined himself to his business as a scrivener. He then lived in the East of London, possibly in Ratcliff, where his father was then living. After the Restoration he moved into the West End, probably to the house known as the John Fletcher's Head, and again set up as a scrivener and bookseller. From his boyhood he had been a collector of

plays, and had written in 1657 a dedicatory epistle to an edition of Marlowe's *Lust's Dominion*. Kirkman was now drawn into the printing of play-books, of which, however, he declares he only printed three, which were his own copies, but his partners (*i.e.*, Nathaniel Brooke, of the Angel in Cornhill, Thomas Johnson, of the Golden Key in St. Paul's Churchyard, and Henry Marsh, of the Princes Arms in Chancery Lane, with whom he was then in business) printed the best plays then extant, though they were other men's copies. The owner of these copyrights issued a warrant, and one of Kirkman's partners, in order to avoid trouble, sold Kirkman his share, and a day or two afterwards sent the searchers to his house where they seized 1,400 play-books. At that time owing to a family bereavement, the death of his father, which took place between August, 1661, and May, 1662, he was unable to attend to business and never recovered any of the books. Being now left in good circumstances, Kirkman decided to give up business, and was induced to trust the partner who had before deceived him with the sale of his stock, but could never get any considerable return for his books. This person, who was undoubtedly Henry Marsh, died of the plague in 1665 considerably indebted to Kirkman, who, in order to recover his money, secured the estate. This accounts for the second imprint of the Princes Arms in Chancery Lane, where once more in 1666 Kirkman set up in business as a bookseller. In 1661 he had printed a catalogue of all the English plays then printed, 690 in number, and this he now issued again, augmented to 806 items. Kirkman was accused by his contemporaries of asking exorbitant prices for his plays and issuing corrupt texts, but Mr. Greg finds no confirmation of this. His name appears for the last time in the *Term Catalogue* of Easter, 1678. [W. W. Greg, *List of English Plays*; D.N.B.; Arber, *Term Catalogue*, i. 310, 554.]

KIRTON (JOSEPH), (?) bookseller in London; King's Arms, St. Paul's Churchward, 1667. Smyth, in his *Obituary*, has this entry (p. 76): "Octr. 1667. This month Joseph Kirton sometime a bookseller at ye Kings Arms in Paul's Churchyard died; buried in St. Faith's."

KIRTON (JOSHUA), bookseller in London, (1) Foster Lane, next to Goldsmith's Hall, 1644; (2) White Horse in Paul's Churchyard, 1638–46; (3) Golden-Spread-Eagle, St. Pauls Churchyard, 1649 (1638–59). Took

up his freedom November 7th, 1636. [Arber, iii. 688.] Originally in partnership with Thomas Warren. Shared with Humphrey Robinson, Richard Thrale and Samuel Thompson the copyrights of T. Whitaker, *q.v.*, consisting of 109 copies. Was one of the six stationers who in 1652 published a list of Popish books under the title of *A Beacon set on Fire*.

KNIGHT (THOMAS), bookseller in London; Holy Lamb Paul's Churchyard, 1629–60. Took up his freedom August 26th, 1627. [Arber, iii. 686.] Succeeded Clement Knight at this address. [Sayle, 591.]

KYNGSTON, *see* Kingston, F.

LAMBERD (WILLIAM), bookseller in London, 1641. Mentioned in a list of stationers dated August 5th, 1641, as paying five shillings as his proportion of the Poll Tax. [*Domestic State Papers*, Charles I, vol. 483. 11.] His address has not been found.

LAMBERT (JOHN), printer in London; Pilkington Court, Aldersgate Street, 1666. Mentioned in the Hearth Tax Roll for the half-year ending Lady Day, 1666. [P.R.O. Lay Subsidy $\frac{252}{32}$.]

LAMBERT (RICHARD), bookseller in York; The Crown Minster Yard, 1660–68. Publisher of Robert Wittie's *Scarborough Spaw*, 1660, 1667. Mentioned in an advertisement of patent medicines in the news-sheets of the year 1663.

LAMBERT (THOMAS), bookseller in London, (1) Horse-shooe, neare the Hospitall gate in Smithfield; (2) neere the Red Crosse in Little Britain. 1633–43. Publisher of ballads, broadsides, and other ephemeral literature. His first imprint is found on the title-page of a pamphlet entitled *A True Discourse of the Two infamous upstart Prophets Richard Farnham .... and John Bull*, 1636. [B.M. G. 20167.]

LAMBETH (THOMAS), stationer in London; Scroope's Court over agaynst yᵉ church in Holborne, 1661. Mentioned in the parish register of St. Andrew's, Holborn, 1661.

LANE (PHIL), (?) bookseller in London. Gray's Inn Gate, 1643. Appears to have been in partnership with Matthew Walbanck at the above address. Their names are found on a pamphlet entitled: *The Proceedings of the Commissioners* .... 1643. [E. 247 (28).]

LANGFORD (TOBY), bookseller in Gloucester, 1646. Mentioned in Hyett and Bazeley's *Manual of Gloucestershire Literature*, vol. i, p. 258, as publisher of Giles Workman's *Private men no pulpit men*, 1646.

LARKIN (GEORGE), bookseller and printer in London; Two Swans without Bishopsgate, 1666–90. Publisher of John Bunyan's *Grace Abounding*, 1666, 8°. Afterwards became a printer. [Gray's *Index to Hazlitt*, p. 435.]

LARNER (WILLIAM), bookseller in London, (1) Golden Anchor, neere Paul's Chain, 1641; (2) The Bible in East Cheap, 1642; (3) Blackmoor in Bishopsgate Street, 1650; (4) Blackmoor near Fleet Bridge, 1652 (1641–59). A noted Puritan and Independent bookseller. In 1642 he published a kind of history of Lilburne's sufferings, which he entitled the *Christian Man's Trial*. He served in the Parliamentary army, but was invalided home and resumed his trade as a bookseller at the sign of the Blackamoor in Bishopsgate Street. He assisted Henry Robinson, Robert and Richard Overton, and John Lilburne to print books secretly, and is believed to have taken an active part in the working of the Coleman Street Press, 1643 (?)–4$\frac{4}{5}$; the Martin Mar Priest Press, 1645–46; the Goodman's Fields Press, 1645, and a press in Bishopsgate Street, 1646. Larner's premises were searched on several occasions, and he was at last thrown into prison, where he remained for many months. No more is heard of him after 1659. [Plomer, *Secret Printing during the Civil War; Library*, October, 1904, p. 374 *et seq.*]

LATHAM (CHRISTOPHER), bookseller in London. 1641–2. Took up his freedom January 18th, 1636. [Arber, iii. 687.] Edward Griffin printed for him. In 1642 he was associated with T. Creake in publishing several political pamphlets. His name disappears after July, 1642.

LATHAM (GEORGE), bookseller in London, (1) Brazen Serpent, St. Paul's Churchyard; (2) Bishop's Head, St. Paul's Church Yard. 1622–58. Took up up his freedom January 31st, 1620, and the same day took over several copyrights from the widow of George Bishop. [Arber, iii. 664, 685.] On November 6th, 1628, he received another assignment from Humphrey Lownes, but these he reassigned to Robert Young on December 6th, 1630. Latham was master of the Company of Stationers in 1650. His death took place on April 21st, 1658 [Smyth's *Obituary*, p. 46], and his will was proved on May 10th following. From this it appears that he had a son George, who was at one time in partnership with him, but who had set up for himself; his daughter Ann married Edward Curle, and another daughter, Mary, was the wife of Timothy Garthwaite, *q.v.* [P.C.C. 244, Wotton.]

LATHAM (J), bookseller (?) in London; Mitre, St. Paul's Churchyard, 1661. Only known from the imprint to the Marquis of Argyle's *Instructions to a son*, 1661.

LAURENSON (G.), (?) bookseller in London, 1649. His name occurs in the imprint to a pamphlet entitled *The King of Scots his message and Remonstrance*, 1649. [E. 562 (8).]

LAWSON (THOMAS), bookseller in Edinburgh, 1645. Died May 11th, 1645. Inventory states: "His haill librarie and books withine his booth, being sold and roupeit, are estimat to the sowme of j[m] ix[c] and ffowrtie marks." [H. G. Aldis, *List of Books*, p. 116.]

LEACH (FRANCIS), printer in London; Faulcon in Shoe-Lane, Fleet Street, 1641–57. Took up his freedom June 30th, 1631. [Arber, iii. 686.] Printer of the news-sheet called *A Continuation of certain special and remarkable passages from both Houses of Parliament*. Administration of his effects was granted to his widow Joane, on July 8th, 1658. [*Admon. Act Book*, 1658.]

LEACH (JOHN), bookseller in Dublin; Castle Street, 1666. Only known from the imprint to: Bladen (Thos.), *Praxis Francisci Clarke* .... 1666. [B.M. 5063. aa. 1.]

LEACH (THOMAS), printer in London; Falcon in Shoe-Lane, Fleet Street, 1658–69. Possibly a son of Francis Leach, *q.v.* Some time in 1662 he was arrested at the instance of Sir John Birkenhead for printing seditious literature "with a base stollen edition of poor Hudibras." [*Domestic State Papers*, Charles II, vol. 49 (19); vol. 67 (30) and (161); vol. 89 (87).] In the Survey taken on July 29th, 1668, he is returned as having "one press and no more, provided by Mr. Graydon, and 1 workman." [Plomer, *Short History*, p. 227.]

LEAKE (WILLIAM), bookseller in London, (1) Crown in Fleet Street, between the two Temple gates; (2) In Chancery Lane, near the Rolls. 1635–81. Son of William Leake, stationer (1592–1634). Took up his freedom July 22nd, 1623. On June 1st, 1635, Widow Leake assigned over to him all his father's copyrights, and in 1638 he obtained from Robert Mead and Christopher Meredith the copyrights that had once belonged to Richard Hawkins. [Arber, iv. 340, 420.] Both these assignments contained several plays. The following issues contain lists of books: Beaumont and Fletcher's *Maid's Tragedy*, 1650, 53 entries; Shakespeare's *Merchant of Venice*, 1652, 16 entries; *The Fort Royal of Holy Scriptures .... by J. H.* .... 1652, number not stated; Beaumont and Fletcher's *King and No King* (sig. l. 4 verso) and Shakespeare's *Othello* (sig. M 4 verso) both issued in 1655, 46 entries; James Shirley, *The Wedding* (sig. A 1 verso) 52 entries; James Shirley, *Grateful Servant* [1660?], 53 entries; Beaumont and Fletcher's *Philaster* [1660?], 60 entries. William Leake died in 1681, and his will is in the P.C.C. (184 North). [W. W. Greg, *List of English Plays*, Appendix.]

LEE, or LEY (WILLIAM), bookseller in London, (1) Paul's Chain, 1640–46; (2) Fleet Street, neere Sergeant's Inne, at the signe of the Golden Buck, 1621–52; (3) Turk's Head in Fleet Street next to the Miter and Phoenix [over against Fetter Lane], 1627–65; (4) Lombard Street, 1659 (1623–65). Three stationers of the name of Lee or Ley took up their freedom between 1601 and 1640, *i.e.*, William Lee, son of Frauncis Lee of Southwark, apprentice to Edward Venge for eight years from March, 1603 [Arber, ii. 270]; William Lee, made free October 2nd, 1620 [*ibid.*, iii. 685]; and William Lee, made free October 2nd, 1637 [*ibid.*, iii. 688]. A William Lee, of Lombard Street, was Master of the Company of Stationers in 1659. [Arber, v. lxv.] One of these men was associated with Richard Rogers in publishing a catalogue of plays in 1656 in an edition of Goffe's *Careless Shepherdess*. [W. W. Greg, *List of Plays*. Appendix II.]

LEE (WILLIAM), junior, bookseller in London; in Chancery Lane, a little above Crown Court, next the Bell, 1658. Probably the stationer whose freedom is recorded on October 2nd, 1637.

LEGATE (JOHN), printer in Cambridge and London; Little Wood Street, 1620–58. Son of John Legate, printer at Cambridge (1588–1620). Admitted Freeman of the Stationers' Company, September 6th, 1619. [Arber, iv. 45.] Appointed printer to the University of Cambridge by Grace, July 5th, 1650, in succession to Roger Daniel, *q.v.* His patent was cancelled for neglect October 10th, 1655, after which he appears to have come to London and settled in Little Wood Street. Smyth in his *Obituary*, p. 49, has this entry, "Nov[r]. 4th 1658, Mr. Legat in Little Wood Street, printer, once printer at Cambridge, since distempered in his senses, died." [R. Bowes, *Biographical Notes on the University Printers*, p. 306.]

LEIGH (JOSEPH), bookseller in London; Upper end of Bassinghall Street, near the Naggs-Head-Tavern, 1662–5. Publisher of broadsides and medical tracts. [Bibl. Lind., 95; Hazlitt, iii. 28.]

LEWIS (STEPHEN) and (THOMAS), booksellers in London; Shoe-Lane, at the signe of the book-binders, 1657–8. Their names are found in the following work: H. Bold's *Wit a sporting in a pleasant grove of new fancies*, 1657.

LEY (WILLIAM), *see* Lee (W.).

LEYBORNE, or LEYBOURN (ROBERT), bookseller and printer in London, (1) Star, Cornhill; (2) Monkswell Street in Lambes Chappel neer Criplegate. 1645–61. Began as a bookseller and publisher of political pamphlets. Printer of the news-sheet called the *Moderate Intelligencer*, 1647–8. In partnership with William Leyborne, or Leybourn, and printed numerous scientific and mathematical books.

LEYBORNE, or LEYBOURN (WILLIAM), bookseller, printer, and mathematician in London; Monkswell Street Cripplegate, 1645–65. Possibly a brother of Robert Leyborne, with whom he was in partnership as a printer from about 1651, and carried on the business until the year 1665. Together they printed books on mathematics, and it is as a mathematician that William Leyborne is best remembered. He was the author of several works on the subject, notably one entitled *Panarithmologia, being a*

Mirror Breviate Treasure Mate for merchants . . . . a work that was long popular and better known as the *Ready Reckoner or Trader's sure Guide.* The year of William Leyborne's death is uncertain, but it is believed to have occurred about 1700.

LEYBOURN, *see* Leyborne.

LIACH (F.), (?) printer in London, 1657. *See* Hazlitt, 4th series, p. 138. Probably a misprint for Leach, F., *q.v.*

LICHFIELD (ANNE), bookseller in Oxford, 1657–69. Widow of Leonard Lichfield, senr., was for a time in business with her son, Leonard Lichfield, junr.

LICHFIELD, or LITCHFIELD (LEONARD), printer in Oxford; Butcher Row [Queen's Street], 1635–57. Son of John Lichfield, and succeeded his father as University printer in 1635. He was a staunch Royalist, and was described in Puritan tracts as the "malignant printer." About 1643–4, he was churchwarden of St. Martin's (Carfax) Church. His printing office was destroyed in the great fire that broke out on October 6th, 1644. His imprint was frequently forged for books printed in London. Amongst the curiosities of his press is an imperfect copy of part of the Epistle of Barnabas in Greek and Latin belonging to an edition printed in 1642. The remainder of the edition was entirely destroyed in the fire, and this copy owes its preservation to the fact that it was wrongly imposed and is supposed to have been taken home by the printer or compositor. [Madan, *Chart of Oxford Printing*, p. 40.] Lichfield died in 1657.

LICHFIELD (LEONARD), junr., bookseller in Oxford. Son of Leonard Lichfield, senr. On the death of his father in 1657 he and his mother, Anne Lichfield, were appointed University printers.

LILLIECRAP, or LILLIECROP (PETER), printer in London, (1) Crooked Billet on Addle Hill; (2) The Five Bells near the church in Clerkenwell Close. 1647–72. Son of Peter Lillicrap, of Queatheack, co. Cornwall. Apprentice to Miles Fletcher, or Flesher, for seven years from April 5th, 1647. At the outbreak of the Civil War he made a discovery of arms, hidden by a Parliament man, and gave information to the High Sheriff of Cornwall, by whom they were seized. Lilliecrap afterwards served in the

Royalist army and was wounded and taken prisoner four times. On the expiration of his apprenticeship he set up for himself as a printer, but was watched with suspicion by the Parliamentary party, and the May before Cromwell died his press was seized by the official printer, Henry Hills, and he was sent a prisoner to the Tower for printing Walter Gostello's *Coming of God in Mercy and Vengeance.* He was in trouble again in 1663 for printing *Farewell Sermons* and other seditious literature, but was discharged from custody after a few weeks. Lilliecrap succeeded Daniel Maxwell as printer of the news-sheet *Mercurius Publicus.* At the survey of the press made in July, 1668, he was returned as employing one press, one apprentice, one compositor and one pressman. [Plomer, *Short History*, p. 227; *Domestic State Papers*, Charles II, vol. 77 (37); 78 (37–40).]

LINCOLN (STEPHEN), bookseller in Leicester, 1663. Gave information against Nathan Brookes, of London, for dispersing a book entitled the *Year of Prodigies.* [*Domestic State Papers*, Charles II, vol. 43 (9).]

LINDESAY (JAMES), printer in Edinburgh; "On the south side of the Cow-gate a little above the College winde," 1643–9. Appointed printer to Edinburgh University. Will registered December 13th, 1649. Probably died or was incapacitated about 1646, as in that year the heirs of R. Bryson printed the University Theses. Lithgow succeeded him as printer to the University on July 5th, 1648.

LINDSEY (GEORGE), bookseller in London; Over against London Stone, 1642–8. Associated with F. Coles. Published the following amongst other political pamphlets: L. (W.), Esquire's *Courts of Justice corrected and amended*, 1642. [B.M. E. 108 (31)]; *Roundhead uncovered*, 1642. [B.M. E. 108 (9)]; *Tub-preachers overturned*, 1647. [B.M. E. 384 (7).]

LITCHFIELD, *see* Lichfield.

LITHGOW (GIDEON), printer in Edinburgh, 1645–62. In 1645 named cautioner in the confirmation of will of R. Bryson, *q.v.* Appointed printer to Edinburgh University July 5th, 1648, in succession to J. Lindesay. Wife, Isobel Harring, probably widow of R. Bryson. Died in December, 1662. Some of his ornaments formerly in possession of Hart and J. Bryson, and afterwards used by A. Anderson. [H. G. Aldis, *List of Books*, pp. 116, 117.]

LITTLEBURY (ROBERT), bookseller in London; Unicorn in Little Britain, 1652–67. One of the overseers to the will of W. Dugard. Mentioned in the Hearth Tax Roll for the half-year ending Lady Day, 1666. [P.R.O. Lay Subsidy, $\frac{252}{32}$.]

LLOYD (HENRY), printer in London, 1662–8. In the return made of the London printers in July, 1668, he is briefly stated to have one press. He printed for William Dugard an edition of Sidney's *Arcadia* in 1662, which was published by George Calvert. His address has not been found.

LLOYD (LODOWICKE), bookseller in London, (1) Next to the Castle Tavern in Cornhill; (2) The Castle in Cornhill, 1655–74. Presumably a son of Llodowicke Lloyd the poet. He is first met with as a bookseller in partnership with Henry Cripps, of Pope's Head Alley, in the publication of Henry Vaughan the Silurist's *Silex Scintillans or Sacred Poems* in 1655. They were also associated in other ventures. Amongst Lloyd's other publications may be mentioned the *Poems* of Matthew Stevenson issued in 1665, and the works of Jacob Boehme. Catalogues of books printed for him will be found at the end of John Norton's *Abel being Dead yet speaketh*, 1658. [E. 937 (6)]; and Samuel Pordage's *Mundorum Explicatio*, 1661. [B.M. 1077, d. 35.] Lloyd's name appears in the *Term Catalogues* for the last time in Easter, 1674. [Arber, *T.C.*, i. 175.] His address is somewhat of a puzzle. In the same book it will be found in the two forms given above, one on the title-page and the other on the "Catalogue of Books" at the end. Humphrey Blunden, *q.v.*, also gave his address as the Castle in Cornhill.

LOCK (T.), printer (?) in London; Sea-cole Lane. 1655–60. Printer for the Rosicrucians. [Gray's *Index to Hazlitt*, p. 458; Ames' *Collection of Title-pages*, No. 2862.]

LONDON (WILLIAM), bookseller at Newcastle upon Tyne, Bridge Foot, 1653–60. Chiefly remembered for his *Catalogue of the most vendible books in England*, published first in 1657, with a supplement down to June 1st, 1658, and a further supplement in 1660 down to Easter term of that year, issued under the title, *A Catalogue of New Books By Way of Supplement to the Former. Being such as have been Printed from that time till Easter Term.* 1660. In this he held out the expectation of another issue of the

catalogue in the following year, but nothing is known of any further supplement. In this catalogue the books were arranged in classes, Divinity coming first, and being followed by History, Physick, etc. In each class the works were arranged alphabetically under the authors. This catalogue has been absurdly attributed to William Juxon, Bishop of London, and later to Thomas Guy the bookseller. [Growoll (A.), *English Booktrade Bibliography*, p. 48.] London also printed several books against the Quakers, which were printed for him by Stephen Bulkley at York.

LOWNDES (RICHARD), bookseller in London, (1) Adjoyning to Ludgate [on Ludgate Hill]; (2) White Lyon in St. Paul's Churchyard; (3) White Lyon, Duck Lane near West Smithfield. [Arber, *Term Catalogues*, i. 557.] 1640–75. Took up his freedom September 26th, 1639 [Arber, iii. 688.] Dealt in miscellaneous literature. Amongst his publications was Francis Quarles' *Barnabas and Boanerges.* 1644.

LUGGAR, or LUGGARD (WILLIAM), bookseller in London, (1) Blind Knight, Holborn; (2) Upon Holborn Bridge; (3) Postern by the Tower. 1599–1658. Apprentice with Henry Carr. Took up his freedom July 21st, 1597. Publisher of mathematical and nautical books. In partnership with William Fisher, *q.v.* Died in 1658. [Smyth's *Obituary*, p. 47.]

LUNNE (ROBERT), bookseller in London; Next the Old Crane, Lambeth Hill [at the end of old Fish Street], 1641–6. Took up his freedom June 15th, 1627. [Arber, iii. 686.] Publisher of George Chapman's play, *Bussy D'Amboise*, 1641, 1646.

MABB (RALPH), bookseller in London; Greyhound St. Paul's Churchyard, 1610–42. Son of John Mabb, goldsmith of London. Apprentice to William Leake for eight years from Christmas, 1603. Took up his freedom January 16th, 1610. [Arber, ii. 269; iii. 683.] Amongst his publications may be mentioned the first edition of John Gwillim's *Display of Heraldrie*, and a play called *The Spanish Bawd*, by James Mabbe.

MABB (THOMAS), printer in London, (1) Ivy Lane; (2) St. Pauls Wharf, next doore to the signe of the Ship [neer the Thames], 1650–65. Thomas Mabb is first found in partnership with A. Coles, the earliest book in which their joint imprint is found being Alexander Ross's translation from John

Wallebius, entitled *The Abridgment of Christian Divinitie*, an octavo printed in 1650. Their office was furnished with a large assortment of type in all sizes, which will bear favourable comparison with that in use in other London printing offices at that time. The partnership appears to have been dissolved some time after August 12th in the following year, and Thomas Mabb is afterwards found printing alone. He was employed by many of the London booksellers, amongst others Henry Atkinson, J. Playfere, W. Sheares, J. Starkey, E. Thomas, and M. Young. In 1663 he is found printing books in conjunction with Richard Hodgkinson. Thomas Mabb was one of the chief witnesses against his brother printer, John Twyn, of Cloth Fair, who was executed at Tyburn for printing a book against the Government, and he afterwards printed an official account of the trial. Amongst other books that came from his press may be noticed Richard Kilburne's *Brief Survey of the County of Kent*, 1657; R. Fletcher's translation of *Martials Epigrams*, 1656; Jo. V. Belcamp's *Consilium & Votum Pro Ordinanda & Stabilienda Hibernia*, 1651, a folio of 38 pages, containing proposals for the settlement of Ireland in the interests of the Adventurers; and John Tatham's *London Tryumphs*, 1658 and 1661, being the author's account of the pageant in connection with the Lord Mayor's annual procession. Mabb probably fell a victim to the Plague of 1665, as no more is heard of him after that date.

MABORNE (F.), *see* Mawborne (F.).

MACOCKE (JOHN), printer in London; Addle or Addling Hill [Thames Street], 1645–92. First entry in the Registers April 5th, 1645. In 1660 he was appointed printer to the Parliament in conjunction with John Streator, and also held the post of printer to the House of Lords with Francis Tyton. He was associated with T. Newcombe in printing *Mercurius Publicus* and the *Parliamentary Intelligencer*. In 1664 he was in trouble for printing law books. [P.R.O. Chan. Proc. before 1714, Reynardson, B. 31, Stationers' Company *v.* Flesher.] On June 4th, 1666, he commenced a news-sheet called the *Current Intelligence*. When the survey of the press was made in 1668 he was found to have three presses, three apprentices and ten workmen; it was, in fact, one of the largest printing houses in London. Macocke was Master of the Stationers' Company in 1680, to which at his death he left a silver cup. [Timperley, p. 575.]

MAGNES (JAMES), bookseller in London; Russell Street near the Piazza in Covent Garden, 1660–79. Publisher of plays and novels, succeeded in 1679 by M. Magnes, probably his widow. [Arber, *Term Catalogues*, i. p. 557.]

MALPAS (JOAN), bookseller (?) at Sturbridge [*i.e.*, Stourbridge] in Worcestershire, 1661. Found in the imprint to the following pamphlet: *Monarchiæ Encomium est sceptrum sive solium Justitia Stabilitum, or A congratulation of the King's Coronation . . . . By Tho. Malpas, Preacher of the Gospel at Pedmore in Worcester-shire. London, Printed by T. Leach, and are to be sold by . . . . Joan Malpas in Sturbridge in Worcester-shire*, 1661.

MAN (EDWARD), bookseller in London; Swan in St. Paul's Church-Yard, 1665. Successor to S. Man, *q.v.*, at this address. His name is found on the following book: *The Princesse Cloria or, the Royal Romance . . . . The Second Edition. London: Printed for Edward Man at the sign of the Swan in St. Pauls Church-yard.* 1665, a re-issue of the unsold copies previously published by William Brooke in 1661.

MAN (SAMUEL), bookseller in London, (1) Swan in Paul's Church yard; (2) Ivy Lane. 1616–74. Apprentice to William Welby. Warden of the Company of Stationers 1643, 1644, and Master in the years 1646, 1654 and 1658. He died in April, 1674, at the age of eighty-seven. [Smyth's *Obituary*, p. 101.] His will was dated December 28th, 1672, and mentions three sons, Thomas, James, and Edward. He left a sum of £320 in the English stock to his wife Anne, and appointed Samuel Gellibrand, *q.v.*, the overseer of his will. [P.C.C. 49. Bunce.]

MARRIOT (JOHN), bookseller in London; [White] Flower de Luce, Fleet Street [St. Dunstan's Churchyard], 1616–57. Published the works of Breton, Donne, Drayton, Massinger, Quarles, and Wither. His son, Richard Marriot, *q.v.*, was for some time in partnership with him, and eventually succeeded to the business.

MARRIOT (RICHARD), bookseller in London; Under St. Dunstan's Church in Fleet Street [White Flower de Luce], 1645–79. In partnership with his father, John Marriot, *q.v.*, for some years. On May 3rd, 1651, his father assigned over to him a large number of copyrights. Amongst his most noted publications was the first edition of Isaak Walton's *Complete Angler*, 1653, printed for him by T. Maxey.

MARSH (HENRY), bookseller in London, (1) Princes Armes at the lower end of Chancery Lane, neer the Inner Temple Gate in Fleet Street; (2) Over against the golden Lyon tavern in Princes Street; (3) Swan Alley, Ludgate Hill. 1641–65. Took up his freedom October 5th, 1635. [Arber, iii. 687.] Associated with Francis Kirkman in publishing plays. He died before the end of the year 1665, and by his will dated September 10th left everything to his mother, Susan Tyton, widow, of St. Andrew's, Holborn. His brother, Michael Marsh, administered the will, but Kirkman took over the business. A list of books on sale by Marsh in 1661 occupies the last three pages of Montelion's *Don Juan Lamberto*, 1661, 4°. Amongst the folios was Ed. Grimstone's edition of *Polybius*; amongst the quartos, Walker's *History of Independency*; and amongst the octavos, Quarles' last poems. [B.M. E. 1048 (6); P.C.C. 100. Hyde.]

MARSHALL (JOHN), bookseller in London; Hand and Pen in Corn-hill over against the Royall Exchange, 1646. William Bentley, *q.v.*, printed for him Dr. Peter Chamberlen's *Voice in Rhama . . . . London*, 1647. [E. 1181. (8).]

MARTIN (EDWARD), bookseller in Norwich; Upper Half Moone in the Market Place, 1646. His name is found on a pamphlet entitled *Hue and Cry after Vox Populi*, 1646. [E. 355. (13).]

MARTIN, or MARTYN (JOHN), bookseller in London; Bell in St. Paul's Churchyard, 1649–80. Partner with James Allestry, *q.v.*, and succeeded him as publisher to the Royal Society. The last entry to him in the *Term Catalogues* is in May, 1680. [Arber, *T.C.*, i., p. 398.]

MARTIN (R), bookseller in London; At the Venice in the Old Bayly, 1641. His name is found on the following work: *Antipathie betweene the French and Spaniard Englished by Robert Gentilys*, 1641.

MARTIN MAR-PRIEST PRESS. The writings of Richard Overton against the Presbyterians, under the pseudonym of Martin Mar-Priest, were printed at a secret press in Bishopsgate Street, supposed to have belonged to William Larner, between April 8th, 1645, and January, $164\frac{5}{6}$. [*Library*, October, 1904, p. 382.]

MASON (EDWARD), (?) printer in London, 1660. Found in the imprint to a pamphlet entitled *Sir Arthur Hesilrigs lamentation & Confession*, 1660. [E. 1016 (4).] The name is probably a pseudonym.

MATHEWES (JOHN), (?) bookseller in London, (?) 1647. Hazlitt, iii. p. 37, records the following: *A True Abstract of a list, In which is set down the severall entertainments allowed by His Majesty to the Officers and other souldiers of his Army . . . . London, Printed for John Mathewes* [about 1647].

MATTHEWS (THOMAS), bookseller in London, (1) ad insigne Galli Gallinacei in cœmeterio Paulino juxta portam Borealem minorem; (2) At the Cock in St. Pauls Church-Yard; (3) White Horse in St. Paul's Church yard, 1651–7. Published amongst other things in 1652 an edition of Ant. Buscher's *Ethicæ Ciceron.*, of which the first edition was printed at Hamburg in 1610. [Schweiger, *Handbuch der classichen Bibliographie*, 1832, p. 252.] The title-page of Matthews' edition is preserved amongst the Ames Collection (No. 2254), but no copy of the book has been seen.

MAWBORNE, or MAWBURNE (FRANCIS), bookseller in York, 1662–6. This bookseller was doubtless in business some years before his name appears in the imprint to the Visitation sermon printed for him by Stephen Bulkley, the York printer, in 1663. In 1666 Mawburne and Bulkley were arrested, the one for printing seditious papers, and the other for selling foreign printed Bibles and seditious papers. Mawburne petitioned Lord Arlington for release from custody, and one John Mascall wrote a letter to Secretary Williamson, dated October 15th, on behalf of the prisoners, in which he described the bookseller as "quiet but weak in business," who "would not wilfully disperse any unlicensed book or pamphlet." On giving bond for his good behaviour Mawburne was released after a few weeks' imprisonment. [*Domestic State Papers*, Charles II, vol. 175 (28); *Library*, January, 1907.]

MAXEY (THOMAS), printer in London; Bennet Paul's Wharf, Thames Street, 1637–1657. Took up his freedom October 2nd, 1637. [Arber, iii. 688.] First book entry June 23rd, 1640. Amongst the famous books that passed through his press was Izaak Walton's *Complete Angler*, 1653, which he printed for R. Marriot. Maxey also printed for William Weekly, bookseller of Ipswich, *q.v.* His name is found in the Churchwardens' books of St. Bennet from 1655. His will was dated January 2nd, $165\frac{6}{7}$, and proved on the 20th of the same month. He left his estate to his wife Anne, who succeeded him in the business. A son Jonathan is also mentioned, and legacies were left to his servants [*i.e.* apprentices] David Maxey, Thomas Putnam, William Godfrey. [P.C.C. 3. Ruthen.]

MAXEY (ANNE), printer in London; Bennet Paul's Wharf, 1657. Widow of Thomas Maxey. Printed several works for William Weekly, bookseller at Ipswich.

MAXWELL (ANNE), printer in London; Thames St. near Baynards Castle, 1665–75. Widow of David Maxwell. In the survey made on July 29th, 1668, she is returned as having two presses, no apprentices, three compositors and three pressmen. [Plomer, *Short History*, p. 227.]

MAXWELL (DAVID), printer in London; Thames Street, near Baynard's Castle, 1659–65. His name appears in the Churchwardens' books of St. Bennet, Paul's Wharf, from 1658–63. Published a newspaper called *Mercurius Veridicus* on June 12th, 1660, but when only two numbers were issued it was stopped by order of the House of Commons. Maxwell died about 1665, when the business passed to his widow, Anne Maxwell.

MAYNARD (JOHN), bookseller in London; George in Fleet Street, 1641. Took up his freedom July 20th, 1635. [Arber, iii. 687.] Associated with Timothy Wilkins in the publication of the writings of John Wilkins, Bishop of Chester. [Hazlitt, ii. 494, 644.]

MEAD (ROBERT), bookseller (?) in London; (?) Crane in St. Paul's Churchyard. [Ch. Meredith's house], 1617–56. Son of Thomas Mead, of Weston, co. Somerset, husbandman. Apprentice to John Standish for nine years from Michaelmas, 1599. Took up his freedom October 3rd, 1608. [Arber, iii. 683.] Warden of the Company of Stationers, 1638, 1642; Master of the Company, 1644, 1645, 1649. In company with Christopher Meredith took over all the copyrights of Richard Hawkins, but they transferred them to William Leake a few months later. [Arber, iv. 420, 452.] No book has been found bearing Mead's name in the imprint.

MEARNE (SAMUEL), bookseller and bookbinder in London; Little Britain, 1655–83. The first heard of Samuel Mearne is in 1655, when in company with Cornelius Bee, *q.v.*, and W. Minshew, he was granted a pass to go to Holland [*Domestic State Papers*, 1655, p. 598]. In 1659 he entered a book in the Registers of the Stationers' Company entitled *Meditations in Three Centuries*, by the Rev. Henry Tabb, so that he was clearly in business as a bookseller at this time. He was appointed a searcher under the Company of Stationers at the Restoration, and an interesting series of papers dealing with this part of his work will be found in the Hist. MSS. Commn. Report 9 [Appendix, p. 72 *et seq.*] Mearne also held a share in the King's Printing Office. [*Library*, N.S., October, 1901, p. 373.] At the desire of Charles II he purchased the collection of pamphlets made by the bookseller George Thomason, but does not appear to have been paid for them, and they were subsequently sold by his successors to King George III. It is, however, chiefly as a bookbinder that Samuel Mearne is remembered. In 1660 he received a patent as bookbinder to Charles II for life at an annual fee of £6 per annum, and several of his accounts for binding books are preserved among the Wardrobe accounts at the Public Record Office. From these it appears that he generally bound his books in red or black Turkey leather. He executed some very choice bindings, the best known being those described as the "cottage" design. Samuel Mearne died in 1683, and his will is in the Prerogative Court of Canterbury. [C. Davenport, *Samuel Mearne, Binder to K. Charles II.* Publications of the Caxton Club. Chicago, 1906.]

MEIGHEN (MERCY), bookseller in London, (?) Under St. Clements Church [Strand], 1642–54. Widow of Richard Meighen. In partnership with G. Bedell. In 1650 Thomas Collins was taken as third partner. The retirement or death of M. Meighen in 1654 caused some confusion. Gabriel Bedell's name is found in connection with R. Marriot and T. Garthwaite, and the imprint J. Crook, G. Bedell & Partners is held to refer to this house, which before the end of the year became Gabriel Bedell & T. Collins.

MEIGHEN (RICHARD), bookseller in London; Under St. Clements Church [Strand], 1615–41. Is found in partnership with Ephraim Dawson, W. Lee, and D. Pakeman in the publication of law books early in 1641, but he

died before the close of this or early in the succeeding year, administration of his goods being granted to his widow, Mercy Meighen, on March 21st, $164\frac{1}{2}$.

MELVILL (DAVID), bookseller in Aberdeen, 1622–43. Buried February 8th, 1643. Son, Robert Melvill. All his books that have been found were printed for him by E. Raban. [H. G. Aldis, *List of Books*, p. 117.]

MEREDITH (CHRISTOPHER), bookseller in London; Crane in St. Paul's Churchyard, 1629–53. Took up his freedom October 4th, 1624. [Arber, iii. 686.] Was associated at one time and another with Edward Brewster, Robert Mead, and Philemon Stevens. Dealt chiefly, if not wholly, in theological books. He died on May 19th, 1653. [Smyth's *Obituary*, p. 34.] His will, dated January 24th, 1652, was proved on September 1st, 1653. He left no son, and bequeathed his copyrights to his brother-in-law, Andrew Kembe, *q.v.* His two houses in St. Paul's Churchyard, the one he occupied (The Crane), and the one occupied by Francis Egglesfield (The Marigold), which he had purchased of Thomas Man, were left to the Company of Stationers (1) To provide an annual sum of £10 to be lent to poor freemen of the Company; (2) To provide bibles for his tenants of the manor of Kempsey, co. Worcester, and school books for the use of the school there. Meredith also owned the house in Paternoster Row called The Chequer. Philemon Stephens, John Legate, and Andrew Kembe were named as executors in the event of the death of the executors nominated [P.C.C. 229. Brent.]

MERREALL (ALEXANDER), bookseller in London; White Hart and Bear in Bread Street, 1662. Mentioned in an advertisement of the Welsh bible in octavo, in *Mercurius Publicus*, February 6th, $166\frac{1}{2}$.

MICHAEL, *see* Mitchel (M.).

MILBORNE, or MILBOURNE (ROBERT), bookseller in London, (1) At the Great South Door of Pauls, 1623–6. [Sayle, 930]; (2) The Greyhound, Paul's Churchyard, 1628–35. [Sayle, 930]; (3) Unicorn, near Fleet Bridge, 1636–9; (4) Holy Lambe in Little Britain, 1641; (5) Britains Burse (?) [New Exchange, Strand]. 1618–41. Took up his freedom March

1st, 1617. [Arber, iii. 684.] He died at the end of 1642 or the beginning of 1643, as on February 23rd in the latter year thirty-four of his copyrights were transferred to Thomas Dainty, and by him re-assigned to the widow of Ch. Meredith. [Stationers' Registers, Liber D.]

MILBOURNE (THOMAS), printer in London; Jewin Street [Aldersgate Street], 1659–67. Took up his freedom July 7th, 1634. [Arber, iii. 687.] Was in trouble in 1666 for printing *The Catholic Apology*. [*Domestic State Papers*, Charles II, vol. 182 (68, 69).] He made overtures for printing the weekly *Gazette*, and undertook that a new fount of type should be cast for it. In the survey taken on July 29th, 1668, he was returned as having two presses, no apprentices and two workmen.

MILLER (ABRAHAM), printer in London; Blackfriars, 1646–53. Eldest son of George Miller. He succeeded to the business on the death of his father in 1646. Printed, amongst others, for E. Dod, Nath. Ekins, William Lee and Christopher Meredith.

MILLER (GEORGE), printer in London; Blackfriars, 1601–46. Son of George Miller, of Kettering, co. Northampton, schoolmaster. Apprentice to Richard Field, successor to Thomas Vautrollier, for seven years from Michaelmas, 1604. [Arber, ii. 281.] Field at his death left him a bequest of twenty shillings to purchase a ring. [Plomer, *Wills*, p. 51.] George Miller and Richard Badger afterwards purchased the business. [Arber, iii. 703.] George Miller died before October 8th, 1646, on which day his will, dated July 20th preceding, was proved in the Prerogative Court of Canterbury. [P.C.C. 147. Twisse.] In it occurs this passage: "*Item* I give to my sonne Abraham the lease of my house in the Blackfriars with the letter and presses copies and all other utensils belonginge to the printinge house to enter all these immediately after my decease." Miller had four other sons, William, John, Symon, and George, all of whom except John are found as booksellers. The will also mentions a daughter Martha, a brother William, and sisters Elizabeth Coe, Ellen Brewster, Elizabeth Archer, and Sarah Foster, the residue being left to his wife Anne. Amongst the witnesses was John Clarke, probably the bookseller of that name.

MILLER (GEORGE), junior, printer in London, 1665. His imprint is found in John Webster's *The White Devil*, 1665. [B.M. 644 f. 76.] He was probably the son of George Miller, printer at Blackfriars.

MILLER (JAMES), bookseller at Edinburgh, (1) In the Cowgate, at the sign of S. John the Divine, at the foot of the Colledge-wynd', 1665; (2) On the North side of the street against the Crosse, at the sign of S. John the Divine, 1671. (1665–72). One of the six booksellers who in 1671 appealed against A. Anderson. Will registered August 2nd, 1672. [H. G. Aldis, *List of Books*, p. 117.]

MILLER (SIMON), bookseller in London; Star in St. Paul's Churchyard, 1653–84. Son of George Miller. Apprenticed April 24th, 1645, to Andrew Crooke. Four books published by him are advertised at the end of Parivale's *Historie of the Iron Age*, 1659.

MILLER (WILLIAM), bookseller in London; Gilded Acron [acorn] in St. Paul's Churchyard, near the little north door, 1661–98. Believed to be the son William mentioned in the will of George Miller, printer at Blackfriars, who died in 1646. William Miller was an important bookseller throughout the reign of Charles II and James II. [Arber, *Term Catalogues*, vols. i. and ii.]

MILLESON (JOHN), bookseller in Cambridge; Over against Great St. Maries, 1642. Only known from the imprint to a pamphlet entitled *A Protestants account of his orthodox holding in matters of religion*, 1642. [Bowes, *Cambridge Books*, p. 29, no. 79.]

MILLION (JOHN), bookseller in London; Man in the Moon, in the Little Old Bayly, 1666. Only known from the imprint to Elkanah Settle's *Mare Clausum: Or a Ransack for the Dutch*, 1666, printed by Peter Lilliecrap, *q.v.* He appears to have been succeeded by Henry Million, possibly a son. [Arber, *Term Catalogues*, i., pp. 57, etc.]

MILLS (RICHARD), bookseller in London; Pestel and Mortar without Temple Bar, 1665–74. Last entry in *Term Catalogues*, Easter, 1674. [Arber, *Term Catalogues*, i. 171.]

MILNER (PETER) (?) bookseller in Warrington, Lancashire, *c.* 1641. In the will of James Milner, of Warrington, co. Lancashire, stationer, proved on the 18th April, 1639, occurs the following passage: "To Peter Milner my servant the half of the books in my shop in Warrington and all such patternes, workloomes, and colers wch I use to paint and drawe worke withall." [*Transactions* of the Historic Society of Lancashire and Cheshire, Vol. 37, pp. 67–115; *Booksellers and Stationers in Warrington, 1639–1657.* By W. H. Rylands, F.S.A.]

MILWARD (WILLIAM), bookseller in London; Without Westminster Hall Gate, 1656. Only known from the imprint to F. Duke's *Fulness & Freeness of God's Grace*, 1656.

MINSHALL (W.), *see* Minshew (W.).

MINSHEW (WILLIAM), bookseller (? in Chester), 1655. In company with Cornelius Bee, and Saml. Mearne, he was granted a pass to go to Holland in 1655. The name may be a misreading for William Minshall, who took up his freedom July 7th, 1634. [Arber, iii. 687.] There were booksellers of the name of Minsh*u*ll in Chester some years later.

MITCHEL, or MICHAEL (MILES), bookseller in London, (1) Within the Gate [*i.e.*, Westminster Hall Gate]; (2) At the first shop in Westminster Hall, 1656–63. He was London agent for T. Jordan, of Gloucester, *q.v.*

MOND (DUNCAN), stationer at Edinburgh, *c.* 1650. "Duncan Mond, stationer in Edinburgh, had a gift of King's printer conferr'd on him, which entirely cut off Tyler." [Watson, 10.] Mr. H. G. Aldis does not confirm this statement, though he quotes it, neither has he apparently come across a single work that bears it out. [H. G. Aldis, *List of Books*, p. 117.]

MOONE (RICHARD), bookseller in London; Seven Stars in St. Paul's Churchyard neer the great north doore, 1653–5. Issued books in conjunction with John Allen, *q.v.* His mark, consisting of a play upon his name, will be found amongst the Bagford fragments. [Harl. 5963 (75).] There was also a Richard Moon or Moone, bookseller in Bristol, who may be identical with the above.

MOONE, or MOON (RICHARD), bookseller in Bristol; Winn Street, 1661–3. In 1663 he was imprisoned for selling seditious literature. Letters were found on his premises from Thomas Brewster and S. M., probably Simon Miller, with whom he admitted having dealings, as well as with Eliz. Calvert, and other London booksellers. [*Domestic State Papers*, Charles II, vol. 81, No. 73, 73 i., ii., iii.] He may be identical with the Richard Moone, bookseller in London, 1653–5.

MOORE (JOSEPH), bookseller in London; Little Britain, 1657–67. Only known from the imprint to a pamphlet entitled *Killing is Murder* .... London. Printed for Joseph Moor .... 1657. [Hazlitt, ii. 150.] There are several stationers of the name of Moore mentioned in the *Transcripts* [Arber, v. 254.]

MOORE (SUSANNA), bookseller in Bristol, 1667. Is mentioned in an information laid by the Mayor of Bristol as having received certain books relating to the Fire of London from Elizabeth Calvert. [*Domestic State Papers*, Charles II, vol. 209 (75).]

MORDEN (WILLIAM), bookseller in Cambridge, 1652–79. Buried March 9th, 167$^{8}_{9}$, in St. Michael's Parish [Venn's *St. Michael Registers*, p. 127; Bowes' *Catalogue of Cambridge Books.*]

MORE (JOHN), Assigns of [*i.e.*, Miles Fletcher, John Haviland, and Robert Young], 1629–61. On January 19th, 15 James I [1618], letters patent were granted to John More or Moore, Esquire, for the sole printing of all books of the Common Law, Statutes, as well as Rastell's and Poulton's Abridgements, for a term of forty years, on the expiration of the patent previously held by Thomas Wight and Bonham Norton, which expired on March 10th, 162$^{8}_{9}$. Whether or not More himself actually printed is uncertain, but he provided a stock of type. On May 1st, 1629, he assigned over all his printing rights to Miles Fletcher and his partners John Haviland and Robert Young, for an annual payment of £60 and a third of the profits. John More died on August 17th, 1638, leaving this annuity to his daughter Martha, the wife of Richard Atkyns, *q.v.* This legacy was the subject of a law suit which ended disastrously for Fletcher, who, after the death of his partners, had made a verbal assignment of his

rights to the Company of Stationers for a cash payment of £200, but subsequently refused to carry it out, alleging that by a decree made in the Court of Chancery the patent was vested in Richard Atkyns. [P.R.O. Chancery Proceedings. Before 1715. Reynardson, Bund. 31, 126.]

MORGAN (JOHN), bookseller in London; Old Bayly, 1642. Only known from the imprint to John Taylor's *Heads of all fashions .... London, Printed for John Morgan, to be sold in the Old-baily, 1642.* [Hazlitt, H. 601.]

MORGAN (JOHN), printer (?) in London, 1660. Hazlitt, ii. (107), records *The Royal Pilgrimage .... By an Eye-witness. London, Printed by John Morgan*, 1660.

MORGAN (THOMAS), bookseller (?) in London, 1660. Only known from the imprint to a pamphlet entitled *Short Representation performed before the Lord General Monk*, 1660.

MORGAN (W), bookseller (?) in London; Near the Blue Boar Ludgate Street, 1661. In Mr. G. J. Gray's Index to Hazlitt there is a reference under this name, but it appears to be a misprint.

MORISON (JOHN), bookseller in Glasgow, 1659–62. One of the debtors in Lithgow's inventory, 1662. [H. G. Aldis, *List of Books*, p. 117.]

MORTLOCK (HENRY), bookseller in London, (1) Phœnix in St. Paul's Churchyard; (2) White Hart in Westminster Hall. 1660–1702. Chiefly a publisher of theological literature.

MOSELEY (ANNE), bookseller in London; Prince's Arms, Paul's Churchyard, 1661–4. Widow of Humphrey Moseley.

MOSELEY (HUMPHREY), bookseller in London; Princes Arms St. Paul's Churchyard, 1630–61. Conjectured to be a son of Samuel Moseley, a Staffordshire man, who was a stationer in London. [Arber, ii. 249; iii. 683.] Took up his freedom May 7th, 1627. [*ibid.*, iii. 686.] His first book entry May 29th, 1630. He became the chief publisher of the finer literature of his age. He published the first collected edition of Milton's Poems, as well as the works of Cartwright, Crashaw, D'Avenant, Denham,

Donne, Fanshaw, Howell, Vaughan, and Waller. He died January 31st, 1660-61, and was buried in St. Gregory's. By his will he appointed his wife Anne and his only daughter Anne his executors, and bequeathed £10 for a bowl to the Stationers' Company. [D.N.B.] An interesting list of books sold by him in 1640, with dates of publication and prices attached, is amongst the *State Papers*, Charles I, vol. 478, no. 16. This consists of 76 items, the greater part being plays, and the average price was sixpence apiece. Printed lists of his publications were issued with many of his books, of which the following have been noted: Sir Aston Cokain's *Dianea*, 1654 (B.M. 12470, bb. 8), containing a list of 180 works, and Richard Brome's *Five New Playes*, 1653 (B.M. E. 1423), which has an added sheet containing 135 items.

MOTTERSHEAD (EDWARD), printer; St. Bennet, Paul's Wharf [near Doctors Commons], 1641-65. Took up his freedom January 20th, 1640. [Arber, iii. 688.] In the Churchwardens' Books of St. Bennet, Paul's Wharf, he is described as cousin germane to Thomas Mottershead of that parish. In partnership with T. Ratcliffe, *q.v.* In 1664 he was arrested at the instance of the Company of Stationers for illegally printing law books. [*Chan. Proc. Before 1714*, Reynardson, bundle 31, Stationers' Co. *v.* Flesher.]

MOULE (GREGORY), bookseller in London; Three Bibles in the Poultry, under St. Mildreds Church, 1649-51. In partnership with T. Brewster in the publication of theological, political, and miscellaneous literature. Moule's name is lost sight of at the end of 1651.

MOULTON (CHARLES), bookseller (?) in London, 1663. Only known from the imprint to: Carleton (Mary), *Historicall Narrative*, 1663. [Hazlitt, iii. 30.]

MOULTON (W.), bookseller (?) in London, 1642. Only known from the imprint to a pamphlet entitled: *His Maiesties Letter, To the Lord Mayor and Aldermen of the Citie of London .... London: Printed for Tho. Hewer and W. Moulton*, 1642. His address has not been found.

MOXON (JAMES), printer in London; (?) Upper end of Hounsditch neere Bishop's Gate, 1647-50. Was evidently a relative, presumably a brother, of Joseph Moxon the typefounder. Their joint names occur in the imprint to a broadside entitled: *Victories obtained .... both by land and sea .... London, Printed by James Moxon and Joseph Moxon for Tho. Jenner .... 1647* [January 23rd.] [B.M. 669, f. 10 (112).]

MOXON (JOSEPH), printer and typefounder in London, (1) Upper end of Houndsditch neere Bishop's Gate; (2) Atlas, by St. Michiel's Church in Corn-hil; (3) Atlas on Ludgate Hill neer Fleet Bridge; (4) Atlas in Warwick Lane; (5) Atlas, Russell Street, Westminster; (6) Westminster Hall, right against the Parliament Stairs. 1647-94. Born at Wakefield, in Yorkshire, August 8th, 1627, and brought up to the trade of a mathematical instrument maker. In 1647 he and James Moxon, possibly a brother, were established in London as printers, for their joint names are found on a broadside entitled *Victories obtained ... both by land and sea .... London. Printed by James Moxon and Joseph Moxon in 1647*. In 1654 Joseph Moxon was living at the sign of the Atlas in Cornhill, and in 1659 he added typefounding to his other callings. He issued his first specimen sheet in 1669. His foundry was fitted with a large assortment of type, mostly from Holland, and included a fount of Irish type. His work as a printer was poor, and he is best remembered for his useful treatise on printing and typefounding, which formed the second part of the *Mechanick Exercises*, and is still a standard work on both these subjects. The date of Joseph Moxon's death is unknown.

MYN, or MYNNE (FRANCES), bookseller in London; St. Paul, Little Britain, 1663-65. Son of Richard Myn, or Mynne. Smyth in his *Obituary*, p. 69, records under date of October 12th, 1665, "Fran. Myn bookseller in Little Britain, son of Richard Myn, buried ex peste."

MYN, or MYNNE (RICHARD), bookseller in London; St. Paul, Little Britain, 1628-50. Took up his freedom June 30th, 1623. [Arber, iii. 685.] Mentioned in a list of secondhand booksellers who, in 1628, were required to send catalogues of their books to the Archbishop of Canterbury. Succeeded by his son, Francis Myn, or Mynne.

NEALAND (REBECCA), bookseller in London; Crown in Duck Lane, 1644. Was perhaps the widow of Samuel Nealand, bookseller, who was in business at the same address from 1618 to 1632. [Arber, iii. 623.] In 1644 she republished a controversial pamphlet entitled *An Historicall Narration .... concerning Gods election ....* which had been issued by Samuel Nealand in 1631 and called in at that time by order of the Archbishop of Canterbury, as containing "divers dangerous opinions." [E. 21 (10).] She is only known from the imprint to this book.

NEALAND (WILLIAM), bookseller in Cambridge, 1655-60. Several entries with his imprint occur in Bowes' *Cambridge Books* between these years. There was also a bookseller of the same name in London during the same period, who may be identical.

NEALAND (WILLIAM), bookseller in London; Crown in Duck Lane, 1649-62. Probably the same as the preceding.

NEDHAM, *see* Needham.

NEEDHAM, or NEDHAM (RALPH), bookseller in London; Bell, Little Britain, 1665-72. Mentioned in the Hearth Tax Roll for the half-year ending Lady Day, 1666. [P.R.O. Lay Subsidy $\frac{252}{32}$]. He died in July, 1672. [Smyth's *Obituary*, p. 96.]

NEILE (FRANCIS), printer in London; Aldersgate Street, 1644-54. Took up his freedom September 4th, 1626. [Arber, iii. 686.] Printer of *The Weekly Intelligencer* [1651-55]. In partnership with Matthew Simmons.

NEILL (JOHN), bookseller in Glasgow, 1642-5. Named as a debtor in inventories of J. Bryson (1642), and R. Bryson (1645). The David Neill in Glasgow mentioned in Lithgow's Inventory (1662) may be a successor. [H. G. Aldis, *List of Books*, p. 118.]

NEVILL (JOSEPH), bookseller in London; Plough, St. Pauls Church Yard, 1660-64. Publisher of R. Baxter's *Treatise of self denial, 1660.*

NEVILL (PHILIP), bookseller in London; Ivy Lane, 1638-42. Son of Philip Nevill, of Smalpace, co. Chester, yeoman. Apprentice to John Grismond I. for eight years from Midsummer, 1630, who at his death in 1638 left him a bequest. [P.C.C. 169, Lee.]

NEWBERY (THOMAS), bookseller in London, (1) Over against the Conduit in Cornhil [near the Royal Exchange]; (2) Three Lions [or Three Golden Lions [Cornhill]; (3) Sweeting's Rents, Cornhill, 1653-8. Probably a descendant of Nathaniel Newbery, bookseller in Cornhill between 1616-32.

NEWCOMBE, or NEWCOMB (THOMAS), printer in London, (1) Parish of St. Bennet, Paul's Wharf, Thames Street; (2) The kings printing house in the Savoy. 1649-81. Son of Thomas Newcomb of Dunchurch, co. Warwick. Apprentice to Gregory Dexter for eight years from November 8th, 1641. [Register of Apprenticeships, Stationers' Hall.] At the expiration of his time in 1649 he married Ruth, the widow of John Raworth, printer, and succeeded to the business. In the same year, on September 1st, the Council of State ordered his committal to Newgate for printing Lilburne's *Outcry of the Young Men and Apprentices of London*, and he remained a prisoner for three weeks. [*Domestic State Papers*, 1649-50, vol. ii., Proc. of the Council of State.] After this he appears to have made his peace with the Government. He printed John Milton's *Pro populo Anglicano Defensio secunda* in 1654, and in the pamphlet entitled *The London Printers Lamentation or the Press Opprest and overprest*, he was bitterly assailed as the printer of much of the Commonwealth literature. At the Restoration he continued in favour and was associated with J. Macock in printing the public journals *Mercurius Publicus* and the *Parliamentary Intelligencer*. He also held a sixth part in the King's Printing House, and became the printer of the Oxford and London Gazettes. In 1664 he was a Common Councillor of the City, and presented a book of homilies to the Church of St. Bennet, Paul's Wharf. [Guildhall MSS., $\frac{877}{1}$.] In the survey taken on July 29th, 1668, he was returned as having three presses and a proof press, one apprentice, seven compositors and five pressmen, in other words, his was one of the largest printing houses in London at that time. [*Domestic State Papers*, Charles II, vol. 243, p. 181.] Some interesting notes about Newcombe at a later date will be found in the Appendix to the 9th Report of the Hist. MSS. Commissioners. His death took place between December 22nd, 1681, and January 11th, $168\frac{1}{2}$, when his will was proved in the Prerogative Court of Canterbury [7 Cottle.] His share in the King's Printing Office he left in trust to pay annuities to ten poor and aged workmen printers or their widows, the residue to go to his son Thomas. He bequeathed the Company of Stationers a piece of plate value £20, and left sums for the poor of Dunchurch, co. Warwick, and those of St. Bennet's, Paul's Wharf. Amongst others mentioned in the will were Henry Herringman, of St. Martin's-in-the-Fields, gent., and Henry Hills, St. Anne's, Blackfryar's, gent.

NEWMAN (DORMAN), bookseller in London, (1) King's Arms in the Poultery neer Grocer's Alley; (2) Surgeon's Arms Little Britain; (3) Ship and Anchor at the Bridge-Foot [near the Bridge Gate] on Southwark side. 1665–93. Another bookseller, the bulk of whose work lies outside the scope of this dictionary. His first imprint is found in Geo. Swinnock's *Christian Man's Calling*, 1665. The rest are given by Mr. Arber in the *Term Catalogues*.

NICHOLAS (AUGUSTINE), printer in London, 16$\frac{49}{50}$. On the 8th March, 1650, the attention of the House of Commons was drawn to a book entitled *The Doctrine of the Fourth Commandment.* Nicholas, who was examined about the matter, stated that he was servant to Gertrude Dawson, who printed the book for James Oakeford. It may be presumed, therefore, that Nicholas was a workman in her service. [*Commons Journals*, vol. 6, p. 378.]

NICHOLLS (JOHN), bookseller in London; Old Bailey, c. 1641. Possibly a brother of Thomas Nicholls.

NICHOLLS (THOMAS), bookseller in London; Bible, Pope's Head Alley, 1637–41. Died in 1641, his will being proved November 9th. In it he refers to his father and mother as still living and a brother John. He nominated his wife Susanna sole executrix, and Miles Flesher and William Hope, overseers. [P.C.C. 141, Evelyn.]

NICHOLSON (ANTHONY), bookseller at Cambridge, 1648–52. An Anthony Nicholson was christened in St. Michael's Church, Cambridge, on August 6th, 1601 (Venn, p. 4), and an Anthony Nicholson paid church rate at Great St. Mary's from 1624–5 to 1634–5. [Foster.] Three books issued by him are noticed in Bowes' *Cambridge Books*, pp. 33, 34.

NICHOLSON (JOHN), bookseller in London; Under St. Martins Church in Ludgate, 1640–2. Took up his freedom December 7th, 1635. [Arber, iii. 687.] Publisher of plays and political pamphlets.

NICHOLSON (ROBERT), bookseller in Cambridge, 1662–73. Published a Latin edition of the Book of Ecclesiastes, 1662. Possibly son, or brother, of Anthony Nicholson, *q.v.*

NICKOLSON, *see* Nicholson.

NICKSON (EDWARD), bookseller (?) in London, 1643. Only known from the imprint to a pamphlet entitled *The Actor's Remonstrance, or Complaint .... London, Printed for Edw. Nickson*, 1643. [E. 86 (8).]

NICOLLS, *see* Nicholls.

NICOLSON, *see* Nicholson.

NIDALE (JAMES), bookseller (?) in London, 1660. Only known from the imprint to a ballad entitled *The Parliament-Complement*, 1660. [Lutt. Coll. ii. 160.]

NORTON (ALICE), printer in London, 1641–2. Printer of political pamphlets and broadsides. It is not clear what relationship, if any, she bore to the other Nortons of this period.

NORTON (JOHN), printer in London, 1621–45. This is probably the John Norton who took up his freedom on July 8th, 1616. [Arber, iii. 684.] There were three stationers of this name at work in London during the first quarter of the 17th century, (1) John Norton, cousin of William Norton, and printer of Sir H. Saville's *Chrysostom*, who died in 1612; (2) John Norton, son of Mark Norton, citizen and grocer of London, apprentice to John Atkinson in 1598 and out of his time in 1605, of whom no more is heard, and (3) the subject of the present article, whose first book entry occurs in the registers on September 18th, 1621. [Arber, iv. 59.] He was in partnership with John Okes, who had succeeded to the business originally established by Thomas Judson in 1586, and in the hands successively of John Harrison the Younger, George and Lionel Snowden, and Nicholas Okes. The position of this printing house is unknown. [Arber, iii. 669 *et seq.*; *Library*, April, 1906, pp. 165, 166.] John Norton was for a time associated with Augustine Mathewes, who died in 1625

NORTON (LEONARD), bookseller in London, 1647. John Norton, the printer who died in 1612, left a legacy to his nephew, Leonard Norton [Plomer, *Wills*, p. 46], but whether he is to be identified with this bookseller is not known. His name appears in the imprint to a pamphlet entitled *Charge .... against Sir John Gayer Lord Mayor*, 1647.

NORTON (LUKE), printer in London, 1642–5. There were two stationers of this name, one of whom took up his freedom March 2nd, 1612, and the other June 1st, 1635. [Arber, iii. 683, 687.] This was probably the later man, who was in partnership with John Field, *q.v.*

NORTON (ROGER), printer in London, 1658. Smyth in his *Obituary*, p. 49, has the following entry: "Rog. Norton, printer, who married Nell Houlker, died very poore," November 27th, 1658. Whether this printer was any relation to Roger Norton of Blackfriars, *q.v.*, is not known.

NORTON (ROGER), printer in London; Blackfriars [(?) Hunsdon House], 1639–62. Son of Bonham Norton, King's Printer 1596–1635, and grandson of William Norton, of the King's Arms, St. Paul's Churchyard, 1561–93. Roger Norton took an active part in the proceedings between his father and Robert Barker the Second in the matter of the King's Printing House, and with his brother John broke into the premises by night and carried off the whole of the stock and printing materials. At the Restoration he petitioned to be appointed King's printer on the grounds that the decree made in the Court of Chancery was illegal, and that he had been of service to His Majesty during the late troubles, both by printing letters and papers and by sheltering those who came from abroad on His Majesty's service. His claim was not allowed. Roger Norton died April 1st, 1662, and his death is recorded by Smyth in his *Obituary* (p. 55): "Mr. Roger Norton printer in Blackffriers died, whose daughter my coz Dr Thos. Clutterbuck marrd." His will was proved April 7th, 1662, and by it he left to Susan his wife his house in Blackfriars excepting the workhouse [*i.e.*, the printing house] and the warehouse, which, with all his printing materials, copyrights and patents, he bequeathed to his son Roger Norton. He had another son, Ambrose, to whom he bequeathed certain lands in Somerset, and several daughters. The rest of his real estate, including lands in Stretton in Shropshire, he left to his wife Susan for life. [*Library*, October, 1901, pp. 353–57; P.C.C. 52, Laud.]

NORTON (ROGER) the Younger, printer in London; Kings printing office in Hebrew, Greek and Latin, (1) Blackfriars [(?) Hunsdon House]; (2) Clerkenwell Green; (3) Little Britain. 1662–86. Son of Roger Norton, printer, of Blackfriars, *q.v.*, and grandson of Bonham Norton. Succeeded to his father's business in 1662. His premises were burnt in the great fire, and he moved to Clerkenwell Green, and later, back to Little Britain, where he built a printing house. In the survey of the press taken in 1668, he is returned as having three presses, one apprentice, and seven workmen.

NOTT (WILLIAM), bookseller in London, (1) Ivy Lane; (2) White Horse in Paul's Churchyard; (3) Queens Arms in the Pell-Mell. 1660–84. Published a book of devotion called *Private forms of Prayer*, 1660, and Anne Wyndham's *Claustrum Regale Reseratum*, 1667. There was a W. Nott, bookseller in Oxford in 1665.

NOTT (W.), bookseller in Oxford, 1665. [Madan, *Chart of Oxford Printing*, p. 30.] He may be identical with the London bookseller, William Nott.

NOWELL (NATHANIEL), bookseller in London; Little Britain, 1664–7. Churchwarden of St. Botolph's without Aldersgate, 1664–5. Died March 9th, 166$\frac{6}{7}$. [Smyth's *Obituary*, p. 74.] His will was proved on March 26th, by which he left everything to his wife Joane. Samuel Mearne and Marmaduke Thompson were witnesses. [P.C.C. 49, Carr.]

NOWELL (WILLIAM), bookseller in Norwich, 1660–1. Published T. Brabourne's *God save the king*, 1660.

NUTHALL (JAMES), bookseller in London, (1) Over against the George, near Holborn Bridge, 1650; (2) In Fleet Street at the sign of the Hercules Pillars, 1651; (3) Minories, next door to the Dolphin, 1660. 1650–60. Publisher of mathematical, surgical and theological books. Amongst these were John Chatfield's *Trigonal Sector*, 1650 [E. 1381 (1)]; T. Vicary's *Surgions Directorie*, 1651 [E. 1265]; and Zachary Crofton's sermon, *The Pursuit of Peace*, 1660. [E. 1025 (19).]

OAKES (EDWARD), printer in London, 1663–8. Set up in business after the Act of 1663. In the survey taken on July 29th, 1668, he is returned as having two presses, no apprentices, and two workmen. [Plomer, *Short History*, p. 227.]

OAKES, or OKES (JOHN), printer in London; Little St. Bartholomews neare Smithfield, 1636–44. Son of Nicholas Okes (1606–39). Took up his freedom January 14th, 1627, and was for some years in partnership with his father. They had a large and old established business, originally founded by Thomas Judson in 1586. John Okes printed for Daniel Frere, Thomas Nabbes' tragedy of *The Unfortunate Mother*, 1640.

OAKES, or OKES (MARY), printer in London; Little St. Bartholomews [Smithfield], 1643–4. Probably the widow of John Okes.

OGILBY (JOHN), author, translator, and publisher in London; Whitefriars, 1600–76. John Ogilby was neither a bookseller nor a printer by trade, but from the facts that he was the promoter of some of the finest books issued during this period, and that he was his own publisher, and even organised lotteries for the sale of his books, he is entitled to notice. He began life as a dancing master, then became schoolmaster to the Earl of Strafford's children. During the troubles of the Civil War he lost everything, was shipwrecked on his way from Ireland, and arrived in London penniless. He proceeded to Cambridge on foot, and was there given Latin lessons by some of the scholars. He also is said to have learnt Greek about the same time. At the Restoration he was made Master of the Revels in Ireland. He was besides given the titles of "king's cosmographer" and "geographic printer." He died September 4th, 1676, and was buried in St. Bride's Church, Fleet Street. Ogilby spared no cost in the production of his books, which were printed by the best men, with the best type, and on the best paper procurable, with illustrations drawn and engraved by the first artists and engravers of the period. A magnificent example of the typography of the period is his translation of the Works of Virgil, printed by Thomas Roycroft in 1658. To facilitate the sale of his books Ogilby was allowed to establish a lottery in which all the prizes were his own works. A copy of the prospectus for one of these lotteries is amongst the Bagford fragments. During the last years of his life he devoted himself to the production of books of geography and topography. [D.N.B.]

OKES, *see* Oakes.

OLIVER (WILLIAM), bookseller in Norwich; Next door to the Castle and Lyon, 1663. Mentioned in an advertisement in *Mercurius Publicus* for the year 1663, and in the same year he published for John Winter, curate of East Dereham, in Norfolk, a sermon called 'Απλῶς και Καλως, *Honest plain dealing*, 1663. [226 g. 23 (9).]

OLTON, *see* OULTON.

OTWELL (JOHN), bookseller in London, 1642. His name occurs as the publisher of one of Pym's speeches in 1642. [E. 200 (65).]

OULTON or OLTON (RICHARD), printer in London; Near Christ-church [Newgate Street], 1633–43. Son of Elizabeth Alde or Allde by a former husband. Succeeded to the business of Edward Alde or Allde and used his device. In 1641 he was joined by G. Dexter, *q.v.*, and in the same year paid a sum of £3 as his share of the poll-tax. [*Domestic State Papers*, Charles I, vol. 483, 11.]

OVERTON (HENRY), bookseller in London, (1) White Horse without Newgate [Sayle, 1121]; (2) Entrance to Pope's Head Alley out of Lombard Street, 1629–48. Took up his freedom June 1st, 1629. [Arber, iii. 686.] Dealt chiefly if not wholly in theological literature, and was one of the syndicate including John Bellamy, A. and J. Crooke, D. Frere, J. Rothwell, R. Sergier, and R. Smith, who published the sermons of the Rev. J. Stoughton.

OVERTON (JOHN), bookseller in London; White Horse in Little Brittain, next door to Little St. Bartholomews Gate, 1667–1703. Published in 1667 an edition of Robert Fage's *Cosmography*.

OWSLEY (JOHN), printer in London; 1658–66. This printer was ruined by the fire of London in 1666. [Plomer, *Short History*, p. 225.] His imprint will be found in Robert Fage's *Description of the whole world*, 1658. [E. 1595 (3).]

OXLAD (FRANCIS), senior, bookseller in Oxford, 1665–67. [Madan, *Chart of Oxford Printing*, p. 30.] His name is found in 1665 on the following: Ryff (Peter), *Questiones Geometricæ*, 1665. [Ames Collection, 3236.]

OXLAD (FRANCIS), junior, bookseller in Oxford, 1667. [Madan, *Chart of Oxford Printing*, p. 30.]

PAGE (DIXY), bookseller in London, (1) Tower Street; (2) Anchor and Marriner in East Smithfield, near the King's slaughter house. 1664–8. In April, 1666, this bookseller, with Thos. Johnson the printer, *q.v.*, was imprisoned for dispersing seditious books, and was bound over in a sum of £500 to be of good behaviour. [*Domestic State Papers*, Charles II, vol. 155 (71).] His second address is from John Newton's *Scale of Interest*, 1668. [Harl. 5987, p. 56.]

PAGE (ROBERT), bookseller (?) in London; Barbican, Three Pigeon Alley [or Court], 1659. His name is found in the imprint to a pamphlet entitled *An ancient and true prophesie*, 1659. [E. 993 (23).]

PAINE (THOMAS), *see* Payne (T.).

PAKEMAN (DANIEL), bookseller in London; Rainbow Fleet Street, 1635–64. Chiefly a publisher of law books, some time in partnership with Ephraim Dawson, W. Lee and Richard Meighen. Died in September, 1664. [Smyth's *Obituary*, p. 61.]

PALMER (RICHARD), (?) bookseller in London, 1643. His name is found in the imprint to the following pamphlet: *Danger wherein the Kingdom of England now standeth, May 2, 1643*.

PALMER (THOMAS), bookseller in London; Crown in Westminster Hall, 1664–73. A "stationer" of this name, whose will was proved in the Prerogative Court of Canterbury [P.C.C. 50, Bath], died at Tewkesbury in Gloucestershire in March, 167$^{9}_{80}$, but he was probably a different person.

PALMER (WILLIAM), bookseller in London; Palm Tree in Fleet Street, 1660–61. Publisher for James Howell and Dr. Peter Heylyn. A list of books sold by him occurs at the end of Howell's *Parly of Beasts*, 1660.

PARIS (NATHANIEL), bookseller in London; The George in Little Britain, 1657–66. Took up his freedom October 3rd, 1639. Associated with T. Dring, *q.v.*, in publishing the Rev. John Gaule's *Sapientia Justificata*, 1657. Churchwarden of St. Botolph's without Aldersgate in the years 1665 and 1666.

PARKER (JOHN), bookseller in London, (1) The Ball, Paul's Churchyard, 1618 [Sayle, 934]; (2) The Three Pigeons, Paul's Churchyard, 1620–48 (?) 1617–48. Son of George Parker, of Honington, Warwickshire, yeoman. Took up his freedom March 1st, 1617. [Arber, iii. 684.] Parker was associated with Henry Fetherston until 1619, and in 1620 he took over the copyrights of W. Barrett which had previously belonged to Gabriel Cawood and W. Leake, amongst which were Shakespeare's *Venus and Adonis* and Lylly's *Euphues*. About this time he bought the shares of several of the adventurers in the Latin stock. Nominated overseer to the will of John Grismond, who died in 1638; Warden of the Company of Stationers, 1641, 1644, 1645; Master of the Company, 1647 and 1648. Died July 30th, 1648. [Smyth's *Obituary*, p. 26.] His will, an interesting document, was dated October 28th, 1647, and proved on August 16th, 1648. The following stationers received rings: Andrew Crooke, Charles Greene, Francis Egglesfield, Octavian Pullen, Richard and Thomas Whitaker, while Miles Fletcher was nominated one of the overseers. [P.C.C. 124, Essex.]

PARKER (PETER), bookseller in London, (1) At the end of Popes Head Alley next Lombard Street, 1665; (2) Under Creed Church, nr Aldgate, 1667. One of the publishers of the first edition of Milton's *Paradise Lost*, 1667. [Masson's *Life of Milton*, vol. vi, p. 516.]

PARKHURST (THOMAS), bookseller in London, (1) George in Little Britain, 1653–6; (2) Three Crowns at the lower end of Cheapside [near the Conduit or near Mercers Chapel]; (3) Golden Bible upon London Bridge, 1666-7. (1653–67). Dealt chiefly, if not entirely, in theological literature. A list of 25 publications on sale by him in 1657 is found at the end of the first part of S. Purchas's *Theatre of Political Flying Insects*, 1657. [B.M. 452, a. 37.] A much longer list, arranged under sizes, was issued with W. Secker's *Nonsuch Professor*, 1660.

PARRY (LEONARD), printer in London; Dogwell Court, Whitefriars, 1660–63. In partnership with Thomas Childe.

PARTRIDGE (JOHN), bookseller in London, (1) Purse Court in the Old Bailey, 1641; (2) Sun in St. Pauls Churchyard, 1644; (3) Cock in Ludgate Street, 1645; (4) Blackfriars, going into Carter Lane, 1648–9 (1623–49).

At the outbreak of the Civil War, Partridge added a trade in astrological books to his other branches of bookselling, and with H. Blunden, *q.v.*, became the publisher of the writings of William Lilly and John Booker. Thomas Brudnell did a good deal of printing for him, and after Partridge's death in 1649 brought an action against his executors to recover a sum of money which he claimed for printing certain books. [P.R.O. Chancery Proc. before 1714, Brudnell *v.* P. Stephens and L. Fawne.] The details of the account are set out in a schedule, and there is also an inventory of the stock of books owned by Partridge at his death. [*Library*, January, 1906, pp. 32–45.] Mr. Sayle states that Partridge used a device of "the sun in splendour." This was not a device, it was only an ornament, a portion of an old wooden block, just as likely to have belonged to the printer as to the publisher.

PASSENGER, *see* Passinger.

PASSINGER (THOMAS), bookseller in London; Three Bibles on London Bridge, 1664–88. Son of Thomas Passinger, of Guildford, co. Surrey. Apprentice to Charles Tyas, or Tyus, bookseller at the Three Bibles on London Bridge for eight years from July 25th, 1657. [Register of Apprenticeships, Stationers' Hall, 1606–66.] On the death of Tyas in 1664, Passinger appears to have succeeded to the business, probably by marrying the widow. He died in 1688 and his will was proved in the Prerogative Court of Canterbury. He left to his kinsman, Thomas Passinger, all his copies and parts of copies and copperplates, as well as his share of books and ballads which he had in partnership with William Thackerye of Pye Corner. He left a bequest of forty shillings to the Company of Stationers and a book of the value of forty shillings to the public library at Guildford. [P.C.C. 82, Exton.]

PATERSON (MICHAEL), bookseller in Glasgow, 1659–62. One of the debtors mentioned in G. Lithgow's *Inventory*, 1662. [H. G. Aldis, *List of books*, p. 118.]

PATERSON (WILLIAM), bookseller in Edinburgh, 1662. One of the debtors mentioned in G. Lithgow's *Inventory*, 1662. [H. G. Aldis, *List of books*, p. 118.]

PAULETT, *see* Pawlett.

PAWLETT, or PAULETT (ROBERT), bookseller in London; Bible in Chancery Lane near the Inner Temple Gate, 1660–67. Publisher of political pamphlets. [Gray's Index to Hazlitt, p. 585.]

PAWLEY (ROBERT), bookseller in London; In Fleet Street, 1661–5. His name is found on the title-page of a book entitled *A Compendious Abridgement of all statutes*, 1661. [Ames Collection, 2992.] He was associated with Henry Twyford in publishing an edition of Hugo Grotius' *De Rebus Belgicis, rendered into English by T. M.*, April 21st, 1665. He may have been a descendant of Simon Pawley, the bookseller, of the earlier part of the century.

PAXTON (EDMUND), bookseller in London; Pauls Chain, over against the Castle-tavern. 1655. His name is found in the imprint to *England's Complete Law judge*, 1655. [E. 860 (3).] An *Edward* Paxton took up his freedom June 7th, 1630. [Arber, iii. 686.]

PAYBODY, or PAYBODIE (THOMAS), printer (?) & bookseller in London; Queens Head Alley, Paternoster Row, 1642–65. Smyth in his *Obituary*, p. 69, records, "15th Octr. 1665 Tho. Paybodie a printer buried *ex peste*." His name is found in the imprint to a pamphlet entitled *An Answer .... upon some .... observations .... against his .... majesty, 1642*, which also has on the title-page a block having the letters T.P. on it, which may have been Thomas Paybody's device. [E. 108 (39).]

PAYNE, or PAINE (THOMAS), printer in London; In Goold-Smiths Alley in Redcross Street [Cripplegate], 1630–50 (?). Took up his freedom March 3rd, 1628. [Arber, iii. 686.] During the Commonwealth he was employed by the Council of State, which on September 19th, 1650, ordered twenty pounds to be given to him "as a gratuity for his sufferings by printing a book for the cause of Parliament, written by Mr. Walker." The Mr. Walker referred to was doubtless Clement Walker, the author of the *History of Independency*, but it was clearly not that book for which the printer was paid, and no further light can be thrown on the passage. [*Domestic State Papers*, Interr. 10, pp. 27–30.]

PERRY (HUGH), bookseller in London; Neere Ivy Bridge in the Strand. 1626–45. Took up his freedom December 15th, 1626. [Arber, iii. 686.] His first book entry in the registers of the Company occurs on the 19th

July, 1627 [*ibid.*, iv. 181.] On the 10th February, 163$\frac{1}{2}$, Thomas Archer assigned over to him several copyrights, in which were included Thomas Middleton's play, *The Roaring Girle*; John Marston's play, *The Insatiate Countess*, and Timberlake's *Travels* [*ibid.*, iv. 248]. Some of these Perry afterwards assigned to Henry Taunton and Francis Coles [*ibid.*, iv. 327, 336.] Between 1642 and 1645 he issued several political pamphlets, after which he is lost sight of.

PIENNE (PETER DE), printer at Cork & Waterford, Ireland, 1644–54. Printed an edition of the *Eikon Basilike* in Cork in 1649. In 1652 he is found printing at Waterford *An Act for the settlement of Ireland.* In that year an order was made by the Council for the affairs of Ireland forbidding the Commissioners of the Revenue at Waterford to pay Peter de Pienne any salary from that time. [E. R. McC. Dix, *Irish Provincial Printing prior to 1701. Library*, October, 1901, pp. 344–5.]

PIERREPOINT (THOMAS), bookseller in London; Sun in St. Paul's Churchyard, 1651–8. Issued in 1655 in conjunction with George Calvert a folio edition of Sidney's *Arcadia.* [B.M., C. 39, h. 10.]

PILKINGTON (STEPHEN), bookseller in London; Next to the Red-lyon Inne in Fleet Street, 1647. His name occurs in the imprint to a pamphlet entitled *Trodden down strength*, 1647. [B.M. 1417. a. 13.]

PITT (MOSES), bookseller in London, (1) White Hart, Little Britain; (2) Angel, St. Paul's Churchyard, over against the little North door. 1666–81. Mentioned in the Hearth Tax Roll for the half-year ending Lady Day, 1666, as a bookseller in Little Britain. [P.R.O. Lay Subsidy $\frac{252}{32}$.] Published in 1667 a *Short Account of the life and death of Pope Alexander VII.* He became one of the most important booksellers of the second half of the seventeeth century. (*See* Arber, *Term Catalogues.*)

PITTS (JOSEPH), *see* Potts (J.).

PLACE (JOHN), bookseller in London, (1) Furnivall's Inn Gate; (2) Greyhound Yard, Holborn. 1645–86. Dealer in law books. Several of his children were baptized at St. Andrew's, Holborn.

PLACE (WILLIAM), bookseller in London; Gray's Inn Gate, 1657–77. Doubtless a relative of J. Place. Also dealt in law books.

PLAYFERE (JOHN), bookseller in London, (1) White Bear in the upper walk of the New Exchange [Strand]; (2) White Lion in the upper walk of the New Exchange. 1664–5. A list of books issued by him in 1665 precedes the *Three Plays* of Sir W. Killigrew and is inserted immediately before the title to *Selindra.*

PLAYFORD (JOHN), bookseller in London; Inner Temple near the church door, 1623–86? Younger son of John Playford, of Norwich, born in 1623. Dealt chiefly in music books. Temporarily in partnership with John Benson and Zachariah Watkins, 1664–5. His printers were Thomas Harper, 1648–52; William Godbid, 1658–78; Ann Godbid and her partner John Playford the younger, 1679–83; John Playford alone, 1684–5. He was the inventor of the "new ty'd notes." In 1672 he began engraving on copper plates. The D.N.B. records no less than seventeen collections of music books published by John Playford, who was succeeded by his son Henry. [D.N.B.]

POCOCK (SAMUEL), bookseller in Oxford, 1662. His name is found in the imprint to P. Du Trien's *Manuductio ad logicum*, 1662. [Ames Collection, 3072.]

POLLARD (ROBERT), bookseller in London; Ben Johnson's Head behind the Exchange, 1655–8. Associated with John Sweeting in the publication of plays.

POPE (WILLIAM), (?) bookseller in London; Neere Essex House, 1642. A political pamphlet entitled *To the Right Honourable the Lords assembled in Parliament* .... bears the imprint *London, Printed for William Pope, and are to be sold at his shop neere Essex House, 1642.* [E. 114 (9).]

POTS, or POTTS (JOSEPH), bookseller (?) in London; In the [great] Old Baily neer the Sessions-House, 1646. His name is found in the imprint to a broadside entitled *Life and Death of the .... Earle of Essex* [October 12th], 1646. [B.M. 669, f. 10 (93).] He was perhaps a descendant of Robert Potts, who was publishing from 1621–3. [Arber, v. 259.]

POUNCET, or POUNCE (JOHN), bookseller (?) in London, (1) Lower end of Budge Row neere Canning [*i.e.*, Cannon] Street; (2) Hand and Bible lower end of Budge Row neer Dowgate. 1646–7. His name is found in the imprints to the two following pamphlets: *Certain Queries touching the ordination of ministers. By. A. W.*, *1647*, 4°, and *Vox Populi*, 1646, 4°. [Hazlitt, i. 440.]

POWEL (EDWARD), bookseller in London; White Swan, Little Britain, 1660. Mentioned in the Hearth Tax Roll for the half-year ending Lady-Day, 1666, as a bookseller in Little Britain. [P.R.O. Lay Subsidy $\frac{252}{32}$.]

POWELL (THOMAS), bookseller in London; Bethlehem [*i.e.*, the precincts of Bethlehem Hospital], 1622–41. A stationer of this name took up his freedom March 1st, 1622. [Arber, iii. 685.] He is named in a list of secondhand booksellers who, in 1628, were ordered to send catalogues of their books to the Archbishop of Canterbury. In 1641 he figures as a publisher of political pamphlets.

PRICE (JOHN), bookseller (?) in London, 1642. His name occurs in the imprint to a pamphlet entitled *Copy of the Queens Letter*, 1642.

PRICE (NEHEMIAH), bookseller (?) in London, 1660. His name occurs in the imprint to W. Prynne's pamphlet *Title of Kings proved to be Jure Devino*, 1660.

PRIDMORE (ISAAC), bookseller in London, (1) The Falcon neer the New Exchange, 1656; (2) The Falcon beyond the New Exchange in the Strand; (3) At the Golden Falcon neere the New Exchange. 1656–9. His name is first met with on an eight-leaf pamphlet entitled *Death in a New Dress, or Sportive Funeral Elegies*, published in August, 1656. [E. 885 (11).] Dealer in plays and broadsides.

PULLEYN, or PULLEIN (OCTAVIAN), the Elder, bookseller in London, (1) The Rose in St. Paul's Churchyard, 1636–66; (2) neer the Pump in Little-Brittain, 1667. Took up his freedom December 14th, 1629. [Arber, iii. 686.] First book entry February 12th, 1636 [*ibid.*, iv. 354.] He is found in partnership with Geo. Thomason from 1639 until about 1643. They occupied one of the houses built by Reginald Wolfe on the site of the charnel house on the North side of the Cathedral between the Great North Door and the church of St. Faith's, known by the name of the Rose. Next to it on the East side was the Three Pigeons, occupied by

Humphrey Robinson, while on the West was the yard of the charnel house, possibly a paved open space near the Great North Door. These premises being destroyed in the fire, Octavian Pulleyn moved into Little Britain "neer the Pump," where he issued Samuel Woodford's *Paraphrase upon the Psalms of David*, 1667. [B.M. 6, a. 3.] Meanwhile Geo. Thomason had apparently set up for himself at the sign of the Rose and Crown in another part of the Churchyard. The date of Octavian Pulleyn's death is unknown.

PULLEYN, or PULLEIN (OCTAVIAN), the Younger, bookseller in London; The Bible in St. Pauls Church yard near the little North door, 1664–7 (?). Probably son of Octavian Pulleyn the Elder. Dealer in French literature in conjunction with John Dunmore. His name is found on a pamphlet entitled *Discours d'un bourgeois de Paris*, 1665. [Ames Collection, 3265.]

PURSLOWE (ELIZABETH), printer in London; East End of Christ Church, 1633–46. Widow of George Purslowe, printer, who died in 1632.

PURSLOWE (G.), printer in London, 1664. Possibly a son of George and Elizabeth Purslowe. His name is found on E. Ford's *History of Parismus*, 1665.

RABAN (EDWARD), printer at Edinburgh, St. Andrews, and Aberdeen, 1620–58; Edinburgh, at the Cowgate, at the signe of A.B.C., 1620; St. Andrews, (1) At the signe of the A.B.C., 1620–22; (2) In the South street of the Citie, 1620; (3) Dwellinge in the Kirke Wynde, 1622; Aberdeen, dwelling upon the Market-place, at the townes Armes, 1622–49. Had also a shop at the end of the Broadgate from 1643. An Englishman. Printer to St. Andrew's University. The first printer in Aberdeen. Succeeded by James Brown in 1650. Died November–December, 1658. Device, Aberdeen City Arms. [H. G. Aldis, *List of Books*, p. 119.]

RAMSAY (PATRICK), printer at Edinburgh, c. 1660–80. Watson, pp. 10–13, says that after the death of Christopher Higgins, the Society of Stationers appointed Ramsay to be overseer of that house, and that about 1680 he set up with John Reid. No book has been found bearing Ramsay's name. [H. G. Aldis, *List of Books*, p. 119.]

RAMZEY (JOHN), Printer at the Hague, 1659. Printed Sir W. Lower's plays, *The Amorous Fantasme*, 1659, and *The Noble Ingratitude*, 1659. It seems probable that he was an exile from Scotland.

RAND (SAMUEL), bookseller (?) in London; Barnards Inn, Holborn, 1642. His name is found on the imprint to H. Peacham's *Art of living in London*, 1642. [E. 145 (20).] There was a bookseller of this name living at Holborn Bridge between 1611 and 1634. [Arber, v. 260.] This may be the same or a successor.

RAND, or RANDS (WILLIAM), bookseller (?) in London, 1659. Hazlitt (H. 169) records an edition of Will. Drummond's Poems, published by him in 1659.

RANDALL (JAMES), bookseller (?) in London, 1641. Mentioned in a list of stationers as one of the "better sort of freemen" who paid twenty shillings as his proportion of the poll tax. The return is dated August 5th, 1641. [*Domestic State Papers*, Charles I, 483 (11).]

RANDS, *see* Rand.

RANEW (NATHANIEL), bookseller in London; Angel in Jewin Street, 1663–7. In partnership with Jonathan Robinson. His name is found in the imprint to the Rev. J. Dyke's *Worthy Communicant*, 1667. [Ames Coll. 3306.] He also published an account of the burning of London, by Samuel Rolls.

RATCLIFFE (THOMAS), printer in London; St. Bennet Pauls Wharf, near Doctors Commons, 1646–67. Took up his freedom January 14th, 1628. [Arber, iii. 686.] About May, 1646, he joined partnership with Edward Mottershead. They had an extensive business, and their initials T.R. and E.M. are met with on the books and pamphlets of this period at every turn. In 1659 Ratcliffe petitioned the Vestry of St. Bennet's to be relieved from serving as a vestryman on the ground that he was above the age of threescore years. [Vestry Books of St. Bennets, Paul's Wharf; Guildhall MSS. $\frac{877}{1}$, p. 182.] The date of his death is unknown. In the survey taken on July 29th, 1668, a Thomas Ratcliffe is returned as having two presses, two apprentices, and seven workmen [Plomer, *Short History*, p. 226], but this and later references probably refer to a son. [G. J. Gray, Index to Hazlitt, p. 639; Hist. MSS., Comm. Report 9, App. p. 73[a].]

RAWLINS (WILLIAM), bookseller (?) in London, 1659. His name occurs in the imprint to a pamphlet entitled *True Relation of the great fight .... near Northwich*, 1659.

RAWORTH (JOHN), printer in London; Parish of St. Bennet Paul's Wharf, 1638–45. Took up his freedom February 6th, 1632. In 1645 he is found borrowing a sum of £25 of the parish of St. Bennet's, for which he paid 5 per cent. interest. He died towards the end of July, 1645, his will being proved August 5th. [P.C.C. 104, Rivers.] In 1648 his widow married Thomas Newcombe.

RAWORTH (ROBERT), (?) bookseller in London; (?) Old Fish Street, near St. Mary Maudlin's Church, 1633–47. His name is found on the imprint to T. Heywood's *English Traveller*, 1633, and Hazlitt in his *Handbook* (p. 246) gives an edition of B. Guarini's *Il Pastor Fido* as published by Robert Raworth in 1647. A Robert Raworth was one of the witnesses to the will of John Raworth.

RAWORTH (RUTH), printer in London; Parish of St. Bennet Paul's Wharf, 1646–8. Widow of John Raworth. In 1648 she married Thos. Newcombe.

RAYNOR, REYNOR, or REINOR (JOHN), (?) bookseller in London, 1659. His name occurs on the imprint to the following pamphlet: *Bloody Almanack .... London, Printed for John Raynor*, 1659. [E. 993. (19).]

RAYNOR, REYNOR, or REINOR (T.), bookseller (?) in London, 1641. His name occurs on the imprint to the following pamphlet: *The Welchman's Answer*, 1641. [Hazlitt, iii. 52.]

RAYNOR, REYNOR, or REINOR (WILLIAM), bookseller (?) in London, 1642. His name occurs on the imprints to the following political pamphlets entitled *Prince Charles His Letter to the Lady Marie His most Royall Sister .... London, Printed for William Raynor*, 1642. [Hazlitt, ii. 681]; *The Truest most joyfull Newes that ever came from Ireland*. [E. 136 (7).]

REA (FRANCIS), bookseller in Worcester, 1651–63. Son of Ann Rea, of Churchill, co. Worcester, apprentice to Francis Ash, *q.v.*, for seven years from January 6th, 1644. His name is found on the imprint to Andrew

Yarranton's *Improvement improved, By a Second edition of The great Improvement of Lands by Clover .... London, Printed by J. C. for Francis Rea, Bookseller in Worcester*, 1663. [B.M. 724, a. 21.]

REA (ROGER), bookseller (?) in London, (1) Golden Cross Cornhill; (2) Gilded Cross, Westminster Street [near Gresham College]. 1660–67. Advertised in the *Kingdoms Intelligencer*, September 9th, 1661, an edition of Sir R. Stapylton's translation of Juvenal's *Mores Hominum*, published in 1660.

REDMAN, *see* Redmayne.

REDMAYNE, or REDMAN (JOHN), printer in London; Lovell's Court Paternoster Row, 1659–88. One of the printers of the *Perfect Diurnal of every dayes Proceedings in Parliament*, which began on February 21st, $16\frac{59}{60}$, and the *Publick Intelligencer* in 1660. At the survey taken on July 29th, 1668, he was returned as having two presses, one apprentice, four compositors, and two pressmen. [Plomer, *Short History*, p. 227.]

REDMAYNE (WILLIAM), bookseller (?) in London, 1648. Hazlitt, iii. 276, records an edition of John Allibond's *Rustica Academiæ Oxoniensis .... Londini, impensis G. Redmayne*, 1648.

REINOR, *see* Raynor.

REYBOLD, *see* Roybould.

REYNOLDS (JOHN), bookseller (?) in London, 1642. Only known from the imprint to a pamphlet entitled *Cornucopia; or Roome for a Ram Head.* [Hazlitt, H. 520.]

REYNOLDS (ROWLAND), bookseller in London; Sun and Bible, Postern Street, neere More-gate, 1667–84. Hazlitt records an edition of Abraham Cowley's *The Mistresse, or Several Copies of Love Verses*, as published by him in 1667. [Hazlitt, i. 105.]

REYNOR, *see* Raynor.

RHODES (MATTHEW), (?) printer in London; (?) Over against St. Andrews Church in Holborn, 1642. His name is found on the imprint to a pamphlet entitled *Declaration or Remonstrance of the Office of a Prince. London, Printed by John Hammond and Math. Rhodes*, 1642. [E. 108 (38).] A bookseller of this name was publishing between 1622 and 1633 [Arber, v. ciii.], but whether he is to be identified with the above is not known.

RICE (AUSTIN), bookseller in London, (1) At the Three Hearts, neer the West end of Pauls; (2) The Crown in St. Paul's Churchyard. 1657–61. Dealer in political pamphlets and broadsides. The addresses given above occur in the two following issues: (1) N. Billingsley's *Brachy-Martyrologie*, 1657. [Ames Coll. 2653]; (2) Edw. Dun, Presbyter, *The Execution of the Covenant, Burnt by the Common Hangman.* [A broadside.] 1661. [Lutt. Coll., 2, 78.]

RICHARDS (GODFRAY), bookseller (?) and author in London; Peacock in Cornhill near the Royal Exchange, 1663. His name is found on the imprint to *The first book of Architecture, By Andrea Palladio. Translated .... by Pr Le Muet .... London, Printed by J. M. and sold by G. Richards .... and by Simon Miller*, 1663. [Hazlitt, iii. 184.]

RICHARDSON (HUMPHREY), bookseller (?) in London, 1643. His name is found on the imprint to a pamphlet entitled *Most excellent and remarkable speech delivered by .... Queen Elizabeth .... London, Printed for Humphrey Richardson. Jan. 28. An Dom. 1643.* [E. 86 (29).]

RIDER (THOMAS), bookseller (?) in London, 1642. Publisher of political tracts and broadsides. [Hazlitt, ii. 449, 489, 558; iii. 36.] His address has not been found.

RIDLEY (BENJAMIN), bookseller (?) in Cambridge, 1647. His name appears on the imprint to a pamphlet entitled *Manifesto from .... Sir T. Fairfax, and the army .... June 27, 1647. Cambridge, Printed for Benjamin Kidley for the use of the Army, under his Excellencie Sir Thomas Fairfax, Anno Dom. 1647.* [E. 394 (15).]

RIDLEY (JOHN), bookseller in London; Castle in Fleet Street near Ram Alley, 1649–53. Originally in partnership with J. Martin, but the partnership was dissolved in 1651, when Martin moved to the Bell in St. Paul's Churchyard.

RISHTON (R.), bookseller (?) in London, 1648. Hazlitt, ii. 103, gives the imprint to a political pamphlet as *Printed for R. Rishton, 1648.* This may be a misreading for *Royston.*

ROBERTS (GEORGE), bookseller (?) in London, 1649. Publisher of political pamphlets. His address has not been found. [Hazlitt, ii. 412, 499.]

ROBERTS (TH[OMAS?]), bookseller (?) in London, 1663. His name occurs on the imprint to Thomas Porter's *A Witty Combat, 1663.* [B.M. 643, c. 8.]

ROBINSON (HUMPHREY), bookseller in London: Three Pigeons, St. Paul's Churchyard, 1624–70. Took up his freedom June 30th, 1623. [Arber, iii. 685.] Became one of the largest and most important booksellers of this period. On March 7th, 1652, in partnership with R. Thrale, Joshua Kirton, and Samuel Thompson, he took over the copyrights of Thomas Whitaker, 109 in number. He was also connected with Humphrey Moseley in the publication of plays, and may be said to have had a share in the chief publications of the time. During the Commonwealth he was in correspondence with Jos. Williamson, afterwards Secretary of State, and this series of letters is amongst the State papers. They give an interesting insight into the many parts that a bookseller of those days was called upon to play [*Domestic State Papers*, 1655–8.] Humphrey Robinson was Master of the Stationers' Company in the years 1661 and 1667. Smyth in his *Obituary* (p. 89), has the following record of his death:—"Nov. 13th, 1670, Die Dominica, circa hora 6. post merid. obiit Hum. Robinson, Bibliopola Trium Columb. in Cœmiter. D. Pauli, reliquens unum fil. et unam filiam. Sepult. in ruinis Eccles. S. Fidei sub. ecclesiam Cathedr. D. Pauli die Lunæ 21 Nov., 1670." His will was dated November 10th, and proved on the 23rd, by which he bequeathed to his daughter Grace his two new built houses in St. Paul's Churchyard. His son, Humphrey Robinson, is described as a fellow of All Souls' College, Oxford. He left a bequest of £10 to the Company of Stationers to rebuild their hall. [P.C.C. 151, Penn.]

On the Hustings Rolls (331, 20) his premises are described as being in "paule crosse churchyard" between the tenement late Richard Bankworth's on the east and the tenement sometime Alice Bing's widow and the yard called the Charnell chappell yard on the West, the churchyard of Pauls on the South and the wall to the churchyard on the North. One of the two houses was in the occupation of Octavian Pulleyn, and was known by the sign of the Rose.

ROBINSON (JOHN), bookseller (?) in London, 1643. His name occurs on the imprint to the following pamphlet: *Widowes Lamentation, 1643.* [E. 88 (26).]

ROBINSON (JONATHAN), bookseller in London; Angel in Jewen Street, 1667–97. In partnership with Nathaniel Ranew.

ROBINSON (RICHARD), bookseller (?) in London, 1648. Issued political pamphlets in that year. [E. 474 (12); E. 475 (5).]

ROBINSON (THOMAS), bookseller in Oxford, 1640–63. Amongst his notable publications was Francis Osborne's *Advice to a Son*, the first part of which was printed in 1655, and the second in 1658. Died April 22nd, 1663. [Smyth's *Obituary*, p. 57.] His will was proved on May 25th. To his son George he left his house in Warwick Lane, London; to his son William certain leases in Oxford, held of Magdalen College; to his son Robert lands at Bladon, in Oxford. Richard Davis, bookseller, of Oxford, was nominated one of the overseers. [P.C.C. 72, Juxon.]

ROGERS (RICHARD), bookseller in London; Paul's Chain near Doctors Commons, 1656. Associated with William Ley in publishing plays.

ROOKES (MARK), bookseller (?) in London; Grub Street neer to the Flying Horse, 1641. Associated with J. Salmon in publishing the following political pamphlets relating to Ireland:—(1) *Bloody Newes from Ireland*, 1641 [E. 179, (9)]; (2) *Treacherous Plot of a confederacie in Ireland*, 1641 [E. 179, (15).]

ROOKES, or ROOKS (THOMAS), bookseller in London, (1) Lamb, at the East End of St. Paul's Church, 1658–66; (2) Lamb and Ink Bottle, at the entrance into Gresham College, next Bishopsgate Street; (3) In Gresham

College, next the stairs entering upon the Exchange near Bishopsgate-Street, 1667; (4) Gresham College, next the stair or warehouse in Moor Fields, against the Cardinal's Cap, 1668. [1658–68?] Issued a catalogue of books that escaped the fire of London. A copy of this is preserved in the Bodleian. [*Bibliographica*, vol. iii, pp. 183–4.] Amongst other books which he published may be noticed Simon Latham's *Faulconry*, 1658. He made a speciality of writing inks, and hence the addition of the ink bottle to his sign. The last three imprints given above probably all refer to the same place.

ROPER (ABEL), bookseller in London, (1) Black Spread Eagle, over against St. Dunstan's Church, in Fleet St., 1641; (2) Sun in Fleet Street, 1650(?)–1667. [1638–80.] Born at Atherston, co. Warwick. Took up his freedom April 3rd, 1637. [Arber, iii. 688.] In company with Thomas Collins, was appointed "printer" to the Council of State, *i.e.*, they were allowed to sublet the printing, and on April 24th, 1660, a sum of £88 was paid to them for printing proclamations. [*Calendar of State Papers*, 1659–60, p. 598.] Abel Roper died early in the year 1680, his will being proved on March 4th, 167$\frac{9}{80}$. He died without issue, and left the interest in his stock of books to his executors for the benefit of his nephew, Abel Roper. Henry Herringman was his cousin, and one of the executors to his will. [P.C.C. 40, Bath.]

ROSSETER (EDWARD), bookseller in Taunton, co. Somerset, 1658. Published a sermon preached by the Rev. John Norman, minister at Bridgewater, at an Ordination at Somerton, co. Somerset, entitled *Christ's Commission Officer. or The Preacher's Patent Cleared.* [Ames Coll., 2781.]

ROTHWELL (JOHN), the elder, bookseller in London; Sun in St. Paul's Churchyard, 1628–49. Dealt almost wholly in theological works. The first entry to him occurs in the Registers on 9th October, 1628. Rothwell served as Warden of the Company of Stationers in 1634 and 1638. Died early in 1649, his will being proved January 11th. He left four sons, John, William, Henry, and Andrew. [P.C.C. 15, Fairfax.]

ROTHWELL (JOHN), the younger, bookseller in London, (1) Sun in Paul's Church Yard; (2) Fountain and Bear in Goldsmith's Row, Cheapside. 1633–60. Son of John Rothwell the elder. Took up his freedom

January 12th, 1631. [Arber, iii. 686.] In 1657 he published a *Catalogue of approved divinity books*. He sometimes used a device showing a bear standing beside a fountain.

ROUNTHWAIT (RALPH), (?) bookseller in London, 1640–63. Smyth records his burial on June 8th, 1663 [*Obituary*, p. 58.] He was probably a descendant of the earlier Ralph Rounthwaite, 1618–26. [Arber, v. 262.] His address is unknown.

ROWLANDSON (THOMAS), bookseller in Gateshead, Yorks. [c. 1664.] His burial is recorded in the parish registers of St. Mary, Gateshead, on August 7th, 1664. [*Notes and Queries*, 10th Series, vol. 6, p. 443.]

ROYBOULD (WILLIAM), bookseller in London; Unicorn in Paul's Churchyard, 1651–60. A list of nineteen works published by him in 1652 occupies the verso of the last leaf of Francis Fulwood's *Churches and Ministry of England . . . . 1652.* [E. 671 (2).]

ROYCROFT (THOMAS), printer in London, (1) Bartholomew Close; (2) Printing House, Charterhouse Yard. 1651–77. Among English printers of the seventeenth century who did credit to their profession, Roycroft is conspicuous. He was the printer of the Polyglott Bible described by Mr. T. B. Reed in his *Old English Letter Foundries* as a lasting glory to the typography of the seventeenth century. The work, consisting of six folio volumes, was carried through in four years, and was the impression of English type, supplied by the four recognised typefounders. Roycroft was also the printer of the handsome editions of the classics published and edited by John Ogilby. On the accession of Charles II he was appointed the King's printer in the Oriental languages, and in partnership with George Sawbridge and others he held a share in the King's Printing House. Roycroft's printing house was totally destroyed in the Fire of London, and many valuable books perished with it. He became Master of the Stationers' Company in 1675. Roycroft died on August 10th, 1677, and was buried in the church of St. Bartholomew the Great. His will is in the Prerogative Court of Canterbury. [P.C.C. 86, Hale.]

ROYSTON (RICHARD), bookseller in London and Oxford; London, Angel in Ivy Lane, 1629–86; St. Bartholomew's Hospital, 1667. His first book entry occurs on January 28th, 162$\frac{8}{9}$. [Arber, iv. 208.] In 1631 he

published T. Heywood's *Fair Maid of the West.* In 1645 he was accused of being a factor for scandalous books and papers against the Parliament, and thrown into prison. [Hist. MSS. Comm., 6th Rep., pp. 71–2.] The first edition of Εἰκων Βασιλικη was published by him in 1648. [Almack, *Bibliography of the King's Book, 1896.*] He was several times called before the Council of State for publishing unlicensed and scandalous books and pamphlets, and was with other booksellers and printers bound in sureties in 1649–50. [*Cal. of Domestic State Papers*, 1649–50, pp. 362, 524.] At the Restoration he was granted the monopoly of printing the works of Charles I, and was allowed a sum of £300 in consequence of his losses by the Fire of London in 1666. [*Cal. of Domestic State Papers*, 1666–7, p. 167.] He was Master of the Stationers' Company in 1673 and 1674. Royston died in 1686, aged 86. By his will, proved on November 16th, he desired to be buried in St. Paul's, but probably the Cathedral was not then finished, and his wishes could not be carried out, so he was buried in Christ Church, Newgate Street. He bequeathed all his copyrights to his grand-daughter Elizabeth Maior, daughter of Mary, the wife of Richard Chiswell, on the understanding that she married with her mother's consent, otherwise the copyrights were to pass to his grandsons, Royston Chiswell, Richard Chiswell, and John Chiswell. Another curious clause in connection with these copyrights was that the holder of them was to be a member of the Church of England. Whether these conditions were fulfilled is unknown, but Elizabeth, the daughter of Mary Chiswell, married Luke Meredith, her grandfather's apprentice. [Timperley, p. 569.] Royston left bequests to the following booksellers of Oxford: George West, Richard Davis, John Crosley and John Wilmot, which seems to bear out the statement that he had a bookseller's shop there. [Madan, *Chart of Oxford Printing*, p. 29.] He also bequeathed a piece of plate of the value of twenty pounds to the Company of Stationers. [P.C.C. 154, Lloyd.] *A Catalogue of some books printed for Richard Royston at the Angel in Ivie Lane, London, and some formerly printed at Oxford*, is found at the end of the second part of William Langley's sermon, *The persecuted Minister*, 1655 [1656.] [E. 860 (4), D.N.B.]

RUDDIARD (JOHN), bookseller (?) in London; Unicorn, Cornhill, under the Royal Exchange, 1662. His name is found in the imprint to the following broadside: *An exact and true relation of the landing of Her Majesty at Portsmovth, 1662.* [B.M., C. 20, f. 2 (50).]

RYDER, *see* Rider, Th.

SADLER (LAURENCE), bookseller in London; Golden Lion in Little Britain, 1631–64. Possibly a son of the Lawrence Sadler found publishing in 1599. [Arber, v. civ.] Smyth in his *Obituary*, p. 60, records "Augt. 2, 1664. Mr. Laur. Sadler, bookseller, died at ye Hague, of ye Plague."

SADLER (THEODORE), bookseller in London, (1) Bible, over against the little North Door of St. Paul's Church, 1660; (2) Next door to the Golden Dolphin, over against Exeter House in the Strand, 1663; (3) Little Britain, 1666 (1660–6.) Probably a relative of Laurence Sadler, *q.v.*, whom he seems to have succeeded. At the outset of his career he was in partnership with T. Davies at the Bible in St. Paul's Churchyard. He is mentioned in the Hearth Tax Roll for the half-year ending Lady Day, 1666, as a bookseller in Little Britain. [P.R.O. Lay Subsidy, $\frac{252}{32}$]

SALMON (JAMES), bookseller (?) Grub Streete, neere to the Flying Horse, 1641. Associated with M. Rookes, *q.v.*, in publishing the following political pamphlets relating to Ireland: (1) *Bloody Newes from Ireland*, 1641. [E. 179 (9)]; (2) *Treacherous plot of a confederacie in Ireland*, 1641. [E. 179 (15).]

SAMUEL (G), bookseller (?) in London, 1651. His name occurs in the imprint to a pamphlet entitled *A Great Fight at Sea . . . . Imprinted at London for G. Samuel*, 1651. [Hazlitt, ii. 550.]

SANDERS (JAMES), bookseller in Glasgow, 1625–42. Sold a bible to the Cathedral authorities in 1625. One of the debtors in J. Bryson's inventory, 1642. [H. G. Aldis, *List of books*, p. 119.]

SANDERS (ROBERT), printer in Glasgow, 1661–96; "Printer to the Toun," 1662; Printer to the City and University, 1672; One of His Majesties printers, 1683. Succeeded Andrew Anderson as printer at Glasgow, and during his thirty years' work produced a large amount of literature. Nephew of William Sanders, Professor of Mathematics in St. Andrew's University. On September 23rd, 1661, the town council of Glasgow granted him an annual subsidy of forty pounds Scots. One of the debtors in Lithgow's inventory, 1662. Prosecuted in 1671 by A. Anderson, and by his heir in 1680 for infringement of their patent. About 1683 purchased

George Swintoun's share of the gift as king's printer. In 1684 was interdicted by the Privy Council from pirating Forbes' Aberdeen almanacs. Died July 12th, 1694. Succeeded by his son Robert. [H. G. Aldis, *List of Books*, p. 119.]

SANDERS (WILLIAM), bookseller (?) in London, 1663. His name occurs in the imprint to a pamphlet entitled *The Tryal of Captain Langston* . . . . *London, Printed for William Sanders, 1663.* [Hazlitt, iii. 146.]

SANDERSONNE (ROBERT), bookseller in Glasgow, 1654. One of the debtors in Andrew Wilson's inventory, 1654. [H. G. Aldis, *List of Books*, p. 120.]

SATTERTHWAITE (SAMUEL), bookseller in London, (1) Black Bull in Budge Row neare to Saint Antholin's Church; (2) Sun on Garlick Hill, 1642–9. Took up his freedom August 6th, 1639. [Arber, iii. 688.] His addresses are found on the imprints to the following books: (1) J. Cotton's *True Constitution* . . . . 1642; (2) Robert Gell's *Stella Nova* . . . . *a sermon*, 1649.

SAWBRIDGE (GEORGE), printer and bookseller in London, (1) Bible on Ludgate Hill; (2) At his house on Clerkenwell Green, 1667. (1647–81.) Appears to have commenced business in partnership with E. Brewster about 1653, in which year their names are found on one of Edward Calamy's sermons, *A Christians Duty and Safety in Evill Times.* [E. 1434 (3).] After the Restoration Sawbridge became a partner with Samuel Mearne, Richard Roycroft and others in the King's Printing House, and held shares in the chief publications of his day. Dunton, in his *Life & Errors*, refers to Sawbridge as "the greatest bookseller that had been in England for many years." He was treasurer to the Company of Stationers during the greater part of his life, and was Master of the Company in 1675. He died a wealthy man in 1681, and was succeeded by his son George. [Arber, *Term Catalogues.*]

SAYWELL (JOHN), bookseller in London, (1) The Starre in Little Britain, 1646; (2) The Greyhound in Little Britain. 1646–58. The first of the above signs is found mentioned in William Hussey's *Just provocation*, 1646. [E. 357 (6).] Saywell sometimes used as a device an engraved plate of a greyhound running.

SCOTT (RICHARD) bookseller in Carlisle, 1656–9. The following books were printed for him: T. Polwhele's *Treatise of Self Denial*, 1659; *The Agreement of the Associated Ministers and Churches of the Counties of Cumberland and Westmorland* . . . . 1656. [E. 498 (3).]

SCOTT (ROBERT), bookseller in London; Princes Arms, Little Britain, 1661–91. In partnership with William Wells, *q.v.*, whom he seems to have succeeded in 1673.

SEAMER (H), bookseller (?) in London; Near the Inner Temple, 1660. His name occurs on the imprint to a pamphlet entitled *Landing of His* . . . . *Majesty* . . . . *at Dover, 1660.* [Hazlitt, iii. 38.]

SEAT, *see* Scot.

SEILE (ANNA), bookseller in London; Fleet St. over against St. Dunstan's Church, 1661–7. Probably the widow of Henry Seile.

SEILE (HENRY), bookseller in London, (1) Tiger's Head, St. Paul's Churchyard, 1622–36. [Sayle, 992]; (2) Tiger's Head in Fleet Street, over against St. Dunstan's church, 1641–61. Took up his freedom April 13th, 1617. Arber, iii. 684.] First book entry August 3rd, 1619. [Arber, iii. 654.] Master of the Stationers' Company, 1657. Died about 1661, when the business passed to Anna Seile, probably his widow.

SEYMOUR (RICHARD), bookseller (?) in London (?) 1642. His name occurs on the imprint to a pamphlet entitled *A Joyful Message* . . . . *to Sir John Hotham* . . . . *Printed for Richard Seymour, Augt. 4th, 1642.* [E. 109 (1).]

SHAW (JOHN). *Discourse Concerning the Object of Religious Worship*, 1665. At the end a Catalogue of books sold by A. Swalle.

SHEARES (MARGARET), bookseller in London, 1664. Probably the widow of William Sheares. She published an edition of the *Remains of Sir W. Raleigh*, 1664. [Hazlitt, ii. 510.]

SHEARES or SHEARS (WILLIAM), bookseller in London, (1) Great South dore of Pauls, 1631; (2) Britains Bursse and neare York House, 1635–59; (3) Bible in Bedford St., Covent Garden, 1642–62; (4) Bible in Paul's Church Yard near Little North Door, 1655; (5) Westminster Hall, 1657.

[1625–62.] Took up his freedom June 9th, 1623. [Arber, iii. 685.] He appears to have had shops in various parts of London, and was the publisher of much of the best literature of the period, including Alexander Brome's *Cunning Lovers*, 1654; John Cleveland's *Poems*, 1659; Phineas Fletcher's *Sicelides*, 1631; Thomas May's version of Lucan's *Pharsalia*, 1651; Quarles' *Divine Fancies*, 1632. Sheares was suspected of having had a hand in printing *Leicester's Commonwealth*, a notorious satire on the House of Lords. [*Domestic State Papers*, Chas. I, vol. 484 (75).] He died September 21st, 1662. [Smyth's *Obituary*, p. 56.]

SHELMERDINE (RALPH), bookseller in Manchester, 1661–3. Son of William Shelmerdine, bookseller in Manchester. [Fishwick, *Lancashire Library*, p. 398, n.] His name occurs in the imprint to the Rev. R. Heyrick's *Sermon*, 1661. [E. 1088 (9).] Also mentioned as a bookseller in an advertisement of patent medicines in *The Intelligencer* and *Newes* of 1663.

SHEPERD, *see* Shepheard.

SHEPHEARD, or SHEPERD (HENRY), bookseller in London, (1) Bible, Chancery Lane [Sayle, 1149]; (2) Bible in Tower Street [on Tower Hill]. 1635–46. Took up his freedom September 15th, 1634. [Arber, iii. 687.] Publisher of plays and political tracts. Associated with W. Lee.

SHERLEY, *see* Shirley.

SHIRLEY, or SHERLEY (JOHN), bookseller in London; Golden Pelican in Little Britain, 1644–66. His name is found on the following among other books: W. Lilly's *Prophecy of the White King*, 1644, and Saml. Parker's *Tentamina Physico-Theologica*, 1665. [Ames Collection, 3267.] Smyth in his *Obituary* (p. 71), has this record, January 23rd, $166\frac{5}{6}$, "Mr. John Shirley, bookseller in Little Britain, hora 10 *sub nocte*, died."

SHIRLEY, or SHERLEY (REBECCA), bookseller in London; Little Britain (? Golden Pelican), 1666. Probably the widow of John Shirley. Mentioned in the Hearth Tax Roll for the half-year ending Lady Day, 1666, as a bookseller in Little Britain [P.R.O. Lay Subsidy, $\frac{252}{32}$.]

SIMMONS (MARY), printer in London; Aldersgate St., 1656–67. Her name occurs in the Hearth Tax Roll for the six months ending Lady-Day 1666. She is returned as having thirteen hearths, a greater number than any other printer on the roll, so that her premises were large. She is probably identical with the Mistress Simmons mentioned as the "Custom House printer" in the return of printing houses made in 1668, and was perhaps the widow of Mathew Simmons. [P.R.O. Subsidy Roll, $\frac{252}{32}$; *Domestic State Papers*, Chas. II, vol. 243, no. 126.]

SIMMONS (MATHEW), bookseller and printer in London, (1) Golden Lyon in Duck-Lane, 1636; (2) Goldsmiths Alley [? Cripplegate]; (3) Next door to the Golden Lion, Aldersgate Street. 1636–54. Took up his freedom January 14th, $163\frac{1}{2}$. [Arber, iii. 687.] Apparently he began as a bookseller, as the 1636 edition of Geo. Gilpin's *Beehive of the Romish church* was printed by M. Dawson and sold by Simmons at the Golden Lyon in Duck Lane. [B.M., 3935, a. 43.] In 1641 he was still in a small way of business, as in the return made on August 5th of those who had paid their proportion of Poll Tax, he is entered amongst those who paid the smallest amount. [*Domestic State Papers*, Charles I, vol. 483 (11).] He appears to have started a press some time after 1641, and quickly rose into favour, his press being largely employed by the Independents. He printed many of John Milton's writings, and amongst the orders of the Council of State are the following: *Sept. 4th, 1649. Mr. Frost to see that Mr. Simmons the Printer is satisfied for printing some books put out under the title of Discoverer. December 26th, 1651. Simmons the printer to attend Frost to give in bond, according to his bargain with Mr. Ledsom, not to sell or part with any of the reams or sheets of paper now in his hands, of the History of Independency.* Simmons was also the printer of the news-sheet entitled *A Briefe Relation of some affairs and transactions, Civill and Military begun Oct. 1., 1649.* He died May 19th, 1654. [Smyth's *Obituary*, p. 38.]

SIMMONS (NEVILL), bookseller in Kidderminster and London, (1) Three Crowns over against Holborn Conduit; (2) Prince's Arms, St. Paul's Churchyard; (3) Three Golden Cocks at the West End of Pauls. 1655–81. Chiefly remembered as publisher for Richard Baxter from 1655 to 1681. [G. Hester, *Nevill Simmons, bookseller and publisher*, 1893. 8°.]

SIMMONS (SAMUEL), printer in London; Next door to the Golden Lion in Aldersgate, 1666–76. Probably son or nephew of Mathew Simmons, *q.v.* Printer of John Milton's *Paradise Lost*, 1667, the copyright of which Milton sold him for £5 and a contingent £15 more, of which £13 was paid. [Masson, *Life of Milton*, Vol. vi. 509 *et seq.*]

SIMMONS (THOMAS), bookseller in London; Bull and Mouth near Aldersgate, 1656–62. Publisher of Quaker books.

SIMMONS (THOMAS), bookseller at Birmingham at the sign of the Bible, 1652. His name is found on the imprint to the Rev. Thomas Hall's discourse on baptism, entitled, *The Font Guarded with XX Arguments*, published on March 26th, 1652. The author addressed it especially to his "friends in the town of Birmingham," and it was on sale in London at the shop of George Calvert. This bookseller may be identical with the Thomas Simmons afterwards found in London as a publisher of Quaker literature.

SIMPSON (EDWARD), bookseller (?) in London, 1647. His name occurs on the imprint to Thomas Smith's *Armies last Propositions to the Commons of England . . . . London. Printed for Edward Simpson, 1647.* [Hazlitt, iv. 168.]

SIMS (JOHN), bookseller in London, (1) Cross Keyes in St. Pauls Churchyard, 1656–64; (2) Cross Keyes, Cornhill, near the Royal Exchange. 1661–6. Married Mary Banckes, of St. Botolph, Aldgate, October 8th, 1661. [Chester's *Marriage Licenses*, 1229.] In T. Brook's *Crown and Glory of Christianity*, 1662, are lists of books sold by J. Sims, H. Crips, and H. Mortlock, the joint publishers.

SKELTON (RICHARD), bookseller in London; Hand and Bible in Duck Lane, 1659. His name is found on the imprint to an edition of Aristophanes . . . . translated by H. H. B. [B.M. 643, b. 47.]

SLATER (F), bookseller (?) in London; Swanne in Duck Lane, 1641. According to Hazlitt his name occurs on the imprint to the pamphlet entitled *Gunpowder Plot . . . . by A. B. C. D. E.* [Hazlitt, i. 194.]

SLATER (THOMAS), bookseller in London; Angel in Duck Lane, 1629–53. Took up his freedom May 6th, 1629. [Arber, iii. 686.] Paid £3 as his proportion of the poll money in 1641. [*Domestic State Papers*, Charles I, vol. 483 (11).] He died before March 7th, 165⅔, on which date his widow, Anne Slater, assigned her rights in his copies to James Fletcher or Flesher. [Stationers' Registers, Liber E.]

SMART (TIMOTHY), bookseller (?) in London; Hand and Bible in the Great Old Bailey, near the Sessions House, 1656. His name is found on the imprint to J. Cotton's *Exposition upon the 13th Rev.* 1656. [E. 893 (2).]

SMELT (MATTHEW), bookseller in London; The Ship [next door to the Castle] in Moorfields, 1667–71. His name occurs on the imprint to G. Thorne's *Cheiragogia Heliana*, 1667.

SMETHWICK (FRANCIS), bookseller (?) in London; Saint Dunstans Churchyard in Fleet Street, under the Dyall, 1642. Son of John Smethwick, one of the publishers of Shakespeare's plays, who died before July 15th, 1641. His father bequeathed him his shop and all the books in it, and the copyrights, including *Hamblett, a play*, *The tameing of a shrew*, *Romeo & Juliett*, and *Love's Labour Lost*, were assigned over to him on August 24th, 1642. In the same year he published an edition of T. Lodge's *Euphues golden legacy*, but a few days after receiving the copyrights he re-assigned them to Miles Fletcher or Flesher. [Stationers' Registers, Liber D.]

SMITH (EDWARD), bookseller (?) in London, (?) 1643. His name occurs on the imprint to a pamphlet entitled *Joyfull Newes from Plymouth . . . . London, Printed for Edward Smith, 1643.* [Hazlitt, ii. 481.]

SMITH (ELEANOR), bookseller (?) in London, 1650. Executrix of Francis Smith. She is mentioned in connection with Vavasour Powell's *Concordance of the Holy Bible*, 1650. [Rowland's *Cambrian Bibliography*, p. 153.]

SMITH (FRANCIS), bookseller in London, (1) Flying Horse Court in Fleet Street; (2) Elephant and Castle, without Temple Bar. 1642–67. There appears to have been several booksellers of this name between 1630 and 1667. Mr. Arber records a Francis Smith as publishing between 1633–6.

[*Transcript*, vol. v.] There was also a Francis Smith who was dead before 1650, leaving a widow Eleanor. He may have been identical with the earlier man. Lastly there was Francis Smith, who in 1659 published, among other things, Capt. W. Bray's *Plea for the people's good cause* [E. 763 (7)], and who was perhaps identical with the Francis Smith better known as "Elephant" Smith of a later period. [Arber, *Term Catalogues*, vol. 1, Index.]

SMITH (G.), bookseller (?) in London, 1642. His name is found on the imprint to the following pamphlet: *Two strange prophesies . . . . London, Printed for G. Smith*, 1642. [Hazlitt, i. 344.]

SMITH (JOHN), bookseller in London; Paul's Alley, 1641–7. Mentioned as one of the "better sort of freemen" in a list of stationers who in 1641 paid 20 shillings as his proportion of the poll tax. [*Domestic State Papers*, Chas. I, vol. 483 (11).] Several stationers of this name took up their freedom before 1640. [Arber, v. 265.]

SMITH (JOHN G.), (?) bookseller in London, 1642. His name occurs on the imprint to a pamphlet entitled *Newes from New England*, 1642. [E. 144 (22.)]

SMITH (NATHANIEL), (?) bookseller in Cambridge, 1647. Several political pamphlets issued in August, 1647, bear the imprint, *Printed for Nathaniel Smith: Cambridge.* No bookseller of this name is known to have been in Cambridge at that time, and it is probably the name of the author of the pamphlet, if it is not altogether fictitious.

SMITH (RALPH), bookseller in London; [Blue] Bible in Cornhil [near the Royal Exchange], 1642–60. Took up his freedom May 6th, 1639. [Arber, iii. 688.] One of the publishers of the Directory for Publick Worship, 1644. A list of books published by him in 1655, all of them theological, is printed at the end of W. Spurstowe's *Wel's of Salvation*, 1655. Another list of twenty books occurs at the end of David Dickson's *Brief Explication of the first Fifty Psalms*, 1653.

SMITH (THOMAS), bookseller in Manchester, 1643–9. Associated with Luke Fawne, *q.v.*, the London bookseller, in the publication of the following books: R. Hollingsworth's *Examination of sundry scriptures*, 1645. [E. 24

(6)]; R. Heyrick's *Queen Esthers Resolve*, 1646; *Deliberate resolution of the ministers of the gospel within the county of Lancaster*, 1647; *Solemn exhortation made to the . . . . churches . . . . within the province of Lancaster*, 1649; R. Hollingsworth's *Main points of church government*, 1649.

SMITH (WILLIAM), printer in Kilkenny and Cork, 1649–67. In 1649 William Smith printed a Proclamation for the Duke of Ormonde at Kilkenny. In 1657 his imprint appears on *The Agreement . . . . of Associated Ministers at Cork*, and in 1660 to James Davies' *History of Charles II.* As his name is found on Cork imprints as late as 1690, there may have been more than one printer of this name, perhaps father and son. [Information kindly supplied by Mr. E. R. McC. Dix.]

SMITHERS (RICHARD), (?) bookseller in London, 1641. His name occurs on the imprint to a pamphlet entitled *An honourable and learned speech made by Mr. Waller*, 1641. [E. 199 (42).] It may be a misprint for Smithurst, *q.v.*

SMITHURST (RICHARD), (?) bookseller in London; Hosier Lane neer Pye Corner [Smithfield], 1641–48. Publisher of political pamphlets. [Hazlitt, ii. 103, 714.] He may be identical with Richard Smithers.

SOWLE (ANDREW), printer in London, (1) Pye Corner Smithfield; (2) Crooked Billet, Holloway Lane, Shoreditch, 1653–67. Son of Francis Sowle, of the parish of St. Sepulchres, yeoman. Born in 1628. Apprenticed on July 6th, 1646, to Ruth Raworth, *q.v.*, for seven years. [Apprenticeship Register, Stationers' Hall.] Although his name is not found in an imprint before 1683, there is no doubt that he was the printer of most, if not all, of the early Quaker literature. In the obituary notice of him that appeared in *Piety Promoted*, Part I, p. 192, it was stated that he engaged himself freely in printing Friends books, and that his printing materials were several times seized and broken to pieces, and on one occasion a thousand reams of printed books were taken from him. On another occasion he was taken before Sir Richard Browne, who threatened to send him "after his brother Twyn," who had been executed in 1664 for printing a seditious book. Andrew Sowle's daughter, Elizabeth, married in 1685 her father's apprentice, William Bradford, who emigrated to America and set up his press in Pennsylvania, and afterwards in New York. Another daughter, Tace Sowle, succeeded her father in his business, and ultimately married Thomas Raylton. Andrew Sowle died in 1695, aged 67.

SPARKE (MICHAEL), senior, bookseller in London. Blue Bible in Green Arbour Court, Old Bailey, 1616–53. Born at Eynsham, Oxfordshire, son of Richard Sparke, husbandman. Apprenticed for seven years to Simon Pauley, a citizen and stationer of London. Took up his freedom June 10th, 1610. Michael Sparke was William Prynne's publisher, and was condemned to stand in the pillory and pay a fine of £500 for publishing *Histrio-mastix*. Michael Sparke was also a vigorous opponent of the monopolies, and was the author of a pamphlet entitled *Scintilla, or a Light broken into Dark Warehouses*, in which he drew attention to what he considered the excessive prices charged for books, particularly Bibles. Sparke at the same time imported Bibles from Holland, which he sold at cheaper rates than those printed in London. This pamphlet has been reprinted by Mr. Arber in the fourth volume of the *Transcript* (pp. 35 *et. seq.*). He was also the author of a pamphlet entitled *A Second Beacon fired by Scintilla* .... 1652, in which he gave many autobiographical details. Amongst the books he published were John Smith's *History of Virginia*, 1624; Captain Luke Foxe's *North West Foxe*, 1635; Mercator's *Atlas*, 1635, and a devotional work with the quaint title *Crums of Comfort.* Michael Sparke lived at Hampstead, and died there on December 29th, 1653. By his will he left a bequest of a seal ring to William Prynne, Esq. He also left bequests to Constance Jones, Elizabeth Macock and Ellen Cotes, the widows of three printers who worked for him. His son Michael was for a time in partnership with him, but was killed in 1645. [P.C.C. 158, Alchin; *Bibliographer*, New York, December, 1902.]

SPARKE (MICHAEL), junior, bookseller in London; Blue Bible in Green Arbour Court, Old Bailey, 1638–45. Son of Michael Sparke, senior, *q.v.* In partnership with his father, but some books, such as Christopher Love's *England's Distemper*, 1645 [E. 274, 15], have his name only as publisher. He died in December, 1645, having been mortally wounded by his brother. His will was proved March 22nd, 1646. [P.C.C. 52, Fines; *Bibliographer*, New York, December, 1902.]

SPEED (SAMUEL), bookseller in London, (1) Printing Press, St. Paul's Churchyard; (2) Rainbow, between the two Temple Gates. 1658–67. Probably the son of Daniel Speed, stationer, who was publishing from 1603 to 1620. [Arber, v. 266.] In 1658 he was associated with Joseph

Barber. In 1664 he issued a catalogue of books entered in the Register of the Company of Stationers between December 25th, 1662, and December 25th, 1663. [*Bibliographica*, vol. iii. p. 183.] In 1666 he was informed against for selling law books that had been printed during the Commonwealth, and was imprisoned and bound over in three hundred pounds not to sell any more of them. [*Domestic State Papers*, Charles II, 156, 105, 106.]

STAFFORD (JOHN), bookseller in London, (1) Blackhorse Alley, near Fleet Bridge; (2) In St. Bride's Church-yard; (3) Over against St. Bride's Church in Fleet Street; (4) ad insigne Georgii, in vico vulgo vocato, Fleet Street propre pontem; (5) In Chancery Lane. 1637–64. In the year 1634 R. Allot entered several books in the registers of the Company to which a marginal note was added to the effect that they were entered in trust for John Stafford. This may mean that he was Allot's apprentice. He took up his freedom September 28th, 1637. [Arber, iii. 688.] Dealt chiefly in theological literature. The fourth address given above is from an imprint only, preserved by Bagford. [Harl, 5919, 261.]

STAMPE (MRS.), bookseller in London; Queens Head, Westminster Hall, 1663. Mentioned as a bookseller in an advertisement of patent medicines in *The Newes*, December 17th, 1663.

STANTON (ISAAC), bookseller in London; White Hart and Bear, Bread Street, 1662. Mentioned in an advertisment in *Mercurius Publicus*, February 6th, 166½, relating to the Welsh bible in octavo.

STARKEY (JOHN), bookseller in London, (1) The Mitre at the North Door of the Middle Exchange, in St. Paul's Churchyard, 1658; (2) The Mitre near the Middle Temple Gate; (3) The Mitre, between the Middle Temple Gate and Temple Bar, 1667 [1658–67.] Son of George Starkey, of Isley Walton, in the County of Leicester. Put himself apprentice to John Saywell, *q.v.*, for eight years from November 6th, 1655. Took up his freedom April 20th, 1664. Published several notable books of travel, amongst which may be mentioned Sir P. Ricaut's *Present State of the Ottoman Empire*, 1667. Hazlitt, ii. 527, gives an interesting account of Samuel Pepys' copy of this work, which contains a list of books

published by Starkey in 1667. He was one of the founders of the periodical bibliography called *Mercurius Librarius*, which began in Michaelmas Term, 1668, and was afterwards succeeded by the *Term Catalogues*. [Arber, *Term Catalogues*, vol. 1, pp. viii–x.]

STATIONERS, COMPANY OF, Edinburgh, 1650. Mr. H. G. Aldis, in his *List of Books printed in Scotland before 1700*, gives one, *A golden chaine of Time*, No. 1415, with the imprint, "Printed at Edinburgh by the Heires of George Anderson, for the Company of Stationers," which he thinks was distinct from the Society of Stationers. [H. G. Aldis, *List of Books*, p. 120.] Amongst the *State Papers*, *Domestic*, for 1651, vol. 15 (18), is an undated and unsigned paper headed *The true ground and reason why the Company of Stationers bought their printing house in Scotland*. In this it is stated that four years before (? 1647) upon an overture from the King's Printer there to sell the Company his patent and printing house, the Company made an agreement with him, which cost them a large sum of money, and that owing to the troubles in both kingdoms they had lost heavily over the transaction. The Company further state that they are "now" [*i.e.*, 1651] withdrawing their stock and materials, in regard that by the late Act full provision is made against importation from that kingdom.

STATIONERS, SOCIETY OF, Edinburgh, 1660–90. This press appears to fall into two periods: First period, 1660–71. Succeeding Higgins, *q.v.* This seems to be the Stationers' Company of London. Watson, p. 10, states that, "Tyler made over his part of the forfeited gift to some Stationers at London, who sent down upon us Christopher Higgins and some English servants with him .... After he died, these London Stationers appoint Patrick Ramsay, *q.v.*, a Scotsman to be overseer of that House .... but the masters living at a distance, and the work coming to no account, they sold this printing house to several booksellers [probably Swintoun, Glen and Brown, *q.v.*] at Edinburgh, who, in a little time after did divide and set up distinct houses." Arber [*Stationers' Registers*, v. xlvii] says that the Company "held for some years a patent for printing in Scotland, granted by the Scotch Parliament. This Scotch Patent .... appears to have been abandoned in 1669 upon the death of Christopher Higgins, the Company's agent at Edinburgh, and the stock and plant sold there for £300." [H. G. Aldis, *List of Books*, p. 121.]

STEDMAN (FABIAN), bookseller (?) in London; In St. Dunstan's Churchyard in Fleet Street, 1665. *An Essay upon the Victory obtained by His Royal Highness the Duke of York, against the Dutch, upon June 3, 1665.* [a broadside.] [Lutt Coll., iii. 90.]

STENT (PETER), printer and engraver in London; Whitehorse in gilt-spur-street, 1643–67. Printer of maps, pictures and copy books. A list of some of his publications will be found at the end of Richard Fage's *Description of the Whole World*, 1658.

STEPHENS (PHILEMON), bookseller in London, (1) Gilded Lyon in Paul's Churchyard, 1647; (2) White Lyon, St. Pauls Churchyard, 1654 [Probably the same house as No. 1]; (3) Chancery Lane, 1669 (1622–70). Took up his freedom May 3rd, 1620. [Arber, iii. 685.] Partner with Christopher Meredith, *q.v.* Master of the Company of Stationers, 1660. Smyth in his *Obituary*, p. 87, thus records his death, "15 July 1670, Philemon Stephens, bookseller in Chancery Lane died at Chelsey; buried at St. Dunstans in ye West." He made a nuncupative will in favour of his wife Dorothy. [P.C.C. 103 Penn.] The house known as the White or Gilded Lion belonged to John Bellamy, and was mentioned in his will. Stephens dealt almost entirely in theological literature. The following works contain lists of his publications: Rev. R. Abbott's *Christian Family builded by God*, 1653; John Trapp's *Commentary upon the twelve minor prophets*, 1654. [See also *Bibliographica*, vol. 3, p. 182.]

STEPHENSON (JOHN), bookseller in London; Sun on Ludgate Hill, 1649–52. Summoned before the Council of State, March 29th, 1649, for selling the Koran, printed by or at the expense of Thos. Ross. [*Calendar of State Papers*, 1649, pp. 59–63.] His name occurs on the imprint to the following book: Raleigh, Sir W., *Marrow of Historie*, 1650. [B.M., 463, h. 4 (2165).]

STORY (EDWARD), bookseller in Cambridge, 1653–74. Nothing of a biographical character appears to be known about this bookseller. Books sold by him in the years 1653, 1668, 1670, 1671, 1674, are noted by Bowes in his *Catalogue of Cambridge books* (pp. 46 *et seq.*).

STRANGHAN (DAVID), (?) *Pseud.* Printer at Aberdeen, 1659. This name is found on the imprint to *Message sent from the King of Scots.* Mr. Aldis thinks it was probably printed by James Brown, *q.v.*, under a feigned name. [H. G. Aldis, *List of Books*, p. 121.]

STREATER or STREATOR (JOHN), (?) bookseller and printer in London; Bible in Budge Row [? Watling Street], 1646–87. Amongst the Bagford fragments [Harl. 5927 (494)] is the following: *Aurefodina Linguæ Gallica, or the Gold Mine of the French language opened . . . . By Edmund Gostlin, Gent., London. Printed for John Streater at the signe of the Bible in Budge-Row, 1646*. No copy of this book can be traced, but if there is no mistake in the date, it would seem to prove that John Streater was a bookseller at the time of the outbreak of the Revolution. His subsequent history is obtained partly from his own petition to Parliament. [Harl. 5928, 13], and from other sources. He served throughout the Civil Wars, and was present at the battles of Edgehill and Newbury, and subsequently went to Ireland as Quarter Master General and Engineer. But in 1653 his views upon public matters changed, and he became a violent opponent of Cromwell, and in August, 1653, was expelled the army and thrown into prison for writing and printing a pamphlet entitled the *Grand Politique Informer*. After a confinement of some months and several appearances before the Judges, he was set at liberty by Judge Rolls. General Desborough urged him to make his peace with Cromwell, and he at length agreed not to print or write anything else against the Government. After Cromwell's death he appears to have been appointed one of the official printers, for on April 11th, 1660, in company with J. Macocke, *q.v.*, he received a warrant for the payment of £528 13*s.* 3*d.* for printing Acts, Orders, etc. [*Domestic State Papers*, 1659–60, p. 596.] In the Act of 1662 was a special proviso exempting Streater from its provisions. He held a patent for printing law-books as one of the assigns of Richard and Edward Atkyns, but in 1664 he was imprisoned with other stationers at the instigation of the Stationers' Company for infringing their privileges [Chan. Proc. Rey. Bundle 31, Stationers' Co. *v.* Flesher.] In 1666 he gave information against Samuel Speed for selling law books printed during the Commonwealth, with the result that Speed was apprehended and fined. Streater was also the author of a pamphlet entitled *The King's Grant of Privilege for sole printing Common Law Books defended and the legality thereof asserted*, 1669.

SUMPTNER (CHARLES), printer in London, 1650. His name is found on the imprint to Daniel King's *A Way to Sion* . . . . London, Printed by Charles Sumptner, for Hanna Allen, at the Crowne in Pope's Head Alley, 1650. [E. 596 (7).]

SWAINE (ROBERT), bookseller in London; Britains Burse, 1629–41. Took up his freedom December 20th, 1628. [Arber, iii. 686.] Mentioned in a list of stationers, dated August 5th, 1641, as one of the better sort of freemen, who paid five shillings to the poll tax. [*Domestic State Papers*, Charles I, vol. 483, 11.]

SWAYLE, or SWALLE (ABEL), bookseller in London; Unicorn, at the West-end of St. Paul's Church-yard, 1665–98. At the end of John Shaw's *Discourse concerning the object of Religious Worship*, 1665, is a catalogue of books sold by Swayle.

SWEETING (JOHN), bookseller in London, (1) Crown in Cornhill, 1639; (2) Angell in Pope's Head Alley, 1639–61. Took up his freedom June 27th, 1639. [Arber, iii. 688.] The following advertisement which appeared in the *Perfect Account* for the week ending Wednesday, January 4th, 1654, will best show the nature of his business: "There is published five new plays in one vollum, viz., The mad couple well matcht; The Novella; The Court Beggar; The City Wit; and the Damoisella; all written by Richard Brown (*sic*) A Collection of those excellent letters to several persons of honour; written by John Donne sometime Dean of St. Paul's London. Likewise a poem called the Shepheards Oracles, delivered in certain Eglogues by Francis Quarls. And the Poems of John Donne . . . . with elegies on the authors death, to which is added divers copies under his own hand never before printed. All which are to be sold by John Sweeting at the Angell in Pope's Head Alley." Sweeting died in 1661, and by his will left a sum of money to the Company of Stationers to be spent on two dinners for all the bachelors that were booksellers and free of the Company. [Timperley, p. 527.]

SWINTOUN (GEORGE), printer and bookseller at Edinburgh, (1) at the Kirk style, at the sign of the Angel, 1649; (2) In the Parliament Yard, 1667. Named among the debtors in Lithgow's Inventory, 1662. Probably one of the booksellers who, in 1671, acquired the business of the Society of Stationers, in which he is believed to have been associated with Robert Brown, Thomas Brown, and J. Glen. [H. G. Aldis, *List of Books*, p. 121.]

SYMMES, *see* Sims.

TAYLOR (JOHN), printer (?) in London, 1660. His name occurs on the imprint to a pamphlet entitled *Rumps last will and testament. London, Printed by John Taylor*, 1660. [Hazlitt, ii. 524.]

TAYLOR (RANDAL), bookseller in London; St. Martin's le Grand neer St. Leonards Church-yard, 1664–7. His name occurs on the imprint to Thos. Philipot's *Original and growth of the Spanish Monarchy*, 1664. [Ames Collection, 3165.]

TAYLOR, or TAYLOUR (WILLIAM), bookseller in Winchester: near the Chequer Gate, 1663. Edward Lane's *Look unto Jesus*, 1663, was to be sold at the above booksellers. [B.M. 696, f. 13.]

TEAGE ( ), bookseller at Bristol; The Dolphin; and at Totnes, Devon, 1662–3. In an undated list of printers and booksellers found selling seditious literature in the reign of Charles II, it is stated that Thomas Bruister was to be found "at Teags house ye signe of ye Dolphin at Bristol." [*Domestic State Papers*, Charles II, vol. 67, 161.] He is also mentioned as a bookseller at Totnes, in Devon, in an advertisement of patent medicines in the *Intelligencer* for the year 1663.

TEW (NICHOLAS) bookseller in London; Coleman Street, 1643–60. (?) Son of William Tew, of London, gent. Apprentice to Henry Bird for nine years from September 6th, 1629. [Register of Apprentices, Stationers' Hall.] Took up his freedom October 1st, 1638. [Arber, iii. 688.] In January, 164$\frac{4}{5}$, he was arrested for printing a "scandalous libel" against Lord Essex and the Duke of Manchester, and confessed that a printing press was brought to his house and used there by Robert Overton and other Independents. In addition to the libel against the generals two other pamphlets have been traced to this secret press. [*Library*, October, 1904, pp. 374 *et seq.*] Edward Dobson, another bookseller, was imprisoned amongst other things for beating Nicholas Tew.

TEY (CHARLES), bookseller (?) in London, (?) 1662. His name is found on the imprint to a pamphlet entitled, *Sad and lamentable newes from several parts of England . . . . Printed for Charles Tay*, 1662. [Hazlitt H. 677.]

TEY (JOHN), bookseller in London; White Lion in the Strand neer the New Exchange, 1650–2. Dealer in plays. T. (J.) *Distracted state a Tragedy*, 1650. [E. 618 (5).]

THACKERAY (WILLIAM), bookseller in London, (1) Black Spread Eagle and Sun, in the Old Bailey, 1666; (2) Sugar Loaf, Duck Lane, 1666–7. Dealt largely in ballads and theological literature. Was mentioned in the will of Thomas Passinger.

THOMAS (EDWARD), bookseller in London, (1) Green Arbour Court, Old Bailey, 1657; (2) Adam and Eve, Little Britain, 1657–82. Succeeded to the business of Michael Sparke, senr. Mentioned in the Hearth Tax Roll for the half-year ending Lady Day, 1666, as a bookseller in Little Britain. [P.R.O. Lay Subsidy, $\frac{252}{32}$.]

THOMAS (JOHN), bookseller in London, 1637–44. Took up his freedom September 28th, 1633. [Arber, iii. 687.] *The Lord Lowden his learned and wise speech*, 1641. [E. 199 (13).] His address has not been found.

THOMAS (MARY), bookseller in London, (?) 1642. Her imprint occurs on a pamphlet entitled *Three proclamations*, 1642. [E. 154 (18).]

THOMAS (MICHAEL), bookseller in Bristol at his shop in the Polzey, 1664–7. Advertisement for recovery of a watch, in the *Newes*, July 14th, 1664. He is also mentioned in an information laid by the Mayor of Bristol in 1667, as having received certain treasonable books concerning the Fire of London from Elizabeth Calvert. [*Domestic State Papers*, Charles II, vol. 209 (75).]

THOMAS (WILLIAM), bookseller (?) in London, 1659. His name occurs on the imprint to a pamphlet entitled *Five strange Wonders*, 1659. [Hazlitt, ii. 1659.]

THOMASON (GEORGE), bookseller in London; Rose, or Rose and Crown, St. Paul's Churchyard, 1627–66. Thomason will always be remembered as the collector of the literature of the Civil War and Commonwealth periods. Nothing is known as to his antecedents before the record of his freedom as a member of the Company of Stationers on June 5th, 1626. [Arber, iii. 686.] His first book entry is recorded in the Registers on November 1st, 1627, and shows him as sharing the copyright with James Boler and Robert Young [*ibid.*, iv. 31, 188, 419]. He is next found in partnership with Octavian Pulleyn, a connection which was apparently dissolved about 1643, when Thomason moved to the Rose and Crown in St. Paul's Churchyard. At the time of the opening of the Long Parliament on November 3rd, 1640, Thomason conceived the idea of collecting and preserving, as far as he could, all the pamphlets printed during the next few years. Not only did he steadfastly carry out the task he had set himself, but he also arranged the collection in the best possible way, that is, chronologically, and made the chronology as precise as possible, by writing on almost every tract the day on which he received it. Thomason failed to get everything, thus many Royalist pamphlets and sheets printed at Oxford are only represented in his collection by a London reprint, and the same remark applies to other provincial or secret presses. It is matter for wonder that he should have collected so much rather than that he should have lost so little. Mr. G. K. Fortescue, Keeper of the Printed Books at the British Museum, gives the figures of the Thomason collection as follows: Pamphlets, 14,942; Manuscripts, 97; Newspapers, 7,216; total, 22,255 pieces, bound in 2,008 volumes. During the Civil War, Thomason sent his collection first into Surrey, afterwards into Essex, and at one time contemplated sending it into Holland, but was fortunately persuaded to give up that idea, and concealed it in his own warehouses, arranging the volumes as tables, and covering them over with canvas. At the Restoration the King commanded his stationer, Samuel Mearne, to purchase the collection, but apparently afterwards went back on his bargain, and not only did not take it into the royal library, but did not repay Mearne for its purchase. Mearne's widow, in 1684, was permitted by the Privy Council to sell it, and the volumes passed into the possession of a relative, Mr. Henry Sisson, a druggist on Ludgate Hill. They were eventually bought for King George III for the paltry sum of £300 and presented by him to the nation in 1762. In 1645-6 Thomason bought up the whole impression of a pamphlet called *Truth's Manifest*, which the Committee of both Houses considered libellous. In 1648 the House of Commons agreed to pay him £500 for a collection of Eastern books, but

he had great difficulty in getting the money. In 1651 he was imprisoned for seven weeks in consequence of his complicity in the Love conspiracy, but was released on giving bail for £1,000. George Thomason died on April 10th, 1666, and Smyth in his *Obituary*, p. 71, adds "buried out of Stationers Hall (a poore man)." His will was proved on the 27th April. By this it appears that he had four sons, George, Edward, Henry, and Thomas, living at the time of his death. Negotiations were then on foot for the sale of his collection of pamphlets, which he bequeathed to Dr. Thomas Barlowe, Provost of Queen's College, Oxford, Thomas Lockey, principal librarian of the "public library," at Oxford, and John Rushworth, of Lincoln's Inn, in trust for the benefit of his three children, Edward, Henry and Thomas, but by a codicil he directed that the sum obtained for them, which he anticipated would be Twelve Hundred Pounds or more, was to be divided equally between his daughter Grace and his son Thomas. [D.N.B.; *Bibliographica*, vol. 3, pp. 291-308; Information kindly supplied by Mr. G. K. Fortescue; P.C.C. 64 Mico.]

THOMASON (HENRY), bookseller in London; Rose and Crown St. Pauls Church yard, 1663-7. Son of the preceding. Sometimes used as a device a copperplate showing a rose crowned.

THOMPSON (GEORGE), bookseller in London; White Horse in Chancery Lane, over against Lincolns Inn [Gate], 1642-60. Dealt in political pamphlets, broadsides and law books.

THOMPSON (JAMES), bookseller in London, 1642-50. Published the following: *Treason discovered from Holland .... London, Printed for J. Thompson*, 1642. [Hazlitt, ii. 692]; *Manual of Godly Prayers*, 1650. [Hazlitt, ii. 494.] His address has not been found.

THOMPSON (JOHN), the elder, bookseller in London, 1641. Mentioned in a list of stationers who had paid their proportion of the poll tax in 1641. [*Domestic State Papers*, Charles I, vol. 483 (11).]

THOMPSON or THOMASON (JOHN), (?) the younger, bookseller (?) in London, 1660. *Proceedings, Votes, Resolves and Acts of the late half quarter Parliament, called the Rump, 1660.* [Hazlitt, ii. 525.] His address has not been found.

THOMPSON (NATHANIEL), printer in Dublin, 1666. Printed an edition of T. Bladen's *Praxis Francisci Clarke*, 1666. [Ames Collection, 3272.] Some interesting notes about him at a later period will be found in the Hist. MSS. Comm. Report 9, app., pp. 69-79.

THOMPSON (THOMAS), bookseller (?) in London, 1642. Took up his freedom July 6th, 1635. [Arber, iii. 687.] His name is found on the imprint to several political pamphlets in 1642. [Hazlitt, 207, 525.]

THOMPSON (SAMUEL), bookseller in London, (1) White Horse, St. Paul's Churchyard; (2) Bishop's Head in Duck Lane, 1664-8. Shared with Humphrey Robinson, *q.v.*, Richard Thrale, *q.v.*, and Joshua Kirton, *q.v.*, the copyrights of Thomas Whitaker, numbering 109 works. His death is thus recorded by Smyth in his *Obituary*, p. 79, "Octr. 26th, 1668. *Die Lunæ hora 12 sub nocte*, Sam Thompson, bookseller in Duck Lane obit, a good husband and industrious man in his profession." In his will, which was proved on November 9th, 1668, he refers to his late losses in the fireing of London, and to the doubtful value of his stock. His son John was a student at Oxford, and Samuel Gellibrand, *q.v.*, was appointed sole executor. [P.C.C. 146, Hene.]

THORN (EDMUND), bookseller in Oxford, 1652-63. Publisher of Clement Barksdale's *Noctes Hibernæ*, 1652.

THORNICROFT, or THORNYCROFT (THOMAS), bookseller in London, (1) Eagle and Child, St. Paul's Churchyard; (2) Eagle and Child, near Worcester House in the Strand. 1663-7. His second address is found in Paul Festeau's *New and easie French Grammar*, 1667. [Eman. Coll. Camb.]

THORPE (WILLIAM), bookseller in Chester, (1) Hand and Bible near the High Crosse; (2) Stationer's Arms in Watergate Street, 1664. A fragment in the Ames Collection (473 h 1, 121) is a portion of an engraved sheet. At the top are three shields, one of them bearing the arms of the Stationers' Company. Between the two uppermost is the date 1664. Below them is a Bible and Hand and the letters W. T., and beneath this the imprint:—"Printed for William Thorpp Bookseller in the City of Chester, and are to be sould by him there, at his shop at the hand and Bible neere the high Crosse, and at the Stationers Armes in the Watergate Street, where alsoe Books both new and old are to bee bound and sold."

THRALE (JAMES), bookseller in London, (1) Cross Keys, Pauls Gate; (2) Under St. Martin's Outwich Church in Bishopsgate Street, 1661-7. In partnership with Richard Thrale, *q.v.*

THRALE (RICHARD), bookseller in London, (1) Cross Keys at Paul's Gate, 1650; (2) Cross-Keyes and Dolphin in Aldersgate Street, over against the Half Moon tavern, 1667. Took up his freedom August 6th, 1623 [Arber, iii. 685.] Master of the Stationers' Company in 1664. On March 7th, 1652, in company with Humphrey Robinson, Joshua Kirton, and Samuel Thompson, he took over the copyrights of Thomas Whitaker. This assignment fills four pages of the register, and numbers 109 books. After the fire he moved into Aldersgate Street, where he published an account of the calamity.

THREIPLAND (JOHN), bookseller in Edinburgh, 1639-45. Probably the John Threipland, servant to Jonet Mayne, to whom she owed a "zieres fie" of forty pounds at her death in April, 1639. A debtor to Widow Hart, 1642; R. Bryson, 1645; T. Lawson, 1645. [H. G. Aldis, *List of Books*, p. 122.]

TOMKINS (NATHANIEL), bookseller (?) in London, 1660. His name occurs on the imprint to a pamphlet entitled *Declaration of Maj. Gen. Harrison, Prisoner in the Tower of London* .... London, Printed for Nathaniel Tomkins, 1660. [Hazlitt, ii. 269.]

TOMLINS (RICHARD), bookseller in London, (1) At his house in Green Arbour, in the Old Bailey, 1644; (2) Sun and Bible near Pye Corner [Smithfield], 1644-56. Took up his freedom March 27th, 1637. [Arber, iii. 688.] His first address is found in a pamphlet entitled *England's troubles anatomized*, 1644. [E. 12 (15).] A list of twenty-eight publications sold by him in 1654 is given at the end of a series of sermons by the Rev. C. Sidenham, entitled *Hypocrisie discovered.* [E. 1504 (3).] The following are among the items: *Pleasant notes upon Don Quixot*, folio; *History of the Seven Champions*, quarto; *The False Jew*, quarto; Erasmus' *Colloquies*, octavo.

TOMLINSON (GEORGE), bookseller (?) in London, 1642. Publisher of political pamphlets. Address not found. [B.M., E. 108 (11, 12).]

TOMPSON (RICH.?), bookseller in London; Bedford Street against the New Exchange. His name occurs on an engraved sheet called the "Fruits of Faith." [B.M., 669, f. 20 (38).]

TOMSON (WILL.), bookseller at [Market] Harborough in Leicestershire, 1655. His name occurs in an advertisement in *Mercurius Politicus*, February 28th, 1655.

TONGE (JOHN), bookseller (?) in Warrington, Lancashire [c. 1653]. In the Registers of the Parish Church of Warrington is the following entry among the burials:—"1653. May 7 John Tounge, 'the stationer.'" Mr. W. H. Rylands when preparing his notes on *Warrington Booksellers and Stationers* had no information about him. [*Transactions of the Historic Society of Lancashire and Cheshire*, vol. 37, pp. 67–115.]

TOPPYN (LANCELOT), bookseller and haberdasher of London; Little Britain, 1641–6. Smyth in his *Obituary* (p. 23), records his death on November 17th, 1646. By his will, proved on November 27th, 1646, it appears that his wife Anne was sister to Dixy Page, *q.v.*, and his sister Elizabeth married Cornelius Bee, *q.v.* [P.C.C. 150, Twisse.]

TOWERS (JOHN), bookseller (?) in London, 1660. His name occurs on the imprint to a broadside entitled *Speech spoken to the Lord General Monk at Goldsmiths' Hall, April 10th, 1660.* [Lutt. i. 86.]

TREAGLE (GEORGE), bookseller at Taunton, 1646–53. Was possibly a relative of John Treagle, who took up his freedom May 7th, 1627. [Arber, iii. 686.] His name is found on the imprints to the following works: G. Newton's *Mans wrath and God's praise*, 1646 [E. 344 (6)]; Francis Fullwood's *Churches and Ministery of England*, 1652 [B.M. 463, h. 4, 2267]; W. Slater's *Civil Magistracy by Divine Authority*, 1653, an assize sermon preached at Winchester.

TRENCH (DAVID), bookseller in Edinburgh, 1662–71. Named among the debtors in G. Lithgow's inventory, 1662. One of A. Anderson's partners in the privilege and appointment as king's printer, 1671. Died 1671. His widow, Janet Mitchell, married Robert Malloch. [H. G. Aldis, *List of Books*, p. 122.]

TROT (ROBERT), printer (?) and bookseller in London; Under the church of Edmond the King in Lombard Street, over against St. Clement's Lane, 1645–9. His name has been met with on the imprints to the following: E. Pagitt, *Heresiography*, 1645; Eikanah Wales, *Mount Ebal levell'd*, 1659. [Ames Collection, 2825.]

TUCKEY (HUMPHREY), bookseller in London; Black Spread Eagle in Fleet Street (between Temple Bar and Chancery Lane, on the north side), 1642–53. Publisher of political tracts and miscellaneous literature.

TURKEY (HENRY), bookseller (?) in London, 1643. Only known from the imprint to the following pamphlet: *Humble petition of the Maior .... of the Citie of London to His Majestie .... London, Printed for Henry Turkey, 1643.* [Hazlitt, ii. 359.]

TURNER (I.), bookseller in London, 1643. Only known from the imprint to a pamphlet entitled, *Elegies on the death of .... John Hampden, Esq. .... by J. S. .... London, Printed by Luke Norton for I. Turner, 1643.* [E. 71 (4).]

TURNER (WILLIAM), printer to the University in Oxford. 1624–43. Took up his freedom on May 24th, 1622 [Arber, iii. 685], and his first book entry is recorded July 18th, 1623. [Arber, iv. 102.] In 1624 he was appointed printer to the University in succession to James Short. In 1631, in company with Michael Sparks, senr., and other London booksellers, he was tried before the Court of Ecclesiastical Commissioners on the charges of printing unlicensed literature and books that were other men's copies. [*Domestic State Papers*, Charles I, vol. 188 (13); 190 (40).] Much dissatisfaction was expressed by Dr. Richard Baylie, the Vice-Chancellor, in a letter to Archbishop Laud, dated January 16th, 1636–7, at the wretched character of the literature that came from Turner's press. Dr. Baylie writes, "He has been urged to print *Joannes Antiochenes*, and adopt some course for advancing the learned press of Oxford, but without any satisfaction .... he prints nothing but almanacks and school-books." [*Domestic State Papers*, Charles I, vol. 344 (20).] This letter may perhaps furnish a clue to the statement made in Wharton's *Remains of Laud* [ii. 174], that Turner had in 1634 abstracted the Savile Greek type. He returned

it in February, $16\frac{39}{40}$. He died about October, 1644, and was succeeded as University Printer by Henry Hall, *q.v.*, who had been one of his apprentices, and who had purchased Turner's presses, letters and utensils. [Madan, *Early Oxford Press*, p. 276; *Chart*, p. 29.

TUTCHEIN (ROBERT), bookseller (?) in London; Phœnix, in the New Rents in S. Paul's Church Yard, 1651. Only known from an imprint preserved amongst the Bagford fragments. [Harl., 5963 (10).]

TUTHILL (JOHN), bookseller in Yarmouth, 1661. His name is found on the imprint to the following pamphlet: Brinsley (John) ΑΓΩΝΟΤΡΟΧΙΑ, *Running of the Christian Race*, 1661. [Ames Collection, 3026.]

TWYFORD (HENRY), bookseller in London, (1) Vine Court in the Middle Temple; (2) Three Daggers in Fleet Street, 1641–75. Took up his freedom January 20th, 1640. [Arber, iii. 688.] Mentioned as one of the "better sort of freemen" in a list of stationers dated August 5th, 1641, as paying ten shillings as his proportion of the Poll Tax. [*Domestic State Papers*, Charles I, vol. 483 (11).] Dealt chiefly in law books, and in 1664 was arrested for illegally selling works of this class, which the Company of Stationers considered as their copyright. [Chan. Proc. Reynardson, Bundle 31, Stationers' Co. *v.* Flesher.]

TWYFORD (TIMOTHY), bookseller in London; At his shop, within the Inner-Temple-Gate, 1660. Possibly a son of the preceding. His name is found on the imprint to the following book: Herne (John), *Law of Charitable uses*, 1660. [Ames Collection, 2933.]

TWYN (JOHN), printer in London; Cloth Fair, 1640–64. Took up his freedom September 4th, 1640. [Arber, iii. 688.] This unfortunate printer, being in a small way of business, apparently did not look too closely at the manuscript supplied to him. At the beginning of the year 1664 he was arrested at the instigation of Sir Roger L'Estrange, for printing, or rather attempting to print, a pamphlet entitled *A Treatise of the Execution of Justice.* He was put on his trial at the Old Bailey on February 20th as a traitor against the King, and the indictment against him was that the book was intended to foment a rebellion. The chief witnesses against him were Joseph Walker, his apprentice, Sir Roger L'Estrange and

Thomas Mabb, a printer, and amongst the jury were Richard Royston, Samuel Thomson, and Thomas Roycroft. Twyn was found guilty, condemned to death, and executed at Tyburn. [*An exact Narrative of the Tryal and condemnation of John Twyn .... London*, 1664; Cobbett's *State Trials*, vol. 6.]

TYLER (EVAN), printer in Edinburgh, 1633–50; Leith, 1651–2; London: Ducket Court, Aldersgate Street, 1656 (?)–67. Took up his freedom July 1st, 1639. [Arber, iii. 688.] The first entry in the Registers under his name occurs on September 11th, 1644. [Liber D, p. 683.] The history of this printer is involved in much obscurity. He apparently had presses in London and Edinburgh simultaneously. Mr. Aldis, in his *List of Books printed in Scotland* (p. 122), says, "Appears to have been in charge of R. Young's Edinburgh business in 1637 .... and in 1641 returned to Edinburgh in partnership with Young. In the following year Young's name dropped out of the imprints and Tyler continued the style of king's printer. In 1651 he moved to Leith, but seems to have returned to London in 1652–3, being succeeded in Leith by C. Higgins .... At the Restoration, Tyler once more returned to Edinburgh, resumed the style of king's printer, and printed there from 1660 to 1672." Amongst the State Papers for the year 1651 is an undated and unsigned paper headed *The true reason why the Company of Stationers bought their printing house in Scotland*, in which occurs the following passage: "About four years before [*i.e.*, 1647] upon an overture from the .... Kings Printer there, to sell the company his Patent and Printing howse, the company made an agreement with him which cost them a large some of money. Since which time, what with the troubles there and in this Commonwealth the Company have extremely suffered there .... The Company are now [*i.e.*, 1651] withdrawing their stock and materials." This at all events would account for Evan Tyler's return to London in 1652. He is mentioned in the Hearth Tax Roll for the half-year ending Lady Day, 1666, as a printer in Ducket Court, St. Botolph's, Aldersgate. [P.R.O. Lay Subsidy, $\frac{252}{32}$.] Tyler was the printer of the unfinished Lithuanian Bible in 1662, which Mr. Steele considers was printed in London. [*Library*, January, 1907.] In contemporary news-sheets Barnard Alsop was stated to be the printer of many things having Tyler's name in the imprint.

TYTON (FRANCIS), bookseller in London; Three Daggers in Fleet Street, neer the Inner Temple Gate, 1649–67. Joint publisher with Thomas Underhill, of Richard Baxter's early works. In 1651 he appears to have held some official position under Government, as on March 31st of that year a payment of £54 14*s.* 7*d.* was made to him for supplying books and papers to the Commissioners for Ireland. [*Calendar of State Papers*, 1651, p. 555.] In 1660 he was appointed "printer" to the House of Lords with J. Macock.

TYUS (CHARLES), bookseller in London; Three Bibles on London Bridge, 1656–64. Dealt in ballads, chap books, and miscellaneous literature. Succeeded by his widow, Sarah Tyus.

TYUS (SARAH), bookseller in London; Three Bibles on London Bridge, 1665. Widow of Charles Tyus. This house was afterwards in the possession of Thomas Passinger.

UNDERHILL (JANE), bookseller in London; Bible and Anchor St. Pauls Churchyard, 1660. Probably widow of Thomas Underhill.

UNDERHILL (THOMAS), bookseller in London, (1) Bible in Wood Street, 1644; (2) Anchor and Bible in St. Paul's Churchyard, 1641–59. Associated with Francis Tyton as publisher of Richard Baxter's early writings. Also associated with Giles Calvert in some publications. His earlier address is found in W. Lilly's *Prophecy of the White King*, 1644.

UNDERWOOD (JAMES), bookseller in London; Near the New Exchange, 1642–3. Took up his freedom June 18th, 1627. [Arber, iii. 686.] Published some political tracts. [Hazlitt, ii. 627, 635.]

UNDERWOOD (THOMAS), bookseller in London, 1643. Took up his freedom September 3rd, 1638. [Arber, iii. 688.] His name appears on the imprint to the following pamphlets: *True Copy of a Welsh sermon*, 1643; *The Welsh ambassadour*, 1643. His address has not been found.

UPHILL (ANTHONY), bookseller (?) in London, 1641. Took up his freedom October 2nd, 1620. [Arber, iii. 685.] Mentioned in a list of stationers dated August 5th, 1641, as one of the "better sort of freemen," who paid twenty shillings as his proportion of the poll tax. [*Domestic State Papers*, Chas. I, vol. 483 (11).]

VALL (THOMAS), bookseller (?) in London, 1657. His name occurs on the imprint to T. Woolsey's *Reasonable Treatise of this age*, 1657. [Hazlitt, ii. 659.]

VAUGHAN (R), printer in London, (1) St. Martin's le Grand; (2) King's College, near Puddledock [Thames Street], 1660–1. In partnership with H. Lloyd. His addresses are found in the following books: (1) *Speech and plea of Archibald, Marquis of Argyle*, 1660; (2) *Last words and actions of John James*, 1661.

VAVASOUR (NICHOLAS), bookseller in London; Little South door of Pauls; (2) Inner Temple, 1623–43. Took up his freedom March 22nd, 1622. [Arber, iii. 685.] Amongst his publications was Sir Henry Colthrop's *Liberties, Usages and Customes of the City of London*, 1642.

VEERE, or VERE (THOMAS), bookseller in London, (1) Upper end of the Old Bayley, near Newgate; (2) Angel in the Old Bailey; (3) Angel without Newgate; (4) Cock in St. John Street, 1667. [1646–80.] Dealt chiefly in ballads and broadsides, in which he was associated with F. Coles, Jo. Wright, and W. Gilbertson.

VERE, *see* Veere, T.

VERIDICUS (TH.), Edinburgh, 1650. [*See* H. G. Aldis, *List of Books*, No. 1412.]

VINCENT or VINSON (ANTHONY), bookseller in London; Old Bailey, 1627–48. Took up his freedom June 21st, 1627. [Arber, iii. 686. Hazlitt, iv. 154, records a speech by Rich. Martin as sold by Ant. Vinson.]

WALBANCKE (MATTHEW), bookseller in London; Gray's Inn Gate, 1618–67. Took up his freedom March 22nd, 1617. [Arber, iii. 684.] Mentioned in a list of dealers in "old libraries," who in 1628 were required to send catalogues of their books to the Archbishop of Canterbury. A publisher of and dealer in law books. He was also the publisher of the news-sheet called the *Exact Diary*. Had a son, Matthew, apprenticed to him on March 1st, $164\frac{9}{50}$.

WALKER (HENRY), bookseller in London, 1641–2. Better known as Walker the Ironmonger. John Taylor, the water poet, wrote a biography of him in 1642, in which he declared that Walker was apprenticed to an ironmonger, and for some years followed that trade, but eventually gave it up to become a bookseller and writer of pamphlets, of which he published as many as four or five hundred thousand copies. Amongst these was one entitled *To your tents, O Israel!* a copy of which he flung into the King's carriage. For this he and the printer were sent to the King's Bench Prison in Southwark, but were subsequently rescued by the mob when on their way to Newgate. After a long hue and cry Walker was recaptured and sent to the Tower. He then made submission. [*The Whole Life and Progress of Henry Walker the Ironmonger . . . . Collected and written by John Taylor*, 1642. 12th July. [E. 154 (29).]

WALKER (JOHN), bookseller in London; Starre in Pope's Head Alley, 1648–50. A stationer of this name took up his freedom October 4th, 1619, but this is probably a different man. His name is found on the imprint to the following pamphlet: *Mercurius Anti-mechanicus, Or, The Simple Cobler's Boy . . . . By Theodore de la Guarden* [*i.e.*, Nath. Ward], London, 1648. [E. 470 (25).]

WALKER (MATHIAS), bookseller in London; (1) 3 Hearts, West End of Pauls, 1664; (2) Under St. Dunstan's Church in Fleet Street, 1667. Chiefly remembered as one of the publishers of the first edition of Milton's *Paradise Lost*, in 1667. His earlier address is found in A. Gordon's *Tyrocynium Linguæ Latinæ*, 1664. [Arber's *Term Catalogue*, vol. i., index.]

WALKLEY (THOMAS), bookseller in London, (1) Eagle and Child, Britain's Burse; (2) Flying Horse, near York House. 1619–58. Took up his freedom January 19th, 1618. On December 1st, 1649, a warrant was issued against him for dispersing scandalous declarations sent from the late King's sons at Jersey. [*Calendar of Domestic State Papers*, 1649–50, p. 557.] He was the publisher of Sir J. Denham's *Coopers Hill*, 1642, Waller's *Poems*, 1647, and much other interesting literature.

WALL (THOMAS), bookseller in Bristol. By the Tolezy in Cornstreet, 1660. Published a sermon entitled, *Plain dealing and Plain meaning . . . . Preacht in the parish church of St. Nicholas, Bristol, April 6th, 1660*. [E. 1026 (5).]

WALLEY, or WALEY (HENRY), bookseller in London; Harts Horn in Foster Lane (?) 1608–55. Grandson of John Walley, or Waley, stationer of London, 1546–86, son of Robert Walley, or Waley, stationer of London, 1578–93. Clerk of the Company of Stationers, 1630–1640. Master of the Company of Stationers in 1655. [Arber, v. 271.]

WALLEY (JOSEPH), bookseller in London, 1666. Stated in a document of that date to be "a great factor for the sectaries." [*Domestic State Papers*, Charles II, 121, 372.] He was possibly a son of the preceding and in business with him.

WALLIS (ELISHA), bookseller in London, (1) Three Black Lyons in the Old Bayley, 1656; (2) At the [Golden] Horse-shoe in the [Great] Old Bayley, 1656–61. His name is found on the imprint to an edition of Robert Burton's *Anatomy of Melancholy*, 1660.

WALTON (ROBERT), printer and print seller in London; Globe and Compasses in St. Paul's Churchyard, between the two north doors, 1647-60. Dealer in maps and prints, and the publisher of Edward Cocker's *The Pen's Triumph*, 1660. A catalogue of prints, etc., on sale by him is given at the end of *A compendious view . . . . of the whole world*, 1659. It is called "a catalogue of some pleasant and useful maps and pictures that are cut in copper, being very neat ornaments for houses, gentlemen's studies and closets, and useful for divers callings, as Painters, Embroyderers, &c." His name is variously given as Walters, Waltor, and Walton.

WARD (FRANCIS), bookseller in Leicester, 1661–3. Gave information against the London bookseller Nathan Brooks for dispersing a book entitled *The Year of Prodigies and Wonders*. October, 1661. [*Domestic State Papers*, Charles II, vol. 43, 7, 8, 9.] Mentioned in an advertisement of patent medicines in the *Intelligencer* of 1663.

WARREN (ALICE), printer in London; Foster Lane (?), 1661–2. Widow of Thomas Warren, printer. Her name is found on the imprint to the second volume of Sir William Dugdale's *Monasticon Anglicanum*, 1661, and the same author's *History of imbanking*, 1662.

WARREN (FRANCIS and THOMAS), printers in London; Foster Lane, 1663–6. Possibly the sons of Thomas Warren, senr., and Alice Warren. They are mentioned in the Hearth Tax Roll for the half-year ending Lady

Day, 1666, as printers in Foster Lane. [P.R.O. Lay Subsidy, $\frac{252}{32}$.] In a list of the several printing houses taken on July 24th, 1668, amongst the master printers returned as ruined by the Fire of London was Mr. Warren. [*Domestic State Papers*, Charles II, vol. 243, 126.] This has reference, doubtless, to the above printing house.

WARREN (THOMAS), senr., bookseller and printer in London, (1) White Horse in St. Pauls Churchyard, 1641; (2) Foster Lane, 1638 (?)–61 (?). Appears to have begun as a bookseller in partnership with Joshua Kirton. Their imprint (No. 1 above) is found on the title-page of James Giffard's *French Schoolmaster*, 1641 [Harl. 5927 (439).] Warren afterwards became a printer and was succeeded by his widow, Alice Warren, in 1661.

WARWICK (WILLIAM), bookseller (?) in Colchester (?), 1663. His name is found on the imprint to a pamphlet entitled: *Some worthy proverbs left behind by Judith Zins-Penninck, To be read in the congregation of the saints .... London, Printed for William Warwick*, 1663. [B.M. 4152, c. 34.]

WATERSON (JOHN), bookseller in London; Crown, at Cheap Gate in Pauls Churchyard (?), 1620–56. Son of Simon Waterson, 1585–1634. Took up his freedom June 27th, 1620. [Arber, iii. 688.] A dealer in plays, is believed to have given up business in 1641. Smyth in his *Obituary*, p. 41, under date February 10th, $165\frac{5}{6}$, records: "John Waterson, once a bookseller, died." He left a son, Simon, who was apprenticed to John Williams, on September 1st, 1645, for seven years. [Register of Apprentices, Stationers' Hall.]

WATERSON (SIMON), bookseller in London; Globe in St. Paul's Churchyard, 1656–7. Son of John Waterson, apprenticed to John Williams, *q.v.*, on September 1st, 1645, for seven years. He was associated with Richard Clavell in publishing an edition of Camden's *Remains*, 1657. [G. 2925.]

WATKINS (R.), bookseller (?) in London (?) 1642. His name occurs on the imprint to a pamphlet entitled *A True and Joyful Relation of Two famous Battels .... Printed for R. Watkins, August 27th, 1642.* [Hazlitt, ii. 516; iii. 290.]

WATKINS (ZACHARIAH), bookseller in London; Near Inner Temple Church, 1663. Advertisement in *The Kingdoms Intelligencer*, April 20th, 1663.

WATKIS (   ), bookseller in Shrewsbury, 1663. Mentioned in an advertisement of patent medicines in the news-sheets of this year.

WATSON (HUMPHREY), bookseller (?) in London (?) 1642. His name occurs on the imprint to a pamphlet entitled *A True Relation of Two Merchants of London ..... Printed for Humphrey Watson*, 1642. [Hazlitt, iii. 145.]

WATSON (JOSEPH), (?) bookseller in London, 1642. His name is found on the imprints to the following pamphlets: *Parliaments last order and determination for the safety and security of Hull*, 1642 [B.M. E. 108 (10)]; *Portsmouth. New discovery of a design of the French*, 1642. [Hazlitt, ii. 489.]

WATSON (WILLIAM), bookseller (?) in London (?), 1641. His name is found on the imprint to a pamphlet entitled *Resolution of the Women of London*, 1641. 4°. [Hazlitt, i. 262.] A stationer of this name took up his freedom July 25th, 1624. [Arber, iii. 685.]

WAYTE (THOMAS), bookseller at York; The Pavement, 1653–95. Joined the Quakers about 1651, and acted as local agent for Friends' publications. Several tracts, all dated 1653, written by George Fox, Richard Farnsworth, James Nayler and William Tomlinson, have the imprint: "Printed for Tho. Wayte at his house in the Pavement in York," or "Printed for Thos. and are to be sold at his house, etc." Wayte's name occurs in a list of "dispersers of Quaker books," drawn up in 1664. He married the sister of Richard Smith, a tanner of York, and his house became a noted meeting place for Friends. Thomas Wayte died in 1695, six years after his wife. [*The First Publishers of Truth*, p. 318 n.]

WEBB (CHARLES), bookseller in London; Golden Boar's Head, St. Paul's Churchyard, 1658–60. Publisher of miscellaneous literature, including plays.

WEBB (DANIEL), bookseller (?) in London, 1660. His name occurs on the imprint to a pamphlet entitled *Brethren in Iniquity*, 1660. 4°. [Hazlitt, iii. 23.]

WEBB (NATHANIEL), bookseller in London, (1) King's Head, St. Paul's Churchyard, 1660; (2) Royal Oak, St. Paul's Churchyard, 1663 (1646–65). In partnership for a time with W. Grantham, *q.v.* Died March 26th, 1665. [Smyth's *Obituary*, p. 62.] His second address is found on a pamphlet entitled *A Modest Discourse concerning the Ceremonies .... used in the Church*, 1660. [E. 1035 (4).]

WEBB (RICHARD), bookseller (?) in London (?), 1642. His name is found on the imprint to John Taylor's *Cluster of Coxcombs*, 1642. [Hazlitt, i. 419.]

WEBB [WILLIAM), bookseller in Oxford, 1629–52. [Madan, *Oxford Chart*, p. 29.] His name is found on a large number of political pamphlets between 1641 and 1652.

WEEKLY (WILLIAM), bookseller in Ipswich, 1657–9. His name is found on the imprints to the following books: C Beck, *Universal Character*, 1657. [E. 1591 (1)]; A. Pringle, *Stay in Trouble*, 1657 [E. 1592 (1)]; M. Lawrence, *Use and Practice of Faith*, 1657 [E. 924 (1)]; Edm. Warren, *Jews Sabbath antiquated*, 1659. [Ames Collection, 2854.]

WELLS (R.), bookseller (?) in London; Royal Exchange in Cornhill (?), 1648. His name is found on the imprint to a pamphlet entitled *Prince Charles his Declaration .... London, Printed for R. Wells, and are to be sold at the Royall Exchange in Cornhill*, 1648. [Hazlitt, ii. 105.]

WELLS (WILLIAM), bookseller in London; Princes Arms, Little Britain, 1641–73. Took up his freedom April 3rd, 1637. [Arber, iii. 688.] Mentioned in a list of stationers who on August 5th, 1641, had paid their proportion of the poll tax. [*Domestic State Papers*, Charles I, vol. 483 (11).] Was in partnership for a time with Robert Scott, *q.v.* Died in January, $167\frac{2}{3}$. Smyth in his *Obituary* records, "Mr. Wells, bookseller in Little Britain (my old acquaintance) died this Satterday morning. Buried at St. Butolphs extra Aldersgate. No sermon."

WENBORN (WILLIAM), bookseller in London; The Rose at the Bridge Foot, 1646. Only known from the imprint to the following pamphlet: Παντᾰλογία. *The Saints Abundance opened. By Thomas Sterry.* [E. 355 (28).]

WEST (G.), bookseller in Oxford (*c.* 1650–95). [Madan, *Oxford Chart*, p. 31; Ames Collection, 3186.]

WEST (SIMON), bookseller in London; Blackamore's Head in great Wood-street, neer Cheapside, 1637–46. Took up his freedom February 6th, 1637. [Arber, iii. 688.] Became a teacher of shorthand and wrote and published a book on the subject entitled *Arts Improvement: or Short and swift Writing .... London, 1647.* [B.M. 1043, c. 45.]

WHALEY (PETER), bookseller in London; Gun in Ivy Lane, 1645. Associated with C. Greene, *q.v.* Had a son Samuel apprenticed on March 1st, $16\frac{49}{50}$.

WHITACRE, or WHITACRES, *see* Whitaker.

WHITAKER (RICHARD), bookseller in London; Kings Arms in St. Paul's Churchyard, 1619–48. Took up his freedom May 3rd, 1619. [Arber, iii. 685.] In partnership with Thomas Whitaker, *q.v.* They had an extensive business, and published much of the best literature of the period. Richard Whitaker was a warden of the Company of Stationers in the years 1643–5. He died on February 5th, $164\frac{7}{8}$. [Smyth's *Obituary*, p. 25.]

WHITAKER (THOMAS), bookseller in London; King's Arms, St. Paul's Churchyard, 1642 (?)–50 (?). In partnership with Richard Whitaker, and carried on the business after Richard's death in 1648. Thomas Whitaker died about 1650, and his widow married Mr. Alexander Brome. On March 7th, $165\frac{2}{3}$, they assigned over all their right and title to the Whitaker copyrights to Humphrey Robinson, Richard Thrale, Joshua Kirton, and Samuel Thompson. This assignment numbered one hundred and nine items, and fills four pages of the Stationers' Register. [*See* also Introduction.]

WHITE (DANIEL), bookseller in London; Seven Stars in St. Paul's Church Yard, 1659–60. His name is found in the following works: P. Cornelius' *Way to the Peace*, 1659; [S. (G.) Poetical Essay, *As an Arrha of a larger Harvest*, 1660; *see* Wharton (G.), *Select and Choice Poems*, 1661.

WHITE (JOHN), bookseller in London; Threadneedle Street, behind the Old Exchange, 1661. His name is found on the imprint to a pamphlet entitled, *Hermas: The Three Bookes of Hermas the Disciple of Paul the*

Apostle . . . . Englished by John Pringle . . . . London, Printed for John White in Threadneedle Street, behinde the Old Exchange, 1661. [Bodleian; Hazlitt, i. 211.]

WHITE (ROBERT), printer in London; Warwick Court, Warwick Lane, 1639–67. Took up his freedom December 7th, 1639. [Arber, iii. 688.] Partner with Thos. Brudenell, in printing the Bible in 1647. They were also joint printers of Sprigge's *Anglia Rediviva*, although only the initials of Robert White occur in the imprint. White was also associated with George Bishop in printing several news-sheets. At the survey of the press taken in 1668 he is returned as having three presses, three apprentices and seven workmen. [Plomer, *Short History*, p. 225.]

WHITING (G), bookseller (?) in London (?), 1652. His name occurs on the imprint to a pamphlet entitled *Black Munday turn'd White*, 1652. [B.M. 718, c. 20 (2).]

WHITTINGTON (GEORGE), bookseller in London; Blew Anchor in Cornhill, neer the Royall Exchange, 1643–9 (?). His name is found on the imprint to the following pamphlet: *Humble petition of many thousands of Young Men*, 1646. [E. 378, 15.] Issued some books in partnership with John Partridge and James Moxon and Hannah Allen.

WHITTLESEY (THOMAS), bookseller (?) in London (?), 1662. His name is found on the imprint to John Heydon's *Holy Guide.* [Hazlitt, iv. 47.]

WHITWOOD (WILLIAM), bookseller in London; Swan, Duck Lane, 1666–7. Dealer in ballads and broadsides.

WILCOX (JOHN), bookseller in London; Crown in St. Pauls Churchyard, 1647. His name is found on the imprint to Thomas Philipot's *Poems*, 1647. [Hazlitt, H. 456.] Probably a misprint for John Williams.

WILDEBERGH (C.), bookseller (?) in London; The Globe in St. Katherines, 1662. His name is found on the following broadside, *An exact and true relation of the landing of Her Majesty at Portsmouth*, 1662. [B.M. C. 20, f. 2 (50).]

WILFORD (GEORGE), bookseller in London; Little Britain, near the Hospital Gate, 1652. His name is found on a pamphlet entitled, *Looking Glasse for a Drunkard*, 1652 [Hazlitt, H. 171.]

WILKINS (TIMOTHY), bookseller in London; George in Fleet St., 1641. In partnership with John Maynard in the publication of the writings of John Wilkins, Bishop of Chester.

WILLIAMS (JOHN), bookseller in London, (1) Crown, St. Pauls Church Yard, 1636–66; (2) Blue Anchor in Little Britain, 1667. Took up his freedom September 15th, 1634. [Arber, iii. 687.] Paid ten shillings as his proportion of the poll tax in 1641. [*Domestic State Papers*, Charles I, vol. 483 (11).] Joint publisher with F. Eglesfield, *q.v.*, of Herrick's *Hesperides*, 1648. The John Wilcox, *q.v.*, recorded by Hazlitt is probably intended for John Williams.

WILLIAMS (RICHARD), bookseller at St. Albans in Hertfordshire, 1649–56. Three stationers of this name took up their freedom before 1640. [Arber, iii. 683, 686, 688.] The following pamphlets have his name on the imprint: *The Divels Delusions*, 1649 [E. 565 (15)]; *Bloudy Fight in Hartfordshire*, 1649. The name R. Williams is also found on the imprint to a political tract in 1642, entitled *Parliaments Declaration concerning the Kings Majesty* [E. 108 (44)], but whether he was the same with the St. Albans bookseller is unknown.

WILLIAMS (THOMAS), bookseller in London; Bible in Little Britain, 1662–7. His name is found on the imprint to a pamphlet by John Humfrey, entitled *Second Discourse about re-ordination*, 1662. [Ames Collection, 3080.] He is mentioned in the Hearth Tax Roll for the half-year ending Lady Day, 1666, as a bookseller in Little Britain. [P.R.O. Lay Subsidy, $\frac{252}{32}$]. His death is recorded by Smyth in his *Obituary*, p. 79.

WILLIAMSON (ANTHONY), bookseller (?) in London; Queens Arms neer the West-end of St. Paul's Church Yard, 1651–9. His name occurs on the imprint to the following pamphlet: *The Grand Debate concerning Presbytery*, 1652. [B.M. 463, h. 4 (2273).]

WILLIAMSON (ROBERT), bookseller (?) in London, 1648–9. His name is found on the imprint to the following amongst other political pamphlets: *Great fight at Chepstow Castle*, 1648. [E. 443, 14.]

WILMOT (JOHN), bookseller in Oxford, 1637–65. [Madan, *Chart of Oxford Printing*, pp. 29, 31.] His name is found on the imprint to Adrian Heereboord's *Philosophia naturalis*, 1665. [Ames Collection, 3237.]

WILSON (ANDRO), bookseller in Edinburgh, (1) Near the Ladies Steps, 1641; (2) At the Plain Stones over against the Stone Shop at the signe of the Great Book, 1649; (3) At the sign of the Bible, 1649 (1641–54. [H. G. Aldis, *List of Books*, p. 124.]

WILSON (HENRY), bookseller (?) in London, 1642. His name is found on the imprint to a political pamphlet entitled *The Virgins Complaint* [Jan. 31], 1642. [*See* Hazlitt, i. 440.]

WILSON (PATRICK), bookseller at Edinburgh, 1643. Issued a broadside entitled *A merrie Ballad, called Christio Kirk on the Green* [25 Nov.], 1643. [669, f. 8, 38.]

WILSON (ROBERT), bookseller in London; Black Spread Eagle and Windmill, St. Martins le Grand, near Aldersgate, 1660 (?)–62 (?). A dealer in Quaker literature. In a letter to Richard Snead, mercer, of Bristol, written in 1661, he says: "I am exposed in this day through many and frequent sufferings to severall difficulties: for very often am I plundered by ye rulers of my goods; burning them at home and abroad." [*Domestic State Papers*, Charles II, vol. 56, 83.] The same year he was committed to the Gatehouse for selling "seditious pamphlets against the Government of the Church of England A list of books seized at his shop in that year was published in *Mercurius Publicus* on November 28th.

WILSON (THOMAS), printer in London; Three Foxes in Long Lane [Smithfield], 1653–7. Joint printer with John Crouch, of the news-sheet called *Mercurius Democritus.* Their printing house was situated in one of the lowest parts of the City of London, and they were largely employed in printing ballads, broadsides, chap books, and such ephemeral literature.

WILSON (WILLIAM), printer in London (?); Three Foxes in Long Lane, 1640–65. Took up his freedom September 4th, 1626. [Arber, iii. 686.; *see* also Harl. MSS., 5919 (281).]

WILTS (J.), bookseller (?) in London (?), 1660. His name appears on the imprint to the following pamphlet: *Two Grand Traytor's Lamentation*, 1660. [E. 1040 (15).]

WINGATE (R), bookseller (?) in London; Golden Hind, Chancery Lane, 1655. Associated with Twyford, Brookes, and J. Place in the publication of a work entitled *The Complete Clark and Scrivenors Guide*, 1655. It is doubtful whether he was a bookseller, and not rather the compiler of the work.

WINNAIN (G), bookseller (?) in (?) London, 1663. This name occurs on a pamphlet entitled, *Articles and charge against the German lady prisoner in the Gatehouse, to be exhibited according to the records of the City of Canterbury* . . . . London, Printed for G. Winnain, 1663. [Hazlitt, iii. 30.] It may possibly be that of a Canterbury bookseller.

WITHRINGTON (C), bookseller (?) in London (?), 1648. His name is found on several political pamphlets issued in that year. [Hazlitt, ii. 103; E. 473 (29).]

WODENOTHE, WOODENOTHE, or WOODNORTH (RICHARD), bookseller and haberdasher in London, (1) Star under St. Peter's Church in Cornhill; (2) Leadenhall Street, next to the Golden Heart, 1645–56. First entry in the Stationers' Registers under his name July 26th, 1645. Is described in the Parish Registers of St. Peter's, Cornhill, as a stationer and haberdasher.

WOOD (RALPH), printer in London, 1642–65. Printer of ballads and popular literature. He was also the printer of Richard Flecknoe's *Poems*, 1660, and John Bunyan's *Sighs from Hell*, 1658. His largest work was apparently the folio edition of the romance called *Cloria*, which he printed for W. Brooke. His address has not been found, but he may have been in partnership with Robert Wood.

WOOD (ROBERT), printer in London, (1) White Hind, without Cripplegate; (2) Near ye Flying Horse in Grub Street. 1642–67. Took up his freedom September 4th, 1637. [Arber, iii. 688.] Printed numerous political pamphlets in which he was associated with J. Greensmith and Edward Christopher. He was possibly a relative of Ralph Wood, and they may have been in partnership together.

WOODHALL (HUMPHREY), bookseller (?) in London, 1617–41. Took up his freedom May 20th, 1617. [Arber, iii. 684.] Mentioned in a list of stationers who paid their proportion of the poll tax on August 5th, 1641. [*Domestic State Papers*, Charles I, vol. 483 (11).]

WOODNORTH, *see* Wodenothe.

WOODNOTHE, *see* Wodenothe.

WREN (JOSEPH), bookseller (?) in London, 1642. *The Poets Recantation .... by John Bond. London, Printed for T. A. and Joseph Wren, 1942* (*sic*). [E. 142 (13).]

WRIGHT (FRANCIS), bookseller (?) in London (?) 1643. Only known from the imprint to a broadside entitled *Good Newes from Plymouth.* [Hazlitt, iii. 64.]

WRIGHT (J), bookseller in London; Next door to the Globe in Little Britain, 1667. His name is found on the imprint to the following book: *Garden of Spiritual Flowers*, 1667. [Ames Collection, 3332.]

WRIGHT (JOHN), senr., bookseller in London; Kings Head in the Old Bailey, 1605–58. Took up his freedom in 1602 and became the publisher of many notable books, including Shakespeare's *Sonnets* and Marlowe's *Faustus.* On January 2nd, 164⅔, he was committed to the Compter in Wood Street for publishing a scandalous book against the Parliament [*Commons Journals*, vol. 2, p. 910], but he quickly made his peace with the Government, and when next heard of, he is found to be one of the official printers to the Parliament. On May 11th, 1643, in company with Thomas Bates, he started a news-sheet called *Mercurius Civicus*, which was distinguished by each issue having on the first page a woodcut, or

sometimes two, intended to illustrate some event mentioned in it. This news-sheet ran till the close of the year 1646. Wright and Bates were also the publishers of another news-sheet, *The True Informer.* John Wright married Katherine, the daughter of Christopher Hatfield, citizen and cutler of London, and is mentioned in his will [P.C.C. 83, Soame.] He had a son, John Wright, junior. John Wright, senior, died in May, 1658, being buried on the 11th of that month. [Smyth, *Obituary*, p. 47; *Library*, April, 1905, pp. 184–207.]

WRIGHT (JOHN), junior, bookseller in London; Kings Head, Old Bailey, 1634–67. Son of John Wright, senior, and in partnership with him. On June 13th, 1642, he took over the copyrights, sixty-two in number, which had belonged to Robert Bird and Edward Brewster. In addition to theological literature it included *The History of Gargantua, A Book of Riddles*, and Robinson's *Citharine book.* [*Stationers' Registers.*] Either he or his father was a large holder in the ballad stock of the Company, and with Fr. Coles, T. Vere, and W. Gilbertson was the chief publisher of this class of literature.

WRIGHT (JONAS), bookseller (?) in London (?) 1642. His name is found on the imprint to the following pamphlet, *Blazing Starre seen in the West at Totneis in Devonshire*, 1642. [Hazlitt, i. 424.]

WRIGHT (M.), printer (?) in London; Kings Head in the Old Bailey, 1658–62. This name, in company with that of Robert Ibbotson, *q.v.*, is found on the imprint to Thomas Gouge's *Christian Directions*, 1661. [Ames Collection, 3019.] Hazlitt has several entries under it. [Gray's Index to Hazlitt, p. 835.] It may apply to another son of John Wright, senior, *q.v.*

YORK (SIMON), bookseller (?) in Dover, 1654. Only known from the imprint to a pamphlet entitled *An Antidote against Anabaptisme .... By Jo. Reading, B.D. .... London, Printed by Tho. Newcombe, for Simon York and Richard Barley, dwelling in Dover*, 1654. [Ames Collection of Title-pages, 2410.]

YOUNG (JAMES), printer in London, 1643–53. Son of Robert Young, printer. On July 22nd, 1644, his father's copyrights, numbering 131 works, were transferred to him. [Stationers' Registers.]

YOUNG (MICHAEL), bookseller (?) in London; Blew Bible in Covent Garden, 1639–64. Published an edition of Sir Thos. More's *History of Edward the Fifth*, 1641. [Hazlitt, i. 295, ii. 143.]

YOUNG (ROBERT), printer in London, 1625–43. An important member of the Company of Stationers. Entered into partnership with Miles Fletcher, or Flesher, and John Haviland, and bought up several large and old-established printing houses in London. On April 12th, 1632, he was appointed King's printer in Scotland in succession to T. Finlason. He appears to have given up his Edinburgh business in 1638, but on June 30th, 1641, with Evan Tyler, was again appointed the Royal printer for Scotland. [Aldis, *List of Books printed in Scotland*, p. 124.] There is also reason to believe that he had the management of the Irish printing office established by the Company of Stationers, and Mr. F. Madan, in his *Chart of Oxford Printing* (p. 29), gives him as having a press in Oxford in 1640. He was dead before September 16th, 1643, and his copyrights, 131 in number, were transferred to his son James Young. The names of two of his workmen, William Warner, corrector of the press, and Robert Chapman, compositor, occur in an order of the House of Lords dated August 16th, 1641, reprinted in Nalson's *Affairs of State*, vol. ii., p. 447. The position of his printing house in London has not been found.

YOUNG (THOMAS), bookseller (?) in London, 1658. Only known from the imprint to a pamphlet entitled *Natural Magick .... In Twenty Books. London, Printed for Thomas Young and Samuel Speed*, 1658. [Hazlitt, ii. 488.]

A DICTIONARY OF THE PRINTERS AND BOOKSELLERS WHO WERE AT WORK IN ENGLAND, SCOTLAND AND IRELAND FROM 1668 TO 1725

BY

HENRY R. PLOMER.

WITH THE HELP OF H. G. ALDIS, E. R. McC. DIX, G. J. GRAY, AND R. B. McKERROW.

EDITED BY ARUNDELL ESDAILE.

THE BIBLIOGRAPHICAL SOCIETY

1968

INTRODUCTION.

THREE important events in the history of the book-trade marked the period covered by this Dictionary:

1. The expiration of the Licensing Act of 1662 in 1695.
2. The paper and pamphlet duties of 1696 and 1713.
3. The Copyright Act of 1709.

The result of the first was that during the closing years of the seventeenth century printing presses were established in many provincial towns, Bristol and Exeter in the West, Chester, York, Newcastle, and Gateshead in the North, Norwich and Ipswich in the East, and with every year their numbers increased until by 1725 all the important towns in the kingdom had their own printers. Almost the first thing these printers did, was to establish a local newspaper, which, though little else than mirrors of the London press, and containing scanty local news beyond a few advertisements and the trials of criminals at the local assizes, served the useful purpose of broadening the outlook of the people and keeping them in touch with the outside world.

The first of the paper duties was imposed by the 8–9 William III, c. 7, called " An Act for granting to his Majesty several duties upon paper, vellum and parchment, to encourage the bringing of plate and hammered money into the Mints to be coined ". It imposed upon all paper, parchment, and books imported an *ad valorem* duty of 25 per cent., a similar duty of 20 per cent. on paper or parchment made, while all stock-in-trade was to pay 17½ per cent.

In 1711 another Act was passed (10 Anne, c. 18) combining duties on paper with a stamp duty on pamphlets and newspapers. The duties on paper took the form of a tax per ream which varied in the case of imported paper from *1s.* to *16s.* per ream, and in the case of British-made paper from *4d.* to *1s. 6d.* per ream. Books, prints, and maps imported were charged 30 per cent. *ad*

valorem; but paper made or imported for printing books in Latin, Greek, Oriental, or Northern languages at Oxford or Cambridge or one of the Scotch universities was to have a complete drawback of the duty.

Naturally these duties raised an outcry of protest from the trade; but the most serious objection to them, and one that was well founded, was, that it enabled the printers in Holland and Ireland, who were under no such heavy duties, to print English books and put them upon the English market at a cheaper rate than the English publisher could do, whereby authors, printers, and publishers suffered heavy losses.

The duties imposed on pamphlets and newspapers by the Act of 1712, were ½*d.* per copy for anything of half a sheet or less; *1d.* per copy on anything from a half to one sheet; and publications from one sheet to six sheets *2d.* The Act had a two-fold object, the increase of the revenue and the limitation of the power of the press. In the latter object it succeeded, as many so-called newspapers were unable to afford the tax and ceased to appear.[1]

Not less far reaching in its effects was the Copyright Act of 8 Anne, c. 19.

Its object was clearly set out in the preamble which commences, " Whereas printers, booksellers, and other persons have of late frequently taken the liberty of printing, reprinting, and publishing or causing to be printed, reprinted and published books and other writings, without the consent of the authors or proprietors of such books and writings, to their very great detriment, and too often to the ruin of them and their families "—and it then enacted that from and after the 10th April 1710, the author or his assignee, whether printer or bookseller, was to have the sole right of printing or reprinting books then in print for twenty-one years and for new books the term was to be fourteen years, after which the copyright returned to the author for another fourteen years. Books were to be duly registered at Stationers' Hall, and there were other clauses respecting the price at which books were to be sold and the presentation of books to certain institutions. The Act was a well-meaning one, and it had the effect of making trade in copyrights a feature of the book-trade in the eighteenth century, but it did little to stop piracy.

[1] For these notes I am indebted to the late John Macfarlane's articles in *The Library*.

The Act of 1662, " For preventing the frequent Abuses in printing seditious, treasonable, and unlicensed Books and Pamphlets, and for regulating of Printing and Printing Presses " put very large powers into the hands of the official licenser and the Master and Wardens of the Stationers' Company, and both by Sir Roger L'Estrange and Samuel Mearne, these were at times oppressively used. A story of other oppressions will be found in *An Account of the Injurious Proceedings of Sir George Jeffreys kt, late Recorder of London, against Francis Smith bookseller*, London, 1680. But in spite of these troubles and the temporary chaos caused by the final lapsing of the Act in 1695, the book-trade flourished. Thus the printing houses were busy, but the names of the printers only appeared in the imprints of books in rare cases, and the average standard of workmanship was low.

Nearly all booksellers were also publishers, and the copyright of books, instead of being vested as formerly in one or two men, was frequently divided amongst all the principal booksellers in London and the Universities. Dunton also records a practice that had recently sprung up of a system of barter or exchange in copies of their books between publishers. Another feature of this time was the issue of books in weekly and monthly parts, which were distributed by the newsvendors and chapmen; while a further and not the least profitable part of their business was the sale of patent medicines and wall-papers.

We are indebted to John Dunton for much of the information contained in this book. Dunton had an excess of vanity and a foolish way of expressing himself; but he was a shrewd observer, and often sums up his contemporaries in a word or phrase that fits them exactly, and his judgements, when stripped of their verbiage, may be accepted.

HENRY R. PLOMER.

REFERENCES

ABBREVIATED IN THE TEXT.

Allnutt. English Provincial Presses. By W. H. Allnutt. Pt. 3 (Bibliographica, ii. 276–308).
C. J. Commons' Journals.
C.P.R. Common Plea Rolls (Record Office).
Cooke. Bibliotheca Cestriensis. By John H. Cooke. 1904.
Creswell. Collections towards the History of Printing in Nottinghamshire. By S. F. Creswell. 1863.
Davies. A Memoir of the York Press. By Robert Davies. 1868.
Dictionary, 1641–67. A Dictionary of the Booksellers and Printers who were at work in England, Scotland, and Ireland from 1641 to 1667, by Henry R. Plomer. *Bibliographical Society*. 1907.
Dredge. Devon Booksellers and Printers in the seventeenth and eighteenth centuries. By J. I. Dredge. 3 pts. 1885–7.
Dunton. The Life and Errors of John Dunton (written 1703, printed 1705) edited, with other tracts by him, by J. Nichols. 1818.
Gent. The Life of Thomas Gent, written by himself. 1832.
Hearne. Remarks and Collections of Thomas Hearne. 1705–22. 10 vols. *Oxford Historical Society*, 1885–1915.
Hyett and Bazeley. The Bibliographer's Manual of Gloucestershire Literature. By F. A. Hyett and W. Bazeley. 5 vols. 1895–1915.
Lawler. Book Auctions in England in the seventeenth century. 1676–1700. By J. Lawler. 1898.
List of Printing Houses in London in 1675. State Papers Domestic. Charles II, 369 (97).
Liverpool Pr. & Doc. Liverpool Free Public Library. Liverpool Prints and Documents. 1908. pp. 333 sq.
Madan. A Chart of Oxford Printing. *Bibliographical Society*. 1904.
Negus. A List of London printers, classified by their political parties, drawn up by Samuel Negus in 1724. Printed in Nichols' Literary Anecdotes, i. 288–312.
Reed. A History of the Old English Letter Foundries. By T. B. Reed. 1887.
Stationers Company Records. (Unprinted.)
Stat. Reg. (Roxb.). A Transcript of Registers of the Worshipful Company of Stationers from 1640 to 1708. [Presented to the Roxburghe Club by G. E. Briscoe Eyre.] 3 vols. 1913–14.
T.C. The Term Catalogues, 1668–1711. Edited by E. Arber. 3 vols. 1903–6.
Times Handlist. *The Times* Tercentenary Handlist of English and Welsh Newspapers, &c. 1920.

Timperley. A Dictionary of Printers and Printing. By C. H. Timperley. 1839. Second edition 1842. The references serve for both editions.

Wallis. A Sketch of the Early History of the Printing Press in Derbyshire. By Alfred Wallis. (Journal of the Derbyshire Archaeological and Natural History Society, III, 137, &c.) 1881.

Watson. History of the Art of Printing. By James Watson. 1713.

Welford. Early Newcastle Typography. By Richard Welford. (Archaeologia Aeliana, 3rd series, III.) 1906.

Wood. The Life and Times of Anthony Wood, ed. A. C. Clark. *Oxford Historical Society.* 5 vols. 1889–92.

A DICTIONARY OF THE PRINTERS AND BOOKSELLERS WHO WERE AT WORK IN ENGLAND, SCOTLAND AND IRELAND FROM 1668 TO 1725

A. (T.), bookseller in Oxford, 1682. [Madan, p. 30.]

ABINGTON, or ABBINGTON (WILLIAM), bookseller in London, (1) Black Spread-Eagle at the West-end of Pauls; (2) Three Silkworms, near the Wonder Tavern, Ludgate Street. 1679–1705. Succeeded Elizabeth Calvert at the first address. First entry in *T.C.*, Trinity, 1679 [I. 359]. Dunton calls him "beauish Abington". He published in 1683 nos. 1 and 2 of *Scotch Memoirs, by way of dialogue between John and Elymas.* [Timperley, p. 565.]

ABREE (JAMES), printer and bookseller at Canterbury. Over against the Three Tuns, (*a*) Castle Street; (*b*) St. Margaret's Parish. 1717–68. Settled at Canterbury in 1717, and began by printing a sheet, containing the names of the mayor, aldermen and common council, who had encouraged the revival of printing in the city. On October 23rd, 1717, appeared the first number of a newspaper called *The Kentish Post or, The Canterbury News Letter.* The early numbers were printed for the proprietors by Thomas Reeve, in quarto form with a cover. It was afterwards printed by James Abree in partnership with W. Aylett and then by Abree alone, and it then took the ordinary form of a small folio, and appeared twice a week. The Kentish news in this sheet was confined to a few inches of space on the last page, and was of very little interest; but many Kentish advertisements were inserted. In 1718 Abree printed Thomas Hardres's *Panegyrical Poem on the Fair and Celebrated Beauties in and about the City of Canterbury*, folio; in 1726–7 several quarto pamphlets in a quarrel between doctors Packe and Grey of

Canterbury, and in 1740 *Poems on Several Occasions*, by an anonymous lady. Abree was also a bookseller and stationer, and sold wall papers and patent medicines. He circulated by his chapmen many books published in weekly or monthly parts, by London publishers. About 1764 he took into partnership George Kirkby, the son of a Canterbury clergyman, in favour of whom he retired in 1768. Kirkby then dropped the publication of the *Kentish Post*, and entered into partnership with another Canterbury printer, James Simmons, who was then publishing a rival sheet, called *The Kentish Gazette, or Canterbury Chronicle.* James Abree died on August 20th, 1768, aged 77, administration of his effects being granted to his daughter.

ACTON (VALENTINE), bookseller in London. Holy Lamb, St. Paul's Churchyard, 1678. T. James printed for him J. Nye's *A Display of Divine Heraldry.* [*T.C.* I. 319.]

ADAMS (JOHN), bookseller at Oxford, 1673. *See Dictionary*, 1641–67. Still in business in 1673, when he published Holyday's edition of Juvenal. [*T.C.* I. 135.]

ADAMS (ROGER), printer at Manchester and Chester. Manchester: At the lower end of Smithy-Door. 1719–33. Printer and publisher of the first Manchester newspaper, the *Manchester Weekly Journal*, first issued in January 1719. Believed to have come from Chester, whither he returned and conducted *The Chester Courant* from 1730 until his death. During his stay in Manchester he reprinted *A Catalogue of the Lords, Knights and Gentlemen that have compounded for their estates*, first printed by Thomas Dring in 1655. This has an introduction signed by the printer and also the advertisement of another reprint, *The Ordinance of Oliver Cromwell for ejecting scandalous ministers.*

ADAMS (WILLIAM), junior, printer in Edinburgh, (1) opposite to the Trone-Church, 1717; (2) in Carubber's Close, 1720. 1717–25. Adams printed *The Caledonian Mercury* from its beginning in April 1720 to the end of 1723.

ADAMSON (JAMES), bookseller in London, Angel and Crown, St. Paul's Churchyard, 1686–94. First heard of in 1686, when he sold the edition of *Reliquiae Wottonianae*, published by Tooke and Sawbridge. In the same year he published a Latin edition of St. Clement's *Epistles to the Corinthians.* [*T.C.* II. 179.] From this time his name is of frequent occurrence in the Term Catalogues.

Amongst other works of note he had a share in Thévenot's *Travels*, 1687; the Latin edition of *The Life of Cardinal Pole*, 1690; and Geo. Ashwell's *De Socino et Socinianismo dissertatio*, 1692. His last book-entry occurs in Michaelmas 1694. [*T.C.* II. 534.]

ADDERTON (WILLIAM), *see Dictionary*, 1641–67.

AINGE (JOHN), bookseller in Bristol. In Temple Street, during the Fair. 1693–97. Advertised in the *Post Boy* of January 6th–8th, 1697, as agent for Powel's *History of Wales, a new edition* by W. Wynne, A.M. An earlier reference to him has been found in some Chancery Proceedings of the year 1693 [Bridges, $\frac{108}{8}$, $\frac{109}{8}$] relating to property in Gloucester, and to business transactions with John Dowly of London, "a wholesale haberdasher of small wares", whose daughter Alice Ainge married. The will of a John Ainge of Lechlade is found in the Calendar of Gloucester Wills, proved in 1717.

AITKEN (WILLIAM), bookbinder in Edinburgh, 1687. Named cautioner in the confirmation of Gideon Shaw's will. [Bann. Misc. II. 294.]

ALEXANDER (JAMES), bookseller in Edinburgh, 1681. A broadside entitled *A true copy of the Indictment . . . against Archibald Earl of Argyle*, bears the imprint, "Edinburgh, Printed for James Alexander, 1681." [Aldis, p. 107.]

ALEXANDER (JO.), bookseller of Bristol, 1682. Only known from a broadside entitled *Sad and lamentable cry of oppression . . . in . . . Bristol*, 1682, 4°. [Haz. I. 53.]

ALKINS (J.), bookseller (?) in London, near Fleet Street, 1704. Only known from a broadside entitled *An account of a most horrid Plot and Conspiracy*, &c. "London, Printed for J. Alkins, near Fleet Street, 1704." [Bibl. Lind. Catalogue of English Broadsides, no. 874.]

ALLAN (ROBERT), bookseller in Edinburgh, at his shop over foregainst the Court of Guard, 1695–6. One of several booksellers who in 1695 sold Sir T. Craig's *Scotlands soveraignty asserted*, and in the following year *A Letter to a Member of Parliament.* [Aldis, p. 107.]

ALLDRIDGE (T.), bookseller in Southwark, 1697. Only known as the publisher in 1697 of a ballad entitled *The True English Prophet.* [Ouvry Catalogue, no. 76; Haz. II. 203.]

ALLEN, MRS., bookseller in Sevenoaks, 1699. Her name appears in the advertisement in the *Flying Post,* December 2nd, of the publication of the Rev. Edward Brown's *Sermon* preached on the occasion of the Kentish Feast on November 16th. It does not appear in the imprint to the Sermon.

ALLEN, or ALLIN (CHARLES), bookseller in Bristol, Broad Street, 1674–81. In 1674 published *Bristol Drollery, Poems and Songs by Mr. C.*, printed in London, doubtless by Edward Horton, who entered it in Stat. Reg. [Roxb. II. 478]. Hazlitt says that the contents have no peculiar connexion with Bristol. [Hdbk., p. 169.] In Hilary 1679 he entered in *T.C.* [I. 342] *Short-writing,* by Laurence Steel of Bristol. His last entry is S. Crossman's *Sermons,* 1681. [*T.C.* I. 438.]

ALLEN (JOHN), bookseller in London, White Horse, Wentworth Street, near Bell Lane, 1669–85. May be the John Allen who was in business in Little Britain in 1667 ; but if so there should be more notices of him in the Term Catalogues. His imprint is found on a poetical broadside entitled *Character of London Village,* 1684. [B.M. 1872. a. 1 (28).]

ALLEN (ROBERT), bookseller in Norwich, St. Stephen's parish, 1702. Mentioned in a list of printers and booksellers contributed by C. J. W. W. to the *East Anglian,* I. 281.

ALLESTREE (HENRY), bookseller in Derby, Market Head, 1719–32. One of a distinguished Derby family of that name, and probably a son of William Allestree, formerly Recorder of the Borough. He was established in business by 1719, when his name occurs in the imprint to the *Nottingham Mercury.* [*Sketch of the early history of the Printing-press in Derbyshire,* by Alfred Wallis, Journal of the Derbyshire Archaeol. and Nat. Hist. Soc., III. 137, &c.]

ALLESTREE (J.). *See Dictionary,* 1641–67.

ALLIN, *see* Allen.

ALLPORT (BENJAMIN), bookseller in London, (1) White Horse, Little Britain ; (2) St. Botolph's, Bishopsgate. 1685–9. Married, October 10th, 1685, Dorothy, daughter of Thomas Dawks, printer, and sister of Ichabod Dawks, printer. After Allport's death she married William Bowyer, printer, *q. v.* [Timperley, p. 660.] The only book that is connected with him is F. André's *Chymical Disceptations,* advertised Easter 1689. [*T.C.* II. 252.]

ALSOP (BENJAMIN), bookseller in London, Angel and Bible over against the Stocks Market [in the Poultry], 1679–85. Probably a descendant of Bernard Alsop (1616–1653). In 1679 he published John Gerhard's *Divine Consolations,* which was advertised in the *Domestic Intelligence* of October 21st. In 1681 he was defendant in an action for assault brought by Bartholomew Sprint against a number of printers and booksellers in London and Oxford, the details of which are wanting. [C.P.R. Trinity 33, Charles II, Roll 2992, m. 256.] Dunton has this account of him : "He was a first-rate bookseller for some years. But see the rambling fate of some men ; for, Ben being a wild sort of a Spark, he left his shop to get a commission in Monmouth's army, and, as Ben told me in Holland, had the Duke succeeded, he had been made an Earl, or a Baron at least : i. e. 'If the sky had fell, he had catched a lark.' I succeeded Captain Alsop in his shop in the Poultry." [Dunton, pp. 147, 214, 262.]

AMERY (JOHN), bookseller in London, (1) Peacock, Strand, over against St. Clement Danes Church ; (2) Peacock, near St. Dunstan's Church, in Fleet-street. 1670–86. Dealer in law books. Described by Dunton as "thinking Amery." [Dunton, p. 292.] First entry in *T.C.*, Easter 1670. [I. 39.] The J. Amery who published the works of Machiavelli in 1695 [*T.C.* II. 541] may have been a son. Amery moved to Fleet Street in 1673. [*T.C.* I. 136, 143.]

ANDERSON (ANDREW), printer, 1653–†1676. At Edinburgh, 1653–7 ; at Glasgow, 1657–61 ; again at Edinburgh, 1661–76. *See Dictionary,* 1641–67.

ANDERSON (ANDREW) and his partners, printers in Edinburgh, 1671–75. This is the copartnery of Andrew Anderson with G. Swintoun, J. Glen, T. Brown, and D. Trench, in the gift of King's printer, which Anderson obtained in 1671. They printed under the style of "His Majesties Printers" 1672–5, and "Andrew Anderson and his partners" 1675. Watson (p. 12) says that on Anderson's death (1676), "After printing of one small Bible by the Widow and Partners in company, they disagreed ; the booksellers apprehending themselves to be wrong'd . . . all of them sold off their shares of the house and gift to Mr. Anderson's widow, except George Swinton." [Aldis, p. 107.]

ANDERSON (HEIR OF ANDREW), Edinburgh, 1676–94.
ANDERSON (HEIRS OF ANDREW), 1680–1700.
ANDERSON (SUCCESSORS OF ANDREW), 1693–1722.
} *See* Anderson (James).

ANDERSON (HEIRS AND SUCCESSORS OF ANDREW), 1694–1717. Over against the north-side of the Cross ; at the printing House in Edinburgh College, 1693. *See* Anderson (James).

ANDERSON (JAMES), printer in Edinburgh, 1676–(?). After the death of Anderson in 1676 his widow (*see* Anderson, Mrs.) conducted the business in conjunction with, or on behalf of, his son and heir James, under the above styles. They were printers to the town and college as well as King's printers. During the Revolution they dropped the latter title and printed by order of the Privy Council until June 1690. Mrs. Anderson came into frequent conflict with the other printers and booksellers in her endeavours to enforce the monopoly conferred by the gift as King's printer. In 1690 she made an unsuccessful attempt, in opposition to Mosman, to obtain the appointment of printer to the General Assembly, but in 1712 succeeded Mosman in his office. [Aldis, p. 107.]

ANDERSON (RELICT OF A.), printer in Edinburgh, 1681. *See* Anderson, Mrs.

ANDERSON MRS., printer in Edinburgh, 1676–1716. *See above,* Anderson (James). Agnes Campbell, wife of A. Anderson. After her husband's death in 1676, she conducted the business. By November 1681, she had married Patrick Telfair, a merchant in Edinburgh. Died July 24th, 1716. Inventory [Bann. Misc. II. 284] names as one of the executors, "Mr. John Campbell, corrector of the said defunct her press". [Aldis, p. 108.]

ANDERSON (JAMES), stationer in Edinburgh, *c.* 1679. Will registered July 1st, 1679. [Bann. Misc. II. 296 ; Aldis, p. 108.]

ANDERTON (WILLIAM), printer in London, 1688–93. Said to have been a North Country man. He was apprenticed to Miles Flesher or Fletcher, and later (?) to one Snowden (*see* below). Became a corrector of the Press. At the Revolution he set up a private printing press. At the Sessions of June 1st–3rd, 1693, he was tried for printing two pamphlets, *Remarks upon the present confederacy and late Revolution in England* and *A French Conquest neither desirable nor practicable.* The principal evidence against him was given by Robert Stephens, the Messenger of the Press, who declared he had known the prisoner for upward of two years as a printer of seditious libels but never could tell where he worked. On May 2nd he had tracked two journeymen printers to a house and there found William Anderton in a secret room in which were a printing press, letters, and all other materials for printing ; and in the press was an Errata, as found in the *Remarks.* Amongst other broadsides found in the room were : *A Caution to the Navy, An Historical Romance upon the Wars, A Second Letter to the Bishop of Salisbury,* which were said to be in the same type as the *Remarks.* Two printers, R. Roberts and one Snowden, a dissenter to whom Anderton was some time an apprentice, also gave evidence. In summing up the evidence everything was aggravated to the utmost, but it was a long time before the jury could be persuaded to find him guilty of high treason. He was sentenced to death and executed at Tyburn on June 16th, 1693. [*Proceedings on the King and Queen's Commissions of the Peace,* B.M. 515. l. 2 (149).—*An account of the Conversation, Behaviour and Execution of William Anderton, printer,* B.M. 515. l. 2 (150).—*Howell's State Trials,* XII. 1240–67.]

ANDREW (JOHN), bookseller in Glasgow, 1676. Named among the debtors in Andrew Anderson's inventory (1676). The "John Androw, in Glasgow", mentioned in G. Lithgow's inventory (1662) may be the same. The will of Bessie Sheills, his widow, was registered December 27th, 1689. [Aldis, p. 108.]

ANDREWE (RICHARD), stationer of London, 1683. Only known from his will, which was proved in the Prerogative Court of Canterbury on September 11th, 1683. As he left bequests to the towns of Desborow and Thorpe in Northamptonshire, he was perhaps a native of that county. He also referred to his son-in-law John Bird, who may be the bookseller of that name who is found renting a stall in Westminster Hall in 1689. [P.C.C. 101, Drax.]

ANDREWS (ROBERT), type-founder in London, Charterhouse Street, 1680–1735. Born in 1650. He served as Steward of the 69th Feast of the Masters and Workmen printers in 1680 and about 1683 succeeded to the foundry of Joseph Moxon, which he transferred to Charterhouse Street. His foundry, largely consisting of Moxon's matrices, was, next to Grover's, the most extensive of his day, and consisted of a large variety of Roman letters and titlings, 11 Hebrew and 5 Rabbinical founts, &c. He was Junior Warden of the Company of Stationers in 1702–3 and 1703–4, and Senior Warden in 1706–7 and 1707–8. Although he accumulated a large quantity of matrices, Andrews does not appear to have been a good workman. Humphrey Wanley describes him as a "blunderer" because he cut the punches for Elizabeth Elstob's Saxon Grammar so badly. According to Timperley Andrews died November 27th, 1735, aged 80, but if that were so, it would make his age 85. His son Silvester carried on the business at Oxford. Thomas James subsequently purchased both foundries. [Reed, pp. 194–7; Timperley, p. 653.]

APPLEBEE (JOHN), printer and bookseller in London, (*a*) a little below Bridewell Bridge in Black-Fryers; (*b*) Fleet Ditch. 1715–1724. Printer of pamphlets and broadsides. In 1715 he printed the *St. James's Evening Post, or Nightly Pacquet*, "for Samuel Jackson, over against Bridewell-Bridge". He was also the printer of a Daily Journal and a Weekly Journal bearing his own name. [Timperley, p. 632.] His printing was very bad, and his type worn and old.

APPLEBY, MRS., bookseller at Gravesend, 1711. Only known from an advertisement of *Seamans Speculum or complete schoolmaster*, by John Davis, in the *Post Man*, March 10th, 17$\frac{10}{11}$.

ARCHER (JOSEPH), bookseller in London, near the Playhouse in Great Russell Street, Covent Garden, 1711. His name occurs in an advertisement of a sale of miscellaneous books by Sam. Illidge in the *Daily Courant* of January 19th, 1711; and in the following month he was mentioned as one of the booksellers receiving subscriptions for R. Bradley's *Treatise of succulent plants*, advertised in the *Post Man* of February 3rd.

ARCHER (THOMAS), bookseller in London, Fleet Street, under St. Dunstan's Church, 1671–3. In partnership with Thomas Burrell he issued in 1671 E. Maynwaring's *Praxis Medicorum* [*T.C.* I. 71], and in 1672 was one of the publishers of the second edition of P. Heylyn's *Aerius Redivivus, or, the History of the Presbyterians*. His last entry was, in Trinity, 1673, *A Pleasant Treatise of Witches*. [*T.C.* I. 142; Haz. II. 654.]

ASHBURN (ROBERT), bookseller in York, 1676. Sold *The* [or *An*] *Appeal from the Cabal*, 1676.

ASHWORTH ( ), bookseller in Durham, 1696. Only known from an advertisement of patent medicines in the *London Gazette*, February 25th, 169$\frac{6}{7}$.

ASPERNE (JO.), bookseller in London, *c.* 1700. Only known from the imprint to a broadside entitled *Duke of Shoreditch; or Barlow's Ghost*, London, Printed for J. Asperne [*c.* 1700]. [Haz. II. 365.]

ASTLEY (THOMAS), bookseller in London, Saint Paul's Churchyard, 1729. Publisher of the *London Magazine*. [Timperley, p. 657.]

ASTWOOD (JAMES), printer in London. Behind St. Christopher's Church in Threadneedle Street, the back-side of the Royal Exchange, 1691–1705. Dunton writes, "He was my near Neighbour and intimate Friend for many years. He printed for me near Sixty books, and was constantly engaged in the 'Athenian Mercury'. . . . Since the death of his son (Mr. John Astwood) he seems no longer to have any commerce with the world and hath nothing so familiar as a life that is (by his retreat from London to a country village) as it were buried in death." [Dunton, p. 245.] As Dunton speaks of him as a "near neighbour" his printing house was probably that in which his son worked, as given above. His name is found in the imprint to T. Hales's *Account of several new inventions*, 1691. [B.M. 534. a. 27.]

ASTWOOD (JOHN), printer in London, behind St. Christopher's Church in Threadneedle Street, the back-side of the Royal Exchange, 1695–8. Son of James Astwood, *q.v.* He printed John Pointz's *Present prospect of . . . Tobago*. Second edition, 1695, 4to, and *A Dialogue between a Country Gentleman and a Merchant*, 1696, 12°. [Haz. I. 194; II. 491.] Amongst those for whom he printed was John Lawrence the bookseller. His address is given in full in an advertisement in the *Post Boy* of May 10th, 1698.

ATHERTON ( ), bookseller in London, *c.* 1700. Dunton [p. 292] mentions, among booksellers and publishers, "grave Atherton".

ATKINS (MAURICE), bookseller in London, (1) King's Head, Westminster Hall; (2) Half Moon in St. Paul's Churchyard; (3) Golden Ball, in St. Paul's Churchyard. 1671–1715. First found in partnership with W. Hensman at the King's Head in Westminster Hall in 1671, when they issued a small octavo entitled *The Ancient rites and monuments of the . . . Cathedral Church of Durham*. [*T.C.* I. 89.] In 1673 he succeeded W. Gilbert at the Half Moon in St. Paul's Churchyard, publishing from there *The Gentleman's Recreation . . . Illustrated with sculptures* and other books. [*T.C.* I. 152, 157.] Then his name disappears from the Term Catalogues until 1707, when he is found at the Golden Ball in St. Paul's Churchyard in partnership with M. Newborough, publishing Boyer's *Wise and ingenious Companion, French and English* and several other works. He was still in business in 1715, when he issued the first edition of Ralph Thoresby's *Ducatus*.

ATKINS, or ATKYNS (RICHARD), patentee of Law Books. *See Dictionary*, 1641–67, Atkyns.

ATKINS (WILLIAM), bookseller at Leicester, 1684. In that year he sold a sermon preached by the Rev. John Newton, then vicar of St. Martin's, Leicester, on the occasion of the execution of certain criminals at the recent assizes. [Haz. IV. 157.]

ATKINSON (ABRAHAM), bookseller at Cambridge or Peterborough (?), 1680. His son Robert, born at Cambridge, educated at Peterborough School, was admitted sizar at St. John's College, Cambridge, February 24th, 16$\frac{79}{80}$, aged 19, his father being apparently still alive. [*St. John's Coll. Admissions*, ed. Mayor, II. 76.]

ATKINSON (GEORGE), bookseller at Chester, 1682. The only book associated with him is John Allen's *Sermon preached at the Assizes held at Chester, April 24, 1682*. [*T.C.* I. 482.] He died during the year 1682, and in Hilary Term 168$\frac{2}{3}$ Awnsham Churchill, the London bookseller, commenced an action against his widow, Mary Atkinson, in the Court of Common Pleas [C.P.R. 3009, m. 113 recto] probably for the recovery of a debt for books or stationery supplied to her husband.

ATKINSON (THOMAS), bookseller in London, White Swan, St. Paul's Churchyard, 1704–7. Chiefly a publisher of divinity. His first and last entries in *T.C.* are in Easter 1704 and Trinity 1707. [*T.C.* III. 403–4, 556.]

ATKINSON (TROYLUS), bookseller in Cambridge, *c.* 1626–75. Lived in Great St. Mary's parish from 1626 when he first appears as paying the Church Rate. He was a wealthy man and died possessed of freehold and leasehold properties as described in his will dated May 23rd and proved November 22nd, 1675. [Gray and Palmer, pp. 115–18.] He died July 20th, 1675. To his son William, *q. v.*, he left the lease of his dwelling-house, book-debts, &c.

ATKINSON (WILLIAM), bookseller at Cambridge, 1675–94. Son of Troylus Atkinson, *q. v.* In 1684 he was defendant in a suit brought by the Sheriff of the County for a debt of £30 [C.P.R. 2994, m. 1151, Trinity 33, Charles II] and again in 4 James II he was defendant in a plea for trespass. [C.P.R. 3068, m. 162 verso.] His will, dated March 7th, 1693, and proved May 28th, 1694, left all household goods and chattels to his wife Mary. [Gray and Palmer, p. 128.]

AULD (WILLIAM), bookbinder in Edinburgh, 1684. Named cautioner in the confirmation of the will of John Calderwood. [Bann. Misc. II. 292; Aldis, p. 108.]

AXE (THOMAS), bookseller, bookbinder, and book-auctioneer in London, (1) Holiday Yard in Creed Lane, near Ludgate Street, 1692; (2) Blue Ball in Duck Lane, 1696. 1692–1703. Dunton [p. 258] describes him as a man "of a great deal of wit and honesty. . . . He was my chief binder for ten years; but honest Tom has met with losses . . . but, notwithstanding . . . I believe Mr. Axe will get money enough: for he is not only a good binder, but sells Books, Globes, Auctions". In 1692 he published an *Epitome of the Whole Art of War*. [*T.C.* II. 394.] His last entry was in Trinity 1696: *Letters and Essays on several subjects . . . in Prose and Verse to John Dryden Esq. . . . Mr. Congreve and other ingenious men of the age. By several Gentlemen and Ladies*. [*T.C.* II. 592]. He was apparently still in business when Dunton wrote in 1703.

AYLMER (BRABAZON) sen. and jun., booksellers in London, Three Pigeons over against (or near) the Royal Exchange, 1670–1709. Dealers in theological works. In the Term Catalogue of Hilary 1670 Aylmer sen. advertised a small schoolbook called *Formulae Oratoriae*, but without giving any address. [*T.C.* I. 27.] His first entry in the Stationers' Register was made on December 12th, 1673, when in partnership with Nath. Ranew and Jonathan Robinson he entered Dr. Bates's *Harmony of the Divine Attributes* [*Stat. Reg.*, Roxb., vol. II, p. 474], and in 1674 *Joannis Miltoni Angli Epistolarum familiarium liber unus* [*ibid.*, p. 481]. He became the assignee of Samuel Simmons and so held the copyright of *Paradise Lost*, one half of which he sold to Jacob Tonson on August 17th, 1683, and the other on March 24th, 1690. [Masson, *Life of Milton*, VI. 786.] Dunton [p. 206] speaks of him as "a very just and religious man. I was partner with him in Keith's *Narrative of the proceedings at Turner's Hall*, and so had an opportunity to know him. He is nicely exact in all his accounts and is well acquainted with the mysteries of his trade." In 1707 the names of Brabazon Aylmer sen. and jun. are found together in several entries in the Term Catalogues. [*T.C.* III. 533–54.] The few subsequent entries in 1708 and 1709 of plain Brabazon Aylmer, at the same address, may imply that the father was dead and the son carrying on the business.

AYSCOUGH (WILLIAM), printer in Nottingham, Bridlesmith Gate, 1710–19. In 1710 he printed for Hildyard of York and Ryles of Hull *Remarks on the several paragraphs of the Bishop of Salisbury's speech in relation to the first article of Dr. Sacheverell's impeachment* [B.M. 111. b. 28]. The second edition of Sir T. Parkyn's *Inn-Play,* 1714 (also perhaps the first, 1713), was printed for him and for Timothy Goodwin of London. In 1717 he printed the *Grammatical Commentaries,* by R. Johnson, Head Master of the Free School in Nottingham; and in 1718–19, for Mrs. Hartshorn at Leicester, *The Certainty . . . of a future General Judgement. A sermon preached at Leicester . . . Mar. 19th, 1718–19,* n. d. Deering in his *Nottinghamia Vetus et Nova,* 1751, 4to, Sec. 2, p. 40, records the following inscription in St. Pèter's Church, in the South aisle: "Here lye the bodies of William Ayscough, Printer and Bookseller of this Town; and Anne his wife, she was daughter of the Rev. Mr. Young, Rector of Catwick in the County of York. He died March 2, 1719: she died Dec. 16, 1732."

B. (B.), printer in London, 1696. Probably B. Beardwell of Swan Yard (*q. v.*). In partnership with J. M. They printed amongst other things Sir Samuel Morland's *Urim of Conscience,* published by A. Roper, E. Wilkinson, and R. Clavel in 1696.

B. (H.), printer in London, 1682. Printed for J. Conyers a poetical broadside entitled *Rome's Thunder Bolt,* 1682. [B.M. C. 40. m. 11 (93).]

B. (J.), printer in London, 1686. Printed for Dorman Newman and R. Bentley.

B. (J.), printer in Exeter, 1688. Printed two broadsides entitled (1) *The General Association of the Gentlemen of Devon to his Highness the P. of Orange,* and (2) *The Speech of the Prince of Orange to some principle Gentlemen of Somersetshire and Dorsetshire, on their coming to joyn his Highness at Exeter, the 15th of Nov. 1688.* [B.M. T. 100*, 201, 202.]

B: (J.), *see* Baker (John), bookseller in London, 1683.

B. (I.), printer in Edinburgh, 1670. Printed an edition of the New Testament, 1670, sold by James Miller.

B. (P.), *see* Bruce (Peter).

B. (R.), *see* Boulter (Robert).

BACK (JOHN), bookseller in London, Black Boy on London Bridge, near the Drawbridge, 1682–1703. Son of John Back of Hinxhill, co. Kent. Apprenticed on May 3rd, 1675, for seven years to Thomas Passenger (*q. v. Dict.* 1641–67).

On taking up his freedom Back set up for himself at the sign of the Black Boy, and, like other London Bridge booksellers, dealt chiefly in cheap popular literature, ballads, broadsides, chap-books and school-books. About 1696 he was appointed bookseller to the Society of Kentish Men, and in addition to selling tickets for the Annual Feast he published the sermons preached at it from 1697 to 1701. He died in the end of June 1703, and was buried in St. Magnus Church on July 3rd [Churchwardens' Accounts of St. Magnus.]

BADMAN (C.), *see* Bateman.

BAGFORD (JOHN), bookseller and printer in London, 1650–1716. Thomas Hearne, the antiquary, believed John Bagford to have been born in Fetter Lane; but other authorities state his birthplace to have been in the parish of St. Anne's, Blackfriars. It is probable that he was originally a shoemaker by trade, but afterwards became a collector of books on commission for booksellers and amateurs, more especially for Robert Harley, Earl of Oxford, Sir Hans Sloane, and John Moore, Bishop of Ely. He was also a bookseller, and during the great frost of January 1716 he had a printing press at work on the Thames. Bagford collected an immense amount of material, both manuscript and printed, for a history of printing, which was also to include bookbinding and paper-making; but it was never published. As a bookseller, he was frequently asked to make up imperfect books, and it was the custom of the book trade to collect title-pages and portions of books for this purpose. A great number of Bagford's title-pages and fragments are from books which could have been bought in his days for a few pence, while it is highly probable that some of them were salvage from the Great Fire of 1666, when immense quantities of books were burnt or damaged; that Bagford wilfully destroyed books, in order to form his collections, is a slander on a man who was universally spoken of as "honest John Bagford" and who, according to Thomas Hearne, was a "despiser of Money". In fact, many of these title-pages show the source from which they were obtained, as they bear the name of the person from whom he received them. Without his industry, many books and editions of books would have perished entirely, being only known to us from the title-page in the Bagford collection. This collection comprises 129 volumes, including three of ballads. The manuscript pieces are contained in 36 volumes, the printed pieces in 63. In addition to title-pages this collection

contains much miscellaneous matter of interest, such as printers' devices, advertisements, and book-plates. In his old age Bagford was admitted to the Charterhouse, and on his death on May 5th, 1716, was buried in the Charterhouse graveyard. [Bibl. Soc. Trans., IV. 185–201; VII. 123–160.]

BAGNALL (JOHN), printer in London, near Fleet Street, 1709, and at Ipswich, 1717–35. The only thing known from his London press is *Sir John Packington's speech in the House of Commons relating to the Harbour of Dunkirk.* [Bibl. Lind. *Broadsides* no. 966.] For his Ipswich press *see* Allnutt, p. 301.

BAILEY, or BAYLY (JOHN), bookseller in London, Judge's Head, Chancery Lane, near Fleet Street, 1708–9. At the latter end of 1708 or the beginning of 1709 he published *A Complete Course of Chemistry* by George Wilson. [*T.C.* III. 629.] Possibly Dunton's "Grammatical Bayley" [p. 293].

BAILEY (WILLIAM), bookseller at Burton on Trent, Lichfield, Tamworth, and Wolverhampton, 1685. His name appears in a list of booksellers selling a patent medicine, given at the end of M. Bromfield's *Brief discovery of the . . . Scurvy,* 1685. [*N. & Q.*, 11 Ser., XI. 45.]

BAKER (   ), bookbinder in London, Warwick Lane, *c.* 1703. Bound for Dunton, who speaks [p. 258] of the excellence of his work.

BAKER (G.), bookseller (?) in London, Bridge Row, north-east corner of the Royal Exchange, 1679. In this year he published a map of the world by Francis Lamb. [*T.C.* I. 364, 372.]

BAKER (J.), bookseller in London, Black Boy, Paternoster Row, 1680–1710. In the *Post Man* for January 13th, 1680, he advertised *The Political State of Great Britain,* but advertised nothing in the Term Catalogues until 1709, when he entered *A Vindication of the Church and Clergy of England from some late Reproaches.* He dealt chiefly in theology. A J. Baker was senior warden of the Company of Stationers in 1686–7.

BAKER (JOHN), bookseller in London, (1) at Mercers' Chapel [i.e. in Mercers' Chapel Porch] at the lower end of Cheapside, 1703–25; (2) Sun and Moon, Cornhill, 1707; (3) near the Bank, in the Poultry, 1709. There was more than one bookseller of this name in London at the beginning of the eighteenth century, and it is possible that the addresses given above are those of two or perhaps three distinct men. First we find a John Baker issuing in

1703 a devotional book from Mercers' Chapel, and Dunton [p. 226] refers to him as at this address. [*T.C.* III. 366.] Then a gap of five years occurs during which no book was entered in the Term Catalogue by J. Baker of Mercers' Chapel, but in July 1707 several books of importance were issued by J. Baker in partnership with R. Burrough at the Sun and Moon [*T.C.* III. 556–8.] Then at the latter end of 1708 or the beginning of 1709 J. Baker of Mercers' Chapel begins advertising again in the Term Catalogue [*T.C.* III. 606]. In 1711 he issued *A Full Account of the Rise . . . of Dr. Asheton's proposal, as managed by the Worshipful Company of Mercers, London, for the benefit of Widows.* In 1722 he started *Baker's News, or, the Whitehall Journal,* "to be continued weekly", the first number of which was dated May 24th.

BAKER (S.), bookseller in London, 1717. Publisher of J. Arbuthnot's *Present State of the Crown-Inn* (2 edd.), 1717. [Esdaile, p. 154.]

BAKER (THOMAS), bookseller in London, Bible and Rose, Ludgate Street, near the West end of St. Paul's, 1708–9. Publisher of theological books and works on book-keeping. [*T.C.* III. 594, 609, 625, 639.]

BAKEWELL (THOMAS), map- and print-seller in London, next the Horn Tavern in Fleet Street, 1670. Publisher of John Ogilby's *England Exactly Described . . . In a compleat Sett of . . . Mapps.* [Haz. III. 179.]

BALDWIN (ANN), bookseller in London, Oxford Arms, Warwick Lane, 1698–1711. Widow of Richard Baldwin. Dunton [p. 260] writes of her: "Mrs. A. Baldwin, in a literal sense was an *help-meet* and eased him of all his publishing work; and since she has been a widow, might vie with all the women in Europe for *accuracy* and *justice* in keeping accompts. . . .'

BALDWIN (RICHARD), bookseller, bookbinder and printer in London, (1) In Ball Court, near the Black Bull, Great Old Bailey; (2) Oxford Arms, Warwick Lane. 1681–98. One of the best-known publishers of his day, his publications consisting largely of political pamphlets and broadsides, satires on social life and on current literature, as well as plays and romances. The newspapers of the last twenty years of the seventeenth century are full of his advertisements and it is surprising that no biography of him exists. Dunton says that Baldwin was a native of Wickham; but there is more than one Wickham in England, and Dunton does not specify the county. Nothing is known as to his parentage, his apprenticeship, or his commencement in business. His name is first met with in the Term Catalogue for Hilary Term 1681, when he advertised a political pamphlet of twenty folio pages entitled *The Certain Way to save England.* [*T.C.* I. 429.] At this time he was also carrying on the business of a bookbinder in Ball Court, near the Black Bull in the Old Bailey, and numbered John Dunton among his customers. In the same year he published a newspaper called *Mercurius Anglicus*, previously printed by Robert Harford. [Timperley, p. 558.] He was also erroneously believed to have been the printer and publisher of the first and second parts of a notorious pamphlet, *No Protestant Plot.* In Michaelmas Term he brought an action in the Court of Common Pleas against Thomas Newcombe, John Towse, Randall Taylor, and Michael Foster, three of whom were stationers, for assault; but the particulars are wanting. [C.P.R. 2996, m. 256 recto.] In *The Impartial Protestant Mercury* of January 10th, $168\frac{1}{2}$, is an account of an assault made on two of Baldwin's apprentices, which incidentally records that it was a long-established custom for bookbinders' servants on Saturday nights to post up the titles of such books as their masters had to bind which were to be published the following week. The title which led to the trouble was a political one, *Rights of the Kingdom, or Customs of our Ancestors*, the result being that one of the lads was forced to give security and a copy of the book was sent to one of the Secretaries of State. On May 1st Baldwin began to issue another newspaper called *The Protestant Courant*, and a complaint was lodged with the Judges of the King's Bench that it reflected upon the Government; but there is no record of what followed. [*London Mercury*, May 15–18, 1682; Timperley, p. 563.] In 1691 he was summoned before the House of Commons for printing and being the author of *The New Observator*, but made his peace by declaring that Dr. Wellwood was the author of the paper. [C. J. X. 558, 562, 566]. During the year 1695 he published a paper called *The Post-Man*, which drew a protest from the editor of *The Post-Boy*, who declared that the author of *The Post-Man* was Monsieur de Fonvive. [*Post-Boy*, Oct. 26–9, 1695]. In 1697 he was sued by the King's Printers for printing speeches. Baldwin continued to publish *The Post-Man* until his death in $169\frac{7}{8}$. Space forbids notice of the many satires published by Baldwin, but Dunton has the following notice of him: "He printed a great deal, but got as little by it as John Dunton. He bound for me and others when he lived in the Old Bailey; but, removing to Warwick Lane,

his fame for publishing spread so fast, he grew *too big* to handle his small tools. Mr. Baldwin having got acquaintance with Persons of Quality, he was now for taking a shop in Fleet street; but Dick, soaring out of his element, had the honour of being a Bookseller but a few months. However to do Mr. Baldwin justice, his inclinations were to oblige all men, and only to neglect himself. He was a man of a generous temper. . . . His purse and his heart were open to all men that he thought were honest; and his conversation was very diverting. He was a true lover of King William; and, after he came on the Livery, always voted on the right side. . . . He was as it were flattered into his grave by a long consumption; and now lies buried in Wickham parish his native place."

BALDWIN (T.), a misprint for T. Bassett (*q. v.*), in *The honesty and true zeal of the King's witnesses justified by Florence Weyer, Gent.*, 1681. [Haz. II. 637; B.M. T. 2* (14). *See T.C.* I. 465, which gives Bassett's name.]

BALL ( ), printer in London, Fetter Lane, 1709. Referred to by J. How as a pirate printer. [*Some Thoughts on the present state of Printing and Bookselling*, 1709, p. 12.]

BALL (JOHN), stationer in Banbury, against the Shambles, 1685. Occurs in a list of booksellers and stationers who sold a patent medicine, given at the end of M. Bromfield's *A brief discovery of the . . . scurvy.* [*N. & Q.* 11 Ser., XI. 45.]

BALLARD (J.), a misprint for S. Ballard (*q. v.*) in one of the editions of *The Clergyman's Vade Mecum.*

BALLARD (SAMUEL), bookseller in London, Blue Ball in Little Britain, 1706–33. Issued in 1706 an edition of *The History of George a Green* [B.M. 1077. e. 32.], and also *The Clergyman's Vade Mecum.* [*T.C.* III. 494.] He was probably related to Thomas Ballard, who was carrying on business in the same street. Samuel was still in business in 1733.

BALLARD (THOMAS), bookseller and book auctioneer in London, (1) Ring in Little Britain; (2) Rising Sun in Little Britain. 1698–1725. Believed to have been the first of an eminent firm of booksellers. He is first found associated with and sharing the premises of G. Conyers at the Ring in Little Britain in 1698, and his first advertised publication was *Youth's Safety, or Advice to the*

Younger Sort. [*T.C.* III. 81.] In 1700 he moved to the "Rising Sun", and Dunton [p. 222] briefly notices him as "a young bookseller in Little Britain; but is grown man in body now but more in mind". Soon after this he appears to have added to his business as a bookseller that of a book auctioneer. In the *Daily Courant* of January 2nd, 1711, he advertised for sale the libraries of Sir Thomas Browne and his son Dr. Edward Browne. Amongst other collections dispersed by him were that of Dr. William Salmon, 1713–14, and the smaller library of Dr. Charles Oliphant, 1720. In March $17\frac{20}{21}$ he issued a catalogue of miscellaneous books. He was succeeded in business by Edward Ballard.

BALLINGER (JOHN), bookseller in Cirencester, 1723–42. Noticed by H. Norris in his *Notes on Booksellers of Cirencester.* [*N. & Q.*, 11 Ser., II. 141.]

BANBURY (BENNET), bookseller in London, Blue Anchor in the New Exchange, 1700. His name occurs in the imprint to Mrs. Centlivre's play, *The Perjur'd Husband*, 1700. [B.M. 644. g. 27.]

BANKS (A.), printer in Edinburgh, 1706. Printed in 1706 a broadside entitled *A List of the Nobility and Gentry . . . for and against the Union.* [B.M. Harl. 5938 (90).]

BANKS (ALEXANDER), bookseller in London, Charing Cross, 1676–85. In an inquiry by a Committee of the House of Lords, February 19th, $167\frac{6}{7}$, into the publication of certain libellous pamphlets, it was incidentally stated that Alexander Banks was one of the compositors of Nathaniel Thompson, one of the printers involved. [*Hist. MSS. Comm.*, 9th Report, App.] Banks subsequently became a publisher of ballads and broadsides. At the time of the Oates conspiracy in 1681, he published *The Hue and Cry after Dr. T. Oates*, and in 1684 he issued a broadside by Thomas Calvert, entitled *A Letter from the Chancellour of Maryland to Col. Henry Meese, concerning the late troubles in Maryland.* His name does not appear in the Term Catalogues.

BANKS (ALLEN), bookseller in London, (1) Flower de Luce, next door to the Three Squirrels, Fleet Street, over against St. Dunstan's Church, 1668–71; (2) St. Peter's Head, West End of St. Pauls, 1672; (3) St. Peters Head, Whitefriars, 1673; (4) Fetter Lane, 1673–82. 1668–82. In 1668 Charles Harper and Allen Banks entered in the Stationers' Registers as their joint

copyright Lukin's *Introduction to the Holy Scriptures* [Trans. Roxb. II. 386], and in the same year they published the English version of Louis Fontaine's satire, *A Relation of the Country of Iansenia.* [B.M. 873. f. 7.] It is not until 1670 that his name appears in the Term Catalogues, and his last advertisement in that publication is in February, 1674. [*T.C.* I. 163.] In 1672 he dissolved partnership with Harper and set up for himself at the sign of St. Peter's Head in the Churchyard; but in the following year he carried the sign into Whitefriars. On March 13th, 1680, he issued a news sheet called *Currant Intelligence.* There was already one publication with this title, and its publisher, John Smith, in his issue of April 6th, 1680, issued a warning to his readers: "This Intelligence having gained reputation as well by its truth as honesty, some persons have maliciously printed another with the very same title . . therefore we think fit to give notice, that the counterfeit 'Currant Intelligence' is printed for Allen Banks in Fetter Lane, but the true one for John Smith in Great Queen Street." Banks's news sheet was very short lived; four numbers can be traced; but he continued publishing up to 1682, when he issued the works of Francis Osborn, beyond which he cannot be traced. He may be identical with the 'Faithful Bancks', mentioned by Dunton. [p. 292.]

BANKS (HAMMOND), bookseller in London, 1714. Married Anne Rogers, sister of William Rogers of Clifford's Inn, London, Gent., and is mentioned in his will proved January 14th, 1714. [P.C.C. 15 Fagge.]

BANNISTER ( ), bookseller (?) in London, Queens Arms in the New Exchange in the Strand, 1711.

BARBER (ABRAHAM), bookseller at Wakefield, Yorkshire, 1700–03. Compiler of a book of Psalm tunes, advertised in 1700 and 1703. [*T.C.* III. 214, 361.]

BARBER (JOHN), printer in London, (1) Queen's Head Alley; (2) Lambeth Hill. 1700–40. Born in 1675 of poor parents, Dunton says [pp. 248, 250] that he was apprenticed to the elder Larkin and afterwards successfully managed the printing office of Henry Clark's widow. He set up for himself in Queen's Head Alley in 1700. Dean Swift befriended him in many ways and makes frequent reference to him in his *Letters to Stella.* It was probably through Swift's influence that Barber was engaged as printer to the ministry of the day, and he printed for Pope, Prior, Dr. King, and Mrs. Manley. Through the patronage of Bolingbroke he obtained the contract for printing the votes of the House of Commons, and became printer of the *London Gazette*, the *Examiner* and *Mercator*. He was also printer to the City of London, and received the reversion of the Royal Printing House after Baskett, but relinquished the latter post for a sum of £1,500. Elected an alderman of Baynard Castle Ward, Barber filled the office of Sheriff, and in 1733 became Lord Mayor. At the time of the South Sea scheme, Barber took large shares and is said to have amassed a considerable fortune. He died on January 22nd, 1740.

BARKER (A.), bookseller in London, Unicorn, Fleet Street, next Sergeant's Inn Gate, 1708. In partnership with C. Smith, he published the Rev. John Harrison's *Exposition of the Church Catechism*, 1708; a catalogue of their other publications is printed on the last page. [*T.C.* III. 567; B.M. 4257. aaa. 47 (2).]

BARKER (BENJAMIN), bookseller in London, (1) White Hart, Westminster Hall; (2) Judge's Head in Westminster Hall. 1701–14. Dealer in general literature. In 1701 he advertised *Advice to the Sceptick* [*T.C.* III. 239]; and in 1702 he published *Three discourses of Sir Walter Raleigh*. He also held a share in Moll's *Atlas Geographus*, 1709. At the end of J. A. Dubourdieu's sermon preached at Chelmsford Assizes, July 15th, 1714, is a list of eight other books published by Barker and C. King at the Judge's Head.

BARKER (CHRISTOPHER) the Third, *see Dictionary*, 1641–67.

BARKSDALE (JOHN), bookseller and bookbinder in London and Cirencester, London: At (or over against) the Five Bells, New Street; between Fetter Lane and Shoe Lane. 1674–1719. Related in some way to Clement Barksdale, the Gloucestershire author. He is first mentioned in the Term Catalogues for Hilary 1674 as the publisher of a translation of Procopius. [*T.C.* I. 177.] Between 1675 and 1678 he published several of Clement Barksdale's translations from Hugo Grotius. Some time between this and 1680 he appears to have moved to Cirencester and set up as a bookseller, publishing in the latter year T. Beye's *Epitaphia*, and in 1681 *Memorials of Alderman Whitmore, Bishop Wilkins &c.*, and there appear to be two impressions of the latter, unless the edition was divided in half, one bearing the imprint of the London publisher, Sam. Lee, at the Feathers in Lumbard Street, 1681, and the other

that of John Barksdale, bookseller in Cirencester, 1681. [Haz. II. 37.] Barksdale was still there in 1698, when he published *The Minister of Cirencester's Address to the Dissenters of his Parish*. [B.M. T. 1047 (13).] There is no evidence to connect him with the John Barksdale, Gentleman, of Middleton-Cheny in Northampton, who died in 1699 and whose funeral sermon was preached by the Rev. Thomas Hilton. [B.M. 4903. ee. 28.] Mr. Herbert Norris, in his *Notes on the Booksellers of Cirencester*, says that J. Barksdale died January 10th $17\frac{18}{19}$. [*N. & Q.*, 11 Ser., XI. 141.]

BARNARD (HENRY), bookseller in London, the Bible in the Poultry, 1693. There is no mention of this bookseller either in the Term Catalogues, in Dunton or in Hazlitt. He is known to have sold: (1) *A Rejoynder to Mr. Daniel Williams his reply to the first part of Neonomianism Unmaskt*, by Isaac Chauncy, M.A. "London, Printed for H. Barnard at the Bible in the Poultry. MDCXCIII." [B.M. T. 1047 (8).] On the last leaf of this is given a list of books printed for Barnard. Briefly stated they are, (2) *Examen Confectionis Pacificae* . . . By Isaac Chauncy, M.A., (3) *The Old Man's Legacy to his Daughters* . . . Written by N. T. deceased, (4) *The Banqueting House* . . . *A Divine Poem* . . . By Benjamin Keach, (5) *Chirurgus Marinus* . . . By John Moyle senr.

BARNES (JOHN), bookseller in London, the Crown in Pall Mall, 1688–1711. In Easter Term, 3 James II (1688), Alexander Pope brought an action against John Barnes for trespass. [C.P.R. 3056, m. 120 r.] He is there described as stationer of Westminster. In 1696 he published *A New Year's Gift for Dr. Birch*. [B.M. T. 1047 (10).] In 1697 a small tract entitled *Fasti Gulielmi Tertii* was issued by him, and he was still in business in 1711.

BARNHAM (ROBERT), bookseller in London, the Goat in Little-Britain, 1701. Only known from his imprint being found on a scurrilous broadside against the Court published in 1701. [B.M. C. 20. f. 2 (214).]

BARRETT (PHILIP), stationer in London (?) 1702. Witnessed the will of Sir William Swann, Baronet, of Greenhithe, Kent, on November 28th, 1702. [P.C.C. 102, Barnes.]

BARRY (EDWARD), bookseller in London, 1681. Only known as the publisher of *Jus Anglorum ab antiquo*. [Haz. II. 203.]

BARTLET (ROGER), bookbinder in Oxford, 1674–82. In Anthony à Wood's Diary occurs the following: "Dec. 24, 1674, Th[ursday], to Bartlet, 4*s.* for binding 7 paper books with stained covers: to Mr. Bartlett for binding my book [i. e. *Hist. et Antiq. Oxon*] 7*s.* 6*d.* a piece 3 in number." [Wood, II. 299.] In a book belonging to Anthony à Wood is a note: "7 Apr. 1681 to Roger Bartlet of Oxon for binding of this book 6*d.*" followed by the bookbinder's signature, "Rog. Bartlet", in evidence of receipt. [*Ib.* I. 249.] He was possibly a relative of T. Bartlett (*q.v.*)

BARTLETT (THOMAS), bookseller at Oxford, 1677. Advertised in 1677 *A Philosophical Essay towards an Eviction of the Being and Attributes of God*, by Seth [Ward], Lord Bishop of Salisbury. [*T.C.* I. 277.] Possibly a relative of R. Bartlet (*q.v.*).

BARTON (GEORGE), bookseller in Boston, Lincolnshire, 1710. Sold E. Kelsall's *Mistakes about moderation detected*, London, 1710. [B.M. 225. h. 12 (2).]

BARTON (HUMPHRY), *see* Burton.

BASKERVILLE (ANTHONY), bookseller in London, the Bible, against St. Clement's Church, 1688–9. His name occurs in the imprint to the Latin edition of Joseph Glanville's *Saducismus Triumphatus*, 1689. Mr. Hilton-Price, in his *Signs of the old Houses in the Strand*, notices him as being there in 1688. [*Middx. & Hert. N. & Q.*, II. 95.] There is no trace of him in the Stationers' Register, or in the Term Catalogues.

BASKERVILLE (LAURENCE), bookseller in London, at the Red Lion in Aldermanbury, 1688. He and John Marsh sold *The British Language in its Lustre, or a copious Dictionary of Welsh and English*, by Thomas Jones, 1688, 8vo. [Haz. I. 240.]

BASKETT (JOHN), King's printer, London, Blackfriars, Oxford and Edinburgh, 1709–42. Nothing seems to be certainly known of Baskett's antecedents. He is first heard of as purchasing the patent of King's printer for Bible printing from the executors of Thomas Newcombe and Henry Hills in 1709, and his name first appeared on a New Testament in 1712. In 1713 he began to print the Book of Common Prayer. Four editions of the Bible appeared with his imprint in 1715. His next publication was an edition in two volumes imperial folio printed at Oxford (the Old Testament in 1717 and New Testament in 1716). Dibdin called this the most magnificent of the Oxford Bibles;

it has also been called "A Baskett-full of Printers errors"; but of its typographical beauty there could be no two opinions. In 1718 Baskett mortgaged his printing materials to James Brooks, stationer, of London. It included "A very large fount of Double Pica, new, the largest in England". It seems possible that this was cut by Caslon I. In 1711 Baskett acquired a third part of Robert Freebairn's gift as King's printer in Scotland, and in 1716 he obtained, in conjunction with the widow of Andrew Anderson, a fresh commission as King's printers in Scotland. Baskett appears to have allowed his share of these privileges to lie dormant until 1725, when he set up a printing-house in Edinburgh and produced some indifferent editions of the Bible during the next three or four years. [Lee (John), *Memorial for the Bible Societies in Scotland*, Edinburgh, 1824 (pp. 179–83 and App. XXXI); *Additional Memorial*, 1826 (p. 153).] Baskett was frequently called upon to defend his title of King's printer in the courts of law, especially in Scotland, where it was stubbornly disputed by John Watson, a printer, and finally settled by a judgement of Lord Mansfield in favour of Baskett. At Cambridge he was seriously disturbed by the proposal of W. Ged to stereotype Bibles and Prayer-books, and succeeded by intrigues in damaging the success of Ged's innovation. In the year 1737 Baskett's printing office was burnt. He died on June 22nd, 1742. He left three sons, Thomas, Robert, and John. His will was proved on the 23rd. Baskett desired that his body might be buried in St. Ann's, Blackfriars. To his son Thomas he left "the messuage or late dwelling house, lately rebuilt, adjoining to the King's Printing House in Blackfryers, the courtyard and other appurtenances . . . also all that other piece of ground whereon part of my dwelling house stood before the fire in January 1737 and whereon part of the printing house now stands". To his son John he left an annuity of £200. "To each of the compositors and pressmen which shall be at work in my printing house at the time of my death, ten shillings, and to each of the boys, five shillings." He directed that his patents were not to be sold but to remain in the family, "during the remainder of the several terms of years therein yet to come." His daughter Elizabeth married — Innys. [P.C.C. 176, Tremley.] Baskett was Master of the Stationers' Company in 1714 and 1715.

BASSET (J.), bookseller in London (?), 1693. Published an edition of the *Counter-Scuffle*, 1693. [Haz. II. 529.]

BASSET (RICHARD), bookseller in London, (1) Mitre, Fleet Street, (*a*) near the Inner Temple Gate, (*b*) over against Chancery Lane, (*c*) within Temple Bar; (2) George, Fleet Street, over against Inner Temple Lane. 1697–1706. Dealer in all kinds of literature and publisher of plays and poems. In most of his publications his name appears jointly with that of Abel Roper, from which it may be inferred that there was some kind of partnership between them. His first and last entries in the Term Catalogues were in Michaelmas 1697 and Trinity 1706. [*T.C.* III. 40, 512.]

BASSET (THOMAS), *see Dictionary*, 1641–67; *also* Baldwin (T.)

BATEMAN (CHRISTOPHER), bookseller and book-auctioneer in London, (1) Bible and Crown, Middle Row, Holborn; (2) Bible and Crown, Paternoster Row, Corner shop. 1698–1730. Probably no bookseller's shop in London was better known in the days of Swift and his contemporaries. Bateman had a large stock of new and second-hand books. He was in addition a book auctioneer of some repute, and the publisher of one or two notable works. He is first heard of as an auctioneer. In or about 1686 he sold a stock of philological and Greek books, and on February 18th, 1698, "the Mathematical and Physical parts of the famous library of Sir Charles Scarburgh, Kt., M.D." [Lawler, p. 183; B.M. 831. i. 5 (9).] Dunton says of him [p. 217]: "There are very few booksellers in England (if any) that understand books better than Mr. Bateman, nor does his diligence and industry come short of his knowledge. He is a man of great reputation and honesty, and is the son of that famous Bateman, who got an alderman's estate by bookselling." We have not been able to identify the father. The aldermen of the name were not booksellers. [Beaven, *The Aldermen of the City of London.*] But possibly "an alderman's estate" is a figurative phrase. Stephen or W. Bateman might be the man, for if they published little, they may have been large retail dealers. Christopher Bateman makes his first appearance as a publisher in Easter Term 1699, when with several other booksellers he issued a translation of La Bruyère's *Characters*. [*T.C.* III. 126.] Amongst other works of which he was the sole or joint publisher, may be noted Sir Hans Sloane's *Voyage to the Islands Madera, Barbadoes, &c.*, 1707 [*T.C.* III. 569], Maittaire's *Historia Stephanorum insignium Galliæ Typographorum*, 1709. [*T.C.* III. 627] and the castrated sheets of Holinshed's Chronicle which he shared with Benj. Cowse in 1722–3, and which were the subject of some dispute. [Nichols, *Lit. Anecd.*, I. 251.]

But it was chiefly as a dealer in second-hand books that he and his shop became famous. Dean Swift was among his customers. Writing to Stella in 1710, he says, "I went to Bateman's the bookseller and laid out eight and forty shillings for books. I bought three little volumes of Lucian in French, for our Stella." Another of his customers about the same time was Zacharias Conrad von Uffenbach, who visited this country in 1710 and published an account of his travels in 1753–4. Extracts from this work have been given in J. E. B. Mayor's *Cambridge under Queen Anne*, 1911, from which the following paragraphs are taken: "11 June [1710] Wednesday—To Paternoster Row, the corner house, to Badman's [*sic*] store of old bound books, which is the best in England. Elsewhere you find few latin books, but here there were two shops full, and the floors piled up with books. The prices were however so high, that I only bought a few English historians, and *Mabillon de re diplomatica*, the last very cheap at 2 guineas." "14th July—I got out at Mr. Badman's [*sic*] in Paternoster Row, and asked the price of Mabillon 'de re diplomatica'. The good man asked only 30*s*. supposing no doubt that the new edition had superseded the old." It is stated that Archbishop Sancroft's nephew sold his MS. papers for 80 guineas to Bateman the bookseller, from whom they were purchased by Bishop Tanner and presented to the Bodleian Library. [D'Oyly's *Life of William Sancroft*, vol. II. p. 90.] Gough says that the MSS. were in 300 vols., but does not give the source of his information. [*Anecdotes*, p. 58.] Finally Nichols [*Lit. Anecd.* I. 424] says: "It was said that Bateman never would suffer any person whatever to look into one book in his shop; and when asked a reason for it, would say, 'I suppose you may be a physician or an author, and want some recipe or quotation; and, if you buy it, I will engage it to be perfect before you leave me, but not after; as I have suffered by leaves being torn out, and the books returned to my very great loss and prejudice.'" Nichols also records [III. 616] that Bateman was holding book auctions as late as 1730.

BATEMAN (STEPHEN), bookseller in London, 1686. Published *Fleta Minor, the laws of art and nature . . . with 44 sculptures*, 1686. [Haz. II. 470–1.]

BATEMAN (W.), bookseller in London, next the King's Head Inn, Old Change, 1684. Advertised Lucian's *Dialogues* in 1684 [*T.C.* II. 73], and in the same year published *The Prerogative of the Monarchs of Great Britain asserted.* [*Ib.* 87.]

BATERSBY, *see* Battersby.

BATES (C.), bookseller in London, Sun and Bible in Giltspur Street, near Pye Corner, 1709–14. A dealer in ballads, broadsides, and all kinds of cheap and popular literature. Most of this was printed without any date, but Hazlitt [I. 436] states that *The Adventures of Five Englishmen*, published by Bates and others, has a date 1714. He is not noticed by either Dunton or Timperley, nor is his name found in the Term Catalogues. Sarah Bates was almost certainly his widow.

BATES (SARAH), bookseller in London, Sun and Bible, Giltspur Street near Pye Corner, 1719–20. Almost certainly the widow of C. Bates. In 1719 she published *The Queen's Royal Cookery* [Haz. III. 294], and in 1720, with Hannah Tracy, an abridged chap edition of Forde's *Montelion*. [B.M. 12403. a. 19.] She published an undated edition of the latter in partnership with A. Bettesworth and C. Hitch, J. Osborn, S. Birt, and J. Hodges, also other undated chap books.

BATLEY (JEREMIAH), bookseller in London, Dove in Paternoster Row, 1717–37. Published an edition of Quarles's *Divine Poems*, 1717. [Haz. II. 506.] Batley was also the publisher of Aubrey's *Miscellanies* in 1721, and shared with S. Chandler the publication of the Rev. P. Morant's *Introduction to the reading of the New Testament* in 1725 [Nichols, *Lit. Anecd.* II. 204], and, with Thomas Cox, Stackhouse's *History of the Bible*, and also published several novels and romances. [Esdaile, pp. 189, &c.] He died September 11th, 1737. [Timperley, p. 684.]

BATTERSBY, or BATERSBY (ROBERT), printer in London, Staple Inn Gate, Holborn, 1670–1705. On June 28th, 1670, Robert Battersby entered Molière's *Tartuffe* in the Stationers' Register [*Stat. Reg.*, Roxb., II. 413.] In February $167\frac{6}{7}$ he was called as a witness before the Committee of the House of Lords, which was inquiring into the publication of certain libellous pamphlets, and deposed that he printed an unlicensed work called *The Ladies Calling*, and that he was warned by Randal Taylor that the Company were making a search on a certain day. Battersby's name does not appear in the Term Catalogue before Michaelmas 1699, when an edition of *Don Quixote* was advertised as printed for several publishers, of whom he was one. In the following year he published a work on Primogeniture. [*T.C.* III. 154, 175.]

Dunton has this record of him [p. 218]: "He printed *The Infant's Lawyer*, and *Ars Clericalis*, and has purchased other Copies that have sold well. He is scrupulously honest; he never abridged another mans Copy, or purchased his Author by out-bidding."

BATTERSBY (WILLIAM), sen., bookseller in London, Thames Inn Gate, Holborn, near St. Andrew's Church, 1671–1701. In Mich. 1671 he advertised Murtadi's *Egyptian History*. [*T.C.* I. 86.] He dealt also in maps, prints, and law books. Some time before the end of the year he took his son William into partnership and their names are jointly found in an advertisement of patent medicine in the *City Mercury*, June 11th, 1694. [B.M. Burney 112 A.] The last entry made by W. Battersby sen. in the Term Catalogues was in Trin. 1701. [*T.C.* III. 263.]

BATTERSBY (WILLIAM), jun., bookseller in London, near Holborn Bars, 1694. In partnership with his father, W. Battersby sen., *q.v.*

BAXTER (THOMAS), bookseller at York, 1697. Only known from the imprint to George Barker's *Sermons upon several texts of Scripture*, 1697. [*T.C.* III. 23.]

BAYLY, *see* Bailey.

BEALE (WILLIAM), bookseller in London, Little Britain, 1690. Published *His Grace the Duke of Schombergh's character*, 1690. [Haz. I. 373.]

BEARDWELL (B.), printer in London, in the Passage going into the Swan Yard next Newgate, 1697. Printer of *The Post Boy* from April 20th, 1697. Dunton says [p. 251]: "Mr. Beardwell and Mr. Moxon were partners all the time I employed them. The former is very generous and obliging."

BEARDWELL (L.), printer in London, next the Red Cross Tavern in Black Friars, 1711–12. He was the printer of *The Post Boy* in 1711.

BECHET, or BECKET (?) (W.), bookseller (?) in London, at the Royal Exchange, 1692. Sold W. Jordan's *Copy Book*. He was more probably a stationer only. [*T.C.* II. 404.] The name Bechet may be a misprint for Becket.

BECKFORD (   ), widow, bookbinder (?) at Oxford, 1681. Probably widow of Ralph Beckford [Madan, p. 30.]

BECKFORD (RALPH), bookbinder at Oxford, 1680 (?).

BEE (CORNELIUS), *see Dictionary*, 1641–67.

BEECHING (EDMUND), bookseller at Cambridge, 1655–89. Lived in St. Michael's parish certainly from 1655 to his death. His will, dated May 28th, was proved June 13th, 1689. To his wife Elizabeth he left all his stock of books, goods, chattels, &c., and debts. The inventory showed his stock of "Books bound & Queres £7 10*s*." By Elizabeth Tillman, whom he married February 22nd, 1655, he had nine children. This was his second marriage, as one of his other sons, John, was christened November 24th, 1651. [Gray and Palmer, p. 127.]

BEIGLIE ( ), Mrs., bookseller in Edinburgh, in the Parliament Close, 1696. Sold John Holland's *Short Discourse . . . Indian and African Company*, 1696. [Aldis, pp. 94, 109.]

BELL (ANDREW), bookseller in London, (1) Pestle and Mortar over against the Horseshoe Tavern in Chancery Lane; (2) Cross-Keys and Bible in Cornhill, near the Stocks Market. 1694–1715. First appears as publisher, in partnership with Jonas Luntley, of Sir George Mackenzie's *The Institutions of the Laws of Scotland*, 1694. [Haz. II. 376.] His connexion with Luntley was brief, as in the following year he published alone *Considerations on the Trade to Newfoundland*. [Haz. III. 174.] Bell's first entry in the Term Catalogues occurs in Hil. 1697 as one of the publishers of Tyrrell's *History of England*. [*T.C.* III. 4], and from that time until 1711 his name occurs frequently as a miscellaneous publisher. In 1702 Dunton [p. 195] sold him the copyright of *The Athenian Oracle*, and in 1707 he started a monthly quarto of poems, songs, &c., entitled *The Muse's Mercury*. Bell was also the publisher of the monthly critical journal, *The Works of the Learned*, and was agent for the Edinburgh booksellers, A. Sympson and R. Freebairn; for the latter he entered in Stat. Reg., March 26th, 1715, *The Rudiments of the Latin Tongue*, by T. Ruddiman. [Timperley, p. 607.]

BELL (E.), bookseller in London, Cheapside, at the corner of Bow Lane, 1698–1722. Advertised in 1698 *An Historical Account of Russia* [*T.C.* III. 64]; in 1722 his name occurs first in a list of publishers of a novel entitled *The Adventures of the Prince of Clermont*. [Esdaile, p. 189.]

BELL (JAMES), stationer in Edinburgh, 1676. Named cautioner in confirmation of Andrew Anderson's will, 1676. [Aldis, p. 109.]

BELLINGER (JOHN), *see Dictionary*, 1641–67.

BELLINGER (R.), bookseller (?) in London, Wych Street, near New Inn Gate, 1685. Only known as the publisher of a *Book of Copies for learners of Round Hand*, a series of engraved plates. He may have been a print-seller rather than a bookseller. [*T.C.* II. 148, 158.]

BENBRIDGE (WILLIAM), bookseller in London, Half-Moon, Huggins Alley, Wood Street, 1683–4. Advertised in Mich. 1683 *The present state of Denmark*, by G. Pierreville, and a translation of Lucian by Ferrand Spence. The last heard of him is in Mich. 1684, when he advertised a sheet, probably engraved, *A Description of Buda in its ancient and present state*. [*T.C.* II. 43, 51, 99.] Of the 5 vols. of the Lucian only 1–3, 1684, were published by Benbridge; 4–5 bear J. Walthoe's name and are dated 1685. [Esdaile, p. 93.]

BENCE (J.), bookseller at Wotton-under-Edge 1725 (?). *A Dialogue between Honest John and Loving Kate, Part the First*, n.d., was sold by him.

BENNET (F.), 1692. Hazlitt [II. 59] records an edition of N. Brady's tragedy *The Rape* as printed for F. Bennet in 1692. This is a mistake for T. Bennet. [*T.C.* II. 411.]

BENNET (THOMAS), London agent for Oxford printers, 1669. [Madan, p. 30.]

BENNET (THOMAS), bookseller in London, Half-Moon in St. Paul's Churchyard; Oxford. 1687–1706. One of the most important booksellers of his time. He made his first entry in the Term Catalogues in Easter 1687 with an edition of Homer's *Iliad* by George Sylvanus. [*T.C.* II. 194.] Dunton was partner with him in the publication of Lecrose's *Works of the Learned*. Bennet had an extensive connexion amongst the clergy, and Bishop Atterbury, who was his friend and patron, has left this account of him: "I need not say how perfect a master he was of all the business of that useful profession wherein he had engaged himself. . . . His natural abilities were very good and his industry exceeding great, and the evenness and probity of his temper not inferior to either of them. Besides he had one peculiar felicity . . . that he was entirely contented and pleased with his lot, loving his employment for its own sake." He published the catalogues of Abp. Tenison's library and of Dugdale's bequest to the Ashmolean. Bennet married Elizabeth Whitewrong, daughter of James Whitewrong of Rothavestead, co. Hereford. He died on August 26th, 1706, and was buried in St. Faith's. His stock was afterwards bought by J. Nicholson, William Newton, Robert Knaplock, and Benjamin Tooke. [*T.C.* III. 563.] Possibly a son of the preceding.

BENNETT (GEORGE), bookseller in Cork, 1714–34. The earliest mentions of Geo. Bennett are in February 1714, when he printed a small single-sheet periodical called *The Idler*, and in 1716, when he was described as a "Bookseller in Cork". His second imprint extant is found in 1719, on a schoolbook entitled shortly *A Tutor to Arithmetic*. He was a member of the Cork Corporation and elected Mayor for 1724. In 1734 he is described as "Alderman" and was appointed in that year to execute all printing that should be wanted for the Corporation. He also printed *The Cork News Letter*, 1723 to 1725.

BENNETT (JAMES), bookseller in London, Paved Alley in St. James's Fields, 1680. Mentioned as a disperser of unlicensed pamphlets. His wife's name was Grace. [*Hist. MSS. Comm. Report* XI. App. pt. i, p. 268.]

BENNETT (JOSEPH), printer in London, St. Giles, Bloomsbury, 1675 (?)–91 A "Josias" Bennett, possibly the same, is mentioned in a list of printing houses drawn up in 1675, as one who had "set up since the Act was in force". [*S.P.D.* Car. II. vol. 369, p. 97.] For Richard Bentley he printed in 1679 a novel entitled *Fatal Prudence* [Esdaile, p. 211], and in 1678 was the printer of *Huntington Divertisement*. [Haz. II. 297.] In 1680 a Joseph Bennett, stationer of St. Giles, gave information against Sir Roger L'Estrange as being a Papist [*House of Lords Journal*, 1680, p. 630], and in 1685 he printed for Charles Brome Dangerfield's *Memoirs*. [Haz. II. 297.] In 1691 he was defendant in a suit brought by a certain John Smith for the recovery of a debt. [C.P.R. Mich. 3, W. & M. 3101, m. 372, verso.]

BENNETT (M.), printer in London, 1701–3. Printed Sir Thomas Craig's *Right of Succession to the Kingdom of England*, 1703. [Haz. III. 50.]

BENSKIN (THOMAS), bookseller in London, (1) St. Bride's Churchyard; (2) Green's Rents near Fleet Bridge; (3) Little Lincoln's Inn Fields. 1681–1704. First heard of in 168$\frac{0}{1}$ as a publisher on the Protestant side during the Popish Plot. On March 10th he issued the first number of *The Protestant Oxford Intelligence*, altered a month later to *The Impartiall London Intelligence, or Occurrences Forraign and Domestick*. On June 6th, 1681, the Earl of Danby moved the Court of King's Bench that Thomas Benskin, the publisher of *The Phanatick Intelligence*, might be ordered to find bail in £1,000 to answer a charge of scandal against the Earl, but the bail was fixed by the Court at £500. In the same year he issued a broadside entitled *The Vindication of . . . James, Duke of Monmouth*. [B.M. 8122. i. 1. (35).] In Michaelmas Term his name first appears in the Term Catalogue as one of the publishers of a work entitled *The History of the Life . . . of Queen Mary*. In 1684 he moved to Little Lincoln's Inn Fields, but between 1682 and 1704 he made little use of the Term Catalogues. He was the publisher of Mrs. A. Behn's comedies *The Round-Heads* and *The City Heiress*.

BENTLEY (F.), bookseller in Halifax, 1695. Publisher of *The Doctrine of the Church of England concerning the Lord's Day*. [*T.C.* II. 548.]

BENTLEY (M.), bookseller in London, 1698. Apparently no relation of Richard Bentley (*q. v.*) The Term Catalogue for Mich. 1697 has an advertisement of L. Hennepin's *New discovery of a vast country in America . . .* printed for M. Bentley, J. Tonson, &c. [*T.C.* III. 39; B.M. (dated 1698) 278. f. 36.]

BENTLEY (RICHARD), bookseller in London, Post House in Russell Street, Covent Garden, 1675–97. The well-known publisher of novels, plays, and romances, hence referred to by Dunton as "novel" Bentley. [*Life & Errors*, p. 292.] His name first appears in the Term Catalogue of Hilary 1675 in partnership with J. Magnes as joint publisher of a tragedy *Andromeda* [*T.C.* III. 197.] and in the following year they advertised and published the romance of *Zelinda*. [Esdaile, p. 329.] As J. Magnes's name appears first in all the imprints, Bentley was evidently the junior partner. In the latter part of 1678 the firm became R. Bentley and M. Magnes and so continued until 1682, when for a few months Bentley was publishing alone, but in the Term Catalogue for Michaelmas 1683 Dryden's *Religio Laici* was published by R. Bentley and S. Magnes [*T.C.* II. 50.] S. Magnes's name occurs for the last time in Mich. 1688, after which Richard Bentley continued the business alone. Some time in 1688 he issued a broadside entitled *The Commissioners' proposals to . . . the Prince of Orange, &c.* [B.M. 1850. c. 6 (6).] In 1692 Bentley reissued some fifty novels of the preceding fifteen years, not all bearing his imprint, as *Modern Novels, in xii volumes*. [B.M. 12410. c. 18–29.] Letters of his in Sir H. Ellis's *Original Letters of eminent Literary Men*, 1843, show that Bentley was both an enterprising and liberal man. Amongst other notable books published by him may be noticed John Evelyn's *Sylva*, and the author, writing to Dr. Richard Bentley in 1697, says that the latter's namesake "had sold off three impressions and was impatient for the fourth." But it is chiefly as a publisher of romances that Bentley is known, and in some "romans à clef" he adopted fictitious imprints. For example, Gabriel de Brémond's *Hattige, or the Amours of the King of Tamaran*, was published "For Simon the African, Amsterdam", 1680; again, *The Secret History of the Duke of Alançon and Q. Elizabeth*, published in 1691, bore the imprint "For Will with the Whisp, at the sign of the Moon in the Ecliptick", sometimes with the addition of "Cologne." [Esdaile, pp. 169, 215.] Bentley's name last appears in the Term Catalogue of Easter 1697 [*T.C.* III. 15] and he died between that date and July 6th, when his will was proved. He made his wife Katherine his sole executrix and he left a son Thomas. Among the witnesses to the will was Robert Everingham.

BENTLEY (THOMAS), bookseller in London, Crown in Little Britain, 1688–95. In 1688, in partnership with B. Walford, Thomas Bentley sold by auction the library of William Cecil, first Baron Burleigh, and the catalogue gives his place of business as above. After this nothing more is known of him until 1695, when he married Mrs. Anne Ridley of Downham in the Isle of Ely. [Cambridge Parish Registers—Marriages—Knapwell, p. 145.] His name does not appear in the Term Catalogues.

BENTLEY (T.), stationer at Cambridge, 1679. Admitted by the Vice-Chancellor and Heads to the trade of stationer in Cambridge, 1679, but on November 1st, 1679, he was "prohibited by the Vice-Chancellor and Heads from selling books in Cambridge till the determination of his controversy with Cambridge stationers".

BENTLEY (WILLIAM), bookseller in London, 1697. Hazlitt records *The Picture of Quakerism drawn to the Life*. . . . By Francis Bugg, London, Printed for and are to be sold by W. Bentley . . . 1697. The only copy in the British Museum of that date does not give Bentley as one of the publishers. [Haz. II. 68.]

BERINGTON (E.), printer in London, Silver Street, Bloomsbury, 1711–24. Only known as the printer of *The Evening Post*, 1711. Mentioned in Negus's List as printer for the Roman Catholics.

BERRY (E.), bookseller and engraver in London, Holborn Court, Gray's Inn, 1672–81. Dealer in maps, charts, prints, playing cards, and topographical

works. In partnership with William Berry. In Michaelmas 1672 they announced *An exact Survey of the United Provinces of the Netherlands*. [*T.C.* I. 119.] In 1681 E. Berry's name is found in the imprint of a work entitled *Jus Anglorum ab Antiquo*.

BERRY (WILLIAM), bookseller and engraver in London, (1) Blue Anchor, Middle Row, Holborn; (2) Globe, Strand, (*a*) near the New Exchange; (*b*) between York House and the New Exchange; (3) Globe, between Charing Cross and Whitehall, near Charing Cross; (4) in Cragg's Court, near Charing Cross. 1671–1703. Dealer in maps, charts, prints, playing cards and topographical works, first heard of in 1671 [*T.C.* I. 80.] In the following year, in partnership with E. Berry, he announced *An exact Survey of the United Provinces of the Netherlands*. [*T.C.* I. 119.] In 1673 he moved from Holborn to the Strand and in 1679 had moved still further west to Charing Cross. He made his last announcement in the Term Catalogues in Michaelmas, 1703. [*T.C.* III. 382.]

BERTRAM (WILLIAM), stationer in Cambridge, in St. Edward's parish, 1693. On January 26th, 1693 the Vice-Chancellor licensed him to keep a "Common Alehouse or Tippling-house" within the Town of Cambridge. [Cooper's *Annals of Cambridge*, IV. 25.]

BETTENHAM (JAMES), printer in London, St. John's Lane, 1712(?)–74. Is believed to have been born in 1683, but no particulars are obtainable as to his life before the year 1712, when he married the step-daughter of William Bowyer the elder. This took place shortly before the fire which destroyed Bowyer's premises. Nichols [*Lit. Anecd.* I. 65] furnishes almost all that is known about him. He refers to Bettenham as "a printer of no small eminence in his profession, which he pursued with unabated industry and reputation till the year 1766, when he retired from business, and died Feb. 6, 1774, of a gradual decay, at the advanced age of 91. To shew the uncertainty of human affairs, this worthy man, after carrying on a respectable and extensive business for more than 60 years, left behind him not quite £400. . . . His first wife died Dec. 8, 1716, aged 30; and he had a second who died July 9, 1735, aged 39." Amongst those who served their apprenticeship in his office was F. Kirkby, the successor of J. Abree the Canterbury printer and the partner of J. Simmons of that city. Bettenham will always be remembered as one of those who helped to finance William Caslon the First

and set him up as a type founder. [Nichols, *Lit. Anecd.* II. 356, 720.] Negus in his list of printers in 1724 described Bettenham as a Non-juror. Most of his work as a printer lies beyond the limit of this volume, but it may be noted that amongst other things he was the printer in 1721 of *Vita Johannis Barwick*. [Nichols, *Lit. Anecd.* I. 217.]

BETTESWORTH (ARTHUR), bookseller in London, Red Lion on London Bridge, 1699–1737. Chiefly a publisher of divinity, though he published many novels, &c., and, like all the booksellers on the Bridge, dealt in some questionable literature. [*See Post Boy*, January 11th, 1711.] His daughter Elizabeth married Charles Hitch, bookseller of Paternoster Row, in partnership with whom her father had published many books. [Timperley, p. 713.]

BEVER (THOMAS), bookseller in London, Hand and Star, within Temple Bar; (*a*) next the Middle Temple Gate, (*b*) by, (*c*) near, Temple Bar. 1689–1712. Made his first entry in the Term Catalogues in Mich. 1689. [*T.C.* II. 283.] Publisher of books on a variety of subjects. Amongst others may be noticed, *Alphonso, King of Naples, A Tragedy*, by Geo. Powell, 1691, and *England's Glory; Or, The Great improvement of Trade in General*, by H. M., 1694. In 1713 he subscribed one guinea to the Bowyer relief fund. Dunton [p. 226] has this character of him: "Mr. Bever, in Fleet Street, had ever the character of being a very merciful, just, and peaceable man, never intermeddling with state matters. He is a constant hearer at St. Dunstan's church. . . . I shall only add, he has a large acquaintance amongst the lawyers, and is himself a very thriving bookseller." The premises he occupied were those once tenanted by Richard Tottell, and bore the same sign.

BICKERTON (S.), *see* Bickerton (T.).

BICKERTON (THOMAS), bookseller in London, (1) Flower de Luce (or Golden Flower de Lucé), St. Paul's Churchyard, 1707; (2) Rose and Crown, Little Britain, 1711; (3) Crown in Paternoster Row, 1719. 1707–20. In partnership with S. Bickerton. Dealer in theological books, and book-auctioneer. On March 26th, 1720 he took over the publication of *The Weekly Packet*, a newspaper issued by the Sun Fire Office, which had previously been published by E. Place.

BILL (CHARLES), printer (?) in London, King's Printing Office, 1687–99. Son of John Bill the Second; held a share of the King's Printing Office by reversion, but he seems never to have exercised the art of printing.

BILL (JOHN) the Second, *see Dictionary*, 1641–67.

BILLING (R.), bookseller (?) in London, White Swan in St. Paul's Churchyard, 1703. Published, with G. Briant, W. Leybourn's *Mathematical Institutions* [*T.C.* III. 370]; but was perhaps a mathematical instrument maker and not a regular publisher.

BILLINGER (J.), *see* Bellinger (J.)

BILLINGSLEY (BENJAMIN), bookseller in London, (1) Printing Press, at the entrance into Gresham College, Broad Street; over against the Church; (2) (*a*) within the South-west Piazza, (*b*) under the Piazza, of the Royal Exchange, Cornhill; over against Pope's Head Alley. 1669–1706. Although carrying on business at the sign of the "Printing Press", Benjamin Billingsley was not a printer but a bookseller. His first entry (with O. Blagrave) in the Term Catalogues was *The Epitome of the Art of Husbandry*. [*T.C.* I. 9.] According to Dunton [p. 230] he suffered for some years from a mental disorder during which time his wife and son managed the business. His name appears in the Term Catalogues for the last time in Trinity Term 1698 [*T.C.* III. 83], but in 1706 he published the ninth edition of Nathaniel Strong's *England's Perfect Schoolmaster*. [Haz. III. 311.] Amongst his numerous publications was *A True Account of the Most Considerable Occurrences that have hapned in the Warre between the English and the Indians in New England*, 1676.

BIRCH (WILLIAM), bookseller in London, (1) Bible, New Cheapside, Moorfields; (2) Blue Bible, at the Lower end of Cheapside, (*a*) at the corner of the Poultry, (*b*) at the corner of Bucklersbury; (3) Peacock in the Poultry, (*a*) near Old Jewry, (*b*) at the lower end of Cheapside; (4) Black Swan, against St. Clement's Church, in the Strand; (5) St. Paul's Alley, over against the little North Door of St. Paul's. 1669–93. His first publication, a theological work, was entered in the Term Catalogue in Mich. 1669. [*T.C.* I. 18.] He was the publisher of J. Crowne's tragi-comedy, *Juliana, or the Princess of Poland*, 1671, also of the Rev. Samuel Clarke's *Marrow of Ecclesiastical History*, 1675. In that year he issued a political broadside on the Royalist side, entitled *The Triumph of Levy*. [B.M. C. 40. m. 11. (35.)] In 1678 he either opened another shop or moved to the Black Swan, against St. Clement's Church in the Strand [*Midd. & Herts. N. & Q.*, vol. II, p. 95]. Birch is last heard of in Easter 1693 when he published Dr. Baldwin Hamey's *Dissertatio Epistolaris De juramento medicorum*, edited by Adam Littleton. [*T.C.* II. 455.]

BIRCHALL (DANIEL), bookseller and printer in Liverpool, Castle Street, 1712–22. In 1712 he published C. Owen's *Hymns sacred to the Lord's Table*, printed for him by S. Terry at Liverpool. By 1722 he had set up a press of his own, for we find him then printing H. Wosterholme's *Sermon . . . for promoting the Charity School.* [Liverpool Free Public Library, *Liverpool Prints and Documents*, 1908, pp. 333–4.]

BIRD (JOHN ?), bookseller in London, Sun in Westminster Hall, 1683–89. This bookseller is perhaps the John Bird, son-in-law to Richard Andrew, stationer, (*q. v.*) who died in 1683. He had a stall in Westminster Hall during Easter Term 1689. Two books were advertised by him in the Term Catalogue. [*T.C.* II. 243, 249.]

BISHOP (GEORGE), printer and bookseller in Exeter. In the Fore Street, opposite to St. Stephen's Church, 1718–20. Son of Philip Bishop, born on January 1st, 1697, and succeeded to his father's business about 1718: but his career was a short one, as nothing more is heard of him after 1720. [Dredge, ff. 19, &c.]

BISHOP (M.), bookseller in Exeter, 1717. Widow of Philip Bishop? The Rev. W. Rayner's *Sermon Preach'd in Ely Chappel at the Consecration of . . . Lancelot Lord Bishop of Exeter*, bears the imprint, "Exon: Printed for M. Bishop . . . 1717." [Dredge, f. 45.]

BISHOP (PHILIP), printer and bookseller in Exeter, (1) Fore Street; (2) High Street; (3) St. Peter's Church Yard. 1688–1716. Philip Bishop, stationer, was admitted a freeman of Exeter by apprenticeship 1688–9. He appears to have lived in St. Martin's parish, as the Register has several entries of his family. [Dredge, f. 10.] The first book recorded by Dredge as published by him was a *Sermon preached in the Cathedral Church of . . . Exon.*, by William Chilcot, M.A., on April 4th, 1697. [*Ibid.*] He appears to have died about 1716 and was succeeded by his widow (?) M. Bishop, and later by his son George. Dunton [p. 237] speaks of him as "a firm adherer to the Established Government, and a declared enemy to Popery and Slavery . . . a man of strict justice, deals much and thrives of his trade".

BIXOU alias TABB (L.), printer in Limerick, 1722–23? Worked with Samuel Terry (*q. v.*) but nothing is known of him beyond the two imprints in which his name occurs.

BLACK (J.), bookseller in London, Holborn, 1694. Hazlitt records: *Dr. Mason's Wonderful Vision. A Further . . . Relation of one Mr. Mason, minister of Water-Stafford, near Buckingham, who pretends Our Saviour appeared to him 16th April 1694* . . . London, printed for J. Black in Holborn. [Haz. II. 68.] It is possible that J. Black is a misprint for J. Blackwell (*q. v.*) but *see* Blake.

BLACKBORNE (J.), bookseller in London, 1681. Only known from his imprint on a pamphlet entitled *The Reformed Papist or High Church Man*, 1681, Fol. [B.M. 1850. c. 6. (43*).]

BLACKBURY (HENRY), stationer in London, 1686. Defendant in a plea of trespass brought by William Roberts in 1686. [Hilary 2–3 James II, C.P.R. 3052, m. 86.]

BLACKWELL (JAMES), bookseller in London, Bernard's Inn Gate, Holborn, 1690–4. In 1690 he published, with R. Taylor, W. Mountford's *The Successful Strangers, A Tragi-Comedy* . . . [*T.C.* II. 301.] Hazlitt also records a poem by E. Ward, *On the Death of the late Lieutenant General Talmach*, 1694, printed for and sold by him. [Haz. III. 313.] The work recorded under J. Black may have been published by James Blackwell.

BLAGRAVE (OBADIAH), bookseller in London, (1) In Cornhill; (2) Printing Press at the entrance into Gresham College, Broad Street; over against the Church; (3) Printing Press, Little Britain; over against the Pump; (4) (*a*) Bear, St. Paul's Churchyard; near the little North Door of the Church, (*b*) Black Bear, or Bear and Star, St. Paul's Churchyard. 1669–91. Probably a member of the family of Blagrave of Reading, as in 1671 he published Joseph Blagrave's *Astrological Practice of Physick*. He is first met with in Easter, 1669, when, with B. Billingsley, he advertised *The Epitome of the Art of Husbandry* [*T.C.* I. 9]. In the following year he had moved to Little Britain, where he remained till 1677 when he is found at the Bear in St. Paul's Churchyard. He was the publisher of John Quarles's *Fons Lachrymarum*, in that year; but he dealt chiefly in works on divinity and mathematics. His last advertisement in the Term Catalogues was in Hilary Term 1691. [*T.C.* II. 352.] He was tersely described by Dunton [p. 292] as "plain Blagrave".

BLAGUE (DANIEL), bookseller and book auctioneer, 1691. Possibly a descendant of John Blague (*see Dictionary*, 1641–67.) He held a book auction on

June 15th, 1691, at Mr. John Martin's at Guildhall Coffee House, a principal feature of which was "a number of Stitched Plays not expressed in the Catalogue" [B.M. 821. i. 9 (10).]

BLAKE ( ), bookseller in London, 1705. Described by Dunton [p. 213] as the "father of the Company of Stationers for age and experience". *See also* Black (J.) who may be identical.

BLAND (THOMAS), printer in London, (1) near Ludgate Street; (2) near Fleet Street. 1706–8. In the British Museum is a copy of the *Postcript to the Post Man*, of May 20th, 1706. This was only printed on one side, but Bland secured copies of it and printed on the back, *The Tryal and Examination of Dr. William Drake for writing Mercurius Politicus*. Hazlitt records the following: *Here is a full and true Relation of one Mr. Rich. Langley, a Glazier . . . that lay in a trance*, London, Printed for T. Bland near Fleet Street, 1708. [Haz. IV. 152.]

BLARE (ELIZABETH), bookseller in London, The Looking Glass on London Bridge, 1707. Widow of Josiah Blare. She carried on the business for a short time after his death in 1706. In 1707 the Company of Stationers entered an action against her in Chancery, for the infringement of their patents in almanacs, &c. [Chan. Proc. before 1714, Bridges $\frac{270}{21}$.]

BLARE (JOSIAH or JOSEPH), bookseller in London, The Looking Glass on London Bridge, 1683–1706. Dealer in chap-books and miscellaneous literature. By his will, proved on December 3rd, 1706, he left to his wife Elizabeth, his shop and house "known by the name or sign of the Looking Glass on the North East side of London Bridge". [P.C.C. 225 Eedes.] He was buried in St. Magnus Church.

BLISS (JOSEPH), printer at Exeter, (1) The Exchange, 1705–10; (2) a little without the East Gate, 1711–19. 1705–19. He printed, *inter alia*: (1) with S. Farley, *A True and Impartial Account of what Occurred at the late Conference in Exon*, 1707 [Dredge, f. 14]; (2) alone, for P. Bishop, Blackall's *Sermon on Almsgiving*, 1708 [J. S. Attwood, *Addenda to Dredge*]; (3) alone, J. Withers's *Truth try'd or Mr. Agate's pretended Plain Truth*, 1709. [*T.C.* III. 610.]

BLITH (FRANCIS), bookseller in Colchester, 1702–11. In Michaelmas Term 1702 he advertised *Serious Advice from a Minister to his Parishioner* [*T.C.* III.

318], and he also published Edward Cresfield's *Duty of the subject to his prince . . . . In a sermon preached at the parish church of Witham in Essex on Tuesday the 30th January* $17\frac{10}{11}$, which was advertised in *The Post Boy*, March 6th, $17\frac{10}{11}$.

BLOME (RICHARD), cartographer in London, at Mr. Kid's in the Corner of Lincoln's Inn Fields, near New [=Clare] Market, 1668–79. Perhaps a descendant or relative of Jacob Blome, *q.v. Dictionary*, 1641–67. On May 29th, 1663, one or the other of them entered in the register *A Geographicall Description of the World, written in French by Sanson, Geographer to ye King of France and translated into English*, and at the same time, although the title was not entered, a translation of the works of Varenius. On the last day of July 1668 Richard Blome entered both these works again in the Register, and an advertisement of Sanson's work appeared in the Term Catalogue for Hilary 1670. Amongst his other publications was an atlas of England and Wales issued during 1673 and the fifth edition of Guillim's *Heraldry* in 1679.

BLOUNT, or BLUNT (CHARLES), bookseller in London; (1) Black-Raven between Worcester House and the Savoy, near the Bear Tavern, Strand; by the New Exchange; (2) The Catherine Wheel, Charing Cross. 1678–84. Publisher of medical books, plays and novels. Amongst the latter may be noticed *The Mock Clelia*, advertised in *Mercurius Civicus*, April 22nd, 1680, and A. Oldys's *Fair Extravagant*, 1681 [*T.C.* I. 461]. In the same number he also advertised a translation of one of the novels of Cervantes, called *The Jealous Gentleman of Estremadura*. His last advertisement was in the issue of Michaelmas 1684. [*T.C.* II. 97.] Blunt moved to the Catherine Wheel about 1680.

BLOW (JAMES), printer in Belfast, 1706–58. Succeeded Patrick Neill. His earliest extant imprint is dated 1706. While very largely of a religious character the output of his press included secular works. Blow was connected by marriage with Geo. Grierson who married his widowed sister. The allegation that Blow printed a Bible in 1704 is now admitted as untenable. Blow did not claim to do so but he certainly did claim in an advertisement of works printed and sold by himself an edition of the Holy Bible in several vols. and the N.T., but no copy is extant or recorded elsewhere. The edition of 1757 commonly called "Blow's Bible" is the earliest one extant from his press.

BLUNT, *see* Blount.

BODDINGTON (M.), bookseller in London, Duck Lane, 1711–25. Published in 1711 in partnership with N. Boddington, Thos. Lydal's *Accomptant's Assistant*. In 1722 the twentieth edition of the first part of Bunyan's *Pilgrim's Progress* was printed by A. Wilde for M. Bodington. [B.M. 4414. de. 27.]

BODDINGTON (NICHOLAS), bookseller in London, Golden Ball, Duck Lane, 1687–1717. This bookseller was perhaps a descendant of George Boddington (1648). He began as a publisher in 1687, when he advertised *The Gentleman's new Jockey or Farrier's approved guide*. [*T.C.* II. 188.] In 1693 he published the thirteenth edition of the First Part of Bunyan's *Pilgrim's Progress* for R. Ponder. In a law suit instituted in 1697 by Nathaniel Ponder, who held the copyright, against Thomas Braddyll, Boddington deposed that he bought ten thousand copies of this edition and paid Braddyll at the rate of five shillings per ream for them, although he had agreed with Ponder that he was to have them at four and sixpence a ream. Boddington gave his age as forty-five or thereabouts. Dunton [p. 209] has the following account of him: "By an industrious management he has gathered a good estate, and makes a considerable figure in the Parish where he lives. He deals much in Bibles, Testaments and Common Prayer Books. He purchased Mr. Keach's *Travels of true Godliness* of me, and deals much in the country." From 1711 he was publishing in partnership with M. Boddington (*q. v.*) who succeeded him.

BODVELL or BODRELL (PETER), *see Dictionary*, 1641–67.

BOLDERO (ARTHUR), bookseller in London, Mitre, Mitre Court, Fleet Street, near the Inner Temple, 1677. Only known by a little octavo called *Poor Robin's Visions*, which he published in 1677. [*T.C.* I. 283; Haz. I. 361.]

BOLTON (S.), bookseller in London (?) 1713. Publisher of the sixth edition of J. Arbuthnot's *Complete Key to Law is a Bottomless Pit*, 1713. [Esdaile, p. 152.]

BONNY (WILLIAM), printer in London and Bristol: Bristol, (1) Tower Lane, 1695; (2) Near the Tolzey, 1699; (3) Small Street, 1703; (4) Corn Street. 1691–1714. Began business as a printer in London and was employed by John Dunton to print Baxter's *Directions to the Unconverted*, Cotton Mather's *Tryals of several Witches*, and Dunton's own *Pleasant art of Money Catching*. He is favourably mentioned for his just dealing by Dunton [pp. 247–8], who suggests

that his migration to Bristol was due to money losses. This took place in the early part of 1695, the Chamber of the City coming to the conclusion that a printing press might be useful in several respects, but not being disposed to allow a "foreigner" to compete with local booksellers in their special business, granted him the freedom on condition that he dwelt in the city and exercised no trade save that of a printer. His first book printed in Bristol was *An Essay on the State of England in relation to its Trade, its Poor and its Taxes*. "By John Cary, Merchant in Bristoll; Bristoll, Printed by W. Bonny for the author and are to be sold in London. . . . Also by Tho. Wall and Rich. Gravett near the Tolzey in Bristol, Novem. 1695." In 1696 he printed (1) a broadside entitled, *The Humble Presentment of the Grand Inquest at Mid-summer Sessions*; (2) *Mr. John Cary's Proposals for the better maintaining and Imploying the Poor of the City of Bristoll*; and (3) *The Banner of Corah, Dathan and Abiram displayed . . . Sermons preach'd at Bristol, by John Moore*. In 1702 he became the editor and publisher of a newspaper called *The Bristol Post Boy* which is believed to have appeared in November, but the earliest known copy of which is that of August 12th, 1704. In one of its issues he announced that he was ready to buy old rope and paper stuff, and to sell Bibles, Welsh Prayer Books, paper hangings, music, maps, blank ale licenses, and blank commissions for private men of war; and in May 1712 he had very good Bridgewater peas and excellent charcoal for sale. *The Post Boy* cannot be traced beyond May 1712. Another of his publications was the Rev. Arthur Bedford's *Evil and Danger of Stage Plays*, 1706. When Dunton wrote (1703) Bonny was "stark blind".

BONWICKE (HENRY), bookseller in London, Red Lion, St. Paul's Churchyard, 1677–1706. Son of the Rev. John Bonwicke and uncle of Ambrose Bonwicke the younger, whose life under the title of *A Pattern for Young Students*, was published by Professor Mayor in 1870. Dunton writes of him [p. 216] "I do not think there is an honester man in London, or one that is more zealous for the church. He served his time with Mr. Benjamin Tooke." He dealt chiefly in works of divinity but published also medical books and books on music. He died in 1706. [Nichols, *Lit. Anecd.* V. 119.] Two letters from him to Strype are printed in *N. & Q.*, August 29th, 1859, p. 343. Rebecca Bonwicke (*q. v.*) may have been his widow.

BONWICKE (JAMES), bookseller in London, (1) Hat and Star, St. Paul's Churchyard; (2) Red Lion, St. Paul's Churchyard. 1699–1714? His relation-

ship to Henry Bonwicke is not clear. His first entry was of a City sermon, in 1699. [*T.C.* III. 134.] After the death of Henry Bonwicke he moved to the Red Lion and was in partnership with Rebecca Bonwicke. They were still publishing in 1711. In 1714 James subscribed for Walker's *Sufferings of the Clergy*.

BONWICKE (REBECCA), bookseller in London, Red Lion, St. Paul's Churchyard, 1706–11? Perhaps the widow of Henry Bonwicke. She was joined after his death by James Bonwicke, and they were still publishing in 1711 and probably later.

BOOMER (T.), bookseller in London, White Horse in Ludgate Street, 1686. His name is found in the imprint to *The Book of Bertram, priest and Monk of Corby*. [*T.C.* II. 164.]

BOSVILLE (ALEXANDER), bookseller in London, The Dial in Fleet Street, 169$\frac{6}{7}$; (2) The Dial and Bible in Fleet Street, 1703. 1696–1709. Publisher, largely of broadsides. Identical with Dunton's "Mr. Boswill" [p. 210]. His first appearance in the Term Catalogue is in Mich. 1696. [*T.C.* II. 599.] In the same year he published Motteux's comedy *Love's a Jest*. [*T.C.* II. 602.] He is last met with in the Term Catalogues in Hil. 1709. [*T.C.* III. 630.] His shop was taken by Edmund Curll in 1711.

BOTHAM (W.), printer in London, Jewin Street, 1700–25. Printed Dampier's *New Voyage round the World* for James Knapton. In 1713 he contributed to Bowyer's relief fund, and in 1724 is mentioned in Negus's List of Printers as "well affected to King George". [Nichols, *Lit. Anecd.* I. 290.]

BOUGES (J.), bookseller (?) in London, Castle in Westminster Hall, 1700. Appears to have had a stall in Westminster Hall in Mich. 1700, when he advertised in the Term Catalogue *A new book, wherein is given the whole . . . Account the Scriptures gives of the Deity, &c.* [*T.C.* III. 212.] It seems doubtful if he was a bookseller.

BOULTER (ROBERT). *See Dictionary*, 1641–67. Still in business in 1679, when he published, or at least sold, Bedloe's *Narrative of the Burning of London*. In 1674–5 the widow of Thomas Underhill transferred to him all her late husband's copyrights, most of these being works of divinity. [*Stat. Reg.*, Roxb., II. 64.] His name appears in the Term Catalogues for the last time in Hil. 1683. [*T.C.* II. 4.] *See* Bowter (R.).

BOURN (SAMUEL), bookbinder in London, *c.* 1700? Described by Dunton [pp. 258–9] as just to those who employed him, but of loose character, and as coming to an untimely end.

BOURNE (CHARLES), printer in York, within the Coffee House Yard, 1721–4. Successor to Grace White. Continued the publication of the *York Mercury*. On June 24th, 1721 he married Alice Guy at St. Michael the Belfry, but he died in August 1724. His widow shortly afterwards married Thomas Gent (*q. v.*).

BOURNE (THOMAS), *see Dictionary*, 1641–67.

BOURNE (ZACHARIAH), bookseller and book auctioneer in London, 1678. Is said by Lawler to have held the third book auction in England, when he sold the library of the Rev. William Greenhill, pastor of Stepney, in February 167$\frac{7}{8}$. [Lawler, *Book Auctions in England*, p. 117; B.M. 821. i. 1. (3).]

BOWEN (J.), bookseller in London, 1681. Hazlitt records *A Poem (by way of Elegie) upon Mr. Stephen Colledge*, 1681, printed for him. [Haz. II. 134.]

BOWERS (JOSEPH), bookseller in London, Crown in Long-Acre, 168$\frac{8}{9}$. His imprint is found in a pamphlet entitled, *A Breviate for the Bishops, By a person of Honour*. [B.M. T. 1702 (5).]

BOWIS (TH.), bookseller in London, 1683. Published a poetical broadside entitled *The Sham Office*, 1683. [B.M. 1875. d. 6 (68).]

BOWLES (JOHN), printseller in London, Black Horse, Cornhill; and [in the Strand] over against Devereux Court, without Temple Bar, 1709. Arber states [*T.C.* III. 701, Index] that John and Thomas Bowles sold G. de l'Isle's map [*Theatrum Historicum*]; the announcement referred to [III. 647] mentions neither, but their names appear on the map itself [B.M. maps 100 (3).].

BOWLES (THOMAS), printseller in London, St. Paul's Churchyard, 1709. *See* Bowles (John).

BOWMAN (FRANCIS), *see Dictionary*, 1641–67.

BOWMAN (THOMAS), bookseller at Oxford, 1664–78. *See Dictionary*, 1641–67. In Trinity Term 1672 he published for R. Bohun, Fellow of New College, *A Discourse concerning the origin and properties of Wind* [*T.C.* I. 112], and in 1678 a book of Songs, composed by H. Bowman, "Philo-Musicus", possibly a relation. [*T.C.* I. 319.] His books were sold by auction at Oxford in February 168$\frac{6}{7}$. [*Life and Times of Anthony Wood*, Oxford Hist. Soc. vol. III, p. 213.]

BOWTELL (WILLIAM), printer in London, (1) Golden Key in Fleet Street, near Mitre Court; (2) Star, Cheapside, near Mercers' Chapel, 1675–9. Bowtell's name occurs in a List of Printing Houses in London, drawn up in March 1675, as one of those who had "set up since the Act was in force" [*S.P.D.* Car. II, vol. 369–97]. His name appears in the Term Catalogue of Trinity Term, 1676, as selling a medical work [*T.C.* I. 246]. Nothing is heard of him after 1679 [*T.C.* I. 342]. Dunton [p. 293] calls him "generous Bowtel". He was possibly a descendant of Stephen Bowtell, 1643–64. [*See Dictionary*, 1641–67.]

BOWTER = BOULTER? (ROBERT), stationer in London and Edinburgh, 1687. Will registered in Edinburgh, July 22nd, 1687. [Aldis, p. 109.] *See* Boulter (R.).

BOWYER (EDWARD), stationer in London, 1686. His name occurs in a lawsuit in this year. [C.P.R. 3042. m. 511, recto.]

BOWYER (JONAH or JONAS), bookseller in London, Rose, Ludgate Street, (*a*) the corner of St. Paul's Churchyard, (*b*) near the West End of St. Paul's Churchyard, 1705–22. Nichols states that this bookseller was no relation to William Bowyer the printer. He succeeded W. Hawes at the Rose in 1705, and his first publication was a divinity book [*T.C.* III. 436.] In 1713 he gave a subscription of two guineas to the Bowyer Fund. Lintot is said to have bought of him a half share in Lauderdale's Virgil for £5 7*s.* 6*d.* [Nichols, *Lit. Anecd.* VIII. 294.] In September 1722 he gave Harley some papers. [*Ib.* I. 9.]

BOWYER (WILLIAM), the elder, printer in London, (1) White Horse in Little Britain; (2) Dogwell Court, Whitefriars. 1699–1737. Son of John Bowyer, citizen and grocer of London, by Mary daughter of William King, citizen and vintner of London. Born in 1663, apprenticed to Miles Fletcher, printer, in 1679, and made free of the Company of Stationers in 1686. By his first wife he had no issue. He married secondly Dorothy, daughter of Thomas Dawks, printer and widow of Benjamin Allport, bookseller. In 1699 he was in business as a printer at the White Horse in Little Britain. In the same year he removed to Dogwell Court, where on January 29th, 17$\frac{12}{13}$ a fire destroyed his printing house with his plant and the MSS. and sheets of many important books. A subscription, amounting to £2,539, by Bowyer's fellow printers and the booksellers, was collected for his relief. Most of the finest books of the

time are the work of the Bowyer press. Negus calls Bowyer a Non-juror. In 1722 he took his son William into partnership. Bowyer died December 27th, 1737, and was buried in the church of Low Leyton, Essex. [Nichols, *Lit. Anecd.*; *D.N.B.*]

BOWYER (WILLIAM), the younger, printer in London, (1) Dogwell Court, White Friars, 1722–67; (2) Cicero's Head, Red Lion Passage, Fleet Street, 1767–77. 1722–77. Only son of William Bowyer the elder, *q.v.*, by his second wife; born on December 19th, 1699. Most of his career lies outside our period, but a brief account may be given of "the most learned printer of the eighteenth century." He entered St. John's College, Cambridge, as a sizar, in 1716, and won a Roper Exhibition there, but did not take a degree. While still at Cambridge he began to assist his father in the work of reading for the press, and in 1722 was taken in as a partner; he continued as "corrector", his father retaining the management. In 1728 he married Anne Prudom, his mother's niece. At the elder Bowyer's death in 1737 he carried on the office alone. In 1729 the firm had been appointed printers of the Commons' Votes, and in 1736 printers to the Society of Antiquaries. The younger Bowyer was soon elected a Fellow of the Antiquaries, and contributed many papers, which were collected and published in 1785 by John Nichols. In 1754 he entered into a partnership with a near relative, James Emonson, which lasted till 1757, when John Nichols, then aged 12, was placed under him, and was soon entrusted with the management of the office, becoming his partner in 1766. He died on November 18th, 1777, aged 77. Nichols's *Literary Anecdotes* is an expansion of a memoir of the two Bowyers with an annotated list of their productions.

BRADDYLL (THOMAS), printer in London, 1680–1704 (?) Braddyll is first heard of in 1680, when he printed for Robert Clavell *The Rights of Bishops to judge in Capital Cases in Parliament cleared*, and in the following year for the same bookseller *The Annals of King James and King Charles the First.* [Haz. II. 50, III. 87.] In 1680 Nathaniel Ponder, in the fourth edition of *Pilgrim's Progress*, accused Braddyll of printing surreptitious and unauthorized editions of the book and spoke of him as a "land pirate". At the same time he appears to have subsequently employed Braddyll to print an edition for him, as appears by a series of documents in a law suit which Ponder brought against Braddyll in 1697. According to the story there told, he gave Braddyll an order to print an edition of ten thousand copies at four shillings and sixpence

a ream, and he accused Braddyll of defrauding him, and further declared that he was the author and printer of the Third Part, in which by transporting a great part of the original work, especially the titles, he hindered the sale of the plaintiff's copies. Braddyll in reply gave a complete answer to these charges, and further stated that while Ponder was a prisoner for debt in the King's Bench Prison he (Braddyll) had spent a sum of £14 on behalf of Ponder's son. He denied having anything to do with the publication of the Third Part of *The Pilgrim's Progress*. Dunton [p. 251] gives the following character of Braddyll: "Mr. Braddyll is a first rate printer and has always been a very active diligent man. He is religiously true to his word and faithful to the booksellers that employ him.... He was once a good friend to Sir R. L'Estrange when matters looked a little dark upon him." In 1704 Braddyll was the printer of the fourth edition of Plutarch's *Morals* for J. Taylor [*T.C.* III. 417] after which nothing more is known of him.

BRADFORD (JOHN) printer in London, (1) Bible in Fetter Lane; (2) Little Britain; (3) New Street, without Bishopsgate; (4) Bible, in Westmoreland Court. 1685–1709. There was more than one printer of this name in London in the latter part of the seventeenth century, and it is difficult to distinguish them. There was first John Bradford, brother of William Bradford the Quaker, and it seems probable that the work entitled, *The Protestant Martyrs: or the Bloody Assizes*, 1685, came from his press. John Bradford was present at his brother William's marriage to Elizabeth Sowle in February 1685, and he is believed to have subsequently gone to America. Another John Bradford is found between 1697 and 1709 printing theological books. [*T.C.* III. 36, 122.] In 1704 he printed *Proceedings at the Old Bailey*, in which his imprint is given as the "Bible in Westmoreland Court". J. How refers to John Bradford as a printer of other men's copies. [*Some Thoughts on the present State of Printing and Bookselling*, p. 12.]

BRADLEY (JOB), bookseller in Chesterfield, 1725–98. In 1725 he sold Charles Cotton's *Wonders of the Peak*. [Haz. III. 49.] Later he became a printer as well as a bookseller, and served the office of Alderman of Chesterfield, where he died in February 1798. [Nichols, *Lit. Anecd.* III. 672.]

BRADLEY (WILLIAM), bookseller in London, Three Bibles, Minories, 1670. Sold *Grammaticus Analyticus*, 1670, a Latin Grammar composed for the use of the Free School in East Smithfield. [*T.C.* I. 43, 49.]

BRADWELL (THOMAS), printer in London, 1681. Defendant in an action for assault brought by Bartholomew Sprint, bookseller, against several printers and booksellers of London and Oxford in 1681. Details are wanting. [C.P.R. Trinity 33 Chas. II. 2992. m. 265.]

BRAGG (BENJAMIN), printer and bookseller in London, (1) White Hart, Fleet Street, over against the end of Water Lane; (2) Blue Ball, Ave Mary Lane, near Ludgate Street; (3) Black Raven in Paternoster Row, over against Ivy Lane End. 1694–1709? Began business as a bookseller in Fleet Street in 1694, amongst his publications in that year being *Miscellaneous Letters and Essays on several subjects . . . by several Ladies and Gentlemen.* [*T.C.* II. 512.] He then disappears from the Term Catalogues for ten years, his next appearance being in Hilary 1704, when he published *An Account of the Proceedings of the Parliament of Scotland*, May 6th, 1703. [*T.C.* III. 391.] He was the printer of a broadside entitled *A New Express from Holland*, July 12th, 1703, [*Bibl. Lind.*, *Broadsides*, No. 840.] He had then moved to Ave Mary Lane, where he published several of Defoe's writings. In 1706 he moved again to Paternoster Row, and between that date and 1709 he published numerous books of all kinds. Dunton, whose *Whipping Post* he printed in 1706, has [p. 210] this character of Bragg: "He was formerly a Bookseller and is now a publisher in Ave Mary Lane. He has been unhappy . . . yet . . . is of a soft, easy, affable temper . . . and being just in his dealings is like to have constant employment." Hazlitt notices several books without dates, with Bragg's imprint. [I. 165, II. 282.]

BRAY (WILLIAM), bookseller in London, (1) in Exeter Court near Exeter Exchange in the Strand; (2) Bell and Dragon, (*a*) at Charing Cross, (*b*) between Charing Cross and Whitehall. 1709–20? His name is first met with in the Term Catalogue for 1708–9 as the publisher of *Reflections on men's prejudices against Religion*. [*T. C.* III. 610]. He may or may not have been related to the Rev. Thos. Bray, Minister of St. Botolph's, Aldgate, whose funeral sermon on a Mr. John Dent he published in 1709. [*T. C.* III. 637.] He also issued an undated reprint of *Terra Australis Incognita*, 1617. [Haz. I. 18.]

BREACH ( ), Mrs., *see Dictionary*, 1641–67.

BRENT (JOHN), printer in Dublin, (1) at the Post-Office-Coffee-House in Fishamble Street; (2) at the back of Dick's Coffee-House (?); and in Cork.

1691-1700? Two imprints of this printer dated at Dublin in 1691 are extant, then he is found in Cork in the same year, but in 1697 he is again in Dublin printing in partnership with J. Brocas (*q. v.*) and S. Powell at the Post-Office-Coffee-House in Fishamble Street. In 1698 we find as an imprint "J. B. & S. P." clearly indicating that either John Brent or John Brocas was in partnership with S. Powell in this year; but in 1699 each of these three printers has his own imprint separately as if they had severed all partnership. There occurs, however, one imprint of "J. B. & S. P." in 1699, and the place of printing is given as "at the Back of Dick's Coffee-House", and this place forms the place of imprint in 1700 without any printer's name and "J. B. & S. P." also occurs in 1700. So possibly John Brent was still at work in 1700.

BREWSTER (ANN), *see Dictionary*, 1641-67. Widow of Thomas Brewster. In the Proceedings in the House of Lords, 167⁶⁄₇, about libellous pamphlets, she was said by Mearne to be of "Cocking's Conventicle", and was more than once in trouble for printing or causing to be printed books against Church and State.

BREWSTER (EDWARD), *see Dictionary*, 1641-67.

BRIANT (G.), bookseller (?) in London, King's Head, Cornhill, near the Royal Exchange, 1703. Published, with R. Billing, W. Leybourn's *Mathematical Institutions* [*T. C.* III. 370]; but was perhaps a mathematical instrument maker and not a bookseller.

BRICE (ANDREW), printer in Exeter, Head of the Serge-Market, in South-gate Street; and in Truro. 1714-73. Only the early part of the career of this well-known printer comes within the scope of this work: but it may be of interest to give an outline of his life as given in Timperley. Andrew Brice was born at Exeter in 1690 of parents neither low nor eminent, who designed him for a dissenting minister and gave him a grammatical education. But at the age of seventeen some other vocation had to be found for him and he was apprenticed to Joseph Bliss the Exeter printer (*q. v.*) for five years. He ran away, married, and enlisted as a soldier; but friends procured his discharge, and in 1714 he commenced business as a printer, having only a fount of Great Primer for everything, including a newspaper, called *The Post-Master, or the Loyal Mercury*, begun in 1718, for which he carved the title in wood. Brice became involved in law suits and for seven years was

confined to his own house as a debtor. He appears to have carried on his printing business nevertheless. He employed women in his printing office. At the time of his retirement from business, he was the oldest master-printer in England. He died November 14th, 1773, aged 83. At one time Brice had a press at Truro, Cornwall, but the business did not succeed and he removed the printing material to Exeter.

BRIDGE (D.), printer in London, 1706, *see* Bridge (S.).

BRIDGE (S.), printer and bookseller in London, (1) in Austen Friars, near the Royal Exchange; (2) Little Moor-Fields. 1699-1724. In Hil. 1699 F. Saunders and T. Bennet advertised the fourth part of the Rev. W. Nicholls's *Conference with a Theist*, pointing out at the same time that the third part, which bore the imprint, "Printed by S. Bridge, and sold by Elizabeth Whitlock," was a surreptitious edition. [*T.C.* III. 106.] In 1700 Bridge succeeded R. Janeway as printer of *The English Post*. At some date, not clearly specified, S. Bridge was joined by D. Bridge, and together they printed, for John Lawrence, Isaac Watts's *Horae Lyricae*, 1706. Samuel Negus in his "List of Printing Houses", 1724, mentions among those well affected to King George, "Bridge, Little Moor-Fields" showing that one of the partners was still at work at that date.

BRIDGES, BRUGES, or BRUGIS (HENRY), *see Dictionary*, 1641-67.

BRIGGS (PHILIP), *see Dictionary*, 1641-67.

BRIGS (B.), bookseller in London, near Paternoster Row, 1707. His imprint occurs on *Lord Haversham's Speech in the House of Peers . . . Nov. 15th, 1705*, printed in 1707.

BRINGHURST (JOHN), printer and bookseller in London, the Book in Gracechurch Street, near Cornhill, 1680-4. Apprenticed to Andrew Sowle; set up a press for himself about 1680. Became a printer of Quakers' books. Amongst the resolutions passed at their Monthly Meeting of February 11th, 1681, was the following: "A book entituled 'the life of Christ magnified in his minister, by certaine testimonyes concerning his faithfull servant Giles Barnardiston' read and given to John Bringhurst to print in octavo in pica." In 1682 he printed *The Present State of Carolina, with advice to the Setlers, By R. F.* [B.M. B. 670 (8)]; also George Fox's *The Devil was and is the old Informer against the Righteous*, 1682 [B.M. T. 407 (10)]; in 1683, *An Abstract*

of a Letter from Thomas Paskell in Pennsilvania [Bodl. Ashm. G. 13 (37)], and Francis Estlacke's *Bermuda's Preacher proved a persecutor, Being a just Tryal of Sampson Bond's book entituled, A Publick Tryal of the Quakers*. An edition of George Fox's *Primer* was printed by him in 1684. Bringhurst's name does not occur in the Term Catalogues.

BRISBANE (WILLIAM), printer in Edinburgh, 1670. Will registered July 28, 1670. [Aldis, p. 109.]

BRISCOE (SAMUEL), bookseller in London, Russell Street, Covent Garden, (*a*) over against Wills's Coffee House, (*b*) at the corner shop of Charles Street. 1691-1705. First heard of in Mich. 1691, as one of the publishers of a translation of Suetonius. [*T.C.* II. 381.] He published numerous plays and also two novels, *The Siege of Mentz* [B.M. 635. a. 5 (1)], and *The Female Gallant*, both issued in 1692. [*T.C.* II. 402.] His name appears in the Term Catalogues for the last time in Hil. 1696. [*T.C.* II. 571.] He was the publisher of the 2nd ed. of Richard Blome's *Art of Heraldry*, 1693. Dunton [pp. 292-3] refers to him mysteriously as "revived Briscoe, who has printed for Dryden, Wycherley, Congreve, &c., and by contracting a friendship with Tom Brown, will grow rich as fast as his author can write or hear from the Dead, so that honest Sam does, as it were, thrive by his misfortunes, and I hear has the satisfaction and goodness to forgive those enemies who are now starving, as a judgment upon them, for attempting his overthrow."

BRISSENDEN (MRS.) bookseller (?) or stationer at Chatham, 1699. Her name appears in an advertisement of Edward Brown's sermon preached on the occasion of the Kentish Feast on November 16, in the *Flying Post* of December 2nd, as one of those from whom the book might be obtained. It does not appear in the imprint.

BRIXEY (JOSHUA), stationer in London, Clement's Inn Gate, 1694-5. His name occurs in an advertisement of the sale of Blank Warrants of the Quarterly Poll Tax in the *London Gazette*, April 30th-May 3rd, 1694. In Easter, 1695, his name appears amongst a number of publishers of *The Law against Bankrupts*. [*T.C.* II. 549.]

BROCAS (ABISHA), *see Dictionary*, 1641-67; also Dredge, pp. 8, 61, 93-4.

BROCAS (JOHN), printer in Dublin, (1) Fishamble Street; (2) Skinner Row; (3) School House Lane. 1696-1707. First met with in 1696 in partnership

with Cornelius Carter in Fishamble Street. In 1697 he is found with J. Brent and S. Powell at the Post Office Coffee House in that street, and they executed some Parliamentary and Government printing. Dunton [p. 522] speaks of Brent, Powell and Brocas as partners, and says that "no man . . . better understands the Noble Art and Mystery of Printing than John Brocas in Skinner Row". He continued in business until 1707.

BROME (CHARLES), bookseller in London, (*a*) Gun, St. Paul's Churchyard, (*b*) at the West End of St. Paul's Churchyard, (*c*) at the West End of St. Paul's in Ludgate Street. 1684-1711. Possibly son of Henry Brome. He succeeded Joanna Brome, the widow of Henry, at the Gun, in 1684. From this time until 1711, his name is constantly in the Term Catalogues, and he was a publisher of all kinds of literature. He is last heard of in the following advertisement in the *Daily Courant* of January 2nd, 1711 [i. e. 17¹⁰⁄₁₁]: "The four following Books printed for C. Brome at the Gun, the West end of St. Paul's Church: (1) *The Compleat Gamster*; (2) *Geographical Cards on Copper plates*; (3) *The Presbyterians, Anabaptists, Independants, Quakers, &c., lively represented on a copper cutt*; (4) *The Dissenters sayings in their own words*."

BROME (HENRY), *See Dictionary*, 1641-67. Still publishing in 1681. [*T.C.* I. 434.] He appears to have died in that year, and was succeeded by his widow Joanna.

BROME (JOANNA), bookseller in London, Gun, St. Paul's Churchyard, 1681-3. Widow of Henry Brome. She occurs frequently in the Term Catalogues from Easter 1681 to Trin. 1683. [II. 437, III. 32.] She was succeeded in 1684 by her son (?) Charles Brome.

BROMWICH (WILLIAM), bookseller in London, Three Bibles, Ludgate Street, 1677-80. In Trin. 1677, he advertised Richard Baxter's *Poor Man's Family Book*. [*T.C.* I. 285.] He published several astrological books for John Partridge in 1679-80, one of which, *Vox Lunaris*, is not entered in the Term Catalogues, in which his name appears for the last time in Hil. 1680. [*T.C.* I. 385.]

BROOKE or BROOKS (JAMES), bookseller in London, Anchor and Crown on London Bridge, 1702-50. In the *English Post* of August 14-17, 1702, this stationer's name occurs as agent for the sale of a remedy for toothache. In 1718 Baskett, the King's printer, mortgaged his letter-presses and other stock at Oxford to Brooke for a loan of £4,000. [*Athenaeum*, September 5th,

1885.] In the same year Brooke is found selling *The Historical Register*, published by the Sun Fire Office. He died December 5th, 1750, leaving a sum of £50 to the poor of the Stationers' Company. [Timperley, p. 680.]

BROOKE (JOHN), bookseller at Coventry, 1671. In 1671, *A Funeral Handkerchief* by the Rev. Thomas Allestree, rector of Ashow, Warwick, was advertised as "printed for J. Wright at the Globe in Little Britain and John Brooke in Coventry", but the imprint ran "London, Printed for the Author. Anno Dom. 1671." [*T.C.* I. 79.]

BROOKE or BROOKS (JOHN), stationer in London, The Ship near the May Pole in the Strand, 1697–1711.

BROOKE (NATHANIEL), *see Dictionary*, 1641–67.

BROOKS (E.), bookseller in London, 1682. Published *A True Account of the Last Speeches . . . of Christopher Vrats, George Boriskie and John Sterne . . . Guilty of the . . . murther of Thomas Thinn Esq.*, 1682. [Haz. I. 422.] Timperley also says that E. Brooks is found in the imprint to *The Loyal Impartial Mercury*. Dunton [p. 292] mentions "military Brooks".

BROOKSBY (ELIZABETH), bookseller in London, Golden Ball, Pye Corner, 1703. Hazlitt [III. 196] records a copy of John Philips's *English Fortune Tellers* with the imprint, "London. Printed for E. Brooksby . . . 1703." She was probably the widow of P. Brooksby.

BROOKSBY (PHILIP), bookseller in London, (1) next door to the Ball, in West Smithfield, near to the Hospital Gate; (2) Golden Ball, West Smithfield, near the Hospital Gate; (3) Golden Harp and Ball near the Bore Tavern in Pye Corner. 1672–96. Dealer in all kinds of popular and cheap literature such as ballads, chap-books, pamphlets, romances and song-books. He did not avail himself much of the Term Catalogues, where his first entry does not appear until Easter 1673. [*T.C.* I. 134.] In the previous year he had published several pieces. [Haz. H. 317, I. 175, III. 30.] In 1683 he had two shops, and amongst the ephemera to be found there were several illustrated poetical broadsides on the great frost and the fair held on the frozen Thames that winter. [B.M. C. 20. f. 2 (160, 161).] His last entry in the Term Catalogues was in Easter 1696. [*T.C.* II. 583.] He was succeeded by his widow Elizabeth. *The Soldier's Fortune*, "printed for T. Brooksby at the Golden Ball, Pye Corner", n.d., is probably a misprint for P. Brooksby. [Haz. H. 566.]

BROOKSBY (T.), *see* Brooksby (Philip).

BROTHERTON (JOHN), bookseller in London, Bible, Threadneedle Street, near the Royal Exchange, 1718–25. Began publishing about 1718, chiefly novels. [Esdaile, pp. 185, 198, 329.] In 1725 he issued *A Short Explication of such Foreign words as are made use of in Musick-Books*. [Haz. II. 410.]

BROUN (ROBERT), *see* BROWN (R.), stationer at Edinburgh, 1649–85? in *Dictionary*, 1641–67.

BROWN, or BROWNE (CHARLES), printer and bookseller in London, 1682–1707. Printer of and dealer in popular literature, such as almanacs, ballads and chap-books. In 1682 he issued a ballad entitled *The Cavalier's Litany*. [Haz. H. 79.] In 1707 he was defendant in an action brought by the Company of Stationers, to uphold their privilege of printing almanacs, &c. [Chan. Proc. before 1714. Bridges $\frac{270}{21}$.]

BROWN, or BROWNE (DANIEL), bookseller in London, Black Swan and Bible, next door to the Queen's Head, without Temple Bar, 1672–1729. He made his first entry in the Term Catalogues in Easter Term 1672, with a small theological book [*T.C.* I. 104.], but quickly rose to an important position in the trade. He also sold books by auction. He was still publishing in 1729, when Bernard Lintot sold him a fourth part of a half share in Webb's *Antiquities of Stonehenge*. [Nichols, *Lit. Anecd.* VIII. 294.]

BROWN (GEORGE), bookseller in Glasgow, 1676. Named among the debtors in Andrew Anderson's inventory (1676). The "George Browne in Glasgow" mentioned in Lithgow's inventory (1662) may be the same person. [Aldis, p. 109.]

BROWN (HUGH), printer in Glasgow, 1712–30. In 1714 Brown got into trouble with the authorities for assuming, without authority, the title of printer to the University in *The Jacobite Curse*. [John McUre: *History of Glasgow* (1830), p. 370.]

BROWN (JAMES), bookseller in Glasgow, 1662 (?)–85. Named among the debtors in Andrew Anderson's inventory (1676). His name appears in the imprints of James Durham's *The Law Unsealed* (Edinburgh, 1676), and James Paterson's *The Scots Arithmetician* (Edinburgh, 1685). The James Browne, Glasgow, in Lithgow's Inventory, 1662, may be the same. [Aldis, pp. 69, 109.]

BROWN, or BROUN (ROBERT), stationer in Edinburgh, 1649–85 (?). *See Dictionary*, 1641–67.

BROWN (ROBERT), printer in Edinburgh, in Forrester's Wynd, 1714–18. In 1714 Brown printed several numbers of *The Edinburgh Gazette*, and James Clark's *Memento mori* (1718) also bears his name.

BROWN (T.), bookseller in London, Green Dragon without Temple Bar, 1682–1705. Published *A recital of the Act . . . respecting the power of the Crown over chattels, hereditaments, &c.*, 1682. [Haz. II. 117.]

BROWN (THOMAS), printer and bookseller in Edinburgh, on the Plain-stones, over against the Stone-shop, 1671–99 [–1722 ?] A Thomas Brown appears among the debtors in Lithgow's inventory (1662). Probably one of the booksellers who in 1671 acquired the printing-house of the Society of Stationers. A partner in A. Anderson's gift as King's Printer, 1671. In virtue of this partnership Brown styled himself "one of His Majesties printers", and his name as printer appears alone in books from 1674 to 1678, and in partnership with others from 1671 to 1681; but from 1687 books bearing his name are printed for, and not by, him. For books bought from him, 1673–7, *see* Fountainhall's Journals, App. 1 and 2. [Scot. Hist. Soc. XXXVI.] In 1695 he sold Sir T. Craig's *Scotland's soveraignty asserted*, and in 1699 Sir George Mackenzie's *Institutions of the Law of Scotland*. The will of Thomas Brown of Eastfield, stationer, burgess of Edinburgh, was registered May 30th, 1722. [Aldis, pp. 91, 109.]

BROWN (WILLIAM), printer and bookseller in Edinburgh, (1) on the north side of the High Street, a little above the Cross, 1714; (2) in the Parliament Close, 1722. 1714–31. Printed in partnership with John Mosman, *c.* 1717–29. In 1724 Brown and Mosman succeeded as assigns of the deceased James Watson, and thereafter they assumed the title of King's Printers. [Lee (John) *Additional Memorial*, Edinburgh, 1826, pp. *105, 153.]

BROWNE (CHRISTOPHER), bookseller in London, Globe, St. Paul's Churchyard, 1691–1707. Dealer in maps and mathematical books. [Haz. II. 403, III. 256; *T.C.* II. 369.] Made his last entry in the Term Catalogues in Trin. 1707. [*T.C.* III. 555.]

BROWNE (ROBERT), bookbinder at Cambridge, in St. Mary's parish, 1667 (?)–81. His will dated August 8th, 1681, and the account of his widow, Rose,

presented the same year, shows value of his stock, &c., at £43 3*s*. 6*d*. He may have been one of the valuers of several inventories, 1667 to 1680. [Gray and Palmer, p. 122.] A Thomas Browne, bookbinder, was living, 1631–55, in one of the houses attached to the west end of Great St. Mary's Church, specially mentioned in a report to Archbishop Laud, September 23rd, 1636. [Gray's *Shops at the West End of Great St. Mary's Church*.]

BROWNE (W.), bookseller in Horsham, 1712. Sold the Rev. Charles Bettesworth's *Sermon preach'd at Petworth . . . on Wednesday, September 3rd, 1712, at a Confirmation* . . . "London, Printed by H. Meere for A. Bettesworth . . . and sold by . . . W. Browne in Horsham, 1712." [B.M. 4473. aaa. 46 (8).]

BROWNING (MERCY), bookseller in Amsterdam, (*a*) op de Beurs-sluys, (*b*) juxta Bursam. 1675–87. Described as a widow. Published in 1675 *An English and Nether Dutch Dictionary*, in 1680 *The Practice of Piety*, and in 1682 Increase Mather's tract on the signs and tokens of the coming of the Messiah. In 1678 she became agent for N. Ponder, the publisher of Bunyan's *Pilgrim's Progress*, and he consigned to her a stock of books for sale which became the subject of a law suit in Chancery; from this we learn that in 1687 she sold her business to Rest Fenner (*q.v.*), a London bookseller who afterwards moved to Canterbury. [Chan. Proc. before 1714, Reynardson, Bundle 428, 132.]

BRUCE (PETER), printer in Edinburgh, Holy-Rood-House, 1687–8. A foreigner who from 1674 onwards was engaged in engineering and other enterprises (including the manufacture of paper and playing cards) in Scotland. In October 1687 he took over James Watson's press in Holyrood Palace, and in December of the same year was appointed royal printer in succession to him. He styled himself "Enginier Printer to his most Excellent Majesty, for his Royal Household, Chapel and Colledge, Holy-Rood-House". His printing house was wrecked by the mob which broke into Holyrood on December 10th, 1688, and Bruce himself was imprisoned till June 1689. Watson says that his printing materials were sold to the Society of Stationers. His paper mill at Restalrig was acquired by James Hamilton in 1690. Some of the Holyrood books of 1687 without printer's name were probably printed by him. [Aldis, p. 109.]

BRUDENELL (   ), printer in London, *c.* 1700. Mentioned by Dunton [p. 252] as a hot-tempered man but "a good Printer and truly honest". Probably a son of John Brudenell; *see Dictionary*, 1641–67. He had a brother Moses Brudenell, a compositor.

BRUGIS (HENRY), *see* Bridges.

BRYAN (STEPHEN), printer in Worcester, next the Cross Keys in Sidbury, 1706–48. Took up his freedom as a stationer on June 3rd, 1706. Three years later while still quite a young man he started *The Worcester Postman*, (no. 1, June 1709); in 1722 the title was changed to *The Worcester Post, or Western Journal.* Bryan died in 1748, but before his death he assigned his paper to H. Berrow, who then gave it the name it has ever since borne, that of *Berrow's Worcester Journal.* [Rev. J. R. Burton, *Early Worcestershire Printers and Books*, 1897.]

BRYSON (MARTIN), bookseller at Newcastle-upon-Tyne, *c.* 1722–55. His name first occurs on *Occasional Hymns*, by Benj. Bennet, Newcastle 1722. He was admitted to the freedom of the Upholsterers', Tinplate Workers', and Stationers' Company of Newcastle July 25th, 1726. His shop was on Tyne Bridge on the west side and near the north end. It was destroyed by the fire of July 24th, 1750, when ten houses and many warehouses adjoining the Bridge were burnt. In May 1751 he took into partnership his apprentice William Charnley, who succeeded to the business on Bryson's retirement in 1755. Bryson went to live at Stockton-on-Tees, where he died August 15th, 1759. The business founded by him was in existence in Newcastle until the year 1881.

BUCK (PETER), bookseller in London, Temple, Fleet Street, near the Inner Temple Gate, 1692–1700. In 1692 he published Congreve's *Incognita* [Esdaile, p. 190]; in 1698 Oldmixon's *Poem to the Earl of Portland*; and in 1700 Dr. Herwig's *Art of curing sympathetically.* [*T.C.* III. 185.] He was possibly a descendant of the Cambridge Bucks.

BUCKLEY (SAMUEL), printer and bookseller in London, (1) Dolphin, Fleet Street, over against St. Dunstan's Church; (2) Dolphin, St. Paul's Churchyard; (3) Dolphin in Little Britain; (4) In Amen Corner. 1696–1741. Began as a bookseller; the first of his publications recorded in the Term Catalogues was *The French Perfumer*, announced in Trin. 1696. [*T.C.* II. 591.] He was also the publisher of Le Comte's *Mémoires* in 1697, and of an edition of *Don Quixote* in 1699. But he is chiefly remembered as a printer. In 1703 he

began to print *The Daily Courant* (no. 1, March 11th, 170$\frac{2}{3}$). This consisted of a single sheet printed on one side only, and was the first daily newspaper. It was first printed by Edward Mallet, but a month afterwards it changed hands. Buckley's imprint appears on the issue of April 22nd, 1703. Dunton [p. 314] refers to him at this time and says: "He is an excellent linguist, understands the Latin, French, Dutch and Italian tongues; and is master of a great deal of wit. He prints the *Daily Courant* and *Monthly Register* (which I hear he translates out of the foreign papers himself)." In 1713 Steele's *Englishman* was printed by Buckley in Amen Corner. Nichols says that Buckley "was afterwards appointed writer of the *Gazetteer*, and was put into the commission of the peace for the County of Middlesex. He was a man of an excellent understanding and great learning, very sincere where he professed friendship; a pleasant companion and greatly esteemed by all who knew him". He died on September 8th, 1741, in his 68th year and is buried in Hornsey Church. [Nichols, *Lit. Anecd.* II. 26, 27.]

BUCKRIDGE (JOHN), bookseller at Marlborough, 1704. Only known as the publisher of *Courage and sincerity . . . A Sermon*, by Robert Wake, Vicar of Ogburn St. Andrew, Wilts., 1704. [*T.C.* III. 422.]

BUDDEN (W.), (?) bookseller in London, near Fleet Bridge, 1685. Only known as the publisher of a broadside: *A strange and wonderful discovery newly made of Houses under ground, at Colton's Field in Gloucestershire.* [*Bibl. Lind., Broadsides, No.* 396.]

BULKLEY, BULKELEY, or BUCKLEY (STEPHEN), *see Dictionary*, 1641–67.

BULL ( ), bookseller at Ashford, Kent, 1699. Mentioned in an advertisement in *The Flying Post* of December 2nd, 1699, of the Rev. Edward Brown's *Sermon preached at the Kentish Feast.* The names of this and other provincial booksellers who sold the work are not given in the imprint to the book.

BULL (SETH), stationer in London, The Minories, 1713. He and his wife Elizabeth are mentioned in the will of Mary Hayes, proved in 1713. [P.C.C. 136, Leeds.]

BULLOCK (J.), bookseller in London, Rose and Crown on Snow Hill, near Holborn Bridge, 1709. Publisher of a poem, *Libertas Triumphans*, in honour of the victory of Oudenarde [*T.C.* III. 620], and also of *Calvin's Ghost* [*T.C.* III. 642], both in 1709.

BULLORD (JOHN), bookseller and book-auctioneer in London, Old Black Bear in St. Paul's Churchyard, 1689–1701. Succeeded Obadiah Blagrave at the above address in 1689. On May 8th of that year he began the sale of *Bibliotheca Selectissima Generosi Angliae nuper defuncti* at Sam's Coffee House in Ave Maria Lane [Lawler, *Book Auctions*, p. 175] and from that time until 1701 he was one of the recognized book-auctioneers of London; amongst the libraries that he sold may be mentioned those of Peter Scott, prebendary of Windsor, Thomas Britton the "Small coal man", Dr. Adam Littleton, John Baron Stawel of Somerton, Robert Littlebury the bookseller, and the Rev. William Hopkins of Oxford. As a publisher he introduced Thomas Durfey to the public in *Collin's Walk through London and Westminster*, 1690, and in 1695 he was agent for the sale of Chauncy's *Hertfordshire.* [*T.C.* II. 544.] His last entry in the Term Catalogues was in Easter 1700. [*T.C.* III. 189.] Bullord is sometimes confused with Thomas Ballard of Little Britain.

BUNCE (THOMAS), printer in London, 1706. Printed Baxter's *Monthly Preparations for Holy Communion* for T. Parkhurst in 1706. [Haz. I. 22.]

BUNCHLEY (SAMUEL), bookseller in London, (1) Blue Ball, Ave Mary Lane; (2) at the Publishing Office (*a*) in Dove Court (*b*) in (*c*) near, Bearbinder Lane, near the Stocks Market. 1707. Made his first entry in the Term Catalogues in Hil. 1707 with one of the pedlars' favourite books, *Essays of Love and Marriage.* [*T.C.* III. 537.] Amongst his other publications was Ned Ward's *Humours of a Coffee House*, issued in penny numbers every Wednesday morning; Bunchley's name did not appear in the advertisement of this, but only his address in Bearbinder Lane. [*T.C.* III. 558.]

BUREAU ( ), bookseller in London, in the Middle Exchange in the Strand, 1683. A lottery of wine was to be drawn for at his shop. [*Lond. Gaz.*, February 4th, 1683.]

BURGES (FRANCIS), printer in Norwich near the Red Well, 1701–6. On September 27th, 1701, there appeared *Some Observations on the Use and Original of the Noble Art and Mystery of Printing*, printed by F. Burges, and said to be the first book printed at Norwich since the sixteenth century. He also started in the same month a newspaper called the *Norwich Post.* Burges died in January 1706, leaving the business to his widow. [Plomer, *English Printing*, 1915, pp. 207–8.]

BURGES (HENRY), *see* Bridges (Henry).

BURGIS (SIMON), bookseller in London, 1689–91. Published *A Full Answer to the depositions . . . concerning the birth of the P. of Wales*, 1689. [B.M. T. 100* (179).] In Hil. 1690 he advertised *The Muses' Farewell to Popery and Slavery*, and in 1691 *Wit for Money; or Poet Stutter.* [*T.C.* II. 301, 360.]

BURLEIGH (FERDINAND), bookseller in London, Amen Corner, 1713–15. Publisher of Steele's *Englishman* and also of *A Letter to a Member of Parliament*, in 1714. Nichols records that Burleigh sold a periodical called *The Balm of Gilead*, which was printed by J. Mayo. [*Lit. Anecd.*, VIII. 494.]

BURNET (C.), bookseller in London, 1696. Published a ballad entitled *The Boon Companion*, 1696. [Haz. II. 587, from Ouvry Cat. no. 75.]

BURRELL (THOMAS), bookseller in London, Golden Ball in Fleet Street, under St. Dunstan's Church, 1670–9. In Mich. 1670 he advertised an edition of Henry Phillippes's *Purchaser's Pattern* [*T.C.* I. 51], and in the following year was joint publisher with Thomas Archer of Maynwaring's *Praxis Medicorum.* In February 167$\frac{6}{7}$ he was examined before the committee of the House of Lords, then inquiring as to the publication of certain libels, and admitted that he had seen one of them, *The Naked Truth*, twenty-five copies of which he declared were "thrown into his shop but he delivered them to Mr. Sawbridge again", but he admitted having sold two or three copies of *The Letter about the Test.* [Hist. MSS. Comm., 9th Report, p. 78.] Amongst Burrell's varied publications may be noted John Ray's *Collection of English Words*, 1673, and Sir H. Spelman's *Villare Anglicum*, 1677. He also published works on gardening. His name does not appear in the Term Catalogues after 1678; but he was the publisher of a sheet called *The English Intelligence* (no. 1, July 21st, 1679) written in the Protestant interest, and also of *The English Currant* (no. 1, September 8th, 1679).

BURRIDGE (RICHARD), journeyman printer, 1717. Reader of *Mist's Weekly Journal.* On March 3rd, 1717 he was convicted of uttering blasphemous words and sentenced to be whipped from the Church in the Strand to Charing Cross, to be fined twenty shillings, and to be imprisoned one month. [Timperley, p. 615.]

BURROUGH (R.), bookseller in London, Sun and Moon, Cornhill, 1705–8. Publisher of historical books; made his first entry in the Term Catalogues in Trin. 1705. [*T.C.* III. 464.] In 1708 he was joined by J. Baker.

BURROWES (SAMUEL), bookseller in London, (1) Crown in Cornhill; (2) Bible and Three Legs, Poultry; (3) Little Britain. 1697–1707. Began as a publisher at the Crown in Cornhill in 1697, when his name appeared amongst those issuing Dr. Adam Littleton's *True method of learning the Latine Tongue by the English.* [*T.C.* III. 7.] His name does not appear again in the Catalogue until Easter, 1702, when he was one of the publishers of John Moyle's *Chirurgus Marinus.* [*T.C.* III. 302.] Finally in 1707 he was one of the publishers of *The Diverting Works of the Countess D'Anois.* [Esdaile, p. 255.]

BURTON ( ), printer in London, St. John's Lane, 1724. Only known from a mention of his name in Negus's list, as well affected to King George.

BURTON (HUMPHRY), bookseller in Tiverton, 1696–1701. Publisher of a sermon, *The Lawfulnesse and use of Organs,* preached by John Newte, Rector of Tiverton, on September 13th, 1696. [B.M. 226. h. 20 (28.)] He was also the local agent for *The Country-mans Conductor in reading and writing,* by John White, master of Chilcot's English Free School in Tiverton, Exeter, 1701. [B.M. 12983. a. 54.] His name is sometimes spelt Barton.

BURTON (PHILIP), bookseller at Preston, Lancashire, 1678. Publisher of Seth Bushell's *The Believer's Groan for Heaven, A sermon . . preached at Preston,* 1678. [*T.C.* I. 308.]

BURTON (RICHARD), *see Dictionary,* 1641–67.

BURTON or BUTTON (SARAH), bookseller at Newcastle-upon-Tyne, 1700–4 (?). Local agent for R. Gilpin's *Assize Sermon at Carlisle,* preached in 1660, London, 1700. The author was "now minister . . . in Newcastle-upon-Tyne". [B.M. 4474. bb. 51.] Wife of Joseph Button (*q.v.*).

BUSH (EDMUND), bookseller in Oxford, 1696–1705. [Madan, p. 31.]

BUTLER (JOHN), bookseller in Worcester, 1702–8. Publisher of Thos. Cooke's sermon, *Workhouses the best Charity,* 1702. Noticed by Dunton [p. 237] as having been "a rising man for some time, has a brisk trade and pays well"

BUTLER (R.), bookseller in London, (*a*) next the Holy Lamb and Three Bowls in the Barbican, (*b*) next door to the Lamb and Three Bowls, 1677–85. Publisher of divinity and books against the Quakers. His last entry in the Term Catalogues was the Rev. N. Taylor's *Practical . . . Exposition of the Catechism,* 2nd ed., in Hil. 1685. [*T.C.* II. 118.]

BUTLER (S.), bookseller in London, Bernard's [i.e. Barnard's] Inn Gate in Holborn, 1707–11. In Povey's *General Remarks on Trade,* July 4–7, 1707 [Burney 140], this bookseller is mentioned as selling "the True Golden Snuff". In the Term Catalogue, Mich. 1708–Hil. 1709, S. Butler's name occurs as publisher of *The Gamester's Law.* [*T.C.* III. 619.] Again in the *London Gazette* of February 8th, 17$\frac{10}{11}$ he appears as one of those selling *A Help to History.*

BUTT, or BUTS (RICHARD), bookseller in London, (1) Bear and Orange Tree in Princes Street, near Drury Lane; (2) Princess Street in Covent Garden [probably the same as (1)]. 1681–96. Publisher of novels and cheap literature. The only reference to him in the Term Catalogues is the entry of Cervantes' *The Jealous Gentleman of Estremadura.* [*T.C.* I. 461; Esdaile, 33.] Timperley [p. 563] records that in 1683 he was publishing *Scotch Memoirs,* and in 1696 he published *Letters written by Mrs. Manley.* [*T.C.* II. 591; Esdaile, 266.]

BUTTER (THOMAS), bookseller in Exeter, near St. Martin's Lane, 1714–20 (?). In a book printed in 1714, Mr. Dredge found the following advertisement: "Sold by *Thomas Butter,* Bookseller near St. *Martin's-lane* in *Exon,* where (besides Books and Stationary Wares of all sorts) is sold the best of Mathematical and Sea Instruments, several sorts of Physical Medicines, as Dr. Daff's Elixir Salutis, Stoughton's Elixir Stomachicum, Spirit of Scurvy-Grass Golden and Plain &c. Also the famous Cephalick or Liquid-snuff, prepar'd for the Queen. With Japan Ink, Indian-Ink, Cake-Ink, Ink-powder, Common Ink; Ink-Glasses, Pounce, shining sand; great variety of paper-hangings for rooms; the best of Stampt-Parchment and Paper, Bonds, &c., at reasonable rates, by Wholesale or Retail." After his death his widow Jane married Daniel Pring jun. by licence on August 31st, 1723; but she continued to carry on the business as Jane Pring until her death sometime before 1731. [Dredge, pp. 44, 67, 98–9.]

BUTTLER (EDWARD), printer in London, 1690. Indicted for printing a libel entitled, *His Majesty's Most Gracious Declaration to all his loving subjects,* a Jacobite broadside found scattered about the streets of London. William Newbolt (*q. v.*) was associated with him, and both were described as "printers". Their printing press was said to have been kept at one Douglas's at Westminster. [Harl. MS. 6846, fol. 371–9.]

BUTTON (JOSEPH), bookseller at Newcastle-upon-Tyne, on the Bridge. 1704–14. In Hil. 1704, he appears as the publisher of *Christus in Coelo,* by Thomas Bradbury. [*T.C.* III. 386.] Some time between this and 1714 he and his wife were parties to an action brought by the Company of Stationers for upholding their privileges. [Chan. Proc. before 1714, Bridges $\frac{270}{21}$.] In 1714, Button published B. Bennet's *Several Discourses against Popery.* See Saywell (J.).

BUTTON (SARAH), bookseller at Newcastle-upon-Tyne, 1704 (?). *See* Burton (Sarah).

C. (A.), *see* Clark (Andrew).

C. (E.), *see* Cotes (Ellen).

C. (F.), *see* Clark (Francis)

C. (L.), *see* Curtis (Langley).

C. (R.), *see* Clavell (Roger); also Cutler (Robert).

C. (W.), *see* Cooper (William).

CADE (JOHN), *see Dictionary,* 1641–67.

CADMAN, or CADEMAN (WILLIAM), bookseller in London, (1) Pope's Head in the Lower Walk of the New Exchange, Strand; (2) Pope's Head in the New Exchange, and Middle Exchange, Strand. 1668–87. On November 9th, 1668 he entered Davenant's comedy *The Rivalls* [B.M. 643. d. 57; *Stat. Reg.,* Roxb., II. 392], and in the Term Catalogue for Mich. 1669 [*T.C.* I. 20] he advertised Frances Boothby's *Marcelia . . . A Tragi-Comedy,* dated 1670. [B.M. 644. g. 20.] He was the publisher of much good literature, and is found in business in 1684, when he appears to have been succeeded at this address by G. Cownly; but his name is found in the Term Catalogues three years later as one of the publishers of Settle's *Emperor of Morocco.* [*T.C.* II. 203.] Dunton [p. 292] calls him "blunt Cademan".

CADWELL (THOMAS), bookseller at Derby, 1685. His name occurs in a list of booksellers and stationers at the end of M. Bromfield's *A brief Discovery of the Scurvy,* 1685, as agent for a patent medicine. [*N. & Q.,* 11 S. XI. p. 45.]

CAIRNS (JOHN), printer and bookseller in Edinburgh, at the lower entry to the Parliament Yard, 1671–80? One of the six booksellers who petitioned the Privy Council against A. Anderson's monopoly in 1671. Watson [p. 14] says that Cairns (who had now Mr. Hyslop's printing-house) was employed by

Sir Thomas Murray to print his digest of the Acts of Parliament, and that he brought Dutch workmen (J. van Solingen and J. Colmar) and materials from Holland for that purpose. Shortly after this Cairns died (1680–1) and his printing house passed to David Lindsay and his partners. [Aldis, p. 110.] Quarles's *Enchiridion* was "printed by John Cairnes for Gideon Shaw" in 1680. [Haz. I. 347.]

CALDECOT ( ), bookseller in Stamford, Lincolnshire, 1690. Only known from the imprint to a sermon by G. Topham, entitled *Pharisaism display'd,* 1690.

CALDECOTT (THOMAS), bookseller in London (?), 1714. Mentioned in the will of his brother-in-law William Rogers of Clifford's Inn, Gent., dated January 14th, 1714. [C.C. 15. Faggs.]

CALDERWOOD (JOHN), stationer in Edinburgh, 1676 (?)–1682. His will and inventory, 1682, are printed in *Bann. Misc.* II. 289. The John Calderwood who appears among the debtors in A. Anderson's inventory 1676 may be the same. The imprint in Richard Simon's *Opuscula critica adversus Isaacum Vossium,* "Edinburgi, typis Joannis Calderwood, M.DC.LXXXV," is fictitious. The book was probably printed at Rotterdam. [Aldis, p. 110.]

CALVERT (ELIZABETH), *see Dictionary,* 1641–67.

CALVERT (GEORGE), *see Dictionary,* 1641–67.

CAM (JOHN), stationer in London, 1688. Defendant in a plea of debt brought by William Johnson, Trin. 4 Jas. II [i. e. 1688]. [C.P.R. 3069. m. 693 verso.]

CAMPBELL (AGNES), *see* Anderson, Mrs., printer in Edinburgh.

CAMPBELL (PATRICK), bookseller in Ireland, Dublin, 1687–1720. Chiefly known from the account of him in *The Dublin Scuffle* by Dunton, whom he opposed during the latter's visit to Dublin in 1698. [*Life and Errors,* pp. 491–639 *passim.*] In 1694 he shared with E. Dobson and M. Gun the publication of a religious work by J. Bayne, a Dissenting minister. His will was proved in the Prerog. Court in 1720.

CANNING (WILLIAM), printer and bookseller in London, Vine Court, (*a*) in the Middle Temple, (*b*) in (or under) the Temple Cloisters. 1686–90. Appears first in Hil. 1686 as a publisher of law books. [*T.C.* II. 160.] In 1687 he published Mrs. Behn's comedy *The Lucky Chance* [*T.C.* II. 188], and N. Tate's *Island*

Princess [*T.C.* II. 200], and was chiefly a publisher of plays and poems. He was at one time a printer, and was arrested for his part in a Jacobite broadside entitled *His Majesty's most gracious declaration to all his loving subjects* [*c.* 1690]. He was stated to be a person " very famous for such work ", who had been tried twice or thrice before for similar offences, and to have kept a private press in Grocers' Alley. [Harl. MS. 6846, fol. 375–9.]

CANTREL (WILLIAM), bookseller in Derby, 1718–27. Mr. Arthur Wallis, in his *History of the Printing Press in Derby*, 1881, says : " It is not unlikely that William Cantrel was the brother of the Rev. Thomas Cantrell, Head Master of Derby School, Lecturer of All Hallowes, and vicar of Elvaston, who dying in 1699, was succeeded by the Rev. Anthony Blackwall in all those offices." William Cantrel published Blackwall's *Introduction to the Classics*, 1718, and also Charles Cotton's *Wonders of the Peak*, 1725. He was also the agent, with H. Allestree, of the *Nottingham Mercury*. As his business was put up to auction in 1727 he was probably then dead.

CARNAN (WILLIAM), printer at Reading, The Bible and Crown in the Market Place, 1723–37. Printer and publisher of *The Reading Mercury*, (No. 1, July 8th, 1723). After his death, his widow married John Newbery, who had worked under her husband and was appointed one of his executors. John Newbery soon afterwards moved to London, where he became famous as the publisher of " penny histories " for children. [C. Welch, *A Bookseller of the last Century*, pp. 6–7.]

CARR (JOHN), bookseller or musical instrument maker in London, (1) under the King's Head Tavern in Chancery Lane end ; (2) at the Middle Temple Gate. 1676–84. Sold Tho. Mace's *Musick's Monument*, 1676. In 1683 he joined J. Playford in the publication of music books. [*T.C.* II. 4.] In the *London Gazette* of October 23rd–27th, 1684 an advertisement of musical books appeared in which his address is given as " at John Carr's shop, at the Middle Temple Gate when built, but as yet under the King's Head Tavern in Chancery Lane end."

CARR (SAMUEL), bookseller in London, King's Head at the West End of St. Paul's Churchyard, 1675–85. His first advertisement in the Term Catalogues was in Trin. 1677 [*T.C.* I. 285], and his last in Mich. 1685, when he issued *Catechismus . . . secundum usum Coll. Regalis Etonensis.* [*T.C.* II. 148.]

CARRON (WILLIAM), printer in Edinburgh, 1680. Joined William Hislop when he set up. He printed for J. Cairns an edition of Jas. Durham's *The Dying Man's Testament*, for G. Shaw, *Funeral of the Mass*, and also *A Discourse unto . . . James Duke of Albany and York*, all in 1680. [Aldis, pp. 59, 110.]

CARRUTHERS (THOMAS), bookseller in Edinburgh, in the Parliament Close, 1695–1700. In 1695 he sold the Earl of Cromarty's *Vindication of Robert III* ; in 1696, A. Pitcairne's *Dissertatio de legibus historiae naturalis* ; in 1699 *Answer to the . . . refutation of Dr. Olyphant's defence* and a medical work ; in 1700 G. Dempster's *The Prodigal Returned*. In the *Edinburgh Gazette*, No. 50, August 14th–17th, 1699, several books are advertised as printed for Thomas Carruthers. [Aldis, p. 110.]

CARSON (JAMES), printer in Dublin, 1713–59. Printer and publisher of miscellaneous literature, including *The Dublin Weekly Journal*, 1725–30. He was styled " the facetious ".

CARTER (CORNELIUS), printer in Dublin, Post Office Coffee House, Fishamble Street, 1696–1727. His name is first found, with John Brocas, in the imprint to a Latin book in 1696, and they were partners in another book in the next year. In 1699 he appears alone as printer of *The Flying Post, or the Postmaster*, and in 1700 of a Dublin edition of the *London Gazette*. His address, given above, is found in these periodicals. In 1710 he printed the *Tatler* and in 1713 the second edition of Bishop Browne's sermon on *Drinking to the memory of the Dean*.

CARTER (WILLIAM), bookseller in London, (1) Green Dragon, St. Paul's Churchyard : (2) Rose and Crown, St. Paul's Churchyard. 1706–11. Publisher of anti-Quaker tracts. A list of some of these will be found at the end of the Rev. Edw. Cookson's *Winding-sheet for Quakerism*, 1711. [B.M. T. 1816 (9).]

CARTERSON (JOHN), bookseller in London, 1690. Published a political play, *The Abdicated Prince*, 1690, without giving an address. [B.M. 643. d. 40.]

CARVER ( ), widow, bookseller (?) in Melton, 1720. Her name occurs in the imprint to the *Nottingham Mercury*, as one of those from whom it might be obtained ; but there is no other evidence that she was a bookseller.

CASTLE (EDWARD), bookseller in London, (1) Angel and Crown, St. Paul's Churchyard ; (2) (*a*) near (or next) Scotland Yard-Gate, by Whitehall,

(*b*) against Scotland Yard, near the Admiralty. 1695–1717. In Easter 1695, he is named as selling *The London Practice of Physick*. [*T.C.* II. 552.] In 1697 he published John Aubrey's *Miscellanies* and shared with A. and J. Churchill an abridgement of John Locke's *Essay on the Human Understanding*. In June 1717 a patent was granted to William Churchill and Edward Castle for the sole furnishing of several offices of His Majesty's Revenue with stationery. [Timperley, p. 615.]

CAWDLE (EDWARD), bookseller in London, of the parish of St. Gregory next Paul's, 1681. Defendant in an action for assault brought against him and others by Israel Aylett, widow, in Mich. Term 33 Chas. II (1681). [C.P.R. 2996. m. 260 recto.]

CHALKIN, *see* Chauklin.

CHALMERS (ANDREW), bookseller in Edinburgh, in the Parliament Close, 1688–91. In June 1688 he had in stock 221 copies of the Irish Psalm Book. In 1691 he was one of several booksellers who sold J. Cockburn's *Eight Sermons*, and in the same year Sir G. Mackenzie's *Moral History of Frugality* and the second edition of W. Sherlock's *Case of Allegiance due to Sovereign Princes*. [Aldis, p. 111.]

CHAMBERLAIN (ABSOLOM), a running bookseller [hawker] in London, Red Bull Playhouse-yard, over against the Pound in St. John's Street, 1684. Known from three broadsides of 1684. [Bodl. Ashm. G. 15 (170) ; Haz. H. 676, II. 423.]

CHAMBERLAIN (J.), bookseller at Bury St. Edmunds, 1685–90. His name occurs in the Term Catalogue for Easter 1685, as publishing *New English Examples to be turned into Latine*, and again in Trin. 1690 as selling Edward Leeds's *Methodus Graecam Linguam docendi*, both for use in Bury school. [*T.C.* II. 128, 322.] No copy of the first edition of either of these books is in the B.M.

CHANDLER (ABRAHAM), bookseller in London, Surgeon's Arms in Aldersgate Street, 1693. Dealt chiefly in theology. [*T.C.* II. 450, 474, 490.]

CHANDLER (SAMUEL), bookseller in London, in the Poultry, *c.* 1720. A well-known Nonconformist divine ; he was forced by the loss of his wife's fortune in the South Sea Bubble to open a bookshop.

CHANDLER (WILLIAM), bookseller in London, Peacock in the Poultry, 1696-9. Published N. Pullen's translation of Jean Mocquet's *Travels into Africa*, 1696, and *Poems on Several Occasions*, 1699, the work of a brother bookseller, Herbert Walwyn (*q.v.*). [*T.C.* II. 588.]

CHANTRY (JOHN), bookseller in London, (1) Pestle and Mortar, without Temple Bar ; (2) at the sign of Lincoln's Inn Square, near Lincoln's Inn Fields, at Lincoln's Inn Back Gate. 1693–1708 (?). In the S.P.D. William and Mary, iv. 11. is a Petition to Parliament from William Fuller, dated February 23rd, $169\frac{3}{4}$, complaining of libels written by William Pettis for Abel Roper and Chantry booksellers. Chantry's name first occurs in the Term Catalogues in 1703 as one of the publishers of John Brydall's *Ars transferendi Dominium*. [*T.C.* III. 285.] Amongst his other publications may be noticed Sedley's *Miscellaneous Works*, ed. 2, 1708. [*T.C.* III. 599.]

CHAPMAN (HENRY), bookseller in London, near Stanhope-Court at Charing Cross, 1685–94. In the Term Catalogue for Trin. 1685 *An Historical Account of the late Troubles during the wars of Paris*, and in Trin. 1694 *The Gentleman's Journal for the War* are advertised as sold by him. [*T.C.* II. 137, 510.] There seems to be some confusion between this publisher and Thomas Chapman (*q. v.*) in the entry of *Spencer Redivivus*, 1687, in *T.C.* [II. 217.]

CHAPMAN (ROBERT), bookseller in Cambridge, 1711. Robert Green's *Demonstration of the Truth and Divinity of the Christian Religion*, 1711, was printed at the University Press for him. [Bowes, *Catalogue of Cambridge Books*, No. 381.]

CHAPMAN (THOMAS), bookseller in London, (1) the Chirurgeons Arms over against the upper Meuse Gate near Charing Cross ; (2) The Golden Key over against the Meuse near Charing Cross ; (3) in Pall Mall over against St. James's Square ; (4) Angel in the Pall Mall. 1687–1709. In 1687 he published *Spencer Redivivus*, a modernization of Book I of the *Faerie Queene* [B.M. 1346. g. 1], the imprint being No. 1 above. In the advertisement in Hil. 1688, not only is the title of this wrongly entered but the publisher's name is given as H. Chapman. [*T.C.* II. 217.] Thomas Chapman dealt largely in plays, and this fact is advertised in another of his publications *The Rule of Behaviour*, in which the Spenser is also mentioned. In 1692, he either moved to another shop in Charing Cross or altered his sign to the " Golden Key " but two years later he moved to Pall Mall, where he was joined by W. Chapman. The last two pages of Le Maire's *Voyage to the Canary Islands*, published jointly by them in 1696, contain a list of plays sold by T. Chapman. [B.M. 1425. a. 4.] His last entry in the Term Catalogues was in 1709. [*T.C.* III. 613.]

CHAPMAN (THOMAS), bookseller in Norwich, 1722. Only known from the occurrence of his name in an advertisement of a patent medicine in the *Post-Man* of February 26th–28th, 170$\frac{2}{3}$.

CHAPMAN (WILLIAM), bookseller in London, Angel in the Pall Mall, 1696. In partnership with Thomas Chapman (*q. v.*).

CHASE (WILLIAM), printer at Norwich, (1) in Dove Lane; (2) at the Printing Press in the Market. 1711–27(?). In 1711 he printed, for Thomas Goddard, Josiah Chorley's *Metrical Index to the Bible*. [B.M. 1017. k. 18 (2).] In 1715–16 he changed his address, *A Form for the Consecration of the New Chapel at Yarmouth*, 1715, being issued from Dove Lane, and the Norwich Visitation Articles of 1716 from the Market. In 1727 he founded *The Norwich Mercury*. The Mr. Chase who died March 1st, 1781 [Timperley, p. 747] may have been his son.

CHAUKLIN, or CHALKIN (HENRY), bookseller at Taunton, 1695–1701. Published some of the sermons and writings of Matthew Hole, vicar of Stogursey, Somerset. His name did not always appear on the title-pages, but it is found on *A Correct Copy of some letters written to J. M.*, which has the imprint, "London. Printed for H. Chauklin, Bookseller in Taunton . . . 1698." [B.M. 472. a. 54.]

CHEESE (RICHARD) jun., printer (?) in London, 1690. A single sheet *Elegy on the Death of His Grace, the Duke of Grafton*, 1690, bears the imprint, "London, Printed by Richard Cheese, junior." [B.M. C. 20. f. 2. (191).]

CHETWIND (PHILIP), *see Dictionary*, 1641–67.

CHILDE (TIMOTHY), bookseller in London, (1) White Hart in St. Paul's Churchyard, 1690–1, 1697–1711; (2) Unicorn, (*a*) St. Paul's Churchyard, (*b*) at the West end of St. Paul's, 1691–7. 1690–1711. Amongst his publications is a rare little book with engravings called *An Accurate description of the United Netherlands . . . with an exact Relation of the Entertainment of . . . King William at the Hague*, 1691. He made his first entry in the Term Catalogues in Mich. 1690. [*T.C.* II. 340.] Sometime in 1691 he moved to the Unicorn and was in partnership with A. Swalle as publisher of classics and history. In 1697, they appear to have dissolved partnership and Childe returned to the White Hart. A list of books published for him is given on sig. b 4[b] of T. Hearne's *Ductor Historicus*, 1704. His last entry in the Term Catalogues was in Easter 1711, when he shared with the Churchills the publication of Moll's *Atlas*. [*T.C.* III. 672.]

CHISWELL (RICHARD). *See Dictionary*, 1641–67. In a manuscript note, dated 1661, in a copy of A. Gölnitz, *Ulysses Belgico-Gallicus*, 1631, Chiswell describes himself as "servant to Mr. John Sherley", i.e. the bookseller of that name, *q. v.* in *Dictionary*, 1641–67. In Mich. 1681, Chiswell was defendant in a suit for debt brought by Richard Hughes. [C.P.R. 2996. m. 260 r.] On January 16th, 1681 he began to publish *Weekly Memorials for the Ingenious, or, an account of books lately set forth in several languages, &c.*

CHOWN (ROBERT), bookseller in Northampton (?), 1684. Hazlitt records a single sheet: *The Speech of Robert Clerk, Esq., Deputy Recorder of Northampton to the Mayor elect For . . . 1684*. London, Printed for Rob. Chown, 1684. [Haz. II. p. 428.]

CHURCHILL (AWNSHAM), bookseller in London, (*a*) Black Swan, Ave Mary Lane; (*b*) at the lower end of Paternoster Row, near Amen Corner. 1681–1728. Son of William Churchill, bookseller of Dorchester. Apprenticed to George Sawbridge. His name first appears in the Term Catalogues in Mich. 1681, as the publisher of a law-book, *The Touchstone of Precedents*. [*T.C.* I. 460.] Another early publication of his was Dr. William Saywell's *Evangelical and Catholick Unity*, which bore the imprint, "Printed for Robert Scott and Awnsham Churchill, at the Black Swan, near Amen Corner, 1682." This Robert Scott was no doubt the bookseller of that name whose shop was in Little Britain. Churchill soon became one of the first publishers of the day, and in 1690 he took into partnership his brother John, the first work recorded under their joint names being *A second Letter concerning Toleration*. [*T.C.* II. 323.] Of their numerous publications, one or two only can be noted. In 1691 they shared in the publication of Sir R. L'Estrange's *Fables of Aesop*. With Jacob Tonson they shared Selden's *Table Talk* in 1696, and in the same year they published alone John Locke's *Several Papers relating to Money*. In 1704 they issued *A Collection of Voyages and Travels*, 4 vols. fol., and between 1704 and 1715 Rymer's *Foedera*, 16 vols. fol. Granger refers to Awnsham Churchill as the greatest bookseller and stationer of his time, while Dunton [p. 204] says of the brothers: "They were of an universal trade. I traded very considerably with them for several years, and must do them the justice to say that I was never concerned with any persons more exact in their accompts and more just in their payments." Awnsham Churchill amassed a considerable fortune and bought an estate in Dorset. He was M.P. for Dorchester between 1705 and 1710. He died unmarried on April 24th, 1728, his will being proved on May 11th. It contains the following clauses: "I give and bequeath my books at Henbury and my bound books in London and Westminster to be divided equally between my three nephews Wm. Churchill, Awnsham Churchill and Joshua Churchill. I give and devise my shop in Dorchester now in possession of the widow Wentworth, to my nephew Wm. Churchill, Esq." He also left a bequest to Mrs. Mary Churchill, widow of his brother John Churchill. [P.C.C. 142. Brook.]

CHURCHILL (JOHN), bookseller in London, Black Swan in Paternoster Row, 1690–1714. Brother of Awnsham Churchill, with whom he was in partnership from 1690 till 1714, soon after which he probably died, leaving three sons, two of them, Joshua and William, being booksellers.

CHURCHILL (JOSHUA), printer in London, 1688–1728. Son of John Churchill (?) Printed for his brother (?) William Churchill a broadside entitled, *A Paper delivered to His Highness the Prince of Orange . . . 1688*. [B.M. T. 100* (199).] He is mentioned in the will of his uncle Awnsham Churchill (*q. v.*), 1728.

CHURCHILL (WILLIAM), bookseller at Dorchester. *See Dictionary*, 1641–67. Father of Awnsham and John Churchill.

CHURCHILL (WILLIAM), bookseller in London, 1688–1736. Son of John Churchill. In 1717 a patent for furnishing stationery was granted to William Churchill and Edward Castle (*q. v.*). He died February 22nd, 1736. [Timperley, pp. 615, 659.]

CLARK, or CLARKE (   ), bookseller at York and Kingston-upon-Hull, 1681–91. His name occurs in an advertisement of the sale of Dr. W. Outram's library in the *London Gazette* of November 17th–21st, 1681. In 1691 "Clarke of York" was sued by Edward Darrell for payment for goods supplied. [C.P.R. Mich. 3 W. & M. Roll 3101.] Probably same as Clarke (Thomas), *q.v.*

CLARK (ANDREW), printer in London, Aldersgate Street, 1670–8. In 1670 he, with E. Cotes, printed for Henry Brome *The History of the Duke of Espernon*. [Haz. I. 147.] He was also the printer of the Term Catalogue of Hil. 167$\frac{4}{5}$ [*T.C.* I. 202], and he is mentioned in the 1675 list of printers in London [*S.P.D.* Car. II. vol. 369, 97], but his name rarely appeared in an imprint except in the form of the initials A. C. He is last mentioned in the Term Catalogue of Easter 1677 [*T.C.* I. 279], but he published in 1678 *The Death and Burial of Mistress Money*, sold by T. Vere and J. Clarke. [Pepys 363 (563); Haz. I. 492.] Nichols records that he succeeded James Flesher as printer to the City of London in 1672, and that in 1679 Samuel Roycroft was appointed to that office. [*Lit. Anecd.* III. 571.] In 1675 he printed a news sheet called *The City Mercury or Advertisements concerning Trade*. [Burney 75 A.] Clark died about 1677 or 1678, and was succeeded by his widow Mary (*q. v.*).

CLARK, or CLARKE (BENJAMIN), printer and bookseller in London, George Yard, Lombard Street, 1674–98. Printer and publisher for the Quakers. In their records at Devonshire House are the following entries: "At a Meeting at Rebecca Travers the 21st of y[e] 7th Month 1674, Agreed upon that hereafter A. S. [i.e. Andrew Sowle] B. C. [? Benjamin Clark] nor no other print any booke but what is first read and approv'd of in this meeting." A. S. and B. C. appear as the Society's publishers in another minute of the 26th, 2nd Month, 1675. In 1680 he published *A Test and Protest against Popery from the conscientious Christian Protestants, called Quakers*. [B.M. T. 407. (4**).] Naturally the Quaker books did not find their way into the Term Catalogues, which was confined strictly to authorized publications; but Benjamin Clark dealt in other literature as well, and his name frequently occurs in the Catalogues between the years 1679 and 1698 as a publisher of school-books, &c. [*T.C.* I. 342, III. 57.] Dunton [p. 292] refers to him as "Thee and Thou Clarke".

CLARK, or CLARKE (FRANCIS), printer in London, 1687–8. Mentioned by Dunton [p. 249] as having printed his *Remains*. In 1687 he was surety for Francis Leach the printer, in a plea of debt brought by Thomas Malthus. [C.P.R. 3056 m. 32 recto, Easter 3. Jas. II.] In 1688 he printed an edition of Thomas Deloney's *Garden of Good Will* for G. Conyers. [Haz. H. 154.] His name does not occur in the Term Catalogues, and his address has not been found, but it may possibly have been the same as that of Henry Clark (*q. v.*).

CLARK, or CLARKE (HENRY), printer in London, near St. Paul's Wharf in Thames Street, 1687–91. Possibly a relative of Francis Clark. This supposition is strengthened by Dunton [p. 249], who speaks of him as chief printer to T. Malthus, with whom Francis Clark had some business transactions. Dunton goes on to say that Henry Clark was diligent and dispatchful in his business. After his death his widow employed Mr. Sedgwick to manage the business and afterwards to better purpose J. Barber. In 1687 he printed a tract entitled *Relief of Apprentices wronged by their masters.* Amongst other publishers who employed Clark to print for them, may be mentioned Dorman Newman, T. Northcott, and J. Taylor.

CLARK, or CLARKE (JOHN), bookseller in London, (1) Bible in the Old Exchange, or, Bible in the Old Exchange, near St. Paul's; (2) Bible and Crown in the Old Exchange; (3) Bible and Crown in the Poultry, near Cheapside. 1697–1723. Publisher of divinity and also of the translation of Le Clerc's *Life of John Locke*, 1705. [*T.C.* III. 481.]

CLARK (MARY), printer in London, Aldersgate Street, 1677–96. Widow of Andrew Clark (*q.v.*). She continued the business until 1696. In 1681 she printed for Charles Harper and Jacob Tonson the 4th ed. of pt. 2 of Cowley's *Works*.

CLARK (S.), bookseller in London, Birching Lane, near the Royal Exchange, 1711. Only found in the Term Catalogue for Easter 1711, when he published three books, one being on trigonometry and another on the art of writing. [*T.C.* III. 673, 674, 676.]

CLARK, or CLARKE (WILLIAM), bookseller in Winchester, 1684–8. In Trin. 1684, his name appears with W. Abington of London, as publisher of the Rev. Henry Anderson's *Religion and Loyalty maintain'd*; and in 1686 and 1688, he published Bishop Ken's *Exposition on the Church Catechism* and *Letter*. [*T.C.* II. 83, 222.]

CLARKE (J.), bookseller in London, Bible and Harp, in West Smithfield, 1680. A poetical broadside by William Farthing was printed for him by T. H. in 1680. [B.M. C. 40. m. 11 (92).]

CLARKE (JOHN), bookseller in London, under St. Peter's Church, Cornhill. *See Dictionary*, 1641–67.

CLARKE (JOHN), jun., bookseller in London, Mercer's Chapel, 1651–78. *See Dictionary*, 1641–67, where the terminal date 1690 is probably incorrect. The latest date on which his name appears in the Term Catalogue is Mich. 1678. [*T.C.* I. 333.]

CLARKE (JOHN), music-seller in London, The Golden Viol, St. Paul's Churchyard, 1681–7. First mentioned in the Term Catalogues in Hil. 1681, and last in Hil. 1687. [*T.C.* I. 432, II. 187.] He dealt solely in music.

CLARKE (JOHN), printer (?) in Oxford, 1714. [Madan, p. 32.]

CLARKE (JOSEPH), bookseller in London, Star, Little Britain, 1670–3. Published the works of William Walker, master of the school at Grantham in Lincolnshire, notably a *Dictionary of English and Latin Idioms*. [*T.C.* I. 50.] His last entry in the Term Catalogue was in Mich. 1673. [*T.C.* I. 155.]

CLARKE (R.), bookseller at Shafton (? Shaftesbury), Dorset, 1719. Received subscriptions for R. Bradley's *Philosophical Account of the Works of Nature*, 1719.

CLARKE (RICHARD), bookseller in London, Rose, St. Paul's Churchyard, 1670–81. Publisher of F. Quarles's *Divine Emblems*, 1670, and in the following year of a Concordance of the Bible. [*T.C.* I. 27, 64.] Junior Warden of the Company in 1676; senior Warden in 1680–1.

CLARKE (THOMAS), bookseller in Kingston-upon-Hull and Newcastle-upon-Tyne, 1675–88. Admitted on July 22nd, 1675 a freeman of the Company of Upholsterers, Tin-Plate Workers and Stationers of Newcastle-upon-Tyne. [*N. & Q.* 10 S. VI. 444.] In 1688, he was sued by Awnsham Churchill the London bookseller in the Common Pleas, on a plea of assault. [C.P.R. 3068 m. 169.] An advertisement of books on sale by him in 1685 is given in *The Way to Good Success*, by N. L. [B.M. 4478. aaa. 124.] *See* Clark, or Clarke ( ).

CLARKE (WILLIAM), bookseller in London, Shakespeare's Head under the Royal Exchange, 1725 (?). Son of John Clarke, schoolmaster, of York, d. 1734. At the end of I. Priest's *Sermon in Defence of the Liturgy*, n. d., is a list headed "The following books, all by Mr. Clarke, are sold by W. Clarke his son, at Shakespeare's Head," &c.

CLAVELL (ROBERT), *see Dictionary*, 1641–67

CLAVELL (ROGER), bookseller in London, Peacock near St. Dunstan's Church in Fleet Street, 1695–8. In the *Post-Boy* of September 17th–19th, 1695, is the

following advertisement: "If any person has any Study of Books, or Library consisting either of Divinity, Law, History, Physick, &c., to dispose of, If they please to send a catalogue of them to Roger Clavel at the Peacock near St. Dunstan's Church in Fleet Street, they shall have the full value for them, and the cost of Carriage Paid." In 1695 he was succeeded by T. Leigh. [*T.C.* II. 633.]

CLAY (F.), bookseller in London, Bible without Temple Bar, 1721–35. Publisher of ladies' novels by Penelope Aubin, Aphra Behn, Madame d'Aulnoy, and others. [Esdaile, pp. 155, 160, 255, &c.]

CLAYTON (WILLIAM), bookseller in Manchester, 1700 (?)–19. Apprentice to E. Johnson of the same town (*q.v.*). Succeeded to the business when his master absconded. [Dunton, p. 238.] His name occurs in a list of those who received subscriptions for R. Bradley's *Philosophical Account of the Works of Nature*, 1719.

CLEAVE (ISAAC), bookseller in London, Star in Chancery Lane, 1678–1711. Makes his first appearance in the Term Catalogues in Hil. 1678 as the publisher of a book against Rome. [*T.C.* I. 306.] In 1681 he became the publisher of a news sheet called *The Popish Mass Display'd*, No. 1 of which appeared on April 20 (with a misprint of the year as 1671). Only two issues are known. [B.M. Burney 81 A.] He was also a publisher of law-books, and Dunton [p. 228] describes him as well known to lawyers of the first rank and having printed several eminent trials. Amongst these latter was *The Tryal of Sir William Parkins knt., for . . . conspiracy to assassinate . . . King William III*, 1696. Cleave was still publishing in 1711, in which year an advertisement in the *Post Man* of February 3rd mentions him as receiving subscriptions for R. Bradley's *Treatise of Succulent Plants.*

CLEMENT (SAMUEL), bookseller in London, (1) Lute, St. Paul's Churchyard; (2) Swan, St. Paul's Churchyard; (3) Sun [*sic*, for Swan ?], St. Paul's Churchyard. 1691–3. Began publishing in 1691, when he issued Guy Miège's *English Grammar* from the Lute in St. Paul's Churchyard. In the next year he moved to the Swan, and in 1693 he entered in the Term Catalogue the 3rd ed. of John Shower's *Serious Reflections on Time and Eternity* with the imprint, "Printed for S. Clement at the Sun in St. Paul's Churchyard" (which we suspect to be a misprint for "Swan"). [*T.C.* II. 458.]

CLEMENTS (HENRY), bookseller in Oxford, 1684–1721. Apprenticed to Richard Davis, bookseller of Oxford. On May 26th, 1681, he married his master's maid. [Wood, II. 541.] Began publishing in 1684. [*T.C.* II. 95.] In 1691, in company with G. West, he published Gerard Langbaine's *Account of the English Dramatick Poets* [*T.C.* II. 358], and in 1693, with West and Crosley, William Somner's *Treatise of the Roman Ports and Forts in Kent.* [*T.C.* II. 476]. On the death of Thomas Bennet, who seems to have been his London agent, Clements took over his business in London at the Half-Moon in St. Paul's Churchyard, in addition to his shop at Oxford. In 1692 Clements was a witness for Clarendon in his libel action against Wood. In his depositions Clements gave his age as about forty-seven. Mr. Clark [*ib.*] gives the date of Clements's death as 1721.

CLEMENTS (HENRY), bookseller in London, Half-Moon, St. Paul's Churchyard, 1707–19. It is not clear whether this bookseller was not identical with the bookseller at Oxford of the same name, as the name appears twice in the proposals for printing *Corpus Omnium Veterum Poetarum Latinorum* in 1709, once for London and once for Oxford. [*T.C.* III. 656.] Mr. Arber refers to the London man as "the younger". Clements succeeded T. Bennet at the Half-Moon in 1707, and became the publisher of many important books, such as Isaac Littlebury's translation of Herodotus in 1708, Dr. William King's *Miscellanies*, 1709, Thoresby's *Ducatus Leodiensis*, 1717, and *Bibliotheca Biblica*, 1717. With Samuel Keble he was appointed printer of the Votes of the House of Commons. He died August 23rd, 1719, when W. and John Innys stated at the end of a catalogue of their publications that they had secured most of the books printed by Mr. Henry Clements "lately deceased". [B.M. 121. i. 1. (18).]

CLEMENTS (RICHARD), printer (?) in Oxford, 1725. [Madan, p. 32.]

CLIFF (NATHANIEL), bookseller in London, (1) Golden Candlestick in Cheapside, near the Old Jewry; (2) (with D. Jackson) Bible and Three Crowns near Mercer's Chapel, 1708–16. Succeeded E. Jaye at the former address in 1708, when he published *A Persuasive to Moderation*. [*T.C.* III. 588.] In the following year with several other booksellers he issued in monthly parts *A New Collection of Voyages and Travels*. About 1710 he entered into partnership with D. Jackson, and together they took over the Bible and Three Crowns in Cheapside near Mercer's Chapel, formerly held by Thomas Parkhurst. Both the partners seem to have died or given up business by 1716, as the firm was then S. Cliff and T. Cox, and in 1718, R. Cruttenden and T. Cox.

CLIFTON (FRANCIS), printer in London, Old Bailey, *c.* 1720. Printer for the Roman Catholics. His trade consisted largely in printing ballads and broadsides that were obnoxious to the Government. Thomas Gent, the York printer, worked for him for some time and consequently was involved in trouble. [Gent, *Life*; Davies, *History of the York Press.*]

COCKERAINE (WILLIAM), *see* Cockram.

COCKERILL, or COCKRIL (THOMAS), bookseller in London, (1) Atlas in Cornhill; (2) Three Legs in the Poultry. 1674–1702. Dealt chiefly in theological and educational works. His first and last entries in the Term Catalogues were in 1674 and 1702. [*T.C.* I. 176, III. 289.] Dunton [p. 214] says of him: "He was always up to the ears among great persons and business (perhaps engaging for a third volume) yet I will do my rival that justice to say he was a very religious charitable man. The printing *The Morning Exercise* and *Charnott's Works* brought him into great credit. . . . His kinsman Mr. Thomas Cockril (*q. v.*) is a living transcript of his uncle's virtues and public spirit".

COCKERILL, or COCKRIL (THOMAS), jun., bookseller in London (?) 1702 ?–1705 ?. Nephew of Thomas Cockerill, sen., whom he survived. See Dunton's account of the latter, written in 1703. The attribution to him as well as to his uncle of some books of 1690 in the Index to *T.C.* appears to be an error. [*T.C.* III. 3,705.]

COCKRAM (WILLIAM), bookseller in Northampton, 1675–7. Published *The State of Northampton from the beginning of the Fire, September 20, 1675 to November 5.* Licensed November 22nd, 1675 [Bodl. Pamph. 135]; and S. Ford's *Fall of Northampton*, 1677.

COGGAN (FRANCIS), bookseller in London, Inner-Temple-Lane, 1699–1707. First mentioned in the Term Catalogues in June 1699, as a publisher of law books. [*T.C.* III. 137.] Dunton [p. 226] says of him, "He is so cautious and wise that he is noted for it . . . and is as well a judge as a seller of books." In 1707 Bernard Lintot bought of him one half of *Love and a Bottle,* for £2 3*s.* He was also the publisher of the second part of V. Bowater's *Antiquities of Middlesex* [Harl. 5961, 128]. He died some time in 1707, and was

succeeded by his widow Margaret Coggan. Her name appears in the Term Catalogues for the last time in 1709. [*T.C.* III. 644.]

COGGAN (MARGARET), bookseller in London, Inner Temple Lane, 1708. Widow of Francis Coggan. She held a share in Dr. John Harris's *Lexicon Technicum,* was also the publisher of a *History of the Reign of Queen Anne,* by Abel Boyer, 1709. [*T.C.* III. 600, 616, 644.]

COLEBROOKE (JOHN), bookseller in Midhurst, Sussex, 1700. In 1700 he sold a *Sermon preach'd at the funeral of George Payne, Junior . . .*, by the Rev. Richard Oliver, curate of Midhurst. [*T.C.* III. 193.]

COLES (FRANCIS), *see Dictionary*, 1641–67.

COLLEY (JOHN), printer (?) in Oxford, 1676. [Madan, p. 30.]

COLLIER, or COLLYER (JOHN), printer and bookseller in Nottingham, (1) Hen Cross; (2) at the Sheep Pens. 1711–25. Mentioned in a list of provincial booksellers in *Notes and Queries* [10 S., vol. v. p. 184], as at work in 1714 and by Allnutt as in 1711. He was the printer of *The Nottingham Mercury* and *The Nottingham Post.* In 1722 he printed a broadside on the method of hiring servants [B.M. 1851. c. 10. (51)], and in 1725 an ed. of Charles Cotton's *Wonders of the Peak.*

COLLIER, or COLLYER (JOSEPH), bookseller in London, (1) Angel on London Bridge, a little below the Gate, or, by the Gate; (2) (*a*) Bible, (*b*) Golden Bible [under the Gate] on London Bridge. 1679–1724. Is first met with in 1679, in partnership with Stephen Foster, at the Angel, when he published *England's Grievances in times of Popery* and a sermon preached in St. George's, Southwark, at the funeral of Mrs. Frances Fenn [*T.C.* I. 366], but shortly afterwards Foster moved to the Sun and Bible on London Bridge. Collier remained at the Angel till after April 10, 1680, as on that date his name and address appeared in an advertisement of Bateman's *Scurvy-Grass* in Smith's *Currant Intelligence*; but in Michaelmas of that year he is found at the Bible [*T.C.* I. 421], where he remained until 1700. [*T.C.* I. 217.] The house was sometimes called The Golden Bible. Treasurer of the Company of Stationers in succession to Benjamin Tooke, 1702–24. Died in 1724. [Timperley, p. 629.] Dunton [p. 219] says of him: "He was my fellow apprentice for many years. . . . He has a great deal of learning, a discerning judgement, is pleasant in his conversation, and sincere in his piety. He

writes an excellent hand, is an accurate accomptant and justly merits the honour the company of stationers did him, in choosing him their treasurer."

COLLINS (ARTHUR), bookseller in London, Black Boy in Fleet Street, 1709–16. Said to have been born about 1690, but probably earlier; his father is said to have been gentleman usher to Queen Catherine of Braganza. Collins is first found as a bookseller in partnership with Abel Roper. He is chiefly remembered as the compiler and publisher of the *Peerage* called after his name. The first edition appeared in 1709, without the compiler's name, but printed for Abel Roper and Arthur Collins. This was a volume of 470 pages, but so great was its success that a revised and enlarged second edition appeared in 1710–11, and a third, sold by Arthur Collins alone, in 1714–16. In expectation of a place under Government, Collins gave up his business in Fleet Street in 1716, but he continued to compile genealogical works, though often "reduced to great straits" for money. At length the king granted him a pension of £400 a year. Collins died in March 1760 and was buried in Battersea Church "aged 70"; if this is correct he published his *Peerage* at the age of 19.

COLLINS (FREEMAN), printer in London and Norwich; Norwich, Red Well. 1682–1713. In 1682 he printed for T. Benskin, London, and C. Yeo, Exon., *A True and Impartial Relation of the Informations against Three Witches, viz. Temperance Lloyd, Mary Trembles, and Susanna Edwards, who were . . . convicted at . . . Exon.* [Haz. I. 127.] Between that date and 1697 he printed other books for Exeter booksellers. [J. I. Dredge, *Devon Booksellers and Printers*, pp. 9, 10.] Dunton says [p. 244] that in 1689, he employed Deputy Collins to print for him. But his name does not appear in the Term Catalogues as a printer until 1703, when he printed for J. Nutt Sir H. Mackworth's pamphlet on Conformity [*T.C.* III. 373], and in the next year he is found printing for Francis Oliver, bookseller in Norwich, the Rev. Thomas Clayton's sermon on *Unity of Worship.* [*T.C.* III. 391.] In 1707 he was elected junior warden of the Stationers' Company. At this time one of his apprentices was Edward Cave, afterwards the founder of *The Gentleman's Magazine,* who was sent down to Norwich to edit *The Norwich Courant.* Later Collins seems to have gone to Norwich himself, and in 1712, to have set up in succession to F. Burgess. His widow Susanna printed till 1724.

COLLINS (GABRIEL), bookseller in London, at the Middle Temple Gate, 1687–90. Possibly son of Thomas Collins. Publisher of Thomas Shadwell's *Tenth*

Satyr of Juvenal, 1687. He was also a publisher of law books. [*T.C.* 200, 341.]

COLLINS (JAMES). *See Dictionary*, 1641–67. Still in business in 1682–3, when Adiell Mill brought an action against him for debt. [C.P.R. 3009, m. 131 r.] In 1681 he had a shop under the Temple Church.

COLLINS (THOMAS). *See Dictionary*, 1641–67. Still in business in 1682. At the end of John Burbury's *Relation of a Journey of . . . Lord Henry Howard*, 1671, published by Collins with J. Ford, is a 24-page list of their publications covering every class of literature. [B.M. 978. b. 1.]

COLMAR (JOHN), printer in Edinburgh, in the Grassmarket at the foot of Heriot's Bridge, 1680–5. One of the Dutch workmen brought over by John Cairns about 1680. In 1685 he printed *Edinburgh's true Almanack*, on his own account; but the greater part of his time he was in partnership with others. *See* Lindsay, David. [Aldis, p. 111.]

COLSON (W.), bookseller at Winchester, 1705. Published the Rev. John Horsnell's *Sermon . . . at the Cathedral of Winchester, at the Assizes . . .* March 8th, 170$\frac{4}{5}$. [*T.C.* III. 477.]

COMBES (CHARLES), sen., printer in Oxford, 1720–8. [Madan, p. 32.]

COMBES (CHARLES), jun., printer in Oxford, 1728 (?)–36. Died in 1736. [Madan, p. 32.]

CONINGSBY (CHRISTOPHER), stationer and bookseller in London, (1) Golden Key, in Fleet Street, 1687; (2) Golden Turk's Head, Fleet Street, 1691; (3) Ink-Bottle, against Clifford's Inn Gate, in Fetter Lane, Fleet Street, 1711. 1687–1711. His first entry in the Term Catalogues, in Hil. 1687, was W. Elder's *Enchiridion Calligraphiae*, a series of engraved plates. [*T.C.* II. 187.] He sold legal forms of all kinds, warrants for land-tax, licences for alehouses, and general literature. He was still publishing in 1711.

CONNIBER (JOHN), printer (? or bookseller) in Barnstaple, co. Devon, 1682. Mr. Dredge inserts this name in his second supplement on the strength of a note made by Mr. J. R. Chanter, who, he thinks, may have met with it in the Corporation Accounts. [Dredge, *Devon Booksellers and Printers.* second supplement, p. 59.]

CONYERS (GEORGE), bookseller in London, (1) Golden Ring, Ludgate Hill; (2) Little Britain, (*a*) over against the Sugar Loaf, (*b*) next the Feathers. 1686–1712. This bookseller had a unique stock, hardly to be found in any other shop in London, for he made a speciality of the publication of cheap practical manuals on every conceivable subject. A glance through the Term Catalogues, of which he availed himself largely, shows him as publisher of books on angling, astrology, building, cookery, drawing, dyeing, gardening, gauging, husbandry, japanning and varnishing, medicine, painting, and perfumery. He also published chap-book abridgements of popular romances, roadbooks, almanacks, &c. In 1713 he contributed to the fund for the relief of William Bowyer, sen. [Timperley, p. 600.] Dunton [p. 230] describes Conyers as a "man free from faction, noise, and anger, a diligent man in his shop, a kind neighbour, and a religious master".

CONYERS (JOSHUA), *see Dictionary*, 1641–67.

COOK or COOKE (JOHN), bookseller in Sherborne, Dorset, 1713–16. Publisher of James Lacy's *Sermon preach'd at the consecration of a church in the parish of Castleton near Sherborne*, 1715. [Mayo, *Bibl. Dorset.*, p. 126.] In 1716 he also published Shuttleworth's *Perswasive to Union.*

COOK (WILLIAM), bookseller in London, Green Dragon, without Temple Bar, 1676. Recorded by Mr. F. G. Hilton-Price in his articles on 'Signs in the Strand'. [*Midd. & Herts. N. & Q.*, III. 13.]

COOKE (J.), bookseller in London, High Holborn, 1720 (?). He published *Life and Character of Mrs. Mary Moders. . . . the Famous German Princess*, n. d. [Haz. III. 30.]

COOKE (WILLIAM), printer in Chester, 1718 (?)–23. Hazlitt records two books printed by him. (1) *Syntax. The Grounds of the Latin Syntax* . . . Chester: Printed by William Cooke for Jos. Hodgson, and . . . sold by Peter Polter. [1720 ?] (2) *A Paraphrase on the xxviij Chapter of Deuteronomy.* By the Rev. McLindsay. Chester: Printed by Wm. Cooke, for the author, 1723. [Haz. I. 415, 492.] He bought Ince's material in or about 1718. [Gent, pp. 83–4.]

COOPER (WILLIAM), bookseller and book-auctioneer in London, (1) Warwick Lane; (2) The Pelican, Little Britain, 1668–88. In a volume of astrological tracts called *The Philosophical Epitaph of W. C., Esquire*, 1673, it appears

that at an early period of his life William Cooper was a religious enthusiast and a great believer in astrology, and that he either suffered from some physical illness, or that his religious beliefs got him into trouble with the authorities. In the dedication to the *Epitaph* he speaks of having been "in a living grave" in 1652, and having been "helped from his long troubles" by Elias Ashmole in 1662. His first entry in the Stationers' Register was made on January 1st, 1667 [i. e. $166\frac{7}{8}$] and was an astrological tract called *A Chymicall dispensatorie, or, the Treasurie of medicines, written in Latine by John Schroder and Englished by William Rowland.* [*Stat. Reg.*, Roxb. II. 383.] To his *Epitaph* he added "A Catalogue of Chemical Books" to which in 1675 he made several additions; this was the first English bibliography of the subject. Cooper was also the first book-auctioneer in England. His first auction was held in 1676, the library dispersed being that of Dr. Seaman. From that time until his death he shared with Edward Millington the foremost place as an auctioneer, amongst the more important libraries that came under his hammer being those of Dr. Samuel Brooke, 1680, Dr. Nathan Paget, M.D., 1681, Walter Rea, 1682, and the stock of Richard Davis, bookseller of Oxford, between 1686 and 1688. Amongst Cooper's publications may be noted Spenser's *View of the state of Ireland*, Ware's *De Scriptoribus Hiberniae*, Usher's *Sylloge veterum Epistolarum Hibernicarum*, an edition of Head's *English Rogue*, and Marlowe's *Lust's Dominion*. Cooper died before Nov. 1689, being succeeded by his widow. [Lawler, p. xxvii.]

CORBET (CHARLES), bookseller in London, Oxford Arms in Warwick Lane, 1683. Does not appear to have been a member of the Company of Stationers, as its records show no sign of his having been an apprentice or taking up his freedom; but he may have been a member of some other company. In 1683 he published a poetical broadside entitled *A New Narrative of the Old Plot* [B.M. 1872. a. 1 (125*)], and in the severe winter of 1683–4 he published two ballads in commemoration of the frost. In the Term Catalogue for Trin. 1683, in company with J. Crowch, he advertised *A Collection of New Songs set within the compass of the Flute. Written and composed by C. F. Gent.* [*T.C.* II. 30.] It seems possible that he was a dealer in music rather than in books.

CORBET (THOMAS), printer (?) at Oxford, 1694. [Madan, p. 32.]

CORBETT (BENJAMIN), bookseller in London, 1686–1701. Son of Waites or Waties Corbett of Elton, Herefordshire. Apprenticed for seven years from

November 4th, 1678 to Robert Everingham, printer. Admitted a freeman of the Company of Stationers on July 5th, 1686. [MS. records of Stat. Co.] He was the publisher of the first review entitled *Weekly Memorials, or Account of Books*, 1688, also of Tooker's *Famous Collection of Papers* [*c.* 1700.] On November 20th, 1701, a Benjamin Corbett who may or may not be identical with the above, wrote to a Mr. Pettiver, saying that he was on the point of sailing for China. [Sloane MS. 4063, f. 128.]

CORBETT (THOMAS), bookseller and book-auctioneer in London, (1) corner of Ludgate Hill, next Fleet Bridge; (2) (*a*) the Child's Coat, down the Ditch side near Bridewell Bridge; (*b*) by Fleet Ditch; (3) Addison's Head, next the Rose Tavern, without Temple Bar. 1715–43. Apparently son of Charles Corbet of the Oxford Arms. Thomas Corbett's name does not appear in the records of the Stationers' Company either as apprentice or freeman. In 1705 he published the fourth edition 'with additions, on a fine paper and Elzevir letter", of *New Miscellaneous Poems.* [*Postman*, Sept. 6th–8th, 1715.] In the same year he also published a sermon called *Great Britain's Happiness under . . . a Protestant King*, by Gershom Rawlins. [B.M. 4474. d. 99.] In 1716 he began selling books by auction at his warehouse, the Child's Coat, down the Ditch side, near Bridewell Bridge. Here on Nov. 7th, 1716, he sold the library of Thomas Cooke of Fulham, and on October 31st, 1717, the library of the Rev. - Kirke of Chester. [*Daily Courant*, Oct. 29th, 1717.] In 1719 he moved to the Addison's Head without Temple Bar, where he continued until his death in 1743. Sir Charles Corbett, the famous lottery agent and bookseller, is believed to have been his son.

CORSELEY (W.), bookseller in Bristol, 1721–35. His name is found in the imprint to a sermon of 1721 by J. Harcourt. [B.M. 226. f. 1 (8).] The dates given above are from a list of provincial booksellers in *Notes and Queries* [10th series, V. 141.]

CORTNEY (   ), bookseller at Salisbury, 1716. Son of John Courtney, *q. v.* (?). Known from an advertisement sheet of prints. [Bodl. Scrapbook, no. 2 (3).]

CORYTON (WILLIAM), bookseller in London, Black Swan on Ludgate Hill. 1711. His name occurs in the imprint to *A Short Character of His Ex. T[homas] E[arl] of W[harton] L[ord] L[ieutenant] of I[reland]*, 1711. [B.M. T. 1815 (3).]

COSGROVE (HENRY), printer in Norwich, 1711. *See* Crossgrove.

COTES (ELLEN), *see Dictionary*, 1641–67.

COTTON (THOMAS), printer in Cork, 1715 (?). *See* Welsh (Andrew).

COTTRELL (JAMES), *see Dictionary*, 1641–67.

COURTENAY (JAMES), bookseller in London, Golden Horseshoe, Saffron Hill, 1671–85. The earliest notice of him is found in the State Papers in the form of a news letter addressed to him from Whitehall, during his absence abroad in 1671. It deals solely with foreign affairs and has no reference to his business. [*Calendar of State Papers*, Charles II, 1671, pp. 332, &c.] In 1679 he published *Female Poems on several occasions, written by Ephelia*, which was printed for him by William Downing. [*T.C.* I. 350.] In 1685 Courtenay sued Thomas Young "bibliopolam", of Shaftesbury, for the balance of his account £30 6*s.* [C.P.R., Hil. 1 Jas. II, Roll 3041, m. 272 v.]

COURTNEY (JOHN), bookseller in Salisbury, 1650–75. *See Dictionary*, 1641–67. In 1675 he had printed for him in London, *Avona: or, A Transient view of the Benefit of making rivers of this Kingdom navigable. Occasioned by observing the Scituation of the City of Salisbury, upon the Avon* . . . By R. G. [Haz. II. 695.]

COWLEY (THOMAS), *see Dictionary*, 1641–67.

COWNLY (GILBERT), bookseller in London, at the Pope's Head in the Lower Walk (or East end of the Lower Walk) of the New Exchange, 1685–91. Succeeded William Cademan at this house in 1685. [*T.C.* II. 129.] Cownly published for the Rev. R. Wolley, *The Present State of France*, 1689 [Haz. III. 270.] The unsold copies were reissued in 1691, with a new title-page, *Galliae Notitia, or the present state of France.* On the verso of the last leaf of a copy of this edition in the B.M. is a list of Cownly's publications, including *Miscellany Poems, with the Temple of Death, by Eminent Hands*, and Segrais' romance, *Zayde.* The latter he apparently took over from Cademan, as Mr. Esdaile notes a copy with the latter's imprint, published in 1678; but he does not record any issue by Cownly, who may merely have bought some of the stock of F. Saunders's second edition, 1690. [Esdaile, p. 304.] About 1690 J. Knight is found in possession of Cownly's premises, but not before; and all the references given in the index to the second volume of the Term Catalogues to Knight as at this address should refer to the Blue Anchor in the Lower Walk, where he carried on business for several years with F. Saunders.

COWPER. *See* Cooper.

COWSE (BENJAMIN), bookseller in London, Rose and Crown, St. Paul's Churchyard, 1714–23. In 1714 Humphrey Wanley approached Cowse and others with a proposal that they should publish *Annales de Lanercost*, Viscount Weymouth having promised his support; but the Viscount died suddenly and the project fell through. In 1721 he published *Laws of British Plantations*. [Haz. A. 261.] Cowse is next heard of in 1723, in connexion with the publication of certain castrated sheets of Holinshed's *Chronicle*, which was advertised in the *Post Boy* of February 16th, 172$\frac{2}{3}$. In this he was associated with Christopher Bateman. [Nichols, *Lit. Anec.*, I. 83, 251.]

COWSEY (J.), bookseller at Exeter, 1682. Only known as selling two of W. Crompton's discourses, *Sovereign Omnipotency* and *The Justice of God Asserted*, both printed for B. Alsop in 1682. [*T.C.* I. 504; Dredge, *Devon Booksellers and Printers*, p. 42.]

COX (   ), bookbinder in London, Sherburne Lane, 1670–1700? Referred to by Dunton [p. 259] as "a grave thriving binder for thirty years, but is now retired . . . and, for all his misfortunes, is a bright example".

COX (BENJAMIN), bookseller in London, Prince's Arms, Ludgate Street, 1685–9. Succeeded Samuel Smith at this address in 1685. [*T.C.* II. 138.] His career was a brief one, as the last entry under his name in the Term Catalogues was an edition of Baxter's *Dying Thoughts*, in Trin. 1689. [*T.C.* II. 281.]

COX (GEORGE), stationer in London, St. Botolph without Aldgate, 1680–2. Died in or before 1682, when the will of his widow Elizabeth Cox was proved in the Prerogative Court of Canterbury. [P.C.C. 16 Drax.]

COX (H.), bookseller in London, Holborn, over against Furnivall's Inn, 1676–9. Successor to Nicholas Cox at this address. Only two entries are recorded in the Term Catalogues, *Recreative pastime by card play*, in Trin. 1676, and *Political and Military Observations*, in Hil. 1679. [*T.C.* I. 247, 342.]

COX (NICHOLAS), bookseller in London and Oxford: (1) London, over against Furnivall's Inn, Holborn; (2) Oxford, near Queen's College. 1673–1721. Manciple of St. Edmund Hall. Author of a work called *The Gentleman's*

Recreation, 1673. It went through many editions. Cox was also the publisher of some plays and historical works. In 1680 he published a catalogue of plays reprinted and brought up to date from that printed in *Nicomede*, 1671. [Wood, I. 20.] In 1685 he appears to have had a shop at Oxford, which Mr. Arber says was near Queen's College. From there he published A. Freyer's *Funeral Sermon on the death of Charles II, preached at Dort*, 1685, and Gerard Langbaine's *Momus Triumphans*, 1688. [*T.C.* II. 143, 240.]

COX (THOMAS ?), bookseller in London, Bible and Three Crowns, near Mercers' Chappel in Cheapside, 1716–18. In partnership with S. Cliff, and afterwards R. Cruttenden (*q. v.*). He may be the Thomas Cox referred to by Timperley [p. 684] as an eminent bookseller and exchange broker, who died on February 3rd, 1754.

CRAWFURD (THOMAS), printer in Glasgow, 1721. In 1721 he printed an edition of *Naphthali, or the Wrestlings of the Church of Scotland*. [John McUre, *History of Glasgow* (1830), p. 371.]

CRAYLE (BENJAMIN), bookseller in London: (1) Bell, St. Paul's Churchyard; (2) Lamb, Fleet Street, (*a*) next, (*b*) near, Whitefriars; (3) Peacock and Bible, (*a*) Ludgate Street, (*b*) West End of St. Paul's Church, (*c*) St. Paul's Churchyard. 1683–90. Began as a publisher in 1683, when he issued Jo. Quarles's poem, *Triumphant Chastity*. [*T.C.* II. 29.] In 1684 he moved to Whitefriars. In 1685 he published *Delightful and Ingenious Novels*, which ran to four editions. [Esdaile, pp. 210–11.] He also dealt in cheap scholastic books. [*T.C.* II. 232.] In 1686 he moved back to St. Paul's Churchyard, and his last entry in the Term Catalogues is Drayton's *England's Heroical Epistles*, Trin. 1690. [*T.C.* II. 326.]

CREED (JOHN), bookseller at Cambridge, living opposite Great St. Mary's Church, on ground where now is the lawn attached to the Senate House, 1670–85. We know of seventeen books, chiefly in Latin and Greek, printed for him from 1670–85. [*T.C.* I. 59–II. 147, and Bowes's *Catalogue of Cambridge Books*.] He was probably succeeded by Thomas Webster (*q. v.*).

CRIPPS (SUSAN). *See Dictionary*, 1641–67. She afterwards married Peter Parker. [Stat. Co.'s Register F, p. 595.]

CROFT (EDWARD), bookseller in London, (1) Two Golden Lions, Poultry; (2) Seven Stars, Little Lombard Street. 1677–8. Was perhaps son of

Edward Croft, who died in 1667. [*See Dictionary*, 1641–67.] In 1677 Edward Croft published *The Right of Tythes asserted*. [*T.C.* I. 294.] In the following year he moved to Lombard Street, and published there a pamphlet on schism and separation. [*T.C.* I. 319.] Nothing more is heard of him.

CROOK (ANDREW), bookseller and King's Printer in Ireland, Dublin, 1681–1731. Son of John Crook (1638–69). In 1681 he was in partnership with his mother Mary Crook (*q. v.*) as a bookseller. In 1685 he took to printing, in partnership with Samuel Helsham. In 1686 he became B. Tooke's assign in the office of King's Printer, and after 1689 was sole King's Printer. He worked till 1731, and died in or about 1732; his will was deposited in the Dublin Prerog.Court.

CROOK (JOHN), jun., printer in Dublin, 1679–84. Son of John Crook, sen. (*q. v. Dictionary*, 1641–67), King's Printer in Dublin, who died in 1669. Apparently he was not old enough or qualified to get his father's place, and it was filled by B. Tooke, from 1669 to 1678 alone, but in 1679 John Crook shared the office of King's Printer with him and so continued till 1683. He died intestate in 1684. Administration was granted to his mother, Mary (or Maria) Crook, widow.

CROOK (MARY), printer in Dublin, 1671–84. Widow of John Crook, sen., King's Printer in Dublin, and mother of John Crook, jun. She was a bookseller in 1671 and also appears as a printer a little later. Her place of business in 1679 was His Majesty's Printing House, and she sold works printed by Tooke, and also by him and her son John when he was Tooke's partner in the office. Her son Andrew joined her in the bookselling business in 1681.

CROOKE (ANDREW), bookseller in London, Green Dragon, in St. Paul's Churchyard, 1630–74. *See Dictionary*, 1641–67.

CROOKE (ELIZABETH), bookseller in London, Green Dragon without Temple Bar, nigh Devereux Court, being the passage into the Middle Temple, 1694–6. Succeeded William Crooke, whose widow she probably was, in 1694. [*Midd. & Herts. N. & Q.* III. 13.] In Hil. 1695 she published a sermon by Thomas Manningham [*T.C.* II. 537.] In 1696 the firm apparently ceased business, and its stock was remaindered; as in Hil. 1696 a notice appeared in the Term Catalogue that "all the books printed for William Crook at the Green Dragon" were to be sold by D. Brown at the Black Swan and Bible without Temple Bar [*T.C.* II. 575.]

CROOKE (JOHN), bookseller in London, and King's Printer in Ireland, 1638–69. *See Dictionary*, 1641–67.

CROOKE (WILLIAM), bookseller in London, Green Dragon, without Temple Bar, 1667–94. *See Dictionary*, 1641–67. Identical with the bookseller living at the Three Bibles on Fleet Bridge in 1664–5. No doubt a son of Andrew Crooke, 1630–74. He printed for Richard Flecknoe and Thomas Hobbes, and published all kinds of literature. Lists of his publications are printed in G. Sibscota, *The Deaf and Dumb Man*, 1670, and *The Moores Baffled*, 1681. He died some time in 1694, and was succeeded by Elizabeth Crooke (*q.v.*) [*Midd. & Herts. N. & Q.*, III. 13.]

CROOM (GEORGE), printer in London, (1) Bride Lane; (2) Blue Ball in Thames Street, near Addle Hill (over against, or near, Baynards Castle); (3) Blue Ball over against Bridewell; (4) On the Thames. 1671–1707. In 1670 or 1671 a private press was discovered by the Company of Stationers at the house of George Croom in Bride Lane; who, being sent for, acknowledged the having a press in his house for printing damask boards. The Company ordered that the press should be taken down and brought to the Hall. [MS. records of Stat. Co.] Nothing more is heard of him until 1682, when he printed *The Loyal London Mercury* (24 nos., June 14th–November 11th). [Timperley, p. 563.] Croom's name appears twice only in the Term Catalogues, first as the printer of *The Tryals of Henry Cornish* [and others], 1685 [*T.C.* II. 150], and 2nd ed. 1707; and in 1689, of a *Manual of Prayers* [*T.C.* II. 284]. On May 9th, 1688 he issued the first number of *The Weekly Test Paper*. [Timperley, p. 571.] Dunton [p. 252] says of him: "Some would insinuate as though he favoured the Jacobites, but I take him for a man of more sense. . . . Mr. Croom is a fair dealer, understands his business. . . . He . . . formerly printed for me *The Tigurine Liturgy* and of late several sheets of the *Post Angel*." During the great frost of 1683–4 Croom set up a printing press on the ice on the Thames, at which he printed a broadside entitled, *Thamasis's* [*sic*] *Advice to the Painter from her Frigid Zone, or, Wonders upon the water*. [B.M. 1875. d. 6 (8).]

CROSKILL (RICHARD), bookseller in London, Lincoln's Inn, New Square, 1706–7. Published *A Trip to Leverpoole, by two of Fate's Children*, 1706. [Haz. IV. 58.]

CROSKILL (THOMAS), bookseller in London, 1675. Only known from *An Answer to the Character of an Exchange Wench*, printed for him in 1675. [Haz. H. 84.]

CROSLEY (JOHN), bookseller at Oxford. *See Dictionary*, 1641–67.

CROSSBY (JOHN), bookseller in Edinburgh, 1700. Robert Russel's *The sin against the Holy Ghost*, 1700, bears the imprint "Edinburgh, printed by James Watson for John Crossby".

CROSSGROVE (HENRY), printer in Norwich, Magdalen Street, 1706–44. Born on August 14th, 1683, at Low Leyton, Essex, son of Patrick Crossgrove, an Irishman, and Elizabeth his wife, widow of John Fellows of London and daughter of Harry Gutteridge of Leyton. In a "Chronological Account of Remarkable Accidents and Occurrences to date", given in Francis Burges's *True Description of the City of Norwich*, ed. 1718, occurs this note: "1706, Sam. Hasbart a distiller, set up a Printing Office in Magdalen St. and sent for Henry Crossgrove from London to be his journeyman." They separated in 1718, according to Gent. The first number of the *Norwich Gazette* was printed by Crossgrove in November 1706. In politics it was a Tory and Jacobite paper. [Timperley, p. 626.] In the *Weekly Journal* for March 12th, 17$\frac{14}{15}$, was inserted a paragraph to the effect that a petition had been signed by the Whigs, calling upon the Government to indict "Mr. Crossgrove the printer" for publishing in the *Gazette* "A Short Account of the State of England, when King James II intended to call his second parliament" taken from Kennet's *History of England*, "but we do not hear that the said printer is sent for in custody, or that he keeps out of the way for the same, it having been only reprinted by him after it had sold above 10 impressions in London". Crossgrove had some correspondence with Strype. In his later years he became Town Councillor for Mancroft Ward. He died on November 12th, 1744.

CROUCH, or CROWCH (EDWARD), printer in London, 1672. *See Dictionary*, 1641–67. Still at work in 1675, when he is mentioned in a list of printing houses in London. [S. P. Dom. Car. II. vol. 369 (97.)]

CROUCH (NATHANIEL), sen., bookseller in London, (1) Bell, next to Kemp's Coffee House in Exchange Alley (over against the Royal Exchange in Cornhill), 1681–2; (2) Bell (*a*) in the Poultry, near Cheapside, (*b*) over against

Grocers' Alley, in the Poultry, near Cheapside, 1683–1708. 1663–1725 (?). Was born about 1632; son of a tailor at Lewes. Apprenticed on May 5th, 1656, to Livewell Chapman for seven years, and then took up his freedom in the Company of Stationers. Under the pseudonym of Richard or Robert Burton, he compiled a number of small books of which Dr. Johnson said that "they seem very proper to allure backward readers". *The History of the Nine Worthies of the World*, 1696, &c., is perhaps the most celebrated. Dunton [pp. 206, 435–6] says of him, "I think I have given you the very soul of his character when I have told you that his talent lies at Collection. He has melted down the best of our English Histories into Twelve penny Books, which are filled with wonders, rarities, and curiosities; for, you must know, his Title-pages are a little swelling". The *D.N.B.* gives a list of forty-six of his compilations. He is believed to have died before 1725, when the name of Thomas Crouch (perhaps his son) is found on one of his books. [*D.N.B.*]

CROUCH (NATHANIEL), jun., bookseller in London, Bell, Poultry, 1697. Probably a son of Nathaniel Crouch, sen., at whose shop he published, with T. Crouch, a divinity book in 1697. [*T.C.* III. 2.]

CROUCH (SAMUEL), bookseller in London, at the Prince's Arms, a corner shop of Pope's Head Alley in Cornhill, 1674–1711. Was in some way related to Nathaniel Crouch (*q.v.*) Samuel made his first entry in the Term Catalogue in Mich. 1674 [*T.C.* I. 187], and became a publisher of school books and cheap literature. In 1679 he started a newspaper called *The True Protestant Domestic Intelligence*. No. 1 was issued on July 9th, 1679. Mr. Arber says that Nathaniel Crouch was the writer of it. [*T.C.* I. 543.] In 1691 Samuel Crouch became surety in £1,000 for a certain John Gardner, in an action brought against the latter for assault. [C.P.R. Mich. 3 W. and M. Roll, 3101 m. 140 recto.] His name occurs frequently in the Term Catalogues up to 1711. Dunton says of him [p. 211], "He is just and punctual in all his dealings: never speaks ill of any man; has a *swinging* soul of his own; would part with all he has to serve a Friend; and that's enough for one Bookseller".

CROUCH (THOMAS), bookseller in London, (1) Bell in the Poultry, 1697; (2) Bell in Paternoster Row, near Cheapside, 1725. 1697–1725? Probably a son of Nathaniel Crouch the elder, at whose shop (above) he published, with N. Crouch jun., a divinity book in 1697 [*T.C.* III. 2.] In 1725 his name is found on one of "R. Burton's" booklets.

CROWCH (J.), music-seller in London, Three Lutes in Drury Lane, 1683–6. With C. Corbet he published in 1683, *A Collection of new Songs*, for the flute, by C. F., and in 1686 with N. Thompson *The Compleat Dancing-Master*. [*T.C.* II. 30, 168.]

CROWNFIELD (CORNELIUS), printer to the University and bookseller at Cambridge, 1698–1743. "A Dutchman, who had been a soldier, and a very ingenious man" [Ames, p. 462]. He was appointed business adviser to the Curators of the University Press in 1698 at the first meeting of that newly formed body, and seems to have been at once sent to Rotterdam to buy type for the University Press. He often visited Holland on business, and there are several references to him in the *Correspondence* of Dr. Richard Bentley, and in Hearne's *Collections*. In a letter from Dr. Barnes to Hearne, May 15th, 1709, "Landlord Crownfield has brought back the frontispiece [to Homer, printed 1711] rarely designed, from Holland". [T. Hearne, *Remarks and Collections*, ed. Doble, II. 198.] He was appointed Printer to the University February 11th, 170$\frac{5}{6}$, but previous to this we find printed for him, A. Tacquet, *Elementa Geometriae, cura Gul. Whiston*, 1703. From the time of his appointment to 1740, when he was succeeded by Joseph Bentham, a large number of important works were printed by him, amongst which may be mentioned, Dr. Bentley's editions of Horace (1711) and Terence (1726), the second edition of Sir Isaac Newton's *Philosophiae Naturalis Principia Mathematica* (1713), Wasse's edition of Sallust (1710), Sir Thomas Browne's *Christian Morals* (1716), *Historiae Ecclesiasticae*, 3 vols., folio (1720), Dr. Knight's *Life of Erasmus* (1726), Conyers Middleton's *Bibliothecae Cantabrigiensis ordinandae methodus* (1723) and his *Dissertation concerning the Origin of Printing in England* (1735), some being beautifully printed with the new type purchased from Holland, on paper specially purchased from the same source [see a note to Newton's *Principia* in Gray's *Newton Bibliography*, p. 7.] On February 25th, 17$\frac{39}{40}$, a resolution was passed to appoint a new inspector, and to allow the present, now infirm, to continue his full salary, and on March 24th, 1740, Joseph Bentham was appointed in the room of Crownfield [Bowes, *Cambridge Printers*, 313]. Crownfield died in 1743 and was buried in St. Botolph's parish on November 4th. His wife Mary had died in 1733. Several children are recorded in the parish registers. Two of his sons, Henry and Thomas, were educated at Clare College, and were subsequently ordained. Previous to his appointment as University Printer he lived in St. Edward's parish, but on his

appointment moved to the house attached to the University Press in Silver Street. Dr. Barnes, writing to Hearne *c.* September 24, 1708, says that he is lodging with Mr. Crownfield at the Printing House [Hearne, *Remarks and Collections*, II. 135.] He was a bookseller as well as a printer; Tacquet was printed for him in 1704 and later in various works printed by him he has a list of "Books Printed for and Sold by Cornelius Crownfield at the University Press in Cambridge".

CRUMP (JOHN), bookseller in London, Three Bibles, St. Paul's Churchyard, 1673–82. Began to publish in 1673 [*T.C.* I. 149.] In 1675 he published a novel entitled *Beraldus, Prince of Savoy*. [B.M. 12510. aaa. 3.] The last entry under his name occurs in Mich. 1682, when he published a political pamphlet called, *The True Loyalist*. [*T.C.* I. 503.]

CRUTTENDEN (HENRY), printer at Oxford, 1681–94. Anthony Wood had a Catalogue of books on sale by John Gellibrand of London dated 1682(?) which was given to him by Cruttenden the printer on the occasion of the execution of Stephen Colledge at Oxford on August 31st, 1681. [Wood, II. 553.] In 1684 he was threatened with proceedings for printing an edition of Cornelius Nepos, which Dr. Timothy Halton the licenser declared contained more than he had licensed. [*Ib.*, III. 86.] In 1687 Obadiah Walker, Master of University College, set up a Roman Catholic press in his house, aided by Cruttenden, who obtained the title of King's printer. [Madan, p. 19.] Cruttenden died in 1694, and Wood notes that he was buried in Holiwell Churchyard on October 12th. [Wood, III. 470.]

CRUTTENDEN (R.), bookseller in London, Bible and Three Crowns near Mercers' Chappel in Cheapside, 1718. Perhaps a son or brother of Henry Cruttenden (*q.v.*). In partnership with T. Cox, in which he appears to have succeeded S. Cliff (*q.v.*).

CULLEN (JOHN) stationer in London, The Buck without Temple Bar, 1710. The shop was bequeathed by Mary Hayes in her will, dated 1710 and proved 1713, and is described as being "heretofore in the occupation of Ephraim Dockwra bookseller decd . . . and now in the occupation of John Cullen citizen and stationer of London", and as having formerly been known as the Pestle and Mortar. The house with this latter sign was occupied in 1694 by Andrew Bell and Jonas Luntley (*q.v.*). [P.C.C. 136 Leeds.]

CUMBERLAND (RICHARD), bookseller in London, Angel in St. Paul's Churchyard, 1693–8. Mathematical and miscellaneous publisher. His first and last entries in the Term Catalogues were in Easter 1693, and Mich. 1698. [*T.C.* II. 458; III. 101.]

CUNYNGHAM (ALEX.), printer in Glasgow, before 1681. His will was registered February 25th, 1681. [Aldis, p. 112.]

CURLL (EDMUND), bookseller in London and Tunbridge Wells, (1) Covent Garden; (2) Peacock without Temple Bar, 1706–10; (3) (*a*) Dial and Bible, against St. Dunstan's Church, (*b*) next the Temple Coffee House in Fleet Street, 1710–23; (4) on the Walk, Tunbridge Wells, 1712; (5) Paternoster Row, 1720 [this and the preceding must be branch shops]; (6) over against Catherine Street in the Strand, 1723–6; (7) next to Wills's Coffee House in Bow Street, Covent Garden, 1729; (8) Burleigh Street, Strand, 1733; (9) Pope's Head, Rose Street, Covent Garden, 1735–47. 1705 (?)–47. Born, according to his own statement [*Curliad*, p. 14] in 1683, but perhaps in 1675, as the *Gentleman's Magazine* [XVII. 592] gives his age as seventy-two at his death in 1747. Curll came early from the West of England to London, and was apprenticed to a bookseller, "Mr. Smith by Exeter Change". Having served his apprenticeship he set up first a stall and then a shop in Covent Garden, where he probably carried on a purely retail trade. In 1706 he first appears in an imprint, publishing at "the Peacock, near St. Clement's Church in the Strand", a "reprint" [*D.N.B.*], really a reissue of the sheets, of Captain Bladen's translation of Caesar's *Commentaries*, published in the previous year by Richard Smith, who may be identified with his old master. In 1707 he pirated Prior's *Poems on Several Occasions*. In 1708 he published, in conjunction with E. Sanger, Dodwell's *Explication ... concerning the Immortality of Human Souls*, and Boileau's *Lutrin*. [*T.C.* III. 595–6.] The latter appears in his list of 1735 as still in stock. Curll declared in 1727 that the former was the first book printed by (i. e. for) him. [*Apology for the Writings of Walter Moyle.*] On September 13th, 1710, he made the first of his very few entries in *Stat. Reg.*, *Some Account of the Family of Sacheverell*, and he himself contributed to the controversy a pamphlet, *The Case of Dr. Sacheverell*, 1710. In this year he left the Peacock for the Dial and Bible close by, previously occupied by A. Boswill, and published there *A Complete Key to the Tale of a Tub*. Two years later he is found subscribing a guinea to the Bowyer

fund, and had prospered enough to have a branch shop at Tunbridge Wells. In 1716 began his long quarrel with Pope. He had had a hand in the publication by James Roberts of *Court Poems*, some of which are attributed in the advertisement to "the laudable translator of Homer". Pope was so annoyed that he arranged a meeting with Curll and Lintot at the Swan Tavern in Fleet Street, and there administered to Curll an "emetic potion"; he then published a satirical account of the affair, *A Full and True Account of a Horrid and Barbarous Revenge by Poison on the Body of Mr. Edmund Curll bookseller*, which was followed by other pamphlets. In the same year Curll first came under the displeasure of authority, being reprimanded at the bar of the House of Lords for breach of privilege in publishing a piratical edition of *An Account of the Trial of the Earl of Wintoun* [*Lords' Journals*, May 1716], and was also tossed in a blanket and beaten by the Westminster scholars for pirating, with many inaccuracies, their Captain's oration over Dr. South. In 1720 he apparently opened a branch shop in the City, in Paternoster Row, but continued to give the Dial and Bible as his address on imprints till at least 1723. In 1721 he was again convicted at the bar of the House of Lords, for an unauthorized edition of the Duke of Buckingham's *Life and Works*; and in 1725 and 1728 he was fined for publishing immoral books; on the latter occasion he was also imprisoned for five months, and used his imprisonment to acquire the copy of the *Memoirs* of John Ker of Kersland, for publishing which (as being defamatory of the Government) he was in the same year condemned to stand in the pillory at Charing Cross; the inconveniences of this he skilfully avoided by circulating among the crowd a leaflet stating that he was suffering for vindicating the memory of Queen Anne. He stated that of the most notorious of the indecent books he had been convicted of publishing in 1728 (*Venus in the Cloister*) he had sold only one chance copy; but this can hardly be true, as it appears, with the rest, in his list of 1735. In spite of all these transactions he is found in 1723–4 and again in 1728 offering his services to the Government. In 1733 his *Copy of the Will of Matthew Tindal*, one of a large series of wills and memoirs which led Arbuthnot to observe to Swift that Curll was "one of the new terrors of death", brought him into a violent quarrel with Eustace Budgell. His feud with Pope had continued intermittently since 1716. In 1726 he printed Pope's *Letters to Henry Cromwell*, of 1708–12, and Pope accused him in the *Dunciad* (Notes, ed. 1729) of, among many other things, clandestinely acquiring the copy

of these letters, a charge which Curll denied. But Pope's attack at large on Curll in the *Dunciad* is so strong that its victim is now generally remembered only as "dauntless Curll" and "shameless Curll". He replied at length in the *Curliad*, 1729, a valuable source of biographical details concerning its author. In spite of these amenities Pope is known to have secretly arranged the publication by Curll in 1735 of his *Literary Correspondence for Thirty Years*, and at the same time to have contrived to have the publication stayed by the Lords on a far-fetched and unsuccessful plea of breach of privilege. His object was to give excuse for and advertise his own authorized edition. Curll published his collection, which degenerated into a miscellany, in 1735–7, and Pope his in 1737–41. Curll had simultaneously moved to Rose Street, Covent Garden, and taken the sign of "Pope's Head", of which sign his device is no doubt a copy. Here he continued to publish, apparently more peacefully, until 1747, on December 11th of which year he died. His will, which was proved on July 21st, 1748, contains the following codicil of July 17th, 1742:

I have no relatives, my son is dead,
He left no issue, and his wife 's re-wed;
Therefore no legacys at all I leave,
But all I've got to my dear wife bequeathe.

[P.C.C. 209 Strahan.]

The son here referred to as dead by 1742 had a separate shop in 1726 and sold his father's books, while the latter was in conflict with the authorities; he appears to have been with him in Burleigh Street in 1733. Curll issued brief select lists of novels and of poems in 1719 [in *The Female Deserters* (printed for James Roberts), and Major Pack's *Miscellanies*], and of theology in 1723 [in Addison's *Miscellanies*], also a list of forty-three books issued from "over against Catherine Street in the Strand", i.e. not before 1723 [a copy is bound after John Hales's *Discourse*, 1720, B.M. 1113. g. 13]. Classified general lists appeared in 1726 [in Ashmole's *Order of the Garter*, 2nd ed., not in B.M.], and in 1735 [separately, B.M. G. 13457/2]. This last contains nearly two hundred items, including not only some of his earliest publications, but also those on account of which he had suffered fines and imprisonment, and is the basis of any bibliography of his productions. It may be compendiously said of Curll that while he possessed all the vices

attributed to him, he also possessed virtues which are too commonly ignored. Some of his publications are in the worst style of a bad period; many are libellous. He was pertinaciously defiant of authority, and malicious toward his enemies. But he is generally truthful, and his chief enemy, Pope, was the aggressor and deserved much worse handling than Curll gave him. The accusations against him of starving his hacks are apparently exaggerated, at least, if not quite false. Curll's classified list of 1735 shows that he was a large publisher of almost every sort of literature, especially of memoirs and of local history. A series of county histories, which he advertised as *Anglia Illustrata*, in 20 vols., and a bibliography of such books, entitled *The English Topographer*, alone give him a claim to gratitude; but comparatively few of his publications are worthless. In short, he was a man of considerable intellect, and an excellent man of business, who was troubled by few scruples. A vivid portrait of him is drawn by Amory in *John Buncle* (ed. 1770, IV, 138, &c.): "Curl was in person very tall and thin, an ungainly, awkward, whitefaced man. His eyes were a light grey, large, projecting, gogle and purblind. He was splay-footed, and baker-kneed. He ... was well acquainted with more than the titlepages of books. ... He was not an infidel. ... He was a debauchee. ... By filling his translations with wretched notes, forged letters and bad pictures, he raised the price of a four shilling book to ten. ... He died at last as great a penitent ... as ever expired." [W. J. Thoms, *Curll Papers* (reprinted from *N. & Q.*); *D.N.B.*; and sources quoted.]

CURTEYNE (AMOS), bookseller at Oxford, 1665–90. *See Dictionary*, 1641–67. Son of Henry Curteyne. Was established as a bookseller as early as 1664, when Anthony Wood bought books of him. [*Life and Times*, vols. i, ii.] He began to publish in 1670, when he advertised Edward Leigh's *Select and Choice Observations concerning all the Roman and Greek Emperors*, and, in partnership with George West and John Crosley, Charles Estienne's *Dictionarium Historicum, Geographicum, Poeticum*. [*T.C.* I. 45, 50, 62.] In 1676 Curteyne published Sir Henry Spelman's *De non temerandis Ecclesiis*. [*T.C.* I. 230.] His name appears in the Term Catalogue for the last time in Easter 1687, when he advertised *Institutio Logicae* by John Wallis and a duodecimo entitled *Of Education*. [*T.C.* II. 193–195.] He died in 1690.

CURTIS (JANE), bookseller in London, 1679–90. Wife of Langly Curtis (*q. v.*).

CURTIS (LANGLY), bookseller in London, (1) Goat Court, (*a*) on Ludgate Hill, (*b*) near Fleet Bridge; (2) Sir Edmonbury Godfrey's Head, near Fleet Bridge. 1668–90. Apparently all these addresses refer to the same shop. On February 16th, 1668 [i.e. 166$\frac{8}{9}$] he entered *The Quaker's Spirituall Cort* [sic] *proclaymed*. [*Stat. Reg.* Roxb., II. 397.] He published several papers in support of Oates and Bedloe, and amongst others *A Pacquet of Advice from Rome*, a weekly sheet the first number of which appeared on Friday, December 3rd, 1678. He and his wife Jane were frequently in trouble with the authorities. On February 7th, 16$\frac{79}{80}$ Jane Curtis was tried for printing a copy of verses reflecting on the Lord Chief Justice entitled *Scroggs upon Scroggs*, and in April 1683, Langly Curtis was ordered to pay £500 and stand in the pillory in Bloomsbury Market for publishing *Lord Russell's Ghost, or the Night Walker of Bloomsbury*. [*London Gazette*, April 21–24, 1683.] In this year he also printed an answer to Elkanah Settle's *Narrative* [Nichols, *Lit. Anecd.*, I. 43], after which nothing more is heard of him in the Term Catalogues, but Hazlitt traces him until 1690. [Haz. I. 456.]

CUTLER (ROBERT), *see Dictionary*, 1641–67.

D. (N.), bookseller (?) in London, Little Britain, 1674. Published a topical pamphlet in 1674. [Haz. I. 264.]

D. (P.), bookseller (?) in London, Little Britain, 1674. Published *News from the Exchange*, 1674. [Haz. III. 146.]

D. (S.), printer in London, 1695–7. Charles Peter's *New Observations on the Venereal Disease*, 2nd ed., was printed in 1695 by S. D. and D. N. [Haz. IV. 160], and in 1697 S. D. alone printed *Miscellanies over Claret*. [Haz. III. 300; Huth.]

D. (W.), bookseller in London. Possibly Walter Davis. These initials are found on many ballads and broadsides during the period of the Popish Plot.

DAGNALL (MATHIAS), bookseller at Aylesbury and Leighton Buzzard, 1658–1736. Probably son of Stephen Dagnall. [*See Dictionary*, 1641–67.] A tablet in the Lady Chapel of Aylesbury Church states that he died September 26, 1736, aged 78. His wife Sarah died in August 1736, aged 76. They left two sons, Matthias and Deverell. He dealt very largely in ballads.

DAGNEL (STEPHEN), bookseller at Chesham, Bucks, 1720. His name is found with that of a score of other provincial booksellers and chapmen, in the

imprint to a ballad entitled *Roger's Delight; or the West Country christning & gossiping*, Northampton, 1720. He was probably son of Stephen Dagnall, bookseller of Aylesbury, and brother of Mathias Dagnall (*q.v.*).

DALTON (ISAAC), printer and bookseller in London, Goswell Street, 1716–18. Published a weekly newspaper, *The Shift shifted*, of which no. 12 appeared on July 21st, 1716; in 1718 he is found printing, for W. Boreham, an edition of Skelton's *Tunning of Elinor Rumming*.

DANCER (NATHANIEL), bookseller and bookbinder in London, Fleet Street, *c.* 1700. Dunton [p. 228] says of him: "He was formerly a binder, but is now a noted bookseller in Fleet-street." His name is not otherwise known, and he was probably only a retail dealer.

DANIEL (M.), bookseller in London, 1671–5 (?). Possibly widow of Thomas Daniel. Published in partnership with T. Ratcliff, Madame de Villedieu's novel, *Love's Journal*. [Esdaile, p. 211.] May be the M. D. who published *The Starr-Prophet Anatomiz'd and Dissected*, by J. S., 1675. [Haz. II. 529.]

DANIEL (THOMAS), printer in London, 1669–70. Possibly successor to Roger Daniel. In company with Thomas Ratcliffe he printed for Philip Chetwind in 1669 the ninth edition of Earle's *Microcosmographie*. One T. D., printer, who may have been Daniel, was associated with William Downing about 1670.

DANVERS (   ), stationer in London, Temple Churchyard, 1689. Known from an advertisement of stolen books in the *London Gazette* of May 6th, 1689.

DARBY (JOHN), sen., printer in London, Bartholomew Close, 1662–1704. *See Dictionary*, 1641–67. In February 1684 he was convicted of printing a libel called *Lord Russell's Speech*; but escaped with a fine of twenty marks. [Nichols, *Lit. Anecd.*, VIII. 367.] Dunton [p. 247] has this notice of him: "I might call him the religious printer. He goes to Heaven with the Anabaptists but is a man of general charity. He printed that excellent speech of my Lord Russell and several pieces of Colonel Sydney, and is a true assertor of English liberties." Timperley [pp. 589–90] says that he died December 11th, 1704, in his 80th year. He was succeeded by his son John. Among his apprentices was Henry Woodfall.

DARBY (JOHN), jun., printer in London, Bartholomew Close, 1704–33. Son of the preceding. Contributed three guineas to the fund raised in

1713 for the relief of William Bowyer after his fire. In 1719 he printed for booksellers at Bath, Bristol, and Oxford, Arthur Bedford's *Serious Remonstrance* against the stage. In 1721–2 he printed for D. Browne the 8-vol. edition of Rushworth's *Historical Collections*. He died at Islington in the early part of 1733, his will being proved on February 3rd, 1732 [i.e. 173$\frac{2}{3}$]. He left an only child, Elizabeth, wife of Isaac Clarke, and desired that his executors should be cautious how they disposed of any of his copies of books or shares of copies, in case any of his grandchildren should become or marry a bookseller.

DARKER (   ), printer in London, *c.* 1690 (?). Dunton [p. 247] mentions "Mr. Darker" as having printed much for him, first in partnership with Mr. Newman in Little Britain, and later alone, till his death. His widow married a Mr. Grantham. He probably died too early to be identified with either Samuel Darker (*q.v.*).

DARKER (SAMUEL), printer in Exeter, 1698–1700. Printed, for Charles Yeo, John Pearce, and Philip Bishop, Richard Dunning's *Bread for the Poor*, 1698. In the same year he entered into partnership with S. Farley, and they printed together till 1700, three pamphlets from their press being known. [Dredge, 10, 11, 62, 94.] In 1700–1 a bookseller of this name is found in London. *See* below.

DARKER (SAMUEL), bookseller in London, (1) Jewen Street; and (2) (simultaneously) Three Legs, at the end of the Old Jewry, in Cheapside, 1700–1. Dealt in theological works. [*T.C.* III. 211, 253.] Possibly identical with the Exeter printer.

DARRACK (THOMAS), printer in London, *c.* 1700–10. Printed John Dunton's *Dissenting Doctors*, 2nd ed., and *Athenianism*, both in 1710, the former at least with Tookey. [Dunton, p. 696; Nichols, *Lit. Anecd.*, V. 80.]

DAVIDSON (JAMES), printer and bookseller in Edinburgh, 1724–64. Printed in partnership with Robert Fleming; the *Acts of the General Assembly* from 1724 to 1764 bear their imprint as printers to the Church of Scotland. In 1728 Davidson and Thomas Ruddiman were appointed conjoint printers to the University.

DAVIES. *See also* Davis.

DAVIES (ELEANOR), bookseller at Oxford, 1683. Sold John Speed's map of Canaan, advertised in Easter 1683. [*T.C.* II. 22.]

DAVIES (T.), bookseller in London, 1681. Publisher of no. 1 of *The Observator Observed, or Protestant Observations upon Anti-Protestant pamphlets*, 1681; nos. 2 and 3 were printed for J. Gilford (*q.v.*). Two books sold by him in this same year are recorded by Hazlitt [II. 90, 363].

DAVIES or DAVIS (THOMAS), bookseller in London. *See Dictionary*, 1641–67. Master of the Company of Stationers, 1668–70.

DAVIS. *See also* Davies.

DAVIS (R.), bookseller (?) in London, Three Ink Bottles, Castle Alley, near the Royal Exchange, 1709. Dealer in maps. In 1709 he sold H. Moll's *Theatrum Historicum*. [*T.C.* III. 647.]

DAVIS (RICHARD), bookseller in Oxford, 1646–88. *See Dictionary*, 1641–67. A catalogue of over a hundred books of all sorts printed for and sold by him is printed on the second leaf of H. Paleston's *Historical Essaies*, 1664. On June 25th, 1688, a portion of his stock was sold by auction. [*London Gazette*, June 11–14, 1688.]

DAVIS (ROBERT), bookseller in Bridgwater, 1716. Mentioned in a list of provincial booksellers contributed by W. C. B. to *Notes & Queries* [10th S., V. 141].

DAVIS (T.), bookseller in London, Red Lion Street, Whitechapel, 1698–1711. Published a divinity book in Hil. 1698. [*T.C.* III. 50.]

DAVIS (THOMAS), bookseller of Denbigh, 1699. Sold school books which he purchased of John Minshull, bookseller of Chester. [*Library*, 2nd ser., IV. 373–83.]

DAVIS (WALTER), bookbinder and bookseller in London, Amen Corner, 1676–87. In 1676 the following advertisement appeared in the Term Catalogue: "I am desired to give notice that, upon the death of Mr. Cutler, Mr. Walter Davis bookbinder, in the Stationers Rents in Amen Corner, is ready to undertake the publishing of new books, in the same manner, and upon the same terms, as Mr. Cutler did. R. Clavell." [*T.C.* I. 264.] His last entry in the Term Catalogues was made in 1686 [*T.C.* II. 165], but Hazlitt records a book with his imprint in 1687. [II. 285.]

DAVIS (WILLIAM), bookseller in London, (*a*) Bull, over against the Royal Exchange; (*b*) Black Bull, Cornhill, near the Royal Exchange. 1699–1705. Publisher of *Poems on several occasions*, said to be by a brother bookseller, Herbert Walwyn, 1699. In 1704 he published a play, *The Faithful Bride of Granada*, and in 1705 a comedy, *The Gamester*. [*T.C.* III. 412, 439.]

DAWES (GEORGE), bookseller in London, Chancery Lane, over against Lincoln's Inn Gate, 1665–85. *See Dictionary*, 1641–67. A list of books printed for and sold by him was inserted at the end of Dr. John Godolphin's *View of the Admirall Jurisdiction*, 2nd ed., 1685. [B.M. 517. b. 21.]

DAWKS (ICHABOD), printer in London, (1) Blackfriars; (2) Wardrobe Court, Great Carter Lane. 1673–1730. Eldest son of Thomas Dawks the younger. Born at Westerham in Kent, September 22nd, 1661. On May 16th, 1673, he went with his father to work at Mrs. Maxwell's printing office, but in the following year they transferred their services to Mrs. Flesher. Ichabod Dawks married on August 3rd, 1687. In 1694 he petitioned the Court of Assistants of the Stationers Company, representing the inconvenience of the press at Chester, and that it was reasonable to suspect that many of the late pamphlets might be printed there, there being no one to overlook it. The court agreed that a representation be made of it to one of the secretaries of State. [Records of the Stat. Co.] He is chiefly remembered as the founder of the newspaper known as *Dawks' News-Letter*, which was distinguished from other papers of the time by being printed on writing paper in script type, with a blank space left for correspondences. It continued until 1715, perhaps later; but copies are rare, and complete sets unknown. Dawks was also the printer of a sheet called *The Protestant Mercury*, issued in 1697. His name rarely appears in the Term Catalogue. He died February 27th, 1730, and was buried at Low Leyton. [*D.N.B.*, Timperley, p. 660; Nichols, *Lit. Anecd.*, I. 3, 72, 118, 373; II. 161; III. 176, 290–1; IV. 9.]

DAWKS (THOMAS), the elder, printer in London, 1635–70. *See Dictionary*, 1641–67. Died at Low Layton in Essex on May 11th, 1670.

DAWKS (THOMAS), the younger, printer in London, (1) Blue Anchor, west end of Paul's; (2) Blue Anchor, Ludgate Street; (3) Blackfriars; (4) end of Thames Street, next Puddle Dock; (5) His Majesty's British Printer, west end of Thames Street; (6) on Addle Hill in Carter Lane. 1652–96 (?). Son

of Thomas Dawks, printer [d. 1670]. Born at Kelmscott in Oxfordshire, October 8th, 1636. Admitted at Merchant Taylors' School, April 2nd, 1649. Began as a printer at the private press of the Master, W. Du Gard, and from 1652 to 1657 was employed as a compositor on Walton's Polyglot Bible; he afterwards worked at John Darby's printing house in Bartholomew Close. He married in December 1660, and his son Ichabod was born at Westerham, Kent, on September 22nd, 1661. On May 16th, 1673, Thomas and his son were working in the office of Mrs. Maxwell, from which they went to Mrs. Flesher's printing house on October 5th, 1673. Thomas Dawks set up as a master printer in Blackfriars in May 1674; in Hil. 1680 he and his son printed a *Methodical History of the Popish Plot*. [*T.C.* I. 384.] In the previous year, however, his address is given as The Blue Anchor at the west end of Paul's and also as in Ludgate Street. These evidently refer to one and the same house, which was doubtless a warehouse or shop for the sale of books, distinct from the printing houses. In the *True Protestant Mercury* of June 22–5, 1681, he advertised his removal to Thames Street, near Puddle Dock, and in 1685 his office was in Addle Hill in Carter Lane. His name occurs for the last time in the Term Catalogues in Easter 1689 [*T.C.* II. 252], but his entries there are few. The date of his death is unknown; but his name occurs as publisher of Dawks' *News Letter* on August 4th, 1696. His daughter Dorothy married first Benjamin Allport and secondly William Bowyer the elder. [*D.N.B.*; Nichols, *Lit. Anecd.*, I. 3, 4; Timperley, p. 660.]

DAWSON (ELIZABETH), bookseller in Cambridge, 1706–28. Widow of Thomas Dawson the younger; she continued to live in the High Street, and died in 1728, her will being, like her husband's, at Peterborough. On October 29th, 1725, the University passed a Grace "for remitting debt for books owed by Elizabeth Dawson".

DAWSON (THOMAS), the elder, bookbinder at Cambridge, 1675–95 (?). Mentioned in the will of Troylus Atkinson (*q.v.*) of 1675 as living in his freehold tenement the "Nag's Head". [Gray and Palmer, *Cambridge Wills*, 115.] *See* next entry.

DAWSON (THOMAS), the younger, bookseller at Cambridge, in the High Street, 1695–1706. Son of Thomas Dawson the elder. His name appears on five works printed for him at the University Press, 1695–1706. In this last year he published the *Lexicon Novi Testamenti Alphabeticum*, by John Dawson, a work

of renown, frequently reprinted, the sixteenth edition being published in 1822. The author, son of Thomas Dawson, and apparently a brother of his publisher, entered Christ's College, July 7th, 1693, as sizar. [Peile's *Biog. Register of Christ's College*, II. 128.] On the title of Censorinus, *de Die Natali*, 1695, the publisher is styled Thomas Dawson, jun. He died 1708, and his will is at Peterborough.

DEACON (B.), bookseller in London, Angel in Giltspur Street, 1699–1704. Dealer in popular literature. In partnership with J. Deacon. Most of their books are undated, but B. Deacon published editions of Richard Johnson's *Tom a Lincoln*, dated 1703, 1704, and 1705. [Esdaile, p. 85.]

DEACON (JOHN), bookseller in London, (1) Rainbow, Holborn, a little above St. Andrew's Church; (2) The Angel in Giltspur Street, without Newgate, 1682–1701. Publisher of all kinds of cheap and popular literature. Made his first entry in the Term Catalogues in Mich. 1682. [*T.C.* I. 509.] About 1694 he moved to the Angel in Giltspur Street, where he continued until 1701, or perhaps later.

DEACON (M.), bookseller in London, Horse-shoe in Giltspur Street, *c.* 1700. Hazlitt records *The Life and Death of Fair Rosamond*, with the above imprint. [Haz. I. 364.]

DEACON (S.), bookseller in London, Angel in Giltspur Street, *c.* 1700. Hazlitt records a copy of *The Garland of Love* with the above imprint. [Haz. I. 266.] Probably the widow of J. or B. Deacon.

DEAN (J.), bookseller in London, (1) Cranbourne Street, in Leicester Fields, near Newport House; (2) at the Queen's Head, between the Royal Grove and Helmet in Drury Lane. 1679–85. A publisher of broadsides. He moved to his second address in 1685. Among dated sheets by him are *The Loyal Conquest*, 1683 [B.M. 1872. a. 1 (32)], *Song of the Light of the Three Nations turn'd into darkness*, 1684 [Haz. II. 431], *Islington Wells, a song* [B.M. C. 20. f. 2 (167)], *The Royal General*, a ballad, 1684 [Bodl. Ashm. G. 15184], and *A Song upon the Rondizvous on Hounsley-Heath*, 1685 [Bodl. Ashm. G. 15187]. Dean's name does not appear in the Term Catalogues.

DEANE (ROBERT), papermaker, Chelmsford, Essex, 1686. Mentioned in a lawsuit in Trin. 2 Jas. II. [C.P.R. 3046, m. 416, verso.]

DEERE or DEEVE (JOHN), bookseller in London, Barnard's Inn Gate, Holborn, 1700–1. Dealer in law-books [*T.C.* III. 176]. He is mentioned as taking in advertisements for *The State of Europe*, 1701 [Burney, 99]. He is probably the person spoken of by Dunton [p. 292] as "unfortunate D—ve".

DEGRAVES (E.), bookseller in London, next the Fountain Tavern in the Strand, 1700. His name occurs in the Term Catalogue for Mich. 1700 as selling some divinity books. [*T.C.* III. 212.]

DEW (R.), bookseller in London, 1682. In 1681 he published *A Vindication of the Character of a Popish Successor* [B.M. T. 94* (13)], and also *Plato Redivivus* [*T.C.* I. 443], and in 1682 *Mr. Emerton's Cause*. [Haz. I. 144.]

DEWALL (JOSEPH), stationer in London, Globe near the New Exchange in the Strand, 1711. Only known from an advertisement of a lost box in the *London Gazette*, March 17th, $17\frac{10}{11}$.

DICEY (WILLIAM), printer at St. Ives, Hunts., near the Bridge, and at Northampton, 1719. Dicey is first heard of at St. Ives, where he began to print the *St. Ives Postboy*, afterwards called *St. Ives Mercury*, in 1719, in partnership with Robert Raikes. In 1720 the partners moved to Northampton and there founded (no. 1, May 2nd) *The Northampton Mercury*, and in 1721 they added (no. 1, January 31st) *The Northampton Miscellany*. In 1722 they founded *The Gloucester Journal*, but Dicey appears to have remained at Northampton, while Raikes became solely responsible for the Gloucester office. Dicey published at Northampton a number of chap-books; the first of these to be advertised in the *Mercury* was *The Force of Nature, or the Loves of Hippolito and Dorinda*, 1720. [B.M. 1078. i. 29 (2).] He also printed and distributed gratis lists of recent books. [R. Austin, *Robert Raikes*, in *The Library*, January 1915; *History of the Northampton Mercury* (*Mercury Extras*, no. 10); P. M. Eastman, *Robert Raikes and Northamptonshire Sunday Schools*, 1880.]

DICKIE (WILLIAM), bookseller in Glasgow, in the Salt Market, 1695–7. Sold the following books: R. Craghead's *Advice to Communicants*, 1695; *Spiritual Songs* [*c.* 1695], Thomas Hall's *Plain . . . Explication . . . shorter catechism*, 1697. [Aldis, p. 112.]

DICKINSON or DICKENSON (HENRY), bookseller at Cambridge, 1672–94. Nine works were printed for him alone or with other booksellers: Sir Isaac

Newton's edition of Varenius, *Geographia*, 1672, Lactantius, *Opera*, 1568, and with other booksellers his name appears as receiving subscribers' names for Torriano's *Italian Dictionary*, 1684, and Ray's *History of Plants*, 1686. His first and last entries in the Term Catalogues were Varenius, 1672, and J. Ellis's *Articulorum xxxix Defensio*, 1694. [*T.C.* I. 120; II. 493.] On "7 Feb. $167\frac{2}{3}$ dyed Mrs. Dickenson, Mr. Wootton's daughter of Malton, the wife of Mr. Dickenson, bookseller". [Alderman Newton's *Diary*, ed. Foster, p. 70.] It is probable that he was father of William Dickinson (*q.v.*).

DICKINSON (WILLIAM), bookseller at Cambridge, 1699–1718. Probably a son of Henry Dickinson (*q.v.*). Lived in the High Street, at what is now no. 1 Trinity Street, or next door, from 1699 to his death, and his widow until $173\frac{2}{3}$. He was one of the Churchwardens of Great St. Mary's, 1706. He died June 26th, 1718, aged 49, and was buried in the churchyard of Great St. Mary's Church. In his will, dated June 24th, 1718, he left to his son Nathaniel and daughter Sara "all my houses and estates in the parishes of St. Andrews and St. Buttolphs". His wife Rose, being executrix, proved the will July 31st following.

DICKSON (FRANCIS), printer and bookseller in Dublin, 1707–14. In 1707 he printed an edition of Defoe's *Caledonia*. In 1708 he joined with S. Powell to print *The Flying Post*, and in 1710 with Aaron Rhames to print an edition of *The Tryal of Dr. Henry Sacheverell*. In 1711 and 1712 he is found alone printing Dr. E. Synge's *Defence of himself* and a sermon by Berkeley on passive obedience.

DIGHT (WALTER), bookseller at Exeter, over against the Guildhall, 1667–93. "Walter Dight's house over against the Guildhall was no doubt the one afterwards occupied by the well-known Gilbert Dyer bookseller." [Dredge, 8.] He published chiefly theological books.

DOBSON (ELIPHAL), sen., bookseller in Dublin, Stationers' Arms, Castle Street, 1682–1720(?). His name appears in the imprint in Laurence's *Interest of Ireland*, 1682, as one of the booksellers, and as publisher of *Logica Elenctica*, by Thomas Goveanus, 1683 [*T.C.* II. 17], and Neal Carolan's *Motives of Conversion to the Catholick Faith, as it is professed in the Reformed Church of England*. [*T.C.* II. 247.] He published many works of value at that time. He was succeeded by his son (*q.v.*).

DOBSON (ELIPHAL), jun., bookseller in Dublin, 1720 (?). Son of Eliphal Dobson, sen. (*q.v.*).

DODD (   ), and Mrs., printers in London, *c.* 1720–4. Dodd married a daughter of Bliss, the Exeter printer. Thomas Gent (*q.v.*) knew and is said to have worked for him. On his death-bed Dodd exhorted his wife to employ Gent as her assistant, which she did. Gent found her printing office in great confusion; he left her service to go to York, where he married in 1724. According to Gent, Mrs. Dodd married again and fell into poverty; it does not appear whether she continued to print or not. [R. Davies, *Memoir of the York Press*, 1868, p. 158; T. Gent, *Life*, 1832, pp. 134, 136–7, 145, &c.]

DODD (A.), bookseller in London, Peacock without Temple Bar, 1714–31. In 1714 in partnership with others he published *The Ladies Tales*, and in 1719 a novel, *Charon, or, The Ferry Boat*. [Esdaile, pp. 254, 185.] Mr. F. G. Hilton Price mentions this bookseller as living in the Strand in 1723 [*Midd. & Herts. N. & Q.* II. 93.] He was still publishing in 1731. [Esdaile, p. 191.]

DODGINS (   ), bookbinder in London, *c.* 1700. Mentioned by Dunton [p. 258].

DOES (   ), bookseller in Sandwich, Kent, 1699. Advertised in *The Flying Post*, December 2nd, 1699, as selling Edw. Brown's sermon preached at the Kentish Feast, November 16th, 1699; he does not appear in the imprint to the book.

DOLLIF (FRANCIS), bookseller at Oxford, near the Mare-maid Tavern, 1681–90. In 1681 he published John Bennion's Assize sermon, *Moses' Charge to Israel's Judges* [Bodl. Wood $\frac{633}{12}$]; an edition was advertised in 1683 by R. Davis [*T.C.* II. 2]; in the index Arber gives this to Dollif. [*T.C.* II. 636.] In 1690 he gave Anthony à Wood a catalogue of "A curious collection of musick books". [Wood, III. 332.]

DOWLEY (   ), bookbinder in London, *c.* 1700. Mentioned by Dunton [p. 261].

DOWNES (GEORGE), bookseller in London, Three Flower de Luces, over against St. Dunstan's Church in Fleet Street, 1676–81. Publisher of law-books. Made his first entry in the Term Catalogues in Mich. 1676, and his last in Hil. $168\frac{1}{2}$. [*T.C.* I. 263, 469.]

DOWNING (JOSEPH), printer and bookseller in London, St. Bartholomew's Close, 1670–1724. He may have been some relation of William Downing the printer, whose name appears in the list of printing houses in London in 1675. But there is reason for believing that Joseph Downing was at work as a printer as early as 1670. Downing was the printer of the piratical edition of Danvers's *Treatise of Baptism*, complained of to a House of Lords Committee in 1677 by Francis Smith [*q.v.*, and Hist. MSS. Comm., Rept. ix, App., p. 78.] In 1707 he issued *A New Catalogue of Books* [B.M. 11900. a. 16 (1)]; and in 1708 he printed a broadside, *Proposals for erecting Libraries in Wales*. [Harl. 5958 (51).] In the same year he published Defoe's *Account of some Remarkable Passages in the Life of a Private Gentleman*. As a bookseller Downing dealt almost entirely in theological literature, and a list of eight of his publications is given at the end of the Rev. John Burrough's *Two Sermons*, which were printed and sold by him in 1714. [B.M. 4454. b. 38 (2).]

DOWNING (W.), printer at Oxford, 1673. Printed in 1673 an edition of Juvenal with the imprint: "Oxford by W. Downing for F. Oxlad Senior." [Haz. II. 323.] Possibly identical with William Downing, of London (*q.v.*).

DOWNING (WILLIAM), printer in London, (1) Great St. Bartholomew's Close; (2) George Court, St. John's Lane. 1675–1720. Possibly identical with the Oxford printer of the name (*q.v.*). First met with in a list of printing houses in London, issued in 1675, when he is referred to as one who had set up since the Act was in force [S.P.D., Car. II, vol. 369, p. 97]. *A Reply to . . . the D. of Buckingham's Letter*, printed by W. D., 1685, may be from his press. In 1690 he reprinted the *Dublin Intelligence*. At the time of the fire at W. Bowyer's premises there were two printers of the name of Downing, who contributed to his relief fund [Nichols, *Lit. Anecd.*, I. 62–3.] In 1720 Edward Ward's *Delights of the Bottle* was printed by W. Downing at the second of the above addresses.

DRANT (T.), bookseller in London, Ship in St. Mary Axe, 1675. In company with T. Lacey he published in 1675 *Syncrisis, or, the most natural and easie method of learning Latin by comparing it with English* [*T.C.* I. 219], and Cocker's *Morals* [*ib.*, B.M. 1077. l. 6 (6)]. Another work which he published in this year was Richard Head's *Proteus Redivivus*. [*T.C.* I. 197.]

DRAPER (RICHARD), bookseller in London, Golden Ball by Aldgate, 1680–2 (?). His name is given as one of those selling *Methodical History of the late . . . Popish Plot*, 1680. [*T.C.* I. 384.] He may be the R. D. who published Francis Osborn's *Works*, 8th ed., 1682. [Haz. I. 311.]

DREW (MATTHEW), printer in London, 1673–5. Head's *Canting Academy*, 1673, was printed for him by F. Leach. [Haz. I. 206.] His name occurs in the List of Printing Houses in London of 1675, as having "set up since the Act [of 1662] was in force". [S.P.D., Car. II, vol. 369, p. 97.] *The Starr-Prophet Anatomiz'd and Dissected*, by J. S., was printed in 1675 for M. D., who may be Drew.

DRING (DANIEL), bookseller in London, Harrow and Crown, Fleet Street; at the corner of Clifford's Inn, 1695–6. Probably a son of Thomas Dring, whom he succeeded at this address. He published two anonymous poems on the death of Queen Mary. [*T.C.* II. 559.] In Trin. 1696 he advertised Abraham Du Quesne's *New Voyage to the East Indies*. [*T.C.* II. 588.]

DRING (THOMAS), bookseller in London, (1) White Lion, Fleet Street, (*a*) at, (*b*) next, Chancery Lane; (2) Blue Anchor, Fleet Street, over against Fetter Lane; (3) Harrow, Fleet Street; (*a*) at the corner of, (*b*) next, Chancery Lane; over against the Inner Temple Gate. 1668–94. Son of Thomas Dring (1649–68, *q.v.*, *Dictionary*, 1641–67). Dealer in law-books, plays, romances, and general literature. In 1673 he moved to the Blue Anchor and in 1674 to the Harrow. He died early in 1695 and in the Term Catalogue for Trinity Term in that year is a notice that some of his stock was to be sold by N. Rolls, D. Brown, and J. Walthoe. [*T.C.* II. 563.]

DRUMMOND (   ), bookseller in London, 1668–9. Only known from a note in the State Papers to the effect "that Mr. Drummond bookseller, now in Holland, can inform where the books, *Vox et Lacramentum* [*Lacrimae*] *Anglorum* and *The Painter* are printed. [S.P.D., Car. II, vol. 251, p. 194.]

DRURY (SAMUEL), bookseller in London, Golden Lion and Lamb, White-chapel, over against the Haymarket, 1702–3. Dealer in theological books His first and last entries in the Term Catalogues are in 1702 and 1703. [*T.C.* III. 283, 366.]

DUCHEMIN (   ), widow, bookseller in London, The Sacrifice of Abraham, over against Somerset House, 1705. Recorded by Mr. Hilton-Price in his *Signs of the Old Houses in the Strand in the 17th and 18th Centuries*. [*Midd. & Herts. N. & Q.* II. 157.]

DUFFIELD (EDMUND), printer (?) in Oxford, 1683. [Madan, p. 30.]

DUMBAR or DUNBAR (ANDREW), bookseller in Edinburgh, at the Tron-Kirk, 1684. His name occurs in the imprint to *Certamen mathematicum, betwixt George Liddell and James Paterson* (Aberdeen. Printed by John Forbes . . . and are to be sold by Andrew Dumbar Book-seller at the Tron-Kirk in Edinburgh). He is believed to have married the widow of William Jaffray, stationer. [Aldis, pp. 112, 115.]

DUNCAN (JAMES), printer and type-founder in Glasgow, near Gibson's-Wynd, in the Salt-Market Street, 1717–*c.* 1750. Up to 1720 he printed in partnership with William Duncan, but after that date he worked alone. In 1718 he is styled a letter-founder, and on October 2nd, 1719, he was appointed printer to the town. [John M'Ure, *History of Glasgow*, 1830, p. 370.]

DUNCAN (WILLIAM), printer in Glasgow, in the Salt Market, 1717–*c.* 1760. Up to 1720 he printed in partnership with James Duncan, but from that date until 1760, or later, he worked alone. [John M'Ure, *History of Glasgow*, 1830, p. 370.]

DUNLOP (JAMES), bookseller in Glasgow, 1676–83. James Durham's *The Law Unsealed*, Edinburgh, 1676, was sold by him and other Glasgow booksellers. His name occurs among the debtors in the inventory of A. Anderson in 1676. The James Dunlope, one of G. Lithgow's debtors in 1662, was probably the same. Will registered September 22nd, 1683. [Aldis, p. 112.]

DUNMORE (JOHN), bookseller in London, near the sign of the Woolpack in Ivy Lane; (2) Three Bibles in Ludgate Street. 1669–81. *See Dictionary*, 1641–67. In 1674 Daniel Elzevir sent him 2,000 copies of Grotius, *De Veritate Religionis Christianae*, which were seized by the Custom House, but afterwards released. [S.P.D., Car. II, vol. 369, pp. 61, 62.] In 1679 he sold the library of Sir Edward Bysshe, the herald. He was the publisher, with Dring, Tooke, Sawbridge, and Mearne of a fine edition of Cicero's *Works*, 1681, printed by E. Horton from the types of J. Grover. [*T.C.* I. 455.]

DUNTON (JOHN), bookseller in London, (*a*) Raven, (*b*) Black Raven; (1) in the Poultry, (*a*) at the corner of Prince's Street, near the Royal Exchange, (*b*) over against the Stocks Market; (2) in the Poultry, over against the Compter; (3) in Jewen Street. 1674–1700 (?). Born at Graffham, Huntingdon, May 4th, 1659, son of the Rev. John Dunton, he was at first intended for the Church, but dis-

appointing his father's expectations was apprenticed in about 1674 to Thomas Parkhurst the bookseller. During his apprenticeship he headed an address of the Whig prentices against one of the Tories, and he seems to have been already somewhat volatile in conduct. After the expiration of his term he set up as a bookseller, at first taking only half a shop. He took to "printing", i.e. publishing, at once; his first books being Thomas Doolittle's *The Lord's Last Sufferings*, 1681 [*T.C.* I. 458], and Stephen Jay's *Daniel in the Den*, a sermon by John Shower, and a collection of his father's funeral sermons, entitled *The House of Weeping*, with a memoir by himself. He made a success with his publications, and opened a shop at the Black Raven, at the corner of Prince's Street, where in 1685 he published *Maggots*, being the anonymous juvenile poems of Samuel Wesley, father of John and Charles. Dunton had in 1682 married Elizabeth, daughter of Dr. Samuel Annesley, a leading Nonconformist preacher. In 1685 his business received a check by the "universal damp upon trade, occasioned by the defeat of Monmouth in the West"; he went to Boston in New England to sell a cargo of books and at the same time recover debts to the extent of £500 owed him there, his business being largely in Puritan theology. Here he visited Elliot, who presented him with twelve copies of his Indian Bible. Dunton returned in 1686, but having given surety for £1,200 for a brother-in-law, was compelled to seek refuge in a tour in Holland and Germany. He returned in 1688 and opened a new shop opposite the Poultry Compter, with the old sign of the Black Raven, and tells us that he remained there ten years "with variety of successes and disappointments." [*Life and Errors*, pp. 151–2.] But his last entry in the Term Catalogues from this house was in 1694, after which he only made one more entry, in 1696, from the Black Raven, Jewen Street. After 1688 Dunton published copiously, some of his ventures being "projects" of his own, noteworthy among these being the *Athenian Gazette*, 1689–95, *The Post-Boy Robbed of His Mail* (a collection of letters), and a laudatory life of Judge Jeffreys. In the course of his career Dunton claims to have printed 600 books (employing a large variety of printers), and to repent of but seven. In 1692 he attained the Livery of the Stationers' Company. His first wife died in 1697; in the same year he married Sarah Nicholas of St. Albans, with whom and her mother he quarrelled over the non-payment of his debts. Soon after his second marriage he visited Dublin with a cargo of books, and became engaged in a quarrel with a bookseller there, Patrick Campbell (*q.v.*), which he

set forth at length with much else in his *Dublin Scuffle*, 1699. Dunton was now compelled to hide from his creditors and so to give up his business; he employed his enforced leisure in much writing, in which growing insanity clearly appears. But in 1703 he wrote *The Life and Errors of John Dunton* (S. Malthus, 1705), in which he gives not only his autobiography, but characters of a vast number of his contemporaries in the book trade, which have been of the greatest value in the compilation of this *Dictionary*. After this he fell further into poverty. In the notes to the *Dunciad* Pope calls him "a broken bookseller and abusive scribbler". He lived till 1733. [*Life and Errors*, ed. with memoir by J. B. Nichols, 1817; *D.N.B.*]

DURRAM or DURHAM (MICHAEL), stationer at Newcastle-upon-Tyne, 1675. Admitted to the Newcastle Stationer's Company, July 22nd, 1675. [Welford, *Early Newcastle Typography*, p. 128.]

DURSTON (THOMAS), printer in Shrewsbury, 1714.

DYER ( ), stationer in London, Rose in Bread Street, *c.* 1700. Partner with Alexander Merreal at the Rose in Bread Street. Dunton [p. 256] says of him: "He was a fair dealer and a pious man. . . . I bought a great deal of paper of him."

DYMOCK (THOMAS), bookseller at Oxford, 1681. In 1681 he was defendant in an action for assault brought by Bartholomew Sprint, bookseller, against a number of booksellers and printers. Details are wanting. [C.P.R., Trin. 33, Chas. II, 2992, m. 256.]

EATON (JOSEPH), bookseller in Liverpool, 1710.

ECKELSTON (EDWARD), bookseller in London, Peacock, Little Britain, 1683. Publisher of Dr. John Barnard's *Theologo-historicus*, 1683. [*T.C.* II. 6.]

EDDOWES (S.), bookseller in London, (1) next the Fleece Tavern, Cornhill, 1682; (2) Blue Anchor, under the Piazza of the Royal Exchange, Cornhill. 1682–93. First entry in the Term Catalogue, a medical book, H. Stubbe's *Select Observations* in Mich. 1682. In 1683 he sold Quevedo's *Visions*, 6th ed., published by Herringman. Last heard of in 1693. [*T.C.* I. 514; II. 34, 473.]

EDLIN (JOHN), printer in London, (1) Dutchy Lane in the Strand, 1719; (2) near the Savoy; (3) (?) Prince's Arms over against Exeter Exchange. 1719–32. Began as a bookbinder. In *The Weekly Packet* of April 18–25, 1719, it is

recorded that last Saturday a fire broke out . . . at Mr. Edlin's a Bookebinder in Dutchy Lane in the Strand". He printed proposals for Stackhouse's *History of the Bible*, "got credit of paper, brushed up his old battered letter, picked up a poor compositor or two . . . and began to be very clamorous for copy". [Stackhouse's *Bookbinder, Bookprinter and Bookseller*, 1732.] Joined by Thomas Edlin. [*Mid. & Herts. N. & Q.* III. 18.]

EDLIN (THOMAS), bookseller in London, 1721–8. One of the publishers of Defoe's *Moll Flanders*, 1721, and *Fortunate Mistress*, 1724. [Esdaile, pp. 202–3.]

EDWARDS (DAVID), printer in London, Nevil's Alley in Fetter Lane, 1694–1701. His imprint is first found on a broadside entitled *The Widow Whiterow's humble Thanksgiving*, 1694. [B.M. T. 1762 (7).] He succeeded A. Baldwin as the publisher of *The New State of Europe* [B.M. Burney 117 B]. In 1696 he was defendant in a suit brought by the Company of Stationers against certain printers and booksellers for printing Primers and Almanacs. In his answer Edwards declared that he printed about thirty or forty gross of black and white Primers for William Spiller. He sold some to a bookbinder named Meade. [Chan. Proc. before 1714, Collins $\frac{486}{100}$, P.R.O.] In 1701 the publication of *The New State of Europe* was taken over by M. Edwards, probably David's widow, at the same address.

EDWIN (JONATHAN), bookseller in London, Three Roses, Ludgate Street, 1671–9. Dealt in all kinds of literature, from sixpenny pamphlets dealing with the lives of pirates and murderers, to folio histories and classics. His first entry in the Term Catalogues was in Mich. 1671, of *Fifty-one Sermons* by Dr. Mark Frank. [*T.C.* I. 84.] In the same year he published a novel, *Amorous Travellers*. [Esdaile, p. 148.] In 1674 he was selling T. Flatman's *Poems and Songs*, published by B. Tooke. Amongst Edwin's more important publications may be noticed an edition of Caesar's *The Welch Common Prayer Book for the use of Churches*, 1678. He made his last entry in the Term Catalogues in Easter, 1679. [*T.C.* I. 348.] He was a staunch Royalist and Churchman, issuing several books against the Presbyterians and Dissenters.

EGLESFIELD (FRANCIS). *See Dictionary*, 1641–67. He made his last entry in the Term Catalogues in 1676.

EGLESFIELD (JOHN), bookseller in London, Marigold, Fleet Street, (*a*) over against the Globe Tavern, (*b*) near Salisbury Court. 1681–6. In all probability related to Francis Eglesfield (1637–76). First heard of in 1681, when he was defendant in an action for assault brought against him by John Jennings. Details are wanting. [C.P.R. Trin. 33 Chas. II, Roll 2992, m. 256.] His name first appears in the Term Catalogues in 1683 [*T.C.* II. 30], and he was the publisher of Henry Bold's *Latin Songs* in 1685 and 1686. [*T.C.* II. 114, 168.]

EGLESFIELD (THOMAS), bookseller in London, (1) Brazen Serpent, St. Paul's Churchyard; (2) Little Britain. 1652–84. Omitted from the *Dictionary*, 1641–67. In 1652 he published Major Cosmo Manuche's *The Royal Lovers, A Tragi-Comedy*, with the first of the above imprints, which had once been the printing house of Reginald Wolfe. In 1683–4 he became surety for Francis Eglesfield, gent., of St. Mary Cray, Kent, doubtless a relative. [C.P.R. Hil. 35–36 Chas. II, Roll 3020, m. 31 recto.]

EIRES (HENRY), bookseller in Warrington, 1704–12. [*N. & Q.*, 10th S., V. 242.]

EKINS (NATH.). *See Dictionary*, 1641–67. He made his last entry in the Term Catalogues in 1673. [*T.C.* I. 143.]

ELLIOTT (ROBERT), printer (?) in Oxford, 1693–6. [Madan, p. 31.]

ELLIS (C.), bookseller in Mansfield, Notts., 1690. Published in Mich. 1690 *Religion and Loyalty inseparable* (a Nottingham Assize sermon), by a namesake and perhaps a relative, Clement Ellis, Rector of Kirby, Notts, "Printed for W. Rogers at the Sun in Fleet Street; and C. Ellis in Mansfield." [*T.C.* II. 329.]

ELLIS (EVAN), printer in London, 1722. According to Gent [p. 118] he printed "the bellman's verses at Christmas".

ELVIES or ELVIS (THOMAS), stationer in London, Strand, 1688. Defendant in an action for the recovery of a debt brought by George Emery. Elvies is also described as a "tanner" of the city of Stafford. [C.P.R. 3068, m. 1640, Trin. 4 Jas. II.]

EVANS (SAMPSON), bookseller in Worcester, 1674–91. First appears in an advertisement for a lost book in Trin. 1674. [*T.C.* I. 183.] His name also appeared in Mich. 1676, as one of the publishers of *Γραφαυταρκεια, or the Scripture's Sufficiency* [*T.C.* I. 250], and in 1681 he published G. Wall's *Sermon preached to the natives of . . . Worcester*. [Bodl. Sermons. 21 (6).] In Mich.

3 William & Mary (1691) an action was commenced against him by Joshua Sharpe and Lucy Singleton for the recovery of a debt. [C.P.R. Mich. 3 W. & M., Roll 3101, m. 400 recto.]

EVELEIGH (ROBERT), bookseller at Exeter, 1668–81. Mr. Dredge [p. 93] only records one book as published by Robert Eveleigh, discourses by Thomas Mall and others, entitled *Of Holy Living*, "London: Printed for William Grantham . . Westminster Hall . . . sold by Robert Eveleigh, Bookseller in Exon." He was still there in 1681, when his name is found in an advertisement of the sale of Dr. W. Outram's library, in the *London Gazette*, November 17th–21st.

EVERINGHAM (ROBERT), printer in London, Seven Stars, Ave Mary Lane, 1680–1700. The earliest notice of this printer that has been found is the imprint of No. 5, &c., of a news-sheet called *Mercurius Civicus*, "Printed by R. E. in Ave Mary Lane for the author. 1680." On October 7th, 1680, he printed a *Weekly Advertisement of Books* [Timperley, p. 560]; in the same year on April 10th there appeared in *Smith's Currant Intelligence* a notice by Colonel Thomas Blood, repudiating Everingham's editions of *The Narrative*. In 1699 he printed *Fruit-Walls Improved*. [Haz. III. 58.] See Whitledge (R.)

EVERSDEN (GEORGE), bookseller in London, Adam and Eve, St. John's Lane. *See Dictionary*, 1641–67.

EVERSDEN (HENRY), *see Dictionary*, 1641–67.

EVETS (EDWARD), bookseller in London, Green Dragon in St. Paul's Churchyard, 1683–1705. His first and last entries in the Term Catalogues were in 1683 and 1705. [*T.C.* II. 20, III. 454.]

EWREY (WILLIAM), bookseller in London, Golden Lyon and Lamb over against the Middle Temple Gate in Fleet Street, 1680 (?)–9. Possibly identical with the W. E. who published *The English Gazette* (afterwards *The Westminster Gazette*), No. 1, December 22nd, 1680, &c., to be sold by T. Fox. In 1689 he published a sermon by W. Wilson, rector of St. Peter's, Nottingham. [B.M. 226. g. 10 (13).] At the end are advertisements of other books sold by him.

F. (E.), printer in London, 1672. Printed T. Willis's *De Anima Brutorum* . . . for R. Davis of Oxford, 1672. [Haz. III. 268.] These initials may be those of

the widow of James Fletcher or Flesher the printer (died 1670), who was still in business in 1675.

F. (F.), bookseller in London, 1679. These initials appear on the imprints to *An Answer to Blundell the Jesuit's Letter*, 1679 [B.M. 515. l. 2 (24)], and *The Deposition . . . of the late . . . Plot*, [1679.] [Bodl.]

F. (N.), bookseller in London (?) 1681. Hazlitt [II. 343] records *A Letter out of Scotland, from Mr. R. Le [Strange] to his Friend H. B. in London. Printed for N. F. in the year* 1681. Folio, 2 leaves.

F. (W.), bookseller in London, 1696. These initials, with those of M. G. (probably Mathew Gilliflower), are found in the imprint to an edition of Quarles's *Emblems* of 1696. [Haz. II. 506.] In all probability they stand for William Freeman.

FABIAN (MARY), bookseller in London, Mercers' Chappel in Cheapside, 1698–1701. Perhaps widow of Thomas Fabian, some of whose publications were also issued by her. Her first and last entries in the Term Catalogues are in Trin. 1698, and Mich. 1701. [*T.C.* III. 87, 276.] She was succeeded at this address by J. Baker.

FABIAN (THOMAS), bookseller in London, Bible in St. Paul's Churchyard, 1676–93. This is perhaps the person alluded to by Dunton [p. 292] as "Lord" Fabian. His name appears for the first time in the Term Catalogues in Easter 1676, when with Abel Roper and others he advertised a folio Josephus. [*T.C.* I. 241.] He was also the publisher of William Drummond's *History of Scotland* in 1681. The bulk of his publications were divinity. Fabian's last entry in the Term Catalogues was made in Mich. 1693. [*T.C.* II. 471.] Mary Fabian may have been his widow.

FAIRBROTHER (S.), printer in Dublin, 1714–34. In 1720 he printed *A Collection of several Statutes* relating to His Majesty's Revenue of Ireland, in 1724 the Charter empowering Erasmus Smith to erect Grammar Schools in Ireland, and in 1725 the 13th ed. of L'Estrange's version of Seneca's *Morals*. In 1723 he was printer to the Irish House of Commons.

FAITHORNE (HENRY), bookseller in London, Rose, St. Paul's Churchyard, 1681–8. Publisher to the Royal Society. He first appears in partnership with J. Kersey, in Hil. 168 0/1. [*T.C.* I. 426.] He published *Weekly Memorials for the Ingenious*, a critical account of recent publications. In 1686 he and his partner advertised proposals for a folio edition of John Ray's *General*

History of Plants. [*T.C.* II. 162.] Some time in 1687 Kersey's name disappears, and Faithorne carried on the business alone until Trin. 1688 [*T.C.* II. 232], after which nothing more is heard of him, unless he be the H. F. who appears in the imprint to *The Muses' Farewel to Popery and Slavery*, 1689. [Haz. III. 200.]

FARLEY (SAMUEL), printer at Bristol, St. Nicholas Street, near the Church, 1712–25. There were two printers of this name, one in Bristol and one at Exeter. Samuel Farley of Bristol was the printer of the *Bristol Postman*, a weekly paper that began to appear in 1712, and was discontinued in 1725.

FARLEY (SAMUEL), printer at Exeter and Salisbury, 1699–1727. In 1699 Samuel Darker of Exeter was joined by Farley, and together they printed several books of local interest until 1701, when Farley is found printing by himself. He appears to have settled in the parish of St. Paul's, Exeter, some time in 1699 and he continued to print in Exeter until 1715, when he removed to Salisbury. In 1705 he was joined by Joseph Bliss, but the partnership only lasted three years. On September 24th, 1714, Farley issued the first number of *The Exeter Mercury, or Weekly Intelligence of News*, but he transferred this to Philip Bishop in 1715, before leaving Exeter. He returned to Exeter in 1723 and started Farley's *Exeter Journal*. In November 1727, the burial of Samuel Farley is recorded in the register of St. Paul's, Exeter. He was succeeded in business by Edward Farley, probably a son. [Dredge, *passim*.]

FARNWORTH (B.), bookseller in Newark, 1715–19. His name is found in an advertisement in the *Evening Post*, December 3rd–5th, 1719.

FARY (ROBERT), bookseller in London. The Bell in Gracechurch Street, 1713. An octavo edition of Phaedrus's *Fables* printed in 1713 bears the imprint "London: Printed by H. Meere, for Robert Fary, Druggist, at the Bell in Gracechurch Street, M.DCC.XIII", and on the back of the title-page three other works, including the *Comedies* of Terence, were advertised as printed for R. Fary.

FAWCET (FRANCIS), bookseller in London, King's Head and Crown, near Durham Yard in the Strand, 1701. Publisher of the Rev. Tho. Knaggs's *Sermon against Atheism*, preached 1700. [B.M. 226. h. 3 (18).]

FAWKNER (J.), bookseller (?) in London, at the Talbot on London Bridge, 1698. Publisher of John Shower's funeral sermon on Mrs. Jane Papillon, who died July 12th, 1698. [B.M. 1418. c. 21.]

FAYRAM (F.), bookseller in London, 1721–9. In conjunction with a number of others he published novels written or translated by Penelope Aubin. [Esdaile, pp. 155–6, 263.]

FELTHAM (ANTHONY), bookseller in London, Westminster Hall, foot of Parliament Stairs, 1691–9. With W. Whitwood he published in 1692 *The Experienced Farrier*, by E. R. Gent. [*T.C.* II. 397.] In 1693 they issued Dr. John Archer's *Secrets disclosed or a Treatise of Consumptions*. [*T.C.* II. 479.] The last entry under his name in the Term Catalogues was the 3rd ed. of Thomas Bray's *Course of Lectures upon the Church Catechism*. [*T.C.* III. 119.] Dunton [p. 292] nicknamed him "smiling Feltham".

FELTON (ANTHONY), *see* Feltham.

FELTON (JOHN), bookseller in Newport, Shropshire, 1679–80. William Thackeray (*q.v.* below and in *Dictionary*, 1641–67) sold him goods to the value of £200 and had to sue him in the King's Bench for the recovery of the money. [C.P.R. Trin. 33 Chas. II, Roll 2995, m. 1876 verso.]

FENNER (ENOCH), bookseller at Canterbury, Bible and Crown behind St. Andrew's Church, 1703–29. Son of Rest Fenner I (?) (*q.v.*). He was in business by himself in 1703, when he published *The Expert English Schoolmaster*, by Thomas Lydal, schoolmaster at Canterbury. [*T.C.* III. 379.] He died in 1729, his will being proved on September 9th. The contents of his shop he directed to be sold, his wife Margaret to have the interest of the proceeds for life. He left a son, Rest Fenner, who succeeded him in the business, and he nominated as his executors Robert Knaplock, William Mount, and Samuel Birt, all booksellers of London. [Probate Registry, Cant. Arch. Reg. 87, f. 36.]

FENNER (REST) I, bookseller and stationer in Canterbury, 1663–1711 (?). It is not clear whether there were three or four booksellers of this name. The first appears in 1663 [*Dictionary*, 1641–67]; the last is too late for our period. In 1678 the stock of Mercy Browning of Amsterdam (*q.v.*) was bought by a Rest Fenner of Canterbury, and an action was brought against him by Nathaniel Ponder for the value of part of it supplied by him. [Chanc. Proc. Before 1714, Reynardson, Bundle 428, 132.] In 1687 and 1689 he published

in conjunction with London publishers a novel, *Cynthia* [*T.C.* II. 193], and N. Greenwood's *Astronomia Anglicana*. [*Lond. Gaz.* July 1st–4th, 1689.] Fenner's name does not appear in the imprint to the latter. The will of Rest Fenner, senior, of Canterbury, stationer, dated January 16th, 1709, was proved on December 29th, 1711; his executors were his sons Rest and Enoch (*q.v.*); the position of his house is not stated.

FENNER (REST) II, bookseller in Canterbury, Mercery Lane, 1681–1711. Son of Rest Fenner I. Apprenticed to his father and took up his freedom as a citizen of Canterbury in 1681. In 1702 R. Ferner [*sic*] jun., Mercery Lane, Canterbury, published with E. Tracy of London, James Brome's sermons, *A Seasonable Warning to all hardened Sinners*, preached at Newington near Hythe. In 1711 he was named executor to his father's will.

FERRABY (GEORGE), bookseller in Hull, 1718–25. His name occurs in the imprint to the *York Mercury* as one of those by whom advertisements for the paper were taken in. [Davies, *Mem. of York Press*, p. 133.]

FICKUS (JOHN), bookseller in Oxford, 1682–6. [Madan, p. 31.]

FICKUS (THOMAS), bookseller in Oxford, Holywell, 1681–4. On August 1st, 1681, Anthony à Wood [II. 549] mentions "Thomas Fickus a stationer newlie set up in Holywell". In Easter 1682 he advertised *Hierocles upon the Golden Verses of the Pythagoreans*, and in Hil. 1684, *Praecipuorum Theologiae Capitum Enchiridion didacticum*, by George Tully, Principal of St. Edmund's Hall. [*T.C.* I. 486, II. 65.]

FIRTH (ISAAC), stationer in London, Little East Cheap, 1707. His name is met with in an advertisement of lost property in Povey's *General Remarks on Trade*, September 29th to October 1st, 1707. [Burney 140.]

FISH (JOHN), bookseller in London, (1) Golden Tun in the Strand; (2) Adam and Eve in Hungerford Market. 1681–1703. He published at the first address given above a broadside entitled *The Speech and carriage of Stephen Colledge* in 1681 [B.M. T. 1.* (109)], and at the latter he advertised a patent medicine in the *Post Man* on February 26th–28th, 170$\frac{2}{3}$.

FISH (WILLIAM), stationer in London, St. Martin's in the Fields, 1686. The sheriffs of London sued to recover against him a debt of £40, in the Court of Common Pleas, Hil. 2–3 Jas. 2. [C.P.R. 3055, m. 1888 recto.]

FISHER (HENRY), bookseller in Wrexham, 1700. Sold school books and devotional works, which he purchased wholesale of John Minshull, bookseller of Chester. [*Library*, 2nd ser., IV. 373–83.]

FISHER (JOHN), printer in St. Ives, Hunts., Tedd's Lane, 1716–18. Printed the first Huntingdonshire newspaper, *The St. Ives Post*. [H. E. Norris in *N. & Q.* 10th S. VIII. 201.]

FISHER (WILLIAM), bookseller in London, at the Postern Gate, Tower Hill, 1657–90. *See Dictionary*, 1641–67. Was still in business in 1690. He took R. Mount into partnership between 1684 and 1687. [*T.C.* II. 108, 195, 321.] An entry by Hazlitt [II. 529] of a book printed for an otherwise unknown William Firder in 1684 may be an error for William Fisher.

FLEMING (ROBERT), printer in Edinburgh, 1724–78. One of the printers to the Church of Scotland. From 1724 to 1764 he printed in partnership with James Davidson.

FLETCHER, or FLESHER (MRS.), printer in London, Little Britain, 1670–8 (?). The widow of James Fletcher. Her name occurs in a list of the printing-houses in London in March 1675. [*State Papers Dom.*, Car. II, vol. 369, 97.] She may be identical with the E. F. (*q.v.*) mentioned in some imprints between 1670 and 1678. She was a daughter of Cornelius Bee, bookseller.

FLETCHER (JAMES), printer in London, 1652–70. *See Dictionary*, 1641–67. The business was continued by his widow (*q.v.* above).

FLETCHER (STEPHEN), bookseller in Oxford and London, 1714–27. Born in 1680 at Salisbury, and apprenticed to F. Oxlad sen. Hearne was one of his customers, and on April 1st, 1716, records that Fletcher was a candidate for the place of verger of the university, which the Statutes required should be filled by a stationer, but he withdrew in favour of "one Pottle", who was neither bookseller nor stationer. [Hearne's *Collections*, Oxf. Hist. Soc. V. 192.] In 1719 he proposed to print *Marmora Oxoniensia*, and consulted Hearne, who dissuaded him from the undertaking. [*Ib.* VII. 6.] In 1721 Fletcher bought the library of Dr. John Keil, giving £220 for it. [*Ib.* VII. 301.] On August 22nd Hearne writes to J. Murray: "Stephen Fletcher (called by some *positive* Fletcher, and by others *pos* Fletcher) is gone to Shirbourne in

Dorsetshire, to get some of Mr. Jo. Pullen's books now selling there." [*Ib.* VII. 395.] Fletcher died in London on September 12th, 1727. From Hearne's notice, it appears that Fletcher had a shop at Westminster as well as at Oxford. Hearne's sketch of his character is not flattering. [*Ib.* IX. 347–8.]

FLETCHER, or FLESHER (THOMAS), bookseller in London, (1) Angel and Crown, St. Paul's Churchyard; (2) Old Change, over against Distaff Lane. 1677–86. In partnership with Jonathan Edwin, he entered in the Term Catalogue of Mich. 1677 John Nalson's *Common Interest of Kings and People*. [*T.C.* I. 293.] In June 1685 John Noakes recovered against him in the Common Pleas a sum of £60. [C.P.R. Trin. 1. Jas. II, Roll 3038, m. 1861 recto.] Fletcher removed to Old Change about 1685. He published one or two medical books. His last entry in the Term Catalogues was in Hil. 1686. [*T.C.* II. 159.]

FORBES (JOHN), the elder and the younger, booksellers and printers at Aberdeen, 1656–1704. *See Dictionary*, 1641–67.

FORD (JOHN), bookseller in London, at the Middle Temple Gate, Fleet Street, 1671–3. Joined Thomas Collins, their first joint entries in the Term Catalogues being *The History and Relation of a Journey of . . . Lord Henry Howard from London to Vienna* [*T.C.* I. 73], and John Wilson's comedy, *The Cheats*, both in Easter 1671. They were also the publishers of Shadwell's comedy *The Miser* in 1672, and in the same year of the *Reliquiae Wottonianae*. In 1673 they published John Evelyn's translation from Rapin, *Of Gardens*, and a miscellaneous *Collection of Poems*. Nothing further is heard of Ford, though Collins continued the business for some years later.

FORREST (EDWARD). *See Dictionary*, 1641–67.

FORREST (JOHN). *See Dictionary*, 1641–67.

FORRESTER (ANDREW), bookseller and bookbinder in London, next door to the Mitre Tavern in King's Street, Westminster, 1676–80. In 1676 he sold Seller's maps, and in 1678 was one of those who sold W. Walgrave's *Decimal Arithmetick*. [*T.C.* I. 301.] He reprinted *A true Narrative of the reception of their Royal Highnesses . . . in Scotland*, 1680. [B.M. T. 100* (158).] His business was carried on later by P. Forrester.

FORRESTER (P.), bookseller in London, King's Street, Westminster, 1687. Probably a son or brother of Andrew Forrester. Hazlitt records a Proclamation by James II as published by him in 1687. This house seems to have been the recognized agency for the publication of Scottish literature.

FORRESTER (SUSANNA), bookseller (?) in London (?) 1685. Perhaps widow of Andrew Forrester. Hazlitt records *A Publication of the Royal Authority of . . . James the Second*, "Edinburgh, printed . . . Reprinted at London by Tho. Newcomb for Susanna Forrester, 1685." [Haz. II. 311.]

FORSTER (JOHN), bookseller in Dublin, Skinner Row, 1704–5. Published in 1704 and 1705 a sermon and a tract by E. Synge. [Bodl. Serm. 19; B.M. 498. a. 28.]

FOSTER (BENJAMIN), bookseller in London, Three Flower de Luces, Poultry, 1672. He advertised James Janeway's *Token for Children*, 1672. [*T.C.* I. 122.]

FOSTER (JOHN), printer (?) in London, Greyhound, Pye Corner, 1697. Only known from the imprint to a ballad about a murderer. [Haz. II. 348.]

FOSTER (MARMADUKE), bookseller in London, Black Swan at Amen Corner, 1685. In partnership with Awnsham Churchill at the above address in 1685, when they published the Rev. Samuel Master's *Discourse of Friendship*. [B.M. 226. g. 12 (17).]

FOSTER (STEPHEN), bookseller in London, (1) Angel on London Bridge; (2) Sun and Bible on London Bridge. 1679–80. Associated with J. Collier, but the partnership was of short duration, as Foster shortly afterwards moved to the Sun and Bible. His last entry in the Term Catalogues was in Hil. 1680. [*T.C.* I. 383.]

FOULKES, or FOWKES (EDWARD), bookseller in London, Saracen's Head, Chancery Lane, 1664–75. *See Dictionary*, 1641–67.

FOWLER (JOHN), bookseller in Northampton, 1714–19. Subscribed for Walker's *Sufferings*, 1714. His name is mentioned in a list of those receiving subscriptions for R. Bradley's *Philosophical Account of the Works of Nature*, 1719.

FOX (JOSEPH), bookseller in London, Seven Stars, Westminster Hall, 1686 (?)–1746. The following notice appeared in the *General Advertiser* of November 25th, 1746: "On Sunday morning [November 23rd] died in the 83rd year of his age, Mr. Joseph Fox, sen. who kept a bookseller's shop in Westminster Hall, upwards of sixty years. He was also eminent for sending written News Letters to most parts of the Three Kingdoms. He is succeeded in both parts of his business by his son, who has been partner with him these Twelve

Years past." In the Term Catalogue of Hil. 1691, A. Roper and J. Fox entered a play called *Sir Anthony Love, or the Rambling Lady*, and two satires on Dr. W. Sherlock, *The Weesils*, and *The Weesil Trap'd*. [*T.C.* II. 347.] In 1696 he sold for the author James Whieston's *Englands Calamities Discover'd* . . . [Haz. IV. 176.] Fox also had a shop in Tunbridge Wells during the season there.

FOX (THOMAS), bookseller in London, (1) Angel in Westminster Hall; (2) White Hart, Fleet Street, over against St. Dunstan's Church. 1679–91. What relation, if any, this bookseller had to Joseph Fox, is unknown. Thomas Fox appears to have begun business in the Hall in 1679, when his name appears in the Term Catalogue as one of the publishers of a *History of Edward II*. [*T.C.* I. 368.] In the same year he is found selling *Cottoni Posthuma* [*T.C.* I. 376], and in 1680 *Behemoth*, a pamphlet in answer to Hobbes. [*T.C.* I. 387.] On Wednesday, December 22nd, 1680, he started *The English Gazette*. After seven numbers had been issued, the title was altered to *The Westminster Gazette*, but the venture came to an untimely end in January 168⁰⁄₁. Fox was also one of the publishers of the *Proceedings* at the trial of the seven bishops in 1688. [*T.C.* II. 251.] His name appears in the Term Catalogues for the last time in Easter 1691. [*T.C.* II. 361.]

FRANCKLIN, or FRANKLIN (RICHARD), bookseller in London, Sun in Fleet Street, 1720–1. Published N. Amhurst's *Familiar Epistle from Tunbridge Wells*, 1720. [Wrenn, I. 8.] He also wrote in 1721 an answer to Amhurst's *Epistle to Sir John Blount*. [Bodl. G. Pamph. 2716.]

FREEBAIRN (ROBERT), printer and bookseller in Edinburgh, (1) his shop in the Parliament Close; (2) his printing-house in Forrester's Wynd. 1705–37. A son of David Freebairn, bishop of Edinburgh. He settled at Edinburgh as a bookseller, and in 1706, having purchased the printing-house which John Spottiswood had imported for the purpose of printing law books, he began to print. Many important books printed in Edinburgh during the next few years bear his imprint. In 1711 he obtained a gift of the office of Queen's printer for forty-one years from the expiration of Andrew Anderson's privilege; one-third of this gift he made over to John Baskett, and one-third to James Watson. At the Rebellion in 1715 he retired to Perth and printed for the Pretender. [W. J. Cowper, *The Pretender's Printer*, 1918, and *The King's Press at Perth*, 1715–16, 1919.] For this his gift was declared forfeit,

but he afterwards returned to Edinburgh and resumed the style of royal printer. His assigns continued printing till 1752.

FREEMAN (   ), bookseller in Durham, 1713–19. Mentioned in the *Memoirs* of Ambrose Barnes [p. 458] as in business at Durham in 1713. In a list of provincial booksellers printed in *Notes and Queries* he is given as still there in 1719. [*N. & Q.* 10th Ser. V. 183.]

FREEMAN (WILLIAM), bookseller in London, (1) Artichoke, Fleet Street, (*a*) next St. Dunstan's Church, (*b*) over against the Devil Tavern, (*c*) near Temple Bar; (2) Bible, Fleet Street, over against the middle Temple Gate. 1682–1713 (?). Began as a publisher in 1682, and from that time onwards did a large and general business. He moved in 1690 or 1691. Dunton [p. 215] says of him, "He is of a courteous affable nature, and very obliging to all he has to do withal; and I found (by that small correspondence I have had with him) he was bred, as well as born, a gentleman." In 1713 he contributed five guineas to the Bowyer Fund. [Timperley, p. 600.]

FRITH (JOHN), bookseller in London, Little Eastcheap, 1682–94. His name is found as publishing a broadside in 1682 [Haz. II. 346], and in an advertisement of the sale of a shop, in the *City Mercury* of June 11th, 1694. [Burney, 112 A.]

FURBY (   ), bookseller (?) at Tenterden in Kent, 1699. His name appears in an advertisement of the publication of the Rev. Edward Brown's Kentish Feast sermon, in *The Flying Post* of December 2nd. It does not appear in the imprint to the book.

FURDER (WILLIAM), bookseller in London, 1684. Known from *The Store-House of Nature expos'd to view*, printed for him in 1684. [B.M. 546. g. 33.]

FYNDAL (   ), printer at Oxford, 1716. A printer at the Theatre in Oxford. There is no evidence that he was a master-printer. Hearne records under date of August 10th, 1716, that a fellow of St. John's, Whately by name, had married Fyndal's daughter. [Hearne's *Collections*, Oxf. Hist. Soc., V. 274.]

G. (J.), printer in London, 1650–88. These initials occur frequently between the dates given. [Haz.] They may possibly stand for J. Grantham (*q.v.*), whose name appears on books of 1682–4.

GAIN, or GAYNE (JOHN), printer in London, 1681–7. In Trin. 33. Chas. II (1681) he was sued by the Stationers' Company for illegally printing primers; but won the case. [C.P.R. 2992, m. 441.] In 1685 he was defendant in an action for debt brought by Elizabeth Jenning, executrix of the will of Jane Jenning. [C.P.R. Mich. 1. Jas. II. 3040, m. 821 recto.]

GALLOT (   ), printer at Oxford, 1673. A compositor of this name is mentioned by Anthony à Wood [II. 261, 264] in connexion with his *Historia et Antiquitates Universitatis Oxoniensis*, 1673.

GALT (JAMES), bookseller in Glasgow, 1675. T. Vincent's *Catechism*, Edinburgh, 1675, was sold by him.

GARDINER (   ), printer in London, Lincolns Inn Fields, 1724. Mentioned by Negus as a Roman Catholic printer.

GARDINER, or GARDNER (FINCHAM), bookseller in London, (1) Three Roses, Ludgate Street; (2) White Horse, Ludgate Street. 1682–4. Mainly a publisher of divinity; but in 1682, he was one of the publishers of Sir William Dugdale's *Antient Usage of . . . Armes*. He is perhaps the person alluded to by Dunton [p. 293] as "prudent" Gardner.

GARDNER (ROBERT), printer in Belfast, 1713–34. This printer was the third who practised the art in Belfast.

GARRET (JOHN), bookseller in London, (*a*) at the foot of, (*b*) going up, the stairs of the Royal Exchange out of Cornhill, 1676–97. Probably the successor of Thomas Jenner; he dealt in maps, gazetteers, &c. Dunton [p. 292] has a reference to "*Indenture* Garret". He may have got the name by selling printed indenture forms. His first and last entries in the Term Catalogues were made in Hil. 1676 and Mich. 1679. [*T.C.* I. 227, III. 39.]

GARRETT (WILLIAM), bookseller in London, 1622–74. *See Dictionary*, 1641–67.

GARTHWAITE (MARY), bookseller in London, Golden Lion in St. Bartholomew's Hospital, 1670. Widow of Timothy Garthwaite. Advertised W. Walker's *Treatise of English Particles* in 1670. [*T.C.* I. 61.]

GASCOIGNE (J.), bookseller in London, Wapping Stairs, 1682. Advertised *A new map of Carolina* in 1682. [*T.C.* I. 513.]

GAVETT (RICHARD), *see* Gravett.

GAYNE (JOHN), *see* Gain.

GEE (ROBERT), bookbinder in Cambridge, 1675–81. In 1675 he was living in a tenement adjoining the dwelling-house of Troylus Atkinson in the parish of Great St. Mary. He died in 1681. The inventory of his goods, dated December 22nd, 1681, ccxlvij*li*. vs. ij*d*. in total, has items "For all his working tools both, for presses for other, bords, past bords v*li*." "For all the books and paper ccij*li*. xviij*s*. ij*d*." [Gray and Palmer's *Cambridge Wills*, 115, 123.] His wife Frances died July 1684. Her goods were valued at £29 9*s*., with no mention of books or shop.

GELLIBRAND (EDWARD), bookseller in London, Golden Ball in St. Paul's Churchyard, 1675–82. Mainly a divinity publisher, but he also published Sir John Temple's *Irish Rebellion*, 1679, and the 4th ed. of Sir William Temple's *Observations on the United Provinces*, 1679 [*T.C.* I. 377], and the 2nd ed. of the latter's *Miscellanea*, 1681. His last entry in the Term Catalogues was in Mich. 1682. [*T.C.* I. 503.] He was probably a son of Samuel Gellibrand, who carried on business at this address until 1675. John Gellibrand (*q.v.*) may have been his younger brother.

GELLIBRAND (JOHN), bookseller in London, (1) west end of St. Paul's Churchyard; (2) Golden Ball, St. Paul's Churchyard. 1680–4. Mainly a publisher of Latin books. His first and last entries in the Term Catalogues are in 1680 and 1684. [*T.C.* I. 385, II. 99.] The Golden Ball does not appear in his address till 1683, and then his name is never found with Edward Gellibrand's in an announcement; but it is reasonable to suppose that they were in partnership, as they used the same address.

GELLIBRAND (SAMUEL), bookseller in London, 1637–75. *See Dictionary*, 1641–67.

GENT (THOMAS), printer in London and York, (1) London, near the Two Fighting Cocks in Fleet Lane: (2) York, Coffee-Yard. 1710–78. Only the early part of this printer's career concerns us, as it was not until the close of 1724 that he set up in York. He was born in Ireland on May 4th, 1693, and was apprenticed to Powell the Dublin printer (*q.v.*) about 1706, but was hardly treated by him and ran away. Arriving in London in August 1710 he at once found employment with Edward Midwinter of Pye Corner, a printer of broadsides and chapbooks, and remained with him till 1713, after which

he worked successively for short periods for Mrs. Bradford, a Quaker printer, and Mears, and then as a "smouter", i. e. casually. On April 20th, 1714, he set out on foot for York, and there entered the service of John White (sen.). He remained in this employment a year, and fell in love with White's granddaughter and maid Alice Guy, whom he was later to marry. He is said to have been dismissed by White upon the latter's learning that he had broken his apprenticeship with Powell; but he himself says that his term being over he wished to visit his parents, and was "offered to be continued". He visited Dublin, where he worked for Hume, and was seized by Powell. In 1716 he was back in London with Midwinter, and in 1717 was made a member of the Stationers' Company. Leaving Midwinter a second time he worked for John Watts and John Wilkins successively, and in 1718 revisited Dublin, where he was again employed by Hume. On his return to London he took service with Francis Clifton, a Roman Catholic printer, and was engaged in a mysterious piece of illicit printing for Atterbury. Soon after this he was with Midwinter again. Clifton had printed for him a satire, *Teague's Ramble*, and in 1722 he cut woodcuts to an abridged *Robinson Crusoe* for Midwinter. In 1722 or 1723 he set up for himself in Fleet Lane and printed *A Collection of Songs*, and (with Hotham) a book of emblems entitled *Divine Entertainments*, with ballads and bills for the cockpits. Meanwhile he continued "smouting" for other master-printers. After his departure from York he had kept up a correspondence with Alice Guy, and the news of her marriage to Charles Bourne, his fellow workman under White, was a severe blow. He wrote a poem, *The Forsaken Lover's Letter to his former Sweetheart*, and gave it to Dodd the printer, who sold thousands of copies. At Dodd's death Gent undertook the management of the press for Mrs. Dodd, but in 1724, on hearing of Bourne's death, he hastened to York and married the widow on December 10th, in spite of the younger White's opposition. He thus became a master-printer, the only one in York, and almost the only one in the North of England. The first books he printed were sermons, Thomas Clarke's *The True Foundations of a Nation's Greatness*, printed for F. Hildyard [1724], and Samuel Johnston's *The Advantage of Employing the Poor*, printed for R. Mancklin [1725]. He also issued *The Original York Journal*, a continuation of *The York Mercury*. White, who was printing at Newcastle-on-Tyne, set up a branch press in York, in opposition to Gent, and though the latter printed actively for many years, his business gradually failed and he fell into poverty,

dying in 1778 at the age of eighty-six. He wrote several topographical works of value, including a *History of York*, 1730, and a life of himself, partially edited in 1832 by Joseph Hunter, from which most of the known details of his life are drawn. He seems to have suffered from a violent and suspicious temper; the *Life* is full of abuse of others and praise of himself. [*Life*; Davies, *York Press*; *D.N.B.*]

GERARD (J.), bookseller in London, Cornhill, 1692. Known as the publisher of a broadside, *A True and Impartial Account of the . . . Earthquake . . .*, 1692. [Haz. I. 264.]

GIBBS (J.), bookseller in London, 1689. Published a pamphlet called, *The Character of a true English Protestant Souldier*, 1689. [B.M. T. 1702 (6).]

GIBBS (ROBERT), bookseller in London, Golden Ball, Chancery Lane, 1650–75. *See Dictionary*, 1641–67. Still in business in 1675, when he entered in the Term Catalogue an edition of Richard Baxter's *Two Disputations of Original Sin*. [*T.C.* I. 204.]

GIBSON (R.), bookseller in London, Roebuck, between the Two Temple Gates, Fleet Street, 1703–4. Advertised in 1703–4 a divinity book, a play, and a political pamphlet. [*T.C.* III. 366, 371, 401.] He may be identical with the subject of the next entry.

GIBSON (ROBERT), bookseller in London, Golden Hat Block in Middle Row, Holborn, 1700. Offered a gratuity of one shilling in the pound, to any one who would help him to the buying of any library or parcel of books. His advertisement appeared in a sheet called *The Infallible Astrologer*, 1700, which also contained a few other booksellers' advertisements. He may be identical with the subject of the preceding entry.

GIFFORD (ANN), bookseller in London, 1722. Possibly widow or one of the daughters of Robert Gifford (*q.v.*). Her name occurs in the imprint to *The Obliging Husband*, 1722.

GIFFORD (ROBERT), printer, bookseller and bookbinder in London, in Old Bedlam, without Bishopsgate, 1689–1721 (?). Publisher of broadsides, chapbooks, and other popular literature. His shop was in the porch or gateway of Bethlehem Hospital. He is first met with in Easter 1689, when he advertised a Jest Book. [*T.C.* II. 257.] He is probably the "Mr. Gifford"

mentioned by Dunton [p. 260] amongst bookbinders that worked for him. "He now keeps a shop in Old Bedlam, and having printed several copies that have sold well he will, if he continues Fair-keeping, get a lumping portion for his daughters." At the beginning and end of *England's Witty and Ingenious Jester*, by W. W. Gent, published by Gifford in 1717, are lists of books printed and sold by him.

GILBERT (THOMAS), bookseller in Oxford, 1669–77. Published the writings of Theophilus Gale, of Magdalen College. [*T.C.* I. 14, 21, 56, 105, 285], and apparently nothing else.

GILBERT (WILLIAM), bookseller in London, Half-Moon, St. Paul's Churchyard, 1672–4. Publisher of popular and cheap literature, amongst which may be noticed a book of songs and catches called *Westminster Drollery* and *A Compendium, containing exact rules to be observed in the composing of two or more parts, either for vocal, or instrumental musick*. His first and last entries in the Term Catalogues were made in 1672 and 1674. [*T.C.* I. 95, 151, 188.]

GILBERTSON (J.), bookseller in London, Sun and Bible on London Bridge, 1684. Advertised in the Term Catalogue of Hil. 1684 an edition of "Joseph ben Gorion's" *History of the Jews*. [*T.C.* II. 65.] At a later date J. Williamson and H. Green held these premises.

GILBOURNE (PERCIVAL), bookseller in London, the Narrow, at the corner of Chancery Lane, in Fleet Street, 1697–8. He sold the 2nd ed. of Lassel's *Travels in and Through Italy*, 1697, and in 1698 he published *The Daily Communicant*. [*T.C.* III. 33, 75.]

GILES (EDWARD), bookseller in Norwich, (1) St. Andrew's parish; (2) near the Market Place. 1678–1703. In 1678 he had on sale the Rev. John Collinges' *Several Discourses concerning the actual providence of God* [*T.C.* I. 329], and in 1680 the same divine's *Defensative Armour against four of Sathans most Fiery Darts*. [B.M. 4409. d. 19.] From 1678 to 1691 he published sermons, &c., by other Norfolk clergy. [*T.C.* II. 26, 41, 68, 93, 134, 378.] In 1695 a catalogue of books printed for him was appended to Martin Finch's *Sermon upon the death of the Rev. John Collinges*. In 1696 he published John Stackhouse's *Mutual Duties of Elders and People*, but the date of the copy in the British Museum is 1698. In the *London Gazette* of December 2nd, 1689, is an advertisement of a sale of books by Edward Millington, the great London auctioneer, at Mrs. Oliver's house in Norwich, and catalogues were to be had of E. Giles. Dunton [p. 237] in a brief notice praising his honesty, speaks of him as alive (1703).

GILLIFLOWER (MATTHEW), bookseller in London, Westminster Hall, (1) The Sun; (2) The Spread-Eagle; (3) Spread Eagle and Crown or Black Spread Eagle; and in Oxford. 1671–1702. One of the most important of the Westminster Hall booksellers. His name appears for the first time in the Term Catalogue in Mich. 1671, when he published, with Richard Lowndes, Sir Robert Cotton's *Cottoni Posthuma*. Amongst the many other interesting works he either sold or published were William Harvey's *Anatomical Exercises* [*T.C.* I. 123], Sir Henry Spelman's *Law Terms*, 1683, Montaigne's *Essays*, 1685–6, and the sixteenth edition of Chamberlayne's *Angliae Notitia*, 1687. In 1688, in company with James Partridge and Samuel Heyrick, he was appointed one of the printers to the House of Lords, a contract which they sublet. Gilliflower is last heard of in 1702. [*T.C.* III. 313.] Oxford appears as his place of imprint in 1700. [Madan, p. 31.]

GILLWORTH (PETER), bookseller at Newcastle-under-Lyme, 1684. Published Cawdry's *Certainty of Salvation*, 1684. [B.M. 4902. cc. 2.]

GITTINS (THOMAS), bookseller in Shrewsbury, 1715–16. Publisher of W. Powell's *Ways that lead to Rebellion laid open*, 1715–16. [B.M. 225. g. 19 (7).]

GLEN (JAMES), printer and bookseller in Edinburgh, 1656–87. *See Dictionary*, 1641–67.

GODBID (ARTHUR), printer in London, near the Grate, Little Britain, 1680–2. Probably a son of William Godbid (*q.v.* in *Dictionary*, 1641–67), and like him printed music. In partnership with J. Playford. Letterpress productions known from their press are: 1680, J. Davies's *Instructions for History*. [*T.C.* I. 382], and *A Seasonable Corrective to the new Project for the Good of England*, broadside, for Clavel [B.M. T. 1* (93)]; 1681, Daniel Nicols's *Sermon preached in the Cathedral of Lincoln*, July 18th, 1681, for Joseph Lawson of Lincoln [B.M. 694. d. 11 (6)], and an address to the King from the Mayor of Gloucester, broadside. [B.M. T. 1* (29).]

GODBID (WILLIAM), printer in London, 1656–77. *See Dictionary*, 1641–67.

GODDARD (THOMAS), printer and bookseller at Norwich, in the Market Place, 1703–19 (?) His name first appears in the Term Catalogues in 1703 as selling

Benjamin Whichcot's *Moral and Religious Aphorisms*. [*T.C.* III. 360.] In 1706 he was the publisher of *The Norwich Postman*, which was printed by S. Sheffield [Timperley, p. 592], and, among other books, of the Rev. J. Chorley's *Metrical Index to the Bible*, 1711, which was printed by William Chase of Norwich (*q.v.*). In 1713 he printed *An Abstract of the several Acts of Parliament relating to Norwich* [Bodl. Gough. Norf. 59 (3)], and his name occurs again in the proposals for printing Richard Bradley's *Philosophical Account of the Works of Nature*, 1719.

GODWIN (JOSEPH), bookseller and printer in Oxford, upper end of Catstreet, 1637–73. *See Dictionary*, 1641–67. Mr. A. C. Clark notes that he died in 1673. He left a son Joseph. [Wood, V. 304.] Mr. Madan [p. 29] enters him as a printer.

GOLDING (EDWARD), bookseller and printer in London, Rainbow Court, Aldersgate Street, 1683–91. During the years 1683–4, his name appears in the Term Catalogues as publishing four books, chiefly of divinity. [*T.C.* II. 50, &c.] He also printed John Blagrave's *Evil Spirit Cast-out*, 1691. [Haz. III. 19.]

GOOD (JAMES), bookseller in Oxford, near the Theatre, 1681–5. Published *Effigies Amoris in English*, 1681, and *A Sermon before the King*, by G. Ironside, 1685. [*T.C.* I. 465, 484; the latter is in Bodl., Mar. 187.]

GOODALL ( ), bookseller (?) in London, Golden Cross, Cornhill, near the Royal Exchange, 1679–80. A Mr. Goodall, a neighbour of Benjamin Harris, gave evidence at the trial of the latter in 1679. In 1680 a pack of cards illustrating the Popish Plot was to be sold by Mr. Goodall at the above address. [*T.C.* I. 384.]

GOODMAN (JOHN), bookseller in London, 1688. Publisher of a broadside, *A True Copy of a Paper delivered by the Lord De . . . shire to the Mayor of Darby*. [B.M. T. 100* (186).]

GOODWIN (JOHN), printer or bookseller at Oxford, 1694. [Madan, p. 31.]

GOODWIN (TIMOTHY), bookseller in London, (1) Maiden-Head, over against St. Dunstan's Church in Fleet Street; (2) Queens' Head, against St. Dunstan's Church in Fleet Street. 1683–1720. This eminent bookseller began publishing in Mich. 1683. [*T.C.* II. 44.] Dunton [p. 284] has this character of him: "He is esteemed a very honest man; and what he engages upon is either very

useful or very curious. Mr. William Rogers, Mr. Harris, and myself were once partners with him in publishing some *Dying Speeches*, and I observed a more than ordinary openness and justness in his dealings . . . He is Dr. Sherlock's bookseller, and printed Abp. Tillotson's Works, in conjunction with Mr. Ailmer." It was Goodwin who started the subscription for the relief of William Bowyer the elder, heading the list of subscriptions with ten guineas. [Nichols, *Lit. Anecd.* I. 60.] In 1694 he changed his sign to the Queens' Head. He died in 1720. [Timperley, p. 622.] The following publications by Goodwin are not recorded in the Term Catalogues: *A true copy of a Paper written by Capt. Thomas Walcot at Newgate*, 1683 [B.M. T. 100* (189)]; *The Speech of Sir George Pudsey*, 1685. [B.M. T. 100* (175).]

GOOLDING (T.), printer in Newcastle-upon-Tyne, on the side, near Henderson's Coffee house, 1715. Only known from the imprint to a booklet entitled *Honesto Willo*. [Welford, *Early Newcastle Typography*, p. 24.]

GOSLING (ROBERT), bookseller in London, (1) Mitre (or Mitre and Crown) against St. Dunstan's Church in Fleet Street; (2) at the Middle Temple Gate. 1707–41. Began publishing in 1707. [*T.C.* III. 555.] Many of his publications are noticed by Nichols. [*Lit. Anecd.* I. 211, et seq.] He is often mentioned by Browne Willis in his correspondence with Hearne. He died on January 4th, 1741. Sir Francis Gosling, the banker, was his son.

GOUGE (J.), bookseller in London, Castle, Westminster Hall, 1700–7. His name first occurs in Trin. 1700, as selling a divinity book. [*T.C.* III. 196.] In 1707 he advertised a metrical translation from Epictetus. [*T.C.* III. 557.]

GOUGH (EDWARD), bookseller in London, Cow-cross, 1682. His imprint is found on William Wood's *Bow-Man's Glory*, 1682. [Haz. I. 467.]

GOVAN (DONALD), printer in Glasgow, 1715–19. Govan had a press within the University, and in 1715 was appointed its printer. On May 1st, 1719, the Town Council authorized a payment to Govan for printing various papers at "the time of the late rebellion." [*Extracts from the records of the Burgh of Glasgow*, 1718–38, p. 59.]

GRAFTON (GEORGE), bookseller in London, (1) Mitre, Fleet Street; (2) Middle Temple Lane. 1687–99. Made his first announcement in 1687. [*T.C.* II. 202.] In 1688 he sold a broadside entitled *The Speech of Sir George Treby to the Prince of Orange*; and in the same year he published Richard Blackbourne's

Three Novels in one. [*T.C.* II. 223.] In 1689 Grafton was one of the booksellers selling the 1687 ed. of Chaucer. [*T.C.* II. 261.] His last entry in the Term Catalogue was in Hil. 1699. [*T.C.* III. 111.] His two addresses apparently represent the same house; it was later occupied by Robert Gosling.

GRANGER (MATTHEW), bookseller in London, 1690. *An Account of what passed in the House of Commons . . . in relation to the Earle of Castlemaine*, 1690, was printed for him. [Haz. IV. 158.]

GRANT (FR.), bookseller in London, 1668. Published *A Strange and true relation of one Mr. John Leech*, 1668. [Haz. II. 703.]

GRANTHAM (J.), printer in London, New Street, between Shoe Lane and Fetter Lane, 1682–4 (?). In 1682 Grantham received advertisements, for insertion in various papers, at the above address. [*The Loyal Impartial Mercury*, September 15th–19th, 1682.] He printed for D. Brown, T. Goodwin, and J. Walthoe at various times. He is last heard of in 1684 [Haz. III. 258], unless he be identical with a J. G. who printed from 1650 till 1688. [Haz.]

GRANTHAM (WILLIAM), bookseller in London, Crown and Pearl over against Exeter Change, in the Strand, 1684. *See Dictionary*, 1641–67. He sold in 1684 an edition of Quarles's *Emblems*. [Haz. III. 207.]

GRAVES (GOWIN), bookseller at Cambridge, living in the parish of Great St. Mary on a site now occupied by the University Senate House lawn, 1684–1725. Mentioned in the wills of his father, William Graves, 1684 (*q.v.*), his mother, Magdalen Graves, 1691, and his brother, William Graves, jun., 1686 (*q.v.*). On his brother's death in 1695 we find him claiming £25 as owing to him, and he was paid £2 0s. 9*d.* for cataloguing his brother's books for sale. [Gray and Palmer's *Cambridge Wills*.]

GRAVES (JOHN), bookseller in London, Bible in Salisbury Street in the Strand, 1681–1715. He never used the Term Catalogues. Hazlitt records his imprint in the following: 1681: *The Character of a Popish Successour Compleat* [Haz. III. 284]; 1695: *Urania. A Funeral Elegy on the Death of Our Gracious Queen*; 1703: *Misery is Virtues Whetstone . . . Remains of . . . Grace, Lady Gethin*; 1715 (with J. Baker): *Memoirs of North Britain*. [Haz. III. 284, II. 386, I. 184, III. 225.]

GRAVES (THOMAS), bookseller in London, next White's Chocolate House in St. James' Street, 1683–1725. In 1683 he published Elkanah Settle's *Supplement to the Narrative.* [Haz. II. 553.] His name does not appear in the Term Catalogues; but he received subscriptions for the Works of Sir Henry Spelman in 1722, and for Francis Mason's *Vindication of the Church of England*, 1725. [Nichols, *Lit. Anecd.* I. 240, 329.]

GRAVES (WILLIAM), sen., bookseller at Cambridge. *See Dictionary*, 1641–67. Graves married Magdalen Tomlinson, April 6th, 1640, at St. Edward's Church, and died 1686. His will, made November 1st, 1684, "being infirm and crasy in body, but of sound and perfect [mind]", was proved September 24th, 1686. The inventory of his goods totalled £667 13*s.* 4*d.*, and amongst the items is "Hall [stall?] and shop, all the stock of books ccccv^{li}." His widow died 1693, and her will, proved March 1st, 1693, is printed along with her husband's by Gray and Palmer, pp. 124, 125. Sons and daughters are mentioned, including William and Gowin (*q. v.*).

GRAVES (WILLIAM), jun., bookseller at Cambridge, 1680–93. Evidently succeeded to his father's business and continued to live in the same house. He published several works from 1680 to 1693. [Bowes, nos. 163(b), 176, 176*, 185, 188, 196; Haz. I. 443, IV. 138.] Mentioned in the wills of his father (*q. v.*) and his mother, Magdalen Graves, 1693 [Gray and Palmer, p. 125.] His will, dated December 25th, 1686, proved February 1st, 1695, by Dr. Wm. Tindall, Fellow of Trinity Hall, contains a curious bequest to Clare College in the event of his wife not having issue which was not executed, for he was bankrupt for twelve weeks before his death, and the administrator, after selling the books and everything else, paid in two instalments 18*s.* 2*d.* in the pound. The inventory of his goods totalled 647^{li} 10^{s} 10^{d}, but their sale realized 838^{li} 15^{s} 1^{d}. A list of the creditors and the dividend, along with the will, &c., is printed by Gray and Palmer, pp. 128–132.

GRAVETT (RICHARD), bookseller in Bristol, near the Tolzey, 1695–1738. Is first heard of as one of the booksellers in Bristol who in 1695 sold John Cary's *Essay on the State of England*. In 1711 his name is mentioned in an advertisement in the *Post Boy* as receiving subscriptions for a forthcoming book. He was Sheriff of the City in 1712–13 and died in 1738. [A. B. Beavan, *Bristol Lists*, p. 292.]

GRAY (S.), printer in London, Amen Corner, near Paternoster Row, 1720. Known from an advertisement for a missing man in *The Daily Courant*, June 30th, 1720.

GREAVES (J.), bookseller at Cambridge, 1663. Published *Ichabod; or, Five Groans of the Church.* [Bowes, no. 121.*]

GREEF (H.), bookseller in Bristol, 1715. Publisher of *The Bristol Weekly Mercury* (no. 1, October 1st, 1715).

GREEN (ABRAHAM), bookseller in London, 1682. Only known as a publisher of broadsides in that year.

GREEN (D.), bookseller in London, 1682. Dryden's *Satyr to his Muse* and *Mac Flecknoe* were published by him in 1682.

GREEN (RICHARD), bookseller at Cambridge, living on the site now occupied by the University Senate House lawn, 1682–94. His name appears on books published from 1682 to 1694, including *Mercurius Rusticus* of 1685 and Dr. Joshua Barnes's edition of Euripides in folio. [Bowes.] He and Luke Meredith, (*q. v.*), married grand-daughters of Richard and Margaret Royston, and in 1698 they employed John Reeves to prosecute a commission of lunacy against their grandmother, and Green gave a bond to cover expenses. On the 24th December, 1698, judgement was given against him for £200. Green died September 1699, and by will left everything to his wife Mary. [Gray and Palmer, p. 132]. He was apparently indebted to Samuel Smith and Benjamin Walford, booksellers of London, at the time of his death. His wife, before satisfying them, also died (1699 or 1700), and they took out letters of administration.

GREEN (ROBERT), bookseller in London, (1) near Ratcliffe Cross, London; (2) Rose and Crown, Budge Row. 1674–85. Dealer in maps and topographical books. His name first appears in Easter 1674, and for the last time in Mich. 1685. [*T.C.* I. 171, II. 148.]

GREENWOOD (JOHN), printer in Manchester, 1693. One of the earliest Manchester printers. R. W. Procter [*Memorials of Manchester Streets*, p. 183] records the following entry in the parish register: "1693. March 1. Jonathan, son to John Greenwood of Manchester, printer, baptized". He adds that in spite of careful search no further information concerning this printer could be found.

GREENWOOD (JONATHAN), bookseller in London, (1) The Crown, in the Poultry; (2) Black Raven, Poultry, near the Old Jewry. 1681–8. Dealt principally in divinity. Made his first entry in the Term Catalogues in Mich. 1681, with Richard Allen's *Instructions about Heart-Work.* [*T.C.* I. 457.] Dunton, who succeeded him at the Black Raven, thus refers to him [p. 227]: "Served his apprenticeship with Mr. Cockril . . . Though he had contracted a large acquaintance and had Dr. Annesley's friendship, who helped him to 'Mr. Allen's Heart-Work' and other saleable copies, yet he concluded trading at last with as small a pittance of the world as he had to begin it." He is last heard of in Mich. 1688. [*T.C.* II. 237.]

GREGORY (J.), bookseller in London, Cornhill, 1690. Published *Great News from the Isle of Wight*, 1690. [Haz. I. 455.]

GRIERSON (GEORGE), bookseller and printer in Dublin, 1709–33 (?). Was the first and most distinguished of several generations of a family of printers. He was first a bookseller (1709–14), but his imprint as printer is found in 1715 and thenceforth frequently. In 1733 he was appointed King's printer in succession to Andrew Crooke. He was twice married, first to the learned and accomplished Constantia Grierson (her maiden name is not certain) and afterwards to a sister of James Blow, the chief Belfast printer. Grierson's press turned out a variety of books on different subjects, including several editions of the Book of Common Prayer, the Bible, some classics, and the Psalms, &c.

GRIFFIN (BENNET), bookseller and printer in London, Griffin in the Old Bailey, 1671–1700. Probably son of Edward Griffin II (1638–52). His name is joined with that of his mother Sarah Griffin as a printer; but Bennet Griffin confined himself to bookselling for a time and published several notable works, including Bacon's *Sylva Sylvarum*, with an epitome of the *Novum Organum*, 1683 [*T.C.* II. 34], and James Wright's *History and Antiquities of the County of Rutland*, 1684. He printed Buchanan's *Latin Poems*, 1686 [*T.C.* II. 173], and an *Epictetus* for Sam. Keble, 1692. [Haz. II. 204.] His name also appears first among the booksellers selling Chauncy's *Hertfordshire*, 1700, after which nothing more is heard of him.

GRIFFIN (SARAH), *see Dictionary*, 1641–67.

GRIGG (G.), bookseller in London, near Charing Cross, 1717. Sold Jer. Owen's *Sermon . . . to . . . Dissenters*, 1717. [B.M. T. 1805 (11).]

GROINE (   ), stationer in London, Black Horse, between the two Temple Gates within the Bar, 1669. Appointed Receiver of Letters for the General Post Office, 1669. [S.P.D. Car. II. 262, 180.]

GROOM (G.), printer in London, 1705–9. He printed editions in 8° of Sternhold and Hopkins's metrical version of the Psalms for the Company of Stationers in 1705 and 1709.

GROSVENOR (RICHARD), bookseller in Wolverhampton, 1685–91 (?) In 1684 or 1685 a broadside entitled *The Loyal Speech of George Plaxton . . . upon the Proclamation of . . . King James the Second* was printed for him at London by J. Leake. [B.M. 8122. i. 1 (41).] Grosvenor is believed to have died in 1691.

GROVE (HUGH), bookseller and printer in Portsmouth, 1718. Mr. F. A. Edwards [*Early Hampshire Printers* (in *Papers of the Hampshire Field Club*), p. 115 n.] refers to a sermon by the Vicar of Portsmouth, printed by Hugh Grove, bookseller in Portsmouth, in 1718 (communicated to him by a Mr. W. H. Long), as preceding the earliest Portsmouth printing previously known by thirty years; but he does not give its author or title. It appears that Grove was both a printer and a publisher.

GROVER (JAMES) and (THOMAS), printers and type-founders in London, (1) Pelican Court, Little Britain; (1) Angel Alley, Aldersgate. 1676–1728. James Grover began as a printer about 1676. [Haz. I. 216.] He probably began as a type-founder at the same time, and in 1679 he cast the types for an edition of *Herodotus* in Greek and Latin which was printed by E. Horton and published by J. Dunmore, R. Chiswell, B. Tooke, and T. Sawbridge, and they were used again in a fine edition of *Cicero* in two folio volumes, also published by Dunmore. Later he was joined by his son Thomas, and after Moxon's retirement from business the Grover foundry, with that of Joseph and Robert Andrews, shared between them the whole of the English trade. The most notable founts in their possession were a pica and long primer Roman from the Royal Press at Blackfriars, Day's double pica Roman and Italic, English Samaritan matrices from which the type for Walton's Polyglott Bible had been cast, and a Greek uncial fount, cut for the specimen of the Codex Alexandrinus which Patrick Young proposed to print, but did not live to accomplish. The date of James Grover's death seems to be unknown: but Thomas died in 1728, after which the foundry remained nearly idle in the hands of Nutt, the printer, husband of one of his daughters, till 1758, when it was sold to John James. [Reed, *The Old English Letter Foundries, p.* 205.]

GROVER (THOMAS), type-founder in London. *See* Grover (James).

GUILLIM, *see* Gwillim.

GUN, GUNN, or GUNNE (MATTHEW), bookseller and printer in Dublin, Bible and Crown, Essex Street, 1694–1710 (?). Described as a bookseller in 1694; in 1695 he published a tract, *The Rector's Case.* [Bodl. G. Pamph. 2194 (15).] In 1696 he printed a quarto tract; but he appears most often as a seller or publisher of books and not as a printer. He bought books largely at Dunton's auction at Dublin in 1698. [Dunton, p. 550.] In 1701 he published *A Full Account of . . . Captain Kidd.* [Haz. I. 245.] He was living in 1710 and perhaps later.

GUNTER (LAURENCE), printer in Edinburgh, 1685. In partnership with J. Colmar. Their imprint appears on N. Paterson's *Panegyrick to Thomas Kennedie*, 1685. [Aldis, p. 69.]

GUY (JOHN), bookseller in London, (1) at the Corner shop of Little Lombard Street and Cornhill; (2) Flying Horse, Fleet Street, between St. Dunstan's Church and Chancery Lane. 1670 (?)–1709. Brother of Thomas Guy (*q. v.*) and a member of the Haberdashers' Company. He began in partnership with his brother, and in Mich. 1677 their joint names appear as sellers of Elisha Coles' *English-Latin and Latin-English Dictionary.* [*T.C.* I. 293.] After the partnership between the brothers was dissolved about 1679, while Thomas continued to occupy the premises in Cornhill, John moved to the Flying Horse in Fleet Street, where he published in Easter Term, 1680, L. Maidwell's tragedy, *The Loving Enemies.* [*T.C.* I. 394.] He either gave up business or ceased publishing shortly after this, as nothing more is heard of him. He died in 1709, his will being proved on July 5th. In this he mentions his sister Anne Varnam and her son Thomas Varnam, who succeeded his uncle Thomas Guy in his shop in 1711. He also mentions a cousin, Joseph Osborne, and he left the residue of his estate to his brother Thomas. [P.C.C. 170, Lane.]

GUY (THOMAS), bookseller in London and Oxford; London, at the Corner shop of Little Lombard Street and Cornhill, 1668–1724. This famous bookseller

was the eldest child of Thomas Guy, lighterman and coalmonger, and was born in 1644 or 1645 in Pritchard's Alley, Fair Street, Horsley Down, Southwark. His father, an Anabaptist, died young, leaving three children, two of whom were boys, Thomas and John. Their mother returned to her native place, Tamworth. Here the children were educated, and the two boys were sent eventually to London and apprenticed to the trade of bookselling, Thomas on September 3rd, 1660, to John Clarke. Thomas, being the elder, was probably apprenticed a few years earlier than his brother John. At any rate Thomas took up his freedom in the Stationers' Company on October 7th, 1668, and shortly afterwards set up in business for himself with a stock worth about £200. Some time about 1675 he was joined by his brother John. It has been erroneously stated by Nichols [*Lit. Anecd.* III. 599–600] that Thomas Guy laid the foundation of his bookselling business by engaging in the unlawful importation of foreign printed Bibles: but what he and his brother did was to buy from the Stationers' Company large stocks of Bibles, &c., which the Company had seized on the wharves. Indeed, the King's printers actually seized these Bibles on the ground that they were illegally imported, then reprinted the first sheet, and issued them again as English Bibles, and thus sought to drive the Universities out of competition. This is made clear by an affidavit by John Guy. [*Hist. MSS. Comm., Rept.* xi, App. p. 274.] Before 1679 Thomas Guy, Peter Parker and Moses Pitt were called in to assist Oxford University in its attempt to put Bibles on the market at a cheaper rate and in better print than the King's printers were then doing. Consequently Pitt was appointed printer and Parker and the Guys managed the selling, with the result that the price of Bibles, Testaments, and Common Prayer Books was reduced very considerably. At the same time it must be confessed that Moses Pitt's earlier attempts at Bible printing were not much better typographically than those that were on the market before. The statement that Guy imported type from Holland is also misleading. It was Bishop Fell who imported Dutch letter, as is well known, for the express purpose of founding the Oxford Press. The assistance of the Guys was not called in until the opposition of the Stationers' Company became so dangerous that the University felt that it should have the help and guidance of some London booksellers, and choice was made of Parker, Pitt, and the Guys. John Guy dropped out of the partnership about 1679 and moved to the Flying Horse in Fleet Street; Thomas Guy's name appears in the

Term Catalogues for the last time in 1707. [*T.C.* III. 576.] According to Dunton [p. 205] Thomas Guy in 1703 occupied a high position among London booksellers and was an eminent figure in the Stationers' Company. A statement that Guy almost starved the bookbinders he employed, may have been only ill-natured gossip. Certainly as early as 1678 Guy had founded at Tamworth an almshouse for six poor women, which he enlarged in 1693 to accommodate fourteen men and women. In 1701 he also built there a town hall, which is still standing. Many of his poorer relations received pecuniary help from him, and in many other ways he showed a generous nature. In 1704 Guy became a governor of St. Thomas's Hospital, and in 1707 built and furnished three new wards. On August 5th, 1717, he offered the Stationers' Company £1,000 to enable them to add to the quarterly charity to poor members and widows. Guy had conceived the idea of providing for the many patients who could not be taken into St. Thomas's Hospital or were discharged thence as incurable. In 1721 he leased from the Governors a piece of ground opposite, and, having pulled down a number of small houses, began the erection of a hospital, ever since known as Guy's. The building, which cost £18,793, was roofed in before the founder's death, which took place on December 27th, 1724, in his eightieth year. Guy's will was proved on January 4th, 1724–5. It was afterwards printed and went through three editions in 1725, being reprinted by the governors of the Hospital in 1732. It dealt principally with the government of the Hospital. [Works quoted; *D.N.B.*]

GWILLIM, or GUILLIM (JOHN), bookseller in London, against Crosby Square in Bishopsgate Street, 1684–1707. According to Dunton [p. 224] John Guillim or Gwillim was originally a clasp-maker. He took up bookselling, attended Bristol fair every year and was a thriving man. He is first mentioned in the Term Catalogues in 1684, when, in company with S. Sprint, he published an astrological work by John Gadbury. [*T.C.* II. 103.] In 1707 he was party to an action brought by the Company of Stationers for the infringement of their patents. [Chan. Proc. before 1714, Bridges $\frac{270}{21}$ P.R.O.]

GWILLIM (PHILIP), printer in London, at his Wharf at the end of Bur Street in East Smithfield, 1717. Possibly son of John Gwillim. He printed in 1717 a pamphlet entitled *A Believer's Evidences for Heaven.* [B.M. 702. f. 2 (5).]

H. (J.), printer in London, 1697–1710. Perhaps John Humphrys (*q. v.*).

HAIGHT (W.), bookseller in London, Bloomsbury, 1689. Only known as publisher of *An Answer to the Bishop of Rochester's First Letter to the Earl of Dorset, &c. . . . By an Englishman*, 1689. [Haz. iii. 126.]

HAIR (J.), *see* Hare.

HALES (THOMAS), printer in London (St. Omer ?), 1696. A Roman Catholic printer, who printed the *Life of the Lady Warner*, " London ", 1696. [Haz. ii. 633.]

HALEY or HALY (FRANCIS), bookseller in London, (*a*) at his shop in Holborn, at the corner of Chancery Lane, (*b*) Chancery Lane near Holborn. 1670–81. Publisher of works on witchcraft. His name first appears in the Term Catalogue for Hil. 1670. [*T.C.* I. 27.] He is last heard of in 1681. Gray's reference to 1690 is a misprint for 1680. [Index to Haz.; cf. IV. 135.]

HALEY or HALY (M.), printer in London, 1683–4. Printed with J. Millet a poetical broadside commemorating the great frost of 1683 (sold by Robert Walton and John Seller). [B.M. C. 20. f. 2 (159).] The same pair put their initials only to a ballad, *An excellent Example to all Young Men*, 1684. [B.M. C. 40. m. 11 (72).]

HALEY (THOMAS), printer in London, 1677–82. Associated with Ann Purslowe in 1677. In 1680 he put his initials to a poetical broadside concerning William Farthing, printed for J. Clarke, and his name is also found in the imprint to a romance, *The Most Excellent History of Antonius and Aurelia*, 1682. [Bodl., Douce A. 271.]

HALL (EDWARD), bookseller in Cambridge, living in the High Street, next [north of] the Green Dragon [on land now occupied by the University Senate House lawn], 1688–1703. His name appears as publisher on books dated 1688–1700. [Bowes, nos. 194, 203, 339, 2905; *T.C.* II. 402, 599; III. 40, 173.] He died in 1703, and his will is at Peterborough. Two years later his premises were occupied by Thomas Webster, bookseller (*q. v.*).

HALL (JOHN), printer at Oxford, 1670 (?)–1707. After Bishop Fell's death John Hall, " who knew how to influence his new masters, and at the same time to make a good hand of it to his own profit and advantage ", raised the prices of all kinds of printing at the Theatre. [Hearne, II. 90.] On the Coronation of William and Mary he was paid £42 15*s.* for printing and binding the verses on the King and Queen, and a further sum of £19 10*s.* for two large Bibles of imperial paper and for binding eight "bookes of (Loggan's) College Cutts" which were probably presented to their Majesties at that time. [Wood, IV. 82.] Hall died just before Christmas 1707. [Hearne, II. 121.]

HALL (JOSEPH), bookseller and bookbinder on Tyne Bridge, Newcastle-upon-Tyne, 1683–99. Publisher of Richard Werge's sermons preached in St. Mary's Church at Gateshead during the years 1683–5, now very rare. [*Memoirs of Mr. Ambrose Barnes*, App., pp. 422, et seq.] In 1691 he published a sermon preached by George Tullie, Sub-Dean of York, before the Mayor of Newcastle. [*T.C.* II. 345.] In 1693 he published the Sermons of John March, Vicar of Newcastle. [*T.C.* II. 473.]

HALL (W.), stationer (?) in London, Angel in Fleet Street, 1684. Sold a "Compendium of Writing, printed on a large Imperial Sheet of Paper".

HALL (WILLIAM), bookseller in Oxford, 1670. *See Dictionary*, 1641–67.

HALSEY (R.), bookseller in London, Cornhill, (*a*) St. Michael's Church Porch, (*b*) Plough and Harrow, near the Royal Exchange. 1700 (?)–1723. Dunton, in 1703 [p. 217], refers to a Mr. Halsey as a "man of good judgement; his great ingenuity and knowledge of the learned Languages have justly entitled him to the friendship of Athens" [i. e. of Dunton's Athenian Society]. In 1711 he appears in an advertisement as one of those from whom catalogues of a book-sale could be procured [*Daily Courant*, January 19th], and in the same year he advertised a preparation called "The Britannick Beautifyer". [*Postman*, February 8th.] In 1703 he published the Rev. J. Hancock's *Febrifugium Magnum*.

HAMMOND (HENRY), bookseller at Bath and Devizes, 1695–1721. Probably in partnership with John Hammond, as their names appear jointly on W. Gough's *Four Sermons*, 1695. [B.M. 4479. a. 40.] In 1697 Henry Hammond published Dr. Pierce's *Bath Memoirs*, printed at Bristol. [*T.C.* III. 26.] In 1719 his name occurs as one of the publishers of the Rev. Arthur Bedford's *Serious Remonstrance . . . against . . . Play . . . Houses*, and he was still publishing in 1721. [*N. & Q.*, 10th Ser., V. 141.] A list of his publications in stock in 1707 is to be found in J. Jackson's *Sermon preached at Bathe*. [Bodl. Serm. II. (1).]

HAMMOND (JOHN), bookseller at Bath and Devizes, 1695–1719. Apparently in partnership with Henry Hammond (*q. v.*). John disappears after 1719,

when his name is found in the proposals for printing Richard Bradley's *Philosophical Account of the Works of Nature*.

HANCOCK (JOHN), sen., bookseller in London, 1643–73 (?). *See Dictionary*, 1641–67. Still in business in 1673.

HANCOCK (JOHN), jun., bookseller in London, (*a*) Three Bibles in Pope's Head Alley, (*b*) at the first shop in Pope's Head Alley, next Cornhill. 1673–1705. Son of John Hancock, senior. Their joint names are found for the first time in Hil., 1673, as publishing certain sermons by William Bridge [*T.C.* I. 126], but the date of his father's death and of his succession to the business is not known. In March 1676–7 he was committed for selling copies of a pamphlet called *The Long Parliament Dissolved*, which he said he had received from Mrs. Brewster, paying her a groat for each copy. On promise of amendment he was released. [*Hist. MSS. Comm., 9th Report*, App., p. 70.] The firm published chiefly divinity, and Hancock's name continues to appear in the Term Catalogues until Easter 1705. [*T.C.* III. 458.] In 1679 the name of "John Hannock", probably a misprint for Hancock, is found as selling Capt. W. Bedloe's *Narrative of the Burning of London*. Dunton [p. 224] refers to him as "an old friend and acquaintance", and states that he "printed" works by Thomas Brooks, and got a considerable estate by bookselling.

HANCOX (THOMAS), bookseller at Hereford, 1674. Publisher of the Rev. T. Good's *Firmianus and Dubitantius, or Certain dialogues concerning Atheism*, 1674.

HANNOCK (JOHN), bookseller in London, 1679. Probably an error for John Hancock, jun. (*q. v.*).

HARBIN (THOMAS), printer in Dublin, 1724–6. In partnership with Pressick Rider, but on one occasion printed alone in 1726. Together they printed, in 1725, an edition of Molyneux's *Case of Ireland*, Lewes' *Origines Hebraicae* and Young's *Poem on the Last Day*, and in 1726 Browne's *English Expositor Improved*.

HARBIN (THOMAS), bookseller in London, (1) Wheatsheaf against the Tun Tavern, near Hungerford Market; (2) Bible and Anchor in the New Exchange in the Strand. 1693–1737. In 1693 he published for John Whittel, *Constantinus Redivivus*. [Haz. II. 643.] On June 11th, 1694, his name occurs in an advertisement of patent medicines in *The City Mercury*. In 1721 he published Sir Francis Hubert's *Life of Edward II*, with the imprint of the Bible and

Anchor. Harbin was also noted as selling ink of good quality. He died November 18th, 1737. [Timperley, p. 660.]

HARBOTTLE (R.), bookseller in London, 1681. He published *Strange News from Hicks Hall*, 1681. [Haz. II. 395.]

HARDEY (RICHARD), bookseller (?) in London, *c.* 1677. Mentioned in some legal proceedings. [Plea Roll, Mich. 29 Chas. II, m. 170.]

HARDING (JOHN), bookseller in London, (1) Bible and Anchor, St. Paul's Churchyard; (2) Bible and Anchor, Newport Street, near Leicester Fields; (3) St. Martin's Lane. 1678–1712. Entered in the Term Catalogue of Mich. 1678 Christopher Nesse's *Christian's walk and work on earth . . . Second edition*. [*T.C.* I. 336.] Dunton became acquainted with John Harding at Sturbridge Fair and dealt with him for several years, finding him [p. 223] "a very honest man, an understanding bookseller and a zealous Church of England man, yet no bigot". In 1684 he moved to Leicester Fields, and among his apprentices was Bernard Lintot, who had been turned over to him from Tho. Linyard. In 1709, among those who received subscriptions for the *Corpus omn. vet. Poetarum Latinorum* was — Harding, in St. Martin's Lane, who is probably identical with John Harding. [*T.C.* III. 657.] In 1713 he subscribed to the fund for the relief of William Bowyer the elder.

HARDING (JOHN), printer in Dublin, 1721–4. In 1721 he printed a *History of the Kings of Scotland*, a substantial volume, and in 1724 Swift's *Drapier's Letters*, for which latter he was prosecuted.

HARE or HAIR (J.), bookseller and musical instrument maker in London, (1) Mutton Court in Maiden Lane, over against Haberdashers' Hall; (2) Freeman's Yard in Cornhill; (3) Golden Viol in St. Paul's Churchyard; (4) Viol and Flute in Cornhill. 1680–1718. The first of the above imprints is found on No. 1 of *Mercurius Publicus*, February 21st–28th, $16\frac{79}{80}$ [Burney, 81A], and may possibly refer to a different man. J. Hare or Hair was by trade a musical instrument maker, but sold all kinds of music books. His name occurs in the Term Catalogues for the first time in Trin. 1696, when he sold *A Collection of New Songs set by Mons. Nicola Matteis*. [*T.C.* II. 589.] He was still in business in 1718, when he published *The Compleat Country Dancing Master*. [Haz. I. 114.]

HAREFINCH (JOHN), printer and bookseller in London, Montague Court in Little Britain, 1682–1690 (?). In 1682 he printed for H. Rhodes a novel called *The Pastime Royal* [Esdaile, p. 282], in 1683 for James Norris, *Hæc and Hic; Or, The Feminine Gender more worthy than the Masculine* [Haz. III. 271], and in 1684, for the same, *Poems and Discourses* by John Norris. [Haz. I. 308.] In the Term Catalogue of Trin. 1688 [*T.C.* II. 236] he advertised Chr. Musgrave's *Motives*. In the following year he printed for William Hensman, the bookseller at the King's Head, Westminster Hall, Nicholas Greenwood's *Astronomia Anglicana*. This work was not advertised in the Term Catalogue but in *The London Gazette*, where the further information is given that the book was to be had at the shop of Rest Fenner in Canterbury. The printer's name was not given. Harefinch died about 1690, and his widow afterwards married a printer named Sharpless. [Records of Stat. Co.]

HARFORD (MRS.), bookseller at Portsmouth, 1695 (?)–1710. Probably widow of Robert Harford, bookseller at Portsmouth (*q. v.*).

HARFORD (ROBERT), sen., bookseller in London, Angel in Cornhill, near the Royal Exchange, 1677–81. Probably son of Ralph and Elizabeth Harford, *see Dictionary*, 1641–67. He made his first entry in the Term Catalogues in Trin. 1677. [*T.C.* I. 285.] He published a news sheet called *Mercurius Anglicus* (no. 1, November 20th, 1679). No. 12 appeared as *The True News or Mercurius Anglicus*; unlike other "Mercuries", which consisted of one leaf, the first eleven numbers consisted of two leaves or four pages; but this was soon found too expensive, and it reverted to the ordinary form in no. 12. It contained a few advertisements, chiefly of books published by Harford. Amongst his varied publications was Edmund Halley's *Catalogus Stellarum Australium* in Mich. 1678. [*T.C.* I. 335.]

HARFORD (ROBERT), jun., stationer and bookseller in London, St. Paul's Churchyard (?), 1685–1714. Defendant in an action for debt brought by William Curtis, judgement being signed against him on November 12th, 1 Jas. II. [C.P.R., Mich. 1 Jas. II, Roll. 3039, m. 414 recto.] "Harford's shop in the Church Yard" is referred to on p. 8 of a pamphlet entitled *The Irish Massacre*, 1714, as a place where pamphlets were sold.

HARFORD or HARTFORD (ROBERT), bookseller at Portsmouth, 1675–95. His name appears in an advertisement of Dr. Sermon's Pills. The business was continued for a long period, the name of Mrs. Harford, bookseller, appearing in 1710. [F. A. Edwards, *Early Hampshire Printers*, 1891.]

HARGRAVE (D.) or (RICHARD), bookseller in London, (1) against Furnivalls Inn Gate; (2) Fleet Street, 1689–1713 (?). In the Term Catalogues for Hil. and Easter 1696, he is mentioned as joint publisher with S. Heyrick of Sir Thomas Raymond's *Reports*. [*T.C.* II. 568, 579.] In one of these entries his initial is given as D., in the other R. In 1713 a Richard Hargrave was connected with the publication of a pamphlet called *The Art of being Honest for a little Time*, which was the outcome of a dispute amongst the parish authorities of St. Dunstan's in the West. It gave the names of all the inhabitants who paid the Scavenger's Rate in 1713–14, and though the trades of the persons named were omitted many stationers and booksellers of that period are named. [B.M. 796. c. 35.] In *The London Gazette*, October 28th–31st, 1689, "Mr. Hargrave" against Furnivall's Inn Gate is mentioned in an advertisement of a sale as one of those from whom catalogues could be obtained.

HARIS (F.), *see* Harris.

HARPER ( ), bookseller at Hallaton, Leicester, 1687. Defendant in an action for trespass brought against him by Henry Hitchcock. [C.P.R., Hil. 2–3 Jas. II (168 6/7), Roll 3052, m. 125 verso.]

HARPER (CHARLES), bookseller in London, The Flower de Luce, Fleet Street, 1670–1709. His name first appears in the Term Catalogues in Easter 1670. [*T.C.* I. 40.] He was a prolific publisher of divinity. A list of books printed for him in 1684 will be found at the end of *The Laws of Jamaica*, 1684. Dunton [p. 210] thus describes him: "I believe him an honest man and a warm votary for High Church. He printed Mr. Wesley's 'Life of Christ', and makes a considerable figure in the Stationers Company." Harper was Junior Warden of the Company in 1699–1700. The Flower de Luce was an old building standing at the corner of Fetter Lane and Fleet Street, and in the first quarter of the seventeenth century was occupied by John Hodgets the bookseller. [*See Dictionary*, 1557–1640.]

HARRIS (BENJAMIN), bookseller and printer in London and Boston, New England; London, (1) Bell Alley, Coleman Street; (2) (*a*) Sweeting's Alley, Cornhill, (*b*) Stationer's Arms, Sweeting's Rents, near the Royal Exchange;

(3) Maiden Head Court in Great East Cheap; (4) Golden Boar's Head in Gracechurch Street, or, at the corner of Gracechurch Street, next Cornhill; Boston, (1) by the Town Pump near the Change; (2) over against the Old Meeting House; (3) Bible, over against the Blue Anchor. 1673–1708. The following sketch of this notorious character is chiefly an abridgement of Mr. P. L. Ford's Introduction to his edition of the *New England Primer*, 1897. Benjamin Harris makes his first appearance as a bookseller in the Term Catalogue for Mich. 1673, when he issued, from Bell Alley in Coleman Street, a work entitled *War with the Devil.* [*T.C.* I. 147.] His chief characteristic at this time seems to have been an ardent Protestantism. At the time of the Popish Plot he threw himself actively into the fray and published a large number of ballads, broadsides, and tracts against the Pope and the Jesuits, as well as printing the *Domestick Intelligence* and other news-sheets with the same object. In 1679 he issued *An Appeal from the Country to the City, for the Preservation of His Majesty's person and the Protestant Religion.* This gave great offence to the Government, and Harris was brought to trial for "printing and sending it", and he was ordered to find security for his good behaviour for three years. Harris himself printed the account of this trial. Unwarned by his experience, Harris in 1681 printed a *Protestant Petition* and was again prosecuted. This time the judge fined him £500 and ordered him to be put in the pillory, a sentence that was duly carried out. After this he left England and went to America, and Dunton, writing from Boston, said, "Old England is now so uneasie a place for honest men that those that can will seek out for another country: And this I suppose is the case of Mr. Benjamin Harris and the two Mr. Hows whom [*sic*] I hear are coming hither". [Dunton, *Letters from New England*, 1867, p. 144.] Harris set up a book and coffee, tea, and chocolate shop "by the Town Pump near the Change" in Boston in 1686. Here too he was quickly involved with the authorities, for in 1690 he issued without permission the first newspaper printed in America, under the title of *Public Occurrences*, which was suppressed by proclamation. Sometime between 1687 and 1690 Harris issued the first edition of *The New England Primer*, of which no copy is known. In Henry Newland's almanac, entitled *News from the Stars*, "printed by R. Pierce for Benjamin Harris at the London Coffee House in Boston, 1691" (and consequently printed late in 1690), the last leaf advertised a second impression of *The New England Primer*, enlarged. In 1691 Harris

formed a partnership with John Allen and became Printer to the Governor and Council, and removed his business to a shop "over against the Old Meeting House", making another move in 1694 to "the Sign of the Bible, over against the Blew Anchor". But evidently things did not prosper with him, and towards the end of 1695 he returned to England and opened a printing office at Maiden Head Court in Great East Cheap, and in 1703 Dunton [p. 217] writes, "He is now both Bookseller and Printer in Gracechurch Street, as we find by his *London Post.*" The last entry under Harris's name in the Term Catalogues was in Mich. 1701, and his death is believed to have taken place about 1708. Partridge in his Almanac says that Benjamin Harris and his son had added a supplement of their own to his almanac in 1704 and 1705.

HARRIS (ELIZABETH), bookseller in London, Harrow in Little Britain, 1699–1711. Widow of John Harris. Dunton says [p. 223] that she printed his *Panegyrick on the Lord Jeffreys, The Great Historical Dictionary, The Present State of Europe,* "and other copies that have sold well".

HARRIS (F.), bookseller in London, 1682. A political pamphlet entitled *War Horns make room for the Bucks with Green Bowes*, bears the imprint, "London, printed for F. Haris, 1682". [Haz. I. 288; B.M. 1077. h. 33.]

HARRIS (GEORGE), bookseller in London, Queen's Head, St. James's Street, 1703–21. Published in 1703 a volume of verse called *Poems on Several Occasions.* [B.M. 11633. e. 52.] In 1721 he was one of the publishers of Paul Chamberlen's series of novels called *Love in its Empire.* [Esdaile, p. 183.]

HARRIS (GABRIEL), bookseller in Gloucester, 1702–22. Published two sermons preached at Colford, Gloucester, one by William Harrison of Stanton, the other by Humphry Jorden of Newland. [*Flying Post*, November 5th, 1702.] *See* Went.

HARRIS (JOHN), bookseller in London, (1) Harrow against the Church in the Poultry; (2) Harrow in Little Britain, 1685–98. This bookseller was the particular friend of John Dunton, who devotes two pages [231–2] of his *Life and Errors* to a description of him. Dunton and he were partners in *Coke's Detection, The Secret History of Whitehall,* Leybourn's *Panarithmologia,* and "thirty other valuable books". Dunton further says, "from the day I left my shop in the Poultry, I put all I printed into John's warehouse and

found him always ready to even accompts, and to discharge his trust to a half-farthing". George Larkin the printer is said to have composed the following couplet on Harris:

> Of all honest Booksellers if you'd have the Marrow,
> Repair to King John, at the Sign of the Harrow.

Harris made his first entry in the Term Catalogues in Mich. 1685. *A pleasant and compendious History of the first Inventers*, 1686, published and probably written by him, has at the end a list of seven books, five religious and all popular, printed for him. [B.M. 1137. a. 37.] He moved to Little Britain sometime in 1695 or 1696, and is believed to have died some time in 1698, his business being continued for some years by his widow Elizabeth Harris.

HARRIS (S.), bookseller in London, 1703. A novel entitled *A Banquet for Gentlemen and Ladies* was published by S. Harris in 1703. [Esdaile, p. 157.]

HARRIS (W.), bookseller in London, next door to the Turn Stile in the Postern, 1690 (?). Published an undated news-quarto, *A Full and True Relation of an English vessel newly taken by a Company of French Pyrats, at next Sessions to be try'd for their Lives.* [Haz. I. 355.]

HARRISON ( ), bookseller in London, Chancery Lane, 1703. Mentioned by Dunton [pp. 229–303].

HARRISON (ISRAEL), bookseller in London, (1) Star, in Chancery Lane; (2) Greyhound, Chancery Lane; (3) under Lincoln's Inn Gate, or Lincoln's Inn Fore-Gate. 1673–1706. Publisher of law books and general literature. Partner with B. Southwood (*q.v.*) in 1673. In 1675 he either changed the sign of the house from the "Star" to the "Greyhound" or moved to other premises with that sign. He also had a second shop under Lincoln's Inn Gate. Dunton describes him [p. 230] as "a diligent man in his shop, a kind neighbour and a religious master".

HARRISON (RICHARD), bookseller in London, New Inn without Temple Bar, 1701. Published John Cory's comedy, *A Cure for Jealousie*, 1701, at the end of which is a "Catalogue of Books printed for R. Harrison . . ." consisting of only three entries. [B.M. 81. c. 19.]

HARRISON (THOMAS), bookseller in London, White Swan, West Corner of the Royal Exchange, Cornhill, 1683–1711. Dunton says [p. 225] that he was apprentice with Samuel Crouch. He is first heard of in the Term Catalogues in Mich. 1683. [*T.C.* II. 39.] In that year he published Manger's *French Grammar*. [*T.C.* II. 53.] He published several tracts against Sacheverell in 1711. [*T.C.* III. 669–70.]

HART (JAMES), printer in Glasgow, 1714. He printed within the University in 1714 *An account of a conference betwixt Mr. John Steel minister at Old Cumnock, and John Adamson a disorderly preacher.* [John McUre: *History of Glasgow* (1830), p. 370.]

HART (JONAS), bookseller in Cambridge. His name appears on two works: *Dissertationes Academicae a Petro Olivier*, 1674, and R. Sheringham's *The King's Supremacy Asserted*, 1682. [Bowes, 151; Haz. IV. 167.] He was probably a relative of William Morden the bookseller (*q.v.*), who in his will, 1678, mentions "brother Andrew Hart and Susanna his wife" [Gray & Palmer's *Cambridge Wills*, 119], Andrew Hart being the executor. He joined with William Morden's son Charles as publisher of Sheringham's work of 1682.

HART or HURT (T.), bookseller in Coventry, 1702–20. Publisher of sermons by E. Davies, n. d., and J. Kimberley, 1702. [B.M. 225. g. 11 (4, 14).] In 1711 he published the Rev. J. Davies's *Book for the Aged*. [*T.C.* III. 667.]

HART (WILLIAM), bookseller in Oxford, 1686. [Madan, p. 31.]

HART or HURT (WILLIAM), printer in London, Great Carter Lane, near Doctor's Commons, 1711. Printer of *The Flying Post*, 1711. In March 1712–13 he printed *The British Ambassadress's Speech to the French King*, "the cursedest libel that ever was seen" on Queen Anne, and was condemned to pillory and fine. [Swift, *Journal to Stella*, March 21st, 1712–13.]

HARTFORD, *see* Harford.

HARTLEY (   ), bookbinder in London, 1668. The searchers of the Stationer's Company took from "Hartley a binder" 35 Psalters, about the year 1668. [Records of Stat. Co.]

HARTLEY (JOHN), bookseller in London, (1) (*a*) over against Gray's Inn Gate in Holborn, (*b*) next Middle Row, Holborn, (*c*) next door to the King's Head Tavern, Holborn; (2) Fleet Street, over against St. Dunstan's Church. 1697–1709. On May 1st, 1697, he advertised in *The Post Boy* J. Gailliard's *Blasphemous Socinian Heresie*, and Hazlitt records under the same year *Regular and Irregular Thoughts on Poets and Orators*. [IV. 104.] Hartley was

the publisher of many important books, including Sacheverell's *Account of the Isle of Man*, 1698, Sir T. Bodley's *Reliquiae Bodleianae*, 1703, Bentley's *Dissertation upon the Epistles of Phalaris*, and an *Universal . . . Dictionary*, in 2 vols., 1709. In 1699 Hartley compiled a catalogue of books in all faculties and languages, from the catalogue of the Bodleian and many other libraries. This catalogue was arranged under subjects, and the seventh part consisted wholly of English books. Hartley reissued this catalogue in 1701, with an index of authors. [B.M. 619. b. 4.] His last entry in the Term Catalogues was in 1709. [*T.C.* III. 629.] He moved to Fleet Street about 1707, when Robert, probably his son, succeeded him in Holborn.

HARTLEY (ROBERT), bookseller in London, over against Gray's Inn, Holborn, 1707–9. Probably a son of John Hartley. In 1707 he published *The Admirable and Indefatigable Adventures of the Nine Pious Pilgrims*. [Esdaile, p. 287.] In 1709 he sold the *Nomenclatura Anglo-Latina*. [*T.C.* III. 627.]

HARTLEY (THOMAS), bookseller in London, Black Boy, behind St. Alban's Church in Wood Street, 1671. Published an edition of *The King's Psalter* in 1671. [Haz. IV. 126.]

HARTLEY (WILLIAM), bookseller in London, *c.* 1703. Dunton [p. 208] has the following description: "He deals much, and has his shop well furnished with ancient books that are very valuable. He prints many excellent translations, and has a good acquaintance among learned men, amongst whom I would reckon the ingenious Mr. Abel Boyer." He did not use the Term Catalogues.

HARTSHORN (   ), bookseller in Leicestershire, 1714. Subscribed to Walker's *Sufferings of the Clergy*.

HASBERT (SAMUEL), printer in Norwich, Magdalen Street, 1706–18. In partnership, which was terminated in 1718, with Crossgrove (*q.v.*). [Gent, p. 77.]

HATLEY (H.), stationer in London, Three Flower de Luces, St. Paul's Churchyard, 1682. In the Term Catalogue for Trin. 1682, appeared the notice of John Ayres's *Practical Penman*, and a ciphering book, both to be had of this stationer and others. [*T.C.* I. 497.] This is no doubt the Major Hatley, noticed by Dunton [p. 255] as "well skilled in Military Discipline, and from being a Captain, is advanced to a Major . . . I dealt with this Military stationer for six years."

HAWES (WILLIAM), bookseller in London, (1) Rose, Ludgate Street; (2) Golden Buck, Fleet Street, over against St. Dunstan's Church; (3) Bible and Rose, Ludgate Street; (4) Rose and Crown, next the Dog Tavern on Ludgate Hill. 1698–1709. Publisher of cheap divinity books. Dunton [p. 208] describes him as "just in Trade, and knows his business very well". In 1705 he moved to the Golden Buck in Fleet Street, being succeeded at the Rose by J. Bowyer. In 1706 he returned to Ludgate Street, and by 1709 had moved to his last address.

HAWKINS (E.), bookseller in London, near Fleet Bridge, 1691–1702. In 1691 he published a rhyming pamphlet entitled *A Last Search after Claret in Southwark*, and its answer *A Search after Wit*. [*T.C.* II. 381.] Another tract of the same kind, called *Bacchanalian Sessions*, by Richard Ames, came from the same publisher in 1693 [*T.C.* II. 454], and in 1702 a broadside elegy on the death of William III. [B.M. C. 20. f. 2 (223).]

HAWKINS (M.), bookseller in London, Angel in St. Paul's Churchyard, 1709. Publisher of an edition of *Hudibras*. [*T.C.* III. 653.]

HAWKINS (S.), and (THOMAS), *see* Howkins.

HAYES (JOHN), printer to the University of Cambridge, 1669–1705. Appointed by Grace of October 14th, 1669. He succeeded John Field who died the previous year. His appointment was made under new conditions, the University by Grace of July 7th, 1669 deciding to lease the printing to him for £100 a year. He died November 28th, 1705, aged 71. During his period of office he printed many works of importance: several editions of the Bible and Prayer Book; Crashaw's *Poemata et Epigrammata*, 1670; Ray's *Proverbs*, 1670, 1678; John Smith's *Discourses*, 1673; Barclay's *Argenis*, 1673; J. Lightfoot's *Horae Hebraicae et Talmudicae*, 1674; Joshua Barnes's *Edward III*, 1688, and *Euripides*, 1694; the Cambridge Concordance to the Holy Bible, 1695, &c. [Bowes, *Cambridge University Printers*, 308, and *Catalogue of Cambridge Books*.]

HAYES (WALTER), bookseller and mathematical instrument maker, in London, Cross Daggers in Moorfields, 1673–85. Publisher of Leybourn's *Line of Proportion or Numbers*, 1673. [Haz. I. 257.] He was one of those who sold W. Walgrave's *Decimal Arithmetick*, advertised in the Term Catalogue for Hil. 1678. [*T.C.* I. 301.] In 1685 he published Dr. John Twysden's *Use of the general Planisphere*. [*T.C.* II. 147.]

HAYHURST (ROBIN), printer in London, 1689, Little Britain [*c.* 1700]. Dunton has two references [pp. 247, 293] to Hayhurst. In speaking of William Bonny the printer, he says that Bonny would have "printed treble to what he did, had not Robin Hayhurst lived so near him", and a little further on in a list of persons, whom he had omitted to describe elsewhere, he refers to "Robin Hayhurst, who lived by printing of false news". In 1689 Hayhurst issued a poetical broadside, commemorating the coronation of William and Mary, printed for him by A. M. [B.M. C. 20. f. 2 (180).]

HAZARD (JOSEPH), bookseller in London, Bible in Stationers' Court near Ludgate, 1716. There is a copy of his advertisement in the Bagford Collection. [Harl. 5961 (314).]

HEAD (GODFREY), letter-founder of London, 1686. Defendant in a plea of trespass brought against him by Charles Fowle. [Hilary 2–3 James II, C.P.R. 3052 m. 86.]

HEAD (RICHARD), *see Dictionary*, 1641–67.

HEATHCOTE (J.), bookseller in London, Baldwin's Gardens, 1680–1725. Published *An Account of the Proceedings at Guildhall . . . for the election of a Sheriff*, 1682. [Haz. II. 364.] He was afterwards the publisher of a *Halfpenny Post*, and was described by Negus as a "High Flyer".

HEATHCOTE (WILLIAM), printer in London, 1718. Committed to Newgate for printing treasonable libels. [*The Weekly Packet*, February 8th–15th, 1718.]

HELDER (THOMAS), *see Dictionary*, 1641–67.

HELME (W.), printer in Dublin, 1721–4. He printed in 1723 Warren's *Abridgement of all the Irish Statutes* of the 4th session of the then Parliament, and in 1724 Downes's *Lives of the Compilers of the Liturgy*.

HELMES (J.), bookseller in London, King's Head, Westminster Hall, 1707–11. His stall had been occupied till 1700 by William Hensman (*q.v.*). In 1707 he was one of the booksellers selling Sir Hans Sloane's *Voyage to . . . Madera, &c.* [*T.C.* III. 569.] Sale catalogues of the library of William Popple, March 1711, were to be had at his stall.

HELSHAM (SAMUEL), printer and bookseller in Dublin, 1681–9. This printer first appears in 1681, when he printed Archbishop Marsh's *Institutiones*

Logicae. He joined Andrew Crook in 1685 and they worked in partnership for three or four years and became assigns of Benjamin Tooke, the King's printer, but Helsham's name appears no more after 1689. In the Term Catalogue for Hil. 1686, his name occurs amongst the booksellers inviting subscriptions for a folio edition of Ray's *History of Plants.* [*T.C.* II. 162.]

HENCHMAN, *see* Hensman.

HENDERSON (ALEXANDER), bookseller in Edinburgh, in the upper end of the Lucken Booths, 1692–1709. Amongst the books in which his name appears, are the following: *The Pastor and the Prelate*, by D. Calderwood, 1692; *Two Sermons* by William Veitch, 1693; Sir T. Craig's *Scotland's Soveraignty asserted*, 1695; and in 1699 a sermon by Andrew Cant. In 1708–9 *The Scots Postman* was sold at his shop. [Aldis, p. 114.]

HENSMAN, HENCHMAN, or HINCHMAN (WILLIAM), bookseller in London, King's Head, Westminster Hall, 1671–1700. Succeeded James Collins at this stall. Publisher of general literature. His first entry in the Term Catalogues was, in Hil. 1671, Francis Quarles's *Boanerges and Barnabas.* [*T.C.* I. 68.] In 1680 he was agent for a Fire Insurance Office. [*True News*, May 5th–8th, 1680.] In 1681 in company with Simon Neal he published a news-sheet called *Mercurius Veridicus* (No. 1, January 7th). His name appears for the last time in the Term Catalogues in Easter 1700. [*T.C.* III. 186.] His stall was occupied some years later by J. Helmes (*q.v.*).

HEPBURN (ANDREW), printer in Glasgow, 1689. Probably a fictitious name. It is found in the imprint to *Late proceedings and votes of the Parliament*, 1689. [Aldis, pp. 77, 114.]

HEPTINSTALL (JOHN), printer in London, 1671–1712. Dunton spoke of him [p. 248] as a "modest humble man, and very ingenious in his calling", and added that he made "the best ink for printers of any man in London". He printed for Edward Giles the Norwich bookseller. He was also a printer of music books, and several of Purcell's works came from his press. In 1713 he contributed four guineas to the Bowyer relief fund. [Nichols, *Lit. Anecd.* I. 62.]

HERRINGMAN (HENRY), *see Dictionary*, 1641–67.

HERRINGMAN (JOHN), bookseller in London, next to the Fountain Tavern in the Strand, 1676. Father (?) of the "kinsman" to whom Henry Herringman

bequeathed all his copies and parts of copies on his attaining the age of twenty-three. He was the publisher of J. Sudbury's *Sermon preached before the King . . . May 7, 1676.*

HEWSON (R.), bookseller in London, Crown in Cornhill, 1689. Chiefly memorable as the publisher of Bartholomew de las Casas' *Popery truly displayed* (not in the British Museum). [*T.C.* II. 273.]

HEYRICK (R.), bookseller in London, 1686. Probably a relative of (or possibly only a mistake for) S. Heyrick. The name is found in the imprint to *Stratagems of War*, by M. D. A. B. D., 1686. [Haz. II. 238.]

HEYRICK (SAMUEL), bookseller in London, Gray's Inn Gate, Holborn, 1662–1700. *See Dictionary*, 1641–67. Elected senior Warden of the Company of Stationers in 1696–7, and again in 1699–1700. From 1684 Richard Sare (*q.v.*) was with him at Gray's Inn Gate, but each published many books independently.

HICKMAN (SPENCER), bookseller in London, Rose in St. Paul's Churchyard, 1670–2. Publisher to the Royal Society. A list of books on sale by him in 1671 fills twenty-four pages at the end of John Burbury's *Relation of a Journey.* [B.M. 978. b. 1.] His last entry in the Term Catalogues was in Hil. 1672. [*T.C.* I. 96.]

HICKS (FRANCIS), bookseller in Cambridge, 1682–99. His name appears on some seven books of 1682–99. [*T.C.* I. 495; II. 336, 559; III. 27, 55; Haz. II. 281, 672.]

HICKS (M.), bookseller in Cambridge, 1699. Probably widow of the preceding. Published *The Sceptical Muse*, 1699. [*T.C.* III. 141.]

HIDE (MICHAEL), bookseller in Exeter, 1663–98. He sold Robert Vilvain's *Theoremata Theologica*, printed for the author, 1663. [Dredge.] On July 10th, 1688 an advertisement of a sale of books at the New Inn, Exeter, appeared in *Public Occurrences*, and catalogues were to be had of Michael Hide. In 1691 he was agent for the proposals for printing *Synodicon in Gallia Reformata.* [*T.C.* II. 388.] Hide probably died in or before 1698, for his stock was advertised for sale in the *Flying Post* of November 10th–12th in that year.

HILDYARD or HILLIARD (FRANCIS), bookseller in York, Bible in Stonegate, 1680 (?)–1731. His name is first found in George Meriton's *Praise of*

Yorkshire Ale, printed for him by J. White in 1685 (3rd ed. 1697). In this year he printed a sale catalogue; so that he must have been in business for some years already. In 1695 he was associated with the Churchills in publishing M. Micklethwait's version of *Olivaires of Castile.* [Haz. III. 159; I. 310.] Ten years later Dunton [p. 237] could speak of him as "the topping man in that city". In the *Post Boy* of February 20th, 1711 he advertised for subscriptions to a *Corpus omnium veterum Poetarum Latinorum.* He was succeeded at his death in 1731 by his son John Hildyard, who died in 1757 and was succeeded by Hon[oria ?] Hildyard and Caesar Ward. [Davies, *passim*; Timperley, p. 841; *Evening Advertiser*, April 7th–9th, 1757.]

HILL (JOHN), bookseller in London, (1) Post Office, Fleet Street; (2) Black Lion, Fleet Street. 1677–8. Published *The Clerk's Manual*, 1677 [*T.C.* I. 290], and in 1678 Part IV, Book iii. of Theophilus Gale's *Court of the Gentiles.* [*T.C.* I. 322.]

HILLAR, *see* Hillier.

HILLIARD, *see* HILDYARD.

HILLIER or HILLAR (NATHANIEL), printer and bookseller in London, Prince's Arms, Leadenhall Street, over against St. Mary Axe, 1700–7. Referred to by Dunton [p. 292] as "independent Hiller". Publisher of Cotton Mather's *More Wonders of the Invisible World*, 1700. [*T.C.* III. 217.] Hazlitt records *Youth's Tragedy, A Poem*, by T. S. "London, Printed and sold by Nath. Hillier, 1707." [Haz. I. 370.]

HILLS (GILHAM), printer (?) in London, 1737. According to Nichols [*Lit. Anecd.* VIII. 168] Gilham Hills, printer, was son of Henry Hills junior, and died in 1737. In this case he must be distinguished from his namesake and uncle, son of Henry Hills senior (*q.v.*). The date of his death makes Nichols's statement probable.

HILLS (HENRY), sen., printer in London, 1641–89. *See Dictionary*, 1641–67. As considerable confusion and error is found in all the accounts of the later life of this printer, the *D.N.B.* for example stating that he died in 1713, the following additional information about him is now recorded. About the year 1670 Henry Hills, sen., became one of the assigns of John Bill the Second and Christopher Barker the Third in the King's Printing House in Blackfriars. He afterwards became a Roman Catholic, with the result that on December 12th, 1688, a mob attacked the printing house in Black-

friars, "spoiled his Formes, Letters, &c., and burnt 200 or 300 reams of paper printed and unprinted." [*English Currant*, December 12th–14th, 1688.] Hills fled for his life to St. Omer, where he died shortly afterwards, his will being proved on January 21st, 1689. Probate was granted to Gilham Hills his son by his first wife; the executors were Elizabeth Hills the widow and Adiell Mill, being one a recusant and the other a bankrupt. His children were Henry Hills jun., Gilham Hills, James Hills, and George Hills, the two latter by his second wife. He also had a son John, who was dead at the time of the making of the will, and a daughter Dorothy, married to a man named Edwin. [*P.C.C.* 6, Dyke.] Both his sons Henry and Gilham became printers and during his father's lifetime, Henry Hills jun. was so-called, in spite of which he has been confused with his father. One of them, presumably the father, was junior warden of the Company of Stationers in 1682–4, and Master in 1687–9.

HILLS (HENRY), jun., printer in London, (*a*) on the Ditch-side, (*b*) near the water-side, in Blackfriars, 1680 (?)–1713. The son of Henry Hills, senior, the King's Printer. His initials "H. H. jun." are found on an undated edition of *Julius Caesar*, printed about 1680, and have been taken to stand for Henry Herringman, jun., but Henry Herringman the publisher left no son. (*See Dictionary*, 1641–67.) In 1683 Henry Hills, jun., printed for W. Davis *An Elegy upon . . . the Lord Capel* [B.M. C. 20. f. 2 (157)], and in the same year, *The Presentment of the Grand Jury of Bristol* [Bodl.]. On the death of his father Henry Hills, jun., succeeded to his father's share in the King's Printing House, and dropped the word "junior", which has been the cause of much confusion. He became notorious for pirating every good poem or sermon that was published, "a circumstance", says Nichols, "which led to the direction in the Act of 8 Anne that fine-paper copies should be presented to the public libraries". [Nichols, *Lit. Anecd.* VIII. 168.] A large number of these pirated duodecimos appeared in 1709 and 1710. In a poem on Lintot's *Miscellanies*, ascribed to Dr. King, occur the following lines,

> While neat old *Elzevir* is reckoned better
> Than *Pirate Hill's* brown Sheets and scurvy Letter.

Henry Hills, jun., died in 1713, and an advertisement appeared in the *Evening Post* of November 12th to the effect that his stock, "consisting of the most eminent Sermons, Poems, Plays, &c., is now to be disposed of, at the Blue Anchor, Paternoster Row. N.B. There can never be any of the same, or any in the like manner, reprinted after these are gone, there being an Act of Parliament to the contrary". Nichols states that Gilham Hills the printer was his son. [VIII. 168.] Many of his cheap reprints, 1708–10, were reissued in two vols. by T. Warner, in 1717, as *A Collection of the Best English Poetry, by several hands.* [B.M. 11603. d. 14, 15.]

HILLS (JOHN), bookseller in London, Exchange Alley in Cornhill, 1676–90. In Mich. 1676 he advertised a set of grammatical cards [*T.C.* I. 256], and in the following year *Tables for all Merchants and Shopkeepers.* [*T.C.* I. 275.] In 1690 he sold a set of *Chronological Tables.* [*T.C.* II. 313.]

HILTON (ROBERT), bookseller at Manchester and Ashbourne, 1678–88. Robert Hilton, bookseller, married in 1678, took the oath of allegiance to Charles II in the following year, had a son baptized in 1681. [R. W. Procter, *Memorials of Manchester Streets*, p. 182.] Apparently moved to Ashbourne, where he published in 1688 *The Gospel-Call in Metre.* [*T.C.* II. 215.]

HINCH (S.), printer in London, 1684. During the Frost Fair held on the Thames in the winter of $168\frac{3}{4}$, four printers, one of whom was the above, printed a broadside in verse, *On the Royal Martyr, King Charles I.*, 'Printed on the Frozen Thames, January the 30th, 1683. By the Loyal Young Printers, viz. G. and A. Melbourn, S. Hinch, and J. Mason.' [Haz. II. 681.]

HINCHMAN, *see* Hensman.

HINDMARSH (H.), bookseller in London, Golden Ball, Cornhill, over against the Royal Exchange, 1696–8. Succeeded Joseph Hindmarsh. Publisher of anti-Quaker literature. [*T.C.* II. 599.] In 1698 he was one of the publishers of Collier's ***Short view of the Immorality and profaneness of the English Stage.***

HINDMARSH (JOSEPH), bookseller in London, bookseller to His Royal Highness, (1) Black Bull in Cornhill, over against the Royal Exchange; (2) Golden Ball in Cornhill. 1678–96. His first entry in the Term Catalogues was ***Loyalty and Peace,*** two sermons by the Rev. Sam. Rolls, Chaplain to the King, in 1678. [*T.C.* I. 329.] At the Sessions at the Old Bailey on April 13th, 1680, Hindmarsh was accused of publishing ***The Presbyterians' Paternoster and Ten Commandments.*** In the same year he issued Oldham's ***Satyrs upon the Jesuits.*** [*T.C.* I. 419.] In 1682 he published Buckingham's ***Essay upon***

Poetry, D'Urfey's *New Collection of Songs and Poems*, Sir R. Talbor's *English Remedy,* a translation from Cicero's *De Natura deorum*, and the Rev. A. Elliot's *Modest Vindication of Titus Oates.* [*T.C.* I. 508–9.] In 1684 he published a poetical broadside entitled *A Letter to Ferguson.* [B.M. 1872. a. 1 (41).] Dr. Richard Midgeley conveyed to him and others in 1693 his copyright in the eight volumes of the *Turkish Spy.* [Nichols, *Lit. Anecd.* I. 413.] In 1685 he moved to the Golden Ball in Cornhill and is last heard of in Hil. $169\frac{5}{6}$. [*T.C.* II. 567.] He was succeeded by H. Hindmarsh.

HINE (R.), bookseller in London, near the Royal Exchange, 1701. Published *A Walk to Smithfield, or A True Description of the Humours of Bartholomew Fair*, 1701. [Haz. H. 31.]

HINTON (THOMAS), printer in Cirencester, in Pye Corner, 1718–24. The first Gloucestershire printer. Probably began printing in 1718. Hazlitt [H. 230] records *The most strangest and unparalleled Account . . . to be justified by several persons living in Campden in Gloucestershire*, n. d. In 1719 he began *The Cirencester Post, or Gloucestershire Mercury* (no. 18, March 16th, 1719) [B.M. P.P. 3424 c.], but the earliest copy recorded by Messrs. Hyett and Bazeley [II. 162] is that of July 25th, 1720. They say, however, that Hinton must have established his press two or three years before Raikes came to Gloucester. This paper was published weekly, and the civil year was used in dating it, so no. 1 must have appeared about the last week of October 1718. His son Thomas was a bookseller at the Talbot in Tetbury in 1720. [Hyett and Bazeley, I. 20.]

HIRST (JOHN), printer and bookseller at Leeds, over against Kirkgate-End, 1718 (?)–30. He printed and sold *The Leeds Mercury* (vol. ii, no. 49, April 5th–12th, 1720, vol. I, no. 1 probably in 1718); and was still at work at Leeds in 1730. [Allnutt, p. 301.]

HISLOP (ARCHIBALD), bookseller and printer in Edinburgh, in the Parliament Yard at the sign of the Bible, 1670–8. Watson [p. 11] says, "Archbald Hyslop, a bookseller, set up, taking in with him William Carron, a very excellent workman, who advis'd Mr. Hyslop to bring new materials from Holland. They printed Thomas à Kempis very neatly, and some other small books; to which is prefix'd sometimes the name of the one, and sometimes the name of the other". No book is known bearing Hislop's

name as printer, but an edition of *The Psalms in meeter* was printed for him in 1670 by A. Anderson, and he was one of those who sold James Kirkwood's *Rhetoricae Compendium* in 1678. There were two bookbinders of this name in Edinburgh. The will of the earlier was registered on July 10th, 1679, and he may have been identical with the bookseller. The other bookbinder died in 1697, his will being registered on June 8th. According to Watson [p. 14] this printing house passed into the hands of John Cairns. [Aldis, pp. 114–15.]

HIVE (T.), bookseller in London, Nag's Head, Jewen Street, 1695 (?). The second edition of John Taylor the Water Poet's ***Verbum Sempiternum,*** 2nd ed., n.d. (Imprimatur dated October 6th, 1693), has the above imprint [Haz. H. 604], but Hive is otherwise unknown.

HODGES (JOHN), bookseller in Derby, 1716. One of the booksellers named in the imprint to Henry Cantrell's ***Royal Martyr a True Christian,*** 1716.

HODGKIN (THOMAS), printer and bookseller in London, next door to the Dolphin Inn, West Smithfield, 1677–1713. This printer is first met with in the proceedings taken by the House of Lords in February 1676–7 to discover the printers and vendors of certain libellous pamphlets. Hodgkin was called before the Committee as a witness in regard to the tract entitled *Some Considerations upon the question whether the Parliament is dissolved by its Prorogation for fifteen months,* but all he could say was that he had been unable to find out who printed it. He was probably only a workman at that time. [*Hist. MSS. Comm.*, *9th Report*, App., pp. 69–78.] In 1686 his name appears as a bookseller, when he sold the *Thirty-six Sermons* of the Bishop of Lincoln. [*T.C.* II. 191.] In 1688 he is recorded as the printer of an edition of Suetonius. [*T.C.* II. 230.] He was also the printer in 1690 of the seventeenth edition of Chamberlayne's *Angliae Notitia,* and continued in business until after 1713, when he contributed to the Bowyer relief fund.

HODGKINSON (S.), printer in Derby, near St. Warburg's Church, 1719–27(?). Printer of *The Derby Postman* (no. 8, January 19th, 1720). The title was changed in 1726 to *The British Spy, or Derby Postman,* and a new series began in 1727. [*N. & Q.*, 3rd Ser., IX. 164.]

HODGSON (JOSEPH), bookseller in Chester, 1712. Only known as the publisher of T. Leche's ***Danger of Bad Principles,*** 1712.

HODGSON (THOMAS), bookseller in London, over against Gray's Inn Gate in Holborn, 1700–2. Noticed by Dunton [p. 215] as a successful bookseller. Amongst his publications was Dr. Sacheverell's ***Account of the Isle of Man,*** 1702. [Haz. III. 218.] His name does not appear in the Term Catalogues.

HOLFORD (JOHN), bookseller in London, (*a*) Pall-Mall, over against St. Alban's Street; (*b*) Crown in Pall Mall. 1681–9. Published ***The Present State of the Protestants in France,*** 1681. [Haz. IV. 40.] In 1684 he advertised in ***The London Gazette*** of November 24th–27th an edition of Lucian. In 1685 he published Edward Eccleston's opera ***The Cataclysm.*** [*T.C.* II. 114.] His last entry was in 1689. [*T.C.* II. 275.] He was probably a relative of S. Holford, who published from the same address at the same time. His two addresses probably describe the same house.

HOLFORD (SAMUEL), bookseller in London, Crown in the Pall Mall, 1685–8. Began to publish about 1685 with Dr. Nehemiah Grew's ***Musæum Regalis Societatis*** [*T. C.* II. 150], and John Holford appears to have been in partnership with him. He sold books on all subjects, and distributed the sale catalogue of Lord Maitland in 1689. He is last heard of in 1694, when with J. Taylor of Paternoster Row he published ***The Swordsman's Vade Mecum.*** [*T.C.* II. 493.]

HOLLAND (ABRAHAM), bookseller in Manchester, Hanging Ditch, 1673–90. Born at Crumpsall in March 1640. In 1673 he married, and he appears in the poll book of 1690. [R. W. Proctor, ***Memorials of Manchester Streets,*** p. 182.]

HOLLAND (J.), bookseller in Chester, 1714. Published ***A General View of Christian Religion,*** by L. Fogg, 1714. [B.M. 4410. f. 17.]

HOLLAND (JAMES), bookseller in London, Bible and Ball in St. Paul's Churchyard, 1705–11. Publisher of sermons; he made his first appearance in the Term Catalogues in Trin. 1705. [*T.C.* III. 463.] He was also the publisher of Nahum Tate's ***The Triumph,*** 1705.

HOLMAN (C.), stationer (?) in London, Hare in Southwark, 1692. Dealer in William Jordan's copy-books. [*T.C.* II. 404.]

HOLT (   ), printer in London, St. John's Lane, 1712 (?)–24 (?). Possibly a son of R. Holt, printer. In 1713 he contributed to the Bowyer Relief Fund, and in Negus's List of Printers in 1724 he is mentioned among those "well affected to King George". [Timperley, p. 631.]

HOLT (ELIZABETH), printer in London, 1689–90. In partnership with W. Horton. In 1689 she printed W. Ravenhill's *Short Account of the Company of Grocers*, and in the same year, in partnership with W. Horton, *Gazophylacium Anglicanum, Containing a derivation of English words*, for Randall Taylor. In 1690 she printed for Thomas Basset, Locke's *Essay concerning Human Understanding*. She is probably the "widow Holt" who was ordered to lay down the trade of printing, *see* Holt (R.). Dunton's reference [p. 292] to "virgin Holt" may be to a daughter.

HOLT (R.), printer in London, 1671–88. In 1671–3 he and Evan Tyler, sometimes as R. H. and E. T., printed in partnership; in 1672 their names appear on Thomas Philipott's *Brief Historical Discourse of Heraldry*. [B.M. 605. b. 7.] In 1686–8 he was in partnership with E. Horton; they printed Sir Roger Manley's *Commentaria de Rebellione Anglicana*, as well as *A Relation of the Conference between William Laud . . . and Mr. Fisher the Jesuit . . .* which they printed for J. Mitchell and R. Hughes. [*T.C.* II. 171.] E. Horton apparently died soon after, for Holt was in partnership with W. Horton in 1688 for the printing of Florio's *Italian and English Dictionary*, and Torriano's *Vocabolario*. [Haz. II. 600.] Holt is believed to have died in 1688, as an order was made in that year by the Company of Stationers that the widow Holt [*see* Holt (Elizabeth)] and others should lay down the trade of printing in obedience to the Act of Parliament. [Records of Stat. Co.]

HOMER (SAMUEL), bookseller in London, St. Paul, Little Britain, 1671. Publisher of a funeral sermon by W. Yole on Mrs. Martha Walmsly in 1671. [*T.C.* I. 85.]

HOOKE (J.), bookseller in London, Flower de Luce, over against St. Dunstan's Church, in Fleet Street, 1718–25. Publisher of the Rev. John Lyly's *False Friend and Inconstant Mistress*, 1718. [Haz. I. 270.] In 1722 he was one of the publishers of a novel called *The Adventures of the Prince of Clermont*, and was still publishing in 1725. [Esdaile, pp. 189, 191.]

HOOKE (NATHANIEL), bookseller in London, King's Arms, Little Britain, 1672. Publisher of Richard Cumberland's *De Legibus Naturae*, 1672 [*T.C.* I. 99], also of vol. iv of M. Poole's *Synopsis* [*T.C.* I. 114], and Dr. Francis Glesson's *De Natura Substantiae Energetica*. [*T.C.* I. 120.]

HOOKER (JOSEPH), bookseller (?) in Exeter, 1688. Advertised catalogues of a book sale at Exeter in *Public Occurrences*, July 10th, 1688. Not mentioned by Dredge.

HOOLE (SAMUEL), stationer in London, Crown, next Ludgate Church, 1689–1712. Received subscriptions for Jean de Launoy's *Epistolae Omnes*, 1689. Dunton [pp. 255, 405] says that he had "traded with him for many years", and praises his charitable disposition. Accordingly he was one of the largest subscribers to the Bowyer Relief Fund in 1713. [Timperley, p. 600.]

HOPE (E.), bookseller in London, North Entrance into the Royal Exchange, 1680 (?)–84. Succeeded to William Hope between 1672 and 1680. He advertised Bateman's *Scurvy Grass* in *Currant Intelligence*, April 10th, 1680, and in 1684 he published the 4th ed. of C. Sutton's *Godly Meditations*. [*T.C.* II. 64.]

HOPE (WILLIAM), bookseller in London, (1) under St. Martin's Outwich, Bishopsgate; (2) at the North Entrance to the Royal Exchange. 1670–2. *See Dictionary*, 1641–67. Still in business in 1672. Succeeded by E. Hope.

HOPPER (GEORGE), printer in London, 1683. Mentioned in the will of Robert Pawlett *alias* Pawley, who died in 1683, as one of his overseers. [P.C.C. 97, Drax.] He may have been only a working printer and not a master.

HORNE (ROBERT). *See Dictionary*, 1641–67. Still at work in 1686. [*T.C.* II. 162.] Succeeded by Thomas Horne.

HORNE (THOMAS), bookseller in London, South Entrance to the Royal Exchange, 1686–1711. Successor to Robert Horne. Began as a divinity publisher in 1686. [*T.C.* II. 175.] In 1694 in company with C. Brome he published *Select Novels* from Cervantes, Petrarch, &c. [*T.C.* II. 505, Esdaile, p. 32.] He was still publishing in 1711. [*T.C.* III. 677.]

HORTON (E.), printer in London, 1671–88. First met with in 1671 as the printer of a broadside entitled, *Great Britain's Beauty, or London's Delight*, by George Elliott, Gent. [B.M. C. 20. f. 2 (89).] Between 1679 and 1688, however, Horton was employed to print some notable editions of the classics, and these books may rank with the best work of that period. The first was a folio Herodotus in Greek and Latin, for which the type was cast by James Grover. This was followed by an edition in two folio volumes of

the Works of Cicero in 1681. From about 1686 he was in partnership with R. Holt (*q. v.*). Neither is mentioned in the list of printing houses of 1675. Also about 1686 Horton levied an execution on Nathaniel Ponder for a debt, which was settled by Thomas Braddyll. He was succeeded by W. Horton between 1686 and 1688.

HORTON (W.), printer in London, 1688 (?)–90. By 1688 he succeeded E. Horton in the partnership with R. and E. Holt (*q. v.*); in 1690 Horton alone printed William Walker's *English and Latin Dictionary*. [Haz. III. 313.]

HOTHAM (MATTHEW), bookseller in London, Black Boy on London Bridge, 1704–25. Successor to John Back. Like all the London Bridge booksellers, he published all kinds of cheap and popular literature, which he circulated up and down the country by chapmen. Hotham died in 1725, and was buried in St. Magnus' Church.

HOW (JOB), printer in London, *c.* 1700. Mentioned by Dunton [p. 250] as "honest Job". Where there is no christian name or address in the imprint it is difficult to distinguish him from John How (*q. v.*).

HOW or HOWE (JOHN), bookseller and printer in London, (1) Sweeting's Alley in Cornhill; (2) Seven Stars, at the South-West Corner of the Royal Exchange in Cornhill; (3) Coach and Horses without Bishopsgate; (4) Ram's Head Inn Yard in Fenchurch Street; (5) Seven Stars, Talbot Court, Gracechurch Street. 1680–1709. He first appeared as publisher of a satirical news-sheet in the Protestant interest, entitled *Catholic Intelligence* (nos. 1–5, March 1st–29th, 1679–80) [B.M. Burney 81], and in the same year sold E. Clark's *Protestant Schoolmaster*. [Haz. III. 43.] In 1683 he published, at the corner of the Royal Exchange in Cornhill, *Catastrophe Mundi, or Merlin revived* [*T.C.* II. 7; Haz. III. 160], and *Rome rhymed to death*, a collection of poems by Rochester and others. [Haz. I. 364.] In 1684 his address appears as "the Coach and Horses without Bishops-gate" on a sheet, *A strange . . . Relation of . . . the . . . Frost*. [Haz. II. 238.] After this he is not heard of again till 1699, when he began a paper, *The Weekly Comedy* (no. 1, May 10th). In the next three years he was actively printing numerous pieces for Edward Ward, including *The London Spy*, and Tutchin's *Observator*; he was settled in Fenchurch Street, but moved in 1702 to Talbot Court, where he is found in 1707 publishing with M. Hotham *Pleasant Intrigues of an English Nobleman . . . at Venice*. [Haz. III. 254.] In 1709 he issued privately a pamphlet entitled *Some Thoughts on the present state of Printing and Bookselling* [B.M. 11901. a. 2 (3)], in which he attacks various fellow-printers for piracy while vindicating himself. Dunton says of him [p. 220], "He was a bookseller for many years, and now follows the trade of printing. . . . He is a true lover of his Queen and Country [i. e. a Whig]. . . . He was a great sufferer in King James's reign, and has had the fate of being a traveller. . . . He is now settled in Gracechurch Street; and, being a great Projector (as we see by the *London Spy* and the *Observator*, &c.), is likely to increase apace." His sufferings and travels here spoken of, possibly due to his political party, account for the gap in our record of him. *See* How (Job).

HOWE (JOSEPH), bookseller in Nottingham, 1689. Sold locally an Assize sermon preached at Nottingham by W. Wilson (London, for Awnsham Churchill). [Creswell, p. 6.]

HOWELL (JOHN), bookseller at Oxford, 1686–99. In 1686 John Howell published *A Collection of Prayers*. [*T.C.* II. 164.] He was still in business in 1699. [*T.C.* III. 148.]

HOWELL (MARY), Oxford, 1698. [Madan, p. 31.]

HOWKINS or HAWKINS (S.), bookseller in London, George Yard, Lombard Street, 1694. Probably identical with a Mrs. Howkins who is frequently referred to at this time, and widow of Thomas Howkins. She dealt largely in patent medicines.

HOWKINS or HAWKINS (THOMAS), bookseller in London, George Yard, Lombard Street, 1684–94. Began as a publisher of mathematical books [*T.C.* II. 98], and also published books on writing and shorthand. His last entry was made in Easter 1693. [*T.C.* II. 459.] In 1694 he was the publisher of *The City Mercury* [Burney 112 A], and in that year S. Howkins, probably his widow (*q. v.*), was in business at the same address.

HOWLETT (   ), printer in London, Lincoln's Inn Fields, 1724. Mentioned in Negus's List as a Roman Catholic printer.

HOYLE (SAMUEL), stationer of London, 1685. Defendant in an action for debt brought successfully against him by Humphrey Brooke, doctor of Medicine, in Trin. 1 James II. [C.P.R. 1 Jas. II, Roll 3038, m. 1666 verso.]

HUBBALD (FRANK), bookseller in London, Duck Lane, *c.* 1700. Noticed very briefly by Dunton [p. 229] as "having been unfortunate in business".

HUD (THOMAS), printer in Manchester, –1692. His burial is recorded in the parish register, September 11th, 1692. [R. W. Procter, *Memorials of Manchester Streets*, p. 182].

HUDDLESTON (GEORGE), bookseller in London, (1) Strand, near the Savoy; (2) Black-a-Moors Head, Exeter Change. 1697–8. Publisher in 1697 of Le Comte's *Memoires of China* [*T.C.* III. 47], and in 1698 of Evelyn's *Gardener's Almanack*, and Thomas Lyster's *Blessings of Eighty-Eight.*

HUDGEBUT (JOHN), stationer in London, (1) Harp and Hoboy in Chancery Lane near Fleet Street; (2) St. Paul's Churchyard; (3) Strand, (*a*) near Charing Cross, (*b*) near St. Martin's Lane. 1680–99. Dealt chiefly in music. In 1680 he published *Youth's Delight, or new lessons for the Flageolet.* [*T.C.* I. 432.] In Hil. 1686 he was sued by Martha, Lady Atcheson, otherwise Atkins, for forfeiture of a bond. [C.P.R. 3055, m. 1911 r.] In this he is described as "Stationer" of St. Paul's Churchyard. He is last heard of in Hil. 1699, when he was in the Strand. [*T.C.* III. 109.]

HUGHES (R.), bookseller in London, Unicorn, over against the Queen's Head Tavern in Paternoster Row, 1684. A Catholic bookseller. In Trin. 1684 he advertised *Critical Enquiries into the various editions of the Bible*, by Father Simon of the Oratory, and in 1686 *The Relation of the Conference between Laud and Fisher.* [*T.C.* II. 82, 171.] In 1692 Viscount Sidney directed the Postmaster-General to stop any letters directed to a Mr. Brett at Mr. Hughes in Paternoster Row and send them to him. [S.P.D., William and Mary, 1692, p. 132.]

HUGHS ( ), bookseller of Beaumaris, 1700. Sold school books and devotional works, which he bought wholesale from John Minshull, bookseller of Chester. [*Library*, 2nd ser., IV. 378.]

HUME or HUMES (THOMAS), printer in Dublin, Copper Alley, 1715–28. He did a great deal of printing, the principal work from his press being Crossley's *Peerage of Ireland*, 1725. In 1715 he was in partnership with A. Meres. In this year, or late in 1714, and again in 1718, Thomas Gent (*q.v.*) worked for him in Copper Alley. He spelt his name with an "s" at first, but omitted the "s" in his later imprints.

HUMPHERIES (RICHARD), bookseller in London, 1690. He published *A Sermon preached at Christ Church, London, Nov. the 2d. 1690*, by David Jones. [B.M. 693. f. 19 (9).]

HUMPHREYS (J.), printer in London, Bartholomew Lane behind the Royal Exchange, 1697 (?)–1724. Two references to a Mr. Humpheries or Humfreys are found in the early part of the eighteenth century, one in the list of printers subscribing to the relief fund for William Bowyer in 1713 and the other in Negus's list of 1724. In the latter Mr. Humpheries is described as being printer to the parish clerks. [Timperley, pp. 601, 631–2.] He printed Sternhold and Hopkins for the Company in 1723. J. Humphrys printed for John Lawrence. He may also be identical with the J. H. who printed for J. Sprint in 1697 and for J. Robinson, J. Laurence, and J. Wyat in 1710.

HUNT (RICHARD), bookseller in London, (1) Lute in St. Paul's Churchyard; (2) Repository in Gresham College. 1683–99. Humphrey Salter's *Genteel Companion*, 1683, was printed for Richard Hunt and Humphry Salter at the Lute in St. Paul's Churchyard. [Haz. IV. 91.] He may possibly be identical with the bookseller of the name who was at Hereford in 1685 (*q. v.*); he does not appear again in London unless he be the Mr. Hunt who in 1693 was advertised as receiver of contributions to the *Philosophical Transactions* [*T.C.* II. 466], and in 1699 published Dr. Edward Tyson's *Orang-Outang.* [*T.C.* III. 137–8.]

HUNT (RICHARD), bookseller in Hereford, 1685. Occurs in a list of booksellers and stationers who sold a patent medicine, given at the end of M. Bromfield's *A brief Discovery of the . . . Scurvy.* [*N. & Q.*, 11th Ser., XI. 45.] Possibly identical with the London bookseller of the name (*q. v.*).

HUNT (WILLIAM), stationer in London, St. Clement Danes, 1688. Defendant in an action for assault brought against him in the Court of Common Pleas. [C.P.R. Trin. 4 Jas. II, 3068, m. 176 verso.]

HUNTER ( ), printer in London, Jewin Street, 1724. Mentioned in Negus's list as "well affected to King George".

HURLOCK (BENJAMIN), bookseller in London, (*a*) over against St. Magnus' Church, (*b*) on London Bridge. 1671–3. Son or grandson of George Hurlock (*q. v.* in *Dictionary*, 1641–67). He first appears in the Term Catalogues in

1671, but may have been at work much earlier; his address is very near George Hurlock's, and both published books for sailors. Like other London Bridge booksellers he dealt mostly in schoolbooks and popular literature, often in association with Passenger. His most important publication was *Military and Maritime Discipline*, 1672, fol. Succeeded by his widow Elizabeth, *q. v.* [*T.C.* I. 73, 75, 76, 86, 88, 111, 133, 134, 157.]

HURLOCK (ELIZABETH), bookseller in London, Rose at the West End of St. Paul's, 1673–5. Succeeded her husband Benjamin (*q. v.*), whose publications she advertised herself as selling in Mich. 1673. In 1675 she published Thomas Miller's *Compleat Modelist*, a nautical book. [*T.C.* I. 157, 224.]

HURT, *see* Hart.

HUSBAND (RICHARD), stationer in London, Upper Shadwell, near the Market, 1680. Sold a pack of cards illustrating the Popish Plot. [*T.C.* I. 384.]

HUSSEY (CHRISTOPHER), bookseller and book auctioneer in London, Flower de luce, over against the Globe in Little Britain, 1678–1705. Began as a publisher of theological and mathematical books in 1678. [*T.C.* I. 308.] He added book-auctions to his other business, and copies of his catalogues of 1691 are in the British Museum, among them being that of the library of the Rev. Ph. Mason, January 4th, 1691–2. [B.M. 821. i. 9 (29).] Hussey's name appears in the Term Catalogues for the last time in Easter 1705. [*T.C.* III. 457.] Dunton [p. 286] speaks of him as "a downright honest man: and has always a large stock of books that are very scarce".

HUTCHINSON (HUGH), bookbinder and bookseller in Durham, 1665–84. Probably son of William Hutchinson. [*See Dictionary*, 1641–67.] Bishop Cosin bought prayer-books and stationery of him in 1665, and in 1670 had his armorial stamp impressed on the backs of all his books by Hutchinson. [*Cosin Correspondence* (Surtees Soc.), II. 268–9, 277–8, 284.] In 1684 he published a sermon, *The Compleat Conformist*, by Archdeacon Grenville.

HUTCHINSON (LEONARD), stationer in London, St. Clement Danes, 1687. Defendant in a suit for the recovery of £60 brought by Hugh Waters. [C.P.R. 3056, m. 589 recto.]

HUTCHINSON (ROBERT), bookseller in Edinburgh, in the Head of the College Wind, 1696. Publisher of *A Satyr against Atheistical Deism* by Mungo Craig, 1696. [Aldis, pp. 94, 115.]

HYTHER (JONAS), bookseller in London, 1682. Published in 1682 *The Speech of . . . Sir George Treby.* [Haz. II. 603.]

I. (M.), bookseller in London, 1668. Hazlitt [IV. 107] records *The Duke of Buckingham's Speech in a late Conference*, "London: Printed for M. I.", 1668.

I. (N.), bookseller (?) in London, 1680. Hazlitt [II. 583] records the following: *An Account of a strange and prodigious Storm of Thunder, Lightning and Hail which happened in and about London on Tuesday the Eighteenth of this instant May* . . . "London, Printed for N. I." 1680, 4°, four leaves, but does not give any reference as to where it is to be found.

ILIVE (T.), printer in London, Aldersgate Street, 1724. Father of Jacob, Abraham, and Isaac Ilive, printers and letter founders. [Nichols, *Lit. Anecd.* I. 309.] Described by Negus as a "High Flyer".

ILLIDGE (SAMUEL), bookseller and book auctioneer in London, under Searle's Gate, Lincoln's Inn, New Square, 1716. Publisher of an edition of Brathwaite's *Drunken Barnaby's Four Journeys* in 1716. He is also frequently mentioned in the newspapers of this period as holding book auctions.

INCE (E.), printer in Chester, 1712–18. His only known imprint is that to Lawrence Fogg's *Two Treatises*, "Chester, Printed by E. Ince for R. Minshull in Bridge-Street," 1712. [Allnutt, p. 299.] Gent [pp. 79, 83–4] says that his materials were bought from his executors in 1718 by one Cook.

INGHALL (WILLIAM), senior, bookbinder and bookseller in London, 1681–2. A broadside entitled *The Character of a Tory* bears the imprint: "London: Printed for William Inghall the Elder, Bookbinder, 1681." [B.M. 816. m. 2 (16).] In the next year Inghall is found publishing *The Irish Evidence.*

INNYS (JOHN), *see* Innys (William).

INNYS (WILLIAM), bookseller in London, Prince's Arms, St. Paul's Churchyard, 1711–32. One of the leading booksellers in London in the first quarter of the eighteenth century. Succeeded B. Walford at this house. He made his first entry in the Term Catalogues in Easter 1711. [*T.C.* III. 659.] In 1713 he subscribed five guineas to the Bowyer fund. He was afterwards joined by John Innys. In 1720 they issued an eight-page miscellaneous catalogue of books printed for them, including Clarendon's *History of the Rebellion*, 6 vols.; Strype's *Life of Archbishop Whitgift*; and Le Neve's *Monumenta*

Anglicana, 5 vols. In 1722 they were among the booksellers receiving subscriptions for a folio edition of Sir Henry Spelman's *Works*. [Nichols, *Lit. Anecd.*, I. 240.] They were also the publishers of many of Sir Isaac Newton's works. They were still at work in 1732. [Roberts, *Cambridge Press*, p. 91.]

ISTED (J.), bookseller in London, Golden Ball against St. Dunstan's Church in Fleet Street, 1711–25. He was advertising books in the news sheets of 1711, and was still publishing in 1725 when he issued the *Miscellaneous Works* of Dr. William Wagstaffe. [Nichols, *Lit. Anecd.* I. 323.]

J. (S.), bookseller in London, 1681. Published in 1681 two sheets, *Mistris Celiers Lamentation for the loss of her Liberty*, and *A Dialogue between the Pope and the Devil, about Owen and Baxter*. [Haz. II. 88, 174.]

J. (T.), printer in London, 1672–82. These initials, which may be those of Thomas James, are found in *A New Help to Discourse*, advertised in Hil. 1672, as printed by T. J. for Peter Parker. [*T.C.* I. 100.] They recur in an edition of Hannah Woolley's *Gentlewoman's Companion*, 1682, "printed by T. J. for Edward Thomas". [*T.C.* I. 468.]

JACOB (WILLIAM), bookseller in London, Black Swan near Bernards-Inn Gate, in Holborn, 1670–80. Publisher of law-books and divinity. His first and last entries in the Term Catalogues were made in Easter 1670 and Trin. 1680. [*T.C.* I. 39, 405.]

JACKSON (DAVID), bookseller in London, Bible and Three Crowns, Cheapside, near Mercer's Chapel, 1700–16(?). Prof. Arber gives under his name in the Index to the Term Catalogues (vol. III) a reference to Parkhurst, whom he apparently succeeded at this address. In 1710 he joined N. Cliff (*q. v.*), and disappeared by 1716. Dunton [p. 293] has a reference to "candid" Jackson, who may or may not be the same person.

JACKSON (JOHN), printer in York, Petergate, 1707. Printed *Catalogus pharmacorum*, 1707. [Bodl. 1692. f. 23.]

JACKSON (N.), bookseller in London, in the Strand, 1693. Published *The Country Miser*, 1693. [Haz. I. 148.]

JAFFRAY (GEORGE), printer in Edinburgh, (1) his Shop, at the Tron Church door; (2) his Printing House within the Head of Peebles Wynd. 1696–1710. "In 1696 George Jaffray set up a small printing-house; it is now extinct."

[Watson, p. 18.] Probably son of William (*q. v.*). No books have been noted bearing Jaffray's name before 1700. [Aldis, p. 115.] He moved to his second house in 1702 or 1703.

JAFFRAY (WILLIAM), stationer in Edinburgh, 1695. Will registered December 30th, 1695; together with those of Margaret Walker, his relict, and Andrew Dunbar, her last husband. [Scottish Record Soc., *Index to Edinburgh Testaments*.] Probably father of George (*q. v.*).

JAKIN (ELLEN), stationer (?) in London, at the end of St. Paul's Alley, in St. Paul's Churchyard, 1680. In 1680 a pack of cards commemorating the Popish Plot was advertised for sale by several dealers, amongst them the above; but she may not have been a stationer. [*T.C.* I. 384.]

JAMES (GEORGE), printer in London, Little Britain, 1712 (?)–35. Author and printer of the *Post Boy*. Perhaps brother of John and Thomas James, type-founders, but *see* Reed, p. 212 note. The inter-relationship of the members of the James family engaged in the trade at this time is obscure. Negus in his list of 1724 describes George as a "High-Flyer". In 1724 he succeeded Alderman Barber as City printer. [Nichols, *Lit. Anecd.* I. 305.] He died in 1735. His sister Elizabeth married Jacob Ilive the printer.

JAMES (THOMAS), bookseller and mathematical printer to the King, Printing Press, Mincing Lane, 1678–1711. Great-grandson of Thomas James, Keeper of the Bodleian Library. Unless he is to be identified with the T. J. (*q. v.*) who printed in 1672, he began printing about 1678. In 1680 he printed for T. Vile a *Weekly Advertisement of Books*. James died in 1711 and his books, which he bequeathed to the public, were offered to and accepted by Sion College. In the College is a portrait of James. [Nichols, *Lit. Anecd.* I. 308.]

JAMES (THOMAS), type-founder in London, Bartholomew Close, 1710–36. Son of the Rev. John James, Vicar of Basingstoke. Served his apprenticeship with Robert Andrews and began business in Aldermanbury, whence he removed to Town Ditch and finally settled in Bartholomew Close. In 1710 he went to Holland, and after considerable trouble returned to England with 3,500 matrices of various founts of roman and italics, as well as sets of Greek and some black letter. William Ged's attempt to introduce stereotype printing failed owing largely to the action of James and his workmen. James's prosperity declined, and he died in 1736, being succeeded

by his son John, who had for some time managed the business. [Plomer, *Short History of English Printing*, 1915, p. 196; Reed, pp. 212–20.]

JANEWAY (ELIZABETH), bookseller in Chichester, 1697. Published *A Sermon preached . . . at the Assizes held at Horsham . . . March 23, 1696/7. By Peter Heald, A.M., Prebendary in the Cathedral Church at Chichester*. [*T.C.* III. 12; Bodl. Sermons, 9.]

JANEWAY (RICHARD), senior, printer, bookseller, and bookbinder in London, (*a*) Queen's Head Alley, (*b*) Queen's Head Court, Paternoster Row, 1680–98(?). Like Benjamin Harris, Langley Curtis, and Nathaniel Thompson, Janeway became notorious as a fanatically Protestant publisher in the time of the Popish Plot. His first entry in the Term Catalogues is in Easter 1680, and is characteristically entitled *The Tryal, conviction and condemnation of Popery for High Treason*. [*T.C.* I. 397–8.] In this year he sold also *A Defence of True Protestants*, spelling his name "Janua". [Title-page only in Bagford Coll., B.M., Harl. 5927 (504).] Janeway quarrelled with other publishers of Protestant news-sheets and retorted in *The Impartial Protestant Mercury* and *The New News Book*, both of which he started in 1681. In that year he also brought an action for assault against Thomas Newcombe, John Towse, Randal Taylor, and Michael Foster, all of them stationers. The details of the case are wanting; but it was probably connected with a search carried out on his premises by the Company of Stationers. [C.P.R. 2296, m. 256 r.] His name drops out of the Term Catalogues in Easter 1690. [*T.C.* III. 318.] He is probably the "honest Dick Janeway", the binder, described by Dunton [p. 257] apparently as dead in 1703. He was probably alive in 1698, as Richard Janeway junior (*q. v.*) describes himself as such in that year.

JANEWAY (RICHARD), junior, printer in London, Dogwell Court, Whitefriars, near Fleet Street, 1698–1724. Probably son of Richard Janeway, senior. In 1698 *The Lancashire Levite Rebuk'd* was "printed by Richard Janeway, junr." He is probably the Janeway given in Negus's list of printers, 1724, as being in White Friars [Nichols, *Lit. Anecd.* I. 291], and also the Janeway who printed occasionally for Dunton both before and after the latter's misfortunes, *c.* 1698 [p. 250]; Negus classes him among the printers "well affected to King George". [Nichols, *Lit. Anecd.* I. 291.]

JANUA (RICHARD), *see* Janeway (Richard), senior.

JAQUES (JOSEPH), bookseller at Midhurst in Sussex, 1712. Sold the Rev. Charles Bettesworth's *Sermon preach'd at Petworth . . . September 3d, 1712, at a Confirmation*, London, 1712. [B.M. 4473. aaa. 46 (8).]

JAUNCY (T.), bookseller in London, Angel, without Temple Bar, 1720. He published two books in 1720: (1) *A New Miscellany of Original Poems . . .* by the most Eminent Hands, viz. Mr. Prior, Mr. Pope, &c.; (2) Longus, *The Pastoral Amours of Daphnis and Chloe . . . The second edition*. [B.M. 11335. a. 2.]

JAYE (ELIPHAL), bookseller in London, (1) Bible on the north side of the Royal Exchange, 1691; (2) Golden Candlestick in Cheapside, 1702; (3) near Mercer's Chapel, 1703. 1691–1703. Advertised Sir Edward Sadler's *History of the Jacobites* in Mich. 1691. [*T.C.* II. 381.] He was the publisher of Edward Ward's *Writings* in 1702 [*T.C.* III. 300–1], and of two of the Rev. Richard Taylor's theological tracts in 1703. [*T.C.* III. 365.] He sometimes held book auctions. [*London Gazette*, August 9th–13th, 1694.]

JEFFERY (EDMUND), bookseller in Cambridge, 1699–1729, living in the High Street two doors south of the Green Dragon, and later, from 1719 to 1729, at what is now No. 1 Trinity Street, succeeding William Dickinson (*q. v.*), and being succeeded by Wm. Thurlburn (*q. v.*). His publications were principally sermons preached before the University. For John Leng's *Sermon* of 1699 we learn that he and R. Clavel of the Peacock in St. Paul's Church-yard, London, paid 16*s.* per sheet for printing the 1,000 copies. [Bowes, *Cambridge Books*, note to no. 105.] A catalogue of some of his publications is to be found in J. Hughes's edition of Chrysostom *de Sacerdotio*, 1710.

JENKINSON (ROBERT), bookseller in London, 1690. Publisher of *The Judgement of the Foreign Reformed Churches concerning . . . the Church of England*, by N. S., 1690. [B.M. T. 1030 (16).]

JENOUR (MATTHEW), printer in London, near St. Sepulchre's Back-Gate in Gilt-Spur Street, 1707–25. Printed Povey's news-sheet, *The General Remark on Trade*, 1707. [Burney 140.] In 1724 Jenour was printing *The Flying Post* and was numbered among those "well affected to King George" by Negus. Later he became "the first establisher of the *Daily Advertiser*", a paper which for many years stood at the head of all the diurnal publications.

"Mr. Jenour was a man of very respectable character, and the *Daily Advertiser* enriched his family". [Nichols, *Lit. Anecd.*, I. 290–1.]

JOHNSON (ANDREW), bookseller in Lichfield and Birmingham, 1694 (?)–1702 (?). Younger brother of Michael and Benjamin Johnson. Apprenticed to the latter at the age of 23, in 1683, for seven years, but never made free of the Company. He assisted his brother Michael at Lichfield, and on his own account published the first Birmingham book, *A Discourse concerning Church-communion* [by A. Jeacocke], 1702, probably at his brother's stall. [Birmingham Pub. Lib., *Cat. of the Birmingham Collection*, 1918, p. 792.] He was a noted boxer, and instructed his nephew Samuel in that art. [Boswell, ed. Hill, V. 229, n. 2; A. L. Reade, in *Times Lit. Suppl.*, January 6th, 1921, p. 11.]

JOHNSON (BENJAMIN), bookseller in London, 1683. Brother of Michael and Andrew Johnson. Born at Cubley in 1658–9; apprenticed to Richard Simpson two years later than Michael, in 1675; took up his freedom in 1683, or two years before him. [A. L. Reade, in *Times Lit. Suppl.*, January 6th, 1921, p. 11.]

JOHNSON or JOHNSTON (EPHRAIM), bookseller in Manchester, 1694–1701. He first appears as one of the publishers of an anonymous work entitled *The doctrine of the Church of England concerning the Lord's Day*, 1695. [*T.C.* II. 548.] He published several controversial pamphlets. [R. W. Procter, *Memorials of Manchester Streets*, p. 183.] In 1700 he sold large numbers of school books and devotional works, which he purchased of John Minshull, bookseller, of Chester. [*Library*, 2nd. Ser., IV. 373–83.] He appears to have left Manchester by 1703, when Dunton says [p. 238]: "He was apprentice to Mr. Johnson of the same town, but his master thinking it necessary to be a knave, and as the consequence of it to walk off, so Mr. Clayton succeeds him, and has stepped into the whole business of that place, which is very considerable."

JOHNSON (J.), printer in London, 1700 (?). Printer of broadsides, amongst others *A full and true discovery of all the Robberies, of that famous English Pyrate Capt. James Kelly . . . executed . . . 1700*. [B.M. 515. l. 2 (786).]

JOHNSON (JAMES), bookseller in London, (1) Chancery Lane; (2) near Fleet Street. 1689–1703. Began business in 1689, when he sold Selden's *Table Talk*. [*T.C.* II. 293.] He also published (1) *Reflections on the Petition and Apology for the Six Deprived Bishops*, 1690; (2) *Murther upon Murther*, printed for J. Johnson, near Fleet Street, 1703. His two addresses may describe the same house.

JOHNSON (MICHAEL), bookseller in Lichfield, Uttoxeter, Ashby-de-la-Zouche, and Birmingham, 1685–1731. Celebrated as the father of Samuel Johnson. Born in 1656, son of William Johnson, yeoman, of Cubley, Derbyshire, who removed to Lichfield and died there in or soon after 1663, and brother of Benjamin and Andrew Johnson (*q. v.*). In 1673 he was apprenticed to Richard Simpson, and in 1685 was made free of the Stationers' Company. The story in Boswell about his apprenticeship at Leek is apocryphal. He remembered in later years the great sale of *Absalom and Achitophel*. In 1687 he published a work, Φαρμακο-Βασανος, by Dr. Sir John Floyer of Lichfield, which was printed for him in London, "to be sold at his shops at Litchfield and Uttoxiter, in Staffordshire; and Ashby-de-la-Zouch, in Leicestershire". At Birmingham, and probably at Uttoxeter and Ashby-de-la-Zouch also, he opened his shop on market days only. He was a man of much learning, but "wrong headed, positive, and afflicted with melancholy," like his greater son, whom he also resembled in stature; he was moreover unmethodical and kept no accounts. He embarked in the manufacture of parchment and lost his money, so that his later years were spent in increasing poverty. But he served many offices in the City of Lichfield, including Sheriff in 1709 and Senior Bailiff in 1725. He married, in 1706, Sarah Ford, of a Worcestershire family, and had two sons, Samuel, and Nathanael; the latter died in early manhood. He died in December 1731. His two brothers, Benjamin and Andrew, were also booksellers. [Boswell, ed. G. Birkbeck Hill, I. 34–7; A. L. Reade, *Johnsonian Gleanings*, and letter, *Times Lit. Suppl.*, January 6th, 1921, p. 11.]

JOHNSON (R.), printer in London, 1682. Identical with the following? Printed *The Tory-Poets, A Satyr*, 1682. [Haz. III. 249.]

JOHNSON (ROBERT), bookseller in London, Holborn, 1701. Identical with the preceding? Published in 1701 *The Jacobites Lamentation for the death of the late King James*. [Haz. III. 126.]

JOHNSON (THOMAS), *see Dictionary*, 1641–67.

JOHNSTON (JOHN), stationer in Edinburgh, –1692. Will registered January 13th, 1693. [Bann. Misc. II. 296.]

JOHNSTON (WILLIAM), stationer in Edinburgh, 1686–8. In 1686 papers of proposals for reprinting the Works of King Charles the First were to be had of him [*T.C.* II. 185]; and in 1688, in partnership with A. Ogston, he published a work entitled: *Bibliotheca Universalis*. [Aldis, pp. 74 and 115.]

JOHNSTONE (EPHRAIM), bookseller in Manchester. *See* Johnson, or Johnston (E.).

JONATHAN (EDWIN), bookseller in London, Three Roses in Ludgate Street, 1672. He published *Two Letters to W. Prynne*, and *Letters relating to the present state of Europe*, both in 1672 [Bodl. Wood, 416; G. Pamph., 1678 (9)]. His device bore the motto "Love and Live".

JONES (ARTHUR), bookseller in London, Flying Horse near St. Dunstan's Church in Fleet Street, 1684–6. His first publication recorded in the Term Catalogues was a work called *The Grandeur of the Law*, 1684. [*T.C.* II. 71.] He also published a large number of broadsides and in 1686 a pack of cards representing the rebellions of Monmouth and Argyle. [*T.C.* II. 159.]

JONES (EDWARD), King's Printer in London, the Savoy; and Dublin. 1688–170$\frac{5}{6}$. The King's printers, Bill, Hills and Newcombe, having printed the *Declaration* made by James II against the Prince of Orange, they were, on the accession of William, replaced by Edward Jones. Dunton [p. 324] speaks highly of his character, and adds "He has got a noble estate 'by authority' and is deservedly famous for printing 'The True News' and publishing the London Gazette". In 1690 he had an office in Dublin. Jones died at his house at Kensington on Saturday the 16th February 1706, and was buried in Hampstead cemetery. Immediately on his decease there was published an elegy on him, *The Mercury Hawkers in Mourning*. [Nichols, *Lit. Anecd.*, IV. 81.]

JONES (H.), bookseller in London, in the Strand, 1681–91. Publisher of political broadsides. The following have been found: (1) *Loyalty vindicated from the calumnies cast upon it by R. J.* [i. e. Richard Janeway], 1681. (2) *Englands Choice*, by Peter Chamberlen, 1682. [Haz. II. 90.] (3) *Elymas the Sorcerer*, by Thos. Jones, 1682. [Haz. II. 311.] (4) *To the King's Most Excellent Majesty*, 1688. [B.M. T. 100* (191).] (5) *An Exact List of the Royal Confederate Army in Flanders*, 1691. [B.M. T. 100* (214).]

JONES (JOHN), bookseller in Worcester and London; London, (1) Dolphin and Crown, St. Paul's Churchyard; (2) Bell, in St. Paul's Churchyard. 1681–99. Messrs. Burton & Pearson in their *Bibliography of Worcestershire* [II. 52] record *Kedarminster Stuff*, "London, printed for John Jones bookseller in Worcester, 1681." Jones, about 1697, opened a shop in London at the Dolphin and Crown in St. Paul's Churchyard, and in the following year issued a *Sermon of Good Works* by J. Jephcott, which has the imprint, "London, Printed for John Jones, Bookseller in Worcester and are to be sold at the Dolphin and Crown in St. Paul's Churchyard, 1698". The last two leaves of this volume contain a list of books printed for and sold by John Jones at the Dolphin & Crown in St. Paul's Churchyard. In 1699 his sign was the "Bell" in St. Paul's Churchyard. [*T.C.* III. 150.] Probably identical with or son of the Jones who was a bookseller at Worcester in 1663. [*Dictionary*, 1641–67.]

JONES (JOHN), bookseller in Oxford, 1702–25. Perhaps the same as "Jones senior," 1718–25, and also the London and Worcester bookseller of the name. [Madan, p. 31.]

JONES (RICHARD), bookseller in London, (1) Jermin's Yard, Aldersgate Street; (2) Golden Lion, Little Britain, near the Lame Hospital Gate; (3) White Horse, Little Britain. 1666–81. *See Dictionary*, 1641–67. He was still at work in 1681.

JONES (THOMAS), bookseller in London; printer at Shrewsbury. 1676–1713. Born at Corwen in 1647, he first practised the trade of a tailor in London. Hazlitt [II. 90] records *The Character of a Quack-Doctor*, London, printed for Thomas Jones, 1676; also, *Ex Nihilo Omnia: or, The Saints Companion*, London, printed by J. Orme for Thomas Jones, 1692. In 1690 Jones also sold books printed in Welsh. [*T.C.* II. 298.] In or before 1696 he set up the first press at Shrewsbury. [Allnutt, p. 297.]

JORDAN (J.), bookseller in London, Angel in Giltspur Street, without Newgate, 1680–2. Publisher of several political broadsides at the time of the Popish Plot. He also received advertisements for *The Loyal Impartial Mercury* in 1682.

JOURDAINE (D.), printer in Plymouth, 1696. Set up the first printing-press in Plymouth in 1696. [Worth, *History of Plymouth*, 1890, p. 464, mentioning no book from the press.]

JOYNER ( ), printer in London, Giltspur Street, against St. Sepulchre's Back Gate, near West Smithfield, 1715. Advertised, in *The British Weekly Mercury*, November 16th–23rd, 1715, *Articles to promote Learning.*

K. (J.), bookseller in London, 1681–9. These initials appear on the following publications: (1) *A New Years Gift for Plotters* (a broadside), 1681 [B.M. 1872. a. I. (122)]; (2) *A New Poem on the Lord Mayor*, 1682 [Haz. II. 364]; (3) *The Clergy's Late Carriage to the King*, printed for H. L. and I. K. [1688] [B.M. T. 100* (194)]; and (4) *The Muses Farewell to Popery and Slavery*, 1689. [Haz. III. 200.]

K. (J.), printer in Edinburgh, *see* Kniblo.

KADWELL ( ), bookseller in Milton, Kent, 1699. His name occurs in the advertisement in *The Flying Post*, December 2nd, 1699, of Edw. Brown's sermon preached at the Kentish Feast. It does not appear in the imprint to the book. The name was probably more often spelt Cadwell.

KEAT (HUGH), bookseller in Evesham, 1678. He published in 1678 a 'Moral Interlude,' entitled; *A Traitor to himself*, by William Johns of Evesham, and the imprint runs, "Oxford, Printed by L. L. [i.e. Leonard Lichfield] and are to be sold by Edward Forrest, Booksellour in Oxford, and Hugh Keat, Booksellour in Evesham, 1678." [B.M. 644. c. 54.] R. Clavell was the London agent for this book. [*T.C.* I. 320.] Keat was no doubt a relative of William Keate (*q.v.*).

KEATE (WILLIAM), bookseller in Stratford upon Avon, 1681–2. Evidently a relative of Hugh Keat of Evesham (*q.v.*). In Hil. 34–35 Charles II, Robert Clavell, the London bookseller, who was also agent for Hugh Keat, brought an action in the Court of Common Pleas, against William Keate of Stratford, to recover various sums of money due to him for goods (presumably books) supplied. [C.P.R. 3009, m. 380, r.]

KEBLE (SAMUEL), bookseller in London, (1) Unicorn, Fleet Street, (*a*) near Ram Alley, (*b*) near Serjeant's Inn; (2) (*a*) Turk's Head, (*b*) Great Turk's Head, Fleet Street, over against Fetter Lane. 1674–1715 (?). A well-known publisher of divinity. Keble's name appears in the Term Catalogues for the first time in Mich. 1674 as the publisher of a translation from H. Grotius, entitled *The Conciliation of Grace and Free-Will* [*T.C.* I. 189], and from that time until 1709 he constantly entered books. In 1706 he published John Bowack's *Second part of the Antiquities of Middlesex.* [Harl. 5961 (128).]

An engraved broadside catalogue of his publications survives. [B.M. 1865. c. 3 (132).] Dunton [p. 297] has the following account of him: "Mr. Keble is a very ingenious, modest, humble man. . . . He printed that useful book called *A Week's Preparation for the Sacrament*, and other excellent books of devotion." In 1704 he took his son William into partnership. In 1715 he was one of those receiving subscriptions for the third volume of Laurence Howel's *Synopsis Canonum Ecclesiæ*, which had been rewritten by the author, after the destruction of the original manuscript in Bowyer's fire in 1713. [Nichols, *Lit. Anecd.* I. 106.]

KEBLE (WILLIAM), bookseller in London, Turk's Head, Fleet Street, 1704. Son of Samuel Keble (*q.v.*). In 1704 he was in partnership with his father, and also published, with W. Freeman and J. Knapton, an edition of Euclid [*T.C.* III. 432], but the later reference to him given in Mr. Arber's Index to that volume is apparently a mistake for Samuel. [*T.C.* III. 650.]

KEBLEWHITE ( ), bookseller in Newport, Isle of Wight, *c.* 1703. "Mr. Keblewite in the Isle of Wight has a good trade, considering the place, but that is not his whole dependence. He has been twice Mayor of the town, and is not only rich, but a grave and discreet Churchman." [Dunton, p. 237.]

KEBLEWHITE (STEPHEN), *see* Kibblewhite.

KEBLEWHITE, or KIBLEWAITE (W.), bookseller in London, Swan, or White Swan, St. Paul's Churchyard. 1694–1702. Dunton [p. 292] distinguishes this bookseller as "London (and sober) Kiblewaite". Keblewhite made his first entry in the Term Catalogues in Hil. $169\frac{3}{4}$ with a book of divinity. [*T.C.* II. 490.] He was publisher for William King, Bishop of Londonderry. He is last heard of in 1702, when he advertised the second edition of Dr. James Keill's *Anatomy of the Human Bodie.* [*T.C.* III. 329.]

KEIMER (S.), printer in London, 1714. Printed for N. Cliff and D. Jackson.

KEINTON (M.), bookseller in London, Rose, in St. Paul's Churchyard. 1678–82. A bookseller of this name was one of the publishers of a book called *Of the Heart and its Right Sovereign.* . . . By J. T., advertised in 1678 and again in 1682, and of *Argumentum Anti-Normanicum.* [*T.C.* I. 302, 496.] This may have been Matthew Keynton, who was at work in 1656 and who was then living at the Fountain in St. Paul's Churchyard. [*Dictionary*, 1641–67.] But the name may be a misprint for M[ary] Keirton (*q.v.*).

KEIRTON (MARY), bookseller in London, 1673. In *Stat. Reg.* 1673, Mary Keirton assigned to Samuel Mearne 151 copies. *See also* Keinton (M.).

KELL (RICHARD), bookseller in London, in or near West Smithfield, 1684–94. Publisher of ballads, broadsides, and chapbooks. Hazlitt quotes several in the Pepys Library, as *Englands Fair Garland . . . Songs*, 1684; *Cupid's Court of Salutations*, 1687. [Haz. I. 423, 481, 484, 490.] In 1694 he published *The Trimmers Confession of Faith.* [B.M. C. 20. f. 2 (202).] He may have been a son of R. Kels [*q.v.* in *Dictionary*, 1641–67].

KELLINGTON (JOB), bookseller in London, Star in Little Britain, 1681 (?)–3. Publisher of the *Works* of the Rev. Isaac Ambrose in 1682 and of Walker's *English Examples of the Latine Syntaxis* in 1683. [*T.C.* I. 488, II. 31.] *See* K. (J.).

KEMP (HOBART), bookseller in London, The Ship in the Upper Walk of the New Exchange, 1671–2. He published *A History of Jewels* in 1671, and Shadwell's *Miser* in 1672. [*T.C.* I. 81, 111.]

KENNEDY (ALEX.), bookseller in Scotland (?) 1681. Three books of 1681 "printed for A. Kennedy" are mentioned by Aldis, who says that they are probably Scottish. [Aldis, p. 115.]

KENT (HUGH), bookseller in Evesham. An error [Haz. II. 317] for Hugh Keat (*q.v.*).

KERSEY (JOHN), bookseller in London, The Rose in St. Paul's Churchyard, 1681–6. In partnership with H. Faithorne. They were publishers of miscellaneous literature and also of *Weekly Memorials for the Ingenious, or, An Account of Books lately set forth in several languages.* [*T.C.* I. 481.] This was a rival publication to that published by R. Chiswell, W. Crook, and S. Crouch. [*T.C.* I. 532.] Kersey either died or gave up business in 1686, and Faithorne continued alone. Their place of business may have been on the site of the house in which George Thomason, the collector of the literature of the Revolution, once lived. *See* K. (J.).

KETTILBY (WALTER), bookseller in London, (1) Bishop's Head, in Duck Lane; (2) St. Paul's Churchyard. 1669–1711. A noted publisher of divinity books. His first appearance in the Term Catalogues was in Mich. 1669, when his address is given as the Bishop's Head in Duck Lane. [*T.C.* I. 17.] In 1670 he was carrying on business both here and in St. Paul's Churchyard. [*T.C.* I. 58], but in 1671 he appears to have given up the Duck Lane premises. Dunton

[p. 209] refers to him as "an eminent Episcopal bookseller", and he published much learned literature, such as Isaac Barrow's *Lectiones Octodecim* [*T.C.* I. 105], and Henry More's *Remarks upon two . . . Discourses.* [*T.C.* I. 228.] A list of his publications is found at the end of Dr. Charles Hickman's *Sermon preached before the . . . House of Commons . . . 19th October 1690.* He was still publishing in May 1711. [*T.C.* III. 660.]

KETTLEWELL (ROBERT), bookseller in London, (1) Hand and Sceptre over against St. Dunstan's Church in Fleet Street; (2) Hand and Sceptre, King Street, Bloomsbury. 1681–94. Probably a relative of the Rev. John Kettlewell, several of whose writings he published. He began as a publisher in 1681 [*T.C.* I. 448], and was for a time in partnership with R. Wells. Some time between 1686 and 1694 he moved to Bloomsbury; after the latter date nothing more is heard of him. [*T.C.* II. 166, 508, 519.] In Trin. 1688 he was defendant in a suit for trespass. [C.P.R. Trin. 4 Jas. II, Roll 3068, m. 187 r.]

KIBBLEWHITE (STEPHEN), bookseller in Oxford, 1714–23. On April 1st, 1716, Thomas Hearne recorded that "Kibblewhyte a bookseller" was one of the unsuccessful candidates for the place of verger in the University. [*Collections*, V. 192.] He was at work in 1723. [Madan, p. 32.]

KIBLEWAITE (W.), *see* Keblewhite.

KIDGELL (JOHN), bookseller in London. (1) Atlas, Cornhill; (2) Golden Ball, Holborn, near Gray's Inn Gate. 1680–84. Dealer in law books; publisher of *Rights of the Kingdom.* He moved to Holborn some time after 1682. His last entry in the Term Catalogues was in February 1684. [*T.C.* II. 63.]

KING (CHARLES), bookseller in London, Judge's Head, Westminster Hall, 1707–25. His name appears for the first time in the Term Catalogues in Trin. 1707 as one of the publishers of Francis Higgins's *Sermon preach'd at Whitehall on Ash Wednesday*, $170\frac{6}{7}$. [*T.C.* III. 553.] A list of eight books published by him with Benjamin Barker is found in an Assize Sermon by J. A. Dubourdieu, 1714. [Bodl. Sermons, 6 (13).] In 1713 Lintot bought of him a third share in Geddes's *Tracts against Popery.* [Nichols, *Lit. Anecd.* VIII. 298.] Charles King was still in business in 1725. The Mr. King mentioned by Dunton [p. 359] as succeeding him at the Black Raven in the Poultry about 1698 may have been this man, but is more probably J. King.

KING (GREGORY), bookseller in London. At the East Corner Piazza House of James Street, Covent Garden, 1677. In Trin. 1677 he advertised a map of England by J. Adams. [*T.C.* I. 282.]

KING (J.), bookseller in London, (1) The Black Raven in the Poultry; (2) The Lute in St. Paul's Churchyard. 1698 (?)–1703. In Trin. 1700 he advertised in the Term Catalogue a sermon preached at Hemel Hempstead by the Bishop of Chester [*T.C.* III. 193] and in 1703 Dr. William Howel's *Elements of History.* [*T.C.* III. 357.] It is doubtful whether he is the Mr. King who succeeded Dunton [*q.v.*, p. 359] about 1698 at his shop in the Poultry.

KINNEIR (D.), printer in Reading. Next door to the Saracen's Head, in High Street, 1723. Printed *The Reading Mercury* in partnership with William Parks (*q.v.*).

KINSEY (J.), book-auctioneer in London. At the Court of Requests, or Wards, over against the Lobby of the House of Commons, 1697. The catalogue of an auction held by him in 1697 is in B.M. He is mentioned by Dunton [p. 232].

KIRKHAM (WILLIAM), bookseller in London, 1681. Defendant in an action for assault brought by Bartholomew Sprint. [C.P.R. Trin. 33 Chas. II, R. 2992, m. 256.]

KIRKMAN (FRANCIS), *see Dictionary*, 1641–67.

KIRKTON (JOSHUA), bookseller in London, *c.* 1679. Will registered in Edinburgh, February 8th, 1679. [Bann. Misc. II. 296.]

KNAPLOCK (ROBERT), bookseller in London, (1) Angel and Crown, St. Paul's Churchyard; (2) Bishop's Head, St. Paul's Churchyard. 1696–1737. One of the chief London publishers of his time. His first entry in the Term Catalogues was an edition of Juvenal and Persius, translated by Dryden, Congreve, Stepney, and Creech, in Mich. 1696. [*T.C.* II. 602.] Dunton [p. 216] says: "He printed Mr. Wesley's Defence of his Letter, &c., and then, to be sure, he is no Dissenter. However he is a very sober honest man, and has not one spot in his whole life, except it be the printing that malicious and infamous Pamphlet." He published many works in all classes of literature and held shares in the most important books. In or soon after 1707 he moved or altered his sign to the Bishop's Head in St. Paul's Churchyard; in that year he appears at the Angel

and Crown as part publisher with John Nicholson of Hickes's edition of the Works of à Kempis; a list of publications is appended to vol. II. Also in 1707 he bought part of the stock of Thomas Bennett, bookseller at the Half Moon. He died on January 1st, 1737. [Timperley, p. 659.]

KNAPTON (JAMES), bookseller in London, (1) Queen's Head, St. Paul's Churchyard; (2) Crown, St. Paul's Churchyard. 1687–1738. This noted bookseller began, like many others, as a publisher of theological books, his first entry in the Term Catalogues being in Mich. 1687. Dunton [p. 295] spoke of him as "a very accomplished person . . . and shews by his purchasing Dampier's Voyages he knows how to value a good copy". In 1688 he began to publish plays and novels in large numbers. It was in 1696 that he first advertised Dampier's *Voyages.* [*T.C.* II. 609.] He held shares in all the most important books that were issued and carried on a flourishing business until his death in 1738. He was Master of the Company of Stationers in 1727 and again in 1728, and was succeeded in business by two of his brothers, John and Paul. [Nichols, *Lit. Anecd.* I. 236, III. 607.]

KNIBLO (JAMES), printer in Edinburgh, 1683–4. In 1683 he printed, in partnership with Lindsay, Solingen, and Colmar, the third part of William Geddes's *The Saints Recreation*; and in 1684, in partnership with Solingen and Colmar, Sir Robert Sibbald's *Scotia Illustrata* and two other books. *See also* Lindsay (David). [Aldis, pp. 64, 67, 127.]

KNIGHT (JOHN), bookseller in Lincoln, 1696–1716. In 1697 he published *Twelve Sermons preached at the Cathedral Church of Lincoln*, by Walter Leighton [*T.C.* III. 23], and in 1699 *An Essay on Virtue and Piety*, by John Carton, Rector of Branston near Lincoln. [*T. C.* III. 130.] He is again found in 1711 as the publisher of a sermon by Sam. Walker, Vicar of Croft, called *Reformation of Manners.* In 1714 he is found among the subscribers to Walker's *Sufferings of the Clergy.* In 1716 he published a sermon by John Clark.

KNIGHT (JOSEPH), bookseller in London, (1) Blue Anchor in the Lower Walk of the New Exchange, Strand; (2) Pope's Head in the Lower Walk of the New Exchange, Strand. 1684–90. In partnership with F. Saunders. They succeeded to the business of Henry Herringman in 1684 and were chiefly publishers of plays. Joseph Knight's name appears for the last time in the Term Catalogues in Easter 1690. [*T.C.* II. 312.]

KNOWLES (THOMAS), bookseller and bookbinder (?) in London, Tower Street, 1682–1700 (?). Published *The Protestant Dissenters' Case*, a folio leaf. He may be identical with the Mr. Knowles noticed as a bookbinder by Dunton [p. 260]: "He is an ingenious and constant man at his Trade; and bound for me that 'History of Living Men' and 'Athenian Oracle' which I lately dedicated and presented to the Prince of Denmark and Duke of Ormond with my own hand."

KNOX (HENRY), bookseller in Edinburgh. In the Luckenbooths, "e regione insigniorum domini Ross". 1696–1716. Probably youngest son of William Knox, bookbinder; baptized May 9th, 1641; M.A. Edin., 1664; entered burgess and guild brother of Edinburgh, 1678; minister of Bowden (transferred from Dunscore) about 1681; ejected by P. C. 1689. In 1696 he is found as a bookseller, selling A. Montgomery's *Cerasum et sylvestre prunum*, and Sébastien Châteillon's *Octupla.* Henry Knox died at Edinburgh, December 27th, 1716, in his seventy-sixth year. [Aldis, p. 115.]

KUNHOULT, or KUNHOLT (GABRIEL), bookseller in London, (1) The King's Head over against the Muse; (2) St. Martin's in the Fields; and at Oxford. 1680–5. Mentioned in an advertisement of patent medicines in *True News*, March 6th–10th, 16$\frac{79}{80}$. In Mich. 1 Jas. II, Mary Wild, widow, recovered against him a debt of £500. [C.P.R. 3040, m. 692 r.] He appears in Oxford in 1681. [Madan, p. 30.]

L. (A.), bookseller in London, 1700. Published the third edition of Joseph Glanville's *Saducismus Triumphatus*, 1700.

L. (H.), bookseller in London, 1688. These initials are found on a broadside, *The Clergy's Late Carriage to the King*, printed for H. L. and I. K. [1688]. [B.M. T. 100* (194).]

L. (J.), printer in London, 1702. Printed in this year for Edward Evets (*q.v.*).

L. (N.), bookseller in London, 1682. A pamphlet entitled *The Charge of a Tory-Plot maintain'd*, 1682, was printed for him and sold by R. Janeway.

LACEY, or LACY (THOMAS), bookseller in London, Golden Lion, Southwark, (*a*) near the Meal Market, (*b*) near the Market Place, (*c*) near St. Thomas's Church. 1672–94. Began publishing in 1672, when he was joint publisher with Robert Pask of Edward Cocker's *London Writing Master.* [*T.C.* I. 120.]

In 1678 he published the first edition of the same author's *Arithmetick.* [*T.C.* I. 323.] Lacey was one of the agents for Bateman's "Scurvy Grass", which he advertised in *The Protestant* (*Domestick*) *Intelligence* of February 24th, 16$\frac{79}{80}$. His name is not found in the Term Catalogues after Mich. 1684; but he published *England's Golden Treasury* in 1694 (license dated 1691). [B.M. 717. b. 55 (1).] Hazlitt [I. 91] records an edition of Cocker's *Morals*, printed for Thomas Lane, 1675. This is apparently an entirely different edition from that in the British Museum with the same date, which has the imprint, "London, Printed by W. D. for T. D. at the Ship in St. Mary Axe, and T. L. at the Golden Lyon near the Meal Market in Southwark stationer." The tenant of the Golden Lion in Southwark was Lacy, and we suspect the Thomas Lane referred to by Hazlitt to be a misreading for Thomas Lacy. At the same time it is clear from the collation that Hazlitt's copy of Cocker's *Morals* belonged to an entirely different edition. The possibility of a misreading of the imprint is strengthened by the fact that in the very next entry Hazlitt records a copy of Cocker's *Arithmetick*, with the name of Thomas Law, at the Golden Lion in Southwark, where a reference to the book itself shows that it is printed by Thomas Lacy.

LADYMAN ( ), bookseller in London, near the Bars at Aldgate, 1691. His name occurs on a sale catalogue of 1691 as one of those from whom copies might be obtained. [B.M. 821. i. 9 (26).]

LAMBERT (RICHARD), bookseller at York, Crown, (*a*) at, (*b*) within the Minster Gate. *See Dictionary*, 1641–67. Working in 1686. He was succeeded by Robert Clarke, who married Susannah Lambert, probably his daughter, in 1690.

LANE (JOHN), bookseller in London, Blue Anchor in Wild Street, 1688. His imprint occurs in a pamphlet by A. Pulton, *Some Reflections upon the Author and Licenser of . . . The Missioner's Arts discovered.* [B.M. T. 1839 (3).]

LANE (THOMAS), *see* Lacey.

LARKIN (GEORGE), senior, bookseller and printer in London, (1) Two Swans without Bishopsgate; (2) Kings Head in Wood Street; (3) Lower end of Broad Street, next to London Wall; (4) Coach and Horses without Bishopsgate; (5) Hand Alley, Bishopsgate Street. 1666–1706. The following may be substituted for the brief account of Larkin given in *Dictionary*, 1641–67.

George Larkin was born about the year 1642. He began publishing and perhaps also printing in 1666, when he issued Bunyan's *Grace Abounding*, and also many things which gave offence to the Government. In the proceedings which took place before the Committee of the House of Lords in 1676, Roger Norton deposed that in 1668 he searched Larkin's house and found there copies of two notorious pamphlets, *The Cobbler of Gloucester* and *Advice to a Painter*. Larkin's name does not appear in the Term Catalogues until Easter 1683, when he printed two books on Uniformity for Edm. Hickeringill. [*T.C.* II. 20.] He afterwards became the intimate friend of Dunton, who makes many effusive references to him in his *Life and Errors* and other writings. To quote from one [p. 245], "Mr. Larkin has been my acquaintance for 20 years and was the first printer I had in London . . . and has lately published an ingenious essay on the Noble Art and Mystery of Printing . . . Mr. Larkin has a son now living of the same name and trade with himself." George Larkin's age is given by Dunton [p. 441] as 64 in 1706; but the date of his death is unknown.

LARKIN (GEORGE), junior, printer in London, Bishopsgate Street, 1703–24. Son of George Larkin, sen. Mentioned by Dunton [p. 250]; also in Negus's *List of Printers*, 1724, as one of those well affected to King George.

LAW (THOMAS), *see* Lacey.

LAWRENCE (JOHN), bookseller in London, Angel in the Poultry, 1681–1711. A noted Presbyterian bookseller. His first entry in the Term Catalogues was J. Houghton's *Collection of Letters for the Improvement of Husbandry and Trade* . . . Mich. 1681. [*T.C.* I. 464.] He shared with Dunton the publication of Lord Delamere's Works, Mackenzie's *Narrative of the Siege of Londonderry*, and Baxter's *Life*. Dunton calls him "an upright honest Bookseller . . . so exact in Trade as to mark down every book he sells". He married a daughter of the Rev. — Roswell. [Dunton, p. 205.] He was still in business in 1711. [*T.C.* III. 673.]

LAWSON (JOSEPH), bookseller in Lincoln, at the Bail, 1681–9. Publisher of Selden's *Of the Judicature of Parliament*; advertised in the Term Catalogue for Easter 1681, a sermon preached in Lincoln Cathedral on July 18th, 1681, by the Rev. Daniel Nicols, and *A General Discourse of Simony*, by the Rev. J. Metford, 1682, John Ineth's *Guide to the Devout Christian*, 1687, and Dr. Brevint's *Christian Sacrament and Sacrifice*, 1689. [*T.C.* I. 443, 470, 509; II. 205, 263.]

LAYCOCK (WILLIAM), bookseller in London, 1696(?)–1703(?). Married (Susannah ?) daughter of William Miller (*q.v.*), and carried on the latter's collection of "stitched books". [Dunton, p. 213.] A sale catalogue of the collection was compiled for him at an unknown date by Charles Tooker.

LEA (PHILIP), bookseller in London, (1) Atlas and Hercules, Poultry, (*a*) in Cheapside, (*b*) right against the Old Jewry; (2) Westminster Hall, next the Common Pleas. 1683–99 (?) In addition to selling books Philip Lea was also a maker of globes and dealer in maps. His name first appears in the Term Catalogues in Trin. 1683. [*T.C.* II. 30.] In 1685 he sold an edition of Euclid [*T.C.* II. 136], and in 1692 *An Epitome of the Whole Art of War*. [*T.C.* II. 394.] His last appearance is a comprehensive advertisement of books, maps, globes, and instruments, in Trin. 1699 [*T.C.* III. 140–1]; the date of his death is unknown, but his widow continued to carry on the business until 1703. [*T.C.* III. 382.]

LEABOURN (ELIAS), bookseller in London, 1680. His name occurs in the imprint to a broadside on the Popish Plot entitled *Reynard's Downfall*, 1680. [B.M. C. 20. f. 6 (8).]

LEACH (DRYDEN), printer in London, Elliot's Court, Little Old Bailey, 1707–24. Son and successor to Francis Leach (*q.v.*), and cousin of Swift and, presumably, of Dryden. Swift speaks of him several times contemptuously in the *Journal to Stella*. He procured him the printing of Harrison's *Tatler* in January 17$\frac{10}{11}$, but a month later Leach lost it. Swift tells us that he was known as printer of the *Postman*, that he had acted Oroonoko, that he married Mrs. Baby Aires of Leicester, and that he was a coxcomb. [Swift, *Prose Works*, II., *Journal to Stella*, 1900, pp. 40, 99, 103, 112.] In 1713 Leach subscribed three guineas to the Bowyer fund. In 1724 Negus classed him among the printers well affected to King George. [Nichols, *Lit. Anecd.* I. 62, 312.]

LEACH (FRANCIS), printer in London, Elliot's Court, Little Old Bailey, 1673–1707. By some oversight, this printer, who was in all probability a son of the Francis Leach, printer, who died in 1658, is not mentioned in the list of printers taken in 1675. He was well known to John Dunton, who gives [p. 247] a rather foolish description of him, from which we may extract what follows: "He is . . . blest with . . . a constant trade; has printed *The Postman*, &c., many years; and I may venture to say, that Francis Leach is the

handsomest Printer in London." His son Dryden (*q. v.*) succeeded him in 1707, the *Postman* for July 1st being the first with his imprint.

LEACH (WILLIAM), bookseller in London, Crown, Cornhill, near the Stocks Market, 1678–91. First appears as a publisher in 1678 [*T.C.* I. 308, 310, 314] with E. Cooke's tragedy *Love's Triumph* and other books. He made his last entry in 1683. [*T.C.* II. 25.] He died intestate in 1691, administration being granted to his principal creditor, Richard Hewson. [P.C.C. Admons, Jan. 1691.]

LEAKE (JOHN), bookseller and printer in London, Crown, Fleet Street, between the Two Temple Gates, 1673–1717 (?). Son of William Leake, with whom he was in partnership until 1679, when William's name appears in the Term Catalogue for the last time. [*T.C.* I. 363.] John Leake then appears to have set up as a printer, and between 1681 and 1693 printed for Awnsham Churchill, Jonathan Greenwood, Arthur Jones, Luke Meredith, Benjamin Needham, and Abel Swalle. [Haz. I. 432; II. 67, 553, 592, 646; III. 125, 233.] He was in all probability the Mr. Leake who in 1713 subscribed to the Bowyer relief fund; he may also be the person mentioned by Dunton [p. 292] as "humble Leek", and the J. L. who printed Sternhold and Hopkins for the Stationers' Company in 1717.

LEAKE (WILLIAM), *see Dictionary*, 1641–67.

LEE, or LEIGH (CHARLES), bookseller in London, 1681–2. Publisher of many political pieces on the Popish Plot, amongst them Pordage's *Medal Revers'd*, 1682. [Haz. III. 291.]

LEE (SAMUEL), bookseller in London and Dublin; London, Feathers, Lombard Street, (*a*) near Pope's Head Alley, (*b*) over against the Post House. 1677–95. Began publishing in 1677, when he brought himself into notice as the compiler and publisher of the earliest known London Directory, *A Collection of the names of the Merchants in and about the City of London*. It was a small octavo, issued at a shilling, and was entered in the Registers of the Company of Stationers by Daniel Major, stationer, on Lee's behalf, the latter not being a freeman of the Company. Major was joint publisher of the work, which was advertised in the Term Catalogue for Mich., Lee's name appearing first. [*T.C.* I. 294.] That the copyright was his is proved by the fact that on November 26th, 1677, a warrant was passed for a grant to him of the sole rights of publication for fourteen years. [S. P. Dom. Entry Book, 334, p. 439.] At the time of the

Popish Plot he published several broadsides, and in Trin. 33, Chas. II [1681–2] Henry Hills brought an action against him in the Court of Common Pleas for slander in saying that there was a principal member of the Stationers' Company who had sent for a Dutch printing-press and letters and printed treasonable and seditious books, and upon being pressed declaring it was Mr. Hills the King's Printer. Hills claimed £1,000 damages. [C.P.R. 2993, Trin. 33, Chas. II. m. 508 recto.] This is Dunton's character of Samuel Lee [p. 214]: "Such a Pirate, such a Cormorant was never before. Copies, Books, Men, Shops, all was one, he held no propriety, right or wrong, good or bad, till at last he began to be known, and the booksellers not enduring so ill a man among them to disgrace them, spewed him out, and off he marched for Ireland where he acted as *felonious-Lee* as he did in London." Lee's name is found for the last time in the Term Catalogues in Hil. 1684. [*T.C.* II. 65.] In Dublin he issued an edition of *The Present State of Europe*, 1693, and one of Dionysius Syrus' *Explication of the History of Jesus Christ*, 1695. [B.M. 3224. b. 18.] He is believed to have died soon after this.

LEIGH (CHARLES), *see* Lee.

LEIGH (JOHN), bookseller in London, (1) Blue Bell, Fleet Street, by Flying Horse Court; (2) Stationers' Hall. 1670–85. Chiefly a publisher of law and divinity. He made his first entry in the Term Catalogues in Easter 1670 [*T.C.* I. 39], was appointed treasurer of the Company of Stationers in 1679, and died 1685–6. [Nichols, *Lit. Anecd.* III. 607.]

LEIGH (THOMAS), bookseller in London, (1) Peacock near St. Dunstan's Church in Fleet Street; (2) Rose and Crown, St. Paul's Churchyard. 1698–1704. Inserted an advertisement for a lost seal in the *Post Boy* of July 21st, 1698. His earliest entry in the Term Catalogues was in Trin. 1698. [*T.C.* III. 74.] Roger Clavell had entered books published at the Peacock in Fleet Street in the Easter Catalogue of the same year. Leigh soon afterwards joined partnership with D. Midwinter at the Rose and Crown in St. Paul's Churchyard; these premises were jointly occupied by them with Richard Chiswell. Leigh's name is not found in the Term Catalogues after 1704 [*T.C.* III. 418], but Midwinter continued the business for many years later.

LENTHALL (JOHN), stationer in London, Talbot, next the Mitre Tavern, against St. Dunstan's Church, Fleet Street, 1709. In partnership with W. Warters (*q. v.*). Sold packs of cards, maps, and general stationery.

LESLIE (HENRY), bookseller in Edinburgh, Blue Bible over against Blackfriars Wynd, 1677. Sold James Kirkwood's *Grammatica delineata . . . editio tertia,* printed in London by G. Godbid in 1677. [Aldis, pp. 57, 116.]

LESLY (GEORGE), bookseller in Edinburgh, in the Parliament Yard, 1678. Publisher, with A. Hislop, of James Kirkwood's *Rhetoricae compendium,* 1678. [Aldis, pp. 58, 116.]

LETT (R.), bookseller in London, 1681. *No Protestant Plot* was printed for him in 1681. [Haz. II. 344.]

LEVI (J.), bookseller in London, Golden Eagle, near the Fountain Tavern in the Strand, 1711. Advertised in newspapers of 1711 as a dealer in French books.

LEWIS (G.), bookseller in Bristol, 1701. Published Dean Hole's *Danger of Deism,* 1701. [*T.C.* III. 268.]

LEWIS (WILLIAM), bookseller in London, Dolphin in Russell St., Covent Garden, 1709–25. An old schoolfellow of Alexander Pope's. Published in 1709 the *Works* of Robert Gould, 2 vols. [*T.C.* III. 645], and in 1711 Pope's *Essay on Criticism.* In 1714, in company with Lintot, he published a reprint of *Miscellanies,* in which pieces by Pope appeared. Lewis was still publishing in 1725.

LICHFIELD (J.), printer in Oxford, 1682–4. Brother of Leonard Lichfield II? [Madan, p. 31.]

LICHFIELD (LEONARD), the second, printer in Oxford, Holywell, 1657–86. *See Dictionary,* 1641–67. Succeeded his father as University Printer in 1657, and was appointed printer of the Oxford Gazette in 1665. In December 1679 he was a candidate for the yeoman bedelship. He died of a fever February 22nd, 1686 [Wood, III. 180], and was succeeded by his son Leonard III.

LICHFIELD (LEONARD), the third, printer and bookseller in Oxford, 1687–1749. Printed for Obadiah Walker (*q. v.*) *Two Discourses of Abraham Woodhead,* which some scholars of the University obtained from the printer sheet by sheet, and printed an answer to it within a month. [Wood, III. 209.]

LILLIECRAP (PETER), printer in London, 1647–72 (?). *See Dictionary,* 1641–67. In the list of printing houses in London of 1675, his business is stated to have been bought in by the Company of Stationers since 1672.

LINDSAY (DAVID), printer in Edinburgh, in the Grassmarket at the foot of Heriot's Bridge, 1681–5. Watson [p. 14] thus relates the history of this press: "Sir Thomas Murray of Glendoick, having carefully digested the Acts of Parliament . . . imploy'd John Cairns, Bookseller in Edinburgh, . . . and he brought Dutch workmen and materials from Holland for that purpose. The Dutch-men's names were Josuah van Solingen and Jan Colmar. Mr. Cairns dying in a short time after they came here, the Dutch-men kept the house a going, and printed the folio Acts of Parliament in 1681. This printing-house, becoming at last the Dutch-men's in property; and Mrs. Anderson endeavouring to stop their working by her gift; David Lindsay, merchant in Edinburgh obtain'd a gift from King Charles II . . . and for his protecting them with his gift, they give him a share of their printing house; he and they printed several books very neatly, under all their names. . . and at last the Dutch-men purchased Mr. Lindsay's gift, and bought back his share of the printing-house. These Dutch-men falling into very considerable debts, by the purchasing of this printing-house, and the ill payment of most of their employers; James Watson . . . paid money for them . . . and they made over the printing-house to him"—and seem to have entered into his employ. The printing privilege prefixed to the Acts of 1681, renews to David Lindsay as undertaker, and John Cairns as printer, the privilege granted to Sir Thomas Murray in 1679; it was confirmed by the Privy Council, March 31st, 1681. Lindsay was appointed one of the King's printers November 23rd, 1682. The succession of imprints at this house was as follows: 1681–3, Lindsay. 1682–4, Lindsay and his partners. 1682, Solingen. 1682–5, Solingen and Colmar. 1683, Lindsay, Kniblo, Solingen, and Colmar. 1684, Kniblo, Solingen, and Colmar. 1685, Colmar. 1685, Colmar and Gunter. [Aldis, p. 116.] Lindsay's advertisement, c. 1681, exists. [B.M. Cup. 651. e. (82.)]

LINDSEY (WILLIAM), bookseller in London, Angel, near Lincoln's Inn, 1694–6. Published weekly an international critical journal, entitled *Miscellaneous Letters.* If we may believe Dunton [p. 229], Lindsey was born to a good estate, and after trading for a few years, retired into the country.

LINTOT, or LINTOTT (BARNABY BERNARD), bookseller in London, (1) Cross Keys in St. Martin's Lane, 1698; (2) Post Office, in the Middle Temple Gate in Fleet Street, 1701–4; (3) Cross Keys (and Crown), (*a*) between the two Temple Gates in Fleet Street, (*b*) next Nando's Coffee House, Temple Bar,

1709–36. 1698–1736. This eminent publisher was born at Southwater, Horsham, on December 1st, 1675. He was the son of John Lintot yeoman and was probably a nephew of the Joshua Lintot who was printer to the House of Commons between 1708 and 1710. Bernard Lintot was bound apprentice to Thomas Lingard in December 1690, was afterwards turned over to John Harding, and became a freeman of the Company in March 1699. In 1698 his name appears on the imprints of Crowne's *Caligula* and Vanbrugh's *Relapse.* He married on October 13th, 1700. He very soon became noted as the publisher of poems and plays by Farquhar, Fenton, Gay, Parnell, Pope, Steele, and other famous authors. In 1712 he published *Miscellaneous Poems and Translations by several hands,* in opposition to Tonson's *Miscellany*; it contained the first version of *The Rape of the Lock.* In 1713 Lintot was the highest bidder for the copyright of Pope's *Iliad,* and became proprietor. The first volume appeared on June 6th, 1715, the last in 1720. Owing to the appearance in Holland of a pirated duodecimo edition, Lintot was robbed of much of his expected profit, being compelled to issue a similar cheap edition in this country. For the *Odyssey,* which he published in 1725–6, Lintot agreed to pay Pope £600, and to supply free of charge copies for Pope's subscribers. Pope insisted that free copies should also be sent to the subscribers found by Broome. This led to a quarrel, and Pope pilloried Lintot in *The Dunciad,* and elsewhere. During the severe frost of 1715–16 Lintot was one of those who set up stalls on the frozen Thames. After the accession of George I he was appointed one of the printers of the Parliamentary votes, and kept this office until 1727. Lintot took his son Henry into business in 1730. He died on February 3rd, 1736, and his will, made in 1730, was proved on February 14th, by his son. Lintot served the office of renter warden of the Company of Stationers in 1715, and in 1729 and 1730 was under-warden. He is described by Swift as large and fair in person and character; Young says that he was choleric. Pope gives an amusing account [Letter CXX, ed. 1730] of Lintot's conversation, in which the latter reveals his arts in managing translators and correctors and critics of tongues unknown to himself. He was noted for posting up the titles of his new books, printed in red. [*D.N.B., T.C.,* &c.]

LINTOT (JOSHUA), bookseller in London, New Street, near St. Martin's Lane, in the Fields, 1708–9. Probably uncle of Bernard Lintot, with whom he published for the House of Commons William Bohun's *Collection of Debates,* 1708–9. [*T.C.* III. 619.]

LITTLEBURY (ROBERT), bookseller in London, (1) Unicorn, Little Britain; (2) King's Arms, Little Britain. 1652–85. *See Dictionary,* 1641–67. Appears in the Term Catalogues for the first time in Hil. 16$\frac{70}{71}$. [*T.C.* I. 64.] On the death of Dr. Edmund Castell in 1685, Robert Littlebury and Robert Scott were chosen to value his library. [Nichols, *Lit. Anecd.* IV. 28–9.]

LLOYD (HENRY), printer in London, 1662–75. *See Dictionary,* 1641–67. In 1672 he printed, for James Magnes, John Cory's comedy, *The Generous Enemies.* [B.M. 644. d. 57.] He was still at work in 1675, for he appears in the list of London printing houses of that year.

LLOYD (O.), stationer and bookseller (?) in London, near the Church in the Temple, 1711. Sold copy books. [*Post Boy,* February 17th, 17$\frac{10}{11}$.]

LLOYD (SIMON), bookseller in Mold, 1699. Sold school books, which he purchased of John Minshull, bookseller of Chester. [*Library,* 2nd Ser., IV. 373–83.]

LOCK (J.), printer in London, in the Long Walk, near Christ Church Hospital, over against the sign of the Drawers, 1673–5. His imprint is found in *Strange and Wonderful News from Ytaly, or, a . . . relation of the Travels, Adventures and Martyrdoms of four eminent Quakers of York-shire,* 1673. [Haz. II. 306.]

LONGFORD (WILLIAM), bookseller in Warminster, 1694. [List of Provincial Booksellers, *N. & Q.,* 11th Ser., I. p. 364.]

LONGMAN (THOMAS), bookseller in London, Ship and Black Swan, Paternoster Row, 1724–55. Son of Ezekiel Longman of Bristol, and founder of the great publishing house; was apprenticed to John Osborn, bookseller of Lombard Street, on June 9th, 1716. Just at the expiration of his term, William Taylor, bookseller, of the Ship and Black Swan in Paternoster Row, died, and Osborn, who was one of the executors, persuaded Longman to purchase the business, which he reopened there soon after, having previously married Osborn's daughter Mary. His subsequent career lies outside the scope of this Dictionary, but an excellent history of the house of Longmans appeared in *The Critic* in 1860 [new ser. XX. 366, &c.].

LORD (HENRY), bookseller in London, Duke of Monmouth, Westminster Hall, 1680–2. First heard of in 1680 when with many other booksellers he sold *A methodical History of the . . . Popish Plot, made in a pack of cards.* [*T.C.* I.

384.] In partnership with Thomas Fox he published in 1682 *The Novels of Geo. Francesco Loredano.* [B.M. 1073. a. 40.]

LORD (THOMAS), bookseller in London, 1681. In 1681 he was defendant in an action for assault brought by Bartholomew Sprint, bookseller, against a number of booksellers and printers in London and Oxford. Details are wanting. [C.P.R. Trin. 33, Chas. II., Roll 2992, m. 256.]

LOVE (JOHN), bookseller in Dumbarton, before 1695–1725. His son John was born in 1695. He died in 1725. [G. Chalmers, *Life of Thomas Ruddiman*, p. 135.]

LOVEDAY ( ), bookseller in Dartford, 1699. His name appears in the advertisement of Edward Brown's *Sermon* preached at the Kentish Feast, November 16th, 1699. [*Flying Post*, December 2nd, 1699.] It does not appear in the imprint to the sermon.

LOVEDAY ( ), bookseller in Evesham, 1714. One of the subscribers to Walker's *Sufferings of the Clergy*.

LOVELL (T.), bookseller in London, Bible, in St. James's Street, 1689–97. His name occurs in Mich. 1689 as one of the publishers of Richard Stafford's *Of Happiness* [*T.C.* II. 282], and again in Hil. 1697 as one of the publishers of Dr. Adam Littleton's *True Method of learning the Latine Tongue*. [*T.C.* III. 7.]

LOWNDES (RICHARD), *see Dictionary*, 1641–67.

LOWNDES (SAMUEL), bookseller in London, (*a*) over against Exeter House, Strand, near the Savoy; (*b*) over against Exeter Exchange, by the Savoy Gates. 1669–1700. One of the leading publishers of the period. Dunton [p. 213] has the following notice of him: "He was Dr. Horneck's bookseller for many years. He printed his 'Great Law of Consideration', his 'Sermons of Judgement' and Discourse on the Sacrament, entituled 'The Crucified Jesus, &c.'—Mr. Lownds was a sincere honest dealer . . ." Lowndes also published for Meric Casaubon, and held shares in all the best copyrights. He is last mentioned in the Term Catalogue in 1700 [*T.C.* III. 186]; and Dunton in 1703 speaks of him in the past tense.

LUCAS (CENTURION), printer in London, 1686–7. Defendant in a suit for trespass brought by Andrew Meeyer in Trin. 2. James II, Adjournment to Mich. [C.P.R. 3046. m. 267, verso.] He may have been only a workman and not a master printer.

LUMISDEN, or LUMSDEAN (CHARLES), bookseller in Edinburgh, in the Lucken-Booths, over against Warristan's Land, 1678–90. "Bought the 15 of Aprill 1678, from Mr. Charles Lumsdean thir six books". [Sir John Lauder, Lord Fountainhall, *Journals*, 296.] A Charles Lumsdean, probably the same, was cautioner for Solingen and Colmar in 1687. [Fountainhall, *Historical Notices*, Bann. Club, II. 804; Aldis, p. 117.]

LUMISDEN (THOMAS), printer in Edinburgh, 1723–48. In 1722–3 Lumisden bought part of the types belonging to the printers to the Church of Scotland (the successors of Andrew Anderson), and the *Acts of the General Assembly* for 1723 were printed by Thomas Lumisden and Company. In 1725 he petitioned the Commissioners of the General Assembly to take off his hands an Irish [Gaelic] translation of the *Confession of Faith* and *Catechism* which he had printed. From 1725 to 1748 he printed in partnership with John Robertson.

LUNTLEY (JONAS), bookseller in London, Pestle, over against the Horse-shoe Tavern in Chancery Lane, 1694. Only known from the imprint to Sir George Mackenzie's *Institutions of the Laws of England*, which he published in partnership with Andrew Bell in 1694. [Haz. II. 376.]

LUTTON (JOHN), bookseller in London, (*a*) Blue Anchor, (*b*) Anchor, Poultry. 1672–4. He published in 1672 an edition of Sir George Downing's *Discourse* (1st ed., 1664). In 1673 he published *Norfolk Drollery*, a small volume of verse by M. Stevenson, and in 1674 he issued Dr. J. Smith's *Grammatica Quadrilinguis*. [*T.C.* I. 112, 127, 155; Haz. I. 390.]

LYFORD (J.), bookseller in London, 1689. Hazlitt [II. 646] records a sheet printed for him in 1689: *The Form of the intended Coronation Oath agreed upon by the Committee.*

M. (B.), bookseller in London, *c.* 1680–82. These initials, when followed by a manifestly fictitious address, stand for R. Bentley and M. Magnes (*q. v.*).

M. (B.), bookseller in London, 1716. Published a sheet, *The Oxford Tragedy*, 1716. [Bodl. Fol. Θ. 662 (7).]

M. (N.), bookseller in London, 1679. Published a broadside in verse entitled *A Consultation between the Pope and a Jesuit, concerning the way how to introduce Popery into England*, 1679. [B.M. C. 20. f. 2 (122).]

M. (T.), bookseller in London, 1678. These initials, which are found in conjunction with T. B. in 1678, may perhaps be those of Thomas Moore.

McEUEN (JAMES), bookseller and printer in Edinburgh, on the north side of the Cross, 1718–32. He printed in partnership with William Brown and John Mosman; and the *Edinburgh Evening Courant*, which in 1718 he obtained an exclusive privilege to publish, bears his name from that year to 1732. McEuen had also an establishment in London. He was succeeded by Alexander Kincaid, whom he had assumed as a partner. [J. W. Couper, *The Edinburgh Periodical Press*, 1908.]

MACKIE (JOHN), bookseller in Edinburgh, in the Parliament Close, 1691–1722 (?). In 1691 he published *A vindicatory schedule . . . cure of fevers*, by Andrew Brown; in 1695 he was one of several booksellers who sold Sir T. Craig's *Scotland's Soveraignty asserted*, and in 1699, in partnership with J. Wardlaw, he published *A Letter giving a description of the Isthmus of Darian*. His will was registered on April 13th, 1722. [Aldis, p. 117.]

McLEAN (ARCHIBALD), printer in Glasgow, "1706" [? 1756]. Keach's *The Travels of Godliness*, 20th ed., bears the imprint: "Glasgow, printed by Archibald McLean, for Alexander Weir, bookseller in Paisley, MDCCVI." This date is most probably a misprint for MDCCLVI. An Archibald McLean printed several books in Glasgow between 1753 and 1757.

MACOCK (JOHN), *see Dictionary*, 1641–67.

MAGNES (H.). An error for J. Magnes. [Haz. I. 224.]

MAGNES (JAMES), *see Dictionary*, 1641–67.

MAGNES (M.), *see* Bentley (R.).

MAGNES (S.), *see* Bentley (R.).

MAJOR (DANIEL), bookseller in London, (1) Flying Horse, Fleet Street; (2) Hand and Sceptre, near St. Dunstan's Church. 1677–80. In 1677 he entered in the Stationers' Register the first London directory, *The Collection of the names of the Merchants living in and about London.* The work was, however, the copyright of Samuel Lee (*q. v.*). Major was also one of the publishers of a broadside on heraldry, entitled *Le Blazon*, 1679. [*T.C.* I. 360.] In that year he moved to the Hand and Sceptre, previously occupied by T. Orrell. His last entry in the Term Catalogues was made in Easter 1680. [*T. C.* I. 393.]

MALLET (A.), bookseller in London, near Fleet Bridge, 1704. Published *An Account of the Behaviour, Confession and last Dying Words of Thomas Sharp*, 1704. [Haz. I. 264.] Other references given to A. Mallet in Gray's Index to Hazlitt should be to D. Mallet (*q. v.*).

MALLET (DAVID), printer in London, (1) Half-Moon Court, adjoining to Ludgate; (2) next door to Mr. Shipton's Coffee House, near Fleet Bridge. 1677–89 (?). One of the lesser London printers. In 1677 he reprinted a scurrilous ballad called *The Four-Legg'd Elder*, originally issued in 1647. [Haz. II. 192.] In 1680 he printed for Elkanah Settle, *The Life and Death of Major Clancie*, which was on sale at his house in Half-Moon Court [*T.C.* I. 382], and in 1687 Sir Charles Sedley's *Bellamira* came from his press. Mallet also printed many broadsides and *Narratives of the Proceedings at the Old Bailey*. His work was very rough, and his type poor. In 1686 he was forbidden by the Company of Stationers to print any more [Records of Stat. Co.], and his name disappears in 1687, but the initials D. M., which may be his, are found as late as 1689 in *England's Happiness Restored*. [B.M. 1872. a. 1 (9).]

MALLET (ELIZABETH), bookseller and printer in London, (1) Black Horse Alley near Fleet Bridge; (2) Hat and Hawk in Bridle Lane; (3) Next door to the King's Arms Tavern by the Ditch-side near Fleet Bridge. 1685–1702. Probably related to D. Mallet, with whom she was associated in the printing business. She was the publisher of *The New State of Europe* (no. 1, September 20th, 1701). [Burney 117 B.] In 1702 she published a novel, *An Historical Account of the Amours of the Emperor of Morocco*. [*T.C.* III. 320.]

MALTHUS (SARAH), bookseller in London, London House Yard, at the West End of St. Paul's, 1700 (?)–1706. Widow of Thomas Malthus. Her only entries in the Term Catalogues were made in 1704: *The Royal Diary* (William III's) and Dunton's *New Practice of Piety*. [*T.C.* III. 397–8.] She was then at London House Yard. Dunton speaks of her kindly in 1703 in his *Life and Errors*, and as if she was then newly set up in business, and she published the book two years later; but by 1706 he had quarrelled with her. He accuses her of slandering him in *The Wandering Spy*; she attached his goods for debt, and he abused her violently in *The Whipping Post*, 1706, calling her "a hedge-publisher", "the famous publisher of Grub-street News", &c. He says that she was a bookseller's daughter. [Dunton, pp. 220, 447, 459, 462–3.]

MALTHUS (THOMAS), bookseller in London, Sun, in the Poultry, 1682–1700 (?). Appears for the first time in the Term Catalogue of Mich. 1682, as the publisher of a *Life of the Duke of Monmouth*. [*T.C.* I. 506.] During 1684 he issued many books, including a cheap abridgement of Exquemelin's *History of the Bucaniers* and several medical works. In 1685, when Dunton was setting out on his voyage to America, he met Malthus at Gravesend, on his way to Holland, "his circumstances being something perplexed". In another passage Dunton refers to Malthus as "very unfortunate". His name appears in the Term Catalogues for the last time in 1686. [*T.C.* II. 169.] But Dunton in 1703 speaks of him as if recently dead. After his death, his business was continued by his widow Sarah (*q. v.*). [Dunton, pp. 86, 220, 447, &c.]

MAN (SAMUEL), *see Dictionary*, 1641–67.

MANHOOD ( ), bookbinder in London, 1684 (?). Mentioned as a bookbinder by Dunton, with whom he did business until Dunton went to Boston. Manhood afterwards gave up business and "went to the Garter Coffee House by the Royal Exchange" [Dunton, pp. 259, 260].

MANKLIN, or MANCKLIN (RICHARD), bookseller in York, 1697–1725. Only known as the publisher (with Hildyard and Baxter) of George Barker's *Sermons*, 1697 [*T.C.* III. 23], and Sam. Johnston's *Advantage of employing the Poor*, 1725, the latter printed for him by Gent. [Davies, pp. 123, 162.]

MANSHIP (SAMUEL), bookseller in London, (1) Black-Bull, over against the Royal Exchange; (2) Ship, Cornhill, near the Royal Exchange. 1687–1713. Made his first entry in the Term Catalogue in Mich. 1686. [*T.C.* II. 177.] Dunton [p. 206] describes him as "Mr. Norris's Bookseller". In 1687 he published a novel called *The Gallant Hermaphrodite*. [Esdaile, p. 185.] He was still in business in 1713, when he contributed to the Bowyer relief fund. [Nichols, *Lit. Anecd.* I. 61.] About 1694 he moved to the Ship. Lists of his books are appended to H. Hills's *Dialogue between Timotheus and Judas*, 1696, and John Norris's *Practical Treatise concerning Humility*, 1707; Cotton's *Montaigne* is the most important book there advertised.

MAPLESDEN, or MAPLISDEN (PETER), bookseller in Newcastle-upon-Tyne, 1676–89. Admitted to the freedom of the city of Newcastle in 1676. [*Memoirs of Mr. Ambrose Barnes*, App., p. 414.] Between 1677 and 1689 he published several sermons for John March, Vicar of Newcastle. [*T.C.* II. 13; Bodl. Sermons 13.] Maplesden was also one of the publishers of Richard Gilpin's *Daemonologia Sacra*, 1677. [*T.C.* I. 287.]

MARCH (JOHN), bookseller in Exeter, (*a*) near the Conduit, (*b*) Bible, a little below St. Martin's Lane in the Fore Street. 1713–26. First met with in 1713, when he published Francis Squire's *Brief Justification of a reputed Whigg*; in 1714 he was a subscriber to Walker's *Sufferings of the Clergy*. In 1716 he printed the same writer's *Brief Exhortation to Protestant Liberty*. [B.M. 225. h. 8 (8).] In 1719 his name occurs in the proposals for printing Richard Bradley's *Philosophical Account of the Works of Nature*. In 1724 he published, with E. Score, Richard Izacke's *Remarkable Antiquities of Exeter*, 2nd ed., which was printed for them in London. March died in 1726, and was succeeded at the same house by Aaron Toyer, jun. [Dredge, pp. 22, 65, 100.]

MARLOW (JOHN), printer in London, Vine, at the upper end of Aldersgate Street, 1674–88. This printer was called before the Committee of the House of Lords in 1676–7, and admitted having printed for Thomas Sawbridge *The Earl of Shaftesbury's Speech*, part of the *Letter from a Person of Quality*, and the pamphlet entitled *The Naked Truth*, the last written by Herbert Croft, Bishop of Hereford, and published in 1675. [Hist. MSS. Comm., *Report* 9, App., pp. 77–8.] Marlow was also the publisher and printer of the first number of *Mercurius Infernus*, 1679. In Easter 3 Jas. II, he was defendant in an action for debt brought against him by Richard Jeff. [C.P.R. 3056, m. 573 v.]

MARRIOT (GEORGE), bookseller in London, Temple, Fleet Street, by the Inner Temple Gate, 1674–77. Makes his first appearance in the Term Catalogues in 1674 as a publisher of law books. [*T.C.* I. 180.] In 1677 he published R. Izacke's *Antiquities of the City of Exeter* [*T.C.* I. 266], and in the same year an edition of Beaumont and Fletcher's *Elder Brother*. [*T.C.* I. 296.]

MARRIOT (RICHARD), *see Dictionary*, 1641–67.

MARRIOTT (ANNE), bookseller in London, 1687–9. The *London Intelligence* of 1689 was printed for Anne Marriott by John Wallis. [Burney, 97 A.] Was she one of the "Mercury women" of whom we hear so much at that time? The initials A. M. on a broadside, *A Speech spoken by Mr. Hayles*, 1687, are probably hers.

MARRIOTT (JOHN), stationer in London, 1700 (?)–1742. Only known from his will, which was proved in the Prerogative Court of Canterbury on November 12th, 1742. [P.C.C. Tremley 331.] He left property in Essex and London and two sons, John and William.

MARSH (JOHN), bookseller in London, Red Lion in Cateaton Street, 1688. In partnership with Lawrence Baskerville he issued an English and Welsh Dictionary under the title of *The British Language in its Lustre*. [Haz. I. 240.]

MARSHALL (JOHN), bookseller in London, Bible in Gracechurch Street, 1695–1725. Probably a relative of William Marshall (*q. v.*), with whom he was associated in 1695 in the publication of a divinity book. [*T.C.* II. 547.] Dunton refers to him as "industrious and thriving John Marshall", and adds, "I heartily wish him success in his new purchase of 'The Western Martyrology'". [Dunton, pp. 216, 292, 355.] In addition to the works of the Rev. Thomas Beverley, John and William Marshall were publishers for Dr. Owen. John Marshall was still publishing in 1725.

MARSHALL (JOSEPH), bookseller in London, Bible in Newgate Street, 1707–25. Son of William Marshall. Was taken into the business about 1707, and was still publishing in 1725. [*T.C.* III. 581.]

MARSHALL (WILLIAM), bookseller and bookbinder in London, (1) Butcher's Hall Lane, 1676; (2) Bible in Newgate Street, 1679–1725; (3) Bible in Gracechurch Street, 1685. 1676–1725. He advertised in Mich. 1676 *The Tomb of Semiramis, hermetically sealed*, "to be sold by W. Marshall Bookbinder in Butcher's Hall Lane". [*T.C.* I. 257.] He dealt chiefly in divinity, and at the time of the Popish Plot published several pamphlets on the Protestant side. In 1695 John Marshall (*q. v.*), a relative, opened a shop at the Bible in Gracechurch Street; but William Marshall also had an interest in that business as early as 1685, as at the end of John Collins's *Doctrine of Decimal Arithmetick*, published by Nathaniel Ponder in that year, is a 12-page catalogue of books newly printed and sold by William Marshall at the Bible in Gracechurch Street. About 1700 he took into business his son Joseph Marshall, and they were still at work at the Bible in Newgate Street in 1725.

MARSTON (JOHN), bookseller in Bury St. Edmunds and Sudbury, 1683–5. In a list of provincial booksellers [*N. & Q.*, 10th Ser., V, February 24th, 1906], John Marston is given as being at Bury St. Edmunds in 1683. In 1685 Dorman Newman, the London stationer, brought an action against John Marston, bookseller, of Sudbury, co. Suffolk, in the Common Pleas, to recover a debt of £166 4*s.* 6*d.*, probably for books supplied. The action was adjourned. [C.P.R. Trin., 1 Jas. II., Roll 3038, m. 1862 r.]

MARTEN, *see* Martin.

MARTIN (BRIDGET), bookseller in Bristol, at the Cross [in Temple Street], 1697. In the *Post Boy* of January 6th–8th, 1697, she advertised for sale, "at the Cross in the same street during the Fair", copies of W. Wynne's edition of Powel's *History of Wales*.

MARTIN, or MARTYN (JOHN), *see Dictionary*, 1641–67. He was at the Bell without Temple Bar till 1670, when he moved to the Bell in St. Paul's Churchyard.

MARTIN (JOHN), bookseller in Edinburgh, 1718–24. *Britannia Triumphans*, 1718, bears the imprint: "Edinburgh, printed by John Mosman and William Brown for the Author, and sold by the said William Brown and John Martin." Martin is also mentioned in the *Acts* of the General Assembly for 1720 and 1724.

MARTIN, or MARTEN (SIMON), bookseller in Leicester, 1705–14. In 1705 he published S. Carte's *Cure of Self-conceit*, a sermon preached at Leicester [Bodl. Sermons 4]; and in 1706 *A Faithful Account of the Lamentable State of a young Man, and his immediate recovery . . . at Cropston in Leicestershire*, was printed for him in London. [Haz. II. 340.] In 1714 he was one of the subscribers to Walker's *Sufferings of the Clergy*.

MARTYN, *see* Martin.

MASON (J.), printer in London, 1684. One of four partners who printed a broadside in verse, *On the Royal Martyr King Charles I*, "printed on the frozen Thames, January the 30th, 1683, by the loyal young printers, viz. E. and A. Milbourn, S. Hinch and J. Mason." They were very likely not master-printers.

MASON (JOHN), bookseller in Edinburgh, 1672. Published *Two Prayers to be taught unto Children*, 1672. [Aldis, pp. 53, 117.]

MATHIE (ALEXANDER), bookseller in Glasgow, 1718. His name occurs in the imprint of William Forbes's *A methodical Treatise concerning Bills of Exchange*, 2nd ed., Edinburgh, 1718.

MATTHEWS (EMANUEL), printer and bookseller in London, Bible in Paternoster-Row, 1700–17. Perhaps a son of John Matthews, printer, of Little Britain. In 1700 a sermon by H. Matthews of Chester was printed for E. Matthews in Paternoster Row. [*Bibliotheca Cestriensis.*] In 1713 he was among the printers subscribing to the Bowyer relief fund, and in 1716 he printed the Rev. J. Owen's *Sermon to Dissenters*. [B.M. T. 1805 (11).]

MATTHEWS (GEORGE), *see* Matthews (John) senior.

MATTHEWS (JOHN), senior, printer in London, (*a*) Pelican, (*b*) Pilkington Court, Little Britain, 1681–1716 (?). In 1681 John Matthews was defendant in an action for assault, brought against him by Bartholomew Sprint. [C.P.R. Trin. 33 Chas. II., Roll 2992, m. 256 r.] In 1701 he printed for Elizabeth Mallet a sheet called *The New State of Europe*. He was also the printer of Defoe's *History of the Union*, 1707. [*T.C.* III. 562.] He contributed three guineas to the Bowyer fund in 1713, and in the next year appears among the subscribers to Walker's *Sufferings of the Clergy*. He died about 1716, three years before the execution of his son John (*q.v.*), and his business passed to his widow, who was then its proprietor. [Gent, p. 91.] A son George is said to have carried it on later. Emmanuel Matthews (*q. v.*) may also have been one of the family.

MATTHEWS (JOHN), junior, printer in London, (*a*) Pelican, (*b*) Pilkington Court, Little Britain, 1719. Son of John Matthews, sen. This unfortunate young man, who was only an apprentice, was in 1719 apprehended and tried for printing a tract entitled *Ex ore tuo te iudico, Vox Populi Vox Dei*, said to be written in support of the Pretender. In the printed account of his trial he is spoken of as a "poor youth" and a "young man"; copies of the libel were found at the printing house of his mother in Little Britain. He was found guilty and executed at Tyburn in 1719, in his eighteenth year. [Howell's *State Trials*, XV. 1327; *Weekly Packet*, October 31st–November 7th, 1719; Timperley, p. 623; Gent, p. 91.]

MAXFIELD ( ), bookseller in London, *c.* 1700. Dunton refers [p. 293] to a bookseller of this name as "conscientious and dutiful Maxfield".

MAXWELL (ANNE), *see Dictionary*, 1641–67.

MAY (GEORGE), bookseller in Exeter, 1680–86. First heard of in 1680, when he published Thomas Long's *Sermon against Murmuring*. [*T.C.* I. 403.] In 1686 he published *God in the Creature . . . a Poem . . .* London, Printed for George May, and are to be sold at the Peacock in St. Paul's Churchyard, 1686 [Haz. I. 192]; and N. Kendall's *Sermon preached at the Assizes at Launceston, 18 March 1685*.

MAYO, MAYOR or MAYOS (JOHN), printer in London, (1) Golden Cross in Thames Street near Queenhithe; (2) over against Water Lane, Fleet Street. 1697–1714. In 1697 he printed and sold Ezekiel Polsted's *Excise-Man* (in the imprint to which his name is spelt Mayos). In *The Postman* of October 25th–27th, 1698, he advertised *An Essay concerning Adepts*. Again, in *The Postman* of January 20th, 17$\frac{10}{11}$, he is found advertising vol. I of *The British Apollo*, and Nichols records that in 1713–14 he printed for F. Burleigh a periodical called *The Balm of Gilead*. [*Lit. Anecd.* VIII. 494.]

MEAD (DANIEL), bookseller in London, Bible, Snow Hill, by the George Inn Gate, 1707–32. Possibly related to the Rev. Matthew Mead, for whom he published two *Discourses* in 1707 and a sermon in 1711. [*T.C.* III. 541, 662.] Hazlitt records a book printed by him in 1715. [I. 472.] He was probably alive in 1732, for Thomas Norris, the London Bridge bookseller, left him a bequest in his will, proved in that year. [P.C.C. Bedford 174.]

MEAD (M.), bookseller and printer (?) in London, Gutter Lane, 1697 (?)–1703. He is probably the M. M. who printed three divinity books in 1697. [*T.C.* III. 3.] In 1701 he put his name with others to two very similar books. [*T.C.* III. 253.] Dunton [p. 252] mentions as then living a Mr. Mead, who printed for him *A Step to Oxford*.

MEAD (RICHARD), bookseller in London, 1684. Only known from the imprint to a broadside entitled *Speech of Hadgi Giafer Aga*, 1684. [B.M. T. 100* (167).]

MEADE ( ), bookbinder in London, Honey Lane Market, 1696. Mentioned by David Edwards as having bought a quantity of primers in 1695. [P.R.O. Chanc. Proc. before 1714, Collins 486/100.]

MEADOWS (W.), bookseller in London, 1719–25. In 1719 he was the publisher of a novel called *Charon, or the Ferry Boat*, and in 1721 he was one of the

publishers of Paul Chamberlen's series of novels called *Love in its Empire*. [Esdaile, pp. 185, 183.] He was still publishing in 1725.

MEARNE (A.), bookseller in London, Little Britain, 1683. Probably Samuel Mearne's widow. *See* Mearne (C.).

MEARNE (CHARLES), bookseller in London, (1) Little Britain; (2) the King's Arms, near Charing Cross. 1680–6. Son of Samuel Mearne. In 1680–81 he was one of several publishers advertising a handsome *Cicero*. [*T.C.* I. 390, 455.] In the next year he appears in partnership with his father in Little Britain, and in 1683 with A. Mearne, probably his mother, advertising the two volumes of John Nelson's *Impartial Collection of the Great Affairs of State*. [*T.C.* I. 471, II. 27.] By 1686 he had moved to Charing Cross, where he then took subscriptions for Ray's *General History of Plants*. In the same year he was one of the partners in the works of Sir Thomas Browne, and this is his last appearance. He seems never to have published alone, but always to have taken shares in large ventures. He has often been held to be a binder, like his father; but Mr. Gordon Duff [*Edinb. Bibl. Soc. Trans.* xi. 47] shows that no bindings can be attributed with any probability to him.

MEARNE (SAMUEL), *see Dictionary*, 1641–67.

MEARS ( ), printer in London, 1713–14. *See* Meere (H.).

MEARS (W.), bookseller in London, Lamb, without Temple Bar, 1713–27. In 1713 he issued a catalogue of plays. [Bodl. 4°, Rawl. 141.] In 1714, in company with D. Brown, he published *The Persian and Turkish Tales*, translated from the French of Pétis de la Croix, and in 1725 Defoe's *New Voyage Round the World*. [Esdaile, pp. 286, 209.] In 1723 he appended a miscellaneous list to T. Salmon's *Chronological Historian*. He was one of the publishers of Defoe's *Tour through Great Britain*, 1724–7, in copies of vol. III. of which appears a list of twenty-four books, many of an historical character, printed for him.

MEERE (H.), printer in London, (1) Black Friar, in Blackfriars; (2) Old Bailey. 1708–24. In the *Observator* of February 7th, 1708, he inserted the following advertisement, printed in the type advertised: "Scriptographia; or, Written Print Hand, (which can't be imitated by any other printer) fit for Bills of Lading, Bills of Sale, Bonds of all Sorts . . . or any other blank Law-Forms. Such as have occasion for any of these, may have them printed on

this, or larger characters of the like, by H. Meere, Printer, at the Black-Fryar, in Black-Fryars, London." In 1713 he printed *The Innocent Epicure* for R. Gosling, and some school-books, including *Terence* and *Phaedrus*, for Robert Fary; he was also the printer of *The Daily Post* and *The British Journal*. In 1724 he was living in the Old Bailey, and is mentioned in Negus's list as a "high-flyer". He is probably identical with the "Mears" in whose printing-office in Blackfriars Gent worked in 1713–14.

MEIN (JAMES), bookseller in Edinburgh, on the North-side of the Street at the Cross, 1684–6. In 1684 he issued *A true Relation of the great Victory . . . by . . . Prester John, against the Turks*, by Jo. Miles, and in 1686 *A Relation of the Procession . . . enjoyn'd by Mahomet Solyman*. [Aldis, p. 117.]

MELLETT (THOMAS), printer in London, 1681. Defendant in an action for assault and trespass brought by Bartholomew Sprint. [C.P.R. Trin. 33 Chas. II, R. 2992, m. 256 r.] Perhaps not a master printer.

MENSON (JOHN), bookseller in Edinburgh, 1671. One of the six booksellers who in 1671 successfully appealed to the Privy Council against A. Anderson's attempted enforcement of his monopoly. [Aldis, p. 117.]

MERCER (THOMAS), bookseller in London, Half-Moon, near the Exchange in Cornhill, 1679–84. His name first appears in Easter 1679 as publisher of Henry Brett's *History of Jesus Christ*. [*T.C.* I. 350.] He figures again, in an advertisement of lost property, in *The Protestant* (*Domestick*) *Intelligencer*, March 19th, 16$\frac{79}{80}$, and is last heard of in 1684, when he published John Jones's *Great Duty of Conformity*. [*T.C.* II. 68.]

MEREDITH (LUKE), bookseller in London, (1) King's Head, West end of St. Paul's Churchyard, 1684–6; (2) Angel, Amen Corner, 1687–92; (3) Star, St. Paul's Churchyard, 1692–1700. 1684–1700. Began in Trin. 1684. [*T.C.* II. 81.] The greater part of his publications were in divinity, but he was the publisher of Langbaine's *Account of the English Dramatick Poets*, 1691. [*T.C.* II. 358.] He married a daughter of Richard Royston, and some time during 1686–7 moved to the Angel, the premises of his father-in-law, who had died in 1686. Meredith succeeded to many of Royston's books, and after his own death in 1700 some were printed for John Meredith in trust for Luke's children, Royston and Elizabeth. [*T.C.* III. 725.] An 8-column list of Royston's copies, as set out in the *Stationers' Register* and certified by the

Clerk to the Company as now the property of the children of Luke Meredith deceased, is appended to Jeremy Taylor's *Antiquitates Christianae,* printed in 1702–3 for the trust.

MERES (A.), bookseller in Dublin, White Hart, Copper Alley, 1715. In partnership with Thomas Hume.

MERREALL (ALEXANDER), stationer and bookseller in London, Rose in Bread Street, 1662–1703. *See Dictionary,* 1641–67. Living in 1703, when Dunton [p. 254] wrote of him thus: "Mr. Merreal at the Rose in Bread Street. He is rich, yet very humble. He has been put up for Sheriff . . . He was the first Stationer I ever dealt with [i. e. about 1681]; and in trading with him for twenty years I ever found him just and kind. It is a question whether he is more his Chapman's Friend, or his own." *See* Sheafe (S.).

METCALFE (THOMAS), bookseller in London, over against the Red Lion Court, Drury Lane, 1694–1711. First appears in 1694 as the publisher of a translation of *Essays supposed to be written by Monsieur* [*Nicholas*] *Fouquet.* [*T.C.* II. 512.] In 1709 he was one of many booksellers who took subscriptions for the *Corpus Poetarum Latinorum.* [*T.C.* III. 657.] He was still in business in 1711.

MIDWINTER (DANIEL), I., bookseller in London, (1) Rose and Crown St. Paul's Churchyard; (2) Three Crowns, St. Paul's Churchyard. 1698–1725. In partnership with Thomas Leigh. They shared the premises formerly occupied by Richard Chiswell, and made their first entry in the Term Catalogues in Mich. 1698. Leigh dropped out of the partnership in 1704, and Midwinter moved to the Three Crowns between 1706 and 1708. Dunton speaks of them as doing a "topping business", and there is no doubt that they were two of the largest booksellers of the day, holding shares in most of the chief undertakings. The date of Midwinter's death is unknown. He was still publishing in 1725, and was succeeded by his son Daniel II.

MIDWINTER (EDWARD), bookseller and printer in London, Star, Pye Corner, 1710–25. His first known publication is *The Northamptonshire Wonder,* "printed and sold by Edward Midwinter", 1710. [Haz. II. 710.] When Thomas Gent first came to London, and again about 1722, he was employed by Midwinter. Midwinter was a printer and publisher of ballads and chap-books, amongst which may be mentioned an abridgement of Defoe's *Robinson*

Crusoe, 1722 [Gent] and in 1724 [Esdaile, p. 208; Haz. II. 362, 710]; but his circumstances were so poor that Gent records that on one occasion, apparently in 1723, he was obliged to remove himself and family to a place called the Mint, a district in Southwark which was then a sanctuary for insolvent debtors. [Davies, *York Press,* p. 158.] Midwinter is mentioned in Negus's list of printers as a "high-flyer". [Nichols, *Lit. Anecd.* I. 311.] He married as his second wife, about 1720, Elizabeth daughter (or perhaps daughter-in-law) of Thomas Norris (*q. v.*). [Gent, *Life, passim,* and sources quoted.]

MILBOURN (ALEXANDER), printer in London, 1684–93. Son of Thomas Milbourn (?). With E. Milbourn (a brother ?), S. Hinch, and J. Mason (*q. v.*) he printed a broadside in the Thames Frost Fair of 1684. At the sessions held at the Old Bailey in April 1693 he was bound over to come up for judgement at the next sessions, for printing a libel. [B.M. 515. l. 2 (148).]

MILBOURN (E.), printer in London, 1684. *See* Milbourn (A.).

MILBOURN (THOMAS), printer in London, Jewin Street, 1659–86. *See Dictionary,* 1641–67. Dunton [p. 244] says that he was married four times, that he had lived in Jewin Street for forty years, and died at the age of 74. By an order of the Company of Stationers made in 1686, he and others were forbidden to carry on the trade of printing. [Records of the Company.]

MILES (E.), printer in London, 1674. Printed a news-tract, *Treason and Murther* [1674]. [Haz. III. 76.]

MILL (ADIEL), stationer of London, Peacock in Amen Corner, 1687–90. First heard of in 1687, when he purchased the business of Robert Scott the bookseller (*q. v.*), "near £10,000 deep", and issued a catalogue of the books in February $168\frac{7}{8}$ [B.M. 821. i. 13 (1)]; but he, "with his auctioneering, atlases, and projects, failed" for £30,000 or more in 1690, and ruined Scott, to whom he could not pay the purchase money, and also his relative, Moses Pitt. He became a debtor in the Fleet. [Roger North, *Lives of Francis North, &c.,* III. 290–1; Moses Pitt, *Cry of the Oppressed,* p. 153.] *See* Hills (H.) sen., and Roberts (R.)

MILLER (J.), bookseller in London, Rose, West End of St. Paul's, 1677. Publisher of an *Alphabetical Martyrology,* compiled by N. T., in 1677. [*T.C.* I. 299.]

MILLER (JAMES), bookseller in Edinburgh, 1665–72. *See Dictionary,* 1641–67.

MILLER (JOHN), bookbinder in Edinburgh, *c.* 1674. Will registered January 21st, 1675. [Bann. Misc. II. 296; Aldis, p. 117.]

MILLER (JOHN), bookseller in Sherborne and Yeovil, 1691–1709. Local publisher or agent for the sale of sermons, &c., by Dorsetshire and Somersetshire divines, also published in London. His name appears in seven such entries between the dates given, a shop at Yeovil being also mentioned in one of 1697. [*T.C.* II. 379; III. 35, 210, 386, 425, 582, 611; the last is B.M. 225. h. 3 (3).]

MILLER (SIMON), *see Dictionary,* 1641–67.

MILLER (SUSANNAH), bookseller in London, The Acorn, in St. Paul's Churchyard, 1698 (?)–1700. Probably daughter of William Miller (*q. v.*).

MILLER (WILLIAM), bookseller in London, Gilded Acorn, St. Paul's Churchyard, 1661–96 (?). *See Dictionary,* 1641–67. Dunton [p. 213] says of him: "He . . . was blessed with a great memory, which he employed for the good of the publick; for he had the largest collection of stitched books of any man in the world, and could furnish the Clergy (at a dead lift) with a printed sermon on any text or occasion. His death was a public loss, and will never be repaired unless by his ingenious son-in-law, Mr. William Laycock, who I hear is making a general collection of stitched books; and as Mr. Miller's stock was all put into his hands, perhaps he is the fittest man in London to perfect such a useful undertaking." A sale catalogue (without date) of this stock of pamphlets was afterwards compiled by Charles Tooker for Laycock. [B.M. 620. a. 1 (1).] Miller advertised largely in the Term Catalogues, and also generally added an advertisement at the end of his imprints. For example, the imprint to the second edition of Captain George St. Lo's *England's Safety,* 1693, runs thus: "London: Printed for W. Miller, at the Gilded Acorn in St. Paul's Churchyard, where gentlemen and others may be furnished with Bound Books of most sorts, Acts of Parliament, Speeches and other sorts of Discourses, and State Matters; as also Books of Divinity, Church Government, Humanity, Sermons on most occasions, &c." A list of his books is to be found in this book. It is the last entered in his name in the Term Catalogues. The exact date of his death is unknown, but his business was

carried on for some time by Susannah Miller, probably the daughter mentioned by Dunton, who married William Laycock.

MILLET (JOHN), printer in London, 1683–92. In partnership with M. Haley. They printed large numbers of ballads, broadsides, and chap-books for various booksellers.

MILLINGTON (EDWARD), bookseller and book-auctioneer in London, (1) Pelican, Duck Lane; (2) Bible, Little Britain; and in Cambridge. 1670–1703. Made his first entry in the Term Catalogues as a publisher of books in Easter 1670, when he published William Seaman's *Grammatica linguae Turcicae.* [*T.C.* I. 31.] It was, however, as a book-auctioneer that he became famous. Dunton [pp. 235–6] calls him "the famous Mr. Edward Millington", and "a man of remarkable elocution, wit, sense, and modesty", and adds: "He was originally a bookseller, which he left off, being better cut out for an auctioneer; he had a quick wit, and a wonderful fluency of speech. There was usually as much comedy in his 'Once, Twice, Thrice,' as can be met with in a modern play: 'Where', said Millington, 'is your generous flame for learning? Who but a sot or blockhead, would have money in his pocket, and starve his brains?' Though I suppose he had but a round of jests. Dr. C. once bidding too leisurely for a book, says Millington, 'Is this your *Primitive Christianity*?' alluding to a book the honest Doctor had published under that title. . . . He died in Cambridge, and I hear they bestowed an elegy on his memory and design to raise a monument to his ashes." Ned Ward, in *A Step to Stirbitch-fair,* gives a similar description of Millington's humour as an auctioneer. He was the chief auctioneer of the time. [B.M. *Catalogue of Sale Catalogues.*] He was holding auctions at Cambridge, in the town itself, at the Eagle and Child, opposite St. Benet's, and at Stourbridge Fair, as early as 1686. [Mayor, *Cambridge under Queen Anne,* pp. 249, 492.] He died in 1703. [Timperley, p. 588.]

MILLION (HENRY), bookseller in London, (1) Bible, Fleet Street; (2) Bible, Old Bailey. 1670–79. Believed to be the son of John Million, *q. v., Dictionary,* 1641–67. His first entries in the Term Catalogues were Cornelius Agrippa's *Female Pre-eminence* and Herbert Palmer's *Memorials of Godliness and Christianity,* Mich. 1670, and his last Moses Rusden's *Full Discovery of Bees,* 1679. [*T.C.* I. 57, 60, 373.] He was in Fleet Street in 1675 [*T.C.* I. 203], and had moved to the Old Bailey by 1679. All his few books were cheap.

MILLS (F.), bookseller in London, Rose and Crown without Temple Bar, 1696. In partnership with W. Turner. Their names are found in the imprint to Le Maire's *Voyages to the Canary Islands*, 1696.

MILLS (RICHARD), *see Dictionary*, 1641–67.

MILNER (JACOB or JAMES), bookseller in Dublin, Essex Street, 1692–1701. The name "Jacob Milner" is first met in 1692 and again in 1693. In 1697 "J. Milner" published Bishop John Stearne's *Tractatus de Visitatione Infirmorum*. [*T.C.* III. 27.] The will of "James Milner" was proved in 1701. All these probably relate to the same man.

MILWARD (EDWARD), bookseller in Lichfield, 1680. He sold John Brinley's *Discovery of the Impostures of Witches and Astrologers*, London, printed for John Wright, 1680. [Haz. II. 62.]

MINIKIN (GEORGE), (?) stationer in London, King's Head in St. Martin's, 1676. Sold a pack of cards representing the counties of England. [*T.C.* I. 237.]

MINSHULL (JOHN), bookseller in Chester, Bridge Street, 1674 (?)–1712. Doubtless related to the William Minshall or Minshull who was carrying on business in Chester in the days of the Commonwealth. [*Dictionary*, 1641–67.] From certain Chancery Proceedings we learn that John Minshull was apprenticed to a London bookseller, Peter Bodvell, and afterwards purchased his freedom from the Company of Stationers of Chester and set up in business for himself about the year 1674. Books published by him in 1682 and 1698 are recorded in J. Cooke's *Bibliotheca Cestriensis*. He sold school-books wholesale to booksellers and stationers in various places, amongst his customers being Ephraim Johnson of Manchester. According to Timperley he died in 1712.

MINSHULL (R.), bookseller in Chester, Bridge Street, 1712. Son of John Minshull. In 1699 he was a student at Trinity College, Dublin, where Dunton visited him [p. 625]. He probably joined his father soon after this, and succeeded him in 1712. He is given in a list of provincial booksellers in *N. & Q.* [10th Ser., v. 142.]

MITCHELL (J.), bookseller in London, Threadneedle Street, 1686. Sold the 4th ed. of the *Conference between Laud and Fisher*. [*T.C.* II. 171.]

MONCKTON (PHILIP), bookseller in London, Star, in St. Paul's Churchyard, 1701–7. A publisher of divinity, which is probably why Dunton [p. 292] refers to him as "Church-Unity Monckton". Made the first and last of his many entries in the Term Catalogues in 1701 and 1707. [*T.C.* III. 263, 537.]

MONCUR (JOHN), printer in Edinburgh, his printing house at the foot of the Bull Close, opposite to the Tron, 1709–12; his house and shop at the Head of the Bank-Close, in the Lawn-market, 1726. 1707–26. In 1709 he printed *The Scots Postman*, and in 1712 *The Evening Post*. On page viii of the edition of Guthrie's *Christian's Great Interest* which Moncur published in 1726 is a list of twenty-nine books printed and sold by him.

MONEY (JOHN), bookseller in London, 1681. Defendant in an action for assault brought by Bartholomew Sprint. [C.P.R. Trin. 33, Chas. II., Roll 2992, m. 256.] He is not known as a publisher.

MONTAGU (RICHARD), bookseller in London, the Book-Warehouse at the corner of Great Queen-street, near Drury Lane, 1718 (?). A list of books and pamphlets sold by him occupies the last leaf of *A Warning-piece for English Protestants*, n. d.

MONTEATH (JOHN), printer in Edinburgh, *c.* 1674. Will registered July 20th, 1674. [Bann. Misc. II. 295; Aldis, p. 117.]

MONTFORD (JOHN), *see* Mountford.

MONTGOMERY (HUGH), bookseller in London, Cornhill, 1703. Only known from Dunton, who says [p. 269], "He was born a Scotsman and served his time with Andrew Bell," and tells us that he was "of a low stature" and that he himself thought so highly of him that he entrusted him with the sale of the whole impression of his *Idea of a New Life*, i. e. *Life and Errors.*

MOORE, or MORE (THOMAS), bookseller in London, Maidenhead, over against St. Dunstan's Church in Fleet street, 1678–84. Publisher of John Wallis's *Defence of the Royal Society*, 1678. [B.M. 740. c. 21 (8).] In 1684 he was defendant in a suit brought by Anthony Trethway in the Court of Common Pleas for the recovery of £300. [C.P.R., Hil. 35/6, Chas. II, 1683–4, Roll 3020, m. 352 verso.]

MOORE (THOMAS), printer in London, 1685. Printed Thomas Wright's *Glory of God's Revenge against Murther and Adultery* for Benjamin Crayle, 1685. [Haz. II. 663.]

MORDEN (CHARLES), bookseller in Cambridge, 1678–89. Son of William Morden, bookseller (*q. v.*) who in his will, March 4th, 1678, left him "all books bound and in quires which I have in Cambridge and those in London and also all my debts" as well as the "Freehold tenement . . . wherein I now dwell . . . in the parish of St. Michael's," &c. We find his name on two works, the third edition of R. Sheringham's *The King's Supremacy Asserted*, 1682, along with Jonas Hart (*q. v.*) a relative, and on *Beaufrons*, 1684. He was buried February 28th, 168 8/9. [Gray & Palmer, 118, 119.]

MORDEN (ROBERT), engraver, printer, and bookseller in London, near the Royal Exchange, 1671–1702. An engraver of maps, charts, prints, playing cards etc., who not only printed his productions but sold them. [*T.C.* I. 10.] His advertisement first appeared in the Term Catalogue of Trin. 1671 [*T.C.* I. 80], and he was still in business in 1702.

MORDEN (WILLIAM), bookseller in Cambridge, 1652–79. *See Dictionary*, 1641–67. In his will dated that year [Gray & Palmer, p. 118] he leaves his business, the freehold house he lived in, along with other bequests, to his son Charles (*q. v.*). In 1661 he subscribed £4 towards the Free and Voluntary Gift to his Majesty, being the largest amount given by a bookseller. Amongst the books published by him are the *Philosophical Works of Henry More*, 1662, editions of J. Ray's *Proverbs*, 1670, 1678, John Smith's *Select Discourses*, 1673, &c.

MORPHEW (JOHN), bookseller in London, near Stationers' Hall, 1706–20 (?). Publisher of political pamphlets, State trials, news-sheets and novels, and one of the principal booksellers of the period. Morphew made his first entry in the Term Catalogues in Mich. 1706, with a shilling book on the war. [*T.C.* III. 522.] He appears to have set up in the premises previously occupied by John Nutt. On October 12th of that year he issued the first number of *The Country-Gentleman's Courant*. He issued the first number as an advertisement without charge. [Nichols, *Lit. Anecd.* IV. 82.] Early in 1707 he issued *Mercurius Oxoniensis, or, The Oxford Intelligencer*, by M. G., and in the same year *The Monthly Miscellany*. Apart from novels and ephemeral tracts he published much interesting literature. In the *Journal to Stella*, December 13th, 1711, Dean Swift wrote, "I forgot to tell you that the printer told me yesterday that Morphew the publisher was sent for by that Lord Chief Justice [the Earl of Macclesfield], who was a manager against Sacheverell, he showed him two or three papers and pamphlets, among the rest mine of the *Conduct of the Allies*, threatened him, asked him who was the author, and has bound him over to appear next term." Morphew was still publishing in 1720, when he issued a second volume of novels by Mrs. Manley. [Esdaile, p. 266.]

MORTIER (DAVID), bookseller in London, Erasmus's Head, in the Strand, 1701. Published, with John Smith and Edward Cooper, C. Le Brun's *Conference upon Expression*, a work illustrated with many engraved plates. [B.M. 1403. d. 48.]

MORTLOCK, or MORTLAK (G.), bookseller in London, 1670–1717. *See* Mortlock (Henry).

MORTLOCK, or MORTLACK (HENRY), bookseller in London, (1) Phoenix, in St. Paul's Churchyard; (2) White Hart, in Westminster Hall. 1660–1709. *See Dictionary*, 1641–67. The first of the above addresses was undoubtedly Henry Mortlock's principal place of business, as the stalls in Westminster Hall were only open during term time and were liable to be cleared away in the event of a State trial or other public function. Henry Mortlock is first met with as a publisher in the Term Catalogue of Easter 1670, when he advertised Phineas Fletcher's *Father's Testament* as on sale at the White Hart in Westminster Hall. [*T.C.* I. 29.] At this time he had a relative, G. Mortlock, in partnership with him, and a list of books sold by them at both their shops is found at the end of Joseph Glanvill's *Essays*, 1676. Dunton has [p. 286] the following note upon Henry Mortlock: "Mr. Mortlack has been Master of the Company of Stationers, and the most indefatigable shop-keeper I have known. He is very exact in trade. He was much assisted by the great Doctor Stillingfleet Bishop of Worcester, and printed [i. e. published] most of his works. He is now pretty much up in years, speaks slow, but speaks seldom in vain." He was one of the most prolific publishers of the time. The last entry under his name in the Term Catalogues is in 1709. [*T.C.* III. 356.] The date of his death is unknown. G. Mortlock was still in business in 1717, when he published Anthony Blackwall's *Introduction to the Classics*. [Nichols, *Lit. Anecd.* I. 133.] John Mortlock, of Nottingham and Newark (*q. v.*) was no doubt a relative.

MORTLOCK (JOHN), bookseller in Nottingham and Newark, 1695. Doubtless a relative of H. and G. Mortlock of London (*q. v.*), as amongst the books sold by him was *An Explanation of the Additional Rules for the Genders of Nouns in the Oxford Grammar,* "by John Twells, Master of the Free School in Newark. London, Printed for Hen. Mortlock . . . and sold by John Mortlock bookseller in Nottingham, and at his shop in Newark, 1695."

MORY (EDWARD), bookseller in London, Three Bibles in St. Paul's Churchyard, 1695–9. Chiefly a publisher of divinity. He made his first entry in the Term Catalogues in Mich. 1691, and his last in Easter 1699. [*T.C.* II. 378 ; III. 128.]

MOSMAN (GEORGE), bookseller and printer in Edinburgh, (*a*) his shop on the South Side of the Parliament Close ; (*b*) his printing house in Hart's Close, over against the Trone-Church. 1669 (?)–1707 or 1708. May be identical with the George Mosman, merchant, who was fined £200 (Scots) by the Privy Council on March 8th, 1669, for being at a conventicle, and who in 1685 was again before the Privy Council for a similar offence. In 1690 George Mosman acquired the printing house of the Society of Stationers, in which he had been a partner, and commenced printing on his own account. In this year he published sermons preached before the King's Commissioner by Gilbert Rule and David Williamson ; the latter has a list of ten books printed for him. By Act of the Privy Council dated November 21st, 1690, he was appointed Printer to the Church of Scotland and her Assemblies, in spite of Mrs. Anderson's opposition. He died in 1707 or 1708, and was succeeded by his widow, who printed the Acts of Assembly from 1708 to 1711. [Aldis, p. 118.]

MOSMAN (JOHN), printer in Edinburgh, 1717–30. Printed in partnership with William Brown, and also as John Mosman and Company. In 1724 Mosman and Brown succeeded as assigns of the deceased James Watson, and thereafter they assumed the style of King's Printers.

MOTTE (BENJAMIN), printer and bookseller in London, (1) Aldersgate Street ; (2) Middle Temple Gate, Fleet Street. 1693–1738. Began as a printer in Aldersgate Street, and is first mentioned in the Term Catalogues in 1693. [*T.C.* II. 469.] In 1694 he described himself as printer to the Company of Parish Clerks [*T.C.* II. 520]. He afterwards added publishing to his business, and was the publisher of *Gulliver's Travels,* which Swift sent to him from Twickenham, where he was staying with Pope, by the hands of Charles Ford. Swift then asked the publisher to deliver a bank-bill of £200 to his friend Erasmus Lewis, on undertaking publication, but Motte preferred to get back some

of his money first, and deferred payment for six months. Motte was also the publisher of *Miscellanies in Prose and Verse* by Swift, Pope, Arbuthnot, and Gay, 1727. Swift maintained friendly relations with Motte, who acted as his London agent. Motte apparently did not give up his printing-office when he took to publishing, as he was included in Negus's list of printers in 1724, as a "high-flyer". He died on March 12th, 1738, and was succeeded by Charles Bathurst, who had been his partner.

MOUNT (RICHARD), bookseller in London, Postern on Tower Hill, 1684–1722. Believed to have come of a Kentish family. His name appears in the Term Catalogues for the first time in Trin. 1684 as one of the publishers of a work on geometry. [*T.C.* II. 84.] Dunton mentions him as dealing chiefly in paper and sea books. In 1697 he was one of those from whom tickets for the Kentish Feast in that year could be obtained. Mount was Master of the Company of Stationers for the three years 1717–19, and Nichols further states that he gave the Clock in the Court Room. He died June 29th, 1722, aged about 70. [*Lit. Anecd.* III. 599.]

MOUNTFORD, or MOUNTFORT (JOHN), bookseller in Worcester, 1690–1710. In 1690 he published *Admiration of Angels at the Salvation of men* [*T.C.* II. 331], and in 1706 G. Wall's *Sermon upon the death of Mrs. Mary Bromley* [Bodl. Sermons, 21 (7)] ; in *The Post Boy* of February 20th, 1710, his name occurs in a list of booksellers from whom proposals for the *Corpus Poetarum Latinorum* could be obtained ; the abbreviated list in *T.C.* [III. 656–7] does not mention him. In 1715 he was one of the subscribers to Walker's *Sufferings of the Clergy.*

MOXON (JAMES), bookseller in London, Strand, Charing Cross, 1668–77 ; in Edinburgh, in Low Ord's Close at the foot of the Cannongate, 1689. 1647–89. *See Dictionary,* 1641–67. The last entries under his name in the Term Catalogues are in Easter 1677 [*T.C.* I. 273, 274], when he was still in partnership with Joseph Moxon. George Walker's *True Account of the Siege of London-Derry,* Edinburgh, 1689, contains an engraved plan with his imprint as given above. [Aldis, p. 118.]

MOXON (JOSEPH), *see Dictionary,* 1641–67.

MOXON (MORDECAI), bookseller in Manchester, 1679–93. In 1683, Adam Martindale arranged with "Mr. Moxon, bookseller in Manchester", for the

publication of a pamphlet. [*Life,* Chetham Soc., 1845, pp. 230–1.] The date of Moxon's decease does not appear, the latest entry referring to the family being the burial of his daughter, March 1693. [R. W. Procter, *Memorials of Manchester Streets,* p. 182.]

MUNNS ( ), bookseller (?) in Cranbrook, Kent. 1699. His name appears in the advertisement in the *Flying Post,* December 2nd, 1699, of the Rev. Edward Brown's sermon at the Kentish Feast. It does not occur in the imprint of the book.

MUSDEN (WILLIAM), stationer and bookseller (?) in London, Hen and Chickens, Cheapside, 1680. Sold a pack of cards representing the Popish Plot. [*T.C.* I. 384.]

N. (C.), bookseller in London, 1675–7. An unknown bookseller who sold the lives of criminals, etc., such as *The Holborn Hector,* "printed for C. N. and are to be sold in the highway to Tybourn", 1675. [Haz. I. 217.]

NEAL (SIMON), bookseller in London, (1) Three Piggeons in Bedford Street, (*a*) in Covent Garden, (*b*) over against the New-Exchange, 1674–87 ; (2) Angel Court, St. Martin's Lane, near the Church, 1687–91 ; (3) in the Long Walk, near Little Britain, 1691–4. 1674–94. Published several plays and romances as well as some historical works. He also dealt in cheap manuals of devotion and Church politics ; but his output is of a secular character to an extent very unusual for the time. His first and last entries in the Term Catalogue are in 1674 and 1694. [*T.C.* I. 163, II. 527.]

NEEDHAM (BENJAMIN), bookseller in London, (1) Black Raven, Duck Lane ; (2) Crown, Duck Lane. 1674–85. Known from the imprints to three books : (1) B. Pererius, *The Astrologer Anatomiz'd,* 1674 ; (2) *Il Putanismo di Roma,* translated by I. D., 1678 ; (3) Elkanah Settle, *Heroick Poem on the Coronation of James II,* 1685. [*T.C.* I. 165, 332 ; II. 127.] He had moved to the Crown by 1678.

NEEDHAM (GWYN), printer in Dublin, Crane Lane, 1718–25. Most of his extant production consists of single sheets.

NEEDHAM (RALPH), bookseller in London, Little Britain, 1665–72. *See Dictionary,* 1641–67. In the Term Catalogue for Trin. 1672, his name occurs as joint publisher with Joseph Clarke of a manual of divinity, compiled by the Archbishop of York. [*T.C.* I. 109.]

NEGUS (SAMUEL), printer in London, Silver Street near Wood Street, 1701 (1722)–24. Chiefly remembered as the compiler in 1724 of a list of the various printing houses in London, classified by their political principles, as "Known to be well affected to King George", "Nonjurors", "Highflyers", &c. He also gave a list of the various newspapers appearing in London, with the names of their publishers or printers. In the introductory epistle he states that he had been a printer for twenty-three years, but a master only two, and that he found great difficulty in making a living. He was rewarded by a carrier's place in the Post Office. Nichols [*Lit. Anecd.* I. 288–312] reprints the whole document.

NEILL (PATRICK), printer in Belfast, 1696 (?)–1702. Said to have come to Belfast in 1696, but his earliest extant imprint is dated 1699, and appears as Patrick Neill & Co., in that year and in 1700, and in 1701 and 1702 as Patrick Neill alone. All the output of his press was Puritan divinity.

NELME, or NELMES (HENRY), bookseller in London, (*a*) Royal Exchange, (*b*) Leg & Star, Cornhill, 1696–7. Apprentice to P. Parker, who left him his business. Dunton [p. 229] says that Nelme came to "an untimely end". He published *Evangelium Medici,* by Dr. Bernard Connor, 1697 [B.M. 1170. c. 20 (1, 2)], and two other religious books, also *An Impartial History of the Plots against . . . King William the Third.* [*T.C.* II. 587, 589.] He also sold, in 1696, "Setts of Cutts for *Bibles* in Folio, Quarto and Octavo, curiously engraven on copper, containing near 200 in number . . . somewhat cheaper than usually, viz. the Folio at 9*s.* the Quarto 7*s.* and 6*d.*, the Octavo and Small Quarto at 6*s.* perfect." [*T.C.* II. 597.]

NELSON (NORMAN), bookseller in London, Gray's Inn Gate in Holborn, 1680. Publisher of and dealer in law books. Also described as a "vintner" in an action for debt brought against him in 1680 by Robert Turner. [C.P.R., Mich. 33, Chas. II, 2996, m. 353.] This seems to be a very late survival of a mixture of trades that was common enough in the sixteenth century.

NEVILL (JOSEPH), bookseller in London, Greyhound in St. Paul's Churchyard, 1660–72. *See Dictionary,* 1641–67.

NEVILL (SARAH), bookseller in London, Archimedes in St. Paul's Churchyard, 1677. Possibly the widow of Joseph Nevill (*q. v.*). Published *The Judgement of Mr. Francis Bampfield.* [*T.C.* I. 270.]

NEWBOLT (WILLIAM), printer in London, 1684–1714. This is no doubt the person described in the London Gazette of September 1st–4th, 1684, as "William Newbolt, aged 22 years, or thereabouts, a well set middle sized man . . . run away from his master on Monday the 1st instant ; and is supposed to be lurking about the City of London. Whoever shall apprehend the said William Newbolt, and bring him to Nat. Thompson, Printer at the Entrance into the Old Spring Garden, near Charing Cross, shall have a Guinea reward, and their Charges born." In 1690 he was indicted for printing *His Majesty's most gracious Declaration to all his loving Subjects*, a Jacobite broadside found scattered about the streets of London. One Edward Buttler was associated with him and both were described as printers. The printing press was said to have been kept at one Douglas's at Westminster. [MS. Harl. 6846, fol. 371–9.] He subscribed in 1714 for Walker's *Sufferings of the Clergy*.

NEWBOROUGH (M.), bookseller in London, Golden Ball, St. Paul's Churchyard, 1707. Probably the widow of Thomas Newborough (*q. v.*). Appears to have taken Maurice Atkins into partnership, and they, with J. Nicholson of the King's Arms in Little Britain, published the third edition of Boyer's *Wise and Ingenious Companion, French and English*, a school book, which they advertised in Easter, 1707. [*T.C.* III. 548.]

NEWBOROUGH (THOMAS), bookseller in London, (1) Star, St. Paul's Churchyard ; (2) Golden Ball, St. Paul's Churchyard. 1686–1707. One of the leading men in the book-trade, and concerned in many of the more important publications of the time. Dunton spoke of him [p. 229] as a good Churchman, "a thoughtful just man, and knows how to encourage a good Author, for none can think that the 'Supplement to the Historical Dictionary', written by the learned Collier, is made at a small charge." Newborough's name is found in the Term Catalogues for the last time in Easter, 1707. He was succeeded by M. Newborough, possibly his widow (*q. v.*), and Maurice Atkins. [*T.C.* III. 537.]

NEWCOMB, or NEWCOME (RICHARD), bookseller and printer in London, Wine-Office Court, Fleet Street, 1691–1713. In 1691 he published *A Voyage round the World, or a Pocket Library*, 3 vols., the translation or editorship of which is ascribed to John Dunton. [*T.C.* II. 338.] His name is also found in 1713 as the printer of a pamphlet entitled, *What sort of a Peace is this?* [B.M. 1850. c. 6 (20*).]

NEWCOMB (THOMAS). *See Dictionary*, 1641–67. He printed numbers of plays for Herringman.

NEWMAN (DORMAN), bookseller in London, (1) King's Arms in the Poultry, near Grocers' Alley ; (2) Surgeons' Arms, Little Britain ; (3) Ship and Anchor (*a*) at the Bridge-Foot, (*b*) near the Bridge Gate, on Southwark Side. 1665–94. *See Dictionary*, 1641–67. One of the largest publishers of his day ; but owing to speculation he went bankrupt in 1694. [*London Gazette*, September 24th–27th, 1694.]

NEWMAN (HUGH), bookseller in London, (1) Kings Arms, Poultry ; (2) Grasshopper in the Poultry. 1692–1703. Served his time with Dorman Newman (*q. v.*), and was nearly related to him. [Dunton, p. 215.] His first entries in the Term Catalogues appear in Easter 1692, when he published *The Life of Richard Baxter* and a poem called *The Jacobite Conventicle*. [*T.C.* II. 402–3.] He continued publishing until Trin. 1703. [*T.C.* III. 355.]

NEWTON (ELIZABETH), bookseller at Portsmouth, 1708.

NEWTON (JOHN), bookseller in London, (1) Three Pigeons in Fleet Street, 1688 ; (2) near the Sugar Loaf in Bell Alley, Coleman Street, 1689–96. 1688–96. Began business in 1688, by the publication of *Religio Laici* and an edition of *Don Quixote*. [*T.C.* II. 233–4.] His second address is found on a poetical broadside of 1689 on the coronation of William and Mary. [B.M. C. 20. f. 2 (181).] He is described by Dunton [p. 233] as a man "full of kindness and good-nature and affable and courteous in trade". His name is not found in the Term Catalogues after Hil. 1698. [*T.C.* III. 55.]

NEWTON (W.), bookseller in London, (*a*) Little Britain, over against Bartholomew Close Gate, (*b*) near the Pump. 1694–1711. Newton's name first appears in the Term Catalogues as the publisher of a divinity pamphlet in Easter 1694. He also sold Dutch editions of the Classics. [*T.C.* II. 500 ; III. 494.] In 1711 his name occurs as one of the publishers of R. Bradley's *Treatise of Succulent Plants*, in an advertisement in *The Post-Man* of February 3rd. He appears to have been in partnership then with Thomas Shelmerdine. Their address is given as in Little Britain ; the two addresses given above therefore probably refer to the same house.

NEWTON (WILLIAM), bookseller in Blandford, Dorset, 1670. Publisher in 1670 of the Rev. John Straight's *Sermon . . . at the Assizes held at Dorchester* in 1669. [Mayo, *Bibl. Dorset.* p. 52.]

NICHOLSON (ANTHONY), bookbinder in Cambridge, Six Bells, 1667–80. Son of Anthony Nicholson [*see Dictionary*, 1641–67], who died in April 1667 [*see* his will in Gray & Palmer, p. 104], at which date Anthony jun. was living at the "Six Bells". The inventory of his goods, dated February 2nd, 1680, mentions "his tooles in the shop x^s." (Gray & Palmer, p. 121). Robert Nicholson, the bookseller, was his brother.

NICHOLSON (JOHN), bookseller in London, (1) King's Arms, Little Britain ; (2) Queen's Arms, Little Britain. 1686–1715. First heard of in the year 1686, when he advertised a pack of heraldic cards. [*T.C.* II. 181.] Ten years later he was associated with T. Newborough in the publication of a Latin Testament for the use of scholars [*T.C.* II. 603], but his place of business is not mentioned until 1697. From that date he was a prolific publisher of works of all kinds and made frequent use of the Term Catalogues. Dunton [p. 209] has this record of him : "His talent lies at projection, though I am thinking his Voyages and Travels will be a little *posthumous*. He is usually fortunate in what he goes upon. He is a man of good sense. . . . He purchased part of my stock, when I threw up all concerns in trade ; and I ever found him a very honest man." Amongst Nicholson's more notable publications may be mentioned Thomas Gage's *New Survey of the West Indies*, which he shared with Newborough, and advertised in Easter 1699 [*T.C.* III. 130], and *The Index Villaris*, published with Newborough and others in 1700. [*T.C.* III. 177.] He also shared in most of the large ventures of the time. He did not change his sign to the "Queen's Arms" in 1702, as might be supposed ; for he still called it the "King's Arms" in 1707, when he published, with Robert Knaplock, Hickes's edition of the Works of à Kempis ; there is a list of books at the end of vol. II of this. In 1715 William Bowyer printed for him Pearson's *Exposition of the Creed*. [Nichols, *Lit. Anecd.* I. 109.]

NICHOLSON (ROBERT), bookseller in Cambridge, 1662–89. [*See Dictionary*, 1641–67.] Son of Anthony Nicholson (d. 1667) and succeeded to his father's business a few years before his death. Alderman Newton's *Diary*, ed. J. E. Foster, under 1687 has "11 Sept. Sunday, Sarah Nicholson, daughter of Robert Nicholson of Cambridge stationer, marryed at Trinity College Chapell by

Dr. Wolfran Stubb unto Robert Dawney of the Citty of Norwich worsted weaver son of Anne Keeling of Norwich widow". With others he drew up the inventory of the goods of John Field, 1668, Robert Gee, 1681, William Graves, 1686, and E. Beeching, 1689. [Gray & Palmer, p. 107.] *A Poem attempting something upon the Rarities of the renowned University of Cambridge* was printed for him in London in 1673. [Bowes, *Cambridge Books*, no. 110 (b).]

NICKS (JOHN), bookseller in London, White Hart in St. Paul's Churchyard, 1722. Published William Burscough's sermon, *The Revolution recommended to our memories, preached at St. Peter's Westminster on Nov. 5th 1715*, 1722. [B.M. 694. f. 7 (17).]

NICOL (JAMES), printer in Aberdeen, his printing house in the north side of the Castle Gate ; his shop in the end of the Broad Gate. 1710–32. In December 1710 Nicol succeeded to the widow of John Forbes, younger, whose daughter he had married, as printer to the town and University. On his retirement from business in 1736 he was succeeded by James Chalmers. [*See* J. P. Edmond, *The Aberdeen Printers*.]

NISBETT (HENRY), bookseller in Derby, 1704–11. In 1704 he published a sermon preached at St. Mary's, Nottingham, by Anthony Blackwall, and in 1706 an edition, also by Blackwell, of Theognis. The latter was printed by J. Heptinstall and sold by Henry Mortlock in London. [*T.C.* III. 535.] Blackwall was "Moderator" at Derby School. In 1711 he printed a sermon preached by H. Harris at Derby on July 9th, 1710.

NOBLE (THOMAS), printer in Edinburgh, 1686. In the employ of James Watson. [Aldis, p. 118.]

NORCOTT, *see* Northcott.

NORMAN (S.), bookseller in London, 1682. *New News from Tory-Land and Tantivy-Shire* was printed for S. Norman in 1682. [B.M. 8122. aaa. 20 (12).]

NORMAN (THOMAS), bookseller in London, Pope's Head in Fleet Street, (*a*) near Fleet Bridge, (*b*) near Salisbury Court. 1679–80. Dealer in plays. His name appears in Mich. 1679, and again in Hil. 1680. [*T.C.* I. 370, 385.]

NORMAN (WILLIAM), bookseller and bookbinder, in Dublin Dame's Street, 1682–1703. In 1682 he sold *A Judgement of the Comet*. In 1683 he is described as "bookbinder to the Duke of Ormond". Publisher of Sir James

Ware's *Hunting of the Romish Fox* in 1684. [*T.C.* II. 74.] In 1686 he is mentioned in a list of those booksellers from whom prospectuses of a reprint of the works of King Charles I could be obtained. [*T.C.* II. 185.] He was printer of the Votes of the House of Commons in Ireland in 1692. [Burney, 104 A.] In 1694 he published a sermon by St. George Ashe, printed by Joseph Ray. He was Master of the Booksellers' Company in Dublin, and was a great amateur gardener. [Dunton, pp. 238, 565–6.]

NORRIS (JAMES), bookseller in London, King's Arms, without Temple Bar, 1682–4. Appears to have been related to the Rev. John Norris, Fellow of All Souls, Oxford, and Rector of Aldbourne in Wilts. Issued a broadside entitled *Erra Pater's Prophesy, or Frost Faire*, 168$\frac{2}{3}$; the whole of this is engraved. [B.M. C. 20. f. 2 (158).] His last advertisement in the Term Catalogues appeared in Mich. 1694, when he issued a translation of Xenophon's *Cyropaedia*. [*T.C.* II. 96.]

NORRIS (THOMAS), bookseller and bookbinder in London, (1) St. Giles without Cripplegate; (2) Looking Glass on London Bridge. 1695–1732. In the course of an action heard in the Court of Chancery Thomas Norris, bookbinder, admitted having bought about five or six hundred psalters and the same number of primers in 1695, but declared that they were printed at Oxford. Some of these he sold to a Mr. Gandy, haberdasher in Milk Street. [P.R.O. Chan. Proc. before 1714, Collins 486/100.] In 1711 Thomas Norris moved to the premises on London Bridge previously occupied by Josiah Blare. There he carried on the joint trades of bookbinder and bookseller, publishing many chapbooks and ballads as well as all kinds of nautical books. He is more than once mentioned in the Churchwardens' Accounts of St. Magnus. In 1720 he was paid three shillings for a Bible, and in 1722–3, being then one of the churchwardens, he made the following entries: "paid myselfe for a large Folio Bible for the Church, very finely bound. Delivered Decr. 24th, 1720 £6 11*s.* 3*d.* Paid ditto for five large common prayer, 4 for the churchwardens, and 1 for the clerk, and new binding two old Bibles £3 13*s.* 9*d.*" Norris retired from business soon after this and settled at Highgate, where he died in 1732, his will being proved on June 7th. He left a son William, and bequests to the following stationers of London, Daniel Mead of Snow Hill, Richard Ware and John Wilford. [P.C.C. 174, Bedford.] Gent [p. 113] says that Norris's daughter (or perhaps daughter-in-law) Elizabeth married, as her second husband, in about 1720, Edward Midwinter, the printer in Pye Corner. Gent calls Norris "a very rich bookseller on London Bridge, whose country seat was at Holloway".

NORRIS (W.), printer and bookseller in Taunton, 1718. Set up the first press at Taunton; the first piece printed and sold by him there was a sermon by F. Squire entitled *The Lawfulness of taking Oaths*, 1718. [Allnutt, p. 301; Bodl.]

NORTH (JOHN), bookseller in Dublin, 1682. Sold *A Judgement of the Comet*, 1682.

NORTHCOT (RICHARD), bookseller in London, next Peter's Alley in Cornhill; and at the Mariner and Anchor upon Fish Street Hill, near London Bridge, 1677–91. May have been related to Thomas Northcott or Norcott (*q. v.*). Richard was chiefly a publisher of theological works between the years named.

NORTHCOTT, or NORCOTT (THOMAS), printer in London, George Yard, Lombard Street, 1684–90. Printer of George Fox's *Journal*. First mentioned in the Monthly Meetings on June 25th, 1684. Dunton [p. 292] refers to him as "friend" Northcot. In addition to Quaker literature, he printed in 1686 Patrick Ker's *Grammatista* [*T.C.* II. 180], and in 1690 *Mankind displayed*. [*T.C.* II. 304.]

NORTON (ROGER), *see Dictionary*, 1641–67.

NOTT, *see also* Nutt.

NOTT (WILLIAM), bookseller in London, Queen's Arms, Old Pall Mall, 1687–90 (?) *See Dictionary*, 1641–67. A copy of *The petition of the Irish Bishops to Lord Tyrconnell* was addressed "For Mr. William Christopher", to be left with Nott, in 1687. [Bodl. MS. Clar. 89, f. 105.] His last entry in the Term Catalogues was in 1689. [*T.C.* II. 274.] For a possible reference to him in 1690 *see* Nutt (J.).

NOWEL (N.), bookseller in London, Duck Lane, 1681–1703. In 1681 he published *Rome's Follies or, the Amorous Fryars, A Comedy*. Dunton describes him [p. 211] thus: "Mr. Nowel is a first-rate Bookseller in Duck-Lane, has a well furnished shop and knows books extraordinary well, which he will sell off as reasonably as any man. I have always reckoned him among our ingenious Booksellers." He does not appear in the Term Catalogues, and was probably a retailer only.

NUTT (ELIZABETH), printer in London, in the Savoy, 1720–31. Printed T. Cox's *Magna Britannia*, 6 vols., 1720–31. She was joined by R. Nutt in 1724, having

printed vols. 1 and 2 alone in 1720. These two volumes were sold by M. Nutt (*q. v.*). "Nutt, in the Savoy," is classed by Negus as a "high-flier".

NUTT (JOHN), printer and bookseller in London, (1) (*a*) near Stationers Hall, or Juxta Basilicam Stationariorum, (*b*) in Stationers' Court; (2) in the Savoy. 1690 (?)–1710 (?). The Rev. Rowland Davies, Dean of Ross, records in his Diary under date April 3rd, 1690: "Then I went to my brother and with him into the City, having at Nott's bought this book and a case for sermons for three shillings." [Camden Soc. Pub. no. 64, 1857, p. 97.] This entry may possibly refer to William Nutt, the bookseller of Pall Mall, although the latest reference to him in the Term Catalogues is 1688–9. On the other hand, if the Dean really made his purchase in the City, then the reference must be to John Nutt, who is not otherwise known to have been established there until 1698. [*T.C.* III. 95.] Dunton again has added to the confusion. He says of "Mr. Nutt": "He was originally a printer, and lived with Mr. Jones in the Savoy for many years . . . and now gives as great content to those that employ him as any publisher whatever." This was written in 1703, but John Nutt, the printer in the Savoy, is not mentioned in the Term Catalogues as a printer until 1708. The fact seems to be that Nutt gave up bookselling about 1708 to resume his earlier trade as a printer. His last entry in the Term Catalogues is Moll's Atlas, 1709, printed by him. [*T.C.* III. 651.] He was apparently succeeded by Elizabeth Nutt (*q. v.*), probably his widow. His most famous publication was Swift's *Tale of a Tub*, 1704 and reprints to 1710.

NUTT (M.), bookseller in London, in Exeter Exchange in the Strand, 1720. *See* Nutt (Elizabeth).

NUTT (R.) *See* Nutt (Elizabeth).

NUTT (WILLIAM), *see also* Nott.

OAKES (EDWARD), printer and bookseller in London, Well-Yard, near West Smithfield, 1663–72 (?). *See Dictionary*, 1641–67. In 1670 he printed (as E. O.), for Francis Haley, *The Opinion of Witchcraft Vindicated*, by R. T., and in 1671 he published with Haley Dean Lloyd's *Legend of Captain Jones*. [B.M. 1077. b. 38.] In the 1675 list of Printing Houses, it is stated that this house had been "bought in" by the Company of Stationers, "since 1672."

OGILBY (JOHN), *see Dictionary*, 1641–67.

OGSTON (ALEXANDER), bookseller in Edinburgh, in the Parliament Close, 1685–8. In 1688 he was threatened for selling anti-popish books, and in the same year Mrs. Anderson seized some octavo Bibles he had imported from London. Amongst his publications were G. Scot's *Model . . . Government . . . East-New-Jersey*, 1685, S. Colvill's *Mock-poem, or whigs supplication*, 1687, and *Bibliotheca Universalis*, 1688. He was succeeded by his widow Martha Ogston (*q. v.*). [Aldis, p. 118.]

OGSTON (JAMES), bookseller in Edinburgh, *c.* 1714. Will registered August 31st, 1714.

OGSTON, afterwards STEVENSON (MARTHA), bookseller in Edinburgh, in the Parliament Close. 1688–1738 (?). Widow of Alexander Ogston, whom she succeeded. Her will, under the name of "Martha Stevenson, relict of Alexander Ogston, bookseller in Edinburgh", was registered on January 20th, 1738. [Aldis, p. 18.]

OKES, *see* Oakes.

OLIVER (   ), Mrs., bookseller in Norwich, 1711–25. Perhaps the widow of Francis Oliver, who ceased publishing in 1712; if so, her publishing in the last year of his activity might be accounted for by his illness. [*N. & Q.*, 10th Ser., V. 184.] It seems very improbable that this Mrs. Oliver is identical with Mrs. Elizabeth Oliver (*q. v.*). No address is given in *N. & Q.*

OLIVER (ELIZABETH), bookseller in Norwich, Cockey Lane, 1689–1704. William Oliver (*q. v.*) was succeeded in 1689 by his widow, at whose house and for whose benefit Edward Millington of London held an auction, probably of Oliver's stock, on December 16th. [*London Gazette*, November 28th–December 2nd, 1689; B.M. 821. i. 2 (4).] Three sermons, by J. Brett, J. Jeffery, and J. Robinson, all of 1704, bear her imprint [Quinton, *Bibl. Norf.*, pp. 54, 235; Bodl. Sermons, 17], after which she disappears. Francis Oliver, presumably her son, began business at the same address in 1704.

OLIVER (FRANCIS), bookseller in Norwich, Cockey Lane, 1704–12. Probably a son of William Oliver, whose widow he succeeded in 1704, between which year and 1712 he is known to have published five books, at least four of them being sermons; most of them were printed for him by Freeman Collins. [*T.C.* III. 391; Quinton, *Bibl. Norf.*, pp. 94, 528–9, 65, 71, 2.] His relationship to the Mrs. Oliver (*q.v.*) who was in business in Norwich from 1711 is obscure.

OLIVER (SAMUEL), bookseller in Norwich, 1692–3. Probably a son of William Oliver. His publications are confined to two years, and consist of Peter

Choavin's *De Naturali Religione*, 1693, and four sermons, one of which was printed for him by John Russell, printer to the University of Cambridge. [Quinton, *Bibl. Norf.*, pp. 444, 548 ; *T.C.* II. 408, 451, 455.]

OLIVER (WILLIAM), bookseller in Norwich, 1663–89(?). *See Dictionary*, 1641–67. Publishing at least as late as 1680, when he had *Three Sermons* by C. Robotham printed for him in London [Quinton, *Bibl. Norf.*, p. 440], and perhaps as late as 1689, at the end of which year the widow Oliver had an auction, probably of her husband's stock. His son John was admitted to St. John's College, Cambridge, on July 8th, 1681. [*Admissions to St. John's College*, II. 84.]

ONELY, *see* Onley.

ONLEY (WILLIAM), printer in London, (1) Little Britain ; (2) Bond's Stables, near Chancery Lane. 1697–1709. A printer of ballads, broadsides, and chap-books for various London publishers. But one of his first productions was a more literary work, the second edition of D'Urfey's *Cinthia and Endimion*, which he printed in 1697 for S. Briscoe and R. Wellington. Dunton's character-sketch of him [p. 248] lays stress on the rapidity of his work and his popularity with the journeymen printers, and tells us that " being very ingenious, by his own projections he keeps two printing houses constantly at work ; one in Little Britain, and the other in Bond's stables, near Chancery Lane ". John How, 1709, asks : " How many copies of other mens has Mr. Onely printed, and whether the booksellers of London, particularly those on the Bridge, were not his customers for the said books ? What Mr. Keble recovered of Mr. Onely when he sued him for printing ' The Week's Preparation ' ? " [*Some Thoughts on the Present State of Printing and Bookselling*, p. 10.] Onley frequently used his initials only, and very rarely dated his books.

ORME (JAMES), printer in London, 1692–8. This printer was employed by several London publishers, including R. Basset, R. Bentley, A. Bosvile, Thomas Jones, Randal Taylor, and R. Wellington. He printed in 1692 Elkanah Settle's *Triumphs of London*, in 1697 Edward Filmer's tragedy, *The Unnatural Brother*, in the same year Mary Pix's comedy, *The Innocent Mistress*, and in 1698 Crowne's tragedy, *Caligula*.

ORME (JOHN), bookbinder in London, 1681–2. In Mich. 33 Chas. II he brought an action in the Court of Common Pleas against William Hare for false imprisonment. [C.P.R. 2997, m. 448 r.]

ORREL (THOMAS), bookseller in London, Hand and Scepter, Fleet Street, 1678. In 1678 he published (1) a play, *The Rambling Justice*, (2) a miscellany of verse, *Oxford Drollery*, and (3) *Words made Visible*. [*T.C.* I. 320, 330, 332.]

OSBORN, or OSBORNE (JOHN), bookseller in London, (1) Oxford Arms in Lombard Street; (2) Paternoster Row. 1711–39. First met with in partnership with T. Varnam, who succeeded to the business of Thomas Guy [*T.C.* III. 667], and in 1725 he is found publishing with his son-in-law, T. Longman, at the Ship in Paternoster Row. Nichols says that he became Master of the Company of Stationers in 1735 and died on March 13th, 1739. [*Lit. Anecd.*, III. 601.]

OSBORN, or OSBORNE (ROBERT), bookseller in Exeter, near the Bear, 1693–6. He was local agent for the sale of two sermons : (1) *The Pastor's Care and Dignity, and the peoples Duty. A sermon preached . . . at Taunton*, by G[eorge] T[rosse], 1693. [Gilling, *Life of Trosse*, p. 127 ; Dredge, 10.] (2) Ποιμνη Φυλακιον, *The Pastor's Charge and the Peoples Duty, A Sermon*, by Samuel Stoddon, 1694. [Dredge, 10.] In 1696 he issued *A Sermon preached in . . . Exeter on the Thanksgiving Day*. [Dredge, 94.] This had a leaf with a list of books printed for him.

OSBORNE (THOMAS), bookseller in London, Gray's Inn, near the Walks, 1702–43. In Trin. 1702 he sold an edition of Glanvil's translation of Fontenelle's *Plurality of Worlds*. [*T.C.* III. 313.] Osborne died in 1743, and was succeeded by his son Thomas. It was the latter who bought the Harleian Library and employed Oldys and Johnson to catalogue it ; his relations with the latter have made him much better known than his father, who was nevertheless one of the leading publishers of his time. [*D.N.B.*]

OSWALD (ANDREW), bookseller in London, Oxinden Street, 1686. Thomas Newcomb printed for him *His Majesties . . . Letter to the Parliament of Scotland*, 1686. [B.M. T. 100* (173).]

OVENS (MARY), bookseller at Kannershmead (?) in Wales, 1699. Sold school-books, which she purchased of John Minshull, bookseller in Chester. [*Library*, 2nd ser. IV. 373–83.]

OVERTON (HENRY), bookseller and printseller in London, White Horse without Newgate, 1707–9. Son of John Overton. His father sold him his stock of maps, prints, and engravings on his marriage in 1707 ; he is mentioned in the

Term Catalogue of 1709. [*T.C.* III. 647.] He had taken his brother Philip (*q. v.*) into partnership 1709.

OVERTON (JOHN), bookseller and printseller in London, (1) White Horse in Little Britain next door to Little St. Bartholomew's Gate ; (2) White Horse without Newgate. 1667–1707. *See Dictionary*, 1641–67. In 1671 he moved to the White Horse without Newgate, the shop previously occupied by Henry Overton (*q.v.*, *Dictionary*, 1641–67), who was perhaps his father. John Overton established a good business in prints, maps, and engravings of all kinds, and was the principal vendor of mezzotints of his day. In 1707, on the occasion of his son Henry's marriage, he sold him his stock-in-trade and retired in his favour. He died in 1713, his will being proved on April 2nd. Besides Henry (*q. v.*) he left three other sons : Thomas, who went to America, James, and Philip (*q. v.*).

OVERTON (PHILIP), bookseller and printseller in London, White Horse without Newgate, 1709. Stated in Arber's index [*T.C.* III. 728] to have sold G. de L'Isle's map (*Theatrum Historicum*) ; the entry of it on the page referred to [III. 647] does not contain his or his brother's name, but the map does.

OWEN (JOHN), bookseller in Oxford and Cambridge, 1701–10. On October 4th, 1701, the University of Cambridge entered into an agreement with John Owen of Oxford, stationer, for the production of an edition of Suidas's *Lexicon* in three volumes folio ; Owen to pay £1 10*s*. 6*d*. per sheet, paying for the first 100 copies when the second 100 were ready for delivery, and so on, six months credit being given for the last 200, the whole stock to remain at the Press as security till paid for. Owen being unable to fulful his part of the engagement, on April 16th, 1703, a Grace was passed for a new contract with Sir T. Jannson in place of John Owen, insolvent. Owen's failure placed the University in difficulties with regard to the work, and correspondence and negotiations respecting it went on for a period of forty years. The work was published by the University Press in 1705, when the degree of LL.D. was given to the editor. Correspondence concerning the work will be found in the *Correspondence* of Dr. Richard Bentley. Other works were arranged for by Owen between 1701–10, and some bear his name as " typographus ", which may only mean " publisher ". In one of these, Simon Ockley's *Introductio ad Linguas Orientales*, 1706, is a long dedication to Elias Abenaker of London, Gent., in which he speaks of his having been induced, by " specious promises ",

apparently by Bentley, ("a Person of an high Character, and a pretending Encourager of Arts and Sciences, and Printing in particular ") to leave Oxford for Cambridge, and acknowledges the "noble assistances you have supplied me with, to raise my Fortune in the World, and put my Affairs into a prosperous and flourishing Condition." In 1703 he published volume I of C. Cellarius' *Notitia Orbis Antiqui, sive Geographia Plenior*, but volume II bears the imprint " Amstelaedami Casparus Fritsch ", and was issued in 1706. He was in Holland in 1706, and was entrusted with books and letters from Rheland and L. Kuster to Dr. Bentley and others. The last book to bear his imprint is a Sallust of 1710. [R. Bowes's *Cambridge Printers*, p. 312, *Cambridge Books*, and *Notes on the Cambridge University Press*, 1701–7, in Camb. Antiq. Soc. Communications, VI., 362–7 ; Bentley's *Correspondence*, ed. Chr. Wordsworth, 1842 ; S. C. Roberts, *Hist. of the Camb. Univ. Press*, pp. 87–9.]

OXLAD (FRANCIS), senior, bookseller and bookbinder in Oxford, 1665–73. *See Dictionary*, 1641–67. Still publishing in 1673, when he published a folio edition of Juvenal. [Haz. II. 323.] Stephen Fletcher was one of his apprentices. [Hearne, *Collections*, IX. 348.]

P. (G.), bookseller in London, 1687. *A true Relation of the Great Thunder . . . at Alvanley* was printed by D. Mallet for G. P., 1687. [Cooke, *Bibliotheca Cestriensis*, p. 24.] G. P. may be George Pawlett or G. Powell, or less probably George Parker, who is only known to have been in business in 1683.

PAGE (DIXY). *See Dictionary*, 1641–67. He was still publishing in 1672, when in company with T. Passinger and B. Hurlock he issued a chap-book, *The History of the Five Wise Philosophers*. [Haz. I. 325.]

PAGE (HUMPHREY), bookseller in Nantwich and Chester, 1685–1711. In 1685 his name occurs in a list of booksellers who sold a patent medicine, given at the end of M. Bromfield's *Brief Discovery of the . . . Scurvy*. [*N.&Q.*, 11 ser. XI. 45.] He was then at Nantwich. He was still in business in 1711, when he published at Chester a sermon by J. Oliver. [B.M. 225. h. 1 (15).]

PALMER (EDMUND), bookseller in Stamford, 1706. His name occurs in a list of provincial booksellers. [*N. & Q.*, 10 ser. V. 242.] He had a son Benjamin, who was entered at St. John's College, Cambridge, on July 8th, 1704, and took his D.D. degree in 1725. [Mayor's *Admissions to St. John's College*, Pt. II, p. 172.]

PALMER (GEORGE), bookseller in London, Black Spread Eagle, without Temple Bar ; [(2) King and Duke of York's Head, Strand, near Arundel House (?)

1670.] Published at the Black Spread Eagle in 1670 *The Lovers' Logick*, an English translation of de Callières' *l'Amant Logicien*. [Haz. II. 162; *T.C.* I. 21.] The second address is given by Arber in the index to vol. i of the Term Catalogues, but without apparent reason, as he gives only the one reference.

PALMER (R.), bookseller in London, Crown, without Temple Bar, 1716. Publisher of a chap-book called *Love's Perpetual Almanack*, . . . by Amorous Gay. [Haz. I. 266.]

PALMER (SAMUEL), bookseller in London, 1685–6. Apprentice to John Dunton and went with him to America. He was "very honest and diligent", but "preferred shooting to bookselling", so about 1686 he gave up the trade, and obtaining a post in the Army, met his death by drowning. [Dunton, pp. 87, 112, 129–130.]

PALMER (SAMUEL), bookseller in Gloucester; and in Tewkesbury, near the Tolsey, 1685. Probably a relative of Thomas Palmer, stationer, of Tewkesbury, who died in March 16$\frac{79}{80}$, *q.v.*, *Dictionary*, 1641–67. His name occurs in a list of booksellers selling a patent medicine given at the end of M. Bromfield's *Brief Discovery of the Scurvy*, 1685. [*N. & Q.*, 11 ser. XI. 45.]

PALMER (SAMUEL), printer in London, Bartholomew Close, 1723 (?)–32. The exact date at which Palmer set up is unknown. He was probably at work in 1700, but we first hear of him as printing Sternhold and Hopkins for the Stationers' Company in 1723. Franklin, when he came to England at the end of 1724, was employed in Palmer's printing house, which he calls famous. [*Autobiography*, ed. J. Bigelow, 1909, p. 91.] He is chiefly remembered as part author of a very bad *History of Printing*. Originally his intention was to write a book about the practical part of the art; but he was deterred by the fears of the trade that he would betray secrets, and turned his work into a history of printing, which was issued in parts but was not completed at the author's death. Although his business was a large one, Palmer eventually became bankrupt, and died on May 9th, 1732. His *History* was continued by George Psalmanazar. The work as a whole was published in 1732. This *History* was worthless, and has been treated with contempt. J. Lewis, writing to Ames, described Palmer as "a good printer, but a bad historian, ignorant, careless and inaccurate". [Nichols, *Illustr. of Lit.* IV. 174.] His merits as a printer caused him to be selected to supervise a private press set up by some

of the Royal Family at St. James's in 1731. The following notice of his death appeared in *The Norwich Gazette*, May 6th–13th, 1732: "Last Thursday died the learned and ingenious Mr. Samuel Palmer, printer of the Grub Street Journal, and author of the History of Printing. He has not left his equal, either as a printer or as a scholar." He printed the *Grub Street Journal* in 1731 and 1732, in partnership with J. Huggonson. [B.M. Burney.]

PALMER (THOMAS), *see Dictionary* 1641–67.

PARDOE (MARK), bookseller in London, Black Raven, Strand, over against Bedford House, 1677–86. Hazlitt records a book as published by him in 1677. The earliest reference to him in the Term Catalogues is in 1680. [*T.C.* I. 385.] A short list of books, several of them scientific, printed for him by 1680 is to be found in *The Novels of Elizabeth*, by Madame d'Aulnoy. [B.M. G. 1516.] In 1682 he published a Latin edition of Hobbes's *Leviathan*. [*T.C.* I. 473.] His last entry in the Term Catalogues was in 1686. [*T.C.* II. 172.]

PARK (JOHN), newsvendor in Edinburgh, at the Fountain Well, 1712. *The Evening Post*, no. 225, May 13th–15th, 1712, has the imprint: "Edinburgh: printed by John Moncur, and sold . . . by John Park at his stand at the Fountain Well, where advertisements are taken in, 1712." [W. J. Couper: *The Edinburgh Periodical Press*, I. 253.]

PARKER (ANDREW), printer in London, Goswell Street, 1724. Parker, of Goswell Street, is included by Negus among printers "known to be well-affected to King George". His Christian name is supplied by Nichols in his Index. [*Lit. Anecd.* VII. 308.]

PARKER (EDMUND), bookseller in London, (1) Bible and Crown in Lombard Street, (*a*) near St. Mary Wolnoth's Church, (*b*) near the Stocks Market; (2) under the Royal Exchange. 1704–23. His name first occurs in the Term Catalogue of Hil. 1704, with two books of divinity. [*T.C.* III. 385.] He contributed to the Bowyer relief fund in 1713 [Nichols, *Lit. Anecd.* I. 61], and was still in business in 1723. [Haz. I. 62.]

PARKER (EDWARD), printer in London, (*a*) Salisbury Court, (*b*) Salisbury Street, 1723–4. Nichols records that "Mr. Parker" printed four sheets of the "*Castrations of Holinshed's Chronicle*" in 1723. [*Lit. Anecd.* I. 252.] Negus in 1724 includes among the printers "known to be well-affected to King George", "Parker Senior, Salisbury Street, and printer of a Half-penny Post".

PARKER (G.), bookseller in London, 1683. Published a poetical broadside entitled *Thompson Tell-lyes, or an answer to Titus Tell-Truth*. This was doubtless a satire on Nathaniel Thompson, the printer of a news-sheet called *The True Domestick Intelligence* at the time of the Popish Plot. [B.M. C. 20. f. 6(13).]

PARKER (PETER), senior, bookseller in London, (1) At the end of Pope's Head Alley next Lombard Street, 1665; (2) under Creed Church near Aldgate, 1667–72; (3) Leg and Star, Cornhill, over against the Royal Exchange, 1673–1703; 1665–1703. *See Dictionary*, 1641–67. In partnership with John and Thomas Guy (*q.v.*), and Moses Pitt was one of the publishers of Oxford Bibles. His removal to Cornhill is dated by entries in the Term Catalogues. [*T.C.* II. 100, 126.] Dunton [pp. 228–9] states that he left his business to his apprentice H. Nelme or Nelmes. This was in 1696; but Nelme "came to an untimely end", and disappears after 1697. Dunton says of Parker, "this bookseller lives by the Royal Exchange", so that it seems that he resumed the business after the failure of Nelmes.

PARKER (PETER), junior, bookseller in London, 1707. Defendant in an action brought by the Company of Stationers, for printing and selling books against their monopoly. Parker pleaded that the Master and Wardens could not claim a benefit apart from the Commonalty of the Company, and that what copies he sold bore the imprint of the Company. [Chanc. Proc. before 1714, Bridges, 270/21.]

PARKER (RICHARD), bookseller in London, Unicorn, under the Piazza of the Royal Exchange, Cornhill, 1692–1725 (?). A publisher of plays and historical works. He made his first entry in the Term Catalogue in 1692. [*T.C.* II. 393.] Dunton [p. 210] speaks of him as "fortunate in all he prints . . . universally known and beloved by the merchants that frequent the Royal Exchange". He subscribed to the Bowyer Fund in 1713.

PARKHURST (THOMAS), bookseller in London, (1) George in Little Britain, 1653–6; (2) Three Crowns (*a*) at the lower end of Cheapside, (*b*) near the Conduit, (*c*) near Mercers' Chapel; (3) Golden Bible upon London Bridge, 1667 (?)–71; (4) Bible and Three Crowns at the lower end of Cheapside, near Mercers' Chapel, 1670; (5) Bible and Three Crowns in the Poultry; 1679. 1653–1711. *See Dictionary*, 1641–67. As the bulk of Parkhurst's life-work was done between 1667 and 1711, the notice previously given may be incorporated with

this. Thomas Parkhurst was bound apprentice to John Clarke, bookseller in London, in 1645, and was made a Freeman of the Company of Stationers on July 3rd, 1654. He began to publish theological books about that date, and a list of twenty-five publications on sale by him in 1657 is found at the end of S. Purchas's *Theatre of Political Flying Insects*. [B.M. 452. a. 37.] Another and longer list, arranged under sizes, was issued with W. Secker's *Nonsuch Professor*, 1660. About 1667 opened the Golden Bible upon London Bridge, in addition to his other shop in Cheapside near Mercers' Chapel, both imprints being given on T. Wadsworth's *Immortality of the Soul explained* [*T.C.* I. 64], but he apparently gave up the London Bridge shop before the end of the year 1671. In 1679 he published for Capt. W. Bedloe *The Excommunicated Prince . . . being the Popish Plot in a play*, the imprint to which was "The Bible and Three Crowns in the Poultry". Probably all his imprints, except the Little Britain and London Bridge ones, refer to one house. Dunton was one of Thomas Parkhurst's apprentices, and spoke well of him as a master. He calls him the most "eminent Presbyterian bookseller in the Three Kingdoms", and adds, "He has printed more practical books than any other that can be named in London." [Dunton, pp. 39, 42, 205, 224, 699.] In 1689 Parkhurst served the office of Under Warden, and in 1703 was chosen Master of the Company of Stationers. He gave up business in 1711, his stock being sold by auction by Thomas Ballard at the Black Boy Coffee House, in Ave-Mary Lane on February 5th and following evenings.

PARKS (WILLIAM), printer in Ludlow, 1719–20; in Hereford, 1721; in Reading, 1723. 1719–23. At Ludlow he printed two sermons by Samuel Jones. [Allnutt, pp. 301–3; information kindly given by Mr. G. P. Mander.]

PARRY (RICHARD), bookseller in Bangor, 1699. Sold schoolbooks and prayer-books which he purchased wholesale of John Minshull, bookseller of Chester. [*Library*, 2nd ser. IV. 373–83.]

PARSHAM ( ), bookseller in Northampton, 1704. An Assize sermon preached at Northampton on July 26th, 1704, by John Pierce, was sold by him. [*T.C.* III. 424.] Possibly identical with James Pasham (*q.v.*).

PARSLOWE, *see* Purslowe.

PARSON, or PARSONS (HENRY), stationer in London, Three Bibles and Three Ink Bottles near St. Magnus' Church on London Bridge, 1711–18. His name occurs in an advertisement of the sale of playing cards in the *Post Man* of February 3rd, 1711. He was also defendant in an action brought against him by John Baskett the printer, judgement being given for the plaintiff on July 8th, 1718.

PARSONS (WILLIAM), stationer in London, 168$\frac{8}{9}$. Defendant in plea of trespass brought against him by John Smith. [C.P.R. Hil., 2–3 Jas. II, 3052, m. 49 v.]

PARTRIDGE (JAMES), bookseller in London, Post Office, between Charing Cross and Whitehall, 1683–94. There seem to have been two stationers in partnership at this address, James and Jo. Partridge. James was sometimes described as "Stationer to Prince George of Denmark", and published several medical works; while three books, two of which are medical and the third a novel, are advertised on the last leaf of *An Historical Account of the Late Troubles, during the wars of Paris,* published by Henry Chapman in 1686, as for sale by "Jo. Partridge" at the above address. But "Jo." may be a misprint. James Partridge's name appears in the Term Catalogues for the last time in 1694. [*T.C.* II. 525.] James Partridge, Matthew Gilliflower and Samuel Heyrick termed themselves Printers to the House of Lords in 168$\frac{8}{9}$; but as none of them were printers by trade, they must have farmed out the office.

PARTRIDGE (JO.), *see* Partridge (James).

PASHAM (JAMES), printer in Northampton, 1721. Printer of a short-lived Tory newspaper, *The Northampton Journal*, in opposition to Raikes and Dicey (*q.v.*). Possibly identical with Parsham (*q.v.*).

PASK, or PASKE (ROBERT), stationer and bookseller in London, (1) Stationers' Arms and Ink Bottle, under Pinners Hall, (*a*) Broad Street, (*b*) Winchester Street by Gresham College, 1669; (2) Stationers' Arms and Ink Bottle, Lombard Street, near Sir Robert Vyners, 1670–72; (3) (*a*) under the Royal Exchange, Threadneedle Street, (*b*) in the Piazza on the North Side of the Royal Exchange, 1676–8. 1669–78. Publisher of some plays, and also the maps and surveys of John Ogilby. His name is found in an advertisement of lost property in *The London Gazette* of November 2nd, 1676, in which the last of the above addresses is found; his removes can be dated from the Term Catalogues.

PASSINGER (SARAH), bookseller in London, Three Bibles on London Bridge, 1689–92. Widow of Thomas Passinger the First (*q.v.*). She was, before her marriage with Passinger, the widow of Charles Tyus, bookseller. In 1689 she advertised a book entitled *Abstractum Chirurgiae Marinae* in *The London Gazette* of July 1st. She died in 1692, and was buried in the south aisle of St. Magnus, the business passing to her nephew Thomas Passinger the Second.

PASSINGER (THOMAS), the First. *See Dictionary*, 1641–67. A list of books sold by him is given at the end of Forde's *Montelion*, 1687. [Bodl. Douce D. 225.]

PASSINGER (THOMAS), the Second, bookseller in London, Three Bibles and Star, on London Bridge, 1692–5. Nephew of Thomas Passinger the First; succeeded to the business on the death of the latter's widow Sarah.

PATON (JOHN), bookseller in Edinburgh, in the Parliament Close, 1716–54. Many issues of *The Acts of the General Assembly* between the years 1716 and 1754, as well as several books printed by Ruddiman, bear his name in the imprint.

PAWLETT (E.), bookseller in London, Bible in Chancery Lane, 1692. Possibly the widow of George Pawlett. Advertised a theological work in 1692. [*T.C.* II. 404.]

PAWLETT (EDWARD), bookseller in Grantham, 1686. Timperley [p. 641] says: "The earliest known sale of books by auction in this country, out of London, is the following: 'A Catalogue of choice books . . . will be sold [*sic*] by auction at Mr. Edward Pawlett's house, bookseller in Grantham, on Wednesday the 4th Day of August 1686.'"

PAWLETT (GEORGE), bookseller in London, Bible in Chancery Lane, 1683–90. Son of Robert Pawlett or Pawley. He was one of the publishers of Sir Henry Spelman's *Glossarium Archaiologicum* in 1687. [*T.C.* II. 189.] He died in 1690; his executors were Abraham Chambers and Jacob Tonson. [P.R.O. Chancery Decree Roll 1356.]

PAWLETT (ROBERT). *See Dictionary*, 1641–67. He died in 1683, leaving to his son George all his copyrights. Roger Norton, printer, was nominated overseer. [P.C.C. 97 Drax.]

PAWLEY, *see* Pawlett.

PEACOCK (JOHN), bookseller in London, 1681. In 1681 he published an edition of the Proceedings of the House of Commons in the Parliament held at Oxford from the 21st to the 28th March, in which he referred to the exorbitant rates paid by booksellers for copyrights. [B.M. T. 94* (17).]

PEARCE (JOHN), bookseller in Exeter, 1697–8. In the Term Catalogue of Hil. 169$\frac{7}{8}$ is entered a work entitled *A Religious Conference between a Minister and Parishioner*, which was to be sold by J. Pearce in Exeter. [*T.C.* III. 1.] Dredge does not mention this, but has the following [ff. 10, 62, 94]: (1) *A Practical Treatise concerning Evil Thoughts* . . . By William Chilcot, 1698; (2) *A Sermon preached in St. Saviour's Church in Dartmouth*, by Humfry Smith, 1698; (3) *Bread for the Poor*, by R. D., 1698. The last three were printed for Pearce, Charles Yeo, and Philip Bishop by Samuel Darker.

PEARSE (FRANCIS), bookseller in London, 1685. Gave a bill for £10 to Thomas Symmons, which afterwards came into the hands of Robert Turner, who sued upon it. The proceedings were adjourned. [C.P.R. Mich., 1 Jas. II, Roll 3039, m. 309 v.] In the same year he published a small book, *The Honourable State of Matrimony made comfortable*, by D. B.

PEARSON (WILLIAM), printer in London, over against Wright's Coffee House in Aldersgate Street, 1700–25. A printer of music. He printed for John Cullen, Henry Playford, D. Brown, and other noted music publishers. In 1723 he printed R. and J. Barber's *Book of Psalmody* for Josiah Rathbone, bookseller at Macclesfield in Cheshire, giving the above address. [J. H. Cooke, *Bibliotheca Cestriensis*, p. 31.]

PEARTREE (OWEN), bookseller in Yarmouth, 1703–6. Publisher of the following books: (1) *A Sermon preach'd at the Cathedral Church of Norwich, . . . by a priest of the Church of England*, printed for O. Peartree in Yarmouth, and J. Sprint at the Bell in Little Britain, 1703. [*T.C.* III. 354.] (2) *The Church Catechism resolved into Questions and Answers*, By B. Love, A.M., the third edition . . . Norwich, Printed by F. Burges and sold by the booksellers of Norwich and Owen Peartree in Yarmouth, 1706. [B.M. 3505. df. 50.]

PEELE (JOHN), bookseller in London, Locke's Head in Paternoster Row, 1722–71. Referred to by Nichols as "a very considerable bookseller". He died on September 8th, 1771. [*Lit. Anecd.* III. 737.] In 1722 he published a sermon by George Stubbes.

PEISLEY, or PIESLEY (ANTONY), bookseller at Oxford, near St. Mary's Church, 1692–1724. Hearne, writing to Dr. T. Smith on February 1st, 1709, informs him that "Peisley the bookseller has bought the whole impression of Ignatius" [*Collections*, II. 166], and in the following year he tells Thorpe that Peisley has bought Leland *De Scriptoribus*. [*Ib.* III. 88.] In 1711 he started a newspaper called *The Surprise*, which Hearne characterized as a "silly paper". The author was believed to be T. Tickell, then Professor of Poetry. In December 1719 Peisley bought the remainder of the library of Dr. Hudson, after the University had taken what they wanted [*Ib.* VII. 85], and in 1721 some books of Dr. Yates, for which he gave £80. [*Ib.* VII. 277.] He died suddenly on August 11th, 1724. Hearne records that he "used to have auctions frequently in Oxford, in the Old Convocation House at the N. East End of St. Marie's Church, and he talked of having one next Lent. . . . He hath one Son of the same trade, about twenty-two years of age, and six Daughters, the eldest of which is married to Mr. Beaver, M.A. and Steward of Corpus Xti College; the other five are unmarried. Mr Peisly had several houses in Oxford and an Estate of about six score Pounds per annum at Clifton, near Dorchester. . . . He died in the fifty-seventh Year of his Age, and was buried in St. Marie's Church this day." [*Ib.* VIII. 252.]

PEMBERTON (J.), bookseller in London, (*a*) Golden Buck, (*b*) Buck and Sun, against St. Dunstan's Church in Fleet Street. 1709–12. One of the publishers of Whitelocke's *Memorials*. [*T.C.* III. 643.] Hazlitt records a work on the Hertfordshire witch, Jane Wenham, published by him in 1712. [II. 280.]

PENDLEBURY (ADAM), bookseller in Oxford, 1684. [Madan, p. 31.]

PENN (JOSEPH), bookseller in Bristol, behind the Rose Tavern, 1709–22. Published *Sermons*, &c., by Strickland Gough, minister in Bristol, in 1709–14. [B.M. 4475. de. 5; 4478. e. 90 (3).] Some books bearing dates 1719–22 are said to have been *printed by* him.

PENNOCK ( ), printer (?) in London, Paternoster Row, 1709. Referred to as a piratical printer by J. How in *Some Thoughts on the present state of Printing and Bookselling*, 1709, p. 12.

PENROSE (JOHN), bookseller in Leeds, 1712. Known from a list of provincial booksellers printed in *Notes & Queries*. [*N. & Q.*, 10 ser. V. 183.]

PEPYAT (JEREMY), bookseller in Dublin, Skinner Row, 1711–15. Published three tracts by E. Synge, Bishop of Raphoe, between 1711 and 1715. [B.M. 4165. c. 26 (4, 5); 4474. aa. 95 (1).]

PERO (JOHN), bookseller in London, (*a*) Black, (*b*) White, Swan, Little Britain, 1694–1703. Made his first entry in the Term Catalogues in Easter 1694. [*T.C.* II. 500.] He was the publisher of *Memoires of the Reign of King Charles I*, by Sir Philip Warwick, 1702 [*T.C.* III. 292], and in 1703, with I. Cleave and E. Tracy, he published an abridgement of La Calprenède's *Cassandra.* [Esdaile, p. 192.] Pero is praised by Dunton [p. 215].

PETERS (FRANCIS), bookseller in London, 1681. Published a pamphlet, *Vox Patriae*, 1681. [B.M. 816. m. 2 (13).]

PEYTE ( ), printer in London, 1717. Gent, under this year [p. 75], speaks of "an old printer, called Father Peyte". Perhaps he was not a master printer.

PHILIPS (JOHN), bookseller in Worcester, 1685. Occurs in a list of booksellers and stationers who sold a patent medicine, given at the end of M. Bromfield's *Brief Discovery of the Scurvy.* [*N. & Q.*, 11 ser. XI. 45.]

PHILLIPPS (JOHN), bookseller in Exeter, 1681. In 33 Chas. II Trinity (C.P.R. 2995) he was sued by George Saffin, sheriff of Exeter, for a debt of £276, and judgement was signed on July 15th, 33 Chas. II.

PHILLIPS (JOSHUA), bookseller in London, (1) Atlas in Cornhill, 1680; (2) Seven Stars, St. Paul's Churchyard, 1680–93; (3) King's Arms, St. Paul's Churchyard, 1694–1706; (4) Black Bull, Cornhill, 1707–9. 1680–1709. First mentioned in the Term Catalogues in Mich. 1680 (the Atlas in Cornhill appearing here only, combined with the Seven Stars). [*T.C.* I. 416.] Published books in various classes of literature. Between Mich. 1693 and Mich. 1694 he altered his sign or moved to fresh premises in St. Paul's Churchyard [*T.C.* II. 487, 527]; he moved to the Black Bull in Cornhill between Easter 1706 and Trin. 1707. [*T.C.* III. 505, 555.] The latest mention of him in the Term Catalogues is in 1709. He often shared copies with H. Rhodes and other booksellers.

PHILPOT, or PHILPOTT (JAMES), printer in Gosport, Middle Street, 1708–36. In 1708 he printed the Gosport *Churchwardens' Accounts*, and in 1710 Essex Waller's farce, *A Trip to Portsmouth.* [Cotton, II. 86.] Noticed by Mr. F. A. Edwards in a list of Hampshire booksellers and printers in *Notes & Queries.* [10 ser. V. 481.] He suggests that this John Philpott may have been the father of James Isaac Philpot of Winchester (*q. v.*).

PHILPOT (JAMES ISAAC), bookseller and printer in Winchester, 1725–32. Son of James Philpot of Gosport (*q. v.*)? Gave 21*s.* to use the trade of printer and bookseller at Winchester, 1725. [*N. & Q.*, 10 ser. V. 482.] A sermon, dated 1732, is known from his press. [Allnutt, p. 303.] In 1732 he had a free loan from the city fund to assist young tradesmen.

PICARD (BENJAMIN), bookseller in London, Three Bibles in the Minories, 1711. Sold J. Davis's *Seaman's Speculum*, and also John Darling's *Carpenter's Rule made Easie* in 1711. [*T.C.* III. 672–4.] Possibly the same as the following.

PICKARD ( ), printer in London, Salisbury Court, 1724. Mentioned by Negus as "well-affected to King George". Possibly the same as the preceding.

PIERCE (THOMAS), bookseller in London (?), 1676. Published in 1676 *A Sad Relation of a Dreadful Fire at Cottenham.* [Haz. III. 29.]

PIESLEY, *see* Peisley.

PIKE (JOHN), bookseller in Shaftesbury, 1675. Published in 1675 a religious tract entitled *A Cluster of Worcestershire Fruit*, by J. P.; printed in London. [Bodl. Pamph. 135.]

PIKE, or PYKE (THOMAS), bookseller in London, (1) Bread Street End, Cheapside; (2) Pall Mall. 1688–94. Publisher of Elkanah Settle's *Insignia Bataviae* . . . 1688. His name is also found in an advertisement of patent medicines in *The City Mercury*, June 11th, 1694. [B.M. Burney, 112 A.]

PINDAR (JOHN), bookseller in Cambridge, 1663 (?)–1703 (?). Published *The Tablet of Cebes, Done out of Greek into English by Robert Warren*, 1699. [Haz. II. 88.] He may be the John Pindar who witnessed the last will and testament of Jonathan Pindar, 1663 [Gray and Palmer, p. 100], and is mentioned in the will of William Morden, 1678, as living in the parish of St. Michael's in a tenement adjoining that of Morden's. [*Ib.* 118.] A John Pindar in 1689 gave £15 towards buying a bell for St. Michael's Church. [Cooper, *Memorials of Cambridge*, III. 342.] As no record of his death appears in the Church Registers it may be that he moved to Great St. Mary's parish to a house by the side of the Market Place, where we know a John Pindar was living from 1699 to his death in 1703, when his widow continued to live there until 1714.

PINDAR (JONATHAN), the First, printer and bookbinder (?) in Cambridge, 1680 (?)–98. Appointed University Printer June 11th, 1686, but in March 1693 another Printer was appointed, and on October 10th, 1698, a Grace was passed for an annuity of £5 each to Hugh Martin and Pindar, "formerly elected printers". [Bowes, *Cambridge Printers*, p. 310.] No books printed at the University Press bear his imprint. Probably a relative of Jonathan Pindar, d. 1663 [Gray and Palmer, p. 100], and of John Pindar (*q. v.*). A Jonathan Pindar appraised the goods of Anthony Nicholson (*q. v.*) 1680, Rose Browne 1687, Robert Gee (*q. v.*) 1681, William Graves (*q. v.*) 1686, and E. Beeching (*q. v.*) 1689. [Gray and Palmer.] John Pindar, Gent., in his will, dated June 25th, proved September 30th, 1680, left property and money to Jonathan Pindar and his wife, and £10 to apprentice their son Jonathan (*q. v.*) and £10 to be paid to him when twenty-one years of age; also to another son John property and reversion of property. In the University Audit Books for 1692–4 are entries for payments made to a bookbinder of this name, who may be the same person. [Bowes, *Cambridge Printers*, p. 311.]

PINDAR (JONATHAN), the Second, printer at Cambridge, 1699–1730. Appointed University Printer September 8th, 1699. "On 28 August 1730, there is a Grace declaring the voidance of the office of Printer to be necessary before certain proposals for printing Bibles and Prayer-Books can be settled, and offering Pindar the continuance of his full salary after his resignation." [Bowes, *Cambridge Printers*, p. 311.] This must be the son of Jonathan Pindar the First, mentioned in John Pindar's will.

PITT (MOSES), bookseller and printer, London and Oxford; London, (1) White Hart, Little Britain, 1668–73; (2) (*a*) Angel, in St. Paul's Churchyard, (*b*) over against the Little North Door of St. Paul's Church, 1673–86; (3) Duke Street, Westminster, 1688; Oxford, The Theatre, 1680–82. 1668–96. Son of John Pitt, yeoman, of St. Teath, Cornwall. On October 1st, 1654, Moses Pitt was bound apprentice to Robert Littlebury, citizen and haberdasher of London, and was made free of the Haberdashers' Company on November 8th, 1661. His first publication was Thomas Brancker's *Introduction to Algebra*, 1668. He continued to publish copiously. Shortly before 1679, when Dr. Fell was looking for some London men to manage the printing and bookselling business on which the University of Oxford was embarking at his suggestion, he chose Moses Pitt as one of them, and it is interesting to read Pitt's own narrative of the transaction as set out in his pamphlet, *The Cry of*

the Oppressed. He there says: "Having undertaken the printing of an Atlas or Description of the Whole World, which will be about Twelve volums in Folio . . . and being much incouraged by Dr. Fell, then Bishop of Oxford, I took of him the Printing House at Oxford called The Theatre, where I have finished four of the volums . . . and have Two volums more almost finished . . . and did also purchase of the Bishop a great quantity of Books, to the value of many thousands of pounds. And did in the latter end of King Charles Time, print great quantities of Bibles, Testaments, Common Prayers &c. in all volums, whereby I brought down the price of Bibles &c. more than half, which did great good at that time (Popery then being likely to over-flow us)." He continued to publish in London throughout these years, and till 1688. The published volumes of the Atlas appeared in 1680–82. Had he confined himself to bookselling Pitt might have completed the publication of *The English Atlas*, and retired a rich man; but he launched out into building speculations, chiefly in Westminster, over which he lost large sums of money and weakened his credit to such an extent that his partners in the bookselling business and Bible trade [*see* Guy (Thomas)] cut themselves loose from him. In Pitt's own words, "they pretended that I ow'd them some hundreds of pounds, and they lock't up my Oxford-warehouse". But it was a relative, Adiel Mill (*q. v.*), who, taking advantage of Pitt's difficulties, advanced him money on exorbitant terms for his building schemes and induced the unfortunate bookseller to hand over to him his "stock of books, atlases, Atlas paper, Copper Plates, Pictures, Printing Press, letters &c.", afterwards forcing him to become a prisoner in the Fleet Prison for debt. Whilst there Pitt wrote a graphic account of the miseries suffered by the prisoners, which he entitled *The Cry of the Oppressed*, 1691. At the same time he endeavoured to raise money for them in various ways. Pitt remained a prisoner from April 20th, 1689, to May 16th, 1691. He married a Miss Upman, perhaps a relative of the Rev. — Upman, to whom he refers in his *Cry.* After his release Pitt wrote *An Account of one Ann Jefferies . . who was fed for six months by . . . fairies*, 1696.

PLACE (JOHN), *see Dictionary*, 1641–67.

PLACE (WILLIAM), *see Dictionary*, 1641–67.

PLAYFORD (E.), bookseller in London, Little Britain, 1685. Part publisher of D. Newhouse's *Whole Art of Navigation*, 1685. [*T.C.* II. 146.] Successor of John Playford the Younger (?).

PLAYFORD (JOHN), the Elder, *see Dictionary*, 1641–67.

PLAYFORD (JOHN), the Younger, printer in London, Little Britain, 1679–85. Son of Matthew Playford, rector of Great Stanmore, and nephew of John Playford the elder. [*See Dictionary*, 1641–67.] From 1679 to 1683 he was in partnership with Ann, widow of William Godbid, the music printer. [*See Dictionary*, 1641–67.] In 1684 and 1685 Playford carried on the business alone; he died in 1685. He printed the sixth and seventh editions of *The Dancing Master*, 1679 and 1686, the latter issued posthumously. [*D. N. B.*]

PONDER (NATHANIEL), bookseller in London, (1) Peacock in Chancery Lane; (2) Peacock, Poultry, (*a*) near Cornhill, (*b*) over against the Stocks Market. 1669–1700 (?). Publisher of Bunyan's *Pilgrim's Progress*. He was the son of John Ponder, a Nonconformist mercer, of Rothwell, in Northamptonshire. On June 2nd, 1656 Nathaniel Ponder was bound apprentice to Robert Gibbs, bookseller, of Chancery Lane, and, at the expiration of his term, set up as a bookseller at the sign of the Peacock in Chancery Lane. His first entry, in the Term Catalogue for Easter 1669, was Dr. Owen's *Brief Declaration and Vindication of the doctrine of the Trinity* [*T.C.* I. 8], and he became the publisher of most of the writings of that Nonconformist leader. Another of his patrons was Sir Charles Wolseley, a Cromwellian. In 1676 Ponder opened a second shop in the Poultry; but shortly afterwards gave up the premises in Chancery Lane, and on August 10th in that year he was committed to prison for publishing Andrew Marvell's *Rehearsal Transpros'd*. [S.P.D. Chas. II, vol. 174, f. 161.] The first edition of Bunyan's *Pilgrim's Progress* was advertised by Ponder in the Term Catalogue for Hil. 1677–8, as an octavo, to be sold for the sum of eighteenpence. Probably no one was more surprised than the publisher at the success achieved by this publication. Three editions were called for within twelve months. Ponder found it difficult to keep pace with the ever-increasing demand for the book, and was obliged to get it printed where and how he could, so that misprints crept in and were not rectified, while the whole production steadily deteriorated with every fresh edition, and surreptitious and unauthorized editions were put on the market by unscrupulous publishers. Ponder did not publish only Nonconformist divinity; in 1685 he published the English translation of Le Vayer de Boutigny's *Tarsis et Zélie*, a romance in folio. About 1680 Ponder consigned to a certain Mercy Browning, a bookseller at Amsterdam, a large parcel of books, for sale on commission. It seems highly probable that she was a connexion of Thomas Browning of Rothwell, a Nonconformist minister for whom Nathaniel Ponder made application for a licence to preach in 1672. This transaction between Mercy Browning and Ponder became the subject of a lawsuit in 1692, Mercy Browning, as Ponder alleged, having sold her stock to a certain Rest Fenner (*q. v.*) without having paid for the books consigned to her by Ponder. A curious point about this lawsuit is that Ponder stated that the consignment was made in 1678, and included two copies of Whitelock's *Memorials of Affairs of State*, which was not published until 1682. [Chancery Proc. before 1714, Reynardson, Bundle 428, 132.] In 1681 Ponder was one of a number of London printers and booksellers against whom a mysterious action for assault was brought by Bartholomew Sprint. [C.P.R. 2992, m. 256 r.] The fourth edition of the *Pilgrim's Progress* had appeared in the previous year, and a part of the impression bore, on the back of the portrait, an "Advertisement", in which in bitter terms Ponder accused Thomas Braddyl of printing unauthorized editions of the work; yet in 1688 he was employing this same printer to print an edition of ten thousand copies, as well as an edition of five thousand copies of the second part, and five thousand copies of Bunyan's *Grace Abounding*. All this we learn from a lawsuit begun by Ponder against Braddyl in the Court of Chancery in 1697. From this we further learn that Ponder was a prisoner in the King's Bench Prison for debt in 1688, and that Braddyl, in addition to settling an execution with which Ponder was threatened, had also supplied Ponder's son with clothes to the value of £14. After this little more is heard of Ponder. Mr. Arber states [*T.C.* III. 730], that he published the 3rd edition of Bunyan's *Mr. Badman* in 1700 from "London Yard, at the West End of St. Paul's Church", but the edition in question is dated 1696, not 1700; the edition of 1700 was issued by the Churchills. Ponder sold an edition of Bunyan's *Holy War* in 1696 [Bodl. Arch. Bodl. A. I. 48]; the last editions of *Pilgrim's Progress* issued by him were Pt. I. edd. 11 and 12, 1688 and n. d. Pt. II. ed. 3 was issued in 1690, and Pt. I. ed. 13 in 1693, by R. Ponder, i. e. presumably his son Robert. One W. P., who may be a relation, figures in Bunyan imprints from 1695 to 1702. He left, besides Robert, who married Mary, the daughter of Robert Guy of Isham, Northants, three daughters, Mary, Susannah, and Hannah. [Chan. Proc. before 1714, Collins 461/31 461/33]. An interesting article on Nathaniel Ponder, written by Mr. W. Perkins, appeared in *The Wellingborough News*, October 2nd, 1903.

PONDER (ROBERT), *see* Ponder (Nathaniel).

PONDER (W.), *see* Ponder (Nathaniel).

POOL, *see* Poole.

POOLE (EDWARD), bookseller in London, (1) Ship, Cornhill, (*a*) next door to the Fleece Tavern, (*b*) over against the Royal Exchange; (2) Exchange Alley. (3) At the Half Moon, (*a*) near, (*b*) under, the Royal Exchange, 1685–1702. Noticed by Dunton [p. 226] chiefly for his religious opinions. His name appears in the Term Catalogues for the first time in Mich. 1685, with a translation of Heliodorus. [*T.C.* II. 145.] He was the publisher of some of Richard Head's works, and in 1692 was one of the publishers of *An Epitome of the whole art of War*. He moved to Exchange Alley between 1690 and 1692, and to the Half Moon by 1700. [*T.C.* III. 196.] He is last heard of in 1702. [*T.C.* III. 310.]

POOLE, or POOL (JOHN), bookseller in London, Clements Inn Gate, 1670–9. This bookseller held shares in various law-books during this period. [*T.C.* I. 39, 53, 359.]

POOLE (JOSEPH), bookseller in London, Blue Bowl, in the Long Walk, by Christ Church Hospital, 1682. Publisher of *A True History of the Captivity and Restoration of Mrs. Mary Rowlandson, in New England*, 1682. [Haz. III. 214.]

POPE ( ), bookseller in Salisbury, 1715. Publisher of *The Necessity of Grace*, a sermon by R. Eyre, 1715. [B.M. 225. h. 2 (10).]

POPE (WALTER), bookseller in Edinburgh, Roxburghe Close, over against St. Giles's Steeple, 1683. In that year a broadside by N. Paterson entitled *Obsequies . . . Alexander, late Lord Bishop of Rosse* were sold by him. [Aldis, p. 118.]

POPPING (SARAH), printer and bookseller in London, Raven, Paternoster Row, 1713–23. Printer and publisher for a time, of the *Observator* (1711, &c.) In 1716 Mrs. Popping was one of the publishers of Pope's satire on Edmund Curll. [Esdaile, p. 289.] In this year she also published Dennis's *True Character of Mr. P[ope] and his Writings*. Her name was in the imprint to Curll's pirated edition of *An Account of the Trial of the Earl of Winton*, also in 1716, for which she was taken into custody for breach of privilege, but was discharged. [W. J. Thoms, *Curll Papers*, pp. 37–9.] In 1723 she advertised Dunton's *Upon this Moment depends Eternity*, but it is believed not to have appeared. [Nichols, *Lit. Anecd.* V. 83.]

PORTEOUS (JOHN), bookseller in Edinburgh, on the south side of the High Street, a little above the Court of Guard, 1699. *The Edinburgh Gazette*, nos. 44 and 50, contain advertisements of books printed for and sold by him.

POTBURY (EDWARD), stationer in Exeter, 1681. Defendant in a suit brought by George Saffin, sheriff of Exeter, for the recovery of a debt. Judgement was signed for the plaintiff on July 12th. [C.P.R. Trin. 33 Chas. II, Roll 2995, m. 1872.] Not mentioned by Dredge, and perhaps only a retailer.

POWELL ( ), Mrs., bookseller in Flint, 1700. Bought one dozen Psalters from John Minshull, bookseller of Chester, for seven shillings. [*Library*, 2nd ser. IV. 373–83.]

POWELL (EDMUND), printer and bookseller in London, Blackfriars, 1708–11. In 1708 his name appears in the Term Catalogue as the printer of *The Improvement of Human Reason* (Hai Ibn Yokdan, translated by Simon Ockley) [*T.C.* III. 595], and he published other works by the translator. Lists of his publications appeared from time to time in *The Female Tatler* in 1709. In 1711 he is mentioned in a list of persons receiving subscriptions for a work entitled *The Grand Curiosity*. [*Daily Courant*, September 29th, 1711.]

POWELL (EDWARD), bookbinder in London, Little Britain, 1698. In the *London Gazette* of December 12th–15th, 1698, is an advertisement of John Brown's work on muscular dissection, with a notice that any subscribers who had not received their copies might have them at Mr. Edw. Powell's, Bookbinder in Little Britain.

POWELL (G.), bookseller in London, Chancery Lane, over against Lincolns Inn Gate, 1685–6. Sold the Coronation Service book used at the crowning of James II. [*T.C.* II. 129.] He was associated with William Powell, who lived at Holborn Court in Grays Inn, in the production of a miscellany entitled *A Memorial for the Learned*, in 1686. [*T.C.* II. 170.] One of these two is probably the man referred to by Dunton [p. 293] as "grave" Powel.

POWELL (STEPHEN), printer in Dublin, 1697–1724. This printer is first found in 1697 in partnership with John Brent and John Brocas. In 1698, 1699, and 1700 he appears under his initials in partnership with one J. B. In 1699 his full name occurs alone in one imprint again. Besides poems, sermons, &c., he printed in 1717 Hugh McCurtin's *Brief Discourse in vindication of the Antiquity of Ireland*.

POWELL (WILLIAM), bookseller in London, Holborn Court, Grays Inn, 1686. Associated with G. Powell (*q. v.*).

POWNEY (ROBERT), stationer in London, Ship and Star, against Katherine Street in the Strand, 1705–25. [Hilton-Price, *Signs of the Old Houses in the Strand in the 17th and 18th Centuries*, in *Midds. & Herts. N. & Q.*, II. 158.]

PRATT (DANIEL), bookseller in London, Bible against York Buildings in the Strand, 1715. Published with D. Mead an edition of *The History of George a Green*. [Haz. I. 472.]

PRESTON ( ), bookseller in Faversham, 1699. His name appears in the advertisement in *The Flying Post*, December 2nd, 1699, of the publication of the Rev. Edw. Brown's sermon preached at the Kentish Feast. It does not appear in the imprint of the book.

PRICE (C.), bookseller in London, next the Fleece Tavern in Cornhill, 1706. Associated with John Senex in publishing *Miscellanea Curiosa*. [*T.C.* III. 513, 523.]

PRICE (THOMAS), bookseller in London (?), 1684. His name is found in the imprint to a pamphlet entitled *A Pair of Spectacles for Mr. Observer*, 1684. [B.M. T. 100* (166).]

PRICKE, or PRYKE (ROBERT), book and print seller in London, (1) in White Cross Street, over against the Cross Keys, 1669–72; (2) Golden Lion, at the corner of New Cheapside, next Bethlehem, in Moorfields, 1669–72; (3) adjoining to Cripplegate within, 1674–6; (4) Golden Ball in St. Paul's Churchyard, 1677–85; (5) Bow Lane, 1698. He translated, engraved, and published a number of foreign architectural and similar books, and also issued Cocker's *Penna Volans* in 1685. He had frequent entries in the Term Catalogues from 1669 to 1672 of books published simultaneously from his first two addresses, but afterwards his entries are only occasional. His copies seem to have passed to S. and J. Sprint, for whom he reissued some in 1698. [*T.C.*, *D.N.B.*]

PRING (JANE), bookseller in Exeter, near St. Martin's Lane, 1723–30 (?) The widow of Thomas Butter (*q. v.*). She married again, on August 31st, 1723, Daniel Pring jun., but she continued to carry on the bookselling business herself until her death, which took place before 1723. [Dredge, ff. 67, 98–9.]

PROCTER (WILLIAM), stationer in London, Bread Street, 1705. In 1704 he received subscriptions for Richard Blome for the latter's *History of the Holy Bible* [*T.C.* III. 396.] Dunton describes him [p. 256] as a fortunate man, who had drawn a sum of £500 per year in the Parliament Lottery; and as a generous creditor.

PROSSER (ENOCH), bookseller in London, Rose and Crown (*a*) in Swithins Alley, (*b*) in Sweeting's Rents, at the East End of the Royal Exchange in Cornhill, 1681. Publisher, in partnership with J. Hancock, of *Memoirs of the Life and Death of Sir Edmund Bury Godfrey*, and *The Plot in a Dream*, by Philopatris, both in 1681. [*T.C.* I. 461, 464.] He was perhaps the E. P. who published a broadside *Elegy on the Death of the Plot*, 1681. [B.M. 1872. a. 1 (30).]

PRYKE (ROBERT), *see* Pricke.

PULLEYN, or PULLEN (CAVE), bookseller in London, Angel in St. Paul's Churchyard, 1681–5. Published (1) *A . . . History of the Succession of the Crown of England*, 1681, and (2) *An Apology for the Builder*, 1685. [B.M. T. 94*. (15); T. 2029 (3).]

PULLEYN (OCTAVIAN), junior, stationer in London, King's Head in Little Britain, 1664–8. *See Dictionary*, 1641–67. An advertisement of his appeared in the *London Gazette* on March 12th, 166$\frac{7}{8}$.

PURSLOWE, or PARSLOWE (ANNE), printer in London, 1675–77. Possibly widow of G. Purslowe [*See Dictionary*, 1641–67.] May be identical with the Mrs. Purslowe whose name occurs in the List of London Printing Houses of 1675. Printer of *Poor Robin's Intelligence* (no. 1), March 23rd–30th, 1676. In the number for April 10th–17th, 1677, T. H. (i. e. Thomas Haley) joins A. P. as printer.

PYKE, *see* Pike.

PYMAN (JAMES), stationer in London, Gracechurch Street, 1692. In Mich. 1692, he became surety in a sum of £50 for one James Daggett. [C.P.R. Mich. 3. W. & M. Roll 3102, m. 757, v.]

RAE (PETER), printer in Kirkbride, 1711–14, and in Dumfries, 1715–20. Peter Rae was minister at Kirkbride and Dumfries, and was the real printer of fourteen books and pieces, mostly theological, but including Rae's own *History of the Late Rebellion*, 1718, which all bear the imprint of Robert Rae, probably his son. Rae is said by Watson [p. 19], to have made his own press, and to be

"making some advance towards the founding of letters". In youth he had followed his father's trade of a clockmaker. [William Stewart, *The Rae Press*, Edinb. Bibl. Soc. Publ. VI. 107–15.]

RAE (ROBERT), *see* Rae (Peter).

RAIKES (ROBERT), printer in St. Ives, Huntingdonshire, Northampton, and Gloucester; St. Ives, 1718–20; Northampton, over against All Saints' Church, 1720–22; Gloucester, (1) against the Swan Inn [in Upper Northgate Street?], 1722–3; (2) in Southgate Street, 1723–43; (3) Black-Friars, 1743–57. 1718–57. Born in 1690, son of a Yorkshire clergyman. Mr. R. Austin states that he was in the employ of Thomas Gent of York in 1718; but Gent did not set up for himself till 1724. In this year Raikes established a press at St. Ives, where he printed the *St. Ives Post Boy*. In 1719 William Dicey (*q. v.*) set up The *St. Ives Mercury*, and in the following year the pair went into partnership, and moving to Northampton, produced the *Northampton Mercury*. In 1722 Raikes and Dicey founded yet another paper, The *Gloucester Journal*, and, to print it, the first Gloucester press. Both names occur on all issues of it till recent times; but Dicey remained at Northampton and Raikes took charge of the Gloucester business. A few popular books, like those published by the firm at Northampton, came from the Gloucester Press; of these the earliest known is John Blanch's *History of Great Britain, from the Tower of Babel*, 1722. Raikes was summoned to the Bar of the House of Commons in 1728 for printing reports of its proceedings. He died in 1757, and was succeeded by his son Robert, the philanthropist and promoter of Sunday Schools. [Roland Austin, *Robert Raikes, the Elder, and the Gloucester Journal*, in *The Library*, 3rd ser., VI. January 1915 (see also *Notes and Queries* 12th ser., X. 261–4); *History of the Northampton Mercury* (Mercury Extras, no. 10), 1901. *See also* Dicey (William).]

RAINY (THOMAS), bookseller in Doncaster, 1693. Only known from Henry Higden's comedy, *The Wary Widdow*, "London, Printed for Abel Roper at the Mitre near Temple Bar, and Tho. Rainy, Bookseller in Doncaster, 1693." [B.M. 644. h. 41.]

RAMSAY (ALLAN), bookseller in Edinburgh, (1) The Mercury in The High Street; (2) in the Luckenbooths. 1716 (?)–58. About 1716 he took up the business of bookselling at his house in the High Street, where he had previously carried on the trade of wig-making. In 1726 he removed to a shop in the

Luckenbooths, and there established the first circulating library in Scotland. His *Poems* (1721) and *The Ever-Green* (1724) were printed for him by Thomas Ruddiman. He continued in business to within about three years of his death, which took place in 1758.

RAMSAY (PATRICK), printer in Edinburgh, *c.* 1660–80. *See Dictionary*, 1641–67, and also below, Reid (John).

RANCE (JOHN), printer in Oxford, 1712–19. In a letter from Hearne to Browne Willis, dated May 1st, 1715, he speaks of "Rance the printer" as "going on" with the remainder of the Index to "Collectanea". [*Collections*, V. 54 *n.*; Madan, p. 32.]

RANDALL, or RANDEL (RICHARD), bookseller at Newcastle-upon-Tyne, 1676–1714. Admitted a freeman of the Newcastle Stationers' Company, December 20th, 1676. [Welford, p. 128.] In partnership with Peter Maplesden he published in 1676 Richard Gilpin's *Daemonologia Sacra* [*T.C.* I. 287], and in 1677 a sermon preached at Newcastle by John March. [Bodl. Sermons, 13.] In 1714 he appears among the subscribers to Walker's *Sufferings of the Clergy*.

RANEW (NATHANIEL), bookseller and book-auctioneer in London, (1) Angel, in Jewin Street; (2) King's Arms in St. Paul's Churchyard, 1663–94. *See Dictionary*, 1641–67. In partnership with Jonathan Robinson (*q. v.*). In 1670 they moved to the King's Arms in St. Paul's Churchyard. The partnership was dissolved in 1671–2, when Robinson moved to the Golden Lion, Ranew remaining at the King's Arms. They published a book together in 1674, however. [*T.C.* I. 166.] In 1678 he sold by auction "at the Harrow, over against the Colledge of Physicians, in Warwick Lane", the libraries of Lord Warwick and Dr. Gabriel Sanger. It appears to have been the only book auction he conducted. [Lawler, *Book-Auctions in England*, p. 124.] His name occurs for the last time in the Term Catalogues in Hil. 1694. [*T.C.* II. 495.] His widow Hannah's will was proved in 1713. *See* Robinson (Ranew).

RATCLIFF (THOMAS), *see Dictionary*, 1641–67.

RATHBONE (JOSIAH), bookseller in Macclesfield, 1723. Published *A Book of Psalmody*, by R. T. Barber. [J. Cooke, *Bibl. Cestr.*]

RATTEN (CALEB), bookseller in Market Harborough, 1708–16. Mentioned in a list of provincial booksellers in *Notes & Queries*. He was evidently the successor to Thomas Ratten. [*N. & Q.* 11th ser., XI. 45.]

RATTEN (GEORGE), bookseller in Coventry, 1701. Only known as the publisher of a sermon by the Rev. M. Heynes, printed in 1701. [B.M. 225. i. 16 (1).] Perhaps father of W. Ratten (*q. v.*).

RATTEN (THOMAS), bookseller in Lutterworth, Kettering, and Market Harborough, 1685. His name occurs in a list of booksellers and stationers at the end of M. Bromfield's *Brief Discovery of the . . . Scurvy*, 1685, as agent for a patent medicine. [*N. & Q.* 11th ser., XI. 45.]

RATTEN (W.), bookseller in Coventry, 1716. Perhaps son of George Ratten (*q. v.*) He sold Joseph Cattell's sermon, *The Destroying Angel recalled*, preached at Rothwell on July 17th, 1715. [B.M. 4474. d. 32.]

RAVEN (JOSEPH), bookseller in London, Searle's Square, Lincoln's Inn, 1700. Published a ballad, *The Welshman's praise of Wales*, 1700. [B.M. C. 40. m. 11 (87).] He also sold a patent medicine called " Elixir Febrifugium Martis ".

RAVENSHAW (SAMUEL), bookseller and book-auctioneer in London, Old Palace Yard, Westminster, 1691. Catalogues of book-sales held by him are in the British Museum. [B.M. 821. i. 9, i. 5 (31).]

RAW, or RAWE (T.), bookseller in London and Bath; London, (1) Bible, St. Paul's Alley, 1679; (2) London Yard, near St. Paul's 1681; Bath, 1685. In Mich. 1679, he advertised *A Full Narrative, or a discovery of the Priests and Jesuits*, but his name did not appear in the imprint. [*T.C.* I. 373.] In 1681 he published in London Yard a poetical broadside, *The Bane to the Devonshire Cant.* [C. 20. f. 6 (19).] In 1685 he published William Leybourn's *Platform for Purchasers, A guide for builders*, which bears his Bath imprint. [*T.C.* II. 136.]

RAWLINS (JOHN), printer and bookseller in London, Anchor in St. Paul's Churchyard, 1674 (?)–1703 (?). The W. and J. R. who printed in 1674 a translation of La Calprenède's *Cleopatra* for P. Parker and T. Guy may be William and John Rawlins. In 1684 John printed an edition of John Wilson's *Cheats* for J. Wright, and in 1686 W. de Britaine's *Humane Prudence* for R. Sare. In 1692 he published *An Account of the great Victory obtained at sea against the French*. Dunton [*p.* 251] says " Mr. Rawlins, near Paternoster row, has printed several Books for me. . . . He is an honest and thriving man, and has an excellent choice of good letter". This might apply to either John or William.

RAWLINS (WILLIAM), printer in London, near Paternoster Row (?), 1674 (?)–1703 (?) *See* Rawlins (John). William was one of the assigns of Richard and Edward Atkyns for printing *Reports des Cases* in 1678. [*T.C.* I. 321.]

RAWSON ( ), stationer in London, Paul's Chain, by Doctors' Commons, 1694. Advertised a patent medicine in the *City Mercury*, June 11th, 1694. [B.M. Burney, 112 A.]

RAY (ELIZABETH or ELIZA), printer in Dublin, 1708 (?)–13. Only known as the printer of *The Church Catechism Explained*, 1713. She was the widow of Joseph Ray and died some time in 1713.

RAY (JOSEPH), printer and bookseller in Dublin, (1) College Green; (2) in Skinner Row, opposite to the Tholsel, 1676–1708. This printer's name is given in an imprint of 1676, but not till 1681 does it occur again. From then till 1708 it is often found. The output from his press was large and included some notable works such as the first ed. of Molyneux's *Case of Ireland stated*, 1698. In 1694 he printed Sir George Ashe's *Sermon preached in Trinity College Chappell*, giving College Green as his address. [Bodl. Sermons, 1 (19).] He printed the *Newsletter* for some months, and later the *Dublin Intelligence*. In 1702 he published Thomas Everard's *Stereometry*. [*T.C.* III. 292, 301.] He died in or about 1708, and his will was proved that year in Dublin. Ray was never the King's printer, but he printed (besides many theological and controversial works for leading divines of the established church) some of the votes of the House of Commons. He was succeeded by his widow Elizabeth (*q. v.*).

REA (FRANCIS), bookseller in Worcester, 1651–85. *See Dictionary*, 1641–67. Still in business in 1685, when he was defendant in a suit brought by William Daniels for payment for certain timber. [C.P.R. Trin. 1 Jas. II, Roll 3038, m. 1777.]

READ (E.), bookseller in London, at the corner of Duke Street, near Lincoln's Inn Fields, 1707. Published *A Supplement to the First Part of The Gentleman instructed*, 1707. [*T.C.* III. 572.]

READ (J.), printer in London, White-Fryers, near Fleet Street, 1709–24. A jobbing printer of broadsides, &c. He was also the printer of a *Half-Penny Post* and a *Weekly Journal*. He is referred to by J. How in *Some Thoughts on the present state of Printing and Bookselling*, 1709, p. 12, as a printer of other

men's copies. Negus mentions him in 1724, as a " well-affected " printer.

READ (R.), bookseller in London, 1682. Publisher of a pamphlet, *London's Liberties*, 1682. [Haz. II. 364.]

REDDISH (W.), bookseller in London, in Griffith's Buildings, near the Royal Cock-Pit, 1697. One of several booksellers selling three theological tracts in 1697. [*T.C.* III. 3.]

REDMAYNE (JOHN). *See Dictionary*, 1641–67.

REDMAYNE (SAMUEL), printer in London, Jewin Street, 1722–4. Possibly a son of William Redmayne. On December 2nd, 1722 he was fined for printing a libel. He is mentioned by Negus in 1724 as a " high-flyer ". [Nichols, *Lit. Anecd.*, VIII. 368; I. 311.]

REDMAYNE (WILLIAM), printer in London, Addle Hill, 1674–1719. Probably successor to John Redmayne. He did a great deal of work for the booksellers, amongst others for D. Brown, S. Coggan, S. Keble, A. Roper, and R. Smith. In 1719 he was imprisoned for printing a libel on the Government. In the *Weekly Packet* of April 4th–11th, 1719, was the following item of news: " Mr. Redmayne the printer is very ill of a fever in Newgate." He died on April 11th. [Nichols, *Lit. Anecd.*, VIII. 368.]

REDWOOD (JOHN), bookseller and printer in Cork, (1) near the Exchange 1715 (?)–21; (2) Castle Street, 1723. 1715–23. He appears as a bookseller in Cork in 1716, or perhaps even in 1715. He so continued till 1721, but is found as a printer in 1723, when his imprint is found in *The Spiritual Week*, and in another devotional book, and in Steele's *Conscious Lovers*.

REEVE (MRS. LITTLE), bookseller in Norwich, 1707. Her name occurs in an advertisement of " Golden Snuff " in the *Daily Courant* of May 30th, 1707.

REEVE (THOMAS), printer in Canterbury, 1717. The first printer in Canterbury. He printed " for the proprietors " the early numbers of the *Kentish Post*, or *Canterbury News Letter*. [F. W. Cock, in *The Library*, July, 1913, 3rd ser., IV. 285–7.]

REID (JOHN), bookseller in Glasgow, 1676. One of the debtors in A. Anderson's inventory of 1676. [*Bann. Misc.* II. 283.]

REID (JOHN), I, printer in Edinburgh, in Bell's Wynd, at the head of the Court of Guard, 1680–1716 (?) Watson says [p. 13] that Reid set up with Patrick

Ramsay about 1680. This is confirmed by a broadside, *Serenissimo . . . Jacobo, Albaniae et Eboraci Duci . . . Congratulatio* . . . XIII *Kal. Mart.* 1680, which has the imprint, " Has praeli sui primitias, ut in publica Gratulatione micam, excuderunt Typographi tyrones, Pat. Ramsaeus, Jo. Rhedus." [Adv. 24 (15a).] In September 1683 Mrs. Anderson gave in a complaint against him to the Privy Council for setting up a printing house in contravention of her privilege; but the Council allowed Reid to print anything not in Tyler's gift, to the terms of which Mrs. Anderson's gift was restricted. In November of the same year Mrs. Anderson brought a further action against him for stealing types from her office. On September 23rd, 1701, he was ordered by the Privy Council to be imprisoned in the Tolbooth till further order, for printing a treasonable paper by a certain Capt. Donaldson, on the death of James II, and the proclaiming of the Prince of Wales in France [*Acts of Privy Council.*] In 1704 his imprint is found on a chap-book, *The New Glous-siershire* [sic] *Garland*. He died about 1716, his will being registered on the 11th May of that year.

REID (JOHN), II, printer in Edinburgh, in Liberton's Wynd, 1699 (?)–1712. Son of the preceding. Watson [p. 18] says that he set up about 1699, but no book of his bearing that date has been found. Reid was connected, as printer, with several of the newspaper enterprises of his time: *The Edinburgh Gazette* (1702); *The Edinburgh Courant* (1707), *The Scots Postman* (1710); and others. After his death in August 1712 his widow, Margaret Reid, carried on business for a short time.

REID (JOHN), III, printer in Edinburgh, in Pearson's Close, a little above the Cross, 1714–21. Son of John II, and Margaret Reid (?) In 1714 Reid printed some numbers of the *Edinburgh Gazette*; and *The Last Speech and Confession of Nicol Muschet*, who was executed on January 6th, 1721, bears his imprint.

REID (MARGARET), printer in Edinburgh, at the foot of the Horse Wynd, 1714–16. Widow of John Reid II (†1712). In 1714–15 she printed some numbers of the *Edinburgh Gazette*, and *An Abstract of an Account of the Proceedings at Perth* was also printed by her, probably in 1716.

REYNOLDS (ROWLAND), bookseller in London, (1) Sun and Bible, Postern Street, near Moorgate, 1667–9; (2) King's Arms, Poultry, 1670; (3) Sun and Bible, Poultry, 1672–5; (4) near Arundel Gate, in the Strand, 1676; (5) Henrietta Street, Covent Garden, 1677; (6) (*a*) next door to the Golden Bottle in the Strand, at the Middle Exchange Door, (*b*) near Salisbury

Exchange, Strand, 1681–4, 1667–91. *See Dictionary*, 1641–67. Publisher of miscellaneous literature, last mentioned in the Term Catalogues in Easter 1684 [*T.C.* II. 76.] In Mich. 3. W. & M. (1691) he was sued by Timothy Hart for debt. [C.P.R. 3101, m. 440.] His frequent removals may perhaps have the same origin.

RHAMES (AARON), printer in Dublin, 1700–34. One of the leading Dublin printers of his time; his descendants continued in Dublin for about two centuries. In 1714 he printed the first extant complete English Bible printed in Ireland. He also printed the earliest heraldic work printed in Ireland. He died in 1734; his will was registered in the Dublin Diocesan Court.

RHODES, or RODES (HENRY), bookseller in London, next door to the Bear Tavern, Fleet Street, near Bride Lane; (2) next door to the Swan Tavern, Fleet Street, at the corner of Bride Lane; (3) Star, Fleet Street, at, or near the corner of Bride Lane, or near Fleet Bridge. 1681–1709. Possibly a son of Matthew Rhodes (1642) a prolific and miscellaneous publisher. He shared with Joseph Hindmarsh and Richard Lane the copyright of *The Turkish Spy*. Rhodes was dead before 1725, when his widow married Sir Thomas Masters, knight. [Nichols, *Lit. Anecd.* VIII. 356.] His various addresses may describe the same house.

RIBOTEAU (H.), bookseller in London, Crown, over against Bedford House, Strand, 1702. Publisher with the widow Mariet of French literature. His name is also found in an advertisement of a book auction in the *Post-man* of November 7th, 1702.

RICHARD (W.), bookseller in London, 1682. Publisher of a political broadside in verse on the Popish Plot entitled *A Letany for St. Omers*. [B.M. C. 20. f. 6 (15).]

RICHARDS (GODFREY), bookseller in London, Golden Ball, Cornhill, over against the Royal Exchange, 1671. Published a book on tonnage and poundage for merchants. [*T.C.* I. 72.]

RICHARDS (HANNAH), bookseller in Nottingham, 1703–4. Probably widow of Samuel Richards (*q. v.*), whom she succeeded in 1703. [Creswell, p. 7.] Published in 1704 the Rev. John Barrett's *Discourse concerning Pardon of Sin*. [*T.C.* III. 409.]

RICHARDS (JOHN), bookseller in Nottingham, 1698–1703. Perhaps a son of Samuel Richards. He published John Ellis's *Sermon preached at the Church of St. Mary in Nottingham*, January 4, 169$\frac{8}{9}$. [*T.C.* III. 106; Creswell, p. 6.]

RICHARDS (SAMUEL), bookseller in Nottingham, 1669–1703. First met with in 1669. In 1674 he published, with T. Guy, *Goodwill towards Men* [*T.C.* I. 185], and in 1686, with L. Meredith, *Rest for the heavy laden*, by Clement Ellis, Rector of Kirkby, Notts. [*T.C.* II. 156.] Dunton says in 1703 [p. 237] that "he pursues his business very closely and is a person of great integrity." He died in this year and his widow or daughter, Hannah Richards (*q. v.*), succeeded him. [Creswell, pp. 5–7.]

RICHARDSON (EDMOND), bookbinder and bookseller in London; (1) Scalding Alley; (2) Naked Boy, Blowbladder Street, over against St. Martin-le-Grand, 1698; (3) Naked Boy, Newgate Street, 1699–1703; (4?) near the Poultry Church. 1680(?)–1703. Dunton says [pp. 257–8] that Richardson "was my kind neighbour in Scalding Alley for many years, bound most of my Calves Leather Books whilst I lived in the Poultry.... Having thrived by his binding trade, he is now a flourishing bookseller in Newgate Street". In 1691 he published *Islington-Wells*, but his first entry in the Term Catalogues was a theological book, in Easter Term 1698. [*T.C.* III. 63.]

RICHARDSON (J.), bookseller in Leeds and Wakefield, 1700–5. Published a volume of sermons in 1705. [*T.C.* III. 462–3.]

RICHARDSON (JOHN), printer in London, near the Mitre Tavern, Fenchurch Street, 1675–1703. His name is first met with in the list of London printing houses of 1675 as one of those who had set up since the Act was in force. He printed the 1685 edition of Cocker's *Arithmetick* for Passinger and Lacy. He also printed for Dunton, who speaks of him [p. 250] as being then (in 1703) a man "pretty much up in years; however his young inclinations are not altogether dead in him; for I am informed his son and he have married two sisters". He was Under-Warden of the Company in 1696–7.

RICHARDSON (STEPHEN), printer at Oxford, Holywell, 1715–55. First mentioned by Hearne in July 1715 as the printer of certain verses on Dr. Radcliffe. He was elected Architypographus, much to Hearne's chagrin. Richardson had two sons, Stephen and John. [Hearne, *Remarks and Collections*, V. 79, IX. 403; Madan, p. 32.]

RICHARDSON (W.), printer in London, 1701. Printed for Eben. Tracy an edition of *Wits Academy*, 1701. [Haz. II. 653.]

RIDER (PRESSICK), printer in Dublin, 1724–5. In partnership with Thomas Harbin he printed in 1725 a new edition of W. Molyneux's *Case of Ireland*.

RILEY (WILLIAM), bookseller in London, next door to the Queen's Head, without Temple Bar, 1670. Sold an edition of T. Clarke's *Phraseologia Puerilis* in 1670. [*T.C.* I. 62.]

RIVINGTON (CHARLES), bookseller in London, (1) Bible and Crown, St. Paul's Churchyard, 1711–42. Born in 1688, the second son of Thurston Rivington, of Chesterfield, he was apprenticed to Matthews, bookseller (*q. v.*), and took up his freedom in 1711. He must have already had considerable capital, though his father did not die till 1734, as he in the same year bought the business of Richard Chiswell, the large bookseller and publisher in St. Paul's Churchyard, who was just dead. He announced Pierre Jurieu's *Practice of Devotion* in Easter 1711 [*T.C.* III. 659] from the Bible and Crown in St. Paul's Churchyard (Chiswell's sign had been the Rose and Crown). The *D.N.B.* states that his first house was in Paternoster Row, and Mr. S. Rivington says that he moved in 1714 to the Bible and Crown at no. 62 on the north side of St. Paul's Churchyard; but he would naturally have succeeded to Chiswell's house in the Churchyard in 1711, instead of going to another in Paternoster Row. He kept up the religious character of Chiswell's business, and later published for the Wesleys and Whitefield. He also did a large business in publishing sermons on commission. He is the hero of the story of the country vicar who ordered 35,000 copies of a sermon to be printed. Rivington agreed after a protest, and, having sold 17, sent him a bill for some £784, but reassured him a day or two later by confessing that he had only printed 100. A list of some of Rivington's early publications is given in Fénelon's *Pastoral Letter*, 1715. He was one of the founders in 1736 of the new "Conger" or booksellers' club for buying and selling shares in copies. He and Osborne share the credit not only of publishing *Pamela*, but of having suggested to Richardson the idea of a collection of letters, which developed into it. He died on February 22nd, 1742, and was succeeded by two sons, John and James, out of a large family; Richardson acted as guardian to his children and trustee for the business till John's majority. [S. Rivington, *The Publishing Family of Rivington*, 1919; *D.N.B.*]

ROBERTS (J.), bookseller in Bridgwater, 1698–1700. In 1698 he published, with S. and J. Sprint, *A Sermon preached at Bridgwater*, by J. B., and in 1699–1700, with J. Sprint, *Religion justified in a sermon preached before ... the Mayor ... of Bridgwater*, by J. H., Minister. [*T.C.* III. 90, 167.]

ROBERTS (JAMES), printer and bookseller in London, (1) near Stationers' Hall, 1706; (2) Warwick Lane, 1713–54. 1706–54. In 1706 J. Gilbert's *Reflections on Dr. Fleetwood's Essay upon Miracles* was printed for J. Roberts near Stationers' Hall. [*T.C.* III. 508, 521.] It is not clear whether he was identical with the printer James Roberts, of Warwick Lane, who was able to subscribe five guineas to the Bowyer Fund in 1713, was classed by Negus as "well-affected", was Master of the Stationers' Company in 1729, 1730, and 1731, and died, aged 85, on November 2nd, 1754, and whom Nichols, in giving these facts [*Lit. Anecd.*, III. 737] calls "a printer of great eminence". He also published books.

ROBERTS (R.), printer in London, 1679(?)–99. He may be the R. R. who with A. M. printed in 1679 *A True Relation of the ... Cruelties lately acted by the Rebels in Scotland*. [Haz. III. 224.] He is first mentioned in the Term Catalogues in Mich. 1685, as printer of *The Mirror of Martyrs*. The advertisement states that it was printed "for R. Roberts"; but in this as in many other cases, it does not imply that he was a regular bookseller. In 1690 one R. R., with M. C., printed for Adiel Mill a folio ed. of the *Letters* of Gerard Vossius. In 1692 Roberts printed the *Votes of the House of Commons in Ireland*. [Burney, 104 A], and in 1699, for J. Nutt, Dr. W. Harris's *Description of the King's Palace and Gardens at Loo*. [*T.C.* III. 154.] Dunton says of "Mr. Roberts" (no doubt this man): "In twenty books that he printed for me he never disappointed me once ... so that what he left to his Widow will wear well"; which shows that he was dead before 1703.

ROBERTSON (JOHN), printer in Edinburgh, 1725–48. Dr. John Lee, in his *Memorial for the Bible Societies*, records several editions of the *Psalms in Metre* and *Confession of Faith* printed at Edinburgh by T. Lumisden and John Robertson between 1725 and 1748.

ROBINSON ( ), bookseller in Great Marlow, 1711. Publisher of the Rev. Richard Millechamp's *Sermon ... at the Funeral of Mr. James Harman ... Augt. 19th, 1711*. His name does not appear on the title page, but was mentioned in a newspaper advertisement of the publication.

ROBINSON (EDWARD), bookseller in Ludlow, 1678–1710. Published William Smith, Rector of Bitterley's *Just Account of the horrid contrivance of John Cupper . . . in poysoning his wife*, 1684. [Bodl. Ashm. 739 (27). ; *T.C.* II. 103.] Mentioned in a list of provincial booksellers as publishing in 1710. [*N. & Q.*, 10th ser., V. 183.]

ROBINSON (JONATHAN), bookseller in London, (1) Angel in Jewin Street, 1667–70 ; (2) King's Arms, St. Paul's Churchyard, 1670–71 ; (3) Golden Lion, St. Paul's Churchyard, 1672–1711. 1667–1711. Publisher for the Nonconformists. Till 1671 he was in partnership with N. Ranew (*q. v.*). There are numerous entries by him in the Term Catalogues. In the *London Intelligence* of January 29th, 168$\frac{8}{9}$, he offered ten shillings reward for a lost MS. of *The Life and Death of Nathaniel Mather of Boston in New England.* He was still publishing in 1711, but was perhaps dead by 1713, when Ranew Robinson (*q. v.*), almost certainly his son, was in business as a bookseller.

ROBINSON (JOSIAH), bookseller in London, Lincoln's Inn Gate, next Chancery Lane, 1672. Published an astrological tract by Thomas Trigge, *The Fiery Trigon Revived*, 1672. [*T.C.* I. 112.]

ROBINSON (RANEW), bookseller in London, 1713. Presumably a son of Jonathan Robinson. Mentioned in the will of Hanna Ranew, widow of Nathaniel Ranew, proved April 15th, 1713. [P.C.C. 89 Leeds.] In the same year he contributed three guineas to the Bowyer Fund.

ROBINSON (ROBERT), bookseller in London, near Gray's Inn Gate, Holborn, 1672–82. He entered a few books in the Term Catalogues in 1672–4, and was still in business in 1682, when his name is found as publisher of *The Moderate Intelligencer*. [Timperley, p. 563.]

ROBINSON (U.), printer in Milton-Ernis, near Bedford, 1719. Printed John Hunt's *Vindiciae verae pietatis*. [Allnutt, p. 302.] A private press ?

RODES (HENRY), *see* Rhodes.

ROE (JEREMIAH), bookseller in Derby, (*a*) Upper end of Sadler Gate, (*b*) near the Market Heads, 1725. About 1725 he issued an advertisement that he sold books and stationery " as cheap as in London ", and that he bought libraries. [Wallis, *Sketch of the Early History of the Printing Press in Derbyshire* (*Derbyshire Arch. & Nat. Hist. Soc. Journal*, III. 142).]

ROGERS (GABRIEL), bookseller in Shrewsbury, 1695. Published a sermon by T. Dawes in 1695. [B.M. 226. f. 21 (8).] He was succeeded by John Rogers.

ROGERS (HENRY), bookseller in London, (*a*) Bible, (*b*) Crown, in Westminster Hall, 1678. With W. Crooke he announced in 1678 Rawlins's comedy *Tunbridge Wells* [*T.C.* I. 310] ; his name alone occurs on the British Museum copy [643. d. 64]. His sign appears as the Bible in the Term Catalogue, and as the Crown on the book.

ROGERS (JOHN), bookseller in Shrewsbury, High Street, 1708–13. Perhaps a son of Gabriel Rogers. Given in a list of provincial booksellers in *N. & Q.* as publishing in 1713. [*N. & Q.*, 10th ser., V. 242.] He sold *A Sermon proving Slowness to Anger the truest Gallantry*, printed for T. Varnum and J. Osborne, London. [n. a. 1713, owner's note in Mr. G. P. Mander's copy.]

ROGERS (WILLIAM), bookseller in London, (1) Maiden's Head in Fleet Street, 1678–9 ; (2) Sun, against St. Dunstan's Church in Fleet Street, 1680–1711. 1678–1711. He became one of the largest publishers of his day, chiefly of theology. One of his chief patrons was Archbishop Tillotson. Dunton [p. 208] was associated with Rogers in publishing some dying speeches.

ROLLS (NATHANIEL), bookseller in London, at his Auction House, Petty Canons Hall, in Petty Canons, (*a*) near the North End, (*b*) on the North Side, of St. Paul's Churchyard, 1692–5. Publisher of schoolbooks. His first entry in the Term Catalogues, in Mich. 1692, was an edition of Eusebius. Another of his publications was Milton's *History of Britain*. His last entry was in 1696. [*T.C.* II. 430, 531, 595.]

ROOKES, or ROOKS (THOMAS), *see Dictionary*, 1641–67.

ROPER (ABEL) I, *see Dictionary*, 1641–67.

ROPER (ABEL) II, bookseller in London, (1) Bell, Fleet Street, (*a*) over against the Middle Temple Gate, (*b*) near Temple Bar, 1688–9 ; (2) Mitre, Fleet Street, 1690–3 ; (3) Black Boy, Fleet Street, over against St. Dunstan's Church, 1694–1707. 1688–1726. Nephew of Abel Roper I, who in a will by which he left him all his copies, expressed a hope that the young man might serve his apprenticeship under him. This wish was not fulfilled, as Abel Roper I died within a year of making his will, on March 4th, 16$\frac{79}{80}$. Abel Roper II is first met with in the Term Catalogue of Trin. 1688. [*T.C.* II. 229.] In 1691 he was sued by Thomas D'Urfey for payment in respect of the latter's comedy *Love for Money*. [C.P.R.

3102, m. 541, r.] In 1694 he joined E. Wilkinson at the Black Boy. [*T.C.* II. 501.] The latter disappears after 1696. Arthur Collins had succeeded Roper at this house in 170$\frac{8}{9}$. In 1707 Roper was the proprietor of the *Post Boy*, and he employed A. Boyer to translate news for the paper. In August 1709 Boyer was discharged and at once set up a rival sheet called *The True Post Boy*. [*Post Boy*, August 16th–18th, 1709.] Dunton [p. 210] says of him : "He rises in the world . . . prints 'The Post Boy', 'The Life of King William', 'The Annals of Queen Anne', and several excellent Abridgements. I have formerly been a Partner with him." He was still in business in 1726 when Bowyer printed Alexander Innes's *Twelve Sermons* for him. [Nichols, *Lit. Anecd.*, I. 348.]

ROSE (GEORGE), bookseller in Norwich, 1675–86. In 1675 he published a sermon preached in Norwich Cathedral by Robert Conold [B.M. 226. g. 10 (4)], and in 1676 *The Divine Physician*, by J. H., M. A. [*T.C.* I. 245.] He was still publishing in 1686.

ROUND (JAMES), bookseller in London, Seneca's Head, Exchange Alley in Cornhill, 1702–45. Began publishing in 1702 [*T.C.* III. 297], chiefly history and school-books, such as W. Willymot's *English Examples to Lilly's Grammar Rules, with the Proprieties, for the use of Eaton School*, 2nd ed., 1711. Round became one of the most important booksellers in London, and was Master of the Company. He died on December 17th, 1745. [*General Evening Post*, December 17th–19th, 1745.]

ROYSTON (RICHARD), *see Dictionary*, 1641–67. *See also* Green (Richard), and Meredith (Luke).

RUDDIMAN (THOMAS), printer in Edinburgh, in Morocco's Close, 1724 ; in the Parliament Close, 1729–57. 1715–57. Ruddiman, who was born in 1674, entered the Advocates' Library as assistant librarian in 1702, and from 1730 to 1752 held the office of Keeper of the Library. In 1707 he added the business of book auctioneer to his other occupations, and from about this time was associated, chiefly in an editorial capacity, with several works printed by Robert Freebairn. He also gave assistance to Ames in the preparation of the *Typographical Antiquities*. His *Rudiments of the Latin Tongue* was first published in 1714, and in the following year his edition of Buchanan's works, in two folio volumes, came from Freebairn's press. In the same year (1715) Ruddiman commenced printer, and took into partnership his younger brother Walter (*q. v.*). As his first undertaking he printed half the second volume of

Patrick Abercromby's *Martial Atchievements of the Scots Nation*, which was published by Freebairn. In 1728 Ruddiman and James Donaldson were appointed conjoint printers to the University of Edinburgh. In 1729 he became proprietor of the *Caledonian Mercury* which he had printed since 1724 and which continued in the family until 1772, when, together with the printing house and materials, it passed into the hands of John Robertson. He died in 1757. [G. Chalmers, *The Life of Thomas Ruddiman*, 1794.]

RUDDIMAN (WALTER), printer in Edinburgh, 1715–70. Younger brother of Thomas Ruddiman (*q. v.*). Born in 1687. From 1706 he worked with Robert Freebairn, printer, and in 1715 was taken into partnership by his brother. Died in 1770.

RUMBALL (E.), bookseller in London, Post House, Russell Street, Covent Garden, 1701. In partnership with R. Wellington he published the second edition of *Five Love Letters from a Nun to a Cavalier*, 1701. [B.M. 10909. a. 9.]

RUMBALL, or RUMBOLD (RICHARD), bookbinder and bookseller in London, Bell and Coffin, Old Change, 1679–84. Published *The Grand Question concerning the Bishops' right to vote in Parliament in cases capital*, 1679, and *A Seasonable Discourse against Toleration*, 1684. [*T.C.* I. 374, II. 91–2.]

RUMBALL, or RUMBALD (WILLIAM), bookseller in London [Bell and Coffin (?)], Old Change, 1680. Probably related to Richard Rumball. He published in 1680 *Don Tomazo, or The juvenile rambles of Thomas Dangerfield*. [B.M. 12614. b. 19.]

RYLES (THOMAS), bookseller in Hull, 1707–16. John White of York printed for him an Assize sermon preached in Lincoln Cathedral by Christopher Hildyard on March 17th, 170$\frac{6}{7}$, n. d. [Bodl. Sermons, 10 (1).] In 1710 he sold one of the pamphlets produced by the arrest and impeachment of Dr. Sacheverell [B.M. III. b. 28.] In 1714 he subscribed to Walker's *Sufferings of the Clergy*. He is met with last in 1716, when his name is found in the imprint to a sermon, preached on July 22nd, by John Clark.

SACKFIELD (JOHN), bookseller in London, Lincoln's Inn Square, 1717. Publisher of Sir Stephen Fox's *Memoirs*, 1717. [Haz. II. 225.]

SADLEIR (ELIZABETH), printer in Dublin, 1715–22. Apparently succeeded Sarah Sadleir. In 1715 and 1716 she printed (for Geo. Gunson) the fourth and fifth editions of Puffendorf's *Whole Duty of Man*. In 1716 she printed Matthew

Henry's *Communicant's Companion*, and in 1721 Burnet's *Exposition of the Thirty-nine Articles* and a large folio edition of Hooker's *Works*.

SADLEIR (SARAH), printer in Dublin, 1712–14. In 1712 she printed a sermon by Peter Hanny, and in 1714 a "twenty-eighth edition" of Cocker's *Arithmetic*, edited by John Hawker.

SADLER (THEODORE), bookseller in London, Little Britain, 1660–9. *See Dictionary*, 1641–67. In 1669 he was examined before Lord Arlington for selling a work called *The Brief Method*. Sadler said the copies were brought to him by a Frenchman in the name of the Superintendent of Somerset House; but that person denied all knowledge of it. [S.P.D. Chas. II, 261, f. 37.]

SALUSBURY (JOHN), printer and bookseller in London, (1) Atlas, Cornhill, near the Royal Exchange; (2) Rising Sun, Cornhill, over against the Royal Exchange; (3) Angel, in St. Paul's Churchyard. 1685–98. Began as a publisher of theological books at the Atlas in Cornhill, about Easter, 1685. [*T.C.* II. 123.] In 1687 he was selling medical books. [*T.C.* II. 206.] In 1689 he moved or changed his sign to The Rising Sun in Cornhill. In 1692 he published the Rev. Thos. Doolittle's *Earthquakes explained and practically improved*. In 1694 he printed a weekly paper called *The Flying Post*, which he sold at 2*d*. and in which he advertised that he was prepared to buy books. He died between August and September 1698, as recorded in *The Flying Post* of October 15th. Salusbury was also the publisher of *The Weekly Memorial*. [Burney, 104 A.] At the time of his death his imprint was The Angel in St. Paul's Churchyard. Dunton calls him "a desperate hypergorgonic Welshman", and "a silly, empty, morose fellow", and adds [p. 210] that he went to law with the Stationers' Company.

SALUSBURY (T.), bookseller in London, (1) (*a*) Black Lion, Post Office, Fleet Street, between the two Temple Gates, (*b*) Temple, Fleet Street, (*c*) next the the Inner Temple, (*d*) near Temple Bar, 1685–92; (2) King's Arms, Fleet Street, 1693–4. 1685–94. His name first appears in the Term Catalogue for Hil. 1685. Publisher of some important works. He is last heard of in Hil. 1694. [*T.C.* II. 494.]

SAMPSON (JACOB), bookseller in London, next door to the Wonder Tavern in Ludgate Street, 1680–2. One of the booksellers who became publishers at the time of the Popish Plot. He published in 1679–80 one book, John Flavell's

Sacramental Meditations, and, with T. Simmons, two pamphlets and a broadside on the Plot: (1) *The Narrative of Lawrence Mowbray*, (2) *The Narrative of Robert Bolron*, (3) *A Full and Final Proof of the Plot*. [*T.C.* I. 381–3; B.M. T. 1* (62).] He also published engraved portraits of celebrities, and he is possibly the person referred to by Dunton [p. 292] as "Card" Sampson.

SANDERS, *see also* Saunders.

SANDERS (RICHARD), bookseller in London, 1681. Publisher of *A New Ballad of London's Loyalty*. [B.M. C. 38. i. 25 (12).]

SANDERS (ROBERT), the Elder, *see Dictionary*, 1641–67.

SANDERS (ROBERT), the Younger. Printer and bookseller in Glasgow, (1) his shop a little above the Grammar School Wynd; (2) his shop a little below Gibson's Wynd; (3) his house in the Salt Mercat a little below the Well. 1695–1730. Son and successor of the preceding. Usually designated "of Auldhouse". One of the King's printers, printer to the City and University. Died January 1730. [Aldis, p. 120.]

SANDYS (EDWIN), printer in Dublin, 1705–18. He printed in 1705 the famous sermon of the Rev. Francis Higgins, and reprinted some English editions; in 1709 he printed *Remarks upon Partiality detected* for T. Servant. In 1713 he reprinted for 'George Grierson' Waller's *Peace on Earth*, in 1715 Phillips's *Cyder*, and Pope's *Temple of Fame*, &c., and in 1718 a *Miscellany of Poems*, &c.

SANGER (EGBERT), bookseller in London, Post House, Middle Temple Gate, Fleet Street, 1707–11. Publisher, in 1707, of *Mercurius Oxoniensis* and of Mrs. Centlivre's comedy, *The Platonick Lady*. In the next year he published, with Curll (*q. v.*), Rowe's translation of Boileau's *Lutrin* and a book by Dodwell. His other publications include William Taverner's comedy, *The Maid the Mistress*, and some historical works. He was still in business in 1711. [*T.C.* III. 669.]

SARE (RICHARD), bookseller in London, Gray's Inn Gate, Holborn, 1684–1723. The son of a clergyman; he was apparently in partnership with S. Heyrick, of this address, but each published independently. Sare's first publication was, with D. Brown, the eleventh edition of Bacon's *Sylva Sylvarum*, in 1684. [*T.C.* II. 105.] He prospered, and published many books. In 1693 he published L'Estrange's translation of Josephus; while it was in the press T. Basset and the other owners of the copyright of the older translation printed an advertisement in protest, and Sare another in reply. [B.M. 806. k. 15 (20*, 20**).]

He supported the Government, and was generally careful in what he published as well as personally blameless; but the casual sale of a copy of *The Rights of the Christian Church Asserted* exposed him to a frivolous prosecution by Samuel Hilliard, Prebendary of Lincoln, which resulted in his acquittal. [S. Hilliard, *A Narrative of the Prosecution of Mr. Sare*, 1709, B.M. 702. f. 2 (3); *A Defence of the Rights of the Christian Church*, 1709, B.M. 858. d. 9.] According to Nichols, Sare was one of the oldest and steadiest friends of the elder Bowyer, and after the fire at his printing-house in 1713 collected over £66 for his benefit. [*Lit. Anecd.* I. 61, 63.] Sare died on February 2nd, 172¾. His funeral sermon, from which much of what we know of him is derived, was preached by Dean Stanhope; it was printed by Bowyer for Richard Williamson, who succeeded to Sare's business. Both the Dean and Dunton [p. 218] warmly praise Sare's amiability and high character.

SARE (THOMAS), bookseller in London, right over against the Black Prince in Duck Lane, 1673. His imprint occurs in the Rev. Richard Steele's *Antidote against Distractions*, 3rd ed., 1673. [*T.C.* I. 137.]

SAUNDERS, *see also* Sanders.

SAUNDERS, or SANDERS (E.), bookseller in London, Crown in the Pall Mall, 1683–92. Associated with S. Holt in publishing an English translation of J. Commelin's *Belgick or Netherlandish Hesperides*, 1683. [*T.C.* II. 19.] In 1692 he was the publisher of *A Collection for the Improvement of Husbandry and Trade*. [B.M. Burney, 105 A.]

SAUNDERS (FRANCIS), bookseller in London, Blue Anchor on the New Exchange in the Strand, 1684–99. Partner with Joseph Knight. They succeeded to the business of Henry Herringman in 1684, and were therefore the leading publishers of plays. The partnership was dissolved about 1688, when Knight moved to the Pope's Head in the New Exchange. Saunders is last met with in the Term Catalogues in Trin. 1699. [*T.C.* III. 149.] Dunton says [p. 214], "He lived in the New Exchange and had the honour to be personally known to very many of the Nobility and Gentry of the first rank in England," and adds that he "lived long a bachelor, being too busy to think of Love".

SAVILE (GEORGE), bookseller in London, 1674. Published *Defensio Legis*, by Fabian Philips, 1674 [Haz. II. 473], which, however, was advertised by William Cooper. [*T.C.* I. 155.]

SAWBRIDGE (GEORGE), the Elder, *see Dictionary*, 1641–67. George Sawbridge, the Younger (*q. v.*), was probably not son of this man but of Thomas Sawbridge, whom he succeeded.

SAWBRIDGE (GEORGE), the Younger, bookseller in London, Three Golden Fleur de Luces, Little Britain, 1692–1711. Succeeded Thomas Sawbridge (*q. v., Dictionary*, 1641–67) at this address in 1692. He published many scientific books. In 1705 he was convicted of printing or publishing a pamphlet entitled *The Case of the Church of England's Memorial*, and sentenced to pay £200 to the Queen and to appear in all the Courts in Westminster with a paper upon his head denoting his offence and to find security for his good behaviour for two years. Dunton [p. 211] has this notice of him: "Mr. George Sawbridge succeeds his father in the trade, and prints many valuable copies. He has good skill in military discipline, and made a very handsome figure in Captain Robinson's company." As Dunton has just described the elder George Sawbridge, he seems to imply that the younger George was his son. If we do not take the words "succeeds his father in the trade" literally, this is possible, and in that case George the elder and Thomas must have been near relatives. But Dunton may have been in error, or have expressed himself confusedly.

SAWBRIDGE (HANNAH), bookseller in London, Bible on Ludgate Hill, 1682–6. Widow of George Sawbridge, the Elder, who died in 1681. Her name occurs in the Term Catalogues as continuing the business till 1686. [*T.C.* II. 160.]

SAWBRIDGE (THOMAS), bookseller in London, (1) next the Anchor, Duck Lane; (2) Three Flower de Luces, Little Britain, 1669–92. For the relationship between George and Thomas Sawbridge *see* above. Thomas Sawbridge began to publish in 1669, with William Leybourn's *Art of Dialling*. [*T.C.* I. 18.] He quickly rose to a high position in the trade, and between 1678 and 1681 was associated with John Dunmore, T. Dring, Charles Mearne, and Benjamin Tooke in the publication of a series of classics which may rank amongst the finest examples of book production of that period. The type for this series came from the foundry of J. Grover. Sawbridge was a prolific publisher. He made his last entry in the Term Catalogues in Mich. 1692 [*T.C.* II. 430], and was succeeded by his son (?) George Sawbridge, the Younger (*q. v.*).

SAYES (W.), printer and bookseller in London, Lovel's Court, Paternoster Row, 1707–14. In 1707 he took in subscriptions for L. Howell's *Synopsis Canonum*, which was advertised in the *Daily Courant* of September 30th. In that he was described as the printer. It appeared in 1708, and was printed for Clavel and others. In 1711 he published the Rev. Charles Palmer's *Danger of a total . . . Neglect . . . of the Lord's Supper*. In 1714 he was one of the subscribers to Walker's *Sufferings of the Clergy*.

SAYWELL (J.), printer at Gateshead, 1710. Founded in this year *The New-castle Gazette, or Northern Courant*. [Allnutt, p. 298; copy in Advocates' Library.]

SAYWELL (WILLIAM), bookseller in London, Red Lion in Winchester Street, 1670. Perhaps a son of John Saywell (*q. v.*, *Dictionary*, 1641–67). He published *The Mystery of Mysteries*, 1670. [*T.C.* I. 47.]

SCORE (EDWARD), bookseller in Exeter, High Street, 1704–24. First appears as publishing, with P. Bishop, Joseph Pitts's *True and Faithful Account of the Religion and Manners of the Mahommetans*, printed by Farley, 1704. [Dredge, p. 13.] In 1714 Score subscribed to Walker's *Sufferings of the Clergy*, and in 1724 he published Richard Izacke's *Remarkable Antiquities of Exeter*, 2nd ed., 1724, which was printed for him in London. The firm was still in existence in 1779, when an Edward Score of Exeter is mentioned by Nichols as selling libraries by auction. [*Lit. Anecd.* VIII. 686.]

SCOTT (JAMES), bookseller in Glasgow, 1676. One of the debtors in Andrew Anderson's inventory, 1676. [Bann. Misc. II. 283; Aldis, p. 120.]

SCOTT (ROBERT), bookseller in London, Prince's Arms, Little Britain, 1661–87. *See Dictionary*, 1641–67. Scott had a large connexion amongst the literary men and aristocracy of his day. Dr. John Cosin, Bishop of Durham, writing to his librarian on December 23rd, 1669, says, "Mr. Scott is now return'd out of France and Holland with a great many good books." [Cosin, *Correspondence*, II. 218.] In 1670 Scott was in correspondence with Viscount Conway over some books. [S.P.D. Car. II, 277, f. 186.] Another of his customers was Sir Joseph Williamson, and among the State Papers is a bill of Scott's amounting to £61 for books supplied to Sir Joseph. Eleven of these had chains attached to them, for which and fixing 14*s.* was charged. But the best biographical notice of this bookseller is that written by Roger North, who says: "Now he [i.e. Dr. John North] began to look after books, and to lay

the foundation of a competent library. He dealt with Mr. Robert Scot of Little Britain, whose sister was his grandmother's woman; and, upon that acquaintance he expected, and really had from him useful information of books and the editions. This Mr. Scott was, in his time, the greatest librarian in Europe; for, besides his stock in England, he had warehouses at Franckfort, Paris and other places and dealt by factors. After he was grown old and much worn by multiplicity of business he began to think of his ease and to leave off. Whereupon he contracted with one Mills [i.e. Adiel Mill, *q. v.*] of St. Paul's Churchyard, near £10,000 deep, and articled not to open his shop any more. But Mills, with his auctioneering, atlases, and projects failed, whereby poor Scott lost above half his means. . . . He was not only an expert bookseller but a very conscientious good man, and when he threw up his trade Europe had no small loss of him. Our doctor, at one lift, bought of him a whole set of Greek classics, in folio, of the best editions." [*Lives of the Right Hon. Francis North . . . the Hon. Sir Dudley North . . . and Dr. John North*, III. 290–1.] His brother-in-law was William Wells, bookseller, with whom he was in partnership for a time. On January 3rd, 167$\frac{6}{7}$, Scott wrote to Williamson, stating that Sir Roger L'Estrange had ordered Wells's shop to be shut up, because he had sold some copies of *L'Escole des Filles*, which he had purchased of Lucas, a bookseller of Amsterdam. Scott considered Sir R. L'Estrange's action as "illegal, unjustifiable, and uncivill". [S.P.D. Car. II, 390, f. 9.] In 1680 Scott commenced a suit against the Company of Stationers in respect of the share in the English stock held by William Wells at the time of his death; Wells's widow had died two years before, leaving Scott her executor. The Company had elected Thomas Rawe in her place, and refused to admit George her son, or to return the £80 originally paid by Wells. [Chan. Proc. before 1714, Bridges 552/10.] Adiel Mill sold off Scott's stock in 1687, and advertised the sale in the *London Gazette* for January 5th–9th. He failed in 1690. The date of Scott's death is unknown. His last appearance is in 1691, when he had a share in the seventeenth edition of Chamberlayne's *Angliae Notitia*. [*T.C.* II. 385.] His last entry before this was of Dr. John Lightfoot's *Works*, 168$\frac{4}{5}$. [*T.C.* II. 110.] He must have sold his stock to Mill soon after this. His publications are not very numerous, and he was mainly a learned second-hand retailer.

SEAR (THOMAS), bookseller in London, Swithin's Alley, near the Royal Exchange, 1676. Only known from a broadside entitled *Bethlehems Beauty*,

London's Charity, and the City's Glory. A Poem on . . . New Bedlam. [B.M. C. 20, f. 2 (106).]

SEARCH (DANIEL), bookseller in London, near Whitefriars' Gate in Fleet Street, 1689. Publisher of *The Harlem Currant*, 1689. [B.M., Burney, 97.]

SEDGWICK (   ), printer in London, *c.* 1691. Dunton tells us [p. 249] that Sedgwick managed the business for the widow of Henry Clark (who died in 1691), but that he was not very successful, and was succeeded by John Barber.

SEILE (ANNE), *see Dictionary*, 1641–67.

SELFE (S.), bookseller in Norwich, Bible and Crown, Cockey Lane, 1701–4. The second edition of Humphrey Prideaux's *Directions for Churchwardens* was printed for him in 1704 by F. Burgess. [*T.C.* III. 395.]

SELL (JOHN), bookseller in London, over against the East India House in Leadenhall Street, 1676. Advertised *A practical Discourse of Gods Sovereignty* in Trin. 1676. [*T.C.* I. 248.]

SELLER (JOHN), senior, bookseller in London, (1) Mariner's Compass, at the Hermitage Stairs in Wapping, 1669–91; (2) Exchange Alley in Cornhill, 1671–3; (3) (*a*) Pope's Head Alley in Cornhill, (*b*) on the west side of the Royal Exchange, 1679–85. 1669–91. Hydrographer to the king, compass-maker, compiler and publisher of maps, charts, and nautical books. In 1667 he makes his appearance in the Royal Society's *Philosophical Transactions*. [I. 478; *D.N.B.*] In 1671 he set up a second shop, in Exchange Alley; his advertisements of mathematical instruments in 1672, and of a book in 1673, give this address only. [*T.C.* I. 100, 151.] In 1676 and 1677 he published from Wapping only; his publications being sold in Exchange Alley, probably at his former shop, by John Hills. [*T.C.* I. 256, 267.] But in 1679 he sold his *Atlas Minimus* both at Wapping and in Pope's Head Alley, Cornhill. [*T.C.* I. 350.] His last appearance in the Term Catalogues [II. 114] is with his *New System of Geography*, 1685. In 1691 he sold his *Sea-Gunner*, printed for him by H. Clark, at the Hermitage in Wapping; he then called himself John Seller, senior. [B.M. 8806. aa. 12.] His chief work was *The English Pilot*, 1671, &c. John Seller, junior (*q. v.*), was probably his son.

SELLER (JOHN), junior, book and map-seller in London, (1) West End of St. Paul's Church; (2) Star, near Mercers' Chapel in Cheapside. 1689. In 1689 he was one of those selling Petty's *Geographical Description of Ireland*.

[*T.C.* II. 289.] He was then at the West End of St. Paul's; the Star near Mercers' Chapel in Cheapside is given as his address in *D.N.B.* Probably son of John Sellers, senior.

SELLERS (R.), bookseller in London, 1683. Only known from his imprint on *Sphinx Lugduno-Genevensis*, 1683. [Haz. III. 237.]

SERVANT (THOMAS), bookseller in Dublin, Bible, Castle Street, 1709. In that year a book entitled *Remarks upon . . . Partiality detected* was printed for him by E. Sandys.

SEYMOUR (JOHN), printer at Putney, 1669–77. On October 7th, 1669, a patent was granted by King Charles II to Captain John Seymour, in consideration of "services to us and to our Royal Father from the beginning to the end of the late troubles and since the restoration, for making several voyages and journeys beyond the seas" to print Latin books, almanacs, &c., for forty-one years. [Patent Roll, 21 Charles II, Pt. VI. 15.] During the proceedings before the Committee of the House of Lords, in 1677, in the matter of seditious publications, Samuel Mearne, Warden of the Company of Stationers, declared that John Seymour had set up two or three presses at Putney, and that there was no one who was obnoxious to the Company but fled to Seymour. [Hist. MSS. Comm., Report 9, App., pp. 75–8.] In the same year there is a record in the archives of the Stationers' Company to the effect that "certain members of the Company, with Randall Taylor the beadle, standing indicted in the Crown Office, for breaking Mr. Seymour's presses, letters and cases, and counsel having advised that the safest way will be to submit to a fine and not to plead against the King; ordered that Randall Taylor do attend the Court of King's Bench, and submit to a fine for himself and the rest, in which the table will bear them all harmless. [Records of Stationers' Company.] Seymour transferred his patent in 1671 to the University of Oxford. [S.P.D. Chas. II, 292, ff. 116, 117.]

SHAD (J.), bookseller in London, 1653. He published one of the many poetical broadsides commemorating the great frost of 1683–4 and the fair on the frozen Thames. [B.M. C. 20. f. 2 (165).]

SHARP (SIR JOSHUA), stationer in London, 1681 (?)–1718. Youngest brother of Archbishop Sharp. He is thus noticed by Dunton: "The next I dealt with was Mr. Sharp (brother to the Archbishop of that name) . . . Mr. Sharp is a person of great honesty—very obliging in his conversation—and thrives so fast in his shop, that 'tis very likely we may see him riding the great horse [i. e. as Lord Mayor]." The prediction of Dunton was in some degree verified. In 1713 Sharp was elected Sheriff of London and knighted. He married Rebecca Harvey, and died December 22, 1718. [Nichols, *Lit. Anecd.* VIII. 354.] Sharp does not appear to have been a publisher. He is just possibly identical with the following.

SHARP (S.), stationer in London, Crooked Lane, 1692. His name occurs in the Term Catalogue of Easter 1692 as one of those who sold William Jordan's copybook. [*T.C.* II. 404.] "S. Sharp" is possibly an error for J. Sharp (*q.v.*).

SHARP (THOMAS), bookbinder and bookseller in London, Blackfriars, 1679. In 1679 he advertised *The Politicks of France* by Mr. P[aul] H[ay], Marquis du C[hastelet], and *A Letter . . . shewing that the Bishops are not to be Judges in Parliament in Cases Capital.* Arber says in his index that Sharp was a bookbinder, but does not give his authority for the statement. [*T.C.* I. 373, 375, 567.]

SHARP (THOMAS), printer in London, Ivy Lane, 1722 (?)–4 (?). In partnership with Thomas Wood, printer of *The Freeholder's Journal.* On June 19, 1722, he was tried and convicted at the Guildhall for printing a supplement to no. 10 of that paper. [Timperley, p. 628.] Negus described him as a High-Flyer. [Nichols, *Lit. Anecd.* I. 311–12.]

SHARPE, *see* Sharp.

SHARPLESS (   ), printer in London (?), 1690 (?). Married the widow of John Harefinch (*q. v.*), who died about 1690. [Records of Stat. Co.]

SHAW (   ), bookseller in Newcastle-on-Tyne, at the Bridge Foot, 1723. He sold, for the anonymous author, in 1723, *Copies in verse for the use of Writing Schools and Hymns for Charity Schools.* [*Memoirs of Mr. Ambrose Barnes*, Surtees Soc., 1867, App., p. 469.]

SHAW (GIDEON), stationer in Edinburgh, in the Parliament Close at the sign of the Blue Bible, 1670–87. Served on the jury at Major Weir's trial in April 1670. One of the six booksellers who in 1671 successfully appealed against Andrew Anderson's monopoly. He married Marion Marshell and had a son, William. Died in 1687. Inventory printed in Bann. Misc. II. 292. [Aldis, 120.]

SHEAFE (SAMUEL), stationer in London, Bread Street, 1712–32. Partner with Alexander Merreal (*q.v.*), whose daughter he married and to whose business he succeeded. In 1713 he contributed five guineas to the Bowyer fund. He died August 4th, 1732. [Timperley, p. 646.]

SHEARES (MARGARET). *See Dictionary*, 1641–67. Still publishing in 1671. [*T.C.* I. 75.]

SHEFFIELD (S.), printer in Norwich, 1706. Printed *The Norwich Postman* in that year.

SHELL (G.), bookseller in London, Stonecutter Court, Shoe Lane, 1684. Published a licentious book in 1684. [*T.C.* II. 62–3.]

SHELMERDINE (RALPH), bookseller in Manchester, 1661–73. *See Dictionary*, 1641–67. Still publishing in 1673, when he issued *The Mystery of Rhetorick unveiled*, by John Smith, Gent. [*T.C.* I. 157.]

SHELMERDINE (THOMAS), bookseller in London, Rose Tree, Little Britain, 1698–1711. In Easter 1698 he advertised the third edition of *Counsellor Manners his last Legacy to his Son, by J. D.* [*T.C.* III. 69.] He was still there in 1711. [*Postman*, February 3rd, $17\frac{10}{11}$.]

SHELTON (JOSEPH), bookseller and book auctioneer in London, Peacock in the Poultry, 1691–6. In 1691 he conducted a book auction. [B.M. 821. i. 9 (14).] In 1694 he held a sale of books in Coventry, co. Warwick, at the house of Samuel Withers (*q. v.*). In partnership with W. Chandler. They issued the English translation of Jean Mocquet's *Travels* in 1696. [*T.C.* II. 589.]

SHEPHERD (F.), bookseller in London, 1682. His imprint occurs on a broadside, *The Last Words and Sayings of the True Protestant Elm Board.* [Haz. III. 243.]

SHERLOCK (RICHARD), bookseller in Oxford, 1684. [Madan, p. 31.]

SHIRLEY (BENJAMIN), bookseller in London, Fleet Street, under the Dial of St. Dunstan's Church, 1676–80. Began to publish in Hil. 1676, with a medical work by James Cooke. [*T.C.* I. 230.] In the following year he issued a *Life* of Sir Walter Raleigh [*T.C.* I. 281], and was one of the publishers of Sir Edward Coke's *Reports.* He is last heard of in 1680. [*T.C.* I. 407.]

SHREWSBURY, or SHROWSBURY (WILLIAM), bookseller in London, Bible in Duck Lane, 1672–1703. His name appears for the first time in the Term

Catalogue of Mich. 1672 as the publisher of J. Smith's *Stereometrie, or, the Art of Practical Gauging.* [*T.C.* I. 118.] He published many scientific and medical books, also a *Life* of Sir Matthew Hale, Lord Chief Justice, of whose treatise, *Contemplations, Moral and Divine*, he published several editions down to 1695. [*T.C.* II. 562–3.] Dunton speaks of him as alive, and says [pp. 221–2]: "He merits the name of 'Universal Bookseller'. . . . He keeps his Stock in excellent order, and will find any Book as ready as I can find a word in the Dictionary. . . . He is a constant frequenter of Sturbridge Fair."

SIMMONS (B.), bookseller in London, Three Golden Cocks, (*a*) at, (*b*) near the West End of St. Paul's, 1681–4. Relative of Nevill Simmons (*q. v., Dictionary*, 1641–67), and succeeded to his business. His first and last entries in the Term Catalogues were made in 1681 and 1684. [*T.C.* I. 457, II. 105.] He was apparently succeeded by Thomas Simmons, who published in 1685 from the Three Cocks in Ludgate Street, an address which probably represents the same house. [*T.C.* II. 112.]

SIMMONS or SYMONS (MARY), printer in London, 1656–75. *See Dictionary*, 1641–67. She must be the Mrs. Simmons in the 1675 List of London Printers.

SIMMONS (NEVILL), the Elder, *see Dictionary*, 1641–67.

SIMMONS (NEVILL), the Younger, bookseller in Sheffield, 1697–1702. His relationship to the elder Nevill Simmons is obscure. Publisher of the Rev. N. Drake's *Sermons*, also of Thomas Jollie's *Vindication of the Surrey Demoniack*, 1698, as well as the writings and sermons of the Rev. Timothy Manlove. [*T.C.* II. 60c, III. 92.] Hazlitt [III. 12] records his imprint in a book of 1702.

SIMMONS (SAMUEL), *see Dictionary*, 1641–67.

SIMMONS, SYMONDS, or SYMMONDS (THOMAS), bookseller in Bury St. Edmunds, 1676–8; and in London, (1) (*a*) Prince's Arms, St. Paul's Churchyard, (*b*) Prince's Arms, Ludgate Street, 1679–84; (2) Three Cocks, Ludgate Street, 1685. 1676–85. Son of Nevill Simmons, and, like him, published for Baxter. He began business at Bury St. Edmunds, where he published a school book, called *English Examples to be turned into Latine*, in 1676 [*T.C.* I. 237]; in the same year and in 1678 he published editions of a grammatical work by Vossius, and of Lucian's Dialogues, both by Edward Leeds, one of the masters of Bury School. [*T.C.* I. 238, 308.] Simmons left Bury St. Edmunds very shortly after this and settled in London at the Prince's Arms in

St. Paul's Churchyard, by 1679, when he published Dr. W. Simpson's *History of Scarborough Spaw*, 1679 [*T.C.* I. 358], and other interesting books. He was also the publisher of several broadsides and pamphlets on the Popish Plot, some with Jacob Sampson (*q. v.*). In 1681 he was defendant in a suit for assault brought against him by Bartholomew Sprint in the Court of Common Pleas. [C.P.R. Trin. 33 Chas. II, 2992, m. 256 r.] Again, in Hil. 34–5 Chas. II, he stood bond for the appearance of Katherine Kirkman, widow [C.P.R. 3009, m. 45 r.], and in 1685 he had some commercial transaction with Francis Pearse, bookseller, which was afterwards the subject of an action in the same court. [C.P.R. Mich. 1 Jas. II, 3039, m. 309 v.] Dunton [p. 224] calls Simmons "a most accomplished bookseller" and praises his domestic virtues. In 1685 Simmons moved to the Three Cocks in Ludgate Street, probably the shop previously occupied by B. Simmons (*q. v.*); but nothing more is heard of him after that date.

SIMPSON (   ), bookbinder in London, *c.* 1690. Dunton [p. 258] says that Simpson, a "grave and antient binder", was recommended to him by Roberts the printer, as "a curious workman and a very honest man". He supposes him to be nearly related to Simpson the bookseller.

SIMPSON (ANDREW), *see* Symson.

SIMPSON (JAMES), bookbinder in Edinburgh, 1670. His wife Anne was one of the witnesses at Major Weir's trial in 1670. [*Ravillac Redivivus*, London, 1678, p. 65; Aldis, p. 120.]

SIMPSON (RALPH), bookseller in London, Harp in St. Paul's Churchyard, 1680–1704. Ralph and Richard Simpson were in partnership at the Harp, and one of them is mentioned in the Term Catalogue for Hil. 1680; but as the imprint to that and several other books is simply R. Simpson, it is impossible to say which of them it was. They were the publishers of some of the works of Sir William Temple, and the first definite mention of Ralph is as joint publisher with Richard of that author's *Miscellanea, the Second Part*, 1690. [*T.C.* II. 337.] In 1692 Richard moved to the Three Trouts in the Churchyard and is last heard of in 1698 [*T.C.* III. 57], but Ralph continued to publish until 1704. [*T.C.* III. 395.] The Simpsons were also publishers of a series of controversial tracts on the siege of Londonderry, one of which, *A Narrative of the Siege of Londonderry*, 1690, is not mentioned in the Term Catalogues, but is in the British Museum. [B.M. T. 1707 (1).]

SIMPSON (RICHARD), bookseller in London, (1) Harp, in St. Paul's Churchyard, 1690–92; (2) Three Trouts in St. Paul's Churchyard, 1692–8. 1690–98. *See* Simpson (Ralph).

SIMPSON or SYMPSON (SAMUEL), bookseller at Cambridge, living on the site now occupied by the Senate House lawn, 1670–1702. His name appears on books from 1670 to 1702. [Bowes, *Cambridge Books*, nos. 142, 150, 193, 290, 314, 354; *T.C.* II. 131.] He probably died before March 170$\frac{2}{3}$, when his house was occupied by another person.

SIMS (JOHN), bookseller in London, King's Head at Sweeting's Alley end of Cornhill, 1656–77. *See Dictionary*, 1641–67. Continued in business until 1677. Dunton [p. 295] alludes to him as "liberal" Sims. He dealt in school books. [*T.C.* I. 127–8, 295.] He was at the address given here, his third, by 1673. He was succeeded by S. Tidmarsh.

SKEGNES (CHRISTOPHER), bookseller in London, Golden Ball in St. Paul's Churchyard, 1686–7. In 1686 and 1687 he entered, either alone or with other booksellers, four books, of which the most important was Thévenot's *Travels*. [*T.C.* II. 175, 182, 193, 198.]

SKINNER (EDWARD), bookseller in Oxford, 1697. [Madan, p. 31.]

SLATER (J.), bookseller in London, on the west side of the Royal Exchange, 1684. In that year he sold a broadside, "curiously cut in copper", of the Fair held on the frozen Thames. [*T.C.* II. 72.]

SLATER, or SLATTER (J.), bookseller at Eton, 1696–1709. Dealer in schoolbooks. In 1696 he advertised an edition of *Aesop* for use in the school at Eton, and he was still there in 1709. [*T.C.* II. 603, III. 627.]

SMALL (MRS.), bookseller in Deal, Kent, 1711. She was one of those who sold John Davis's *Seaman's Speculum*. [*T.C.* III. 672; *Post Man*, March 10th, 17$\frac{10}{11}$.]

SMELT (MATTHEW), *see Dictionary*, 1641–67.

SMITH (CHARLES), bookseller in London, (1) Black Swan, over against the Horn Tavern in Fleet Street, 1671; (2) Angel, Fleet Street, near the Inner Temple Gate, 1675–81. 1671–81. Made his first entry in the Term Catalogues in Easter 1671. [*T.C.* I. 71.] Publisher in 1675 of Edward Phillips's *Theatrum Poetarum*. [*T.C.* I. 212.] In 1681 he issued a translation of Rousseau de la Valette's novel *Casimir, King of Poland*. [*T.C.* I. 450.] In that year he was defendant in an action for trespass and assault, brought against him by Lemuel Bradley. [C.P.R. 33 Chas. II, 2992, m. 242 v.]

SMITH (CHARLES), bookseller in London, Buck, between the two Temple Gates in Fleet Street, 1707–9. [*T.C.* III. 567, 613, 652.]

SMITH (E.), bookseller in London, Bible (*a*) under the Piazza, (*b*) in the South Portico, of the Royal Exchange, Cornhill, 1686–9. Publisher, with others, of G. de Malynes' *Consuetudo vel Lex Mercatoria* in 1686. [*T.C.* II. 184.] He made his last entry in 1689. [*T.C.* II. 277.]

SMITH (E.), bookseller in London, 1707 (?)–9. [*T.C.* III. 576, 654.] Possibly, but not probably, identical with the preceding.

SMITH (FRANCIS), bookseller in London, (1) Elephant and Castle, without Temple Bar; (2) Elephant and Castle, Cornhill, near the Royal Exchange, 1659 (?)–1688 (?). *See Dictionary*, 1641–67. Commonly called "Elephant" Smith. This bookseller became notorious for his strong political and religious views, for which he was persecuted without mercy by the Government. There is little doubt that he was the Francis Smith who in 1659 published Captain W. Bray's *Plea for the Peoples Good Cause* [B.M. E. 763 (7)], and he has left on record two pamphlets, in which is recorded his subsequent history. The first of these is entitled *An Account of the injurious Proceedings of Sir George Jeffreys . . . against Francis Smith, bookseller . . . Sept. 16, 1680; upon an Indictment then exhibited against the said Francis Smith, for publishing a pretended Libel, entituled, An Act of Common Council for Retrenching the Expenses of the Lord Mayor and Sheriffs of the City of London, &c.* [1680 ?]. [B.M. 1872. a. 1 (36).] The second was called *An Impartiall Account of the Trial of Francis Smith . . . for printing and publishing . . .* [*Clod-Pate's Ghost, by*] *Tom Ticklefoot. As also of the Tryal of Jane Curtis . . . for publishing . . . a Satyr upon Injustice, or Scroggs upon Scroggs*, 1680. [B.M. 6495. i. 32.] Briefly summarized these are the facts which Smith records: In the year 1659 his windows were broken and his lodgers frightened away, because he was suspected of being disaffected to General Monk and the Royalists. In 1660 he was three times a prisoner in the Messenger's hands about a book called *The Lord's Loud call to England*, and his charge and damage were £50. At the time of Venner's rising (1657) the mob broke into his house and destroyed his property, threatening to kill him and using him so badly that for some time afterwards he was not able to turn himself in his bed. In August 1661 he was thrown into the Gatehouse for printing *Mirabilis Annus*, and by that he lost his shop and trade for two years, amounting to upwards of £300. On another occasion he was "so often and dayly harassed too and fro by Mr. L'Estrange's order" that he became dangerously ill and delirious. During the plague (of 1665) he was living with his family at Dorking. In 1666 Lilliecrap, a printer and one of L'Estrange's spies, went to his shop and warehouse near Temple Bar, and took away as many books as two porters could stand under, few of which he ever recovered. In 1671 Smith was persecuted under the Conventicles Act, and lost his shop and trade for more than six months. Altogether he reckoned he had lost at least £1,400 during the previous twenty years. Smith stated before a Committee of the House of Lords in 1677 that Samuel Mearne and Robert White, acting presumably for the Company, had seized an impression made for Smith of Danvers' *Infant Baptism*, and, in spite of an order by Lord Arlington, refused to give it up; a large edition was meanwhile printed by Joseph Downing for Thomas Sawbridge and Randal Taylor, with Smith's name and sign; Mearne knew of this piracy, but took no steps to seize the edition. [Hist. MSS. Comm., Report 9, App., p. 78.] Smith was the publisher of *Smith's Protestant Intelligence, Domestick and Foreign*. The first number appeared on February 1st, 16$\frac{80}{81}$. It recorded the publisher's indictment for publishing a pamphlet entitled *A Speech lately made by a noble Peer of the Realm*. The Grand Jury threw out the bill. This news-sheet contained very little foreign news and only occasionally inserted advertisements. Smith's last entry in the Term Catalogues was in Mich. 1679; but we know that he was in business as late as 1683. Obediah Smith (*q.v.*), probably his son, published at the Elephant and Castle in 1672–3. *See also* Downing (Joseph). A Francis Smith, stationer, was buried at Farnham in Surrey on July 6th, 1688, and was probably the notorious "Elephant" Smith.

SMITH (J.), bookseller in London, Aldersgate Street, 1710. Publisher of a broadside on the Sacheverell controversy entitled *A Rod for a Fool's back*, 1710. [B.M. T. 100* (233).]

SMITH (J.), printer in London, Fleet Street, 1715. Printed *A short Account of the state of England when King James design'd to call his second Parliament*, 17$\frac{14}{15}$. [B.M. T. 100* (235).]

SMITH (JOHN), printer in London, Great Queen Street, 1679–83. Chiefly known as the printer and publisher of *The Currant Intelligence*, begun in 1679. He was also the publisher of *The Jockey's Intelligencer of Horses and Coaches* in 1683.

SMITH (JOHN), bookseller in London, Lion and Crown in Russell Street, in Covent Garden, 1701. One of three booksellers publishing C. A. Brun's *Conference . . . upon Expression*, 1701, a book with many engravings.

SMITH (JOHN), bookseller in Coventry, 1683. Publisher of Jonathan Kimberley's Warwick Assize Sermon, *Of Obedience for Conscience sake. . . .* [*T.C.* II. 37.]

SMITH (OBEDIAH), bookseller in London, (1) Elephant and Castle, without Temple Bar, 1672–3; (2) Black Swan, Fleet Street, 1673–80(?); and in Daventry, 1684–1704. 1672–1704. Probably a son of Francis ("Elephant") Smith, who also lived at the Elephant and Castle without Temple Bar. In 1673 Obed. Smith moved to the Black Swan in Fleet Street. [*T.C.* I. 102, 157.] Somewhere about 1680 he appears to have left London and settled at Daventry; in 169$\frac{4}{5}$ he published there C. Allestree's sermon, *The Desire of All Men* [Bodl. Serm. 1 (8)], and he was still living there in 1704. [*T.C.* III. 424.]

SMITH (RALPH), bookseller in London, 1642–84. *See Dictionary*, 1641–67. Still in business in 1684. [*T.C.* II. 108.]

SMITH (RICHARD), bookseller in London, (1) Angel and Bible, (*a*) near the May-Pole, Strand, (*b*) without Temple Bar; (2) Fore-walk of Exeter Change in the Strand; (3) Bishop Beveridge's Head in Paternoster Row. 1698–1720. Began business as a publisher in 1698, and issued several of the writings of William Beveridge, Bishop of St. Asaph. He moved to Exeter Change in 1708, and afterwards opened a shop in Paternoster Row, which he named, after his patron, Bishop Beveridge's Head. At the time of the fire at the elder Bowyer's printing office, Richard Smith had in that press Bishop Bull's *Important Points of Primitive Christianity* as well as an edition of Bishop Bull's *Works*; all of which were destroyed. Bowyer made good the paper, although Smith had released him from any obligation to do so, and also paid Smith the same dividend as other sufferers received. [Nichols, *Lit. Anecd.* I. 55–6.] Smith died before 1721, and was succeeded in the business by his widow Mary Smith. [Nichols, *Lit. Anecd.* I. 219.] Dunton has two references to a Mr. Smith, but there is nothing to show to whom they apply.

SMITH (SAMUEL), bookseller in London, St. Paul's Churchyard, 1681–1703. Apprentice with Moses Pitt. Afterwards in partnership with Benjamin Walford, and bookseller to the Royal Society. Dunton declared that Smith dealt in foreign books and spoke French and Latin with fluency. Smith is said by Moses Pitt in his *Cry of the Oppressed* [p. 153] to have gone down to Portsmouth with Pitt's oppressor, Adiel Mill, and taken possession of certain property there.

SMITH (W.), bookseller in Cambridge, 1706–31. His name appears on Poor Law Overseers' Forms (in the Great St. Mary's Church Books), 1708–31. A Mr. Smith, bookseller, appears in the Rate Book of St. Botolph Church, March 172⅝, for 10*s*. In 1706 there appears to have been a charge against him "for selling books and strong drinks", and depositions of Cambridge stationers were made February 4th and March 23rd concerning this charge.

SMITH (WILLIAM), *see Dictionary*, 1641–67.

SMITHURST (BENJAMIN), bookseller, in Launceston, 1693–1700; (?) and in Plymouth, 1714. 1693–1714 (?). It seems highly probable that the Benjamin Smithurst who compiled a Peerage and Baronetage in 1689, under the title of *Britain's Glory*, was none other than the Benjamin Smithurst who in 1693 and 1700 published sermons by John Hill and J. R., Cornish clergy. [*T.C.* II. 475, III. 169.] Smithurst, bookseller in Plymouth, subscribed in 1714 for Walker's *Sufferings of the Clergy*. His identity with Benjamin is not more than probable.

SNOWDEN (THOMAS), printer in London, 1678 (?)–1680. Probably the T. S. who printed for Thomas Moore in 1678. His full name is only known from *An Account of the New Sheriffs holding their Office*, 1680. [B.M. 816. m. 9 (61).]

SOLINGEN (JOSHUA VAN), printer in Edinburgh, 1680–5. One of the Dutch workmen brought over by John Cairns about 1680. Afterwards in partnership with Lindsay (*q.v.*), Kniblo, and Colmar. [Aldis, p. 120.]

SOLLERS (J.), bookseller in London, Cornhill, 1684. His name appears in 1684 as a publisher of an elementary work on Geometry. [*T.C.* II. 84.]

SOLLERS (ROBERT), bookseller in London, (1) Flying Horse, St. Paul's Churchyard, 1677; (2) King's Arms, Ludgate Street, 1678; (3) King's Arms and Bible, St. Paul's Churchyard, 1679–82. 1677–82. His name appears first in the Term Catalogue for Easter 1677. He dealt in plays, novels, poems, and divinity. Dunton [p. 292] refers to him as "*Country* Sollars", perhaps implying that he supplied the chapmen or else that he went to country fairs himself. It is possible that he had a shop at Rochester in Kent, as Edward Brown's sermon at the Kentish Feast of November 16th, 1699, was advertised in the *Flying Post* of December 2nd, to be sold, amongst others, by "Mr. Sollers in Rochester". His name, however, does not appear in the imprint to the book.

SOUTHALL (RICHARD), bookseller in Stafford, 1722. Publisher of a sermon by W. Jervis entitled *The duty of praying for Princes*, 1722, 8vo. [B.M. 225. h. 10 (3).]

SOUTHBY (JOHN), bookseller in London, (1) The Plough in Cornhill; (2) The Harrow in Cornhill, 1684–91. Began as a publisher of theology in Trin. 1684 [*T.C.* II. 80], in which year he either moved, or changed his sign from the "Plough" to the "Harrow". In 1690 he issued *The Great Question, or, how Religion, Property and Liberty are to be best secured.* [B.M. T. 1707 (2).] The announcement of this in Trin. 1691 [*T.C.* II. 371] is the last that is known of him.

SOUTHBY (RICHARD), bookseller in London, Golden Fleece in Fleet Street, 1693. Advertised a set of tables of the sovereigns of Europe, and also a treatise on the law of bankruptcy. [*T.C.* II. 440, 478.]

SOUTHWOOD (BENJAMIN), bookseller in London, (1) Star, next to Serjeant's Inn in Chancery Lane, 1673–5; (2) New Inn Gate, without Temple Bar, 1679. 1673–9. Began business as a publisher in 1673 when, in partnership with Israel Harrison, he reissued J. Smith's *England's Improvement Reviv'd* of 1670. Harrison dropped out of the partnership after this, and Southwood continued alone as a publisher of a few divinity books and political pamphlets. He gave evidence before the Committee of the House of Lords in 1676–7 that he had received from Dr. Carey the MS. of *The Long Parliament Dissolved*, which he gave to Nathaniel Thompson to print. [Hist. MSS. Comm., Report 9, App., p. 72.] His last entry in the Term Catalogues was in 1679. [*T.C.* I. 356.]

SOWLE (ANDREW), *see Dictionary*, 1641–67.

SOWLE (TACE, or TACY), printer and bookseller in London, next door to the Meeting House in White-Hart Court in Gracious [Gracechurch] Street; and at the Bible in Leadenhall Street, 1695–1746. Printer for the Quakers. Daughter of Andrew Sowle; born January 29th, 166⅚. She succeeded her father, who died in 1695. Dunton [pp. 222–3] says: "She is both a Printer as well as a Bookseller, and the daughter of one; and understands her Trade very well, being a good Compositor herself. . . . She keeps herself unmarried." Three years later, however, in 1706, she married Thomas Raylton. Her mother, Jane Sowle, and from 1715 the latter's assigns, continued the business. Tace survived her husband twenty-three years and died in 1746.

SPEED (ANNE), bookseller in London, Three Crowns in Exchange Alley, over against Jonathan's Coffee House in Cornhill, 1705–11 (?). Probably wife of Thomas Speed (*q.v.*). Her chief publications were sermons and theological tracts. Her first entry in the Term Catalogues was made in Mich. 1705. [*T.C.* III. 476.]

SPEED (SAMUEL), bookseller in London, 1658–70. *See Dictionary*, 1641–67. Still in business in 1670, when a catalogue of books sold by him occurs at the end of D. Lloyd's *State Worthies*. [B.M. 615. b. 2.]

SPEED (THOMAS), bookseller in London, (1) Crown, Poultry, 1689; (2) Three Crowns, Cornhill, near the Royal Exchange, 1690–1714 (?). 1689–1714. He was probably son or brother of Samuel Speed. His name first appears in the Term Catalogue for Easter 1689, when he advertised two books on shorthand by Thomas Shelton, and Thomas Farnaby's *Index Rhetoricus*. [*T.C.* II. 263.] Dunton [pp. 218–9] says: "He has the honour to print for Sir William Dawes, Dr. Smith and other eminent churchmen. He is a very modest quiet man." His name occurs in the Term Catalogues for the last time in Mich. 1707. [*T.C.* III. 577.] A list of eleven books printed for him is to be found at the end of L. Smith's *Knowledge and Virtue*, 1702. [Bodl. Serm. 19 (4).] In 1714 he was among the subscribers to Walker's *Sufferings of the Clergy*. Anne Speed (*q.v.*) published at the second of Thomas's addresses in his lifetime.

SPENCER (JOHN), printer in London, 1684. He appears as defendant in an action for debt brought by Sara Reeve, widow. [C.P.R. Trin. 1 Jas. II, 3036, m. 195 r.] He was probably not a master.

SPICER (JOHN), bookseller in London, 1682. Only known from a poem, *The Conspiracy of Aeneas and Antenor against the State of Troy*, printed for him in 1682. [B.M. 11631. bbb. 3.]

SPILLER (WILLIAM), bookseller in London, 1696. David Edwards, a printer, in the course of some Chancery proceedings, stated that he had printed about thirty or forty gross of black and white primers at the instigation of William Spiller. [Chan. Proc., before 1714, Collins 486/100.]

SPOTTISWOOD (JOHN), printer (?), Edinburgh, 1706. "In 1706, Mr. John Spotiswood Advocate, and professor of the Law, brought home a neat little house [*sic*] for printing his law books: But in a little time after, dispos'd of it to Mr. Robert Freebairn bookseller." [Watson, p. 18.] No books bearing Spottiswood's name in the imprint have been noted.

SPRINT (BARTHOLOMEW), bookseller in London, 1681. Only known as plaintiff in an action for assault, brought by him against a number of booksellers and printers in London and Oxford. The details are wanting, and nothing is known of his relation to the other Sprints, booksellers of London. [C.P.R. Trin. 33 Chas. II, 2992, m. 256.]

SPRINT (BENJAMIN), bookseller in London, Blue Bell, Little Britain, 1709–37. Son of Samuel Sprint, who left him half his books, bound and unbound, and half his copyrights, desiring him to continue with his brother John; he was in the business by 1709, and the brothers were in partnership till 1727 at least, when they issued the fourth edition of the Works of Scarron. [Esdaile, p. 301.] Benjamin Sprint died September 20th, 1737. [Timperley, p. 660.]

SPRINT (JOHN), bookseller in London, Blue Bell, Little Britain, 1698–1727. Son of Samuel Sprint. Entered the business in 1698. In 1713 he contributed three guineas to the Bowyer fund. He was joined by his brother Benjamin (*q. v.*) in 1709, and they were still together in 1727. Dunton [p. 230] praises him highly.

SPRINT (SAMUEL), bookseller in London, (1) Golden Ball, Duck Lane; (2) Bell, Little Britain; (3) Blue Bell, Little Britain. 1670–1707. Began business in Duck Lane in 1670, in partnership with George Calvert. [*T.C.* I. 35.] In 1672 he set up for himself at the Bell, in Little Britain, and in 1676 his sign became the Blue Bell in Little Britain. In 1698 he took his son John into partnership. They were the publishers of the *Index Villaris*, and in 1700 a translation of the Works of Scarron, "illustrated with copper cuts." Samuel Sprint died in 1707, his will being proved on April 28th. He left three sons, John, Benjamin, and Samuel. To his son Benjamin he left half his books, bound and unbound, and half his copyrights, and desired him to continue in partnership with his brother John. [P.C.C. 94, Poley.] He served the office of Under Warden of the Company in 1700–1, and Upper Warden in 1704–5. Dunton [p. 209] says of him : " Mr. Samuel Sprint, senior, thrives much in trade, and is punctual and honest : he has been very fortunate in several engagements. He printed ' Mr. Fox of Time ', ' Mr. Doolittle on the Sacraments,' and was engaged the same way for Mr. Steele, and other eminent authors."

STAGG (JOHN), bookseller in London, Westminster Hall, 1716 (?)–46. The following notices in the *General Advertiser* of September 20th and 27th, 1746, contain all the information met with concerning this bookseller : " Yesterday morning [September 19th], died, at his house in Old Palace Yard, Westminster, after a long and tedious indisposition in the 52nd year of his age, Mr. John Stagg, who has been near 30 years an eminent bookseller in Westminster Hall." " Last night [September 26th] the corps of Mr. John Stagg, . . . was interr'd . . . in the Cloysters belonging to Westminster Abbey."

STANDFAST (RICHARD), bookseller in London, Westminster Hall, 1711–25. Published *A Caveat against Seducers* in 1711, by Richard Standfast, Rector of Christchurch, Bristol, possibly his father.

STARKEY (JOHN), bookseller in London, 1658–89. *See Dictionary*, 1641–67. Still at work in 1689. A list of books printed for him appears at the beginning of *Jesuitical Aphorismes*, 1679. G. Grafton was at Starkey's house, the Mitre in Fleet Street, by 1687 [*T.C.* II. 202] ; Starkey at this time appears to have been in partnership with Chiswell. [*T.C.* II. 248, 255, 274.]

STATIONERS, SOCIETY OF, in Edinburgh, *see Dictionary*, 1641–67.

STEPHENS (ANTHONY), bookseller in Oxford, near the Theatre, 1685. *Miscellany Poems and Translations by Oxford Hands* was printed for him in this year. [B.M. 11641. bbb. 38.]

STEPHENS (J.), bookseller in London, Hand and Star, between the Two Temple Gates in Fleet Street, 1722. Published a sermon by George Parry in 1722.

STEPHENS (JOHN), bookseller in Oxford, 1704–9. On June 13th, 1709, his goods and effects were seized by his brother. John Stephens is described by Hearne as " a careless, negligent prating fellow ", who had several things

printed for him at the " Theater-Press ", but paid no University dues. [*Collections*, II. 211–12 ; Madan, p. 31.]

STEPHENS (PHILEMON), *see Dictionary*, 1641–67.

STEPHENS, or STEVENS (ROBERT), printer in London, 1668 (?)–1700 (?). This man, who does not appear to have exercised his trade as a printer, was appointed " messenger " and " constable " by the Company of Stationers and was in consequence cordially hated by his brother printers, who gave him the nickname of " Robin Hog ". He was employed to hunt out secret presses, and figures in nearly all the prosecutions of that period. He sometimes met with resistance. Francis Smith states that in December 1679, " Mr. Stevens and a constable came to his shop with a general search warrant, but as it did not state his name or crime, he dared them at their peril to touch him or anything in his shop." In 1681 Stephens was defendant in an action for assault brought against him by S. Lee. [C.P.R. 2994, m. 1093 v.] In 1692, having discovered a private press at the house of Thomas Topham, in Shoreditch, Stephens was allowed £4 for his expenses and service, with liberty to prosecute the landlord of the house for the £5 due by the Act for his own benefit. [Records of the Stationers' Company.] Moses Pitt, in his *Cry of the Oppressed*, also mentions the activities of Robert Stephens.

STEWART (GEORGE), bookseller in Edinburgh, 1716–34. *The Freeholder* of April 10th, 1716, was printed for and sold by him ; and in 1722, 1724, and 1734 he sold books printed by Ruddiman.

STEWART (ROBERT), bookseller in Glasgow, 1662 (?)–76. One of the debtors in A. Anderson's inventory of 1676. The Robert Stewart in Glasgow, debtor to G. Lithgow in 1662, is probably the same. [Aldis, p. 121.]

STOKOE (LUKE), bookseller in London, (1) Golden Key and Bible at Charing Cross ; (2) Golden Key, against the Mews Gate, Charing Cross ; (3) Coventry Court, Haymarket, 1700 (?)–27. In 1700 " L. Stoley " is recorded by Arber [III. 182] as publishing a divinity book at the first of the addresses given above. This appears to be an error for L. Stokoe. In conjunction with George Harris he published a small volume of verse called *Poems on Several Occasions. Together with some Odes in Imitation of Mr. Cowley's Stile and Manner* in 1703. In 1725 he took subscriptions for Francis Mason's *Vindication of the Church of England*, and in 1727 he issued two sale catalogues. [Nichols, *Lit. Anecd.* I. 329, III. 664.]

STOLEY (L.), *see* Stokoe (L.).

STONE (AMY), bookseller in Nantwich, 1699–1710. In 1699 she sold grammars and devotional books, which she purchased wholesale of John Minshull of Chester. [*Library*, 2nd ser. IV. 373–83.] In the same year and again in 1710 her name appears in the imprints to sermons by J. Oliver, Prebendary of Chester. [Cooke, *Bibl. Cestr.*, p. 26 ; B.M. 226. g. 13 (8).]

STORY (EDWARD), bookseller in Cambridge. *See Dictionary*, 1641–67. To that notice should be added that he was buried in Great St. Mary's February 5th, 169$\frac{2}{3}$. By his will he bequeathed his real and personal estate to his son Edward Story (M.B. and Fellow of Magdalene College), and, if he should die without issue, to trustees to erect ten almshouses in the town of Cambridge. The son died without issue about 1710, and the almshouses were erected about 1729. These almshouses, like those founded by bequest of another bookseller, Henry Wray (*q.v.*, *Dictionary*, 1557–1640) are still in existence, and used for the object for which they were founded. [Cooper's *Memorials of Cambridge*, III. 175, 310.]

STORY (JOHN), bookseller in Newcastle-on-Tyne, 1685–6. Took up his freedom in the Newcastle Stationers' Company on July 25th, 1685. [Welford, *Early Newcastle Typography*, p. 128.] In the following year he issued George Stuart's *Joco-Serious Discourse*. [*T.C.* II. 178.]

STRAHAN, or STRACHAN (GEORGE), bookseller in London, Golden Ball, Cornhill, over against the Royal Exchange, 1699–1740 (?). Began publishing in 1699 [*T.C.* III. 128], and became one of the leading publishers in London. Nichols [*Lit. Anecd.*] notes several of the important books which Strahan published. In or about 1740 he was one of six booksellers contracting with the Society for the Encouragement of Learning. [Nichols, *Lit. Anecd.* II. 96.]

STREATER, or STREATOR (JOHN), *see Dictionary*, 1641–67.

STREATER (S.), printer in London, 1677. Only known from Giles Fletcher's *Israel Redux*, 1677. [Haz. II. 222.] Possibly a misprint for J(ohn) Streater.

STREATOR (JOSEPH), printer in London, 1688. Only known from the imprint to *Sylvia's Revenge*, 1688. [Haz. II. 715.] Perhaps successor to John Streator, who disappears in the previous year.

STURTON (JOHN), bookseller in London, at the Post Office at the Middle Temple in Fleet Street, 1696–8. Publisher, with A. Bosvill, of *The Delights of*

Holland, by William Mountague, 1696. [Haz. III. 173.] Sturton advertised *Timoleon, or the Revolution*, in the *Post Boy*, March 2nd–4th, 169$\frac{7}{8}$.

SULLEY (GERVAS), bookseller in Nottingham, 1703. Published in 1703 *A Sermon Preached before the Mayor . . . of Nottingham*, December 3rd, 1702. [Creswell, p. 7 ; Bodl. Serm. 4.]

SWAFFIELD (J.), bookseller, Lion and Lamb, Whitechapel, 1703–4. His name appears in the Term Catalogue for Hil. 170$\frac{3}{4}$, as publishing divinity books. [*T.C.* III. 385, 395.]

SWALE (JOHN), bookseller in Leeds, 1714. One of the subscribers to Walker's *Sufferings of the Clergy*.

SWAYLE, or SWALLE (ABEL), *see Dictionary*, 1641–67.

SWINTON (PETER), printer and bookseller in Knutsford, 1684. In 1684 he printed the funeral sermon on Sir Robert Leicester of Tabley. [Cooke, *Bibl. Cestr.* p. 23 ; *N. & Q.*, 10th ser. v. 183.]

SWINTOUN (GEORGE), printer and bookseller in Edinburgh, 1649–83. *See Dictionary*, 1641–67. Swintoun appears to have continued till at least 1683. His name is found on the title page of a *Confession of Faith* of that date in the British Museum. [Ames III. 643.]

SWINTOUN (JOHN), printer in Edinburgh, 1675–81. Printed several books between these dates. In 1679 he was joined with Thomas Brown in printing two books. Swintoun was " one of His Majesties printers ". [Aldis, p. 121.]

SYMMONDS, SYMMONS, *see* Simmons.

SYMON (EDWARD), bookseller in London, corner of Pope's Head Alley, in Cornhill, 1720. Published the sixth edition of H. Phillip's *Purchaser's Pattern*, 1720.

SYMONDS, SYMONS, *see* Simmons.

SYMSON (ANDREW), printer and bookseller in Edinburgh, in the Cowgate, near the Foot of the Horse-Wynd, 1699–1706. Published the second edition of Sir George Mackenzie's *Laws of Scotland*, 1699. " In 1700 Mr. Matthias Simpson, a student in divinity, set up a small house ; but he, designing to prosecute his studies, left the house to his father, Mr. Andrew, one of the Suffering Clergy, who kept up the house till about a year ago [1712], that he died." [Watson, p. 18.] His *Tripatriarchicon ; or, the lives of . . . Abraham, Isaac and*

Jacob, which appeared in 1705, bears the imprint "Edinburgh: Printed by the Author"; and in 1706 *Some just Reflexions on a . . . Pasquill* came from his press with the date misprinted 1606. [Aldis, p. 121.]

T. (A.), printer in London, 1681. Printed a broadside in verse, *A Diaologue* [*sic*] *between the E. of Sh—— and L. Bell—— in the Tower, concerning the Plot*, 1681. [B.M. C. 20. f. 6 (20).]

TABB (L.), *see* Bixou.

TAILER (THOMAS), bookseller in Oxford, 1684–91. [Madan, p. 31.]

TANNER (PETER), stationer in London, Middle Temple Lane, 1691–9. In 1691 he was sued by the Rev. Roger Rogerson for a debt of £33. [C.P.R. Mich. 3 W. & M. 3101, m. 117 r.] His name occurs in connexion with a money-lending office in the *Post Boy* of March 4th, 1699.

TAYLOR, *see also* Tailor.

TAYLOR ( ), bookseller of Whitchurch, Salop, 1700–19. Sold school books and devotional works, which he bought wholesale from John Minshull of Chester (*q.v.*). [*Library*, 2nd ser. IV. 373–83.] He subscribed to Walker's *Sufferings of the Clergy* in 1714, and in 1719 he was one of those who received subscriptions for R. Bradley's *Philosophical Account of the Works of Nature.*

TAYLOR (JOHN), bookseller in London, Globe, (1) at the West End of St. Paul's Churchyard, 1683–7; (2) Ship, St. Paul's Churchyard, 1687–1713. 1683–1713. One of the largest publishers of the period; the references under his name in the Term Catalogues, beginning in Mich. 1683 [*T.C.* II. 55], are very numerous. In 1687 he moved to Benjamin Tooke's premises, the Ship in St. Paul's Churchyard. About 1700 he took his son William into partnership, but in 1711 William set up for himself in Paternoster Row. John Taylor was a contributor to the Bowyer fund in 1713; but the date of his death is unknown. Dunton [p. 207] wrote of him: "Mr. John Taylor deals very much and is very honest. . . . His principles are moderate." Timperley [p. 588] says that he instituted an annual sermon at the Baptist Church in Lincoln's Inn Fields, to commemorate his escape from death in the great storm of 1703.

TAYLOR (RANDAL), *see Dictionary*, 1641–67. Still in business in 1700. [*T.C.* III. 170.]

TAYLOR (THOMAS), bookseller in London, (1) next door to the Beehive on London Bridge, 1671; (2) Hand and Bible in the New Buildings on London Bridge, 1673–6. 1671–6. In Mich. 1671 he advertised Hodder's *Arithmetick.* [*T.C.* I. 91.] In Easter 1673 he used his second address, which may describe the same house. [*T.C.* I. 235.] He dealt chiefly in theology. He is referred to by Dunton [p. 292] as "Bridge" Taylor.

TAYLOR (WILLIAM), bookseller in London, (1) Ship in St. Paul's Churchyard; (2) Ship in Paternoster Row. 1700–23. Son of John Taylor. Joined his father in the business in St. Paul's Churchyard about 1700. Made his first entry in the Term Catalogue in 1710. He moved to the Ship in Paternoster Row in 1711, and afterwards took the adjoining premises. He is best remembered as the publisher in 1719 of Defoe's *Robinson Crusoe,* by which he is said to have cleared £1,000. He died in 1723, and appointed as one of his executors John Osborne; the latter induced his son-in-law Thomas Longman (*q.v.*) to purchase the business, which is still flourishing, and still uses the device of the Ship.

TEBB (THOMAS), bookseller in London, Duck Lane, near Little Britain, 1708–15. In the *Daily Courant* for November 10th, 1707, Tebb advertised an edition of Lilly's *Grammar,* and in 1708 he published for John Jackson a translation of Aesop, with cuts from the Frankfort edition. [*T.C.* III. 597.] Hazlitt [I. 5] records a book with his imprint, dated 1715.

TERRY (JOHN), bookseller in London, Three Swans, Paternoster Row, 1689. Only known from an advertisement of Dr. Manton's *Three Volumes of Sermons,* published in this year by Thomas Parkhurst and J. Robinson.

TERRY (ROBERT), bookseller in London, 1710–11. Advertised a sale of books by auction in the *Daily Courant* of January 13th, 17$\frac{10}{11}$.

TERRY (SAMUEL), printer at Liverpool; Dale Street, Cork; and Limerick. 1712–25. First heard of in 1712 as printing Charles Owen's *Hymns* for Birchall at Liverpool. In the same year he commenced *The Liverpoole Courant.* He was still in Liverpool in 1720 [Allnutt, p. 299], but he is found printing in Cork in 1721 and perhaps in 1722. He is then found at Limerick in this latter year, and in 1723, probably printing two works in partnership with L. Bixou *alias* Tabb, and again alone in 1725, when he printed a sermon by the Bishop of Limerick. The principal items from his Cork press were *Pietas Corcagiensis,*

or a view of the Green-Coat Hospital, with plates [Bodl. Ireland, 141], an edition of Dr. Bisse's *Beauty of Holiness in the Common Prayer,* and an edition of Puckle's *Club.*

TERRY (T.), bookseller in London, without Newgate, 1687. Published John Smith's *Compendium of Fair Writing* in that year. [*T.C.* II. 200.]

THACKERAY (THOMAS), bookseller in London, 1693. One of four booksellers publishing a chapbook, John Booker's *Dutch Fortune-Teller,* in 1693. [*T.C.* II. 487.] In Arber's Index the entry is given in error to W. Thackeray. He also published two ballads, *A Warning for Married Women* and *Doctor Faustus,* with A. M[ilbourn] and W. O[nley]. [B.M. C. 22 f. 6 (24, 132).] Son of W. Thackeray (?).

THACKERAY (WILLIAM), bookseller in London, (3) Angel in Duck Lane, 1664–92. *See Dictionary,* 1641–67. Still publishing in 1692. [*T.C.* II. 415.] He moved to this (his third) address some time between 1669 [*T.C.* I. 15] and 1675 [*T.C.* I. 218]; in the intervening years he gives his address in the Term Catalogues simply as "in Duck Lane". The mass of his publications consisted of ballads and other chapbooks; they were published by a syndicate in which he was a partner, and were not advertised in the Term Catalogues. T. Passenger, F. Coles, T. Vere, J. Wright and J. Clarke were the other regular members; W. Whitwood appears more seldom. An advertisement of books sold by Thackeray appears at the end of Forde's *Montelion,* 1687. Succeeded by T. Thackeray (*q.v.*)?

THOMAS (EDWARD), *see Dictionary,* 1641–67.

THOMAS (HUGH), bookseller of St. Asaph, 1699. Sold grammars and devotional works which he purchased wholesale of John Minshull of Chester. [*Library,* 2nd ser. IV. 373–83.]

THOMAS (JOHN), printer in London, 1681. Defendant in an action for trespass and assault brought by Bartholomew Sprint. [C.P.R. Trin. 33 Chas. II, 2992, m. 256 r.]

THOMPSON, *see also* Tompson, and Tomson.

THOMPSON (J.), bookseller at Mansfield, 1703. Published an edition of *Cynthia,* a novel. [*T.C.* III. 376.]

THOMPSON (J.), printer in London, in the Strand, 1725. Printed a series of broadsides relating to the trial of Jonathan Wild. [Haz. I. 455.]

THOMPSON (MARY), printer in London, 1688. Widow of Nathaniel Thompson (*q.v.*). Printed for the Roman Catholics A. Pulton's *Reflections upon the anonymous Author and the Licenser of . . . The Missioner's Arts Discovered,* 1688. [B.M. T. 1839 (3).]

THOMPSON (NATHANIEL), printer and bookseller (?) in Dublin and London, (1) next the Cross Keys in Fetter Lane; (2) at the entrance into the Old Spring Garden, near Charing Cross. 1666–88. *See Dictionary,* 1641–67. Printer for the Nonconformists, and also for the Roman Catholics. In 1673 he is found in London printing a Romanist book in partnership with T. Ratcliffe. [*T.C.* I. 136.] He was constantly in trouble with the Company. In 1676 he was committed to Newgate for printing seditious pamphlets. In 1677 the Company ordered that he should be indicted at the next Quarter Sessions for printing part of a Mass Book in French. [Records of the Stationers' Company.] In the Report of the Proceedings of the House of Lords Committee in February 167$\frac{8}{9}$ it was stated that Thompson had printed a pamphlet, *The Long Parliament Dissolved,* the type having been examined with Thompson's types and found to agree in everything. [Hist. MSS. Comm., Report 9, App., pp. 69–78.] He next started a news-sheet called *Domestick Intelligence,* but in 1679 he altered the title to *The True Domestick Intelligence.* It was a rival sheet to that issued by Benjamin Harris, with whom Thompson was always at war. In 1680 he was committed to the Gatehouse for being privy to the conspiracy of the apprentices to levy war against the King [*Protestant Domestic Intelligence,* April 2, 1680], and in 1684 he was again in trouble for printing *The Prodigal Returned Home.* An account of the proceedings against him on that occasion was published as a broadside by A. Banks. [B.M. 515. l. 2 (94).] In 1686 *The Compleat Dancing Master* was announced [*T.C.* II. 167–8] as printed for him; it is doubtful whether this implies that he was a bookseller. Thompson was dead in 1688, when the Stationers' Company ordered his widow to lay down the trade of printing in obedience to the Act of Parliament. [Records of the Company of Stationers.]

THOMPSON (SAMUEL), *see Dictionary,* 1641–67.

THOMPSON (WILLIAM), printer in Stamford, 1717; and in Bury St. Edmunds, 1719. 1717–19. With Thomas Bailey he printed the *Stamford Mercury.* [Allnutt, pp. 299, 303.]

THOMSON (PETER), bookbinder in Aberdeen, 1698–9. A payment to him is recorded in the Marischal College accounts for 1698–9. [J. P. Edmond, *Aberdeen Press*, LV; Aldis, p. 121.]

THORN (NATHANIEL), bookseller in Exeter, St. Peter's Churchyard, 1717 (?)–71. Began to publish about the year 1717, when he issued *A Sermon Preach'd in Ely Chappel at the Consecration of . . . Lancelot, Lord Bishop of Exeter, . . .* February 24, $17\frac{16}{17}$, by William Rayner. [Dredge, p. 45.] In 1722 he was one of the publishers of Izacke's *Remarkable Antiquities of the City of Exeter*. He married Mary Simpson by licence dated February 1st, $172\frac{7}{8}$. [Dredge, p. 101.] He was still in business in 1771.

THORNCOMB (ANDREW), bookseller in London, 1685. In 1685 he printed Rochester's *Poems*. [Haz. II. 520.] In 1686 he was in Boston, Mass. Dunton met with him there and has recorded [pp. 97–8] a favourable impression of him. He is probably also the same person mentioned by Dunton [p. 293] as "musical" Thorncomb.

THORNICROFT (THOMAS), bookseller in London, Sun, St. Paul's Churchyard, 1663–72. *See Dictionary*, 1641–67. In business till 1672; in this and the preceding year he advertised two books from this third address. [*T.C.* I. 89, 98.]

THORNTON (JETHRO), bookseller in Derby, 1675. Only known from the appearance of his name in an advertisement of a stolen horse. [*London Gazette*, January 6th–10th, $167\frac{5}{6}$.]

THORNTON (ROBERT), bookseller and printer in Dublin, 1682–1701. First appears as a stationer or bookseller in Dublin in 1682, where the Dublin edition of Dryden's *Medal* was printed for him. He published in September to December 1685 *The News Letter*, and in 1691 *The Dublin Intelligence*. In 1692 he appears as a printer, with *The Civil Articles of Lymerick*. In 1693 he was "stationer to their Majesties".

THORP, or THORPE (GEORGE), bookseller in Banbury, 1703–6. Successor to William Thorpe. His first entry in the Term Catalogues was a sermon by Benjamin Loveling, Vicar of Banbury, preached on December 3rd, 1702, and published early in 1703.

THORP, or THORPE (WILLIAM), bookseller in Banbury, 1682–95. In 1682 he published a sermon by J. Knight called *The Samaritan Rebels Perjured* [B.M. 1358. c. 3], in 1686 Edward Pocock's translation of *Hai Ebn Yockdan*

[*T.C.* II. 166], and in 1694 *The Husbandman's Manual*. [*T.C.* II. 517.] He was succeeded by his son George.

THOURSTON, *see* Thurston.

THRALE (BENJAMIN), bookseller in London, Bible, (*a*) Poultry, near Cheapside, (*b*) at the lower end of Cheapside, 1677–9. Perhaps son of Richard Thrale. In 1677 and 1679 he advertised two cheap and ephemeral books. [*T.C.* I. 292, 345.]

THRALE (RICHARD), bookseller in London, in Bishopsgate, 1650–73. *See Dictionary*, 1641–67. Is found still in business in 1673 in Bishopsgate, where he had published before 1668 with James Thrale (*q.v.* in *Dictionary*, 1641–67). [*T.C.* I. 60, 133, 138.]

THURLBURN, or THURLBOURNE (RICHARD), bookseller in Cambridge, 1707–24. His name appears on Robert Cannon's *Sermon before the Queen at Newmarket*, Cambridge, 1707; and S. White's *Commentary on Isaiah*, 1708, and as receiving subscribers' names for *Corpus Omnium Veterum Poet. Lat.*, in 1709. [Bowes, *Cambridge Books*, no. 375; *T.C.* II. 613, III. 659.] He was witness to a conveyance of property in 1724, now preserved in the University Registry.

THURLBURN, or THURLBOURNE (WILLIAM), bookseller in Cambridge, 1724–68. His name appears on books from 1724. [Bowes, *Cambridge Books*, no. 419.] In 1729 he succeeded Edmund Jeffery, bookseller (*q.v.*), at what is now No. 1 Trinity Street, and moved in 1757 to No. 2, where he remained until his death in 1768. He was succeeded at No. 1 by William Woodyer, bookseller. Both houses were purchased by Thurlburn in 1737. One of his daughters married James Essex, jun., the architect and builder. [*See D.N.B.*]

THURSTON, or THOURSTON (JAMES), bookseller in Nantwich, 1684. His name appears in the imprint to Zachary Cawdrey's funeral sermon on Lord Delamer, entitled *The Certainty of Salvation*, 1684. [B.M. 4902. cc. 2; *T.C.* II. 93.]

THURSTON (MATHIAS), bookseller in Nantwich, 1682–8. In 1688 he was sued by Lawrence Baskervile, for a debt for goods supplied to him in 34 & 35 Chas II. [C.P.R. East. 3 Jas. II, 3056, m. 409 v.]

TIDMARSH (SAMUEL), bookseller in London, King's Head in Sweeting's Alley End, next house to the Royal Exchange in Cornhill, 1679–89. Made

his first entry in the Term Catalogues in Trin. 1678. [*T.C.* I. 322.] Chiefly a publisher of the usual divinity, but in 1681 he published Dr. J. Peter's treatise on certain mineral springs near Lewisham. [*T.C.* I. 450.] In 1689 he published a third edition of Peter's *Artificial Versifying, a new way to make Latin verses*. [*T.C.* II. 280.] Referred to by Dunton [p. 292] as "travelling" Tidmarsh, no doubt because he attended country fairs.

TILLET (THOMAS), bookbinder at Cambridge, 1695–1702. In 1695 he bound copies of *Lachrymae Cantabrigienses in Obitum . . . Reginae Mariae*, printed at Cambridge by John Hayes, $169\frac{4}{5}$, the fine paper copies in velvet, satin, and vellum, the ordinary copies in vellum or merely stitched. He also bound the University Verses of 1698, also printed by Hayes, and the Verses of 1702, printed by Crownfield.

TILLIER (T.), printer (?) and bookseller in Chester, 1688. Randle Holme, Chester Herald, published in 1688 his *Academy of Armory*, in which appear certain verses signed "T. Tillier, Typog." Holme [III. 484] gives the arms of Tillier as "a Talaria or Mercuries Shooe Sable, Winged Argent, in a Field Azure." A broadside entitled *An Account of a late Horrid and Bloody Massacre in Ireland* has the imprint "London: Printed for T. Tillier, 1688." [Allnutt, pp. 293–4; Bodl.]

TILLOTSON (J.), bookseller in London, 1690. Only known as having published two sermons by Archbishop John Tillotson in that year. The relationship, if any, between the bookseller and the archbishop has not been traced.

TODD ( ), printer in London, Fleet Street, 1724. Classed by Negus as a "highflier".

TOMLINS (RICHARD), bookseller in London, (3) in Giltspur Street, 1670; (4) Bible, St. Paul's Churchyard, 1672. 1637–72. *See Dictionary*, 1641–67. Was still publishing in Easter 1672. [*T.C.* I. 106.]

TOMLINSON ( ), widow, bookseller in Liverpool and Warrington, 1685. Her name occurs in a list of booksellers and stationers at the end of M. Bromfield's *A Brief Discovery of the . . . Scurvy*, 1685, as agent for a patent medicine. [*N. & Q.* 11th ser. XI. 45.]

TOMPSON, *see also* Thompson.

TOMPSON ( ), bookseller in London, Westminster Hall, 1689. His name occurs in an advertisement of patent medicines in the *London Gazette* of December 26th, 1689.

TOMPSON (DANIEL), printer in Dublin, Coles Alley, Castle Street, 1714–15. Four or five books printed by him are extant, one being Thomas Sheridan's Latin Grammar.

TOMPSON (RICHARD), bookseller in London, Sun, Bedford Street, 1669. *See Dictionary*, 1641–67. Sold Alexander Browne's *Ars Pictoria*. He may be identical with — Tompson, bookseller, who had a stall in Westminster Hall some years later. The second address given by Arber [*T.C.* I. Index] is evidently a confusion with R. Tonson, who carried on business under Gray's Inn Gate.

TOMSON, or THOMPSON (WILLIAM), bookseller in [Market] Harborough, 1655–69. *See Dictionary*, 1641–67. In 1669 he published Joseph Bentham's *Disswasive from Error much Increased*.

TONGE (GEORGE), bookseller in Warwick, 1682. In this year Evan Tyler of London (*q.v.*) left him £50.

TONSON (JACOB) I, bookseller in London, (1) Judge's Head in Chancery Lane, near Fleet Street, 1678–98; (2) in Gray's Inn Gate, next Gray's Inn Lane, 1700–10; (3) Shakespeare's Head, opposite Catherine Street in the Strand, 1710–20. 1677–1720. Younger brother of Richard Tonson (*q.v.*) and second son of Jacob Tonson, "a barber-surgeon in Holborn". He served his apprenticeship with Thomas Basset, to whom he was articled in 1670, and took up his freedom on December 20th, 1677. He settled at once at the Judge's Head, and in Hil. 1678 shared with his brother and with Bentley and Magnes the publication of Préchac's novel, *The Heroin Musqueteer*, his name only appearing on the third and fourth volumes. [*T.C.* I. 300, 320, 330; Esdaile, p. 291.] He soon began to publish plays, and in 1679, with Abel Swalle, of whom a probably fabulous tradition asserts that he borrowed the purchase money, he published his first book for Dryden, *Troilus and Cressida*. In 1684 he started the celebrated *Miscellany Poems*, edited and largely written by Dryden, and commonly called *Tonson's Miscellany*. Another very important acquisition by Tonson was *Paradise Lost*, which he purchased in two instalments in 1683 and 1690. Between 1698 and 1700 [*T.C.* III. 57, 171] he moved from Chancery Lane to Gray's Inn Gate, no doubt succeeding his brother, whose name disappears from the Term Catalogues in 1689. The latter's son Jacob probably joined his uncle now; he had possibly been latterly keeping up a retail business at Gray's Inn Gate. Tonson followed up his earlier successes by publishing for the rising school of literary men. In 1705 he published *Remarks on Several Parts of Italy* for Addison, whom he had met in Holland; Steele seems to have acted for him as a "publisher's reader". He also published *Cato*, 1713. In 1709 he secured Pope's Pastorals for his sixth *Miscellany*. From about 1700 he was secretary to the newly founded literary Kitcat Club, and it shortly took to meeting at his house. In 1710 he made his second move, to the Strand. [*Tatler*, October 14th.] He retired about 1720, in favour of his nephew, and lived till 1737 at Ledbury. Tonson was accused by Dryden of meanness, and is caricatured by him in the well-known lines:

> With leering look, bull-fac'd, and freckled fair
> With two left legs, with Judas-coloured hair,
> And frowzy pores, that taint the ambient air.

Dunton comments [p. 216] on the harshness of Tonson's critical judgements. [*D.N.B.*; Nichols, *Lit. Anecd.* I. 292–5.]

TONSON (JACOB) II, bookseller, bookbinder and printer in London, (1) Gray's Inn Gate; (2) Shakespeare's Head, opposite Catherine Street in the Strand, 1700 (?)–35. Nephew of Jacob Tonson I (*q. v.*), and probably son of Richard. He may have succeeded his father soon after 1689, but is first known as in partnership with his uncle after 1700. It was Jacob II who in 1712 bought half the rights in the *Spectator*, vols. i–vii, from Addison and Steele. In or about 1720 he succeeded his uncle, and continued to publish important literary works for Steele, Pope, Theobald, &c. From his will it appears that he was a bookbinder, a stationer and a printer, as well as a bookseller; his printing business was in partnership with John Watts, in Covent Garden they are given as "well-affected" by Negus in 1724. He died on December 2nd, 1735, and was succeeded by his son Jacob III. [*D.N.B.*; Nichols, *Lit. Anecd.* I. 295–7.]

TONSON (RICHARD), bookseller in London, Gray's Inn Gate, 1675–89 (?). Elder brother of Jacob Tonson I. Made his first entry in the Term Catalogues in Hil. 1675 with a duodecimo, *The Courtiers Calling*. [*T.C.* I. 198.] In 1676 he published Otway's tragedy *Don Carlos*, and in the following year the same author's *Titus and Berenice* and Charles Davenant's *Circe, a Tragedy*. In 1678 in company with his brother Jacob he published Mrs. Behn's comedy *Sir Patient Fancy*. He also published several law-books. In 1683 a list of the brothers' joint publications is found in *An Account of De Quesne's Expedition*. He is last heard of in Easter 1689. [*T.C.* II. 263]. Jacob Tonson took over

the shop between 1698 and 1700; possibly Richard had only left publishing to his brother and confined himself to retail bookselling.

TOOK ( ), printer in London, Old Bailey, 1724. Classed by Negus as a "highflier".

TOOKE (BENJAMIN) I, printer in Dublin, 1669–85 (?); bookseller in London (1) Anchor, Duck Lane, 1669; (2) Ship, St. Paul's Churchyard, 1670– ; (3) Middle Temple Gate, Fleet Street. 1669–1716. According to Timperley, this celebrated bookseller was born about 1642, and is supposed to have been the son of the Rev. Thomas Tuke, vicar of St. Olave's, Old Jewry; but the bookseller always spelt his name as Took or Tooke. He served his apprenticeship with John Crooke, and was admitted a freeman of the Company of Stationers in February 166$\frac{5}{6}$. He succeeded Crooke in 1669 as King's Printer in Dublin, and, like him, combined the office with bookselling in London. The last entry in the Term Catalogues of a book printed by him in Dublin was made in 1685. He began as a London bookseller by advertising two books, one in partnership with George Sawbridge, from the Anchor in Duck Lane, in 1669; in the next year he moved to St. Paul's Churchyard, where his business rapidly throve. He is best remembered as Dean Swift's bookseller, and through Swift's good offices he obtained several offices of profit, including that of Printer to the Queen in 1713. He also published for other leading men of letters in Ireland. In 1689 he was junior warden of the Company of Stationers, and was for some years Clerk of the Company and Treasurer from 1677 to 1702, when he resigned in favour of Joseph Collyer. He was one of the largest publishers of the time, and held shares in all the most important undertakings. He died in 1716, leaving a son Benjamin to carry on the business.

TOOKE (BENJAMIN) II, bookseller in London, Middle Temple Gate, Fleet Street, 1703–23. Son and successor to Benjamin Tooke I. Dunton [p. 212] speaks well of him, and adds "near Temple Bar" to his name; he was therefore probably already in partnership with his father. "He died May 24th, 1723, leaving a considerable estate to his younger brother Andrew Tooke, who was for many years Master of the Charterhouse Schools." [Nichols, *Lit. Anecd.*, III. 627.]

TOOKER (ARTHUR), bookseller in London, Globe and Half Moon, Strand, *a*) near the New Exchange, (*b*) over against Salisbury House, (*c*) over against

Ivy Bridge, 1669–80. Associated with R. Tompson in the publication of Alexander Browne's *Ars Pictoria* in 1669. (B.M. copy has his engraved trade label.) In 1680 he was selling a *Travelling Map of England*. [*T.C.* I. 405.]

TOOKEY (R.), printer in London, behind the Royal Exchange, 1695 (?)–1724. Dunton [pp. 250, 696] referred to him as a "pretty modest obliging Printer". He contributed one guinea to the Bowyer fund in 1713, and is mentioned by Negus in 1724 as "well-affected".

TOOTH (BARBER), bookseller in London, near York House in the Strand, 1673. Published *The Citizen's Companion*, 1673. [*T.C.* I. 153; Haz. I. 96.]

TRACY (EBENEZER), bookseller in London, Three Bibles on London Bridge, 1695–1719. Successor to Thomas Passinger the Second. Began publishing in 1695. [*T.C.* II. 547.] Published many ballads, chapbooks and nautical manuals. He was also the proprietor of a patent medicine called the "Balsam of Chili", the virtues of which he set out in a pamphlet published in 1696. [*T.C.* II. 579.] In 17$\frac{14}{15}$ he paid a fine of £12 for exemption from serving the office of churchwarden of St. Magnus. He was succeeded by his sons H. and J. Tracy. There was another house called the Three Bibles, "the corner house of the square, about the middle of London Bridge", occupied by John Stuart, stationer, who dealt in playing cards and wall-papers, and who also sold a "Balsam of Chili", in rivalry with the Tracys.

TRENCH (DAVID), *see Dictionary*, 1641–67.

TUCKYR (ROGER), bookseller in London, Golden Leg, the corner of Salisbury Street, in the Strand, 1700. Published the third edition of Joseph Glanvil's *Saducismus Triumphatus*, 1700.

TURNER (JOSEPH), bookseller in Sheffield, 1701–15. Published *The Silvan Dream or, The Mourning Muses, a Poem*, 1701. The author is believed to have been John Philips, who was probably a Sheffield man. [B.M. 11631. h. 4.] In 1715 he published for J. and J. Green the third edition of *A Collection of choice Psalm Tunes*; it was printed for him by W. Ayscough at Nottingham. [Creswell, p. 14.]

TURNER (MATTHEW), bookseller in London (*a*) near Turnstile, in Holborn, (*b*) Holy Lamb in Holborn, (*c*) near Turnstile, 1673–93. His name first appears in the Term Catalogue for 1673. In 1678 he is found publishing Ravenscroft's *King Edgar and Alfreda*. His name is mentioned in the course of the trial

of Francis West for selling a book called *The Errata to the Protestant Bible, or the truth of the English Translation examined*. [*Proceedings . . . in the Old Bayly, on . . . the 12th . . . of October 1693*; B.M. 515. b. 2 (152).] His three addresses probably refer to the same house.

TURNER (ROBERT), bookseller in London, Star, St. Paul's Churchyard, 1676. Sold a pack of cards representing the counties of England and Wales. [*T.C.* I. 247.]

TURNER (WILLIAM), bookseller in London, (1) Rose and Crown, without Temple-Bar; (2) White Horse, without Temple Bar; (3) Angel at Lincoln's Inn Back Gate. 1696–1705. In partnership with F. Mills. Their names are found in 1696 in the imprint to the English translation of Le Maire's *Voyages to the Canary Islands*. In 1703 he published two plays, *The Stolen Heiress* and Cibber's *She wou'd and She wou'd not*. [*T.C.* III. 336.] In 1705 Dr. Samuel Cobb's poem on the Duke of Marlborough's victories, entitled *Honour Retrieved*, was published by Turner as well as several plays. His last entry in the Term Catalogues was a comedy called the *Basset Table*, in 1705. [*T.C.* III. 482.] He was at the Angel by 1703.

TUTHILL (J.), bookseller in Great Yarmouth, 1678. Publisher of *The Victory of Faith over Satan . . . in . . . the Life and Death of Hannah Purgal*. [*T.C.* I. 309.] Probably the John Tuthill of 1661 (See *Dictionary* 1641–67).

TWYFORD (HENRY), *see Dictionary*, 1641–67.

TYLER (EVAN), printer and bookseller in Edinburgh, Leith and London, 1633–82. *See Dictionary*, 1641–67. At the Restoration Tyler once more returned to Edinburgh, and printed there from 1660 to 1672, when he finally left Scotland, and A. Anderson succeeded him as Royal Printer. He returned to London and was Master of the Company of Stationers in 1671. He died December 5th, 1682; in his will, proved December 29th, he left £50 to George Tonge of Warwick, bookseller. Tyler is there described as "printer and bookseller".

TYTON (FRANCIS), *see Dictionary*, 1641–67.

UNETT (ANN), bookseller in Wolverhampton, 1714. Widow and successor of George Unett.

UNETT (GEORGE), bookseller in Wolverhampton, 1691 (?)–1714. Succeeded R. Grosvenor, and succeeded by his widow, Ann Unett (*q. v.*). [Information kindly supplied by Mr. G. P. Mander.]

UNETT (RICHARD), bookseller in Ridware Hamstall, Staffordshire, 1681. Had a son Richard, born at Hamstall Ridware or Ridware Hamstall, and admitted to St. John's College, Cambridge, on June 2nd, 1681. [J. E. B. Mayor, *Admissions to St. John's College, Cambridge*, II. 83.]

UNSWORTH (ANN), bookseller in Manchester, 1696. Henry Pendlebury's series of sermons entitled *Invisible Realites*, 1696, was printed for her in London. [B.M. 4453. b. 18 (1).]

UNWIN (MATTHEW), printer in Birmingham, 1716–17; and in Leicester, 1741. 1716–41. [Allnutt, pp. 300, 303.]

VADE (JAMES), bookseller in London, Cock and Sugar Loaf, Fleet Street, 1677–81. Began publishing in 1677. [*T.C.* I. 296.] For Edward Ravenscroft he published a comedy called *The English Lawyer* in 1678 and in the next year no less than eighty pamphlets on the Popish Plot. In 1681 Vade was defendant in the action for assault brought by Bartholomew Sprint, bookseller, against a number of printers and booksellers in London and Oxford. [C.P.R. Trin. 33 Chas. II, 2992, m. 256.]

VAILLANT (PAUL), bookseller in London, over against Bedford House in the Strand, 1686 (?)–1739. "Paul Vaillant was of a respectable Protestant family at Samur in the French province of Anjou. At the time of the Revocation of the Edict of Nantes he escaped and in 1686 settled as a foreign bookseller in the Strand, opposite Southampton Street, where himself, his sons Paul and Isaac, his grandson [Paul II died February 1st, 1802], and Mr. Elmsly successively carried on the same trade in the same house till nearly the end of the eighteenth century." [Timperley, p. 811.] As Timperley is also the authority for the statement that Paul Vaillant died on October 14th, 1739, aged 67 years, and as Vaillant would only have been 14 in 1686, it seems more likely that 1696 was the date at which he opened his shop in the Strand. He began to use the Term Catalogues in Trin. 1707, when he was one of the publishers of John Mill's Greek Testament. [*T.C.* III. 557.]

VALLANGE, or VALLANCE (JOHN), bookseller in Edinburgh, (1) at the Plain-Stones; (2) on the North Side of the High Street a little above the Cross, 1691–1713 (?). In 1691 he was one of the publishers of J. Cockburn's *Eight Sermons*. Macqueen's *The Magistrate's Dignity, Duty and Danger*, 1693, was also to be sold by him, and his name appears in several other books down to at least 1708. He changed his house in or before 1701. The will of John Vallance of Chesters, bookseller, burgess of Edinburgh, was registered April 9th, 1713. [Aldis, p. 122.]

VAN HAEGHEN (FRANCIS), bookbinder and printer (?) in Aberdeen, before 1669. "Issobell Spens relict of the deceased Francis Vanhaggan, bookbinder in Aberdeen." [Register of Privy Council, Scotland, 1669, p. 45.] This may be the F. V. whose initials appear in James Leslie's Ὁ Αςτηρ [*sic*] Ὀρθρινὸς Ἀπολαμπεῖ, printed at Aberdeen in 1661. [J. P. Edmond, *Aberdeen Printers*, p. 214.]

VARENS (   ), bookseller in London, Seneca's Head, near Somerset House in the Strand, 1711. Sold the "True Cephalick and Head Snuff", and other patent medicines, according to an advertisement in *The Post Man*, January 11th, 17$\frac{11}{12}$.

VARNAM (THOMAS), bookseller in London, Lombard Street, 1711–25 (?). Was a nephew of John and Thomas Guy, and is mentioned in the will of the former. In partnership with J. Osborne he succeeded to Thomas Guy's business in Lombard Street, and his name is first found in the Term Catalogue of Easter 1711. [*T.C.* III. 675.] He subscribed to Walker's *Sufferings of the Clergy* in 1714.

VAUGHAN (CHARLES), bookseller in Bella (?) Wales, 1700. Sold grammars and devotional books, which he bought wholesale of John Minshull, bookseller of Chester. [*Library*, 2nd ser. IV. 373–83.]

VAUGHAN (ROGER), bookseller in London, (1) Little Britain, (2) Bishop's Court in the Old Bayly, 1673–7. In 1673 he sold with J. Williams, jun., *The Pope Shut out of Heaven's Gates*; he also published a pamphlet, entitled *The Northumberland Monster*. [B.M. 551. d. 18 (30).]

VERE (THOMAS), *see Dictionary*, 1641–67.

VEZEY (LAWRENCE), printer in London (?), 1720. Is mentioned in *The Original Weekly Journal* of June 25th, 1720, in connexion with the execution of John Matthews (*q.v.*). Two journeymen printers, William Phelps and Richard Riley, are also mentioned.

VINCENT (ROBERT), bookseller in London, Clifford's Inn Lane, Fleet Street, 1691–1713. Hazlitt records a book as published by Vincent in 1691. [Haz. III. 160.] In 1693 he published Wright's comedy, *The Female Virtuosos*. He was also a publisher of law-books. In 1713 his name occurs in the list of contributors to the Bowyer fund.

W. (H.), printer in London, 1699. He printed an edition of the New Testament for the Company of Stationers in 1699. [*T.C.* III. 142.]

WADE (S.), bookseller in London, Bible, under the Piazza of the Royal Exchange, Cornhill, 1693. His name appears in the Term Catalogue for Easter 1693 as one of those who sold John Shower's *Sacramental Discourses*. [*T.C.* II. 450.] The house was previously in the occupation of Ralph Smith.

WALBANCK (ELIZABETH), bookseller in London, (1) Southampton Court, Old Southampton Buildings, Gray's Inn, Holborn; (2) near the Three Tuns Tavern, Holborn. In Hil. 1674 she published *March's Actions for Slander*. [*T.C.* I. 165.] In 1677 she is mentioned in an advertisement of a house to let in *The London Mercury* of March 7th. [B.M. Burney, 99.] These two addresses may represent the same house as that occupied by George Walbanck.

WALBANCK (GEORGE), bookseller in London, near Gray's Inn Gate in Holborn, 1669. Possibly son and successor to Matthew Walbanck (1618–67). In Easter 1669 he advertised *An Address to the hopeful young Gentry of England*. [*T.C.* I. 10.] He was succeeded by Elizabeth Walbanck, perhaps his widow, in 1674. [*T.C.* I. 164.]

WALE (JEFFREY), bookseller in London, Angel, St. Paul's Churchyard, 1703–7. His name first appears in 1703 as publisher of the works of the Rev. J. Forbes. [*T.C.* III. 371.] He became bankrupt in 1707. [*London Gazette*, November 13th, 1707.]

WALFORD (BENJAMIN), bookseller and book-auctioneer in London, (1) The Bear in Ave-Mary Lane; (2) The Prince's Arms, St. Paul's Churchyard. 1689–1710 (?). Apprenticed to Robert Scott. When Scott sold his business to Adiel Mill, Walford continued in his service. In 1689 he began to sell books by auction at the Bear in Ave-Mary Lane; one of the largest libraries which came under his hammer is believed to have been that of Lord Maitland. [Nichols, *Lit. Anecd.* III. 665–6.] In 1691 he held a sale of books for the creditors of Adiel Mill (of whom Scott (*q. v.*) was probably the largest). [B.M. 821. i. 9 (16).] His name does not appear in the Term Catalogues until 1693, when he became publisher, with others, of *The Counter Scuffle*. He had then joined partnership at the Prince's Arms with S. Smith, publisher to the Royal Society, to which office Walford succeeded on Smith's death. They were among the leading publishers of the day. Walford retired from business or died between 1709 and 1711, being succeeded at the Prince's Arms by W. Innys. Dunton states (p. 207) that Walford "was a very ingenious man and knew books extraordinary well".

WALFORD (J.), bookseller in London, St. Paul's Churchyard, 1710. Publisher of a broadside for Sacheverell in 1710. [B.M. T. 100* (232).] This may be a printer's error for B. Walford.

WALKER (MATHIAS), bookseller in London, under St. Dunstan's Church in Fleetstreet, 1672. Only known as the publisher of Sir Christopher Wyvill's *Pretensions of the Triple Crown examined* in 1672. [*T.C.* I. 120.]

WALKER (OBADIAH), printer in Oxford, University College, 1687–8. The Roman Catholic Master of University College. Shortly before Bishop Fell's death in 1686 Walker asked him for the control of the University Press, but Fell replied that "he would first part with his bed from under him". In spite of this, Fell bequeathed his patent for printing to Walker and two others. In May of that year Walker procured a Royal licence to print some forty Romanist books. According to Wood he had Abraham Woodhead's *Two Discourses*, 1687, "printed at Lichfield's, and some scholars . . . getting the book sheet by sheet . . . [there] came out an answer to it in a month following. Whereupon Mr. Walker being sensible that he was falsly dealt with, he set up a press in his owne lodgings (the back part of Univ. Coll.) and there printed Church Government (part 5)." The practical printer who worked this press was Henry Cruttenden (*q. v.*). At the Revolution Walker fled, but was arrested before leaving England. He died in 1699. [Wood, III. 198, 209, 218–21, 282, &c.; Hist. MSS. Comm., Report 7, App., pp. 691–2; Madan, p. 19; *D.N.B.*]

WALKER (R.), bookseller in London, under Gray's Inn Gate, Holborn, 1676. Only known as the publisher of *Modus transferendi Status*, 1676. [*T.C.* I. 259.]

WALL (FRANCIS), bookseller in Bristol, on the Tolzey, 1721. Probably son or grandson of Thomas Wall. Only known from his name appearing in W. C. B.'s list of provincial booksellers. [*N. & Q.*, 11th ser. I. 304.]

WALL (THOMAS), bookseller in Bristol, (*a*) Tolzey, (*b*) Corn Street, near the Tolzey, 1660–79. *See Dictionary*, 1641–67. In 1673 he published a map of Bristol. [*T.C.* I. 135.] Dunton [p. 236] says, "He is well accomplished for his trade, which is very considerable. He was first a Goldsmith but made an exchange of that way for this of bookselling. . . . For those two years that I kept Bristol Fair, I was treated very kindly at his house."

WALLIS (JOHN), printer in London, (*a*) near the Green Dragon in Fleet Street (*b*) Whitefriars, 1682–1700. Printer of broadsides and news-sheets. In 1682 he printed for Randal Taylor a sheet headed *A Description of His Majesties True and Loyal Subjects scandalously called Toreys* [Haz. II. 600], and in 1683, for Joanna Brome, *Remarks on the Preface to the Protestant Reconciler.* [B.M. T. 1030 (7).] In 1688 he appears as printer of *A New Fairing for the merrily disposed or, the Comical History of . . . W. Phill——.* [Bagford (Harl. 5961); Haz. II. 458.] In the same year he became the printer of *The Universal Intelligence* (no. 1, Tuesday, December 11th, 1688) [Burney, 96], and for Anne Marriott he printed about the same time *The London Intelligence.*

WALLUP (G.), bookseller in London, 1690. Only known from the imprint to a poem, *Caesarem & Fortunam vehis*, 1690. [B.M. C. 40. m. 11 (1).]

WALSALL (SAMUEL), bookseller in London, (1) Golden Frying Pan, Leadenhall Street, 1680–4; (2) Heart and Bible, near the West-end of the Royal Exchange in Cornhill, 1684–5. 1680–5. Began to publish in 1680 with *A Translation of the Sixth Book of Mr. Cowley's Plantarum.* [*T.C.* I. 394.] His later books were chiefly in divinity. His last entry in the Term Catalogues was in Mich. 1685. [*T.C.* II. 142.]

WALTER (J.), bookseller in London, (1) Hand and Pen, next the White Hart Inn, in High Holborn, near Drury Lane; (2) Golden Ball in Pye Corner. 1700(?). Publisher of chap-books, e.g. *The New Year's Garland, The Merchant Lady's Garland* [Bodl. Douce PP. 183], and *The . . . History of Titus Andronicus.*

WALTHOE (JOHN), bookseller in London, (1) Black Lion, Chancery Lane, (*a*) over against, or near, Lincoln's Inn, (*b*) over against St. John's Head Tavern, 1683–8; (2) Vine Court, Middle Temple, adjoining to the Cloisters, 1690– ; (3) Pump Court, Middle Temple Cloister; and in Stafford. 1683–1733. Began publishing in Mich. 1683. [*T.C.* II. 50.] In 1684 he published two novels from the French entitled *The Triumph of Friendship* and *The Force of Love* [*T.C.* II. 96], and from that time onward he continued to be a prominent publisher of similar books. Dunton, however [p. 208], who speaks very well of him, does not mention these, but notes that " he prints and deals much in Law Books ". Walthoe contributed five guineas to the Bowyer

fund, and was in business as late as the year 1733. He moved from Chancery Lane to Vine Court between 1688 and 1690. [*T.C.* II. 238, 342.] As he gave very vague and abbreviated descriptions of his quarters in the Temple it is difficult to decide when he made his second change.

WALTON (ROBERT), printer in London, Globe (and Compasses) in St. Paul's Churchyard, 1647–87. *See Dictionary*, 1641–67. He was still in business in 1687. [*T.C.* II. 200.] An advertisement of " several things made and sold " by him is in Bodl. [Gough Maps, 46, fol. 169.]

WALWYN (HERBERT), bookseller in London, Three Legs in the Poultry, (*a*) over against, (*b*) in, the Stocks Market, (*c*) at the corner of the Old Jewry, 1698–1702. First appears in 1698, as one of the publishers of John Conant's *Sermons.* [*T.C.* III. 62.] He was the author of *Poems on several Occasions*, 1699. [B.M. 11633. df. 20.] Dunton [p. 218] praises Walwyn's poetical powers in extravagant terms, and adds that he was well informed on many subjects and clever at " forming of titles ".

WARD (JOHN), bookseller in Leicester, 1711–19. In company with William Ward, bookseller in Nottingham, perhaps his father or brother, he sold Henry Felton's funeral sermon on the Duke of Rutland, preached February 23rd, 17$\frac{10}{11}$. [*T.C.* III. 662.] He was still there in 1719.

WARD (ROBERT), printer in York, 1725. With John White he set up a press in opposition to Gent's, and printed a rival newspaper. *The York Courant.* [Gent, pp. 160–3.]

WARD (THOMAS), bookseller in London, Inner Temple Lane, 1711–20. Published a *History of the reign of Q. Anne*, 1711, and also was one of the booksellers who sold the second edition of John Brightland's *Grammar of the English Tongue* in that year. [*T.C.* III. 675.] In 1720 he was one of the publishers of the *Works* of Machiavelli. [Esdaile, p. 264.]

WARD (WILLIAM), printer and bookseller in Nottingham, 1710–38. His first known publication was S. Berdmore's Assize sermon of 1710; between that year and 1738 he is found publishing several more sermons of local interest by the same and other divines. In 1717 his name occurs as printer on a single imprint, that to Sir Thomas Parkyns's *Practical . . . Introduction to the Latine Tongue*; but in 1735 and 1738 he had his printing done in London.

WARDLAW (JAMES), bookseller in Edinburgh, on the North-side of the Street, opposite to the middle of the Lucken-Booths, 1691; (2) in the Parliament Close, at the South door of the New Kirk, 1697–9; (3) on the North side of the Street a little below the Cross, at the sign of the Bible, 1699; (4) the first Stair below the Post Office, a little below the Cross, 1701. 1691–1701. In 1691 he published the defence of James Clark, in 1695 a medical work by Archibald Pitcairne entitled *Apollo staticus*, and in 1697 *A Poem upon the . . . Royal Company of Scotland trading to Africa.* In 1699 he was joint publisher with J. Mackie of the *Letter giving a description of the Isthmus of Darian.* [Aldis, p. 123.]

WARNE, or WARN (R.), bookseller in Chippenham, 1707–14. In the *Observator* of April 12th, 1707, is an advertisement of B. Fox's *Agrippa almost Persuaded*, published by Warne. In 1714 he subscribed for Walker's *Sufferings of the Clergy.*

WARNER (JAMES), (?) printer in Edinburgh, 1688–9. A Dutch book, with a title beginning *Crimineel proces*, has the fictitious imprint, " Gedrukt tot Edenburg in Schotland, by James Warner, Drukker van 't hoge Hof des Parlements, 1688." Two other quarto tracts, entitled *Crimineel-Proces . . .*, printed in 1688 and 1689 respectively, bear similar imprints. These were in all probability printed in Holland. [Aldis, p. 123.]

WARNER (WILLIAM), bookseller in London, 1687. Defendant in an action for assault brought by Sir John Coel. [C.P.R. East. 3 Jas. II, 3056, m. 42 v.]

WARREN (THOMAS), printer in London, 1693–8. Doubtless a descendant of either Francis or Thomas Warren, who were printers in Foster Lane between 1663 and 1668. [*Dictionary*, 1641–67.] He printed, for N. Rolls, John Lewkenor's *Metellus his Dialogues*, pt. 1, 1693, and a number of reprints of plays by Dryden and others in 1697–8, " for Henry Herringman " (i. e. for his widow, *see* Herringman), and for others.

WARTER (WILLIAM), stationer in London, Talbot, (*a*) under the Mitre Tavern, Fleet Street, over against Fetter Lane, (*b*) next the Mitre Tavern, against St. Dunstan's Church, Fleet St., 1684–1709. Son of John Warter, gent., and Jane his wife. In partnership with J. Lenthall (*q. v.*). His first entry in the Term Catalogues was *An exact and lively Map or Representation of the Booths . . . upon the Ice on the River of Thames . . . in . . . 1683.* [*T.C.* II. 62.] In 1689–90

he was defendant in a suit in the Court of Common Pleas for the recovery of a sum of money lent or entrusted to him. [C.P.R., 1 W. & M., 3082, m. 495 v.]

WATERS (EDWARD), printer in Dublin, 1708–36. Printed a considerable variety of books at four or five addresses in Dublin. A reprint in 1712 of Swift's *Conduct of the Allies* and three books by Peter Brown, Bishop of Cork, were among his most notable productions.

WATERTON (RICHARD), bookseller in London, next door to the Blue-Anchor, 1691. Publisher of *An Impartial Account of the Late Famous Seige . . . of the City of Mons* [1691]. [B.M. T. 1707 (11), the imprint partially cut away by the binder.]

WATSON (J.), printer in Maidstone, High Street, near the Conduit, 1725. Printed *The Maidstone Mercury* (no. 25, May 27th, 1725).

WATSON (JAMES), the Elder, printer in Edinburgh, (1) in the Grassmarket at the foot of Heriot's Bridge; (2) Holy-Rood-House. 1685–7. Originally an Aberdeen merchant. In 1685–6 he acquired the printing house of van Solingen and Colmar [*see* Lindsay (D.) and his partners], and occupied the same premises in the Grassmarket, though no book of Watson's with this imprint has been found. In February 1686, his premises having been broken into by the populace and his workmen (including Thomas Noble) ill-treated, he was taken under Royal protection and his press set up in the precincts of Holyrood Palace. He was also appointed Printer to the Royal Family and Household, and granted other privileges. Watson died in 1687, his will being registered on December 21st. He left a son, James Watson the Younger, and was succeeded by Peter Bruce. [Aldis, p. 123.]

WATSON (JAMES), the Younger, printer in Edinburgh, (1) in Warriston's Close, over against the Luckenbooths; (2) in Craig's Close on the North-side of the Cross; (3) his shop next door to the Red Lion, opposite to the Lucken Booths. 1695–1722. Son of the preceding. Commenced printing in 1695. Imprisoned in 1700 for printing *Scotland's Grievance respecting Darien.* Mrs. Anderson in 1701 attempted to shut up his office, but was defeated on Watson's appeal to the Privy Council. In 1711, on the expiry of Mrs. Anderson's gift, he was appointed Queen's printer in conjunction with Freebairn and Baskett; this gift was forfeited in 1716, and a new one issued in favour of Baskett and Mrs. Anderson. In 1713 he published his *History of the Art of Printing.* The

Preface is the only valuable part of this work; it contains notices of many contemporary Scottish printers, and has been edited separately by Mr. W. J. Couper (1913). Died September 24th, 1722. His widow, afterwards Mrs. Heriot, died in August 1731. [Aldis, p. 123; W. J. Couper, "James Watson, King's Printer", *Scot. Hist. Rev.*, April 1910, and "Watson's History of Printing", *Library*, October 1910.]

WATSON (RALPH), senior and junior, booksellers in Bury St. Edmunds, 1686–1714. The elder is in W.C.B.'s list of provincial booksellers as in business in 1686. [*N. & Q.* 11th ser. I. 304.] His name occurs in an advertisement in *The Post Man*, February 26th–28th, 170$\frac{2}{3}$, as selling a plaster. He published school-books for the use of Bury school in 1705, and in Easter 1707 Francis Hutchinson's sermon preached at the Assizes in that town on March 25th, 1707. [*T.C.* III. 468, 543.] "Ralph Watson junior" subscribed in 1714 for Walker's *Sufferings of the Clergy*. It is not clear when he succeeded his father.

WATTS (JOHN), printer in London, Little Queen Street, Lincoln's Inn Fields, 1700 (?)–63. This was one of the most important printing houses in London in the first half of the eighteenth century, and was the school in which many eminent printers learnt the art. Nichols says: "The fame of Mr. John Watts for excellently good printing will endure as long as any public library shall exist. The duodecimo editions of Maittaire's Classicks 'ex officinâ Iacobi Tonson et Iohannis Watts' would alone have been sufficient to have immortalized his memory, both for correctness and neatness. But there are many works of still higher importance; Clarke's Caesar for example; and several beautiful volumes of English Classicks." [*Lit. Anecd.* I. 292.] Among those who worked in this office was Thomas Gent (*q. v.*) and Chalmers, the father of James Chalmers, printer to the City of Aberdeen; but the best known of all was Benjamin Franklin, who on finding himself stranded in London, first entered the printing office of Palmer and afterwards that of Watts, where he acted as compositor during the remainder of his stay in London. John Watts was one of the patrons of William Caslon the first, and lent him £100 to make a start. He died September 26th, 1763, aged 85. [Nichols, *Lit. Anecd.* III. 739.]

WATTS (JOSEPH), bookseller in London, (1) Gilded Acorn, St. Paul's Churchyard, 1685; (2) Half-Moon, St. Paul's Churchyard, 1685; (3) Angel, St. Paul's Churchyard, 1686–92. 1685–92. Began to publish in 1685, when he issued Sir William Davenant's *Gondibert*, bk. III, canto vii. [*T.C.* II. 114.] He made entries fairly frequently in the Term Catalogues between this and 1692, when he disappears.

WAVER (   ), bookseller in Oxford, 1677. Sold a map of England, designed by J. Adams. [*T.C.* I. 282; Madan, p. 30.]

WAYTE (THOMAS), bookseller at York, 1653–95. *See Dictionary*, 1641–67.

WEALE (J.), bookseller in Bedford, 1721. Only known from a list of provincial booksellers in *Notes & Queries* [10th ser., V. 141].

WEBB (WILLIAM), bookseller in Chichester, 1700–14. Sold the funeral sermon on George Payne, junior, of Midhurst, preached by Richard Oliver on March 6th, 1699/1700. [*T.C.* III. 193.] In 1712 he sold a sermon preached at Petworth by Charles Bettesworth. [Bodl. Sermons, 2 (17).] He was still in business in 1714, when he published a sermon by M. Woodford. [B.M. 225. h. 3 (15).]

WEBSTER (THOMAS), bookseller in Cambridge, 1701–22. His name appears on a sermon by Dr. John Cornwall, preached May 18th, 1701. [Bowes I, *Cambridge Books*, no. 349.] He lived (1) on the site of what is now the Senate House lawn, moving in 1704 to (2) a house in the High Street facing Great St. Mary's Church, two doors to the right of the "Green Dragon" (previously occupied by John Creed, bookseller), where he died in 1722.

WEEKS (   ), bookseller (?) at Maidstone, 1699. His name appears in an advertisement in *The Flying Post*, December 2nd, 1699, of the publication of Edward Brown's sermon preached at the Kentish Feast on November 16th, 1699. It does not appear in the imprint to the book.

WEIR (ALEXANDER), bookseller in Edinburgh, 1670. His wife Margaret was sister[-in-law ?] of Major Weir, and a witness at his trial in 1670. [Aldis, p. 123.]

WEIR (JOHN), bookseller in Edinburgh, 1681. Published in 1681, in partnership with T. Brown and J. Glen, a translation of Scudéry's *Les Femmes Illustres*. [Aldis, pp. 62, 123.]

WELBURN (CHRISTOPHER), bookseller at York, 1691. Published George Halley's *Sermon preached at the Castle of York, to the condemned prisoners on March 30, 1691*. [*T.C.* II. 357.]

WELD (JOHN), bookseller in London, Crown, betwixt the two Temple Gates in Fleet Street, 1685–1700. Began to publish in 1685, with a copy-book by John Chalmer and Dr. Abercromby's *Discourse of Wit*. [*T.C.* II. 137.] In 1686 he published an anonymous work on witchcraft. [*T.C.* II. 159.] At the end of R. Adams's *Earthly and Heavenly Building*, 1690, is an advertisement of four books printed for him. The last entry under his name in the Term Catalogues was Bishop Burnet's *The Life of God in the Soul of Man*, 1700. [*T.C.* III. 203.]

WELLINGTON (M.), bookseller in London, 1718–22. *See* Wellington (Richard) I.

WELLINGTON (RICHARD) I, (1) Lute, St. Paul's Churchyard, 1693–9; (2) Dolphin and Crown, St. Paul's Churchyard, 1699–1709 (?). 1693–1709 (?). Made his first entry in the Term Catalogues in 1693. [*T.C.* II. 475.] In 1704 the Company of Stationers brought an action in Chancery against him and John Minshull of Chester, for importing and selling *The Psalms in Metre*. Wellington professed ignorance of the Company's privilege. [Chan. Proc. before 1714, Hamilton 320/40, 319/77; *Library*, 2nd ser., IV. 373–83.] Wellington was the publisher of many plays, romances, and the like. He was publishing in 1709. [*T.C.* III. 654.] He moved to the Dolphin and Crown between Trin. and Mich. 1699. [*T.C.* III. 141, 154.] Edd. 2 (?)–5, 1696–1705, of Mrs. Behn's collected *Histories and Novels* were printed for R. Wellington; ed. 6, 1718, printed by J. D. for M. Wellington; ed. 7, 1722, printed by J. D. for M. P.; and ed. 8, 1735, for R. Wellington among others. [Esdaile, p. 160] Nichols [*Lit. Anecd.* II. 304] mentions Richard Wellington as the publisher in 1740 of Edward Spelman's translation of Xenophon. From these facts it would seem probable that there were three booksellers of the name: (1) Richard I, who died between 1709 and 1718; (2) "M." (perhaps his widow, and subsequently wife of some bookseller with a surname beginning with P.), who published the sixth and seventh editions of Mrs. Behn in 1718 and 1722; and (3) Richard II, who was at work in 1735–40. Dunton [p. 212] says that Wellington "has the intimate acquaintance of several excellent pens, and therefore can never want copies; and trust him for managing and improving them. He has a pretty knack at keeping his word and I expect to see him master of the Company at least, if not a gold chain about his neck, before he dies".

WELLS (GEORGE), bookseller in London, Sun, St. Paul's Churchyard, 1677–87. This bookseller published some interesting books. He is first met with in 1677 as selling a French Liturgy. In 1678 he published the second edition of Paul Festeau's *Nouvelle Gramaire* [sic] *Anglois*. [*T.C.* I. 323.] In the following year (1679) he was joint publisher with J. Robinson of Dr. A. Tuckney's *Praelectiones Theologicae*, and in 1680 they were also the publishers of a French and English vocabulary, compiled by Jacob Villiers, master of a French school in Nottingham. [*T.C.* I. 386.] In 1682 Wells alone published *Antiquitates Ecclesiae Orientalis*, by Cardinal Barberino and other writers [*T.C.* I. 473], and shared with Littlebury and Scott in the publication of Chamberlayne's *Angliae Notitia*. Wells was also the publisher of Isaac Barrow's *Lectiones* and of a French version of a sermon of Calamy's [*T.C.* II. 60], and held a share in Torriano's Italian Dictionary, 1684. [*T.C.* II. 66.] In 1686, in company with Abel Swalle, he published a translation from the French of Varrilas' *History of William de Croy*. [*T.C.* II. 177.] Another work of considerable value published by Wells was *The Universal Historical Bibliotheque, or an Account of most of the considerable books, printed in all languages, in . . . January and February*, 168$\frac{6}{7}$. This work ran to three issues and then ceased. Finally, in Mich. 1687, he was part-publisher of Florio's *Vocabolario Italiano e Inglese*. [*T.C.* II. 214.]

WELLS (JOHN), bookseller and bookbinder in London, St. Paul's Alley, 1687–1716 (?). Defendant in an action for trespass brought by — Gardner, widow. In this he is described as bookbinder. [C.P.R. Hil. 2–3 Jas. II (1686–7), 3052, m. 49 v.] In Easter 1691 he entered in the Term Catalogue *The Title of a Thorough Settlement examined*. [*T.C.* II. 361.] Perhaps identical with the John Wells who in 1716 published *The Case of the Five Rioters*. [Bodl. Fol. Θ. 662 (31).]

WELLS (R.), bookseller in London, Hand and Sceptre, Fleet Street, over against St. Dunstan's Church, 1686. In partnership with Robert Kettlewell in June 1686, when they published several theological pamphlets. [*T.C.* II. 166.]

WELLS (WILLIAM), bookseller in London, *see Dictionary*, 1641–67; also *T.C.* I. 10–120.

WELLS (WILLIAM), bookseller in Oxford, 1719–32. [Madan, p. 32.]

WELSH (ANDREW), printer in Cork, Castle Street, 1715 (?)–25. This printer's name is first found, jointly with Thomas Cotton's, upon a folio sheet, probably of 1715, *The Freeholder's Answer to the Pretender's Declaration*. It was sold by John Redwood (*q. v.*). Welsh printed alone a similar sheet in 1722 [*Bibl. Lind. Broadsides*, 1221] and John Knapp's Cork Almanack for

1723 and again for 1724. He was then in Castle Street. In 1725 he printed a stout 4to in French, M. Laval's *Les Veritez &c. de la Religion Chrétienne.*

WENT (SAMUEL), bookseller in Stroud, 1722. He and G. Harris sold J. Blanch's *History of Great Britain from the Tower of Babel,* printed at Gloucester by Raikes and Dicey.

WEST (   ), bookseller in London (?), 1703. Mentioned disparagingly by Dunton [p. 356], who says that he had been apprenticed to Samuel Manship, but "sued out his indentures".

WEST (GEORGE), bookseller in Oxford, *c.* 1650–1707. Mr. Madan [p. 32] says that West died in 1695; but he and Antony Peisley were Oxford agents in 1697 and 1699 for two auction catalogues, *Bibliotheca selectissima* (M. Harding's) and *Bibliotheca Andertoniana.* [B.M. 821. i. 2 (11, 12).] In 1700–1 Bullord, for whom he sold the latter, was employing Dollive; but West was in business as late as 1707, for on September 17th of that year Hearne [II. 46] speaks of a book being "bought of old George West the bookseller".

WHALLEY, or WHALEY (JOHN ?), printer in Dublin, 1700–24. He was an almanac maker in Dublin in 1691, but in 1700 he had become, in addition, a printer, and printed his own almanac for that year. He continued to print occasional broadsides till 1717. He has been described, not unreasonably, as a quack. He died in or about 1724, and his will is lodged in the Dublin Diocesan Court.

WHISTLER (EDWARD), bookseller and bookbinder in Oxford, 1710–22. In March 1716 he was elected Inferior Beadle of Arts. Hearne refers to him [V. 189] as a "very silly conceited Fellow, but fit enough for some dull Heads of Houses", and further records that he was University Verger and a bookbinder. He was still living in 1722. [Madan, p. 32.]

WHITE (GRACE), printer in York, Coffee House Yard, near the Star in Stonegate, 1716–21. Second wife and widow of John White, senior. Besides books she founded and printed the *York Mercury* (no. 1, February 23rd, 171$\frac{8}{9}$, which was edited and sold by T. Hammond, the Quaker bookseller, till Gent quarrelled with him. Mrs. White died in January 1721, and was succeeded by Charles Bourne, her husband's grandson. [Davies, pp. 132–9.]

WHITE (HENRY), bookseller in London, Three Bibles, Minories, 1677–80 (?). In 167$\frac{6}{7}$ he advertised John Ryther's *Looking Glass for the Wise and Foolish, Godly and Ungodly.* [*T.C.* I. 265.] Succeeded in 1680 by John White (*q. v.*).

WHITE (JOHN), bookseller in London, Three Bibles, Minories, 1680. Probably identical with the John White who on Bulkley's death went to York and settled there as a printer. He may have been the son of Henry White, but all that is known of his business in London is the publication of J. Ryther's *Hue and Cry of Conscience* in 16$\frac{79}{80}$. [*T.C.* I. 380.] Dunton [p. 292] mentions "Presbyterian (alias Minories) White" and, after a number of other names, "Hue and Cry White"; he may be thus distinguishing Henry and John.

WHITE (JOHN), senior, printer at York, Coffee-House-Yard, over against the Star in Stonegate, 1680–1716. The year that Stephen Bulkley died (1680) John White, "late of London," settled at York. He was perhaps the John White who is found at the Three Bibles in the Minories in 1680; but he must have had some previous acquaintance with York and the family of Thomas Broad the printer, as the first thing he did upon his arrival was to marry Broad's daughter Hannah on November 9th, 1680, upon which Alice Broad, the widow, retired from business in favour of White. In November 1688, soon after the landing of William of Orange, White had the boldness to print at York the Prince's famous manifesto, which had been refused by all the printers in London, King James having issued a proclamation threatening with severest punishment all who should circulate or even dare to read it. For this daring act White was sent prisoner to Hull Castle, where he was confined until the town surrendered. He was afterwards rewarded by William III with the appointment of "Their Majesties Printer for the City of York and the five Northern Counties", dated May 26th, 1689. In 1714 he was elected one of the City Chamberlains. He died January 10th, 17$\frac{15}{16}$, aged 80, and was buried in the church of St. Michael le Belfrey. He was twice married; his son by his first wife was the John White (*q. v.*) who became a printer and bookseller at Newcastle-upon-Tyne. His second wife Grace survived him and carried on the business until her death in 1721. Thomas Gent, who afterwards carried on White's business at York, was in 1714–15 a workman under him. [Davies, pp. 131.]

WHITE (JOHN), junior, printer in Newcastle-upon-Tyne, (1) in the Close, 1708 (?) –11; (2) on the Side, 1712–69; and in York, in Stonegate, near St. Helen's Church, 1725–35. 1708 (?)–69. Son of John White, senior; born about 1689. In 1708, according to Davies, and in any case by 1711, he set up by himself the second permanent press at Newcastle. In 1711 he began to print *The Newcastle Courant* (no. 1, August), perhaps a continuation of *The Newcastle Gazette,* or *The Northern Courant,* which Saywell had printed for Button, and which disappears

about this time. His output consisted, besides the usual local sermons and pamphlets, in chap-books and ballads, of which he was a large producer; one of these, *The Second Part of Jack and the Giant,* is dated 1711. [B.M. 1076. l. 18 (23).] Woodcuts soon became a feature of his books, and he printed two handsome works of local interest, Henry Bourne's *Antiquitates Vulgares,* 1725, and *History of Newcastle-upon-Tyne,* 1736. In 1739 White found presses and pressmen to print off the Sallust, and Scougal's *Life of God in the Soul of Man* from the stereotype plates made by Ged (*q. v.*), which had been refused by other printers. White apparently disliked his niece Alice Bourne's marriage with Gent, by which she took his father's York business out of the family, and was on bad terms with Gent, who calls him "our unmerciful uncle". In 1725, the year following the marriage, whether or not, as Gent supposed, out of animosity, he set up a rival press in York, with the aid of one Robert Ward, who was probably its practical manager. They printed a newspaper, *The York Courant* (no. 1 calculated to be for August or September 1725), and some books. In September 1734 White was elected sheriff of the city of York; but in 1735 he sold his business to Alexander Staples. He continued to print at Newcastle; in 1761 he took a partner, and in 1769 he died, in his eighty-first year, "the oldest master printer in England". [Welford, pp. 18–23; Davies, pp. 233–6, &c.; Nichols, III. 688; Gent, pp. 160–3.]

WHITE (LAWRENCE), bookseller in London, White Cross Street, 1679. His name is found in the imprint to a broadside on the Popish Plot in 1679. [Haz. II. 486.]

WHITE (MARGARET), bookseller in London, 1683. She published in 1683 *Crossing of Proverbs,* by B. R., Gent. [Pepys; Haz. I. 477.]

WHITE (ROBERT), printer in London, 1639–77. *See Dictionary,* 1641–67. He was still at work in 1677.

WHITLEDGE (ROBERT), printer, bookseller, and bookbinder in London, (1) Bible in Creed Lane within Ludgate; (2) Bible and Ball in Ave Mary Lane. *c.* 1695 (?)–1713. A publisher of Welsh books. In *The Post Man* of January 25th, 1711, he advertised *The Welsh Common Fold at Bristol Fair.* Dunton [p. 250] tells us that he was a printer and in partnership with Everingham, and that the pair "loved themselves into two Journeymen printers again". Perhaps he had by 1711 set up afresh as a bookseller. He contributed to the Bowyer fund in 1713.

WHITLOCK (ELIZABETH), bookseller in London, near Stationers' Hall, 1695–9. Doubtless widow of John Whitlock. Her name first appears in the Term Catalogues in Hil. 1696. [*T.C.* II. 567.] She published several theological pamphlets and *A Compleat List of the Knights, Citizens and Burgesses of the New Parliament,* 1698. [B.M. 1850. c. 6 (16).]

WHITLOCK (JOHN), bookseller in London, near Stationers' Hall, 1683–95. His name first appears in the Term Catalogue for Mich. 1683. [*T.C.* II. 39.] In 1684 he advertised a novel, *The Grand Vizier* [*T.C.* II. 96], and then he disappears from the Catalogue for ten years. In 1694 he reappears as selling *The Parish Clerk's Vade Mecum.* [*T.C.* II. 520.] In 1695 he issued *Solon Secundus: or, some defects in the English Laws* [B.M. 8122. aaa. 20 (15)], and in the same year *An exact Journal of the victorious Expedition of the Confederate Fleet . . . under . . . Admiral Russell.* [*T.C.* II. 557.] Whitlock appears to have died shortly after this, and he was succeeded by Elizabeth Whitlock, presumably his widow.

WHITWOOD (WILLIAM), bookseller in London, (1) Swan, Duck Lane; (2) Golden Lion, Duck Lane, next Smithfield; (3) Golden Bell, Duck Lane; (4) Middle Exchange, Strand; (5) next the Cross Keys, Strand, near Ivy Bridge; (6) next the George Inn, Little Britain; (7) Angel and Bible, near the George Inn, Little Britain; (8) next to the Bible, Duck Lane; (9) Golden Dragon, next door to the Crown Tavern, Duck Lane, near West Smithfield; (10) Rose and Crown, Little Britain. 1666–99. This bookseller, who started business in 1666 and was therefore only briefly noticed in the *Dictionary,* 1641–67 (*q. v.*), was chiefly remarkable for the number of times in which he changed his place of business. He was at the Golden Bell in 1676, and in 1680 had moved into the Strand, where he published Richard Izacke's *Remarkable Antiquities of the City of Exeter.* [*T.C.* I. 419.] In 1682 he was back in Little Britain, and his last entry in the Term Catalogues shows that between 1697 and 1699 he once more altered his sign to the Rose and Crown. He was a miscellaneous and prolific publisher and used the Term Catalogues freely. Dunton [p. 292] calls him "rolling and honest Whitwood", a phrase which may imply that he was a "rolling printer", i.e. a printer of engravings, but which may merely allude to his constant removals, though some of his addresses given above probably refer to the same house.

WHITWORTH (JOHN), bookseller in Manchester, Smithy Door, 1697 (?)–1727. Successor to Zachary Whitworth. According to the inscription on the family gravestone at Cross Street Chapel, John Whitworth died August 2nd, 1727, aged sixty-four. [R. W. Procter, *Memorials of Manchester Streets*, p. 183.] His son Robert, born in July 1707, was the printer of *The Manchester Magazine*, and eventually became a bankrupt.

WHITWORTH (ZACHARY), bookseller in Manchester, Smithy Door, 1690–7. In the Poll Book of 1690 Zachary is accredited to the amount of one shilling. On November 30th, 1697, he was buried. He was succeeded by John Whitworth. [R. W. Procter, *Memorials of Manchester Streets*, p. 183.]

WIAT. *See* Wyat.

WICKER (TOBIAS), stationer in London, 1683. In Hil. 34–5 Chas. II (1682–3) he was sued by George Bradshaw for debt. [C.P.R., 3009, m. 50 r.]

WICKINS (JOHN), bookseller in London, (1) White Hart, Fleet Street, over against St. Dunstan's Church, 1679–84; (2) Mitre, Fleet Street, 1684–95 (?). 1679–95. Began to publish in 1679, when he issued a translation of Mervault's *History of the Siege of Rochel*. [*T.C.* I. 369.] In 1680, in company with T. Basset, he published William Petyt's *Miscellanea Parliamentaria*. [*T.C.* I. 421], and also, with Heyrick and Dring, *A Collection of Letters*, relating to the Popish Plot, and published by order of the House of Commons. [*T.C.* I. 425.] Hazlitt [III. 189] records his imprint in 1695.

WIDDOWES (GILES), bookseller in London, (1) Maiden's Head, Aldersgate Street, 1669; (2) Green Dragon, St. Paul's Churchyard, 1670–5. 1669–75. His name first appears in the Term Catalogue for Mich. 1669, when, with Cademan of the Pope's Head, he published Frances Boothby's tragicomedy, *Marcelia*. Amongst his publications at this time was John Josselyn's *New England's Rarities discovered . . . Illustrated with cuts*, 1672 [*T.C.* I. 112], and the same author's *Account of two Voyages to New England*, 1674. Both these books contain lists of his publications. [*T.C.* I. 177.] Widdowes used as his device a dragon with the letters G. W. above it. His last book entry was made in Trin. 1675, and his death occurred soon afterwards. He was succeeded by his widow, Margaret Widdowes (*q. v.*).

WIDDOWES (MARGARET), bookseller in London, Green Dragon, St. Paul's Churchyard, 1676–80 (?). Widow of Giles Widdowes; her name appears for the first time in the Term Catalogue for Hil. 1676, and is met with up to Easter 1679. *The Complete Catalogue of all the stitcht Books and single sheets printed since the first discovery of the Popish Plot*, 1680, was sold at the Green Dragon in St. Paul's Churchyard. [*T.C.* I. 228, 354, 386, 406, 419.] She encouraged Dunton, while still an apprentice, in his amour with Rachael Seaton.

WILCOX (J.), bookseller in London, 1721–62 (?). He sold the sixth edition of N. Cox's *Gentleman's Recreation* in 1721. Benjamin Franklin, while working in Palmer's office, lodged next door to Wilcox's shop, and was allowed, for a fee, to use the stock as a lending library. [Franklin, *Autobiography*, ed. J. Bigelow, 1909, p. 91.] This bookseller may perhaps be identical with the John Wilcox, Gent., who in 1762 took part in a certain insurrectionary movement in the Company of Stationers. [Timperley, p. 709.].

WILDE (ALLINGTON), printer in London, Aldersgate Street, 1722–31. Son of John Wilde. In 1722 he printed an edition of Mandeville for Conyers, Norris, and Bettesworth. He died in 1731. His daughter Martha was the first wife of Samuel Richardson.

WILDE (JAMES), bookseller in Hereford, 1714. Subscribed to Walker's *Sufferings of the Clergy*.

WILDE (JOHN), printer in London. Aldersgate Street, 1693–1709. Samuel Richardson was bound apprentice to John Wilde in 1706. Dunton thus writes of him [p. 252]: "He has a very noble Printing House in Aldersgate Street. Whilst I employed him, he was always very civil and obliging. I brought him to be concerned in printing 'The Present State of Europe', in which he is yet employed." Wilde printed many almanacs for the Company of Stationers. He was succeeded by his son Allington Wilde. [Timperley.]

WILDE (JOSEPH), bookseller in Dublin, Castle Street, 1672–83. In 1672 Benjamin Tooke printed for him Dr. John Stearn's *De Obstinatione*, edited by Henry Dodwell, Fellow of Trinity College. [*T.C.* I. 113.] In the same year he published Dudley Loftus's translation of Dionysius Syrus on St. Mark. [B.M. 3227. c. 13.] His imprint occurs on a few books for the next four years, and then again in 1682 and 1683. Perhaps related to Richard Wilde, of London and Dublin.

WILDE, or WILD (JOSEPH), bookseller in London, Elephant (*a*) near, (*b*) at, Charing Cross, 1698–1700. He sold Daniel Baker's *Poems upon Several Occasions*, 1698, and Charles Hopkins's poem, *The Art of Love*, 1700. [*T.C.* III. 55, 173.]

WILDE, or WILD (RICHARD), printer, bookseller, and book-auctioneer in London and Dublin; London, (1) Bible and Crown, Ludgate Hill, 1686–8; (2) Map of the World, St. Paul's Churchyard, 1689–90 (1696–7?); Dublin, 1694–5, 1698. 1686–98. First known as London publisher of *Grammatica Anglo-Romana*, by Sam. Shaw of Ashby-de-la-Zouch; Michael Johnson of Lichfield shared this publication with him. [*T.C.* II. 180.] He dealt specially in anti-Quaker pamphlets. He did not use the Term Catalogues after 1690. [*T.C.* II. 331.] In 1694 and 1695 he appears as a printer at Dublin, printing in the latter year an Act of Parliament (6 W. & M. cap. 2), though not King's Printer. He was again in London between that year and 1698, when he followed Dunton to Dublin and conducted his auction there for him. Dunton gives, in the *Dublin Scuffle*, a long and laudatory account of Wilde, in the course of which he tells us that he was "descended from an antient family in Herefordshire, and brought up to Learning . . . was bound apprentice to George Sawbridge", that he remained a bachelor, had met with losses but preserved his integrity, that he was a "great Williamite", and was therefore called in derision "Protestant Dick". [*Life and Errors*, &c., pp. 550, 617–19, &c.] He was perhaps related to Joseph Wilde of Dublin.

WILDE (W.), printer in London, 1687–96. A jobbing printer. He was probably the W. W. who, with one J. R., printed in 1687 an edition of Forde's *Montelion* for Thackeray and Passenger [Bodl. Douce D. 225], as in 1696 his full name is found on the imprints of the same author's *Parismus* [B.M. 12450. f. 5], and Deloney's *Gentle Craft* [Bodl. Douce D. 237], and also of the undated fourteenth edition of Deloney's *Jack of Newbury*, printed for Passinger and Thackeray. [B.M. 1077. g. 35 (1).]

WILFORD (JOHN), bookseller in London, Three Flower de Luces, Little Britain, 1722–32. Perhaps a descendant of George Wilford, bookseller in Little Britain in 1652; *see Dictionary*, 1641–67. Hazlitt mentions one or two books published by him between 1724 and 1727. He is mentioned in the will of Thomas Norris, the London Bridge bookseller, who died in 1732. [P.C.C. Bedford, 174.]

WILKIN (RICHARD), bookseller in London, King's Head in St. Paul's Churchyard, 1693–1720. Referred to by Dunton [p. 234] as a "bookseller of good reputation". He began to publish in 1693 [*T.C.* II. 475], and from that time until 1720 he published much, chiefly in theology.

WILKINS (FRANCIS), printer in London, near Fleet Street, 1700. Only known from the imprint to a broadside, *Act anent the Aliment of poor prisoners* (October 9th, 1696, Scotland), 1700. [B.M. T. 100* (221).]

WILKINS (JOHN), bookseller in London, (1) Maiden's Head, New Cheapside, in Moorfields, 1670; (2) Exchange Alley, by the Exchange Coffee House, over against the Royal Exchange, 1672. 1670–72. Publisher in 1670 of a small *History of the Administration of Cardinal Ximenes*, and in 1672 of *Index Biblicus Multijugus*, 2nd ed., and George Scortreth's *Warning Piece for the Slumbering Virgin*. [*T.C.* I. 56, 122–3.]

WILKINS (JONATHAN), bookseller in London, Star in Cheapside, next Mercers Chappel, 1680–1703 (?). With Nathaniel Ponder and Samuel Lee he issued a broadside illustrating the mock procession of the Pope, &c., which paraded the streets of London on November 17th, 1680, in commemoration of the Fire of London. [B.M. C. 20. f. 6 (26).] He was also the publisher of other broadsides. He is perhaps the person referred to by Dunton [p. 292] as "*Apprentice* Wilkins (commonly called so from his being a good servant and a bad master)."

WILKINS (MATTHEW), printer in Great Milton, Oxfordshire, 1715 (?). [Allnutt, p. 299.]

WILKINS (RICHARD), bookseller in Limerick, *c.* 1660–*c.* 1680. In 1686, being then fifty, he was Dunton's landlord at Boston, whither, the latter tells us, he had fled for conscience' sake. He is not included by Dunton in his list of the Boston booksellers, so he had apparently adopted some other trade. [Dunton, pp. 131, 136.]

WILKINS (WILLIAM), printer in London, Little Britain, 1700–51. The favourite printer of the Whig party. He printed *The Whitehall Evening Post* and several other London newspapers. Gent was employed by him for a time. [Davies, p. 148.] He died in 1751, and bequeathed a portrait of Dr. Benjamin Hoadly to the Stationers' Company. [Timperley, p. 680.]

WILKINSON (CHRISTOPHER), bookseller in London, Black-Boy in Fleet Street, 1669–93. Began publishing with T. Basset in 1669, their first entry in the Term Catalogues being Peter Heylyn's *Help to English History*. [*T.C.* I. 24.] Wilkinson became one of the most important publishers in London, issuing books on all subjects. The last entry under his name was in Easter 1693.

He was succeeded by E. Wilkinson, probably his widow. [*T.C.* II. 458, 486.] Robert Newberry, Wilkinson's apprentice, being then about thirteen, ran away from him on January 2nd, $16\frac{79}{80}$, and was described in an advertisement; he is not otherwise known.

WILKINSON (E.), bookseller in London, Black Boy in Fleet Street, over against St. Dunstan's Church, 1693–6. Successor and probably widow of Christopher Wilkinson. Made a first book entry in the Term Catalogue for Mich. 1693, and carried on the business until 1696, when it was taken over by Abel Roper, who had been a partner in the business for some time.

WILKINSON (JAMES), bookseller and printer (?) at Portsmouth, near the [Point] Bridge, 1711–55. Publisher of J. Davis's *Seaman's Speculum.* [*Post Man*, March 10th, $17\frac{10}{11}$; *T.C.* III. 673.] In 1755 Archibald Maxwell's *Portsmouth* was "printed and sold by W. Horton, J. Wilkinson and R. Carr; but this may mean only that the book was sold by them. [F. A. Edwards, *Early Hampshire Printers* (Hampshire Field Club Papers, 1891), p. 126.]

WILLIAMS (JOHN), senior, bookseller in London, (1) Crown, St. Paul's Churchyard, 1636–66; (2) Blue Anchor in Little Britain, 1667; (3) Crown, Cross Keys Court, Little Britain, 1670–6; (4) Crown, St. Paul's Churchyard, 1676–83. 1636–83. *See Dictionary*, 1641–67. His later career can be traced in the Term Catalogues. [*T.C.* I. 27–406.] He died in $168\frac{2}{3}$, for his will, to which Benjamin Tooke was one of the witnesses, was proved on March 14th. He was succeeded by his son John Williams, junior.

WILLIAMS (JOHN), junior, bookseller in London, (1) Crown, Cross Keys Court, Little Britain, 1672–4; (2) Crown, St. Paul's Churchyard, 1684. 1672–84. Between 1672 and 1674 he published several books from the house in Little Britain at which his father was in business, but apparently on his own account. [*T.C.* I. 96, &c.] In 1684 his name, without the "junior", is found as publishing at the house in St. Paul's Churchyard where his father had latterly published till his death in the previous year. Nothing is known of his career for the intervening decade.

WILLIAMS (JOHN), bookseller in Ruthin, 1699. Sold school-books which he purchased of John Minshull, bookseller of Chester (*q. v.*). [*Library*, 2nd ser., IV. 373–83.]

WILLIAMS (T.), printer at Oxford, 1718. Printed a broadside on Edward Biss. [Bodl. Fol. Θ. 662 (9).]

WILLIAMS (THOMAS), bookseller in London, (1) Bible, Little Britain, 1662–70; (2) Golden Ball, Hosier Lane, 1672–5 (–8 ?). 1662–78. *See Dictionary*, 1641–67. He continued to publish until 1678. His last and perhaps most substantial publication was Wilson and Bagwell's *Complete Christian Dictionary*, 1678. [*T.C.* I. 323.] In 1679 his assigns were Chiswell, Tooke, and Sawbridge. He married the daughter of Richard Cotes, printer; his eldest son Thomas died in 1671. [Smyth, *Obituary*, pp. 79–91.]

WILLIAMS (W.), bookseller (?) in London, White Swan, Blackfriars, 1677. Published *Poetical Piety*, apparently his own composition. [*T.C.* I. 281–2.]

WILLIAMSON (GAVIN), bookbinder in Edinburgh, 1681. Will registered December 27th, 1681. [*Bann. Misc.* II. 296; Aldis, p. 124.]

WILLIAMSON (JOHN), bookseller in London, (1) Sun and Bible, or Bible, next the Golden Cock, on London Bridge, 1670–8; (2) Cannon Street, 1677. 1670–78. Began to publish in 1670, when he issued Wingate's Arithmetic. [*T.C.* I. 60.] He was also the publisher of Hans Bloome's *Description of .... Architecture* in 1674. [*T.C.* I. 166.] He was succeeded at the house on London Bridge by Stephen Foster in 1679. The Cannon Street address appears with the other on one imprint of 1677. [*T.C.* I. 279.]

WILLIS (J.), bookseller in London, Three Crowns, Henrietta Street, Covent Garden, 1701. Published *The Beau in a Wood, A Satyr.* [*T.C.* III. 245.]

WILLIS (WILLIAM), bookbinder in London, King Street, Westminster, 1684. Defendant in a suit for trespass. [C.P.R. Trin. I Jas. II, 3036, m. 346 r.]

WILLSON (H.), bookseller in Boston, Lincolnshire, 1721. [W. C. B.'s list of provincial booksellers in *N. & Q.*, 10th ser., V. 141.] *See* Wilson (Henry).

WILMER (THOMAS), printer in London, 1709. Printer of Richard Gibson's almanac, *Astrologus Britannicus*, 1709, for the Company of Stationers. He also printed in 1714 for William Webb, bookseller in Chichester, a sermon by Matthew Woodford. [B.M. 225. h. 3 (15).]

WILMOT ( ), printer in London, Fenchurch Street, 1724. Included by Negus among the "well-affected" printers. Possibly identical with William Wilmot, the Dublin printer.

WILMOT (JOHN), senior and junior, booksellers and stationers in Oxford, in St. Mary's parish, near Lincoln College, 1637–1718. *See Dictionary*, 1641–67.

This name is found in Oxford at intervals during this period. It must obviously describe two, and possibly three, generations. [Madan, pp. 29–31.] Wood frequently dealt at the shop, and in 1676 made notes for a catalogue from books bought by Wilmot of a Dr. Lockey. His references to Mr. John Wilmot cover the years 1659–81. [I. 295, IV. 9.] The name is found in the Term Catalogues in 1671 and 1705. [*T.C.* I. 79–80, III. 482.] Hearne's "Mr. Wilmot bookseller in Oxford" [VII. 257, &c.] probably means Samuel, who may have been another son of "old Mr. Wilmot". [VII. 174.]

WILMOT (SAMUEL), bookseller in Oxford and in London (?), 1715 (?)–33. Hearne has many references to this bookseller. In one of these he notes the prices (some excessive) which Wilmot was asking for secondhand books. [Hearne, V., &c.] Possibly identical with the Samuel Wilmot who published some sermons in London in 1729.

WILMOT (WILLIAM), printer in Dublin, 1724–7. He printed in 1724 two books, two pamphlets against Wood's halfpence, an almanac, and other pieces, and in 1727 Whalley's *Advice from the Stars*, &c. He died intestate in this year. He may be the — Wilmot whom Negus mentions as printing in London in 1724.

WILSON (GEORGE), printer in Wolverhampton, 1724 (?)–48. His name does not appear till 1744; but he may have been the anonymous printer of some tracts by Edward Elwall in 1724–6, and of advertisements in 1734–6 of an annual Charity Sermon preached at Wolverhampton. He died in 1748, and was succeeded by his widow Mary Wilson. [Information kindly given by Mr. G. P. Mander.]

WILSON (H.), printer in Maidstone. *See* Wilson (R.)

WILSON (HENRY), bookseller in Boston, Lincolnshire, 1719. *A Strange and Wonderfull Account of . . . a Fiery Meteor . . . seen at . . . Boston* was printed at Stamford for him. [Bodl. Arch. Bodl. A. II. 152, 35.] Presumably identical with H. Willson, 1721.

WILSON (JOHN), bookbinder in Glasgow, 1696–1726. His name occurs as a subscriber of £100 to the Darien Company in the list published in 1696. [Aldis, p. 124.] John Wilson, bookbinder, is also mentioned in the Records of the Burgh of Glasgow under date February 14th, 1726.

WILSON (R.), printer (?) and bookseller at Maidstone, 1701 (?)–7. Published the *Life of James II*, by F. Brettoneau, in 1704, and *Gods Providence the*

support of Government, by J. Bernard, Vicar of Ospring in 1707. The "H. Wilson", given by Cotton (2nd ser.) as a printer and bookseller at Maidstone in 1701 is probably an error for this R. Wilson.

WINDSOR (JOSIAH), printer in Dublin, 1667–9. He printed an *Oratio* for Peter Butler in 1667, and a poem in 1669.

WINGFIELD (JOHN), bookseller in London, Crutched Friars, near the Church. 1669–71. Publisher of nautical and mathematical books during these years. [*T.C.* I. 19, 80.]

WINTER (JOHN), printer in London, 1668 (?)–72 (?). He was examined in 1668 for printing Roman Catholic books; and he was further prosecuted by the Company of Stationers for working as a printer without licence. His press was thereupon partly demolished. Upon the Queen's intercession it was afterwards returned to him, but in the list of printing houses of 1675 his business was said to have been "bought in by the Company since 1672". [S.P.D. Chas. II, 261 (37); Records of the Stationers' Company; Haz. I. 114, II. 581.]

WINTER (WILLIAM), bookseller in Dublin, 1682. One of those selling *A Judgement of the Comet*, 1682.

WITHERS (SAMUEL), bookseller (?) at Coventry, Trinity Churchyard, 1694. In the *London Gazette* of May 10th–14th, 1694, is the following advertisement: "In the City of Coventry at the House of Mr. Samuel Withers in or near Trinity Church Yard on Wednesday the 23rd Inst. will be sold by auction a Catalogue of English Books . . . by Joseph Shelton. Catalogues may be had gratis at Bemford's Coffee House in Coventry, and at the place of sale." It seems probable that Samuel Withers was a Coventry bookseller. The auctioneer, Joseph Shelton, was a London bookseller.

WOLLASTON (JOHN), bookseller at Bishop's Castle, Salop, 1713. Only known from W. C. B.'s list of provincial booksellers. [*N. & Q.*, 10th ser., V. 141.]

WOOD (THOMAS), printer in Oxford and in London, 1715–42. [Madan, p. 32.] The Oxford and London imprints with this name seem to refer to the same man. He is probably the T. W. who in 1720 printed in London for a number of booksellers the works of Machiavelli. [Esdaile, p. 264.] Negus enters him as "well-affected"; and Nichols notes that he was the printer of the fifth volume of Thuanus' *Historiae* for Samuel Buckley in 1733. [*Lit. Anecd.* II. 26.] He was for a time in partnership with T. Sharpe.

WOODEN (JOHN), bookseller in Oxford, 1698. [Madan, p. 31.]

WOODFALL (HENRY), printer in London, without Temple Bar, 1724– . Mentioned in Negus's list as " well-affected ". Nichols adds this note : " This was the first, I believe, of a name which has now for almost a century been conspicuous in the Annals of Typography. That the more immediate subject of this note was a man of wit and humour, is evident from the famous old ballad of *Darby and Joan* which he wrote when an apprentice to the printer of that name. At the age of forty he commenced master, at the suggestion, and under the auspices of Mr. Pope, who had distinguished his abilities as a scholar whilst a journeyman in the employment of the then printer to this admired author. Of his personal history I know little farther, except that he carried on a considerable business with reputation ; and had two sons, Henry, a printer in Paternoster Row, and George a bookseller at Charing Cross, both of whom I well remember ". [*Lit. Anecd.* I. 300.] Woodfall was apprentice to one John Darby : as he was forty by 1724, this must have been to the elder Darby, who died in 1704.

WOODWARD ( ), bookbinder in London, *c.* 1680–95 (?). Dunton [p. 262] tells us that he bound for him, and suggests that he specialized in binding folios ; he also says that Woodward was related to one Mitchel, a bookbinder of St. Christopher's Alley, probably J. Mitchell, of Threadneedle Street (*q. v.*). It may be noticed that James Woodward lived in St. Christopher's Alley rather later.

WOODWARD (JAMES), bookseller in London, (1) (*a*) St. Christopher's Alley, Threadneedle Street, near St. Christopher's Church, (*b*) St. Christopher's Churchyard, behind the Royal Exchange, 1707–9 ; (2) Scalding Alley, near the Royal Exchange. 1707–23. First met with in Mich. 1707, when he advertised *The Mathematical and Philosophical Works* of John Wilkins, Bishop of Chester. [*T.C.* III. 571.] In 1708 he published Motteux's *Rabelais*. [*T.C.* III. 600.] He was still in business in 1723. [Nichols, *Lit. Anecd.*, I. 256.]

WOOLFE (NICHOLAS), bookseller in London, (*a*) end of Bread Street in Cheapside. (*b*) next the Red Lion in Cheapside, 1676–8. In Easter 1676 he advertised *Poems*, by T. Duffet [*T.C.* I. 236], and in 1678 *New Songs and Poems à la Mode*, by P. W. [*T.C.* I. 303.] His two addresses may well refer to the same house.

WOTTON (MATTHEW), bookseller in London, (1) Three Pigeons, Fleet Street, 1687 ; (2) Three Daggers, Fleet Street, 1687–1725 (?). 1687–1725 (?). This well-known publisher is first met with in Hil. 1687, when, in company with George Conyers, he advertised Thomas York's *Practical Treatise of Arithmetick*. [*T.C.* II. 187.] From that time his output of books increased rapidly. He published law-books, histories, travels, and medical works, and also romances and chap-books, such as *The History of the Seven Wise Masters*, Greene's *Dorastus and Fawnia*, and *A Thousand Notable Things*. A list of books printed for him is given at the end of Richard Willis's *Sermon before the Lord Mayor*, 1702. [Bodl. Sermons 21.] In most of his later publications he only held a share with Chiswell, Tooke, Sawbridge, Conyers, and others. Writing in 1703 Dunton [p. 210] spoke of Wotton as "a very courteous, obliging man. His trade lies much among the lawyers . . . I hear he is a rising man ". He was still publishing in 1725, and was succeeded by his son Thomas.

WRIGHT ( ), bookseller in Nantwich, 1699. Sold grammars and books of devotion which he bought wholesale from John Minshull, bookseller of Chester (*q. v.*). [*Library*, 2nd ser., IV. 373–83.]

WRIGHT (JOHN), junior, bookseller in London, (1) King's Head, Old Bailey, –1667 (?) ; (2) next door to the Globe in Little Britain, 1667 ; (3) Globe in Little Britain, 1667–77 ; (4) Crown, Ludgate Hill, 1678–93. 1634–93. *See Dictionary*, 1641–67. He must surely also be identical with the J. Wright there given as publishing " next door to the Globe in Little Britain " in 1667. He succeeded his father in 1658, and carried on and increased a large business. It was mostly in ballad-stock and chap-books, in partnership with Coles, Vere, and others, and he therefore did not use the Term Catalogues much, but made a certain number of entries in them between 1669 and 1693. [*T.C.* I. 23, II. 458.] In 1681 he was with Chiswell defendant in an action for debt. [C.P.R. Mich. 33 Chas. II, 2996, m. 260 r.] In the Parish Register of Leeds is recorded the death on March 6th, 167$\frac{5}{6}$ of " Mary daughter of Mr. John Wright bookeseller in London ", which may refer either to his sister or daughter. [*Thoresby Soc. Publ.* X. 160.]

WRIGHT (JOHN), bookseller in Chatham, 1711. One of those selling J. Davis's *Seaman's Speculum*, 1711. [*T.C.* III. 672 ; *Postman*, March 10th.]

WRIGHT (ONESEPHORUS), bookseller in Kammershmead, in Wales, 1699.

Sold school-books and psalters which he purchased wholesale of John Minshull, bookseller of Chester (*q. v.*). [*Library*, 2nd ser., IV. 373–83.]

WRIGHT (THOMAS), stationer in London, Fore Street, near London Wall, 1683–4. He became surety for William Hitch, in the Court of Common Pleas in Hil. 35–36 Chas. II [i. e. 168$\frac{3}{4}$]. He is not known to have been a publisher.

WYAT, or WYATT, or WIAT (JOHN), bookseller in London, (1) Golden Lion, St. Paul's Churchyard, 1690–1 ; (2) (*a*) Rose, (*b*) Rose and Crown, St. Paul's Churchyard, 1691–1711 (–20?). 1690–1720 (?). Publisher for the Nonconformists. Dunton [p. 207] says of him : " Mr. Wiat, if *Trim Tram* have any truth in it, is an honest and ingenious Bookseller ; but, indeed it is character enough for him, that he was Mr. Robinson's [Robert Robinson's] Apprentice. He prints Mr. Dorrington's Books." In 1714 he subscribed for Walker's *Sufferings of the Clergy*. He used the Term Catalogues fairly regularly.

WYER (ENOCH), bookseller in London, (1) White Hart, St. Paul's Churchyard, 1677–8 ; (2) Westminster, 1686. 1677–86. Began to publish in 1677 [*T.C.* I. 274], but he does not seem to have made much use of the Term Catalogues, and his name does not appear in it after Mich. 1678. [*T.C.* I. 334.] Amongst his publications was a novel called *Capello and Bianca*, 1677. [*T.C.* I. 289.] In some proceedings brought against him in 1686 he is described as of Westminster. [C.P.R. 3052, m. 88.]

YATES ( ), bookseller in London (?), Duck Lane, 1686–1703 (?). Catalogues of a book-auction held at Grantham by Edward Pawlett (*q. v.*), in 1686, were to be had of him. Dunton [p. 217] says that Yates had had losses, but was again (in 1703) deservedly prosperous.

YEO (CHARLES), bookseller in Exeter, High Street, 1682–1706. First appears as publisher or local agent for the sale of *A . . . Relation of . . . three witches, viz. Temperance Lloyd . . . convicted at . . . Exon, August 14th, 1682.* In the previous year he had married Margery Hooper, who survived him. His latest known imprint is of 1704 ; but there is extant a letter of 1706 from R. Clavell to Walker, author of *The Sufferings of the Clergy*, speaking of Yeo as then very ill. [Walker MSS., Bodl.] He must have died between this date and 1709. [Dredge.]

YEO (MARGERY), bookseller in Exeter, over against St. Martin's Lane, in the High Street, 1709–28. Widow and successor of Charles Yeo (*q. v.*). She is

first found publishing in partnership with her son Philip in 1709. The last record of her is on April 19th, 1728. [Dredge.]

YEO (PHILIP), bookseller in Exeter, against St. Martin's Lane, in the High Street, 1709–16. Son of the preceding. In these years he published a few books from the same house as his mother, at first being in partnership with her.

YOUNG (THOMAS), bookseller in Shaftesbury, 1685. Sued by James Courtney, bookseller, of London, for the balance of his account, £30 0s. 6*d*. [C.P.R. Hil. I. Jas. II, 3041, m. 272 v.]

ADDENDA

ATKINS (GEORGE), bookseller in Chester, 1682. *See* Atkinson (G.).

BAILEY (THOMAS), printer in Stamford, 1710–19 (?) and in Bury St. Edmunds, 1716–19 (?). [Allnutt, p. 299.] Probably the printer of the *Stamford Mercury* (1715, &c.) and of the *Bury St. Edmunds Mercury* (1716, &c.) [*Times Tercent. Handlist*], and of *A strange . . . account of . . . a fiery Meteor . . at . . . Boston*, which was printed anonymously at Stamford, and "sold by the printers in Stamford and at their printing office at Bury St. Edmunds in Suffolk". [Bodl. Arch. Bodl. A. II. 152 (35).] His partner was W. Thompson.

BAKER (CHARLES), bookseller in London, *c.* 1690–1700. Published a ballad, *The Seamans Complaint for his Unkind Mistress of Wapping.* [B.M. C. 22. f. 6 (175).]

BALDWIN (EDWARD), stationer in London, near Ratcliff Cross, 1714. Subscribed for Walker's *Sufferings of the Clergy.*

BENTLEY (K.) A misprint in Etherege's *Comical Revenge*, 1697. *See* Bentley (R.)

BISSEL (JAMES), bookseller in London, Bible and Harp, near the Hospital Gate in West Smithfield, *c.* 1690–1700. Published a ballad, *The Victualar's Wifes Kindness.* [B.M. C. 22. f. 6 (202).]

BLITHE (JAMES), bookseller in Colchester, 1714. Successor to Francis Blith. He subscribed for Walker's *Sufferings of the Clergy* in 1714.

BODINGHAM ( ), widow, printer in London, 1722. Gent [p. 119] bought a fount of pica from her.

BOUCHIER ( ), bookseller in Peterborough, 1714. Subscribed for Walker's *Sufferings of the Clergy* in 1714.

BROWN (JONAH), bookseller in London, 1714. Subscribed for Walker's *Sufferings of the Clergy* in 1714.

BULLINGER (JOHN), bookseller in London, in Clifford's Inn Lane, 1677. Published *A Touchstone for Gold and Silver Wares*, by W. B., of London, Goldsmith.

BURGES (EDWARD), bookbinder and bookseller in Canterbury, the Precincts, 1690–1714. He married Mary Page in 1690, and is then described as a bookbinder. In 1700 he was a widower and married Martha King. [Canterbury Marriage Licences, col. 92. Kindly communicated by Dr. F. W. Cock.] He subscribed for Walker's *Sufferings of the Clergy* in 1714.

CADWELL. *See* Kadwell.

CAMPBELL (ALEXANDER), printer in Dublin, 1718. In that year he was working for Hume. [Gent, p. 82.] Perhaps he never became a master printer.

CLEMENTS (HENRY), booksellers in Oxford and London. *See* above. These two appear respectively as "senior" and "junior" in the subscription list to Walker's *Sufferings of the Clergy*, 1714. They were therefore probably father and son.

CONYERS (JOSHUA), *see Dictionary*, 1641–67. He was at work in 1689. From 1686, and perhaps earlier, he was at the Black Raven, above or near St. Andrew's Church in Holborn, also described as the first shop in Fetter Lane, Holborn. [*T.C.* II. 178, 269; ballad of *Sir Walter Raleigh sailing in the Lowlands*, B.M. C. 22. f. 6 (76).]

COOKE (WILLIAM), printer and bookseller in Chester, the Bishop of Canterbury, near the Eastgate, 1718 (?)–25. In 1725 he started *The Chester Weekly Journal.* [Cooke, p. 31.]

COOPER (EDWARD), book or print seller in London, Three Pigeons, Bedford Street, 1701. With John Smith and David Mortier he published C. Le Brun's *Conference . . . upon Expression*, a book with many plates.

CULLIMORE (LUKE), bookseller in Portsmouth, on the Point, *c.* 1702–14. Temp. Queen Anne. [*N. & Q.* 10th S. V. 242.]

DAVIS (S.), printer in Coventry, 1721. [Allnutt, p. 302.]

DENNISSON (C.), bookseller in London, Stationers' Arms within Aldgate, *c.* 1690. A publisher of ballads and chap-books.

EXELL (JOHN), printer in Wotton-under-Edge, 1704. Cotton, 2nd ser., p. 304.

FIRDER (WILLIAM). *See* Fisher.

FREER (JOHN), bookbinder in London, 1714. Subscribed for Walker's *Sufferings of the Clergy* in 1714.

GAMMON (WILLIAM), bookseller in London, Smithfield, *c.* 1690–1700. Published a ballad, *Newes from More-Lane.* [B.M. Rox. III. 212.]

GAYLARD (ROBERT), bookseller in Dorchester, 1714. Subscribed for Walker's *Sufferings of the Clergy* in 1714.

GILBERT (STEPHEN), printer in London, 1716. Printed Sternhold and Hopkins for the Company.

GUNNE (RICHARD), bookseller in Dublin, 1714. No doubt the successor of Matthew Gun. He subscribed for Walker's *Sufferings of the Clergy* in 1714.

GUNSON (GEORGE), bookseller in Dublin, 1715–16. Elizabeth Sadleir printed for him in three years the 4th and 5th editions of Puffendorf's *Whole Duty of Man.*

HAMMOND (THOMAS), bookseller in York, opposite the Market Cross in the Pavement, 1719–25. Described as "junior". A Quaker. Joint founder with Grace White of the *York Mercury.* He apparently wrote the paper; and Gent, who speaks very disparagingly of him, turned him off.

HINTON (THOMAS), junior, bookseller in Tetbury, the Talbot, 1720. He sold E. L. Griffin's *Some Copies of Original Instruments and Papers*, 1720, published by his father at Cirencester. [Hyett and Bazely, I. 20.]

HODGSON (JOSEPH), bookseller in Chester, 1711–12. *See* above. He also published John Cowper's Assize sermon of 1711, presumably in the same year. [Cooke, p. 29.]

HYDE (JOHN), bookseller in Dublin, Dame Street, 1719. Published E. Synge's sermon, *The Reward of Converting Sinners.*

J. (K.), printer in London, 1702. In that year he printed Sternhold and Hopkins for the Stationers' Company.

KELL (RICHARD). *See* above. His address, the Blue Anchor, near Pye Corner, occurs on a ballad, *The Farmers Reformation.* [B.M. C. 22. f. 6 (118).]

KENRICK (WILLIAM), bookseller in London, Black Spread Eagle in the Old Bailey, *c.* 1690–1700. Published a ballad, *Loves Mistery.* [B.M. Rox. III. 254.]

KENT (E.), printer in Plymouth, in Southside Street, near the New Key, 1717 (?)–25. Printed *The Plymouth Weekly Journal, or General Post* (no. 36, August 29th–September 5th, 1718—February 28th, 1725). [*Times Handlist.*]

LAWRENCE (MARY), bookseller in Dublin, on the Merchants' Quay, near the Old Bridge, 1700. Aaron Rhames printed a book for her in this year.

MARIET ( ), widow, bookseller in London, 1702. With H. Riboteau, dealt in French books.

MITCHELL (J.). Also a binder. *See* Woodward ( ).

NEWBERY (ROBERT), bookseller (?) in London, *c.* 1690 (?). *See* Wilkinson (C.).

OLIVER (E.), bookseller in London, Golden Key on Snow-hill, over against St. Sepulchre's Church, near the Saracen's Head, *c.* 1690. Dealer in chap-books and ballads; known from the imprint to a ballad, *The Country Miss now come in Fashion.* [B.M. C. 22. f. 6 (100).]

PASSINGER (CHARLES), bookseller in London, Seven Stars on London Bridge, 1695 (?). Perhaps successor to Thomas Passinger the Second. He published ballads.

READ (G.), printer in Gateshead, 1713–14. Printed two sermons in these years, the earlier being without his name. [Welford, p. 24.]

RICHARDSON (SAMUEL), printer in London, 1724 (?)–61. The famous novelist. His work lies almost entirely outside our period, and he will be dealt with in a future volume. He was at work in 1724, and was classed by Negus as a "highflier".

SHERMERDINE. *See* Shelmerdine.

SOWLE (JANE), printer in London, 1706–15. *See* Sowle (T.).

TRACY (H.) and (J.), booksellers in London, 1719–(?). *See* Tracy (E.).

UNETT (RICHARD), bookseller in Wolverhampton, (?)–1739. Son of George and Ann Unett, and succeeded his mother. He died in 1739 and was succeeded by his sister Sarah, who carried on the business till 1767.

WENTBRIDGE (V.), bookseller in London, Duck Lane, *c.* 1690. Known as publishing a ballad, *The Maid's Complaint.* [B.M., C. 22. f. 6 (148).]

INDEX OF PLACES OTHER THAN LONDON

For the convenience of users of the Bibliographical Society's *Dictionaries* I have included in this index the names of all the provincial printers and booksellers given in Mr. Plomer's *Dictionary, 1641–1667*, except such as were already included in the index to the earlier *Dictionary, 1557–1640*. The index of the latter and the present one taken together should therefore, so far as the provinces are concerned, cover the whole period from 1557 to 1725. The few men who traded in the provinces before the earlier date may conveniently be found in Mr. Gordon Duff's *English Provincial Printers . . to 1557*, Cambridge, 1912. Names occurring in the 1641–1667 *Dictionary* alone, or in the present work merely as cross-references, have been distinguished by an asterisk. The few persons mentioned, for various reasons, in the two *Dictionaries* as trading abroad have been listed on page 342; but it must of course be understood that neither this *Dictionary* nor Mr. Plomer's earlier one is intended to include foreign printers or publishers of English books as such.

For the sake of brevity many non-significant variations of spelling, such as "Clark or Clarke", have been ignored and only that form given which is placed first in the text. The dates are added merely for convenience of reference. When the period during which a man worked at a particular place is clear from the text I have given this as his date. Otherwise the date is that of his *total* activity. I have omitted all query-marks as the index is not intended to be used apart from the text of the *Dictionary*.

R. B. McK.

INDEX OF PLACES OTHER THAN LONDON

A.—England, Scotland, Ireland, and Wales.

CHESTER : * W. Minshew, 1655 ; * W. Thorpe, 1664 ; * P. Bodvell or Bodrell, 1666–70 ; J. Minshull, 1674–1712 ; G. Atkinson, 1682 ; G. Atkins, 1682 (*see add.*) ; H. Page, 1685–1711 ; T. Tillier, 1688 ; J. Hodgson, 1711–12 (*see also add.*) ; R. Minshull, 1712 ; E. Ince, 1712–18 ; J. Holland, 1714 ; W. Cooke, 1718–25 (*see also add.*) ; R. Adams, 1730–3.

CHESTERFIELD : J. Bradley, 1725–98.

CHICHESTER : E. Janeway, 1697 ; W. Webb, 1700–14.

CHIPPENHAM : R. Warne, 1707–14.

CIRENCESTER : J. Barksdale, 1678–98 ; T. Hinton, 1718–24 ; J. Ballinger, 1723–42.

COLCHESTER : * W. Hall, 1663 ; * W. Warwick, 1663 ; F. Blith, 1702–11 ; J. Blithe, 1714 (*see add.*).

CORK : * P. de Pienne, 1649 ; * W. Smith, 1657–90 ; J. Brent, 1691 ; G. Bennett, 1714–34 ; T. Cotton, 1715 ; J. Redwood, 1715–23 ; A. Welsh, 1715–25 ; S. Terry, 1721–2.

COVENTRY : J. Brooke, 1671 ; J. Smith, 1683 ; S. Withers, 1694 ; G. Ratten 1701 ; T. Hart or Hurt, 1702–20 ; W. Ratten, 1716 ; S. Davis, 1721 (*see add.*).

CRANBROOK, Kent : Munns, 1699.

DARTFORD : Loveday, 1699.

DEAL, Kent : Mrs. Small, 1711.

DENBIGH : T. Davis, 1699.

DERBY : J. Thorton, 1675 ; T. Cadwell, 1685 : H. Nisbett, 1704–11 ; J. Hodges, 1716 ; W. Cantrel, 1718–27 ; S. Hodgkinson, 1719–27 ; H. Allestree, 1719–32 ; J. Roe, 1725.

DEVIZES : J. Hammond, 1695–1719 ; H. Hammond, 1695–1721.

DONCASTER : T. Rainy, 1693.

DORCHESTER : W. Churchill, 1659–88 ; J. Churchill, 1688–1728 ; R. Gaylard, 1714 (*see add.*).

DOVER : * R. Barley, 1654 ; * S. York, 1654.

DUBLIN : * R. Hughes, 1648–51 ; * J. Crooke, 1660–9 ; * S. Dancer, 1662–8 ; * J. Leach, 1666 ; N. Thompson, 1666–88 ; J. Windsor, 1667–9 ; B. Tooke, 1669–85 ; M. Crook, 1671–84 ; J. Wilde, 1672–83 ; J. Ray, 1676–1708 ; J. Crook, 1679–84 ; S. Helsham, 1681–9 ; A. Crook, 1681–1731 ; J. North, 1682 ; W. Winter, 1682 ; R. Thornton, 1682–1701 ; W. Norman, 1682–1703 ; E. Dobson, sen., 1682–1720 ; P. Campbell, 1687–1720 ; E. Jones, 1690 ; J. Brent, 1691–1700 ; J. Milner, 1692–1701 ; S. Lee, 1693–5 ; R. Wilde, 1694–5, 1698 ; M. Gun, 1694–1710 ; J. Brocas, 1696–1707 ; C. Carter, 1696–1727 ; S. Powell, 1697–1724 ; M. Lawrence, 1700 (*see add.*) ; J. Whalley or Whaley, 1700–24 ; A. Rhames, 1700–34 ; J. Forster, 1704–5 ; E. Sandys, 1705–18 ; F. Dickson, 1707–14 ; E. Ray, 1708–13 ; E. Waters, 1708–36 ; T. Servant, 1709 ; G. Grierson, 1709–33 ; J. Pepyat, 1711–15 ; S. Sadleir, 1712–14 ; J. Carson, 1713–59 ; R. Gunne, 1714 (*see add.*) ; D. Thompson, 1714–15 ; S. Fairbrother, 1714–34 ; A. Meres, 1715 ; G. Gunson, 1715–16 (*see add.*) ; E. Sadleir, 1715–22 ; T. Hume or Humes, 1715–28 ; A. Campbell, 1718 (*see add.*) ; S. Needham, 1718–25 ; J. Hyde, 1719 (*see add.*) ; E. Dobson, jun., 1720 ; J. Harding, 1721–4 ; W. Helme, 1721–4 ; P. Rider, 1724–5 ; T. Harbin, 1724–6 ; W. Wilmot, 1724–7.

DUMBARTON : J. Love, 1695–1725.

DUMFRIES : P. Rae, 1715–20.

DURHAM : * W. Hutchinson, 1655 ; H. Hutchinson, 1665–84 ; Ashworth, 1696 ; Freeman, 1713–19.

EDINBURGH : * J. Harrower, 1600–54 ; * Widow Hart, 1621–42 ; E. Tyler, 1633–72 ; * A. Wilson, 1641–54 ; * P. Wilson, 1643 ; * J. Lindesay, 1643–9 ; * T. Lawson, 1645 ; * G. Lithgow, 1645–62 ; * Heirs of R. Bryson, 1646 ; * J. Gray, 1647 ; * Heirs of G. Anderson, 1649–53 ; G. Swintoun, 1649–83 ; * R. Brown, 1649–85 ; * D. Mond, *c.* 1650 ; * Company of Stationers, 1650 ; * J. Hill, 1652 ; A. Anderson, 1653–7, 1661–76 ; * C. Higgins, 1655–60 ; * J. Glen, 1656–87 ; P. Ramsay, *c.* 1660–80 ; * Society of Stationers, 1660–90 ; * W. Paterson, 1662 ; * D. Trench, 1662–71 ; * J. Miller, 1665–72 ; G. Mosman, 1669–1707 ; I. B., 1670 ; W. Brisbane, 1670 ; J. Simpson, 1670 ; A. Weir, 1670 ; A. Hislop, 1670–8 ; G. Shaw, 1670–87 ; J. Menson, 1671 ; A. Anderson and partners, 1671–5 ;

J. Cairns, 1671–80 ; T. Brown, 1671–99 (–1722 ?) ; J. Mason, 1672 ; J. Miller, *c.* 1674 ; J. Monteath, *c.* 1674 ; J. Swintoun, 1675–81 ; J. Anderson, 1676– ; J. Bell, 1676 ; J. Calderwood, 1676–82 ; Heir of A. Anderson, 1676–94 ; Mrs. Anderson, 1676–1717 ; H. Leslie, 1677 ; G. Lesly, 1678 ; C. Lumisden or Lumsdean, 1678–90 ; J. Anderson, *c.* 1679 ; W. Carron, 1680 ; J. Colmar, 1680–5 ; J. van Solingen, 1680–5 ; Heirs of A. Anderson, 1680–1700 ; J. Reid I, 1680–1716 ; J. Alexander, 1681 ; Relict of A. Anderson, 1681 ; J. Weir, 1681 ; C. Williamson, 1681 ; D. Lindsay, 1681–5 ; W. Pope, 1683 ; J. Kniblo, 1683–4 ; W. Auld, 1684 ; A. Dumbar or Dunbar, 1684 ; J. Mein, 1684–6 ; L. Gunter, 1685 ; J. Watson, sen., 1685–7 ; A. Ogston, 1685–8 ; T. Noble, 1686 ; W. Johnston, 1686–8 ; W. Aitken, 1687 ; R. Bowter (= Boulter ?) 1687 ; P. Bruce 1687–8 ; J. Warner, 1688–9 ; A. Chalmers, 1688–91 ; M. Ogston, afterward Stevenson, 1688–1738 ; J. Wardlaw, 1691–1701 ; J. Vallange or Vallance, 1691–1713 ; J. Machie, 1691–1722 ; J. Johnston, –1692 ; A. Henderson, 1692–1709 ; Successors of A. Anderson, 1693–1722 ; Heirs and Successors of A. Anderson, 1694–1717 ; W. Jaffray, 1695 ; R. Allan, 1695–6 ; T. Carruthers, 1695–1700 ; J. Watson, jun., 1695–1722 ; Mrs. Beiglie, 1696 ; R. Hutchinson, 1696 ; G. Jaffray, 1696–1710 ; H. Knox, 1696–1716 ; J. Porteous, 1699 ; A. Symson, 1699–1706 ; J. Reid II, 1699–1712 ; J. Crossby, 1700 ; R. Freebairn, 1705–37 ; A. Banks, 1706 ; J. Spottiswood, 1706 ; J. Moncur, 1709–12 ; J. Baskett, 1711–42 ; J. Park, 1712 ; J. Ogston, *c.* 1714 ; M. Reid, 1714–16 ; R. Brown, 1714–18 ; J. Reid III, 1714–21 ; W. Brown, 1714–31 ; T. Ruddiman, 1715–57 ; W. Ruddiman, 1715–70 ; G. Stewart, 1716–34 ; J. Paton, 1716–54 ; A. Ramsey, 1716–58 ; W. Adams, 1717–25 ; J. Mosman, 1717–30 ; J. Martin, 1718–24 ; J. McEuen, 1718–32 ; T. Lumisden, 1723–48 ; J. Davidson, 1724–64 ; R. Fleming, 1724–78 ; J. Robertson, 1725–48.

ETON : J. Slater or Slatter, 1696–1709.

EVESHAM : H. Keat, 1678 ; Loveday, 1714.

EXETER : A. Brocas, 1655–74 ; M. Hide, 1663–98 ; W. Dight, 1667–93 ; R. Eveleigh, 1668–81 ; G. May, 1680–6 ; J. Phillips, 1681 ; E. Potbury, 1681 ; J. Cowsey, 1682 ; C. Yeo, 1682–1706 ; J. B., 1688 ; J. Hooker, 1688 ; P. Bishop, 1688–1716 ; R. Osborn, 1693–6 ; J. Pearce, 1697–8 ; S. Darker, 1698–1700 ; S. Farley, 1699–1727 ; E. Score, 1704–24 ;

J. Bliss, 1705–19 ; P. Yeo, 1709–16 ; M. Yeo, 1709–28 ; J. March, 1713–26 ; T. Butter, 1714–20 ; A. Brice, 1714–73 ; M. Bishop, 1717 ; N. Thorn, 1717–71 ; G. Bishop, 1718–20 ; J. Pring, 1723–30.

FAVERSHAM, Kent : Preston, 1699.

FLINT : Mrs. Powell, 1700.

GATESHEAD : * T. Rowlandson, *c.* 1664 ; J. Saywell, 1710 ; E. Read, 1713–14 (*see add.*).

GLASGOW : * J. Sanders, 1625–42 ; * J. Neill, 1642–5 ; * Heirs of G. Anderson, 1648 ; * R. Sandersonne, 1654 ; A. Anderson, 1657–61 ; * J. Falconer, 1659–62 ; * J. Morison, 1659–62 ; * M. Paterson, 1659–62 ; R. Sanders, 1661–96 ; R. Stewart, 1662–76 ; J. Brown, 1662–85 ; J. Galt, 1675 ; J. Andrew, 1676 ; G. Brown, 1676 ; J. Reid, 1676 ; J. Scott, 1676 ; J. Dunlop, 1676–83 ; A. Cunyngham, –1681 ; A. Hepburn, 1689 ; W. Dickie, 1695–7 ; J. Wilson, 1696–1726 ; A. McLean, "1706" ; H. Brown, 1712–30 ; J. Hart, 1714 ; D. Govan, 1715–19 ; J. Duncan, 1717–*c.* 1750 ; W. Duncan, 1717–*c.* 1760 ; A. Mathie, 1718 ; T. Crawfurd, 1721.

GLOUCESTER : * T. Jordan, 1644–64 ; * T. Langford, 1646 ; S. Palmer, 1685 ; G. Harris, 1702–22 ; R. Raikes, 1722–57.

GOSPORT : J. Philpot, 1708–36.

GRANTHAM : E. Pawlett, 1686.

GRAVESEND : Mrs. Appleby, 1711.

GREAT MARLOW : Robinson, 1711.

GREAT MILTON, Oxfordshire : M. Wilkins, 1715.

GREAT YARMOUTH : *see* Yarmouth.

HALIFAX : F. Bentley, 1695.

HALLATON, Leicestershire : Harper, 1687.

HAMSTALL RIDWARE, *see* Ridware Hamstall.

HARBOROUGH, *see* Market Harborough.

HEREFORD : T. Hancox, 1674 : R. Hunt, 1685 : J. Wilde, 1714 ; W. Parks, 1721.

HORSHAM : W. Browne, 1712.

A DICTIONARY OF THE PRINTERS AND BOOKSELLERS WHO WERE AT WORK IN ENGLAND SCOTLAND AND IRELAND FROM 1726 TO 1775

THOSE IN

ENGLAND BY H. R. PLOMER

SCOTLAND BY G. H. BUSHNELL

IRELAND BY E. R. McC. DIX

THE BIBLIOGRAPHICAL SOCIETY
1968

INTRODUCTION

THE "galley"-proofs of the English section of this volume were read by Mr. Plomer in the weeks immediately preceding his last illness. Arrangements had then already been made for the Scottish and Irish sections, but it was some time before they could be carried out. With the completion of the volume the Bibliographical Society has the satisfaction of having issued in dictionary form information as to printers and publishers in Great Britain and Ireland from the beginning of English printing to 1775, a period of just three centuries, considerably longer than that for which similar information is available for any other country. The inception of the work and the form given to it were due to Edward Gordon Duff, who in 1905 offered for publication by the Society *A Century of the English Book Trade: short notices of all printers, stationers, bookbinders and others connected with it from the issue of the first dated book*[1] *in* 1457 *to the incorporation of the Company of Stationers in* 1557. Papers by Mr. Plomer were frequently quoted from in this, and he was so stirred by the example set him that by 1907 he had produced off his own bat a similar dictionary for the little known period from 1641 to 1667, as "an attempt to fill the gap between the Stationers' Registers and the Term Catalogues so ably edited by Mr. Edward Arber". This also was offered to and published by the Bibliographical Society in 1907. Although both Mr. Duff and Mr. Plomer had deliberately framed their dictionaries to cover periods for which official information was not available, or scanty and not at that time in print, it was inevitable that a call should at once be made for the gap between 1557 and 1641 to be filled, and to the *Dictionary* covering that period which appeared in 1910, edited by Dr. McKerrow, Mr. Plomer was by far the largest contributor. After this, in 1922, he produced a further volume covering the years 1668 to 1725 in which, save for some little editing by Mr. Arundell Esdaile, the English entries were entirely his own, while for Scotland he relied on Mr. Harry Aldis and for Ireland on Mr. E. R. McC. Dix, the entries for all the three countries being amalgamated in a single alphabet.

[1] The Psalter printed by Fust and Schoeffer at Mainz.

In the present *Dictionary*, at the request of Mr. Dix, a separate alphabet is used for each of them. Mr. Aldis having died, the Scottish section was entrusted to Mr. G. H. Bushnell, librarian of the University of St. Andrews.

Mr. Plomer, before he undertook his share in all this dictionary work, had written an excellent *Short History of English Printing*, but including his contributions to the second of the five volumes (that for 1557–1640) his task for the dictionaries was to supply information as to English members of the book trade during more than two centuries, and it is evident that he could not do this from detailed personal knowledge equally distributed over the whole period. His own personal knowledge, from the books themselves, from documents at the Record Office and from wills at Somerset House, was probably more detailed for the second half of the period covered by Mr. Duff's *Century* than for the later ones dealt with in his own continuations. As will be illustrated later on by a list of the more noteworthy of his single papers and articles, he had produced new information as to many of the men of later years. But in the main he relied on the sources of information of which a list is given on pp. xix–xxi. He was interested in the history of printing and publishing for its own sake, and only very slightly (except in the case of Shakespeare) for the sake of the authors whose works the printers and publishers produced. Hence bibliographers who start from their interest in authors and books of approved literary merit, and expect that the printers and publishers who were concerned with these should receive special attention, have not infrequently been disappointed with the information that these successive dictionaries provide. Some rumours of this dissatisfaction have been largely responsible for the delays in issuing the present volume; but in the end Mr. Plomer's section of it appears substantially as he left it. He had developed his own method, and though some pains were taken to obtain further information by working through advertisements in contemporary newspapers and consulting other sources, the additional facts thus gleaned seemed rather scrappy and unimportant, and attempts to incorporate them into Mr. Plomer's entries disturbed the balance of these without materially improving them. Thus, as already stated, despite the curtailment of his revision of the proofs by his illness and death, it finally seemed best to allow his work to go out with only a minimum of editing. After this decision had been taken, and when all Mr. Plomer's section had been for some months in page proofs, a series of articles

covering some of the same ground appeared in *Notes and Queries* (18 July 1931–13 Feb. 1932). At the stage which had then been reached it was impossible, even if it had been legitimate, to incorporate the new information in these articles satisfactorily into Mr. Plomer's entries. Fortunately one of the contributors, Mr. Ambrose Heal, had already allowed Mr. Plomer to use many of his notes for this Dictionary, so that in this case it may be hoped that the loss is only slight.

II

Henry Robert Plomer, to whom all English bibliographers are greatly indebted for a life largely devoted to their service, was born at Upper Rohais, Guernsey on 13 December 1856. He came of a Canterbury family which his antiquarian zeal and skill enabled him to trace back vaguely to Plomers in the fourteenth century, who had really been plumbers, and spelt their names as they pleased, and with some certainty and detail to a William Plumer, probably born about 1567, apprenticed on 4 June 1580 to William Barley "of the citie of Caunterb^{y}, Fletcher", i.e. a maker of arrows, though the decadent occupation with which the master was associated in the city records is not likely to have been that to which the boy was brought up. It was probably as an addition to his unknown main occupation that this William Plumer became, in or before 1598, a lay clerk or singing man in the Cathedral, and held this office till 1625. He seems to have died the following year. His son Francis (1601–64) was also a lay clerk in the Cathedral, but married the daughter of a brewer and was a brewer himself. Next come two Thomas Plomers, the first (1647–79) a grocer, the second (1678–1720) a victualler and wheelwright; after these three Georges, the first (1715–66) a proctor in the ecclesiastical courts and Mayor of Canterbury 1758–9; the second (1759–1836) a solicitor who practised in London at 4 Essex Court in the Temple, but returned to Canterbury and was made an alderman in 1810; the third (1793–1844), of no known occupation save for his membership of the East Kent Yeomanry. Yet a fourth George, George Daniel Plomer (1816–75), distinguished from his predecessors by having a second name, who also seems to have lived on his private income, was the father of our Henry Robert Plomer, who was thus eighth in descent from the Elizabethan William, and like a curiously large proportion of his ancestors, the third son of his father. George

Daniel Plomer (born in Watling Street, Canterbury) had been brought up at Dublin by his Irish mother, Louisa Margaret (Stevens), and himself married (10 August 1838) a Dublin woman, Charlotte Amy Burrows. In the early years of their marriage two sons were born to them in Dublin; their third, Henry Robert, came twelve years after the second.

It would have been an impiety to forgo an opportunity of putting in print this severely abridged epitome of the genealogical details which my old friend took much pains to work out.[1] I should perhaps apologize for the meagreness of my summary. It is clear from it that the fortunes of the family were most prosperous in the days of its two legal members, the first and second George Plomer, on their shares in whose estates George of the East Kent Yeomanry, and George Daniel Plomer seem to have lived. Some remnant of the family property came to Henry Robert Plomer, but at nineteen he started earning his living as a bank-clerk. One day, after I had known him some years, he disclosed to me that while in the bank he had added to his income by making up their annual accounts for various tradespeople. In the course of doing this he had formed a high opinion of the profits to be made from a livery stable. In an unlucky hour (except for bibliography) he gave up his clerkship, took to himself a partner in whose knowledge of horses he had faith, and put a good deal of his money into the business. His venture met with no success and ended in his finding himself out of work and with a reduced private income. He was a resourceful man, and I believe at this time earned some money by writing short stories for small newspapers, but he got on a track more suited to his tastes when he was given some copying work at the Record Office and Somerset House for the British Record Society. He also returned to bibliography, which he must have begun early, since before he was thirty he had contributed to *Notes and Queries*, in two articles, *A Catalogue of English Almanacs of the Sixteenth* (and *Seventeenth*) *Century, with Bibliographical Notes.* In 1892 he published locally with Messrs. Cross and Jackman *A Short Account of the Records of Canterbury.* In 1894 he talked to the Library Association about Robert Wyer, a minor sixteenth-century printer, and wrote to me in the autumn offering for publication by the Bibliographical Society

[1] In a typewritten monograph entitled: George Plomer, Alderman of Canterbury (1756–66), Mayor 29 September, 1758–28 September, 1759, his Ancestors and Descendants. By Henry R. Plomer. "Every man has a history worth knowing", Emerson. pp. iv. 52, kindly lent me by Mrs. Plomer.

a bibliography of early English books about the plague. This seemed rather a gruesome subject for a young society, so it was suggested that he should give a fuller treatment to Robert Wyer, and he did so in a paper read before the Society on 21 January 1895. This was a bitter cold night (the Society then met at 8 p.m.) and the attendance was so small that the faithful few, leaving the platform unoccupied, sat round a gorgeous fire at 20 Hanover Square, and had the pleasure of listening to an admirable paper, which by way of honour was rather unfortunately given separate publication in our small quarto series, in which nothing else quite ranges with it. One volume of *Bibliographica* had then already been issued; to the remaining eight numbers Mr. Plomer contributed five papers, and was soon in much demand as a quick and faithful copyist at the British Museum.

For the next few years Mr. Plomer was the Bibliographical Society's "handyman"; he spent August 1895 at the Bodleian, making notes for us of the titles of its English books printed between 1501 and 1556 for the unhappily named *Handlists of English Printers* (i.e. of books printed by them), extracted entries from Gordon Duff's note-books for the same purpose, and read several excellent papers. In 1900 appeared in Messrs. Kegan Paul & Co.'s *English Bookman's Library* his *Short History of English Printing 1476–1898*, of which a second and cheaper edition followed in 1915. After 1900 most of his papers appeared in *The Library*, to the forty numbers of the Second Series of which he made no fewer than twenty-six contributions, and another thirteen (mostly in the earlier volumes issued before the War) to those of the Third. For the Society he compiled in 1903 *Abstracts from the Wills of English Printers and Stationers from 1492 to 1650*. Meanwhile his main business was that of a copyist who knew his way about the British Museum, the Record Office, and Somerset House, and until rotography superseded copying he was seldom out of work, and was rather pleased at times to be left free to pursue researches of his own. The Bibliographical Society, while restricted to 300 members and a guinea subscription, had but a slender income, and *The Library* during its first thirty years seldom made a profit, so his market for the results of his researches was not a rich one; but his finds gave him great pleasure and he did more than anyone before him, or anyone of his own day, to show what results could be obtained by record searching.

During the War Mr. Plomer helped for some time in the recruiting office at Canterbury and seems to have found plenty of opportunities for research, producing for the Kent Archaeological Society two volumes of its *Kent Records*, in 1915 Vol. 5, *Churchwarden Accounts of St. Nicholas, Strood*, and in 1916, Vol. 6, *Calendar of Wills and Administrations 1396–1558, now preserved in the Probate Registry at Canterbury*; also in this latter year *The Kentish Feast: Notes on the Annual Meeting of the Honourable Society of Natives of the County of Kent, 1657–1701*, published, like his pamphlet of 1892, by Messrs. Cross and Jackman. He ended this Kentish work in 1920 with an *Index of Wills in the Probate Register at Canterbury, 1396–1558 and 1640–1650*, printed by the British Record Society in the *Index Library* (no. 50).

In May 1920 Mr. Plomer had returned to London after spending 1919 at Oxford collecting material for his second *Dictionary* (1668–1725). Work was at first plentiful and he had a particularly good year in 1922 in which the 1668–1725 *Dictionary* was published. After that his income from copying dropped heavily, presumably because of the increased use of rotography, and with his wonted industry and resourcefulness he published three books in two years: in 1924 *English Printers' Ornaments* for Messrs. Grafton & Co., and in 1925 *Wynkyn de Worde and his Contemporaries* (Grafton), and a little book on *William Caxton* for the "Roadmakers Series" published by Leonard Parsons. His earning powers, however, were now much diminished and an influentially supported memorial was prepared for presentation to the Prime Minister, asking for a pension to be granted to Mr. Plomer from the Civil List in recognition of his many contributions to the history of printing and publishing. Before it could be presented, by the death of his elder brother, George Daniel Plomer, his unearned income was considerably increased and, though disappointed at the loss of the recognition which a Civil List Pension would have conferred on his work, he at once asked that the memorial should be abandoned lest his claim should keep out a needier applicant.

For the next year or two he struggled bravely with the compilation of the present Dictionary and in 1927 produced, in collaboration with Mr. Tom Peete Cross, a "*Modern Philology* Monograph" on *The Life and Correspondence of Lodowick Bryskett*, printed in Chicago. In July 1928 I received from him for printing in *The Library* a short paper on *The Importation of Low Country and*

French Books into England, 1480 and 1502–3, continuing and annotating one printed five years earlier. When it appeared in September I had to add a postscript beginning: "As this article waits to be printed off, news comes of the death of its author in his 72nd year, on 20 August", followed by "a first acknowledgement of the debt which both *The Library* and the Bibliographical Society owe to the researches of Henry Robert Plomer, whose industry and enthusiasm won the respect of all who knew his work". He had been a sadly ill man for several weeks before his death, but this last paper of his was fully up to his standard, so he kept his brain clear and his interest in his subject keen to the very end. Earlier in the summer he had told me, when he feared a long illness, that the veto which he had put on the memorial to the Prime Minister urging his claim to a Civil List Pension was now withdrawn, lest he should have to encroach on the provision he could make for his family. The pensions for the year had then been awarded, but a grant promptly made by the Committee of the Royal Literary Fund defrayed all the expenses which were worrying him and gave him on his deathbed the assurance that the "recognition" which he had felt himself bound in honour to forgo a little earlier had been gladly granted him as soon as his wish was known. He was single-minded in his devotion to the researches which he had pursued for over forty years and a most loyal friend and fellow worker.

Mr. Plomer in October 1884 married Ellen Esther, daughter of Thomas Young of Essex. They had three children, Nelly Elizabeth, Cyril Henry Maurice, and Harriet Amy Kathleen, all living at the time of his death. Mr. Cyril Plomer, who was an early volunteer in the War and before the end of 1914 was under fire in the trenches in France in the 13th London Regiment, is married and has one son, Peter George Daniel Plomer.

III

The following is a list, based on one drawn up by Mr. Plomer in 1924, of papers and articles contributed by him to periodicals and the Transactions of Societies on bibliographical subjects. I have added the dates of the periods which they cover, and the arrangement is chronological, reckoning by the earliest year in each period.

(1313–1611) References to Books in the Reports of the Historical Manuscripts Commission.
Bibliographica, III. 142–56. (1896–7.)

(1369–1547) Books mentioned in Wills.
Transactions of the Bibliographical Society, VII. 99–121. (Read: October 19th, 1903.)

(14th and 15th cent.) Some early Booksellers and their Customers.
3 *The Library*, III. 412–8. (October, 1912.)

(15th and 16th cent.) The Importation of Books into England in the Fifteenth and Sixteenth Centuries.
4 *The Library*, IV. 146–50. (September, 1923.)

(1480–1503) The Importation of Low Country and French Books into England 1480 and 1502–3.
4 *The Library*, IX. 164–8. (September, 1928.)

(1482) Richard Pynson, Glover and Printer.
4 *The Library*, III. 49–51. (June, 1923.)

(1485–1509) Some notices of Men connected with the English Book-trade from the Plea Rolls of Henry VII.
3 *The Library*, I. 289–30. (July, 1910.)

(1492–1498) The Law Suits of Richard Pynson.
2 *The Library*, X. 115–33. (April, 1909.)

(1492–1505) Bibliographical notes from the Privy Purse Expenses of King Henry VII.
3 *The Library*, IV. 291–305. (July 1913.)

(*c.* 1506–1562) New Documents on English Printers and Booksellers of the sixteenth century.
Transactions of the Bibliographical Society, IV. 153–83. (Read: November 15th, 1897.)

(1508–1547) Robert Copland.
Transactions of the Bibliographical Society, III. 211–25. (Read: June 15th, 1896.)

(1517–1569) Notices of English Stationers in the Archives of the City of London.
Transactions of the Bibliographical Society, VI. 13–27. (Read: October 15th, 1900.)

(1519–1667) Notices of Printers and Printing in the State Papers.
Bibliographica, II, 204–26. (1895–6.)

(1523–1616) The Long Shop in the Poultry (Notes on its printing tenants: R. Banckes, R. Kele, J. Allde, H. Rockett, Catherine Rockett, N. Bourne).
Bibliographica, II. 61–80. (1895–6.)

(*c.* 1534–1535) John Rastell and his Contemporaries.
Bibliographica, II. 437–51. (1895–6.)

1540 (1560) Anthony Marler and the Great Bible.
3 *The Library*, I. 200–6. (April, 1910.)

(1543–1554) An Exeter Bookseller (Martin Coffin), his friends and contemporaries.
3 *The Library*, VIII. 128–35. (April, 1917.)

(1553) An Inventory of Wynkyn de Worde's house, the Sun in Fleet Street, in 1553.
3 *The Library*, VI. 228–34. (July, 1915.)

(1553–1556) The Protestant Press in the Reign of Queen Mary.
3 *The Library*, I. 54–72. (January, 1910.)

(1553–1593) Richard Tottell.
Bibliographica, III. 378–84. (1897–8.)

(1557–1728) The Booksellers of London Bridge.
2 *The Library*, IV. 28–46. (January, 1903.)

(1560–1589) Henry Denham, Printer.
2 *The Library*, X. 241–50. (July, 1909.)

(1565–1609) Thomas East, Printer.
2 *The Library*, II. 298–310. (July, 1901.)

(1566–1583) Henry Bynneman, Printer.
2 *The Library*, IX. 225–44. (July, 1908.)

(1570) Plays at Canterbury in 1570.
3 *The Library*, IX. 251–4. (October, 1918.)

(1571–1576) Some Elizabethan Book-sales.
3 *The Library*, VII. 318–29. (October, 1916.)

(1574) The 1574 Edition of Dr. John Caius' *De Antiquitate Cantebrigiensis Academiæ libri duo.*
4 *The Library*, VII. 253–68. (December, 1926.)

(1581–1592) Stephen Vallenger.
2 *The Library*, II. 108–12. (January, 1901.)

(1584–1674) The Eliot's Court Printing House, 1584–1674.
4 *The Library*, II. 175–84. (December, 1921.)

(1584–1650) Eliot's Court Press: Decorative Blocks and Initials.
4 *The Library*, III. 194–209. (September, 1923.)

(1590–1599) Edmund Spenser's Handwriting.
Modern Philology. (November, 1923.)

(1593–1609) The Printers of Shakespeare's Plays and Poems.
2 *The Library*, VII. 149–66. (April, 1906.)

(1596) A Secret Press at Stepney in 1596.
2 *The Library*, IV. 236–42. (July, 1903.)

(1599) The Edinburgh edition of Sidney's Arcadia.
2 *The Library*, I. 195–204. (March, 1900.)

(1599) An Examination of some existing copies of Hayward's "Life and Raigne of Henrie IV".
2 *The Library*, III. 13–23. (January, 1902.)

(1602–1604) Bishop Bancroft and a Catholic Press.
2 *The Library*, VIII. 164–76. (April, 1907.)

(1603–1642) The King's Printing House under the Stuarts.
2 *The Library*, II. 353–75. (October, 1901.)

(1616–1637) Some notes on the Latin and Irish Stocks of the Company of Stationers.
2 *The Library*, VIII. 286–315. (July, 1907.)

(1620–1640) The Oxinden Letters.
2 *The Library*, VI. 29–62. (January, 1905.)

(1630–1638) St. Paul's Cathedral and its Bookselling Tenants.
2 *The Library*, III. 261–270. (July, 1902.)

(1637) Some Petitions for Appointment as Master Printer called forth by the Star-Chamber decree of 1637, &c.
3 *The Library*, X. 101–16, 129. (April, 1919.)

(1637) More Petitions to Archbishop Laud (The Makers of Embroidered Bindings; Cutting the price in a Greek book; Bookselling by Exeter Ironmongers; A Seizure of Books).
3 *The Library*, X. 129–38. (July, 1919.)

(1638–1734) The Church of St. Magnus and the Booksellers of London Bridge.
3 *The Library*, II. 384–95. (October, 1911.)

(1639–1680) Stephen Bulkley, Printer.
2 *The Library*, VIII. 42–56. (January, 1907.)

(1640–1797) Westminster Hall and its Booksellers.
2 *The Library*, VI. 380–90. (October, 1905.)

(1641–1647) Some Dealings of the Long Parliament with the Press.
2 *The Library*, X. 90–7. (January, 1909.)

(1642–1660) An Anonymous Royalist Writer: Sir Edmond Peirce.
3 *The Library*, II. 164–72. (April, 1915.)

(1643) A Cavalier's Library. (Edward, 2nd Viscount Conway).
2 *The Library*, V. 158–72. (April, 1904.)

(1643–1646) An Analysis of the Civil War Newspaper, "Mercurius Civicus".
2 *The Library*, VI. 184–207. (April, 1905.)

(1643–1646) Secret Printing during the Civil War.
2 *The Library*, V. 374–403. (October, 1904.)

(1644–1648) A Printer's Bill in the Seventeenth Century (T. Brudnell).
2 *The Library*, VII. 32–45. (January, 1906.)

(1667–1700) A Chester Bookseller (John Minshull).
2 *The Library*, IV. 373–83. (October, 1903.)

(1688–1697) A Lawsuit as to an early edition of the *Pilgrim's Progress*.
3 *The Library*, V. 60–9. (January, 1914.)

(1717–1768) John Abree, Printer and Bookseller of Canterbury.
3 *The Library*, IV. 46–56. (January, 1913.)

(1792–1848) A glance at the Whittingham Ledgers.
2 *The Library*, II. 147–63. (April, 1901.)

(1803–1897) Some Private Presses of the Present Century.
2 *The Library*, I. 407–34. (September, 1900.)

(1808–1809) On the value of Publishers' Lists.
2 *The Library*, III. 427–33. (October, 1902.)

It is in these papers and articles, almost every one of which brought to light new facts, that Mr. Plomer is seen at his best, and it may be doubted whether any other bibliographer has a finer record.

In conclusion I must express my regret for the long delay in bringing out this volume. Its subject was altogether off my beat, and when confronted with the need of making numerous small decisions I was frequently tempted to postpone them in the hope of obtaining further light. I am very grateful to my fellow-secretary, Dr. McKerrow, for finally helping me to finish it up.

A. W. POLLARD.

ENGLISH PRINTERS, BOOKSELLERS, STATIONERS, ETC.

REFERENCES

ABBREVIATED IN THE TEXT OF THE ENGLISH PORTION

Add. MSS. Additional Manuscripts, British Museum.
Antiquarian Magazine and Bibliographer.

B.M. British Museum.
Benham Memoirs. Memoirs of J. Hutton, by Daniel Benham, 1856.
Berwick upon Tweed Typography, 1735–1900, by J. L. Hilson, 1918.
Bibliographica, 1895–7.
Bibliotheca Somersetensis, by Emanuel Green, 1902.
Booksellers Signs in Fleet Street by W. G. Page—*Karslake, Book Auction Records*, Vol. 13.
Bowes. Cambridge Books by R. Bowes, 1894.
Bowes. University Printers, by R. Bowes, 1884.
Boyne. The Yorkshire Library, by W. Boyne, 1869.
Burton. Early Worcester Printers and Books. In *Assoc. Architect. Societies' Reports*, XXIV, 197–213, 1897.

Calendar of Middlesex Sessions Records.
Chamberlain's Accounts for City of Bath.
Cresswell. Collections towards the History of Printing in Nottinghamshire, by S. Cresswell, 1863
Curwen. A History of Booksellers, by H. Curwen, 1873.

D.N.B. Dictionary of National Biography.
Davies. A Memoir of the York Press, by Robert Davies, 1868.
Decision of the Court of Sessions upon Literary Property, 1774.
Dickons. Catalogue of books published at Bradford, by J. K. Dickons, 1895.
Dictionary, 1668–1725. A Dictionary of Printers and Booksellers who were at work in England, Scotland and Ireland from 1668 to 1725, by Henry R. Plomer, 1922.
S. P. Dom. Domestic State Papers, George II.
Dredge. Devon Booksellers and Printers, by J. I. Dredge. 3 parts, 1885–7.

Earwaker. Local Gleanings. Ed. by J. P. Earwaker, 1879.
Edwards. Early Hampshire Printers, by F. A. Edwards, 1891.

Foster's Alumni Oxoniensis, by Joseph Foster, 1887–91.

G. E. C. Complete Baronetage, 1907.
Gay and Fox. The Register of baptisms, &c. of the parish of Falmouth, by J. E Gay and Mrs. H. Fox, 1915.
Gentleman's Magazine.
Gerring. Notes on Printers and Booksellers, by C. Gerring, 1900.
Griffiths. Oxford Wills, by John Griffiths, 1862.

Halifax Books and Authors, by J. H. Turner, 1906.
Hearne. Remarks and Collections, 1705–22. 10 vols. *Oxford Historical Society*, 1885–1915.
Hill. Boswell's Life of Johnson, ed. Birkbeck Hill.
Hill. Bookmakers of Old Birmingham, by T. Hill, 1907.
House of Harrison, 1887.
Hyett and Bazeley. The Bibliographer's Manual of Gloucestershire Literature, by F. A. Hyett and W. Bazeley. 5 vols., 1895–1915.

J.C.B.L. or J.C.B. John Carter Brown Library, Providence, U.S.A.
Journal of Friends Historical Society.

Knight. Shadows of the Old Booksellers, by C. Knight, 1865.

Lackington. Memoirs of the first forty-five years of the life of James Lackington. Written by himself [1791].
Lancashire Printed Books, by A. J. Hawkes, 1925.
Latimer. Annals of Bristol in the 18th Century by J. Latimer, 1893.
Letters between the Rev. James Granger and many of the most literary men of his time. Edited by J. P. Malcolm, 1805.
Letters of the late Rev. Mr. Laurence Sterne, 1775.
Library.
Library World.
Life of Thomas Gent.

Mayo. Bibliotheca Dorsetiensis, by C. H. Mayo, 1885.
Memoirs of John Almon, Bookseller of Piccadilly, 1790.
Monkland. Supplement to the "Literature and Literati of Bath", by G. Monkland, 1855.
Musgrave's Obituary. Obituary prior to 1800. Compiled by Sir W. Musgrave, 1899, &c.

N. and Q. Notes and Queries.
Nichols. Literary Anecdotes of the Eighteenth Century, by John Nichols, 1812–15.
Norris. Booksellers and Printers of Cirencester, by H. E. Norris, 1912.
Norris. Notes on St. Neots Printers, by H. E. Norris, 1901.
Nowell. Early Printers in Norwich, by C. Nowell, 1919.

Oldest English Newspaper. Worcester, 1890.

P.C.C. Prerogative Court of Canterbury.
P.R.O. Public Record Office.
Parkers of Oxford. An Address by Mr. J. C. Parker, 1919.
Piper. Notes on Sussex Printing, by A. C. Piper. The Library, 3rd ser., v. 257–65.
Procter. Memorials of Manchester Streets, by R. W. Procter, 1874.
Publishing House of Rivington, The, by Septimus Rivington, 1919.

Reed. A History of the Old English Letter Foundries, by T. B. Reed, 1887.
Richardson, Mrs. Wiltshire Newspapers past and present.
Roberts. Cambridge University Press, by S. C. Roberts, 1921.
Rowe-Mores. Dissertation upon English Typographical Founders and Foundries, 1778.

Straus. Robert Dodsley, by R. Straus, 1910.
Surtees. History of Durham, by Robert Surtees, 1816–40.

Timperley. A Dictionary of Printers and Printing, by C. H. Timperley, 1839 and 1842.

W.M.C. Wilford's Monthly Catalogue, 1713–1913.
Wells. History of the Bristol Times and Mirror, by C. Wells, 1913.
Welch. The City Printers, by Charles Welch. Nov. 1916 (Bibl. Soc. Trans. xiv. 175–244).
Welford. Early Newcastle Typography, by Richard Welford. (*Archaeologia Aeliana*, 3rd series, III), 1906.
Welsh. A Bookseller of the Last Century (John Newbery), by Charles Welsh, 1885.
Winship. Harvard College Library, U.S.A. (sometimes referred to under "W." only).

Yarmouth Printing and Printers, by F. J. Farrell, 1912.

A DICTIONARY OF THE PRINTERS AND BOOKSELLERS WHO WERE AT WORK IN ENGLAND. 1726–1775

By HENRY R. PLOMER.

ACKERS (CHARLES) and (JOHN), printers in London, St. John's Street, Clerkenwell, 1728–59. In 1728 Charles Ackers printed for J. Billingsley, James Ralph's poem, *Night*, in type probably obtained from Caslon. The dedicatory epistle has a factotum signed F. H. He was afterwards joined by John Akers, or Ackers, whose marriage is found recorded in the *Penny London Post* of January 15th, 174$\frac{7}{8}$: "On Tuesday was married at St. John's Clerkenwell Mr. John Ackers, an eminent printer in Swan Alley, St. John Street, to Miss Dolly Bell, a celebrated beauty, daughter of Mr. Bell an eminent broker in Aldermary churchyard, Bow Lane, a young lady of great merit, with a handsome fortune." The joint names of C. & J. Akers is found in the imprint of J. Warburton's *London and Middlesex illustrated*, published in 1749. Charles Ackers was for many years J.P. for Middlesex, and was the printer of the *London Magazine* from its foundation. He died on June 17th 1759. [Nichols, *Lit. Anecd.* III. 714, VIII. 478.] Amongst his apprentices was Henry Baldwin (*q.v.*) The date of John's death has not been found.

ACKERS or AKERS (JOHN), *see* Ackers (Charles) and (John).

ADAMS (ELIZABETH), printer in Chester, 1733 (?)–56. Possibly the widow of Roger Adams [*see Dictionary* 1668–1725] whose business she continued to carry on. She was the printer of Adam's *Weekly Courant* and in 1747 of *An Alphabetical List of the Names of all the Freemen of the City of Chester*, [B.M. 4477. f. 79 (2)]. Two years later she was both printer and publisher of a series of papers, under the title of *Manchester Vindicated*, that had appeared in the *Manchester Magazine* and *Chester Courant*, [Timperley 1842, ed. 679.] A further series of reprints from the *Chester Courant* came from her press in 1750 with the title *The Chester Miscellany*, [B.M. 292. c. 37.] In 1756 her name appeared in the *London Gazette* of October 9th as selling a patent medicine. In or before 1748 her son John was joined with her in the management of the business.

ADAMS (JAMES), bookseller and stationer in London: (1) Near Three Kings' Court, Lombard Street, 1738; (2) Adam and Eve, near yᵉ Vine Inn without Bishopsgate, *c.* 1750. 1738–50 (?) Issued a trade card about the year 1750. [A. Heal's Collection.]

ADAMS (JOHN), printer in Chester, 1748. Son of Elizabeth Adams (*q.v.*). In or before 1748 he joined his mother in the management of the printing-office and the publication of the various newspapers of which they were the owners.

ADAMS (OLIVER), printer in Plymouth, co. Devon, 1758–64. Printer of the *Plymouth Magazine* in 1758. His name occurs in a list of subscribers to Calcott's *Collection of Thoughts*, 1764. [Dredge, p. 36.]

ADAMS (ORION), printer in Oxford (?), Chester &c., 1726–97. Referred to in the letters of Daniel Prince to John Nichols as "an old itinerant type". The son of Roger Adams, printer in Chester. For some years in partnership with T. Boden. He was a master printer, and worked at Manchester, Chester, Plymouth, and Dublin, and occasionally as a journeyman in various London and provincial offices. Towards the end of his life he fell into poverty and became a distributor of play-bills to an itinerant company. After he had attained his 70th year, he frequently walked from London to Chester and back. He died in great poverty in an obscure lodging near Chester in April 1797, aged 80. [Nichols, *Lit. Anecd.* III. 708, IX. 572. *Gentleman's Magazine*, LXVII. 445 (the same article).]

ADLARD and BROWN, printers in London, Fleet Street, 1769. Their imprint is found in two folio volumes entitled *England Displayed*, a work by P. Russell and Owen Price, issued in monthly parts and profusely illustrated with maps and engravings. [B.M. 10348. l. 1.]

AKENHEAD (DAVID), bookseller in Newcastle-upon-Tyne, 1776. Possibly a son or grandson of Robert. His name appears in 1776 amongst a list of those receiving subscriptions for a suggested publication of the *Lectures* of the Rev. J. Murray; but the work does not seem to have been issued.

AKENHEAD (ROBERT), bookseller and publisher in Newcastle-upon-Tyne; Bible and Crown upon the Bridge, 1722–51. Dr. Welford in *Early Newcastle Typography* [p. 127] mentions him as the founder of a newspaper called the *Newcastle Mercury* (?) in 1722, and in a list of booksellers, states that he was in business from 1722 to 1751.

AKENHEAD (ROBERT), Junior, bookseller and publisher in Newcastle-upon-Tyne, 1750. Son of Robert Akenhead (1722–51), publisher of several of Dr. Askew's writings.

ALBIN (JOHN), printer, bookseller, and publisher in Spalding, Lincolnshire, 1775–1800. Possibly a descendant either of Henry Albin who on October 13th, 1716, married Jane Dale, widow, in the parish church of Spalding, or of Robert Albin who on November 11th in the same year married Elizabeth Groom in the same church. The editor of the *Lincolnshire Free Press* supplies the following information. John Albin was a printer and bookseller in Spalding about the year 1775. He was succeeded by his son, Thos. Albin, who in 1801 and 1802 published the *Provincial Literary Repository*. White's *Lincolnshire Directory* of 1842 gives Thos. Albin, junr., in business in the Market Place, adding the description "circulating library and publisher". He died in 1883. Nichols, in his *Literary Anecdotes*, III. 672, under date of 1800, records the death of John Albin the founder, and adds that he was the principal bookseller in Spalding.

ALLARD (W.), printer in London, 1770. *The History and Art of Printing* [Luckombe] bears the imprint, "W. Allard and J. Browne for J. Johnson, London, 1770".

ALLEN (EDMUND), printer in London, Bolt Court, Fleet Street, 1726–80. Son of the Rev. Thos. Allen, rector of Kettering, and author of *Archaeologia, Universalis* [*Northampton Mercury*, December 16, 1751.] The neighbour and friend of Samuel Johnson, frequently alluded to in Boswell's *Life*. Nichols refers to him as a "very excellent printer", a character that is amply borne out by the two folio volumes of Dr. Lye's *Dictionarium Saxonico- et Gothico-Latinum*, printed by him in 1772. He died July 28th, 1780.

ALLEN (GEORGE), printer (?) and publisher in London, 59 Paternoster Row, 1775–6. His name is found as one of the publishers of a sermon by the Rev. Wm. Scott, entitled *O Tempora! O Mores!* printed in 1774. The other publishers were Robinson, Crowder, and Bew. Two thousand five hundred copies had been sold when this, the sixth edition, bearing the date 1775, was issued. [J. C. B. L.] In 1775 the *Covent Garden Magazine* and *Annals of Gaming* were advertised as sold by him. On April 29th, 1776, according to Timperley, he was sentenced to three months imprisonment for printing a pamphlet called the *Rat-Trap*. By "printing" Timperley probably meant "publishing". [Timperley, 1842, p. 736.]

ALLESTREE (HENRY), bookseller in Derby, 1719–35. *See Dictionary*, 1667–1725. Still in business in 1735.

ALLISON (MATTHEW), printer in Falmouth, 1753. On the Market Strand, 1750–94. Advertised as selling Bibles, Stationery, &c., in a book of 1750. [Attwood, Addenda to Dredge.] Printed a *Sermon preached at Truro in Cornwall* by Samuel Walker, A.B. The second edition, 1753, 8vo. [Dredge, p. 25.] His name is found also as selling Thomas Vivian's *Exposition of the Catechism* in 1770 [*Ib.*, p. 29] and *Peter's Sermons*, 1776 [*Ib.*, p. 30.] Buried in the parish church of Falmouth on February 9th, 1794, aged 79. [S. E. Gay and Mrs. H. Fox, *The Register of Baptisms, &c., of the parish of Falmouth*, 1915, part II, p. 895.] The Ann Alison whose burial is recorded on October 15th, 1789, aged 58, was perhaps his wife. [*Ib.*, p. 885.]

ALLIX (J.), bookseller and publisher in London, Glanville Street, Rathbone Place, 1768. His name occurs in 1768 in the imprint to the London edition of Anthony Benezet's *A Short Account of that part of Africa, inhabited by the negroes*. [J. C. B. L.]

ALMON (JOHN), bookseller and publisher in London, Piccadilly, 1763–1805. Almost better known as a writer of slashing political pamphlets than as a publisher and seller of books: but in both fields he won for himself a distinctive place. He was the son of John Almon of Liverpool, and was born there on December 17th, 1737. Having lost both his parents at an early age, he was apprenticed in March 1751 to Mr. Robert Williamson, printer, bookseller, and bookbinder, in Liverpool. At the expiration of his time he went abroad, and on his return in 1759 took up work as a journeyman printer. At the same time he began to contribute articles on public matters to the newspapers. In 1761 the printer of *The Gazetteer* engaged him to conduct that paper. In this year Almon made the acquaintance of John Wilkes, and a warm friendship at once sprang up between the two men. In 1763 he set up as a bookseller in Piccadilly and was appointed bookseller to the Opposition club the "Coterie". His support of Wilkes brought him into trouble with the Government, and in 1770 he was fined for selling a paper containing a reprint of Junius's letter to the King. Amongst his best known publications were the *New Foundling Hospital for Wit*, and *The Parliamentary Register*. In 1781 he retired from business, and soon after lost his wife. In 1784 he married the widow of William Parker, printer of the *General Advertiser*, and then returned to London and plunged into business again. In 1786 he was tried for libel and fled to France; but returning to England died at Boxmoor in Hertfordshire on December 12th, 1805. Timperley says that much of his misfortune was due to a too-trusting disposition, and that he was swindled and robbed by unworthy servants. [*Memoirs of John Almon, bookseller of Piccadilly*, 1790: Timperley, 1842 ed., pp. 713, &c., *D.N.B.*]

AMEY (ROBERT), pamphlet seller in London, Craigs Court, Charing Cross, and Westminster Hall, Court of Requests, 1737–53. His name is first found in the imprint to a pamphlet entitled *The Poet and the Muse*, published in 1737. It is next found in *Observations upon the manifesto of his Catholick Majesty, with an answer* [B.M. T. 1110 (2).] In the following year he was in trouble for selling the *London Evening Post* of Tuesday, April 1 [Dom. S. Papers, Geo. II. Bundle 50–81]. The British Museum has a copy of a pamphlet entitled *Reasons for an immediate war against France*, which bears the imprint, "London; Printed for R. Amey, against Craigs Court, Charing Cross; and sold by A. Dodd without Temple Bar. M.DCC.LX." This date is probably a printer's error, as the pamphlet was advertised in the monthly register of books published in the *Gentleman's Magazine* for 1740. In 1745 Amey was one of the publishers of Christopher Middleton's *Rejoinder to Mr. Dobbs' reply to Captain Middleton* and his address was given as "R. Amey in the Court of Requests". [J. C. B. L.] In 1746 his name appears in an imprint of a pamphlet entitled *Captain Temple West's Defence against Vice-Adm. Lestocks Charge* [Winship]. He was succeeded by J. Barnes (*q.v.*) whose name is found in an advertisement of *The Court and City Register* in January 1753.

ANDERSON (WILLIAM), bookseller and publisher in London, at the Oxford-Theatre, Paternoster-Row, 1759. Dealer in chap-books. Whether he had any business connexion with Woodgate and Brooks (*q.v.*) is unknown; but he published some of the works advertised in their catalogue. Amongst these were the Rev. H. W. Dulworth's *The Royal Assassins* and *The History of the Conquest of Mexico*, both dated 1759.

ANDERTON (Miss), bookseller in Taunton, co. Somerset, 1765–79. A book called *The Wisdom of Divine Providence* was advertised as for sale in 1765 by M. Anderton and others in the West Country, and in 1779 another entitled *The Importance of Truth, &c.* bears the imprint "Sold by Miss Anderton".

ANDERTON (T.), bookseller and bookbinder in Manchester, Shakespeare's Head, near the Market Cross, 1756–62. Mentioned by a correspondent in *Notes and Queries* as in business in 1756. [*N. & Q.* 2 S. I. 364.] In 1762 published the *Manchester Chronicle or Anderton's Universal Advertiser*. [Procter & Timperley.]

ANDREW ( ), bookseller in Evesham, co. Worcester, 1749-63. In 1749 he was one of the agents for the distribution of the catalogues of the Birmingham bookseller, T. Warren. He was still in business in 1763, when his name is found in an advertisement in the *London Evening Post* of a house to be sold on October 6th.

ANDREWS (BENJAMIN), bookseller in London, Charing Cross, 1749. His name occurs in the Poll-Book of that year, for the city of Westminster.

ANDREWS (W.), printer at Chichester in Sussex, 1770. In this year his imprint is found on T. Joel's *An easy Introduction to English Grammar*, printed for the use of Mr. T. Joel's School by W. Andrews. [*Notes on Sussex Printing*, by A. C. Piper; *Library*, July, 1914, p. 257 *et seq.*]

ANDREWS (WILLIAM), printer at Exeter and Plymouth, co. Devon; Exeter, 1763–4, Plymouth, 1765. 1763–5. Printer of the first number of the *Exeter Mercury, or West Country Advertiser* in 1763. In 1764 his name is found in a list of subscribers to Calcott's *Collection of Thoughts*, which he also printed. In the same year he was appointed printer of the *Exeter Flying Post*, but retired from it in November 1765 and went to Plymouth, "there being then no printer there". [Dredge, *Addenda*.]

ANGEL (J.), book or pamphlet seller in London, near the New Church in the Strand, 1759. Only known from the imprint to a pamphlet entitled *The honest grief of a Tory*, published in that year. [J. C. B. L. and W.]

ANGUS (THOMAS), printer in Newcastle-upon-Tyne, Trinity Corner, St. Nicholas's churchyard, 1774–6. This printer appears to have begun business in 1774, in which year he issued the *Freemason's Companion*. He entered into partnership with Thomas Robson, and amongst other things that issued from their press was Hilton's *Poetical Works*. The partnership seems to have been dissolved in 1776. [Welford, p. 39.]

ANSDELL or ANSDALE (JAMES), bookseller and publisher in Liverpool, Derby Square, 1728–77. In Wilford's *Monthly Catalogue* for May, 1728, this bookseller appears as one of the publishers of the Rev. Robert Wright's *Humble Address to the Lords . . . concerning the Longitude*, and he was also the publisher of the Rev. Thomas Maddock's *Sermon preached at St. George's Church in

Liverpool . . . 9th of October* 1746. [B.M. 225. i. 1 (15).] His name continues to be found in the Liverpool Directory until 1777, when he was succeeded by Robert Ansdell. It is possible that the above description applies to two men of the same name, as in a manuscript collection of transcripts of the monumental inscriptions in the churchyard of St. Peter's parish church, Liverpool, is that of James Ansdell, died February 10th, 1758, aged 70.

APPLEBEE (JOHN), printer and bookseller in London, Bolt Court, Fleet Street (1740), 1715–50. *See Dictionary*, 1668–1725. Applebee was still at work in 1740 in Bolt Court, Fleet Street, where he printed *A general remonstrance to the whole people of England . . . concerning the ensuing elections. . . .* [B.M. T. 1110 (11).] In 1748 he was printer to the Middlesex Court of Sessions. [*Cal. of Midd. Sessions Records*, Jan. 174⅞—December 1751, p. 13.] He died about the year 1750, his business being carried on by his widow Elizabeth. There is also a George Appleby, printer, mentioned in the Poll-Book for the City and Liberty of Westminster for 1749 as living in Clements Lane.

ARCHDEACON (JOHN), printer to the University of Cambridge, 1766–95. A native of Ireland, after some previous connexion with the Cambridge University Press, as shown by the Nichols-Bowyer Letters printed in Nichols's *Literary Anecdotes*, II. 459, he succeeded Bentham as Inspector of it on October 29th, 1766, and on December 15th as University Printer. In 1768 his salary was fixed at £140, without any contingent advantages. The principal works issued during Archdeacon's tenure of office were: the facsimile of the *Codex Bezae*, edited by Thos. Kipling, 2 volumes, folio, 1793; Gray's *Commemoration Ode*, set to music by Dr. Randal, 1769; Jas. Nasmith's *Catalogue of the Parker MSS.*, 1777; the *Italian Dialogues* of Agostino Isola, 1774, whose grand-daughter was brought up by Charles and Mary Lamb and became the wife of Edward Moxon the publisher; T. Tanner's *Notitia Monastica*, 1787; Peckard's *Life of Nicholas Ferrar*, 1790; S. T. Coleridge's *Fall of Robespierre*, 1794, and various Bibles and Prayer-Books. He died at Hemingford Abbots September 10th, 1795, aged 70. But two years previously his successor, John Burges, was appointed (1793), and their names appear together until Archdeacon's death. [R. Bowes, *University Printers*, 1884, and *Cambridge Books*, 1894; S. C. Roberts, *Cambridge University Press*, 1921.]

ARCHER (W.), printer in Bath, 1768. His name occurs in the imprint to a volume of *Poems* by T. Underwood published in that year. [B.M. 1162. k. 4.] From August 4th, 1768 to September, 1769, he owned the *Bath Chronicle* in

succession to Cornelius Pope for whom he had managed it. During this time he was joined by R. Cruttwell (*q.v.*).

ARIS (SAMUEL), printer in London, Creed Lane, 1724–55. Mentioned in Samuel Negus's List [1724] as well affected to King George. In 1730 he printed the third edition of *Remarks upon Dr. Clarke's Exposition of the Church-Catechism*, and also D. Waterland's *The Nature, Obligation and Efficacy of the Christian Sacraments*, with the Supplement "issued in the same year. Each of these was printed for John Crownfield at the Rising Sun in St. Paul's Church-Yard, and sold by Cornelius Crownfield, printer to the University of Cambridge." [B.M. T. 697 (2), (3), (4).] In printing these books Aris shows a good assortment of type in all sizes as well as a fount of nonpareil Greek used in the foot-notes. His head-pieces, ornaments, and initial letters were heavy and not particularly artistic. He was still in business at the end of 1755, when he received a bequest of ten pounds from his neighbour Samuel Birt, bookseller. [P.C.C. 304 Paul.]

In the *Public Advertiser* of January 8th, 1775, is a notice of the death of "Mr. Samuel Aris, Printer of the *Birmingham Gazette*". Hutton states in his *Memoires* that Aris was one of only three booksellers in Birmingham in 1750.

ARIS (THOMAS), printer in Birmingham, High Street, 1741–61. Printer and publisher of the *Birmingham Gazette or General Correspondent*, the first number of which appeared November 16th, 1741. In this he stated that he first went to Birmingham in May 1741, but owing to his house not being ready he returned to London, until Michaelmas. Meanwhile another printer from London, R. Walker, who for some years had been publishing a newspaper called the *Warwick and Staffordshire Journal*, started a paper at Birmingham, possibly a continuation of the *Journal*. Walker, however, soon retired, and Aris continued to print until his death, July 4th, 1761. [J. Hill, *Bookmakers of Old Birmingham*, pp. 52–3.]

ASHBURNER (ANTHONY), bookseller in Kendal, co. Westmoreland, 1763. Took up his freedom in 1763–4. Was perhaps son or relative of Thomas Ashburner of Kendal. [J. P. Earwaker, *Local Gleanings*, I. 31.]

ASHBURNER (THOMAS), printer in Kendal, co. Westmoreland, Fishmarket, 1730–76. Believed to have succeeded Thomas Cotton (*q.v.*) Printer of the *Kendal Weekly Mercury*, which succeeded the *Kendal Courant*, in 1733. This second Kendal newspaper continued until 1745. Was also printer of *The Agreeable Miscellany or something to please every mans taste*. In 1777 he issued a sheet almanac, called the *Kendal Diary*.

ASHFORD or AYSHFORD (JOHN), bookseller and publisher in London, Westminster Hall, 1726–8. In Wilford's *Monthly Catalogue* for March 1726 he advertised a *History of the amours of the Marshal de Boufflers*. Again in 1728 his name, amongst others, is found in the imprint to the first volume of Dr. Richard Rawlinson's *New Method of studying History*, and amongst other books sold by him in that year was Joseph Mitchell's *Ratho, a poem to the King*. The position of his stall is not known. He was afterwards a clerk in the City, and in 1732 was accused, but acquitted, of a felony.

ASHURST (SAMUEL), stationer in London, Paternoster Row, 1736(?)–53. Son of Samuel Ashurst, citizen and merchant of London. The date when he first set up in business is not recorded, but he prospered, and in 1736–7 was Master of the Company of Stationers. According to Timperley, p. 688 (1842 ed.) Samuel Ashurst died on November 8th, 1753.

ASHMEAD ( ), bookseller (?) in Tewkesbury, co. Gloucester, 1753. Mentioned in an advertisement as one who sold the *Daily Register*.

ASTLEY (THOMAS), bookseller and publisher in London, Dolphin and Crown, St. Paul's Churchyard, 1726–59. Mentioned in Wilford's *Monthly Catalogue* for September, 1726, as the publisher of the Rev. Tobias Swinden's *Enquiry into the Nature and place of Hell*. He also dealt in plays and miscellaneous literature. In 1732 he was sharing copyrights with Stephen Austin and Weaver Bickerton (*q.v.*). In 1742 the sign of his house was The Rose in St. Paul's Churchyard. On April 3rd, 1747, in company with Edward Cave of St. John's Gate, he was arrested for printing an account of the trial of Simon Lord Lovat. After a strict examination by the House of Lords, he was discharged upon paying the fees. Thomas Astley died on February 28th, 1759. [Nichols, vols. III and V.]

ATKINS (THOMAS), stationer in London, Queens Head and Half Moon against Bread Street in Cheapside, *c.* 1744. Issued a trade card with portrait of Queen Anne. Succeeded by Charles Powell. [A. Heal's Collection.]

ATKINS (TIMOTHY) (?), bookseller and publisher in London, Dr. Sacheverell's Head, near St. Paul's, 1729. This imprint appears on the title-page of a satirical poem by "Jacob Gingle, Esq.", entitled *The Oxford Sermon versified*. It was probably fictitious. [W.] The imprint "London, printed for Timothy Atkins 1729" appears in *Dean Jonathan's Parody on the 4th Chap. of Genesis*.

ATKINSON (JOSEPH), bookseller and publisher in Newcastle-upon-Tyne, Groat Market, 1769–88. A correspondent to *Notes & Queries* [10 S. VI. 443] states that he was in business in 1769, and that he died on August 6th, 1788, and was buried in St. John's Churchyard. In the *Newcastle Chronicle* of 1776 is a list of books published by him.

ATKINSON (THOMAS), bookseller and publisher in York, Minster Yard, 1758. Publisher of a pamphlet entitled *An Answer to a Letter addressed to the Dean of York*, 1758. [Davies, *History*, p. 256.]

AUSTEN or AUSTIN (STEPHEN), bookseller and publisher in London, (1) Angel and Bible, in St. Paul's Churchyard, 1730; (2) Newgate Street, 1747. 1730–50. Dealt chiefly in law-books and theology. Amongst his more important undertakings were W. Wotton's *Discourse concerning the Confusion of Tongues*, printed in 1730 and edited by William Bowyer, and *A New History of the Bible*, by the Rev. Thomas Stackhouse. Second edition, 1742. A list of his publications is given at the end of *A Sermon occasioned by the Distemper among the Cattle*, printed in 1747. [B.M. 695. f. 10 (23).] He died in December 1750, and his widow Elizabeth, in 1770, married John Hinton the bookseller. [*Decision of the Court of Session upon . . . Literary Property*, 1774, p. ii.] Another Stephen Austen, possibly his son, was carrying on business as a bookseller in Ludgate Hill in 1766, when he published a pamphlet entitled *The Celebrated Speech of a Celebrated Commoner* [W. Pitt].

AUSTIN (STEPHEN), printer in Hertford, 1768–76. Apprenticed to George Kearsley, of Ludgate Hill. In 1768 began as a printer and schoolmaster at Hertford, and in 1772 started a newspaper called the *Hartford Mercury*, which afterwards became the *Hartford, Bedford, and Huntingdon Mercury*. Stephen Austin was succeeded by his son Stephen, and the firm have always made a speciality of oriental printing.

AXTEL (T.), bookseller and publisher in London, Royal Exchange, 1774–6. Publisher of political and other pamphlets. In 1774 his name is found in the imprint of *A Faithful Account of the . . . transactions relating to a late affair of honour*, the publication of which he shared with R. Snagg of Paternoster-Row. In 1776 Axtel was sentenced to three months imprisonment for printing (? publishing) another tract called *The Crisis*. [Timperley, 1842, p. 736.]

AYRES, *see* Eyres.

AYSCOUGH (ANNE), printer in Nottingham, 1719–32 (?). Widow of William Ayscough; probably carried on the printing business until her son George (*q.v.*) was old enough to manage it. Charles Deering (*Nottinghamia vetus et nova*, 1751) says she died on December 16th, 1732, but there seems to be some error in this, as the Rev. S. F. Creswell in his *Collections*, [p. 25] records a theological pamphlet as sold by Anne Ayscough in Nottingham in 1737.

AYSCOUGH (GEORGE), printer, bookseller, and publisher in Nottingham, 1734–46. Son of William Ayscough. [1710–19]. The Deering manuscript states that Ann Ayscough was made guardian of her son George, then 17 years of age, in 1732. According to the Rev. S. F. Creswell [p. 23] he was in business as a printer two years later, when he issued *The excellent use of Psalmody . . .* by R. W. In 1746 he sold a sermon preached by the Rev. Richard Arnold, rector of Thurcaston, co. Leicester. [B.M. 226. i. 2 (21).]

AYSHEFORD, *see* Ashford.

BADHAM (C.), bookseller and publisher in Hereford, 1769–76. Agent for the monthly parts of Smollett's *History of England*, in 1769. He was still in business in 1776.

BAGNALL (JOHN), *see Dictionary*, 1668–1725.

BAILEY (JAMES), Master of the Company of Stationers, 1768.

BAILEY or BAILY (   ), bookseller, Bury St. Edmunds, 1725. Mentioned in a list of provincial booksellers. [*N. & Q.* 10 S. v, February 24th, 1906, p. 141.]

BAILEY or BAYLEY (RICHARD), bookseller and publisher in Lichfield, 1729–53. Probably a descendant of William Bailey (1685, *see Dictionary*, 1668–1725), and doubtless related to S. Bailye, a printer in Coventry. In 1729 he sold the Rev. W. Baker's sermon preached in the Cathedral at Lichfield on July 21st, 1728, called *The Credibility of Mysteries*. In 1743 he sold a sermon of Rev. W. Denham's entitled *On the Ascension* [B.M. 225. g. 20 (14)], and again his name occurs on a sermon preached at St. Chad's on October 1st, 1747, by the Rev. M. Horbery. [B.M. 225. f. 16 (3).] In 1753 he or another of his name appears in an advertisement of those selling copies of the *Daily Advertiser*.

BAILEY or BAILYE (S.), printer and bookseller in Coventry, co. Warwick, 1743. Probably related to William Bailey who kept a bookseller's shop at Burton-on-Trent, Lichfield, Tamworth, and Wolverhampton in 1685 [*see*

Dictionary, 1668–1725], and also to Richard Bailye, bookseller in Lichfield in 1743, in which year he printed the Rev. W. Denham's sermon *On the Ascension*. [B.M. 225. g. 20 (14).]

BAILEY (THOMAS), printer in Stamford, co. Lincoln, 1710–28. *See Dictionary*, 1668–1725, p. 324. Still in business in 1728.

BAILEY or BAYLEY (THOMAS), printer in London, Petticoat Lane, 1763. Only known from his having printed a tract by Sarah Osborn entitled *The nature, certainty and evidence of true Christianity. In a letter from a gentlewoman in New England, to her dear Friend* . . . 1763. [J. C. B. L.]

BAILEY (W.), printer in London, 28 Great Tower Street, 1775. Printer and publisher of a pamphlet entitled "*The rise, progress and present state, of the dispute between the people of America, and the Administration. By the Bishop of* . . ." The imprint runs, "London: Printed and sold by W. Bailey, at 28, Great Tower-street; where Tradesmens bills are printed neat and reasonable, and printing in general perform'd." [J. C. B. L.]

BAILYE, *see* Bailey.

BAINBRIDGE (   ), bookseller in Barnard Castle, Durham, 1764. Mentioned by a correspondent to *Notes & Queries* [10 S. VI. 443].

BAKER (   ), bookseller in Tonbridge, co. Kent, 1765. His name appears in an advertisement of the sale of *Registrum Roffense*, in the *Gazetteer and Daily Advertiser* for August 26th, 1765.

BAKER (J.), bookseller, "over against Hatton Garden", 1726– . There is an advertisement in the *London Journal* of February 5th, 1726, of *A Practical Treatise*, a medical book, printed for and sold by J. Baker and others.

BAKER (THOMAS), bookseller and printer in Southampton, 1767–76. His name is first found in the imprint to a "*Manual of religious Liberty*. By an author, as yet, unknown", published in 1767. This imprint wound up in a somewhat unusual way: and "sold by all the booksellers in England and Corsica". He kept a circulating library two doors above Butcher Row in the High Street. He was the printer of the *Southampton Guide*. [Edwards, *Early Hampshire Printers*, p. 118.]

BAKER (SAMUEL), bookseller, publisher, and book-auctioneer in London, York Street, Covent Garden, 1736–78. The original founder of the modern firm of Sotheby. Little seems to be known of his early history, but he was

established in London as a bookseller before 1739, in which year he was appointed by the Society for the Encouragement of Learning, one of its six booksellers, and several letters written by him relating to it are preserved in the British Museum. [Add. MS. 6190, 59, 67, 73, 74.] In 1744 he began to hold sales of books by auction, and was joined by George Leigh in 1775. In January 1775 an advertisement in the *Public Advertiser* states that an edition of *Orlando Furioso*, elegantly printed by Baskerville, was to be had of Baker and Leigh, York Street, Covent Garden, and again on the 12th July *Archaeologia*, published by the Society of Antiquarians of London, was to be had "at their house in Chancery Lane and of S. Baker & G. Leigh". Samuel Baker died on April 24th, 1778, aged 66, and was buried in the churchyard of St. Paul's, Covent Garden. [Timperley, 1842, p. 742.]

BAKER (WILLIAM), printer in London, (1) Cullum Street; (2) Ingram Court. 1763–85. The son of a schoolmaster at Reading. Originally intended for the Church; but the plans falling through, William Baker was apprenticed to Mr. Kippax, a printer in Cullum Street, after whose death he succeeded to the business. He afterwards moved to Ingram Court, and died on September 29th, 1785. William Baker was a man of considerable attainments, with a knowledge of Greek, Hebrew, French, Latin, and Italian, and he was the author of two works that had some vogue in their day. One of these, printed in 1770, was entitled *Peregrinations of the Mind through the Most General and Interesting Subjects which are usually agitated in Life*, and the second was *Theses Graecae et Latinae Selectae*, 1780. The first was reprinted in 1811 with a life of the author. [Nichols, *Lit. Anecd.* III. 715.]

BAKER (W. and D.), publishers in London, 1753. *The Court and City Register*, was issued by their firm, in conjunction with several others. [The *Public Advertiser*, January 12th, 1753.]

BAKER and LEIGH, booksellers and auctioneers. *See* BAKER (SAMUEL) and LEIGH (GEORGE).

BAKEWELL (ELIZABETH), bookseller and publisher in London, opposite Birchin Lane, Cornhill, 1759. In partnership with H. Parker. They were the publishers of Richard Rolt's *Lives of the Reformers*, 1759, fol., a work remarkable for the fine portraits with which it is illustrated.

BAKEWELL (THOMAS), map and print-seller in London. 1. Next door to the Horn Tavern in Fleet Street. 2. Against the end of Birchin Lane in Cornhill, *c.* 1750. Issued two trade cards, one with a medley of illustrations. [A. Heal's

Collection.] Sold maps for exportation and "Pictures in Oyl for Chimney Pieces". Succeeded by Elizabeth Bakewell (*q. v.*).

BALDWIN (HENRY), printer in London, Britannia Printing Office, White Fryers, Fleet St., *c.* 1766. Amongst the numerous works printed by this firm were *Read's Weekly Journal* and the *Daily Chronicle.*

BALDWIN (ROBERT), bookseller and publisher in London, The Rose, 47 Paternoster Row, 1749–1810. Nephew and successor to R. Baldwin. For many years an important publisher of political and other pamphlets. Died March 30th, 1810. Timperley records that "his industry and integrity were almost proverbial". He was succeeded by Robert, the son of an older nephew. The literature sold by the house of Baldwin both in Warwick Lane and Paternoster Row during the seventeenth and eighteenth centuries is a mirror of the political and social history of those times; much of it is now scarce. The life story of the men themselves is very difficult to unravel, and it is to be hoped that before long some bibliographer will publish a full history of the firm and its work. Amongst the numerous works published by Robert, the following have been noted: 1753, *Memoires of Bolingbroke, History of England,* "sold by R. Baldwin junior", the *London Magazine*; 1765, *Plays of Shakespeare,* by Samuel Johnson, in temporary partnership with several others; 1775, *The Ladies Complete Pocket Book,* with three other publishers.

BALLARD (EDWARD), bookseller and book-auctioneer in London, Rising Sun, Little Britain, 1726–96. Succeeded Thomas Ballard at the above address. As he was born in the house he was probably son of Thomas. In 1768 he issued a catalogue of his stock, consisting of nearly ten thousand volumes in all classes of literature. Died January 2nd, 1796, aged 88. [Nichols, I. 423.] His will, which was proved on February 20th, 1796, only mentions his sister Elizabeth. In addition to his copyright, he held a share in the *Daily Advertiser.* [Nichols, III. 405; P.C.C. 60; Harris.] There was also a firm of S. & E. Ballard who in 1758 published John Leusden's *Liber Psalmorum.*

BALLARD (THOMAS), *see Dictionary,* 1668–1725. Still in business in 1728 when he advertised a sale of books at St. Paul's Coffee House. [*Daily Journal.*]

BALLINGER (J.), bookseller in Cirencester, 1726. Probably successor of W. Ballinger, who in 1723 had sold there an Assize Sermon by Wm. Shaw, printed by Raikes and Dicey at Gloucester. In 1726 sold the *Lives of six notorious Murderers executed at Kingston for the murder of T. Ball,* printed by Raikes. [R. Austin, Cat. of Gloucestershire Collections.]

BALLY (WILLIAM), bookseller in Bath, Milsom Street, 1720–74. Took up his freedom as a citizen of Bath in 1720. [Chamberlain's Accounts.] On March 27th, 1732, he paid £10 for 99 years' lease of a messuage, lying between the backway to the Swan Inn, north, John Willet's house, south, for the lives of himself and his sons William and John. [Council Minutes.] About the year 1773, it may have been later, R. Cruttwell printed a new edition of *The New Bath Guide,* to which is prefixed a plan of the City, bearing the imprint, "Printed for and sold only by W. Bally and A. Tennent, booksellers in Milsom Street, Bath". In 1774 his name is found in an advertisement in the *Bath Chronicle* as one of the booksellers selling Dr. Gill's *Exposition of the New Testament.* William Bally died on August 29th, 1774, and was buried in St. Michaels, on September 3rd. [*Bath Chronicle,* and Parish Register.] The business was carried on by his widow, M. Bally, who in November 1774 opened a circulating library and reading-room, where in addition to all the London and provincial newspapers, readers might consult Faulkner's *Dublin Journal.* The firm was still in existence in 1778. [P. Thicknesse, *Bath Guide,* 1778, p. 56.]

BANCKS (T.), bookseller in Warrington, 1761–74. Mentioned by a correspondent in *Notes & Queries* as at work in 1761. His name is found again in an advertisement in Adam's *Weekly Courant* for January 1774. [*N. & Q.* 11 S. I. 364.]

BANNISTER (WILLIAM), stationer in London, Queen's Arms, near York Buildings in the Strand, 1728. In Wilford's *Monthly Catalogue* for April 1728 occurs the advertisement of a pamphlet entitled *The Objections of a Late Anonymous Writer against the Book of Daniel,* which was to be sold by the above stationer.

BARBER (JOSEPH), bookseller in Newcastle-upon-Tyne, Amen Corner, 1740–81. A native of Dunshauglin near Dublin, and well known as an ancestor of the late Bishop Lightfoot. He appears to have begun business in 1748, and in 1776 his name has been found in a list of booksellers receiving subscriptions for a suggested edition of the lectures of the Rev. J. Murray; but the work does not seem to have been issued. There is a memorial to him and his family in the Cathedral ground, Newcastle. The firm ultimately became Barber and Son. [Information supplied by R. A. Peddie; *N. & Q.* 10 S. VI. 443.]

BARKER (BENJAMIN), bookseller in London, Bowling Alley, Westminster, 1701–58. *See Dictionary,* 1668–1725. His name is found in the Poll-Book for the

City and Liberty of Westminster for 1749, and he was still publishing in 1758, when his name is found in the imprint to Johannes Leusden's *Liber Psalmorum.* [J. C. B. L.]

BARKER (C.), bookseller in Chester, 1774. His name occurs in an advertisement in Adam's *Weekly Courant* for January 1774.

BARKER (S.), bookseller, Russel Street, Covent Garden, 1735. His name is among others in an advertisement in the *Daily Journal* of February 4th, 1735, as taking subscriptions for Otway's *The Orphan,* in the issue for February 13th, for his *Caius Marius.*

BARNES (JOHN), bookseller and publisher in London, (1) *London Gazette,* Charing Cross, 1749; (2) opposite the Haymarket; (3) in the Court of Request, 1753. His name occurs in the Poll-Book for that year, and he was the publisher of O'Connor's *Considerations upon the Trade to Africa,* issued in the same year. In 1753 he moved to a house opposite the Haymarket, and also had a stall in Westminster Hall in the Court of Request in succession to Robert Amey (*q. v.*); both these later addresses being found in the imprint to the second edition of *A Candid Narrative of the Rise and Progress of the ... Moravians. By Henry Rimius.* [J. C. B. L.]

BARRETT (JOHN), bookseller in Oxford, 1744–53. On February 6th, 174$\frac{3}{4}$ he was appointed "privilegiatus bibliopola" by the University [Foster's *Alumni*]. Amongst his publications in 1751 was Warton's *Ode to Music* which he shared with other booksellers. He lived at No. 12 Amsterdam Court, High Street, where he died in 1753; administration of his goods being granted on April 7th, 1753. [Griffiths.]

BARROW (ANTHONY), Junior, bookbinder in London, at the Sign of the Crown in Panton Street, by Leicester Fields, *c.* 1727. Described himself as "French bookbinder" and in the *Daily Post* for April 22nd, 1727, advertised for sale, "a new choice Parcel of the best Italian Books, lately imported, with some Latin Books of antient Editions".

BARSTOW (BENJAMIN), bookseller and publisher in York, Ousegate, 1744–50, in partnership with S. Stabler. They succeeded to the business of Thomas Hammond. Caesar Ward printed for them the Rev. John Plaxton's *Sermon,* preached at the Parish Church of St. Michael the Belfry, on Sunday, November 17th, 1745. [Davies, *History,* p. 252.]

BARTLET, or BARTLETT (A.) (?), pamphlet seller in London, at the Royal Exchange, 1739–40. One of a number of booksellers and others who sold William Seward's *Journal of a Voyage from Savannah to Philadelphia and from Philadelphia to England* ... 1740. [J. C. B. L.] Probably identical with Mrs. Bartlett at the same address.

BASKERVILLE (JOHN), type-founder and printer in Birmingham, London, and Cambridge, 1706–75. This eminent type-founder, whose skill was equal to that of William Caslon, was born at Sion Hill, Wolverley, Worcestershire, on January 28th, 1706, of lowly parents. He developed great skill in handwriting and the cutting of monumental inscriptions. When about twenty years of age he began to teach writing and book-keeping in a little court near the High Town, Birmingham, and later kept a school in the Bull Ring. When John Turner commenced the japanning of snuff boxes, Baskerville created a complete revolution in the manufacture of japanned goods. Starting in business at 22 Moor Street in 1740, where he remained until 1749, he quickly became so prosperous that in 1745 he was able to take a lease of an estate of eight acres, which he named Easy Hill, and there he built a house and suitable buildings wherein he continued the japanning business. He also purchased a pair of cream-coloured horses, and a coach with panels characteristically painted with representations of branches of his business. About 1750 Baskerville interested himself in type-founding and spent a large amount of money in experiments before he succeeded in producing a type to his taste, eventually publishing the fruit of his experiments in the Virgil of 1757, followed by Milton's *Poetical Works* in 1758. In that year the University of Oxford contracted with Baskerville for a complete alphabet of Greek types in Great Primer. This type is described by Reed in his *Old English Letter Foundries* as "stiff and cramped", while Rowe Mores described it as "execrable". It was generally considered a failure, and Baskerville wisely gave up the attempt to cut foreign or learned founts, and for the future confined his attention to English. His ambition was to print a Common Prayer Book, and a Bible; but the privilege of printing these belonged to the Universities, so he applied to the University of Cambridge to help him in the matter. He was accordingly elected one of the printers to the University for ten years from December 16th, 1758, and an agreement was drawn up setting forth the number of copies to be printed of the Prayer Book and the Bible, under the supervision of the Inspector of the University Press, and the payment to be made, with sufficient security required. In June 1759 he had his printing presses installed in Cambridge, and had written a letter to the Vice-Chancellor from Birmingham, dated May 31st, to say that he had sent everything requisite to begin the printing. During 1760 the Book of Common Prayer was issued in four varying forms, two more in 1761, and one in 1762. His edition of the Bible in folio was issued in 1763. In 1762, by a special arrangement with the University Press, he printed an edition of the Common Prayer in foolscap octavo. But Baskerville's connexion with the Cambridge University Press did not prove happy. Although he had succeeded in fulfilling the ambition of his life, he was bitterly disappointed, and when the Bible was completed handed over his presses and material to his journeyman, Robert Martin (*q.v.*). In 1669, having quarreled with Martin, he took back his types and printed successfully himself, until his death on January 8th, 1775. His types were dispersed after his death. Use was made of them for two editions of Voltaire's *Works*, printed at Kehl during the years 1785–9. His wife Sarah continued the printing business until April, 1775, and two books bear her imprint. She continued the type-foundry until February 1777.

BASKERVILLE (SARAH), widow of John Baskerville, printer at Birmingham. See Baskerville, John.

BASKETT (JOHN), *see Dictionary*, 1668–1725.

BASKETT (MARK), printer in London and Oxford, 1742–67. Probably son of Thomas Baskett and grandson of John Baskett, the King's Printer. Held a share in the King's Printing Office, which in 1770 came into the hands of Charles Eyre. He also held a lease of the Clarendon Printing House in Oxford. This expired in 1765 when, after a spirited competition with Charles Eyre, and Messrs. Wright and Gill of London, Mark Baskett surrendered all title to the house, &c., to the last named, who secured the contract. In a contemporary record it is said that Mark Baskett neither understood nor gave any attention to the business of printing, leaving the care of it to his servants, who were a set of idle and drunken men, and that his printing-house was more like an ale-house. [Add. MS. 6880.] The first Bible bearing his imprint was that of 1761. The date of his death is unknown; but as he is mentioned in the will of his uncle Robert, who died in 1767 [P.C.C. 253 Legard], he was evidently still alive in that year.

BASKETT (ROBERT), printer in London and Oxford, 1742–4. Son of John Baskett. His name is found in Bible imprints, between 1742 and 1744: but he was not a printer, only enjoying a share of the patents during his life. He is perhaps identical with the Robert Baskett, Esq., of Epsom in Surrey, who made his will on August 2nd, 1766. He makes no mention of the printing business; but nominated his nephew Mark Baskett of Dorking, one of his trustees and executors. This will was proved on July 15th, 1767. [P.C.C. 253 Legard.]

BASKETT (THOMAS), printer in London and Oxford, 1742–61. Son of John Baskett. Succeeded his father as King's Printer and also to the business of Bible Printing at the Clarendon printing office in Oxford. He died March 30th, 1761 [Timperley, 1842, p. 706], leaving a son Mark Baskett, who is called nephew in the will of Robert Baskett, proved on July 15th, 1767.

BASNETT (J.), stationer in Bath, 1770. Dealer in maps and plans. The plan of the city of Bath prefixed to the *Strangers' Assistant and Guide to Bath*, printed in 1773, bears the imprint: Sold by J. Basnett, Stationer, Bath. In all probability he was also a bookseller, but not a publisher.

BASSAM (ROBERT), bookseller and publisher in London, 53 St. John's Street, West Smithfield, 1750? The imprint of this publisher has been found in an undated copy of a novel entitled *The Discreet Princess*, &c. A work with the title *The Discreet Princess or the Adventures of Finetta. A Novel*, is in the British Museum, but only has the imprint: "London. Printed in the Year 1755." [B.M. 12510. c. 40 (2).]

BATHOE (SAMUEL), bookseller in London, the Strand, 1768. There seems to be some uncertainty as to the Christian name of Bathoe the bookseller. Nichols gives it as "Samuel" in one place and "William" in another. Timperley plumps for Samuel and copies Nichols's note on "William", who is said to have died October 2nd, 1768.

BATHOE (WILLIAM), bookseller and publisher in London, near Exeter Change in the Strand, 1749–68. His name occurs in the Poll-Book for the City and Liberty of Westminster, as living in Church Lane in 1749. He was one of the publishers of the *Court & City Kalendar*, and his name is found in the imprint to a political pamphlet entitled *Opposition to the late Minister*. Nichols records his death as taking place on October 2nd, 1768.

BATHURST (CHARLES), bookseller and publisher in London, (1) at the Cross Keys, against St. Dunstan's Church; (2) at the Middle Temple Gates, Fleet Street. 1737–86. Successor to B. Motte (*q. v.*). Was reputed to be a baronet. He was bookseller to Dr. John Taylor, F.S.A., and is mentioned in a letter to Dr. Ducarel written by Taylor in 1753, and also in a letter from Wm. Bowyer to the Rev. S. Pegge relating to some books. He was interested in most of the important publications issued during his lifetime. He died July 21st, 1786, aged 77. [Nichols, II. 256.]

BATLEY (J.), bookseller and publisher in London, The Dove, Paternoster Row. [*See Dictionary*, 1668–1725.]

BATTLY (HENRY), bookseller (?) and publisher in Ipswich, Butter Market, 1763. The *Confession of Richard Ringe and Margery Beddingfield*, a broadside, bears the imprint: "Ipswich: Printed for Henry Battly in the Butter Market." [1763.] [B.M. 1891. d. 1 (14).] It is very doubtful if he was a bookseller.

BAXTER (GALPINE), stationer in London, No. 58 Cornhill, third door from Gracechurch Street, *c.* 1770. Issued a trade card about this date. [A. Heal's Collection.]

BEATNIFFE (RICHARD), printer, bookseller, and publisher in Norwich, 1 Cockey Lane, 1773–1818. Born at Louth in Lincolnshire in 1740. Apprentice to Mr. Hollingworth, a bookseller at Lynn. Publisher of the first edition of the Rev. Thos. Pyle's *Sixty Sermons*, in 1773. He appears to have succeeded W. Chase at the above address, although Timperley says that he took the business of Jonathan Gleed but gives no date, and as we hear nothing of Gleed after 1754, at which date Richard Beatniffe would have only been fourteen years old, there seems to be a mistake on Timperley's part. Beatniffe was the author, printer, and publisher of *The Norfolk Tour*, which appeared first in 1772. He died on July 9th, 1818. [Timperley, 1842, p. 868.] Issued a small trade card with a representation of the Bible at the top, without date. [A. Heal's Collection.]

BECKETT (J. B.), bookseller in Bristol, 1774. Mentioned in a list of provincial booksellers by a correspondent in *Notes & Queries* [11 S. II. 23].

BECKET and DE HONDT, *see* Becket (Thomas).

BECKET (THOMAS), bookseller and publisher in London, Tully's Head in the Strand (east corner of the Adelphi, or near Surrey Street), 1760–76. Apprentice to Andrew Millar in the Strand. Set up for himself at Tully's Head near Surrey Street in the Strand on January 14th, 1760, and placed an advertisement in the *London Chronicle or Universal Post* of January 8–10, in connexion with an edition of *Roderick Random*. He imported French literature and published periodical lists of new books from France. Amongst his earliest publications was a romance called *Chrysal or the Adventures of a Guinea*, which was first advertised in April 1760. This work went through several editions before the end of the century. Before the end of the year 1760 Becket took into partnership Peter Abraham De Hondt, and the firm published large numbers of romances, plays, and poems. They were the leading prosecutors in the famous copyright case against Alexander and James Donaldson for printing an edition of Thomson's *Seasons* in 1768, which ended so disastrously for the booksellers. In 1775 Boswell wrote to Johnson asking what Becket meant by saying, in the *Public Advertiser* of January 20th, that he had the original of *Fingal* in his shop in 1762, but could not get enough subscribers to encourage him to publish it, and returned the manuscript to the proprietor. About this time Becket is described as "Bookseller to their Royal Highnesses the Prince of Wales, Prince William and Prince Edward". Sterne in one of his letters says of him: "Becket I have ever found to be a man of probity." [*Letters of the late Rev. Mr. Lawrence Sterne*, 1775–8, p. 164.]

BEDFORD (J.), publisher and bookseller, The Crown, St. Paul's Churchyard, 1765. There is an advertisement in the *Gazetteer and Daily Advertiser*, September 16th, 1765, of *The Life of Christ*, printed for, and sold by, J. Bedford & C. Sympton, Fleet Street.

BEECROFT (JOHN), bookseller and publisher in London, Paternoster Row, 1740–79. Son of John Beecroft, of the City of Norwich, gentleman. Held shares in most of the important publications of his day. He was for many years agent to the University of Cambridge. Master of the Company of Stationers in 1773. Died at Walthamstow, November 12th, 1779. [Timperley, 1842, p. 745.] He shared in the publication of Theobald's *Shakespeare* in 1775.

BEEVOR (H.), bookseller in London, Little Britain, 1768. His name appears in the imprint to the third volume of Almon's *Political Register*, 1768.

BELL (ARCHIBALD), bookseller and publisher in London, (1) No. 8, near the Saracen's Head, Aldgate; (2) near the Stone Pump, Aldgate, 1773. His name occurs in the imprint to a volume of *Poems* said to have been written by a negro slave named Phillis Wheatley in 1773. [B.M. 992. a. 34.] On the last leaf two other works are advertised by the same publisher. *The Memoirs of Miss Williams*, and *The Church-Members' Directory*, both issued in the same year. No doubt both addresses refer to the same house.

BELL (JOHN), bookseller and publisher in London, near Exeter Change, Strand, 1768 (?)–1831. Succeeded Mrs. Bathoe at the above address. Amongst the most enterprising and successful booksellers in London during the second half of the eighteenth century. Timperley sums up his character as "one of the most marked men of his day: he possessed a masculine understanding which a long course of observation, and a particular quickness and facility in observing, had very highly cultivated, so as to have given him a judgement as just and exact as his powers of conception were vigorous and acute". At least he showed much better judgement of the public desire than his brother publishers, by the issue of books in small sizes, which created some friction. Andrew Millar, writing to his manager, T. Cadell, says: "It is as bad as robbery for Bell to supply the market with every book." The bulk of his work lies outside the limits of this Dictionary, but his duodecimo edition of Shakespeare's *Works* began to appear in 1774, and his *British Theatre* in 1776. He was one of the first to engage William Bulmer, the printer from Newcastle. On October 20th, 1769, he married a Miss Doree of Ongar in Essex. [*London Chronicle*, October 19th–21st, 1769.]

BELL (NATHANIEL), bookseller in York, Pavement, 1739–78. This bookseller was a member of the Society of Friends and published numerous books for them. In 1757 he was elected one of the City Chamberlains and died in 1778.

BELLAMY (T.), bookseller and publisher in Kingston-upon-Thames, 1754–7. In 1754 his name occurs in an advertisement of *The Young Attorney and Gentleman's Assistant*, and in 1757 he published the Rev. D. Bellamy's *Family Preacher*.

BENNET (J.), bookseller in London, The Crown, in Crown Court, St. Ann's, Soho, 1765. There is an advertisement in the *Gazetteer and Daily Advertiser* of July 20th, 1765, of him and others selling *The Practical Surveyor*.

BENSLEY (T[HOMAS ?]), printer and publisher in London, 2 Swan Yard, Strand, 1775. Possibly father of Thomas Bensley the noted printer of a later date. In the *Public Advertiser* of July 10th, 1775, he advertised a translation into

English from the French, of a sermon preached by the Rev. A. J. Roustan, pastor of the Helvetick Church in Soho, upon the occasion of its dedication. The translation was entitled: *Considerations on the Present State of Christianity*.

BENTHAM (JOSEPH), printer to the University of Cambridge, 1740–78. The son of Samuel Bentham, vicar of Witchford, near Ely. Was appointed Inspector, March 28th, 1740, and University Printer, on the resignation of Cornelius Crownfield (*q. v.*), December 14th, 1740: and from his appointment until the death of Crownfield (1743) both names appear on the titles of books issued during that period. He belonged to the Stationers' Company, and was an alderman of the town, living in the house attached to the University Press. He died June 1, 1778, and was buried in Trumpington church. During his tenancy of office the University was engaged, from 1741 to 1758, in a law-suit brought by Baskett to restrain their printing of Law Books, but the Court of King's Bench decided in favour of the University. Many works of importance were printed during his term of office (see R. Bowes, *Cambridge Books*; S. C. Roberts, *Cambridge University Press*), and later (1771) the University printed the *History of Ely Cathedral* by his brother, the Rev. James Bentham. He had the curious experience of having John Baskerville (*q. v.*) appointed one of the University Printers specially to print editions of the Prayer Book and Bible, whilst he was doing the same at the University Press.

BERINGTON (E.), *see Dictionary*, 1668–1725. Still at work in 1726.

BERROW (HARVEY), printer in Worcester, near the Cross, 1748–77. Berrow had been apprenticed to the printing trade in London and came to Worcester as assistant to Stephen Bryan who, before his death in 1748, assigned over to him the newspaper then known as the *Worcester Post or Western Journal*, which has ever since been known as *Berrow's Worcester Journal*. Berrow died in June 1777, and his widow, E. Berrow, carried on the business for two years, and then transferred it to a nephew, J. Tymbs. [Rev. J. R. Burton, *Early Worcestershire Printers and Books*, 1897; *The Oldest English Newspaper*, Worcester, 1890, p. 14.]

BERRY (CHRISTOPHER), bookseller and publisher in Norwich, Dove Lane, near the Market-Place, 1751–76. An advertisement by this bookseller appeared in the *Ipswich Journal* of 1751, and in 1773 he published a work by Joseph Phipps entitled *The Original and Present State of Man*, in which the writer upheld the doctrine and teaching of the Quakers. [B.M. T. 198. 4.]

BETTESWORTH (ARTHUR), bookseller in London, Paternoster Row, 1726–38. *See Dictionary*, 1668–1725. In 1738 Kent's *Directory* records Arthur Bettesworth and Company. Arthur Bettesworth's will was proved on June 9th, 1739. He left his copies of books to his son Thomas who was then under age, but his stock in co-partnership he left to be divided between all his children equally.

BETTINSON (HANNAH), printer in Sherborne, co. Dorset, 1746. With J. Bettinson, perhaps her son, carried on the printing of the *Sherborne Mercury*, after the death of her husband William Bettinson (*q. v.*). [C. H. Mayo, *Bibl. Dorset.*, p. 76.]

BETTINSON (J.), printer in Sherborne, co. Dorset, 1746. Successor to William Bettinson as printer of the *Sherborne Mercury*. [C. H. Mayo, *Bibl. Dorset.*, p. 76.]

BETTINSON (WILLIAM), printer in Sherborne, co. Dorset, 1731–46. Printer of the *Sherborne Mercury*. Said to have come from London. In partnership with G. Price. The first number appeared on February 21st, 1736–7. Died at Sherborne, and was buried September 5th, 1746. [C. H. Mayo, *Bibl. Dorset.*, p. 76.]

BETTS ( ), bookseller and publisher in London, 1736. In 1736 he published, *Rudiments of Latin Grammar Explained*. [Nichols, *Lit. Anecd.* II. 86.] The only copy in the B.M. bears the imprint: "Lovain, Printed in the Year MDCCXXXVI", and makes no mention of the publisher. [B.M. 12934. e. 4.]

BEVINS (EDWARD), bookseller, bookbinder, and stationer in London, Bible and Dove, corner of Brownlow Street, near Great Turnstile in Holbourn (*sic*) *c.* 1740. Issued a trade card about that time. [A. Heal's Collection.]

BEW (JOHN), bookseller and publisher in London, 28 Paternoster Row, 1774 (?)–1775 (?). A dealer in popular and ephemeral literature, such as *The Ambulator*, an alphabetical Guide to London and the neighbourhood, which he published in 1774; Arcandum's *Astrology*, something after the style of *Old Moore's Almanac*; and a *Lecture on Mimicry* by G. S. Carey. [B.M. 1080. h. 29 (3).] In January 1775, he issued a periodical entitled the *St. James Magazine*, but whether this was a continuation of Robert Lloyd's publication between 1762–4, is unknown.

BICKERTON (WEAVER), bookseller and publisher in London and Eton, London, (1) Devereux Court, Temple Bar; (2) Lord Bacon's Head, without Temple Bar. 1728–32. Nichols records that this bookseller was one of the proprietors

of the *Grub Street Journal* which was first published in 1730. He appears to have shared a number of copyrights with Thomas Astley and Stephen Austin, as a catalogue of books printed for them jointly is found at the end of William Ellis's *Practical Farmer*, published in 1732. [Nichols, III. 631, IV. 602.] He was one of the temporary partners in publishing the translation of Bayle's Dictionary, January 1735, and there is an advertisement of "Sale of a Library at W. Bickertons, Lord Bacon's Head" in the *Daily Journal* of January of the same year. Bickerton had a branch shop at Eton. The date of his death is unknown.

BILLINGSLEY (S.), bookseller in London, Judge's Head, Chancery Lane, 1726. Possibly a relative of Benj. Billingsley. [*See Dictionary*, 1668–1725.] One of the publishers of the Rev. William Webster's *Clergy's Right of Maintenance Vindicated*, advertised in Wilford's *Monthly Catalogue*, January, 1726.

BINGLEY (WILLIAM), bookseller and publisher in London, (1) opposite Durham Yard, in the Strand; (2) 34 Newgate Street. 1767–99. Born in New Romney, co. Kent. In 1767 his name is found in the imprint of a Quaker tract by J. Phipps entitled, *Observations on a Late Anonymous Publication. . . . In Vindication of Robert Barclay*. Publisher of No. 47 of the *North Briton*, May 10th, 1768. Was committed to Newgate, where he remained for seventy-two days, for refusing to answer interrogations upon oath, which he declared he never would, without torture. Was afterwards transferred to the King's Bench Prison for debt. No. 117 of the *North Briton* bears the imprint "by W. Bingley a prisoner in the King's Bench and sold at his shop, No. 34, Newgate St." In 1770 he reprinted *A Short Narrative of the Horrid Massacre in Boston*. Became bankrupt in 1771. Afterwards went to Ireland, where he set up as a bookseller. Returned to England in 1783, and was given employment by John Nichols, the printer, who in his *Literary Anecdotes* [III. 631–4.] speaks of him as a man of "strong understanding, though not much assisted by literature; and was of the strictest integrity: but unfortunately possessed an habitual irritability of temper, which proved a perpetual discomfort". He wrote a long account of his own sufferings under the title of *A Sketch of English Liberty*, to which was prefixed a portrait of the author. He died October 23rd, 1799, aged 61, and was buried in St. Bride's, Fleet Street, with the following inscription:

Cold is that heart that beat in Freedom's cause,
The steady advocate of all her laws.

Unmoved by threats or bribes his race he ran,
And lived and died the Patriot !—the Man.

He was twice married, but left no sons.

BINNS (JOHN), bookseller and publisher in Leeds, 1766–96. Eldest son of Nathaniel Binns, bookseller of Halifax. Learnt the trade under his father. Went to London when he was twenty, and worked for S. Crowder of Paternoster Row. He set up for himself in the town of Leeds about 1766, publishing his first book catalogue in 1767. In November 1770, he married, at Dewsbury, Miss Halliley of Kirkheaton. [*London Evening Post*, November 22nd, 1770.] Timperley [p. 791] records that John Binns "was most indefatigable in business, and his bibliographical knowledge was excelled by few". He died at Grantham, on a journey from London, on May 6th, 1796, and was buried in St. Peter's Church, Leeds, being succeeded by his eldest son John.

BINNS (NATHANIEL), bookseller and bookbinder of Halifax, 1750(?)–1801. Father of John Binns (*q. v.*). Timperley says that he died in January 1801 at an "advanced age" [p. 791].

BIRD (THOMAS), bookbinder in London, at the Old Angel and Bible, No. 5 Ave Marie Lane, 1749. Issued a trade card in that year. [A. Heal's Collection.]

BIRT (SAMUEL), bookseller and publisher in London, The Bible, Ave Mary Lane, 1728–55. One of the foremost of London publishers, he held shares in all the most important publications of his day, and dealt largely in law-books. In January 1728 an advertisement appeared of religious books "printed for S. Birt" and others. In 1736 he became the publisher of the Rev. Samuel Wesley's writings. [Nichols, II. 84, 85.] He died in November, 1755, leaving no issue, his wife and his son having died before him. In his will he leaves legacies to the following London booksellers and printers who were his neighbours: Samuel Aris, of Creed Lane; Richard Baldwin, senior; Daniel Browne; Edward Owen; and Henry Whitridge; and also to the following provincial bookseller, Edward Score, junior, of Exeter. [P.C.C. 304 Paul.]

BIRT (WILLIAM), bookseller and publisher in London, near Fountain Court in the Strand, 1757. His name occurs in the imprint to a pamphlet entitled, *The Constitution. With an Address to a Great Man*, 1757, 8vo. [B.M. E. 2214 (2).]

BISHOP (JAMES), bookseller in Maidstone, Kent, 1741. Mentioned by a correspondent. [*N. & Q.* 10 S. v, March 1906, p. 183.]

BISHOP (ROBEY), stationer in London, Bible, Upper end of Castle Street, opposite Gt. Newport Street, near Newport Market, *c.* 1768. Issued a trade card about that date. [A. Heal's Collection.]

BIZET (WILLIAM), pamphlet-seller (?), and publisher in London, in St. Clement's Church-yard, 1757. Only known from the occurrence of his name as publisher on a pamphlet entitled *A Letter to the Right Honourable Lord A. . . .*, 1757, 8vo. [B.M. E. 2214.]

BLACK (ALEXANDER ROBERT), bookbinder and stationer in London, George Yard, Tower Hill, *c.* 1775. Issued a trade card, engraved by Clowes, about this date. [A. Heal's Collection.]

BLACKMAN (S.), bookseller and publisher in Reading, Berks., 1767. His name occurs in the imprint to the Rev. John Williams's *Concordance to the Greek Testament*, 1767, 4to.

BLACKSTONE or BRACKSTONE (JAMES), bookseller and publisher in London, Globe in Cornhill, 1743–53. Publisher of a sermon on the death of the Rev. Daniel Neal, in 1743; also of the second edition of Neal's *History of New England* in 1747 [J. C. B. L.], and also an *Abridgement of the Life of the Rev. Cotton Mather*. In 1753, he was taking advertisements for the *Public Advertiser*.

BLADON (SAMUEL), bookseller and publisher in London, Paper Mill in Paternoster Row, 1733–99. In 1753 he joined with A. Millar in the publication of Bishop Burnet's *History*. Publisher of the Works of Dr. James Houston, and of political tracts such as *The Conduct of the Ministry impartially examined, in a Letter to the Merchants of London*, which bears as imprint: London: Printed for S. Bladon, in Pater-noster-Row, MDCCLVI. Price one shilling. [B.M. 1093.e. 53.] In 1773 he issued *Considerations on the State of the Sugar Islands, and on the Policy of Enabling Foreigners to Lend Money on Real Securities in those Colonies*. [J. C. B. L.] In 1775 with several others he published *The Fables of Mr. Gay*. Timperley [p. 804] states that Bladon was a skilled accountant and was frequently an arbitrator in complicated accounts. Died July, 1799. [Nichols, III. 718.]

BLAKE (   ), bookseller in Maidstone, co. Kent, *c.* 1775. Issued an engraved trade-card, without date. [A. Heal's Collection.]

BLAKENEY (J.), bookseller in Windsor, 1774. His name occurs in the imprint to a guide book entitled *Windsor and its Environs*, printed in London in 1774. [B.M. 579. b. 51.]

BLANDFORD (N.), bookseller and publisher in London, London Gazette, Charing Cross, 1726–30. In 1726 he is found selling Johnson's *The Female Fortune Teller*, and *Hecuba, a Tragedy*. In 1728 he shared with Warner and Whitridge in the publication of the *Daily Journal*. In 1729 he published *An Epistle to His Royal Highness Frederick, Prince of Wales*, by Henry Stephens of Merton College, Oxford. [W. M. C. August, 1729.] He was apparently succeeded by J. Barnes (*q. v.*).

BLISS (ROBERT), bookseller in Oxford, 1770–5. Privilegiatus bibliopola, June 16, 1770. [Foster, *Alumni*, p. 124.] In 1775 there is an advertisement in the *Public Advertiser* of the sale of "*Table of evidence of the Authority of the Sacred Canon* by Mr. Bliss at Oxford."

BLUNT (J.), bookseller in Ross, Hereford, 1741–53. Mentioned in a list of provincial booksellers by a correspondent. [*N. & Q.*, 11 S. I. 364.] His name also appears in a list of those selling the *Daily Register* for 1753.

BLUNT (J.), bookseller and publisher (?) in London, 1754. Probably a fictitious imprint, found on the title-page of a pamphlet entitled a *Counter-Address to the Public*, 1753. [B.M. 21. d. 4.]

BLYTH (FRANCIS), printer, bookseller, and publisher in London, (1) John's Coffee-House, Royal Exchange; (2) 87 Cornhill; (3) Warwick Court, Warwick Lane, Newgate Street. 1766–88. Blyth was one of the publishers of *The Charters of North America* in 1766, when he gave his address as John's Coffee-House, Royal Exchange [J. C. B. L.]. He next moved to No. 87 Cornhill, sometimes described as "at the Royal Exchange", and was there joined by H. Beevor (*q. v.*), their names being found on a reprint of the "Act" for the establishment of a College or University in Rhode Island, U.S.A. In 1770 Blyth was the publisher of a pamphlet dealing with the conduct of the Bishop of Winchester. [B.M. 517. g. 28 (4).] Later on he set up as a printer in Warwick Court, Warwick Lane, and took over the printing of two newspapers, the *London Packet* and the *Public Ledger*. He died on May 27th, 1788, not 1787, as stated by Timperley. [*Gents. Mag.* LVIII. 563.] He was succeeded by John Crowder (*q. v.*).

BOAD (H.), bookseller in Colchester, 1735–6. In an advertisement in the *Country Journal or Craftsman* of December 27th, 1735, announcing the publication of Sam. Humphreys's *Old and New Testament*, this bookseller is named as one from whom it could be had; but his name does not appear in the imprint of the book. In conjunction with J. Kendall of the same town he was local agent for a book entitled *A New English Accidence*, in 1736.

BODDELEY (THOMAS), printer and bookseller in Bath, 1740–56. According to a correspondent [*N. & Q.*, 10 S. v. 141] this printer was at work in 1740. In 1742 he printed Wood's *Essay towards a Description of Bath*; in 1744 he became the printer and publisher of the *Bath Journal*, which he carried on until 1756, when he made it over to his brother-in-law, John Keene, and for many years it was known as *Keene's Journal*. [Monkland, G., *Supplement to the literature and Literati of Bath*, 1855, p. 96.] The Journal became incorporated with the *Bath Herald* in March, 1916. [Information kindly supplied by Messrs. W. Lewis & Sons, Ltd. of Bath.] In 1753 he published a Guide to Bath and Bristol under the title of *The Tradesmans and Travellers Companion*. A third edition appeared in 1755; a fourth was "printed for J. Keene", without date, but after 1759.

BODDINGTON (JOSEPH), stationer in London, at the Angel and Bible in Fenchurch Street, next Gracechurch Street, *c.* 1760. Probably a descendant of M. and Nicholas Boddington (1687–1725), *see Dictionary* 1668–1725. Issued a trade card about 1750, a copy of which is in the Banks Collection. Appears to have moved to the above address from Tower Street. [Information supplied by Mr. A. Heal.]

BODEN (NICHOLAS), printer in Birmingham, Great Charles Street, 1769–70. Published a folio Bible (part of which was printed in Baskerville's office) in conjunction with Orion Adams in 1769. Carried on a printed warfare with Baskerville, whom doubtless the issue of this Bible caused to return from retirement to printing, by issuing a rival Bible. [*N. & Q.*, 10 S. x. 184.] Mentioned in Sketchley's *Birmingham Directory* for the year 1770.

BOLTON (   ), bookseller at Chatham, Kent, 1761. In 1761 he sold a print called *The Royal Protestant Hero*. [*Public Advertiser*, January 2nd, 1761.]

BOND (R.), bookseller and publisher in Gloucester, Westgate Street, 1753–71. The name of Bond of Gloucester occurs in 1753 in a list of those selling the *Daily Register*. Timperley [1842 ed., p. 820] records the death of a Richard Bond, whom he describes as at one time "a master printer of some eminence at Gloucester", whose business had failed, and who died a pensioner of William Bowyer, junior. He may be identical with the above.

BONNER (S.), bookseller and printer in Bristol, Castle Street, 1746–89. Little seems to be known about this Bristol tradesman. A correspondent [*N. & Q.*, 11 S. I. 304] notes him there in 1746, but the only mention of him in Messrs. Hyett and Bazeley's *Bibliography* is the statement that in 1789 Bonner and Middleton's Journal was taken over by S. Bonner. [III. 279.]

BONWICK (JAMES), *see Dictionary*, 1668–1725. Still publishing in 1726. [Wilford's *Monthly Catalogue.*] *See* Bonwick, R.

BONWICK (REBECCA), bookseller (?) in London, Red Lion, St. Paul's Churchyard, 1726–35. *See Dictionary*, 1668–1725. *See* Wilford's *Monthly Catalogue*. Advertised in *London Journal* of February 5th, 1726, *Religio Unica Reipublicae Salus*, Impensis R. and J. Bonwicke, Red Lion, St. Paul's Churchyard. January 9th, 1735 "*New Voyages to N. America*, Printed for J. and J. Bonwicke" and others. [*Daily Journal.*]

BOOTH (MARTIN), bookseller and publisher in Norwich, 1767–83. Probably was in business before 1767, in which year he published the *Seventeen Sermons* of the Rev. Nath. Torriano, rector of Aldham, Suffolk. [B.M. 4455. g. 14.] In 1774 his name occurs in the imprint to *Some Memoirs of the Life of John Glover, late of Norwich* [B.M. 4903. bbb. 20 (1).] and between 1775 and 1783 he held periodical sales by auction. He died on September 28th, 1783. [Nichols, *Lit. Anecd.* III. 672.]

BOREMAN (THOMAS), bookseller and publisher in London, (1) on Ludgate Hill, near the Gate; (2) The Cock on Ludgate Hill; (3) Guildhall, 1733–45 (?). Publisher of miscellaneous literature. In 1733 he issued *A Compendious Account of the Whole Art of Breeding . . . the Silk Worm.* In 1736 his imprint appeared on a pamphlet entitled *Political Dialogues*, [B.M. T. 2028 (5).] and in 1740 he published *A Survey of the County of Down*, which had been previously published in Dublin by Edward Exshaw of Cork Hill. [B.M. 968. I I.] About this date Boreman began to issue a series of books for children which he entitled *Gigantick Histories*. One of these, *A Little History of St. Paul's*, bore the imprint: "Printed for Tho. Boreman, Bookseller near the two giants in Guildhall London 1741." J. G. Nichol put a query about these children's books in *N. & Q.* for December 3rd, 1859 [2 S., VIII. 450.], but no reply was ever made. [P. Merritt, Boston, Mass.]

BOTHAM (W.), printer in London, Bartholomew Close, 1700–48. *See Dictionary*, 1668–1725. He died in 1748. [Musgrave.]

BOTTOMLEY (JAMES), printer in Manchester, 1763. Only known from the entry of his marriage in the parish register. Procter in his *Memorials* suggests that he was only a workman (p. 201).

BOUCHER (G.), bookseller in Peterborough, 1714–55. *See Dictionary* 1668–1725, p. 324. He was still in business in 1755. See *N. & Q.* 10 S. V. 242.

BOUQUET (J.), bookseller and publisher in London, White Hart, Paternoster Row, 1753–4. For some years in partnership with John Payne. They were the publishers of William Lauder's attack on Milton, which was founded on forged documents. A letter from the publishers is printed in vol. IV of the *Monthly Review*, p. 99. His name is found in the imprints to several anti-Jewish pamphlets, published at this time. [B.M. T. 2231 (17).] In 1754 he published one of the many pamphlets that appeared in defence of the conduct of the Rector and Fellows of Exeter College, Oxford. [B.M. 517. g. 2 (3).]

BOURN (B.), bookseller and publisher in London, Ludgate Street, 1749. In that year he published a pamphlet relating to the reform of schools. [Information supplied by Mr. G. A. Winship.]

BOWLES (CARINGTON), book, map, and print-seller in London, (1) Black Horse in Cornhill 1754–64; (2) next the Chapter House in St. Paul's Churchyard, 1764–93. 1754–93. Son of John Bowles of Cornhill. Born 1724. In partnership with his father from 1754 until about 1764. They were joint publishers of a map of Hertfordshire [Sir H. G. Fordham, *Hertfordshire Maps*, 1901, p. 55.]. From 1764 until his death in 1793, Carington Bowles carried on the business of Thomas Bowles (*q. v.*) in St. Paul's Churchyard, and at the time of his father's death in 1779 he was "possessed of a plentiful fortune". He died intestate in 1793, administration of his goods, &c., being granted on July 5th to his only child Carington, and the business was continued as Bowles and Carver.

BOWLES (JOHN), book, map, and print-seller in London, (1) Opposite the Stocks Market, 1724–39 (or earlier); (2) Mercer's Hall in Cheapside, 1728; (3) Black Horse in Cornhill 1740(?)–1775. 1720–79. Born in 1701. Brother of Thomas Bowles (*q. v.*). Is believed to have commenced business about 1720. In 1724, he was one of the publishers of the fourth edition of *Britannia Depicta*.

In 1728 he issued *The New Principles of Gardening* from Mercer's Hall. He and his brother Thomas, though they had separate shops, were interested in the same publications. One of the maps in which both their imprints is found is De l'Isle's *Theatrum Historicum*, which was originally published in 1709, but the copy on which their names are found had evidently been in circulation for some years as there are traces of erasure of earlier names above which the Bowles imprints have been re-engraved [B.M. Maps 1000 (3)]. From 1754 John Bowles' second son Carington was in partnership with him and the firm was then known as John Bowles & Son. They issued an elaborate trade card, showing part of a map of England. He died in 1779, and his will was proved in the Prerogative Court of Canterbury. [335 Warburton.] In 1780 the business was in the hands of Robert Wilkinson [Sir H. G. Fordham, *Hertfordshire Maps* 1914, p. 76.]

BOWLES (THOMAS), book, map, and print-seller in London, next to the Chapter House in St. Paul's Churchyard, 1712(?)–1767. Brother of John Bowles (*q. v.*) and evidently his senior by some years. Began publishing about 1712, perhaps earlier, as his imprint is found on an undated map of Asia engraved by Moll, and dedicated to William Lord Cowper, Lord High Chancellor, who held that office from 1705 till 1718. Again Moll's map of the North Part of Great Britain dated 1714 also has Thomas Bowles' imprint. [B.M. K.T. 4. Tab. 17 (3) (12).] About 1725 he began to engrave maps and illustrations to books. He shared with his brother John the publication of many books and maps, and was generally referred to as the great print-seller. He died on April 8th, 1767. [*Gentleman's Magazine*, vol. 37.] His will was proved in the Prerogative Court of Canterbury on May 15th. After his death John Bowles bought the business for his son Carington Bowles (*q. v.*).

BOWLING (JAMES), printer in Leeds, Yorks, 1767–76. In the year 1767 James Bowling revived the *Leeds Mercury*, of which he was proprietor, editor, and printer. [Timperley, p. 850.] *The Memoirs of General Fairfax*, printed in 1776, bear the following imprint: Leeds, printed by T. Bowling, and sold by J. Hartley, and G. Nicholson in Bradford, price two shillings. [J. N. Dickon's Catalogue of Books, Pamphlets, &c., published at Bradford, 1895.] Died in May 1813.

BOWYER (JONAH), bookseller in London, Rose, Paternoster Row, 1726. *See Dictionary*, 1668–1725.

BOWYER (WILLIAM I and II), *see Dictionary*, 1668–1725.

BOYDEL (J.), bookseller and publisher in London, Russel Court, Covent Garden, 1739. His name is found in conjunction with that of F. Noble, in the imprint to a poem called *The Green Cloth*, published in that year. There is no evidence to connect him with John Boydell, the engraver and print-seller, who came to London about the same time. [B.M. 11602. i. 17 (7).]

BRACKSTONE, *see* Blackstone.

BRADLEY (JOB), *see Dictionary*, 1668–1725.

BRASSETT (J.), bookseller at Poole, co. Dorset, 1744. His name occurs in an advertisement in the *Salisbury Journal* of Tuesday, April 10th, 1744. Issued a trade-card. [A. Heal's Collection.]

BRETT (GEORGE), printer, stationer, and book or pamphlet-seller in London, Three Crowns on Ludgate Hill, 1744–5. His name is found in the imprint to two pamphlets by Christopher Middleton, the first, *A Reply to the Remarks of Arthur Dobbs, Esq.*, 1744, and the second, *Forgery Detected*, 1745. Possibly a relative of John Brett (*q. v.*). Issued a well-engraved trade-card. [A. Heal's Collection.]

BRETT (JOHN), pamphlet-seller in London, (1) St. Clement Danes, corner of Milford Lane; (2) at the Golden Ball, over against St. Clement's Church, 1739–45. Dealer in pamphlets of all kinds. In the year 1739 he was summoned before the Court of King's Bench in respect of a libel called *Common Sense, or the Englishman's Journal* of June 23rd. [Dom. S. P. Geo. II. Bundle 48 (14).] Brett was again in trouble with the authorities in 1740 for selling the *London Evening Post* of April 1st [*Ib.*, Bundle 50/82], and in 1745, when proceedings were instituted against several printers, booksellers, and others in London, for printing and publishing obscene literature, Brett and his wife admitted having obtained some of the books in question from Thomas Read's printing-house, and others from the printing-house of Leake in Angell Street, St. Martin's-le-Grand. They were ordered to enter into sureties to appear at the next Term of the Court of King's Bench. [*Ib.*, Bundle 65/82–3.] Brett is believed to have had a son Thomas.

BREWER (THOMAS), stationer of London, Ludgate Hill, 1712–55. Son of Ralph Brewer, citizen and girdler. Master of the Company of Stationers, 1745–6. Died June 14th, 1755, aged 76. In 1712 he contributed to the Bowyer relief fund. [Timperley, p. 600.]

BRICE (ANDREW), *see Dictionary*, 1668–1725.

BRICE (G.), bookseller and publisher in Leicester, 1744–6. In 1746 he sold a *Sermon* preached by the Rev. Rich. Arnald, rector of Thurcaston in co. Leicester, on October 9th. [B.M. 225. i. 2 (21).]

BRINDLEY (JAMES), bookseller, publisher, and bookbinder in London, (1) Hospital Gate, Little Britain, (2) 29 New Bond Street. (?) 1726–58. Began business as a bookbinder before 1728 in Little Britain, but soon afterwards set up as a publisher in New Bond Street. In 1736 he described himself as bookseller and bookbinder to the Royal family. The Society for the Encouragement of Learning appointed him one of six booksellers to retail their publications. He published Mr. Pemberton's *View of Sir Isaac Newton's Philosophy* in 1728, and W. Cavendish, Duke of Newcastle's *General System of Horsemanship*, which he edited himself, in 1743. In 1744 he began to issue an edition of the classics in duodecimo, very well printed, which became known as *Brindley's Classics*. In 1750 J. Hart the printer printed for him a new edition of Sir T. Urquhart's translation of the works of Rabelais, with numerous plates. On June 17th, 1751, he was in correspondence with Dr. Birch. Brindley was also the publisher of some of Eliza Haywood's novels. He died some time in 1758, and was succeeded by a relative, James Robson. [Nichols, III, 634; V. 5. 323.] The premises are now occupied by Messrs. Ellis & Elvey, booksellers.

BRINDLEY ( ), Mrs., bookseller (?) in London, 1758. The second edition of a pamphlet entitled *The Reply of the Country Gentleman to the Answer to his Military Argument. By The Officer*, 1758. 8°. [B.M. E. 2049 (13)] has this name in the imprint. She may have been the widow of J. Brindley.

BRISTOW (W.), bookseller and publisher in London, St. Paul's Churchyard, next the Great Toyshop, 1760–5. Is first met with in 1760 as a publisher of pamphlets [J. C. B. L.]. In 1763 his name is found in the imprint to James Scott's poem *Every Man the Architect of his own Fortune*. Whether he was any relation to the bookseller of the same name in Canterbury is not known.

BRITON (A.), bookseller (?) and publisher in London, near Temple Bar, 1749. Probably fictitious. Occurs on a pamphlet called *An Occasional Letter from a Gentleman in the Country to his Friend in Town. Concerning the Treaty negotiated at Hanau in* . . . 1743. 8°. [B.M. E. 2042 (10).]

BROADFOOT ( ), bookseller at Ashford in Kent, 1737–50. Publisher of the *Gentleman and Builder's Repository*, 1737. Still in business in 1750.

BROMAGE (J.), bookseller and publisher in London, Temple Bar, 1749. His name occurs in the imprint to *Poems on Several Occasions*, issued in 1749. [B.M. 1346. g. 2.]

BROMLEY (J.), printer in Nantwich, co. Cheshire, opposite the Crown, 1774–5. Printer of a book entitled *Some Account of the fore-part of the Life of Elizabeth Ashbridge*. [J. P. Earwaker, *Local Gleanings*, I. 114.] Also of C. Comyn's *Trial of George Birbrick* in 1775.

BROMLEY (JOHN), stationer in London, Spread Eagle in King Street, opposite Bedford Street, Covent Garden, *c.* 1760. Successor to D. Job. Issued a trade card about this date. [A. Heal's Collection.]

BROOKE (J.), bookseller and publisher in London, The Golden Head, under St. Dunstan's Church, Fleet Street, 1751. Publisher of *An Apology for the Robin-Hood Society*, 1751. [B.M. T. 1113 (2).]

BROOKE (JAMES), stationer in London, Anchor and Crown, near the Square, on London Bridge. *See Dictionary*, 1669–1725. Mentioned in a London Directory, 1740–4. Issued a trade card showing his device. [A. Heal's Collection.]

BROOKLAND (JOSEPH), printer in Oxford, Oxford Theatre Printing-House, 1693–1729. Apprentice to John Hall, the Oxford printer, in 1693. Printer and agent for Thomas Hearne, the antiquary, and manager or head printer at the Printing-House. [Hearne, *Remarks and Collections*, X. 25, 104.]

BROOKS (SAMUEL), bookseller and publisher in London, Golden Ball in Paternoster Row, 1760. In partnership with H. Woodgate. The Rev. W. H. Dilworth wrote for them a number of shilling histories, one of these being a Life of Peter the Great, under the title of *The Father of His Country*, which appeared in 1760. [B.M. 10795. a. 53.] At the end of this are advertised sixteen of Dilworth's writings, followed by a *Catalogue of Chapmen's Books*, consisting of 143 items ranging in character from jest books and penny histories, such as *Amadis de Gaul* and *Parismus*, to Bunyan's *Pilgrim's Progress*, Russell's *Seven Sermons*, and *The Week's Preparation*. Last of all is a *Catalogue of Plays*, sold at sixpence each. Henry Woodgate went bankrupt in 1766 and

died on July 19th of that year. [Lloyd's *Evening News*.] What happened to Brooks is unknown. Timperley mentions a Samuel Brookes who died in 1805, aged fifty, who may have been a son of the above. [Timperley, 1842, p. 820.]

BROSTER (P.), bookseller in Chester, 1774–5. His name is found in an advertisement in Adam's *Weekly Courant* of January, 1774. Published catalogues of his stock.

BROTHERTON (JAMES), bookseller and publisher in London, (1) Next door to Tom's Coffee-House in Cornhill, (2) Royal Exchange. Probably a relative of John Brotherton (*q. v.*), whom he appears to have succeeded in the Cornhill business. In 1761 James was advertising quack medicines [*Public Advertiser*, January 1st], and his name appears in Kent's *Directory* for 1768. About the year 1770 he was joined by John Sewell (*q. v.*), and they became the publishers of several books and pamphlets dealing with the American colonies [J. C. B. L.]. In 1775 they issued, in partnership with Robson and Walter, a *History of Jamaica*. A work with a similar title had been published by T. Lowndes in the preceding year. James Brotherton either died or retired from business in 1775, and Sewell continued to carry it on alone.

BROTHERTON (JOHN), bookseller and bookbinder in London, (1) The Bible, Cornhill, (2) Bible in Threadneedle Street, over against the Merchant Taylors' Hall. 1718–53. *See Dictionary*, 1668–1725. In 1750 his name is found in a pamphlet by William Richardson, *An Essay on the Causes of the Decline of the Foreign Trade*, and again in 1753 he sold the *Anglo-French Dictionary*, [*Public Advertiser*, January 8th]. Issued a trade card as a bookbinder, on which the second address is found. [A. Heal's Collection.]

BROWN (A.), bookseller in Bristol, 1732–76. "Sold by Mr. Brown in Bristol" is found on the imprint in *The West Country Farmer, &c.*, 1732. Mentioned in an advertisement of a work called *Examples of the Ancient Sages*, by P. Bernard, Esq. [*Publ. Advertiser*, January 1st, 1761], and was still there in 1776. [*Glouc. Journal*.]

BROWN (ARTHUR), bookseller in Honiton, co. Devon, 1763–73. His name is first met with in an advertisement in the *Exeter Flying Post* of September 2nd, 1763. In 1764 he subscribed for twenty copies of S. Bamfield's *Astronomy* (Dredge, p. 35). In 1773 his name is found in the imprint of *The Mariner's Instructor*.

BROWN (WILLIAM), bookseller and publisher in London, The corner of Essex Street in the Strand, 1765–97. Apprentice with W. Sandby whom he succeeded about 1765. He issued several catalogues. He died February 14th, 1797, aged 63, and was succeeded by Robert Bickerstaffe. [Nichols, III. 634–5.] Amongst his publications was a pamphlet issued in 1770, entitled an *Epistle to Lord Holland* [Winship].

BROWNE (DANIEL), bookseller in London, (1) Black Swan without Temple Bar, (2) Crane Court, Fleet Street, 1744. 1672–1753. *See Dictionary*, 1668–1725. It is evident that there was more than one publisher of this name at the Black Swan, possibly father and son, the latter moving to Crane Court in 1744 and continuing there until 1753, when with those other publishers, his name is found in the imprint to Whiston's *Sacred History of the World*.

BROWNE (J.), printer in London, 1770. William Doyle's *Some Account of the British Dominions beyond the Atlantic*, published in 1770, bears the imprint: "London: Printed for the author by J. Browne", and in the same year he shared, with W. Allard, Luckombe's *History and Art of Printing*.

BRYAN (STEPHEN), *see Dictionary*, 1668–1725.

BRYCE, *see* Brice.

BRYDON (ROBERT), bookseller and bookbinder in Dover, Kent; King Street, 1773–6. Successor to P. Newport of Snargate Street. [*Kentish Gazette*, January 30th, 1773.]

BRYSON (MARTIN), *see Dictionary*, 1668–1725.

BUCKLAND ( ), bookseller and publisher in Truro, co. Cornwall, 1776. Publisher of *Sermons* by the late Rev. Charles Peters, M.A., 1776. Dr. Philip Bliss described this as "the scarcest single volume of sermons" he knew. [Dredge, p. 30.]

BUCKLAND (JAMES), bookseller and publisher in London and Chelmsford, co. Essex: London, The Buck, Corner of St. Paul's Court, Paternoster Row, 1736–90. The earliest reference found to this bookseller is an advertisement in the *Daily Journal* of February 18th, 1735, of a sale of books by auction by James Buckland, Bookseller at Hamlin's Coffee House in Swithin Alley; but the sign of his house was the Buck. About 1736 he appears to have set up a branch shop at Chelmsford in Essex, where he published Moody's *Impartial Justice*. He dealt largely in theological works, amongst others the writings of

John Glover of Norwich. In 1775 he was one of the partners in the publication of *Fables by Mr. Gay*, which were advertised in the *Public Advertiser* of January 10th. Timperley records that he was "a bookseller of eminence", a "remarkable gentlemanly-looking personage in the dress of George II's days" and that "he kept up the old custom of posting up the titles of the latest books, on a long board, which hung by his doorway". This custom is alluded to by Gay in the following lines:

High raised on Fleet-street Posts consigned to Fame,
This work shall shine and walkers bless my name.

Buckland died on February 21st, 1790, aged seventy-nine [Timperley, p. 765], his will being proved on the 23rd. He left a son James, and amongst the other legatees was a Richard Lobb, presumably the bookseller of that name in Chelmsford. He recommended his executors to take the advice of Thomas Longman of Paternoster Row respecting the disposal of his stock and copies. [P. C. C.] [*N. & Q.* January 5th, 1878, and December 15th, 1877.] Issued a trade card with his device. [A. Heal's Collection.]

BUCKLEY (SAMUEL), *see Dictionary*, 1668–1725.

BUCKRIDGE (JOHN), bookseller and publisher in Marlborough, co. Wilts., 1704–45. *See Dictionary*, 1668–1725. His name occurs in an advertisement of the second edition of Stackhouse's *Bible* in 1745.

BULKELEY (G.), bookseller in Chester, 1774–5. His name is found in an advertisement in Adams' *Weekly Courant*, 1774.

BULL (LEWIS), bookseller and publisher in Bath, (1) The Walks, (2) Opposite Gyde's Rooms on the Lower Walks, *c.* 1773–90. Succeeded to the old-established business of James Leake (*q. v.*) on the Walks. In the *Strangers Assistant and Guide to Bath*, printed by R. Cruttwell in 1773, in a list of those who let lodgings, is found the name of "Mr. Bull, bookseller and jeweller", an unusual combination of trades. On October 22nd, 1774, a notice appeared in the *Bath Chronicle* intimating that "Bull, jeweller, goldsmith, and toyman, is removed from his late shop in the Grove, to a more commodious one adjoining to his library, opposite Gyde's Rooms on the Lower Walks". In the same year he and others advertised the sale of Gill's *Exposition of the New Testament*, and he is also mentioned as agent for The Pectoral Balsam of Honey. The first book traced as being published by him was Lady Miller's *Poetical Amusements at a villa near Bath*, of which the first volume was printed by Cruttwell in 1774, and appeared in January 1775. Bull retired from business, owing to ill health,

in 1790. In the Hunt Collection of prints, &c., relating to Bath and its neighbourhood, in the Bath Reference Library are two undated book-plates of Bull. One, a small oval cut to plate-mark with lettering: The Public Library —Bull, Bookseller and Stationer, on the Lower Walk, Bath; the other an elaborate design: (plate-mark) $6\frac{1}{2}'' \times 4\frac{5}{10}''$. Inscription, "Bull's Circulating Library, Bath." History, Antiquities, Voyages, Travels, Lives, Memoirs, Philosophy Anatomy and Physic, Coins, Novels, Poetry, Plays.

BURBAGE (GEORGE), printer and bookseller in Nottingham, 1747–1807. Started business as a bookseller about 1747. In 1772 he commenced the *Nottingham Chronicle*, which in 1775 became merged with its rival the *Nottingham Journal*, conducted by Samuel Creswell. At the latter's death in 1786, George Burbage became sole proprietor of the Journal, and at his death on December 13th, 1807, it passed to his apprentice George Stretton, who had married his master's daughter and succeeded to his business.

BURD (J.), bookseller and publisher in London, near the Temple Gate, Fleet Street, 1760–1. Publisher of pamphlets, amongst which may be noted *The Clockmaker's Outcry against the Author of the Life and Opinions of Tristram Shandy*, 1760. [B.M. 11840, bbb. 45.]

BURDON (JOHN), bookseller and publisher in Winchester, College Street, near the College, 1773–1802. F. A. Edwards in his *Early Hampshire Printers* describes John Burdon as a "printer"; but this seems to be a mistake, as is also the statement that his name appears in the imprint to T. Warton's *Description of the City, College, and Cathedral of Winchester*. The British Museum copy has the name of T. Burdon in the imprint, and the date of publication is there given as 1760. In 1773 he issued a catalogue of the library of the Rev. Dr. Perkins of Southampton [Nichols, *Lit. Anecd.* III. 673]. On August 21st, 1775, William Sollers of Blandford began a sale of the library of the Rev. Christopher Twynihoe and amongst those from whom catalogues might be had was "Mr. Burdon" of Winchester. [B.M. 824. b. 17 (4).] In 1776 he issued a catalogue of his stock. His son Charles was for a time associated with him in the business, but died in 1803 at the early age of 24. John Burdon died in 1802. [*N. & Q.* 10 S. VI. 31.]

BURDON (T.), bookseller in Winchester, St. Michaels, 1760–5. His name appears in the imprint to T. Warton's *Description of the City, College, and Cathedral of Winchester*, printed without date, but ascribed by the British

Museum to 1760. On April 16th, 1765, he married Jane Widmore, widow, at St. Michael's church. His subsequent history is unknown, nor is it clear what relation he was to John Burdon.

BURNET (GEORGE), bookseller and publisher in London, (1) Without Temple Bar; (2) Bishop Burnet's Head in the Strand. 1758–75. His name is found in the imprint to a pamphlet entitled *The Reply of the Country Gentleman to the Answer to his Military Arguments. By the Officer.* 1758. 8°. [B.M. E. 2049 (13).] In 1764 there was a G. Burnet at Bishop Burnet's Head in the Strand, who was probably identical with the above. His imprint is found in that year on Dr. John Ogilvie's poem *Providence* [B.M. 643. k. 8 (8)], again as George Burnet in 1765, and in 1775 he and some others published Stanhope's *Paraphrase on the Gospels*.

BURNHAM (T.), bookseller and publisher in Northampton, Gold Street, 1775–6. Mentioned in advertisements of books in the *Northampton Mercury* of 1775. In 1776 he published the first work of Thomas Lewis O'Beirne, afterward Bishop of Ossory and Meath, a poem called *The Crucifixion*, which was printed in London. [B.M. 161. m. 15.]

BURROUGH, or BURROUGHS (T.), printer and publisher in Devizes, 1744–74. His name is first met with in an advertisement in the *Salisbury Journal* of Tuesday, April 10th, 1744. In 1755 he issued a prospectus for printing the Rev. Wainhouse's sermon preached at the Abbey Church of Bath. In 1774 he printed and published a pamphlet entitled *America vindicated from the High Charge of Ingratitude and Rebellion*.

BURTON (WILLIAM), printer in London, 1728. In the *Weekly Journal* of September 28th, 1728, is the following note: "Wednesday Mr. Burton the printer, who was committed to Newgate for reprinting Mist's *Journal* of Aug. 24. was admitted to Bail before the Lord Chief Justice Raymond." He was probably only a journeyman.

BUSSEY (S.), (?) bookseller and publisher in London, in Ivy Lane, 1725. A pamphlet entitled *Mr. Forman's Letter to the Right Honourable William Pulteney Esq.* bears the following imprint: "London: Printed for and Sold by S. Bussey, in Ivy Lane. MDCCXXV."

BUTLER (ESTHER), printer in Birmingham, New Street, 1758–70. Widow of Henry Butler (*q.v.*). Took over the business on his death and was still at work in 1770, when her name appears in the Birmingham Directory.

BUTLER (H.), bookseller in London, Bow Church, and at the Foundry, 1744. His name occurs in the imprint of Wesley's *Moral and Sacred Poems*. [Dredge.]

BUTLER (HENRY), printer in Birmingham, New Street, 1726–58. Is believed to have been in business as early as the year 1713 as entries relating to his children are found in the parish registers of St. Martin and St. Peter. His shop in New Street stood next to a tavern called the Fountain and he continued there until his death. His business was taken over by his widow Esther Butler (*q. v.*). [Joseph Hill, *The Bookmakers of Old Birmingham*, pp. 38–9.]

BUTLER (THOMAS), bookseller in London, Pall-Mall, 1754. Made a speciality of prints of race-horses with their pedigrees. Being at Newmarket on October 6th, 1753, he was set upon and beaten by a crowd and his business was boycotted. In the following year he published a pamphlet entitled *The Case of Mr. Thos. Butler*, London, 1754, in which he gave an account of his treatment. [*Public Advertiser* of Saty. Mar. 23rd.] Amongst his other publications was the *Proceedings of the Commons of Ireland*.

BUTTON (JOSEPH), bookseller in Newcastle, 1733, in which year he subscribed to *Thuanus*.

CABE (E.), bookseller and publisher in London, Ave Mary Lane, 1758–70. Publisher of a pamphlet entitled *A Letter of Consolation to Shebbeare*, 1758. He was still in business in 1770, when he published a sermon on the death of the Rev. George Whitefield, the famous preacher. [J. C. B. L.]

CADELL (THOMAS), bookseller and publisher in Bristol, Wine Street, 1739–75. Father of Thomas Cadell, the successful London publisher (*q. v.*). A correspondent in *Notes and Queries* states that he was in business from 1739–75. [10 S. V. 141.] In the latter year his name occurs in an advertisement in the *Public Advertiser* as one of the publishers of a work called *Divine Maxims*.

CADELL (THOMAS), bookseller and publisher in London, Strand, 1742–1802. Son of Thomas Cadell, a bookseller in Wine Street, Bristol, where he was born in 1742. In 1758 he was sent to London and apprenticed to Andrew Millar. Nichols has described him as a man "eminently characterized by the rectitude of his judgement, the goodness of his heart, the benevolence of his disposition, and the urbanity of his manners". He rose rapidly in his profession, was admitted as a partner in the firm in 1765, and succeeded to the business on the retirement of Millar in 1767. On April 1st, 1769, he married the daughter of Mr. Thomas Jones of the Strand. [*Middlesex Journal*, No. 1. Tues. April 4, 1769, third leaf, col. 3.] Like his predecessor he was a generous patron of authors. Cadell was one of the coterie of booksellers who met at the Chapter Coffee House and arranged the publication of several great undertakings, including *The Works of the English Poets* to which Dr. Johnson wrote the prefaces, Blackstone's *Commentaries*, Gibbon's *Decline and Fall*, and Cook's *Voyages*. From 1780 to 1784 William Strahan was his partner and was succeeded in that position by his son Andrew. Cadell retired from business in 1793 and was elected Alderman of the Ward of Walbrook in 1798. He died in 1802 at his house in Bloomsbury, and one of his last acts was to present a stained-glass window to the Company of Stationers, of which he had been a liveryman for thirty-seven years. [Timperley, 1842, pp. 804, 805.]

CAIRNESS (FRANCIS), bookseller in London, Heming Row, 1749. His name occurs in the Poll-book for the City and Liberty of Westminster in that year.

CALDICOTT (S.), bookseller in London, Bell Savage Yard, 1761. In 1761 he published a pamphlet *The Case of the Orphans and Creditors of John Ayliffe Esq.*, who had been convicted at the Old Bailey in 1759 of forgery. [C. H. Mayo, *Bibl. Dorset.*, p. 175.]

CAMPBELL (A.), printer in London, Printing House, New Palace Yard, Westminster, 1726–8. In partnership with John Cluer of Bow Church Yard and Printer of Cluer and Creake's *Second Pocket Volume of Opera Songs*, published in 1726. There is an advertisement of a *History of Scotland*, printed for J. Cluer and B. Creake by A. Campbell at the printing house in King Street, Westminster [*Daily Post* 1728, January 1st], and during the same year he printed for John Roberts of Warwick Lane a pamphlet entitled *The Controversy concerning Free-will and Predestination*. [B.M. 1019. l. 6 (4).]

CAMPBELL (ALEXANDER), bookseller in Carlisle, 1776. Died in the course of the year 1776, and was succeeded by Mrs. Campbell, who inserted an advertisement in the *Cumberland Packet*, asking her late husband's creditors to send in their claims.

CARLOS (JAMES), bookseller and publisher in Norwich, Dove Lane, 1730–46. In the *Country Journal* of May 2nd, 1730 (page 3, col. 2), he advertised *A Reply to the Answer unto the Letter written to a Quaker in Norfolk*, and in 1746 his name is found in the imprint of the Rev. J. Francis's *Sermon preached at*

Norwich. [B.M. 225. i. 2 (18).] He was perhaps related to the Rev. James Carlos, A.M., Rector of Blofield, who in 1773 published a *Sermon* preached by him on the occasion of the visitation. [*Bibl. Norfolciensis*.]

CARLTON ( ), bookseller and publisher in Gainsborough, Lincoln, 1728. Publisher of a work entitled *Dialogues between Two Young Ladies*, advertised in the *Stamford Mercury*.

CARNAN (THOMAS), bookseller and publisher in London, 65 St. Paul's Churchyard, 1737–88. This bookseller is chiefly remembered for his attack upon the monopoly of the Stationers' Company in almanacs, which he overthrew in 1779 after a strenuous fight. He is believed to have been the son of William Carnan, printer in Reading [*see Dictionary*, 1668–1725], who died in 1737 and whose widow married John Newbery, her husband's apprentice. When Newbery removed to London, Carnan appears to have gone with him and was intimately associated with him in his business. Carnan was also connected by marriage with Christopher Smart the poet. Carnan's name first appears in the imprint to a periodical called *The Midwife*, published in 1751. On the death of John Newbery in 1767 he continued the business in partnership with Francis Newbery, the nephew of John. Soon after this he began to publish almanacs, in defiance of the monopoly of the Company of Stationers, and his arrest was an annual affair which gave rise to the story that at that season of the year he always kept a clean shirt in his pocket, that he might make a decent appearance in Court. In November, 1773, the Company brought an action against him in the Court of Chancery for publishing *A Diary for the year 1774 by Reuben Burrow, late Assistant Astronomer at Greenwich*, which they maintained was an infringement of their patent. Carnan boldly replied that King James had no right or property in almanacs and therefore could not pass it on to others; but the Company obtained an injunction against him which was set aside by the judges of the Court of Common Pleas, who decided against the validity of the patent. The Company then prevailed upon Lord North to bring in a Bill to legalize their monopoly, to which Carnan replied by presenting a petition against the Bill, which was thrown out by the House of Commons on May 10th, 1779. Carnan was equally opposed to the monopoly of what was known as the Chapter Coffee House booksellers, the princes of the London trade. No wonder that he is passed over in silence by John Nichols in his *Anecdotes* and *Illustrations* save for the mere record of his death on July 29th, 1788.

[C. Welsh, *A Bookseller of the Last Century*, 1885; P.R.O. Chan. Proc. 1770–1800, *c.* 12$\frac{29}{42}$; Journals of H. of C., 1779.]

CARNAN & Co., booksellers, Reading, 1765. Their names appear in an advertisement of the sale of *Paraphrase of the Psalms*, in which Dodsley and Newbery were interested.

CARNEGY (T. J.), printer in London, 1775. Printed for Hawes, Clarke, and Collins, the publishers, Dr. Percival Pott's *Chirurgical Observations*. [B.M. 1172. h. 4 (1).]

CARPENTER (E. T.), bookseller and publisher in London, 4 West Harding Street, Fetter Lane, 1775. Publisher in 1775 of a pamphlet entitled *The Speech of the Right Hon. John Wilkes Esq., relative to the American Taxation Bills*. [J. C. B. L.]. His name is advertised as selling "Germanicus, a Tragedy". [*Public Advertiser*, November 7th, 1775.]

CARPENTER (HENRY), (?) pamphlet publisher in London, Fleet Street, 1741 (?)–55 (?) Many satirical pamphlets, such as the *Court-Spy or Memoirs of St. James* [B.M. 12330 f. 7.] were published by the above between these years and advertised in the daily and weekly press, and as the name has not been found in any book of importance, the person referred to was probably one of the numerous pamphlet sellers scattered up and down the City.

CARR (R.), bookseller, publisher, and printer in Portsmouth, Hants, (1) Grand Parade; (2) Milton's Head, near the Grand Magazine, 1751–77. In the *Monthly Review* for February 1751, in a list of recent publications mention is made of the Rev. John Sturcks's discourse entitled *Christ's Appearance in the Flesh*, delivered at Portsmouth on December 25th, 1750, as sold by Carr in Portsmouth. Under the date of 1755, Mr. Edwards in his *Early Hampshire Printers* records a copy of Mr. Archibald Maxwell's poem entitled *Portsmouth, a descriptive poem in two books*, as having the imprint, "Printed, and sold by W. Harton, J. Wilkinson, and R. Carr; by B. Collins in Salisbury; and by W. Owen bookseller near Temple Bar, London". Some twenty years later Carr appears to have added printing to his business, as in 1777 he printed a *Catalogue of the Pictures at Cowdray House*.

CARTER (JOHN), bookseller and publisher in London, (1) Blackmore's Head, opposite to the Royal Exchange in Cornhill; (2) near the Royal Exchange, 1739–41 (?). A publisher of Americana. In 1739 he published William Berriman's *A Sermon preach'd before the Honourable Trustees for establishing the Colony of Georgia in America*. He had perhaps been in business a year or two at this time, as in the *Weekly Miscellany*, published on Saturday, November 8th, 1740, appeared the following item of news: "On Tuesday last [Nov. 4] was married at Eaton [=Eton], by the Rev. Dr. Bland, Dean of Durham, Mr. John Carter, an eminent bookseller near the Royal Exchange, to Miss Dixon, daughter of Mrs. Dixon, housekeeper to the Rt. Hon. Sir Robert Walpole at Houghton, a young lady of great beauty, merit and fortune." In 1741 his name is found in the imprint to a pamphlet entitled *A Geographical and Historical Description of the Principal Objects of the Present War in the West Indies*. [B.M. T. 2032.]

CARTER (JOSEPH), printer in London, 1728. Apprentice with Nath. Mist. Committed for being concerned in the printing of Mist's *Journal* of August 24th, 1728, and sentenced to stand in Westminster Hall, with papers on his head. [Coram Rege Roll, Hilary, 2 Geo. II, Roll 108 (Rex m. 29); State Papers Dom. Geo. II, vol. 8, 74.] He was probably only a journeyman.

CASLON (THOMAS), bookseller and publisher in London, Stationers' Court, 1750(?)–83. Younger son of William Caslon the First, the type-founder; by his first wife. Timperley (p. 749) says his name appeared "conspicuously on the title-pages of the day"; but it is unknown when he first set up in business. He became Master of the Stationers' Company in 1782, and died March 29th, 1783. In 1765, in conjunction with the Tonsons, Strahan, and others, he published *The Art of Cookery*. [*Gazetteer & Daily Advertiser*, July 27th], and was one of the partners in the publication of Johnson's *Shakespeare* in the same year. [*Ib.*, October 3rd.] In 1775 he shared in the publication of Gay's *Fables* [*Public Advertiser*, January 10th.]

CASLON (WILLIAM, I), type-founder in London, Chiswell Street, 1720–66. William Caslon the First was born at Cradley Halesowen, Shropshire, and in course of time apprenticed to an engraver. His subsequent career was romantic. He was working as an engraver of gunlocks in a shop in Vine Street Minories, and apparently in his spare time cut punches for letters. Some confusion exists as to who discovered his skill in this direction or the exact date of his discovery, but somewhere about 1716 he became known to three important men in London—Jacob Tonson, John Watts, and William Bowyer. Dutch type was at that time the best that printers could procure, and it was both ugly and badly cast, so that the discovery of an Englishman who had the gift of punch-cutting was one to be made the most of. Accordingly Bowyer and Watts interviewed the young engraver, took him to the foundry of James in Bartholomew Close, and offered to put up a sum of money to give him a start if he cared to become a type-founder. With the £500 thus provided William Caslon set up as a letter founder in a garret in Helmet Row, Old Street. Although 1720 is said to be the year in which the first fount of type came from his foundry, it is extremely doubtful if he would have begun with so difficult a task as a fount of Arabic, and it is much more likely that the fount of Double Pica mentioned in the list of types possessed by John Baskett in 1718 was his earliest work. We have at least the authority of John Nichols that Caslon cut a beautiful fount of English (Roman) in 1722, which is seen in an edition of the works of Selden published in 1726. In a very short time the skill of William Caslon as a punch-cutter made his foundry famous. From Helmet Row he moved to Ironmonger Row, and finally in 1734 to much larger premises in Chiswell Street, from which he sent out his first specimen sheet. This further enhanced his success, and his type was eagerly sought after in all parts of the country, and even the skilful John Baskerville of Birmingham was unable to compete with him in public favour. William Caslon the First died at Bethnal Green on January 23rd, 1766. He was succeeded by his son William Caslon the Second, who died in 1788.

CASS (JOHN), bookseller in Wells, Somerset, 1753. Mentioned in a list of provincial booksellers by a correspondent in *Notes and Queries* [11 S. I. 364.]

CATER (WILLIAM), bookseller and publisher in London, facing or opposite Red Lion Street, High Holborn, 1759–76. Was established at the above address in 1759, when he published J. N. Moreau's *Mystery reveal'd* and was joint publisher with John Ward and others of John Brine's *Knowledge of Future Glory*. [J. C. B. L.] In 1765 he advertised "Books for Sale" for which catalogues might be obtained from Brotherton in Cornhill. In the public journals of the year 1767 he advertised a medical work by P. Motteaux entitled *A Commentary on Dysentery*. No copy of this book has been found. In the following year his name occurs in Kent's *Directory* and he was still in business in 1776.

CATLIN (MYLES), bookseller in Northampton, Huntingdon, Kimbolton, Godmanchester, St. Ives, and St. Neot's, 1744–8. Although this bookseller's name has not been found in any imprint, it is more than probable that with so ex-

tensive a business he published something. He died before September 5th, 1748, and was succeeded by John Ellington. Catlin's widow carried on the business at Godmanchester for a time.

CAUSTON (HENRY), printer in London, Finch Lane, 1764–1806. Son of Richard Causton, a printer who lived in the parish of Clerkenwell. Took up his freedom in the Company of Skinners on November 6th, 1764. Succeeded to the business of Henry Kent (*q. v.*). Sir Joseph Causton, grandfather of the present head of the firm, was the son of Robert Causton, who is believed to have been a nephew of the above Henry Causton. There was a very clear family connexion with the Skinners' Co., various brothers and sons being members of it. Henry Causton held the office of Master in 1798 and his son Henry was apprenticed in 1788. Henry the elder died April 20th, 1806. [Information kindly supplied by Lady Causton and the Clerk of the Skinners' Co.; *Gentleman's Magazine*, LXXV. 391.]

CAVE (EDWARD), printer in London, St. John's Gate, 1691–1754. Born on February 27th, 1691, at Newtown in Warwickshire. Sent to a school in Rugby kept by Dr. Holyoke, where he showed considerable talent and was considered fit for a university education. Fate was against him. He was accused of robbing Mrs. Holyoke's henroost, and afterwards, upon a further accusation of obstructing the discipline of the school, he left and after a short experience as assistant to a collector of excise Cave left Rugby to seek his fortune in London. He was first bound apprentice to Freeman Collins, printer in the Old Bailey, and a deputy-alderman. In two years he had attained so much skill and ability that he was sent down to Norwich to manage the *Norwich Courant*. After the death of his master, he settled in Bow, where he married a young widow, and obtained a situation as journeyman in the printing office of Alderman Barber. Through his wife's influence he also obtained a place in the post office. He next began to write news letters, and sent news to various country papers and did a considerable amount of other literary work. Amongst other things he began to furnish the country papers with reports of the proceedings in Parliament. Dr. Johnson who wrote a Life of Cave, notes how he obtained these reports. He says, "Cave had interest with the doorkeepers; he and the persons employed under him got admittance; they brought away the subject of discussion, the names of the speakers, the side they took, and the order in which they rose, together with notes of the various arguments adduced in the course of the debate." They would then adjourn to a

tavern and having compared notes, these were handed to an "abler hand" to put into form. But the members of the House of Commons looked upon this as a breach of privilege and in 1727 both Cave and Robert Raikes, the publisher of the *Gloucester Journal*, were imprisoned and fined for this offence. Thereupon Cave resorted to other methods, but continued his News Letters, and at length saved sufficient money to set up as a printer in St. John's Gate, Clerkenwell. In January 173$\frac{0}{1}$ he printed and published the first number of the *Gentleman's Magazine*, which became so popular that by 1739 its sale was over ten thousand and a few years later had risen to 15,000. He quickly collected round him the chief literary men of the day, and amongst his early friends was David Henry (*q. v.*), who in 1736 married Cave's sister Mary. Another was Dr. Johnson, who contributed to the Magazine for some years, and of whose *Life of Richard Savage* he published the second edition. Their friendship continued until Cave's death on January 10th, 1754. In appearance Cave was a tall and stout man. In his later years he suffered much from gout. His character was marked by great resolution and perseverance, and the success of the *Gentleman's Magazine* was due entirely to his able editorship. After Cave's death the magazine was continued by David Henry and Richard Cave. In addition to the *Gentleman's Magazine* Cave was the printer of many of Johnson's writings and several other notable works, such as Mackerell's *History of Kings Lynn*, 1738. His work as a printer was good and his types clear. He was Dodsley's first printer and is mentioned by Boswell in his *Life of Johnson*.

CHACE, Mr., bookseller, *see* Chase.

CHALMERS (JAMES), bookseller in Newcastle-on-Tyne, 1775–81. His name occurs in 1776 in a list of those receiving subscriptions for the Rev. J. Murray's *Lectures*, a work that does not seem to have been published. A correspondent to *Notes and Queries* states that he died on January 1st, 1781, whilst visiting Mr. Younghusband's near Belford. [*N. & Q.* 10 S. VI. 444.]

CHANDLER (RICHARD), bookseller and publisher in London, York, and Scarborough: London (1) Flower de Luce without Temple Bar; (2) The Ship, without Temple Bar: York, Coney Street, 1732–44. This bookseller was possibly related to Abraham or William Chandler (1696–9); *see Dictionary*, 1668–1725. He is first met with in the pages of Fog's *Weekly Journal*, where in the issue of May 27th, 1732, it is said that he succeeded John Hooke, deceased, and moved to the Flower de Luce without Temple Bar just previously. About the year

1734 he was joined by Caesar Ward, who at once became the senior partner, the firm being always known as Ward and Chandler, and not Chandler and Ward, and in that year "Richard Chandler and Co." wrote to Dr. Thomas Birch saying that they were supplying Dr. Gilbert Burnet with copies of *The General Dictionary*. [Sloane MS. 4302. 161.] In the *London Evening Post*, covering from Tuesday, January 16th to Thursday January 18th, 1739 [? 17$\frac{39}{40}$], they inserted a notice to this effect "That the *York Courant*, late in the occupation of Alexander Staples, is now printed and published by Ward and Chandler, booksellers, at the shop late Mr. Mancklins, deceased, in Coney Street, they having purchased the printing office, lately belonging to the said Staples." This notice further stated that advertisers living in or near London could hand in their advertisements at the Ship without Temple Bar, where copies of the paper could be obtained. It was about this time that they opened a branch business at Scarborough. Early in 1743 the firm completed in twelve volumes octavo *The History and Proceedings of the House of Commons from the Restoration to the end of the last Parliament in 1741*. Although none of the imprints bear Ward's name, he appears to have been joint editor with Chandler. Early in 1744 Chandler committed suicide,[1] and next year Caesar Ward became a bankrupt. [*London Gazette*, June, 1745.] Drake the historian and other friends set him on his feet again and he continued to print and publish the *York Courant*, and in 1749 he was printing for John Hildyard (*q. v.*). The Ship without Temple Bar passed into the hands of William Sandby (*q. v.*).

CHANDLER (S.), printer in London (?), 1763. Printer of *Letters between the Hon. Andrew Erskine and James Boswell, Esq.*, 1763.

CHANDLER (SAM.), bookseller in London, Cross-Keys in the Poultry, 1726–8. *See Dictionary*, 1668–1725. Continued to sell books until August, 1726. In November of the same year Wilford in his *Monthly Catalogue* advertised two theological books as sold by J. Chandler at the above address, and in 1727 the Rev. Samuel Chandler's *Reflexions on the Deists* was "Printed for *John* Chandler at the Cross Keys in the Poultrey." In 1728 *An Essay on the Passions* is advertised to be sold by Sam. Chandler in the Poultry, among others.

CHANEY (JA.), printer, 1738. His imprint has been found on a pamphlet entitled, *The Voice of Liberty*, 1738, but no address is given and nothing more is known of this printer. [Winship.]

[1] *Life of Thomas Gent*, p. 192.

CHANGUION (FRANCIS), bookseller in London, Juvenal's Head, near Somerset House in the Strand, 1742. In the issue of *The Champion, or the Evening Advertiser*, of August 19th, 1742, appears an advertisement of "New Books. Just imported" by the above. It consists of seventeen works all foreign.

CHAPELLE (HENRY), bookseller and stationer in London, Grosvenor Street, 1741–64. His name occurs in the imprint to a pamphlet entitled *A Geographical and Historical Description of the Principal Objects of the Present War in the West Indies*, 1741. [B.M. 932.] He died before September 5th, 1764, on which day his will was proved in the P.C.C. [Simpson 340.] He left a son Anthony, but makes no mention of his business, which was carried on by his widow Mary Chapelle.

CHAPMAN (J.), printer in London, 42 Fleet Street, 1775. Printed for I. Williams, publisher in Fleet Street, a poem entitled *The Drama*. [B.M. 644. k. 18 (13).]

CHAPMAN (SAMUEL), bookseller in London, The Angel, Pall Mall, 1723–8. Doubtless a relative of Thomas and William Chapman. [*Dictionary*, 1668–1725.] He is chiefly remembered as the publisher of the novels and plays of Eliza Hayward, for which he was pilloried by Pope in the *Dunciad*. [Nichols, *Lit. Anecd.* III. 649.] In 1726 he published Richard Savage's *Miscellaneous Poems and Translations*. 1728. *The Illegal Lovers* is advertised as printed for S. Chapman and others. [*Daily Post*, January 5th.]

CHARLETON (R.), bookseller and publisher in London, at the corner of Sweeting's Alley next the Royal Exchange in Cornhill, 1733–5. Publisher of *A Reply to the Vindication of the Representation of the Case of the Planters of Tobacco in Virginia*, in 1733 [J. C. B. L.], and of *Moral Reflections on the Ministry of Cardinal Alberoni*, in January, 1735, with Dodd and Cook. [*Daily Journal*, January 13th, 1735.] Perhaps he died in January, as *A Faithful Narrative of the Murder of Squire Y— W—* is advertised as "printed for Mrs. Charlton at the Royal Exchange and A. Dodd." [February 13th, 1735, *Daily Post*.]

CHARNLEY (WILLIAM), bookseller and publisher in Newcastle-upon-Tyne, (1) Bridge End, (2) The Great Market. 1749–1803. Served his apprenticeship with Martin Bryson and became a member of the Newcastle Company of Stationers on January 25th, 1749, being admitted by servitude. In May, 1751, he was taken into partnership by Bryson, and on July 22nd, 1766, he married a daughter of John Tidy of Staindrop. He was the publisher of numerous books.

In 1755, he succeeded to the business on Bryson's retirement. Having had his premises washed out by a flood he moved to safer quarters in The Great Market in 1777. Charnley died on August 7th, 1803, aged 76, and was succeeded by his son Emerson Charnley. [Welford, *Early Newcastle Typography*; *Newcastle Journal*, 1766; Timperley, 1842, p. 816.]

CHASE (WILLIAM), *see Dictionary*, 1668–1725. There is an advertisement of "Catalogue of Books to be sold by William Chase, bookseller, Cokey Lane, Norwich", in the *Gazetteer and Daily Advertiser* of July 27th, 1765. Mr. Chace, bookseller, subscribed for seven sets of the *Novum Test. Græcum*. [Lond. 1768.]

CHASTELL ( ), book or pamphlet seller in London, Compton Street, 1755. His name is found in the imprint to the second edition of J. Palairet's *Concise Description of the English and French Possessions in North America*, published in that year. [J. C. B. L.]

CHATER (JOHN), bookseller in London, King Street, Cheapside, 1767–8. In the issue of the *Daily Chronicle* of March 31st, 1767, he advertised a sale of books; but he does not seem to have been a publisher. His name occurs in Kent's *Directory* for the year 1768. In partnership for a time with T. Vernor.

CHAULKIN (HENRY), bookseller in Taunton, 1695–1750, *see Dictionary*, 1668–1725. He was still in business in 1750 when with others he sold the 4th edition of *Divine Institutions*.

CHIRM (SYLVANUS), bookseller, bookbinder, and stationer in London, at the Golden Hart, Aldersgate Bars, near Charterhouse Square, *c.* 1770. Issued a trade card about that date. [A. Heal's Collection.]

CHOLMLY, or CHOLMONDELEY (N.), bookbinder in London, (1) Bennets Court in the Strand; (2) Corner of Thavie's Inn, Holborn (?). 1730–2 (?). The *London Evening Post* of Tuesday, December 1st, 1730, reported that an anonymous letter, threatening to kill him, had been dropt at his door and that on the previous night he had been assaulted in Rounds Court by two Irishmen. He may be identical with the N. Cholmondeley at the Corner of Thavies Inn, Holborn, who in 1732 published *A Conference between his Excellency Jonathan Belcher . . . and the chief Sachemo of several Indian Tribes . . . at Falmouth, in Casco Bay in New England*. [J. C. B. L.]

CHRICHLEY (J.), printer in London, the *London Gazette*, Charing Cross, 1731–5. Printer of a pamphlet entitled *The Letters of Atticus*, 1731. 8°. [B.M. E. 2022 (6).] His name also appeared in the imprint to the *Weekly Miscellany* from March 3rd, 1733, till January 25th, 1735. He was one of the printers employed by Dodsley. [Straus, *Robert Dodsley*.]

CHRISTIE (ALEX.), bookseller in Liverpool, South Side, Old Dock, 1776. Mentioned in the *Liverpool Directory* of 1777.

CHURCH ( ), bookseller in Nantwich, co. Cheshire, 1756. In 1756 he was agent for the sale of Schofield's *Middlewich Journal, or Cheshire Advertiser*.

CLACHER (WILLIAM), printer in Chelmsford, Essex, 1776–1813. Proprietor and printer of the *Chelmsford Chronicle*. Died in May, 1813, aged 80. [Timperley, 1842, p. 850.]

CLARIDGE (T.), printer and bookseller at St. Neot's, Huntingdon, 1768–80. His imprint is found on a poll-book for the County of Huntingdon in 1768. He was still in business in 1776 [H. E. Norris, *Notes on St. Neot's Printers*, 1901] and, according to a correspondent in *Notes and Queries*, in 1780. [*N. & Q.* 10 S. XII. 164.]

CLARK, or CLARKE (ABRAHAM), bookseller in Manchester, 1756–74. In 1756 his name is found in the list of agents selling Schofield's *Middlewich Journal, or Cheshire Advertiser*. His name occurs in an advertisement in Adam's *Weekly Courant* of January, 1774. He died May 20th, 1775, aged 60, and was buried in St. Ann's churchyard.

CLARK, or CLARKE (ARTHUR), printer in Scarborough, Yorkshire, 1733. Nephew of Thomas Gent, the York printer. In his *Life*, p. 182, Gent records, "1733 My nephew Arthur Clarke was sent with materials to furnish a printing office in Scarborough" and says further "that it was established about June 16th, 1734, in a House in Mr. Bland's Lane formerly call'd his cliff."

CLARKE (EDWARD), bookseller in Gateshead, Durham, 1772. Mentioned by a correspondent to *Notes and Queries* as at work in that year. [*N. & Q.* 10 S. VI. 443.]

CLARK, or CLARKE (JOHN), bookseller and publisher in London, (1) Duck Lane; (2) Bible under the Royal Exchange. 1697–1760. *See Dictionary*, 1668–1725. May have been identical with John Clarke, publisher in the Old

[or Royal] Exchange. In the *London Journal* of January 3rd, 1726, he advertised *The Compleat Clerk in Court*, and in 1728, in partnership with others, *New Principles of Gardening*. [*Daily Post*, January 3rd.] In 1751 he published the Rev. W. Webster's *Two Sermons upon the Sabbath* [B.M. 225. g. 9 (3)], and in 1753 he joined with the Rivingtons in *An Impartial Examination of Bishop Burnet's History* [*Public Advertiser*, January 5th]. Master of the Company of Stationers in 1760 [Arber, lxviii]. See also Hett, R.

CLARK, or CLARKE (JOHN), printer in London, 1728. One of the workmen employed by Nathaniel Mist, printer. He was committed with others, for printing the issue of Mist's *Journal* of August 24th, 1728. [Dom.S.P. George II., 8. 74.]

CLARKE (SAMUEL), printer in London, Bread Street, Cheapside, 1765–89. Printer of books for the Quakers. Was for a time in partnership with William Richardson, nephew of Samuel Richardson, the printer and novelist. Timperley [p. 763] speaks of him as "a most amiable man: in temper he was cheerful and serene; in manners mild and unassuming; his benevolence was boundless." He retired from business in 1768 and died in 1789.

CLARK (S.), and RICHARDSON (W.), printers in London, 1765. Printers of George Fox's *Journal* in that year.

CLARK, or CLARKE (W.), bookseller and publisher in London, Red Lion, Paternoster Row, *c.* 1750–76. In partnership with L. Hawes and R. Collins, who carried on business for many years at No. 32 Paternoster Row. No particulars can be gleaned as to the history of the firm. In 1765 they were among the publishers who combined in publishing Johnson's *Shakespeare* [*Gazetteer and Daily Advertiser*, October 3rd], and Gay's *Fables*, in 1775. [*Public Advertiser*, January 10th.]

CLARKE (W.), publisher and bookseller in London, under Royal Exchange 1753. Publisher of the *Companion to the Almanack*, which was advertised as printed for him and T. Jefferys. [*Public Advertiser*, January 1st, 1753.] Perhaps this is the same as, or a misprint for, J. Clarke, who was "Under the Royal Exchange" at the time.

CLARKE (WILLIAM), bookseller in Winchester, *c.* 1730. The following is extracted by Mr. A. C. Piper from the Winchester City Records (Tenth Book of Ordinances) "16 April 1734. Agreed and ordered . . . that — Clarke, widow of William Clarke heretofore of this city, bookseller, decd. shall have the Marks in the room of Widow Walker decd. to commence from Michaelmas last past." [*The Book Trade in Winchester. Library*, 3rd Series, vol. vii, p. 193.]

CLAY (F.), *see Dictionary*, 1668–1725. In 1735 he was selling *A Collection of Treaties and Declarations of War.* [*Daily Journal*, January 15th.]

CLAY (JOHN), bookseller in Daventry, co. Northampton, Rugby in Warwickshire, and Lutterworth in Leicestershire, 1744–75. Although this bookseller is heard of in three counties, and was in business for more than a quarter of a century, nothing appears to be known about him except the solitary fact that he died in 1775, and was succeeded by his son Thomas, which appears from the files of the *Northampton Mercury.*

CLAY (THOMAS), bookseller in Daventry, co. Northampton, 1775–6, *see* Clay (J.).

CLAYTON (WILLIAM), bookseller in Manchester, 1700–32. *See Dictionary*, 1668–1725. In 1731 he was associated with Charles Rivington in the publication of Tillemont's *Ecclesiastical Memoirs*, and in 1732 was the publisher of Wright's *Tables.*

CLEAVE (W.), bookseller in Totnes, co. Devon, 1773. His name occurs in the imprint to the *Mariner's Instructor*, published in that year.

CLEMENTS (RICHARD), bookseller and publisher in Oxford, 1728–56. Presumably this is a son of Henry Clements. [*See Dictionary*, 1668–1725.] He is found among others selling *Les Voyages de Cyrus* in 1728. [*Daily Post*, January 1st.] In 1735 there is an advertisement of the sale of *The Literary Magazine*, by R. Clements, Oxford, and W. Thurlstone, Cambridge. [*Daily Journal*, April 4th.] In 1751 both firms were joined by Barrett and Dodsley in the sale of *Odes for Music* (Warton). [Straus, *Robert Dodsley.*] Clements was still in business in 1756.

CLIFF (JOHN), printer in London, Queen Street, near Cheapside, 1726. In that year he was appointed printer to the Lottery.

CLIFTON (R.), bookseller in Durham, 1764. Mentioned in a list of provincial printers. [*N. & Q.* 10 S. VI. 443.]

CLUER (ELIZABETH), printer in London, Bow Churchyard, 1728–31. Widow of John Cluer. Carried on the business after her husband's death. Afterwards married Thomas Cobb (*q. v.*).

CLUER (JOHN), printer in London, Maiden Head, lower end of Bow Churchyard, 1726–1728 (?). This printer had been in business for some years before 1726, and is believed to have been a printer of chap-books and penny histories. He died some time in 1728, and from an advertisement printed in Fog's *Journal* of October 19th, 1728, the business was carried on for a while by his widow Elizabeth, who claimed that she had the same hands to act for her as her late husband employed; but in 1731 she married her foreman, Thomas Cobb (*q. v.*), who thus succeeded to the business. In 1738 Thomas Cobb assigned it over to his brother-in-law, William Dicey of Northampton. [*Daily Journal*, December 24th, 1736.] John Cluer was also a dealer in music, and in company with B. Creake he issued in 1724 a *Pocket Companion for Ladies and Gentlemen containing all the Opera Songs*, which appeared in parts.

COBB (THOMAS), printer in London, Printing Office Bow Churchyard, 1726–36. In 1726 Cobb was foreman to John Cluer (*q. v.*) whose widow he married in 1731. In 1736 he assigned the business to his brother-in-law, William Dicey of Northampton (*q. v.*). [*Daily Journal*, December 24th, 1736.]

COCKING (THOMAS), printer in Bristol, Small Street, 1767–83. Messrs. Hyett & Bazeley, in their *Bibliography of Gloucestershire*, record two works as printed by this printer. The first is *Clifton, a Poem*, 2nd ed., 1767. The British Museum has a copy of a poem with the same title printed at Bristol in 1775 by G. Routh; but there is nothing to indicate that it is not the first edition. [B.M. 11631. g. 2 (13).]

CODERC (J. P.), bookseller in London, Pliny's Head in Little Newport Street, near Leicester Fields, 1728–9. Dealer in French literature. In 1728 he was one of those who published an edition of Voltaire's *Henriade*, and also the *Works* of Le Comte Boullainviller (W. M. C.), and in the same year his name appeared in an advertisement offering to take subscriptions for "A New Edition of a Hebrew Bible". [*Daily Journal*, January 1st.]

CODRINGTON ( ), bookseller and publisher in Bridgewater, co. Somerset, 1745. His name is found in an advertisement of the second edition of Stackhouse's *Bible* in 1745.

COE (S.), bookseller in Chesham, Bucks, 1740. Mentioned in a list of provincial booksellers. [*N. & Q.* 10 S. v, February 24th, 1906, p. 142.]

COGAN (FRANCIS), bookseller and publisher in London, at the Middle Temple Gate, 1730–54. Possibly son of Francis Coggan (1699–1707). His name

appears in the imprint of Eliza Haywood's *Love-Letters on all Occasions*, published in that year, and also on the London edition of Dean Swift's periodical, *The Intelligencer*, which also appeared in 1730. He was also a publisher of law books. His business was not a success, and he became bankrupt in 1754.

COLE (THOMAS), bookseller in Greenwich, Kent, 1770. His name occurs in a list of provincial booksellers as at work in that year. [*N. & Q.* 11 S. I. 304.]

COLE (WILLIAM), bookseller, publisher, and engraver in London, (1) At the "Crown" in Great Kirby Street, near Hatton Garden; (2) Newgate Street, opposite Warwick Lane. 1765–92. Probably related to Benjamin Cole the engraver (1725–67), who was official engraver of the Grand Lodge of Freemasons between 1745 and 1767. William was a publisher of works on Freemasonry and author of a work called *The Defense of Freemasonry*, and between 1766 and 1778 he printed lists of Masonic Lodges. Both Benjamin and William issued engraved trade cards, that of Benjamin being reproduced in Mr. Ambrose Heal's *Trade Cards of Engravers*, 1927 (Plate vii).

COLES (JOHN), stationer in London, (1) Sun and Mitre, against Chancery Lane, Fleet Street; (2) over against St. Dunstan's Church. 1750–7. Issued a printed list of blank warrants and other stationery. Mr. Heal possesses two bill-heads of this stationer, one dated 1750 and the other 1757, the latter being for parchment supplied to Mr. Bickham, the engraver. John Coles was Master of the Company of Stationers in 1762. The firm was continued as J. Coles & Son, the address then given being 21 Fleet Street. [A. Heal's Collection.]

COLLIER, *see* Collyer.

COLLINS (BENJAMIN), printer, bookseller, and publisher in Salisbury, 1729–85. Brother of William Collins, bookseller (*q. v.*), with whom he is said to have been associated in the proprietorship of the *Salisbury Journal* in 1729, on the assumption that the initials B. C. seen in the heading of the issue of July 6th, 1730, refer to him. But if his age at the time of his death is correctly given as sixty-eight, he was born in 1717, and could only have been twelve years of age in 1729. He was certainly in business in 1735, as his name is found in the imprint to the "Bible" annotated by Samuel Humphreys printed in that year, and it seems probable that when the *Salisbury Journal* was resumed in 1736 by "William Collins & Comp." the "Comp." was Benjamin, who on the death of his brother in 1740 took over the management of the paper. In 1743 he established business relations with John Newbery of the Bible & Sun in

St. Paul's Churchyard, the great publisher of juvenile literature. The first address in Salisbury at which he is found is the Bible & Crown in Silver Street, the premises previously occupied by his brother William; but in 1741 he moved to a "corner shop fronting the Poultry Cross"; in 1748 yet another move was made, "to the New Canal, formerly called the Ditch", a house which has been identified as that in which Samuel Farley printed the *Salisbury Postman* of 1715–16. In 1758 an action was brought against him for selling copies of the *Spectator* printed in Scotland, but the proceedings were dropped. [*Considerations on the Nature and Origin of Literary Property*, 1767, 8vo, p. 27.] In 1766 he printed for Francis Newbery the first edition of Goldsmith's *Vicar of Wakefield*. Benjamin Collins also held shares in such noted publications as the *Gentleman's Magazine*, *The Rambler*, and the *London Chronicle, or Universal Evening Post*. He also carried on an extensive banking business in Salisbury. Some interesting notes from his ledgers are printed at the end of C. Welsh's *A Bookseller of the Last Century*, 1885. He died at his house on the New Canal on February 15th, 1785. [For the particulars of this article I am indebted to Mrs. Herbert Richardson of the Red House, Wilton, Salisbury, to whom I tender my cordial thanks.]

COLLINS (ROBERT), bookseller and publisher in London, Red Lion, Paternoster Row, 1750 (?)–1786. In partnership with L. Hawes and W. Clarke. The firm carried on business for several years and was succeeded by Thomas Evans (*q. v.*), but no particulars have been found respecting it. Robert Collins died on May 3rd, 1786. [Nichols, VIII. 480.] In 1775 the firm shared in the publication of Gay's *Fables*. [*Public Advertiser*, January 10th.]

COLLINS (WILLIAM), bookseller in Salisbury, Silver Street, 1730–64. Publisher of a sermon entitled *Humanity and Alms-giving* preached by the Rev. John Price, rector of Newton Tony, Wilts, upon the day the brief for the relief of the German and French protestants at Copenhagen was read, October 26th, 1729. [B.M. T. 1034 (13).]

COLLYER (J.), bookseller and publisher in London, Ivy Lane, 1745–61. This name appears in the imprint to Thomas Pascoe's *True and Impartial Journal of a Voyage to the South Seas*, published in 1745. In 1761 he was one of Dodsley's partners in *The Death of Abel*. [Straus, *Robert Dodsley.*]

COLLYER (M.), pamphlet-seller in London, at the Royal Exchange, 1756. This name is found on the imprint to a pamphlet, *A Fourth Letter to the People of England. The Second Edition*, by John Shebbeare. [B.M. 8132. a. 5.]

COLLYER (THOMAS), printer and bookseller in Nottingham, near the Hen Cross, 1734–54. Probably related to John Collyer (1711–25), whom he appears to have succeeded. In 1734 he printed a devotional work called *Serious Advice of a Parent to his Children*. [Creswell, p. 23.] Continued in business until 1754 when he was succeeded by Samuel Creswell (*q. v.*).

COLSON (WILLIAM), bookseller and publisher in Winchester, 1705–41. *See Dictionary*, 1668–1725. On March 13th, 1741, it was agreed and ordered by the City Council that William Colson, bookseller, an aged man and a person who heretofore lived in good repute, should be placed an almsman in Christ's Hospital. [A. C. Piper: *The Book Trade in Winchester*. *Library*, 3rd Series, vol. vii, p. 193.]

COMBES (CHARLES), senior, printer in Oxford, 1722–31. *See Dictionary*, 1668–1725. The following additional information about this printer has been kindly supplied by Mr. F. Madan. Charles Combes, senior, was born in the year 1666. On May 23rd, 1720, John Baskett appointed him manager of the Bible Side of his printing-house at Oxford, and a schedule of the stock and printing materials was attached to the deed. The documents were printed in the *Athenaeum* of September 5th, 1885. Combes was appointed "Privilegiatus bibliopola" of the University on October 11th, 1722. [Foster, *Alumni*.] He was also master printer of the Bible Side of the Clarendon Press. He died in St. Ebbe's parish, December 3rd, 1731, and his will is among those of the Archdeaconry Court at Oxford.

COMBES (THOMAS), bookseller in London, Bible and Dove, Paternoster Row, 1726–8. Was perhaps a relative of Charles Combes, senior, or Charles Combes, junior, printers at Oxford. [*See Dictionary*, 1668–1725.] In 1726 in partnership with Anthony Peisley, bookseller in Oxford, he published the Rev. Digby Cotes's *New Ecclesiastical History of the Seventeenth Century*. [Wilford, *Monthly Catalogue*, January 1726.]

COMYNS, or COMINS (EDMUND), bookseller in London, (1) over against King's Arms in Little Britain (1730); (2) under (or at) the South entrance of the Royal Exchange. 1730–58. Dealer in educational books (see advertisement in the *Country Journal*, May 2nd, 1730). Between 1740 and 1745 he published several pamphlets relating to America, written by John Ashley. [J. C. B. L.] Succeeded in 1758 by Thomas Hope, who transferred the business to the sign of the Bible and Anchor opposite to the North gate of the Exchange at the

corner of Bartholomew Lane in Threadneedle Street. [Advertisement in *Cambridge Journal*.]

CONANT (NATHANIEL), bookseller and publisher in London, Fleet Street, 1766–80. Son-in-law and successor to John Whiston. Publisher in 1775 of a pamphlet entitled *Some Reasons for approving of the Dean of Gloucester's Plan for separating from the Colonies*, and in 1780 of Uno von Troil's *Letters on Iceland*. [J. C. B. L.]

CONYERS (GEORGE), bookseller in London, 1686–1727. *See Dictionary*, 1668–1725. Was one of the shareholders in John Selden's *Opera Omnia* advertised in Wilford's catalogue of January 1726.

COOKE (A.), bookseller in London, Mincing Lane, Fenchurch Street, 1765. He advertised as selling a Bible. [*Gazetteer and Daily Advertiser*, August 11th, 1765.] He ran a circulating library and published an elaborate trade card advertising his stock of books. [A. Heal's Collection.]

COOK, or COOKE (E.), bookseller and publisher in London, Royal Exchange, 1735. There is an advertisement of *Moral Reflections on the Ministry of Cardinal Alberoni* as printed and sold for E. Cook and others. [*Daily Journal*, January 13th, 1735.]

COOKE (JOSHUA), bookseller in Sherborne, co. Dorset, *c.* 1732. His name is found in the imprint of *The West Country Farmer*, published without date. [Addenda to Dredge.] What his relationship was to other booksellers of this name in Sherborne has not been ascertained.

COOK, or COOKE (JOHN), bookseller and publisher in Sherborne, co. Dorset, 1713–46. *See Dictionary*, 1668–1725. In 1726 his name is found in the imprint of a *Sermon* preached by the Rev. Thos. Naish at the cathedral in Salisbury on November 30th, and in 1746 he was the publisher of the Rev. Robert Dagge's *Sermon* preached at the Assizes in Dorchester. [B.M. 225. f. 16 (1).]

COOK, or COOKE (JOHN), bookseller and publisher in Uppingham, co. Rutland, 1729–44. Publisher of a work called *Medicina Musica* written by Richard Browne, apothecary in Oakham, co. Rutland. [B.M. 1191. e. 14.] His name is next found in the *Proposals* issued by the Rev. Francis Tolson, vicar of Easton Maudit in Northamptonshire, in September 1739, for a work called *Hermathenae* [B.M. 11631. bbb. 30], as one to whom subscriptions for the work

might be sent. The copy of the work in the British Museum has only an engraved title-page with no imprint. It should probably also have a printed title-page giving the names of the printers and publishers.

COOK, or COOKE (JOHN), bookseller and publisher in London, (1) The King's Arms without Temple Bar, opposite Devereux Court, 1756; (2) opposite St. Clement's Church in the Strand, 1757; (3) Shakespeare's Head, Paternoster Row, 1766. 1756–66. In partnership with J. Coote made a speciality of jest-books and chronicles of crime, which he advertised extensively in provincial newspapers. He also published the *Ladies' Magazine*. [*Gazetteer and Daily Advertiser*, August 1st, 1765.]

COOK, or COOKE (RICHARD), bookseller in Carlisle, 1739. Only known from the fact that his name occurs, like that of John Cook, in an advertisement of the issue by subscription of Francis Tolson's *Hermathenae*, 1739. [B.M. 11631. bbb. 30.]

COOK, or COOKE (S.?), Mrs., pamphlet-seller and publisher in London, Royal Exchange, 1743. Her name appears in the imprint to a pamphlet entitled *Enthusiasm display'd*, a reprint of a tract attributed to Oliver Cromwell. [B.M. 113. m. 65.] In 1764 a pamphlet entitled *Clodius, a Poem* bore in the imprint the names of S. Cook and J. James. Possibly widow of E. Cook.

COOK (W.), bookseller in London, Pope's Head Alley, Cornhill, 1765. His name occurs with Dodsley's and others as issuing "proposals" for Poems. [*Gazetteer and New Daily Advertiser*, July 2nd, 1765.]

COOKE (WILLIAM), bookbinder in London, Bible and Dove in Fetter Lane, 1765. Receipted account for binding, dated May 11th, 1765. [A. Heal's Collection.]

COOPER (JOHN), stationer in London, Bible and Crown within Bishopsgate, *c.* 1750. Issued a trade card about that date. Succeeded by Joseph Woodgate (*q. v.*). [A. Heal's Collection.]

COOPER (MARY), widow of Thomas Cooper, 1743–61. Mrs. Cooper was associated with Dodsley in several of his publications, including *The Oeconomy of Human Life* (1750), of which she published the first edition anonymously for him. When *The Appendix, or Second Part to the Oeconomy of Human Life*, a spurious addition, was published, Mrs. Cooper sold both parts as genuine, despite Dodsley's advertised denials of its genuineness, and in January 1751

issued a second edition of the Appendix which she sold bound up with the genuine first part. She was succeeded in her business in 1761 by John Hinxman of York, who moved to London. [Mumby.]

COOPER (THOMAS), printer and publisher in London, (1) in Paternoster Row, (2) corner of Ivy Lane; (3) in Ivy Lane, next Paternoster Row; (4) Globe in Ivy Lane near Paternoster Row (all these probably refer to the same house). 1732–40(?). One of the most prolific printers and publishers of the pamphlet literature of the eighteenth century. From 1732 till 1761 his name and that of his widow and lists of their publications are to be found in the columns of the London and provincial newspapers. The exact date of Thomas Cooper's death is unknown, but his widow Mary Cooper's name begins to appear alone in imprints about 1743, and she continued the business until her death in 1761. T. Cooper was the printer of the *Daily Courant*, 1735.

COOTE (J.), bookseller and publisher in London, (1) King's Arms, opposite Devereux Court in the Strand; (2) King's Arms, Paternoster Row. 1757–74. A native of Horsham in Sussex. For many years in partnership with John Cooke (*q. v.*). In 1758 his name is found in the imprint to a pamphlet entitled *The Folly of appointing Men of Parts to great Offices of State*, a satire on Government officials. Coote was fond of dramatic composition and was the author of an opera and five farces. [Timperley, 1842, p. 834.] He is also found publishing the *Royal Magazine* in 1765. [*Gazetteer and Daily Advertiser*, August 1st.] On June 5th, 1774, among "Dividends to Creditors" is one promised July 1st for "John Coote, late of Paternoster Row, Bookseller." Presumably he went bankrupt the previous year and retired. He died on October 20th, 1808. [Nichols, III. 719.]

COPPERTHWAITE (G.), bookseller and publisher in Leeds, co. York., 1763–71. His name is found in the imprint to a poem entitled *Every Man the Architect of His Own Fortune*, by James Scott, 1763, 4to. [B.M. 11630. d. 8 (1).] In 1769 he published Elizabeth Moxon's *English Housewifery*, which was printed for him by Griffith Wright of Leeds. A correspondent in *Notes and Queries* [11 S. I. 363] records him as still in business in 1771.

CORBETT (CHARLES), bookseller and publisher in London, Addison's Head, next the Rose Tavern without Temple Bar, 1732–52. Son of Thomas Corbett, was born on February 16th, $17\frac{09}{10}$, at St. Mary's Hill, London. Succeeded his father in the business before June 17th, 1732. Dealt in plays, political tracts, children's books, and shared in many large undertakings, such as the *Complete*

System of Geography (1747), Boyer's *Dictionary* and Bayle's *Dictionary* (1734). Charles Corbett was also the publisher of the *British Magazine*, which commenced in March 1746. It was run on the same lines as the *Gentleman's Magazine*, but was sold at threepence instead of sixpence. He had a private house in Islington, where he died after a lingering illness on February 24th, 1752. He was spoken of as "a man well respected by his acquaintance". [*Read's Weekly Journal or British Gazetteer*, Saturday, February 29th, 1752.] He married Ann, daughter of Nathan Horsey of Norfolk, and left one son Charles, who succeeded him in the business and assumed the title of baronet. [G. E. C., *Complete Baronetage*, 1907, II. 184.]

CORBETT (SIR CHARLES), bookseller, publisher, and keeper of Public Lottery Office in London, Addison's Head opposite St. Dunstan's Church in Fleet Street, 1752–1808. Son of Charles Corbett and grandson of Thomas Corbett. Succeeded to the business on the death of his father, having previously been a clerk in a lottery office in London. Nichols in his *Lit. Anecd.* [III. 769] says that he used "to astonish the gaping crowd by the brilliancy of his nocturnal illuminations". This was part of his advertisement of the Lottery Office which he added to the business on taking it over. He also continued the publication of the *Whitehall Evening Post*, which his father had started in 1747. In 1757 complaint was made in the House of Lords of certain paragraphs that had appeared in that paper, and Corbett appeared at the Bar of that House and admitted the publication and said he believed them to be matter of public interest. On March 7th, after begging pardon on his knees, he was discharged from custody. [*House of Lords Journals*, XXIX. 70.] Nichols further states that he was ruined in business by an unfortunate mistake in the sale of a ticket which was worth £10,000, but the story is so vague that little credence can be attached to it. But whatever the circumstances, Charles Corbett appears to have fallen on evil times, and gave up business about the year 1771. In September 1774 he assumed the title of Baronet, and a notice of him appears in G. E. C.'s *Complete Baronetage*, but here again the information is vague and inconclusive and it is impossible to gather whether his claim was good or not. His assumption of the title did not improve his fortunes, and he died in great poverty on May 15th, 1808, in Compton Street, and was buried on May 26th in St. Anne's, Soho. He had a son, Thomas, who died seven days after in the same house, and was buried on the same day. [G. E. C., *Complete Baronetage*, 1907, II. 184.]

CORBETT (THOMAS), bookseller in London, Addison's Head, or The Painted Head of Joseph Addison, without Temple Bar. *See Dictionary*, 1668–1725.

CORNEY (THOMAS), bookseller in Penrith, *c.* 1726. Mentioned in a list of provincial booksellers. No details. [*N. & Q.* 10 S. V. 242.]

CORNISH (D.), bookseller and publisher in London, 1775. One of the partners in the publication of Gay's *Fables*.

COSLEY, or COSSLEY (WILLIAM), bookseller and publisher, in Bristol, Tolzey, 1726–50. Published a sermon preached by the Rev. J. Hart at the Mayor's chapel at Bristol on Sunday, February 13th, 1726, entitled *Liberty of Conscience*. [W. M. J.] Mentioned in an advertisement of the second edition of Stackhouse's Bible in 1745. Towards the end of the year 1750 he was succeeded by John Crofts (*q. v.*).

COTTON (JOHN), bookseller in Shrewsbury, 1746–65. In a list of Shrewsbury booksellers contributed to the pages of the *Shropshire Notes and Queries*, May 6th, 1898, he is noted to have paid a sum of 17*s*. 4*d*. to the Saddlers' Company, probably for admission on June 6th, 1746. His name occurs in the imprint to a *Sermon* preached at St. Chad's on October 1st, 1747, by the Rev. Matthew Horbery. [B.M. 225. f. 16 (3).] In 1761 he is found in partnership with Joshua Eddowes. [*N. & Q.* 10 S. V. 242.] In 1765, the *Life and Death of Phillip Henry*, bears the imprint: "Salop, printed by J. Cotton and J. Eddowes."

COTTON (THOMAS), printer in Kendal, 1731. Printer of the *Kendal Courant*. *See* Nicholson (C.), *Annals of Kendal*.

COTTRELL (THOMAS), letter-founder in London, Nevil's Court, Fetter Lane, 1757–85. Served his apprenticeship with William Caslon the second. A dispute arising in the foundry over the price of certain work, Cottrell, who was one of the ringleaders, was dismissed in company with Thomas Jackson (*q. v.*). He set up a foundry in Nevil's Court. In 1758 Cottrell was entrusted by Rowe Mores with the fount of Anglo-Saxon type which had been used in printing Miss Elstob's *Rudiments of Grammar*, and was asked to repair and fit it for use. This fount had been entrusted to Mores' care by William Bowyer in 1753 for presentation to the University of Oxford. Cottrell carried out the work satisfactorily, and the fount eventually reached Oxford, but was never used. In 1759 Cottrell was engaged in casting various sizes of roman and a fount of Engrossing. His first specimen sheet was undated, but is believed to have been

issued about the year 1760, and a few years later an octavo specimen book was issued which bore a strong likeness to Caslon's. Cottrell died in 1785 in poor circumstances. He is described as obliging and friendly. [T. B. Reed, *Old English Letter Foundries*, pp. 288–92.] The foundry passed into the hands of Thomas Thorne, who moved it to Barbican.

COWBURNE (THOMAS), printer in Liverpool, Atherton Street, 1766. His name occurs in the *Liverpool Directory* for 1766. It is not found in that for 1777.

COX, or COCKS ( ), printer in London, Paternoster Row, 1770. A severe fire broke out in the premises of Messrs. Johnson and Payne, booksellers in Paternoster Row, in the early morning of January 8th, 1770. It spread with great rapidity, and amongst the adjacent buildings destroyed was that of Mr. Cocks, printer. [Timperley, 1842, p. 721.]

COX (H. SHUTE), bookseller in London, (1) Ludgate Hill, 1745; (2) Paternoster Row. 1745–55. His name appears in the imprint to the Rev. V. Perronet's *Discourse on Romans xii. 13*, 1745. [B.M. 225. f. 14 (6).] Publisher of Rev. F. Ayscough's *Discourse against Self-Murder*, 1755, and of *The Adventures of Signor Gaudentia di Lucca*, in partnership with Innys, Richardson, and Manly. [*Public Advertiser*, January 12th.]

COX (NICHOLAS), bookseller in Oxford, St. Peters-in-the-East, 1726–31. Born in 1649. Manciple of St. Edmund Hall and St. John's College; well known as a bookseller. Died May 12th, 1731. [Hearne, X. 415. Information supplied by Mr. F. Madan.]

COX (THOMAS), *see Dictionary*, 1668–1725. Still in business in 1754. He was one of the publishers of Bayle's *Dictionary* in 1735. [*Daily Journal*, January 13th.]

COX and BIGG, printers in London, Savoy, 1775–6. Their names appear in the imprint to a pamphlet by E. Miller entitled *Three Letters to the Prisoners in Northampton Gaol*, 1775. [*Northampton Mercury*.] On March 2nd, 1776, their office was destroyed by fire. [Timperley, 1842, p. 736.]

CRAIGHTON, or CREIGHTON (ELIZABETH), bookseller and publisher in Ipswich, Suffolk, Butter Market, 1728–76. Sister of William Craighton (*q. v.*). In the year 1728 she published the Rev. B. Blomefield's sermon entitled *Of contending earnestly for the Faith*, and in the following year a pamphlet by William Matthews entitled *Observations upon a Pamphlet entitul'd, The Letter which Pope Gregory XV. wrote to Charles I etc.*, which was printed for

her by J. Bagnalls. She held an interest in the *Ipswich Journal* which she made over to a nephew, William Jackson, and their names are found together as joint printers in 1765 [*N. & Q.* 10 S. V. 183]; but in 1771 William Jackson became bankrupt, and Elizabeth Craighton afterwards became partner with William Shave, and another nephew, Stephen Jackson, in the management of the *Ipswich Journal*.

CRAIGHTON, or CREIGHTON (HENRY), bookseller in Sunderland, 1770–6. Died November 16th, 1776. [*Newcastle Courant*.] [*N. & Q.* 10 S. VI. 443.]

CRAIGHTON (WILLIAM), printer and bookseller in Ipswich, Stationer's Arms, Butter-market, 1733–65. According to a correspondent in *Notes and Queries* [10 S. V. 183], there was a bookseller of this name at work in 1733. This may refer to Elizabeth Craighton. In 1736 William's name appears in a list of those receiving subscriptions for Wilkins's *Concilia*. On February 17th, 1739, he started the *Ipswich Journal*. He gave up the bookselling business in 1759, when it was taken over by John Shave (*q. v.*), but he continued the printing business until his death, when the paper was continued by W. Jackson, who went bankrupt in 1771. A dispute arose as to an annuity to be paid to Mrs. Craighton, which led to the publication of some broadsides and pamphlets, one of which, issued by John Shave, was headed: *To the Public. A more particular account of the transactions relating to the right of publishing the "Ipswich Journal" than has as yet appeared*, and was in a *Narrative*, published by Messrs. Wallis Garrard and Leggatt. [B.M. 1304. m. 1 (12).] His imprint is found in a *Sermon* preached by the Rev. John Chubb, Rector of Whatfield and Vicar of Debenham, before the Incorporated Society of Sons of the Clergy in the parish church of St. Mary at Tower, Ipswich. [B.M. 225. i. 8 (16).]

CRANE (SAMUEL), bookseller and publisher in Liverpool, Dale Street, 1776. Mentioned in the *Liverpool Directory* for 1777. Publisher of a work called the *Universal Cash Book*.

CRANSTON (W.), bookseller in Alton, Hants, 1740–1. Mentioned in a list of Hampshire Booksellers contributed to *Notes and Queries* by F. A. Edwards. [*N. & Q.* 10 S. V. 481.]

CRAVEN (W.), bookseller in Dartmouth, co. Devon, 1763–78. In 1763 his name is found in the *Exeter Flying Post* as "Bookseller, Dartmouth". One of the publishers of a work entitled *The most General School-assistant*, by G. Dyer, master of Tacker's-Hall School in Exeter, MDCCLXX, 8vo. [Dredge.]

CREAKE (B.), bookseller and publisher in London, The Bible, Jermyn Street, 1726–8. Publisher of a work on Epitaphs, which was issued in monthly parts under the title of *Sepulchrorum Inscriptiones* in 1726. [W.M.C. April to September.] There is an advertisement of his selling *Diamonds cut Diamonds*, fifty-two songs by Mr. Carey, in the *London Journal* of February 12th, 1726. In 1728 he published Dr. Alex Innes's theft of Dr. A. Campbell's *Enquiry into the Original of Moral Virtue.* [W.M.C. February.] And also a *History of Scotland* with J. Cluer [*Daily Post*, January 1st], and *Arithmetic in all its Parts* with J. Hazard. [*Daily Journal*, January 3rd.]

CREIGHTON, *see* Craighton.

CRESSWELL (SAMUEL), printer, bookseller, and publisher in Nottingham, (1) Market Place; (2) New Change. 1753 (?)–1786. The exact date upon which this bookseller began business has not been found; but on September 1st, 1753, he was summoned to appear before the magistrates of the city for selling the *Leicester Journal.* He was let off with a reprimand. [*Public Advertiser*, September 19th, 1753.] He lived in St. Mary's parish, of which he was at one time sexton. He purchased from George Ayscough *The Courant*, and changed its name to the *Nottingham Journal.* [Timperley, 1842, pp. 702, 721.] Amongst his many publications may be noticed an English Grammar compiled by Samuel Hammond, a schoolmaster in Nottingham, entitled *A New Introduction to Learning*, and printed without date. It went through many large editions. [B.M. 827. d. 39 (4).] Samuel Cresswell died August 25th, 1786. [Nichols, III. 673.]

CROFTS (JOHN), bookseller in Bristol, Tolzey, 1750. Successor to W. Cosley (*q. v.*). In the following year he drew the £10,000 prize in the Lottery. [*London Evening Post*, December 21–4, 1751.] May be identical with the J. Crofts of Monmouth (*q. v.*).

CROFTS (J.), bookseller in Monmouth, 1726–8. Dealer in chap-books. In 1728 he sold Dr. George Brown's *Arithmetica Infinita.* Was perhaps identical with John Crofts of Bristol (*q. v.*).

CROKAT, or CROKATT (JAMES), bookseller and publisher in London, (1) Golden-Key, near the Inner-Temple-Gate in Fleet Street, 1726; (2) Prujeian Court, over against Surgeons Hall in the Old Bailey. 1726–52. Is first met with in 1726 as the publisher of the Rev. W. Webster's pamphlet *The Clergy's Right of Maintenance.* [Wilford's *Monthly Catalogue*, January, 1726.] In 1734

he gave evidence before a Committee of the House of Commons on the Copyright question, when he stated that, being at Preston in Lancashire, he was in a bookseller's shop when a bale of books arrived from Dublin which were all (pirated) English books. [*House of Commons Journals.*] In 1740 he brought forward a project for a *Universal History*, five volumes of which were published in 1740–1, the sixth in 1742, and the seventh in 1744. [Timperley, 1842, p. 667.] He began to issue a periodical entitled *The Publisher* in 1745, and in 1752 another called *The Repository.* He was also part proprietor of the *Daily Advertiser*, and secretary or manager of the Society of Booksellers. Nichols says he was the greatest literary projector of the age; and died worth —nothing! Issued a small trade card with the sign of the key. [A. Heal's Collection.] There was also a James Crokatt whose address is given as the Black Horse, near Fleet Bridge, 1742, who may be the same.

CROMPTON (JOSEPH), bookseller in Birmingham, Colmore Row, 1770. His name occurs in the *Birmingham Directory* for that year.

CROPLEY (W.), bookseller and publisher in London, Dryden's Head in Paternoster Row, 1762. In partnership with H. Payne. Amongst their publications was J. Cunningham's *The Contemplatist*, 1762, 4to.

CROUCH (THOMAS), bookseller in London, Bell, over against Queen's Head tavern in Paternoster Row, 1697–1728. *See Dictionary*, 1668–1725. Advertisement of patent medicine, *Daily Post*, January 17th, 1726. Died before January 6th, 1728, when he was succeeded by J. Isted. [*London Journal*, last page, 1st col.]

CROUSE (JOHN), printer and publisher in Norwich, 1761–96. Is first heard of in 1761 when he took over Crossgrove's *Norwich Gazette*, the title of which he altered to the *Norwich Gazette and Weekly Advertiser*, and later to the *Norfolk Chronicle or Norwich Gazette.* He was the printer of numerous sermons, and in 1768 he published an anonymous *History of the City and County of Norwich* in two volumes. In November 1785 W. Stevenson joined him, and in 1794 J. Matchett, Stevenson's son-in-law, joined the firm. John Crouse died in October 1796, and the business was carried on by Stephenson and Matchett. [C. Nowell, *Early Printing in Norwich*, 1919.]

CROWDER (STANLEY), bookseller and publisher in London, (1) The Looking-Glass, over against St. Magnus Church, London Bridge, 1755–60; (2) The

Golden Ball in Paternoster Row, 1760–70. 1755–70. Apprentice to Sir James Hodges the bookseller on London Bridge, and appears to have occupied the same premises from 1755 until the tenants of the Bridge received notice to quit in 1760. He appears to have been a short time in partnership with H. Woodgate (*q. v.*), and the firm was then known as S. Crowder and Company. They afterwards moved to Paternoster Row, where Nichols says they carried on a wholesale trade. In 1768 they took seven sets of the *Novum Test. Graecum.* The partnership was dissolved in 1769, and Crowder carried on the business alone; but he met with misfortune, his premises being entirely destroyed by fire during the year 1770. He then applied for and obtained the post of Clerk to the Commissioners of the Window Tax for the City of London. In 1775 S. Crowder of Paternoster Row was publishing the *Ladies Complete Pocket Book* with Carnan and R. Baldwin, and was one of the partners in Gay's *Fables* the same year. [*Public Advertiser*, January 10th.] He died on May 23rd, 1798. [*N. & Q.* 6 S. VII. 461; Timperley, 1842, p. 721; Nichols, III. 720.]

CROWNFIELD (CORNELIUS), I, printer to the University of Cambridge, 1698–1743. *See Dictionary*, 1668–1725.

CROWNFIELD (CORNELIUS, II, and JOHN), booksellers, Cambridge, *c.* 1743–60. This Cornelius Crownfield was probably the son of Adrian Crownfield (living in St. Botolph's parish in 1715, but dead when Cornelius I, the printer, made his will, 1741). John was the son of Cornelius I, the printer. *See* also next entry. G. Bally's *Solomon de Mundi Vanitate* was printed for them by J. Bentham, 1743, and *Advice to a Young Student*, with a method of study for the first four years (by Daniel Waterland), the third edition of 1760, with the Alma-Mater block on the title-page.

CROWNFIELD (JOHN), bookseller at the Rising Sun, St. Paul's Churchyard, *c.* 1728–(?), and at Cambridge, *c.* 1730–44. Son of Cornelius I the University printer. Born 1710. *Supplement to the Treatise, entituled, Nature, Obligation, &c.* (by D. Waterland), 1730, and D. Waterland's *Doctrinal Use of the Christian Sacraments*, 1736, were both printed in London for him, and Zach. Grey's *Review of Neal's History of the Puritans*, 1744, was printed by J. Bentham, the Cambridge University Printer, also for him. He evidently was joined in business by his cousin, Cornelius Crownfield II, as we find them together *c.* 1743 and 1760. (*See* previous entry.)

CRUDEN (ALEXANDER), bookseller and publisher in London, The Bible and Anchor, Under the Royal Exchange, 1732–8. Chiefly remembered as the compiler of the *Biblical Concordance.* His career as a bookseller was a brief one. He opened a shop under the Royal Exchange in 1732. He is said to have begun his *Concordance* in 1736, and published it in 1737. The Queen, to whom he presented a copy, died on November 20th. The book did not turn out a financial success and Cruden gave up his bookselling business soon afterwards. His name occurs in Kent's *Directory* for 1738. For the remainder of his life he devoted himself to the reformation of the morals of the nation. He was a man of weak intellect and was on more than one occasion put under restraint. He died at Islington on November 1st, 1770. [Timperley, 1842, pp. 722–3.]

CRUTTWELL (RICHARD), printer, bookseller, and publisher in Bath, 1773–99. In 1773 he printed for two booksellers in the city, W. Taylor and A. Tennent, *The Strangers Assistant and Guide* to Bath, which was a great advance on those previously published by Boddeley and Keene. It contains a very useful list of those who let lodgings, in which the names and addresses of the principal booksellers in the city are found. In 1775, he printed for L. Bull, another bookseller in Bath, the first volume of Lady Miller's *Poetical Amusements at a Villa near Bath.* He became the proprietor and editor of the *Bath Chronicle*, and was the printer of the Bible with Bishop Wilson's notes published in 1785. Richard Cruttwell died at Cheltenham on June 1st, 1799. In his obituary notice in the *Gentleman's Magazine* his character is summed up in these words: "His friendship was warm, sincere and active; his heart tender and affectionate; his religion pure and practical."

CRUTTWELL (WILLIAM), printer and stationer in Sherborne, co. Dorset, 1764–1804. In 1764, in opposition to the Whig newspaper, the *Sherborne Mercury*, William Cruttwell published *Cruttwell's Sherborne Journal.* From an advertisement in the later numbers he sold Bibles, Prayer Books and Sealing Wax, from which it may be concluded that he was bookseller and stationer as well as a printer. He died in 1804, aged 62, so that he must have begun the publication of the paper almost immediately after he set up in business. [C. H. Mayo, *Bibl. Dorset.*, p. 78.]

CULLIMORE (LUKE), bookseller in Portsmouth, 1702–31, *see Dictionary*, 1668–1725, p. 325. Sold a book called *Reasons for uniting the Church and Dissenters . . . To which is annexed a Liturgy.* [Advertisement in *Grub Street Journal*, August 5th, 1731.]

CURLL (E.), *see Dictionary*, 1668–1725.

CURRY (MICHAEL), printer to John Wilkes, 1760 (?)–1788. Employed by John Wilkes in his private printing office. Afterwards gave information against his employer, for which treachery no one in London would employ him, as his offence was a violation of the freedom of the press. Curry afterwards retired to Norwich, where he died. [*Gentleman's Magazine*, LVIII, Jy–Dec., 1788, p. 752.]

CURTIS (T.), bookseller, 1775. He issued *The Royal Calendar* in 1775, with T. Cadell and a number of others.

DAGNALL (STEPHEN), bookseller in Chesham, Bucks, 1720–6. *See Dictionary*, 1668–1725. Still in business in 1726. [*N. & Q.* 10 S. v. 142.]

DAGNALL (THOMAS), printer and bookseller in Aylesbury, co. Bucks, 1776. Was probably a descendant of Mathias Dagnall, bookseller in Aylesbury, 1658–1736, *see Dictionary*, 1668–1725. He died December 12th, 1792. [*Nichols*, III. 674.]

DAPPE ( ), bookseller, London, Great Ryder Street, 1753. "The First vol. of Dalton's Museum" is to be obtained at Mr. Dappe's in Great Ryder Street, and at Mr. Dodsley's. [*Public Advertiser*, January 9th, 1753.]

DARBY (EDWARD), bookseller in Market Drayton, co. Shropshire, 1756. Agent for Schofield's *Middlewick Journal or Cheshire Advertiser* in that year.

DARBY (JOHN), junior. *See Dictionary*, 1668–1725. His executors were still carrying on business in 1753, as they shared in the issue of *Thesaurus Linguae Latinae Compendiarius* at that date. [*Public Advertiser*, January 5th.]

DARBY (P.), printer at Halifax, co. Yorks, 1760–3. The earliest example of this printer's work is *A Pocket-Companion for Harrowgate Spaw*, published in 1760. [J. N. Dickons, *Catalogue*, p. 231.] Amongst his other work was a small treatise entitled *Halifax and its Gibbet Law*, printed for John Bentley [Boyne's *Yorkshire Library*, p. 93], and in the same year Nathaniel Fletcher's *Tradesman's Arithmetic*. [J. H. Turner, *Halifax Books and Authors*, p. 43.] In 1763 his name occurs in an advertisement of books in the *Leedes Intelligencer*.

DAVENHILL (WILLIAM), bookseller and publisher in London, No. 8 in Cornhill, 1768–76. Publisher of works relating to America: (1) *The Journal of a Two Months' Tour . . . among the Frontier Inhabitants of Pensylvania*, 1768. (2) The second edition of Governor Hutchinson's *History of the Province of Massachuset's Bay*, 1768. In two advertisements in the *Public Advertiser*, January

12th and January 28th, 1775, his address is given as 19 Cornhill, and Royal Exchange, respectively. He was still in business in 1776.

DAVENPORT ( ), bookseller and publisher in London, Paternoster Row, 1760–8. In partnership with Joseph Johnson (*q. v.*). They were the publishers of *The Monthly Record of Literature*, in 1767. [Timperley, 1842, p. 836.]

DAVEY (P.), bookseller and publisher in London, 1756–8. In 1756 he was one of the partners in the edition of Ben Jonson's works, and in 1758 his name is found in the imprint to the *Supplement to the English Introduction to Lily's Grammar, &c.*

DAVEY or DAVY (ROBERT), (?) printer in Norwich, 1746–8. In 1746 an edition of *The Busybody, a Comedy* was issued bearing the imprint "Norwich: Printed for Robert Davy . . ." and again, in 1748, C. Parkin's *Reply to Dr. Stukeley* bears the imprint "Norwich: Printed for the author by Robert Davy . . ."

DAVIDSON (J.), bookseller and publisher, London, 1753. His name appears as one of the partners in the publication of *Thesaurus Linguae Latinae Compendiarius*. [*Public Advertiser*, January 5th, 1753.]

DAVIES (THOMAS), bookseller and publisher in London, 8 Russell Street, Covent Garden, 1760(?)–1785(?). The friend of Dr. Johnson. Frequently referred to in Boswell's *Life*, and there described as a man of good understanding and talents. Davies was educated at Edinburgh University and was for several years an actor. He set up as a bookseller in 1762, and it was in his shop that Boswell was introduced to Johnson: "At last on Monday, the 16th of May (1763) when I was sitting in Mr. Davies' back parlour, after having drunk tea with him and Mrs. Davies, Johnson unexpectedly came into the shop: and Mr. Davies having perceived him through the glass door in the room in which we were sitting, advancing towards us, he announced his awful approach to me, somewhat in the manner of an actor in the part of Horatio, when he addresses Hamlet on the appearance of his father's ghost, 'Look, my lord, it comes'." In 1768 Davies issued a Catalogue containing some 8,000 titles [B.M. 128. i. 16 (3)]. Added at the end was a list of his publications or rather of the works in which, at that time, he was a part shareholder. It included such works as Burnet's *History*, both in folio and octavo]; *Celebrated Authors*, 2 vols.; *Clarissa*, 8 vols.; the works of Congreve, Dryden, Gay, Jonson, Otway, Shakespeare, and Waller. He also republished many notable Elizabethan and Jacobean writings, and between 1769 and 1785 he was in

correspondence with the Rev. James Grainger, whose *Biographical Dictionary* he published. [*Letters between the Rev. James Grainger M.A. and the literary men of his time*. Edited by J. P. Malcolm, 1805, 8vo, pp. 22 *et seq.*] Davies was also an author, and Boswell's opinion of his writings was that they had "no inconsiderable share of merit". In 1780 he wrote a *Life of Garrick*. Johnson's opinion of his friend was expressed thus: "Sir, Davies has learning enough to give credit to a clergyman." The date of his death is unknown.

DAVIES, *see also* Davis.

DAVIS (CHARLES), bookseller in London: (1) Covent Garden; (2) Hatton Garden, 1726; (3) Holborn, opposite Gray's Inn; (4) Against Gray's Inn Gate in Holborn; (5) Paternoster Row. 1723–55. In business in 1723 when he held a book-auction sale in Covent Garden, the catalogue of which is in the British Museum. [128. i. 3 (9).] In 1726 his name occurs in Wilford's *Monthly Catalogue* as part publisher of the second edition of W. Somner's *Treatise of Gavelkind*. [W.M.C. March, 1726.] He continued to do a considerable publishing and bookselling business until his death on August 31st, 1755. He was succeeded by his nephew Lockyer Davis (*q. v.*). Timperley, probably on the authority of Nichols, says that Charles Davis was "one of the earliest booksellers who retailed libraries by marked catalogues". [p. 695.]

DAVIS (LOCKYER), bookseller and publisher in London: (1) Over against Gray's Inn Gate in Holborn; (2) Lord Bacon's Head, near Salisbury Court, Fleet Street. 1753–91. Succeeded his uncle Charles Davis (*q. v.*). For some years he was in partnership with Charles Reymer or Rymer. They were printers to the House of Commons. Davis and Reymer published in 1757 Dr. John Brown's *Estimate of the Manners and Principles of the Times*, which according to J. H. Burton ran into seven editions in a few months and was reprinted at Boston (N. E.) In 1766 they published a work called the *English Connoiseur*. In 1770 the partnership was dissolved and Davis carried on alone, and issued numerous catalogues between 1770 and his death on April 23rd, 1791. His knowledge of books was extensive, and his opinion was sought by almost all the literary men of his day. He was buried in the church of St. Bartholomew the Great, where there is a tablet to his memory.

DAVIS (ROBERT), bookseller and publisher in London, corner of Sackville Street, Piccadilly, *c.* 1764–75. Nichols, in *Lit. Anecd.* [IX. 276], prints a letter from P. Thicknesse relating to certain MSS. purchased by this bookseller from the library of Lord Masham, but gives no clue to the date of the transaction.

Nichols also says that soon afterwards Davis retired from business and settled at Barnes. Amongst his publications in 1764 was *Museum rusticum et commerciale*. In 1775 there is an advertisement of the sale of a "Bible, printed for R. Davis, L. Davis, T. Carnan, and F. Newby, junior". In 1765 the same firm had previously produced a Bible. [*Gazetteer and New Daily Advertiser*, July 1st.]

DAVIS, *see also* Davies.

DAVY, *see* Davey.

DE HONDT (PETER ABRAHAM), bookseller and publisher in London, near Surrey Street, in the Strand, 1765. In partnership with T. Becket (*q. v.*). In 1761 *The Genuine Letters of Baron Fabricius* was published by them from Tully's Head in the Strand. In 1765 they are found advertising a Translation of a French Book, on July 12th, and "New Books imported by" them on August 5th. [*Gazetteer and Daily Advertiser.*]

DELL & Co. (HENRY), bookseller, London, Corner of Brook Street, Holborn, 1765. He advertises second-hand books in the *Gazetteer and Daily Advertiser* of July 27th, 1765.

DENOYER, *see* Dunoyer.

DIAL (S.), (?) bookseller and publisher in London, Covent Garden, 1742. A fictitious imprint found on the title-page of the following pamphlet: *A Key to some late important transactions: In several letters from a certain great man, No body knows where, wrote No body knows when, and directed to No body knows who.* [B.M. 101. g. 44.]

DICEY (CLUER), printer and publisher in London, The Maiden-head in Bow Church Yard, and Northampton, 1736–64. Son of William Dicey (*q. v.*). The old-established business of John Cluer, printer and publisher of chap-books, in Bow Church Yard, was in the hands of Cluer Dicey in 1736. In 1764 he was in partnership with Richard Marshall and they issued a catalogue in which they gave their address as Aldermary Church Yard, London. This catalogue is quoted by Mr. C. Gerring in his *Chapter on Chap-books*. Part III *Notes on Printers and Booksellers*.

DICEY (ROBERT), bookseller in Northampton, Market Hill, 1746–9. Succeeded to his father's business in 1747, but in the previous year on 22nd September he was the publisher of the *Sermon* on behalf of the Northampton County Infirmary, preached by the Rev. Henry Layng, M.A. [B.M. 1658 (5).]

DICEY (THOMAS), printer in Northampton, Market Hill, 1758. His name occurs in the *Poll-Book* for that year, which was printed by Cluer Dicey & Son.

DICEY (WILLIAM), printer in London and Northampton. London: At their Warehouse against the South door of Bow Churchyard, at the further end of the churchyard from Cheapside. *See Dictionary*, 1668–1725. In 1730 he was in partnership with his brother-in-law, Thomas Cobb, who married the widow of John Cluer, at the above address. In 1736 Cobb assigned and sold the business to him, and he then took his son Cluer Dicey (*q. v.*) into partnership, and together they issued a very beautifully engraved trade card, as an advertisement of their printing and engraving business. [A. Heal, *The Trade-Cards of Engravers*, plate VIII, 1927.] William Dicey was still in business in Northampton in 1754, when his name is found in an advertisement of the *Young Attorney and Gentleman's Assistant*. He appears to have handed over the management of the London business to his son Cluer Dicey (*q. v.*).

DICKENSON (J.), (?) bookseller and publisher in London, Witch Street, 1733–54. Publisher of a poetical satire on Pope's *Dunciad* called *The State Dunces* . . . 1733, fol. [B.M. 643. m. 15 (19)], and in 1735 *The Previous Question in Politics*, a sixpenny pamphlet.

DICKENSON (WILLIAM), printer in London (?) and Dublin, 1756. In the *London Gazette* of September 11th, 1756, is the second notice of his bankruptcy, in which he is described as "William Dickenson, formerly of the parish of St. James, Clerkenwell, in the county of Middlesex, late of Dublin in Ireland, printer".

DICKINSON (B.), (?) bookseller and publisher in London, Inigo Jones's Head, over against Exeter Exchange in the Strand, 1736. His name occurs in the imprint to a poem entitled *The Forsaken Fair*, published in 1736. [B.M. 11602. i. 17 (4).]

DILLY (CHARLES) and (EDWARD), booksellers and publishers in London, 22 Poultry, Rose and Crown, 1732–1807. These brothers came of a yeoman family of Southill in Bedfordshire. Edward, the elder of the two, was born there on July 25th, 1732, and his brother on May 22nd, 1739. Edward was apprenticed to a bookseller in London and afterwards set up for himself at No. 22 Poultry, and dealt largely in theological literature. He also published the works of Catharine Macaulay the historian. He was afterwards joined by his brother Charles, whom he took into partnership, and their house became one of the most noted meeting-places of literary men in London. Both Boswell and

Johnson frequently dined there. Nichols describes Edward Dilly as a great talker. He died on May 11th, 1779. He was responsible for the publication of the *English Poets*, the issue of which was brought about by the publication of Bell's duodecimo edition. Dr. Johnson was asked to contribute the Lives, which he did for the small fee of two hundred guineas, a sum which he fixed himself. The publishers later gave him a further £100. On the death of his brother, Charles succeeded to the business and published, among other things, Boswell's *Life of Dr. Johnson*. He was Master of the Stationers' Company in 1803, and died on May 4th, 1807, being succeeded by Joseph Mawman. [Nichols, III. 190–3.] Edward Dilly issued a trade card as successor to Mr. John Oswald. [A. Heal's Collection.]

DINNING (JOHN), bookseller and publisher in Taunton, co. Somerset, 1725–6. Mentioned in an advertisement as selling a catalogue for a book-sale in 1725, and in the following year his name is found in the imprint of a work entitled *An Appeal to Justice*, where he is described as "publisher of *Brice's Journal* in Taunton".

DIX or DICKS (J.), bookseller and publisher in London, Without Temple Bar, 1731. Publisher of a pamphlet entitled *A Letter to William Pulteney Esq.* . . . 1731, 8vo. [B.M. E. 2023 (4).]

DIXWELL (I.), bookseller and publisher in London, St. Martin's Lane, near Charing Cross, 1761–76. His name is found in the imprint to numerous pamphlets about this time. He was still in business in 1776. He seems to have specialized in medical books.

DOD or DODD (ANNE) (Mrs.), book and pamphlet-seller in London: (1) Without Temple Bar; (2) Peacock, near Temple Bar, 1728; (3) near Essex Street in the Strand, 1726–43. Dealer in news-sheets and pamphlets of all kinds. Her name appears in an advertisement of *The General History of the West Indies*, as printed for A. Dodd and four others. [*London Journal*, Feb. 26th, 1726.] She was frequently proceeded against by the authorities. In one of her petitions she said she had been left a widow with a large young family, and was just able to feed them by selling papers. Whenever a public character was satirized or condemned by the press, the unfortunate newsvendor, who was probably quite ignorant of the contents of the journals, was fined and imprisoned, as if he or she had been the author of the offending article. In connexion with the *London Evening Post*, Mrs. Dod was said to have taken thirty quires of this paper weekly, from John Purser, printer (*q.v.*). [S. P. Dom. Geo. II, Bundle 23

(82); Bundle 48 (13, 14).] Mrs. Dod's name is constantly found in the imprints of eighteenth-century pamphlets.

DOD or DODD (BENJAMIN), bookseller in London, Bible and Key in Ave Mary Lane, 1745–64. Bookseller to the Society for Promoting Christian Knowledge. One of his earliest publications was *The History of Lambert Simnel and Perkin Warbeck*. This contained six pages of advertisements of books said to have been published by J. Watts, at the printing office in Wild Court, and sold by B. Dod. This included a large number of plays, novels, and classical works. [B.M. 9505. cc. 12.] His executors joined in the publication of Johnson's *Shakespeare*. [*Gazetteer and Daily Advertiser*, October 3rd, 1765.]

DODSLEY (ROBERT), bookseller and publisher, poet and dramatist, in London, Pall Mall, Tully's Head, 1735–64. One of the most remarkable men in the bookselling world of the eighteenth century. The friend of Dr. Johnson, who called him "Doddy", and of Alexander Pope, who set him up as a bookseller. Born at Mansfield in 1703, was the son of a schoolmaster of that town, who took some care with his education. His circumstances were very poor, and the best his parents could do for him was to find him a place as footman with a society man, Charles Dartineuf, and afterwards with the Hon. Mrs. Lowther. But, as Charles Knight observes in his *Shadows of the Old Booksellers*, young Robert Dodsley was a "youth of observation and discretion" with an active mind, a love of literature and the drama, and a facile pen, that soon lifted him from the mean station of a footman. This period of his life he recorded in a poem called *The Muse in Livery*, published in 1732. He also wrote a play called *The Toy-shop* while he was in the service of Dartineuf, and this coming under the notice of Alexander Pope, the poet, he induced Rich to stage it. The play was a success, and when published later it went to eleven editions. Pope further gave or lent him £100 to start as a bookseller, and accordingly, in 1735, Robert Dodsley opened a shop in Pall Mall under the sign of Tully's Head. The street was not then the fashionable thoroughfare it afterwards became; but Dodsley was not wholly dependent on casual customers, and, no doubt partly through Pope's introduction and his own love of literature, his shop soon became known to scholars and literary men. In 1738 he first made the acquaintance of Dr. Johnson, who brought with him a poem entitled *London*. This Dodsley agreed to publish, and from that time forward he had no stauncher friend than the doctor. It was Dodsley who induced Johnson to undertake the *Dictionary*. In 1739 the publication of *Manners*, by

Whitehead, caused the author and publisher to be summoned to the Bar of the House of Lords. Only Dodsley appeared. The pamphlet was voted "A wicked reflection on several Lords of the House", and Dodsley was imprisoned for a week, but liberated thanks to his powerful friends. In 1743 he began to publish Young's *Night Thoughts*, and in 1744 after a successful publication of Mark Akenside's poem *The Pleasures of Imagination*, he arranged with Akenside to edit *The Museum, or Literary and Historical Register*, a fortnightly journal which ran for thirty-nine numbers. Dodsley published several of Swift's works at this time. Among other authors whose works he issued were Lord Orrery, William Whitehead, Christopher Pitt, Joseph Warton, Gilbert West, Lyttleton, Percy, and Shenstone. Robert Dodsley is best known as the founder of the *Annual Register* and the publisher of a *Select Collection of Old Plays*, in 1744. Isaac Reed, when republishing the Collection in 1780, bore this witness to Dodsley's ability: "The first edition of the present volumes was one of many excellent plans produced by the late Mr. Robert Dodsley; a man to whom literature is under so many obligations that it would be unpardonable to neglect this opportunity of informing those who may have received any pleasure from the work, that they owe it to a person whose merits and abilities raised him from an obscure situation in life, to affluence and independence. He was a generous friend, an encourager of men of genius; and acquired the esteem and respect of all who were acquainted with him." As a writer of plays, Robert Dodsley met with some success. *The King and the Miller of Mansfield?* was founded upon the ballad he had known in his boyhood, and was published in 1737, and his tragedy of *Cleone* was produced at Covent Garden in 1758, Johnson being present on the first night. In 1750 Robert Dodsley took into partnership his younger brother James, who succeeded him in the business on his death, September 25th, 1764. He was buried in the churchyard of Durham Cathedral. [C. Knight, *Shadows of the Old Booksellers*; Straus, *Robert Dodsley*.]

DOMVILLE (W.), bookseller and publisher in London, Royal Exchange, 1770–5. Publisher, with others, of Dr. William Doyle's *Some Account of the British Dominions beyond the Atlantic*; published without date, but assigned to the year 1770. His name again occurs in the imprint to a pamphlet entitled *Colonising*, which appeared in 1774. [J. C. B. L.] In 1775 he joined in the publication of Ainsworth's *Dictionary*. [*Public Advertiser*, January 27th.]

DONALDSON (ALEXANDER), bookseller in Edinburgh, 1750–63 [*see Scottish Section*], and in London: (1) in partnership with his brother John between

Norfolk Street and Arundel Street, Strand, 1763–73, and (2) by himself at 48 St. Paul's Churchyard, 1773 till about 1788. He speedily became known for selling cheap reprints of books which were in his opinion out of copyright, disregarding the courtesy copyright observed between members of the trade. He boasted that he was selling his publications from 30 to 50 per cent. under their prices. Boswell has recorded Dr. Johnson's violent outburst against him as "a fellow who takes advantage of the law to injure his brethren"; and when it was pointed out to him that Donaldson was encouraging literature by reducing the price of books, so that poor students might buy them, Johnson retorted, "Well, sir, allowing that to be his motive, he is no better than Robin Hood, who robbed the rich in order to give to the poor". In 1764 he published *Some Thoughts on the state of Literary Property humbly submitted to the consideration of the Public,* in which he protested that "the booksellers of London have endeavoured of late to monopolize books of all kinds, to the hurt of all the other booksellers in England, Scotland, and Ireland". He followed this up shortly after with a similar pamphlet. In 1768 he reprinted Thomson's *Seasons,* the copyright of which had just been sold by Andrew Millar's executors, but the sale of the reprint was stopped by the Court of Chancery, until in 1774 the judgement was reversed by the House of Lords. Meanwhile in 1773 a London bookseller named Hinton brought an unsuccessful action against Donaldson for selling Stackhouse's *History of the Bible,* a book first published in 1732. One of the counsel for Donaldson was James Boswell. [*Hinton* v. *Donaldson,* B.M. 6573. 9. 11.] After moving to 48 St. Paul's Churchyard, he issued a four-page quarto list of his publications. [A. Heal's Collection.] Donaldson bought property near Edinburgh in 1786, and died there 11th March, 1794. (*See* R. T. Skinner's *A Notable Family of Scots Printers,* 1928.)

DONALDSON (JOHN), bookseller in London, Norfolk Street and Arundel Street, Strand: (1) in partnership with his brother Alexander (*q. v.*), 1763–73, (2) alone. (*See Scottish Section*).

DOORNE (STEPHEN), bookseller in Faversham, Kent, 1770–5. Mentioned by a contributor to *Notes & Queries.* [10 S. v, March 10th, 1906, p. 183.] His name occurs in the imprint to an edition of a pamphlet entitled *A Proposition for the present Peace and future Government of the British Colonies in North America,* 1775, which is in the John Carter Brown Library in America. None

of the provincial booksellers are named in the imprint to the edition in the British Museum [103. i. 63].

DORMER (J.), printer in London: (1) Three Kings and Half-Moon next Ludgate; (2) The Green Door in Black and White Court, Old Bailey. 1733–5. Printer of pamphlets, amongst which may be noticed *A Collection of State Flowers,* 1733 [B.M. 11602. i. 17 (1)], and *The Norfolk Gamester,* 1734. He was perhaps related to T. Dormer (*q. v.*). In 1735 was published *The Bath, Bristol, Tonbridge and Epsom Miscellany,* printed by T. Dormer. [*Daily Journal,* May 1st, 1735.] Perhaps "T" is a misprint?

DORMER (T.), bookseller and publisher in London, next the Castle Tavern in Fleet Street, 1732. This name is found in the imprint to a pamphlet entitled *The Norfolk Sting,* 1732, 8vo. [B.M. T. 1109 (2).]

DOWNHAM (E.), bookseller and publisher in London, Pope's Head Alley, Cornhill, 1751. In partnership with F. Stamper (*q. v.*).

DOWNING (JOSEPH), printer in London, Bartholomew Close, 1670–1734. *See Dictionary,* 1668–1725. Died August 31st, 1734. [Timperley, p. 652.]

DOWNING (M.), bookseller in London, Bartholomew Close, 1735–53. In all probability the widow of Joseph Downing, who had died on August 31st, 1734. She dealt in theological literature and was still living in 1753, when her name is found in a list of those selling *Expository Notes on the New Testament.* [*Public Advertiser,* January 6th, 1753.]

DOWSE (J.), bookseller and publisher in London, opposite Fountain Court in the Strand, 1753. Publisher of pamphlets.

DRAPER (SOMERSET), bookseller and publisher in London, 1743–53. In 1743 he obtained the publication of the Bishop of Chichester's *Sermon* preached before the Society for the Propagation of the Gospel in Foreign Parts, at their annual meeting on Friday, February 18th, 174$\frac{3}{4}$. [B.M. 694. f. 14 (8).] His name appears with several others as part proprietor in *Thesaurus Linguae Latinae Compendiarius.* [*Public Advertiser,* January 5th, 1753.]

DREW (JOSEPH), printer and bookseller in Exeter: (1) Opposite Castle Lane; (2) Printing office, near Eastgate. 1745–8. Began as a bookseller about 1740, but later on took up printing. Nothing more is heard of him after 1748, in which year he published *A Letter to Mr. Z —Y, M—ge,* bearing the imprint: "Exon. Printed and Sold by Joseph Drew, Bookseller nr. Eastgate." [Dredge, pp. 47 and 70.]

DUFRESNOY (SAMUEL), bookseller in London, parish of Great St. Helen's, 1733–41. By his will, dated June 17th, 1733, and proved on February 11th, 1741, it would appear that he had been in business, probably as a dealer in foreign books, for some years, and he mentions that his son Samuel was in partnership with him. [P. C. C. 48 Trenley.] Paul Vaillant was one of the witnesses.

DUNBABIN (JOHN), bookseller and publisher in Liverpool, Castle Street, 1776. Mentioned in the *Liverpool Directory* for 1777.

DUNCOMB (E.), bookseller and publisher in London, Butcher Hall Lane, 1748–53. Publisher of pamphlets, amongst which may be noticed *The Life and Surprising Adventures of James Wyatt,* a sailor, first issued in 1748, and the fifth edition of which appeared in 1753.

DUNCOMBE (JOHN), publisher, 1757. In 1757 he collected and published *Horace in English Verse.* Dodsley had an interest in the publication. [Straus.]

DUNN (JOHN), printer and publisher in Whitehaven, 1771–5. His name is found in the imprint to a volume of verse compiled in 1771 by G. A. Stevens and entitled *The Choice Spirit's Chaplet.* [B.M. 11621. aaa. 21.]

DUNOYER (H.), bookseller and publisher in London, Lisle Street, 1772. This name occurs in the imprint to the first part of the Rev. Wm. Mason's poem, *The English Garden,* 1772. [B.M. 643. k. 10 (1).] It may be that of the widow of P. Dunoyer.

DUNOYER (P.), bookseller in London, Erasmus Head, The Strand, 1728–55. Dealer in foreign literature; no biographical particulars obtainable. In 1728 he received subscriptions for a new edition of a Hebrew Bible [*London Journal,* January 1st], and was selling *Remarques Théologiques* on January 4th [*Daily Journal*]. Received proposals for the Rev. Richard Grey's *Memoria Technica.* [Nichols, i. 423.] In 1755 his name is found in the imprint to J. Palairet's *Concise Description of the English and French Possessions in North America.* [J. C. B. L.]

DURHAM (T.), bookseller and publisher in London, (1) Plato's Head, near Round Court, Strand; (2) Golden Ball, Savoy, over against Exeter Change; (3) against Ivy Bridge; (4) Charing Cross. 1753–75. In 1753 he was in partnership with D. Wilson at Plato's Head, from which address they published *The Works of Christina Queen of Sweden.* [*Public Advertiser,* January 5th, 1753.]

Mentioned by F. G. Hilton-Price in his *Signs of Old Houses in the Strand.* [*Middlesex and Herts. Notes & Queries,* III. 18.] He is also mentioned in Kent's *Directory* for 1768 and was still in business in 1775. He held shares in most of the important publications of the time, and in 1762 his name is found in the imprint to an interesting item of Americana, *An Account of the Spanish Settlements in America,* printed in Edinburgh and sold by the leading booksellers in London. [J. C. B. L.]

DURSTON (THOMAS), bookseller and publisher in Salop (probably Shrewsbury is meant), 1714–47. Mentioned in an advertisement of lost horses [*London Evening Post,* October 24th, 1728]. As late as 1747 he was agent for Adam's *Weekly Courant,* a newspaper printed at Chester, and in that year his name is found in the imprint to a sermon preached at St. Chad's, by the Rev. Matthew Horbery. [B.M. 225. f. 16 (3).]

DYER (SAMUEL), bookseller in Tiverton, 1716–26. His imprint is found in a book entitled *A Brief Exhortation* in 1716, and again as the publisher of one of the Rev. Samuel Westcott's sermons in 1726.

DYMOTT (RICHARD), bookseller in London, opposite Somerset House, in the Strand, 1766–72. Published catalogues of his stock and also advertised himself as bookbinder to the Duke of Gloucester. In or about 1766 he published William Stork's *An Account of East Florida.* [J. C. B. L.]

EADE (J.), bookseller in London, King Edward's Stairs, 1726. He was part proprietor in Joshua Kelly's *Modern Navigator's Complete Tutor,* which was advertised in the *London Journal* of February 5th, 1726.

EARL (CHRISTOPHER), printer in Birmingham, Dale Street, 1770–8. Described in Sketchley's *Birmingham Directory* for 1770 as "printer and publican", an interesting instance of the survival of two trades that are frequently found joined in the sixteenth century. He was still in business in 1778. [*N. & Q.* 10 S. v.]

EAST (WILLIAM), printer at Waltham in Leicestershire, 1748–54. Printer of music. [Allnutt in *Bibliographica,* II. 308.]

EASTON (EDWARD), I, bookseller and publisher in Salisbury, 1725 (?)–53. Publisher of the Rev. Thomas Naish's sermon preached in the Cathedral on November 30th, 1727. [B.M. 694. h. 2 (17).] He died in 1753, and by his will left to his son Edward his stock-in-trade and utensils. [P.C.C. 314 Searle.]

EASTON (EDWARD), II, bookseller and publisher in Salisbury, 1742–95. Son of Edward Easton I. In partnership with his father, whom he succeeded in 1753. In 1754 his name is found in the imprint to a poem entitled *Two Epistles on Happiness*. [B.M. 840. k. 2 (8).] He died in 1795 at the age of 75.

EATON (WILLIAM), bookseller and publisher in Yarmouth, (1) on the Quay; (2) near the Bridge. 1728–76. His first place of business was situated at the south-west corner of Row No. 5 and the Quay, known as Gurney's Bank Row. [F. J. Farrell, *Yarmouth Printing and Printers*, 5.] As early as 1728 he published a *Grammar* for the use of the Grammar School in Yarmouth. In 1755 he moved to another shop "nearer the Bridge". [*Ipswich Journal*, September 1755.] His name occurs in the imprint to the Rev. Thomas Bowman's sermon entitled *The Principles of Christianity*, printed at Norwich in 1764. [B.M. 4474. a. 71 (2).]

EDDOWES (JOSHUA), printer and bookseller in Shrewsbury, 1749–75. In a list of Shrewsbury booksellers contributed to the pages of the *Shropshire Notes & Queries* on May 6th, 1898, Joshua Eddowes is described as a bookbinder, who, on May 26th, 1749, paid 17*s*. 4*d*. to the Company of Saddlers of Shrewsbury, probably for his admission. He was the youngest son of Ralph Eddowes of Shrewsbury, and was born on April 15th, 1724. He was a notable dealer in old books, and eventually added printing to the other branches of his trade. In 1761 he appears to have been in partnership with John Cotton. [*N. & Q.* 10 S. v. 242.] In 1772 he printed two sermons preached by the Rev. T. Humphries, vicar of St. Chad's, Shrewsbury. In 1775 he shared in the publication of *Divine Maxims* with several London and country booksellers. [*Public Advertiser*, Jan. 3rd.] His son, William, afterwards joined him in the business. Joshua Eddowes died on September 23rd, 1811, aged 85. Hunter, the antiquary, described him as "a very respectable friendly man". [Add.MS. 24569.]

EDLIN (THOMAS), printer in London, Prince's Arms over against Exeter Change in the Strand; (2) Story Passage, St. James's Park. 1721–8. *See Dictionary*, 1668–1725. In the *Country Journal* of September 28th, 1728, he advertised the speedy issue of a new periodical called *The Flying Post, or the Weekly Medly*, of which No 12, for December 21st, is in the Burney Collection, 267. It bore an imprint as above with the addition, "and sold at his Shop in Story Passage near St. James's Park". Issued an elaborate trade card from the Prince's Arms. [A. Heal's Collection.]

EDMONDS (HUGH), Stationer in London, Paper Mill near Barnard's Inn, Holborn, *c.* 1760. Issued a trade card engraved by Sherborne about that date. [A. Heal's Collection.] His address is interesting as showing the presence of a paper-mill in London, which was probably situated near the stream that ran from Hampstead and gave its name to the street.

EDWARDS (A.), bookseller in London, Cockspur Street, 1775. His name is found in an advertisement for the sale of *A History of the West Indies*. [*Public Advertiser*, October 28th, 1775.]

EDWARDS (WILLIAM), bookseller in Halifax, Yorks., 1758–1808. Distributed the newspaper called the *Leedes Intelligencer*. Published catalogues of his stock which Nichol's described as "astonishingly rich in scarce, valuable books". He died on January 10th, 1808, aged 86. [Nichols, III. 422.]

EGELSHAM (WELLS), printer in London, 1753–86. His name is found in the imprint to several issues of the *Public Advertiser* in that year. Timperley [*Encyclopaedia*, 1842, p. 759] has the following notice of him: "1786, April 4. *Died*, Wells Eglesham, a worthy journeyman printer, a character not unknown in the regions of politics, porter and tobacco in London. He was bred to the profession, and worked as a compositor, till disabled by repeated attacks of a formidable gout. For some years he was employed in the service of the elder Mr. Woodfall, and his name appeared for some time as the ostensible publisher of the *Public Advertiser*. In 1769 he published a little volume of humorous poetry under the title of *Winkey's Whims*. In 1779 he was the author of a *Short Sketch of English Grammar*, 8vo. A great variety of his fugitive pieces appeared in the public prints. . . . He died overwhelmed with age, infirmities and poverty, leaving an aged widow, who obtained a small pension from the Co. of Stationers, and survived till 1811."

EGERTON (PARK), bookseller in London, near Whitehall, 1730. Timperley says that James Thomson the poet, when he first came to London, lodged with this bookseller, and that he finished his poem *Winter* in a room over the shop. [p. 676.]

ELLINGTON (J.), bookseller in Huntingdon, 1755. Mentioned by a correspondent in *Notes & Queries* as in business in that year. [*N. & Q.* 10 S. v. 183.]

ELMSLEY (PETER), bookseller and publisher in London, facing Southampton Street, Strand, 1770–6. One of the best known and most important booksellers in London. Succeeded to the business of Paul Vaillant (*q. v.*). Amongst his customers he numbered the Duke of Grafton, the Hon. Topham Beauclerk, Mr. Stuart Mackenzie, Gibbon the historian, Mr. Cracherode, and John Wilkes. Gibbon offered him his *History* to print, but Elmsley declined it. Nichols speaks of him as possessing consummate ability and sound judgement and as a man of the strictest integrity. [Nichols, v. 325.] In 1775 he was selling books from the Clarendon Press. [*Public Advertiser*, February 15th, 1775.] On March 2nd, 1776, he lost a large quantity of books in a fire that began in the printing house of Cox and Bigg in the Savoy, and spread to the adjoining premises. Elmsley died on May 3rd, 1802, aged 67.

EMERSON, *see* Emonson.

EMM ( ), bookseller in Bishop Auckland, co. Durham, 1764. Mentioned by a correspondent to *Notes & Queries* as carrying on business in that year. [*N. & Q.* VI. 443.]

EMONSON, or EMERSON (JAMES), printer in London, St. James's, Clerkenwell, 1754–80. Nothing appears to be known as to the early career of this printer. The earliest notice of him is the agreement of 1754, by which he became a partner with John Bowyer the printer; but he was a friend of the Bowyer family before this, as, in a letter printed by Nichols, he speaks of having known Bowyer's grandfather and father. The partnership turned out a failure, and if one may accept the story as given by Bowyer himself in certain letters to Bishop Warburton which Nichols says were never sent, the quarrel arose over the purchase of new type for the second part of that prelate's *Divine Legation*. What Bowyer meant by the "second part" we have not been able to discover; but as the printer's name is not mentioned in the imprint to any edition an appeal to the book does not help. Bowyer's partner was not willing to incur the expense and refused to pay for the type, with the result that Bowyer resigned the printing of the book, but, without consulting his partner, agreed to correct the proofs. Unfortunately Bowyer in his agreement with Emonson stipulated that he was not to be asked to correct proofs, and when by accident a portion of Warburton's proof fell into Emonson's hands the incident created much unpleasantness between the two men and the partnership was dissolved soon afterwards. This happened about July 1757. Emonson then set up for himself at the above address. Timperley says he was the proprietor of *Lloyd's Evening News*, but there is no confirmation of this. He died June 6th, 1780, and was succeeded by John Rivington, a grandson of Charles Rivington the publisher of Paternoster Row (*q. v.*). [Nichols, II. 260, 387; Timperley, p. 746; Rivington, *The Publishing Family of Rivington*, 1919, p. 79.]

ENEFER (W.), bookseller and publisher in Harwich, 1769. In 1769 his name occurs in an advertisement of John Gibson's *Seasonable Hints on Midwifery*.

ETHERINGTON (CHRISTOPHER), bookseller, printer, and publisher in York, (1) Pope's Head, Coney Street; (2) The Pavement; (3) Coppergate, 1770–5. Began as a bookseller at the sign of Pope's Head in Coney Street. In 1772 he is found with a printing office in Coppergate, from which on December 18th he issued the first number of a weekly newspaper called the *York Chronicle*. This turned out a failure, and in January 1777 he became bankrupt and nothing more is known of him. [Davies, p. 331.] He had a son Thomas who became a bookseller at Rochester, Kent. [Timperley, 1842, p. 832.] In 1775 he published, with J. Bell of the Strand, Lord Chesterfield's *The Principles of Politics*. [*Public Advertiser*, February 1st, 1775.]

EVANS (THOMAS), bookseller and publisher in London, Paternoster Row, 1770–1803. Chiefly remembered by the assault made on him by Oliver Goldsmith, in connexion with a letter that appeared in the *London Packet*, which reflected on Miss Horneck. The poet came off second best as Evans was a rough character. He began as a porter to W. Johnston the bookseller in Ludgate Street. He afterwards acquired the *Morning Chronicle* and the *London Packet*, and eventually succeeded to the business of Messrs. Hawes, Clarke & Collins in Paternoster Row. He died on July 2nd, 1803. [Nichols, III. 720.] He bequeathed his property to Christopher Brown, father of Thomas Brown, of Longman, Brown, Greene & Longman. [Curwen.]

EVANS (THOMAS), bookseller and publisher in London, Strand, 1774–84. Chiefly remembered as the publisher of the collection of old ballads that bears his name. During his short-lived career he published and edited many fine books. He was apprenticed to Charles Marsh (*q. v.*), and set up for himself about 1774. He must not be confused with the other Thomas Evans, bookseller, who was attacked by Oliver Goldsmith. Thomas Evans died in 1784, his will being proved on May 18th. He appointed his "dear and excellent friend Thomas Cadell of the Strand" his executor, while Isaac Reed and William Fell were two witnesses. The will makes no mention of his business. His son Robert Harding Evans was the celebrated auctioneer. [P.C.C. 256 Rockingham.]

EVANS (WILLIAM), bookseller in Bristol on St. James Back, 1733–45. In an advertisement in the *Country Journal or Craftsman* of December 27th, 1735, announcing the publication of the Rev. Samuel Humphrey's, *Old and New Testament,* this bookseller is named as one of those from whom it could be had; but his name does not appear in the imprint. Also in 1745 in connexion with the second edition of Stackhouse's *Bible.*

EVERDEN (GEORGE), bookseller in Portsmouth, Hants, Bible and Crown, 1725. Mentioned by a correspondent to *Notes & Queries* in a list of provincial booksellers. [*N. & Q.* 10 S. v. 482.]

EVERINGHAM (ELINOR), printer in London, Seven Stars, Ave Maria Lane, 1712. *See* Everingham (Robert).

EVERINGHAM (J.), printer in London, Dean Street, Fetter Lane, 1761. Possibly a relative of Robert Everingham, printer (1680–1700). His name is found in the imprint to a pamphlet entitled *The American Negotiator,* 1761. [J. C. B. L.]

EVERINGHAM (ROBERT), printer in London, Seven Stars in Ave Maria Lane, 1680–1700. *See Dictionary,* 1668–1725. It was this printer who, in 1681, used Moxon's Irish type in which he printed Damet's Irish *New Testament.* [Reed, *Old English Letter Foundries,* p. 189.] He was in partnership with R. Whitledge, and Dunton has left it on record that he often employed them and looked upon them as honest and thriving men. He further says that they became journeymen printers again; but Everingham's business was carried on at the same address by his widow in 1712, when she printed for Dr. John Richardson *The Book of Common Prayer, Irish and English.* [Reed, *ibid.*]

EYRE (CHARLES), printer in London, *see* Strahan, W.

EYRES or AYRES (JAMES), bookseller and printer in Winchester, 1720 (?)–58. A correspondent to *Notes & Queries* stated that about 1720 he printed a sermon on St. Peter's repentance and was still in business in 1758. [*N. & Q.* 10 S. v. 482.]

EYRES (JOHN), printer in Warrington, next door to the White Bull in the Horse-Market, 1731–56 (?). In the parish register for May 1731 is entered the birth of Thomas son of John Eyres, printer, "and in May 1734 the birth of William son of John Eyres printer". Printed a broadside concerning tolls, which is preserved in the Free Library at Warrington. [J. Kendrick, M.D., "Eyres' Warrington Press", *Warrington Guardian,* 1881.]

EYRES (MARGARET), bookseller in Liverpool, Preston Row, 1776. Mentioned in the *Liverpool Directory* of 1777.

EYRES (THOMAS), *see* Eyres, William, 1756–76.

EYRES (WILLIAM), printer in Reading, co. Berks., 1727–34. In the year 1727 he printed a sermon by the Rev. Joseph Slade, of St. Lawrence, Reading, which was sold by Benjamin Shirley of that town. [B.M. 226. f. 10 (11).] A correspondent to *Notes & Queries* mentions him as still there in 1734. [*N. & Q.* 11 S. I. 364.]

EYRES or AYRES (WILLIAM), printer in Winchester, *c.* 1739. Amongst the anti-Quaker tracts recorded in J. Smith's *Bibliotheca Anti-Quakeriana,* is one entitled *A dispute between a journeyman tanner of Carisbrooke, and a Quaker,* which is said to have been printed by William Ayres in Winchester about the year 1739.

EYRES (WILLIAM), printer and bookseller in Warrington, near the Market-Gate, in the Horse Market, 1756–76. Son of John Eyres. Born May 1734. In company with his elder brother, Thomas, started on March 23rd, 1756, *Eyres Weekly Journal, or Warrington Advertiser.* The partnership between the brothers did not last long, Thomas Eyres moving to Prescot in 1779. William Eyres printed many ballads and chap-books, and the woodcuts used in these are still in existence. On the other hand he was largely patronized by such writers as Dr. John Taylor, Pennant the naturalist, and Holland Watson, whose *History of the House of Warren* was described by Gilbert Wakefield as "perhaps the most accurate specimen of typography ever produced by any press". He died in 1809. [J. Kendrick, M.D., "Eyres Warrington Press", *Warrington Guardian,* 1881.]

FADEN (WILLIAM), printer in London, (1) Wine Office Court, Fleet Street; (2) near Shoe Lane. 1749–67 (?). Although chiefly remembered from his association with Samuel Johnson, William Faden deserves recognition as the printer of the first edition of Joseph Ames's *Typographical Antiquities* in 1749. On March 20th, 1750, appeared the first number of *The Rambler,* "well and accurately printed by William Faden, on a sheet and a half of fine paper". [Timperley, 1842, pp. 678–9.] Faden's name is next found in the imprint to the Rev. William Dodd's *Church Catechism explained,* published in 1754. [*Monthly Review,* October 1754, p. 313.] In 1760, in company with R. Stevens, he began a new venture, the *Universal Chronicle, and Westminster Journal,* but he was

only the publisher of this. Dr. Johnson's *Idler,* a series of short papers on social life and manners, was contributed to this publication. On December 17th, 1759, William Faden received a royal licence for fourteen years to print another periodical called the *Public Ledger.* This licence he printed in the *Universal Chronicle,* as well as in the first number of the new paper, issued on January 12th, 1760. The imprint only gives the name of the publisher, "W. Bristow", who kept a kind of trade bureau or registry, next the Great Toy Shop in St. Paul's Churchyard. After March 8th, 1760, the *Universal Chronicle* was published by Stevens alone. Dr. Johnson when on his death-bed in 1784 inquired if any of the family of Faden the printer were living, and on being told that the geographer near Charing Cross was Faden's son, he said to his informant, "I borrowed a guinea of his father, near thirty years ago: be so good as to take this and pay it for me". William Faden's work as a printer was good, and his press-work excellent. His roman and italic founts were regularly cast, and possibly came from the Caslon foundry. His books were distinguished by their freedom from "errata".

FARLEY (EDWARD), I, printer in Exeter, 1725–9. Son of Samuel Farley who died in 1732. In the latter half of 1725 Samuel Farley transferred his *Exeter Journal* to Edward Farley. In August or September 1728, Edward was committed to Exeter gaol and heavily ironed for transferring to his paper something that had appeared in *Mist's Journal* in London on August 28th. The case came on in July 1729, when only two witnesses could be found by the Crown, one a man of bad character and the other Farley's son-in-law, who would only speak on compulsion. The Attorney-General recommended that the prosecution should be dropped. An order was accordingly made for Farley's release, but it came too late, as the unfortunate printer had died in gaol two months before. [S. P. Dom. Geo. II, Bundle 13, 86; *London Evening Post,* May 17–20.] Edward Farley had a son, Samuel, who died a few weeks after his birth. [Mrs. Richardson, *Wiltshire Newspapers—Past and Present.*] In all probability Edward Farley, the printer of the *Genealogical History of the . . . Family of Courtenay,* 1735, was another son.

FARLEY (EDWARD), II, printer in Exeter, Shakespeare's Head, near Eastgate, 1735. In his *Devon Booksellers and Printers,* p. 23, Mr. Dredge records a copy of the *Genealogical History of the . . . Family of Courtenay* with this imprint: "Exon: Printed by Edward Farley at Shakespeares Head, near Eastgate, 1735." Probably son of Edward Farley, I.

FARLEY (ELIZABETH), printer in Bristol, Small Street, 1754–67. Printed a Poll-Book in 1754. [Hyett and Bazeley, III. 58.] Sometimes traded as E. Farley & Son, at others as E. Farley & Co. She was the widow of Felix Farley, and in the will of Samuel Farley II was bequeathed one shilling. She is last heard of in 1767.

FARLEY (E. & SON), printers in Bristol, Small Street, 1758–9. *See* Farley, Elizabeth.

FARLEY (FELIX), printer in Bristol, Exeter, and Bath: Bristol, (1) Shakespeare's Head, upper end of Castle Green [or] without Westgate, (2) Small Street; Exeter, St. Peter's Churchyard, 1741; Bath, Shakespeare's Head without Westgate, 1733–41. 1718–53. Son of Samuel Farley (1699–1732). Mr. Charles Wells in his *History of the Bristol Times and Mirror,* p. 5, suggests that Felix and his brother Samuel were in a partnership with their father as "printers" from "1718 if not earlier". In 1733 Felix was at Bath using the same sign as at Bristol. His imprint is found on a poem *To the Fore-Chairman that carried Her Majesty,* February 1732. By a Gentleman of Bath. A correspondent in *Notes & Queries* [10 S. v. 183] notes him as printing in Exeter in the year 1741. He held a share in the proprietary rights of the *Bristol Journal* until 1752, when he started *Felix Farley's Bristol Journal.* In 1744, *Moral and Sacred Poems,* collected by Wesley, bears the imprint "Bristol. Printed and sold by Felix Farley". According to Mr. Charles Wells, Felix Farley died in 1753 shortly before his brother. [C. Wells, *History of the Bristol Times and Mirror.*]

FARLEY (FELIX) & Co., printers in Bristol, 1744. Messrs. Hyett and Bazeley, in their *Bibliographer's Manual,* III. 341, record an entry as above, but they have no record of any book printed by the firm in that year. The "Company" was probably Felix's brother Samuel.

FARLEY (HESTER), printer in Bristol, Castle Green, 1774–5. Daughter of Felix Farley. For a short time proprietress of the *Bristol Journal.* In September 1775 she sold her interest to Messrs. George and William Routh and Charles Nelson. [C. Wells, *History of the Bristol Times and Mirror* (1913).] Another work bearing her imprint is *An Account of the Hospitals . . . in Bristol* which she printed for T. Mills, bookseller in Wine Street, in 1775.

FARLEY (SAMUEL), II, printer in Bristol, Castle Green, 1718 (?)–54. Son of Samuel Farley (1699–1732), and brother of Felix Farley. In partnership with his father, and with his brother successor to the business; but in 1752 a quarrel appears to have broken out between the brothers, and Felix Farley set up a rival newspaper called *Felix Farley's Bristol Journal*. In 1741 they set up a press at Bath which seems to have been carried on by Samuel Farley III. Samuel Farley II died some time between September 7th, 1753, and February 9th, 1754, when his will was proved in the Prerogative Court of Canterbury. [P.C.C. 38 Pinfold.] He bequeathed one moiety of all his goods and chattels, excepting the materials and utensils of his printing business, to Mary Beaufoy and Elizabeth Nelson, her daughter, of Evesham, co. Worcester, equally. His printing business he left to Sarah Farley, daughter of Edward Farley, late of the City of Exeter, printer, provided she carried on the business. He also directed that she should join the Quakers and take a Quaker for her husband. To Elizabeth Farley, wife of Felix Farley, late of Bristol, to her son Samuel and her two daughters he left a shilling each, as he did also to his sister Elizabeth, wife of John Thorn.

FARLEY (SAMUEL), III, printer in Bristol, Castle Green, 1754–74; Bath, Market Place, 1756. Son of Felix Farley (*q. v.*) and grandson of Samuel Farley I. In partnership with his mother Elizabeth Farley (*q.v.*). In 1756 he is found at Bath, issuing a weekly paper called *Farley's Bath Journal*, two issues of which for Monday, October 11 and 18, are in the British Museum.

FARLEY (SARAH), (?) printer in Bristol, 1754. Daughter of Edward Farley II, late of the city of Exeter, printer. Samuel Farley II left her his printing business, but it is not clear whether she carried it on. [P.C.C. 37 Pinfold.]

FARRAR or FERROUR (T.), bookseller in Boston, co. Lincoln, 1758–9. Advertisement in the *Cambridge Journal*. In 1759 he was succeeded by Caleb Preston, a bookseller from London. [*Ibid.*]

FAYRAM (FRANCIS), bookseller in London. At the South entrance of the Royal Exchange, 1726–8. *See Dictionary*, 1668–1725. He advertised books for sale—including *Optical Lectures* by Newton, printed for Francis Fayram—in the *Daily Post*, January 3, 1728.

FEALES (W.), bookseller and publisher in London, (1) Rowe's Head, over against Clement's Inn Gate; (2) the corner of Essex Street, Strand, 1731–40. Publisher of a collected edition of plays called *The English Theatre*, and also of numerous single plays, including Otway's *The Orphan*, in conjunction with other publishers. The addresses given above may refer to the same shop.

FEATHERSTON (J.), bookseller in Hexham, Northumberland, 1764. Mentioned in a list of provincial booksellers as at work in that year. [*N. & Q.* 10 S. VI. 443.]

FELL (ISAAC), bookseller and publisher in London, 14 Paternoster Row, 1762–9. In partnership with J. Wilson (*q. v.*). In 1762 they published a pamphlet entitled, *The Ministers of State*. In 1769 Fell was the publisher of the *Middlesex Journal* and of Almon's *Letter to Grenville*.

FENNER ( ), Mrs., bookseller in Canterbury, Kent, 1732–41. Believed to be the widow of Enoch Fenner (1703–29).

FENNER (MARY), printer and publisher in Cambridge and London, Turk's Head, Gracechurch Street, 1734–57 (?). Widow of William Fenner (*q. v.*). After her husband's death in 1734, she continued to print at Cambridge until 1738, when the lease of the premises was abandoned after much acrimonious correspondence between the parties concerned. She appears to have printed only one work at Cambridge, viz. Dr. Bentley's *Boyle Lectures*, for W. Thurlbourn, in 1735. She is next found in London, at the Turk's Head in Gracechurch Street, from which address she published in 1743 E. Latham's *Sermon at Kidderminster*, and Dr. Doddridge's sermon entitled *Compassion to the Sick*, preached at Northampton, September 4th, 1743, in favour of a proposed County Infirmary. [B.M. T. 1034 (10).] Her son William Fenner II, also a printer and publisher, gave his address as the Turk's Head in Lombard Street, and M. (possibly Mary) Fenner published from that address in 1757 *A Letter from a Member of the Marine Society* [B.M. E. 2049 (4)]. [Notes supplied by G. J. Gray.]

FENNER (REST), III, bookseller and bookbinder in Canterbury, Kent, behind St. Andrew's Church; and Ramsgate, Kent, 1729–41 (?). Son of Enoch Fenner (1703–29). Served his apprenticeship in London. On the death of his father he succeeded to the business in Canterbury, and opened a branch shop in Ramsgate. He is believed to have been the last of his name to carry on the business. The date of his death is not known, but he was still living in 1741.

FENNER (REST), bookseller in Ramsgate, Kent, 1736–7. Possibly a branch shop of Rest Fenner III, of Canterbury. His name is found in the imprint to *The Gentleman and Builder's Repository*, published by a London firm in 1737.

FENNER (WILLIAM), I, printer in London and Cambridge, 1725–34. Chiefly remembered by his association with the first attempt at stereotyping in this

country. In 1729 he entered into partnership with William Ged, Thomas James, the founder (*see Dictionary*, 1668–1725), John James and James Ged, to develop printing from stereotype plates, and in 1730 they appealed to the University of Cambridge for permission to print Bibles and Prayer Books by this method, a lease being granted to them on April 23rd, 1731. The plates were first made in London, but afterwards in Cambridge. But the partnership was not a success, and only four works were printed. Fenner died insolvent in 1734, but his widow continued until 1738, when the lease was abandoned. In 1732 certain London stationers brought an action against Fenner for printing Bibles, but on August 4th, 1733, an order was obtained to dissolve the injunction against the defendant. Although the action was taken against Fenner, it was really an attack on the printing rights of the University. Thus the first attempt to work from stereotype plates was made at Cambridge. [Bowes, *Cambridge University Printers*; Roberts, *Cambridge University Press*.] Whether this printer and his son were connexions of the Canterbury family of booksellers has not been discovered.

FENNER (WILLIAM), II, printer (?), bookseller, and publisher in London, (1) Turk's Head in Lombard Street; (2) Angel and Bible in Paternoster Row, 1756–1809. Son of William Fenner I. In partnership with J. Waugh (*q. v.*). Their joint names occur as printers of the Rev. John Taylor's *The Lord's Supper*, 1756. The house may have been also known as the Turk's Head in Gracechurch Street. Between 1756 and 1759, Fenner removed into Paternoster Row, leaving Waugh at the Turk's Head. The new address is found in the imprint to the Rev. John Taylor's *Examination of the Scheme of Morality*. [B.M. 699. e. 12 (6).] Soon after this he retired from business, but was Master of the Company of Stationers in 1786. He died October 30th, 1809. [Timperley, 1842, p. 836.]

FENWICK (HENRY), printer in London, (1) Snow Hill; (2) Little Moorfields, 1769–76. Succeeded Charles Rivington in 1772 as Printer to the City of London. [C. Welsh, *City Printers*; Nichols, III. 571.]

FERGUSON (J.), bookseller in Norwich, Cockey Lane, 1741–74. In 1774 his name is found in the imprint to *Some Memoirs of the Life of John Glover, late of Norwich*. [B.M. 4903. bbb. 20 (1).]

FERRABY (GEORGE), bookseller in Hull, 1718–36. *See Dictionary*, 1668–1725. His name is found in the imprint to a sermon preached by the Rev. John

Mawer on the *Nature and design of the Lord's Supper*, on Good Friday, 1736. [B.M. 225. g. 14/5.]

FERROUR (T.), *see* Farrar (T.)

FIELD (THOMAS), bookseller and publisher in London, (1) near St. Paul's; (2) at the White-sheaf the corner of Paternoster Row, Cheapside, 1755 (?)–75 (?). Publisher for the Nonconformists. The second imprint is found in Richard Baxter's *Causes and Danger of slighting Christ*, 1765. In 1775 he published, with the Fullers and C. Rivington, *An Exposition of the Old and New Testament*. [*Public Advertiser*, January 12th, 1775.] Issued a trade card engraved by F. Garden, with bill on back dated 1760. [A. Heal's Collection.]

FIELDER (ELIZABETH), *see* Mason, W.

FIELDER (WILLIAM), *see* Mason (W.).

FISHER (JOSEPH), bookseller, London, against Tom's Coffee House, Cornhill. He advertised sermons for sale in The *Daily Courant*, May 25th, 1735.

FISHER (THOMAS), printer and publisher in Rochester, Kent, 1765 (?)–93. In business before 1768, in which year he published the Poll Book for the City of Rochester for Members of Parliament. In 1770 he published a pamphlet entitled, *A Plea in favour of the Shipwrights belonging to the Royal Dockyards*. by W. S. [B.M. 10368. c. 7 (24).] But his most important undertaking was *The History and Antiquities of the Town of Rochester*, which he printed in 1772. The editor was the Rev. S. Denne of Wilmington, and an interesting series of letters written by Denne to the printer, concerning this and other business, and extending over several years, is among the Egerton manuscripts in the British Museum. [Bibl. Eg. 926.] Amongst Thomas Fisher's many activities was the printing and publishing of *The Kentish Traveller's Companion*, the first edition of which appeared in 1776. Denne in his correspondence also refers to a *Kentish Almanac* and *The Lady's Kentish Journal* as being two of Fisher's publications. He was for many years a member of the Common Council, and appears to have retired from business about 1793, being succeeded by — Gillman.

FITZER (S.), bookseller in London, Three Bibles in the Minories, 1726. Dealer in nautical and mathematical books. [W. M. C., November 1726.]

FITZGERALD (J.), bookseller in Newcastle-upon-Tyne, 1749–54. Mentioned in a list of Newcastle booksellers by Mr. Welford in his *Early Newcastle Typography* [p. 128].

FLACTON (JOHN), bookseller and publisher in Canterbury, St. Alphege, 1738–90 (?). Son of John Flacton, bricklayer, and brother of William Flacton (*q.v.*). Took up his freedom in 1738, and afterwards joined his brother in his bookselling and publishing business. The date of his death is unknown. [Karslake, *Book Auction Records*, 1918.]

FLACTON (WILLIAM), bookseller and publisher in Canterbury, St. Alphege, 1730–98. Son of John Flacton, bricklayer. Took up his freedom in 1730. Joined by his brother John (*q.v.*). They published Seymour's *Survey of Kent*, 1776. William Flacton was an amateur musician, and was for a time organist of Faversham. The firm were publishers of music, and also held book-auctions. William Flacton died in January, 1798, aged 88. [Karslake, *Book Auction Records*, 1918.]

FLEETWOOD (R.), bookseller in Liverpool, 1746–62. 1746. His name is found in the imprint to "*A Sermon* Preached at St. George's Church, in Liverpool . . . On the Ninth of October 1746. . . . By Thomas Maddock, Lecturer in the said Church". 4to. [B.M. 225. I. 1 (15).] According to a correspondent in *Notes & Queries*, he was still in business in 1762. [*N. & Q.* 11 S. I. 364.]

FLEMING (JAMES), bookseller in Newcastle-upon-Tyne, The Bible on Tyne Bridge, 1741–66. R. Welford in *Early Newcastle Typography* (p. 128) briefly records that he was in business between 1741 and 1765. The *Newcastle Courant* records his death from palsy on January 7th, 1766. [*Newcastle Courant*, Saturday, January 11th, 1766.]

FLETCHER (JAMES), senior, bookseller and publisher in Oxford, The Turl, 1730–95. Born at Salisbury in 1710, and possibly brother of Stephen Fletcher [1714–27. *See Dictionary*, 1668–1725]. Was appointed "Privilegiatus bookseller" on January 13th, 17 29/30. [Foster's *Alumni*.] He leased his shop in the Turl from the City in 1731. Took his son, James, into business in 1769. They also had a shop in Westminster Hall in Term time, as well as a branch shop at the Oxford Theatre in St. Paul's Churchyard. From this latter address they published, in 1754, a satirical work called *The History of the Robinhood Society*. [B.M. 741 a. 12.] James Fletcher was the Rev. Thos. Warton's publisher, and his shop in the Turl was resorted to by all the literary men of the day, as well as by undergraduates seeking books. An eight-page catalogue of his publications in 1757, containing upwards of 100 titles, occurs at the end of the Rev. James Snowden's *Sermon*, preached at the Parish Church of St. Peter in the East, in Oxford, on Friday, February 11th. James Fletcher died in Oxford in 1795, aged 85.

FLETCHER (JAMES), junior, bookseller in Oxford, The Turl, 1756–96. Son of James Fletcher, senior. Became "privilegiatus bookseller" on February 13th, 175 6/7. [Foster's *Alumni*.] For some years in partnership with James Rivington, of St. Paul's Churchyard. In partnership with his father. Died May 20th, 1798, aged 67. [Timperley, 1842, pp. 798–9.] A book by Wesley is advertised as printed by William Pine, Bristol, and sold by Fletcher & Co., St. Paul's Churchyard. [*Gazetteer and New Daily Advertiser*, July 3rd, 1765.]

FLETCHER (MARY), widow, bookseller and publisher in Oxford, 1729–51. Occurs in imprints as publisher between these years. Presumably the widow of Stephen Fletcher (1714–27), and mother of James Fletcher senior. She lived near St. Mary's Church. [Hearne, x. 260.]

FLETCHER (T.) and HODSON (F.), printers in Cambridge, New Printing Office, Market Hill, 1762–77. Printers of the *Cambridge Chronicle*, the first number appearing October 30th, 1762. This was the second newspaper printed in Cambridge. The number of January 3rd, 1767, appeared as the *Cambridge Chronicle and Journal*, the proprietors having purchased the *Cambridge Journal* (established 1744) from the proprietor, Sarah James. In addition to printing the newspaper between 1763–76, they printed many works, including several editions of *The New Bath Guide* and other works by Christopher Anstey, A. Isola's *Italian Dialogues*, Fovargue's *New Catalogue of Vulgar Errors*, works by Robinson the dissenting minister, Roger Cotes, Caesar Morgan, &c. The *Cambridge Chronicle* of December 24th, 1779, contains the following notice from the *Gazette* of December 20th, under "Bankrupts": "Thomas Fletcher of Cambridge, Printer, to surrender Dec. 21 and Jan. 4, at 10, and Jan. 29, at 5, at Guildhall, London."

FLEXNEY (WILLIAM), bookseller and publisher in London, near Gray's Inn Gate, Holborn (?), corner of Southampton Buildings, Holborn, 1760 (?)–1808. Succeeded Thomas Trye (*q.v.*) in this old-established house, which had been founded by Richard Sare in 1684. Flexney was the original publisher of Churchill's *Poems*, and also of Warburton's pamphlet, an *Enquiry into the Nature and Origin of Literary Property*, 8vo., published in 1762. He died on January 7th, 1808, aged 77. [Timperley, 1842, p. 834.]

FORD (RICHARD), bookseller and publisher in London, Angel in the Poultry, near Stocks Market, 1720 (?)–40 (?). Publisher of sermons and miscellaneous literature. Amongst the more important works which bear his name in the

imprint, is Daniel Neal's *History of New England*. [J. C. B. L.] His name appears in Kent's *Directory* for 1738.

FOWLER (   ), bookseller in Northampton, 1727–44. Sold the Rev. Thomas Marshall's sermon preached at Northampton on Wednesday, March 8th, 1726–7, at the Assizes, entitled, *Good Laws the greatest Blessing to any Nation*. [W. M. C., April, 1727.]

FOX (J. and J.), booksellers (1) in London, Half-Moon and Seven Stars, Westminster Hall; (2) at Tunbridge Wells, 1736–76. *See Dictionary*, 1668–1725.

FOX (SAMUEL), bookseller in Derby, 1755–8. His name occurs in a list of those selling John Barrow's *Psalm-Singer's Choice Companion*, the Third Edition, advertised in the *Whitehall Evening Post*. [January 2nd, 1755.] In 1758 he issued a catalogue of books, including the library of the late Dr. Holland of Chesterfield. [Timperley, 1842, p. 703.]

FOX (WILLIAM), bookseller in London, Holborn, 1773–7. Published catalogues of his stock during those years. [Nichols, *Lit. Anecd.* III. 643.]

FRANCE (W.), bookseller in London, at the Meuse [or Mews] Gate, 1731. His name occurs in the imprint of a pamphlet entitled, *A Short History of Standing Armies in England*, 1731. [B.M. 1398. d. 27.]

FRANKLIN or FRANCKLIN (RICHARD), printer, bookseller, and publisher in London, Tom's Coffee House, Covent Garden, 1726–56. *See Dictionary*, 1668–1725. In 1726 he became the printer and publisher of *The Craftsman*, a periodical, started and maintained by Nicholas Amhurst under the pseudonym of Caleb D'Anvers, which became notorious for its outspoken attacks on the Government of the day. Franklin was frequently prosecuted and imprisoned for libel; and while he deserves some measure of sympathy as a "martyr" to the liberty of the press, his disgraceful treatment of his journeyman, Henry Haines (*q. v.*), whom he used as a "cat's paw" and left to starve in gaol, was a great blot on his character. In his later years, Richard Franklin lived at Strawberry Hill, occupying the cottage in the enclosure which Horace Walpole called the "Flower Garden". Writing to Richard Bentley on July 17th, 1755, Walpole says, "Can there be an odder revolution of things, than that the printer of *The Craftsman* should live in a house of mine?"; and again in a letter to John Chute he writes, "I had a little private satisfaction in very naturally telling my Lord Bath how happy I have made his old printer, Franklyn". [*Letters*, 1857 ed., II. 451; III. 18.]

FREDERICK (WILLIAM), bookseller and publisher in Bath, No 18 The Grove, *c.* 1742–76. This bookseller and James Leake were two of the chief men in the book-trade in the West of England during the latter half of the eighteenth century, and their names figure in the imprint of all the most important publications of the period. Frederick is said to have been educated at the Bath Grammar School, but as no list of scholars for the century can be found it has been impossible to verify the statement. He is also said to have been a pupil of Leake, but this again is difficult to verify. His business was at No 18 The Grove, and the first volume in which his name is found is Wood's *Essay towards a Description of Bath*, printed by T. Boddeley for W. Frederick, bookseller in Bath, 1742, a second part of which appeared in 1743. Amongst his numerous other publications the following of local interest may be noted: *An Essay on Electricity*. By Benjamin Martin. Bath. Printed for the author, and Mrs. Leake, and Mr. Frederick, booksellers 1746. *A Practical Essay on the Use and Abuse of Warm Bathing in Gouty Cases*. By William Oliver, 2nd edition. Bath. Printed by T. Boddeley for James Leake and William Frederick, booksellers 1753. *A Treatise on the Medicinal Qualities of the Bath Waters*. By J. N. Stevens. Bristol . . . Sold by J. Leake, and W. Frederick, booksellers in Bath 1758. *The Nature and Qualities of Bristol Water*. . . . By A. Sutherland. Bristol . . . Sold by . . . W. Frederick in Bath 1758. *An Attempt to ascertain and extend the Virtues of Bath and Bristol Waters*. By Alex Sutherland, 2nd edition. London. Printed for W. Frederick and J. Leake, booksellers in Bath, 1764. In 1757 William Frederick was agent for the lottery in London, and sold tickets for it [*Bath Advertiser*, April 2nd, 1757], and on January 14th, 1758, he advertised for sale an edition of the Delphin Classics [*ibid.*]. On October 2nd, 1766, William Frederick was elected a member of the Corporation in the room of Thomas King, deceased. [Council Minutes, September 22nd.] He died in August 1776, and was buried in the Abbey. [*Bath Abbey Registers*, II. 462.]

FREEBAIRN (ROBERT), *see Dictionary*, 1668–1725.

FREEMAN (JOHN), (?) bookseller in London, near St. Paul's [1748]. Probably a fictitious imprint, found on the title-page of a pamphlet entitled, *An Apology for a late Resignation*, attributed to Lord Chesterfield. Another imprint of this kind is that of R. Freeman, junior, near St. Paul's, found on a pamphlet of this date. [B.M. T. 1615. 1 and 3.]

FREER (GEORGE), bookseller in London, Bible, Bell Yard, Temple Bar, 1747–54. Publisher of the fourth and sixth editions of Burgh's *Britain's Remembrancer*. [B.M. T. 1112 (2).]

FRENCH (J.), bookseller, and publisher, London, 28 Poultry, 1775. He was one of the partners in *Divine Maxims* [*Public Advertiser*, January 3rd, 1775]. Issued a trade card engraved by Hall. [A. Heal's Collection.]

FRENO (ZACH), bookseller (?) in Plymouth, *c.* 1763. This name is found in the imprint to a work called *Observations on the late Act of Parliament. (n.d.)*

FROST (CHARLES), bookseller, binder, and publisher in Chelmsford, 1769–76. His name is first met with in an advertisement of John Gibbons, *Seasonable Hints on Midwifery*, 1769, a very rare book. In what part of the town he was then resident has not been discovered, but early in January 1771 he opened a shop in the Market Place and advertised it largely in the *Chelmsford and Colchester Chronicle*. In these advertisements he stated his intention of opening a circulating library in connexion with his business, and a week or two later he published his first catalogue and the terms of subscription, which were 16*s*. per year, 5*s*. per quarter, or threepence per volume. As a further attraction to the inhabitants he published almost immediately, *The Ladies' most elegant and convenient Pocket-Book for the year* 1771. Frost's next step was to secure the services of one of Messrs. Toft and Lobb's workmen, named W. Clacher, and to issue a rival newspaper to theirs. The new venture was called *The Chelmsford Chronicle and Essex Gazette*, and the first number appeared on April 5th, 1771. The latter part of the title was soon after dropped. A fortnight later this enterprising young bookseller took another serious step, and married a Miss Westley, of Chelmsford, on April 19th, 1771. He then bought the binding tools of Messrs. Toft and Lobb and set up bookbinding. In 1776 he and S. Gray another bookseller of the same town, advertised *Fables for Youths*.

FULLER (JOHN), bookseller and publisher in London, (1) Dove in Creed Lane (1743–51); (2) Paternoster Row, 1749; (3) Bible and Dove, Ave Mary Lane; (4) Blow-bladder Street, Cheapside, 1749–76. In the *Monthly Review* for October 1749 is a short notice of *A New Essay with relation to the Doctrine of the Trinity*, a small pamphlet, priced at sixpence, and sold by J. Fuller, in Paternoster Row. In 1755, in company with S. Neale (*q. v.*), he published Sarah Jackson's *The Director, or Young Woman's Best Companion*, a volume of medical and cookery recipes, which came out in weekly parts. In this he

advertised a lending library. He was also the publisher of numerous discourses and sermons, and was still in business in 1776, when his name is found in Kent's *Directory*. There was another J. Fuller publishing in 1775, possibly his son. *An Exposition on the Old and New Testament* is advertised as "Printed for J. Fuller, senior, T. Field, C. Rivington, and J. Fuller, junior". [*Public Advertiser*, January 12th, 1775.] Issued elaborate trade cards from the Bible and Dove, and also from Blow-bladder Street. [A. Heal's Collection.]

FURSMAN (J.), bookseller in Ashburton, co. Devon, 1770–3. Sold a work entitled, *The most general School-Assistant* . . . by G. Dyer, master of Tacker's Hall school in Exeter. MDCCLXX. 8vo. [Dredge.] Also *The Mariner's Instructor*, in 1773.

G. (L.), printer in London (? Lawton Gilliver), 1733. *The First Satire of the Second Book of Horace, imitated in a dialogue between Alexander Pope . . . and his learned counsel* . . . February 17th, 1733.

GALES (THOMAS), bookseller in Sheffield, 1756 ?–1809. Died at Eckington, near Sheffield, September 21st, 1809, aged 73. [Nichols, *Lit. Anecd.* III. 478.] His son, Joseph Gales, emigrated to America, and set up as a printer in Washington.

GAME, (THOMAS), (?) bookseller in London, Bible facing the East end of the New Church in the Strand, 1733. His name occurs in the imprint to a *Compendious Account of the whole art of breeding the Silk-Worm*, published in that year.

GAMIDGE (S.), bookseller and publisher in Worcester, Leech Street, 1758–68. The following title appeared in a bookseller's catalogue some years ago: *A full and true account of the Murders, Robberies, and Burnings committed at Bradforton and Upton Snodbury; An account of the Bishop of Oxford to the Prisoners*, 74 pp. 8vo. For S. Gamidge, Worcester, 1758. In 1765, *Plain Trigonometry* was printed for S. Crowder and S. Gamidge, Worcester. [*Gazetteer and New Daily Advertiser*, July 4th, 1765.] In 1771 he issued a catalogue of books. Amongst his other publications was a little chap-book called the *Garland of Trials*, printed without date but with the imprint, "Printed for S. Gamidge at his Warehouse, Leech Street, Worcester." [B.M. 1070. i. 29 (14).] According to a correspondent in *Notes & Queries* he was still in business in 1768. [*N. & Q.* 10 S. v. 242.]

GANT (W.), bookseller and publisher in Bristol, 1775. His name occurs in the imprint to one of the issues of *A Proposition for the Present Peace and Future*

Government of the British Colonies in North America, 1775. A copy of this is in the John Carter Brown Library at Providence. The imprint to the copy in the British Museum does not give the names of any of the provincial booksellers who sold it. [B.M. 103. i. 63.]

GARDINER, *see* Gardner.

GARDNER or GARDINER (E.), bookseller in London, (1) The Ship, in Lombard Street; (2) Gracechurch Street. 1749–58. His name is found in the imprint to various pamphlets published at this time. One of these was a *Sermon*, preached at Boston, U.S.A., on Thursday, August 24, 1749, by Thomas Prince, and reprinted in London in 1750. [J. C. B. L.] A Mrs. Gardner was selling tracts in Gracechurch Street in 1765. Presumably his widow. [*Gazetteer and Daily Advertiser*, September 25th, 1765.]

GARDNER (HENRY), bookseller and publisher in London, opposite St. Clement's Church, in the Strand, 1774–6. Possibly son of T. Gardner (*q. v.*). In 1774 his name is found in the imprint of a pamphlet entitled, *America vindicated from the High Charge of Ingratitude and Rebellion*. In 1775 a dictionary was printed for and sold by H. Gardner and three others. [*Public Advertiser*, January 3rd, 1775.] His name is found in Kent's *Directory* for 1776. He died February 29th, 1808. [Nichols, III. 644.]

GARDNER, (THOMAS), printer and publisher in London, Cowley's Head, without Temple Bar, Strand, 1735–56. In the *Country Journal or Craftsman* for April 26th, 1735, is an advertisement of a proposed issue of an *Exposition of the Common Prayer*, for which he amongst others was prepared to receive subscriptions. In 1739 a certain Thos. Barker of Witham in Essex desires that letters may be directed to him "To be left at Mr. Thos. Gardner's, Printer, without Temple Bars in ye Strand, London". In that year he published, but did not print, *An Examination of a pamphlet entitled His Catholic Majesty's Manifesto*. [B.M. T. 1110 (1).] In 1743 he printed a pamphlet entitled *Old England's Te Deum*, for William Shropshire, the bookseller (*q. v.*). [S.P. Dom. Geo 2, Bundle 62 (62).] In 1756 he began the publication of a periodical called *The Universal Visitor*. In Boswell's *Life of Johnson* occurs the following passage: "JOHNSON. Old Gardner the bookseller employed Rolt and Smart[1] to write a monthly miscellany called *The Universal Visitor*. There was a formal written contract, which Allen the printer saw. They were bound to write nothing else; they were

[1] Richard Rolt and Christopher Smart.

to have, I think, a third of the profits of this sixpenny pamphlet; and the contract was for ninety-nine years. I wish I had thought of giving this to Thurlow, in the cause about literary property. What an excellent instance would it have been of the oppression of booksellers towards poor authors (smiling)! DAVIES, zealous for the honour of the trade, said, Gardner was not properly a bookseller. JOHNSON. Nay, sir; he certainly was a bookseller. He had served his time regularly, was a member of the Stationer's Company, kept a shop in the face of mankind, purchased copyright, and was a *bibliopole* sir, in every sense."

GARNET (JOHN), printer in Sheffield, 1737–53. Printer of chap-books, the earliest known being *The Perjur'd Lover, or Tragical Adventure of Alexis and Boroina. . . . By a Young Gentleman of Sheffield.* Printed at Sheffield by J. Garnet; pr. 1s. [*Gentleman's Mag.*, September, 1737; Allnutt in *Bibliographica*, II. 306.]

GARRATT (WILLIAM), printer and bookseller at King's Lynn, co. Norfolk, 1740–62. In 1740 he issued *The Curiosity or, Gentleman and Ladies Repository*, 8vo. [Bodl.; Allnutt in *Bibliographica*, II. 306.] In 1747 he printed some Poor Law Overseers forms. The following notice of his death has been found in the *Gazetteer* of September 26th, 1762: "A few days since died at King's Lynn in Norfolk, aged 65, Mr. William Garratt, printer and bookseller of that town."

GAYDON (A.), bookseller in Barnstaple, co. Devon, 1734. Published a sermon preached in the parish church of Barnstaple on May 5th, 1734, on the occasion of the death of the vicar. [Dredge, *Devon Booksellers and Printers*, p. 4.]

GAYDON (JOHN), senior, bookseller in Barnstaple, co. Devon, 1732. Nothing appears to be known concerning this bookseller, except the entry of his death in the Barnstaple Parish Register: "1732. Mr Iohn Gaydon, sen^r, buried the 14th of December."

GAYDON (JOHN), junior, bookseller in Barnstaple, co. Devon, 1732–5. His name is found in the imprint to No. 2 of *The West Country Farmer*, published in 1732. [Dredge, p. 86.] According to a correspondent in *Notes & Queries* he was still in business in 1735. [*N. & Q.* 10 S. v. 161.] He was possibly the son of John Gaydon, senior.

GENT (THOMAS), *see Dictionary*, 1668–1725.

GIBBON (SAMUEL), bookseller and publisher in London, Middle Temple Gate, 1740. Only known from his connexion with the publication of the early sheets of John Bridges' *History of Northampton*. According to Nichols all the papers and plates were delivered to this "stationer", who shortly afterwards became bankrupt, and the plates were dispersed and the publication of the *History* was not resumed for some years. In 1753, *A Rational Double Grammar* was advertised as sold by Samuel Gibbons, junior, near the Church in the Temple. [*Public Advertiser*, January 6th, 1753.]

GILES, or GYLES (FLETCHER), merchant tailor, bookseller, and publisher in London, over against Gray's Inn in Holborn, 1721–41. Publisher of law-books and theological works. Dr. Conyers Middleton, writing to Bishop Warburton in 1739, stated that he had asked Giles to take in subscriptions for his *Cicero*; but he seemed cold in the affair, and gave not the least hint of any inclination to be further concerned in it. [Add. MS. 32457, p. 143.] Warburton on the contrary found Giles an honest but very busy man. He became the publisher of the *Divine Legation*, and is frequently mentioned in the bishop's correspondence. Almost his last undertaking was the purchase of the Thurloe MSS. and also the *Reports* of Lord Chief Justice Raymond. Giles died on November 8th, 1741, apparently unmarried. In his will, which was proved on the 12th of that month, he directed that his stock of books should be sold by auction, and referred to himself as a merchant tailor. [P.C.C. 305 Spierway.]

GILFILLAN (JOHN), printer in York, (1) Thursday Market; (2) Coffee Yard. 1741–52. According to a correspondent in *Notes & Queries*, the above printer was at work in 1741. [*N. & Q.* 11. S. I. 364.] He was the printer of the *York Journal or the Weekly Advertiser*, and on January 22nd, 1745, he was ordered to appear before the House of Commons, for printing matter reflecting on one of the Members, but on apologizing was allowed to go. [*Commons Journal*, XXV. 36, 96.] In 1747 he printed for John Hildyard, bookseller in York, the Rev. Jaques Sterne's charge to the clergy of the Archdeaconry of Cleveland, entitled *The Danger arising from the Increase of Papists*. [B.M. 694. k. 19 (5).] His last dated publication, says the historian of the York press, was another charge to the clergy by the Archdeacon, delivered at the visitation in 1751 and printed in 1752. [Davies, *Memoirs*, p. 325.]

GILLIVER (LAWTON), bookseller and publisher in London, (1) Homer's Head against St. Dunstan's Church in Fleet Street; (2) Westminster Hall. 1728(?)–

38(?). Chiefly remembered as one of Alexander Pope's numerous publishers. No biographical or other details are obtainable. He is not mentioned by Timperley, and is only briefly alluded to in Knight's *Shadows*. At one time Gilliver appears to have been in partnership with J. Clarke, and at another time with Dodsley: but such partnerships were only in the proprietorship of books and not in the actual business. He had a share in the publication of Bayle's *Dictionary*. [*Daily Journal*, January 13th, 1735.] As an elaborate piece of caution, Pope assigned the copyright of *The Dunciad* to Lords Bathurst, Burlington, and Oxford, who afterwards assigned it to Lawton Gilliver. [*Camb. Hist. of Lit.*] In 1729 Gilliver obtained an injunction against Watson for printing a pirated edition of *The Dunciad*.

GILLMORE ( ), bookseller and publisher in Marlborough, 1745. His name is mentioned in an advertisement of the second edition of Stackhouse's *Bible*, in that year.

GILMAN (RICHARD), bookseller in Oxford, Gravel Walk near Magdalen, 1665 (?)–1730. Born at the time of the Revolution, as he told Hearne in 1728 that he was eighty-four years of age. Known as "Vanity Gilman" from his vain, weak temper. Died February 27th, 17$\frac{28}{30}$. His will was proved August 16th, 1731. [Griffiths.]

GINGER (W.), bookseller and publisher in London, 1775. *Miscellaneous Poems* were printed for him in 1775. [*Public Advertiser*, January 12th, 1775.]

GITTINS (THOMAS), bookseller in Shrewsbury, 1727. Publisher of the Rev. William Powel's sermons against swearing, preached at Llanly Mynach in Shropshire, 1727. [W. M. C.]

GLEED (JONATHAN), bookseller and publisher in Norwich, Cockey Lane, 1742 (?)–1753 (?). Was probably in business before 1742, when he and James Carlos, another Norwich bookseller, advertised in the *Norwich Gazette*, *A Brief Examination of Dr. Warburton's "Divine Legation"*. In 1746 his name occurs with those of Carlos and Thomas Goddard, as publishers of a sermon preached by the Rev. John Francis in Norwich on August 3rd and 10th. [B.M. 225. I. 2 (18).] Gleed was also the publisher of the Rev. H. Hubberd's *Sermon*, preached at Ipswich in aid of a charity on July 19th, 1750. [Bowes, 493.] He was succeeded by Richard Beatniffe (*q. v.*).

GOADBY (ROBERT), printer, bookseller, and publisher in Bath, Wade's Passage, 1740–5; Yeovil, 1748–9; Sherborne, 1749–78. 1740–78. A well-known printer, bookseller, and publisher in the West of England. Born in 1721, and educated at Repton School, co. Derby, to the masters of which he afterwards dedicated his translations from Cervantes. His knowledge was considerable, and he was well versed in several languages. He appears to have set up as a bookseller, first at Bath in Wade's Passage, from which he published in 1741 two humorous novels entitled *Scipio and Bergansa* and *Rinconete and Cortadillo*, translated from the Spanish of Cervantes, which went through at least three editions. In 1745 he gave up his business in Bath, sold his entire stock and went to the Hague. He returned to England in 1748, and once more took up the trade of a printer and bookseller, in Yeovil. There he began to issue a weekly newspaper called *The Western Flying Post or Yeovil Mercury*, and amongst other things he printed and sold a theological work in 1748, with the title *Mercy and Truth*, of which a copy is in the Bodleian Library. [*See* Rev. L. Southcomb's *Christian's peculiar character*, 1752.] In 1749 he moved his presses to Sherborne and united his paper with Bettinson's *Sherborne Mercury*, under the joint title of *The Western Flying Post or Sherborne and Yeovil Mercury*, the first number of which appeared on January 30th, 1749. He was the conductor of several miscellaneous publications, which he sold cheaply in the West of England. Robert Goadby died on August 12th, 1778, aged 57, and was buried at Oborne, a village near Sherborne. By his will he left a bequest of 40*s*. a year to the vicars of Sherborne for an annual sermon on May Day. [Nichols, III. 723-4.]

GOADING, *see* Gooding (John).

GODDARD (THOMAS), bookseller and publisher in Norwich, 1703–46. *See Dictionary*, 1668–1725. In the year 1746, in company with James Carlos and Jonathan Gleed, he sold a *Sermon* preached by the Rev. John Francis in Norwich on the 3rd and 10th of August. [B.M. 225. I. 2 (18).]

GODWIN (JOHN), bookseller in London, at Shakespeare's Monument, No. 171, opposite the New Church in the Strand, 1775. Issued a trade card, a copy of which bears a receipt for the purchase of a travelling-case by the Earl of Winterton, dated 1775. [A. Heal's Collection.]

GOLDSMITH (W.), bookseller and publisher, London, 20 Paternoster Row, 1772, 1775. In 1772 he issued Chatterton's *The Execution of Sir Charles Bawdin*,

two years after the poet's death. [Mumby, *Romance of Bookselling*.] In 1774 he took part in publishing Oliver Goldsmith's *The Grecian History*. He was one of the partners in a Dictionary. [*Public Advertiser*, January 3rd, 1775.]

GOODENOUGH ( ), bookseller and publisher in Warminster, 1745. His name occurs in an advertisement of the second edition of Stackhouse's *Bible* in 1745.

GOODING (JOHN), printer in Newcastle-on-Tyne, Burnet House Entry, 1743-51. Printer for the Wesleyans. Succeeded William Cuthbert as printer of the *Newcastle Journal* and the *General Magazine*; but his chief work was the printing of sermons. He is not heard of after 1751. [Welford, p. 33.]

GOODMAN (ROBERT), bookseller in Norwich, on the Upper walk in the Market Place, 1742. Sold *The Present State of Great Britain and Ireland*, the Ninth Edition, 1742.

GOODSMAN (DAVID), bookseller and publisher in London, 17 the Strand, 1775. In the *Public Advertiser* of August 11th, 1775, appeared an advertisement of a new edition of George Buchanan's *Paraphrase of the Psalms* as printed by Alexander Grant in Bridges Street for David Goodsman, 17 Strand. The copy in the British Museum has this imprint, "Londini: Ex Ædibus Alexandri Grant, Bridges Street, prostat apud Davidem Goodsman, Strand, M,DCC,LXXV. [B.M. 3089. b. 15.] Nothing further appears to be known of this bookseller.

GORE (JOHN), bookseller in Liverpool, Dale Street, 1762–76. Publisher of the *Liverpool General Advertiser*. He is mentioned in a list of provincial booksellers as in business in 1762. He died on December 17th, 1803. [Timperley, 1842, p. 817.]

GOREHAM (H.), printer and publisher in London, (1) next the Leg Tavern, Fleet Street; (2) The Bible in Wine Office Court. 1737–40 (?). In 1737 he printed *A History of Priesthood*. He afterwards printed the notorious paper, *The Country Journal or Craftsman*, in 1739, and was prosecuted by the Government. [S. P. Dom. Geo. II, Bundle 50 (58).] He advertised in 1742 a work entitled *The Female Robber*, to be published in parts at 2*d*. each. No doubt it was the same person who was the subject of an undated ballad now preserved in the British Museum. [B.M. 11621. k. 5 (144).] Goreham gave his address as The Bible in Wine Office Court.

GORHAM (EDWARD), bookseller and publisher in Maidstone, Kent, 1736–56. His name occurs in an advertisement in the *Kentish Gazette* in 1736, and he was still in business in 1756.

GOSLING (FRANCIS), bookseller and publisher in London, Mitre and Crown, over against Fetter Lane, 1742–57. Son of Robert Gosling. Better known as head of the great banking firm, but was for a short time a bookseller. He was the publisher of Browne Willis's *Survey of the Cathedrals*, which on quitting the trade in 1757 he handed over to Osborne. [Nichols, VI. 198.] His father had published the second edition of the same author's *Notitia Parliamentaria* in 1730.

GOSLING (R.), printer in London, 1735. *The Young Clerk's Tutor* is advertised as "Printed by R. & E. Nutt and R. Gosling [assigns of Edw. Sayer, Esq.] for John Osborne, the Golden Ball". [*Daily Journal*, January 2nd, 1735.]

GOSLING (ROBERT), bookseller and publisher in London, Middle Temple Gate in Fleet Street, 1726–41. *See Dictionary*, 1668–1725.

GOUGH ( ), bookseller in Whitchurch, 1738. Agent for Daffy's 'Elixer'. [J. P. Earwaker, *Local Gleanings*, I. 237.]

GORDON ( ), printer in London, 1757. He printed *The History of Health and how to preserve it* for Dodsley in 1757. [Straus.]

GOUGH (JOSEPH), stationer in London, No. 6 Gracechurch Street, 1774. Issued a trade card in that year. [A. Heal's Collection.]

GOULD (SAMUEL), bookseller and publisher in Dorchester, 1733–83. It is said by a correspondent to *Notes & Queries* that this bookseller was in business for half a century. He is mentioned in an advertisement in the *Salisbury Journal* of Tuesday, April 10th, 1744. He was the publisher of Hutchins's *History of Dorset*, and some letters from him in connexion with the publication are in the Bodleian Library at Oxford. The *History* contains a plate engraved at his expense, and the first copy of the work is said to have been shown in his shop window. [*N. & Q.* 10 S. V. 492.] Gould died on February 22nd, 1783, and Dr. Cummings wrote his epitaph in which he referred to the bookseller as "Superintendent of the Amusements of Dorchester".

GOVER (JOHN), bookseller in Gosport, Hants, 1735–44. A correspondent to *Notes & Queries* states that he was in business in 1735. [*N. & Q.* 10 S. V. 481.] His name appears in an advertisement in the *Salisbury Journal* of Tuesday, April 10th, 1744.

GOVER (T.), printer in London, in Bridewell Precinct, Fleet Ditch, 1735. Printer of a folio pamphlet entitled, *An Appeal to the Publick; or Burchett and Lediard compar'd*. [B.M. 597. k. 11 (1).] Judging by this example, Gover, who probably was at work for some years, possessed some good founts of type and was a careful workman.

GRABHAM (JOHN), and PINE (WILLIAM), printers in Bristol, Wine Street, 1759–60. In 1759 J. Grabham printed *An Extract of the Christian's Pattern*, by John Wesley. [Winship.] In vol. III, p. 61, of *The Bibliographer's Manual of Gloucestershire Literature*, Messrs. Hyett and Bazeley record the printing by this firm of a *Letter . . . to the Commissioners for rebuilding a stone bridge over the Avon. By Bystander.* 1760. Grabham appears to have dropped out of the partnership soon afterwards.

GRAHAM (A.), bookseller in Alnwick, co. Northumberland, 1746–86. Mentioned in a list of provincial booksellers as in business in 1746. [*N. & Q.* 10 S. VI. 443.] Publisher of William Wood's Sermon preached at Darlington, 9 Oct. 1746 [Burman. *Alnwick Typography* 1748–1900, in *Hist. Berwick's Nat. Hist. Club*, vol. 23.] and of a pamphlet entitled, *Queries, Problems and Theorems upon the Doctrine of the Holy Trinity, Inscribed to the Rev. Mr. Nimmo, Minister of the Associate Congregation, in the Close, Newcastle. By FitzAdams*, n.d. [B.M. 4372. g. 2 (10).] Said to have been still in business in 1786. [*N. & Q.* 10 S. V. 141.]

GRAHAM (JAMES), bookseller in Sunderland, co. Durham, 1767–76. This name appears in the imprint to the pamphlet entitled, *Queries, Problems and Theorems*, with which A. Graham of Alnwick was concerned. In 1776 he published a catalogue of his stock.

GRAHAM (JOSIAH), bookseller and publisher in London, (1) under the Inner Temple Gate opposite Chancery Lane [*c.* 1737]; (2) the corner of Craven Street in the Strand [*c.* 1757]. Publisher of *The Modern Englishman* and also Horace Walpole's *A Letter from Xo Ho, a Chinese philosopher of London*. [B.M. 8133. k. 10.]

GRANT (ALEXANDER), printer in London, Bridges Street, 1775. He printed *Georgii Buchanani Paraphrasis* for David Goodsman. [*Public Advertiser*, August 11th, 1775.] [B.M. 3089. b. 15.]

GRANT (THOMAS), bookseller and publisher in Bristol, St. James's Back, 1755. Publisher of a pamphlet entitled *The Bristol Watch Bill*, 1755. [Hyett and Bazeley, III. 59.]

GRAY ( ), bookseller in Lancaster, 1761. Mentioned in a list of provincial booksellers as in business in that year. [*N. & Q.* 11 S. I. 363.]

GRAY (JOHN), bookseller and publisher in London, Cross-Keys in the Poultry, 1732 (?)–1741 (?). Partner with and successor to Samuel Chandler (*q. v.*), and was also in partnership with R. Hett. Amongst his publications was, *An Abridgement of the Philosophical Transactions*, 1720–32. Gray afterwards became a dissenting minister and held a living at Ripon in Yorkshire. [Nichols, V. 305.] It was doubtless to this bookseller that Johnson's tragedy of *Irene* was offered in 1741. [R. Straus, *Robert Dodsley*, p. 95.] Steele's *The Christian Hero* was printed for him in 1735. [*Daily Courant*, February 4th, 1735.]

GRAY (R.), bookseller in Redruth, co. Cornwall, 1753. Sold the Rev. S. Walker's *Sermon pr. at Truro . . . June 3, 1753. Second edition.* [Dredge.]

GRAY (SAMUEL), printer in Northampton, Abingdon Street, 1758. Mentioned in the Poll-Book for that year. He is perhaps identical with the printer of the same name who is found in Chelmsford, Essex, twenty years later.

GRAY (SAMUEL), printer in Chelmsford and Maldon, co. Essex 1773 (?)–6. This printer must have been established in Chelmsford before November 1773, on which date he opened a shop at Maldon in Essex, opposite the town hall, and in his advertisement speaks of himself as "late of Chelmsford"; but in 1776 he printed at Chelmsford Holden's *Paraphrase on Isaiah* [R. A. Peddie, *Library World*, September 1904], so that he probably had a printing-office in both places. He may be identical with the printer of the same name found in Northampton twenty years earlier.

GRAY, or GREY (SAMUEL), printer in London, 1720–8. *See Dictionary*, 1668–1725. The following paragraph appeared in the *Weekly Journal* for December 21st, 1728: "We hear that Mr. Samuel Grey, Printer, will be made Messenger of the Press, in the room of Mr. Kent, Deceased."

GREAVES ( ), Mrs., pamphlet seller in St. James's Street, 1728. Her name appears in the imprint to a translation of Fontenelle's *The elogium of . . . Peter I Czar of Muscovy*, published in 1728.

GREEN (RICHARD), printer at Oxford (?), 1700–46. Hearne (X. 375) described him as a grave, sober man, in 173$\frac{0}{1}$. Died June 28th, 1746, aged 57, at his house in Holywell, Oxford. [*Lloyd's Evening Post*, June 29, July 2, 1746.]

GREEN (THOMAS), bookseller and publisher in London, (1) "near" or "at Charing Cross", 1729–31; (2) against Falstaffe's Head, near Charing Cross, 1734; (3) Over against the Mews Gate, Charing Cross. 1728–35. Sold the library of Sir Richard Gibbs, knt., in 1729. Nichols thought the catalogue was one of the earliest issued with fixed prices. [Nichols, III. 626.] In the same year he published S. Strutt's *Defence of the late learned Dr. Clarke's Notion of Natural Liberty*. [W. M. C., December], and in 1734, a pamphlet entitled *The Necessary Respondent*. [B.M. 4105. aaa. 4.] His name is found in an advertisement of firms selling *Les Voyages de Cyrus*, at Charing Cross. [*Daily Journal*, January 1st, 1728.] In 1735 catalogues of books to be sold by Herman Noorthouck were to be had at Green's, Charing Cross, among other places. [*Ibid.*, January 21st, 1735.]

GREEN (W.), printer, publisher, and bookseller in Chelmsford, and Bury St. Edmunds, 1731–69. Began as a bookseller and publisher in Chelmsford, Essex, where in 1731 he issued Dr. T. Lobb's, *Treatise of the Small-Pox*. In 1755 he moved to Bury St. Edmunds in Suffolk, and opened a shop in Cook's Row [*Ipswich Journal*], and amongst his publications there was C. Potter's *Pretended Inspiration of the Methodists*. [B.M. 4473 c. 6 (9).] In 1760 he added printing to his other activities, as W. Seymour's *Odes on the Four Seasons* bears the imprint: "Bury St. Edmunds, Printed and sold by W. Green, 1760". Nichols records that Mary, the sister of Dr. Macro of Bury St. Edmunds, upon her brother's death in 1767 applied to the above-named bookseller to spare no expense in getting the notice of his death inserted in every newspaper. [Nichols, IX. 365.] He was still there in 1769, when he published a work by John Harrison, botanist, entitled, *A New Method of making the Banks of the Fens impregnable*.

GREENVILLE, or GRENVILLE (WILLIAM), bookseller in Winchester, co. Hants, 1765–75. Mentioned by F. A. Edwards in a list of Hampshire booksellers and printers, contributed to *Notes & Queries*. [10 S. V. 482.] In 1765 he had on sale *A Collection of Anthems performed in the Cathedral Church . . . in Winchester*. [B.M.]

GREEP (HENRY), printer in Bristol, The Red-Bible in Castle Street, 1732. Sold mineral waters procured from Wiltshire. [Advertisement in *Fog's Weekly*, February 19th, 1732.]

GREG, GREGG, or GRIGG (G.), bookseller in London, next to Northumberland House, Charing Cross, 1717(?)–1735(?). His name is found in an advertisement of an Anodyne necklace, in the *Daily Post* of January 1st, 1726. He is perhaps identical with the G. Grigg who published Jer. Owen's *Sermon to Dissenters* in 1717 [*see Dictionary*, 1668–1725, p. 134]. In 1728 Greg is again mentioned in connexion with an advertisement of a lost dog. [*Mist's Weekly*, January 6th, 1728.] The shop was afterwards taken by Charles Marsh (*q. v.*), who recorded the event in a poem in which these lines occur:

> There lately Grubstreet authors might you spy
> Exposed to sale . . .
> Here grew the poppy o'er G. J—b's brow,
> And Dunciad heroes might have slept till now,
> But home-bred faction and domestic strife
> Sever'd old Greg from his too youthful wife.

There is an advertisement of a sale of medicine at Mr. Greg's, bookseller, next to Northumberland House, Charing Cross. [*Daily Journal*, February 18th, 1735.] Greg's widow died in Leicester Street, near Leicester Square, in February 1749, and her next of kin were advertised for in the *Whitehall Evening Post* of February 21st.

GREGORY (JOHN), printer and bookseller in Leicester, 1757–89. Printer of the *Leicester Journal*, which began in 1757. Descended from an ancient family, settled at Raveness, in co. Derby. Timperley speaks of him as a man of great openness of heart and of upright conduct. He was an alderman of the city of Leicester and served the office of Mayor in 1781 [p. 764]. Died March 22nd, 1789. [Nichols, III. 678.]

GRETTON (J.), bookseller and publisher in London, Old Bond Street [or] Opposite to the Duke of Grafton's in Old Bond Street, 1758–62. Publisher of a newspaper called *The Patriot*, and also of numerous pamphlets.

GREY, *see* Gray.

GRICE ( ), bookseller in Ormskirk, 1738. Agent for Daffy's "Elixer". [J. P. Earwaker, *Local Gleanings*, I. 237.]

GRIFFIN (WILLIAM), bookseller, printer, and publisher in London, (1) Fetter Lane; (2) Garrick's Head, Catherine Street, Strand. 1764 (?)–1776 (?). This publisher, whom we should like to think was connected with Bennet Griffin [1671–1700], was probably in business before the year 1764, when he issued Dr. Theobald's *Every Man his own Physician*. The imprint of that work runs: "Printed and sold by W. Griffin in Fetter Lane"; but the collected *Essays* of Oliver Goldsmith, which he published in the following year, were printed for

him, although at the end of the volume is "A list of Books, Printed and sold by W. Griffin". In addition to the medical work above noticed, the list included several plays. In 1767 Griffin moved to Catherine Street in the Strand, under the sign of Garrick's Head. In the year following on February 5th he published Goldsmith's comedy *The Good-natur'd Man*, produced on January 29th. It was sold out immediately and went into a fourth edition by February 22nd. In 1770 Griffin also published that delightful work, *The Deserted Village*, which went through six editions within the year. Goldsmith received £250 from Griffin for *The Grecian History* (June 22nd, 1773) published by Griffin and others in June 1774, and 600 guineas for his *Animated Nature*. [K. Balderston's *Census of Goldsmith's Letters*, 1926, pp. 33, 34.] Griffin also published his *Miscellaneous Works* 1775, and his translation *The Comic Romance of Monsieur Scarron*, the same year. In 1773 Griffin's name is found in the imprint of Dr. M. A. Clarke's *Directions for the Management of Children* [B.M. T. 294 (16)], and in 1775 he was the proprietor and publisher of the *Morning Post*, a London newspaper that still flourishes.

GRIFFITHS (RALPH), bookseller and publisher in London, (1) The Dunciad, in Ludgate Street; (2) The Dunciad, St. Paul's Churchyard; (3) The Dunciad, in Paternoster Row; (4) The Strand. 1747–1803. As the promoter of the *Monthly Review*, and the persecutor of Oliver Goldsmith, the name of this bookseller has become famous. Timperley says that he was originally a watchmaker, but he abandoned that trade and came to London, where he set up as a bookseller in 1747. In May 1749 he founded the *Monthly Review*, a critical magazine, which gained a good deal of support. While acting as usher for Dr. Milner at Peckham, Oliver Goldsmith met Griffiths, and early in 1757 began to contribute miscellaneous articles to the Magazine. The agreement was that Goldsmith should lodge at Griffiths's house, and receive a small salary. From April to September, 1757, Goldsmith contributed twelve articles to the *Monthly Review*, amongst them being reviews of Smollett's *History of England* and Gray's *Odes*. Griffiths's treatment of his reviewer was harsh in the extreme. He kept him short of food and money, accused him of being a thief, and threatened him with imprisonment. Goldsmith left this employment in 1758. Johnson on being asked which of the two literary journals, the *Monthly* and *Critical Reviews*, was the best, replied that the *Monthly Review* was done with the most care. In 1760 Griffiths published *A Catalogue of all Books and Pamphlets published for ten years past, with their prices, and references to their characters in the Monthly Review*. Business did not prosper with him and he became bankrupt, his *Review* being sold for the benefit of his creditors. He afterwards recovered the property and from that time became prosperous and wealthy, kept two carriages, and obtained the degree of Doctor of Laws from an American college. He died September 28th, 1803. [Timperley, 1842, p. 816.]

GRIG, *see* Greg.

GRIGG (WILLIAM), bookseller in Exeter, co. Devon, (1) near The Conduit in the Fore Street; (2) in the Exchange opposite the Broad Gate in Exeter. 1765–89. He was selling *The Wisdom of Divine Providence*, in 1765 [*Gazetteer and Daily Advertiser*, October 3rd, 1765.] Sold the fourth edition of *Life and Death of Philip Henry*. [Dredge, p. 28.] In 1769 his name is found in the list of subscribers to the Rev. John Gerrard's *Poems*. His name occurs in a list of Exeter booksellers as late as 1789.

GROENEWEGEN (J.), bookseller in London, at the sign of Horace, Strand, 1715–28. He advertises the sale of Latin and French books in the *Daily Post* of January 4th, 1728. About 1715 he is found in partnership with Vandenhoek and they issued a trade card. [A. Heal's Collection.]

GROVE (HUGH), bookseller in Portsmouth, Hants, 1718–44. *See Dictionary*, 1668–1725. Still in business in 1744, when his name appears in an advertisement in the *Salisbury Journal* of April 10th.

GUNTER (S.), bookseller and publisher in Chesterfield, 1725. Publisher of Charles Cotton's *The Wonders of the Peak*, 1725, 8vo. [Creswick, p. 22.]

GURNEY (JOSEPH), bookseller and publisher in London, 54 Holborn, 1769–1772. Dealer in law-books. His name is found in the imprint to the Rev. R. Hall's *Sermon* printed at Coventry about 1772 [B.M. 4473. e. 10 (6)], also in *The Whole Proceedings in the . . . Action brought by . . . George Onslow . . . against the Rev. Mr. Horne*, 1770. [B.M. 1131. d. 3.]

GYLES, *see* Giles.

HABERKORN (JOHN), printer in London, Gerrard Street, Soho, 1755–65. In 1755 he printed for several booksellers J. Palairet's *Concise Description of the English and French Possessions in North America*. [J. C. B. L.] Printer of the first volume of James Stuart's *Antiquities of Athens*, and in 1765 editor of *Psalmodia Germanica*. [B.M. 176. f. 2 (1).]

HAINES (HENRY), printer in London, (1) Russell Street, Covent Garden, (*see* R. Francklin); (2) Hart Street, Covent Garden; (3) upper end of Bow Street, Covent Garden. 1726–38. Journeyman to R. Francklin, and associated with *The Craftsman* from its first issue in December 1726. When in July 1731 Francklin was thrown into the King's Bench prison for publishing what was known as the "Hague letter", he obtained Haines's consent to his [i.e. Haines] name being placed in the imprint, assuring him that there were several gentlemen of great fortunes supporting the paper and defending all prosecutions, who would make him a suitable present, in case any corporal punishment should be inflicted on him. The second part of *An Argument against Excise* by "Caleb D'Anvers" [i. e. Nicholas Amhurst] is said to have been printed by Haines "at Mr. Francklins, in Russell St., Covent Garden" [*London Evening Post*, January 18th, 1733], as is also a pamphlet entitled *The Politicks on both sides*, published in 1734. Things went on satisfactorily for a few years more, though Haines was by no means comfortable in his position, and at last became so nervous that he determined to have his name removed from the paper; but Francklin agreed that Haines should take a house in his own name and take over all the printing material belonging to Francklin and that he should keep these as security against all future damages. Haines then moved the printing-office to premises in Hart Street, Covent Garden, and all went well until the unlucky issue of July 2nd, 1737. On being arrested he endeavoured in every way to shield his employers and was remanded on bail in £600. Being unable to find such an amount, he appealed to Francklin to go bail for him; but Francklin coolly told Haines's wife that "He knew nothing of her husband, and desired he might not be troubled any more with her impertinences". Mrs. Haines died six months afterwards, and Haines was only released by the bail of two friends of his own. Further trouble befell him by the publication of *The Craftsman* of December 10th, 1737. He applied again to both Mr. Francklin and Mr. Amhurst, and avers that they did nothing, but "cuff'd him about from one to the other, for about six weeks". Haines told Francklin that he was prepared to stand the consequences if Francklin would pay him his wages, one guinea a week, whilst he was in prison: but, so he says, Francklin proposed as an alternative that he should run away, as it would be cheaper to him to pay three hundred pounds, the amount of his bail, than probably a guinea a week for his life. Haines refused this. Then Francklin removed the printing materials from the house in Hart Street, and for the next two years Haines remained in close confinement in the King's Bench prison, his employers having left him to starve. In a satirical poem written in 1738 entitled *A Supplement to One Thousand Seven Hundred and Thirty Eight*, there is a reference to "Poor *Haines*'s ears in pain for *Caleb*'s wit."

HALL (FRANCIS), bookseller in Isleworth, co. Middlesex, 1760–1. In the *London Daily Chronicle* of April 8th–10th, 1760, this bookseller advertised a catalogue of books on sale by him, and in the next issue of that paper (April 10th–12th) Benjamin Franklin's famous pamphlet, *The Interest of Great Britain with regard to her Colonies considered.* His name does not appear in the imprint, the publisher being T. Becket of Tully's Head in the Strand, so that the advertisement was only to call public attention to the fact that he had this pamphlet in stock. In 1761, he issued another catalogue of books, which he advertised in *Lloyd's Evening Post* of July 10th–13th.

HAMILTON (ARCHIBALD), I, printer in London, Falcon Court, Fleet Street, 1736–93. A native of Edinburgh, where he is said to have been bred to the profession of a printer. In 1736 he left the city, to escape the consequences of having been a partaker in the Porteous riots, and came to London, where for a time he acted as manager to William Strahan. He afterwards set up for himself and made his press successful by the excellence of his work. In 1756 he started the *Critical Review* in opposition to Griffiths's *Monthly*, to which Oliver Goldsmith was a contributor. One of his most successful undertakings was Smollett's *Compleat History of England*. He was also for a time in partnership with W. Jackson of Oxford, in the management of the University Press. He died, a rich man, on March 9th, 1793, his will being proved on April 17th. He had one son, Archibald Hamilton II (*q. v.*), who died before him. He bequeathed his printing business to his grandsons, Archibald and Samuel. [P.C.C. 205 Dodwell.]

HAMILTON (ARCHIBALD), II, printer in London, near St. John's Gate, 1792. Son of A. Hamilton I. Printer of *The Town and Country Magazine*. He also had an office between Highgate and Finchley and afterwards at Golders Green. He died on October 6th, 1792, leaving two sons, Archibald and Samuel, who not only succeeded to their father's business, but also to that of their grandfather, Archibald Hamilton I (*q. v.*).

HAMMOND (THOMAS), junior, bookseller and publisher in York, High Ouzegate, 1730–40. His name is found in the imprint to the Rev. J. Clarke's

sermon, *The Foundation of Morality*, printed in York by Thomas Gent, about the year 1730. [B.M. 698. e. 8 (4)]. He was still there in 1740. [*N. & Q.* 11 S. I. 364.]

HANSARD (LUKE), printer in Norwich and London, 1752–1828. Son of Thomas Hansard, a manufacturer of Norwich. He was apprenticed to Stephen White, printer of Cockey Lane, Norwich, and was for a time in John Crouse's office. Some time afterwards he left Norwich and went to London, where he became a compositor in the office of John Hughs. He became managing director and a partner in the firm in 1774. He died on October 30th, 1828. As he printed the Journals of the House of Commons, the reports of the proceedings have long been referred to as "Hansard".

HARBERT (J.), printer and publisher in London, the White Lamp, in Tavistock Court, Covent Garden, 1732. Printer of a pamphlet entitled *The History of the Abdication of Victor Amadeus II*, 1732. [B.M. 1057. a. 32.]

HARDING ( ), bookseller in Portsmouth, 1767. In that year his name is found in the imprint to a *Manual of Religious Liberty*, which was to be had of all the booksellers in England and Corsica. [J. C. B. L.]

HARDING (SAMUEL), bookseller and publisher in London: (1) At the Post House on the Pavement in St. Martin's Lane; (2) Bible and Anchor on the Pavement, &c., 1735. 1726(?)–1755. His name is first met with in an advertisement of a sale of books in the *Daily Post*, of January 10th, 1726. One of his most important publications was Stephen's *Thesaurus Linguae Latinae*, in four folio vols., issued in 1735. He died at Edgware in January 1755, and his daughter is said to have carried the *Daily Advertiser* to the family of Jenour on her marriage. [Nichols, IX. 490.] Issued a trade card while at the Bible and Anchor. [A. Heal's Collection.]

HAROLD (E.), printer in Marlborough, 1774. In that year he printed *A Letter to the Right Rev. Shute [Barrington] Bp. of Landaff*. [Allnutt in *Bibliographica*, II. 306.]

HARPER (THOMAS), bookseller and publisher in London, The Angel, without Temple Bar, 1738. In that year he published *The Usefulness of the Stage to Religion and to Government.* [W. G. B. Page's, *Booksellers' Signs of Fleet Street*; Karslake, *Book Auction Records*, vol. XIII.]

HARRIS (GABRIEL), senior, bookseller and publisher in Gloucester, 1702–38. *See Dictionary*, 1668–1725. In 1728 he published the Rev. Josiah Woodward's *Fair Warnings to a Careless World*. He was still in business in 1738, when his name is found in a list of provincial booksellers. [*N. & Q.* 10 S. V. 183.] Gabriel Harris, junior, was perhaps his son, and was in partnership with him. A Gabriel Harris was still there in 1783.

HARRIS (JOHN), bookseller in London. Principal assistant to Thomas Evans, Goldsmith's adversary. He then went to John Murray, and afterwards to Newbury, whom he succeeded. [Curwen.]

HARRIS (M.), bookseller and publisher in London. At the Sign of the Bee Hive, over against St. Clement's Church, Strand, 1735. Publisher of a weekly pamphlet, *The Bee Revived*, of which No. XCVII was the current number for January 4th, 1735. [*Daily Journal*.] He also published *A Key to the Times*. [*Ib.*, January 13th, 1735.]

HARRIS (T.), printer in London, The Cloysters, by West Smithfield, 1756. His name appears as printer of a *Form of Prayer, to be used in all Churches and Chapels*, 1756. By what authority, if any, he printed this is unknown.

HARRIS (T.), bookseller and publisher in London, The corner of Angel-Court in Shoe-Lane, over against the Three Tuns, near Fleet Street, 1739. Publisher of a pamphlet called *Mr. Walpole's Case, in a Letter from a Tory Member of Parliament*, 1739. [B.M. 8133. bb. 55.]

HARRIS (THOMAS), bookseller and publisher in London, Looking-Glass on London Bridge, 1741–5. Like all the London Bridge booksellers, Harris dealt in chap-books, ballads, and penny histories, one of his publications being a reprint of *The True History of the Life and Sudden Death of old John Overs, the rich Ferry-man of London*, 1744, price sixpence. He may be the Thomas Harris who in 1746 printed at Carlisle *The Genuine dying speech of the Reverend Parson Coppock*. [Copy in Bodl.] In 1745 he became bankrupt. In 1763 he was living in Ironmonger Row, Old Street, and the *Kentish Gazette*, reports that on November 27th, when returning from the Minories, he was attacked by footpads and severely injured, but the date of his death is not known. There is an advertisement of sale by auction of a valuable library by Thomas Harris at Janeways Coffee House, Cornhill, in 1753. [*Public Advertiser*, January 9th, 1753.]

HARRIS (THOMAS), printer at Carlisle, 1746. *See* supra.

HARRIS (W.), bookseller in London, St. Pauls' Churchyard, 1770–5. Publisher of sermons by John Wesley and others between these dates.

HARRISON (JAMES), printer in London: (1) Warwick Lane; (2) Opposite Stationers' Hall. 1766–9. Brother of Thomas Harrison. Apprenticed to Edward Say, printer in Warwick Lane. Is said to have married his master's daughter. Died in 1769. His wife carried on the business at 2 Red Lion Court, Fleet Street, until her son James was old enough to take it up. [*The House of Harrison*, pp. 1–6.]

HARRISON (JOHN), bookseller in Newcastle-upon-Tyne, 1736–59. Admitted freeman of the Newcastle Stationers' Company on July 26th, 1736. [Welford, p. 128.]

HARRISON (THOMAS), printer in London, Warwick Lane, 1738. A native of the town of Reading, co. Berks. Came to London with his younger brother James. Apprenticed to Mr. Edward Owen, of Amen Corner, Ludgate Hill, printer, on June 1st, 1738, and was later on taken into partnership. The *London Gazette* was printed by them for many years. After the death of Owen in 1783, he was joined by S. Brooke. Thomas Harrison was Master of the Stationers' Company in 1784, and died on November 4th, 1791. [*The House of Harrison*, pp. 1–6.]

HARROD (WILLIAM), printer and bookseller in Market Harborough, co. Leicester, 1768–1806. In the first-named year he printed for Rowland Rouse, a native of the town, *A Collection of the Charities and Donations given ... to the town of Market Harborough*. [B.M. G. 3381.]

HARROP (JOSEPH), printer and bookseller in Manchester, at the sign of the Printing Press, opposite the Exchange, 1749–76. Printer and publisher of the *Manchester Mercury*, the first number of which appeared on March 3rd, 1752. He died on January 20th, 1804, aged 76, and was buried in St. John's Churchyard, Byrom Street. He published *The History of Man* in 6*d*. numbers. Harrop's *Bible* was published by his son and successor. [Curwen].

HART (HARRIS), printer in London: (1) Popping's Court, Fleet Street; (2) Crane Court. 1765(?)–1787. What relation this printer was to John Hart (*q.v.*) is unknown. He possibly succeeded to the business in Popping's Court on the retirement or death of John. Amongst the books printed by him was Payne's *Elements of Trigonometry*, 1772. He died May 24th, 1787. Timperley describes him as "a very worthy and industrious man", and adds that he moved his business to Crane Court a few years before his death. He left no children, and the bulk of his property he bequeathed to the children of his sister Elizabeth. [P.C.C. 270. Major.]

HART (JOHN), printer in London: (1) Bartholomew Close, West Smithfield, (1737); (2) Popping's Court, Fleet Street. 1737–64. Began business in Bartholomew Close, where he printed the second vol. of the *Works* of John Bunyan in folio, in 1737. Some time before 1746 he moved into Popping's Court, and printed in that year a *Sermon preached in the Parish Church of Greenwich in Kent on May 4th, 1746*, by the Rev. Robert Pool Finch, after the victory at Culloden. In 1754 he printed for the publishers, J. Lewis in Paternoster Row, and A. Keith at the Bible and Crown in Grace Church Street, two theological tracts by Anne Dutton. He was still there in 1761, when he printed two more theological tracts for the same A. Keith, and J. Fuller in Blow-bladder Street, near Cheapside, which were also from the same pen. [*London Mercury*, November, 1923.] About 1745 he was joined by T. Hart, perhaps a brother, who remained with him until 1765.

HART (T.), printer and type-founder in London: (1) Bury Court, Love Lane, Wood Street; (2) Popping's Court. 1732–85. In an interesting article upon "William Strahan and his Ledgers", contributed by Mr. R. A. Austen Leigh, to *The Library*, he states that some years ago a handbill was discovered by Mr. H. L. Bullen, of the Typographical Library and Museum of the American Typefounders' Company, headed *A Specimen of the Printing Letter, by T. Hart and W. Strahan, in Bury Court, Love Lane, Wood Street.* The bill was undated, and was assigned by Mr. Bullen to a period between 1737 and 1739. This appears to be somewhat too early, as at that time Hart was employed by William Bowyer. About 1745 he is found at John Hart's, in Popping's Court, so that this short partnership with William Strahan would seem to fit in between 1740–5. He remained with John Hart until 1765, when he rejoined Strahan, with whom he continued until 1785. [*Library*, 4th Ser., Vol. III, No. 4, March 1923, pp. 265–6.]

HARTSHORNE ( ), bookseller in Leicester, 1714–35. *See Dictionary*, 1668–1725.

HARTLEY (J.), bookseller and publisher in Bradford, co. Yorks., 1776. Joint publisher with G. Nicholson of *The Memoirs of General Fairfax*, in that year. [Dickons, J. N., *Catal. of Books, &c., published at Bradford*, p. 47.]

HARWARD (SAMUEL), bookseller and printer in Tewkesbury, Gloucestershire, 1760–1809. The first Tewkesbury printer. Printed a large number of chapbooks, some of which were collected by Joseph Haslewood. A list of these and others printed at Harward's press, was given in the second volume of Bennett's *Tewkesbury Register and Magazine*, 1840–9 [pp. 191–2]. This list was reprinted, without any additional information, in the *Gloucestershire Notes and Queries* for 1887, pp. 226–8. In 1771 he had on sale a catalogue of books issued by the Worcester bookseller S. Gamidge. [*British Chronicle, or Pugh's Hereford Journal*, August 8th, 1771; Burney Collection.] He afterwards moved to Cheltenham. Harward died in August 1809. He is said to have kept five shops, and to have left behind him very considerable property and a large and valuable collection of books. [Timperley, 1842, p. 835.] Issued a trade card. [A. Heal's Collection.]

HARWICK ( ), bookseller at Lynn, co. Norfolk, 1728. Dr. Robert Hill, Rector of Stankow, Norfolk. *A Discourse on the Fourth Commandment* . . . sold by Mr. Harwick, bookseller in Lynn. [W. M. C. I.]

HASLEWOOD (BENJAMIN), bookseller and publisher in Bridgnorth, Shropshire, 1730–93. One of the younger sons of William Haslewood, attorney-at-law and town-clerk of Bridgnorth, who had eleven children and died in 1746. Benjamin, who is described in the Haslewood pedigree as stationer and gentleman, was born October 22nd, 1710, and became a burgess of the town in 1730. He was probably then in business; but the earliest mention of him that has been found is in an advertisement in the *Northampton Mercury* of 1749, where he is named as an agent for the distribution of the sale catalogues of T. Warren, the bookseller of Birmingham. Benjamin Haslewood married Sarah, daughter of John Wells of Bridgnorth, clothier. He was elected bailiff of the town in the years 1754, 1766, 1773, and 1786. He died April 27th, 1793. He was the publisher of John Barrow's *Psalm Singer's Choice Companion*. [*Whitehall Evening Post*, January 2nd, 1755], and in 1772 and 1776 of *Sermons* by the Rev. T. Humphries of Shrewsbury. [B.M. 4408. dd.] [Information from R. J. R. Haslewood, Esq.]

HASLINGDEN (JOHN), bookseller in Manchester, Cannon Street, 1760–76. Procter, in his *Memorials of Manchester Streets* (p. 201), speaks of him as an "occasional publisher".

HASSELL (LIONEL), printer in Chelmsford, Essex, 1769–71. Printer of the *History of Essex*, a work in six volumes, the second of which was finished in

1769, the first and third in 1770, the fourth in 1771, and the fifth in 1772. The last volume which also bears the date 1772, was printed by M. Hassell. [R. A. Peddie, *Library World*, September 1904]. Hassell was also the printer of a *Sketch of the Materials for a New History of Cheshire*, in 1771.

HATCHETT (T.), bookseller and publisher in London, Cornhill, 1735. One of the partners in the publication of *A General Dictionary*. [*Daily Courant*, January 23rd, 1735.]

HAWES (L.), bookseller in London, Red Lion, Paternoster Row, 1750–76. In 1752 in partnership with C. Hitch (*q. v.*), and in 1753 they published *Compleat Tables for Measuring Timber* [*Public Advertiser*, January 5th, 1753], and were one of the firms taking subscriptions for part LXXXV of *Chambers' Cyclopaedia* [*Ib.*, January 6th]. In 1755 they had a share in publishing Johnson's *Dictionary*, and in 1763 were joint publishers, with R. and J. Dodsley, of a pamphlet entitled *The Case of going to War, for the sake of . . . Trade*, an abridgement of a work by Dean Tucker. [B.M. E. 2055.] In an advertisement of the publication of "Postlethwayt's *Dictionary*" the firm is described as L. Hawes and Co. [*Gazetteer and New Daily Advertiser*, July 3rd, 1765.] In the same paper October 3rd, 1765, L. Hawes, Clark, and Collins are named among the publishers of Johnson's *Shakespeare*. They were also partners in the publication of Gay's *Fables*. [*Public Advertiser*, January 10th, 1775.]

HAWES (ROBERT), printer in London: (1) 34 Lamb Street, near Spittle Square; (2) Corner of Dorset Street, Crispin Street, Spittlefields; (3) The Foundry in Moorfields. 1774–89. In the year 1774 he printed, for several London and country booksellers, *Some Memoirs of the Life of John Glover, late of Norwich*. [B.M. 4903. bbb. 20 (1).] In 1775 he printed and published an edition of John Wesley's *A Calm Address to our American Colonies*, and in 1776 John Fletcher's *Vindication* of that Address. Amongst other "Americana" that came from his press were *A Narrative of Mr. Ebenezer Punderson, Merchant, who was drove from North America*, 1776; T. Rankin's *Brief Narrative of the Revival of Religion in Virginia*, third edition, 1778; and John Wesley's *Some Account of the late Work of God in North America*, the second edition, 1778. Copies of these books are in the John Carter Brown Library, Providence, U.S.A. Robert Hawes also had a type foundry in Moorfields between 1775 and 1789.

HAWKES ( ), bookseller in Wells, co. Somerset, 1742. In that year he had on sale copies of a *Tour through . . . Great Britain*, which he advertised in the local press. [*Norwich Gazette*, May 1, 1742.]

HAWKINS (GEORGE), bookseller in London, Milton's Head in Fleet Street, 1741–80. His name is first found in the imprint to a rare pamphlet by Samuel Keimer called *Caribbeana*, published in 1741. In 1743 his name is found in a list of subscribers to the second volume of Dr. Care's *Historia Literaria*. He was also publisher of *Remarks on Dr. Middleton's Examination of the . . . Bishop of London's Discourses, concerning Prophecy*, MDCCL. 8vo. [B.M. T. 1631 (3).] In 1756 he was appointed bookseller to the Prince of Wales, and in 1775 he was one of the publishers of *The Court and City Register*. [*Public Advertiser*, January 27th, 1775.] Died in 1780 at a very advanced age. [Nichols, III. 607.]

HAWORTH (R.), printer in Bury St. Edmunds, *c.* 1740. Printer of a pamphlet entitled *The History of a Schoolmaster, or the renowned Pedagogue of Nibbiano*, n.d. 8vo. [B.M. 12330. c. 11.]

HAYDON ( ), printer and bookseller in Plymouth, 1770. His name is mentioned in the imprint to the Rev. T. Vivian's *Exposition of the Catechism*, 1770. [Dredge, p. 29.]

HAYWOOD (ELIZABETH), authoress and publisher in London, at the sign of Fame in Covent Garden (1742?). On the verso of the last page of the first vol. of her novel (a translation from the French), *The Virtuous Villager*, 1742, is an advertisement headed, "New Books, sold by Eliza Haywood, publisher, at the sign of Fame in Covent Garden'. Two books only are named. How long she remained in this business is uncertain.

HAZARD (JOSEPH), 1716–35. *See Dictionary*, 1668–1725. Still in business in 1735, when he published *Devotions for the Altar*, and shared in the publication of the second volume of Bayle's *Dictionary*. [*Daily Journal*, January 3rd and 13th, 1735.]

HAZARD (SAMUEL), printer and publisher in Bath: (1) Cheap Street, 1772; (2) King's Mead Square, 1774. 1772–1806. His imprint is first found in Daniel Lysons's *Practical Essays*, which appeared in 1772. He was then living in Cheap Street, from which he removed in 1774 and took over the business of T. Mills. [*Bath Chronicle*, January 6th, 1774.] Amongst his other work we find the following: *The Priest Dissected, a poem* [by C. Anstey], printed by S. Hazard and sold by Dodsley, Pall Mall . . . and by Frederick Tennent and Hazard at Bath. [1774]. 4to. (an advertisement of this book appears in the *Bath Chronicle*, May 26th, 1774, under the heading, "Anatomy"); *An Election Ball.* [By C. Anstey.] Printed for the author by S. Hazard, Bath, fo. 1776, 2nd ed. 4to. 1776; a Latin version of this, *Ad C. W. Bampfylde Arm. Epistola poetica familiaris . . . An Election Ball.* Auctore C. Anstey, Bathonæ Impensis Auctoris excudebat, S. Hazard, 1776; *Epistle to Mrs. M*ll*R.* [by C. Anstey], Bath, printed and sold by S. Hazard in King's Mead Square, 1776, 4to.; *The Way to Christ . . .* by Jacob Behmen, Bath, printed by S. Hazard, 1775. 8vo.; *A Practical Discourse of God's Sovereignty*, by Elisha Coles, Bath, printed and sold by W. Gye, also by S. Hazard, printer and bookseller in King's Mead Square, 1776. In the list of subscribers to this work S. Hazard's name appears for 150 copies. Hazard's name also occurs with others, in an advertisement in the *Bath Chronicle* of January 26th, 1774, as selling Gill's *Exposition of the New Testament*, and two months later (March 24) as agent for Dr. Hill's Medicine, "Pectoral Balsam of Honey, Volatile Spirit of Fever, &c., &c. Sold by Mr. Cruttwell printer in Bath, and Messrs. Frederick Taylor, Bull, Tennent, and Hazard". In the *Bath Directory* for the year 1792, his address is given as Cheap Street, and in that of 1800 he is described as "Printer, Bookseller, and Circulating Library". He died on Saturday, September 20th, 1806, and the business was continued by his son-in-law, John Binns. [Information supplied by Miss Elsie Russ, librarian, Municipal Libraries, Bath.]

HEAD (I.), bookseller in Helston, co. Cornwall, 1753. One of those who sold the Rev. S. Walker's *Sermon pr. at Truro . . .* June 3rd, 1753. [Dredge.]

HEATH (JOSEPH), bookseller and publisher in Nottingham, near the trees in the market-place, and Mansfield, 1744–60. Publisher of one of the Rev. J. Sloss's *Sermons*. [Creswell, p. 28.] In 1753 he had a shop in Mansfield. [*ib.*, p. 30.] His name occurs in an advertisement in the *Cambridge Journal* in 1760. Issued a trade card. [A. Heal's Collection.]

HENDERSON (C.), bookseller and publisher in London, Royal Exchange, 1756–64. Amongst his publications may be noted N. Horrebow's *Natural History of Iceland*, 1756, and a weekly issue of the *History of Religion* in 1764.

HENDERSON (THOS.), printer and publisher at Greenwich, 1748. In 1748 he printed and published a *Sermon* preached by the Rev. John Butley, in the Church of Greenwich, before the various associations of Antigallicans, on June 15th. [B.M. 226. I. 2 (29).]

HENRY (DAVID), printer in London and Reading, 1725(?)–1792. He was a native of Scotland. Born at Fovron, sixteen miles from Aberdeen, December

26th, 1710. His father intended him for the Church and put him to college at Aberdeen; but the boy had an independent spirit and left the college and came to London before he was fourteen. He is said to have found a job in the same printing house in which Benjamin Franklin was employed; but very soon after his arrival in London he made the acquaintance of Edward Cave, and was probably employed by Cave when, in 1731, he started his printing-house in St. John's Gate, Clerkenwell. In 1736, so the story goes, Henry married Cave's sister Mary. In 1745 he set up a press at Reading, in Frier's Street, and there published the *Winchester Journal*. [*N. & Q.* 10 S. v. 482.] In 1749 there was a D. Henry, a publisher in Wine Office Court, Fleet Street, whose name is found on many plays and poems and who may have been the same. On the death of Edward Cave, David Henry became publisher of the *Gentleman's Magazine* in partnership with R. Cave, a nephew of the original founder. Henry was a man of considerable literary ability, and his name will always be remembered as the editor and publisher of *An Historical Account of all the Voyages round the World*, in 1774, and of *The Voyages of Captain Cook*. He was also an authority on agriculture and in 1772 he wrote and published *The Complete English Farmer*. Henry is said to have been first or second cousin to Patrick Henry, the first Governor of Virginia. He died at Lewisham in 1792. [Timperley, 1842, pp. 775–6.]

HETT (RICHARD) I, bookseller and publisher in London, Bible and Crown in the Poultry, 1726–66. Publisher for the Dissenters. In partnership with J. Clark (*q. v.*), and later on with J. Oswald. Treasurer of the Stationers' Company. In the London press of 1726 several advertisements appeared of religious tracts published by J. Clark and R. Hett, and in 1728 their names are found as publishers of a book by Jones, on *The New Testament*. [*Daily Post*, January 2nd.] Hett's name is found in Kent's *Directory* for 1738, and in 1753 he was taking subscriptions for Chambers's *Cyclopaedia*. [*Public Advertiser*, January 6th.] There is some confusion in Nichols's account of this bookseller, as to the date of his death. In one place [vol. III, p. 607] he says that Hett died in 1766, and in a footnote to the same page that he died in 1780, leaving two sons.

HETT (RICHARD) II, printer in London, Wild Court, 1752–76. Son of Richard Hett I, successor to J. Watts in Wild Court. His imprint is found in the Rev. John Williams's *Concordance to the Greek Testament* in 1767. Like his father he was largely employed by the Dissenters.

HEWERS (ELIZABETH), bookseller in Colchester, 1726–7. Agent for the *Ipswich Journal* until December 16th, 1727. Her death took place about that time, as in July 1728 the name of Mrs. Burnham, daughter of Eliz. Hewers, appears in the imprint to the *Ipswich Journal*.

HEWIT ( ), bookseller in Knutsford, co. Cheshire, 1738. Agent for Daffy's "Elixer". [J. P. Earwaker, *Local Gleanings*, I. 237.]

HEYDINGER (C.), printer and bookseller in London, in the Strand, opposite the Theatre Royal, Drury Lane, in Bridges Street, 1774–8. Dealer in French and German books, and works on exploration in Polar regions. A. J. Roustan, minister of the Helvetic Church in London, on the occasion of its dedication preached a sermon on December 17th, 1775, a copy of which is in the British Museum and bears the following imprint: "A Londres, chez C. Heydinger, Imprimeur et Libraire dans le Strand. M.DCC.LXXVI." Above this is his very artistic mark. [B.M. 4424. f. 7.] The English translation was published by T. Bensley on July 10th, 1775. The church was situated in Stidwell Street, Soho. Heydinger's business was a failure and he died in distressed circumstances in 1778. [Timperley, 1842, p. 744.]

HIBBART (A. W.), bookseller and publisher in Bath, 1776. This name occurs in the imprint to C. Anstey's *Ad C. W. Bampfylde Arm. Epistola poetica familiaris*, published in that year.

HICKEY (BENJAMIN), bookseller and publisher in Bristol, Nicholas Street, 1742 (?)–1752 (?). Is stated by a correspondent in *Notes and Queries* to have been in business in 1742. [*N. & Q.* 11 S. II. 23.] In 1748 he advertised on the covers of Hooke's *Bristollia*, and in 1750 published that writer's *Essay on the National Debt*. In 1751 he had on sale the Rev. John Sturch's discourse entitled *Christ's Appearance in the Flesh*, delivered at Portsmouth, Hants. on Christmas Day, 1750. [*Monthly Review*, February, 1751, p. 313.] He is not noticed in Latimer's *Annals of Bristol*, and the date of his death is unknown.

HIGGINSON ( ), bookseller in Warrington, 1738. Agent for Daffy's "Elixer". [J. P. Earwaker, *Local Gleanings*, I. 237.] Mrs. Higginson, probably his widow, is mentioned in a list of provincial booksellers as there in 1761. [*N. & Q.* 11 S. I. 364.]

HILDYARD (FRANCIS), *see Dictionary*, 1668–1725.

HILDYARD (JOHN), bookseller in York, Bible in Stonegate, 1731–57. Son of Francis Hildyard, whom he succeeded in 1731. In 1735 he advertised in the *Daily Post: A Discourse on the usefulness of Oriental translations of the Bible*. [*Daily Post*, February 13th.] In 1751 he issued a catalogue of 30,000 books, very well printed and arranged. [B.M. 11904. c. 3.] He died in 1757. [*Evening Advertiser*, April 7–9, 1757.]

HILDYARD (S.), bookseller in York, 1740. Mentioned in a list of provincial booksellers in *Notes and Queries*. [10 S. V. 242.] Probably a misprint for (J.) Hildyard.

HILL (E.), publisher in London, 1737. This name is found in the imprint to the second edition of Pope's *The Impertinent, or a Visit to the Court; A Satyr.* [Isaac.]

HILL (GEORGE), printer in Cirencester, co. Gloucester, 1741–59. In partnership with J. Davis (*q. v.*), issued a newspaper called *Cirencester Flying Post and Weekly Miscellany*, the first number of which must have appeared in the first week of 1741. Copies are very rare. It bore the imprint "Cirencester: Printed by G. Hill and J. Davis, where advertisements are taken in". In 1742 he printed A. Palmer's *The Gospel New Creature*, third edition, with an advertisement at the end of books sold by G. Hill at the Printing Office at Cirencester. In 1758 he was churchwarden of his parish. [H. E. Norris, *Booksellers and Printers of Cirencester*, pp. 3, 4.]

HINCHCLIFFE (WILLIAM), bookseller and publisher in London, Dryden's Head, under the Royal Exchange, 1726(?)–38(?). His name is found in 1726, in the imprint to the second edition of *Poems Amorous, Moral and Divine*, advertised in Wilford's *Monthly Catalogue*, for March. He was one of the partners in the publication of vol. II. of Bayle's *Dictionary*. [*Daily Journal*, January 13th, 1735.] In 1738 his name occurs in Kent's *Directory*.

HINDE (LUKE), printer and publisher in London, The Bible, George Yard, Lombard Street, 1750–67. Printer and publisher for the Society of Friends. His name is found on the imprint of *Sufferings of the People called Quakers*, 1753. [*Bibliography of Worcestershire*, p. 57.] Succeeded in business by his wife Mary (*q. v.*).

HINDE (MARY), printer and publisher in London, George Yard, Lombard Street, 1767–74. Widow of Luke Hinde. Printed amongst other things, Penn's *No*

Cross. No Crown, and the writings of Joseph Besse. A Catalogue of her publications, filling forty octavo pages, is in the Friends' Library in Devonshire House. [Tracts 143, last item.] She was succeeded in the business by James Phillips.

HINGESTON (MILESON), bookseller and publisher in London, Temple Bar, 1768–76. His name occurs in 1768 as a subscriber to the Greek Testament of that year and in 1772 in an advertisement of Wm. Payne's *Elements of Trigonometry.* In the same year Richard Gough, the antiquary, writing to the Rev. Michael Tyson a gossipy letter about books, says, "I have despatched my Mercury to Hingeston and White after Ray without success." [Nichols, VIII. 586.] He was one of the partners in the publication of Theobald's *Shakespeare.* [*Public Advertiser,* July 21st, 1775.] His name is found in Kent's *Directory* for 1776. When he retired from business he held a position in the Ordnance Office, where he died March 25th, 1806. [Timperley, 1842, p. 825.]

HINTON (JOHN), bookseller and publisher in London: (1) Bow Street, Covent Garden, 1739?; (2) King's Arms, St. Paul's Churchyard; (3) Newgate Street, near Warwick Lane; (4) King's Arms, Paternoster Row. 1739?–81. A bogus *Craftsman* was circulating in London in the early part of January 173 8/9, and the publishers of D'Anvers's paper inserted an advertisement in the *London Evening Post* of January 9–11, warning readers against the fraud. They stated that it was published by "one Hinton", at the upper end of Bow Street, Covent Garden, but as there were two Hintons in London at that time, it is not clear to which they were referring. John Hinton was the publisher of a periodical called the *Universal Magazine,* one of the most successful of the early magazines. He was the principal plaintiff in a copyright action over Stackhouse's Bible, brought against Alexander Donaldson and other booksellers in Edinburgh in 1773. Hinton had acquired this copyright by marrying the widow of Stephen Austin, the original holder. John Hinton died on May 21st, 1781. [Nichols, III. 441.]

HINTON (THOMAS), bookseller and publisher in London, at the White Horse in Water Lane, Black Fryars, 1726. *Conjugal Love Revealed,* is advertised as "Printed for Thomas Hinton at the White Horse in Walter Lane, Black Fryars, where also may be had *The Adventures of Priests and Nuns*". [*London Journal,* February 12th, 1726.] He may possibly have removed to Bath in 1730 and set up as a printer. See next entry.

HINTON (THOMAS), printer in Bath, 1730. The following entries appear in the Chamberlain's Accounts for the City of Bath in the years 1729–30: "Paid Thomas Hinton the Printer as by bill £1 8*s.* 0*d.* Paid Thomas Hinton for printing of bills per order £1 1*s.* 0*d.*"

HINTON (W.), bookseller in London: (1) At the King's Arms in High Holborn next the Three Cups Inn; (2) Sergeant's Inn Gate, Fleet Street. 1731–2. Publisher of a pocket annual called *The Ladies' Miscellany* in 1731, and in 1732 of a news-sheet called *The Universal Spy, or the Royal Oak Journal reviv'd.* May possibly have been the Hinton referred to in an advertisement in the *London Evening Post* in 1739 as publishing a bogus edition of *The Craftsman. See* Hinton, J.

HINXMAN (JOHN), bookseller and publisher in York, Stonegate, 1757–60. In 1759 he published a catalogue of books as the stock of the late Mr. John Hildyard, deceased; but Timperley (p. 841) says that Hildyard was succeeded by John Todd (*q. v.*). In 1760 Hinxman published the first two volumes of *Tristram Shandy* at York. [*Cambridge History of Literature.*] Soon afterwards he went to London and took over the business of Mrs. Mary Cooper. [Mumby, *The Romance of Bookselling.*]

HIRST (JOHN), printer and bookseller in Leeds, 1730. Mentioned in a list of provincial booksellers and printers as in business in Leeds in 1730. [*N. & Q.* 10 S. v, March 1906, p. 183.]

HITCH (C.), bookseller in London, Paternoster Row, 1733–64. In 1735 Johnson's *Lobo* was "printed for A. Bettesworth and C. Hitch". Later in partnership with L. Hawes. They dealt largely in novels such as *The Inhuman Husband, The Batchelor of Salamancha, The History of Hippolyto and Aminta.* A catalogue of some of their publications in 1752 is found at the end of the twelfth edition of John Locke's *Some Thoughts Concerning Education.* Printed for S. Birt, &c., 1752. [B.M. 8307. C. 21.] Hitch was Master of the Stationers' Company in 1758. He died September 20th, 1764.

HODGE (MATTHEW), bookseller and bookbinder in Tiverton, co. Devon, near the Market Cross, 1759. Issued an advertisement of his stock of stationery, including Bibles and Prayer Books, which was printed by Goadby of Sherborne in 1759. [A. Heal's Collection.]

HODGES (SIR JAMES), bookseller in London: (1) The Looking-Glass over against [or under] St. Magnus Church; (2) At the Looking-Glass on London Bridge.

1730(?)–1758(?). Is believed to have succeeded Thomas Norris at this house about 1730. His early history is unknown. Like all the booksellers on London Bridge he dealt largely in chap-books and penny histories such as *Robin Hood's Garland, Amadis of Gaul, The History of Reynard the Fox, Tom Thumb,* and a host of others. At the same time he sold literature of a higher order, such as works on navigation and books on popular science, e.g. *The Laboratory or School of Arts,* which dealt with glass-making, cutlery, &c. Another of his numerous publications was *The Art of Painting in Miniature,* and in 1737 he issued a collection from the poets entitled *The Muses' Library,* made by Elizabeth Cooper. In 1750 Hodges was elected deputy for Bridge Ward Without, and later he held the position of town clerk of the City of London. In 1758 he was knighted by George II, on presenting an address.

HODGES (JOHN ?), bookseller in Manchester, 1728. In Wilford's *Monthly Catalogue* for January 1729 there was advertised under "New Pamphlets", *The Charge of . . . Samuel Lord Biopsh (sic) of Chester, to the Clergy of his diocese in his primary Visitation, begun at Chester, June 19, 1728.* Printed for J. Hodges, bookseller in Manchester, and sold by J. Roberts in Warwick Lane." Mr. Axon, in *Notes and Queries,* referred to this pamphlet, but gave the publisher's name as Thomas Hodges. R. W. Procter, in his *Memorials of Manchester Streets,* p. 195, says, "We have failed in our search for further traces of this publisher".

HODGES (P.), bookseller in Hereford, 1740–69. A correspondent to *Notes and Queries* states that this bookseller was in business in 1740. In 1749 he had on sale an edition of Addison's *Miscellaneous Works,* and in 1753 his name is met with in an advertisement of John Barrow's *Psalm Singer's Choice Companion.* [*Whitehall Evening Post,* January 2nd, 1755.] Hodges was also the Hereford agent for the monthly parts of Smollett's *History of England,* issued in 1769.

HODGSON (JAMES), bookseller and publisher in Halifax, co. Yorks., 1737–8. Mentioned in a list of provincial booksellers in *Notes and Queries* as in business in 1737. [10 S. V. 183]. In 1738 he was the publisher of the Rev. Thomas Wright's *Antiquities of Halifax.* [Boyne's *Yorkshire Library,* p. 93.]

HODSON (FRANCIS), printer in Cambridge, 1762–1812. During the years 1762–77 he was partner with T. Fletcher (*q. v.*) in printing the *Cambridge Chronicle* and many works. The partnership was dissolved, and in 1778 Hodson appears alone as the printer of the *Chronicle.* He also printed the works of

Robert Robinson and W. Hayley, besides Poll Books, &c. Died October 17th, 1812, and was succeeded by his son James.

HODSON and JOHNSON, printers in Salisbury, on the New Canal, 1774–6. Their names occur in the imprint to John Ryland's *Compendious View of the Principal Truths of the . . . Gospel of Christ,* 1774. [B.M. 4372. de. 6 (3).]

HOGBEN ( ), bookseller in Smarden, Kent, 1756. Mentioned in an advertisement of a London publication in the *Kentish Gazette* in that year.

HOGBEN ( ), bookseller at Rye, co. Sussex, 1756. Perhaps identical with Hogben of Smarden, in Kent, or a relative. Mentioned in an advertisement of a London publication in the *Kentish Gazette.*

HOLBECHE (A.), bookseller in London, Moorfields, 1735. In 1735 this bookseller is named as one who received subscriptions for a proposed *Exposition on the Common Prayer Book.* [*Country Journal,* April 26th.]

HOLDER (P.), publisher in London, (?) 1734. Found in the imprint to a ballad entitled *The Knight and the Prelate,* 1734. [Information kindly supplied by Col. Isaac.]

HOLLINGWORTH ( ), Mrs., bookseller in Lynn, co. Suffolk, 1742. Her name appears in the *Norwich Gazette* of Saturday, May 15th, 1742, in an advertisement of Defoe's *A Tour through . . . Great Britain.*

HOLLINGWORTH (T.), bookseller and publisher in Lynn, co. Suffolk, High Street, facing the Grass Market, 1748(?)–1769(?). His name appears in an advertisement in the *Ipswich Journal* of February 4th, 174 8/9. As Nichols, in his *Literary Illustrations* (VI. 523), states that Hollingworth was in business for more than forty years, he had probably been established some years earlier. He was the publisher of the second edition of Nathaniel Kinderley's *The Ancient and Present State of the Navigation of the Towns of Lynn, Wisbeach, Spalding, and Boston . . .* 1751, his name appearing on the title-page. [B.M. 8775. c. 28.] In 1769 he published *A New Method of making the Banks in the Fens impregnable,* by John Harrison, botanist. Nichols further states that Hollingworth always had four apprentices. One of these, Richard Beatniffe, bookseller of Norwich, has not left a favourable account of his master's character. Hollingworth had one daughter, whom he offered in marriage to Beatniffe, with the business; but the offer was declined. He was probably in business later than 1769.

HOLLIWELL (THOMAS), printer in Birmingham, Moor Street, 1770. Mentioned in the *Birmingham Directory* of that year.

HOLLOWAY (ROBERT), bookseller and publisher (?) in London (?), 1776. Timperley [p. 736] records that he was sentenced to three months imprisonment for publishing a pamphlet called *The Rat-Trap*. This publication has not been traced. He may have been the author and not a bookseller.

HOLMBE (WILLIAM), printer in Manchester, 1741. The record of his burial in that year was found by R. W. Procter in the registers of the collegiate church; but he could not gain any further information about this printer, who may have been only a journeyman. [*Memorials*, p. 196.]

HOOD (E.), bookseller in London, Ludgate Street, 1765. He is advertised as selling *A Defence of Freemasonry* in the *Gazetteer and New Daily Advertiser*, September 20th, 1765.

HOOD (H.), bookseller in London, Tooley Street, Southwark, 1735. Mentioned in an advertisement in the *Country Journal*, April 26th, 1735.

HOOKE (ANDREW), printer in Bristol, Shannon Court, Corn Street. A native of Bristol, and a man of some literary attainments. Was at one time wealthy, but lost his fortune in speculation. In 1742, he printed and published a paper called *The Oracle*, and sometimes the *Bristol Oracle and Country Advertiser*, the first number of which was issued on February 3rd. He is said to have been a prisoner in Newgate when he started it; but the authority for this statement is not given. He was afterwards prosecuted by the Attorney-General for evading the advertisement duty; but what punishment, if any, he received is not recorded. In 1748 he became the compiler of *Bristollia, or Memoirs of the City of Bristol*, which was issued in parts in blue paper covers at the price of one shilling each. His London agent was James, afterwards Sir James, Hodges, a noted bookseller on London Bridge. Only two parts were published. Hooke is also said to have taught geography at a house in Exchange Alley, near the Exchange, which afterwards became the West Indian Coffee House. In August 1749 the Town Council granted him a pension of £30 a year and a further £20 was allowed him by the Merchants' Society. Hooke died on February 2nd, 1753, aged 65. His widow carried on a printing and bookselling business for some years at the Maiden Tavern in Baldwin Street. [J. Latimer, *Annals of Bristol in the Eighteenth Century*, 1893, pp. 51, 240, 279.]

HOOK, or HOOKE (H.), bookseller and publisher in London, Fleet Street, 1732. Possibly successor to J. Hooke at the Flower de Luce in Fleet Street. Publisher of a work called *Reason against Coition*, at the end of which is a list of other books sold by this bookseller. Most of these were of an ephemeral character.

HOOKE (J.), bookseller in London, Flower de Luce, Fleet Street, 1718–29. *See Dictionary*, 1668–1725. He continued to publish until (?) 1729 [W. M. C.]

HOOKHAM (J.) and (T.), booksellers and publishers in London, Great Queen Street, Lincoln's Inn Fields, 1765. Publishers of *De Arte Graphica* in that year. [*Gazetteer and New Daily Advertiser*, July 6th.]

HOOKHAM (THOMAS), bookseller in London, (1) New Street, Hanover Square; (2) New Street, opposite Maddox Street; (3) 15 Old Bond Street, opposite Stafford Street; (4) New Bond Street, corner of Bruton Street. 1772–5. Chiefly remembered for his circulating library. Issued various trade cards, with the different addresses given above, but the dates of which cannot be determined. Mr. Heal has a bill-head dated from New Street, Hanover Square, in 1772. [A. Heal's Collection.]

HOOKHAM (THOMAS JORDAN), bookseller in London, 100 New Bond Street, *c.* 1775. Successor to T. Hookham. Issued a trade card showing his circulating library. [A. Heal's Collection.]

HOOPER (SAMUEL), bookseller and publisher in London, (1) Gay's Head near Beaufort Buildings, Strand; (2) 25 Ludgate Hill, 1773; (3) Ludgate Circus; (4) High Holborn. 1756–93. An important publisher with a large trade. In 1756 he was issuing a political periodical called *The Constitution*. [B.M. E. 2049 (1).] Another pamphlet in the same volume, *Things as they are*, bears the imprint of S. Hooper and A. Morley, showing that they were in partnership at that date. At the end is an advertisement of their publications which included an edition of Thomas Betterton's *History of the English Stage*, which was not the edition of 1741. How long this partnership lasted is not clear. Samuel Hooper's most important publication was Frances Grose's *Antiquities of England and Wales*, which was in the press from 1773 to 1778. He died February 20th, 1793. [Timperley, 1842, p. 777.]

HOOTON (CHARLES), printer in Salisbury, 1729–30. Printed the Rev. J. Price's sermon, *Humanity and Almsgiving*. Sarum, printed by Charles Hooton for William Collins, bookseller in Silver Street, MDCCXXX. [B.M. T. 1034 (13). Allnutt in *Bibliographica*, II. 299.]

HOPE (THOMAS), bookseller and publisher in London, Bible and Anchor, opposite [or] behind the North Gate of the Royal Exchange, 1758–61. Successor to Edmund Comyns (*q. v.*) in 1758. In 1760 he published an edition of Walton and Cotton's *Complete Angler*, edited by John Hawkins. Only the previous year a second edition of the same work as edited by the Rev. Moses Browne, vicar of Olney, Bucks., had been placed on the market, and some acrimonious advertisements were inserted in the newspapers by the rival publishers. Another of Hope's miscellaneous publications was *The Bird Fancier's necessary Companion*, issued in 1761.

HOPKINS ( ), (?) bookseller in Warwick, 1733. His name occurs in a list of country booksellers who sold the London newspaper, the *Daily Register*, in that year.

HOPKINS (FRANCIS), bookseller, bookbinder, and printer, Cambridge, *c.* 1722–58. Printed many Law Overseers Forms during this period, and sold "Bibles, Common-Prayers, and shop books of all sorts". He bound books for the University Press, and supplied books to the University Library during this period.

HOPKINSON (J.), bookseller and publisher in Warwick, 1735–43. In 1735 he was named in an advertisement amongst a list of persons selling Richard Spencer's *Laws and Customs of the Lead Mines*. His name occurs in the imprint to the Rev. W. Denham's sermon, *On the Ascension*, printed at Coventry in 1743 [B.M. 225. g. 20 (14)], and again in 1745 on the Rev. William Gardner's "*Sermon* preached before the University of Oxford . . . on . . . July 7, 1745" [B.M. 225. f. 14 (2)].

HOPPS (JOHN), bookseller in Manchester, 1740–76. According to the inscription on his tombstone in Flixton Church, he was born at a village called Helwith, near Richmond in Yorkshire, on March 4th (O.S.), 1740.

HORDEN ( ), bookseller in Peterborough, 1770 (?). Mentioned as a bookseller who issued catalogues. He died April 5th, 1799. [Nichols, III. 679.]

HORSFIELD (J.), bookseller and publisher in London, the Half Moon in St. Paul's Churchyard, 1726–60. Advertised in the *Daily Journal*, May 3rd, 1726, the Rev. Luke Milbourne's *Vindication of the Church of England*. He was still publishing in 1760.

HORSFIELD (ROBERT), bookseller and publisher in London, (1) the Crown in Ludgate Street; (2) 5 Stationers' Court, 1764–76. Possibly a relative of J. Horsfield, who was carrying on the trade of a bookseller in 1726 at the Half Moon in St. Paul's Churchyard. In 1764 Robert Horsfield published *Letters between Col. Robert Hammond . . . and the Committee of Lords and Commons at Derby House. . . .* [B.M. E. 2055 (9).] He had a share in the publication of *Postlethwayt's Dictionary*. [*Gazetteer and New Daily Advertiser*, July 3rd, 1765.] *Geographia* was published by him from Stationers' Court. [*Public Advertiser*, January 4th, 1775.]

HORTON (W.), printer in Portsmouth, co. Hants, near Point Gate, 1751–5. Printed amongst other things a pamphlet entitled *The Geese in Disgrace* (1751); *The Famous Bull Unigenitus*, translated into English (1753); *Portsmouth*, a poem, by A. Maxwell, 1755. [Edwards's *Early Hampshire Printers*, p. 115.]

HOTHAM ( ), bookseller in York, 1752. His name occurs in the imprint to J. Orton's *Sermon on the death of the Rev. P. Doddridge*, on October 26th, 1751 [B.M. S. 1655 (6)]. He is not noticed by Robert Davies in his *History*.

HOWGATE (SAMUEL), bookseller in Leeds, co. Yorks. His death is recorded in the *Leedes Intelligencer* of May 26th, 1761, and the statement was made that he was succeeded by Joseph Ogle.

HOWGRAVE (FRANCIS), printer in Stamford, 1738–51. In the first-named year he was the printer of a pamphlet entitled *A Vindication of a certain Reverend Gentleman &c.* [B.M. 1414. e. 35.]

HUGGONSON (J.), printer in London, (1) Bartholomew Close; (2) near Sergeants' Inn, Chancery Lane; (3) Sword and Buckler Court over against the Crown Tavern on Ludgate Hill, 1741. 1730 ?–1741 (?). His name has been found as printer of the following pamphlets: *The Truth of the Christian Faith*, by B. M., 1730, and *The Plain Truth, a Dialogue between Sir Courtly Jobber . . . and Tom Telltruth* . . . 1741. [B.M. E. 2032. (5).] *Daily Journal*, April 11th, 1735. *The Real Crisis* is advertised as printed for him.

HUGHES or HUGHS (H.), printer and publisher in London, 1775. Possibly son of John Hughs (*q. v.*). He was one of the partners in the publication of *The Court and City Register* in 1775, and in the same year he printed for T. Payne *An Essay on the Genius of Homer*. [*Public Advertiser*, January 27th and July 10th.]

HUGHS (JOHN), printer in London, (1) Holborn, near the Green Gate; (2) near Great Turnstile, Lincoln's Inn Fields. 1730–71. Born at Thame in Oxfordshire in 1703. Son of a dissenting clergyman. Educated at Eton, and served a regular apprenticeship to a stationer in London. Became one of Robert Dodsley's printers. In 1740 Hughs incurred the displeasure of the Government for printing a pamphlet entitled *Considerations on the Embargo on Provisions of Victual.* In 1749 he printed an edition of Michael Drayton's *Works*, which was advertised in the *Whitehall Evening Post* of March 23–5. In 1763, or near that date, he was appointed printer of Parliamentary papers, it is said through the interest of Lord North. In 1765 he printed Percy's *Reliques*, and, according to Nichols, most of Dodsley's publications were printed by him. John Hughs died on September 30th, 1771, at the age of 68. He left one son, also a printer. [Timperley, 1842, p. 726.]

HULSE (RALPH), bookseller in Sandbach, co. Cheshire, 1756. In 1756, agent for Schofield's *Middlewich Journal or Cheshire Advertiser.*

HUMBLE (EDWARD), bookseller in Newcastle-upon-Tyne, near the Pack Horse in the Side, 1775–1820. Born about the year 1753. In 1776 he married Maria the daughter of Joseph Barber, another Newcastle bookseller. [*Newcastle Courant*, November 2nd, 1776.] He had an extensive and flourishing business, and shortly before his death became proprietor of the *Durham County Advertiser.* He died on June 11th, 1820, in his sixty-seventh year. [Timperley, 1842, p. 878.]

HUMPHREY (P.), bookseller and publisher in Chichester, co. Sussex, 1766–74. His name is found in the imprint to *The Antiquities of Arundel*, published in 1766, and again in 1769 in W. Clifford's *Farmer's Guide.* He was still in business in 1774. [A. C. Piper, "Notes on Sussex Printing," *Library*, July, 1914, p. 264.] Another Humphrey is mentioned as a bookseller in Halstead (?) in 1725, in a list of Provincial Booksellers in *Notes & Queries.* [10 S. v. 183.]

HUNT (JAMES), bookseller and publisher in Hereford, 1726. Dealer in chapbooks. Possibly a descendant of Richard Hunt [1685, *see Dictionary*, 1668–1725]. He was associated with John Hunt, perhaps a brother.

HUNT (JOHN), bookseller and publisher in Hereford, 1726. Associated with James Hunt, *q. v.*

HUTTON (JAMES), bookseller and publisher in London, Bible and Sun, next Rose Tavern without Temple Bar, 1735–95. Publisher for the Nonconformists.

Born in London, September 3rd, 1715. Educated at Westminster School. About 1735 he was apprenticed to Mr. William Innys, the bookseller. At the expiration of his apprenticeship he opened a bookseller's shop at the above address, and having been converted by the Wesleys a short time before, he began to hold religious meetings there. Soon afterwards he joined the Moravians and published many of the writings of Count Zinzendorf. He was bookseller to George Whitefield and published his journal. He afterwards gave up his business and was for many years Secretary to the Moravian Society, and devoted the later years of his life to preaching and charitable work. He died at Oxted Cottage, Surrey, on May 3rd, 1795. [D. Benham, *Memoirs*, 1856; Timperley, 1842, p. 786; Nichols, III. 436–7.]

HUTTON (WILLIAM), bookseller in Birmingham, 1750–1815. Born in Full Street, Derby, September 30th, 1723. His father was a master woolcomber, but two years after the birth of William he failed and became a journeyman. In 1728 William was sent to school, but the education he received was small, as at seven he was bound apprentice to a silk mill in Derby. At fourteen he entered on a second apprenticeship to his uncle George Hutton, and from the age of twenty-one to twenty-seven he worked as a stocking-maker. He evinced a curiosity for books, and having bought three volumes of the *Gentleman's Magazine*, he contrived to bind them himself. He then in 1749 walked to London and back to buy bookbinder's tools, and in April 1749 opened a shop at Southwell, Nottinghamshire, and sold books. In 1750 he paid a visit to Birmingham with a view of seeing whether there was any opening for a bookseller in that city. Although there were three booksellers there already, he thought there might be room for another in a small way. He rented half a shop at a shilling a week. By the end of the first year he found himself better by twenty pounds. In spite of persecution by the overseers of the parish, who ordered him to procure a certificate of respectability, he began to make headway. In 1751 he opened the first Circulating Library in Birmingham. On the advice of his friend, Robert Bage, he went into the paper trade. In 1755 he married and began to launch out in various directions. He bought a paper-mill, but after losing about £1,000 relinquished it. Then he started to buy land, and in 1772 bought a house in High Street, Birmingham. In 1781 he published a *History of Birmingham*, and was elected a Fellow of the Society of Antiquaries of Scotland. In 1791 riots broke out in Birmingham, and his house was sacked, and a valuable library destroyed. In his later years he wrote poetry, and also a *History of the Roman Wall.* He died in 1815, aged 92.

HYATT (B.), bookseller in Bedford, 1773. Only known from a list of provincial booksellers in *Notes & Queries.* [*N. & Q.* 10 S. v, February 24th, 1906, p. 141.]

ILIVE (ABRAHAM), *see* Ilive (Jacob).

ILIVE (ISAAC), *see* Ilive (Jacob).

ILIVE (JACOB), printer and typefounder in London, Aldersgate Street, over against Aldersgate Coffee-house, 1730; (2) London House, Aldersgate, 1746. 1730–63. Son of T. Ilive, printer [1724]. With his two brothers, Abraham and Isaac, set up a letter-foundry in Aldersgate Street about 1730. It was only a small one, and no specimen of its types is known. Rowe-Mores in his *Dissertation upon English Typographical Founders and Foundries*, 1778, says that it produced a nonpareil Greek fount, and founts of roman and italic in various sizes. He gave up letter-founding in 1740, when the contents of the foundry were sold to John James. Ilive, however, continued in business as a printer until his death in 1763. It is said that he was disordered in his mind. He held extreme religious views, and wrote and published several pamphlets in support of them. In consequence of an attack upon Bishop Sherlock in one of these he was imprisoned for two years [1756–8] in Clerkenwell Bridewell, and during his confinement wrote *Reasons offered for the Reformation of the House of Correction in Clerkenwell*, published in 1757. He was also the author of a literary forgery, *The Book of Jasher*, said to have been translated by Alcuin. He finished up a remarkable life with an attack upon the Company of Stationers, which failed in its object. [T. B. Reed, *A History of the Old English Letter Foundries*, pp. 346–9.]

ILLIDGE (SAMUEL), *see Dictionary*, 1668–1725. Still in business in 1728, when he published E. Hatton's *Mathematical Manual.* [W. M. C., June.]

INGMAN, or INMAN ( ), bookseller in Doncaster, 1736–63. In 1736 his name appears in the imprint to a sermon by the Rev. John Mawer [B.M. 225. g. 14 (5)], and in 1739 his name is given as one receiving subscriptions for Francis Tolson's *Hermathenae.* Inman was still in business in 1763, when he figures in a list of booksellers in the *Leedes Intelligencer.* His surname was frequently spelt "Ingman"; his Christian name has not been found.

INJURED (A.), (?) bookseller and publisher in London, near Temple Bar, 1739. Cruden's pamphlet, *Mr. Cruden greatly injured*, published in 1739, bears the imprint "London: Printed for A. Injured near Temple-Bar: and sold by the pamphlet sellers of London and Westminster". Evidently a pseudonym to conceal the real publisher.

INNYS (W. and J.), *see Dictionary*, 1668–1725. William Innys was still in business in 1756, when, in partnership with J. Richardson, he published *Two Sermons*, preached by the Rev. William Totton. [B.M. 225. i. 6 (4).] They also published *The Adventures of Signor Gaudentio di Lucca* from Paternoster Row. [*Public Advertiser*, January 12th, 1753.] Master of the Stationers' Company, 1747–8.

IRELAND (JOHN), bookseller in Leicester Market Place, 1769–1810. A man strictly independent in his principles, of great probity, and much respected. He died April 17th, 1810. [Nichols, III. 680.]

ISTED (J.), bookseller and publisher in London, Golden Ball, between St. Dunstan's Church and Chancery Lane, 1711–32. *See Dictionary*, 1668–1725. In 1726 he published Sir John Floyer's *Commentary on Hippocrates.* [W. M. C., March.] In the *Daily Post* of January 8th, 1728, is an advertisement of a medical work "now sold by J. Isted (Mr. Crouch, bookseller in Paternoster Row, being now dead)". Isted was still in business in 1732.

IVES (JOHN), amateur printer at Yarmouth, 1772–6. Son of John Ives, merchant at Yarmouth, born in 1750. The delicate state of his health prevented his receiving a classical education. At an early age he developed a taste for archaeological studies. He collected seals and occupied himself with a printing-press, at which he printed a few trifles, the earliest of which was *A Pastoral Elegy on the death of Thomas Martin, F.S.A.* He died in 1776 and was buried in Bolton Church. [F. J. Farrell, *Yarmouth Printers and Printing.*]

JACKSON (ANDREW), bookseller in London, Clare Court, Drury Lane, 1740–78. Published "modernized" edition of some of Chaucer's *Canterbury Tales*, under the title of *Matrimonial Scenes*, in 1751. He retired from business about a year before his death, which occurred on July 25th, 1778, in his eighty-third year. [Nichols, III. 625–6.]

JACKSON (H.), bookseller in London, 198 Oxford Street, 1775. He advertised the sale of *Wit à la Mode* in the *Public Advertiser* of January 22nd, 1775.

JACKSON (J.), bookseller and publisher in London, (1) Pall Mall, near St. James's House; (2) bottom of St. James's Street; (3) St. James's Street, near the Palace. 1728–61. Publisher of pamphlets, etc., which he advertised in *Mist's Weekly.* In 1728 his name is found in the imprint to a pamphlet entitled *Liberty, or the Meeting of Parliament.* [W. M. C., January; Winship.]; in 1729 he published a dramatic opera *Love and Revenge.* [W. M. C., November.] At one time he was in partnership with J. Jolliffe. In 1761 he sold patent medicines.

JACKSON (JOHN), printer in York, Petergate, 1740–70. Son of John Jackson the Elder. Obtained the freedom of the city by patrimony in 1734. First set up his press in Grape Lane, adjoining to Coffee Yard. In 1740 he began a weekly journal which he called the *York Gazetteer*, and was also a publisher of books that he printed. He was succeeded about 1771 by his son Francis. Eventually this printing-office passed to William Storry and his son. [Davis, *History of York Press*, pp. 312–20.]

JACKSON (STEPHEN), printer at Chelmsford and Ipswich, 1773–5. Is said to have succeeded Samuel Gray (*q. v.*) when he went to Maldon. He is possibly identical with the Stephen Jackson, nephew of Mr. Craighton, who became the proprietor of the *Ipswich Journal* about 1775, and was in partnership with John Shave the bookseller (*q. v.*). He had a brother William, a printer in Ipswich about this time.

JACKSON (WILLIAM), printer in Oxford, 1753–95. He was proprietor and publisher of the *Oxford Journal* from its first establishment in 1753. He was lessee of the Oxford Bible Press, and was partner for a few years with Archibald Hamilton in the University Press. He afterwards became a banker, and was one of the founders of the Old Bank, Oxford, now amalgamated with Barclays. He died April 22nd, 1795, over 70. [Nichols, III. 679, and 398.]

JACOB (J.), bookseller and publisher in Peterborough, co. Northampton, 1775–95. Publisher of a pamphlet entitled *Political Productions*, 1775. He was still in business in 1795. [*N. & Q.* 10 S. V. 242.]

JALLASSON ( ), type-founder and printer in London, Prujeans Court in the Old Bailey, 1728. The printer of a new edition of the Hebrew Bible in that year. He offered "to pay 2*s.* 6*d.* for every fault that shall be found in the sheets exposed after printing". [*Daily Journal*, January 1st, 172$\frac{8}{9}$.]

JAMES (ELIZ.), Mrs., printer and pamphlet-seller in London, at the Royal Exchange, 1736–62. Widow of George James, and succeeded him in the office of printer to the City of London until 1750. In 1762 her name occurs in the imprint to a pamphlet entitled *A Letter to . . the Lord Mayor . . . of London, concerning the Peace now in agitation between Great Britain and France*, 1762. 8vo. [B.M. E. 2054 (1).] In 1764 the name of J. James, perhaps her son, is found coupled with that of S. Cook at this address.

JAMES (J.), *see* James (Eliz.).

JAMES (S. and J.), printers, Cambridge, *c.* 1750–73. *The Book of References to the Map of Sutton and Mepall Levels*, done from a Survey taken in 1750. [R. Bowes, *Cambridge Books*, No. 498.] They printed various Poor Law Overseer Forms, 1763–73.

JAMES (SAMUEL), bookseller in London, at the Bible in Gutter Lane, Cheapside, *c.* 1770. Ran a circulating library, a view of which appears on his engraved trade card of about this date. [A. Heal's Collection.]

JAMES (SARAH), wife of Thomas James, printer, Cambridge. *See* Walker, Robert.

JAMES (THOMAS), printer in Cambridge, *c.* 1744–58. Died 1758, and was buried in St. Michael's Church-yard, October 31st. *See* Walker, Robert.

JAMES, (THOMAS), type-founder in London, joint holder of lease to print by stereotype at Cambridge, 1730–8. *See* Fenner (W.) and *Dictionary*, 1668–1725.

JEFFRIES (FRANCIS), bookseller in London, Ludgate Street, 1728. Dealer in ephemeral literature under such titles as *The Adventures of the Priest and Nuns*; *The Adventures of the Bath*, &c. [W. M. C., September 1728.] In 1753 J. Jeffries, of Ludgate Street, was one of the partners in the publication of *Gentlemen's and Tradesmen's Pocket Assistant*. Perhaps a son of the above? [*Public Advertiser*, January 5th, 1753.]

JEFFREYS (T.), bookseller and publisher, London, corner of St. Martin's Lane, 1753–65. He published *A Companion to the Almanack* in partnership with W. Clarke [*Public Advertiser*, January 1st, 1753], and was advertising the sale of *The Practical Surveyor* in the *Gazetteer and Daily Advertiser* of July 20th, 1765. Messrs. Jeffreys and Faden of Charing Cross advertised the sale of an *Atlas*, March 8th, 1775, in the *Public Advertiser*.

JENKINSON (JOHN), printer and bookseller in Huntingdon, 1768–1807. The first to set up a press in Huntingdon. Jenkinson sold the business to Thomas Lovell in 1807, but lived a long time after in poor circumstances. An A. Jenkinson is found there in 1774. [*N. & Q.* 11 S. VI. 207.]

JENKINSON (J. and J.), booksellers in Yealand, Westmoreland, 1762. Mentioned in a list of provincial booksellers. [*N. & Q.* 11 S. I. 364.]

JENOUR (JOSHUA), bookseller (?) in London, Fleet Street. Master of the Company of Stationers in 1772. Died 1774. [Arber, V, p. lxix.]

JENOUR (MATTHEW), 1797–86. *See Dictionary*, 1668–1725. Became Master of the Stationers' Company in 1769, and died in 1786. [Nichols, III. 727.]

JEPHSON (CHARLES), printer and bookseller in London, next door to the Vine and Rummer tavern in West Smithfield, 1736–48. Printer of the *Weekly Miscellany* (Hooker's), 1735. Was perhaps related to the Rev. Alex. Jephson, rector of Craike in the diocese of Durham, whose *Discourse concerning the . . . observation of the Lord's Day* was published by him March, 1736–7. He printed for J. Hodges, of the Looking-Glass on London Bridge, *The History of the Life and Adventures of Don Alphonso Blas*, in 1742, and in 1748 the second edition of *The Young Mathematician's Companion*, an octavo of 354 pages, containing many diagrams and numerals. His name occurs at the end of these books.

JOB (DANIEL), stationer in London, Spread Eagle in King Street, opposite Bedford Street, Covent Garden, *c.* 1750. Issued a trade card. Probably succeeded by John Bramley, who is found at the same address about 1760. [A. Heal's Collection.]

JOHNSON ( ), bookbinder in London, 1726 (?). In a catalogue of books issued by L. Davis and C. Reymer in 1768 occurs this entry: "4748. Spectator, printed in 16 vols. large print, elegantly bound by Johnson £2 8*s.* 1724."

JOHNSON ( ), bookseller in Maidstone, Kent, 1737. Publisher of the *Gentleman and Builder's Repository*, 1737.

JOHNSON (A.), bookseller in London, Westminster Hall, 1759. Miss Robson, assistant librarian of the John Carter Brown Library, Providence, R. I., sends the following title: "J. J. *Candid Reflections on the Expedition to Martinico* . . . London: Printed for A. Johnson in Westminster Hall, M.DCC.LIX. (Price one shilling.)"

JOHNSON (ANDREW), bookseller in Birmingham. *See Dictionary*, 1668–1725. He died in June 1729. See A. L. Reade, *Reades of Blackwood Hill*, 1906, pp. 217 sqq., also J. Hill, *Bookmakers and Booksellers of Birmingham*.

JOHNSON (E.) and Co., booksellers and publishers in London, (1) Old State Lottery Offices, No. 4 Ludgate Hill, 1776 (?); (2) Ludgate Place, 1793 (?)–1796. Publishers of a collection of songs called *The Lottery Song Book*, about 1776. [B.M. 11641. b. 42.] A much larger edition appeared in 1777. E. Johnson was also the proprietor of a Sunday newspaper, *E. Johnson's British Gazette and Sunday Monitor*, the first number of which is believed to have been published some time in the year 1779. It was still alive at the beginning of the nineteenth century.

JOHNSON (JOSEPH), bookseller and publisher in London, (1) Paternoster Row, 1760–70; (2) St. Paul's Churchyard, 1770–1809. 1760–1809. One of the leading booksellers and publishers in London in the second half of the eighteenth century. He was the son of a farmer at Everton near Liverpool, and was born November 15th, 1738. He was apprenticed to George Keith, a bookseller in London, and at the expiration of his time set up for himself at the Golden Anchor in Fenchurch Street, in partnership with a B. Davenport, and issued from that address a pamphlet entitled *Free and Candid Thoughts on the Doctrine of Predestination*, by T. E. His shop became the head-quarters of the bookselling of Protestant Dissent. He dissolved partnership with Davenport about 1768 and joined John Payne. Their premises in Paternoster Row were totally destroyed by fire in 1770. Friends came to Johnson's relief, and he set up again in St. Paul's Churchyard. He is best remembered as the publisher of William Cowper's *Poems*. The poet had a very warm regard for him and spoke highly of his help. The volume was published in octavo at the price of three shillings. Johnson was opposed to the growing taste for luxurious books, which had enhanced the price and formed an obstacle to the study of good literature. Johnson was also publisher for the Rev. John Newton, Dr. Priestly, Horne Tooke, Maria Edgeworth, and Erasmus Darwin. He was a very sympathetic and generous man, often purchasing manuscripts of persons in distress, which he had no intention of publishing. He encouraged Fuseli to paint a Milton Gallery to be published after the manner of Boydell's *Shakespeare*. In 1797 he suffered for his faith, being imprisoned for nine months in the King's Bench for publishing the political works of Gilbert Wakefield. After a long illness he died on December 20th, 1809. His life was written by J. Aitken in the *Gentleman's Magazine*. [Timperley, 1842, p. 835; Knight, *Shadows*, n.d.]

JOHNSON (MARY), bookseller in Manchester, 1738. Mentioned in list of provincial booksellers. [*N. & Q.* 11 S. I. 364.]

JOHNSON (MICHAEL), bookseller in Lichfield, 1685–1731. *See Dictionary*, 1668–1725; also Hill's *Boswell*, i. 79 sqq.; A. L. Reade's *Gleanings* and *Reades of Blackwood Hill*, *passim*; and *N. & Q.* 7 S. IV. 403.

JOHNSON (NATHANAEL), bookseller in Lichfield, son of Michael Johnson. Died 1737. *See* Hill's *Boswell*, i. 90, and Johnson's *Letters*, i. 84. [The letters signed Ball and Walmesley do not relate to the Lichfield Johnsons; but the receipts signed Nath. and Sarah Johnson are authentic. L. F. P.]

JOHNSON (SARAH), widow of Michael Johnson, bookseller in Lichfield, 1737–49. Her name occurs among the country subscribers to the *Harleian Miscellany*, 1744, and in 1749 in a list of booksellers who were distributing the sale catalogues of Thos. Warren, the bookseller of Birmingham. [*Northampton Mercury*.] She died aged 90, Jan. 1759.

JOHNSON (THOMAS), printer in Liverpool, Crowder Court, Water Street, 1775 (or earlier)–7. Mentioned in the *Liverpool Directory* of 1777. He was also a member of the firm of Thomas Johnson and Co., printers, in Fenwick Alley.

JOHNSON (THOMAS), bookseller at Rotterdam, 1735. Advertised in *The Craftsman* of March 22nd, 173[illegible]: Bishop Burnet's *History*, 3 vols.; sold for 7*s*. 6*d*. Milton's *Poetical Works* in two pocket volumes, "with a new sett of pretty cutts and Mr. Addison's Notes, for five shillings." There was also a T. Johnson, near Christ's Hospital in Newgate Street, issuing pamphlets in 1742.

JOHNSTON (WILLIAM), bookseller in London, Golden Ball, St. Paul's Churchyard, 1748–73. One of the foremost booksellers and publishers in London. He boasted that his name was on three-quarters of the books in the trade as part proprietor. He began business in the year 1748 by purchasing the stock of John Clarke, with his copyrights, which cost him £3,000. In partnership for a time with George Robinson. Johnston retired from business in 1773, and in 1774 gave evidence before a Committee of the House of Commons respecting copyright.

JOLLYFFE (JOHN), bookseller and publisher in London, (1) St. James's Street; (2) Pall Mall. 1731–76. Dealer in pamphlets, the earliest met with being *An Appeal to the Nation*, 1731. In 1735 he was taking subscriptions for Otway's *The Orphan*, in Pall Mall. [*Daily Journal*, February 4th, 1735.] In 1741 his name is found in the imprint of a pamphlet, *A Geographical and Historical Description of the Principal Objects of the Present War in the West Indies*, 1741, 8vo [B.M. E. 2032]. In 1749 he was the publisher of the Rev. William Henry's *Sermon*, preached on the occasion of the Thanksgiving. [B.M. 225. f. 19 (19).] He was one of the partners in the publication of *The Court and City Register* in

1753 [*Public Advertiser*, January 12th, 1753], and also in 1775 [*Ib.*, January 27th, 1775]. His name is found in Kent's *Directory* for 1776. He was for a time in partnership with J. Jackson (*q. v.*).

JONES (J.), bookseller and publisher in London, Old Palace Yard, Westminster, 1729. Publisher of plays. In 1729 he issued *Hurlothrumbo, Or the Super-Natural. As it is acted at the New-Theatre in the Hay-Market. Written by Samuel Johnson from Cheshire.* [W. M. C., May 1729.]

JONES (MICHAEL), bookseller in Brecon, 1772. Mentioned in an advertisement of books and patent medicines in the *British Chronicle or Pugh's Hereford Journal*, September 3rd, 1772.

JONES (WILLIAM), bookseller and publisher in Coventry, 1774. Publisher with others of J. Jones's *Remarks on the English Language*, Birmingham, 1774, 4to. [B.M. 12316. f. 25 (2).]

JOPSON (JAMES), printer in Coventry, (1) Hay Lane; (2) over against the Black Bull Inn, in High Street; Northampton, Gold Street. 1741–59. Printer and publisher of the *Coventry Mercury, or the Weekly Coventry Journal*, the first number of which appeared on Monday, July 20th, 1741. The title was altered in 1743 to *Jopson's Coventry and Northampton Mercury, or the Weekly Coventry Journal.* At the death of Mr. Jopson in 1759, the paper was continued by his widow. It is now known as *The Coventry Standard.* [Information supplied by an undated pamphlet called *The Coventry Standard, a short account of its development from . . . 1741 to the present time.*] Probably the J. Jopson who in 1741 published J. Barker's *Twelve Songs*, issued in that year, fol. [R. A. Peddie.]

JORDAINE (JOHN), printer, Millbrook, 1756. His name is found in the imprint of a bill.

JOYNSON (PETER), printer in Chester, 1747. Mentioned in the Poll-Book for that year.

KEARSLEY (GEORGE), bookseller and publisher in London, (1) Golden Lion, Ludgate Street; (2) Fleet Street, opposite Fetter Lane [Johnson's Head, Fleet Street, or 46 Fleet Street] (1773–6). 1758–97. Publisher of pamphlets from about the year 1758. He was also the publisher of John Wilkes's notorious periodical *The North Briton.* He was arrested with several others for issuing No. 45, but was discharged. In 1773 he removed from Ludgate Hill to Fleet Street and

was still there in 1776. [Timperley, 1842, pp. 710–13.] He published *The Beauties of Johnson* in 1781, and the ninth edition (1797) bears his name among others. In some of his imprints he gave as his address, "No. 46, near Sergeants Inn in Fleet Street", which probably was the same as "opposite Fetter Lane". Issued an engraved trade card showing St. Dunstan's Church and Temple Bar. [A. Heal's Collection.]

KEATING ( ), bookseller in Stratford-on-Avon, 1749–72. His name occurs in a list of those distributing the sale catalogue of T. Warren of Birmingham, in 1749, and in the imprint to the Rev. Talbot's *Narrative of the Proceedings relative to Jonathan Britain.* Bristol [1772]. [B.M. 1093. b. 60.]

KEATING (HENRY), bookbinder in London, 1743. Was concerned in publishing the pamphlet called *Old England's Te Deum*, but refused to give sureties on the ground of inability to find any one to go bail for him. He was therefore committed to Newgate in November 1743. [S. P. Dom. Geo. II, Bundle 62. 59 c.]

KEEPING ( ), (?) bookseller in Frome, Somerset, 1747. Mentioned in an advertisement of the second edition of Stackhouse's *Bible* in 1747.

KEITH (GEORGE), bookseller and publisher in London, (1) in Mercers' Chapel, Cheapside; (2) Bible and Crown in Gracechurch Street. 1749–75. An extensive publisher of religious tracts who may have been a descendant of the Rev. Geo. Keith the controversialist. It is also possible that he was apprentice to John Marshall the bookseller, whose address was the Bible in Gracechurch Street, and who published one at least of the Rev. Geo. Keith's books. George Keith's name is also found in the imprints to two secular works, the first published in 1749 and entitled *A Letter to the Author of an Examination of the Principles; and an Enquiry into the Conduct of the Two B—rs*; the other, printed in 1762, and entitled "*Poems on several subjects. . . .* By John Ogilvie A.M." [Winship.] He married a daughter of Rev. John Gill, D.D. One of his apprentices was Joseph Johnson the noted bookseller in St. Paul's Churchyard. In the John Carter Brown Library is a copy of the Rev. J. Gill's *A Reply to the Defence of the Divine Right of Infant Baptism, by Peter Clark . . .*, which has at the end two lists of books: (1) Books written by John Gill, D.D., and sold by G. Keith . . . ; (2) Books printed and sold by G. Keith. He was still publishing in 1777.

KELLINGTON (THOMAS), printer in Wakefield, 1758. Mr. Allnutt says he was a freeman of York in 1758. [*Bibliographica*, II. 307.]

KELT (RICHARD), bookseller in London, the Poultry, 1744. Name found in imprint of a sermon, 1744.

KENDALL (JOHN), senior and junior, booksellers and publishers in Colchester, Essex, 1736–73. In 1736, in conjunction with H. Boad, of the same town, the elder Kendall's name occurs as agent for the sale of *A New English Accidence.* He was also the publisher of a sermon by Richard Canning, M.A., minister of St. Lawrence, Ipswich, preached December 18th, 1745, on the occasion of the Rebellion. [B.M. 225. f. 13 (7).] In 1749 John Kendall, junior, and Thomas Kendall advertised in the *Ipswich Journal.* It was probably John Kendall, junior, who sold *The New and Easy Method to learn French*, written by Claude Gay in 1773, noticed in Smith's *Catalogue of Quaker Books.*

KENDALL (THOMAS), bookseller and publisher in Colchester, near the Red Lyon, 1749–73. In partnership with John Kendall, junior (*q. v.*). He is mentioned in a list of provincial booksellers as still in business in 1773. [*N. & Q.* 11 S. I. 304.]

KENT (HENRY), printer and publisher in London, Finch Lane, near the Royal Exchange, 1732 (?)–1771 (?). This printer is best remembered for his *Directory for the City of London*, which he began to publish in 1732, and which held its position until ousted by *Kelly's Post Office Directory.* About 1750 Kent succeeded Elizabeth James as printer to the City of London. Amongst other work from his press was a translation from Cervantes, entitled *Two Humorous Novels.* The translation was made by Robert Goadby (*q. v.*), and was printed for Ward and Chandler in 1741. Kent became a member of the Common Council, and was deputy for the Ward of Broad Street. He is believed to have retained the office of City Printer until 1771. His business passed to Henry Causton (*q. v.*). [C. Welch, *The City Printers*, p. 52.]

KERBY (JOHN), bookseller in London, Bond Street. Died November 11th, 1803. [Nichols, III. 727.]

KEYMER (H.), bookseller and publisher at Colchester, co. Essex, 1764. This name occurs in the imprint to a sermon entitled *The Principles of Christianity*, preached by the Rev. Thomas Bowman, Vicar of Martham, co. Norfolk, 1764. The initial may be a misprint for R. or W. Keymer (*q. v.*).

KEYMER (ROBERT), bookseller and publisher in Hadleigh, co. Suffolk, and Colchester, co. Essex, 1750 (?)–1776 (?). The Keymer family seem to have been settled in Colchester in the seventeenth century. Robert Keymer was doubtless a member of this family, several of whom followed the trade of booksellers and publishers at the "Bible and Star" near the White Hart Inn in St. Peter's parish. Together with William Keymer, possibly his son or brother, his name occurs in the imprint of the *Seventeen Sermons* of Nath. Torriano, Rector of Aldham, 1767. [B.M. 4455. g. 14; R. A. Peddie, *Library World*, September 1904.] In 1768 he began publishing a Memorandum or Pocket Book annually. He was still in business in 1771. Robert Keymer had a branch shop at Hadleigh in Suffolk, and was advertising in the *Ipswich Journal* as early as 1750. [Notes supplied by G. Rickword, Librarian, Colchester Public Library.]

KEYMER (WILLIAM), bookseller and publisher in Colchester, co. Essex, Bible and Star, near the White Hart, 1750–1813. Believed to have been the son of Robert; was born in 1731, and was advertising sales of books at the Colchester Moot Hall as early as 1750. In 1760 a William Keymer, probably the same, aged 28, of St. Peter's parish, had license to marry Ann Edwards, 30, of St. Runwald's parish. Keymer held sales of books at Wallace's Coffee House, and added to his bookselling business that of a chemist. In 1761 he published P. Bernard's *Examples of the Ancient Sages*. [*Public Advertiser*, January 1st, 1761.] He continued the Hadleigh business until 1762. In 1764 he was agent for the sale of Dr. Collignon's *Enquiry into the Structure of the Human Body*, and in 1767, in company with Robert Keymer (*q. v.*), possibly his father or brother, he published the *Seventeen Sermons* of the Rev. Nath. Torriano, Rector of Aldham in Suffolk. [B.M. 4455. g. 14; R. A. Peddie, *Library World*, September 1904.] In 1765 he moved to St. Runwald's parish to premises said to have belonged to the Keymer family for one hundred years. He died May 29th, 1813, aged 82. [Notes supplied by G. Rickword, Librarian, Colchester Public Library.] He was succeeded in business by his son, W. K., junior, on whose retirement in 1821 it passed into other hands.

KING (CHARLES), bookseller in London, Judge's Head in Westminster Hall, 1707–35. *See Dictionary*, 1668–1725. Dissolved partnership with Benjamin Barker (*q.v.*), but they shared in books as, in 1733, their names both appear in the advertisement of *The Travels of the Chevalier Darvieux*. [*London Evening Post*, February 8th–10th, 1733.] Charles King died in 1735. His daughter married Joseph Fox, junior. [*Craftsman*, October 18th, 1735.]

KING (JOHN), bookseller in London, Moorfields, *c.* 1760. Nichols says of him that he "made the curiosity of his customers a foundation of a collection for his own use, and refused to part with an article where he found an eagerness in a purchaser to have it". [*Lit. Anecd.* III. 625.] His stock of books was sold by Baker in 1760.

KING (T.), bookseller and publisher in London, near Bethlehem, Moorfields, 1768. Possibly son and successor of John King (*q. v.*). In 1768 he published for Charles Frederick, Esq., a collection of verse which he called "Idalian buds", and this, under the title of *Idalia, or, the Utile dulci*, was to be continued occasionally, and contributions for it were to be sent to the author at the above address. [B.M. 643. m. 16 (25).]

KING (WILLIAM), (?) printer in London, 1728. Apprentice with Nathaniel Mist, printer. Committed for being concerned with the printing of *Mist's Journal* of August 24th, 1728. [S. P. Dom. Geo. II, Bundle 8. 74.]

KINNERSLEY (THOMAS), publisher in London, 1758. Publisher of the *Grand Magazine*, the first number of which appeared on August 1st, 1758. In this he reprinted large extracts from Johnson's *Rasselas*, and was sued by Robert Dodsley for doing so. [Straus, *Robert Dodsley*.]

KIPPAX (   ), printer in London, Cullum Street, 1760 (?). Amongst his apprentices was William Baker, printer, who succeeded to his business. [Nichols, III. 715.]

KIRGATE (THOMAS), printer, Strawberry Hill Press, 1765–89. Was taken on by Horace Walpole on March 18th, 1765, and proved the best and most reliable of his printers, most of the later issues of the press bearing his imprint. [*Journal of the Printing-office at Strawberry Hill*. With notes by Paget Toynbee, M.A., 1923.] *See* Strawberry Hill Press.

KNAPLOCK (ROBERT), *see Dictionary*, 1668–1725.

KNAPP (G.), bookseller in Peterborough, co. Hunts., 1767. Mentioned in a list of provincial booksellers as in business in 1767. [*N. & Q.* 10 S. v. 242.] In 1768 his name occurs in the imprint to a *Sermon* preached by the Bishop of Peterborough before the House of Lords. [B.M. 694. i. 18 (12).] In 1769 he had on sale a book by John Harrison, botanist, entitled *A New Method of making the Banks of the Fens impregnable*, which was advertised in the newspapers. Copies of this book are scarce.

KNAPTON (JAMES), *see Dictionary*, 1668–1725.

KNAPTON (JOHN), and (PAUL), booksellers and publishers in London, (1) The Crown, St. Paul's Churchyard; (2) Crown in Ludgate Street. 1735–1770 (?). Brothers to James Knapton (1687–1736), and successors to his business. This eminent firm were connected with the chief publications of the day. George Vertue, the engraver, whose works they published, complained that after making large sums of money by him, they employed cheaper men and tried to jockey him out of the business. [Add. MSS. 23089, ff. 68, 69.] In the *Daily Courant* of January 3rd, 1735, is an advertisement of *Monuments of Kings of England*, printed for James, John, and Paul Knapton, the Crown in Ludgate Street. John Knapton died in 1770. [Nichols, III. 607.] On February 14th, 174$\frac{0}{1}$, Paul Knapton married a Miss Elizabeth Chalwell, of Coleman Street, at Stevenage in Herts. [*Daily Press*.] John Knapton was Master of the Stationers' Company in 1742, 1743, and 1745.

KNELL (ROBERT), printer in London, 1728. One of the workmen employed by Nathaniel Mist, printer. Committed for printing the issue of *Mist's Journal* of August 24th, 1728. [S. P. Dom. Geo. II, Bundle 8. 74.] He was sentenced to the pillory.

KNOX (JOHN), bookseller in London, The Strand, 1740 (?)–1775. Born in Scotland in 1720. Became a bookseller in London and amassed a fortune. After his retirement he devoted himself to philanthropic work in connexion with his native country. He made certain proposals for the improvement of the Fisheries, which he published in 1784. He died at Dalkeith, near Edinburgh, on August 1, 1790.

LA BUTTE (RENÉ), a native of Angers in Anjou, came to England as a printer, and was with Bowyer of London. Composed Wm. Gardiner's *Tables of Logarithms*, 1742. Went to Cambridge with Walker and James (*q. v.*) who began in 1744 the *Cambridge Journal*, the first newspaper issued in Cambridge. Through Dr. Conyers Middleton he was established as a French teacher in Cambridge, and continued with great success till the time of his death in 1790. [Bowes, *Cambridge Books*, no. 748.] The University printed the second edition of his *French Grammar* in 1790. His nephew, N. H. Lunn, was a Cambridge bookseller and removed to London in 1797, where, having inherited a fortune from his uncle, La Butte, he engaged in the publication and sale of Classical books, which unfortunately, owing to the disturbed times, proved his ruin. He died in 1815, and Dr. Samuel Parr wrote a notice of him in the *New Monthly Magazine*.

LACKINGTON (JAMES), bookseller in London, (1) Featherstone Street, 1774; (2) Chiswell Street, 1775–6. This remarkable man was born at Wellington, in co. Somerset, in 1746. His parents were poor, his father, a journeyman shoemaker by trade, being an habitual drunkard. With no schooling, he began life by selling pies for a local baker, and to this he joined the sale of almanacks. At the age of fourteen he was apprenticed to a shoemaker at Taunton. He joined the Methodists, and often rose soon after midnight in the winter in order to attend their meetings. Although he could not write and could only read with difficulty, he composed songs, which were printed, and sold in the streets of Bristol. In 1770 he married, and he then moved to London; but his wife was in poor health and their poverty was such that they often lived on potatoes. In June 1774 he opened a shop in the parish of St. Luke as a shoemaker and bookseller, his stock of books consisting of a bagful which he had bought for a guinea. In 1775 his wife died, but he soon married again, and from that time success attended him in everything he undertook. His subsequent career does not fall within the limits of this volume, but it may be briefly summarized. His principle was to sell everything cheap and to do no business except for cash. He became a rich man, and in 1791 published his *Memoirs* which reached their eighth edition in three years. In 1798 he retired, making over his business to his cousin George Lackington. In some respects He resembled John Dunton, both in his shrewdness and outspoken opinions of his brother booksellers. He died in November 1815. Mr. Ambrose Heal has a number of trade cards, some of them showing the Temple of the Muses from both inside and out.

LACY (JAMES), bookseller and publisher in London, Ship between the Temple-gates, 1726–32. Dealer in law books. In 1726 he published *The Compleat Clerk in Court*. [W. M. C., February.] He died in 1732.

LACY (J.), bookseller and publisher in London, the corner of St. Martin's Court, St. Martin's Lane, near Leicester Fields, 1757–65. In 1757 he published the *Trial of . . . Admiral Byng*, and other pamphlets on the same subject. He was selling a medical book in 1765. [*Gazetteer and New Daily Advertiser*, July 2nd, 1765.]

LACY (J.), bookseller and publisher in Northampton, in the Drapery, from some time before 1776. Probably in business some years earlier than 1776, in which year he issued a prospectus for P. Whalley's *History of Northamptonshire*, a work based on the collections of Dr. John Bridges. The work did not appear until 1791, and it then bore J. Lacy's name in the imprint.

LANE (ISAAC) & Co., printers, in Newcastle-upon-Tyne, 1734–6. Head of the Side, Durham, 1740 (?). Shared with Leonard Umfreville the printing of *The North Country Journal; or, Impartial Intelligencer,* which began to appear in 1734. In 1735 the company printed a sermon by the Rev. J. Thompson, preached in St. John's Church, Newcastle, upon the death of Lady Jane Clavering. [Welford, p. 64.] Shortly afterwards Lane removed to Durham, where about 1740 he printed Bishop Chandler's *Visitation Articles.*

LANE (WILLIAM), printer and publisher in London, (1) Minerva printing office; (2) Leadenhall Street. 1763 (?)–1814. Timperley [p. 853] says that he published novels and was instrumental in the establishment of circulating libraries throughout the country. "No man knew the world better, and none better how to manage and enjoy it." Lane died in March 1814. His name occurs as a bookseller in Leadenhall Street in Kent's *London Directory* of 1776. In the *Gentleman's Magazine* for 1774 his name occurs as publisher of Hugh Stopley's *Christiani Cultus,* but no copy of that work has been seen. Bill-head and trade card, the former dated 1793. [A. Heal's Collection.]

LANGFORD (C.), *see* Langford (J.)

LANGFORD (J.), pamphlet seller in London, pamphlet shop opposite St. Clement's Church in the Strand [or] successor to Mrs. Dodd, bookseller opposite St. Clement's Church in the Strand, 1756–65. The only pamphlet traceable to him was *The Genuine Defence of Admiral Byng,* advertised in the *Public Advertiser* in February 1757. In the same paper there is a mention of a C. Langford of Temple Bar as publisher of *The Genuine Memoirs of the Life and Adventures of Robert Francis Damien,* and of T. Langford at the Peacock in the Strand as publishing Admiral Byng's speech. As Mrs. Anne Dodd's address was "the Peacock, near Temple Bar", it is highly probable that the changes of initials and the variants in the address were made to deceive the authorities, unless it can be proved that C. J. and T. Langford were members of the same family. Langford, bookseller, Strand, is advertised as selling "An Ode to the People of England" in 1765. [*Gazetteer and New Daily Advertiser,* August 12th, 1765.]

LANGFORD (T.), *see* Langford (J.)

LARKIN ( ), see Osborne (W.)

LATHROP (RICHARD), printer and bookseller in Shrewsbury, 1739–47. A correspondent in *Shropshire Notes and Queries* of May 6th, 1898, says that the booksellers and stationers of the city were affiliated to the Sadlers' Company. He gives a list of the booksellers, in which Richard Lathrop is stated to have paid 17*s.* 4*d.*, perhaps for his admission, on June 22nd, 1739. His name is found in the imprint to a sermon preached by the Rev. Matthew Horbery at St. Chad on October 1st, 1747. [B.M. 225. f. 16 (3); *N. & Q.* 11 S. I. 364.]

LAW (BEDWELL), bookseller and publisher in London, Ave Maria Lane, 1756–98. In 1756 he was one of the partners in an edition of the works of Ben Jonson. He died May 25th, 1798, and was succeeded in business by his son Charles Law. [Nichols, III. 422.]

LAW (JOHN), bookseller and publisher in London, St. Martin's Churchyard, 1763. Shared with John Rivington the copyright of two poems by George Coryate of Salisbury, entitled *Descriptio Angliae,* 1763. [B.M. 577. h. 26 (4).]

LAWRENCE (MONTAGUE), stationer in London, at the Globe near Durham Yard in the Strand, *c.* 1770. Issued a trade card about this time. [A. Heal.]

LAWTON (JOHN), bookseller and publisher in Chester, 1767–71. Two items published by him have been found. The first is *Il Penseroso, an evening contemplation in St. John's Church-yard, Chester,* 1767, of which there is a copy in Harvard College. [Winship.] The second is a sketch of the materials for a *New History of Chester,* 1771. [*N. & Q.* 10 S. XII. 128.]

LAYLAND ( ), bookseller in Wigan, co. Lanc., 1738. Agent for Daffy's "Elixer". [J. P. Earwaker, *Local Gleanings,* I. 237.]

LEACH (DRYDEN), printer in London, 1759–63. Son and successor to Francis Leach, of Eliot's Court. He had large interests in several newspapers, and on December 10th, 1763, obtained a verdict and £300 damages from three of the king's messengers for taking him into custody as the supposed printer of Wilkes's famous paper, no. 45 of *The North Briton.* There were altogether twelve actions commenced by various printers and printers' journeymen in connexion with the action of the Crown, but Timperley says that this verdict determined all the rest. The whole damages amounted to £2,000. His name also occurs in the imprint of Wanley's *Catalogue of the Harleian Collection of Manuscripts* [Timperley], and of Capell's *Prolusions* (1760).

LEACROFT (SAMUEL), bookseller and publisher in London, the Globe, Charing Cross, 1771–6. Successor to Charles Marsh (*q. v.*). Was previously in the employ of Lockyer Davis Publisher of miscellaneous literature. He died in 1795. [Nichols, III. 646.]

LEAGE (J.), (? pamphlet seller) in London, opposite the Queen's Head in the Great Old Bailey, 1753. His name occurs in the imprint to a pamphlet entitled *Some Considerations on the Naturalization of the Jews,* 1753, 8vo. [B.M. T. 2231.13.]

LEAKE (HENRY) I, bookseller and publisher in Bath (*c.* 1720). In an article on Bath booksellers, Mr. R. E. M. Peach says that there were two brothers, Henry and Samuel Leake, booksellers, in that city at the beginning of the eighteenth century, and that Henry was the father of James Leake (*q. v.*).

LEAKE (HENRY) II, bookseller and publisher in Bath, son of James Leake, the elder, born 1741. He was evidently a partner in 1764 of his brothers James and Samuel (*Bath Chron,* Nov. 22, 1764, advt.). In 1766 he published Underwood's *Poems,* printed by W. Archer.

LEAKE (JAMES) I, bookseller and publisher in Bath, 1724 (?)–1764. Son of John Leake, of London (see *N. & Q.* 12 S. XI. 224–5). Began business as a publisher in Bath about the year 1724, when his name is found in the imprint to Dr. George Cheyne's *Essay of Health and Long Life.* He followed this up with Guidot's *Treatise on the Bath Waters* in 1725. For many years he shared with Frederick the position of leading bookseller in Bath, and his name is usually found in the imprints of the most notable books published there. On April 23rd, 1721, the Bath Abbey Registers record the marriage by license of James Leake to Hannah Hammon, or Hammond, possibly a daughter or sister of one of the two Hammonds, booksellers of Bath between 1695–1721. Leake may possibly have succeeded to their business. He died on May 29th, 1764, aged 79, and was succeeded by his son, James Leake, junior. One of the visitors to Bath left this unflattering description of James Leake: "He is the Prince of all the Coxcomical fraternity of booksellers; and not having any learning himself, he seems to be resolved to sell it as dear as possible to others." [Letter from the Earl of Ossory to Councillor Kemp, Hist. MSS. Comm.]

LEAKE (JAMES) II, bookseller and publisher in Bath, 1765 (?)–1790. Son of James Leake, the elder. Born May 29th, 1724. Succeeded to his father's business. Married the daughter of C. Hitch, 4 Apr. 1765 [*Gent. Mag.*] Elected Sheriff in 1772, Alderman in 1781, and Mayor in 1783. The business eventually passed to Lewis Bull (*q. v.*).

LEAKE (JOHN), printer in London, Angell Street, St. Martin's-le-Grand, 1745–8. On April 9th, 1745, he was ordered into custody for publishing obscene literature, and on being examined said that the first books he ever printed he printed for David Lynch living in New Street near Shoe Lane. The book for which he was then being questioned he said was printed by Thomas Harper, and published by Thomas Read printer. [S. P. Dom. Geo. II, Bundle 65. 85.] John Leake was employed in 1748 to print 1000 orders of General Quarter Sessions, respecting the rates for maintaining vagabonds. [*Middlesex Session Records,* vol. lix, p. 87.]

LEAKE (SAMUEL), bookseller in Bath, *c.* 1726. Son of James Leake, the elder, born 1739; in partnership in 1764 with his brothers Henry and James.

LEDSHAM (THOMAS), bookseller and publisher in Chester, 1746–9. His name is found in the imprint to a Sermon preached at Lancaster on July 31st, 1746, on the occasion of the Assize, by the Rev. William Smith. [B.M. 225. f. 16 (9).] In 1749 he was one of those who distributed the Sale Catalogues of T. Warren, bookseller of Birmingham.

LEE (ARTHUR), printer at Lewes in Sussex, 1745. Joined with William Lee (*q. v.*) in printing and publishing the *Sussex Weekly Advertiser.* [*Notes on Sussex Printing,* by A. C. Piper, *Library,* July 1914, 3rd Ser., V., pp. 261 *et seq.*]

LEE (J.), bookseller at Chichester, 1749. Mentioned in a list of provincial booksellers. [*N. & Q.* 10 S. V, February 24th, 1906, p. 142.]

LEE (JOSEPH), bookseller and bookbinder in Lynn and Swaffham, co. Suffolk, Lynn (next door to the White Lyon), 1749. His name is found in an advertisement in the *Ipswich Journal,* February 11th, 174$\frac{8}{9}$.

LEE (WILLIAM), printer and publisher in Lewes, co. Sussex, 1745–56. The *Sussex Weekly Advertiser* for the year 1745 was printed by William and Arthur Lee. [*Notes on Sussex Printing,* by A. C. Piper, *Library,* July 1914, 3rd Ser., V., pp. 257 *et seq.*] In 1756 William Lee's name is found in the imprint to the sermons preached by the Rev. Nathaniel Torriano, on the occasion of a public fast.

LEECH (J.), bookseller and publisher in Knutsford, co. Cheshire, 1753–6. His name appears with that of J. Shipton in the imprint to the Rev. John Holland's *Sermons and Prayers* . . . London, 1753. [B.M. 4455. aaa. 2.] In 1756 he was agent for the sale of Schofield's *Middlewich Journal or Cheshire Advertiser.*

LEES (RICHARD), bookbinder in Manchester, 1738. Mr. R. W. Procter, in his *Memorials of Manchester Streets*, p. 196, states that his name is found in the register of the Collegiate Church in 1738.

LEGASSICKE (R.), bookseller in Totnes, Devon, 1739. Sold the *Sermons* of Prebendary Z. Mudge, but his name is not found in the imprints.

LEIGH (GEORGE), bookseller and book auctioneer in London, York Street, Covent Garden. In 1774 he was taken into partnership by Samuel Baker the elder. On Baker's death in 1778 he carried on the business alone till 1780, when Baker's nephew, John Sotheby, joined him. He died in 1815. Nichols, in his *Literary Anecdotes*, III. 630, has left this portrait of him: "This genuine disciple of *the elder Sam* is still (1812) at the head of his profession. . . . His pleasant disposition, his skill and his integrity, are as well known as his famous *snuff-box*, described by Mr. Dibdin as having a not less imposing air than the remarkable periwig of Sir Fopling of old . . . When a high priced book is balancing between £15 and £20 it is a fearful signal of its reaching an additional sum, if Mr. Leigh should lay down his hammer, and delve into this said crumple-horn-shaped snuff-box."

LENTHALL (JOHN), stationer, London, at the Talbot and Buck near St. Dunstan's Church, Fleet Street, 1728. He advertised *Fine Pictures in Cards* in the *London Journal*, January 3rd, 1728.

LEPARD (W.), bookseller in London, (1) Hand and Bible, Battlebridge; (2) Tooley Street, second house from the Bridge Foot. 1758–66. Between these dates his name is found in the imprints of the works of the Rev. John Gill, preacher at Horsleydown. The two addresses may refer to the same house. Issued trade cards. [A. Heal's Collection.]

LEVER (JOHN), printer, publisher, and printseller in London, at Little Moorgate, next to London Wall, near Moorfields, 1765–70. A publisher of some curious literature. He published in 1765 *The Husband forced to be Jealous*. [*Gazetteer and Daily Advertiser*, July 27th, 1765.] In 1766 he reprinted *The Legend of Captain Jones*, a poetical satire, no doubt directed at Captain John Smith, which had been composed by one David Lloyd and printed more than a century before, the first edition being dated 1631. It had gone through several editions since then and a second part dealing with an imaginary voyage by the Captain to Patagonia had been added. Miss Robson, of the John Carter Brown library in Providence, Rhode Island, states that their copy has at the end two pages and a half containing a list of books printed and sold by John Lever. The

two leaves are missing from the copy in the British Museum. Lever was also the printer of another work, *The Strange Voyage and Adventures of Domingo Gonsales*, in 1768. At the end of this is a list of fifteen books, including works on architecture and gardening, as well as the second edition of Thevenot's *Art of Swimming*. [B.M. 635. e. 31.] In 1770 he published the second edition of the *Life of Ambrose Gwineth*. [B.M. T. 1090 (7).]

LEWIS (JOHN), printer in London, Bartholomew Close, 1746–54. Reprinted in 1746 a sermon preached at the South Church in Boston, N.E., by the Rev. Thomas Prince in July 1745. [B.M. 225. f. 14 (9).] In 1754 there was a firm of J. & J. Lewis printing for the Dodsleys.

LEWIS (M.), printer and publisher in London, 1 Paternoster Row, 1756–76. Printer to the Moravians. In 1756 appeared the Rev. John Gambold's sermon preached at the Brethren's Chapel in Fetter Lane, on the Fast Day, with the imprint: "London, Printed, and sold at the Brethren's Chapels, and by M. Lewis in Paternoster Row, near Cheapside, 1756. [Price Four-pence.]" On the last page of this is a list of eight other publications of the United Brethren. Amongst miscellaneous books and pamphlets printed at this press may be noticed: *The second edition of the Old Woman's Loyalty: or, a few lines made on the birth of the Illustrious Prince of Wales*, 1762, and the Rev. A. M. Toplady's attack on John Wesley, *An old Fox tarr'd and feather'd*, by an Hanoverian, 1775. The type and ornaments in these pamphlets was quite ordinary, and the press was probably what would be called a "jobbing" one.

LEWIS (MRS. MARTHA), bookseller in Bristol, on the Tolzey, 1728–47. Her name is found in an advertisement of patent medicine in Farley's *Exeter Journal*, November 8th, 1728. A bookseller of the name of Lewis in Bristol is also mentioned in an advertisement of the second edition of Stackhouse's *Bible* in 1747. Possibly the same as the above.

LEWIS (R.), bookseller in Worcester, 1753–71. His name is first met with in a list of booksellers who sold the London newspaper, the *Daily Register*, in 1753, and again in an advertisement of books in the London press of 1769. He is said to have been still in business in 1771. [*N. & Q.* 11 S. I. 264.]

LEWIS (THOMAS), bookseller in London, Great Russell Street, Covent Garden, 1750 (?)–1802. Son of William Lewis (*q.v.*). Publisher of the *Midnight Rambler*, 1772. Died August 7th, 1802. Timperley says he used to relate that his father was a school-fellow with Alexander Pope [p. 812].

LEWIS (WILLIAM), bookseller in London, Russell Street, Covent Garden, 1709–27. *See Dictionary*, 1668–1725. In 1726 he published a collection of voyages by Captain Robert Boyles [W. M. C., March 1726], and in 1727 was a subscriber to Hearne's *History of Glastonbury*. Succeeded by his son, T. Lewis (*q. v.*).

LEWIS and WHITE, printers in London, Birchin Lane, 1756. Printed for W. Innys and J. Richardson, of Paternoster Row, *Two Sermons*, by the Rev. William Totton, M.A., 1756, 4to. [B.M. 225. I. 6 (4).]

LEY (CHARLES), bookseller in Kelvedon, co. Essex, near the Angel Inn, 1773. Only known from an advertisement in the *Chelmsford Chronicle* of that year.

LICHFIELD (HENRY), printer in Oxford, 1726. Brother of Leonard Lichfield the third (1687–1749). Hearne records that he was married on October 20th, 1726, to — Gillman, widow of Thomas Gillman: both were of the parish of St. Peter's in the East, Oxford. He was aged about 41, she about 61, "both of them peevish, cross people." [Hearne, IX. 211.] His first wife, a Miss Betts, died on April 28th, 1726. [Madan.]

LICHFIELD (LEONARD), III, *see Dictionary*, 1668–1725.

LIGHTFOOT (T.), bookseller in Sunderland, 1760. His name occurs in a list of provincial booksellers. [*N. & Q.* 10 S. VI. 443.]

LINDE (ANDREAS), bookseller and publisher in London, Catherine Street, Strand, 1754–8. Described himself as Bookseller to Her Royal Highness the Princess Dowager of Wales. Amongst his publications was the well-known *Golden Treasury* of C. H. v. Bogatzky, which first appeared in an English form in 1745.

LINDEN (JAMES), printer in Southampton, High Street, 1768–76. Printer of the *Southampton Guide* in 1768. Issued the first newspaper printed in the county, *The Hampshire Chronicle*, the first issue of which appeared in August 1772. [F. A. Edwards, *Early Newspaper Press of Hampshire*, 1889.]

LINDLEY, *see* Lindsey.

LINDSEY, or LINDLEY (JOHN), bookseller in Pontefract, co. York, 1769. His name is found in an advertisement of patent medicines in the *Chelmsford Chronicle* of November 10th, 1769, and also in the *London Chronicle* of that year as one of those by whom E. Moxon's *English Housewifery* was sold.

LINN (JOHN), bookseller in Newcastle-upon-Tyne, 1739. Mentioned by Welford in his List of Printers, Booksellers, &c. [*Early Newcastle Typography*, p. 128.]

LINTOT (BERNARD), *see Dictionary*, 1668–1725.

LINTOT (HENRY), bookseller and publisher in London, Cross Keys, against St. Dunstan's Church in Fleet Street, 1730. The following is mainly extracted from Timperley [p. 703]: Henry Lintot, son of the great London bookseller Bernard Lintot, was born about August 1709, and became a freeman of the Company of Stationers by patrimony on September 1st, 1730, after which he joined his father in the business, on whose death in 1736 he succeeded to the business in London and also became High Sheriff for the county of Sussex. He was twice married, but left no male heirs. In 1739 he published the third edition of John Keill's *Introduction to the true Astronomy*, at the end of which is bound up a fourteen-page catalogue of books printed for Bernard Lintot. In this the titles of the books are given at much greater length than in the second edition of this work which was published by Bernard in 1730, and also contains a few additional titles. This was probably one of a number of remainder copies of this catalogue, which Henry got rid of after his father's death in this way. Henry Lintot died in 1758.

LISTER (J.), bookseller and publisher in Oxford, 1772–3. His name is found in Oxford imprints at this time. [Madan.]

LISTER (JAMES), printer in Leeds, co. York., New Street End, 1736–53. Belonged to the Society of Friends, for whom he printed extensively. He also printed for James Hodgson, the bookseller, the Rev. Thomas Wright's *Antiquities of . . . Halifax*. Lister died in 1753. [*Journal of Friends' Hist. Soc.* V. 60.]

LLOYD (W.), (?) bookseller in London, Chancery Lane, 1738. His name occurs in the imprint to two poetical pieces entitled *The Rival Wives* and *The Rival Wives answer'd*. [B.M. 840. m. 1. (12. 13).]

LOBB (R.), bookseller and publisher in Chelmsford, Essex, 1771. This bookseller was possibly a son of Richard Lobb (d. 1749 ?), but little seems to be known about the family, and nothing certain can be learned as to the connexion between the Lobbs of Chelmsford and those of Bath. Mr. J. A. Howarth, the librarian of the Public Library at Chelmsford, has been unable to trace the name either in the Rate Books or Poll Books of that town. In 1771, R. Lobb and T. Toft of Chelmsford are mentioned in an advertisement of books on sale.

LOBB (RICHARD), bookseller and publisher in Chelmsford, Essex, 1745–9. In the Parish Register of Chelmsford under January 22nd, 1739, is the following entry: "Marriages—Richard Lobb and Frances Greene (lic)." Published several sermons by Nathaniel Ball, Master of the Grammar School in Chelmsford, between 1745 and 1749. Died either in 1749 or 1750, his business being continued by his widow Frances. [*Ipswich Journal*, July 28th, 1750.]

LOBB (SAMUEL), bookseller and publisher in Chelmsford, Essex, and Bath, Somerset, 1728–31. A relative of the Rev. Theophilus Lobb, who, removing into Essex, took with him the children of a brother lately deceased, of whom perhaps this was one. He is first found at Chelmsford in 1728, when he advertised in the *London Journal* of May 4th the Assize Sermon, preached there on March 21st by the Rev. A. A. Sykes. In 1730 he appears to have moved to Bath and his name is found in the Council Book under July 17th, as that of a "bookseller". About this time he published a *Description of Bath*, a poem [B.M. 643. m. 15 (5).] In 1731 he sold the Rev. Theophilus Lobb's *Treatise of the Small-Pox*. The date of his death has not been found.

LONGMAN (THOMAS), bookseller in London, Ship and Black Swan, Paternoster Row, 1726–75. *See Dictionary*, 1668–1725. The firm was carried on after the death of the founder under the same title. The name occurs in numerous advertisements of high-class publications up to 1775. In 1728 the firm was interested in the publication of Chambers's *Encyclopaedia*. Longman's share when it was first published cost £50, and was probably 1/64th part; but he bought up other shares, and by 1740 the Stationers' Book assigns him 11 out of 64 shares, a larger number than was ever held by any other proprietor. On the death of Osborn, his father-in-law, in 1746, Longman took Thomas Shremrell into partnership, but this only lasted two years. In 1754 a nephew, Thomas Longman (II), became a partner, after which the title-pages of their books ran: "Printed for T. & T. Longman at the Ship in Paternoster Row." The firm was associated with Dodsley, Millar, and others in the publication of Johnson's *Dictionary*. On June 10th, 1765, only two months after its publication, Thomas I, the elder, died. He had no children and left half the partnership stock to his nephew, and the rest of his property to his widow. Thomas Longman (II), the nephew, was born in 1731, entered the firm aged 15 as an apprentice, and at his uncle's death was only 25. Under his management the old traditions were kept up, and the business relations with the American Colonies were increased. At the outbreak of War, Longman had a large sum

laid out in that particular business, but several of his correspondents liquidated their debts in full even subsequent to the Peace of 1783. Longman married a Miss Harris and had by her three sons, of whom Thomas Norton Longman, born in 1771, began to take his father's place in the firm about 1792. In 1794 Owen Rees was admitted a member and the title of the firm was altered to Longman & Co. Thomas Longman (II) died February 5th, 1797. [Curwen.]

LORD (   ), bookseller and publisher in Barnsley, Pontefract, and Wakefield, Yorks., 1736–54. In 1736 his name appears in the imprint to a sermon preached by the Rev. John Mawer, and printed by and for Alexander Staples of York, and he was agent for the *York Courant* for many years [Davies, *Hist. of York Press*, pp. 238, 243, 314], but in no instance is his Christian name revealed. In 1754 he advertised Mayleston's "Pectoral Tobacco" as on sale at his shops in Barnsley, Pontefract, and Wakefield.

LOWNDES (THOMAS), bookseller and publisher in Fleet Street, 1756–84. Born 1719. Began business in Fleet Street in 1756. A publisher of plays. Died November 7th, 1784, and was buried in St. Bride's. [Timperley, 1842, p. 752.] A native of Cheshire. He had an extensive circulating library in Fleet Street. He was a strong minded, uneducated man, rough in his manners, but of sterling integrity; and is supposed to have been delineated by Miss Burney in her novel *Cecilia* under the name of Briggs. [Nichols, III. 646.]

LUCKMAN (T.), printer, bookseller, and publisher in Coventry, co. Warwick., 1756 (?)–1776. Amongst his publications during those years were a *Sermon* by the Rev. T. Edwards [1756 ?] [B.M. 225. g. 10 (11)]; *The Royal Spiritual Magazine*; *A Book of Accounts for the use of Surveyors*, advertised in *Lloyd's Evening Post*, Monday October 24th. 1768, p. 395; Rev. Joseph Brown's *Family Testament.* No biographical details are available.

LYE (S.), bookseller in London, Leadenhall Street, 1735. In that year he received subscriptions for an *Exposition on the Common Prayer Book.* [*Country Journal*, April 26th.]

LYMANS (JAMES), (?) bookseller in London, 1756. This name is found in the imprint to a small volume of *Orders*, &c., of the House of Commons printed in that year.

LYNCH (BRIDGETT), pamphlet-seller in London, 1745. *See* Lynch (Thomas).

LYNCH (THOMAS), pamphlet-seller in London, 1745. He and his wife, Bridgett, were bound over for selling obscene literature. [S. P. Dom., Geo. II, Bundle 65.]

LYON (A.), bookseller and publisher in London, Russell Street, Covent Garden, 1733. Publisher of an edition of Voltaire's *Letters concerning the English Nation*, 1733. *See also* D. Lyon. "Mr. Lyons'" name is found as selling catalogues for Herman Northouck in the *Daily Journal*, January 21st, 1735.

LYON (B.), bookseller and publisher in Bath, near the North Gate, 1729. The earliest printer in this city. Printer for Capt. Thomas Goulding, an eccentric character who kept a shop opposite the Pump House, where he sold jewelery and toys and probably his own literary ventures. Lyon also printed for Spurrell and Dixon. [Green, *Bibl. Soms.*, vol. I, pp. xxxv, 215.]

LYON (DAVID ? or DANIEL ?), bookseller and publisher in London, Russell Street, Covent Garden, 1726–30. In partnership with James Woodman. Their stock was sold in 1730. Lyon afterwards became secretary to the Society for Encouragement of Learning. [Nichols, II. 95; III. 616.]

LYON (G.), bookseller and publisher in London, in Ludgate Street, 1743. Publisher of a pamphlet on theatrical matters entitled "*Tyranny triumphant.* By Patrick Fitz-crambo, Esq.", 1743, 8vo. [B.M. 641. d. 30 (5).]

M. (A) Andrew Millar (?), bookseller and publisher in London, 1731–2. Publisher of a political satire on Sir Robert Walpole entitled *Sir Robert Brass, or the Intrigues, serious and amorous, of the Knight of the Blazing Star*, 1731. [B.M. 162. n. 65.] These initials also occur in an advertisement of books in *Fog's Weekly Journal* of April 1st, 1732 [Second leaf recto, col. 3].

M. (J.), bookseller (?) in Paternoster Row, 1744. Sold a work entitled *Authentic Papers relating to the Expedition against Carthagena*, 1744. The initials may stand for J. Morgan (*q. v.*), or J. Mechell (*q. v.*).

MABERLEY (M.), bookseller in Gosport, Hants, 1750. Named in a list of provincial booksellers. [*N. & Q.* 10 S. v. 481.]

MACE (JOHN), bookseller and publisher at Hull, co. Yorks., 1740 (?)–1758 (?). His name is met with in the imprint to John Clark's *Introduction to the making of Latin*, published in 1740, and in 1750 he published the same writer's edition of *Eutropius.* The author of these works was a schoolmaster in the city. Mace was agent for the *York Courant.* Mr. Allnutt, in his valuable notes on pro-

vincial booksellers and printers in *Bibliographica* [II. 306], says that John Mace became a Freeman of York in 1758. Neither Davies nor Timperley say anything about him. He was probably in business before 1740, and later than 1758.

MACKLEW (   ), bookseller in London, The Haymarket, 1765. He advertised as selling *An Ode to the People of England* in the *Gazetteer and Daily Advertiser*, August 12th, 1765.

MACY (B.), bookseller in London, on Hermitage Bridge, 1726. One of the partners in *The Modern Navigator's Tutor.* [*London Journal*, February 5, 1726.]

MALLISON (   ), printer in Falmouth, 1753. His name is found in the imprint of a sermon in 1753. [Dredge.] Perhaps an error for M. Allison (*q. v.*).

MALTUS (   ), bookseller in Northwich, co. Cheshire, 1756. In 1756 he was an agent for the sale of Schofield's *Middlewich Journal or Cheshire Advertiser.*

MANBY (RICHARD), bookseller and publisher in London, west end of St. Paul's, or Ludgate Hill, 1733–69. One of the foremost publishers of the age. For some years he was in partnership with W. Innys, and together they published Dr. Conyer's Middleton's *Letter from Rome*, the third edition of which appeared in 1733. Manby was also one of the publishers of Middleton's *History of the Life of Cicero.* Writing to Warburton from Cambridge, on October 27th, 1739, about this work he says: "I gave the same number of receipts [for subscriptions] to Manby who expressed a great desire to undertake the whole management of it and made proposals . . . so convenient . . . that I have agreed to throw the work into his hands." [Add. M.S. 32457, f. 143.] Richard Manby was Master of the Company of Stationers in 1765. He died at Walthamstow on April 13th, 1769, and was succeeded in business by Mr. John Pridden. [Nichols, III. 602.]

MANISTY (R.), bookseller in Durham, Market Place, 1764–6. Mentioned in lists of provincial booksellers [*N. & Q.* 10 S. v, March 10, 1906, p. 183; *ib.*, 10 S. VI, 443], and also in an advertisement in the *Newcastle Journal* of 1766.

MANKLIN, or MANCKLIN (RICHARD), bookseller and publisher in York, Coney Street, 1697–1739. *See Dictionary*, 1668–1725. Still in business in 1726, when he published a sermon preached by the Rev. Samuel Johnson before the Mayor and Aldermen of York. [W. M. C., January, 1726, p. 5.] He died in

1739, and Messrs. Ward and Chandler took over his premises, making them the publishing office of the *York Courant*. [*London Evening Post*, January 18th, 1739.]

MANNING ( ), MRS., bookseller in Bideford, co. Devon, 1763–4. Her name is found in the *Exeter Flying Post*, 1763. [Addenda to Dredge.] [*Western Antiquary*, V. 164.]

MARCH (JOHN), bookseller in Exeter, at the Bible, a little below St. Martin's Lane, 1726. His name appears in the imprint of *Render to all their Dues*, printed by "Andrew Bryce at Exeter and sold by John March". [Dredge.]

MARCH (JOHN), printer in London, Tower Hill, 1733–98. For many years a printer of considerable importance. He printed for Messrs. Mount and Page, booksellers on Tower Hill, various sermons, notably one for establishing the colony of Georgia in America, preached by Samuel Smith on February 23rd, 17$\frac{30}{31}$, and published in London in 1733. [J. C. B. L.] Issued a trade card. [A. Heal's Collection.] Became warden of the Company of Stationers in 1754 and Master in 1790. He died April 15th, 1798. [Nichols, III. 441 and 602.]

MARCHBANK (ROBERT), printer at Newcastle-on-Tyne, Custom House Entry, 1761. Only known from three works: two ballads in the British Museum with the imprint: Newcastle, printed and sold by Robert Marchbank in the Custom House Entry, and a work by John King, usher in the Grammar School, entitled *Sententiae ex diversis Auctoribus excerptae*. Mentioned by Brand in his *History*, I. 98. [Welford, p. 37.]

MARGETTS (R.), bookseller in London, Bishopsgate Street, 1735. In that year he received subscriptions for an *Exposition on the Common Prayer Book*. [*Country Journal*, April 26.]

MARINER ( ), bookseller in London, (1) Covent Garden, 1770 (?); (2) Compton Street, Soho. 1770–2. Publisher of *The Whisperer*, for which he was imprisoned ten months in the King's Bench, early in January, 1772. The first number of this periodical was published on February 17th, 1770, and Timperley declares that those who sold it were frequently sentenced to imprisonment. [p. 721.]

MARSH (CHARLES), bookseller and publisher in London, (1) Charing Cross, near Northumberland Avenue; (2) Old Round Court, Strand, 1730 (?)–67. He was apparently in business about 1730, as in 1734 he was a member of a "free and

easy" called the Grand Kaibar, and wrote an *Ode* for it which, with others, he printed at the end of his tragedy called *Amasis*, in 1738. [B.M. 11775. f. 25.] Marsh took over the shop previously kept by G. Greg or Grig (*q. v.*) next to Northumberland House at Charing Cross, which he described in the following lines:

Next to your spiral turret, that surveys
What pious times did to the martyr raise;
An house (a very little one) there stands;
* * * * *
There lately Grubstreet authors might you spy
Exposed to sale.
* * * * *
Here grew the poppy o'er G. J—b's brow,
And Dunciad heroes might have slept till now,
But home-bred faction and domestic strife
Sever'd old Greg,[1] from his too youthful wife.
This . . . house I took . . .

He was altogether a very singular and eccentric character, and was described by a correspondent to J. Nichols as "proud, insolent and conceited". Marsh was the author of a tragedy called *Amasis* which he dedicated to the Princess of Wales in 1738. He was also the publisher of an edition of Shakespeare's *Winter's Tale*, with his own emendations, and author of a poem called *The Library, an Epistle from a Bookseller to a Gentleman his Customer, desiring him to discharge his Bill*, 1766. He published periodical catalogues of his stock, and in 1771 was succeeded by S. Leacroft (*q. v.*). [Nichols, III. 647.]

MARSHALL (JOHN), bookseller in London, Bible in Gracechurch Street, 1695. *See Dictionary*, 1668–1725. Still in business in 1726, when he published the Rev. D. Mayo's sermon *The Intercession for the Fruitless Fig-tree*. [W. M. C., January, 1726, p. 5.]

MARSHALL (JOSEPH), bookseller and publisher in London, Bible in Newgate Street, 1707–34. *See Dictionary*, 1668–1725. Still in business in 1734.

MARSHALL (JOSEPH), bookseller in London, St. Clement's Churchyard, 1776. Mentioned in Kent's *Directory* of that date.

MARSTON (J.), bookseller in London, Denmark Street, Ratcliff Highway 1726. One of those for whom was printed *The Modern Navigator's Compleat Tutor*. [*London Journal*, February 5th, 1726.]

[1] The late master of the shop.

MARTIN (B.), bookseller (?) in Wallingford, co. Berks, 1776. His name occurs in the imprint to T. Pentycross's *W. Henham-Hill, a Poem*, 1776. [Winship.] The copy in the Harvard Library once belonged to Horace Walpole.

MARTIN (CHARLES), printer, bookseller, and bookbinder, Angel and Bible, Guildford, co. Surrey, 1769. He printed more than one of the writings of the Rev. Joseph Greenhill, Rector of East Horsley and East Clandon, in the county of Surrey. Issued a trade card engraved by Mathias Darley. [A. Heal's Collection.]

MARTIN (ROBERT), printer in Birmingham, 1763 (?). Apprentice to John Baskerville. In 1763 after the publication of the folio *Bible*, Baskerville came to an agreement with Martin, and gave him the use of all his printing materials, and Martin printed with them between 1766 and 1769: *The Christian's Useful Companion*, 1766, 8vo.; Somervile's *Chace*, 1767; an edition of Shakespeare's *Works*, in nine volumes, in 1768; and a *Bible* with cuts in 1769, as well as editions of the *Lady's Preceptor*. In 1769 Baskerville resumed work, and Martin appears to have set up as a bookseller. [Reed, *Old English Letter Foundries*, p. 281.]

MARTIN (SIMON), bookseller and publisher in Leicester. *See Dictionary*, 1668–1725. Was still in business in 1737, when he published the Rev. R. Arnald's *Sermon* preached at the Visitation held at St. Martin's, Leicester, on April 22nd.

MARTIN (STEPHEN), printer in Bath, Brick House, just without Westgate, 1755–7. Editor and publisher of the *Bath Advertiser*, the first number of which appeared on October 18th, 1755.

MARTIN (THOMAS), bookseller and publisher in Leicester, 1746–57. His name occurs in the imprints to the following works: a *Sermon* by the Rev. Richard Arnald, Rector of Thurcaston, preached October 9th, 1746 [B.M. 225. i. 2 (21)]; a *Sermon* preached by the Rev. Chas. Stokes, Rector of Knaptoft, in St. Mary's Church, Stamford, on October 4th, 1750 [B.M. 225 i. 6 (12)]; and a *Sermon* preached in the parish church of Monk's Kirby, co. Warwick, by the Rev. J. Ancell, February 11th, 1757 [B.M. T. 1619 (10)].

MASON (SAMUEL), bookseller and publisher in London, (1) Love Lane in Wood Street; (2) near St. Alban's Church in Wood Street. 1741–2. Publisher of Americana, notably sermons, and a pamphlet by G. Whitefield, *A Vindication and Confirmation of the remarkable Work of God in New-England*, 1742. [J. C. B. L.]

MASON (WILLIAM), stationer in London, Bell and Star, opposite the Royal Exchange, Cornhill, 1760. Issued a trade card printed on both sides, one in English and the other in French, in that year. [A. Heal's Collection.] Succeeded by William and Elizabeth Fielder.

MATHEWS (EMANUEL), printer and bookseller in London, The Bible, Paternoster Row, 1700–26. *See Dictionary*, 1668–1725. Still in business in 1726. [W. M. C., January, 1726, p. 5.]

MATHEWS (JAMES), bookseller in London, 18 Strand, 1774–81. Father of Charles Mathews, the famous actor, who was born at the shop on June 28th, 1776. According to Nichols, James Mathews was a vendor of patent medicines and a Wesleyan preacher, with a chapel of his own at Whetston in Middlesex. He was possibly the son of Emanuel Mathews, the printer and bookseller (1700–26). His name occurs in the imprint to a sermon by Jonathan Edwards, preached in Boston, Mass., which was reprinted in London in 1774. His name also appears in Kent's *Directory* for 1776, in which year he published Daniel Leonard's *Massachusettensis*, first printed in Boston. He was still in business in 1781, when his name is found in the imprint to David Bostwick's *Vindication of Baptism*.

MATTHEWS (BENJAMIN), bookseller and publisher in Bath, (1) Merchants Court; (2) Book Warehouse, corner of Cheap Street. 1725–55. In a list of provincial booksellers published in *Notes and Queries*, this bookseller is mentioned as in business in 1725 [10 S. V. 141]. In 1750 he published the Rev. William Roberts's *The Divine Institution . . . the fourth edition*. [Dredge, *Devon Booksellers and Printers*, p. 25]; and in 1751 he issued a pamphlet on the curative properties of the water at Glastonbury in Somerset, under the title, *Wilt thou be made whole?* [B.M. 234. i. 2]. According to an advertisement in the *Bath Chronicle* of 1755, he held periodical sales by auction, kept a circulating library, and was a dealer in second-hand books.

MATTHEWS (R.), bookseller in Cambridge, near Great St. Mary's Church, *c.* 1758–73. Published S. Ogden's *University Sermons*, 1758. His name appears as a bookseller, stationer, and bookbinder on Poor Law Overseer forms from 1763 to 1773. He died 1778 and was succeeded by John Deighton, who was afterwards elected Printer to the University (1802). This was before Deighton succeeded John Woodyer at 1 Trinity Street.

MAUD (N.), bookseller and publisher (?) in London, 6 Old Bailey, 1775. This name is found in the imprint to an interesting piece of Americana, a small octavo pamphlet with the title *Resistance no Rebellion*, published in the above year. N. Maud may possibly indicate the author and not the publisher. The name has not been met with elsewhere.

MAULE (JOHN), bookseller at Cranbrooke, Kent, 1737–56. Publisher of the Rev. D. Dobel's *Seventh-day Sabbath*, 1737. Is believed to have removed to Chatham in 1756.

MAURICE ( ), Mrs., bookseller in Plymouth, Plymouth Dock, 1770. Mentioned in a list of provincial booksellers. [*N. & Q.* 11 S. I. 364.]

MAYNARD ( ), Mrs., bookseller in Devizes, 1765. Her name occurs in an advertisement in the *Gazetteer and Daily Advertiser*, February 12th, 1765, as selling *The Complete Letter Writer.*

MEADOWS (W.), bookseller and publisher in London, The Angel, Cornhill, 1719–53. *See Dictionary*, 1668–1725. In 1748 his shop in Cornhill was destroyed in a great fire that broke out in Exchange Alley on March 25th. [*Penny London Journal.*] In 1753 Meadows's name is found as selling an *Anglo-French Dictionary*, with several others. [*Public Advertiser*, January 8th, 1753.]

MEAISEY (J.), bookseller in Winchester, St. Maurice, 1765 (?)–1768 (?). From an entry in the parish register it appears that he was a widower, aged 40 in 1765, when he married Mary Ayres, widow, so that presumably he had been in business for some years. He is mentioned in a list of provincial booksellers as still in business in 1768. [*N. & Q.* 10 S. V. 242; VI, 31.]

MEARS (W.), *see Dictionary*, 1668–1725. In 1728 he was receiving subscriptions for a new edition of the Hebrew Bible. [*Daily Post*, January 1st, 1728.] Succeeded in business by John Nourse (*q. v.*).

MECHELL (J.), printer and bookseller in London, King's Arms, Fleet Street, 1740 (?)–54. His imprint occurs on a pamphlet entitled *Judgement signed in the Cause between . . . Sir Robert Walpole and Mr. Whatley* . . . 1740. At the end are two pages of publisher's advertisements, and also one page of books to be had at John Noon's (*q. v.*). Another of Mechell's publications bore the title: *The New-Comers; or the Characters of John the Carter, Sandy Long-Rib, Daniel Raven and Old Will with the Spencer wig. To which is added Will Trimmer formerly of the St. Stephen's Club.* [Winship.] In this he added to his address, "opposite the Leg-Tavern". In September 1754 he started a periodical called *The Entertainer*, by Charles Mercury, Esq. [Timperley, 1842, p. 691.]

MEERE, MEARS, MEERES, or MERES (CASSANDRA), printer and publisher in London, Old Bailey, near Ludgate, 1725–6. Widow of H. Meere (1708–24). Continued to print the *Daily Post* until February 1st, 1726, when the imprint bears the name of R. Nutt, her son-in-law. The business subsequently came into the hands of John Meeres, or Meres, a kinsman (*q. v.*).

MEERE, MEARS, MEERES, or MERES (JOHN), printer and publisher in London, Old Bailey, 1738–61. The relationship of this printer to Hugh Meere (1708–24) is not very clear, nor is there any certain evidence as to the date upon which he took over the two newspapers, the *Daily Post* and the *London Evening Post*. S. Neville's name appeared in the imprints to both down to the year 1735, and possibly later. John Meres was certainly established in the Old Bailey in 1738, for in that year he got into trouble for inserting a paragraph in the *Daily Post* reflecting on the King of Sweden. As he refused to find sureties for good behaviour, he was committed to Newgate, where he quickly thought better, and his two sureties were Robert Gosling, bookseller of St. Dunstan's in the West, and George Strahan, bookseller of St. Michael's, Cornhill. [S. P. Dom., Geo. II, Bundle 46, nos. 4, 5, 6, 7.] In 1740 he was again in trouble for printing in the *Daily Post* a paper reflecting on the embargo on provisions. On December 2nd he was called to the Bar of the House of Commons, and committed to the custody of the Sergeant at Arms, and was not released until February 10th, 174$\frac{0}{1}$ and with Mrs. Nutt (*q. v.*), a pamphlet-seller, was cautioned for selling the *London Evening Post*. John Meres died in 1761, and was succeeded by his son, also named John, who gave up the *Daily Post* in 1772.

MEGGITT ( ), bookseller and publisher in Wakefield, co. Yorks., 1769. His name occurs in an advertisement of the tenth edition of E. Moxon's *English Housewifery*, in the pages of the *London Chronicle* of that year.

MEIGHAN (THOMAS), bookseller and publisher in London, Drury Lane, 1726–53. Possibly this publisher was a descendant of Mercy and Richard Meighen, who were booksellers in London in the previous century [*see Dictionary*, 1641–67]. Thomas Meighan was probably a Roman Catholic, as in the *British Journal* of February 5th, 1726, is the following item of news: "Last week one Mr. Meighan a Popish bookseller in Drury Lane was taken into custody of a messenger by a warrant from one of His Majesties principal Secretaries of State, for printing and publishing a libel against the Reformation, intitul'd *The Conversion and Reformation of England compared.* He hath since been admitted to bail." In the *Weekly Journal* for July 9th, 1726, is the notice of his conviction. He confessed that the book was printed at Antwerp and sent over. Meighan was the publisher of G. P. Domcke's *Philosophiae Mathematicae Newtonianae*, in 1730. He died in December 1753, his will being proved on the 29th of that month. He left his stock in trade and the residue of his goods to his wife Martha, and nominated Thomas Parker of Jewin Street, printer, one of his executors. [P.C.C. 323 Searle.]

MELLOR ( ), bookseller in London, Lombard Street. *See* Parker (E.)

MERCER (W.), bookseller in Maidstone, 1765. He, with other Kent booksellers, is advertised as selling *Registrum Roffense.* [*Gazetteer and Daily Advertiser*, August 26th, 1765.]

MERRILL (J.), bookseller in Cambridge, *c.* 1750. Published J. Mitchell's *Treatise on Artificial Magnets*, 1750. Query if he joined T. Merrill (*q. v.*) in partnership.

MERRILL (JOHN and JOSEPH), booksellers and publishers in Cambridge, *c.* 1773–95. Probably succeeded T. and J. Merrill at 3 Trinity Street (*q. v.*), and published several works, being succeeded by John Deighton, 1795. John, an Alderman of Cambridge, died October 17th, 1801, aged 70, and his brother Joseph died October 23rd, 1803, aged 70. Both buried in Great St. Mary's Church. Joseph was a wealthy man, and left large sums to Addenbrooke's Hospital, the old Charity School, for maintaining the water conduit and pipes, and the Jackenett Almshouses, which are still in existence in King Street. *See also* J. Merrill.

MERRILL (THOMAS), bookseller, publisher, and binder in Cambridge, *c.* 1736–82. Lived on the Regent Walk. He bound many books for the University Library between 1736 and 1748, and published many works, including Heathcote's *Historia Astronomiae*, 1747, and Roger Cotes's *Harmonics*, 1749. In 1752 he purchased from the University Press 75 sets of Kuster's edition of Suidas. He is supposed to have removed in 1769, when the houses on the Senate House site were vacated, and in 1779 and 1782, according to some deeds of property, he was then at what is now No. 3. Trinity Street. During 1758 to 1775 the names of T. and J. Merrill appear together on several works as publishers, and they also were agents for selling the publications of the University Press. Presumably they were succeeded by J. and J. Merrill, 1775–95, to whom John Deighton succeeded in 1795.

MERRILL (T. and J.), booksellers and publishers in Cambridge, *c.* 1758–75. *See* Thomas Merrill.

MESPLET (FLEURY), printer in London, 24 Crown Court, Little Russell Street, Covent Garden, 1773. A French refugee who came over to England in the early part of 1773, and set up a press at the above address. His imprint is only found in one book, *La Louisiane ensanglantée*, written by Colonel Chevalier de Champigny: "Chez Fleury Mesplet, No. 24 Crown Court, Little Russell Street, Covent Garden. MDCCLXXIII". Not satisfied with the limited support he received, he applied to Benjamin Franklin, and was advised by him to emigrate to America, which he did towards the close of 1773, or early in 1774. He landed at Philadelphia, but subsequently moved into Canada, and became the first printer at Montreal. A memoir of him was published in 1906 by R. W. McLachlan, Honorary Curator of the Numismatic and Antiquarian Society of Montreal. Copies of Mesplet's book, printed in London, are in the Carter Brown Library at Providence, R. I., and in the Library of Congress at Washington.

MEYER (W.), bookseller and publisher in London, May's Buildings, St. Martin's Lane, 1749–53. Amongst the books he sold was Thomas Crosby's *Book-keeper's Guide*, 1749, and his name also occurs in the imprint to Lambert's *Curious Observations upon the Manners, Customs . . . of the several nations of Asia, Africa, and America*, published in 1751. [J. C. B. L.] Another edition of this appeared in 1753 with the names of Woodfall and W. Russel added. [*Public Advertiser*, January 10th, 1753.]

MICKLEWRIGHT (C.), printer, bookseller, and publisher in Reading, 1742–50. In partnership with John Newbery. After the latter's removal to London he continued the business in Reading, and amongst his publications was an account of the trial of a criminal called Thomas Chandler, written by Edward Wise, an attorney of Wokingham, Berks. *An Explanation of Scripture Prophecies* bears the imprint: "Reading. Printed and Sold by J. Newbery and C. Micklewright.'

MIDDLETON (THOMAS), printer in Newcastle-on-Tyne, Printing Office, St. Nicholas Churchyard, 1740–1. Only known from two publications issued in those years, one of which was a volume of poems by the Rev. Wm. Bewick of Hexham. His name is not found in any later book, and what became of him is unknown. [Welford's *Early Newcastle Typography*, p. 32.]

MIDDLETON ( ), bookseller in Mortlake, co. Surrey. In 1761 he was selling (?) a catalogue of books issued by Francis Hall, bookseller at Isleworth. [*Lloyds Evening Post*, July 10–13, 1761.]

MIDWINTER (DANIEL) II, bookseller and publisher in London, St. Paul's Churchyard, 1726–57. Son of Daniel Midwinter I. Succeeded to the business in St. Paul's Churchyard, which he carried on until his death in 1757. By his will, which was dated June 20th, 1750, he bequeathed £1,000 to Christ's Hospital, and £1,000 to the Stationers' Company, who were to pay £14 annually to the parishes of Hornsey and St. Faith to put out two boys or girls to some kind of trade. He left bequests to the following booksellers in Edinburgh: William Miller, Andrew Martin, John Trail, and John Paton. Amongst the witnesses to his will, were Thomas Longman and John Rivington. [P.C.C. 59 Herring.]

MILES (THOMAS), bookseller and publisher in Arundel, Sussex, 1746–56. His name occurs in the imprint to a *Sermon* preached at the churches of Southstoke and Arundel on December 18th, 1745, by the Rev. Daniel Gittings, Rector of Southstoke. [B.M. 225. f. 13 (10).] Again, in 1756, he published another *Sermon* by the same preacher on the Fast Day, appointed in consequence of the earthquake at Lisbon.

MILLAN, or MILLEN (JOHN), bookseller and publisher in London, (1) Locke's Head in New Street, between Marylebone Street and Piccadilly, 1727; (2) Whitehall, 1727–44; (3) near the Admiralty Office, 1739; (4) near Scotland Yard; (5) St. Martins-in-the-Fields, Charing Cross. 1727–84. A publisher of note, and an extensive dealer in second-hand and new books. He is chiefly noted as the publisher of several of the works of James Thomson, the poet. He sold the copyright of these to Andrew Millar (*q. v.*) for a hundred guineas. He was also the publisher of heraldic works such as *Arms of the English Nobility, with Supporters, Crests, Mottoes, and Tables of Dates to Family Honours*; *Lists of Baronets, with Dates, Arms, Crests, &c.*; and similar works for Scotland. Another of his publications was Kane's *Campaigns*. In 1743 he was examined by the Government with reference to a pamphlet called *A True Dialogue*, which he admitted buying at Mrs. Cooper's in Paternoster Row. As only two copies were found in his shop the prosecution was dropped. [S. P. Dom. Geo. II, Bundle 62, 59c.] Richard Gough, the antiquary, writing in 1772, says that he had penetrated the utmost recesses of Millan's, that he had found the bookseller enjoying a hand at whist with some friends, and that when he asked Millan if he had Dillenius in sheets, the bookseller replied that "he had none in sheets or blankets". Gough wound up his description of the premises by calling them "a future Herculaneum" where we shall hereafter root out many scarce things, now rotting on the floor". John Millan died February 15th, 1784, aged 80. [Timperley, pp. 750, 784.]

MILLAR (ANDREW), bookseller and publisher in London, (1) Buchanan's Head, near St. Clement's Church; (2) opposite Catherine Street, Strand. 1728–68. Is said to have been born in Scotland in 1707. In all probability he was apprenticed to a bookseller in Edinburgh, as when he came to London in 1728 he appears to have brought with him the unsold sheets of Archibald Pitcairn's *Poemata*, which was published there by an unknown publisher in 1727 or early in 1728. The preface to the Edinburgh edition was dated, "Edinburgi postridie Kal. Januarias MDCCXXVII", which according to the Old Style was really 172⅞. These unsold sheets were issued by Andrew Millar in 1729 with a new title-page which bore the words "Editio secunda", and the imprint to which ran: "Londini, Apud A. Millar, ad insigne Buchanani capitis, juxta S. Clementis ecclesiam, in the Strand MDCCXXIX". But there is an even earlier record of his settlement in London. In *Fog's Weekly Journal* for December 21st, 1728, is an announcement of the publication of T. Consett's *Present State . . . of the Church of Russia*, and this names "Andrew Millar over against St. Clement's Church in the Strand" as one of the booksellers selling it. The title-page of the book bears the date 1729, but it was on the market before December 21st, 1728, and Millar was evidently established at the Buchanan's Head before that. His premises were not those previously in the occupation of the Tonsons, father and son, but another house on the same side of the street, midway between the shop of Pownall the stationer and Tonsons's premises at the corner of Dutchy Lane. [*N. & Q.* 12 S. VII. 321.] The Pitcairn volume already alluded to contained several laudatory poems to Sir William Bennett, of Grubbet, one of the early patrons of James Thomson, the poet, whom very possibly Millar knew before he left Edinburgh. One of his earliest ventures was the purchase in 1729 of Thomson's tragedy of *Sophonisba*, and of a poem called *Spring* by the same author. The purchase price was £137 10s. [The Cases of the Appellants and Respondents in the Cause of Literary

Property . . . 1774.] He bought copyrights very largely, and Dr. Johnson has left a testimony to the generous nature of Millar's dealings with authors. To Boswell he said, "I respect Millar, Sir; he has raised the price of literature." On the other hand, as Charles Knight has pointed out in his gossipy volume, *Shadows of the Old Booksellers*, "Millar made more thousands by Fielding's novels than he paid hundreds to the needy and extravagant author. If Thomson's *Liberty* were a bad bargain, *The Seasons* must have been 'a little estate'. Millar had acquired from John Millan on June 16th, 1738, the remainder of the poems that went to form *The Seasons* and other works by the same author, paying him £105 for those copyrights, and in 1751 he paid Fielding £1,000 for the manuscript of *Amelia*. Andrew Millar was one of the chief undertakers of Dr. Johnson's *Dictionary*, and of Hume's *History of England*. The publication of the first volume of the *History* at Edinburgh did not meet with the success the author had hoped; but Millar agreed to take over the publication, with the result that the book became a success, and the author was able to say, when in 1761 the last volume was published, that the copy-money he had received exceeded anything formerly known in England, and he had become not only independent but opulent". [Knight, *Shadows*.] Millar was also the publisher of some good editions of the older writers, such as Bacon and Milton, and he spared no efforts to obtain the best texts. One of his chief helpers was Dr. Thomas Birch, with whom he had much correspondence on literary matters. Some of Millar's letters are now in the British Museum. [Add. MSS. 4314, 6190.] In November 1766 began the great copyright action of Millar *v.* Taylor. In 1763 Millar had published an edition of 2,000 copies of *The Seasons* of James Thomson, and while he still had a thousand copies unsold, Robert Taylor printed another edition, and by so doing infringed Millar's copyright. He at once brought an action; but he did not live to hear the successful end of it. The case was brought up in Trinity Term, on Tuesday, June 7th, 1768, and adjourned till the following Term. Andrew Millar died the next morning. Andrew Millar's right-hand man for many years was Thomas Cadell, who had been his apprentice. Whilst Millar was at Bath a few months before his death he wrote a long letter to Cadell on business matters. This letter is now in the British Museum. In it he complains bitterly of Bell, who was issuing cheap editions of plays and poems, "It is as bad as robbery for Bell to supply the market with every book." He recommends Cadell to employ Bowyer or Hett to print the Bishop of Oxford's *Sermon*, of which he intended to print 1,000, and he finished up by expressing his satisfaction at the way in which

Hume's *History* was selling. "I alwaies knew", he says, "it would get the better of prejudice, for there is real substantial merit in the work." This letter hardly bears out the oft-repeated statement that Andrew Millar retired from business in 1767. If the *Autobiography of Dr. Alexander Carlyle* is to be believed, Millar was nicknamed "Peter Pamphlet", from his resemblance to a character in Murphy's *Upholsterer*. By his will he left legacies to David Hume and to the two sons of Henry Fielding.

MILLER (THOMAS), bookseller and publisher in Bungay, co. Suffolk, 1755–1804. Born in Norwich, August 14th, 1732. Not only dealt in books, but was a great collector of engraved portraits and coins, of which he published a catalogue in 1782. Miller also issued a token with his profile on it, now known to collectors as the "Miller halfpenny". During the later part of his life he was quite blind. He died on July 25th, 1804, being succeeded by his son. [Nichols, III. 680, 681.] There was also a Thomas Millar, bookseller in Halesworth, co. Suffolk, who died in June 1802, aged 82; but what was his relationship to the above is not known. [*Ib.*]

MILLS (T), bookseller and publisher in Bath, *c.* 1770–5. In 1770 T. Mills of Kingsmead St., bookseller and stationer, had his premises broken open and certain articles stolen. Dorney's *Contemplations*, 1773, were printed by W. Gye for T. Mills, bookseller, in King's Mead Square. He was one of the partners in the publication of *Divine Maxims*. [*Public Advertiser*, January 3rd, 1775.]

MINORS (RALPH), bookseller and publisher in London, St. Clement's Churchyard, Strand, 1739–42. Publisher of *An Essay for the Better Regulation and Improvement of Free-thinking, in a Letter to a Friend*, 1739. Attributed to John Hildrop. At the end is an advertisement of other publications by Minors. [Winship.] In 1742 he published for the same author, *Free-thoughts upon the Brute-creation . . . In Two Letters to a Lady*. [B.M. 1103. f. 17 (1).] On the back of the first leaf is a list of five other publications, chiefly theological.

MINORS, or MYNORS (WILLOUGHBY), bookseller in London, Clare Court, Drury Lane, 1744. Possibly a relative of R. Minors, who was in business as a bookseller and stationer in St. Clement's Churchyard, Strand, in 1739. W. Minors started a subscription library at the above address in November 1744, charging three shillings per quarter, or half a guinea a year, for which readers were allowed two books at a time.

MIST (NATHANIEL), printer in London, Great Garter Lane, 1725–31. He printed *Mist's Weekly Journal*, the new series of which started in 1725 and ran for 151 numbers. Pope referred to it in the following line:

"To Dullness Ridpath is as dear as Mist." [*Dunciad.*]

About 1731 Mist fled abroad owing to the commencement of an action for libel against him. *Fog's Weekly Journal* was then published instead in 1732.

MITCHELL (J.), bookseller in Penzance, co. Cornwall, 1753–6. One of those who sold the Rev. S. Walker's *Sermon preached at Truro* . . . June 3rd, 1753 [Dredge], and also, in 1754, Borlase's *Antiquities of Cornwall.* In 1756 he published *Practical Lectures in Education*, &c.

MITCHELL (P.), bookseller and publisher in London, North Audley Street, 1775. *A Letter from Sir Robert Rich*, printed for P. Mitchell, North Audley Street. [Advertisement, *Public Advertiser*, May 13th, 1775.]

MONK (EDMUND), printer and bookseller in Chester, 1775. Proprietor and printer of the *Chester Courant.* Died February 1800. [Timperley, 1842, p. 802.] What connexion this printer was to J. Monk (*q. v.*) is not known.

MONK (J.), printer in Chester, Newgate Street, 1771–5. Printer of Adam's *Weekly Courant* to which he succeeded on December 17th, 1771. What connexion this printer was to E. Monk (*q. v.*) is not known.

MONTAGU (RICHARD), book and pamphlet-seller in London, (1) Wild Street, near Drury Lane; (2) Book Warehouse, The *General Post* Office, end of Great Queen Street. 1728–49. First heard of in December 1728, when he petitioned for the post of messenger to the printing-press. [S.P.Dom. George II, Bundle 9, 71.] In 1748 he published a pamphlet entitled *Observations on the Probable Issue of the Congress at Aix-la-Chapelle.* [B.M. E. 2042 (3).]

MOON (JOHN), printer in Preston, co. Lancashire, Market Place, 1745–62. In partnership with James Stanley (*q. v.*); but in 1762 he appears to have printed and published *The Guild Merchant* alone.

MOORE (A.), pamphlet-seller and publisher in London: Near St. Paul's, 1722–47. In 1722 Thomas Woolston published a work with the title *A Free Gift to the Clergy*, which bore this imprint, "London: Printed for the author, given to the clergy gratis and sold by A. Moore, near St. Paul's (Price one shilling)." Reprinted at Philadelphia and sold by S. Keimes, 1724. [Winship.] Mentioned

in Wilford's *Monthly Catalogue* for March 1726. In 1746 an M. Moore published from this address, *A new Ballad on Lord D–n–l's altering his Chapel at Gr–e into a Kitchen.*

MOORE (ISAAC), printer and type-founder in Bristol and London (London, Queen Street, near Upper Moorfields), 1764–75. Originally a whitesmith in Birmingham. Turned his attention to letter-founding, and was appointed manager to Joseph and Edmund Fry, who had set up as letter-founders in Bristol in 1764. Mr. T. B. Reed, in his *Old English Letter Foundries*, quotes from a catalogue of P. Renouard's to the effect that it contained *A Specimen by Isaac Moore, Bristol*, issued in 1768. In the same year the foundry was moved to London and set up in Queen Street, near Upper Moorfields, and in the Sohmian Collection of Stockholm Mr. Blades discovered a broadside specimen sheet by Isaac Moore and Co., showing romans from five-line to brevier. In 1770 another was issued. The firm chose as its model the type of Baskerville; but this had given place to those of Caslon, and, in spite of much puffing, the new firm had to conform to public taste. Whether Isaac Moore was in the firm in 1775 is not known; but in that year Messrs. I. Moore & Co., letter-founders and printers, printed a pamphlet entitled *Considerations on the State of the Coffee Trade.* [J. C. B. L.]

MOORE (JOSEPH), printer in Poole, co. Dorset. Born April 2nd, 1736. Began printing in 1765 and was succeeded by his nephews. [C. H. Mayo, *Bibl. Dorset.*, p. 284.]

MOORE (W.), printer and publisher in London, 22 Fleet Street. His claim to notice rests on the publication of what Timperley describes as "a violent party paper, written in opposition to the government under Lord North's Administration". It was called *The Whisperer*, and the first number was dated February 17th, 1770. Ninety-five numbers had appeared by December 7th, 1771. According to the above authority, the author and printer "were often pursued by bills of indictment and warrants for their apprehension". [Timperley, 1842, p. 721.]

MORAN (C.), bookseller in London, Covent Garden: (1) Under [or in] the Great Piazza; (2) Tavistock Row, Covent Garden. 1761–9. Publisher of numerous pamphlets, amongst which were, *The Meretriciad* by Edward Thompson, 1761; *Vindications of the Whigs*, 1765; *Court of Cupid*; Trinculo's *Trip to the Jubilee*, by Thompson, 1769. The copies now in the Harvard Library formerly belonged to Horace Walpole, who has supplied some of the references. [Winship.]

MORE (A.), *see* Moore (A.)

MORGAN (J.), bookseller and publisher in London: (1) The Strand; (2) Paternoster Row. 1737(?)–1761(?) Publisher of numerous pamphlets, the earliest found being entitled *The Contrast to the Man of Honour*, London, printed for J. Morgan in the Strand, 1737. This is a poem relating to the politics of the time, and a copy of it is in the Harvard Library, U.S.A. [Winship]. Twenty years later he is found publishing, from Paternoster Row, *A Letter to his Grace the D[uke] of N[ewcastl]e* [B.M. E. 2214 (7)]; *Six Letters from A[rchibal]d B[owe]r to Father Sheldon*, 1756; *The Right Honourable Annuitant Vindicated*, 1761 [B.M. E 2052 (7)].

MORLEY (A.), bookseller in London, Gay's Head, near Beaufort Buildings, Strand, 1756–76(?). In partnership with S. Hooper (*q. v.*)

MORS (THOMAS), book- and map-seller in London, at the sign of the Lute on the north side of St. Paul's Churchyard, *c.* 1760. Issued a trade card about that date. [A. Heal's Collection.]

MOSELEY (H.), bookseller in Kidderminster, co. Worcester, 1748–9. Mentioned in list of provincial booksellers [*N. & Q.* 10 S. v. March 1906, p. 183.] as in business in 1748, in which year his name is found as sharing in the publication of a *Sermon.* [*Bibliography of Worcestershire*, p. 57.] In 1749 he was agent for the distribution of the Catalogues of T. Warren, bookseller of Birmingham.

MOUNT (WILLIAM) and PAGE (THOMAS), booksellers and publishers in London, on Tower Hill, 1722–86. On the death of Richard Mount [1684–1722] he was succeeded by his son William, who carried on the business until his death in 1769. Before 1733 he had taken into partnership his son-in-law Thomas Page, who died in 1762, and the business was then taken over by John the son of William Mount and Thomas Page the son of Thomas. John Mount died in 1786, and his partner very soon afterwards. This firm dealt largely in nautical books. William Mount was Master of the Company of Stationers in the years 1733–5. [Timperley, 1842, p. 719.]

MOUNTFORD (J.), bookseller in Worcester, 1748. Possibly successor to S. Mountford (*q. v.*) Mentioned in list of provincial booksellers as in business in that year. [*N. & Q.* 10 S. v. 242.]

MOUNTFORD (SAMUEL), bookseller and publisher, in Worcester, High Street, 1725–48. Mentioned by a correspondent in *Notes and Queries* [10 S. v. 1906,

p. 242] as in business between these dates. In 1728 he published the Rev. Jas. Brooke's sermon, *The Duty and Advantage of Singing to the Lord*, and in 1744 a sermon by the Rev. Richard Meadowcourt, M.A., Canon of Worcester. [B.M. 225 f. 13 (2).] Again, in 1746, his name is found in the imprint of another sermon by the same preacher. [B.M. 225. f. 16 (19).] In 1748 *A Sermon preached by the Bishop of Worcester* bears the imprint "Worcester: Printed and sold by M. Olivers and S. Mountford in High St." [*Bibliography of Worcestershire*, p. 57.]

MUMFORD (H.), bookseller and publisher in London, Fleet Street, 1747. In that year he published a pamphlet on theatrical matters entitled *A Letter to a certain Patentee*, n.d. 8vo. [B.M. 641. d. 30 (11).]

MUNBY ( ), bookseller in Hull, 1736. His name is found in the imprint to a sermon preached by the Rev. John Mawer on *The Nature and Design of the Lord's Supper.* [B.M. 225. g. 14 (5).]

MURCH (FIDELIO), printer and bookseller in Barnstaple, co. Devon, near The Cross in High Street, 1763–95. In 1763 an advertisement in the *Exeter Flying Post* states that Fidelio Murch, near The Cross in High Street, Barnstable, Bookseller and Printer, lends books to read. He was one of the publishers of a work entitled, "*The most General School-assistant* . . ., by G. Dyer, master of Tackers-Hall School in Exeter, M.DCC.LXX." 8vo. [Dredge.] In 1791 he printed an advertisement card for the Barnstaple Bank, and in 1795 was succeeded by — Syle.

MURRAY (JOHN), bookbinder and publisher in Nottingham, 1738. His name occurs in the imprint to the Rev. James Sloss's *Vindication of the Answer to the sixth question in the Assembly's Shorter Catechism*, which is wrongly dated 1728. [Creswell, p. 22.]

MURRAY (JOHN), bookseller and publisher in London, The Ship, 32 Fleet Street, opposite St. Dunstan's Church, 1768–93. The founder of the great publishing house of Murray was John MacMurray, a lieutenant of Marines, who retired from the service on half-pay and invested his savings in buying a bookselling business. This was William Sandby's shop at the above address. John Murray was born in Edinburgh in 1745. Amongst his early friends was William Falconer, the poet, whom Murray invited to join him in his new trade, but nothing came of it. On commencing business, he dropped the prefix "Mac". His earliest issues as a publisher were new editions of

Walpole's *Castle of Otranto*, and Lyttelton's *Dialogues of the Dead*, and the Rev. Dr. Cartwright's legendary tale of *Armine and Elvira*. For some years his success as a publisher was very moderate. But about the year 1775 he came into a small fortune on the death of an uncle, and from that time forward proved successful. The bulk of his work lies outside the limit of this Dictionary. He died in 1793 and was succeeded by his son John II.

NANKIVELL (J.), bookseller in St. Austell, co. Cornwall, 1752–3. His name occurs in the imprints to the following two sermons: *The Christian's Peculiar Character*, preached by the Rev. L. Southcomb, Rector of Rose-Ash, on January 1st, 1752, and printed by R. Goadby at Sherborne, co. Dorset [B.M. 4473. aaa. 46 (9)], and the Rev. Sam. Walker's sermon preached at Truro on June 13th, 1753. [Dredge, p. 25.]

NEALE (S.), bookseller at Chatham, 1754–5. Joint publisher with J. Fuller (*q. v.*) of Sarah Jackson's *The Director, or Young Woman's Best Companion*, 1755, 8vo, a useful work containing recipes for cookery and cures for illness. [B.M. 1037. e. 37.]

NEVETT & Co., printers in Liverpool, Princes Street, 1766–76. Mentioned in the *Liverpool Directory* of 1766.

NEVETT (WILLIAM), printer in Liverpool, Falcon Alley, Castle Street, 1776. Successor to Nevett & Co.

NEVILLE (S.), printer in London, in the Old Bailey, near Ludgate, 1735. The *Daily Post*, February 13th, 1735, bears his imprint. *see* Nutt (Richard).

NEWBERY (FRANCIS), bookseller in London: (1) The Crown, Paternoster Row; (2) St. Paul's Churchyard. 1767–76. Son of John Newbery. Born at Reading, July 6th, 1743. Educated at both Oxford and Cambridge Universities; but took no degree. Appears to have been in business at the Crown in Paternoster Row in 1765, and perhaps earlier. On the death of his father he took up the business in St. Paul's Churchyard, in 1767. Married Mary, the sister of Robert Raikes, printer, of Gloucester. Died July 17th, 1818. Francis Newbery was a lover of music, his favourite instrument being the violin. There was also a Francis Newbery, a nephew of John. On the death of the founder of the house, disputes arose over the business, and Newbery the nephew opened a shop and began to publish books at 20 Ludgate Street. He was for a time publisher of the *Gentleman's Magazine*. He died in January, 1780.

NEWBERY (JOHN), bookseller in Reading and London, Bible and Sun, St. Paul's Churchyard, 1730–67. Son of Robert Newbery, born in 1713. Succeeded (by marrying his widow) to the business of William Carnan, publisher and editor of the *Reading Mercury* and *Oxford Gazette*, who died in 1737. In 1744 he transferred his business to London and set up at the Bible and Sun in St. Paul's Churchyard. He made a speciality of books for children, which he issued in a cheap form and advertised largely. Newbery began to publish a periodical called *The Public Ledger* in 1759, to which both Johnson and Goldsmith contributed. He died in 1767 and was succeeded by his son Francis (*q. v.*). [*Records of the House of Newbery*, 1911.]

NEWPORT (PETER), bookseller in Dover, co. Kent: (1) St. James's Street; (2) Snargate Street, near Five Posts Lane. 1760(?)–1772. In business before 1760, in which year he founded a circulating library in the town. In the *Kentish Post* of October 31st, 1761, there appeared "Verses found written in a book belonging to Mr. Newport's Circulating Library at Dover". One verse of it will be enough:

> Thy shop, O Newport, richly stor'd
> With every pleasing Lay
> Shall to my raptured mind afford
> New pleasures every day.

In 1768 Newport moved to larger premises in Snargate Street, and his advertisement in the *Kentish Gazette* of November 4th, 1769, stated that his library contained seven thousand volumes. He was also a dealer in second-hand books. Newport retired from business in 1772 and his stock was brought by Robert Brydon.

NEWTON (S.), bookseller in Manchester, 1748–61. A pamphlet published by J. and J. Rivington in 1748 and entitled: *An Apologetical Epistle to the Author of Remarks on two pamphlets . . . against Dr. Middleton's introductory discourse . . .*" has the addition to the imprint "and S. Newton, bookseller in Manchester", and on the last page is an advertisement of another pamphlet entitled: *A full, true, and comprehensive view of Christianity*, Printed for S. Newton, bookseller in Manchester." This was perhaps a relative of the Thomas and William Newton mentioned by Procter. In 1750 he published *The Chester Miscellany*, a volume of reprints from the *Chester Courant*, while in a list of provincial booksellers he is given as in business in 1761. [*N. & Q.* 11 S. I. 364.]

NEWTON (THOMAS), bookseller in Manchester, Exchange Street, 1749–1762(?). The earliest mention of this bookseller is in a list of those who in 1749 distributed the sale catalogue of T. Warren, bookseller of Birmingham. One of the sons of Thomas Newton, proprietor of the Coffee House near the Exchange in that city. In 1755 his name appears in an advertisement of the third edition of John Barrow's *Psalm Singer's Choice Companion*. [*Whitehall Evening Post*, January 2nd, 1755.] He died in February, 1758, at the early age of thirty-seven. He and his brother William (*q. v.*) were, says Mr. Procter, considered dealers of mark by the book-buyers of their period.

NEWTON (WILLIAM), bookseller of Manchester, Exchange Street, 1762–75. In partnership with his brother Thomas, and succeeded to the business. Married a Miss Parren in April 1762. [R. W. Procter, *Memorials of Manchester Streets*, p. 197.] He advertised the sale of the *Universal Magazine*. [*Public Advertiser*, January 2nd, 1775.]

NICHOL, *see* Nicol.

NICHOLS (JOHN), F.S.A., printer in London, Red Lion Passage, 1766–1826. Son of Edward Nichols, of Islington, and Anne his wife. Born at Islington February 2nd, 174$\frac{4}{5}$. Educated at a school kept by John Shield. Apprenticed to William Bowyer, the printer, in 1757, before he was thirteen years of age. His industry and integrity won the esteem of his master, and in 1766 he was taken into partnership and eventually succeeded to the business. In 1775 he issued a supplement to Hawkesworth's *Life of Swift* in his edition of Swift's works, and in 1778 became associated with the *Gentleman's Magazine*, of which he remained editor for nearly fifty years. The bulk of his life-work lies outside the scope of this volume. He was Master of the Stationers' Company in 1804, and died October 26th, 1826.

NICHOLS (THOMAS), printer in London, outside Temple Bar, 1730. He was the printer of an edition of S. Prichard's *Masonry Dissected* in that year, but the copy in the British Museum [4738. c. 48] does not give his name.

NICHOLSON (G.), bookseller and publisher in Bradford, 1776. Joint publisher with J. Hartley of *The Memoirs of General Fairfax*, in that year.

NICHOLSON (JOHN), bookseller and publisher, Cambridge, 1752–96, of Mountsorrel, Leicestershire. When Robert Watts died (February 1751–2), leaving the business to his daughter, Mary Anne, Nicholson married the daughter the following 28th March, and continued the business, and the circulating library in the same house, until his death, August 8th, 1796. He was known by the name of "Maps", and his portrait, painted by Reinagle, hangs in the Cambridge University Library a reduced reproduction is in Gray's *Cambridge Bookselling*, 1925). This occasioned the *Lines on seeing the portrait of Old Maps*, printed in the *Cambridge Tart*, 1823. Nicholson was also the subject of the *Tripos Verses* of 1781 (reprinted in the *Cambridge Calendar* of 1802). He published many works by Roger Cotes, T. Cockman, and others, and he used to supply themes or declamations, or compositions on occasional subjects, or sermons, but strictly concealed the names of the parties concerned. It was to oblige "Maps" that, in 1786, Porson added some notes to Hutchinson's edition of Xenophon's *Anabasis*, about to be published. A good deal of information about him is in Christopher Wordsworth's *University Life in the xviijth century* (1874).

NICKSON (JOSHUA), printer in Malton, co. Yorks., 1750. In that year he printed the Rev. Thomas Comber's *Modest and Candid Reflections on Dr. Middleton's Examination of the Bp. of London's Use and Intent of Prophecy*. [Allnutt in *Bibliographica*, II. 308.]

NICKSON (NICHOLAS), printer in York: (1) Coffee House Press, Coffee Yard, 1758–9; (2) Feasegate, 1767; (3) Thursday Market, 1773; (4) Blake Street, 1776. 1754–77. Successor to John Gilfillan. Became a freeman of York in 1754. His most important work was Dr. Burton's *Monasticon Eboracense*, published in 1758. He was still in business in 1777. [Davies, p. 326 *et seq.*]

NICOL or NICHOL (GEORGE), bookseller in London: (1) Opposite York Buildings, Strand; (2) Pall Mall. 1769–1829. Apprenticed to his uncle David Wilson, in the Strand, and was taken into partnership about 1769, when their joint names appear in the imprint to Stephen Hales's *Statical Essays*, fourth edition, and also, in the same year, in the imprint to R. W. Johnson's *New System of Midwifery*. On the death of his uncle he removed his business to Pall Mall, where he gathered round him a large and distinguished *clientèle* and was appointed bookseller to King George III. On September 8th, 1787, George Nicol married the niece of William Bulmer. Subsequently he took his son William into the business, and the firm became G. and W. Nicol. He died June 25th, 1829, aged 88. Amongst other work, he compiled a catalogue of the library of the Duke of Roxburghe. John Nichols, in his *Literary Anecdotes*, states that George Nicol was a member of the Booksellers' Club that met at the Shakespeare Tavern. [vol. VI, p. 434.] He was also one of the executors to the will of Mr. James Dodsley, who left him a legacy of £1,000. [Timperley, p. 911.]

NICOL or NICOLL (w.), bookseller in London: (1) Paper Mill in St. Paul's Churchyard; (2) No. 51, St. Paul's Churchyard; 1761–75. Publisher of political pamphlets, many of which were printed for him by W. Strahan. Subscribed for seven sets of the Greek Testament of 1768. In 1769 he published an edition of Joe Miller's *Jests*. In 1775 W. Nichol was one of the partners in the publication of *The Works of Congreve*. [*Public Advertiser*, January 7th, 1775.]

NISBET (DAVID), bookbinder in Newcastle, *c.* 1760, *see* Scottish Section.

NOBLE (FRANCIS and JOHN), booksellers and publishers in London: (1) Holborn; (2) Dryden's [Otway's] Head in St. Martin's Court; 1739–92. Commenced a circulating library in Holborn in 1739(?), said to be one of the first four that were established in London. In 1746 they issued a catalogue which shows that they specialized in books for children, and were also dealers in second-hand books. In 1765 *The History of Miss Clarinda Cathcart* is advertised as "Printed for and sold by Francis Noble at his Circulating Library opposite Gray's Inn Gate, Holborn, and John Noble, near Leicester Square. [*Gazetteer and Daily Advertiser*, October 7th, 1765.] In 1775 the addresses are given as F. Noble, Middle Row, Holborn, and J. Noble, St. Martin's Court, near Leicester Fields. [*Public Advertiser*, February 24th, 1775.] They did not always publish together, and seem to have been separate firms. Francis Noble issued a trade card engraved by Ravenet, showing the interior of his library. This card, judging from the costumes, appears to have been issued between 1745 and 1750. He was then apparently alone at Otway's Head. [A. Heal's Collection.] He died in 1792. [Timperley, 1842, p. 776.]

NOBLE (SAMUEL), bookseller (?) in London, Pope's Head in Carnaby Street, near Cardigan Market, *c.* 1775. Ran a circulating library. Issued trade cards without date, but somewhere round about the above year. He was succeeded by Charles Geary. [A. Heal's Collection.]

NOMAN (T.), (?) Printer in London, near Fleet Street, 1738. A broadside entitled *The Prince in Custady* (sic) *or, a trip from St. Jamese* (sic) *to the Earl of Grantham's house in Arllbemarl-street* (sic), was published without date, but some time during the year 1738, and bore the imprint "London: Printed by T. Noman, near Fleet Street". It was evidently the work of a third-rate printer, many italic letters being mixed with the roman. The name of the printer is probably fictitious. This broadside was brought to the notice of the Government, but what resulted is unknown. [S.P. Dom., Geo. II, Bundle 46 (120).]

NOON (J.), bookseller and publisher in London, White Hart, near Mercer's Chapel in Cheapside, 1726(?)–1763. Publisher of theological and philosophical works. He advertised *The Examination of Mr. Barclay's Principles* in 1726. [*London Journal*, December 2nd, 1726.] At the end of Moses Lowman's *Appendix to a Dissertation on the Civil Government of the Hebrews*, issued in 1741, is a list of books printed for J. Noon, consisting of nine items, all theological. In 1747 he published a Life of Thomas Chubb, the Freethinker, and in 1751 C. Bulkley's *Vindication* of Shaftesbury. He was the publisher of the writings of the Rev. John Jackson, Rector of Sessay, a noted controversialist. As a set off to so much theology, Noon is found associated with Andrew Millar in publishing *An Account of the Behaviour of Mr. James Maclaine*, who was executed on October 3rd, 1750. [Winship.] Noon died January 18th, 1763, aged 83.

NOORTHOUCK (HERMAN), bookseller, London. In Russell Court, against the Chapel, near Covent Garden, 1735. He advertised second-hand books in the *Daily Journal*, January 21st, 1735.

NORRIS (T.), *see Dictionary*, 1668–1725.

NORRIS (W.), printer and bookseller in Taunton, 1718–55, *see Dictionary*, 1668–1725. Still in business in 1755, when his name is found in an advertisement in the *Bath Advertiser*. Apparently succeeded by T. Norris.

NORTON (WILLIAM), printer in Manchester, 1761. Only known from the entry of his marriage in the parish register. Procter, in his *Memorials*, suggests that he was perhaps a workman only (p. 201).

NOURSE (JOHN), bookseller and publisher in London, Lamb without Temple Bar, 1730(?)–1780. Successor to W. Mears at this address. Dealt in French literature, and made a feature of scientific works. In 1736 in partnership with Brotherton, and together they issued an edition of the works of Horace. Nourse was one of the booksellers appointed by the Society for the Encouragement of Learning, *q. v.* In an advertisement in the *Public Advertiser*, January 9th, 1775, J. Nourse is described as "Bookseller to His Majesty". John Nourse died in 1780. [Nichols, II. 95, III. 732.] He was succeeded by Francis Wingrave (*q. v.*).

NUTT (BENJAMIN), printer in London, Savoy, 1710(?)–1747. Possibly son and successor of John Nutt, printer, 1690(?)–1710(?). He died March 15th, 1747. [Timperley, 1842, p. 674.]

NUTT (EDWARD), bookseller in London, Royal Exchange, 1725–1730(?). Nichols mentions him, but gives little information, and his relationship (if any) to the family of printers in the Savoy has not been found. In 1728 his name occurs in a list of those selling *The Exaltation of Christmas Pye*. [*Daily Post*, January 1st, 1728.] In 1735 Mrs. Nutt, of the Royal Exchange, is found selling a theological book. [*See* Nutt, Sarah.]

NUTT (ELIZABETH), printer in London. In the Savoy, 1720–38. *See Dictionary*, 1668–1725. She was still living in 1736 [Nichols, VIII. 368], and may be identical with the Elizabeth Nutt who is described as "widow" in the administration of Joseph Nutt of the precinct of St. John Baptist, Savoy, granted on May 2nd, 1738. [P.C.C. 128, Brodrepp].

NUTT or NOTT (JAMES), printer in London, St. Botolph's, Aldersgate, 1729. Was examined on April 29th, 1729, regarding the printing of the *London Journal* of Saturday, April 26th, 1729 (No. 508). He admitted it was printed at Mr. Wilkins's in Little Britain, and that he printed it during Wilkins's absence from town. [S.P. Dom., Geo. II, Bundle 11 (39, 41.)] His relationship (if any) to the other families of this name has not been discovered.

NUTT (RICHARD), printer in London: (1) Old Bailey; (2) Savoy. 1724(?)–1780. Possibly son of John Nutt, printer, 1690(?)–1710(?). Son-in-law of Hugh Meres or Meeres, printer (*q. v.*). In partnership with Elizabeth Nutt in 1724. In 1726 he took over the printing of the *Daily Post* from C. Meere or Mears, and continued to print it until 1732, when the name of S. Neville is found in the imprint. In 1735 *The Young Clerk's Tutor* was advertised as printed by R. and E. Nutt and R. Gosling (assigns of Edward Sayer, Esq.) for John Osborn, Golden Ball. [*Daily Journal*, June 2nd, 1735.] Richard Nutt was also printer of the *London Evening Post* for many years. On July 10th, 1755, he was tried and convicted of publishing in that paper a libel on the Government over the signature "True Blue". He was sentenced to stand in the pillory at Charing Cross for one hour, to be imprisoned in the King's Bench Prison for two years, to pay a fine of £500, and to find sureties for his good behaviour for five years. He died in Bartlett's Buildings, Holborn, on March 11th, 1780, aged 86. [Nichols, III. 733; *Gentleman's Magazine*, 1755, XXV. 329 and 569.]

NUTT (SARAH), pamphlet-seller in London, Royal Exchange, 1735–40. Possibly the widow of Edward Nutt (*q. v.*). In 1735 she sold *The Religious ... and Moral Conduct of Matthew Tyndale*. Later on, in 1740, she was in trouble with the

authorities for selling the *London Evening Post*, and admitted that she had been selling it for two years (i.e. since 1738).

OLIVER (J. and W.), *see* Oliver (John).

OLIVER (JOHN), printer and publisher in London, Bartholomew Close, 1740(?)–1775. Printer to the Society for Promoting Christian Knowledge, and also to the corresponding society engaged in promoting English Protestant working schools in Ireland. Printed also largely for the Methodists and other Nonconforming bodies. About 1767 he took into partnership W. Oliver, possibly a son, and the firm became J. and W. Oliver. Their printing was always good, and amongst the works that issued from this press may be mentioned the second edition of *An Earnest and Affectionate Address to the people called Methodists*, by A. B., in 1745; John Wesley's sermon on the death of George Whitefield in 1770; and a pamphlet by Thomas Green, called *A Dissertation on Enthusiasm*, printed in 1775. John Oliver died on January 19th, 1775, aged 73. [Nichols, III. 733.]

OLIVER (W.), *see* Oliver (John).

OLIVERS (M.), *see* Olivers (Thomas).

OLIVERS (THOMAS), bookseller in Worcester, 1746. Mentioned in a list of provincial booksellers. [*N. & Q.* 10 S. V. 242.] An M. Olivers is mentioned in the same list as in business in 1748. A sermon published in 1748 bears the imprint "Worcester: Printed and sold by M. Olivers and S. Mountford in High Street". [*Bibliography of Worcestershire*, p. 57.]

OSBORN (JOHN), *see Dictionary*, 1668–1725. In 1735 his name is found alone, publishing from The Golden Ball, Paternoster Row. [*Daily Journal*, January 29th, 1735.] In 1739 John Osborn (late of Paternoster Row) printed an edition of Shakespeare's *Works*, "as a copy that lay in Common". The Booksellers did not venture to claim an exclusive right by law or equity, but bought up the copies which Osborn had printed, for a pension. [*Observations on the Case of the Booksellers of London and Westminster.*]

OSBORNE (THOMAS), bookseller, publisher, and book-auctioneer in London, Grays Inn, 1738–67. Son and successor of Thomas Osborne (1702–43). He has been variously described as "coarse, dull, and uneducated", and as "a very respectable man". Pope sneered at him in *The Dunciad*. Johnson said he was impertinent and knocked him down with a folio. On the other hand, a well-known Nonconformist minister employed him as a publisher and spoke well of him. On the whole, perhaps the Rev. Thomas Toplady was of a more charitable frame of mind than either Johnson or Pope. Osborne succeeded to a good business and he improved it. Nichols says that "he filled one side of Gray's Inn with his lumber, and without knowing the intrinsic value of a single book, contrived such arbitrary prices, as raised him to his country house, and dog and duck huntings ". [Nichols, III. 625.] If we may judge by his acts, Osborne knew a good deal more than some of his fellow tradesmen gave him credit for. At any rate he secured the valuable library of Edward Harley, Earl of Oxford, in 1742, for the sum of £13,000. He sold this again in February 1744. He took considerable care in the preparation of the catalogue and secured Dr. Johnson to write the *Proposals* and compile the first volume. He incurred the jealousy and enmity of the trade by making a charge for the catalogue and for putting what they considered too high a price on the books. Dibdin, in his *Bibliomania*, spoke of Osborne as "the most celebrated bookseller of his age, and gave it as his opinion that his charges were "extremely moderate". His correspondence was by no means that of an uneducated man, and his handwriting was small and neat. Thomas Osborne died in 1767, his will being proved on August 26th. It is of little interest. He left his house in Warwick Court to his wife, and he owned other premises in Paved Court, Fulwood's Rents, Holborn, in which he kept part of his stock. He left no heir, and desired that his business should be sold to pay his legacies. To the Benchers of Gray's Inn he bequeathed a ring each. [P.C.C. 315, Legard.]

OSBORNE (WILLIAM), printer in London, the Minories, 1732. On April 14th, 1732, the postmaster at Greenwich wrote to Charles Delafaye: "The enclosed is a ballad sung in Greenwich yesterday, though I believe I have spoyl'd his singing for the present, haveing committed him to the House of Correction. I find Osborne the printer of them is just sett up in ye minories and his principall buisnes [*sic*] is to print such low, seditious stuff .... P.S. I am told the printer prints some affaires for the Custom House." [S. P. Dom. George II, Bundle 26, 65.] Being examined on May 19th, the printer confessed that he had sold the ballad of *The Forlorn Lover* and also had printed and sold one entitled *Britain's Joy for the return of the Duke of Ormond*, and added that this was also printed by Larkin, now a printer in Petticoat Lane, Whitechapel. [*Ib.*, Bundle 26, 74.]

OSWALD (JOHN), bookseller and publisher in London: (1) White's Alley, Chancery Lane; (2) Rose and Crown in the Poultry, 1726–53. In 1726 he published the

Rev. Robert Fleming's *Fulfilling of the Scriptures* [W.M.C., November], and he apparently made theological works his principal business; but amongst his publications in 1747 was Daniel Neal's *History of New England*, the second edition. [J. C. B. L.] In 1753, with Gardner and G. Woodfall, he published *The True Protestant* from the Rose and Crown, Poultry. [*Public Advertiser*, September 1st, 1753.]

OTRIDGE (WILLIAM), bookseller and publisher, in London, opposite the New Church in the Strand, 1772–1812. This name is found in the imprint to a pamphlet by Francis Hargrave, *An Argument in the Case of James Sommersett, a Negro*, 1772. [J. C. B. L.]. In 1775 he and three others published and sold a Dictionary. [*Public Advertiser*, January 3rd, 1775.] Died at Turnham Green, November 9th, 1812. [*Gentleman's Magazine*, LXXXII, p. 500.]

OWEN (EDWARD), printer in London: (1) Amen Corner, or Warwick Lane, (?)1732; (2) near Chancery Lane, Holborn, 1743–70. One of the printers of the *London Gazette*. In partnership with T. Harrison (*q. v.*). For T. Astley, the publisher, he printed in 1732, *Full Instructions for Country Gentlemen* and *The Gentleman's Pocket Farrier*. In 1755 Samuel Birt (*q. v.*) left him a legacy of ten pounds. [P.C.C. 304, Paul.] Amongst his publications for 1743 was *Memoirs of the first settlement of the Island of Barbados, and other Carribee Islands*, which bore the imprint " for E. Owen, near Chancery Lane, Holborn". He printed numerous pamphlets that are now scarce, such as *A Definition of the Treaty of Aix-la-Chapelle*, 1749; *Two memorials of the Abbé de la Ville*, 1747. In 1751 he printed a tract by Howard for Dodsley. [Straus.]

OWEN (WILLIAM), bookseller and publisher in London, Homer's Head, near Temple Bar, 1748–93. In 1748 his name is met with in the imprint to a little pamphlet entitled *The Remembrances. By George Cadwallader, Gent, Consisting of the Twelve First Numbers from the Weekly Paper, Published under the above-mentioned Title.* [B.M. P.P. 3557. o.] In the Poll-Book for the City and Liberty of Westminster, printed in 1749, occurs the name of a "W. Owen, bookseller," in St. James's Street, but there is nothing to show whether the two were identical. On July 6th, 1752, William Owen was tried and acquitted at the Guildhall of the City of London for selling a pamphlet setting out the hardships suffered by Alexander Murray at the hands of Parliament for interfering at an election. The House of Commons voted *The Case of Alexander Murray Esq.*, "an impudent, malicious, scandalous and seditious libel", but the jury found that William Owen did not publish it. The proceedings are

printed in the *State Trials*. In 1753 W. Owen and W. Goadby, the bookseller in Sherborne, Dorset (*q. v.*), published *An Account of the Fairs held in England and Wales*; but owing to the alteration in the calendar, made in the preceding year, when the New Style was adopted, they were not satisfied with it, and destroyed the unsold copies. They were encouraged to make another attempt, and, obtaining the help of a Government official, and also a Royal licence for fourteen years, they published in 1756 *An Authentic Account, published by the King's Authority, of all the Fairs in England and Wales*, which bore the imprint "London: Printed for W. Owen at Homer's Head, Temple Bar, and R. Goadby at Sherborne in Dorsetshire, M.DCCLVI". [B.M. 577. b. 4.] They also published a Book of Roads, and both these works went through several editions up till 1859. William Owen was Master of the Stationers' Company in 1781, and died on December 1st, 1793. [Timperley, 1842, p. 781.] William Owen was also the publisher of many pamphlets of a political character, such as *A History of Patriotism*, which are now very scarce.

PAGE (JOHN), bookseller in Chester, 1747. Mentioned in list of provincial booksellers. [*N. & Q.* 10 S. v, February 24th, 1906, p. 142.] Possibly son and successor of Humphrey Page, 1685–1711, *see Dictionary*, 1668–1725.

PAGE (THOMAS), booksellers and publishers in London, Tower Hill, 1730(?)–1781. There were several booksellers of this name, who succeeded each other at the above address. One of them is believed to have been son-in-law to William Mount (*q. v.*), by whom he was taken into partnership. Timperley states that he died on March 15th, 1733 (p. 651). In the *London Evening Post* for February 13th–15th, 1733, is the notice of the marriage of Sally, daughter of Thomas Page, stationer, of Tower Hill, to Daniel Croggs, paper merchant, of Bread Street; but whether she was the daughter of the man who died in 1733 or of the Thomas Page, bookseller, who died April 5th, 1762, is not clear. A third Thomas Page, "bookseller", died at the above address in 1781. The firm dealt chiefly in nautical books.

PAGE (THOMAS), bookseller in Ipswich, Suffolk, 1763. Mentioned in list of provincial booksellers as in business in that year. [*N. & Q.* 11 S. I. 363.]

PAINTER (J.), bookseller in Truro, co. Cornwall, 1753–70. One of those who sold the Rev. S. Walker's *Sermon preached at Truro . . . June 3, 1753.* [Dredge.] In 1770 his name is found in the imprint of *An Exposition of the Catechism*. [Dredge.]

PALAIRET (JOHN), (?) bookseller and publisher in London, Duke's Arms in the Strand [almost facing Catherine Street], 1743–4. He was the publisher of a highly successful pamphlet entitled *Serious Considerations on the several High Duties which the Nation in general (as well as its Trade in particular) labours under, &c. &c. By a Well wisher to the Good People of Great Britain.* The first edition appeared in 1743, and was almost immediately followed by another, and three other editions were published during the year 1744.

PALMER (ELIZABETH), bookseller and bookbinder in Gloucester, 1744–51. Possibly a descendant of Samuel Palmer (1685). Agent for *The Political Cabinet*, a monthly review. In 1751 she was one of the publishers of the Rev. Anselm Bayly's *Antiquity . . . of Christianity*. [B.M. 225. g. 9 (1).]

PALMER (JOHN), bookseller and publisher in Bristol, (1) Nicholas Street; (2) Wine Street. 1748–71. In 1748 his advertisement is found on the covers of Hooke's *Bristollia*. During the election of 1754 he published a pamphlet called *The Bristol Contest*. [Hyett and Bazeley, p. 58.] In 1757 he published the Bishop of Bristol's *Sermons*; in 1766 J. Newton's *Reply to a letter to the Rev. Caleb Evans of Bristol*. [B.M. 4223. aaa. 14.] In 1771 he was taking in advertisements for Pugh's *Hereford Journal*. He was apparently dead before 1777, when Mrs. Palmer was carrying on the business. [*N. & Q.* 10 S. v. 141.]

PALMER (JOHN), bookseller in Gloucester, 1728–53. Publisher of the Rev. Peter Senhouse's *Sermon* preached in Gloucester Cathedral on September 20th, 1727. [W. M. C., May 1728.] Possibly a descendant of Samuel Palmer (1685). In 1753 his name occurs in a list of booksellers selling the London newspaper the *Daily Register*.

PARIS (JOHN), bookseller in St. Benedict's parish, Cambridge, *c.* 1759–79. Published H. Malden's *Account of King's College Chapel, with a short history of King's and Eton*, 1760. He was one of the two constables of the town indicted and convicted at the town sessions, on April 26th, 1759, for disobeying the orders of the high constable to meet at the Town Hall (in pursuance of the directions of the Vice-Chancellor and Mayor) on February 27th, being Shrove Tuesday, to assist in apprehending all persons guilty of throwing at cocks on that day. [Cooper's *Annals*, IV. 302.] An advertisement in the *Cambridge Chronicle*, June 21st, 1777, and June 19th, 1779 announces his appointment as agent and receiver for the county for the Royal Exchange

Assurance Office. On November 15th, 1777, the same paper advertised the publication by John and Thomas Paris of William Cole's *Nature and Properties of Light and the Theory of Comets.*

PARKER (   ), bookseller in Coventry, co. Warwick., 1767–76. His name occurs in the imprint to the Rev. Henry Homer's *An Enquiry into the Means of Preserving and Improving the Publick Roads of this Kingdom,* printed at Oxford in 1767. He was still in business in 1776.

PARKER (CHARLES), bookseller and publisher in London, upper part of New Bond Street, 1767–76. Publisher of travels, satirical poems, and broadsides. Two somewhat rare items were: *Remarks on a passage from the river Balise, in the Bay of Honduras, to Merida ; the capital of the Province of Jucatan. In the Spanish West Indies,* 1769; and *American Resistance Indefensible, A Sermon,* 1776. Price sixpence. Both are in the John Carter Brown library, Providence, U.S.A. Parker published catalogues of his stock in 1771, and again in 1776. [B.M. 11904. e. 7, 9.] Bill-head dated 1768 in the possession of Mr. A. Heal.

PARKER (EDMUND), bookseller in London, Bible and Crown, Lombard Street, 1704–39. *See Dictionary,* 1668–1725. Still in business in 1726. [W. M. C., February 1726.] He died on December 16th, 1739. He was unmarried, and administration of his effects was granted to his brother, the Rev. Edward Parker. [P.C.C., Admons. 1740 ; *Weekly Miscellany,* December 22nd, 1739.] He was succeeded in his business by a Mr. Mellor, who within a year died of a violent fever. [*Weekly Miscellany,* December 13th, 1740.]

PARKER (HENRY), book and printseller in London, (1) 82 Cornhill; (2) opposite Birchin Lane, 36 Cornhill. 1759 (?)–1775. Timperley [p. 835] calls him "an eminent stationer and printseller". In 1759 he was in partnership with E. Bakewell, and amongst their publications in that year was Richard Rolt's *Lives of the Reformers,* notable for the fine series of portraits that it contained. The following advertisement is in the *Public Advertiser,* January 31st, 1775 : "Henry Parker, Book and Printseller, has removed from 82 Cornhill to 36, the Corner of Birchin Lane." Henry Parker retired from business in 1775, and died at Stoke Newington, aged 84, on August 28th, 1809. He was for many years deputy of Cornhill Ward.

PARKER (JOHN), bookseller and publisher (?) in London, near the Cocoa-Tree in Pall Mall, 1700 (?)–1735. This bookseller was evidently in business at the beginning of the century, as in 1713 he took as an apprentice Henry Baker,

who afterwards became a famous naturalist and Fellow of the Royal Society. Baker has left it on record that his seven years' apprenticeship with John Parker were among the happiest of his life. He speaks of his former master as "an honest, good-natured man, who treated him with the utmost kindness". [Timperley, 1842, p. 732.] In the London *Daily Post* of February 11th, 1726, occurs an advertisement inserted by John Parker, that the second part of Mr. Baker's *Poems* were ready for the subscribers and could be had of him. They were also advertised in Wilford's *Monthly Catalogue* for February 1726 as follows: "Original Poems, serious and humourous. The second Part. By Mr. Henry Baker. Sold by *J. Brotherton* in *Cornhill,* and *T. Worral* in *Fleet-street.* Price 1*s.* 6*d.*" The author was evidently Parker's former apprentice. The first part of the *Poems* had been published by J. Roberts in Warwick Lane a year earlier, and there is no evidence that Parker had anything to do with the publication, beyond acting as agent for the sale of the second part. Parker died about 1735, and was succeeded at the above address by Robert Dodsley.

PARKER (SACKVILLE), bookseller and publisher in Oxford, 1730 (?)–1796. Son of Samuel Parker, who married the daughter of Henry Clements, bookseller in Oxford. Sackville Parker was born in 1707. Apprenticed to Richard Clements, son of Henry. Known to his intimates as "Sacky" or "Sack" Parker. He matriculated. His shop was at the corner of Logic Lane, next to University College. In 1752 he published the Rev. William Hawkins's *Sermon* preached at St. Mary's on January 30th. [B.M. 694. f. 4 (6).] In 1784 he received a visit from Dr. Johnson, who found him very ill and was much upset at parting from him. Sackville Parker died at Oxford in his eighty-ninth year on December 10th, 1796. [*The Parkers of Oxford,* an address by Mr. J. C. Parker in 1914.]

PARKER (THOMAS), printer in London, Jewin Street, *c.* 1753. Mentioned in the will of Thomas Meighen, proved on December 29th, 1753. [P.C.C. 323 Searle.]

PARKER (WILLIAM), bookseller and publisher in London, King's Head, St. Paul's Churchyard, 1732–40. In 1729 his imprint occurs in a work entitled *Six Sermons.* Publisher of a *Sermon* by Thomas Macro, D.D., entitled *Charity of Temper,* 1732. [B.M. 225. f. 19 (7).] In 1740 he published *An Explanation of Scripture Prophesies.*

PARKHOUSE (J.), bookseller at Tiverton, co. Devon., 1740 (?)–1819. The earliest work in which his name has been found is *A Paraphrase . . . on the Epistles . . . to the Romans and Galations,* by the Rev. Timothy Edwards, Vicar of Okehamp-

ton, Devon, in 1752. It is also found in the imprint to the Rev. William Roberts's *Divine Institution,* published without date but assigned to the year 1750. [Dredge, p. 24.] He had evidently been in business for some years before that, as Timperley says that his daughter, afterwards Mrs. Hannah Cowley, the dramatist, was born at Tiverton in 1743. For many years J. Parkhouse was engaged in preparing a *Talmudic Lexicon.* He died in April 1819. [Timperley, 1842, p. 870.]

PARKHOUSE (PHILIP), bookseller in Tiverton, Devon., 1750 (?)–1753. No doubt a relative of J. Parkhouse, with whom he shared the publication of Roberts's *The Divine Institution.* His name is found in the imprints of other publications during the years 1752–3.

PARRADISE (   ), bookseller in Calne, co. Wilts., 1747. Mentioned in an advertisement of the second edition of Stackhouse's *Bible* in 1747.

PARSONS, (R.), bookseller in Newcastle-under-Lyme, co. Stafford., 1734–42. Voted for Gower and Ward at an election on May 1st, 1734. In 1742 he published a map of Staffordshire. [Sims.]

PARSONS (S.), bookseller and publisher in Newcastle-under-Lyme, Stafford., and Congleton in Cheshire, 1747–65. The earliest mention of this bookseller that has been found is in the imprint to a *Sermon* preached at St. Chad's on October 1st, 1747, by the Rev. M. Horbery. [B.M. 225. f. 16 (3).] In 1755 the third edition of John Barrow's *Psalm-singer's Choice Companion* was on sale at his shop in Newcastle-under-Lyme, while in 1756 he appears as agent for Schofield's *Middlewich Journal or Cheshire Advertiser.* He still kept his shop in Newcastle in 1765, according to a list of provincial booksellers. [*N. & Q.* 10 S. v. 183.]

PARTINGTON (R.), printer in London. In 1748 the Court of Sessions for Middlesex instructed the County Treasurer to pay this printer two guineas for printing two reams of certificates. [*Cal. of Midd. Sessions Records,* January 1748/9, December 1751, p. 83.]

PARVISH (SAMUEL), bookseller in Guildford, Surrey, 1731. Only known from an advertisement of the following: *Reasons for Uniting the Church and Dissenters . . . To which is annexed a Liturgy* . . . 1731. [Advertisement in *Grub Street Journal,* August 5th, 1731.]

PASHAM (JOHN), bookseller and stationer in Northampton, 1744–9. Possibly son of James Pasham (1721). Publisher of the Rev. H. Layng's *Sermon* preached in the parish church of All Saints, Northampton, on Monday, September 22nd, 1746, on behalf of the County Infirmary. He also contributed one guinea to the funds of the Institution. [B.M. T. 1658 (5).]

PASHAM (J. W.), printer in Bury St. Edmunds, Suffolk, 1776–83. Printer of the *Bury Flying Weekly Journal.* Afterwards moved to London and settled in Blackfriars. Died September 16th, 1783. [Nichols, VIII. 482.]

PASHAM (T.), printer at Stratford-upon-Avon, 1745. In that year he printed *Short Remarks on Dr. Perry's Analysis made on the Stratford Mineral Water.* By William Baylies, junior.

PATERSON (SAMUEL), bookseller, publisher, and book-auctioneer in London, (1) opposite Durham Yard, Strand; (2) Essex House, Essex Street, Strand; (3) King Street, Covent Garden. Born March 17th, 1728. Losing his father at the age of twelve he was sent to France. When little more than twenty, he opened a shop in the Strand and dealt in foreign literature. About the same time he married a Miss Hamilton, niece of the Countess of Eglinton, and connected with several noble families in Scotland. His first publication was a volume of poems by Miss Charlotte Ramsay. In 1753 he started as a book-auctioneer at Essex House in Essex Street, and in 1757 he rescued the manuscripts of Sir Julius Caesar, Judge of the Admiralty Court in the reigns of Elizabeth and James I, from the cheesemonger to whom they had been sold as waste paper, prepared a catalogue of them, and sold them by auction in December. A copy of this, with the names of the purchasers and the prices, said to have been added by Bishop Heber, is in the British Museum [824. b. 17 (10)]. Amongst other notable libraries that came under his hammer were those of Topham Beauclerk, Alderman Fleetwood, and Benjamin West. He was famous for his catalogues, and on the death of Dr. Johnson (who had stood godfather to one of his sons) he was asked to catalogue his library, but was then in Holland. Samuel Paterson was also the author of an account of a tour through Holland and Flanders under the pseudonym of *Coryat Junior,* in 1767. There is an advertisement in the *Public Advertiser,* March 13th, 1775, of "A Dividend to Creditors of Samuel Paterson, late of Essex Street, Strand, Bookseller". In or about 1788 he accepted the post of librarian to the Marquis of Lansdowne. He died November 29th, 1802. [Nichols, III. 438.]

PAYNE (HENRY), bookseller and publisher in London, Pall Mall, 1760–1. For some time in partnership with W. Cropley. Publisher of theological literature.

PAYNE (J.), bookseller in Brackley, Northamptonshire, 1772. William Payne's *Elements of Trigonometry* was advertised in the *General Evening Post* of January 2nd, 1772, to be sold by "T. Payne at the Mews-Gate in London" (*q. v.*) and the above. They were perhaps relatives of the compilers. His name does not occur in the imprint of the book.

PAYNE (JOHN), bookseller and publisher in London, (1) Pope's Head, Paternoster Row, (2) The Feathers, Paternoster Row. 1745–87. It is not known if any relationship existed between this bookseller and those of the Brackley family. He appears to have set up about 1740, and was a member of the club which met in Ivy Lane of which Dr. Johnson was the founder in 1749; in March 1750 appeared the first number of the periodical called *The Rambler*, John Payne having agreed to give Johnson two guineas for each paper as it appeared and to give him also a share of the profits. He also published *The Adventurer*, No. xviii of which he was selling on January 6th, 1753 [*Public Advertiser*], also the early numbers of *The Universal Chronicle*, No. 5 of which (May 6th, 1758) is entitled *Payne's Universal Chronicle*. Johnson's *Idler* first appeared in No. 2. In 1765 there is an advertisement of the sale of the *Universal Museum*, printed for J. Payne, The Feathers, Paternoster Row. [*Gazetteer and New Daily Advertiser*, July 1st, 1765.] In 1744 John Payne had entered the service of the Bank of England, and from 1780 to 1785 was accountant-general.

PAYNE (OLIVER), bookseller in London, Horace's Head, Round Court, Strand, 1733–9. Son of Oliver and Martha Payne of Brackley, Northamptonshire, and brother of Thomas Payne. According to Timperley [1842, p. 799], who, however, gives no authority for his statement, this bookseller received an annuity from the Marquis of Douglas for a manuscript said to have been stolen from the Vatican. He is also said to have been the first bookseller to print catalogues. He advertised in 1735 "To sell books at the prices marked". [*Daily Journal*, January 13th, 1735.] His brother Thomas was for some years his assistant; but Oliver Payne got into serious financial difficulties and was adjudged bankrupt in March 173$^{8}_{9}$, whereupon Thomas Payne set up for himself at Charing Cross.

PAYNE (THOMAS), bookseller in London, (1) next the Mew's Gate near St. Martin's Church in Cheapside; (2) near the South Sea House, Bishopsgate Street. 1730–90. "Honest Tom Payne"—so acclaimed by Nichols in his *Literary Anecdotes* [VI. 439–41], for forty years a celebrated bookseller, was born at Brackley in Northamptonshire, and baptized on May 26th, 1719. Apprenticed to his brother, Oliver Payne (*q. v.*). After the latter's bankruptcy he set up for himself, but imitated Oliver's practice of issuing printed catalogues of his stock, with the prices affixed, the earliest of his own catalogues being issued on February 29th, 174$^{0}_{1}$. In 1745 Thomas married Elizabeth Taylor, whose brother, also a bookseller in London, carried on business in Castle Street, next the Mew's Gate. Payne succeeded to both the business and the premises, which became afterwards known as the Literary Coffee-House. Nichols has recorded his character as one who was warm in his friendships, a convivial, cheerful companion, whose one pursuit in life was "fair dealing". His shop was the rendezvous of all the literary men of the day. Thomas Payne retired from business in 1790, when he was succeeded by his son Thomas, who had been in partnership with him for more than twenty years. He died on February 2nd, 1799. Many of his catalogues are in the British Museum.

PAYNE (THOMAS), bookseller and stationer in Wrexham, co. Denbigh., *c.* 1730. Issued a trade card about this date. [A. Heal's Collection.] In 1735 he was agent for the sale of *Adam's Weekly Courant*. [J. P. Earwaker, *Local Gleanings*, I. 237.]

PAYRAM (F.), bookseller and publisher, London, 1726. He published "*Acta Regia*, no. vi", in partnership with C. Rivington, J. Darby, and others. [*London Journal*, February 26th, 1726.]

PEARCE, or PEARCH (GEORGE), bookseller and publisher in Cheapside, 1768–71. Publisher of Dr. Charles Beatty's *Journal of a Two Months' Tour* amongst the inhabitants on the frontiers of Pennsylvania, which was printed in London in 1768. At the end he advertised several other books. [J. C. B. L.]

PEARCH, *see* Pearce.

PECK (DAVID), bookseller and publisher in York, St. Helen's Square, 1768–1780 (?). His name occurs in the imprint to *An Accurate Description and History of the Cathedral . . . of St. Peter, York*, published in 1768. [Davis, p. 265.] He was succeeded by Henry Sotheran.

PEELE (JOHN), bookseller and publisher in London, Locke's Head in Amen Corner, Paternoster Row. *See Dictionary*, 1668–1725.

PELLET (JOHN), bookseller in London, (1) "ad insigne Capitis St. Evremont in Foeni Foro apud Westm"; (2) in the Haymarket, 1726. An edition of the commentary of Petrus Petitus on the three books of Aretaeus was printed by "Will. Bowyer impensis Johannis Pellet . . ." in 1726, 4to, also an edition of Xenophon. [W. M. C., June.]

PEMBERTON (HENRY), bookseller in London, Fleet Street, 1739 (?)–1748. Son of John Pemberton the elder (*q. v.*), and probably in the business before his father's death, after which event he and his brother John carried on the business. Henry died unmarried, on March 29th, 1748, his will being proved on that day. [P.C.C. 97, Strahan.] He desired to be buried in St. Dunstan's in the West. He made no reference to his business, but he left the residue of his estate to his brother Thomas. As he does not mention his brother John, he was also perhaps dead before 1748. Henry's death was recorded in the *Penny London Post*.

PEMBERTON (JOHN), bookseller and publisher in London, Golden Buck in Fleet Street, 1709–39. *See Dictionary*, 1668–1725. In 1726 he published *A Mechanical Essay on Singing, Music, and Dancing*. [W. M. C., November.] In 1729 he was granted a share in printing the Votes of the House of Commons, but not being a printer he farmed this to others. In 1735 the firm became J. and J. Pemberton, he having taken his eldest son John into the business, and it is so styled in Kent's *Directory* for 1738. According to the *London Daily Post*, John Pemberton the elder died on July 9th, 1739, his will being proved on the 28th of the same month. He left to his widow Rebecca his Livery Share in the English Stock of the Company of Stationers. He left four sons and one daughter. Two of the sons, John and Henry, succeeded to the business. A bequest was also left to Robert Gosling, bookseller, of St. Dunstan's in the West. [P.C.C. 162, Henchman.] As John junior is not mentioned in the will of his brother Henry (*q. v.*), proved in 1748, he may have died in the interval.

PEMBERTON (JOHN), junior, bookseller and publisher in London, The Buck in Fleet Street, 1739 (?)–1744 (?). Son of John Pemberton the elder. During his father's lifetime the firm was known as J. and J. Pemberton. They were the publishers for the House of Commons, and also for the Society for the Pro-

pagation of the Gospel in Foreign Parts. After the death of his father in 1739, John the younger was joined by his brother Henry, and their joint imprint is found in books until 1744; but as there is no mention of John in the will of Henry, proved in 1748, it may be presumed that he died or retired between 1744 and 1748.

PENN ( ), widow, bookseller in Bristol, Wine Street, 1733. Mentioned in a list of provincial booksellers in *Notes & Queries* as in business in that year. [*N. & Q.* 11 S. I. 304.] She was probably the widow of Joseph Penn (1709–22).

PEN, or PENN (JOHN), bookseller and publisher in London, (1) next the Castle Tavern in Fleet Street; (2) in Westminster Hall; (3) Bible and Dove in Fleet Street. 1726–9. In Wilford's *Monthly Catalogue* for November, 1726, is the following under *New Miscellaneous Pamphlets*: "*Farther Advice to the Clergy of St. Albans, respecting the augmentation of small livings within that Archdeaconry*. By the Reverend Mr. Archdeacon Stubbs. Sold by John Penn next the Castle-Tavern in Fleet-Street, and John Penn in Westminster Hall. Price 1s." No copy of this has been found, nor is the original extant. The author was Philip Stubb, Archdeacon of St. Albans. Later on he wrote *More Advice to the . . . Clergy . . . of St. Albans*, without date, but after May 23rd, 1729. In this, Pen's address is given as at the Bible and Dove in Fleet Street. [B.M. 109. c. 2.]

PENN ( ), bookseller at Tunbridge, co. Kent, Tunbridge Walks, 1731. In 1731 sold the Bishop of London's caveat against aspersing Princes and their administration. [Advertisement in *Fog's Weekly*, July 31st, 1731.]

PENNINGTON (WILLIAM), printer in Kendal, co. Westmoreland, 1776. Printer of an annual called *The Kendal Diary*.

PENNY (ROBERT), printer in London, (1) Wine Office Court, Fleet Street, 1735; (2) Mark Lane, 1746; (3) Allhallows Staining, 1761. Printer of Samuel Humphrey's edition of the Bible, the first volume being advertised in *The Country Journal or Craftsman* of December 27th, 1735. In this advertisement the names of many provincial booksellers who were distributing agents were given, but they were omitted from the title-page. The second volume of the work appeared in 1737, and a third in 1746. In 1735 Penny is also found as the printer of James Miller's *A View of the Town*. In 1746 he printed for E. Comyns, of the Royal Exchange, and a couple of Liverpool booksellers, Thomas Maddocks's *Sermon* preached at St. George's Church in Liverpool on October 9th. [B.M.

225. i. 1 (15).] Timperley says that he was printer to the East India Company [p. 709]. Robert Penny died between September 15th, 1761, the date of his will, and October 26th, in the same year, the date upon which it was proved in the Prerogative Court of Canterbury. He was apparently unmarried, and he left as his executors a nephew, Thomas Penny, son of Thomas Penny, of White Parish, near Salisbury, Mr. Marshall Sheepy, his partner, and William Gilbert, who for nearly twenty years had been his overseer and servant. The witnesses were Tho. Hart and Joseph Lockley. [P.C.C. 366, Cheslyn.]

PERKINS (THOMAS), bookseller and publisher in London, near the Royal Exchange, 1733. Publisher of a pamphlet written by John Bruce, entitled *The Conduct of the Emperor and Muscovites*, 1733, 8vo. [B.M. E. 2025 (6).]

PHILLIPS (JAMES), bookseller in London, George Yard, Lombard Street, 1775–6. Bookseller to the Society of Friends, and successor to Mary Hinde at the above address.

PHILLIPS (R.), printer in London, in Tart's Court, West Smithfield, 1725–50. Printer of broadsides, ballads, and other ephemeral literature. [*Antiquarian Magazine and Bibliographer*, v. 221–2.]

PHILPOTT (JAMES ISAAC). *See Dictionary*, 1668–1725. Still in business in 1744, when on April 10th he inserted an advertisement in the *Salisbury Journal*.

PHIPPS (J.), bookseller and publisher in London, at the Britannia Printing Office, Whitefriars, 1759. His name occurs in the imprint to a work dealing with the stage, entitled *Theophilus Cibber to David Garrick Esq.*, 1759, 8vo. [B.M. 80. i. 15.]

PICKARD (EDWARD), bookbinder and publisher in London, (1) St. George the Martyr, Southwark; (2) Old Bailey, 1739. On October 23rd, 1739, this bookbinder was examined in connexion with the publication of *The Craftsman*. [S.P.Dom. Geo. II, Bundle 50/63.] He may have been a relative of Pickard the printer found in Salisbury Court in 1724. [*See Dictionary*, 1668–1725.]

PICKERING (J.), bookseller in Stockton, co. Durham, 1763–6. Mentioned in a list of provincial booksellers as in business in the year 1763 [*N. & Q.* 10 S. vi. 443], and in an advertisement in the *Newcastle Journal* in 1766.

PICKSTONE (THOMAS), bookseller and stationer in Reigate (Surrey) opposite the Town Hall, *c.* 1770. Issued a trade card, now in the possession of the Allingham family. [A. Heal.] His successor, an Allingham, took over the business about 1776.

PIERCY (J. W.), printer and bookseller in Coventry, co. Warwick., Broad-gate, 1770–6. In 1771 he printed for G. Keith, the London publisher, *Two Discourses at the Ordination of Mr. George Moreton at Kettering*, November 20th, 1771 [B.M. 4473. e. 10], and in 1775 the following imprint is found on the title-page to a pamphlet entitled *Two Letters from the American Continental Congress held at Philadelphia, Sept. 5, 1774*, "Coventry: Printed and sold by J. W. Piercy, in Broad-gate. Price Two-pence." [J. C. B. L.]

PIESLEY ( ), bookseller in Oxford, 1735. Presumably a descendant of Antony Peisley or Piesley. [*See Dictionary*, 1668–1725.] His name is found in an advertisement of the sale of the library of the Bishop of Winchester in the *Daily Journal*, February 18th, 1735.

PIKE (M.), bookseller and publisher in London, 1734. Possibly a relative of Thomas Pike or Pyke (1688–94). Publisher of Lord Wharton's *Puppies, or just as they were sinking their Eyes open'd ; an excellent new ballad*. [Britwell Library.]

PILBOROUGH (JOHN), printer and bookseller at Colchester, 1733–71. In 1733 he printed the *Sermons* of the Rev. John Tren, and in 1735 received subscriptions for a proposed *Exposition on the Common Prayer Book*. [*Country Journal*, April 26th.] He was still in business in 1771, when his name is found as a bookseller in the *Chelmsford and Colchester Chronicle*.

PINDER and WARDLAW, booksellers and stationers in London, in Lincoln's Inn, New Square, *c.* 1750. Issued a trade card about this time. [A. Heal's Collection.]

PINE (WILLIAM), printer in Bristol, Wine Street, 1753–1803. Partner with Joseph Fry of Bristol, letter-founder, whom he joined in 1764. They modelled their early founts on those of Baskerville ; but the public verdict had been given in favour of the types of Caslon, and Fry's foundry had to recast the whole of the stock. Between the years 1767 and 1771 William Pine printed several editions of Wesley's *Hymns*. In 1774 he issued a *Bible* in pearl type, and in 1776 he printed for T. Mills, bookseller in Wine Street, the third edition of John Fry's *Essay on Conduct and Education*. [B.M. 11602. ee. 1 (7).] In 1782 Pine severed his connexion with Fry's type-foundry. He died in 1803, aged 64. [T. B. Reed, *Old English Letter Foundries*, pp. 298 ff.] *See* Grabham (John).

PIQUENET (C. D.), bookseller and publisher in London, Berkeley Square, 1775. Publisher of a work entitled *Peeps into Seats and Gardens* in that year. [*Public Advertiser*, January 10th, 1775.]

PITT ( ), bookseller in Blandford, co. Dorset., 1744. Mentioned in an advertisement in the *Salisbury Journal*, Tuesday, April 10th, 1744.

PITT, or PYTT (JOHN), printer in Gloucester, Westgate Street, 1771–98. In 1771 this printer was taking advertisements for Pugh's *Hereford Journal*. Amongst his output was a broadside published in 1775, *An Address to the Ladies of Gloucester*, and later on several broadsides concerning the Cathedral. His latest work appears to have been *An historical account of the Cathedral of St. Peter's, Gloucester*, printed in 1798. [Hyett and Bazeley, I. 267–8; II. 398.]

PLOWMAN (HENRY), stationer in London, Plough in Cheapside in the Poultry, 1727. Dealt in surveyors' warrants, licences for alehouses, receipts for land tax, &c., besides the usual stationer's stock. His advertisement will be found in the *Daily Post* of January 6th, 1727.

PLUMMER (CHARLES), printer in Whitby, Yorks., 1770(?)–1776. Is said to have set up the first printing-press in the town at the west end of the Bridge, and printed mainly handbills and tracts.

PLUMMER (J.), stationer, bookseller, and publisher in London, The Rising Sun, 100 Fenchurch Street, *c.* 1775. *Tables of Products for performing multiplication* were printed for him in 1775. [*Public Advertiser*, July 10th, 1775.] Issued a broad-sheet advertisement of his stock, which included "Fine Asses Skin pocket books". [A. Heal's Collection.]

POOLE (J.), printer and bookseller in Chester, Foregate Street, 1775–8. In partnership with C. Barker and others, established the New General Printing Office in Foregate Street. He is mentioned in a list of provincial booksellers as being there in 1778. [*N. & Q.* 10 S. v. 142.] J. Poole and P. Broster were the first booksellers in Chester to publish catalogues of their stock.

POPE (CORNELIUS), printer in Bath, 1760–8. Pope served his apprenticeship with Boddeley of the *Bath Journal* and on October 16th, 1760, founded the *Bath Chronicle*, a paper now amalgamated with the *Bath Herald* and known as the *Bath Chronicle and Herald*. Publisher and printer in 1764 of C. Lucas's *Cursory Remarks on . . . Bath and Bristol Waters*. Pope was also the printer for the booksellers in Bath of an edition of the *New Bath Guide*, which mentions that "the Streets every night are extremely well lighted by lamps".

The last Bath Guide printed by Pope was the 5th edition, *c.* 1768. He left Bath in that year.

POTE (G.), bookseller and publisher (?), 1754. A fictitious imprint found on a satire entitled *The Ragged Uproar; or the Oxford Roratory*, 1754. J. Pote of Eton (*q.v.*) repudiated all connexion with it. [*Monthly Review*, September 1754, p. 235.]

POTE (JOSEPH), bookseller, printer, and publisher in London and Eton: London, (1) The Golden Door, over against Suffolk House, Charing Cross, 1726–8; (2) Isaac Newton's Head, the corner of Suffolk Street near Charing Cross, 1729–30. Eton, 1730–87. Joseph Pote began his career as a bookseller and publisher in London, like many of his contemporaries, by publishing a *Sermon*. This was by Richard Coliere, Vicar of Kingston-on-Thames, and is advertised in Wilford's *Monthly Catalogue* of November 1726; in the same issue Pote is named as one of the booksellers taking subscriptions for J. Morgan's *History of Algiers*. Early in the following year he issued a catalogue of his stock. [Nichols, III. 660.] In 1728 Pote published the Rev. John Chapman's *Objections of a late Anonymous Writer . . . considered*, and in 1729 Entick's *Evidence of Christianity*; *The Foreigner's Guide to London*, and an English translation of Perrault's *Contes des fées*. Either in that year or in 1730 he moved to Eton and set up a press there. What induced him to make this change does not appear to be known; but during the year 1730 he published a compilation of his own, a *Catalogus Alumnorum*, which bears the imprint: *Etonae apud Josephum Pote 1730*. In 1737 he undertook the publication of Dr. William Cave's *Historia Literaria*, and a correspondent having asked why it was necessary to print the work by subscription, Pote pointed out that if it were published without such a guarantee, it would be at once pirated either abroad or in Ireland, with the certain result of ruining the venture [*A Letter to A. . . . B. . . .* By Joseph Pote, 1737]. The work was published in two handsome folio volumes, printed at the Oxford University Press, the first in 1740 and the second in 1743. From his own press came *The History and Antiquities of Windsor*, with notes on the Knights of the Garter, illustrated with copper-plates, and published in 1749. Joseph Pote died March 3rd, 1787, and was succeeded by his son Thomas. His daughter married John Williams, bookseller, of Fleet Street, and publisher of the *North Briton*.

POTTENGER, or POTTINGER (JAMES), bookseller and publisher in London, (1) King's Arms, Great Turnstile, Lincoln's Inn Fields; (2) Royal Bible in

Paternoster Row, 1757–69. Publisher of satires and plays. In 1757 he issued a small octavo pamphlet entitled *A Letter from Lewis xv to G . . . l M . . . t.* In 1761 his name appears in the imprint to Doctor Howard's *Royal Bible*, and another of his publications was an undated edition of Mrs. Glasse's *Book of Cookery*. He was also the author of several plays and poems.

POTTER (PETER), bookseller and publisher in Chester, 1732–9. In 1732 he published Robert Wright's *New and Correct Tables* [*N. & Q.* 10 S. XI. 127], and he was also the publisher of C. Leadbetter's *Royal Gauger* in 1739.

POTTINGER, *see* Pottenger.

POWELL ( ), bookseller in Yarmouth, co. Norfolk, 1757. Mentioned in a list of provincial booksellers as in business at that date. [*N. & Q.* 11 S. I. 364.]

POWELL (CHARLES), stationer in London, No. 97 Cheapside, *c.* 1770. Successor to Thomas Atkins. Used the same trade card. Found in *London Directory* of 1777. [A. Heal's Collection.]

POWELL (EBEN), bookseller in London, Bible and Dove in Crooked Lane, *c.* 1760. Issued a small trade card without date, but showing his sign. [A. Heal's Collection.]

PRAT (W.), printer in London, (1) Eagle Court, Westminster; (2) New Round Court, Strand, 1749–58. His name is first met with in the Poll Book for the City and Liberty of Westminster in 1749 as a "printer", living in Eagle Court. He printed *The Reply of the Country Gentleman to the answer to his Military Arguments, by the Officer.* The second edition, 1758, 8vo. [B.M. E. 2049 (13).]

PRESCOTT (JOHN), printer in Manchester, Old Millgate, 1771. [Mentioned by correspondent in *N. & Q.* 10 S. V. 183.] Printer of the *Manchester Journal.* Afterwards removed to Bedford near Leigh. [Procter, p. 201.]

PRESCOTT (M.), bookseller at Preston, Lancs., 1728. On the occasion of a Confirmation held at Preston by the Bishop of Chichester in 1728, a manual was prepared for the candidates, entitled *The Nature of Confirmation*, which bore the imprint: "London, printed for M. Prescot, bookseller at Preston . . ." [W. M. C., June 1728.]

PRESCOTT, or PRESCOT (W.), bookseller and publisher in Preston, Lancashire, 1709 (?)–1728 (?). The earliest mention that has been found of this publisher is in the imprint to a *Sermon* preached at the Assizes on April 7th, 1710, by the Rev. Samuel Peploe, Bishop of Chester. [B.M. 694. g. 24 (13).]

PRESTON (CALEB), bookseller in Boston, co. Lincoln., 1759. In 1759 he took over the business of T. Ferrour or Farrar, of Boston. He referred to himself as of London, so that he had perhaps been apprenticed to the trade there. [*Cambridge Journal.*]

PREVOST (N.), bookseller and publisher in London, (1) at the Ship in the Strand; (2) over against Southampton Street in the Strand, 1728. Is first heard of in 1728, when he advertised books for sale in the *Daily Post* of January 4th. In 1730 he published a catalogue of Italian and Spanish books. [B.M. 824. d. 30 (1).] His name is found in an advertisement in the *Grub Street Journal*, October 26th, 1732, as selling two books published by F. Cogan. In 1733 he subscribed for four copies of Stephen's *Thesaurus* in seven volumes. He married Susanna Vaillant, sister of Paul and Isaac Vaillant.

PRICE (A.), (?) bookseller and publisher in London, near Temple Bar, 1749–55. Probably fictitious. Occurs on several political pamphlets published between 1749 and 1755. [*see* A. Briton.]

PRICE (G.), printer in Sherborne, co. Dorset., 1737. Joint printer with W. Bettinson of the *Sherborne Mercury*, 1737. Said to have come from London.

PRICE (THOMAS), bookseller and publisher in Gloucester, (1) Tewkesbury in the Tolzey; (2) Cheltenham, New Inn. 1735–69. One of those who published the editions of *The Old and New Testament*, annotated by Samuel Humphreys in 1735; but his name does not appear in the imprint. [*County Journal*, December 27th, 1735.] In 1748 his name is found in the imprint of a *Sermon* printed at Worcester in 1748 [*Bibliography of Worcestershire*, p. 57], and again in 1753 in a list of those provincial booksellers who were agents for the London newspaper, the *Daily Register*. In 1756 he was selling the third edition of John Barrow's *Psalm-singer's Choice Companion*, which was advertised in the *Whitehall Evening Post* of January 2nd. Finally, in 1769 he was agent for the monthly parts of Smollett's *History of England.*

PRIDDEN (JOHN), bookseller and publisher in London, The Feathers, near Fleet Bridge. 1748–1807. A native of Shropshire. Born on July 20th, 1728, at Old Martin Hall, in the parishes of Ellesmere and Whittington. Left home and came to London on March 25th, 1748. The date of his first setting up as a bookseller and publisher is unknown, but about the year 1756 he published a very amusing collection of satires, under the title of *The Scots Scourge, or Pridden's Supplement to the British Antidote to Caledonian Poison.* The humour of the

work was intensified by the illustration, which might have been done by Rowlandson or Hogarth. On March 27th, 1757, he married Anne, daughter of Mr. Humphrey Gregory, of Twemloves, near Whitchurch. In 1759 he published *The Comptroller.* In 1769 he published a catalogue of his stock, which consisted chiefly of seventeenth and eighteenth century literature. [B.M. 128. i. 19 (5).] He died on March 17th, 1807. [Timperley, 1842, pp. 827–8.]

PRINCE (DANIEL), bookseller in Oxford, corner of New College Lane, 1750–96. Succeeded his uncle, Richard Clements, and is described as "'bookseller', privilegiatus 19 Sept. 1750." [Foster's *Alumni.*] Married Anne, daughter of Dr. William Hayes, organist of Magdalen College. One of his most notable publications was Bridges' *Northamptonshire* between 1762 and 1769. He subscribed for twenty sets of the Greek Testament of 1768, when most of the large London booksellers were taking seven. Between 1780 and 1796 he wrote many letters on literary and antiquarian subjects to Richard Gough, the antiquary, which are printed in Nichols's *Literary Anecdotes.* At the time of his death on June 6th, 1796, he was one of the oldest booksellers in England. He was succeeded in his business by Joshua Cooke. [*The Parkers in Oxford*, 1914; Nichols, *Lit. Anecd.*, pp. 426, 694.]

PRIOR (WILLIAM), bookseller, paper-maker, and publisher in South Stoneham, Winchester, co. Hants, 1743 (?)–1756 (?). Mentioned in a list of provincial booksellers as at work in 1743, but he was probably in business some years before, as according to the Registers of Winchester Cathedral he married Jane Roe of North Stoneham on May 2nd, 1736. [Harl. Soc. Publications, XXXVI. 137.] A William Prior, probably the bookseller, was Mayor of Winchester in 1756. [*N. & Q.* 10 S. V. 482.] His name occurs in the imprint to the Rev. B. Simpson's *Sermon* preached at Winchester on the occasion of the Assizes which began there on February 29th, $174\frac{3}{4}$. [B.M. 225. i. 1 (8).]

PRYSE (STAFFORD), bookseller in Shrewsbury, 1775–6. Annually attended the fair at Chester and put up at the Red Lion, where he sold "Welsh and other books". [Advertisement in *Chester Courant.*]

PUE (JOHN), printer in Manchester, 1760. Only known from the entry of his marriage in the parish register in that year. Procter suggests that he may have been only a workman. [Procter, p. 201.]

PUGH (C.), bookseller and publisher in Hereford, 1762 (?)–1776. His name occurs in the imprint to a pamphlet entitled *A Letter to the . . . Lord Mayor . . . of the*

City of London. From an old servant. The author was George Heathcote, who dated it from Hereford, October 6th, 1762. [B.M. E. 2054 (2).] In 1771, sold a catalogue of books on sale by S. Gamidge of Worcester. [*British Chronicle, or Hereford Journal*, August 8th, 1771.] Was the printer and publisher of the *British Chronicle, or Pugh's Hereford Journal.* Still in business in 1776.

PUNCHARD (C.), bookseller and publisher at Ipswich, 1774. In that year his name appears in the imprint of *Some Memoirs of the Life of John Glover, late of Norwich.* [B.M. 4903. bbb. 20 (1).]

PURSALL (THOMAS), (?) bookseller in Congleton, co. Chester, the Black Lyon near the Market Cross, 1756. The creditors of a bankrupt named Joseph Amery, of Astbury, co. Cheshire, were to meet at the above address (which may have been an Inn) on December 1st, 1756. He was also agent for the sale of Schofield's *Middlewich Journal, or Cheshire Advertiser.*

PURSER (JOHN), printer in London, (1) Whitefriars; (2) Shoe Lane, near Holborn. 1728 (?)–1744 (?). This was one of the many newspaper printing-offices that set up in the neighbourhood of Fleet Street in the early part of the eighteenth century. As most of these were purely business undertakings and none of their trade-books have survived, it is almost impossible to trace their activities. Purser's name is found on March 14th, 1728, in the imprint to the *Daily Journal*, which before that bore no printer's name. It was a half-sheet only, and contained both foreign and domestic news, scrappy and imperfect and often misleading. It also contained advertisements of sales by auction and many publishers' advertisements. It was not long before the printer was in trouble with the Government. On the Coram Rege (Rex) Roll for Michaelmas Term of that year is the record of his indictment for inserting false and slanderous statements, but it was not pressed. On May 1st, 1731, he took over the printing of *Fog's Weekly Journal*, another London newspaper, whose fearless editors were the terror of evil-doers, whether public or private. In the course of the year 1737 he was examined about something that appeared in it, and then said that the publisher was named John Brett, and that the author of the article to which exception was taken was a certain John Kelly. [S. P. Dom., Geo. II, Bundle 41/29.] Again in 1739 he was bound over to be of good behaviour, and one of his sureties on that occasion was Thomas Read, a brother printer. [S. P., Dom., Geo. II, Bundle 48/14.] He printed a Latin Book of Pope's for Dodsley and Killpatrick in 1744. [Straus.] He also printed large numbers of pamphlets.

RACAYROL (A.), bookseller in London, Green Street, Leicester Fields, 1728–30. Dealer in French literature. In 1728 he advertised the sale of *Remarques Théologiques*. [*Daily Journal*, January 4th, 1728.]

RADNAL ( ), bookseller in Bewdley, co. Hereford, 1771. In 1771, distributed copies of a catalogue of books on sale by S. Gamidge, bookseller of Worcester. [*The British Chronicle, or Pugh's Hereford Journal*, August 8th, 1771.]

RAIKES (ROBERT), I, printer in Gloucester, *see Dictionary*, 1668–1725.

RAIKES (ROBERT), II, printer in Gloucester, *see Dictionary*, 1668–1725.

RAILTON ( ), bookseller in Carlisle, 1755. His name occurs in an advertisement of a patent medicine in the *London Evening Post* of December 25th, 1755.

RANDALL (J.), bookseller and publisher in London, Pall Mall, 1775. Published *Peeps into Seats and Gardens* with Ridley and Piquenet. [*Public Advertiser*, January 10th, 1775.]

RANGER (H.), bookseller and publisher in London, Temple Exchange Passage, Fleet Street, 1775. Publisher of *Harris's List of Covent Garden Ladies*. [*Public Advertiser*, January 2nd, 1775.]

RATHBOURNE, or RATHBONE (JOSIAH), bookseller and publisher in Macclesfield, 1723–56. *See Dictionary*, 1668–1725. Still in business in 1756, when his name appears in an advertisement of Schofield's *Middlewich Journal, or Cheshire Advertiser*.

RATTEN (CALEB), bookseller in Market Harborough. *See Dictionary*, 1668–1725.

RATTEN (JOHN), bookseller in Coventry, 1744–76. In partnership with J. Brooks. Possibly a descendant of W. or G. Ratten. *See Dictionary*, 1668–1725.

RATTEN (WILLIAM), bookseller in Coventry, 1716–26. *See Dictionary*, 1668–1725. A correspondent in *Notes & Queries* records him there in 1726. [*N. & Q.* 10 S. v. 142.]

RAVEN (WILLIAM), bookseller in London, St. Andrew's, Holborn, 1745. Possibly a descendant of James Raven, of Lincoln's Inn (1700). Nothing is known of his history or business beyond the fact that he was unsuccessful and was declared a bankrupt in 1745. [Timperley, 1842, p. 673.]

RAYLTON (T. S.), bookseller and publisher in London, 1740–9. Publisher for the Society of Friends. In partnership with Luke Hinde. It is not known whether this publisher was Tacy Sowle, or one of her children. [*The Friend*, XVI. 415.]

RAYMOND (J.), bookseller and publisher in London, (1) at Charing Cross, 1749; (2) near the Haymarket, 1752. 1749–53. Publisher of pamphlets. His first address is found in the imprint to *A Dialogue between Thomas Jones, a Life-guard-man, and John Smith, late a Serjeant* &c. In 1753 he published *An Exposition of Motives*, from the Haymarket. [*Public Advertiser*, January 5th, 1753.]

RAYNER (E.), pamphlet-seller in London, at the new pamphlet shop, near Charing Cross (or) next the George Tavern, Charing Cross, 1731–1732 (?). This name is found in 1731 in the imprint to an anonymous poem addressed to the Right Hon. William Pulteney, Esq. [B.M. 643. m. 15 (13).] In the next year it is found on the title-page of *Vanelia, or The Amours of the Great*. The premises were those of William Rayner, printer (*q. v.*); but what relationship, if any, there was between E. and W. there is nothing to indicate.

RAYNER (WILLIAM), printer and publisher in London, (1) next the George Tavern, Charing Cross, 1731; (2) Faulcon Court, near St. George's Church, Southwark, 1736–9; (3) parish of St. Andrew, Holborn, 1736. 1731 (?)–1740 (?). In a curious periodical called *The Friendly Writer*, published by a pretended Quakeress named Ruth Collins between September 1732 and the following February, is given a detailed account of the prosecution of this printer for libelling Sir Robert Walpole. This account, which appears in the "third book or number for November 1732, p. 11, states that his offence was for publishing pictures with the title *Robin's Reign, or Seven's the Main*, which had originally appeared in *The Craftsman*" a year and a half before he was brought to trial, which would make the date of the publication 1731, not 1733 as given by Timperley. He was probably in business some years earlier, but in 1731 a list of books "printed for and sold by" him at the first address, appears at the end of a pamphlet entitled the *History of Mortimer*, published by J. Millan. [B.M. T. 2024 (3).] In 1736 he was the printer of a news-sheet called *Rayner's Morning Advertiser*, and on August 11th in the same year he was examined as to the publication of a pamphlet entitled *A Second Letter from a Member of Parliament to his Friend in the Country*, and also a ballad called *The Pacifick Fleet*. He denied being either the printer or the publisher of them; but admitted that

his wife was employed by Mr. Michael Walker, an attorney, who was the author of the *Second Letter*, to fold and stitch about five hundred copies of that publication, and that he helped to distribute them. [State Papers. Dom., George II, Bundle 39/75.] Rayner was also said to have been the proprietor of the notorious journal *The Craftsman*, and to have employed Norton Defoe, the second son of Daniel, to write for it, paying him one guinea a week since the latter end of May or the beginning of June 1739. [*Ib.*, Bundle 50/53.] Amongst other activities of his press were the lives of notorious criminals, one of which, *The Life of Gill Smith*, executed in 1738 for the murder of his wife, is in the library of the British Museum. [518. f. 33.] The date of his death has not been found.

READ (JAMES), printer, *see Dictionary*, 1668–1725. *Read's Weekly Journal* was still being published in 1739, and bore the imprint of J. Read, in Whitefriars.

READ (JOHN), printer in Chester, 1747. Mentioned in the Poll Book for that year. But the position of his printing-house is not given.

READ (THOMAS), printer in London, (1) behind the Sun Tavern in Fleet Street; (2) Dogwell Court, Whitefriars, Fleet Street. 1726 (?)–1753 (?). One of the many busy printing-offices in the neighbourhood of Fleet Street in the eighteenth century. James Read (*q. v.*) was also connected with it. It was probably established before 1726, when the printer inserted an advertisement of *A True Copy of the Paper which Mrs. Catherine Hayes delivered to a Friend* in the *Daily Journal* of May 10th, 1726. The firm published many things, such as *Collections of Trials*, issued in parts; Seymour's *Survey of London and Westminster*, and *The English Traveller*, in three volumes, illustrated with maps of the various counties. Read was also the printer of many pamphlets. In 1739 he stood bail for John Purser, a fellow printer (*q. v.*) *Youths' Friendly Monitor* was printed and sold by T. Read, Dogwell Court, in 1753. [*Public Advertiser*, January 12th, 1753.]

REASON (W.), bookseller and publisher in London, Fleur de Lis Court, 1735. Publisher of *A Poem on the Marriage of the Prince of Orange with Princess Anne*. [*Daily Courant*, January 23rd, 1735.]

REDMAYNE (G.), printer in London, Creed Lane, Ludgate Street, 1765. He was the printer of the *Westminster Journal* in 1765.

REDMAYNE (WILLIAM), printer in London, Little Britain, 1747–8. Only known from his obituary notice in the *Penny London Post* for January 23rd,

1747/8: "Last week died at Charlton in Kent . . . Mr. William Redmayne printer in Little Britain. He was a person greatly respected amongst his profession for his solid judgement . . . and universally beloved amongst his acquaintance as a good companion and an honest man." He was possibly the son of Samuel or William Redmayne. [*See Dictionary*, 1668–1725.]

REDWOOD (J.), bookseller and bookbinder in Norwich, against the Three Feathers near St. George's, Tombland, 1735–42. In an advertisement in the *Country Journal or Craftsman* of December 27th, 1735, announcing the publication of Sam. Humphrey's *Old and New Testaments*, this bookseller is named as one of those from whom it could be had; but his name does not appear in the imprint. He was also agent for Thomas Astley, the publisher, at the Rose in St. Paul's Churchyard, and advertised his publications in *Cross-Grove's News*.

REED (HENRY), bookseller in Newcastle-upon-Tyne, 1747–54. Was admitted to the Newcastle Stationers' Company April 30th, 1747. [Welford, p. 128.]

REEVES (JOHN), printer in London, Savoy, 1767. Stated by Nichols to have been an eminent Law Printer, who died in December 1767. [*Lit. Anecd.* III. 737.]

REEVES (W.), bookseller and publisher in London, Shakespeare's-Head in Fleet Street, 1753–9. He was one of the partners in the publication of *The Court and City Register* in 1753. [*Public Advertiser*, December 1st, 1753.] Publisher of a book dealing with theatrical subjects, entitled *Theophilus Cibber to David Garrick Esq.*, 1756–9. [B.M. 80. i. 15.]

REILY, or REILLY (R.), printer in London, Little Britain, 1730. In 1730 he printed for J. Stagg in Westminster Hall and other booksellers Claudius Arnoux's *Parallels of the Sounds and Syllables of the French and English Languages*, 1730. [B.M. 627. i. 5.] He is believed to have gone over to Ireland, where in 1736 he printed *Advise to a Son: A Poem*, by William Hammond. Dublin, printed by R. Reilly, 1736. [Copy in the Britwell Library.]

REYMER, or RYMER (C.), printer in London, *c.* 1759. Partner with Lockyer Davis (*q. v.*), printer of the Votes of the House of Commons. Another book printed by him was *The Brothers*, a tragedy, for Robert Dodsley. [Straus.]

REYNOLDS (T.), (?) bookseller in London, in the Strand over against the Fountain Tavern, 1731–3. This name is found in the imprint to a poem entitled *The City Triumphant*, 1733. [B.M. 804. m. 1 (23).]

RHODES (THEOPHILUS), bookseller in Plymouth. His name occurs in the imprint of an Assize Sermon, printed in 1754.

RICE (C.), bookseller in London, 123 Mount Street, Berkeley Square (removed from Berkeley Square), *c.* 1775. Ran a circulating library. Issued a trade card about this date. [A. Heal's Collection.]

RICHARDS (DANIEL), stationer in London, near St. Andrew's Church in Holborn, *c.* 1742–1802. Senior member of the Court of Assistants of the Stationers' Company; Master in 1778. Known as father of the parish of St. Andrew's, where he kept a stationer's shop for more than sixty years. Died in September 1802, aged eighty-seven. He issued a trade card. [A. Heal's Collection.]

RICHARDS (ROBERT), bookseller and publisher in London, (1) Clare Market; (2) corner of Barnard's Inn, Holborn. 1749–53. His name is found in the Poll-Book for the City and Liberty of Westminster in 1749 as living in Clare Market. In 1753 he published a pamphlet, entitled *The Case of the Jews considered.* [B.M. T. 2231 (16).]

RICHARDSON (H.), bookseller in Waltham Cross, Herts., 1740. Noticed in a list of provincial booksellers. [*N. & Q.* 10 S. v. 242.]

RICHARDSON (JOHN), bookseller and publisher in Durham, Market Place, 1750–63. In 1750 it was proposed to issue by subscription a collection of the *Poems* of Christopher Smart, and amongst the provincial booksellers who received subscriptions was the above; but how long before that he had been in business is not known. His name occurs in the imprint to the Rev. W. Forster's *Sermon* preached in the Cathedral of Durham on July 24th, 1755. [B.M. 226. f. 3. (8).] After the death of the well-known Durham antiquary, Dr. Christopher Hunter, in 1757, his library was sold to Richardson, who was said to have paid £360 for it. [Surtees, *History*, II. 288.] He was still in business in 1763, when his name is found in a list of booksellers in the *Leedes Intelligence.*

RICHARDSON (J.), bookseller and publisher in Paternoster Row, 1753–63. *The Adventures of Signor Gaudentio di Lucca* was published by W. Innys and J. Richardson, of Paternoster Row, R. Manby, and H. Shute Cox. [*Public Advertiser*, January 12th, 1753.] In partnership with W. Innys in 1756, when they published *Two Sermons* by the Rev. William Totton. [B.M. 225. i. 6 (4).]

RICHARDSON (SAMUEL), printer, publisher, and author, in London, (1) Fleet Street; (2) Salisbury Court; (3) White Lyon Court. 1719–61. Born in 1689 in Derbyshire, to which county his father had fled when the Duke of Monmouth was executed, young Samuel's early education was only such as was to be had at a dame's school. Leigh Hunt has left it on record that Richardson was later on a scholar at Christ's Hospital, but his statement is erroneous. [A. L. Reade in *N. & Q.* 10 S. xii. 301–3, 343–4.] Richardson appears to have been a strange lad, averse to active sport, and very much of a prig, probably due to his being thrown largely into the society of servants. It is said of him that while still a child he wrote a silly letter to a widow of about sixty, full of those virtuous sentiments that he afterwards embodied in the *Familiar Letters* and in his novels. The women servants gathered round him to listen to the sentimental semi-moral tales that, even as a boy, came easy to him. From this stage he passed to writing love-letters for his female friends. He was at length sent up to London and apprenticed to John Wilde, a printer in Aldersgate Street, in 1706. During the seven years of his apprenticeship he worked hard and had little leisure; but such as he had he devoted to reading and in corresponding with a wealthy gentleman, whose name is unknown, but who promised to help the young printer to advancement. This would-be benefactor died without carrying out his promises, and the correspondence between them was burnt. Richardson is careful to tell us that whilst he was thus employed, in order not to waste his master's goods he used to buy his own candles. After his apprenticeship was ended Samuel Richardson continued to work with Wilde for another six years as journeyman and corrector of the press, and thus became a thoroughly practical printer. In 1719 he set up in business for himself in Fleet Street, and shortly afterwards married Martha Wilde, the daughter of his late master. Amongst the work put into his hands at this time was the printing of the *True Briton*, a newspaper that was making itself notorious. His name did not appear in the imprint of the first six numbers; after which he severed his connexion with it. Edmund Curll also stated in evidence before a Committee of the House of Commons, that he believed that Richardson was the printer of *Mist's Journal* of August 24th, 1728, which aroused the King's anger. [State Papers Dom., Geo. II, Bundle 8/33.] About this time he made the acquaintance of Charles Rivington, the founder of the great publishing house in Paternoster Row, and this ripened into a close friendship which continued until Rivington's death in 1742. It was at the instigation of Charles Rivington and John Osborne, another publisher

in the "Row", that Richardson wrote the series of *Familiar Letters* that were published by them in 1740. The idea as set out in the title-page was not only to show the styles and forms to be observed in writing such letters, "but how to think and act justly and prudently in the common concerns of human life." This was the germ of Richardson's novels: *Pamela*, 1740; *Clarissa*, 1748; *Sir Charles Grandison*, 1753. The popularity of these works was enormous. They were even quoted from the pulpit, and while Henry Fielding ridiculed them, he nevertheless derived from Richardson more than the mere form of his parodies. These works Richardson printed at his own press; but in 1753 he was invòlved in a lawsuit with the printers of Dublin over a barefaced piracy of *Sir Charles Grandison.* The story is familiar, and need not be repeated here. Richardson lost his first wife in 1731, and soon afterwards married Elizabeth Leake, daughter of John Leake, London printer [*N. & Q.* 12 Ser. xi. 224]. In 1742 his friend Charles Rivington died, and Richardson being nominated an executor of the will, took upon himself the guardianship of his late friend's two sons, John and James. For many years he was the printer of the *Journals* of the House of Commons, and in other ways his business had increased so largely that he found it necessary to build a new and larger printing-house in White Lyon Court in 1755. He soon afterwards entered into partnership with Catherine Lintot, the daughter of Henry Lintot, who held a moiety of the Patent for printing lawbooks. Samuel Richardson died in 1761. Although two sons had been born to him, both had died in infancy, and the business passed to his nephew, William Richardson. He was Master of the Stationers' Company in 1754. [Nichols, IV. 578–95; Knight, *Shadows of the Old Booksellers*; Austin Dobson, *Samuel Richardson*, 1902.]

RICHARDSON (STEPHEN), printer in Oxford, St. Giles, 1715–55. Father of Stephen and Zaccheus Richardson, of Magdalen Hall. His will was proved September 20th, 1756. [Madan.]

RICHARDSON (THOMAS), printer in Oxford, 1749. He is mentioned as a compositor in the colophon of Edward Rowe-More's *Nomina et insignia Gentilicia*, Oxon, 1749. [Madan.]

RICHARDSON (WILLIAM), printer in London, Castle Yard, Holborn, 1760. 1701–88, *see Dictionary*, 1668–1725. Nephew of Samuel Richardson, printer and novelist. For a time he was in partnership with S. Clarke, a Quaker, who retired from business about 1768. William Richardson took over his uncle's business in 1761, having previously acted as its overseer. In 1764, W. Richardson and S. Clarke were the printers of *Observations on Marriage* for Dodsley. [Straus]. In 1765 their names were still found in the *Gazetteer and Daily Advertiser*, August 26th. William Richardson died at Dagenham in Essex in May, 1788. [Nichols, VI. 620, VIII. 506.]

RICHARDSON (ZACCHEUS), printer in Oxford, 1756–78. Son of Stephen Richardson. Appointed Privilegiatus "printer" on September 20th, 1756. [Foster's *Alumni.*] Died in 1778, his will being proved on November 1st in that year. [Griffiths.]

RICHARDSON and URQUHART, booksellers and publishers in London, Royal Exchange, 1765–75. A firm of some repute as publishers. In 1765 their imprint is found on *A Letter to the Earl of* —, and they were publishing the *Westminster Gazette* in 1775.

RIDER (JOHN), printer in London, Little Britain, 1760–1800. Nichols says he was the author of a *History of England* to the year 1763 inclusive, in fifty pocket volumes, and that he was also the compiler of *A Commentary of the Bible, An English Dictionary*, and other works; but no copies of these works have been traced. John Rider died on April 1st, 1800. [Nichols, III. 737.]

RIDGWAY (WILLIAM), stationer in London, at the White Bear, corner of Warwick Court, Holborn, *c.* 1755. Mr. Heal has a bill-head used by this stationer with the date 1755.

RIDLEY (JOHN), bookseller and publisher in London, St. James's Street, 1765–82. Publisher of many pamphlets on political matters, including several relating to America and the American War. Amongst the latter were: *The Memoirs of Lieut. Henry Timberlake*, describing his travels amongst the Cherokee Indians and his visit to this country with one of the chiefs in 1762; Doyle's *Account of the British Dominions beyond the Atlantic*; and an anonymous tract on *The Constitutional Right of the Legislature of Great Britain to tax the British Colonies in America*, published in 1768. He also published Sophie Hume's *Caution to such as observe Days and Times* in 1766, a poetical essay by William Woty called *Particular Providence* in 1774, and *Johnsoniana* in 1776. [B.M. T. 667 (7).] His shop must have been well known, and he probably did a high-class business, but no record of him has survived. He died November 28th, 1782. [Timperley, 1842, p. 749.]

RILEY (GEORGE), bookseller, publisher, and stationer, in London, Curzon Street, Mayfair, 1772(?)–1779. Timperley [p. 908] says that he came from

York and was "many years a printer and bookseller", but he is not mentioned in Davies' *History of the York Press*. When he first set up in London is unknown; but in 1772 he is found publishing numbers of books in a small form, ostensibly "for the use of schools'. Riley's *Royal Spelling Cards*, "originally composed for the Amusement of the younger branches of the Royal Family," were eagerly bought up, whilst another of his publications was *Choice Emblems for Youth*, first published in 1772, which went through several editions. He was also the publisher of Wheble's *Lady's Magazine*. He kept an extensive stock of stationery of all kinds, according to an advertisement which he placed at the end of *Heathen Mythology made easy* which he published in 1779. [B.M. 1210. h. 1 (2).] Riley died at Greenwich on January 19th, 1829, aged eighty-six, and was nearly the oldest proprietor of a newspaper in the kingdom.

RIVINGTON (CHARLES), bookseller in London, Bible and Crown, St. Paul's Churchyard, 1726. *See Dictionary*, 1668–1725.

RIVINGTON (CHARLES), junior, printer in London, (1) White Lyon Court; (2) Steyning Lane. 1746–90. Third son of Charles Rivington, publisher (1711–42). Articled to Samuel Richardson the printer and publisher (*q. v.*), on August 9th, 1746, and afterwards succeeded to his printing business. He was appointed City printer in 1771, and resigned in 1772. Timperley says that "he carried on an extensive business for thirty-two years in Steyning-Lane, in a noble house which had formerly been the residence of a Lord Mayor" (p. 770). He died June 22nd, 1790. [S. Rivington, *The Publishing Family of Rivington*, p. 40.]

RIVINGTON (JOHN), bookseller and publisher in London, St. Paul's Churchyard, 1740–92. Son of Charles Rivington I, the founder of the house. For a time he was under the guardianship of Samuel Richardson. He and his brother James carried on the business until 1756, when the partnership was dissolved; James ultimately went to America. John was a quiet, sedate man. In 1760 he was appointed bookseller to the Society for Promoting Christian Knowledge. In 1775 he was master of the Stationers' Company. He married Elizabeth Miller, a daughter of Robert Gosling (*see Dictionary*, 1668–1725), and sister of Sir Francis Gosling, bookseller and banker (*q. v.*). By her he had a numerous family. His sons Francis and Charles were taken into the business, and carried it on after their father's death in 1792. Another son, John, was a printer. [S. Rivington, *The Publishing Family of Rivington*, 1919; Nichols, III. 400.]

RIVINGTON (JOHN), printer in London, St. John's Square, Clerkenwell. Son of John Rivington, publisher, and grandson of Charles Rivington. Succeeded James Emonson at the above address in 1780. He died in 1785. It is not clear that he was identical with the John Rivington, junior, who was the publisher of *Lloyd's Evening Post* in 1778. [S. Rivington, *The Publishing Family of Rivington*, 1919.]

ROACH (WILLIAM), bookseller and stationer in London, Bible and Crown, next the Black Swan Inn, near Fetter Lane End, Holborn, *c.* 1750. Issued a trade card about this date. [A. Heal's Collection.] May be identical with the Mr. Roach, bookseller, who in 1795 was sentenced to twelve months' imprisonment for publishing an immoral book. [Timperley, 1842, p. 789.]

ROBERTS (JAMES), *see Dictionary*, 1668–1725.

ROBINS (THOMAS), bookseller (?) and publisher (?) in London, Fleet Street, 1740. Possibly a fictitious imprint found on the title-page of a political pamphlet entitled *The D[uke] of A[rgyl]e's letter . . .*, 1740. [B.M. T. 1110 (10).]

ROBINSON (   ), printer in London, employed at Strawberry Hill, 1758. The printer of a book by Spence, 1758. [Straus.]

ROBINSON (GEORGE), bookseller and publisher in London, Addison's Head, 25 Paternoster Row, 1764–1801. Described by Nichols as "one of the most eminent booksellers of his time". He was born at Dalston in Cumberland, and came to London in 1755. Apprenticed to John Rivington. In 1764 he started as a wholesale bookseller in partnership with J. Roberts, who died about the year 1776. Robinson was much helped by T. Longman, who lent him money. He prospered in his business, and in 1780 had the largest wholesale trade in London, and in the purchase of copyrights he became the rival of the most formidable of the old-established houses. Among his publications were: *The Critical Review, The Town and Country Magazine, The New Annual Register, The Modern Universal History*, Bruce's *Travels*, and much other literature. He paid his authors well, believing that in this he was carrying out the true spirit of bookselling. In 1784 he took into partnership his son George and his brother John, who succeeded him in business. He died June 6th, 1801. It is recorded that in 1770 an information was laid against him by T. Nuthall, for publishing the *Letters of Junius* [Treasury Papers, B. 479 (15)]. [Nichols, III. 445–9, VI. 282.]

ROBINSON (JACOB), bookseller and publisher in London, (1) Next the One Tun Tavern, near Hungerford Market in the Strand, 1737; (2) Golden Lyon in Ludgate Street, 1742–58. 1737 (?)–1758 (?). An extensive publisher of miscellaneous literature. His first address appears in the imprint to a volume called *The Artless Muse*, published in 1737, a copy of which is in Harvard College. In 1743 he was bound over in a sum of £400 to appear in the Court of King's Bench for publishing a libel called *Old England's* "Te Deum" [State Papers Dom., Geo. II, Bundle 62/59[a]], and in the same year he published a pamphlet on theatrical matters entitled *Theatrical Correspondence in Death: an Epistle from Mrs. Oldfield in the Shades to Mrs. Br[a]ceg[ir]dle, upon Earth*. [B.M. 641. d. 30 (6).] He was still publishing in 1758. Succeeded by George Kearsley in 1760.

ROBINSON (JOHN), bookseller in London, (1) at Horseleydown; (2) at Shad, Thames. 1765–72. He published a *Sermon* with Keith and Lepard in 1765 [*Gazetteer and New Daily Advertiser*, July 2nd, 1765], and in the same year his name appears in the imprint to a discourse by the Nonconformist divine, John Gill, entitled *Baptism a Divine Commandment*; a second edition was published in 1766. He also sold the *Sermon* preached by Rev. S. Stennett on Gill's death in 1771 in which the second address is found.

ROBINSON (RANEW), bookseller in London, Golden Lion, St. Paul's Churchyard, 1726. *See Dictionary*, 1668–1725. R. Robinson was one of the partners in the publication of *The Works of the Learned John Selden*. [*London Journal*, February 12th, 1726.]

ROBSON (JAMES), bookseller and publisher in London, 29 New Bond Street, the Feathers, 1759–1806. Born at Sebergham, Cumberland, in 1733. Was sent to London at the age of sixteen and apprenticed to a relative, J. Brindley, of New Bond Street, whom he succeeded in 1759. He held shares in the chief publications of his day, and issued periodical catalogues of his stock. In 1772 he described himself as bookseller to the Princess Dowager of Wales. In 1788 he purchased the Pinelli library, which he sold by auction in London in 1789 or in 1790. James Robson died on August 25th, 1806. He was one of the group of booksellers who met at the Shakespeare Tavern, and his chief amusement was fishing. He had two sons who died in childhood, a third, James, was killed by a fall from his horse at the age of twenty-one; a fourth, George, took holy orders and held a prebend in the cathedral of St. Asaph.

ROBSON (I. & CO.), booksellers in Newcastle-upon-Tyne, 1776–88. Mentioned in a list of provincial booksellers. [*N. & Q.* 10 S. VI. 444.]

ROCKET (DUDLEY), bookseller in Bradford, Yorkshire, 1737. Mentioned in list of provincial booksellers. [*N. & Q.* 10 S. V. 141.]

ROE, or ROWE (JEREMIAH), bookseller in Derby, 1725–54. *See Dictionary*, 1668–1725. Still in business in 1754, when his name appears in an advertisement of *The Young Attorney and Gentleman's Assistant*.

ROGERS (ANDREW), bookseller and publisher in Stamford, co. Lincoln., 1744–50. From an advertisement in the *Northampton Mercury* of December 24th, 1744, it appears that this bookseller came from London about that time and opened a shop in the High Street, Stamford. He also had a branch shop in Oundle at the White Swan Inn which he opened on Saturdays. His name occurs in 1746 in a list of subscribers to the second edition of Elizabeth Justice's *Voyage to Russia*, and in 1750 he was the publisher of a *Sermon* preached at St. Mary's Church, Stamford, by the Rev. Charles Stokes.

ROGERS (ELIZABETH), bookseller in Bury St. Edmunds, opposite the Cross, 1755–74. Began to advertise in the *Ipswich Journal* in 1755. In 1769 her name occurs in an advertisement of John Gibson's *Seasonable Hints on Midwifery*, which appears to be a very rare book. She was also one of those who sold *Some Memoirs of the Life of John Glover, late of Norwich*, 1774, 12mo. [B.M. 4903. bbb. 20 (1).]

ROGERS (JOHN), bookseller in Shrewsbury, 1729. One of the creditors of Richard Muckleston, an insolvent debtor, late of Shrewsbury. [Middlesex Sessions Book, no. 877, pp. 63, 65.]

ROGERS (SAMUEL), bookseller in Witham, Essex, 1769. Held periodical sales of books, which he advertised in the provincial press.

ROSS (J.), printer in Durham, 1733–6. A work entitled *Durham Cathedral* bears the imprint: "Durham, Printed by J. Ross for Mrs. Waghorn," 1733, 8vo [Bodl.]. Three years later the imprint "Durham, Printed by J. Ross" is found on the title-page of Dr. Christopher Hunter's anonymous pamphlet, *An Illustration of Mr. Daniel Neal's History of the Puritans*, 1736, 8vo. [B.M. 4135. aaa. 89.]

ROSS (S.), (?) printer in Newcastle-upon-Tyne, Angel in the Flesh Market, 1732. In Smith's *Catalogue of Friends' Books* he records a copy of John Milton's

Considerations touching the likeliest means to remove hirelings out of the Church, reprinted by S. Ross, 1732, 8vo. Ross was probably a prominent Quaker, and the book was probably printed for him rather than by him.

ROUTH (GEORGE), printer in Bristol, in the Maiden Tavern, 1775–78. The above imprint is found on a poem called *Clifton*. Messrs. Hyett and Bazeley record a poem with a similar title, the second edition of which was printed at Bristol by T. Cocking in 1767. There is nothing in Routh's publication to indicate that it is a reprint. His name occurs in a list of provincial booksellers as still in business in 1778. [*N. & Q.* 10 S. v. 141.]

ROUTHS and NELSON, booksellers and printers in Bristol, 1775–6. This firm is mentioned in a list of provincial booksellers as in business in 1775. In that year they bought the *Bristol Journal*, a continuation of *Farley's Bristol Newspaper*, from Hester Farley. The firm may have consisted of George and William Routh, with a partner named Nelson. [Hyett and Bazeley, vol. III; *N. & Q.* 11 S. I. 304.]

ROWLAND (J.), bookseller in London, Angel Court, Long Ditch, Westminster, 1771. In 1771 he made proposals for printing a work called *Examples of the Ancient sages*, by P. Bernard. [*Public Advertiser*, January 1st, 1761.]

ROWLEY (JOHN), bookseller and publisher in Chester, 1745. In that year he published a *Sermon* preached at the Assizes held in the city, by the Rev. John Hulse, A. M. [B.M. 225. i. 1 (10).]

ROWLES (WILLIAM), bookseller in Deptford, Butt Lane, 1756. Mentioned in list of provincial booksellers. [*N. & Q.* 10 S. v. 183.]

RUDDER (SAMUEL), printer and publisher in Cirencester, co. Gloucester., 1749–1801. Born at Stout's Hill, in the parish of Uley, where the family had been settled for some generations. Son of Roger Rutter, or Rudder, a noted vegetarian, and baptized at Uley on December 5th, 1726. Mr. Roland Austin in his account of this printer, which appeared in *The Library* for July 1915, and on which this notice is founded, suggested that Rudder was probably apprenticed to George Hill, printer of the *Cirencester Flying Post and Weekly Miscellany*. At the expiration of his apprenticeship he opened a bookseller's shop in Dyer Street, Cirencester. The earliest date at which his business is mentioned is November 7th, 1749, in the pages of the *Gloucester Journal*, where amongst the agents for "Mr. Jackson's Tincture" is the name of "Mr. Samuel Ruddey, bookseller in Cirencester", the misspelling being a printer's error. Like those of most provincial booksellers of that period his stock consisted of many things besides books, sugars, coffees, teas, wall-papers, and even linen cloth. Before the year 1752, Rudder had added the business of a printer to that of a bookseller, and during that year he printed for the Rev. Charles Davies, Master of the Swansea Free Grammar School, Busby's *English Introduction to the Latin Tongue examined*, the title-page of which bears the date 1753, and about the same time *The Young Astronomer's Assistant, and Countryman's Daily Companion*, compiled by William Hitchman, shoemaker of Poulton near Cirencester, besides a collection of election papers issued between August 9th and October 17th, 1753. Rudder's chief claim to remembrance rests on his work as an historian of the county of Gloucester. He began with *The History of Fairford Church*, which he printed in 1763. This went through no less than eleven editions during his life, and was frequently reprinted. Sir Robert Atkyns's *The Ancient and Present State of Gloucestershire*, first published in 1712, was the first and only work of reference relating to the county then extant; but a large part of the edition having been destroyed in the fire which consumed William Bowyer's premises in 1713, the work had become scarce, and in February 1767 Rudder sent out proposals for a *New History*, but before he could get his material together a second edition of Atkyns's was printed in 1768. Rudder took considerable pains to collect reliable and valuable information for his work; but from one cause and another *The New History of Gloucestershire* did not appear until 1779. He followed up this work in 1780 with his *History of Cirencester*. Rudder died on March 15th, 1801. Mr. Austin says of him: "Rudder introduced the personal element into his books by his observations and reflections on matters arising out of the various subjects dealt with, and did not hesitate to differ from traditions and accepted notions. His remarks in the prefaces show independence of spirit, and he must have been a man of marked individuality."

RUDHALL (JOHN), bookseller in Oxford, 1726–8. Mentioned as "bibliopola" in Bliss's slips under date of September 30th, 1726. As Bliss was Keeper of the University Archives the entry may probably be relied upon, and it receives confirmation from an entry in Wilford's *Monthly Catalogue* for May 1728, where a sermon by the Rev. Peter Senhouse was advertised "to be sold by J. Rudhall, bookseller in Oxford." Timperley [p. 817] suggests that he was the father of John Broughton Rudhall, a bookseller and printer in Bristol, who is found there in 1772. [*N. & Q.* 11 S. I. 304.]

RUSSEL (WILLIAM), bookseller and publisher in London, Horace's Head by Temple Bar, 1751–55. Publisher, with John Clarke, of the Rev. W. Webster's *Two Sermons upon the Sabbath*, 1751 [B.M. 225. g. 9 (3)], and in 1755 the fourth volume of Carte's *History of England*. [Nichols, II. 505, 506.]

RUSSELL (J.), bookseller in Guildford, at the Bible, 1761–1804. Born in 1711, he was four times Mayor of Guildford. [Dr. G. C. Williamson's *Guildford in other days*.] He is found issuing a trade card about 1761, and is also known from a bill-head dated 1761. [A. Heal's Collection.] His name occurs in a list of provincial booksellers as still in business in 1772. [*N. & Q.* 10 S. v. 183.]

RUSSELL (DR. WILLIAM), printer in Edinburgh and London, 1757–1770 (?). Born at Windydoors, in the county of Selkirk in Scotland. Was apprenticed for five years to Messrs. Martin and Weatherspoon, booksellers and printers in Edinburgh. Afterwards came to London to follow a literary life, but found himself compelled to apply to William Strahan the printer, who employed him for a time as corrector of the press. In 1769 he became overseer in the printing office of Messrs. Brown and Aldred. At the same time he pursued his literary studies and was the author of several essays in prose and verse which met with success, and he finally gave up his employment as a printer and devoted himself to historical studies. He was the author of *A History of Modern Europe* in 1792, and also *A History of America*. He died December 25th, 1793.

RYALL (J.), bookseller in London, Hogarth's Head, opposite Salisbury Court, Fleet Street, 1755–6. In partnership with Robert Withy. They described themselves as "book and print-sellers". In 1755 they published the seventh edition of William Romaine's *Discourse on Earthquakes*, and in the following year a useful work on English coins, consisting of twelve plates of English silver coins with letterpress. [B.M. 603. i. 23.]

RYAL (N.), bookseller and publisher in Westminster Hall, 1735. In the newspapers of that year he advertised an edition of Thomas Otway's play of *Caius Marius*, and also received subscriptions for E. Ravenscroft's comedy *The Anatomist*. [*London Evening Post*, July 12th, 1735.]

RYLES (THOMAS), bookseller in Hull, Yorks., 1707–36. *See Dictionary*, 1668–1725. Still in business in 1736, when his name is found in the imprint to John Clark's edition of the *Colloquies* of Erasmus.

SADLER (ADAM), printer in Liverpool, 1728–41. Believed to have been the fourth printer to set up in the city. In 1728 he printed a small book called *The Lawyer, or Complete Knave*. Although it bore no date on the title-page it is clear from internal evidence, such as the names of Judges, that it was printed during that year. Altogether he printed seven books, the last in 1741. [*Lancashire Printed Books*, 1925, p. xvii.]

SADLER (JOHN), bookseller and printer in Liverpool, 1740–65. Began to print in 1740 in association with Guy Green. His best known work was a volume of songs called *The Muses Delight*, printed in 1754. Mr. A. J. Hawkes states that the head and tail and other wood-cut ornaments were in his belief specially designed for the work. Sadler printed a series of letters by Joseph Clegg criticizing the Corporation, and had to apologize. His son (John II) invented the process of transfer printing on china. He joined Green, who had lately succeeded to Sadler's father's painting business, and in 1752 they produced the first Liverpool Transfer ware. Published an edition of Thomas à Kempis's *Following of Christ* in 1755. He is mentioned in a list of provincial booksellers as still in business in 1761. [*N. & Q.* 11 S. I. 365.]

SAINT (THOMAS), printer in Newcastle-upon-Tyne, Pilgrim Street, 1761–88. Admitted to the Newcastle Stationers' Company on April 30th, 1761, and was in partnership with John White, their joint names appearing in the imprint to two books in 1763. He was descended from a family of merchants and yeomen at Morpeth, and served his term of apprenticeship with the firm of Bryson and Charnley. On the death of J. White, Thomas Saint carried on the business. Printed the works of Dr. Hutton and Thomas Bewick. During his lifetime he was the sole printer of the *Newcastle Courant*, which had been founded by John White in 1711. Thomas Saint died July 31st, 1788, and was buried at Morpeth. [R. Welford, *Early Newcastle Typography*.]

SANDBY (WILLIAM), bookseller and publisher in London, Fleet Street, the Ship, opposite St. Dunstan's Church, 1746–68. Son of Dr. Sandby, Prebendary of Worcester, Timperley speaks of him as a "bookseller of high eminence". He was also the publisher of numerous works, amongst which may be mentioned an edition of the Rev. William Smith's translation of Longinus *On the Sublime*; an *Assize Sermon*, preached by the same divine in 1746; *A little known French Grammar* by J. D'Gairtier; and *An account of the Spa in Germany*. He was married three times, and lost one wife in October 1756 after a lingering illness. [*Read's Weekly Journal*, October 16th, 1756.] In 1768 he sold his business to John Murray (*q. v.*). In a letter to the poet Falconer offering him a share in the business, Murray says: "The shop has been long continued in the trade; it retains a good many old customers." Sandby died at Teddington on November 2nd, 1799, in the eighty-second year of his age. [Timperley, 1842, p. 802.] Issued an engraved trade card with his sign. [A. Heal's Collection.]

SANDERS (P.), printer in London, Crown Court, Butcher Row, without Temple Bar, 1732. Printer of the *Grub Street Journal* in that year.

SANDERS (T.), bookseller and publisher in London, Little Britain, 1726. His name is found in the imprint to the second edition of the Rev. Robert Millar's *History of the Propagation of Christianity* printed in that year. [B.M. 4570. b. 15.]

SANDERSON (PATRICK), bookseller and publisher in Durham, "Mr. Pope's Head," 1764–75. Mentioned in a list of provincial booksellers as being in business in 1764. [*N. & Q.* 10 S. VI. 443.] In 1767 he compiled and published *The Antiquities of the Abbey or Cathedral Church of Durham*, which was printed at Newcastle. Issued a trade card. [A. Heal's Collection.]

SARJEANT, (H.). *See* Serjeant.

SAY (CHARLES GREEN), printer in London, (1) Newgate Street; (2) 10 Ave Maria Lane, Ludgate Street. 1753–75. Son of Edward Say. Taken into business about 1753. In 1760 he was summoned before the House of Commons as printer of *The Gazetteer* for printing the proceedings. With regard to this incident the writer of the biographical notice of the Earl of Marchmont in *Biographical, Literary, and Political Anecdotes*, 1797, III. 405, says: "the printer of the Gazeteer (Say) was brought upon his knees before the House, for only saying in his paper, that the thanks of the House had been given to Sir Edward Hawke, for his Victory over Conflans in the month of November 1759." In 1770 information was laid against him for printing the *Letters of Junius*. [*House of Commons Journal*, XXVIII. 741–5.] He died in November 1775.

SAY (EDWARD), printer in London, Ave Maria Lane, 1727–69. In business in 1727, when he printed a work entitled *Excidium Angliae, or, A View of the . . . consequences attending the Smuggling of Wool*. [B.M. 712. d. 16 (35).] But he is chiefly remembered as the printer of a weekly paper called *The Gazetteer*. In 1763 he became Master of the Stationers' Company, and died in May 1769. His will was proved on the 6th of that month. He left an annuity to his wife Frances, and the residue of his estate to his son Charles Green Say (*q. v.*). [P.C.C. 184, Bogg.]

SAYER (ROBERT), bookseller and publisher in London, (1) Golden Buck, opposite Fetter Lane; (2) 53 Fleet Street. 1752–75. Made a speciality of books on carpentry. His advertisements are found in the London press from 1752 to 1769. [*St. James's Chronicle*, November 25th, 1769.] Later on he was in partnership with J. Bennett. They advertised *A New Atlas* in 1775. [*Public Advertiser*, January 19th, 1775.]

SCHOFIELD (JAMES), printer in Manchester, (1) down the Fountain Court at the back of the Exchange, 1754; (2) Middlewich, co. Cheshire, 1756; (3) Rochdale, 1758–60; (4) Scarborough co. York., 1798. First found in Manchester in partnership with M. Turnbull in 1754. They were the printers of the *Manchester Journal*. [Timperley, 1842, p. 691.] In 1756 he moved to Middlewich and became the printer of the *Middlewich Journal, or Cheshire Advertiser*. [Burney Collection, 477.] There was also a Schofield a bookseller in Rochdale who advertised books between 1758 and 1760. Procter in his *Memorials of Manchester Streets*, p. 201, says that he afterwards became a bookseller in Scarborough and died there in 1798.

SCORE (EDWARD), junior, bookseller in Exeter, over against the Guildhall, 1740–79. Probably the son of Edward Score, 1704–24. His name is found in the imprints to many books between these years. Issued a small label of patent medicines. [A. Heal's Collection.]

SCOTT (G.), printer in London, 1775. Only known from the imprint to *A Table of Evidence of the authority of the Sacred Canon*, which was advertised in the *Public Advertiser* on April 14th, 1775, as on sale at Oxford and Cambridge.

SCOTT (JOHN), bookseller, printer, and publisher in London, Black Swan, Paternoster Row, 1748 (?)–1776 (?). Is believed to have set up first in Cornhill, where he was burnt out in 1748. He published many pamphlets of a political character, such as *A Letter to the People of England upon the Militia*, 1757. [B.M. E. 2048 (2).] Later on he appears as a printer for J. Robson the publisher.

SEDGELEY (THOMAS), bookseller and bookbinder in Oxford, 1727–34. Dr. Philip Bliss, Keeper of the Oxford University Archives, notes that T. Sedgeley was an Oxford bookseller in 1727. In 1734 a Mr. Sedgeley bound a Bible for Holywell Church. [Madan.]

SEELEY (B.), bookseller and publisher in Buckingham, 1747–76. In the *Northampton Mercury* he advertised a *Sermon* preached at Buckingham on

July 5th, 1747. He was still in business in 1776. A correspondent to *Notes & Queries* says that he was a writing-master. [*N. & Q.* 10 S. V. 141.]

SENDALL (THOMAS), bookseller in Bristol, Lock's Head, Wine Street, 1728. Established the first circulating library in the city in March 1728. [J. Latimer, *Annals of Bristol in the Eighteenth Century*, 1893, p. 163.]

SENEX (JOHN), bookseller in London, Globe in Salisbury Court, Fleet Street, 1719–41. Although chiefly known as an engraver and maker of Globes and Maps, John Senex kept a bookseller's shop at the above address from 1719. He was admitted a Fellow of the Royal Society in 1728, and died on January 1st, 1740. *Hooker's Weekly Miscellany* of January 3rd contained an obituary notice, and described him as "a sincere, worthy, honest man, and greatly valued by men of learning".

SENEX (M.), bookseller and publisher in London, 1749–53. Associated with S. Birt (*q. v.*) in the publication of the third edition of a pamphlet by Edward Bentham, of Oriel, entitled *A Letter to a Young Gentleman of Oxford*, 1749, 8vo. [B.M. 1111. h. 18 (2).] In 1753 he was one of those taking subscriptions for Chambers's *Cyclopaedia*. [*Public Advertiser*, January 6th, 1753.]

SERGENT (E.), printer in Preston, Lancs., 1762. In 1762 the account of the festivities held in the city on the occasion of the Jubilee of the Guild Merchant of Preston bore his imprint. [B.M. 577. e. 28/2.]

SERJEANT or SARJEANT (H.), bookseller and publisher in London, without Temple Bar, 1775. He published with J. Smith a Masonic book. [*Public Advertiser*, January 10th, 1775.]

SERJEANT (WILLIAM), stationer in London, Bible in Great Newport Street, near Newport Market, 1730. Issued a trade card in that year. [A. Heal's Collection.]

SEWELL (JOHN), bookseller in London, Cornhill, 1754 (?)–1802. For some years partner with John Brotherton, whom he succeeded in 1775. Nichols says that his shop was the resort of "the first mercantile characters in the City, particularly those trading to the East Indies". He died November 19th, 1802, aged sixty-eight. [Nichols, III. 737, 738.]

SEYFFERT (C. G.), bookseller and publisher in London, (1) Dean Street, Soho; (2) Pall Mall. 1758–60. A dealer in foreign books between those dates, and also a publisher of pamphlets.

SEYMOUR ( ), bookseller and publisher in London, Threadneedle Street, 1765. In the *Gazetteer and Daily Advertiser* of August 3rd, 1765, is the advertisement of a medical book published by him in conjunction with a Mr. Turpin.

SHARP, or SHARPE (JOHN), bookseller and publisher in Warwick, 1769–91. On June 24th, 1769, he advertised for a bookbinder in the *Oxford Journal*. In 1772, sold copies of the Rev. Wm. Talbot's *Narrative of his Proceedings relative to Jonathan Britain* [B.M. 1093. b. 60], and in 1774, J. Jones's *Remarks on the English Language*. [B.M. 12316. f. 25 (2).] Nichols records him as in business as late as the year 1791. [*Lit. Anecd.* III. 686.]

SHATWELL (P.), bookseller and publisher in London, Strand, 1775. His name occurs as publisher of a medical book in an advertisement in the *Public Advertiser* on January 3rd, 1775.

SHAVE (JOHN), bookseller and publisher in Ipswich, Suffolk, Stationer's Arms, Butter Market, 1745–98. Apprentice and successor to W. Craighton (*q. v.*), who gave up the bookselling and stationery business in 1759, but continued to carry on his trade as a printer. John Shave's first advertisement appeared in the *Ipswich Journal* of June 14th, 1759. In 1761 he announced in the *Public Advertiser* the publication of P. Bernard's *Examples of Ancient Sages*. Another work issued by him was *The Complete Assessor's Duplicate* in 1765, and two years later his name occurs in the imprint to the *Seventeen Sermons* of the Rev. Nathaniel Torriano, Rector of Aldham. [B.M. 4455. g. 14.] John Shave was also a bookbinder and copperplate printer, to which, probably after the death of Craighton, he added that of letterpress printing in partnership with Stephen Jackson. He retired in November 1793, and died sometime in June 1798, being succeeded by P. Forster. In a list of provincial booksellers in *Notes & Queries* mention is made of a T. Shave as in business as a printer "in Ipswich in 1767", but this is a mistake for J. Shave. [Information kindly supplied by C. R. McColvin, Esq., librarian of Ipswich Public Libraries.]

SHAW ( ), widow, bookseller in Newcastle-upon-Tyne, 1724. Probably widow of Ralph Shaw. [Welford, p. 128.]

SHAW (J. W.), printer and publisher in London, Fleet Street, opposite Anderton's Coffee House, 1775–76. On January 20th, 1775, he began to issue a weekly periodical entitled *The Crisis*, a bold and outspoken indictment of the King and his Government for the American war. No. 3 was in the form of a letter to the King, and was so strongly worded that the Houses of Parliament ordered it to be burnt at the hands of the common hangman. This publication ran till October 12th, 1776, when the authors brought it to a close and stated their determination of quitting this country for America.

SHAW (WILLIAM), bookseller in York, Low Jubbergate, 1741. Only known from a Poll Book for the Election of Members of Parliament in 1741, which was printed for him by John Gilfillan. [Davies, *History*, p. 321.]

SHEEPEY (MARSHALL), printer, publisher, and bookseller in London, (1) Watling Street, near Bow Lane, 1748; (2) under the South-West Piazza of the Royal Exchange, 1749; (3) Threadneedle Street, 1748–53. Publisher of *Sheepey's Daily Journal*, a pocket-book and calendar. An advertisement in 1753 runs: "Marshall Sheepey, Bookseller and Publisher has removed from under the Royal Exchange into Threadneedle Street, between the Royal Exchange and the New England Coffee Houses and opposite the end of Sweeting's Alley." [*Public Advertiser*, January 10th, 1753.] He shared in the publication of *The Gentlemen's and Tradesmen's Pocket-Book* from the new address. [*Ib.*, January 5th, 1753.]

SHEPHERD (A.), bookseller and publisher in London, Great Turnstile, Holborn, 1757. Publisher of a pamphlet entitled *A Letter to Admiral Smith*, 1757, 8vo. [B.M. E. 2048 (5).]

SHEPHERD (T.), bookseller in London, 147 Minories, 1772. Publisher of a sheet called *The Midnight Rambler* for 1772.

SHERWOOD (T.), bookseller in Devizes, 1744. Mentioned in an advertisement in the *Salisbury Journal* of Tuesday, April 10th, 1744.

SHEWELL (THOMAS), bookseller and publisher in London, Paternoster Row, 1747. This name occurs in the imprint to a *Sermon*, preached by the Rev. Matthew Harbery at St. Chad's on October 1st, 1747. [B.M. 226. f. 16 (3).] He was in partnership with Thomas Longman for several years.

SHIPTON (J.), bookseller and publisher in Knutsford, 1753. In 1754 his name occurs with that of J. Leach (*q. v.*) on the imprint to the Rev. John Holland's *Sermons... and Prayers*, London 1753, 8vo. [B.M. 4455. aaa. 2.]

SHOVE (J.), bookseller and stationer in London, at the Mitre opposite Furnival's Inn, *c.* 1760. Issued a trade card showing his sign about this date. [A. Heal.]

SHROPSHIRE (WALTER), bookseller and publisher in London, New Bond Street, 1768 (?)–1785. Possibly a son of William Shropshire (*q.v.*). In 1767 and 1768 he issued catalogues of his stock, which consisted of about 2,000 books. He died October 17th, 1785, at Hendon. [Timperley, 1842, p. 757.] By his will, which was proved on October 29th, it is evident that he had retired from business some years before his death, as his premises in Bond Street were then in the occupation of an engraver and printseller named William Dickinson. He left no son to succeed him, and his share in the *Morning Chronicle, or Daily Advertiser* he left to his eldest daughter Elizabeth. [P.C.C. 529, Ducarel.]

SHROPSHIRE (WILLIAM), bookseller and publisher in London, (1) St. George, Hanover Square, Bond Street: (2) over against the Duke of Grafton's in New Bond Street. 1732 (?)–1750 (?). This publisher was established in 1732, and possibly earlier, as the name of W. Shropshire is found in the imprint to a pamphlet with the title *Faithful Memoirs of the Life and Actions of James Butler, late Duke of Ormonde*, published in that year. [B.M. 10817. c. 22 (3).] On November 12th, 1743, there appeared a pamphlet called *Old England's* "Te Deum ", which was on sale not only at the various pamphlet shops but also at the Magpye alehouse in Giltspur Street. William Shropshire admitted having caused it to be printed by Mr. Thomas Gardner, a printer in the Strand, and said that the copies when printed were sent to Mr. [i.e. John] Robinson, a bookseller in Ludgate Street, who had promised to publish them. Shropshire further said that he had received the manuscript from Sir James Harrington with instructions to get it printed: but he did not know who was the author of it. [S. P. Dom., Geo. II, Bundle 62, 61.]

SHUCKBURGH (ANNE (?)), bookseller and publisher in London, at the Sun between the Temple Gates in Fleet Street, 1761–1765 (?). This was possibly the widow of John Shuckburgh, whose name was Anne. She was the publisher of H. Carey's *Chrononhotonthologus* in 1765.

SHUCKBURGH (JOHN), bookseller and publisher in London, (1) between the two Temple Gates in Fleet Street; (2) at the Sun, near the Inner-Temple Gate in Fleet Street; (3) at the Sun next to Richard's Coffee-House, Fleet Street. 1727 (?)–1761. Published numerous pamphlets. J. Shuckburgh was selling *A Trip thro' London* from "Between the Two Temple-Gates, Fleet Street," in 1728. [*Daily Post*, January 3rd, 1728.] In 1734 John Whiston, of the Boyle's Head, bought of him the library of Bishop Kidder for £180. In 1753 he published *A Proposal for the Amendment and Encouragement of Servants* from

the Sun next to Richard's Coffee-House, Fleet Street. [*Public Advertiser*, January 11th, 1753.] He died on April 4th, 1761, his will being proved on the 14th of the same month. It made no mention of his business, but it named three sons, Samuel, William, and John, and a daughter Anne, named after his wife, whom he appointed executrix. [P.C.C. 148, Cheslyn.]

SHUCKFORTH ( ), bookseller at Diss, co. Norfolk, 1742. Sold the third edition of Defoe's *A Tour through ... Great Britain*, published in May 1742.

SHUTT, or SHUTE (WILLIAM), bookseller in Tiverton, Devon, 1725–32. His name is found in the imprint of a sermon in 1725. [Dredge.] Agent for London book auctions. [See *Farley's Exeter Journal*, March 8th, 172$\frac{7}{8}$, last page, col. 2.] In 1729 he became the publisher of *A Necessary Guide to Landlords and Tenants*. [W. M. C., December 1729, p. 145.] In 1732 his name is found in the imprint of *The West Country Farmer &c.*

SIBBALD (JOHN), bookseller and publisher in Liverpool, Castle Street, 1766–76. Mentioned in the *Liverpool Directory* for the above year.

SILVER (JACOB), bookseller and publisher in Sandwich, Kent, 1726 (?)–1739 (?). Mentioned in an advertisement in the *Kentish Post* of Wednesday, March 23rd, 17$\frac{25}{26}$, as selling *The Merchant's and Trader's Daily Practice in Writing, Arithmetick &c.* by Thomas Lydal, Teacher of Merchants' Accompts &c. at Margate. In the same year he published a *Sermon* preached by the Rev. de Gols, Rector of St. Peter's, Sandwich. On March 17th, 173$\frac{8}{9}$ he advertised in the *Kentish Post* a sale of books. The date of his death is unknown, but he appears to have been succeeded by Samuel Jacob (*q. v.*).

SILVER (SAMUEL), bookseller and publisher in Sandwich and Margate, Kent, 1751 (?)–1776 (?). Believed to have been successor to Jacob Silver, of Sandwich, and in 1751 became administrator of the goods of John Silver, saddler. In 1753 he published *The Lover's Manual, a Choice Collection of Poems*, and also a pamphlet entitled *Some Short and Plain Arguments from Scripture*. [B.M. 11643. aaa. 22; 4372. g. 2 (2).] He afterwards moved to Margate, where he set up a circulating library and Register Office for lodgings in Cecil Square in 1773, but his business failed and he became bankrupt in 1776, as appears by an advertisement in the *Kentish Gazette* of June 8th, in which persons were instructed to pay any debts they owed the bankrupt to Mr. Sawkins, attorney, at Margate.

SIMMONS, or SYMMONDS (MRS.), bookseller in Sheffield, 1731. In 1731 he sold the Rev. J. Clegg's *Sermon* preached at the ordination of John Holland, junior, at Chesterfield, co. Derby., August 11th, 1731. [*London Evening Post*, December 25th.] Perhaps identical with S. Simmons, and widow of Nevill Simmons (1697–1702).

SIMMONS (JAMES), printer in Canterbury, Kent, 1768–1807. Son of a barber, was born in 1740. Apprenticed to T. Greenhill, stationer, of London. Founded the *Kentish Gazette*, which superseded Abre's *Kentish Post*. Took into partnership George Kirby. They established a circulating library in the city in 1780. James Simmons became an Alderman and also Member of Parliament for Canterbury, and owing to his generosity the city acquired the Dane John Gardens. He died at Westminster on January 22nd, 1807, aged sixty-six. Amongst the notable works printed and published by Simmons and Kirby was the first edition of Hasted's *History of Kent*, 1778.

SIMMONS (S.), bookseller and publisher in Sheffield, 1738. In 1738 he sold the Rev. J. Clegg's *Sermon* preached at the High Pavement in Nottingham, entitled *The Things that make for Peace*... [Creswell, p. 26.] Possibly identical with Mrs. Simmons.

SIMPSON, or SYMPSON (C.), bookseller and publisher in London, the Bible Warehouse, Chancery Lane, 1753. His name occurs in connexion with several anti-Jewish pamphlets about this time. [B.M. T. 2231 (30).]

SIMPSON (J.), bookseller and publisher in London, Shakespeare's Head, Paul's Alley, 1761. In that year he published *Genuine Memoirs of the late celebrated Mrs. Iohn D. ...* [*Lloyd's Evening News*, July 1st, 1761.]

SIMPSON, or SYMPSON (JOSEPHUS), printseller in London, The Dove, Russell Court, Drury Lane, *c.* 1750. Issued a trade card about this date. [A. Heal's Collection.]

SINGLE (J.), (?) bookseller or pamphlet-seller in London, near St. Paul's, 1758. This name, probably fictitious, appears in that year in the imprint to the notorious *Seventh Letter to the People of England*, for which the author, John Shebbeare, was sentenced to stand in the pillory, which he did with an umbrella over him. [B.M. 8132. a. 93 (9).]

SKETCHLEY (JAMES), printer and publisher in Birmingham, 1763–76. Is believed to have been originally an auctioneer, but in 1763 he printed and published *Sketchley's Birmingham Directory*. Mr. Joseph Hill, in his *Bookmakers of Old Birmingham*, says that from being the printer of his own sale bills he became a publisher, magazine editor, and journalist. In 1764 appeared no. 1 of the *Birmingham Register*, printed in Birmingham by and for J. Sketchley, and sold in Coventry by T. Luckman, printer; and in the following week *The Coventry Museum*, printed by T. Luckman, and sold in Birmingham by J. Sketchley. In size, character, contents, type &c., these two journals were identical. From 1769 to 1774 Sketchley was connected with the newspaper which ultimately became *Swinney's Chronicle*. He is believed to have died about 1781.

SKETCHLEY (JAMES), printer in Bristol, 27 Small Street, 1775. Mentioned by Messrs. Hyett and Bazeley in vol. III, p. 343, in a list of Bristol printers as at work in that year.

SKETCHLEY (SAMUEL), bookseller and stationer in Birmingham, 74 Bull Street, 1770. Joint publisher with J. Sketchley of *Sketchley and Adams's Tradesman's True Guide and Universal Directory* in 1770.

SLACK (THOMAS), printer and publisher in Newcastle-upon-Tyne, Union Street, 1755–84. First heard of as manager to Isaac Thompson, printer. He appears to have been a very capable business man, and became the founder and printer of the *Newcastle Chronicle*. Slack was also the author of several works of a mathematical character, which he published in the name of S. Thomas. [Sykes, *Local Records*, I. 333.] His best-known work was the *Newcastle Memorandum Book*, which continued to be published annually until 1893. His wife was also a writer of books of an educational character under the pen-name of "A. Fisher", and together they built up a large and successful business. Thomas Slack died on January 13th, 1784, aged sixty-five, and leaving no heir, his business passed to his son-in-law, Solomon Hodgson. [Welford, pp. 36, 37.]

SLADE (   ), (?) bookseller in Wincanton, co. Somerset., 1745. Mentioned in an advertisement of the second edition of Stackhouse's *Bible* in 1745.

SLATER (   ), junior, bookseller in London, Holborn, 1756. In the *London Evening Post* of August 3rd, 1756, is the announcement of his marriage to Miss Preston of Ramsgate, at St. Lawrence's Church, Thanet. He may be identical with Henry Slater (*q. v.*).

SLATER (MRS.), bookseller at Chesterfield, co. Derby., 1731 (?)–1738 (?). Sold the Rev. J. Clegg's *Sermon* preached at the ordination of Mr. John Holland, junior, at Chesterfield, August 11th, 1731 [*London Evening Post*, December 25th], and in 1738 another *Sermon* by the same preacher [Creswell, p. 26].

SLATER (HENRY), bookseller and publisher in London, Golden Key, the corner of Clare Court in Drury Lane, 1749–55. His name is found in the Poll Book for the City and Liberties of Westminster in 1749 as living in Clare Court. In 1750 he published *A Genuine Account of Earthquakes, especially that at Oxford*. He may be identical with the previously mentioned Slater, junior.

SLOW, or SLOE (S.), bookseller and publisher in London, over against Devereux Court without Temple Bar, 1732–3. Publisher of the *Life of Robert Wilkes, comedian* in 1732, and in 1733 *Mr. Taste's Tour*. He sometimes advertised in *Fog's Journal*.

SMALLEY (   ), bookseller in Preston, co. Lancs., 1762. Sold *The Guild-Merchant of Preston*, an account of the entertainments &c., held in that year.

SMART (   ), bookseller (?) in Ludlow, co. Shropshire, 1771. In 1771 he distributed copies of a catalogue of books on sale by S. Gamidge, bookseller of Worcester. [*The British Chronicle, or Pugh's Hereford Journal*, August 8th, 1771.]

SMART (WILLIAM), bookseller and publisher in Northampton, 1744–9. In 1746 his name occurs in the imprint to a *Sermon* preached by the Rev. Henry Layng, M.A., in the parish church of All Saints, Northampton, on behalf of the County Infirmary. [B.M. T. 1658 (5).] Again in 1749 he published a *Sermon* by the Rev. John Nixon.

SMITH (A.), bookseller in Halifax, Yorks., 1763. Only known from a list of booksellers given in the *Leeds Intelligence* of that year.

SMITH (MRS. ELIZ. (?)), pamphlet-seller under the Royal Exchange, 1728. Her name appears in the imprint to a translation of Bernard de Fontenelle's *The Elogium of . . . Peter I. Czar of Muscovy*, printed in 1728. In the same year she was, with others, tried at the King's Bench for publishing [i.e. selling] *Mist's Journal*. [Coram Rege Roll. 108, Rex. 27, Hilary, 2 Geo. II.]

SMITH (ELIZ.), bookseller in Plymouth and Tavistock, 1753. One of the publishers of Dr. Thomas Salmon's *Personal Union of the Divine and Human Nature*, 1753, 4to. [Dredge, p. 48.]

SMITH (G.), printer in London, Johnson's Court, Fleet Street, 1743. About May 12th, 1743, he published an evening paper called, *The Express, or Evening Gazette*, which he advertised in the *Daily Gazetteer*.

SMITH (J.), bookseller and publisher in London, Inigo Jones's Head in the Strand, 1726–8. He was the publisher of Dr. Wells's *Paraphrase . . . on the Books of Isaiah, Jeremiah &c.*, 1728.

SMITH (J.), printer in London, Well Close Square, 1765–8. Two pamphlets dealing with America were printed at this press, the third edition of the *American Negotiator* issued in 1765, and Thomas Hutchinson's *History of the Province of Massachusetts Bay* in 1768.

SMITH (JAMES), bookseller in Dorking, Surrey, 1746. Mentioned in a list of provincial booksellers as in business in that year. [*N. & Q.* 10 S., March 10th, 1906, p. 183.]

SMITH (JAMES), stationer in London, (1) Wheatsheaf, near the Royal Bagnio in Newgate Street, 1723; (2) Wheatsheaf in Newgate Street, 1744. 1723–44. Probably both addresses refer to the same house. Bill-head used by this stationer, with the date 1744. [A. Heal's Collection.]

SMITH (JOHN), bookseller in Daventry, co. Northampton., 1739–44. His name occurs in an advertisement of the intended publication of Francis Tolson's *Hermathenae* in 1739. He is believed to have died before 1744.

SMITH (JOHN), map and print-seller in London, Hogarth's Head, near Friday Street, Cheapside, *c.* 1750. Issued a large and ornate trade card, without date, with a portrait of Hogarth at the top. [A. Heal's Collection.]

SMITH (JOHN), printer (?) in London, 1755. Author of a technical work called *The Printer's Grammar*, which Timperley describes as an unfinished work. It is, however, useful as giving the various sizes of type in use in the eighteenth century.

SMITH (JOSEPH), stationer and paper-hanging maker in London, Rose and Crown, in the corner of Angell Street, St. Martin's le Grand, *c.* 1770. Issued a trade card about this date. [A. Heal's Collection.]

SMITH (R.), bookseller in Northampton, 1770–6. His name occurs in 1770 in the imprint to the Rev. John Ryland's *Death-bed Terrors of an Infidel*. [B.M. 4015. aa. 51 (2).]

SMITH (S.), bookseller and publisher in London, 17 Paternoster Row, 1775–6. Issued *Bacchus and Venus* with T. Lewis. [*Public Advertiser*, January 9th, 1775.]

SMITH (SAMUEL), stationer and bookseller in London, The Sun and Wheatsheaf, No. 6, near Staples Inn, Holborn, *c.* 1770. Successor to William Roach (*q. v.*). Issued a trade card. [A. Heal's Collection.]

SMITH (T.), bookseller and publisher in Canterbury, Kent, 1753–88. One of the leading booksellers in the city for many years. Died January 14th, 1788. Amongst his publications was a *Catalogue* of the sale of the books belonging to John Knowles, Recorder of Canterbury. [Nichols, VIII. 473.]

SMITH (THOS.), bookseller in Tavistock, co. Devon., 1753. One of the publishers of the Rev. Thomas Salmon's *The Personal Union of the Divine and Human Nature*, 1753, 4to. [Dredge, p. 48.]

SMITH (WILLOUGHBY), printer in Hereford, By Street, 1739. Printer of the *Hereford Journal*, a small folio of four pages. He may be identical with the W. Smith who in 1740 published the first newspaper in Preston, Lancashire, called *The Preston Journal*.

SMITHURST (B.), bookseller in Plymouth, 1739. One of the publishers of Prebendary Mudge's *Sermons*. [Advertisement in the *Weekly Miscellany*, April 28th, 1739.]

SNAGG (R.), bookseller and publisher in London, (1) 129 Fleet Street; (2) 29 Paternoster Row. 1774–5. Dealer in books for children, and usually advertised his business premises as the "Little Book Warehouse". Amongst his publications in 1775 was an edition of the *Works* of Congreve in two volumes, advertised in the *Public Advertiser* of January 7th, and *The Complete Florist*, advertised in the same journal on April 15th.

SNELLING (   ), bookseller in London, Fleet Street, 1770. Mentioned in the will of the Rev. Charles Godwyn, of Oxford. [Nichols, VIII. 226.]

SNELSON (EDMUND), printer and publisher in Nantwich, co. Cheshire, 1775–6. Printer of *Sermons* by the Rev. John Smith, Rector of Nantwich.

The SOCIETY FOR THE ENCOURAGEMENT OF LEARNING, publishers in London, 1736–49. The Society was started in 1736 "To assist authors in publication and to secure them the entire profits of their own works." The

President was the Duke of Richmond, and the Committee of Management included Paul Whitehead and James Thomson as representatives of Professional Authorship. Its affairs were never flourishing, and although Thomson was on the Committee he would not leave Millar, who had published his *Seasons* in 1730. Among the books published by the Society were Carte's *Original Letters*, Roe's *State Papers* and *Bibliotheca Britannica*. Knight states that at its close it left its patrons £2,000 in debt. On the other hand, William Jerdan, in a pamphlet published in 1838, says that at the close of the business the promoters of the scheme gave the balance of their profits, £24 12*s.*, to the Foundling Hospital.

SOLLERS (WILLIAM), bookseller and book auctioneer in Blandford, co. Dorset., 1775. In August 1775 he sold the library of the Rev. Christopher Twynihoe, late of Turnworth, near Blandford. [B.M. 824. b. 17 (4).]

SOTHERAN (HENRY), bookseller and publisher in York, Stonegate, 1764 (?)–1776 (?). His name occurs in the imprint to Dr. Charles Collignon's *Enquiry into the Structure of the Human Body*, Camb. 1764, 8vo. In partnership with John Todd for some years. They issued numerous catalogues of books between 1767 and 1770, but the partnership was dissolved by 1776 when Todd is found issuing catalogues alone, and Sotheran moved into the premises in St. Helen's Square vacated by Daniel Peck. [Davies, *History*, pp. 265, 266.]

SOUTHERN (J.), bookseller and publisher in London, St. James's Street, 1775. He issued a medical *Disquisition* with two others in 1775. [*Public Advertiser*, January 3rd, 1775.]

SPAVAN (GEORGE), bookseller and publisher in London, (1) opposite St. Clement's Church in the Strand; (2) Crown in Ivy Lane in the Strand. 1745–50. Publisher of pamphlets of all kinds, and also of *The Musical Miscellany*, a collection of songs. On one occasion he was indicted for dealing in questionable literature. [State Papers Dom., Geo. II, Bundle 65/86.]

SPENCE (JOHN), bookseller in Exeter. His name occurs in the imprint of *The Practice of Inoculation &c.* (1765). [*Bibliotheca Cornubiensis*, 1029.]

SPENCER (JOHN), printer in Exeter, in Gandy's Lane, 1761–5. Printer of several controversial pamphlets in a dispute between Dr. Andrew and Mr. Pitfield, the first being *A Short Reply to the Falsehood and Slander published against Dr. Andrew* . . ., Exeter, printed by J. Spencer, 1761. In 1765 he gave

his address as Fore Street in the imprint to the Rev. Richard Harrison's *Sermon* preached at Honiton on August 25th after the great fire there. [Dredge, p. 50.]

SPILSBURY (JOHN), stationer and engraver in London, Russell Court, Covent Garden, *c.* 1750–*c.* 1795. Was drawing-master at Harrow School. Issued a trade card. [A. Heal's Collection.]

SPILSBURY (THOMAS), printer in London, (1) Newcastle Court, Fleet Street; (2) Snow Hill. 1769 (?)–1795. On Friday, October 13th, 1769, a serious fire broke out in Fleet Street, and the *Middlesex Journal* of that date stated that amongst the buildings destroyed was Spilsbury's printing house in Newcastle Court. How long Spilsbury had been in business there we do not know, nor where he went after the disaster. The next heard of him is in 1781, when, on the death of William Strahan, junior, he took over the premises in Snow Hill. He had a good connexion, and printed for the Rev. W. Herbert. He died December 1st, 1795. Nichols spoke of him as a man of the strictest integrity, and says that he was the first in this country to print French accurately.

STAGG (J.), bookseller in London, Westminster Hall, 1726–46 (*see Dictionary*, 1668–1725). Still in business in 1746.

STAMPER (F.), bookseller and publisher in London, Pope's Head Alley, Cornhill, 1750–?. In partnership with E. Downham, published cheap literature such as chap-books, ballads, trials, and other ephemeral literature. Their imprint is found upon the title-page of *The Adventures of Capt. De la Fontaine* . . ., 1751, 8vo. [B.M. 10825. c. 31.]

STANDEN (JOHN), printer in London, (1) D'Anvers Head, Chancery Lane; (2) Caleb D'Anvers Head in the Old Bailey, 1739. Printer of the *Country Journal or Craftsman* of Saturday, October 13th, 1739. This contained a notice that he had moved to the Old Bailey, a few doors from the printing office of the *Daily Post* and *London Evening Post*. Standen was also the printer of political pamphlets.

STANDFAST (R.), bookseller in Westminster, Westminster Hall, 1726. *See Dictionary*, 1668–1725. Still in business in 1726, when he published *Parergon juris canonici Anglicani*. [Wilford.]

STANLEY (JAMES), printer in Preston, Lancashire, Market Place, 1745. In partnership with John Moon. They issued a newspaper called *The British Courant, or Preston Journal*, the first number of which appeared in 1745.

STAPLES (ALEXANDER), printer and publisher in York, Coney Street, 1734–9. Son of Robert Staples, of London, bookseller. In September 1734 he bought the stock and printing business, including the *York Courant*, from John White. He is said by Gent to have been ruined by Dr. John Burton, but there is no confirmation of this. In 1739 Staples sold the business to Messrs. Ward and Chandler. Amongst his other work was the Rev. J. Mawer's *Nature and Design of the Lord's Supper*, printed in 1736. [B.M. 225. g. 14 (5); Davies, p. 241.]

STAPLES (J.), bookseller and publisher in London, Stationers' Court, Ludgate Street. He was the publisher with others of the third edition of a pamphlet entitled *Things as they are* in 1758. [B.M. E. 2049 (6).]

STARK (ROBERT), stationer and paper-hanging maker in London, on Ludgate Hill, *c.* 1770. Issued a trade card about this date. [A. Heal's Collection.]

STEEL (DAVID), bookseller and publisher in London, (1) Bible and Crown, King Street, Little Tower Hill, 1765; (2) 1 Union Row, the lower end of the Minories, Little Tower Hill, 1765–84. Publisher of nautical books, such as Steel's *Naval Remembrances*, 1784. His name is also found in the second edition of Bougainville's *History of a Voyage to the Malouine* (*or Falkland*) *Islands*, published in 1773.

STEEL (M.), bookseller in Bury St. Edmunds, 1757–75. This name occurs on some Poor Law Overseers Forms in this year. [Information supplied by G. J. Gray, of Cambridge.] In 1775 a Mrs. Steel, possibly identical with the above, was carrying on the business of a bookseller and publisher.

STEPHENS (A.), bookseller and publisher in London, the Bible in the Butcher Row, 1745. This name occurs in the imprint to a *Sermon* by the Rev. John Peters, M.A., preached in the Chapel in Spring Garden on Sunday, October 27th, 1745. [B.M. 225. i. 2 (10).]

STEPHENS (J.), bookseller in London, Fleet Street, 1735. He was one of the booksellers advertised as taking subscriptions for Otway's *Caius Marius*. [*Daily Post*, February 13th, 1735.]

STEVENS (E.), publisher and bookseller in London, 1775. One of the partners in the publication of *The Court and City Register*. [*Public Advertiser*, January 27th, 1775.]

STEVENS (JOHN), bookseller in London, in Shepherd's Land in Humerton [i.e. Homerton] in the parish of St. John's, Hackney, 1745. In Easter term of

that year he was bound over in a sum of £200 to appear in the Court of King's Bench to answer a charge of publishing obscene literature. [S. P. Dom., Geo. II, Bundle 65/101.]

STEVENS, (PAUL), bookseller and publisher in London, the Pasteboard Warehouse facing Stationers' Hall, in the parish of St. Martin's, Ludgate Hill, 1752–63. His name occurs in a list of those for whom *The Gentlemen's and Tradesmen's Pocket Assistant* for 1753 was printed. [*Public Advertiser*, January 5th, 1753.] He died in February 1763, *not* 1768, as stated by Nichols [III. 739], his will being proved on the 19th of that month. He left a legacy to his brother Robert, but made no mention of his business. [P.C.C. 34, Secker.]

STEVENS (ROBERT (?)), bookseller and publisher in London, Paternoster Row, 1761. May be identical with Robert Stevens, mentioned in the will of Paul Stevens (*q. v.*) or his brother, but his trade is not disclosed in the will. In 1761 he published a pamphlet written by Thomas Roch, citizen of Canterbury, entitled *An Address to the Electors of the City of Canterbury*, 1761, 8vo.

STICHALL (BENJAMIN), bookbinder in London, the Bible in Blackamoor Street, Clare Market, 1745. His name occurs in the imprint to the Rev. John Peters's *Sermon* preached at the Chapel in Spring Garden on Sunday, October 27th, 1745. [B.M. 225. i. 2 (10).]

STOKES ( ), bookseller in Dudley, co. Staffs., 1730–7. Mentioned in a list of provincial booksellers. [*N. & Q.* 10 S. v, March 10th, 1906, p. 183.]

STOKES (CHARLES), bookseller and publisher in London, Red Lyon, Fleet Street, 1728 (?)–1741. According to an advertisement in *Mist's Journal* for August 3rd, 1728, "the right and true opthalmick tobacco" was to be had at his shop. The only book that has been found with his name in the imprint is one of the editions of Conyer Middleton's *Dissertations*. He died June 10th, 1741, and a short obituary notice of him appeared in Hooker's *Weekly Miscellany* for June 11th, 1741, in which it was stated that he was a collector of medals and other curiosities.

STONE (J.), bookseller and publisher in London, near Gray's Inn, 1735. Issued *The Life of the late Czar* in 1735. [*Daily Post*, February 13th, 1735.]

STRAWBERRY HILL PRESS, near Twickenham, Middlesex, 1757–89. On June 25th, 1757, Horace Walpole set up a private printing press in a cottage on his estate at Strawberry Hill, near Twickenham, for his own amusement. He was not a practical printer, and never professed to be one; but he kept a journal of the works printed, the names of the printers whom he employed, the wages he paid them, and other matters connected with the venture, besides superintending the typographical details of each book, procuring vignettes, and otherwise giving them a personal touch. His journal of the press was printed in 1923, with notes by Dr. Paget Toynbee, so the less need be said here. The first printer engaged was William Robinson, an Irishman, whom he paid a guinea per week, and the firstfruits of the press were two Odes by the poet Gray, *The Progress of Poetry* and *The Bard*, the manuscript of which Walpole happened to see in Dodsley's shop and carried off. These appeared in August 1757. He followed them up in 1758 with P. Hentzner's *Journey into England*, of which only 200 copies were printed. From the outset he had trouble with his printers, Robinson was an eccentric and erratic character, who left him in 1759. He then engaged Benjamin Williams, who came to him on March 5th, 1759, and was discharged on the 25th. On June 19th in the same year he tried a third printer, James Lister; but he only stayed a week. A month later he took on Thomas Farmer, who for a time proved more satisfactory, and remained with him until December 2nd, 1761, when he ran away. By this time Walpole was beginning to tire of his hobby. Writing to Dalrymple on February 23rd, 1764, he said: "The plague I have had in every shape with my own printers, engravers, the booksellers &c., beside my own trouble have almost discouraged me from what I took up at first as an amusement, but which has produced very little of it." [*Journal*, p. 76.] His fifth printer was Thomas Pratt, whom he turned away at the end of the year 1764. Finally, on March 18th, 1765, he engaged Thomas Kirgate, who proved more satisfactory, and remained with Walpole until 1789, when he abandoned the venture. Amongst some of the notable books printed by Walpole were, in addition to those mentioned, the *Memoirs of Grammont*, the *Life of Lord Herbert of Cherbury*, and several of his own works, such as *The Anecdotes of Painting in England*, the first two volumes of which appeared in 1762 with the imprint of Thomas Farmer, the third in 1763 without any printer's name, and the fourth in 1780 with the imprint of Thomas Kirgate. From 1775 to 1778 the press was idle. The last work issued from the press was *Bishop Bonner's Ghost*, of which two copies were printed on brown paper. Considering that the whole staff consisted of a man and a boy the output of the press was highly satisfactory, and Walpole spared no expense in order to obtain the best results, his type being mainly obtained from the famous Caslon foundry.

STRAHAN (ALEXANDER), stationer in London, (1) Golden Ball, corner of Three Tuns Passage, 1696; (2) Golden Ball, near St. Michael's Church in Cornhill, 1749. 1696–1749. Evidently related to George Strahan (*see Dictionary*, 1668–1725). House destroyed by fire in 1748. Bill-head used by this stationer. [A. Heal's Collection.]

STRAHAN (GEORGE), *see Dictionary*, 1668–1725.

STRAHAN (WILLIAM), printer in London, (1) Bury Court, Love Lane, Wood Street; (2) New Street. 1737–85. Son of Alexander Strahan, a customhouse officer. Born March 24th, 1715. Apprenticed to a printer in Edinburgh. Came to London about 1737 and entered into partnership with T. Hart, a printer. A specimen sheet of their type was recently found by Mr. H. L. Bullen of the Typographical Library and Museum of the American Typefounders' Company. [*Library*, Fourth Series, March, 1923.] On July 20th, 1738, William Strahan married Margaret Penelope, daughter of William Elphistone an Episcopalian clergyman, and on October 3rd in the same year he was admitted to the freedom of the Stationers' Company by redemption. His first publication is believed to have been *The Life of James Fitz James, Duke of Berwick*. There is no evidence that he was ever in partnership with either Andrew Millar or Thomas Cadell, but he held shares in many publications in which they were also shareholders. The partnership with Hart seems to have been of short duration, as in 1739 he is found paying journeyman's wages to the amount of £4 10*s*. weekly, which represented the employment of four or five men. In 1742 his printing office was in Wine-Office Court, off Fleet Street, and in 1748 he is found in New Street. He soon had an extensive business, amongst those for whom he printed being Andrew Millar, Thomas Longman, Charles and John Wesley, and other prominent publishers and writers such as the Knaptons and the Rivingtons. Amongst his personal friends was Benjamin Franklin, who had offered a post to Strahan's friend David Hall. At one time there was a suggestion of a marriage between Strahan's son and Franklin's daughter, but nothing came of it. At that time (1760) Strahan was said to be making £1,000 a year. He was part proprietor of a newspaper called *The London Chronicle, or Universal Evening Post*. In 1762 he secured a share in the patent for Law printing, and in 1766 he became a partner in the King's Printing House. Mr. Charles Eyre, upon whom the Patent devolved, not being a practical printer, entered into an agreement with Strahan by which, for a sum of £5,000, he was to have a third share of the Patent, and was appointed manager at a salary of

£300 per annum. Strahan had a new office built adjoining his own house in New Street, and some idea of the magnitude of his business may be gathered from his own statement that there were sometimes as many as nine presses at work at one and the same time. William Strahan became M.P. for Malmesbury in 1774, and sat for Wootton Bassett in 1780, but lost his seat in the election of 1784. He died July 9th, 1785. He had three sons, William, George, and Andrew. William set up for himself as a printer. The second son, George, became Vicar of Islington, and the third son, Andrew, succeeded to the business. One of his daughters married in 1779 John Spottiswoode, and two of her sons inherited the Strahan business. From entries in his Ledgers it is evident that Strahan obtained most of his type from the Wilson type-foundry of Glasgow, and in the list of his apprentices is found that of Andrew Wilson, one of the sons of Alexander Wilson; but later on he gave some of his orders for type to William Caslon. In addition to his Government work, many famous books were printed by William Strahan. Most notable of all was Johnson's *Dictionary*. Five firms of booksellers were financially interested in this venture, J. and P. Knapton, T. and T. Longman, C. Hitch and L. Hawes, Andrew Millar, and R. and J. Dodsley. The work was begun in 1747, and was published on April 15th, 1755. William Strahan was also the printer of Gibbon's *Decline and Fall*.

STUART, or STEWART (WILLIAM), bookseller at Wigan, Preston, and Manchester, 1742 (?)–1762 (?). Son of James Stewart, of Ormskirk. A bookseller of this name at Wigan in Lancashire was agent for the catalogues issued by T. Warren, the bookseller of Birmingham, in 1749. He may be identical with the stationer mentioned in *The Guild-Merchant of Preston* as steward of the Trade Assembly, who refused to allow the editors to see the list of subscribers, and who had tried in "a mean and artful manner" to obtain the list of the guests at the Mayor's banquet on August 30th, 1762. He published an account of the proceedings.

STUART (W.), bookseller and publisher in London, 1775. One of the partners in the publication of *The Court and City Register*, and of the Rev. Mr. Harvey's *Meditations*. [*Public Advertiser*, July 10th, 1775.]

STUART (ZACHARIAH), bookseller and publisher in London, the Lamb, Paternoster Row, 1759 (?)–1774 (?). Successor to Mr. Cox. [Bill-head in Mr. A. Heal's possession.] Publisher of the following Americana: Richard Gardiner's *Account of the Expedition to the West Indies against Martinico*, 1759, and a

second edition of the same work in the following year, *America Vindicated from the high charge of Ingratitude and Rebellion*, which was printed at a local press at Devizes in Wilts. [J. Carter Brown Library.] He issued *The Candid Review* in 1765. [*Gazetteer and Daily Advertiser*, August 13th, 1765.] He subscribed for seven sets of the Greek Testament of 1768.

SUMPTER (E.), bookseller and publisher in London, Bible and Crown in Fleet Street, 1763–84. His name occurs as publisher on certain issues of the notorious paper issued by John Wilkes, the *North Briton*, in the years 1763–5. Twenty years later his name is found in the imprint to John Harman's *Remarks upon the Life of the Rev. George Whitefield*.

SWALE (JOHN), bookseller in Leeds, 1714–42. *See Dictionary* 1668–1725. In 1726 he advertised a theological work in Wilford's *Monthly Catalogue* for June, and was still in business in 1742, when his name is found in the imprint to a work by the Rev. Dr. T. Barnard, M.A., master of the Free School in Leeds.

SWAN, or SWANN (ROBERT), printer in London, Crown Court, corner of Salisbury Square, Strand, near St. Martin's Lane, 1748–? 1807. This printing-house was established about 1748, and numerous broadsides and pamphlets were printed there. On August 20th, 1807, it was destroyed by fire. Whether it was then in the hands of Robert or one of his descendants is not established, as Timperley merely speaks of the proprietor as Mr. Swan [p. 831].

SWINNEY (MYLES), printer, type-founder, bookseller, and journalist in Birmingham, 21 New Street, and 75 and 76 High Street, 1770–1812. Began as a printer about 1770, and is said to have been a workman in Baskerville's type-foundry. In 1771 he began to print the *Birmingham Chronicle and Warwickshire Journal*, which was a continuation of the *Warwickshire Weekly Journal*. In this he used Baskerville type: but in 1785 he began type-founding on his own account, and aimed at utility rather than beauty of form. In addition to the *Chronicle* he issued a magazine called *The British Museum, or Universal Register*, and in 1773 a *Directory* of Birmingham. He was also a publisher. He died in 1812. [J. Hill, *Bookmakers of Old Birmingham*, pp. 63, 64, 71, 75–9.]

SYMMONS, *see* Simmons.

SYMON (EDWARD), *see Dictionary*, 1668–1725. Still in business in 1741, when he acted as stationer to the South Sea House and Post Office. Died Tuesday, June 16th, 1741, his will being proved on the 26th of the same month. He left no heir, but mentions a brother John. He owned property at Eversholt, co. Beds. [P.C.C. 165, Spurway.]

SYMPTON (C.), bookseller and Publisher in London, Stonecutter Street, Fleet Market, 1765. He issued *A Life of Christ* with J. Bedford. [*Gazetteer and Daily Advertiser*, September 16th, 1765.]

TANS'UR (WILLIAM), bookseller in St. Neots, co. Hunts., 1743–83. Was born at Dunchurch in Warwickshire in 1700. After many years wandering about the country as a teacher of music, William Tans'ur spent the last forty years of his life as a bookseller in the town of St. Neots, where he died on October 7th, 1783, aged eighty-three. In his *Beauties of Poetry*, published in 1776, he has one headed: "William Le Tans'ur recommends these Books to all his Social friends. The Bookseller's Shop." That he dealt in second-hand books is evident from the following specimen from this poem:

The Art of *War* is taught by valiant *Bland*,
Ellis and *Hill* teach to improve your land:
Markham and *Gibson*, cures your horses ills,
And *Owen's Treatise* all your *Vermin* kills.

He concludes thus:

These *Books*, and Thousands more, of late invention,
And *Manuscripts*, more than I here can mention;
Are selling cheap, (Books also neatly Bound,)
The Like elsewhere is scarcely to be found:
Obedient to your *Orders*, Sirs, I stand,
And am your humble servant, at command.

W. L. T.

TAYLOR ( ), bookseller in Nantwich and Drayton, 1738–9. Agent for Daffy's "Elixer". [J. P. Earwaker, *Local Gleanings*, I. 237.] In 1739 his name occurs in a list of booksellers selling John Kelly's *Nature Delineated*. R. Taylor, whose name is found in 1775 in the imprint to *Sermons* by the Rev. John Smith, Rector of Nantwich, was probably a descendant. [*Ib.*, I. 114.]

TAYLOR (R.), bookseller and publisher in Berwick-upon-Tweed, 1753–76. Publisher of Stephen Jackson's *A Thought on Creation*, 1753. Is believed to have set up a printing-press later. [J. C. Hilson, *Berwick-upon-Tweed Typography*, 1753–1900.]

TAYLOR (T.), bookseller and publisher in London, (1) at the Rose in Exeter Exchange, 1741; (2) at the Meuse Back-gate, 1748. 1741 (?)–1748 (?). In 1741 he published a political pamphlet called *The Inventory of the Goods, and Chattels of the P—r, W—s*, and in 1748 his name is again found in the imprint to *The Life and Surprising Adventures of James Wyatt*. [Carter Brown Library and Harvard.]

TAYLOR (W.), bookseller and publisher in Bath, Church Street, 1760–73. Mentioned in a list of provincial booksellers as in business in 1760. In 1773 Richard Crutwell, the printer, printed for him and another bookseller in the city, A. Tennent (*q. v.*), a *Guide to the City*. [B.M. 579. c. 3 (3).]

TEBB (THOMAS), bookseller and publisher in London, Flower de Luce, Little Britain, 1708–28; *see Dictionary*, 1668–1725. In 1727 his name appears in Wilford's *Monthly Catalogue* in an advertisement of the fourth edition of Aesop's *Fables*, and again in the same publication of the following January in connexion with the third edition of *The Female Orators*.

TENNENT (A.), bookseller and publisher in Bath, Milsom Street, 1773. Publisher with W. Taylor of a *Guide to the City*, which was printed for them by Richard Crutwell (*q. v.*). They also advertised in it T. Guidott's *Collection of Treatises relating to the City and Waters of Bath*. [B.M. 579. c. 3 (3).]

TESSEYMAN (WILLIAM), bookseller and publisher in York, (1) Bookbinder's Alley; (2) Minster Yard. 1763 (?)–1811. Successor to Francis Mawburne. Began to publish about 1763, when his name is found in the imprint to an edition of William Mason's *Elegies*. He also published the first edition of the same writer's poem, *The English Garden*. Tesseyman died in 1811, and a catalogue of his stock was published in 1813. [Davies, *Memoir*, p. 64 n. &c.; Timperley, 1842, p. 843.]

THOMAS (MORRICE), printer in Oxford, 1738. Only known from the fact that his Administration bond, dated June 7th, 1738, is amongst the Oxford University Archives. [Madan.]

THOMPSON (ISAAC), bookseller and publisher in Newcastle-upon-Tyne, without Pilgrim Street Gate, 1737–76. Is believed to have been born in Lancashire of Quaker parents. At an early age he went to Newcastle, where he set up as a land agent and surveyor. He was of studious habits, and in 1731 published a collection of poems. In 1739 he became a printer and started the *Newcastle Journal*, the first number of which appeared on April 7th of that year. About 1747 he began another periodical called *The Newcastle General Magazine*, which ran till 1760. His next venture was a weekly publication called *The Literary Register, or Weekly Miscellany*, begun in 1769. Isaac Thompson died on January 6th, 1776. He left three sons, only one of whom, John, was for a short time in the printing business. [Welford.]

THOMPSON (J.), bookseller and publisher in London, near the Sessions-House in the Old Bailey, 1729–46. In 1729 J. Thompson published a pirated edition of Gay's *Polly* with the Music at the end, which caused Bowyer to insert an advertisement in the *Evening Post*, threatening "Prosecution with the utmost severity" against anyone who sold it. [Nichols, *Literary Anecdotes*.] Amongst the publications of the year 1746 was a small pamphlet entitled "*The Life and Behaviour of John Skinner*, who was executed August 29th, 1746 . . .", which bears the imprint "London: Printed for J. Thompson, Publisher, near the Sessions-House in the Old-Bailey; and may be had at the Pamphlet-shops, and of the News-sellers".

THOMPSON (R.), (?) bookseller in London, 1738. In that year he published a ballad called the *Negociators , or Don Diego brought to reason : an excellent new ballad*, of which a copy is amongst the State Papers of George II, with an unsigned note suggesting that the authors, printers, and publishers should either be sent to the House of Correction as loose, idle, disorderly persons under the Statutes 39 Elizabeth and 17 James I: or, those who hawked them should be called upon to show their licences, and, failing to do so, should be sent to the House of Correction as provided by the Statute 3 and 4 Anne, *c.* 4. [S. P. Dom., Geo. II, Bundle 46/119.] Another copy of this ballad is in the Harvard Library.

THOMPSON (WILLIAM), printer and bookseller in Stamford, co. Lincoln., 1726, *see Dictionary*, 1668–1725.

THOMPSON, *see also* Tomson.

THORN (MRS), bookseller in Braintree, Essex, 1773 (?). Her name appears in the imprint to Coese's *Objections against any Human Authority in Religion*. [R. A. Peddie, *Library World*, September 1904.]

THORN (BARNABAS), printer and bookseller in Exeter, (1) St. Peter's Churchyard, 1756; (2) opposite the Guildhall, 1775. 1742–91. In partnership with Andrew Brice, whom he appears to have succeeded in 1742, when his name first appears in the imprint to the Rev. Samuel Johnson's *An Explanation of Scripture Prophecies*. [Dredge, p. 23.] During the next forty years he was a prolific publisher of sermons and other works. In 1775 he printed the eighth edition of *An Exmoor Scolding*, previously printed by R. Thorn in 1771. In the local press of the year 1791 appeared an advertisement by T. Brice stating that he had succeeded to the business of Mr. Thorn.

THORN (NATHANAEL), bookseller in Exeter, 1726–42. *See Dictionary*, 1668–1725. Continued in business until 1742, and was succeeded by Barnabas Thorn.

THORN (R.), printer and publisher in Exeter, co. Devon., in Fore Street, opposite the Guild Hall, 1771–89. In 1771, in partnership with A. Brice, he printed and sold *An Exmoor Scolding*, and in 1786 his name is found in the imprint to a work called *Pogonologia . . . an Essay on Beards*. He appears to have died in 1789, being then mentioned as "the late Mr. Thorn of Fore Street".

THORN (W.), bookseller and publisher in London, in St. Clement's Churchyard, 1740. His name is found in the imprint to Thomas Wilson's *An Essay towards an Instruction for the Indians* published in that year. [J.C.B.L.]

THURLBORNE ( ), bookseller in Cambridge, 1735–51. *See Dictionary*, 1668–1725. In 1735 catalogues of T. Osborn's Book Sale are advertised as "to be had at Mr. Thurlborne, Cambridge". [*Daily Journal*, February 18th, 1735.] He also sold the *Literary Magazine*. [*Ib.*, April 4th, 1735.] In 1751 Barrett, Clements, Thurlborne, and Dodsley were partners in Warton's *An Ode for Music*. [Straus.]

TILLY (J.), printer and publisher in London, Rose and Rainbow Court, Aldersgate Street, 1743. In that year his name occurs in the imprint to a pamphlet entitled *Enthusiasm Display'd*, a reprint of a sermon preached in 1649 and attributed to Oliver Cromwell. [B.M. 113. m. 65.]

TIPPELL ( ), printer at Halesworth, co. Suffolk, 1751. Printed the *Ordinances and Statutes for Warner's Almshouses at Boynton, co. Suffolk*. [B.M. 1304. m. 1 (11).]

TODD (JOHN), bookseller in York, Bible in Stone Gate, 1757–1811. Successor to J. Hilyard. In 1767 he was in partnership with H. Sotheran, and for several years they held many book sales and issued numerous catalogues. Timperley (p. 841) says: "Few country booksellers had exerted themselves with greater ardour and perseverance in the laborious pursuit of catalogue making . . . than Mr. Todd.' Todd also kept a State Lottery Office and was a dealer in patent medicines. He died on March 29th, 1811, and was succeeded by his two sons.

TOFT (TIMOTHY), printer and bookseller in Chelmsford, co. Essex, 1755 (?)–1769 (?). Local agent for J. Buckland of the Buck in Paternoster Row in 1755. In 1758 he issued a catalogue, which he advertised in *Lloyd's Evening Post* of Friday, March 10th. He set up a printing-press about 1758, and his imprint is found in David Ogborne's *Merry Midnight Mistake, a Comedy*. [B.M. 1346. f. 11 (3).] He was afterwards in partnership with R. Lobb, and was still in business in 1769.

TOMSON (WILLIAM), printer in Northampton, Bradshaw's Lane, 1758. Mentioned in the Poll Book printed in that year.

TONSON (J. and R.), *see Dictionary*, 1668–1725.

TORBUCK (JOHN), printer and bookseller in London, Clare Court, Drury Lane, 1737–41. In 1737 he published a work called the *Church of England's Complaints against Careless Non-residents &c.* This printer had some share in printing the journals or votes of the Parliament, but the reference has been lost. There was a bookseller and auctioneer of the same name in Dublin some years later who may be the same.

TORBUCK (MISS), pamphlet seller in London, Exeter Change, 1745. In April 1745 information was given against her for selling obscene literature. [State Papers Dom., Geo. II, Bundle 65/74.]

TOUCHIT (A.), bookseller (?) in London, Westminster, 1759. Published a pamphlet entitled *The Case of Mary Edmondson. By a Gentleman of the Law*, in that year. The name may be fictitious, or that of one of the numerous pamphlet sellers.

TOVEY (BARNES), bookseller and publisher in London, (1) at the Dove in Bell Yard, Temple Bar; (2) in Palace Yard; (3) in Westminster Hall. 1750–1806. Partner with and successor to John Worrall (*q. v.*). Tovey had a stall in Westminster Hall in the year 1750. Amongst his publications was a form of the Coronation of George III in 1761. According to Nichols, he retired in 1775, and lived until 1806. [*Lit. Anecd.* III. 741.]

TOWERS (JOSEPH), printer, bookseller, and author in London, (1) Piccadilly, 1758; (2) 3 Fore Street near Cripplegate, 1769. 1749–75. In 1749 a *John* Towers, printer, of Piccadilly, is mentioned in the Poll Book for the City and Liberty of Westminster. He may have been related to the above, who was the printer and publisher of a pamphlet entitled *The Expedition against Rochefort . . . considered. By a Country Gentleman*, 1758, 8vo. [B.M. E. 2050 (1).] In 1775 *A Letter to Mr. Samuel Johnson* was printed for J. Towers, Fore Street. [*Public Advertiser*, February 12th, 1775.] The author of this was the Rev. J. Towers.

TOWNSEND (JOHN), printer and publisher in London, at the corner of White Friar's Gateway in Fleet Street, 1758–9. He was the printer and publisher of *A Journal of the campaign on the coast of France*, 1758, 8vo. [B.M. E. 2050 (6).] In the following year he reprinted a pamphlet by Richard Clarke called *A Warning to the World*, first printed at Charles Town, U.S.A.

TOWNSON (   ), bookseller in Berkhampstead, co. Herts., 1735. One of those from whom Samuel Humphrey's edition of the *Old and New Testament* could be had; but his name only appears in the advertisement and not in the book itself. [*Country Journal*, December 27th, 1735.]

TOWNSON (MATTHEW), bookseller, bookbinder, and publisher in Manchester, St. Mary's Gate, 1772. Mentioned in the *Manchester Directory* for 1772 and 1773, where his name is given as both Thompson and Townson.

TOZER (   ), bookseller in Modbury, co. Devon, 1770. Sold the Rev. Thomas Vivian's *Exposition of the Catechism*, . . . 1770, 12mo. [Dredge, p. 29.]

TOZER (AARON), bookseller and publisher in Exeter, co. Devon., the Bible, 1727–65. In 1727 Andrew Brice, the Exeter printer, printed a *Sermon* for Aaron Tozer, junior. [Dredge.] He was also the publisher of the Rev. John Lavington's *Sermon* preached at Exeter on November 8th, 1743. [Dredge, p. 47.] Another *Sermon* by the Rev. John Kiddell, preached on May 6th, 1747, is in the British Museum [T. 1034 (21)]. In 1765 he was advertising a book called *The Wisdom of Divine Providence*. [*Gazetteer and Daily Advertiser*, October 3rd, 1765.]

TREMLETT (THOMAS), bookseller in Dartmouth, co. Devon., 1756. Only known from his imprint in a work called *Practical Lectures on Education*, published in this year.

TREWMAN (ROBERT), printer and bookseller in Exeter, co. Devon., behind the Guildhall, 1764–76. First heard of in 1764, when his name appeared in a list of subscribers to Calcott's *Collection of Thoughts*. [Dredge, p. 28.] In the following year he printed a *History of Exeter*, and continued in business until 1789. In 1775 a T. Trewman, perhaps a misprint for R. Trewman, advertised the sale of imported books in the *Public Advertiser*, January 25th. The firm was still flourishing in 1819.

TRIMER, or TRIMMER (   ), bookseller in Derby, 1749–53. Agent for Dr. Powell's Cure for Tooth-ache. Distributed in 1749 the sale catalogues of T. Warren of Birmingham (*q. v.*), and in 1753 his name occurs in a list of country booksellers who sold the London newspaper, *The Daily Register*.

TROTT (W.), bookseller and publisher in London, the Seven Stars, Russell Court, 1728. One of the partners in the publication of *The Illegal Lovers*. [*Daily Post*, January 5th, 1728.]

TROWNSON (JOHN), bookseller at Totnes, co. Devon., 1750–73. Sold the Rev. William Robert's *Divine Institution*. The fourth edition (*c.* 1750). [J. I. Dredge, *Devon Booksellers and Printers*, p. 25.] His imprint is also found in *The Mariner's Instructor*, published in 1773.

TRYE (THOMAS), bookseller and publisher in London, near Gray's Inn Gate, 1737–*c.* 1760. Succeeded to the business of Richard Williamson at the above address. Dealt largely in theological works, and was publisher for the Rev. Josiah Tucker and Dr. Edward Synge. He was also the publisher of numerous works on trade, *e.g.*, *Reflections on opening the Trade to Turkey*, 1753 [B.M. T. 788 (7).], and a pamphlet against cock-fighting on Shrove Tuesday. On the death or retirement of Trye about 1760 the business was carried on by William Flexney (*q. v.*). [Nichols, I. 266; Timperley, 1842.]

TURBOT (R.), bookseller in London, Fleet Street, 1735. His name occurs among others taking subscriptions for Otway's *The Orphan* and *Caius Marius*. [*Daily Post*, February 13th, 1735.]

TURNBULL (MICHAEL), bookseller in Newcastle-upon-Tyne, 1755–76. Began business in October 1755. Stated by Welford to have remained in business until 1779. Succeeded by his widow. [*Early Newcastle Typography*, p. 128.]

TURNER (D.), bookseller in Hempsted, Herts., 1739. Mentioned in a list of provincial booksellers as in business in 1739. [*N. & Q.* 10 S. v, March 1906, p. 183.]

TURNER (JOSEPH), bookseller and publisher in Cirencester, co. Gloucester., 1735. The following imprint is recorded by Mr. H. E. Morris in his *Booksellers and Printers of Cirencester*, 1912: "Sold by Joseph Turner in Cirencester, 3rd edition 1735," but he omits the title. In 1736 Turner published Harrison's *Scriptural Exposition of the Church Catechism*, which he advertised in the columns of the *Weekly Miscellany* of Saturday, May 29th.

TURPIN (HOMAN), bookseller in London, Golden Key (104) St. John's Street, West Smithfield, 1764–87. Issued catalogues of his stock. Made a speciality of manuscript sermons. His stock in 1772 is said to have numbered 10,000 volumes, and his catalogue filled 178 octavo pages, to which were added four extra pages of New Books, &c. Still in business in 1787, as shown by a bill-head in Mr. A. Heal's collection.

UMFREVILLE (LEONARD), printer in Newcastle-upon-Tyne, 1733–6. Printer of *The North Country Journal, or Impartial Intelligencer*, which he started in the year 1734. In 1736 the firm was "Leonard Umfreville and Company". He was succeeded in 1737 by Thomas Umfreville & Co. [Welford, pp. 63, 65, and 128.]

UMFREVILLE (THOMAS), printer of Newcastle-upon-Tyne, 1737–43. Brother of Leonard. Succeeded to the publication of *The North Country Journal, or Impartial Intelligencer* in March $173\frac{6}{7}$, on his brother's death, and continued it until 1739. He gave up business in or about 1743, when he became parish clerk of St. John's, Newcastle. He died in June 1783. Mr. Welford adds: "the publications of the Umfreville press are not important." [Welford, p. 26.]

UNETT (S.), bookseller (?) in Wolverhampton, 1749–55. A Mrs. Unett was in 1749 agent for the distribution of the sale catalogues of T. Warren, bookseller in Birmingham. She may be identical with the S. Unett whose name occurs in a list of those selling the third edition of John Barrow's *Psalm-Singer's Choice Companion*, advertised in the *Whitehall Evening Post* of January 2nd, 1755.

UNWIN (MATTHEW), bookseller and publisher in Loughborough, co. Leicester.; and Ashby de la Zouch, co. Derby, 1728. In that year he advertised in the *Stamford Mercury* a work called *Dialogues between Two Young Ladies*. This was probably Matthew Unwin who was at Birmingham in 1716, and at Leicester in 1741. *See Dictionary*, 1668–1725.

URIEL (P.), bookseller in London, Inner Temple Lane, 1775. He advertised the sale of *Reports of Cases* in the *Public Advertiser*, January 28th, 1775.

UWINS (ANTHONY), bookseller in Andover, Hants, 1725–7. Mentioned in a list of provincial booksellers. [*N. & Q.* 10 S. v. 481].

VAILLANT (ISAAC), and (PAUL I), booksellers in London, over against Bedford Street in the Strand, 1705–50. Sons of François Vaillant. Isaac went to

Rotterdam for a few years prior to 1726 in connexion with his foreign business. He retired in 1750 and died in 1753. Paul I was publisher of *La Distribution de la Somme* (the lists of grants to poor refugees) from 1705–8. A copy is in the Guildhall Library. He died in 1738.

VAILLANT (PAUL) II, bookseller in London, 87 Strand. Son of Paul I and grandson of Francois, the founder of the business. Apprenticed to his cousin Nicholas Prevost, bookseller, on November 3rd, 1730. Admitted freeman of the Company of Stationers on February 7th, 1737–8. In 1739 he went to Paris to superintend the famous edition of *Cicero* edited by the Abbé Olivier. In 1750 he succeeded to the business of his uncle Isaac (*q. v.*). He went to Paris again in 1759 to arrange for a new edition of *Tacitus* by the Abbé Brotier. In that year he was elected Sheriff of London, and was present at the execution of Earl Ferrers at Tyburn. He served the offices of Under Warden, Upper Warden, and Master of the Company of Stationers in the years 1768, 69, 70, and was known as the "Father" of the Company. Published a general catalogue of his stock in 1762. Died February 1st, 1802. An interesting booklet on the Vaillant family has been published by the Rev. W. B. Vaillant, M.A. Oxon., of Weybridge, from which and from notes supplied by him the above notices have been compiled. The firm during the eighteenth century issued a beautifully engraved trade card, embodying the sign of the Ship. [A. Heal's Collection.]

VALANS (   ), bookseller in Liverpool, Lancashire, 1756. Agent for the sale of Schofield's *Middlewich Journal or Cheshire Advertiser* in 1756.

VANDENBURGH, or VANDENBERGH (SIMON), bookseller in London, Piccadilly, 1772–79. Nichols records him as carrying on the Philobiblion Library in Piccadilly between 1772 and 1779. [Nichols, III. 665.]

VANDENHOEK (ABRAHAM), bookseller and publisher in London, Virgil's Head against the new church in the Strand, 1727–34. In partnership with J. Groenegen (*q. v.*) until 1727. Dealt largely in French literature. Issued a *Bibliotheca Selecta* between 1727 and 1728. Gave up business in England and went to live at Hamburg about 1734. His shop was then taken by John Wilcox who, on the title-page of a catalogue printed in 173$\frac{4}{5}$, makes the above statement about his predecessor. Issued a trade card showing his sign. [A. Heal's Collection.]

VERNON (   ), bookseller at Holms Chapel, co. Cheshire, 1756. Agent for Schofield's *Middlewich Journal or Cheshire Advertiser* in 1756.

VERNOR (THOMAS), bookseller in London, (1) 31 Newgate Street; (2) Ludgate Circus; (3) St. Michael's Alley, Cornhill. 1766–76. A partner in the firm of Thomas Vernor and Company, who were established in business as stationers' before 1769. Nichols gives the name of the firm as Vernor and Chater, and says that they were issuing catalogues in 1766; but according to Kent's *Directories* for that period, John Chater was carrying on a separate business as a bookseller in King Street, Cheapside. It was not until 1772 that the firm appears as Thomas Vernor and Co., booksellers in St. Michael's Alley, Cornhill. As Chater's name does not appear in the *Directory* for that year, he may have sold his business to Thomas Vernor. [Nichols, III. 665.]

VERRALL (EDWARD), bookseller in Lewes, co. Sussex, 1734–66. Mentioned in the Lewes Poll Book of 1734. Publisher of *The Antiquities of Arundel.*

VERTUE and GOADBY, printers and stationers in London, Royal Exchange, 1734 (?)–1750 (?). This firm consisted of Mrs. Vertue the widow of Vertue, and Samuel Goadby, one of his apprentices. The partnership developed into a domestic as well as a business one, as they were married shortly afterwards. *See* Goadby (S.). Amongst their publications was *A Letter written by Sherlock Bishop of London to the Clergy and peoples of London and Westminster on occasion of the Earthquake.* A copy in the British Museum has a manuscript note to the effect that 52,000 copies were printed of it at four shillings a hundred. [B.M. T. 1655 (10).]

VINEY (ROBERT), bookseller in London, at the Bible in Cannon Alley, St. Paul's, 1736–50. This imprint is found on the title-page of a pamphlet entitled *The Golden Fleece* published in the year 1736. [B.M. T. 47 (2).] Issued an oval trade card showing his sign, undated, but about 1750. [A. Heal's Collection.]

VOWELL (JOHN), stationer in London, Watling Street, 1767–81. Master of the Company of Stationers in the years 1767 and 1771. [Arber, *Transcript.* V, p. lxviii.]

WAGHORN (MRS.), bookseller and publisher in Durham, 1733–6. Possibly widow of J. Waghorn (*q. v.*). Published a work entitled *Durham Cathedral*, of which there is a copy in the Bodleian. In 1736 her name is found in the imprint to a sermon preached by the Rev. John Mawer on *The Nature and Design of the Lord's Supper.* [B.M. 225. g. 14 (5).]

WAGHORN (J.), bookseller in Durham, 1727–30. Received subscriptions for Thomas Mangeys's proposed edition of the works of Philo Iudaeus, advertised

in Wilford's *Monthly Catalogue* for March. The work was not published until 1742.

WAINWRIGHT (HUMPHREY), bookseller at Bunny, co. Notts., 1727–8. Publisher of Sir Thomas Parkyns *Προγυμνασματα, The Inn-Play: or Cornish-Hugg-Wrestler*, 1727, 4to. He was advertising a third edition in 1728. The play was then "printed for Thomas Weekes". [*Daily Journal*, January 8th, 1728.]

WAIT (T.), bookseller (?) and publisher in London, 1735. This name is found in the imprint to a pamphlet entitled *Whats to be expected from a new Parliament?* [Harvard.]

WALKDEN (RICHARD), printer, bookseller and stationer in London, at the Bell on London Bridge, near St. Magnus's Church, 1735–80. Famous for the manufacture of ink powder. Issued a trade card dated 1754. Succeeded by his son, John Walkden, who carried the sign to no. 7 in the Borough, Southwark. He also issued a trade card, but without date. [A. Heal's Collection.] Richard Walkden died in 1780. [Timperley, p. 803.]

WALKDEN (JOHN), *see* Walkden (Richard).

WALKER (JEFFREY), bookseller and publisher in London, 1729–52. Publisher of an unauthorized edition of Gay's *Beggar's Opera* in that year. [*Evening Post*, April 10th, 1729.] Jeffrey Walker was notorious for his pirated editions: 1729 *Polly*, 1735 *The Whole Duty of Man*, 1736 Nelson's *Festivals*, 1752 *Paradise Lost*, in all of which cases Injunctions were brought against him.

WALKER (JOHN), bookseller in London, Paternoster Row, 1750. He began as a book-auctioneer and afterwards became a wholesale bookseller. [Nichols, III. 666.]

WALKER (R.), printer in Oxford, *c.* 1755. In partnership with W. Jackson, who printed *An Account of the Inquisition.* (Oxford, no date, about 1755). [Madan.]

WALKER (ROBERT), printer in London and Cambridge; London, (1) Shakespeare's Head, Turnagain Lane, Snow Hill, 173$\frac{4}{5}$; (2) Exchange Alley; (3) Shakespeare's Head in Cornhill, 1744; (4) at the British Oil Warehouse in the Little Old Barley, near St. Sepulchre's Church, 1748; (5) Shakespeare's Head between the Savoy and Somerset House in the Strand; (6) Fleet Lane, 1746; Cambridge, (1) the New Printing Office; (2) next the Theatre Coffee-House. 1729 (?)–1758 (?). The early history of this printer is not clear. In 1729 he

published *Thomas Redivivus, or a compleat history of the life and marvellous actions of Tom Thumb*, in three volumes which bears the imprint "printed for R. Walker 1729". [Copy lately at Britwell.] He first made himself notorious by issuing a duodecimo edition of Shakespeare's plays in opposition to Tonson's; this was about 1734. He is next heard of at Cambridge, where in 1744 in company with Thomas James, he issued the *Cambridge Journal and Flying Post*, the first newspaper published in Cambridge. Until the appearance of the printers of this journal, the University Printers had possessed a monopoly under their grant of Letters Patent of July 20th, 1534, and the year 1744 is therefore the first in which any printer who did not receive his appointment from the University is known to have been established in the town. [R. Bowes, *Early Cambridge Newspapers.*] In order to help the sale of the paper Walker and James issued Conyer Harrison's *History of the Life and Reign of Queen Anne*, 1744; *The Life and Adventures of Simon, Lord Lovat*, 1746; and Jacob Hooper's *Impartial History of the Rebellion and Civil Wars in England*, 1749. James died in 1758, and presumably Walker had either died or retired when in 1764 the *Journal* was printed by Sarah James (near the Senate House). She retired, owing to ill-health, in 1766, and assigned the *Cambridge Journal* along with the stock of printing materials, stationery, and patent medicines, to Messrs. T. Fletcher and F. Hodson (*q. v.*), at the New Printing Office on Market Hill, and it was amalgamated with their *Cambridge Chronicle* (1762), appearing January 3rd, 1767, as *The Cambridge Chronicle and Journal*, and has continued to be issued weekly to the present day. [G. J. Gray.] Walker retained his business in London, where he had at least three shops at the same time, all under the sign of the Shakespeare's Head. The date of his death is unknown.

WALL (MRS. FRANCES), bookseller in Bristol, on the Tolzey, 1728–48. In 1728 issued an advertisement of patent medicine in Farley's *Exeter Journal*, November 8th. In 1745 the name of Wall as a bookseller in Bristol occurs in an advertisement of the second edition of Stackhouse's *Bible.*

WALL (THOMAS), bookseller in Chichester, co. Sussex, 1746. In 1746 his name occurs in the imprint to a sermon preached by the Rev. Daniel Gittins, Rector of Southstoke, on December 18th, 1745. [B.M. 225. f. 13 (10).]

WALLER (M.), bookseller and publisher in London, opposite Fetter Lane, Fleet Street, 1775. He published *Jus Parliamentarium.* [*Public Advertiser*, May 2nd, 1775.]

WALLER, T., publisher in London, Mitre and Crown, opposite Fetter Lane, Fleet Street. Published Dr. Dodd's *Beauties of Shakespeare*, 1752.

WALLIS (JAMES), bookseller in Plymouth, 1763–89. His name is first met with in an advertisement in the *Exeter Flying Post* of September 2nd, 1763. It occurs again in 1764 in a list of subscribers to Calcott's *Collection of Thoughts*. [Dredge, p. 36.] He was also one of the publishers of a work entitled *The Most General School-Assistant*, by G. Dyer, master of Tacker's Hall School in Exeter, in 1770. [Dredge, p. 29.] Still in business in 1789, when he was agent for Newbery's publications.

WALLIS (JOHN) and STONEHOUSE, publishers and booksellers in London, Yorick's Head, Ludgate Street, 1775. They published *A Second Answer to John Wesley*. [*Public Advertiser*, October 28th, 1775.] They were advertising *A Chronology and History of the World* [*Ib.*, June 5th, 1775].

WALPOLE (HORACE), *see* Strawberry Hill Press.

WALTER (JOHN), bookseller and publisher in London, (1) Homer's Head, Charing Cross; (2) corner of Spring Gardens. 1750–1803. Apprenticed to Robert Dodsley. He afterwards set up for himself as a bookseller at Charing Cross, where he carried on business for forty years. He was also a director of the Phoenix Fire Office. He died July 25th, 1803. [Nichols, VI. 443.] A trade card bearing on the back a receipt dated 1750 is in Mr. Heal's possession. In 1759 he advertised: "John Walter bookseller from Mr. Dodsley takes this method to aquaint his friends and the publick that he has opened a shop at Homers Head in the New Buildings Charing Cross." Dodsley left him £1,000 in his will. [Straus]. In 1765 *Fables in Verse* was published by him. [*Gazetteer and Daily Advertiser*, July 24th, 1765.] In 1775 he advertises: "J. Walter Bookseller removes from Homer's Head, Charing Cross, to the Corner of Spring Garden." [*Public Advertiser*, January 16th, 1775.]

WALTHOE (JOHN), bookseller and publisher in London, over against the Royal Exchange in Cornhill, and in Richmond, 1683–1748, *see Dictionary*, 1668–1725. In 1729 he published a *Sermon* preached by the Rev. John Browne, M.A., Rector of Beeby in Leicestershire. On Friday, March 25th, 1748, a fire broke out in Exchange Alley, Cornhill, which proved to be the worst that had occurred since the fire of London. Amongst the sufferers was Mr. Walthoe in Cornhill, whose shop was burned down. Walthoe was one of the booksellers who fought for perpetual copyright. In 1736 he obtained an injunction against Walker for the pirating of Nelson's *Festivals*, a publication of 1703. [Collins.] Walthoe, junior, was one of the partners in the publication of Bayle's *Dictionary*, 1735. [*Daily Journal*, January 13th, 1735.]

WARBURTON ( ), bookseller in London, 1759. One of the London booksellers who fought for perpetual copyright. In 1759, when the length of copyright was uncertain, he was granted a Patent by Royal Licence for *Pope's Works*, then outside the terms of Statute protection. [Collins, *Booksellers and Authors in the Days of Johnson*.]

WARD (AARON), bookseller and publisher in London, King's Arms in Little Britain, 1726 (?)–1747 (?). A member of the "Printing Conger", an association of London booksellers who endeavoured to secure a monopoly of the trade and to fix prices. In 1726 he was one of the partners in the publication of *The Works of the Learned John Selden*. [*London Journal*, February 12th, 1726.] He was the publisher of a *Sermon* by John Kiddell, preached before an assembly of ministers at Exeter on May 6th, 1747. [B.M. T. 1034 (21).]

WARD (ANNE), printer in York, (1) Coney Street; (2) Kidd's Coffee House. 1759–89. Widow of Caesar Ward. Continued the publication of the *York Courant* for thirty years after the death of her husband. She is believed to have been the printer of the first edition of Sterne's *Life and Opinions of Tristram Shandy* in 1759. In 1767 she printed the catalogue of John Todd, the bookseller in Stonegate, and in 1775 the first edition of Mason's *Poems of Gray*. Mrs. Ward died on April 10th, 1789, leaving the business to her son-in-law, Mr. George Peacock. [R. Davies, *Memoirs of the York Press*, 1868.]

WARD (CAESAR), bookseller in York, Coney Street, *see* Chandler (Richard). Issued several engraved trade cards in conjunction with Chandler, these being the work of J. Haynes, of York. [A. Heal.] They also issued an undated trade card from the Ship between the Temple Gates in Fleet Street [*Ib.*]. Went bankrupt in 1745. [Timperley, p. 673.]

WARD (EDWARD), printer in Bristol, (1) Castle Street, 1749; (2) Broad Street, 1751; (3) Corn Street, 1757; (4) King's Arms, Tolzey, 1758; (5) opposite the Post Office, 1759–60. 1749–60. Messrs. Hyett and Bazeley, in their *Bibliographer's Manual*, mention several works of local interest printed by Edward Ward at these various addresses.

WARD (J. W.), bookseller in Nottingham. *See Dictionary*, 1668–1725. Still publishing in 1745. [*N. & Q.* 10 S. V. 184.]

WARD (JOHN), bookseller and publisher in London, King's Arms in Cornhill, 1749–59. Was perhaps related in some way to Aaron Ward, as they both used the same sign. John Ward dealt largely in theological literature; but he was also the publisher of Cadwallader Colden's *History of the Five Indian Nations of Canada*, published in 1755. Nichols records that he was executor to the will of Dr. John Ward, who died October 17th, 1758, and that he died soon after the Doctor. [*Lit. Anecd.* V. 523.]

WARD (MARY), printer in Bristol, Corn Street, 1774–76. In 1776 her name is found in the imprint to *An Account of the Bristol Education Society*. [B.M. 8365. a. 7.]

WARD (T.), bookseller and publisher in London, Inner Temple Lane, *see Dictionary*, 1668–1725. He was still in business in 1726, and was publishing Law Books and *Reports of Cases*. [*London Journal*, February 26th, 1726.]

WARD (WILLIAM), printer and publisher in Sheffield, Yorks., 1736–63. Printer of the *Sheffield Public Advertiser*, 1736. [Timperley, 1842, p. 866.] In 1763 his name occurs in the imprint to William Mason's *Elegies*.

WARD (WILLIAM), bookseller and publisher in Nottingham. *See Dictionary*, 1668–1725.

WARE (CATHARINE), bookseller and publisher in London, Bible and Sun, Ludgate Hill, 1761. In partnership with Richard Ware (*q. v.*).

WARE (JOHN and SONS), printers in Whitehaven, King Street, co. Cumberland, 1776. Printers of the *Cumberland Pacquet*.

WARE (RICHARD), bookseller and publisher in London, Bible and Sun, Warwick Lane at Amen Corner (the end of Paternoster Row), 1724–56. Dealer in Bibles, Common Prayers, and Testaments. One of his illustrated publications was called *The Historical Part of the Holy Bible . . . Described in . . . Two Hundred Historys, Curiously engraved by J. Cole*, and was published about 1724. Timperley speaks of him as a bookseller on London Bridge, but this was a mistake. He died in August 1756 at Harefield in Middlesex. [Read's *Weekly Journal*, August 21st, 1756.]

WARENER, *see* Warrener.

WARNE (R. (?)), bookseller at Chippenham, Wilts., 1742 (?)–1745 (?). *See Dictionary*, 1668–1725. Still in business in 1742, when he sold the Rev. Samuel Johnson's *Explanation of Scripture Prophecies*. In 1745 his name occurs in an advertisement of the second edition of Stackhouse's *Bible*.

WARNER (T.), bookseller and publisher in London, Black Boy, Paternoster Row, 1726 (?)–1729 (?). Publisher of lists of the Privy Council, members of Parliament, and useful literature of that kind. He also published satires such as *The Tavern Scuffle, or the Club in an Uproar*, by "Saynought Dryboots". At one time he printed the *Flying Post*, but an advertisement in the *Daily Post* of January 1st, 1728, states that "Warner of Paternoster Row is discharged and that the *Flying Post* will be published by J. Roberts of Warwick Lane". He then transferred his services to the *Daily Journal*. He was probably in business both earlier and later than the dates given above.

WARREN (EDWARD), printer in Manchester, 1755. Briefly referred to by R. W. Procter in his *Memorials* as possibly only a journeyman. [Procter, p. 201.]

WARREN (THOMAS), bookseller and printer in Birmingham, (1) near St. Martin's Church, Mercer's or Spiceall Street, 1727; (2) against the Swan Tavern, 1731; (3) over against the Swan Passage, 1732; (4) no. 1 Corn Cheaping, 1742. 1727–42. His name first appears in Wilford's *Monthly Catalogue* for November 1728 as one of the publishers of the Rev. John Reynold's *Practical Discourse of Reconciliation*; the title-page of the book was dated 1729, and it contained a leaf containing a list of books sold by Thos. Warren. After his removal in 1731, he set up as a printer and began the publication of the *Birmingham Journal*, only one copy of which, the issue of Monday, May 21st, 1733, is known to exist. As it is numbered 28, the first number must have appeared on November 14th, 1732. Samuel Johnson stayed about six months in Warren's house as the guest of his friend, Edmund Hector, and is believed to have helped Warren in his business. Soon after this, in June 1733, he translated Father Jerome Lobo's *Abyssinia*, which, however, was not published until 1735. It was printed at Warren's printing-office. In 1736 Johnson married the widow of Harry Porter, who had previously occupied the premises. In 1742 Warren became bankrupt, and he died in 1767. [Joseph Hill, *Bookmakers of Old Birmingham*, pp. 39 et seq.]

WARRENER, or WARENER (JAMES), bookseller and publisher in Bath, 1728. In the *Daily Post Boy* of November 10th, 1728, his name is given as one who sold the *Monthly Chronicle*. He is also mentioned as the publisher of *An Essay on the Nature . . . of the Passions* in the January issue of Wilford's *Monthly Chronicle* for that year.

WATERS (T.), bookseller and publisher in London, South Audley Street, 1775. Began to advertise as a publisher about this time. [*Public Advertiser*, April 14th, and November 1st, 1775.]

WATSON (MRS.), bookseller in Bury St. Edmunds, 1729. In Wilford's *Monthly Catalogue* for July 1729 her name is given as one of those receiving subscriptions for a projected issue of Mr. Templeman's *Survey of the Globe*.

WATSON (J.), *see Dictionary*, 1668–1725.

WATSON (JAMES), bookseller and publisher in London, (1) over against Hungerford Market; (2) Wardrobe Court, Great Carter Lane. 1728–1735 (?) On December 5th, 1728, the Secretary of State issued a search warrant in connexion with certain "scandalous and seditious libels", about to be printed and published by James Watson. [S. P. Dom., Geo. II, Bundle 9.] He also dealt in such literature as *The Adventures of the Priests and Nuns*, and *The Adventures of the Bath*. In 1735 he was selling *The Syren* in Wardrobe Court. [*Daily Journal*, April 4th, 1735.]

WATSON (M.), bookseller in Bury St. Edmunds, co. Suffolk, 1750. Mentioned in a list of provincial booksellers. [*N. & Q.* 10 S. v, February 24th, 1906.]

WATSON (S.), bookseller and publisher in Bury St. Edmunds, co. Suffolk, 1745–8. Mentioned in a list of provincial booksellers as in business in 1745. [*N. & Q.* 10 S. v, February 24th, 1906.] Publisher of a *Sermon* preached by the Rev. Henry Goodall, Archdeacon of Suffolk, on April 28th, 1748. [B.M. 693. f. 17 (5).]

WATTS (JOHN), printer, *see Dictionary*, 1668–1725.

WATTS (ROBERT), bookseller in Cambridge, *c.* 1745–1752. Lived on the western side of Trumpington Street, adjoining the old Provost's Lodge, King's College. He was the first person who established a circulating library in Cambridge. It was opened about 1745, and comprised a large stock of standard mathematical and classical books. He died February 5th, 1752, and was buried in St. Edward's Church. He bequeathed his stock-in-trade to his only daughter Anne, who on March 28th, 1752, married John Nicholson ("Maps") of Mountsorrel, Leicestershire, who carried on the business on the same premises until his death in 1796.

WAUGH (JAMES), bookseller in London, the Turk's Head, Lombard Street, 1747–52. His name is found in 1747 as publisher of Doddridge's *Life of Col. Jas. Gardiner*. Again in 1752 as publishing a work called *The Christian's Triumph over Death*, and in 1757 a collection of *Psalms and Hymns*.

WEATHERLEY (ROBERT), printer in Plymouth, 1759–78. Mentioned in a list of provincial booksellers as in business in the year 1759. [*N. & Q.* 11 S. I. 364.] He was still in business in 1778. [Dredge.]

WEBLEY, or WEOBLEY (A. and HENRY), booksellers and publishers in London, Bible and Crown in Holborn, near Chancery Lane, 1762 (?)–1770 (?). This firm made a speciality of books on architecture and trade manuals; but they also dealt in general literature. They issued a catalogue in 1762 in which the following items appear: Palladio's *Architecture*, by Leoni, Folio; Ware's *Compleat Body of Architecture*, Folio; *Fifteen large prints of the Churches and other Buildings built by Sir Christopher Wren, with four large and magnificent views of his Majesty's Palace at Whitehall, as intended by Inigo Jones*. The price asked for these was three guineas each. Other publications to which special attention was directed were: *The Cabinet and Chairmaker's Real Friend and Companion*; Moxon's *Mechanick Exercises*; and Lock and Copland's *Ornaments of Chimneys, &c.* In the Holborn rate books the name is generally spelt as Weobley, and their shop was apparently situated between Fenwick Court and Cursitor Street. The name disappears about 1770, when Isaac Taylor, the engraver, is found at the Bible and Crown. Issued a book-list. [A. Heal.]

WEEKES (THOMAS), bookseller in London, at the White Hart in Westminster Hall, 1728. He published the third edition of *The Inn-Play*. [*Daily Journal*, January 8th, 1728.]

WELCH (R.), bookseller at Lymington, Hants, 1744. His name occurs in the *Salisbury Journal* of Tuesday, April 10th, 1744.

WENMAN (J.), publisher in London, 144 Fleet Street, 1775. He published the *Classical Magazine*. [*Public Advertiser*, November 1st, 1775.]

WEST (   ), bookseller in Stourbridge, 1771. In 1771 he distributed copies of a Catalogue of books on sale by S. Gamidge, bookseller of Worcester. [*The British Chronicle, or Pugh's Hereford Journal*, August 8th, 1771; Burney.]

WEST (S. (?)), bookseller and publisher in London, near St. Paul's, 1731. Query, if not fictitious. Occurs in imprint to Eustace Budgell's pamphlet *A Letter to his Excellency Mr. Ulrick D'Ypres . . . Fourth Edition*, 8vo. [B.M. E. 2022 (4).]

WESTCOTE (R.), bookseller and publisher in Windsor, 1761. Publisher of *The Ceremonial at the Installation of Knights of the Garter*.

WHEBLE (JOHN), bookseller and publisher in London, 24 Paternoster Row; (2) no. 22 opposite St. Dunstan's Church, Fleet Street; (3) Pine Apple, City Road. 1758–1820. Born in 1746 at Gatcombe, Isle of Wight. Apprentice to J. Wilkie in 1758. Publisher of the *Middlesex Journal and Lady's Magazine*. In 1772 he was indicted for printing the Parliamentary debates, and was taken before the magistrates of the City of London, one of whom was John Wilkes. He was at once discharged, and on June 30th Edward Troine Carpenter, printer of Hosier Lane, was tried for an assault in seizing and taking Wheble prisoner. He died at Bromley in Kent in September 1820, aged seventy-five. Issued a trade card while he was at the Pine Apple, City Road. [A. Heal's Collection.]

WHISTON (JOHN), bookseller and publisher in London, Mr. Boyle's Head in Fleet Street, 1734–80. Son of the Rev. William Whiston, translator of Josephus, born July 30th, 1711. Apprentice to Fletcher Gyles, bookseller in Holborn. Set up for himself about 1734 and adopted the sign of Mr. Boyle's Head (i.e. the Hon. Robert Boyle) possibly at the suggestion of his father, who was Boyle Lecturer in 1707. Whiston's shop quickly became well-known. His connexion lay chiefly amongst the clergy, and amongst the distinguished men who might have been seen there were the Bishop of Gloucester, William Warburton; the Dean of Lincoln, Dr. William George; the Rev. Dr. Plumtre; the Rev. John Jortin, author of the *Life of Erasmus*; Horace Walpole, and others. In 1747 he was called in to catalogue the library of Bishop Moore, which had been bequeathed to Cambridge University by King George I in 1715, and which had been lying neglected for want of room to shelve it. He also acted for Eton College in the disposal of the library of Nicholas Mann, Master of the Charterhouse, who died in 1753. He published numerous books, particularly his father's writings. In 1759 he was compelled to retire from business in consequence of a nervous breakdown, caused it is believed by a fright, as the result of a practical joke. For a time he was in an asylum: but the business continued to be carried on by Benjamin White who had been in partnership with him for some years. The partnership was dissolved about 1766, and the business was then taken over by Whiston's son-in-law, Nathaniel Conant. Whiston made his will in 1766, and nominated Lockyer Davis and William Manby, booksellers, his executors. He also left mourning rings to Mr. Sandby, William Owen, Thomas Payne, booksellers in London, and to Thos. Merrill and Jas. Fletcher, booksellers in Cambridge. [P.C.C. 297, Collins.] He lived until 1780.

WHITE (BENJAMIN), bookseller in London, (1) Mr. Boyle's Head, 64 Fleet Street; (2) Horace's Head, Fleet Street. 1725 (?)–1794. It is not clear when he began business, but he is found in partnership with John Whiston for some years, and they issued several sale catalogues together. It is doubtful whether the partnership lasted beyond 1766 or 1767, as about that time Whiston's son-in-law, Nathaniel Conant, succeeded to the business at Mr. Boyle's Head. White then moved to Horace's Head and carried on an extensive business for many years, making a speciality of books on Natural History. Nichols says he was brother of Gilbert White, the naturalist, and published the first edition of *Selborne*. He died at Lambeth on March 9th, 1794. [Nichols, III. 127.]

WHITE (JOHN), bookseller in York and Newcastle-upon-Tyne. *See Dictionary*, 1668–1725.

WHITE (STEPHEN), printer in Norwich, Bible and Crown, Magdalen Street, 1769–71. Mentioned in a list of provincial booksellers. [*N. & Q.* 11 S. I. 364.]

WHITE (T.), bookseller in Arundel, co. Sussex, 1766–74. Publisher of *The Antiquities of Arundel*, 1766.

WHITEFIELD (NATHANIEL), bookseller in Rotherhithe, King's Stairs, 1770. Mentioned in a list of provincial booksellers. [*N. & Q.* 11 S. I. 364.]

WHITFELD, *see* Whitfield.

WHITFIELD (HENRY), bookseller and publisher in Plymouth, co. Devon., 1759. Publisher of *Observations on the Air and Epidemic Diseases* in that year. [Dredge, p. 82.]

WHITFIELD, or WHITFELD (J.), bookseller and publisher in Plymouth, co. Devon., 1770. Mentioned in a list of provincial booksellers. [*N. & Q.* 11 S. I. 364.]

WHITFIELD (PETER), printer in Liverpool, and author, 1748–56. His press seems to have been a private one used for printing his own writings. [*Lancashire Printed Books*, pp. 30, 31.]

WHITING (J.), bookseller in Romsey, Hants, 1768. Mentioned in a list of provincial booksellers. [*N. & Q.* 10 S. v. 242.]

WHITRIDGE (HENRY), bookseller in London, (1) under the Royal Exchange; (2) corner of Castle Alley near the Royal Exchange, 1727–55. Dealer in law books. The second address, which probably refers to the same place as the first, is given in the imprint to *The Elogium of . . . Peter I, Czar of Muscovy*, a pamphlet of forty-six pages. He is mentioned in the will of Samuel Birt, who died in 1755. [P.C.C. 304, Paul.]

WHITTINGHAM (WILLIAM), bookseller, printer and publisher in Lynn, co. Norfolk, 1768–97. Publisher of a poem on *Poverty* in 1768. In the following year his name appeared in the imprint to a work by John Harrison, the botanist, entitled *A New Method of making the Banks in the Fens impregnable*. Nichols says he was the editor of Blomfield's *History of Norfolk* and other topographical work. He died April 29th, 1797. [Nichols, III. 689.]

WICKSTEED (E. or C.), bookseller in Wrexham, Denbigh., 1730. Mentioned in a list of provincial booksellers. [*N. & Q.* 11 S. I. 364.] Issued a trade card. The same plate was used by Thos. Payne, bookseller in Wrexham, but which was the first is not quite certain. [A. Heal.]

WICKSTEED (E.), bookseller in London, (1) in the Temple, (2) Bible and Bell in Ave Maria Lane, 1735–53. He was one of the partners in the publication of Bayle's *Dictionary*, vol. ii. [*Daily Journal*, January 13th, 1735], and of *Thesaurus Linguae Latinae Compendiarius*. [*Public Advertiser*, May 1st, 1753.] A catalogue of Books sold by him occurs at the end of Ledbetter's *Mechanick Dialling*, 1737.

WIGHTMAN (THOMAS), bookseller in Grantham, co. Lincoln., 1726. Sold the *Grasier's Companion and Petition for Redress, by a Lincolnshire Grasier*, 1726. [B.M. 712. g. 16 (37).]

WILCOX (J.), bookseller in London. *See Dictionary*, 1668–1725.

WILDE (ALLINGTON), printer in London, Aldersgate Street, 1731(?)–1770. Son of Allington Wilde (1722–31). In 1735 *Letters written by a Turkish Spy* was advertised as printed for S. Ballard, A. Wilde, R. Willock, and others. [*Daily Post*, February 13th, 1735.] He was Master of the Company of Stationers in 1762, and lived to be the oldest master printer in England. Died in Aldersgate Street on December 28th, 1770. [Nichols, III. 739.]

WILDE, or WILD (JAMES), bookseller and publisher in Hereford, 1714–1757 (?). In the previous *Dictionary* (1668–1725) this bookseller was briefly mentioned as a subscriber to Walker's *Sufferings of the Clergy* in 1714. In 1728 he published the Rev. Thomas Payne's *Constant regard to the true ends of Government . . . in a Sermon preached at St. Peter's in Hereford, September 30, 1728, being the day of the Mayor's admission.* [W. M. C., November 1728.] He is mentioned in a

list of provincial booksellers as at work in 1748. [*N. & Q.* 10 S. V. 183.] He is found selling a sermon at both Hereford and Ludlow in 1748. [*Bibliography of Worcestershire*, p. 57.] In 1755 he had a shop at Ludlow, as appears from an advertisement of John Barrow's *Psalm-Singers' Choice Companion* in the *Whitehall Evening Post* of January 2nd. The exact date of his death or retirement has not been found.

WILDE (T.), bookseller in Stourbridge, 1748. Mentioned in a list of provincial booksellers as in business in that year. [*N. & Q.* 10 S. V. 242.] His name is found in the imprint of a sermon printed in Worcester 1748, in the publication and sale of which he joined. [*Bibliography of Worcestershire*, p. 57.]

WILDEN ( ), bookseller in Tenbury, 1771. Distributed a catalogue of books on sale by S. Gamidge, of Worcester, in that year.

WILFORD (JOHN), bookseller and publisher in London, (1) Three Luces [or] Flower de Luces, Little Britain; (2) Stationers' Court near Ludgate; (3) behind the Chapter Coffee-House in St. Paul's Churchyard. 1722–64. The following may be substituted for the meagre notice that appeared in the *Dictionary*, 1668–1725. John Wilford was perhaps a descendant of George Wilford, bookseller in Little Britain in 1652 [*see Dictionary*, 1641–67]. Hazlitt mentions several books and pamphlets published by him between 1724 and 1727: but perhaps his most useful work was the *Monthly Catalogue of Books* which he began in 1723, and continued down to 1729. This has been found of great use in the compilation of this *Dictionary*, but Wilford's *Catalogue* was squeezed out by other publications. In 1728 he was in trouble with the authorities for publishing *Mist's Weekly Journal* of September 7th and 14th, in which the proceedings of the Government in connexion with the South Sea Scheme were adversely criticized. What his punishment was is not stated. In his defence he said he took upon himself the publication in order to rescue it out of bad hands. After this he altered the title to *Fog's Weekly Journal*. Somewhere about 1730 he and another man named Edlin (*q. v.*) were approached by the Rev. Thomas Stackhouse in connexion with his *History of the Bible*, and the woes of the unfortunate author were recorded by him in a pamphlet entitled *Bookbinder, Bookprinter, and Bookseller refuted*, 1732. Wilford was the publisher of numerous pamphlets which sprang up as the result of Alexander Pope's poem, *Essay on Man*. In 1735 he became the publisher of the *Daily Post Boy*, and in 1741 he began to issue in monthly parts a work entitled *Memorials and Characters*, which came to be known as Wilford's *Lives*.

WILKES (JOHN), printer and publisher in Winchester, co. Hants, and London, Ave Maria Lane, 1762–1810. Is said to have begun as a bookseller in Winchester, but is only briefly mentioned by F. A. Edwards in *Early Hampshire Printers*, p. 114. On December 8th, 1771, he married Rebecca Lover, of St. Lawrence's, Winchester, and in 1773 he published *The History and Antiquities of Winchester* in two volumes. He was the originator and proprietor of the *Encyclopedia Londoniensis*, in connexion with which he was fined for piracy. In his later years he lived at Milland House, Sussex, where he died in March 1810. [*Gentleman's Magazine*, LXXX. 394; *N. & Q.* 10 S. VI. 31.]

WILKIE (JOHN), bookseller and publisher in London, (1) Fleet Street, 1757; (2) Bible, afterwards no. 71 St. Paul's Churchyard, 1757–85. Succeeded Richard Baldwin. Hilton Price gives his earliest date as 1757. Publisher of the *Ladies Magazine* in 1759, also the *London Chronicle*. October 3rd–November 24th, 1759. Wilkie also published *The Bee*, a weekly paper for which Goldsmith wrote. In 1763 he issued a pamphlet entitled *The Anatomy of a late Negociation*. [B.M. E. 2055 (2).] He was one of the partners in the publication of Gay's *Fables* in 1775. [*Public Advertiser*, January 10th, 1775.] He died July 2nd, 1785. [Nichols III. p. 607.] Issued a trade card. [A. Heal's Collection.]

WILKIN (R.), bookseller and publisher, 1735. One of the partners in the publication of *New Voyages to North America*. [*Daily Journal*, June 9th, 1735.]

WILKINSON ( ), bookseller in Portsmouth, 1744. His name appears in an advertisement in the *Salisbury Journal* of Tuesday, April 10th, 1744.

WILKINSON ( ), printer at Ripponden (?), 1746. Recorded by Mr. Allnutt on the strength of an imprint to *Tim Bobbin's View of the Lancashire Dialect*, 1746. Nothing further has been found to confirm this.

WILKINSON (L.), bookseller in Appleby, 1766. Mentioned in an advertisement in the *Newcastle Journal* of that year.

WILLIAMS ( ), bookseller and publisher in Carmarthen, 1772. Mentioned in an advertisement in the *British Chronicle or Pugh's Hereford Journal*, 1772.

WILLIAMS (JOHN), bookseller and publisher in London, (1) Ludgate Hill, 1760–61; (2) under St. Dunstan's Church, Fleet Street; (3) next (or near) the Mitre Tavern, Fleet Street, 1763–74. 1760–74. A "Wilkes and Liberty" man, and published numerous pamphlets on the subject. As he was one of those who sold no. 45 of the *North Briton* in 1765 he was condemned to stand in the

pillory for one day in Old Palace Yard, and Timperley records a short but vivid picture of the scene. He says that opposite the pillory were erected four ladders with cords running from one ladder to another. On these were hung a jack boot, an axe, and a Scotch bonnet. The boot and bonnet after remaining some time were burnt, the top of the boot having been previously chopped off no doubt with the axe. A gentleman with a purple purse, ornamented with ribbons of an orange colour, began a collection in favour of Mr. Williams and raised no less than £200. Williams was again in trouble in 1774 for publishing a paragraph in the *Morning Post* reflecting on the character of Charles J. Fox. The Court of King's Bench ordered him to pay a fine of £100 and the costs of the action, and to be kept in prison for a month. Williams married the daughter of Joseph Pote, the printer, of Eton. His subsequent history is unrecorded. [Timperley, pp. 713, 732, 760; B.M. E. 2053 (3).]

WILLIAMS (THO.), bookseller in Tring, Herts., 1726. Mentioned in a list of provincial booksellers. [*N. & Q.* 10 S. V. 242.]

WILLIAMSON (RICHARD), bookseller and publisher in London, Gray's Inn Gate, 1723–37. Successor to the business of Richard Sare (1684–1723). In 1729 he published White-Kennett's *Providence of God*, and in 1730 Dr. George Stanhope's translation of the Greek devotions of Bishop Andrews. In his later years Williamson was appointed Deputy Receiver General of the Post Office. He died January 7th, 1737, and was succeeded by Thomas Trye (*q. v.*). [Timperley, p. 659; *Kentish Post, or Canterbury News Letter*, January 12th, 1736–7].

WILLIAMSON (ROBERT), printer, bookseller and bookbinder in Liverpool, 1751–76. John Almon, the well-known London publisher, was one of his apprentices from 1751–8. [See *Memoirs of John Almon*, 1790, 8vo, p. 13.] On May 28th, 1756, he began to publish the *Liverpool Advertiser and Mercantile Chronicle*. [Timperley, 1842, p. 696.] Succeeded by Alice Williamson in 1777.

WILLIS (JOHN), bookseller in Newbury, co. Berks., 1769 (?)–1771 (?). On July 19th he married a Miss Smith, of Newbury. [*Reading Mercury*.] Made a speciality of plays. Mentioned in a list of provincial booksellers as still in business in 1771. [*N. & Q.* 11 S. I. 364.]

WILLIS (RICHARD), bookseller and publisher in Nottingham, Bearwood Lane, 1734. In company with George Ayscough who printed the work he published, *The Excellent Use of Psalmody . . .* By R. W. [Creswell, p. 23.]

WILLOCK (R.), bookseller in London, Sir Isaac Newton's Head, Cornhill, 1735–65. In 1735 he was one of the partners in the publication of Bayle's *Dictionary*. [*Daily Journal*, January 13th, 1735]. In 1765 he advertised the sale of *The Philosophical Commerce of Arts*. [*Gazetteer and Daily Advertiser*, July 12th, 1765.]

WILMOT (L.), bookseller and publisher in Oxford, 1741. In that year he published Dr. R. Sanderson's *Logicae Artis Compendium*, Oxford, 1741. [Madan.]

WILMOT (SAMUEL), *see Dictionary*, 1668–1725. Still in business in 1745, when he entered into an agreement with Robert Dodsley, the London publisher, to hand over the copyright in Joseph Spence's *Essay on Mr. Pope's Odyssey* to Dodsley. [Straus, *Robert Dodsley*.]

WILMOT ( ), bookseller in Pembroke, 1771. Advertised in the *British Chronicle, or Pugh's Hereford Journal* in 1771.

WILSON (D.), bookseller and publisher in London, Plato's Head near Round Court in the Strand, 1751–77. In partnership with George Nicol and in 1753 with T. Durham (*q. v.*). The firm was known as D. Wilson & Co. In 1751 published *A Narrative of the Transactions of the British Squadrons in the East Indies*. D. Wilson died at an advanced age in July 1777. [Nichols, III. 671.]

WILSON (GEORGE), printer in Wolverhampton, 1744, *see Dictionary*, 1668–1725. He reprinted *The Voyages and Adventures of Captain Robert Boyle*, in 1744.

WILSON (J.), bookseller and publisher in London, Paternoster Row, 1762–66. In partnership with Isaac Fell. They published in 1762 a pamphlet entitled *The Minister of State*, and in 1766 an edition of Anstey's *New Bath Guide*.

WILSON (JOHN), bookseller and publisher in Bath, (1) Horse Street; (2) Wine Street. 1726–45. Dealer in chap-books and publisher of the *Gloucester Journal*. Was ordered to appear before the House of Commons for publishing its proceedings, but was discharged. [*H. O. C. Journal*.] In 1743 he was one of the publishers of Charles Thomson's *Travels*. He is mentioned in a list of provincial booksellers as still in business in 1745. [*N. & Q.* 10 S. V. 141.]

WILSON (JOS.), bookseller in Leeds, Yorks., 1749–61. Published catalogues (copies of which are in the Bodleian), and still in business in 1761, when his name is found in an advertisement in the *Leedes Intelligence*.

WILSON (MARY), printer in Wolverhampton, 1755. Printed in that year a theological work entitled *The Lama Sabachthany: or Cry of the Son of God*. [Allnutt in *Bibliographica*, II. 307.] Possibly widow of George Wilson.

WILSON ( ), bookseller in York, Pavement, 1755. This name occurs in an advertisement of a patent medicine in the *London Evening Post* of December 25th, 1755. The firm afterwards became Wilson and Spence. [Nichols, III. 689.] A trade card was issued by a T. Wilson living in High Ousegate, but there is no date to show whether he is identical with the above. [A. Heal's Collection.]

WILSON, or WILSONN (ROBERT), stationer in London, (1) Birchin Lane; (2) Crown, corner of Nicholas Lane, Lombard Street; (3) 22 Lombard Street. 1752–77. A bill-head used by this stationer, and dated 1752, is in Mr. A. Heal's Collection. The last two addresses refer to the same house.

WIMPEY (J.), bookseller and publisher at Newbury, co. Berks., 1761. In 1761 he was the publisher of the Rev. Thomas Penrose's *Discourse delivered in the Parish Church of Newbury on Sunday November 2nd, 1760*.

WINBUSH (JOHN), bookseller and pamphlet-seller in London, at the sign of the King's Speech at Charing Cross, $174\frac{7}{8}$. The *Penny London Post*, in its issue of January 8th, $174\frac{7}{8}$, records the death of this bookseller, and adds that he had kept the shop "for many years", and that he also held the post of Clerk to the Post Office. Winbush made his will on December 28th, 1747. From this we learn that his only son Edmund had predeceased him. There had evidently been some family quarrel, as the testator only left to his son's widow one shilling, and a like amount to his grandson John. Mention is also made of his daughter, Ann Wayte, who may have been the wife of T. (Wart or Wayte). The residue of all his property he bequeathed to his wife, Hannah, whom he appointed sole executrix. The will was proved on January 5th, $174\frac{7}{8}$. [P.C.C. 31, Strahan.]

WINDER (THOMAS), bookseller in Tenterden, co. Kent, 1737. Publisher of the Rev. Daniel Dobel's *Seventh-day Sabbath*, 1737.

WINGRAVE (FRANCIS), bookseller and publisher in London, Lamb, without Temple Bar, 1780. Successor to John Nourse. [Timperley, p. 746.]

WINPENNY (R.), bookseller in Bristol, Castle Street, 1744. His name appears in an advertisement in the *Salisbury Journal* of Tuesday, April 10th, 1744.

WISE (J.), bookseller in Newport, Isle of Wight, 1768. Mentioned in a list of provincial booksellers as being in business in that year. [*N. & Q.* 10 S. V. March 1906, p. 183.]

WITHERS (EDWARD), bookseller and publisher in London, (1) opposite Chancery Lane, Fleet Street; (2) next the Inner Temple Gate in Fleet Street; (3) the Seven Stars, near the Temple Gate in Fleet Street. 1737–57. Was associated with a publication long attributed to Lord Chesterfield, *The Oeconomy of Human Life*, a collection of moral axioms, that sold well and was frequently pirated. E. Withers published an *Appendix* to the *Oeconomy*, but this, like many other additions of the original work, was spurious. [Straus, *Robert Dodsley*, pp. 173, 175.] He was also the publisher in 1753 of *A Serious and Friendly Address to the Reverend Mr. John Wesley . . .*, by the Reverend John Parkhouse. [B.M. 695. g. 10.] The above three imprints may refer to the same house. Withers issued a trade card showing his sign on a cartouche at the top. [A. Heal's Collection.]

WITHY (ROBERT), book and printseller in London, (1) the Dunciad in Cornhill; (2) Hogarth's Head opposite Salisbury Court, Fleet Street. 1755 (?)–1766. Was probably in business several years before 1755, when he is found in partnership with J. Ryall (*q. v.*). They published the seventh edition of William Romaines's *Discourse on Earthquakes*, and in 1756 a work on English coinage. Robert Withy was an agent for advertisements in 1761, when he was living at the second of the two places mentioned above, as his late house was being rebuilt. [*Daily Advertiser*, January 24th, 1761; *London Evening News*, January 27th, 1761.] In 1765 he published with three others *A General History of the World*. [*Gazetteer and Daily Advertiser*, August 26th, 1765.]

WOLFE (J.), printer in London, Great Carter Lane, 1728. In 1728 he was the printer of *Mist's Journal*. In the *Weekly* for Saturday, August 3rd, it is reported: "Thursday one Mr. Wolfe, Printer of Mist's Journal was a third time taken into custody by one of His Majesty's Messengers, for the said paper." Probably only a journeyman.

WOLLASTON (FRANCIS), bookseller in Birmingham, 1750–4. This was one of the "eminent" booksellers mentioned by William Hutton. Joseph Hill states that there is little or nothing on record about the Wollastons' connexion with the book-trade, and ascribes this to the fact that they were neither printers nor publishers. [*Book-makers*, p. 47.] Succeeded by Pryn Parkes.

WOLLEY (E.), bookseller and publisher in Worcester, 1726–40. Dealer in chap-books. In 1727 he sold the ninth edition of Chillingworth's *Works*. He was still there in 1740 when he published Dr. Meadowcourt's *Sermon* preached in the Cathedral on November 5th, 1739. [B.M. 695. g. 10 (12).]

WOOD (J.), bookseller in Bradford, co. Yorks., Ive Gate, 1760. Mentioned in a list of provincial booksellers as in business in that year. [*N. & Q.* 11 S. I. p. 304.]

WOOD (THOMAS), printer in Shrewsbury, on Pride Hill, 1772–1801. Printer of the *Shrewsbury Chronicle* from 1772. His name has also been found in the imprint to a pamphlet on the *Profanation of the Sabbath* printed in 1777. [B.M. 4372. cc. 21 (4).] He died in April 1801, aged fifty-four. [Timperley, p. 808.]

WOOD (WILLIAM), I, bookseller and printer in Lincoln, 1729 (?). Has not been met with before 1729, when he printed the visitation articles, a copy of which is in the Bodleian Library.

WOOD (WILLIAM), II, bookseller and printer in Lincoln, ? 1771–87. Presumably son of William I. In 1771 he printed and published *An Historical Account of the Antiquities in the Cathedral Church of St. Mary's, Lincoln*. An interleaved copy of this in the British Museum [4707. e. 18] contains a manuscript note to the effect that Wood was but a weak and ignorant man, and that he employed a coach-painter named Abbott to write the description of the Minster, and that most of it was a crib from Browne-Willis's *Survey*. Wood resigned his business in 1787, having bought an estate at Langworth, where he died on December 6th, 1804, aged sixty-two. [Nichols, III. 689.]

WOODFALL (GEORGE), bookseller in London, (1) Charing Cross, at the King's Arms; (2) corner of Craig's Court, 1760; (3) no. 6 Silver Street in Whitefriar's, 1771. 1748–71. Son of Henry Woodfall. Dealer in pamphlets between 1748 and 1771. There was another of the same name, son of Henry Sampson Woodfall, but he was not born until 1767.

WOODFALL (HENRY), printer in London, Paternoster Row, 1737–1764 (?). Nichols in his *Literary Anecdotes*, I. 300, says that Henry Woodfall, who was a printer without Temple Bar, and died about 1747, "had two sons [i.e.] Henry a printer in Paternoster Row and George a bookseller at Charing Cross, both of whom I well remember." But there seems to be considerable confusion between Henry Woodfall and Henry Sampson Woodfall (*q. v.*). In 1855 there appeared in *Notes & Queries* some short extracts from the ledgers of Henry

Woodfall between 1734 and 1748, but whether these refer to Henry Woodfall, who died about 1747, or to his son, there is nothing to show. But it is clear that the printer had a large business and printed for all the chief publishers of the day, and his prices compared favourably with those of other London printers. One of the Henrys became Master of the Company of Stationers in 1766 and died in 1767. [Arber, *Transcript*. v. lxviii.]

WOODFALL (HENRY SAMPSON), printer in London, Ivy Lane, Paternoster Row, 1758–1805. Born at the sign of the Rose and Crown in Little Britain on June 21st, 1739. The son of Henry Woodfall, but of which of the two Henries is not clear. Educated at St. Paul's School, and at the age of nineteen is said to have entered his father's business and to have been entrusted with the printing of a paper called *The Public Advertiser*. This periodical has been made famous for all time by the publication of a trenchant series of political letters signed "Junius." The author of these was, by the aid of the printer, able to conceal his identity. For a long time the letters were attributed to the pen of Sir P. Francis. The printer was tried in 1770 for printing them, but the result amounted to an acquital. Woodfall disposed of the *Public Advertiser* in 1793, when his printing-office was destroyed by fire. He died December 12th, 1805.

WOODGATE (HENRY), bookseller and publisher in London, Golden Ball, Paternoster Row, 1759–66. In partnership with Samuel Brooks (*q. v.*). They dealt largely in chap-books and plays. The Rev. W. H. Dilworth wrote several histories for them. The business does not seem to have been a success, as in 1766 Woodgate became bankrupt, and died on July 19th of that year. [*Lloyd's Evening News*.] Issued a trade card about 1760. [A. Heal's Collection.]

WOODGATE (JOSEPH), stationer in London, Bible and Crown within Bishopsgate, 1760. Successor to J. Cooper and succeeded by Armitage and Roper (*q.v.*). Issued a trade card engraved by Morison in 1760. [A. Heal's Collection.]

WOODMAN (JAMES), bookseller and publisher in London, Russell Street, Covent Garden, 1723–8. In the early part of the year 172$\frac{2}{3}$ he issued a catalogue of books obtained from France. [B.M. 128. i. 2 (13).] Woodman's name occurs in the imprint to Eliza Haywood's novel, *The Injur'd Husband*, published in 1723. In 1726 he was apparently joined by D. Lyon. Amongst their publications was *A History of France*, in five volumes, and a sumptuous edition of L'Abbé de Vertot's *History of the Knights of Malta* in 1727, and in 1728 they published the *Life of F. de Salignac*. [*Daily Post*, January 1st, 1728.]

WOODWARD (T.), bookseller in London, Half Moon against St. Dunstan's Church in Fleet Street, 1726–35. Possibly a relative of James Woodward. [1707–23; *see Dictionary*, 1668–1725]. In 1728 he advertised the sale of *Les Voyages de Cyrus*. [*Daily Post*, January 2nd, 1728.] In 1735 he published with J. Peele *The Works of Tacitus*. [*Daily Journal*, March 1st, 1735.]

WOODWARD (T.), bookseller in Bedford, 1773. Mentioned in a list of provincial booksellers as in business in that year. [*N. & Q.* 10 S. v. 141.]

WOODYER (JOHN), bookseller and publisher in Cambridge, 1759–82. Succeeded Wm. Woodyer (*q. v.*) at no. 1 Trinity Street in 1759, and publications were continued to be issued by Thurlbourne and Woodyer until Thurlbourne's death in 1768, when Woodyer took over the house and published under his own name. He was churchwarden of Great St. Mary's Church, 1760–1 and 1776–9. In 1773 *Alphonso: or the Hermit* was printed for R. Woodyer (the author?) and sold by J. Woodyer. In the *Cantabrigia Depicta*, 1763, it is stated that "A. Newman sets out from Thurlbourne and Woodyers' every saturday for Chesterfield" &c., with newspapers. In the same work some new plates were added, engraved by T. Woodyer. He was bankrupt in 1782, T. Cordell of London being one of the assignees, and the property was purchased by John Deighton who moved to the house and continued the business.

WOODYER (WILLIAM), bookseller and publisher, Cambridge, *c.* 1756–9. Succeeded Wm. Thurlbourne (*see Dictionary of Printers and Booksellers*, 1668–1728) at no. 1 Trinity Street, when Thurlbourne bought the two houses in 1757, and moved to no. 2. But they were in partnership, as works were published by Thurlbourne and Woodyer during 1756–9. Wm. Woodyer was succeeded in the partnership by John Woodyer (*q. v.*) in 1759.

WOOLLEY (HENRY), bookseller in Northampton, in the Drapery, 1746–9. In 1746 his name occurs in the imprint to a *Sermon* preached by the Rev. Henry Layng, M.A., in the parish church of All Saints, Northampton, on behalf of the County Infirmary. [B.M. 1658 (5).] Held periodical book sales.

WOOLRIDGE (R.), bookseller in Shaftesbury, co. Dorset., 1744–1775 (?). His name occurs in an advertisement in the *Salisbury Journal* of Tuesday, April 10th, 1744, a "Mr. Woolridge of Shafton" was amongst those who sold the catalogue of the library of the Rev. Christopher Twynihoe, sold by auction on August 21st, 1775, by William Sollers, of Blandford. [B.M. 824. b. 17 (4).]

WORLEY (RICHARD), bookseller in Boston, co. Lincoln., Butcher Row, near the Church, 1758. Only known from an advertisement in the *Cambridge Journal* of April 29th, 1758. There was also a bookseller of the name of W. Worley in Pinchbeck, co. Lincoln. Both were dealers in popular literature called *Shilling Histories*.

WORRALL (JOHN), bookseller and publisher in London, the Bible and Dove in Bell Yard, near Lincoln's Inn, 1736–63. Began life as a bookbinder. Dealt chiefly in law books. In 1728 there is the following advertisement: "Books to be sold by auction at Daniel's Coffee House in Temple Bar by J. Worrall, Bookseller at the Bible and Dove in Bell Yard." [*Daily Journal*, September 1st, 1728.] He was the compiler of two useful catalogues of books in the year 1736. The first, *Bibliotheca Legum Angliae*, went through several editions. He followed this up with *Bibliotheca Topographica Anglicana*. There is a copy of the second work in the British Museum with prices set against each item by a former owner, and with a manuscript note on one of the fly-leaves at the end to the effect that he had done this in order that a country antiquary might not be imposed on, as well as to show which were too dear. Worrall was also the publisher of books on *Natural History*, and in 1763 he published an *Introduction to the Laws of England*.

WORRALL (THOMAS), bookseller and publisher in London, Judge's Head or Judge Coke's Head over against St. Dunstan's Church in Fleet Street, 1729–67. Brother of J. Worrall. He published Robert Dodsley's poem *Servitude* in 1729, and in 1730 a pamphlet entitled *Some Objections against the Treaty of Seville*, at the end of which is a page of advertisements of books lately printed for him. Worrall subsequently went out of his mind, and died September 17th, 1767. [Nichols, III. 741.]

WOTTON (THOMAS), bookseller and publisher in London, Three Daggers and Queen's Head against St. Dunstan's Church, Fleet Street, 1726–66. Son of Matthew Wotton (1687–1725). Best known as the compiler of the *Baronetage*. He was also the publisher of many other well-known books, such as Rushworth's *Historical Collections*. He was Warden of the Company of Stationers in 1754, and Master in 1757. On his retirement from business he settled in Surrey, where he died April 1st, 1766. [Nichols, III. 440.]

WREN (J.), bookseller and publisher in London, over against the New Exchange Buildings in the Strand, 1764–5. Publisher of the third edition of Cadwallader

Colden's *History of the Five Indian Nations of Canada*; also of a collection of political essays by John Trenchard and T. Gordon in two volumes, 12 mo, and an astronomical work by J. B. de Freval, *The History of the Heavens*. In 1765 he issued *The Contrast, or the Behaviour of Two Criminals*, a most extraordinary medley of natural religion and spiritualism. [B.M. 4372. cc. 21 (3).]

WRIGHT ( ), bookseller in London, no. 132 in the Strand, 1740. Timperley says that he established the first circulating library in London in 1740, and that Batho, Bell, Lowndes, and the Nobles were his most successful rivals. There is an undated trade card of Wright's Circulating Library in Exeter Court, Strand. [A. Heal's Collection.]

WRIGHT (GRIFFITH), printer in Leeds, co. York., New Street End, 1754 (?)–1818. Printer of the *Leedes Intelligence*. Amongst other works from his press were *A Collection of Hymns and Spiritual Songs*, 1769, made by John Edwards, minister of Leeds [B.M. 3436. bbb. 28], and in the same year *An Historical Account of . . . Pontefract* and Elizabeth Moxon's *English Housewifery*. [*See* Copperthwaite, G.] Wright died October 28th, 1818. [Timperley, p. 869.]

WRIGHT (J.), printer in London, 1735–7. His name is found in the imprint of *An Essay on Reason* by Harte: "J. Wright for Lawton Gilliver 1735." [Britwell Library.] Presumably the Wright who printed Pope's *Letters* in 1737.

WRIGHT (THOMAS), printer in London, (1) Chancery Lane; (2) Peterborough Court; (3) Essex Street, Strand. 1766–97. One of Archibald Hamilton's assistants. Set up for himself in Chancery Lane about 1766. Died March 3rd, 1797. [Nichols, III. pp. 398–9.] T. Wright, of Essex Street, Strand, possibly the same man, was interested with Richardson and Urquhart in publishing the *Westminster Magazine* in 1775. [*Public Advertiser*, January 2nd, 1775.]

WRIGHT (THOMAS), printer in Oxford, 1765–98. Messrs. Wright and Gill, stationers, of Abchurch Lane, London, offered £850 a year for Baskett's lease in Bible printing in Oxford, which came to an end at Lady Day, 1765. This was accepted by Convocation on December 10th, 1765, and sealed on December 17th. [Bodl. M.S. 27889; B.M. Add. MS. 6880; Nichols, III. 604.]

SCOTTISH PRINTERS, BOOKSELLERS AND BOOKBINDERS, 1726–1775

REFERENCES ABBREVIATED IN THE TEXT

Brown's Bookstall. [Issued by Alex. Brown & Co., Booksellers, Aberdeen, Jan. 1892–Dec. 1913.]

Chalmers' History. A historical and statistical account of Dunfermline. By Peter Chalmers. 2 vols. Edinb., 1844–59.

Chalmers' Ruddiman. The life of Thomas Ruddiman. . . . By George Chalmers. London, 1794.

Constable's Lit. Corr. Archibald Constable and his literary correspondents. By Thos. Constable. 3 vols. Edinburgh, 1873.

Cotton. Typographical Gazetteer. By Henry Cotton. 2nd Series. Oxford, 1866.

Couper. The Edinburgh Periodical Press. . . . By W. J. Couper. 2 vols. Stirling, 1908.

Creech's Fugitive Pieces. Edinburgh Fugitive Pieces. By William Creech. Edinburgh, 1815.

D.N.B. Dictionary of National Biography [and Supplements].

Duncan. Notices and documents illustrative of the literary history of Glasgow during the greater part of last century. Ed. by W. J. Duncan. (Maitland Club, Glasgow, 1831.)

Henderson's Annals. The Annals of Dunfermline. By Ebenezer Henderson. Glasgow, 1879.

Kay's Portraits. A series of original portraits. . . . With biogr. sketches and illustr. anecdotes. By John Kay. 2 vols. Edinburgh, 1837–8.

Maxwell. Dumfries. A history of Dumfries and Galloway. By Sir H. Maxwell. (County hist. of Scotland.) Edinburgh, 1896.

Murray. Foulis Press. Robert & Andrew Foulis and the Glasgow Press . . . by David Murray. Glasgow, 1913.

Murray. Letters of Foulis. Some letters of Robert Foulis. By David Murray. Glasgow, 1917.

Registers. The registers of marriages, burgesses, &c., referred to are all publications of the Scottish Record Society.

Reid. Glasgow Past and Present: illustrated in . . . the reminiscences and communications of Senex [i.e. Robert Reid]. Glasgow, 1851.

Scot. N. & Q. Scottish Notes and Queries.

Southey's Life of Bell. The Life of the Rev. Andrew Bell. By R. and C. C. Southey. 3 vols. London, 1844.

Timperley. A Dictionary of Printers and Printing. By C. H. Timperley. 1839. Second edition 1842. The references serve for both editions.

SCOTTISH PRINTERS, BOOKSELLERS AND BOOKBINDERS

By GEORGE H. BUSHNELL

ADIE (JOHN), printer in Edinburgh, 1772. In Old Kirk Parish. Married Betty, daughter of John Millar, turner, April 19th, 1772. [*Edinb. Marr. Reg.*, 1751–1800.] Probably a journeyman.

AIKMAN (EUTHRED or EUPHRID), journeyman printer in Edinburgh. In Old Grayfriar's Parish, 1768–70. Married Jacobina, daughter of James Chisholm, smith in Calton . . . May 20th, 1770. [*Edinb. Marr. Reg.*, 1751–1800.]

AINSLIE (JAMES), printer in Edinburgh, 1758–92 (?) In Old Grayfriar's Parish, 1764. Married, first, Anna, daughter of John Moir, April 9th, 1758; second, Christian, daughter of John Halden, skinner, April 29th, 1764. His daughter Mary married Archibald Lethem, printer, May 11th, 1792. The stationer of the same name who married Agnes, daughter of Andrew Lookup, architect in Jedburgh, June 11th, 1787, may have been his son. [*Edinb. Marr. Reg.*, 1751–1800.]

AINSLIE (PATRICK), printer (journeyman?) in Edinburgh, 1728. In South-West Kirk Parish. Married Mary Drummond, servant to James Cassie, vintner, November 10th, 1728. [*Edinb. Marr. Reg.*, 1701–50.] Possibly father of James Ainslie (*q.v.*).

AITKEN (JOHN), bookseller and stationer in Edinburgh, 1718–86. Parliament house, 1734. Possibly a son of Wm. Aitken (*see Dictionary*, 1668–1725). Entered in the Edinburgh Guild Register as a stationer, September 10th, 1718, and as a bookseller April 4th, 1733. On both occasions he was described as "prentice to Robert Freebairn". In 1734 he sold copies of *A Treatise concerning the origin and progress of fees . . . being a supp. to Spotiswood's Introd. to . . . stile of writs*; Edinb., Ruddiman. His will was registered July 5th, 1786. [Scot. Rec. Soc., *Edinb. Test.*] Apparently he is not to be confused with the printer of the same name (*q.v.*). Omitted from *Dictionary*, 1668–1725.

AITKEN (JOHN), printer in Edinburgh, 1774. Married Herriot, daughter of Archibald Black, gardener at Nisbet, near Dunce, November 13th, 1774. [*Edinb. Marr. Reg.*, 1751–1800.] Possibly a journeyman. Not to be confused with the bookseller of the same name (*q.v.*).

ALEXANDER (MUNGO), bookbinder in Glasgow, 1737. Burgess and Guild Brother, by right of his wife Janet, daughter of John M'Lean, merchant, June 17th, 1737. [Scot. Rec. Soc., *Burgesses and G.B. of Glasgow*, 1573–1750.]

ALFIONI ( ), (?) printer in Edinburgh, 1745. The imprint to *Translations and Paraphrases of several passages of Sacred Scripture . . . May 18th, 1745*, reads: "Edinburgh, Alfioni, 1745".

ALISON (ALEXANDER), printer and bookseller in Edinburgh, *c.* 1714–46. Printer of John Nicol's *Copy of three letters* . . . Edinb., 1714. In partnership with Robert Fleming (*see Dictionary* 1668–1725), from about 1741 to 1746. In 1732 W. Cheyne (*q.v.*) printed for him *The Fort-Royal of the Scriptures; or, A Vade-mecum Concordance. . . .* Various works appeared from the joint press of Fleming and Alison, including *Essays Moral and Spiritual*, 1741, which was printed for A. Kincaid; and *The Christian Monthly History, or an account of the Revival and Progress of Religion abroad and at home* . . . November 1743–46. In 1740 he printed alone Ebenezer Erskine's *Christ the Resurrection*, for David Duncan and James Beugo in Dunfermline.

ALLARDICE (ALEXANDER), printer in Edinburgh, 1754. Married Barbara Ross, June 16th, 1754. [*Edinb. Marr. Reg.*, 1751–1800.] Probably a journeyman.

ALSTON (GAVIN), printer in Edinburgh, *c.* 1763–79. Jackson's Close *c.* 1763–69; Old Fishmarket Close, 1773–74; Tolbooth Kirk Parish, 1779. About 1763 or a little earlier he set up as a printer in Jackson's Close, in partnership with John Gray (*q.v.*). The earliest book noticed which bears their joint imprint is dated 1763 (Andrew Welwood's *Meditations*). On April 17th of the same year Alston married Jean, daughter of John Barclay, merchant. He was later married to Strickland Crockat, relict of . . . Ramsay, on November 25th, 1779. [*Edinb. Marr. Reg.*, 1751–1800.] The partnership was dissolved between 1769 and 1774. In 1769 they printed jointly Archibald Hall's *An Humble Attempt to Exhibit a Scriptural View of the Constitution . . . of the Church*, but in 1774 Gray printed alone James Scot's *Collection of Sermons*. In the same year Alston printed the very rare Gaelic ed. of Isaac Watts's *Children's Catechism*. His name has not been noticed on any book later than 1776, when he printed W. Perry's *Only Sure Guide to the English tongue*, but he was in business until 1779 if not later.

ANDERSON (GEORGE), printer in Edinburgh, 1768. In College Kirk Parish. Married Marion Lauder, relict of David Alexander, farmer in parish of Glenholm, October 2nd, 1768. [*Edinb. Marr. Reg.*, 1751–1800.]

ANGUS (ALEXANDER), publisher, bookseller and printer in Aberdeen, 1744–1802. Castlegate, 1765; Narrow-Wynd, 1791. Son of the Rev. John Angus of Kinellar. Born 1721. Partner in the firm of Alex. Angus & Son, which he founded about 1744. He had a numerous family, most of whom died young, but his sons John and Andrew were taken into the business. The firm continued to exist until the death of John in 1828, when the last survivor, Andrew, gave up business. In 1765 they published Scougal's *Reflections*. For many years they were "the Leigh & Sotheby and the King and Lochee of that part of the world, and sold a great many libraries by auction". [Nichols' *Lit. Anecdotes*, v. 3, p. 690.] The shop was a well-known lounge and meeting place for the better class citizens. One book auction which commenced on November 18th, 1765, contained 1,728 lots and lasted for eighteen nights. A printed catalogue of this sale was issued. By 1781 they employed a professional auctioneer, Mr. J. Walker. In 1779 they had a circulating library, which, by 1790, had grown to 3,384 vols. Baillie Burnett in a letter to a friend in 1791 described their shop as "the showiest shop in town—a large new door, and two of the very largest windows in the City". During the nineteenth century the shop was pulled down and the Town-House built on its site. Amongst their publications are: *The Trial of Katherine Nairn and Lieut. Patrick Ogilvie*, 1765; Spalding's *Memorialls of the trubles in Scotland*, 1792; *Inquiry into the life of . . . Dr. William Guild . . . by James Shirrefs*, 1799; and a number of sale catalogues. *A Catalogue of books for a circulating library . . . which was lent at ten shillings a year* . . . was issued in 1765. Alex. Angus, died in 1802. [*Brown's Bookstalls*, v. 1; Lawrance, *An Old Bookselling Firm, Alex. Angus & Son*, 1923; &c.]

ANGUS (ANDREW), bookseller, publisher, &c. in Aberdeen, 1754–1830. Son of Alexander Angus, and partner in the firm of Alex. Angus & Son. Librarian of the Advocates' Library at Aberdeen in 1811. Retired from business on the death of his brother John in 1828. *See under* Angus (Alexander).

ANGUS (JOHN), bookseller, publisher, &c. in Aberdeen, *c.* 1750–1828. Son of Alexander Angus, and partner in the firm of Alex. Angus & Son. Died in 1828. *See under* Angus (Alexander).

ARMSTRONG (MARTYN JOHN), (?) publisher in Edinburgh, 1774–5. In Kay's *Portraits*, vol. 1, p. 247, it is stated that Martyn John Armstrong, in company with his son, published surveys of several counties of Scotland in 1774–5.

AULD (ROBERT), printer in Edinburgh, 1765–6 (?) In partnership with William Auld (*q. v.*) and William Smellie for about two years, but withdrew from the firm in 1766. Said to have continued for a time to print independently.

AULD (WILLIAM), printer in Edinburgh, 1761–90 (?). Morocco's Close, 1761–5; Turk's Close, Lawn-market, 1773–4. Possibly a son of William Auld, bookbinder (*see Dictionary*, 1668–1725). Printed with Walter Ruddiman, junior, and Company in 1761. From 1765 he was in partnership with William Smellie (*q.v.*) and Robert Auld (*q.v.*), but in 1769 disputes began between them, and in 1771 Auld withdrew from the partnership. He was one of the publishers of the *Edinburgh Weekly Journal*, against which an action was brought in 1765, and Auld was cited as meriting the most severe censure. The judge dealt leniently with him however. Two years later he appeared again, this time on a charge of contempt of court, but again he was let off with a rebuke. [*Scots Mag.* 29, p. 339.] On July 17th, 1768 he married Alexandrina, daughter of Captain James Ogilvy, shipmaster in St Andrews. [*Edinb. Marr. Reg.* 1751–1800.] In 1772 he commenced to publish the *Scots Farmer*, but this periodical did not live long. As a rival to *Ruddiman's Weekly Magazine*, he founded the *Gentleman and Lady's Weekly Magazine* in 1774, but this did not meet with sufficient support and was dropped on March 29th, 1775. In 1776 he commenced to issue the *North British Intelligencer or Constitutional Miscellany*, and continued to print it for four volumes. He printed until about 1790.

BAIN (JOHN), typefounder, 1742–90 (?), see p. 371.

BAIN (JOHN), bookseller in Edinburgh, 1747. In South-South-East Kirk Parish. Married Mrs. Catherine Cant, daughter of Ludovic Cant of Thurstone, January 4th, 1747. [*Edinb.* Marr. Reg., 1701–50.]

BAIN (JOHN), printer in Edinburgh, *c.* 1760. In New Grayfriar's Parish. His widow, Margaret Watson, married Andrew Houston January 7th, 1770. His daughter Margaret married David Reid, glover, April 18th, 1797. [*Edinb. Marr. Reg.*, 1751–1800.]

BAIN (JOHN), journeyman bookbinder in Edinburgh, 1771. In New North Kirk Parish. Married Jean, daughter of James Stewart, March 31st, 1771. [*Edinb. Marr. Reg.*, 1751–1800.]

BAIN (JOHN), type-founder in Edinburgh, 1773–4. In the Calton. His name appears in the *Edinburgh Directory*, 177$\frac{3}{4}$. Possibly a son of John Bain of St Andrews (*q.v.*).

BALFOUR (JOHN), bookseller and printer in Edinburgh, *c.* 1745–95. In the College, 1754–66; Head of Anchor Close, 1773–4. In 1766 Balfour took the place of Robert Auld (*q.v.*) in the firm of Auld and Smellie. Previously he had served his apprenticeship with Gavin Hamilton (*q.v.*), whose daughter he married. He was the son of Mr. Balfour of Pilrig. Probably Hamilton took him into partnership about 1745. In 1749 the firm became Hamilton, Balfour and Neill. Hamilton retired in 1766 and Balfour joined the firm of Auld and Smellie. In 1769 disputes arose and Auld withdrew from the firm. Balfour and Smellie continued in partnership for some years, but probably about 1778 the partnership was dissolved. In 1780 his name appears alone in imprints to various works. About 1781 he took his son Elphingstone Balfour into partnership with him. He purchased from the descendants of Gavin Hamilton the paper-mills at Collington and this business was carried on by his sons. The bookselling business was abandoned early in the nineteenth century. His daughter Louisa married James Millar, writer, August 5th, 1786, and his son John married Peggy Grieve, December 22nd, 1783. In addition to printing, publishing, paper making and bookselling he sold libraries by auction. His name occurs in the imprints to a great number of books published over a period of nearly fifty years. He died on October 16th, 1795, and was succeeded by his son Elphingstone Balfour. He left many descendants, and the name of Balfour has only recently disappeared from Edinburgh's roll of printers. [*The Printing House of Neill*, 1918; Constable's *Literary Correspondence*; &c.]

BALLANTYNE (GEORGE), bookseller in Glasgow, *c.* 1770. Described as "the younger, of Waterhaughs". His wife was Alleta M'Leod, whose will was registered June 11th, 1776. [Comm. Rec. Glasgow, *Reg. Test.*, 1547–1800.]

BANNERMAN (WILLIAM), running stationer in Edinburgh, 1763–71. Tron Kirk Parish 1763; College Kirk Parish 1771. Apparently he was twice married. Married first, Isobel, daughter of William Dick, cowfeeder at Hermons, St Jermins, May 29th, 1763; second, Margaret, daughter of William Ross, stationer, July 14th, 1771. [*Edinb. Marr. Reg.*, 1751–1800.]

BARR (JAMES), papermaker, Gorbals of Glasgow, 1761. His name occurs in the list of subscribers to James Durham's *Christ crucified*, 6th ed., Glasgow, M'Lean & Galbraith, 1761.

BARRY (JOHN), bookseller and publisher in Glasgow, 1744–8. Robert Urie (*q.v.*) printed an edition of the *Spectator* in 1744 for Andrew Stalker (*q.v.*) and John Barry. [Murray, *R. & A. Foulis*, 1913, p. 20.] His name occurs as a Glasgow bookseller in the imprint to MacLaurin's *Account of Sir Isaac Newton's discoveries* . . . London, 1748.

BAXTER, (DANIEL), bookseller in Glasgow, 1744–50. Son of David Baxter. Burgess and Guild Brother as eldest living son of deceased David Baxter, bookbinder, B. & G.B., March 5th 1747. [Scot. Rec. Soc., *Burgesses and G.B. of Glasgow*, 1573–1750]. A list of books "printed in Scotland and sold by Daniel Baxter" is found at the end of Hutcheson's *Reflections upon laughter* . . . 1744. He was the publisher of the *Reflections*, another ed. of which was printed for him by Robert Urie (*q. v.*) in 1750.

BECK (ALEXANDER), glazier and stationer in Perth, 1739. Married Eupham Graham, daughter of Robert Graham, town-clerk in Perth and afterwards of N.K. Parish, Edinburgh, September 30th, 1739. [*Edinb. Marr. Reg.*, 1701–50.]

BELL (ALEXANDER), type-founder in St Andrews, *c.* 1742. In Southey's *Life of Dr. Bell* the statement is made that Alexander Wilson (*q.v.*) was greatly assisted in his type-founding experiments, by Bell. Curiously enough no mention is made of Wilson's well-known partner John Bain (*q.v.*), and no other notice of Bell's participation in the work has been found. He is locally remembered as "Baillie Bell the Barber". His son was the famous Dr. Bell, founder of the "Madras" system of education in this country and whose name is perpetuated in those of many schools in England and Scotland.

BELL (DAVID), bookbinder in Edinburgh. In North-West Kirk Parish, 1752. In New North Kirk Parish, 1764. Married first Jane Watt, December 10th, 1752; second Christian Taylor, April 8th, 1764. [*Edinb. Marr. Reg.*, 1751–1800.] His will was registered June 6th, 1798. [Scot. Rec. Soc., *Edinb. Test.*] Possibly the same as David Bell, bookseller (*q.v.*).

BELL (DAVID), bookseller in Edinburgh. In New North Kirk Parish, 1759. Married Margaret, daughter of James Wright, November 11th, 1759. [*Edinb. Marr. Reg.*, 1751–1800.] Possibly the same as David Bell, bookbinder (*q.v.*).

BELL (GEORGE), bookbinder in Edinburgh. Before 1737. His will was registered on April 27th, 1737. [Scot. Rec. Soc., *Edinb. Test.*]

BELL (JOHN), bookseller and publisher in Edinburgh, *c.* 1760–1806. Addison's Head, 1773; Writers' Court, 1773–4. For several years during the latter part of the eighteenth century he was called the Father of the bookselling trade. He was one of the original promoters of the Society of Booksellers of Edinburgh and Leith and was the first Praeses of that Society. From about 1760 to 1771 he was in partnership with Alex. Kincaid (*q.v.*) as Kincaid & Bell. William Creech (*q.v.*) was apprenticed to this firm, and on its dissolution in May 1771, he succeeded Bell in partnership with Kincaid, as Kincaid & Creech. In 1768 Kincaid & Bell sold by auction the Collection of William M'Farlane of M'Farlane. In 1762 Bell's name occurs in the imprint to John Mair's *Brief survey of the terraqueous globe*, and from then onwards his name is met very frequently in Edinburgh books. His name occurs in 1779 in the list of Assize at the trial of Basil Alves on January 29th. About 1790 or a little earlier he entered into partnership with Bradfute as Bell & Bradfute. In 1802 this firm was supplying the Advocates' Library. They published a number of works between 1790 and 1806, including such periodicals as *Constitutional Letters*, 1792, and *Annals of Medicine*, about 1800. William Blackwood, the eminent bookseller and publisher commenced his apprenticeship with this firm at the age of 14 (? in 1790). Bell died in September 1806, at about seventy years of age. A well-drawn character sketch and account of his career appeared in the *Edinburgh Evening Courant*, October 11th, 1806.

BELL (JOHN), printer in Edinburgh, *c.* 1770–84. In Tolbooth Parish, 1781. Married Jean, daughter of . . . Ballantyne, merchant in Peebles, April 2nd, 1781. [*Edinb. Marr. Reg.*, 1751–1800.] His will was registered June 29th, 1784. [Scot. Rec. Soc., *Edinb. Test.*] Not to be confused with the well-known bookseller, to whom he may have been related, however.

BEUGO (GAVIN), printer and bookseller in Dunfermline, 1762. (1) Collier Row; (2) High Street. "Had a bookshop and small printing press in the Collier Row, afterwards in the High Street (east of the Cross) as early as 1762." [Henderson's *Annals*, p. 477.] M'Kerrow, in his *History of the Secession Church*, 1845, p. 144, mentions a Gavin Beugo, probationer in the Established Church, as joining the Secession, July 1739. This was evidently the Gavin Beugo named in Rogers' *The Book of Robert Burns*, vol. I, p. 35, as "a licentiate of the Church, resident in Edinburgh", descended from a Linlithgow family, and father of John Beugo, who is well known as the engraver of Nasmyth's portrait of Burns. [Beveridge, *Bibl. of Dunfermline*, 1901, p. xvi.] He may have been the same as the above. No books bearing his imprint have been found. *See* Beugo (James).

BEUGO (JAMES), bookseller in Dunfermline, 1729–52. His name is first found in the imprint to the Rev. Ralph Erskine's *The Main Question of the Gospel Catechism, what think ye of Christ?* 2nd ed. Edinb., 1729: "Printed for, and sold by James Beugo, Book-seller in Dunfermline". From that year until 1749 he sold numerous sermons, mostly pamphlets, by that prolific author, for whom he probably acted as publisher. Most of the earlier ones were printed in Edinburgh and some of them bear Alexander Alison's imprint. In 1747 and 1748 Glasgow was the place of printing, and in 1749 Edinburgh again. In 1740 he sold George Whitefield's *The Marriage of Cana* . . . Edinb. From 1730 his name appears on a number of works by the Rev. Ebenezer Erskine, on whose *Gospel Treasure in Earthen Vessels*, Edinburgh, 1752, it is last found. In the *Acts and Proceedings of the Associate Synod* (April 1747) . . . Edinburgh, James Beugo is mentioned as Ruling Elder from Dunfermline (p. vii). [Beveridge, *Bibl. of Dunfermline*, 1901, p. 115, note.] He may have been the father of Gavin Beugo (*q.v.*).

BEVERIDGE (ANDREW), stationer in Edinburgh, 1741. Entered in the *Edinburgh Guild Register*, as a Stationer, December 9th, 1741.

BEVERIDGE (ROBERT), bookseller in Dunfermline, 1729. Only known from the Rev. Ralph Erskine's *The Strength of sin, and how the Law is the strength thereof* . . . Edinb., 1729. "Printed for, and sold by Thomas Beveridge, Merchant in Braughty in the Parish of Fosway, and by Robert Beveridge, Merchant in Dunfermline."

BEVERIDGE (THOMAS), bookseller in Braughty, in the Parish of Fosway, 1729. In 1729 the Rev. Ralph Erskine's *The Strength of sin, and how the Law is the strength thereof* . . . Edinburgh, was "Printed for, and sold by Thomas Beveridge, Merchant in Braughty in the Parish of Fosway, and by Robert Beveridge, Merchant in Dunfermline."

BISSET (JOHN), bookseller in Perth, 1762–94. His name occurs in the imprint to John Mair's *Brief survey of the terraqueous globe* . . . Edinburgh, 1762. He was one of the subscribers to the building of the bridge at Perth in 1776. His will was registered November 26th, 1794. [Comm. Rec. St Andrews: *Reg. Test.*, 1549–1800.]

BLAIR (J.), of Ardblair, printer in Edinburgh, *c.* 1736. In 1736 was published *Proceedings in the submission betwixt W. R. Freebairn, his majesty's printer, and Mr. J. Blair of Ardblair, and Mr. J. Nairn, of Greenyards, aspiring to be King's Printers*, Edinburgh, folio. [Timperley, p. 655.]

BOGLE (WILLIAM), bookseller in Edinburgh, 1764. Married Hamilton, daughter of Lauchlan Hunter (*q.v.*), bookseller and bookbinder, April 8th, 1764. [*Edinb. Marr. Reg.*, 1751–1800.]

BOWER (PATRICK), bookseller in St Andrews, 1723–1814. Arch-beadle of the University of St Andrews, which office he held for nearly seventy years. At his death on July 7th 1814 he was one of the oldest and most respected booksellers in Europe. He was in his ninety-second year. [Timperley, p. 853.] The will of his eldest son, John, was registered June 7th, 1775. [Comm. Rec. St Andrews; *Reg. Test.* 1549–1800.] For the four years 1786–1790 Robert Tillas or Tullis served his apprenticeship with Bower. Tullis later became Printer to the University of St Andrews. He also founded the paper-mills at Markinch and issued the first Fife newspaper, from his office at Cupar. In 1820 Tullis had a shop in Market Street, St Andrews, which was probably the place of business which had formerly belonged to his old master, Patrick Bower.

BOYD (PATRICK), bookbinder in Edinburgh. Before 1764. His will was registered March 1st, 1764. [Scot. Rec. Soc., *Edinb. Test.*] May have been succeeded in business by George Moodie (*q.v.*), bookbinder, who on November 17th, 1776, married his daughter Jean. [*Edinb. Marr. Reg.*, 1751–1800.]

BOYD, (W.), printer in Dumfries, *c.* 1773–77 (?). Printed in partnership with Robert Jackson (*q.v.*). [Maxwell, *Dumfries*, p. 379.]

BOYLE (JOHN), bookseller, papermaker, and publisher in Aberdeen, 1760–92 (?). In 1776 Allan Ramsay's *Poems* . . ., were "printed and sold by J. Boyle". Succeeded Francis Douglas (*q.v.*). With Robert Hyde founded a paper mill at Stoneywood in 1771, but in the same year Boyle sold his half-share in this business to Hyde. An article on John Boyle appeared in the *Aberdeen Book-Lover* for November, 1925. [Information kindly supplied by Mr. G. M. Fraser, Aberdeen.]

BRIDGES (JOHN), *see* Briggs.

BRIGGS or BRIDGES (JOHN), bookseller in Edinburgh, Luckenbooths, 1727–33. Sold copies of John Currie's *Jus populi Divinum* . . . 1727; Currie's *The Overture considered* . . . 1732. Ebenezer Erskine's *Rainbow of the Covenant* . . . 1731, was "Printed for and sold by John Bridges in the Luckenbooths". In 1733 Currie's *A Sermon preached in the Church of Kirkaldie* . . . was "Printed for John Briggs and sold at his shop in the Lucken-booths".

BROUN, *see* Brown.

BROUNE or BROWN (JAMES), bookbinder in Glasgow, 1661–1730 (?). Bookbinder, burgess, as serving apprentice with Robert Sanders [*see Dictionary*, 1641–67], January 24th, 1661. Guild Brother, by same right, January 20th, 1670. [Scot. Rec. Soc. *Burg. and G. B. of Glasgow*, 1573–1750.] Died before November 15th, 1736. The will of his widow, Janet Hunter, was registered on that date and on January 16th, 1738. [Comm. Rec. Glasgow; *Reg. Test.*, 1547–1800.]

BROWN, MRS. (AGNES), bookseller and printer in Glasgow, 1734. Wife of James Brown (*q.v.*). *See under* Brown (John). Her maiden name was apparently Agnes Martin.

BROWN (ALEXANDER), stationer in Biggar, before 1764. His daughter Jean married Archibald Robertson, journeyman baxter, March 17th, 1764. [*Edinb. Marr. Reg.*, 1751–1800.] Brown was then dead.

BROWN (JAMES), bookseller and printer in Glasgow, 1734–99 (?). His will was registered April 26th, 1799. *See under* Brown, (John).

BROWN (JAMES), bookseller in Edinburgh, 1758–74 (?). In Tolbooth Parish, 1758: Parliament close, 1773–4. Burgess. Married Agnes, daughter of Dr. Alexander Martine, physician, March 5th, 1758. [*Edinb. Marr. Reg.*, 1751–1800.] His name is found in the *Edinburgh Directory* 177¾.

BROWN (JAMES), stationer in Glasgow, *c.* 1748. Prentice master of James Robb (*q.v.*), stationer, August 25th, 1748. [Scot. Rec. Soc., *Burgesses and Guild Brothers of Glasgow*, 1573–1750.] May be identical with the bookseller and printer of the same name, 1734–99?

BROWN, MRS. (JANET), printer and bookseller in Edinburgh, *c.* 1731–44. In the Parliament Closs, 1741. Widow of John M'Pherson (*q.v.*), printer. Married William Brown, bookseller, June 5th, 1715. [*Edinb. Marr. Reg.*, 1701–50.] Her imprint appears on Alexander Macdonald's *A Galick and English vocabulary*, Edinburgh, 1741. It is probable that she succeeded to her husband's business about 1731. On January 1st, 1744, she married James Stewart. [*Ib.*]

BROWN (JOHN), bookseller, stationer and printer in Glasgow, 1715–66. Burgess and Guild Brother, July 4th, 1715. Married Marion, daughter of James Sheirer, weaver. [Scot. Rec. Soc., *Burgesses and G. B. of Glasgow*, 1573–1750.] In 1734 Alexander Carmichael, Alexander Miller, John, James and Mrs. Brown were printing in company. Mrs. Brown's name disappears in 1735, and those of John and James in 1736, the firm then becoming Alexander Carmichael and Alexander Miller. [Murray, *R. & A. Foulis*, 1913, p. 15.] In 1755 Brown published an edition of William Guthrie's *The Christian's Great Interest*. [*Ib.*, p. 32.] John and James Brouns sold the seventh (? Scottish) edition of Bunyan's *Pilgrim's Progress* in 1735. [Esdaile, *English Tales and Romances*, p. 175.] The will of John Brown, bookseller, was registered April 28th, 1766. [Comm. Rec. Glasgow: *Reg. Test.*, 1547–1800.] He is not to be confused with the Edinburgh printer of the same name. Omitted from *Dictionary*, 1668–1735.

BROWN (JOHN), bookseller and printer in Edinburgh, 1731–34 (?). Cowl's Closs, Canongate-head, north-side of the street, 1734. His name occurs in the imprint to Ebenezer Erskine's *The King held in the Galleries*, Edinburgh ... 1734. Married Janet Sharp (Hutchison) widow of Patrick Hutchison, cook, February 12th, 1731. [*Edinb. Marr. Reg.*, 1701–50.] Possibly father of the John Brown, printer in Edinburgh, who married Isobel, relict of James Hutchison, and daughter of Robert Wight, baker, on February 5th, 1780. [*Ib.*]

BROWN (JOHN), bookbinder in Glasgow, 1741. Burgess and Guild Brother. Prentice-master of Patrick Davie (*q.v.*), who was admitted Burgess May 20th, 1741. [Scot. Rec. Soc.; *Burgesses and G.B. of Glasgow*, 1573–1750.]

BROWN (WILLIAM), printer and bookseller in Edinburgh, 1714–31. Married Janet M'Pherson, June 5th, 1715. [*Edinb. Marr. Reg.*, 1701–50.] His widow succeeded him about 1731 and printed as Mrs. Brown for some years. *See also Dictionary*, 1668–1725.

BROWN (WILLIAM), bookbinder in Edinburgh, 1768–93 (?). In New North Parish, 1768. Opposite to the back-stairs, 1773–4. Married Katherine Jackson, November 6th, 1768, by whom he had a daughter Isobel, who was married on April 4th, 1793, to William Wilson, merchant. [*Edinb. Marr. Reg.*, 1751–1800.]

BRUCE (JOHN), printer in Edinburgh, *c.* 1750–69. Probably father of the John Bruce, printer, who married Katherine Andrew, July 4th, 1797. [*Canongate Reg. Marr.*, 1564–1800.] His will was registered June 6th, 1769. [Scot. Rec. Soc., *Edinb. Test.*] In 1765 he printed, as J. Bruce and Company, William Hunter's *The Black Bird; a choice collection of the most celebrated songs.*

BRYCE (JOHN), printer and bookseller in Glasgow, *c.* 1750–1786. Shop near the middle of the Salt-mercat, 1763. Salt-market opposite Gibson's Wynd, 1782. In 1755 printed in partnership with David Paterson (*q.v.*). In the following year they printed a new ed. of John Owen's ... *Grace and Duty of being*

Spiritually minded, of which some copies were "on a fine writing paper ... neatly bound in calf, letter'd and gilt": followed by several other of his works in similar style. They were also booksellers and publishers, and in 1758 issued Peter Williamson's *French and Indian cruelty*: "Printed ... for the benefit of the unfortunate author". The partnership was dissolved either in 1759 or in 1760:[1] Bryce then occupied a shop in the Salt market and Paterson went to Edinburgh. Between 1760 and 1785 Bryce printed at least three editions of the *Westminster Confession*, as well as a goodly number of other works including the *Act of the Associate Presbytery for renewing the National Covenant of Scotland* ... 1763; a new ed. of *Joshua redivivus or* ... *Letters by Samuel Rutherfoord* [sic] ... 1765; George Muir's *Synod of Jerusalem* ... 1778; and Brown's *The Young Christian* ... 1782. The last-mentioned contains a list of the books he had for sale. Bryce was married in Edinburgh on September 27th, 1767, to Margaret, d. of Andrew Gibson. [*Edinb. Marr. Reg.*, 1751–1800.]

BRYMER (ALEXANDER), bookseller in Edinburgh, 1733–42 (?). Entered in the Edinburgh Guild Register as a bookseller, by right of John Brymer, father, merchant, August 1st, 1733. The imprint to the *Scots Magazine* for 1740 reads: "Printed by Sands, Brymer, Murray and Cochran". A note inside the volume describes A. Murray and J. Cochran as the printers and W. Sands and A. Brymer as booksellers. In 1743 the magazine was "Printed by James Cochran and Company". From 1744 it was "Printed by W. Sands, A. Murray, and J. Cochran". *See under* Murray (Alexander).

BRYMER (ROBERT), running stationer in Edinburgh. In South-West Kirk Parish, 1755. Married Mary, relict of James Hamilton, gardener, October 5th, 1755. [*Edinb. Marr. Reg.*, 1751–1800.]

CADEL (BAILLIE), (?) bookseller in Haddington in 1747. Sold copies of Rev. Ralph Erskine's *A Sermon preached immediately before the Administration of the Sacrament of the Lord's Supper, at Dunfermline, July 19, 1747*; Glasgow: Printed for J. Newlands ... 1747.

CAMERON (DUNCAN), copper-plate printer in Edinburgh, 1760. Married Agnes, daughter of John Gib, indweller in Dundee, June 6th, 1760. [*Canongate Reg. Marr.*, 1564–1800.]

CAMPBELL (COLIN), bookbinder in Edinburgh, 1733. Bookbinder by right of Robert Campbell, father, May 16th, 1733. [*Edinb. Guild Reg.*]

[1] In 1759 their joint imprint appeared upon James Durham's *Exposition of the Book of Job.*

CAMPBELL (DUNCAN), junior, gardener in Glasgow, *c.* 1750–80. Near the Gallowgate toll. In 1756 an ed. of John Willison's *Fair and impartial testimony* was "printed for and sold by John Finlay, wright, at his house in Shuttle Street; and by Duncan Campbell, junior, gardner, at his house near the Gallowgate toll". [Murray, *Foulis Press*, p. 26; Reid, *Glasgow Past and Present*, v. 3, p. 218.]

CAMPBELL (JOHN), running stationer in Edinburgh. In North Kirk Parish, 1754. Married Alison, daughter of John Johnston, February 17th, 1754. [*Edinb. Marr. Reg.*, 1751–1800.]

CAMPBELL (SAMUEL), bookbinder in Edinburgh, 1773–80. West-bow, 1773–4. In New North Kirk Parish, 1780. His daughter Jean married Thomas Allan, bookbinder, May 13th, 1780. [*Edinb. Marr. Reg.*, 1751–1800.] His name is found in *Edinburgh Directory*, 177¾.

CANT (JAMES), bookseller and publisher, Dunkeld, *c.* 1770–1812 (?). Born about 1736, probably in Perth. Became a Government official and held the position of Surveyor of H. M. Customs at Perth. Editor of the 2nd. ed. of *The Muses Threnodie*. A member of the Glassite Church and a very active church worker. A contributor to the *Perth Magazine*, 1772–3. The publication of *The Muses Threnodie* was commenced in this magazine, but did not satisfy Cant, who published the work in book form in 1774. About 1770 he took over Robert Morison's book shop at Dunkeld. He was no doubt a bookbinder as well as bookseller. *See* Morison (Robert).

CARLILE, CARLISLE, CARLYLE (ALEXANDER), bookseller in Glasgow, 1742–52. In 1742 Robert Urie (*q.v.*) printed an edition of Terence which was issued in three forms: (1) for R. Urie & Company themselves; (2) for Robert Foulis; and (3) for Alexander Carlile, with the imprint *Typis Alexandri Carlile*. [Murray, *R. & A. Foulis*, 1913, p. 9.] He is mentioned in the list of subscribers to John Welch's *Miscellany Sermons* ... 1744, where his name is spelt Carlisle. His will was registered November 1st, 1752 [Comm. Rec. Glasgow: *Reg. Test.*, 1547–1800]—name spelt Carlyle.

CARMICHAEL (ALEXANDER), bookseller and printer in Glasgow, 1724–36. Glasgow College, 1730–3. Son of Gerschom Carmichael. About 1726 set up as printer and bookseller in partnership with Andrew Stalker (*q.v.*). In 1730 he appears as a printer within Glasgow College. In that year he printed a second edition of his grandfather's theological treatise *Believer's Mortification of sin*

by the Spirit, which bears the imprint: Glasgow-College, printed by Mr. Carmichaell and Company, 1730. [B.M. 4410. g. 17.] Two years later he printed for Andrew Stalker (his former partner), as University Printer, three works of Cicero, and in 1733, a fourth, for Andrew Stalker and Gavin Hamilton of Edinburgh. Apparently his appointment as University Printer only lasted from 1730 to 1733, for in 1734 Alexander Carmichael, Alexander Miller, John, James and Mrs. Brown were printing in partnership, but not apparently in connexion with the college. [Murray, *R. & A. Foulis*, 1913, p. 15.] In 1735 he sold a seventh (Scottish) edition of the *Pilgrim's Progress*, [Esdaile, p. 175], and in that year Mrs. Brown's name disappeared from the imprint. John and James Brown do not appear in 1736, the firm then becoming Alexander Carmichael and Alexander Miller. [Murray, *R. & A. Foulis*, p. 5; R. Duncan, *Documents illust. of the lit. hist. of Glasgow*, p. 155.] It is possible that he maintained some connexion with the college, for his partner Alexander Miller was afterwards the College Printer. He was admitted Burgess and Guild Brother, November 26th, 1724. [Scot. Rec. Soc., *Burgesses and G. B. of Glasgow*, 1573–1750.]

CARMICHAEL (JOHN), running stationer in Edinburgh. New Kirk Parish, 1760. Married Elizabeth, daughter of Peter Watson, miller at Barieshole in Fife, November 2nd, 1760. [*Edinb. Marr. Reg.*, 1751–1800.]

CARMICHAEL (ROBERT), printer in Edinburgh. In South-West Kirk Parish, 1750. Married Catherine, daughter of James Scott, February 18th, 1750. [*Edinb. Marr. Reg.*, 1701–50.] Probably a journeyman.

CATANACH (JOHN), printer in Edinburgh, *c.* 1728–35. Printed Alexander Bruce's *An Explication of the xxxix Chapter of the Statutes of King William*, Edinburgh, 1728. Entered in the Edinburgh Guild Register as a printer, by right of ... Watson, his spouse, daughter of James Watson, printer, August 5th, 1730. His will was registered April 25th, 1735. [Scot. Rec. Soc., *Edinb. Test.*]

CAVERHILL (T.), (?) bookseller in Jedburgh, 1747. Sold copies of Rev. Ralph Erskine's *Sermon preached immediately before the Administration of the Sacrament of the Lord's Supper, at Dunfermline, July 19, 1747*. Glasgow: "Printed for J. Newlands ... 1747."

CAW (ALEXANDER), bookbinder in Edinburgh, 1776–84. In New North Kirk Parish. He was twice married, first to Helen, daughter of Andrew Hendrie, miller at Buchanty, Perthshire, December 29th, 1776; and afterwards to Elizabeth, daughter of David Watt, miller at Stockbridge, May 29th, 1784. [*Edinb. Marr. Reg.*, 1751–1800.] He was probably in partnership with John Caw (*q.v.*) who may have been a brother.

CAW (JOHN), bookseller and bookbinder in Edinburgh. In New North Kirk Parish, 1779. Married Cecilia, daughter of John Finney, sometime miller at the Water of Leith, April 21st, 1779 [*Edinb. Marr. Reg.*, 1751–1800]. *See* Caw (Alexander).

CHALMERS (JAMES) 1st, printer, publisher and bookseller in Aberdeen, 1736–64. Son of the Rev. James Chalmers, Professor of Divinity in Marischal College, Aberdeen. In 1736 he succeeded James Nicol (*see Dictionary*, 1668–1725), and became printer to the town and university. He commenced printing and publishing the *Aberdeen Journal or North British Magazine* in 1746. This is said to have been the first periodical in the ordinary sense of the term issued north of the Forth. The *Journal* was discontinued after the first number, however. The explanation seems to be that Chalmers held the position of Assistant Commissioner to the Royal Army and was obliged to attend to business for a considerable time in Inverness, and was thus prevented from continuing the *Journal*. After some two years he returned to Aberdeen and resumed its publication. [Grant, *Newspaper Press*, v. 3, p. 521.] He is said to have suffered considerably for his attachment to the House of Hanover. In 1751 he printed *The Works of the Rev. Benjamin Whichcote, D.D.*, in 4 vols.; and in 1762 an octavo ed. of Buchanan's *History*. He was the father of several children including George, one of the most voluminous writers of his time, and James, who succeeded to the business on his death in 1764.

CHALMERS (JAMES), 2nd, printer in Aberdeen, 1764–1810. Born in March 1742. Succeeded his father, James Chalmers, 1st (*q.v.*). Educated at Marischal College, Aberdeen. Worked as a printer in London and Cambridge in his youth in order to gain experience. He is said to have worked for Watts in London and to have had Benjamin Franklin as a fellow-workman. Under him the firm was known as J. Chalmers & Co. In 1769 he married Margaret, youngest daughter of David Douglas of London. By her he had four sons and six daughters. One of his daughters, Catherine, became the wife of William Brown, bookseller in Aberdeen, on February 17th, 1795. [*Brown's Bookstalls*, v. 1, p. 35.] He introduced the large and important addition of national and local public lists in the *Aberdeen Almanac* in 1771. He was the printer of many

Chap-books, most of which have become rare. He died June 17th, 1810. [Timperley; *Scot. N. & Q.*, v. 1, p. 4; &c.]

CHALMERS (WILLIAM), journeyman printer in Edinburgh, 1747. In South Kirk Parish. Married Margaret, daughter of James Chalmers, Minister at Elie and afterwards in S.E. Parish, May 24th, 1747. [*Edinb. Marr. Reg.*, 1701–50.]

CHEYNE (ALEXANDER), bookseller in Aberdeen, 1764. In partnership with George Fowler at that date.

CHEYNE, CHYNE (WILLIAM), printer in Edinburgh, 1731–50 (?). Foot of Craig's Close, opposite to the Cross, 1734. Printer, by right of John Chyne, Chirurgeon, his father, November 24th, 1731. [*Edinb. Guild Reg.*] The earliest book printed by him which has been noticed is an edition of Forbes (Patrick) and Love (Christopher) *The Fort Royal of the Scriptures* . . . Edinburgh, 1732. In 1734 he commenced to print and publish *The Thistle*, No. 1 of which bears the date February 13th, 1734. This weekly publication was continued for two years, the last number being issued on February 11th, 1736. Two years later, in January, 1738 he printed the first number of *Letters of the Critical Club*, which was "sold by A. Martin and other booksellers in town". This journal appears to have come to an end in six months. [Couper, *Edinb. Period. Press.*] He was still printing in 1749, in which year the following books appeared from his press: Alexander Bayne's *Notes for Students of Municipal law;* and *Collection of the Laws in favour of the Reformation in Scotland.* The first was sold by Gideon Crawfurd (*q.v.*) and the second printed for A. Stevenson (*q.v.*).

CHRISTIE (WILLIAM), bookbinder in Edinburgh. Back-stairs, 1773–4. His name appears in the *Edinburgh Directory*, 177¾. He was probably a relative (possibly father) of the Alexander Christie, bookbinder, who married Margrete Manson, June 20th, 1786. [*Canongate Marr. Reg.*, 1564–1800.]

CLARK or CLERK (ROBERT), bookseller, bookbinder, publisher, in Edinburgh, 1738–1810. Son of John Clark, printer, and said to have been descended from Alexander Clerke, Lord Provost of Edinburgh at the commencement of the seventeenth century. He was born in 1738 and at about seventeen years of age married Barbara, daughter of John Williamson, farmer at Bellside, near Linlithgow. Apparently before his marriage he served his apprenticeship as bookseller and probably as printer, perhaps with his father. It is believed that through his marriage he obtained sufficient money to set up as a bookseller on

his own account. He succeeded in establishing a good business and also employed a good many bookbinders. As a publisher he also did well, publishing amongst other works, *The Builder's Jewel*, a book of considerable importance in its day. About 1765 he purchased a house in the Cowgate, "Kincaid's Land", where he resided for some years. In 1782 he bought a property at Newhaven, known from its size as "The Whale". In 1800, having sold his stock, and "The Whale" being without a tenant, he let his Edinburgh house and retired to Newhaven. He died in 1810, at the age of seventy-two, and was buried in the Grayfriar's Churchyard. Of his eight sons, six died in infancy. Robert, the eldest, died in 1786, and Alexander, the only remaining son, was a solicitor in Edinburgh. [Timperley, pp. 837–8; Kay's *Portraits*, 2, p. 29.]

CLEGHORN (WILLIAM), bookbinder in Edinburgh. In North West Kirk Parish, 1755. In Old Church Parish, 1777. Married Barbara Weir, daughter of John Weir, sometime weaver in Toryburn, November 16th, 1755. Their daughter Barbara became the wife of Alexander Brown, bookseller, April 13th, 1777. [*Edin. Marr. Reg.*, 1751–1800.]

CLERK, *see also* Clark.

CLERK (WILLIAM), bookbinder in Edinburgh. In New North Kirk Parish, 1774. Married Isobel, daughter of John Drummond, gentleman's servant at Lasswade, September 11th, 1774. [*Edinb. Marr. Reg.*, 1751–1800.]

COCHRAN (JAMES), printer in Edinburgh, 1739–85. Entered in the Edinburgh Guild Register as a printer, by right of William Cochran, writer, father, March 21st, 1739. The imprint to the *Scots Magazine*, 1740–2 reads: "Printed by Sands, Brymer, Murray and Cochran". In 1743 it was printed by James Cochran and Company. From 1744 onwards the imprint became "Printed by W. Sands, A. Murray, and J. Cochran". He married Margaret, younger daughter of Patrick Robertson, sometime factor to Emilia, Lady Dowager of Lovat, May 26th, 1745. [*Edinb. Marr. Reg.*, 1701–50.] His will was registered May 26th, 1785. [Scot. Rec. Soc., *Edinb. Test.*]

COKE (WILLIAM), bookseller and stationer in Leith, 1764–1819. On the shore. Commenced business as a bookseller in 1764, but his stock, consisting principally of minor publications and common articles of stationery, was not very extensive. By perseverance and economy his trade gradually increased, although it is somewhat doubtful if he ever attained to easy circumstances. He was a most indefatigable person, however, for he sometimes travelled to Edinburgh three or four times in one day for the purpose of supplying the

orders of his customers, and he would have performed the journey to obtain a sixpenny pamphlet. A calculation was made from his own information respecting these journeys and it was found that he had walked a distance equal to more than twice the circumference of the world. David Ramsay, who published the *Courant*, used to compare him to a squirrel in a cage, always endeavouring to get to the top. He was a ready-money dealer and whatever he purchased was paid for in cash and carried away with him at once. His temper is said to have been a rather irritable one. A son went to sea and was never heard of again, but three of his daughters long survived him. His death took place on May 18th, 1819, when he was over eighty years of age. It was noticed in the journals of the day thus: "At Leith, on the 18th May, Mr. William Coke, bookseller, who carried on business, in the same premises, for the long period of fifty-five years, and was the father of the bookselling profession of Scotland." According to the *Edinburgh Directory* for 177¾ he was a constable of Leith in 1773. [Timperley, p. 870; Kay's *Portraits*, v. 2, pp. 30–1.]

COLLINS (EDWARD), paper-maker at Dalmuir, *c.* 1775. Supplied paper to Andrew Foulis the younger. [Murray, *Foulis Press.*]

COLQUHOUN (JAMES), junior, printer in Edinburgh, 1744–5. In South-West Kirk Parish. Probably the son of an elder James Colquhoun whose daughter in 1723 married a William Paris. Married Janet, daughter of John Tait, shoemaker in Kirkbraehead, November 4th, 1744. Another printer of the same name married Sarah, daughter of William Simpson, indweller in South Leith, May 19th, 1745. [*Edinb. Marr. Reg.*, 1701–50.]

COLVILLE (THOMAS), printer and publisher in Dundee, *c.* 1770–1819. In 1775 succeeded to the business of Henry Galbraith & Co. (*q.v.*), and commenced publishing *The Edinburgh Weekly Amusement.* In 1783 he published the first *Dundee Register and Directory.* Ten years later Dr. Small's *Statistical Account of town and parish* appeared from his press. About 1796 he commenced *The Dundee Repository*, a monthly publication which ran the length of two volumes, and in January 1799 he published *The Dundee Magazine and Journal of the Times.* This was also a monthly publication. From January 8th, 1802, until May 24th, 1805, he printed *The Dundee Weekly Advertiser and Angus Intelligencer*, the first number of which actually appeared on January 16th, 1801. After severing his connexion with this paper he started a rival one, *The Dundee Mercury*, which was published weekly on Wednesdays, but about 1813 this failed. In partnership with his son Alexander, as Thomas Colville & Co., he endeavoured to establish a monthly periodical *The Dundee Magazine* in 1816, but again met with failure, for the magazine lasted one year only. He died on August 22nd, 1819. [*Dundee Magazine*, December, 1800; *Scot. N. & Q.*, v. 3, p. 98; &c.]

COMB (JOHN), bookbinder in Edinburgh, 1772. In Tron Parish. Married Margaret, daughter of William Drysdale, brewer in Alloa, November 15th, 1772. [*Edinb. Marr. Reg.*, 1751–1800.]

COOK (JOHN), corrector of Ruddiman's press in 1737. [Chalmers' *Life of Ruddiman*, 1794, p. 450.]

COOK (WILLIAM), journeyman bookbinder in Edinburgh, 1758. In Tron Parish. Married Anne Blair, relict of James Ratrey, writer in Perth, December 10th, 1758. [*Edinb. Marr. Reg.*, 1751–1800.] Probably father of the later binder of the same name, who married Elizabeth Whitlaw, August 25th, 1790. [*Ib.* 1751–1800.]

COOPER (R.), printer in Edinburgh, 1734. The imprint to William McGibbon's *Six Sonatas for two German Flutes*, reads: "Edinburgh: Printed by R. Cooper for the Author, 1734".

COPLAND (JAMES), journeyman bookbinder in Edinburgh, 1773. In Old Kirk Parish. Married Janet, daughter of James Hook, April 18th, 1773. [*Edinb. Marr. Reg.*, 1751–1800.]

COWAN (LAWRENCE), printer in Edinburgh, 1747–65. In South Kirk Parish, 1747–53. Old Kirk Parish, 1765. Was three times married. Married (1) Elizabeth Frogg, February 8th, 1747; (2) Margaret Anderson, June 17th, 1753; (3) Margaret Myles, April 14th, 1765. [*Edinb. Marr. Reg.*, 1701–50; 1751–1800] No book bearing his name in the imprint has been noticed.

CRAWFORD (WILLIAM), bookbinder in Edinburgh, 1744. Mentioned in the list of subscribers to John Welch's *Miscellany Sermons . . .*, Edinburgh, R. Drummond & Co., 1744.

CRAWFURD (GIDEON), bookbinder and bookseller in Edinburgh, 1720–49 (?). Parliament Close, 1738–49. Bookbinder, March 10th, 1725; bookseller, June 1st, 1737. [*Edinburgh Guild Register.*] Married (1) Christian, daughter of John Ramsay, shipmaster in Kirkcaldy, June 30th, 1720; (2) Christian, daughter of Thomas Henderson, farmer in Dundas, September 21st, 1735. [*Edinb. Marr. Reg.*, 1701–50.] Subscribed to John Welch's *Miscellany Sermons . . .* 1744.

Sold copies of Alexander Bayne's *Notes for Students of municipal law*, Edinb., Wm. Cheyne, 1749.

CREECH (WILLIAM), bookseller and publisher in Edinburgh, 1745–1815. Born at Newbattle, April 21st, 1745. Son of the Revd. William Creech. Educated at Edinburgh University. He was originally intended for the medical profession, but his tastes led him to become an apprentice to Alexander Kincaid (*q.v.*), who had previously befriended his mother, and who was then in partnership with John Bell (*q.v.*). On his mother's death in 1764, Creech went to live with Kincaid, and he remained with the firm of Kincaid and Bell until 1766. In that year he went to London to obtain wider experience. With the same object in view he spent most of the following year in Paris and Holland. About the beginning of 1768 he returned to Edinburgh but did not settle down for long, and in 1770 made an extensive tour of the continent in company with Lord Kilmaurs, the eldest son of the Earl of Glencairn. On his return in the following year he was taken into partnership by Kincaid, the firm of Kincaid and Bell having been dissolved in May 1771. The Company of Kincaid and Creech was only a bookselling firm, for Kincaid retained his private rights as King's printer. The firm lasted until May 1773, when Kincaid, whose activities as printer and magistrate seem all along to have made his partnership more or less a nominal one only, withdrew from the business, which was afterwards carried on by Creech alone for over forty years. Creech was thus fortunate in becoming sole owner of a business which already had a long established reputation. The shop itself was situated at the top of the High Street, commanding a view of the Bay of Musselburgh. Kincaid had succeeded to it after it had been established as a bookseller's shop by James McEuen (*see Dictionary*, 1668–1725). Allan Ramsay at one time occupied the premises above the shop for his circulating library. For over a hundred years this famous shop was the resort of the most distinguished literary characters in Scotland; a picture of it is given in Creech's *Fugitive Pieces*. Firmly established as a bookseller, Creech turned his attention to publishing. He became the original publisher of the works of Dr. Blair, Dr. Beattie, Dr. Geo. Campbell, Dr. Cullen, Dr. Gregory, Mackenzie, Adam Ferguson, Dugald Stewart and many other famous men. His connexion with Robert Burns is well known. Of periodicals he published *The Mirror* and *The Lounger*, the former from January 23rd, 1779 to May 27th, 1781, and the latter from February 5th, 1785 to January 6th, 1787. He was one of the founders of the Speculative Society of Edinburgh in 1764. At

various times he was a town councillor and he filled the office of Lord Provost from 1811–13. He was one of the founders of the Society of Booksellers of Edinburgh and Leith, and he took an active part in the formation of the Chamber of Commerce. At the time of his death he was Praeses of the Committee of the Society for Propagating Christian Knowledge in Scotland. His death took place in his 70th year, on January 14th, 1815. [*D.N.B.*, Kay's *Portraits*; Creech's *Fugitive Pieces*; &c.]

CRICHTON (ALEXANDER), 1st, printer in Edinburgh, 1754. Probably a journeyman. Married Margaret Jack, October 20th, 1754. [*Edinb. Marr. Reg.*, 1751–1800.] May have been the father of the next.

CRICHTON (ALEXANDER), 2nd, printer in Edinburgh, 1784. In Old Kirk Parish. Probably a journeyman. Married Helen, daughter of David Ross, December 25th, 1784. [*Edinb. Marr. Reg.*, 1751–1800.] *See under* Alexander Crichton, 1st.

CRICHTON (JAMES), running stationer in Edinburgh, 1752. In South-East Kirk Parish. Married Mary, daughter of John Denholm, wright, April 19th, 1752. [*Edinb. Marr. Reg.*, 1751–1800.]

DALLAS or DOLLAS (MARMADUKE), printer in Edinburgh, 1713–60 (?). In South-East Kirk Parish. Probably a son of Marmaduke Dallas, litster and Burgess, and Janet Dallas, who were married on November 25th, 1712. [*Edinb. Marr. Reg.*, 1701–50.] Married Elizabeth Veitch, December 12th, 1736, [*Ib.*]. Died before November 26th, 1769, on which date his daughter Elizabeth married Robert Kinloch, glover. [*Ib.*, 1751–1800.]

DARLING (WILLIAM), printer and bookseller in Edinburgh, 1767–82. In New North Kirk Parish, 1767; Old Grayfriar's Parish, 1773; Bridge Street, 1773–4; Tolbooth Parish, 1782. Married three times: (1) Elizabeth Goodsman, June 7th, 1767; (2) Ann Ross, January 31st, 1773; (3) Patricia Rolland, December 7th, 1782. [*Edinb. Marr. Reg.*, 1751–1800.] His name appears as a bookseller in the *Edinburgh Directory*, 177¾ (*Suppt.*).

DAVIDSON (ALEXANDER), bookseller in Edinburgh, 1720–34. In the Parliament-house, 1734. In North Kirk parish, 1730. His name occurs in the imprint to Spotiswood's *Practical observations upon divers titles of the law of Scotland . . .* "Edinburgh, Printed and sold by A. Davidson" . . ., and other booksellers in town, 1734. Bookseller and prentice to George Stewart, bookseller (*see Dictionary*, 1668–1725), September 7th, 1720. [*Edinb. Guild Reg.*] Married

Elizabeth Forbes, daughter of Robert Forbes of Waterfoull, June 7th, 1730. [*Edinb. Marr. Reg.*, 1701–50.]

DAVIDSON (ALEXANDER), printer in Inverness, 1774–85 (?). In 1774 he printed an ed. of Macfarlane's Gaelic version of *The Psalms*. At this time he seems to have worked in partnership with the bookseller William Sharp (*q.v.*). He also printed an ed. of *The Shorter Catechism* in Gaelic, in 1778; and an ed. of Ronald Macdonald's *Collection of Poems*, Edinburgh, 1782, bears his name in the imprint, so that presumably he was also a bookseller.

DAVIDSON (JAMES), printer and bookseller in Edinburgh, 1719–64. Bookseller, July 22nd, 1719. [*Edinb. Guild Reg.*] Married (1) Janet, daughter of John Lithgow, Minister at Swinton, September 12th, 1718; (2) Elizabeth, daughter of John Brown, merchant, November 22nd, 1721. [*Edinb. Marr. Reg.*, 1701–50.] Member of the Society of Improvers in the knowledge of Agriculture in Scotland, 1743. *See Dictionary*, 1668–1725.

DAVIE (PATRICK), bookbinder in Glasgow, 1741. Burgess and Guild Brother as serving apprenticeship with John Brown, bookbinder, May 20th, 1741, gratis. [Scot. Rec. Soc., *Burgesses and G. B. of Glasgow*, 1573–1750.]

DEANS (HUGH), bookseller in Edinburgh. Prentice to William Brown [*see Dictionary*, 1668–1725], bookseller, May 4th, 1726. [*Edinb. Guild Reg.*] No book bearing his name in the imprint has been found.

DECHMAN (JAMES), merchant in Glasgow, 1738. One of a number of merchants who, in 1738, sold copies of Isaac Ambrose's *War with devils*, Glasgow—College. . . . Printed for Archibald Ingram (&c.).

DEWAR, MRS. (ELIZABETH), compositor, *c.* 1760. Daughter of Robert Foulis (*q.v.*). Trained as a compositor in the printing office. Married Robert Dewar. [Murray, *R. & A. Foulis.*]

DICK (ANDREW), printer in Edinburgh, *c.* 1726. His will was registered on December 11th, 1727. [Scot. Rec. Soc., *Edinb. Test.*] His name has not been noticed in the imprint to any book.

DICKIE (WILLIAM), bookseller in Edinburgh, *c.* 1712–40. Burgess. Married Janet Dundas, daughter of John Dundas, merchant, burgess, November 1st, 1713. He was dead before January 11th, 1741, on which date his daughter, Grizel, married John Chalmers, writer. [*Edinb. Marr. Reg.*, 1701–50.] May be identical with the Glasgow bookseller of the same name, 1695–7. [*Dictionary*, 1668–1725.]

DICKSON (JAMES), bookseller, stationer and publisher in Edinburgh, 1765–1800. West side of the front of the Royal Exchange entry, 1773. Commenced business as a bookseller in 1765, after being preceptor to the family of James Kerr of Boughtrigg, a jeweller who represented Edinburgh in Parliament from 1747–54. In 1772 (Dec. 27th), he married Margaret, daughter of Charles Greig of Burntisland and sister of Admiral Sir Samuel Greig. He was elected a member of the Town Council as Kirk Treasurer in 1774 and until 1786 his name repeatedly occurs in the lists of magistrates and Town Council, and also in the Annals of the Chamber of Commerce. He was a town constable in 1773. In 1773 he was in partnership with Charles Elliot (*q.v.*) Their joint imprint occurs on the title page of Walter Steuart's *Collections and Observations Concerning the Worship . . . of the Church of Scotland*, Edinb. 1773. The partnership seems only to have been of short duration, however, and cannot have lasted later than 1776. His name occurs until 1794 in the imprints to many books, of some of which he seems to have been the publisher. He died at Stockbridge on July 8th, 1800.

DOBIE (JOHN), running stationer in Edinburgh, 1740–2 (?). In North-West Kirk Parish, 1740. Married Margaret, daughter of James Main, October 26th, 1740. He must have died before November 20th, 1743 as his widow, Margaret Main, married George Nairn (*q.v.*) running stationer, on that date. [*Edinb. Marr. Reg.*, 1701–50.]

DON (JOHN), printer in Edinburgh, 1768. In New North Kirk Parish, 1768. Probably a journeyman. Married Margaret, daughter of deceased Robert Forbes, merchant in Frazersburgh, August 28th, 1768. [*Edinb. Marr. Reg.*, 1751–1800.]

DONALDSON (ALEXANDER), printer and bookseller in Edinburgh and London, 1750–94. Became a bookseller in Edinburgh in 1750. Son of James Donaldson, weaver. Entered in the Edinburgh Guild Register as a Burgess and Guild Brother, by right of his father, August 29th, 1750. Married Anna, daughter of Andrew Marshall, merchant, January 10th, 1751. His grandfather was Captain James Donaldson, merchant and publisher in Edinburgh (1663–1719) who from 1699 to 1705 published the second *Edinburgh Gazette*. He removed to London in 1763 (*See* English Section, p. 78). In 1764 he established the *Edinburgh Advertiser*, acting as editor and publisher until December 31st, 1773. He retired from London shortly before 1789, and subsequently resided at Broughton Hall, a property he had acquired on June 3rd, 1786. His death

took place in Edinburgh on March 11th, 1794, and he was buried in Grayfriar's Churchyard. An account of his relations with Dr. Johnson and of his publications is given in R. T. Skinner's *A Notable Family of Scots Printers*, 1928. His shop in London was situated in the Strand, two doors east from Norfolk Street. The printing house in Edinburgh was in the Castle Hill, and the shop was on the South side of the High Street, opposite the Mercat Cross. His sign was the Pope's Head.

DONALDSON (JAMES), printer, bookseller and publisher in Edinburgh, 1751–1830. Founder of the Donaldson Hospital. Born in the West Bow, Edinburgh, on December 10th, 1751. Succeeded his father, Alexander Donaldson (*q.v.*) as editor of the *Edinburgh Advertiser* in January 1774. Made a Burgess and Guild Brother, February 21st, 1782. Married Jean, daughter of Dr. Thomas Gillespie, physician, September 29th, 1792. Director of the Chamber of Commerce from 1790 almost continuously to 1819. A manager of the Public Dispensatory from 1799 to 1818. Elected a director of the Bank of Scotland in 1807. His town residence was at 85, Princes Street. Died at Broughton Hall on October 19th, 1830. By his will he left to six trustees the sum of £240,000 for the purpose of endowing a hospital for boys and girls, to be called "Donaldson's Hospital". Donaldson's printing-office occupied almost the whole of what was called the Stripping Close, Castle Hill. His foreman for thirty-four years was James Macaulay, and his journeymen were George Robertson, James Lamb, Robert Lamb, and John Bryce. The pressmen were James Thomson and Joseph Thomson. William Begg, Robert Miller, James Thomson and James Campbell served as apprentices in the case department. For nearly half a century Henry Elder acted as publisher of the *Advertiser*. The last issue of the *Advertiser* bearing Donaldson's name is dated March 7th, 1820. The issue for March 10th was "Printed and published by Claud Muirhead". [Skinner, *A Notable Family of Scots Printers*, 1928.]

DONALDSON (JAMES), bookbinder in Edinburgh, 1753. In North-West Kirk Parish. Not to be confused with James Donaldson, founder of the Donaldson Hospital, though it is possible that he was connected with the famous family. On January 7th, 1753 he married Jean, daughter of the deceased Andrew Ritchie, schoolmaster at Aberdour. [*Edinb. Marr. Reg.*, 1751–1800.]

DONALDSON (JOHN), manufacturer in Edinburgh and bookseller in London, *c.* 1730–80 (?). Corner of Arundel street, Strand. Grandson of Captain James Donaldson publisher of the second *Edinburgh Gazette*, and son of James

Donaldson, linen manufacturer. Described as "Manufacturer at Drumsheugh near Edinburgh, son to the defunct (Treasurer James Donaldson), only executor dative qua nearest in kin". In partnership with his brother Alexander (*q.v.*) in a bookselling business in London. This partnership was dissolved on June 24th, 1773, Alexander removing to 48 St. Paul's Churchyard, and John remaining at Arundel Street. On December 24th, of that year John advertised that he never intended to remove, nor had he "any concern in any other shop". [Skinner, *A Notable Family of Scots Printers*, 1928.]

DOUGLAS (FRANCIS), printer, publisher and bookseller in Aberdeen, 1748–69. End of the Broadgate, 1759–60. With William Murray set up a printing and publishing business in 1750. Previously a bookseller only. They printed jointly in 1755, *Letter to the Author of the Edinburgh Review . . . Rebellion of 1745*. From October 3rd, 1752 until February 22nd, 1757 they published *The Aberdeen Intelligencer*, but after the latter date it was incorporated in its more successful rival *The Aberdeen Journal*. From about 1759 Douglas seems to have printed alone. In 1760 he printed *A Dissertation on the chief obstacles to the improvement of land*. In 1761 he commenced *The Aberdeen Magazine*: "each number consists of 56 pp. and contains a good deal of interesting local gossip. It is the first magazine which appeared from the local press". [*Scot. N. & Q.*, v. 1, pp. 4–5.] In 1768 he printed Alexander Ross's *The Fortunate Shepherdess, a pastoral tale*. Succeeded by John Boyle (*q.v.*).

DOUGLAS (ROBERT), stationer in Edinburgh. In Old Kirk Parish, 1765. Married Isobel, daughter of James Ker, merchant, November 3rd, 1765. [*Edinb. Marr. Reg.*, 1751–1800.]

DRUMMOND (ALEXANDER), printer in Edinburgh, 1775. In Lady Yester's Parish. Married Janet Tulloch, widow of David Tylor, shopkeeper, May 7th, 1775. [*Edinb. Marr. Reg.*, 1751–1800.]

DRUMMOND (GAVIN), bookseller in Edinburgh, 1728–48. Son of Gavin Drummond of Ochterarder. Entered in the *Edinburgh Guild Register* as a bookseller, August 21st, 1728. Married Lilias, daughter of James Dunning, in Corrievechter, June 2nd, 1731. [*Edinb. Marr. Reg.*, 1701–50.] Sold copies of *Select Trans. Soc. Agric. Scotland* . . . 1743. His will was registered October 28th, and November 18th, 1748. [Scot. Rec. Soc., *Edinb. Test.*]

DRUMMOND (JOHN), bookbinder in Edinburgh, 1749. His daughter Anna married John Christie, June 4th, 1749. [*Edinb. Marr. Reg.*, 1701–50.]

DRUMMOND (R.), printer in Edinburgh, 1743–4 (?) In the Swan-close, 1744. Printed as R. Drummond (or Drumnond) and company. Married Margaret, daughter of John Hepburn, merchant in Prestonpans, November 6th, 1743. [*Edinb. Marr. Reg.*, 1701–50.] The following books, issued in 1744, bear his imprint: *A Collection of Farewell Sermons*; Renwick and Shield's *Informatory vindication of a poor, wasted, misrepresented remnant*, (reprinted); and John Welch's *Miscellany Sermons*.

DRUMMOND (WILLIAM), *of Callander*, bookseller in Edinburgh, 1733–76. Entered in the *Edinburgh Guild Register* as a bookseller, May 27th, 1733. His will was registered, July 4th, 1776. He is not to be confused with the printer of the same name (*q.v.*).

DRUMMOND (WILLIAM), printer and bookseller in Edinburgh, 1744–74 (?). Printer of an edition of Shield's *A Hind let loose* . . . Edinburgh, 1744. His address in 177¾ is given in the *Edinburgh Directory* as "At the Cross".

DUNBAR (ALEXANDER), running stationer in Edinburgh. In Old Kirk Parish, 1763. Married Elizabeth, daughter of John Gibson, wright, October 30th, 1763. [*Edinb. Marr. Reg.*, 1751–1800.] This must have been a second marriage, for on March 20th, 1763 his daughter Janet married Thomas Weston, running stationer. [*Ib.*]

DUNCAN (   ), printer in Edinburgh, 1735. In partnership with . . . Webster. Their joint imprint appears on Mrs. Ross's *Memoirs of Spiritual exercises written with her own hand*, Edinburgh, 1735.

DUNCAN (DAVID), bookseller in Edinburgh, 1731–42. Near the foot of the West-Bow, 1731–3. Grass-Market, 1742. Sold copies of Ebenezer Erskine's *Rainbow of the Covenant* . . . 1731; Erskine's *A Sermon* . . . 1733; and John Currie's *A Sermon preached in the Church of Kirkaldie* . . . 1733. Bookseller in Edinburgh, 1739. [*N. & Q.* 10 Ser. vol. 5, p. 242.] Erskine's *Christ the Resurrection* . . . Edinburgh, 1740, was printed for David Duncan and James Beugo in Dunfermline, by A. Alison (*q.v.*). Published Rev. Ralph Erskine's *Redemption by Christ, shewn to be of God*. . . . Edinburgh, 1742, in the imprint to which his address is given. "House in the Grass-Market, opposite to the Corn-Market, South Side of the Street, the second Door up the Timber-ravel'd Fore-Stair."

DUNCAN (DAVID), printer in Glasgow, 1743.

DUNCAN (JAMES), senior, printer in Glasgow, 1717–*c.* 1754. In 1754 he printed Wedderburne's *Heaven upon earth, or history of the Transfiguration of Jesus Christ*; and Livingstone's *Brief historical relation of his life at Killinchie, Ireland, 1630 . . . See Dictionary*, 1668–1725, where dates are given as 1717–*c.* 1750.

DUNCAN (JAMES), junior, printer and bookseller in Glasgow, *c.* 1769–1802. Saltmarket. In 1770 he printed an ed. of *Translations and Paraphrases of several passages of Sacred Scripture. . . .* From that date onwards his name is found in the imprints to many books. With Robert Chapman he was appointed Factor to the creditors of R. & A. Foulis in 1776. [Murray, *R. & A. Foulis*, p. 117.] In 1784 Andrew Foulis the younger was ordered to pay for the printing utensils of the firm of Foulis, the price of them as estimated by James Robertson and James Duncan, printers in Glasgow. [*Ib.*, p. 119.] Amongst the assets of R. & A. Foulis was "the Library of Books which belonged to Dr. James Moor . . . as valued by James Duncan and Robert Chapman at £102 sterling". [*Ib.*, p. 127.] His name occurs in the imprint to a Gaelic ed. of Alex. Macdonald's *Poems and Songs*. [Reid, *Glasgow Past and Present*, v. 2, p. 181.]

DUNCAN (JOHN), bookbinder in Edinburgh. In New Grayfriar's Parish, 1773. Married Barbara, daughter of deceased William Herriot (*q.v.*), bookbinder, February 14th, 1773. [*Edinb. Marr. Reg.*, 1751–1800.]

DUNCAN (WILLIAM), printer in Glasgow, 1717–65. His will was registered September 20th, 1765. [Comm. Rec. Glasgow; *Reg. Test.*, 1547–1800.] The bookbinder who was admitted Burgess on July 29th, 1718 and Guild Brother (by purchase) on October 5th, 1747, may be identical with this printer. [Scot. Rec. Soc., *Burgesses and G. B. of Glasgow*, 1547–1750.] *See also Dictionary*, 1668–1725.

DUNCAN (WILLIAM), bookbinder at Crosscauseway. Before 1770. His will was registered June 14th, 1770. [Scot. Rec. Soc., *Edinb. Test.*]

DUNDAS (WILLIAM), bookbinder in Edinburgh. In South-South-West Kirk Parish, 1748. Married Ann Hay, daughter of John Hay, merchant, November 20th, 1748. His daughter Elizabeth married William Davidson, June 29th, 1797. William Dundas was then dead. [*Edinb. Marr. Reg.*, 1701–50; 1751–1800.]

DUNING, (?) DUNNING (ALEXANDER), bookseller in Edinburgh, 1726. Prentice to James Davidson (*see Dictionary*, 1668–1725), bookseller, November 16th, 1726. [*Edinb. Guild Reg.*] Probably a relative of Matthew Duning (*q.v.*).

DUNING, (?) DUNNING (MATTHEW), bookseller in Edinburgh, 1731. Entered in the *Edinburgh Guild Register* November 24th, 1731, as a bookseller. Probably a relative of Alexander Duning (*q.v.*).

ELLIOT (CHARLES), bookseller and publisher, Edinburgh and London, 1770–90. Parliament Close, Edinburgh, 1773–4. Parliament Square, Edinburgh, 1777. Strand, London, 1784–7. Sold the books printed by George Elliot, from about 1770–80, when he succeeded to the business of William Sands (*q.v.*), whose daughter, Christian, he had married on September 5th, 1780. [*Edinb. Marr. Reg.*, 1751–1800.] In 1773 he was in partnership with James Dickson (*q.v.*). He was the first Scottish publisher to buy copyrights, and made William Smellie an offer of 1,000 guineas for the copyright of his *Philosophy of Natural History*, plus fifty guineas for each subsequent edition, besides the employment of printing the work. He refused even to sell shares in copyrights, although that was the usual practice of the day. It was in his shop that James Sibbald (*q.v.*), served a kind of free apprenticeship in 1779, before setting up in business for himself in the following year. In or about 1784 he opened a shop in the Strand; the imprint to books published in 1787 reading "for C. Elliot, T. Kay & Co., No. 332, opposite Somerset House, Strand". He was the publisher of the ten-volume edition of the *Encyclopaedia Britannica*. In 1799, having come into possession of what remained of Allan Ramsay's Circulating Library, he made it known that at his rooms at the Cross magazines and reviews could be seen "including nearly one hundred newspapers weekly, some of which are carefully preserved, but the greater part is sold at low prices second hand". His will was registered on January 28th, 1790. In 1807 John Murray, then the most distinguished London publisher, married his sister. George Elliot, "bookseller in Kelso", for whom James Ford's *National Ingratitude* was printed at Edinburgh in 1777, may have been a connexion.

ELLIOT (WILLIAM), bookbinder in Edinburgh, 1770–1. In New North Kirk Parish. Married Janet Clerk, August 12th, 1770; May 5th, 1771. [*Edinb. Marr. Reg.*, 1751–1800.]

ELPHINSTONE (JAMES), publisher (?printer) in Edinburgh, *c.* 1750. Brother in-law of Strahan the printer. A friend of Samuel Johnson. He undertook to publish *The Rambler* in Edinburgh (as well as the London ed.). The Edinb. ed. of *The Rambler* bears the following imprint: "Edinburgh: printed for the author; and sold by William Gordon and C. Wright, at their shops in Parliament-close."

FAIRBAIRN (JOHN), bookbinder in Edinburgh, 1761. In Tolbooth Parish. Married Katherine, daughter of George Barklay, farmer in the Parish of Carnock, June 28th, 1761. [*Edinb. Marr. Reg.*, 1751–1800.]

FARIE (ROBERT), bookseller in Glasgow, *c.* 1770. He died on March 30th, 1800. [Nichols' *Lit. Anecd.* vol. 3, p. 691.]

FARQUHAR (ROBERT) 1st, bookseller in Aberdeen, 1692–1753. Died in 1753 at the age of 61, and is buried in St. Nicholas Churchyard, Aberdeen. He was succeeded in business by his nephew, Robert, some of whose family rose to distinction in the navy. Described as "quondam Bibliopola". [*Brown's Bookstall's*, vol. 1, p. 93.] His will was registered May 21st, 1753. [Comm. Rec. Aberd., *Reg. Test.*, 1715–1800.] Bookseller, Aberdeen [*see Scottish N. & Q.* v. 1, p. 134.] *See next entry*. Omitted from *Dictionary*, 1668–1725.

FARQUHAR (ROBERT) 2nd, bookseller in Aberdeen, 1753–62 (?). In the Castlegate. Succeeded his uncle, R.F. 1st (*q.v.*) in 1753. He is said to have been the first to hold a book auction in Aberdeen [*Brown's Bookstalls*, vol. 1.] Apparently he was also a printer. He issued a printed catalogue of a six nights' sale which commenced on November 8th, 1762. There were 840 lots in this sale and it is probable that it was held on his retirement from business.

FELL (ROBERT), printer in Edinburgh. In Old Kirk Parish, 1764. Married Margaret, daughter of Alexander Hutton, merchant, December 16th, 1764. [*Edinb. Marr. Reg.*, 1751–1800.] Probably a journeyman.

FERGUSON (ALEXANDER), printer in Edinburgh, 1745–8 (?). In North-East Parish. Married (1) Margaret May, May 10th, 1745; (2) Rosina Jamison, July 10th, 1748. [*Edinb. Marr. Reg.*, 1701–50.] Burgess of Edinburgh.

FINLAY (JOHN), wright in Glasgow, 1756. Shuttle Street. In 1756 an ed. of John Willison's *Fair and impartial testimony* was "printed for and sold by John Finlay, wright, at his house in Shuttle Street; and by Duncan Campbell, junior, gardner, at his house near the Gallowgate toll". [Murray, *Foulis Press*, p. 26.]

FITCH (ALEXANDER), journeyman bookbinder in Edinburgh. In Old Grayfriar's Parish, 1771–3. Married (1) Margaret, daughter of Robert Burns, November 3rd, 1771; (2) Isobel, daughter of Hugh Spence, December 12th, 1773. [*Edinb. Marr. Reg.*, 1751–1800.]

FLEMING (GEORGE), printer in Edinburgh, 1739. Entered in the *Edinburgh Guild Register* as a printer, August 8th, 1739. May have been a relative of Robert Fleming, the well-known Edinburgh printer. No book bearing his imprint has been found.

FLEMING (JOHN), *of Strathaven*, proof reader to Foulis Press, *c.* 1750–70. A relative of Professor William Fleming. Dr. Wodrow in his reminiscences of the Foulis Brothers records the "incessant and incredible attention and diligence" of John Fleming. [Murray, *Foulis Press*.]

FLEMING (ROBERT), printer in Edinburgh, 1719–79. In Pearson's Close, 1729–*c.* 1752. First stair below the Laigh Coffee House, opposite to the Cross, north side of the street, 1753–78. Old Fishmarket Close, 1779. Prentice to Andrew Simpson (i.e. Symson; *see Dictionary*, 1668–1725), December 9th, 1719 [*Edinb. Guild Reg.*] Married (1) Anne Brown, relict of Alexander Beg, September 3rd, 1758; (2) Elizabeth, daughter of George Weir of Kerse, September 29th, 1765. [*Edinb. Marr. Reg.*, 1751–1800.] From 1729–34 printed *The Echo, or Edinburgh Weekly Journal*. Printed the *Edinburgh Evening Courant*, 1732–79. For a long period he was one of the leading printers of Edinburgh, and during his career was associated at one time or another with several other eminent printers. Was at first bookseller and printer on his own account, but in 1741 had A. Alison as partner. In 1745 was printing in company with Alexander Kincaid. At various periods his imprint was simply "R. Fleming and Company," and in or about 1778 David Ramsay appears as his partner and successor as printer of the *Courant*. [Timperley, p. 699; Couper, *Edinb. Period. Press*, &c.] *See also Dictionary*, 1668–1725.

FORBES (DANIEL), running stationer in Edinburgh, 1766. In Tron Parish. Married Katherine, daughter of deceased George Dow, farmer in Gleneagles, March 2nd, 1766. [*Edinb. Marr. Reg.*, 1751–1800.]

FOREST (G.), (?) bookseller in Linton, 1747. Sold copies of Ralph Erskine's *Sermon preached immediately before the Administration of the Sacrament of the Lord's Supper, at Dunfermline, July 19, 1747*. "Glasgow: Printed for J. Newlands . . . 1747."

FORREST (THOMAS), printer in Edinburgh, 1774–7. In Old Grayfriar's Parish, 1774. Married Isabel, daughter of deceased Francis Thomson, February 27th, 1774. [*Edinb. Marr. Reg.*, 1751–1800.] He was a poet in addition to being a printer, and printed his own *Mirthful Songs* in Gaelic, 1777. This is a small 12mo. of which only three perfect copies are known. He may have been a son of Thomas Forrest, bookbinder.

FORREST (WILLIAM), printer in Edinburgh, 1767–74. In Old Grayfriar's Parish, 1767. Foot of West-bow, 1773–4. A printer whose address is found in the *Edinburgh Directory* for 177¾. His daughter Mary married Alexander Bolton, January 18th, 1767. [*Edinb. Marr. Reg.*, 1751–1800.]

FORSYTH (JAMES), bookbinder in Edinburgh, 1747–86 (?) Opposite Meal-market, 1773–4. Married Ann, daughter of Alexander Gray, gardener, September 9th, 1747. [*Edinb. Marr. Reg.*, 1701–50.] Was married again, to Jean Tait, December 18th, 1774. Had at least three daughters, (1) Isobell, who married John Brown, merchant, March 10th, 1778; (2) Anne, who married Charles Nasmyth, March 8th, 1782; (3) Marion, who married Thomas Neilson, merchant, December 22nd, 1786. [*Edinb. Marr. Reg.*, 1751–1800.] His name appears in the *Edinburgh Directory*, 177¾.

FOTHERINGHAM (JOHN), merchant and bookseller in Aberdeen, 1769. Netherkirkgate. An edition of Isaac Ambrose's *War with Devils* was printed at Aberdeen in 1769 " by George Johnston for John Fotheringham . . .".

FOULIS (ANDREW), printer and bookseller in Glasgow, *c.* 1746–75. In partnership with his brother Robert (*q.v.*). Died September 18th, 1775.

FOULIS (ELIZABETH). *See* Dewar, Mrs. Elizabeth.

FOULIS (ROBERT), printer and bookseller in Glasgow, 1741–76. In the College, 1741–7; High Street and Shuttle Street, 1747– (?). Born April 20th, 1707. Son of Andrew Faulls, maltman, and Marion Paterson. In 1720 he was apprenticed to a barber, in which trade he established himself in 1727. He remained at this business until 1738. In 1741 he established himself as a bookseller in premises within the College, where he was subsequently joined by his brother Andrew. Book auctions were held in the evenings. His first publication was an edition of Cicero, *De natura Deorum*, which appeared in 1741. In the following year he became a printer, and in that year issued several works including a Juvenal. He was appointed University Printer in 1743. Towards the end of 1746 or in 1747 his brother Andrew was taken into partnership and "henceforward they carried on the business of booksellers, literary auctioneers, and printers, under the style of Robert and Andrew Foulis". Most of the productions of the Foulis Press are very well known. The great Homer was produced in 1756 and 1758, and this was followed in 1759 by Thucydides. Herodotus appeared in 1761. The firm possessed a binder's shop and Robert personally supervised the binding of many of the volumes. Red morocco was commonly employed in binding. Robert Foulis died on June 2nd, 1776. His first wife was Elizabeth Moor, who died in 1750. A few years later he married Euphan Butcher, who died in 1774, leaving two children, Andrew, the younger, and Euphemia. On the death of Robert Foulis his son Andrew, who was then about twenty years of age, carried on the business, unaware that it was insolvent. Trustees were soon afterwards appointed to wind up the estate. From 1777 to 1781 Andrew was in partnership with James Spotiswoode of Glenfernat, a bookseller and paper-maker. In 1782 a fresh company was formed as Andrew Foulis & Company, the other partners being Alexander Tilloch, Hugh Anderson, and James Harvey. [Murray, *R. & A. Foulis*, 1913.]

FOWLER (GEORGE), bookseller in Aberdeen, 1764. In partnership with Alexander Cheyne at that date.

[FOX (PETER)]. *De Miraculis quae Pythagorae, Apollonio Thyanensi, Francisco Assisio, Dominico, & Ignatio Lojolae tribuuntur . . . Auctore Phileleuthero Helvetio* . . . Edinburgi typis Petri Foxi, 1755. This is a spurious imprint.

FREEBAIRN (ROBERT), printer and bookseller in Edinburgh. In 1740 he printed John Major's *Historia, editio nova* . . . This book is typographically interesting since the tailpiece on p. iii is an impression from the actual block used in 1608 by Thomas Finlayson, the Edinburgh printer, 132 years earlier. *See Dictionary*, 1668–1725.

FULTON (GEORGE), printer in Glasgow, Edinburgh, and Dumfries, 1752–1831. Born February 3rd, 1752. Served his apprenticeship to a printer in Glasgow and afterwards worked as a journeyman with . . . Willison in Edinburgh. He also worked as a printer at Dumfries. Compiled and published a *Pronouncing Dictionary*, which was used in almost all the schools in the kingdom. For over twenty years he was a teacher of English in Edinburgh. He retired to a villa called Summerfield, near Newhaven, about 1806. He was twice married, one of his wives (the other not traced) being Jacobina Tod, daughter of James Tod, a schoolmaster in Edinburgh. At his marriage on March 15th, 1772, he was still described as a printer. It is probable that he gave up printing about the year 1785. He died in his eightieth year, on September 1st, 1831. [Timperley, p. 918.]

GALBRAITH (HENRY), printer and publisher in Dundee and Edinburgh, *c.* 1750–75. About 1750 set up a printing office in Dundee as Henry Galbraith & Co. In 1755 commenced publishing the ***Dundee Weekly Intelligencer***, but its existence seems to have been brief. Printed and published in 1759 the *Theological Works of Isaac Ambrose*, in one folio volume, and about the same time Ostervald's *Bible*. He married Marion, daughter of Alex. Burton, May 30th, 1756. [*Edinb. Marr. Reg.*, 1751–1800.] Appears as a printer, Bull's Close, Edinburgh, in the *Edinburgh Directory* for 177¾. Thomas Colville succeeded to the Dundee business about 1775.

GALBRAITH (JOSEPH), printer in Glasgow, 1761. In partnership with Archibald M'Lean, with whom he printed the 6th ed. of James Durham's *Christ Crucified*, for James Wilken, merchant in Paisley, in 1761.

GARDINE or GARDEN (JAMES), printer in Edinburgh. Before 1773. Apparently in partnership with his son William (*q.v.*). His will was registered July 28th, 1773. [Scot. Rec. Soc., *Edinb. Test.*]

GARDINE or GARDEN (WILLIAM), printer in Edinburgh. Before 1773. Son of James Gardine, with whom he seems to have been in partnership. His will was registered on the same date as his father's. [Scot. Rec. Soc., *Edinb. Test.*]

GARDINER or GARDNER (GEORGE), printer in Edinburgh, 1754. In South West Kirk Parish. Married Ann Milln, relict of John M'Crabie (*q.v.*), printer, September 8th, 1754. [*Edinb. Marr. Reg.*, 1751–1800.] Probably a journeyman. No book bearing his imprint has been noted.

GED (JAMES), printer in Edinburgh, London, and Jamaica, *c.* 1740–9. Son of William Ged, *senior*. Apprenticed to a printer in Edinburgh. Helped his father to produce the famous *Sallust*. After the disappointments attending the non-success of his father's projects he gave up printing and engaged in the 1745 Rebellion as a captain in Perth's regiment. He was taken prisoner at Carlisle and condemned, but for his father's sake, and by Dr. Smith's interest with the Duke of Newcastle, he was pardoned. Afterwards he returned to the printing trade as a journeyman with James Bettenham (*see Dictionary*, 1668–1725), a printer in London, and later set up as a master printer himself. Being unsuccessful, he emigrated to Jamaica in 1748, where his younger brother William was already established as a printer. His tools and other belongings he left behind to be shipped by a false friend, who most ungenerously retained them for his own use. Ill fortune seems to have dogged the footsteps of himself and his father, and even in Jamaica he did not long enjoy success and comfort, for he died there in 1749. In spite of this, however, his name, with that of his father, was destined to live in the halls of fame.

GED (WILLIAM), senior, goldsmith and printer (stereotype). London and Edinburgh, *c.* 1680–1749. By 1725 Ged had begun plate-making. In 1727 he entered into a contract with a person who had a little capital, but who, on conversing with a printer, got so intimidated that at the end of two years he had only laid out £22. In 1729 Ged entered into a new contract with William Fenner, stationer, Thomas James, type-founder, and John James, architect. On April 23rd, 1731, these partners having applied to the University of Cambridge for the privilege of printing Bibles and Common Prayer Books, with blocks instead of single types, a lease was sealed to them on that date, but only two Prayer Books were finished, so that the attempt had to be given up. It appears that one of the partners was actually averse to the success of the plan and engaged such people for the work as he thought most likely to spoil it. A casual workman who had been engaged is said to have stated that both Bibles and Prayer Books had been printed, but that the compositors, when they corrected one fault, made purposely half a dozen others, and the pressmen, when the masters were absent, battered the letter in aid of the compositors. In consequence of these base proceedings the books were suppressed by authority and the plates sent to the king's printing-house and from thence to Caslon's foundry. After much ill usage Ged, who appears to have been a man of great honesty and simplicity, returned to Edinburgh. His friends were anxious that a specimen of his art should be published, and this was at last accomplished by subscription. His son James (*q.v.*), who had been apprenticed to a printer, with the knowledge and consent of his master, set up the formes during the night, after the other compositors had gone, for his father to cast the plates from. By this means the famous *Sallust* was printed in 1739. A second issue, the only difference being the date, was published in 1744. In 1742 appeared Henry Scougal's *Life of God in the Soul of Man*; Newcastle, printed and sold by John White, from plates made by William Ged, goldsmith in Edinburgh. He was the father of James Ged and William Ged, *junior*. He died October 19th, 1749. [Nichols, *Biogr. Memoirs of Wm. Ged*, 1781; *Biogr. Mems. of Wm. Ged*, Newcastle, 1819; Timperley, &c.]

GED (WILLIAM), junior, printer in Jamaica, 1748 (?)–67. Apprenticed in Scotland, probably Edinburgh. Son of Wm. Ged, senior and brother of James Ged. Established as a printer in Jamaica by the year 1748, when he was joined by his brother James. He died in 1767.

GEORGE (JAMES), bookbinder in Edinburgh. In New Kirk Parish, 1760.

Married Margaret, daughter of deceased James Watson, February 24th, 1760. [*Edinb. Marr. Reg.*, 1751–1800.]

GIBB (WILLIAM), bookseller in Edinburgh, 1773–4. Parliament House. His name is found in the *Edinburgh Directory* for 177$\frac{3}{4}$, but no books bearing his name have been noted.

GILCHRIST (PETER), running stationer in Edinburgh, 1745. Married Jane Paterson, widow of Thomas M'Corkendale, running stationer, February 17th, 1745. [*Edinb. Marr. Reg.*, 1701–50.]

GILMOUR (JOHN), bookbinder in Glasgow, 1749–73. Burgess and Guild Brother. Bookseller and merchant, prentice master of William Marshall (*q.v.*), May 25th, 1749. [Scot. Rec. Soc., *Burgesses and Guild Brothers of Glasgow*, 1573–1750.] His will (as that of a bookbinder) was registered September 13th, 1773. [Comm. Rec. Glasgow, *Reg. Test.*, 1547–1800.]

GLASS (ALEXANDER), printer in Edinburgh, *c.* 1743–6. South Niddry Street. Printed a broadside, *King Crispin*, for R. Martin, about 1745. [Lindsay Library: *Cat. Engl. Broadsides.*] He was twice married, first to Janet Paterson, servant to Alex. Jolly, writer, on October 30th, 1743. His second wife, whom he married on April 27th, 1746, was Margaret, daughter of William Neilson. [*Edinb. Marr. Reg.*, 1701–50.]

GLASS (THOMAS), bookseller in Dundee, *c.* 1750–1763. His will was registered April 11th, 1759, and February 17th, 1763. [Comm. Rec. Brechin.; *Reg. Test.*, 1576–1800.] Murray, Sands & Cochran, printers in Edinburgh, printed for him, in 1752, a neat little edition of Burnet's *Travels*, with very clear and beautiful types.

GLASSFORD (JOHN), merchant in Glasgow, *c.* 1720–83. A well-known Glasgow merchant, who traded largely abroad and who owned a fleet of ships. In 1738 he sold copies of Isaac Ambrose's *War with Devils*, but he was not a bookseller in the strict sense of the term.

GLEN (HUGH), printer in Edinburgh, 1746. In North-East Kirk Parish. Married Margaret, daughter of Andrew Beattie, sailor in Dunbar, May 11th, 1746. [*Edinb. Marr. Reg.*, 1701–50.]

GOODALL (JOHN), journeyman printer in Edinburgh, 1757. In Old Kirk Parish. Married Janet, daughter of deceased Adam Steel, October 9th, 1757. [*Edinb. Marr. Reg.*, 1751–1800.]

GORDON (ALEXANDER), bookbinder in Aberdeen, before 1742. The will of his widow, Isobell Largoe, was registered October 15th, 1742. [Comm. Rec. Aberdeen, *Reg. Test.*, 1715–1800.]

GORDON (G.), bookseller in Edinburgh, 1763. Parliament Square. The imprint to *Decii Junii Juvenalis Aquinatis, et A. Persii Flacci Satyrae* reads: "Edinburgi: Impensis G. Gordon, Bibliopolae in Area Parliamentaria, apud quem Venales prostant, 1763."

GORDON (WILLIAM), bookseller in Edinburgh, *c.* 1743–94. Parliament Close, 1773–4. His name is first found in the imprint to *Select Transactions of the Society . . . Agriculture in Scotland . . .* Edinburgh, 1743. The imprint to the Edinb. ed. of *The Rambler* reads: "Printed for the author; and sold by William Gordon and C. Wright at the shops in the Parliament-close." A bookseller of this name married Margaret, daughter of Robert Dick, writer, 1759. This is no doubt the same man. His second daughter, Mary, married Charles Stewart, W.S., April 11th, 1795. [*Edinb. Marr. Reg.*, 1751–1800.] His name is found in the *Edinburgh Directory* for 177$\frac{3}{4}$. His will was registered January 6th, 1794. [Scot. Rec. Soc., *Edinb. Test.*]

GORRIE (ALEXANDER), printer in Edinburgh. In Tolbooth Parish, 1762. Married Mary, daughter of George Easton, November 8th, 1772. [*Edinb. Marr. Reg.*, 1751–1800.] His name has not been noted in the imprint to any book and it is probable that he was either an ordinary workman in one of the large printing establishments, or else that he was a journeyman.

GRAHAM (DOUGAL), printer and chapman in Glasgow, *c.* 1753–79. Born at Raploch, near Stirling in or about 1724. Author of the well-known *History of John Cheap the Chapman*. Known as the "Skellat" Bellman of Glasgow. His *Full, particular and true Account of the late Rebellion in the Year 1745 and 1746 . . .* was advertised in the *Glasgow Courant* for September 29th, 1746. He is said to have become a printer about 1753 and to have set up his own works in type without committing them to writing. He died on July 20th, 1779. [MacGregor, *Coll. writings of Dougal Graham*, 1883.]

GRAHAM (JOHN), printer in Edinburgh, *c.* 1740. His will was registered June 9th, 1758. [Scot. Rec. Soc., *Edinb. Test.*] A daughter, Margaret, married John Monro, shoemaker, June 9th, 1765. [*Edinb. Marr. Reg.*, 1751–1800.] No book bearing his name in the imprint has been noted.

GRAHAM (JOHN), running stationer in Edinburgh, 1757. In Old Kirk Parish. Married Mary, daughter of deceased James Tawes, May 15th, 1757. [*Edinb. Marr. Reg.*, 1751–1800.]

GRAHAM (JOHN), bookbinder in Edinburgh, 1759–74. Opposite the Meal market, 1773–4. Married Isobel, daughter of William Robertson, burgess, January 28th, 1759. [*Edinb. Marr. Reg.*, 1751–1800.] His name occurs in the *Edinburgh Directory* for 177$\frac{3}{4}$.

GRAHAM (SAMUEL), bookbinder in Edinburgh, 1719–59. Bookbinder, right of John Graham, stabler, father, November 18th, 1719. [*Edinb. Guild Reg.*] Prentice-master to Laghlan [i.e. Lauchlan] Hunter (*q.v.*), June 27th, 1733. *Ib.*]. Burgess of Edinburgh. Married Barbara Mitchell, daughter of John Mitchell, April 22nd, 1744. [*Edinb. Marr. Reg.*, 1701–50.] His will was registered May 16th, 1759. [Scot. Rec. Soc., *Edinb. Test.*]

GRANT (ALEXANDER), printer in Edinburgh, 1772. In New North Kirk Parish. Married Magdalen, daughter of William Aitken, smith in Lady Yester's Parish, December 13th, 1772. [*Edinb. Marr. Reg.*, 1751–1800.]

GRANT (JAMES), bookbinder in Edinburgh, 1703–45 (?). Burgess. Married (1) Elizabeth, daughter of John Durington, tailor, October 24th, 1703 [*Edinb. Marr. Reg.*, 1701–50]; (2) Elizabeth, daughter of Robert Wallace of Kairnhill, February 24th, 1711. [*Canongate Reg. Marr.*, 1564–1800.] His only daughter, Anna, married Robert Reid, writer in Edinburgh, March 23rd, 1746. [*Edinb. Marr. Reg.*, 1701–50]. Not the same as James Grant, printer and publisher (*q.v.*). Omitted from *Dictionary*, 1668–1725.

GRANT (JAMES), printer and publisher in Edinburgh. In May 1736 a deed of copartnery was signed by Thomas and Walter Ruddiman and James Grant, jointly to produce the *Caledonian Mercury*. Walter became the cashier, and Grant was "to collect the foreign and domestic intelligence; to attend to the press and to publish the paper". [Chalmers' *Ruddiman*, p. 142.] The agreement was to hold good until April 17th, 1746, but in the meantime the Rebellion broke out, and on November 1st, 1745, Grant renounced his part in the business. He became a lieutenant in the Rebel army and printed several treasonable papers for them. [Scot. Hist. Soc., *List of Persons concerned in the Rebellion*, p. 249.] He finally found safety in France. [Chalmers' *Ruddiman*, p. 143.] His daughter Jean married Alexander Henderson, merchant, December 6th, 1741. [*Edinb. Marr. Reg.*, 1701–50.] He may have been the father of

the printer of the same name who married Helen Tait on July 22nd, 1788. [*Ib.*, 1751–1800.]

GRAY (DAVID), bookbinder and stationer in Edinburgh, 1718–32. Entered in the *Edinburgh Guild Register* as stationer, September 10th, 1718. His will was registered (as that of a bookbinder), October 4th, 1732. [Scot. Rec. Soc., *Edinb. Test.*]

GRAY (DAVID), printer in Edinburgh, 1759. In Foulis Close, a little above the City Guard, north side of the street. Printer of Rev. Ralph Erskine's *Christ the People's Covenant . . .* 1759, from the imprint to which the above address is obtained. Possibly son of David Gray the bookbinder (*q.v.*).

GRAY (GEORGE), bookbinder in Culross, 1766.

GRAY (JOHN), printer and bookseller in Edinburgh. Jackson's Close, 1763–9; opposite the Guard, 1773–4. Burgess. In 1763 or earlier commenced to print in partnership with Gavin Alston (*q.v.*); their joint imprint appearing in that year on Andrew Welwood's *Meditations*. In the same year, on May 22nd, he married Margaret, daughter of Rev. James Fisher, minister of the Gospel at Glasgow. [*Edinb. Marr. Reg.*, 1751–1800.] The partnership with Alston lasted until about 1769, in which year they printed jointly Archibald Hall's *Humble Attempt to exhibit a Scriptural View of the Constitution . . of the Church.* In 1774 he printed alone the Rev. James Scot's *Collection of Sermons*. His name appears in the *Edinburgh Directory* for 177$\frac{3}{4}$, but no book of later date bearing his imprint has been noted.

GRAY (WILLIAM), bookseller in Prestoun, Glasgow, 1739. Mentioned in *Notes & Queries*, 10 ser., v. 5, p. 243. May be the same as the bookseller in Lanark, 1740.

GRAY (WILLIAM), bookseller in Lanark, 1740. In 1740 *The Voice of the Dead to the Living; or Paul's Ghost*, was printed at Glasgow "for William Gray, bookseller in Lanerk". Possibly to be identified with the bookseller in Prestoun, Glasgow, 1739.

GRAY (WILLIAM), bookbinder in Edinburgh, 1740–4 (?). A little without the West Port, 1744. Entered in the *Edinburgh Guild Register* as a bookbinder, by right of David Gray, merchant, Father, June 27th, 1744. Married Christian, daughter of William Galloway, corkcutter, June 15th, 1740. [*Edinb. Marr. Reg.*, 1701–50.]

GRAY (WILLIAM), bookseller in Edinburgh. Magdalen's Chappel, within the Cowgate Head, 1749; Front of the Exchange, *c.* 1758–78. Sold copies of James Fraser's *Treatise on justifying Faith* . . . 1749. In 1758 he advertised that "at his circulating library in the front of the east wing of the Exchange [he intends to have] in future six of the London magazines and three of its newspapers ready for the perusal of the citizens who are willing to pay 2*s.* per quarter for the privilege". [Couper, *Edinb. Per. Press*, p. 130.] He seems to have built up a large business, for during the next twenty years his name is found in the imprints to many works. He is mentioned in the list of Assize at the trial of Basil Alves on January 29th, 1779. He died before April 11th, 1785, on which date his daughter Margaret married William Galloway. [*Edinb. Marr. Reg.*, 1751–1800.]

GREENFIELD (ARCHIBALD), papermaker in Edinburgh. At Giffordhall, *c.* 1750. Died before February 2nd, 1755, on which date his daughter Margaret married Patrick Stewart. [*Edinb. Marr. Reg.*, 1751–1800.]

GREIG (JOHN), bookseller in Edinburgh, 1734. His name occurs in the imprint to Rev. Ebenezer Erskine's *The King held in the Galleries*, Edinburgh . . . 1734.

GRIEVE (ALEXANDER), bookbinder in Edinburgh, 1771–94. In College Kirk Parish, 1771. Bell's Wynd, 1773–4. In Old Kirk Parish, 1794. Married Barbara Low, daughter of George Low, porter in Gilmertoun, parish of Liberton, July 28th, 1771. His daughter Agnes married Charles Allan, bookbinder in Edinburgh, June 24th, 1794. [*Edinb. Marr. Reg.*, 1751–1800.]

GULLEN (JOHN), paper printer in Edinburgh, 1761. Married Euphan, daughter of David Clerk deceased, shipmaster in Limekilns, January 11th, 1761. [*Edinb. Marr. Reg.*, 1751–1800.]

GUTHRIE (JOHN), bookseller in Edinburgh, *c.* 1768–1824. Linen Hall, Cowgate, *c.* 1768–1813; Nicolson Street, 1814–24. Born in the parish of Boltriphinie, Aberdeenshire, in 1748. He lost both parents when very young and was left to the care of an uncle, who abandoned him before he had reached the age of twelve years. In this forlorn situation he managed to scrape together a few pence with which he procured a small stock of needles, pins, &c., and commenced travelling as a pedlar. The rest of his boyhood was passed in this manner, his capital gradually increasing. In early manhood he gave up travelling and opened a bookstall in Edinburgh at the Linen Hall, Cowgate. By nature a most industrious man, he was never idle at his stall, but was con-

stantly engaged in useful work such as knitting stockings, making onion nets, and so on. Moderately successful at his stall, he was soon able to open a shop at the Netherbow. He next moved to Nicolson Street, where he took William Tait into partnership with him. On February 8th, 1790, he married Elizabeth Huline [*Edinb. Marr. Reg.*, 1751–1800], but apparently they did not have any children. He was an Episcopalian and a very religious and philanthropic man. Believing only in cash transactions, he earned for himself the sobriquet of "Ready-Money John". He died on May 10th, 1824, and the business was carried on by his partner and successor under the old name of Guthrie and Tait. [Timperley, p. 890; Kay's *Portraits*; &c.]

HALL (JAMES), papermaker at New Paper Miln of Cathcart, 1763. Married Isobel, daughter of Robert Lang, Comptroller of His Majesty's Customs at Glasgow (? date). His wife's will was registered February 28th, 1763. [Comm. Rec. Glasgow, *Reg. Test.*, 1547–1800.]

HAMILTON (ARCHIBALD), printer in Edinburgh and London, *c.* 1730–93. Born in Edinburgh (?) about 1719. He left that city in 1736 and went to London, where he became associated with Strahan, whose printing office he superintended for some time, in the capacity of manager. He made the acquaintance of Smollett, whose *History of England* alone proved a little fortune both to the printer and the bookseller. In 1756, with Smollett's assistance, he commenced the *Critical Review*, which, with the Rev. Joseph Robertson, he carried on with considerable success until the time of his death, on March 9th, 1793, in his 74th year. [Nichols, *Lit. Anecd.* III, 398.] The *Town and Country Magazine*, which he printed, had the largest sale of any monthly publication of the time, 14,000 copies being sold. Thomas Wright, printer in London, was first employed in his office. Hamilton left one daughter and had a son, Archibald, who predeceased him, but who left two sons, Archibald and Samuel, both printers. [Timperley, p. 795, &c.]

HAMILTON (GAVIN), bookseller and printer in Edinburgh, *c.* 1733–66. In the College. His name is first found in books printed in 1733. In that year R. Fleming and Company printed for him *An Enquiry into the Original of Moral Virtue . . . by Archibald Campbell*; and his name also appears in a Glasgow printed edition of one of Cicero's works. In 1739 he sold copies of J. Anderson's *Selectus Diplomatum et Numismatum Scotiae Thesaurus*, Edinburgh, Ruddiman. The exact date when he entered into his first partnership, with John Balfour (*q.v.*), does not seem to be known, but he seems to have been alone as

late as 1743. Probably Balfour, who was his apprentice, was taken into partnership soon after that year. Hamilton was the son of Dr. William Hamilton, Principal of the University, and Sir William Hamilton, *Bart.*, was a relation. He was thus one of the best connected booksellers of his day. He carried on business as a papermaker at Bogsmill in the neighbourhood of Collington, on the Leith Water, a few miles from Edinburgh. After the dissolution of the firm Hamilton retained the sole proprietorship of the paper-mill and was afterwards succeeded in that business by his sons. The sons later sold the mill to Balfour, in whose family it remained for many years. In 1749 a deed of copartnery, dated December 7th, was signed by Hamilton, Balfour (both booksellers), and Patrick Neill, printer. This deed was in a sense the foundation-stone of the present-day firm of printers, Neill & Co. The capital was only £320 (equal to £1000 of the present day), of which Hamilton and Balfour furnished three-fifths and Neill two-fifths, the profits to be divided in proportion. Neill was paid £30 extra for managing the business. This partnership lasted for sixteen years. In 1754 the firm was appointed printers to the University. One of Hamilton's daughters married her father's partner, John Balfour. Another daughter, Louisa, married the Rev. James Woodrow, minister at Dunlop, April 22nd, 1759. In 1766 Hamilton retired from the business, and Balfour joined the firm of Auld and Smellie. The house of Hamilton and Balfour was concerned in the publication of Hume's works and of many English works, such as those of Pope. They were the publishers of Blair's *British Poets* in forty-four volumes. [*The Printing House of Neill*, 1918; Constable's *Lit. Correspondence*, &c.]

HAMILTON (JOHN), merchant in Glasgow, *c.* 1730–80 (?). In 1738 Isaac Ambrose's *War with Devils*, Glasgow College, was "Printed for Archibald Ingram, John Hamilton [&c.] . . . merchants, and are to be sold by them". Hamilton was one of several merchants who petitioned as a creditor against James Douglas, in 1763. He was a member of the company formed in 1750 to establish the "Glasgow Arms Bank". In 1780 his name appears as that of a shareholder (£5 5*s.* 0*d.*) in the Tontine Coffee Room. [Reid, *Glasgow Past and Present*, v. 1.]

HAMILTON (ROBERT), paper merchant in Edinburgh, 1773–4. West Bow. His name is given in the *Edinburgh Directory*, 177¾.

HAMILTON (WILLIAM), bookseller in Edinburgh, 1730– (?). Possibly a relative of Gavin Hamilton (*q.v.*). Entered in the *Edinburgh Guild Register* as a

bookseller, by right of William Hamilton, Father, Keeper of Holyrood, May 6th, 1730.

HARDIE (SAMUEL), printer in Edinburgh, 1728. Married Ann, daughter of deceased Patrick Christy, dyer, November 22nd, 1728. [*Canongate Reg. Marr.*, 1564–1800.]

HAY (EBENEZER), journeyman printer in Edinburgh. In Tolbooth Parish, 1764. Married Mary, daughter of David Goodwillie, shoemaker in Dalkeith, January 7th, 1764. [*Edinb. Marr. Reg.*, 1751–1800.]

HAY (GEORGE), printer in Edinburgh, 1750. In South Kirk Parish. Probably a journeyman employed by Ruddiman. Married Isobel Guthrie, servant to Thomas Ruddiman, February 23rd, 1750. [*Edinb. Marr. Reg.*, 1701–50.]

HEGGIE (DAVID), bookseller in Kirkcaldy. Before 1765. His will was registered January 26th, 1765. [Comm. Rec. St Andrews; *Reg. Test.*, 1549–1800.]

HENDERSON (PATRICK), running stationer in Edinburgh, 1764. In New Kirk Parish. Married Helen, daughter of John Murray, workman, May 20th, 1764. [*Edinb. Marr. Reg.*, 1751–1800.]

HENDERSON (THOMAS), bookseller in Edinburgh, 1733–4. Prentice to James McEuen, 1733. Entered in the *Edinburgh Guild Register*, June 27th, 1733. His will was registered December 10th, 1734. [Scot. Rec. Soc., *Edinb. Test.*]

HERIOT or HERRIOTT (CHARLES), bookseller and bookbinder in Edinburgh. In Old Grayfriar's Parish, 1768. Parliament House, 1773–4. Married Ann, daughter of John Wilson, bookseller (*q.v.*), September 25th, 1768. [*Edinb. Marr. Reg.*, 1751–1800.]

HERIOT (THOMAS), bookseller in Edinburgh, 1724–40 (?). Parliament Close, 1728. Entered in the *Edinburgh Guild Register*, July 15th, 1724. Married Jean Smith, widow of James Watson, printer, July 6th, 1725. [*Edinb. Marr. Reg.*, 1701–50.] Jean Smith or Heriot died in August 1731. [Aldis, p. 123.] In 1728 John Catanach (*q.v.*) printed "For Mr. Thomas Heriot" *An Explication of the xxxix Chapter of the Statutes of King William . . . by Sir Alex. Seton . . . with Notes by Alex. Bruce.* He seems to have died about 1740.

HERRIOT (WILLIAM), bookbinder in Edinburgh. In North-West Parish, 1750. Later in Old Kirk Parish. Married Elizabeth Watt, daughter of John Watt, miller at Peppermill, June 3rd, 1750. He died before 1773. His daughter

Barbara married John Duncan, bookbinder (*q.v.*), February 14th, 1773. Another daughter, Elizabeth, married George Thomson, a corporal in the 46th Regt., July 14th, 1784. [*Edinb. Marr. Reg.*, 1701–50; 1751–1800.]

HERRIOT (Mrs.), bookbinder in Edinburgh, 1773–4. Old Fish-market Close. Her name occurs in the *Edinburgh Directory*, 177¾.

HOOD (Andrew), printer in Edinburgh, 1760. In Old Kirk Parish. Married Ann Thom, relict of John Scott, smith, December 21st, 1760. [*Edinb. Marr. Reg.*, 1751–1800.] Probably a journeyman. May have been a relative of Arthur Hood (*q.v.*).

HOOD (Arthur), printer in Edinburgh, 1731. In South-South-East Kirk Parish. Married Margaret, daughter of David Inglis, merchant in Hamilton, April 22nd, 1731. [*Edinb. Marr. Reg.*, 1701–50.] Probably a journeyman.

HOOD (Thomas), printer in Edinburgh, 1766. In Lady Yester's Parish. Married Katherine, daughter of deceased George Gordon, indweller in Peeble's Wynd, November 16th, 1766. [*Edinb. Marr. Reg.*, 1751–1800.]

HORN (John), bookseller in Dunfermline, 1764. His name is recorded in Erskine Beveridge's *Bibliography of Dunfermline*, 1901, p. xix.

HOUSTON (John), papermaker in Edinburgh. Before 1768. At Giffordhall, in Tron Parish. His daughter Margaret married Robert Innes, wright, May 1st, 1768. Houston was then dead. [*Edinb. Marr. Reg.*, 1751–1800.]

HOWIE (J.), (?) bookseller at Lochgoin, *c.* 1774. Concerned in obtaining subscriptions for the publication in 1774 of Michael Shields' *Historical Relation of the State and Actings of the Suffering Remnant in Scotland*, which was to be published by John Bryce (*q.v.*), of Glasgow. The prospectus was dated April 1st, 1774.

HUNTER (Charles), bookbinder in Edinburgh, 1757–74. In Tolbooth Parish, 1757. Hammermen's Close, Cowgate, 1773–4. Married Katherine Theodor, daughter of Robert Morrison, writer, May 22nd, 1757. [*Edinb. Marr. Reg.*, 1751–1800.] His name occurs in the *Edinburgh Directory* for 177¾.

HUNTER (Henry), printer in Edinburgh. Before 1760. His daughter Ann married David Millar, on November 16th, 1760. [*Edinb. Marr. Reg.*, 1751–1800.] No book bearing his name in the imprint has been noted.

HUNTER (Lauchlan), bookseller and bookbinder in Edinburgh, 1733–*c.* 1770. In Old Kirk Parish, 1764. Prentice to Samuel Graham (*q.v.*), bookbinder, June 27th, 1733. [*Edinb. Guild Reg.*] Bookseller, August 6th, 1740. [*Ib.*] Prentice-master of John Wood (*q.v.*), bookseller. [*Ib.*] He was still living on April 8th, 1764, when his daughter Hamilton married William Bogle (*q.v.*) [the second of that name]. [*Edinb. Marr. Reg.*, 1751–1800]. Sold copies of Hume's *History of the House and Race of Douglas*, 1743.

HUNTER (Robert), printer in Edinburgh. In Old Grayfriar's Parish, 1772. Married Margaret, servant, daughter of Robert Richardson, maltman in Perth, November 15th, 1772. [*Edinb. Marr. Reg.*, 1751–1800.] Probably a journeyman.

HUTCHESON (Alexander), printer and bookseller in Glasgow, 1731–80 (?). In the Salt-mercat, 1743. In 1743 he was printing in company with Robert Smith (*q.v.*). Their joint imprint is found upon Samuel Rutherford's *Trial and Triumph of Faith*, 1743. He seems to have been mainly a bookseller, and probably did not actually own a press himself. His will was registered November 14th, 1780. [Comm. Rec. Glasgow, *Reg. Test.*, 1547–1800.] He was admitted Burgess and Guild Brother (as a bookbinder), as second living son of deceased James H., cordiner, B. & G. B., June 22nd, 1731. [Scot. Rec. Soc., *Burgesses and Guild Brothers of Glasgow*, 1573–1750.]

HUTCHISON (Elizabeth or Elspeth), bookbinder in Kinross. Before 1765. Her will was registered November 11th, 1765. [Comm. Rec. St Andrews, *Reg. Test.*, 1760–9.]

HUTTON (John), papermaker in Edinburgh. Parliament Close, 1773–4.

HYDE (Robert), papermaker in Aberdeen, 1770–2. Originally a dyer. In 1770 John Boyle and Robert Hyde obtained a charter from James Moir of Stoneywood, the famous Jacobite, of land for a mill at Stoneywood, and in 1771 the mill was erected. Later in that year Boyle sold his half-share to Hyde, who sold it again to Alex. Smith, wigmaker in Aberdeen. In 1772 Hyde sold his remaining half-share to Thomas Sparke, a merchant in Aberdeen, who, in 1773, disposed of his share to Smith, who then became sole owner. The mill later fell into the hands of Alex. Pirie, who was the first member of the famous family of papermakers to be associated with the business. [Information kindly supplied by Mr. G. M. Fraser, Aberdeen.]

IMRIE (David), printer in Edinburgh, 1758–64. In Old Grayfriar's Parish. No book bearing his imprint has been noted, and it is probable that he worked for one of the large firms then in Edinburgh. He was twice married, first, on June 4th, 1758, to Mary, daughter of deceased Adam Waddle, and secondly, on May 6th, 1764, to Margaret, daughter of deceased Alexander Finlayson. [*Edinb. Marr. Reg.*, 1751–1800.]

INGRAM (Archibald), calico-printer, banker, bookseller, Glasgow, 1704–70. Born in 1704. Not a bookseller in the strict sense of the word but a merchant who occasionally sold books. Isaac Ambrose's *War with Devils* . . . Glasgow College . . . 1738, was "Printed for Archibald Ingram, John Hamilton [&c.] . . . and are to be sold by them . . .". Ingram was a wealthy man and held the office of Provost of Glasgow from 1762–4. Together with his brother-in-law, John Glassford of Dougalston, he supplied Robert Foulis with funds for the purchase of pictures for his famous Academy of Fine Arts. "Archibald Ingram takes his place amongst the notable men who figure in *The Caldwell Papers* as correspondents of Baron Mure; and the beautiful monument to his memory in the Directors' room of the Merchants' House—one of the most graceful pieces of sculpture in the city—testifies to the appreciation in which he was held by those who knew him. The Royal Exchange, the meeting-place of his successors, the merchants of to-day, looks out upon the street which bears his name". [Murray, *R. & A. Foulis*, 1913, p. 64.]

JACK (John), bookseller at Borrowstonness (Bo-ness), 1774–6. Took subscriptions for Michael Shields' *Historical Relation of the State and Actings of the Suffering Remnant in Scotland*, in 1774. Purchased for sale two dozen copies of the Rev. James Renwick's *Choice Collection of Sermons* . . ., Glasgow, Bryce, 1776.

JACKSON (Robert), printer and publisher in Dumfries, *c.* 1773–1811. In partnership for a time with W. Boyd. Printed and published the *Dumfries Magazine*, 1776–7. This magazine was dropped in 1777 and a newspaper, *The Dumfries Weekly Journal* was commenced. Jackson was provost of Dumfries, 1797–9, 1800–2, 1806–8, and 1809–11. [Maxwell, *Dumfries*, p. 371, &c.]

JAFFREY (J.), bookseller in Stirling, 1747. Sold copies of Rev. Ralph Erskine's *Sermon preached immediately before the Administration of the Sacrament of the Lord's Supper, at Dunfermline, July 19th, 1747*; Glasgow: Printed for J. Newlands . . . 1747.

JAMES (John), type-founder, *see* Ged (William).

JAMES (Thomas), type-founder, *see* Ged (William).

JAMIESON or JAMESON (Robert), bookbinder and bookseller in Edinburgh, 1771–80. In Tolbooth Parish, 1771; Parliament Square, 1778. Originally a bookbinder only. Married Isobel, daughter of deceased Alexander Jamison, shipmaster in Alloa, December 8th, 1771. [*Edinb. Marr. Reg.*, 1751–1800.] Sold copies of W. Perry's *Only Sure Guide to the English Tongue*, printed by Gavin Alston . . . Edinburgh, 1776. His name occurs as publisher of the 2nd ed. of the Rev. Wm. Shaw's *Analysis of the Gaelic*, Edinburgh, W. & T. Ruddiman, 1778. The latest occurrence of his name seems to be in the imprint to the 1780 London ed. of Shaw's *Gaelic Dictionary*.

JARDINE (John), journeyman printer in Edinburgh. In New North Kirk Parish, 1765. Married Janet, daughter of John Goldie, shoemaker in Selkrig [i.e. Selkirk], March 3rd, 1765. [*Edinb. Marr. Reg.*, 1751–1800.]

JERVEY (Mathew), printer in Edinburgh, 1757. In Old Grayfriar's Parish. Married Lucy, daughter of deceased Andrew Johnston, druggist, May 1st, 1757. [*Edinb. Marr. Reg.*, 1751–1800]. (?) a journeyman.

JOHNSTON (William), bookseller in Newlands–Borland, 1741. Sold copies of the Rev. Ralph Erskine's *Sermon preached before the Associate Presbytery . . . Aug. 28, 1739, in the Parish of Kinross;* Edinburgh, printed by R. Fleming and A. Alison . . . 1741.

JOHNSTONE (George), printer in Aberdeen, 1769. *See* Johnstone (George), printer in Perth. In 1769 he printed an edition of Isaac Ambrose's *War with Devils*. [Information kindly supplied by Mr. G. M. Fraser.]

JOHNSTONE (George), printer in Perth and Edinburgh, *c.* 1770–(?). Printed in 1770 *The Bloody Tribunal*, in which he takes the credit for establishing a printing press in Perth, and also mentions that a paper manufactory had been started in the neighbourhood. From 1772 to 1774 he printed for Robert Morison (*q.v.*) the *Perth Magazine*. He is said to have left Perth for Edinburgh in 1775. He may be identical with the printer of the same name in Aberdeen, 1769. A George Johnston, printer, appears in Montrose in 1784. [Cotton, *Typ. Gaz.*, 2nd ser., p. 145.]

KAY (John), printer in Edinburgh. In South-West Kirk Parish, 1752. Married Isobel M'Intosh, relict of Henry Buchanan, January 5th, 1752. [*Edinb. Marr.*

Reg., 1751–1800.] Probably a journeyman. No book has been noted bearing his name in the imprint.

KERR or KER (DAVID), printer in Edinburgh, 1770. In New Grayfriar's Parish. Married Marion, daughter of Alexander Rainie, slater in Prestonpans, November 11th, 1770. [*Edinb. Marr. Reg.*, 1751–1800.]

KIDD (JOHN), printer in Edinburgh, *c.* 1776–(?). In College Kirk Parish. Married Henrietta, daughter of James Paterson, tailor, January 24th, 1778. [*Edinb. Marr. Reg.*, 1751–1800.]

KINCAID (ALEXANDER), printer, bookseller, and stationer in Edinburgh, 1734–77. Opposite the foot of the old fish-market, 1773–4. Prentice to James McQueen [i.e. McEuen], bookseller, March 20th, 1734. [*Edinb. Guild Register.*] In 1738 he sold copies of *An Essay on the Antiquities of Gt. Britain & Ireland*, printed by Ruddiman. Commenced printing about 1740 and in 1743 printed *Select Transactions of the Society . . . Agriculture in Scotland.* In 1744 he became His Majesty's Printer and Stationer for Scotland. Married the Hon. Caroline Kerr, daughter of Lord Charles Kerr, October 13th, 1751. [*Edinb. Marr. Reg.*, 1751–1800.] For many years he befriended William Creech (*q.v.*), who became his assistant, partner, and successor in the bookselling business. His name appears as the printer of many books during the period 1750–77. "In 1770 he brought an action against Colin Macfarquhar for printing a Bible, with notes, called Ostervald's Bible," [Timperley, p. 722.] For some years Robertson printed in partnership with him, and about 1768 Bell was a member of the firm. Long a prominent citizen of Edinburgh, he served as Baillie and later as Lord Provost of the city. He died on January 21st, 1777, aged 66 years. His will was registered March 7th, 1777, and April 24th, 1778. [Scot. Rec. Soc., *Edinb. Test.*]

KNOX (   ), printer in Glasgow, 1752. Printed an edition of the *Westminster Confession*, at Glasgow in 1752.

KNOX (GEORGE), bookseller in Ayr, *c.* 1760. His will was registered March 23rd, 1767, September 13th, 1768, and November 1st, 1770. [Comm. Rec. Glasgow, *Reg. Test.*, 1547–1800.]

LAING (CHARLES), paper manufacturer in Edinburgh, 1763. In parish of Galston. Married Alison, daughter of deceased Robert Johnstone, mason, November 6th, 1763. [*Edinb. Marr. Reg.*, 1751–1800.]

LAING (WILLIAM), bookseller and publisher in Edinburgh, 1764–1832. Born in Edinburgh, July 20th, 1764. Educated at a grammar school there. He served an apprenticeship for six years to a printer, but abandoned this trade on account of weak eyesight. In 1785 he commenced business on his own account as a bookseller. He is said to have been a modest, unassuming, well-read man. His publications included some excellent editions of Greek authors. For fifty years he carried on business as a bookseller, and prior to his death, on April 10th, 1732, was the oldest bookseller actually in business in Edinburgh. In 1821 his son David, the well-known Scottish antiquary, was taken into partnership. He died at Lauriston, near Edinburgh, and left a widow and nine children. [Timperley, p. 921; various accounts of David Laing, &c.]

LANG (JAMES), bookbinder in Glasgow, 1734. Burgess and Guild Brother as eldest living son of deceased Robert L., merchant, July 31st, 1734. [Scot. Rec. Soc., *Burg. & G. B. of Glasgow*, 1573–1750.]

LAURIE (GEORGE), stationer and bookbinder in Glasgow, 1704–27. Prentice master (stationer) of John Robieson (i.e. Robertson), April 6th, 1704. Described as Burgess and Guild Brother. Prentice master of James M'Lean, bookbinder, December 20th, 1727. Described as bookbinder. [Scot. Rec. Soc., *Burg. & G.B. of Glasgow*, 1573–1750.] Omitted from *Dictionary*, 1668–1725.

LEARMONT (JAMES), bookbinder in Edinburgh, 1730. Entered in the *Edinburgh Guild Register* as bookbinder, August 19th, and September 30th, 1730, by right of John Learmont, merchant, father.

LEECHMAN (JAMES), bookbinder in Edinburgh, 1766. In New Kirk Parish. Married Marion, daughter of James Anderson, farmer in Gilmerton, in Liberton Parish, November 16th, 1766. [*Edinb. Marr. Reg.*, 1751–1800.] Probably the father of the binder who is entered as Leishman in the *Canongate Marr. Reg.*, August 6th, 1794.

LEGGET (FRANCIS), stationer in Edinburgh, 1759. In Tron Parish. Married Janet, daughter of deceased John Simpson, writer in Canongate, July 1st, 1759. [*Edinb. Marr. Reg.*, 1751–1800.]

LEIPER (JAMES), merchant and bookseller in Aberdeen, 1747–8. A merchant who sold copies of the *Aberdeen Journal* during the years 1747–8. [*Scot. N. & Q.* I. 4.]

LESLIE (JOHN), printer in Edinburgh, 1770. In Lady Yester's Parish. Married Anne, daughter of deceased Alexander Robin, weaver in Torreburn, June 10th, 1770. [*Edinb. Marr. Reg.*, 1751–1800.]

LIDDEL (JOHN), bookseller in Falkirk, 1734. His name occurs in the imprint to Ebenezer Erskine's *The King held in the Galleries*; Edinburgh, 1734.

LINDSAY (HENRY), paper maker, Woodend, near Huntingtower *c.* 1760–1820(?) Son of David Lindsay, merchant and banker in Perth, and Catherine Anderson. In partnership with his brother-in-law, James Morison (*q.v.*) in the paper works of Woodend. Supplied the firm of Morison & Son, Perth.

LIVINGSTONE (JOHN), printer in Edinburgh, 1764–85(?). In Grayfriar's Parish, 1764. Later in the Canongate. Married Anne, daughter of James Gordon, November 18th, 1764. He had a daughter Agnes who married James Weir, painter, November 14th, 1785. [*Edinb. Marr. Reg.*, 1751–1800.]

LOGAN (ROBERT), bookbinder in Edinburgh. In Old Kirk Parish, 1765. Foot of West-Bow, 1773–4. Married Jean, daughter of George Simpson, January 20th, 1765. [*Edinb. Marr. Reg.*, 1751–1800.] His name appears in the *Edinburgh Directory*, 177$\frac{3}{4}$.

LOW (DAVID), printer in Edinburgh, 1747. In South-West Kirk Parish. Married Janet, daughter of Robert Brown, maltman in South Leith, August 23rd, 1747. [*Edinb. Marr. Reg.*, 1701–50]. Probably a journeyman. May have been related to Carnegie Low, who was a bookbinder in Edinburgh in 1792, and to John Low, a journeyman printer in the same town in 1786.

LUKE (GEORGE), printer in Glasgow. Before 1754. Son of deceased George Luke, merchant in Glasgow, *alias* Bristol John. His will was registered July 4th, 1754. [Comm. Rec. Glasgow, *Reg. Test.*, 1547–1800.]

LUKE (HENRY), bookbinder in Glasgow. Before 1729. His will was registered April 29th, 1729. [Comm. Rec. Glasgow; *Reg. Test.*, 1547–1800.] Probably a relative of George Luke, *alias* Bristol John, merchant in Glasgow.

LUMISDEN (THOMAS), printer in Edinburgh, 1722–49. Fish Market, 1727–49. Printer, April 6th, 1722, by right of Charles Lumsden, minister. [*Edinb. Guild Reg.*] Married Katherine, daughter of John Brown, merchant, burgess, July 27th, 1729. [*Edinb. Marr. Reg.*, 1701–50.] In 1749 printed, as Thomas Lumisden and Company, *Alarm to the Householders and Heritors of the City of Edinburgh: In Copies of Proposals sent off by some in the City, for procuring an*

Act of Parliament, to impose a Poors-Rate thereon. . . . See also Dictionary, 1668–1725.

LUNDIE (JAMES), bookseller in Dundee. Before 1769. His will was registered February 16th, 1769. [Comm. Rec. Brechin, *Reg. Test.*, 1576–1800.]

LYLE (JAMES), printer in Edinburgh, 1773–86. In New Kirk Parish, 1773. Married (1) Jean, daughter of deceased William Reay, merchant and late Provost of Haddington, November 7th, 1773; (2) Margaret, daughter of deceased Thomas Caverhill, merchant in Jedburgh, March 21st, 1786. [*Edinb. Marr. Reg.*, 1751–1800.] No book bearing his imprint has been found. Possibly a journeyman.

M'ALPINE (WILLIAM), printer in Greenock, *c.* 1776–(?). In 1779 he printed an edition of the *Shorter Catechism* in Gaelic.

M'ARTHUR (W.), bookseller in Paisley, 1774. His name occurs on the prospectus, dated April 1st, 1774, for the publication of Michael Shields' *Historical Relation of the State and Actings of the Suffering Remnant in Scotland*, by John Bryce of Glasgow.

M'AULAY (DONALD), running stationer in Edinburgh, 1763. In Tolbooth Parish. His daughter May married Donald Mackenzie, soldier in George Beauclerk's regiment, March 6th, 1763. [*Edinb. Marr. Reg.*, 1751–1800.]

M'CALLUM (   ), printer in Glasgow, 1751. He appears as the printer of William Wilson's *True and impartial Relation of the Persecuted Presbyterians in Scotland* . . . Glasgow, 1751.

M'CANNAN (ALEXANDER), printer and bookseller in Edinburgh, 1773–4. Crosscausey. His name is found in the *Edinburgh Directory* for 177$\frac{3}{4}$ (Supplement).

M'CASLAN or M'ASLAN (ALEXANDER), printer, bookseller, and publisher in Edinburgh, 1771–93 (?). Opposite to the Chapel of Ease, 1779. Printing office, Hastie's Close, back of Adam Square, South Bridge Street, 1793. Publisher of a sermon by A. Ambrose, entitled *Looking unto Jesus*, 1771. Printed *The Gospel-Mystery of Sanctification*, by Rev. Walter Marshall, Edinburgh, 1779. After the imprint there is a note which reads: "N.B. Religious, instructive and entertaining Books lent out to read, at 10*s.* per year, 5*s.* 6*d.* per half-year, 3*s.* per quarter; 1*s.* 6*d.* per month, or one penny per night. Printed catalogues of the Books to be had at A. M'Caslan's Shop, opposite to the Chapel of Ease, Cross-causey, Edinburgh." In 1793 he commenced printing and publishing

The Observer, or a Delineation of the Times, No. 1 of which bears the date September 28th, 1793. The price was 6*d.* monthly. "It is unknown how long this magazine lasted." [Couper, *Edinburgh Period. Press,* II. 207.]

M‘CLEISH (JAMES), stationer in Edinburgh, 1773–4. Candlemaker Row. His name is found in the *Edinburgh Directory* for $177\frac{3}{4}$.

M‘COLL (HUGH), journeyman printer in Edinburgh, 1770. Married Helen, daughter of deceased Thomas Winter, land surveyor in Kildees, February 11th, 1770. [*Edinb. Marr. Reg.,* 1751–1800.]

M‘CORKENDALE (THOMAS), running stationer in Edinburgh. Before 1745. His widow, Jane Paterson, married Peter Gilchrist (*q.v.*), running stationer, February 17th, 1745. [*Edinb. Marr. Reg.,* 1701–50.]

McCOUL (JAMES), bookseller in Glasgow, 1739. His name is mentioned in *N. & Q.,* 10 ser. v. 243.

M‘CRABIE (JOHN), printer in Edinburgh. Before 1754. His widow Ann Milln, married George Gardiner (*q.v.*), printer, September 8th, 1754. [*Edinb. Marr. Reg.,* 1751–1800.] Probably a journeyman or a workman in one of the printing establishments in Edinburgh, as no book bearing his imprint has been noted.

MACDONALD (A.), bookseller in Edinburgh, *c.* 1768. Name occurs in the imprint to a Gaelic ed. of Duncan Macintyre's *Poems and Songs,* Edinburgh, 1768.

MACDONALD (ROBERT), stationer and bookseller in Glasgow, 1770. His name occurs in the imprint to a Gaelic ed. of Duncan Macfadyen's *Spiritual Hymns,* Glasgow, 1770. His daughter Margaret married James Dow, November 13th, 1797. [*Edinb. Marr. Reg.,* 1751–1800.] Died before 1797.

McEUEN or McQUEEN (JAMES), bookseller and printer in Edinburgh, 1718–34. Prentice master of Thomas Henderson (*q.v.*), June 17th, 1733. *Edinb. Guild Reg.*]. Prentice master of Alexander Kincaid (*q.v.*), March 20th, 1734. [*Ib.*] *See also Dictionary,* 1668–1725, where his dates are given as 1718–32.

MACEWEN (JOHN), bookbinder in Edinburgh, 1767. In Lady Yester's Parish. Married Isobel, daughter of deceased John Stalker, farmer in parish of Monivard, July 5th, 1767. [*Edinb. Marr. Reg.,* 1751–1800.]

MACFARQUHAR (COLIN), printer in Edinburgh, 1767–75. Married Jean, daughter of Mr. James Scrator, accomptant in Glasgow, December 13th, 1767. [*Edinb. Marr. Reg.,* 1751–1800.] In 1770 Alexander Kincaid, His Majesty's

printer for Scotland, brought an action against him for printing a Bible, with notes, called Ostervald's Bible. [Timperley, p. 722]. He was concerned in the production of the 1771 edition of the *Encyclopaedia Britannica,* and shared in the payment of £200 to William Smellie for editing it. On July 18th, 1775, there came on before the Court of Session in Scotland a cause between Mr. James Dodsley, bookseller of London, and Messrs. Elliot and Macfarquhar of Edinburgh, booksellers. The action was brought for reprinting Lord Chesterfield's *Letters to his Son,* which had cost Dodsley £1,575. Their Lordships decided in favour of Mr. Dodsley, by continuing the interdict which he had obtained against Messrs. Elliot and Macfarquhar, by a majority of nine against five. [Timperley, p. 735.]

MACGREGOR (DUNCAN), running stationer in Edinburgh, 1775–8. On November 19th, 1775, Finlay Mackenzie, shoemaker, married Mary, daughter of Duncan M‘Grigor, running stationer. Duncan Macgregor, running stationer, married Jennet, daughter of John Robertson, barber, February 8th, 1778. [*Edinb. Marr. Reg.,* 1751–1800.]

M‘KINLAY (DANIEL), running stationer in Edinburgh, *c.* 1760–83 (?). On August 16th, 1783, his daughter Elizabeth married James Harris, weaver. [*Canongate Reg. Marr.,* 1564–1800.]

M‘LAREN (WALTER), papermaker at Lasswade, *c.* 1770. Died before April 27th, 1798, on which date his daughter Margaret married Henry Tod, seevewight [*sic*]. [*Edinb. Marr. Reg.,* 1751–1800.]

McLEAN (ARCHIBALD), printer in (1) Glasgow, *c.* 1738–68; (2) Paisley, 1769–73; (3) Edinburgh, 1773–84 (?) Printed in Glasgow in partnership with John Robertson in 1739. [Duncan: *Notices and docs. illustr. of the lit. hist. of Glasgow,* 1831, p. 155.] It is not clear when the partnership was dissolved, but by 1748 Robertson was printing alone. Between 1753 and 1756 McLean printed several books, and in 1757 an edition of the *Westminster Confession.* Keach's *The Travels of Godliness,* 20th ed., bears the imprint: "Glasgow, printed by Archibald McLean, for Alexander Weir, bookseller in Paisley, MDCCVI." This date is no doubt a misprint and may mean 1756 or 1766. In or about 1769 he seems to have removed to Paisley, where, in that year, in partnership with Alex. Weir, he produced the first book printed in that town. This was the Rev. George Muir's *An Essay on Christ's Cross and Crown,* 2nd ed. According to the title-page it was "printed by A. Weir and A. M‘Lean, and sold at the

shop of A. Weir, near the Cross. In the same year a 3rd ed. of Ascanius was printed by the firm "for James Donaldson & Co., Fergusley, near Paisley". They also appear to have been the printers of *A Prophecy concerning the Lord's Return,* which was "printed for and sold by George M‘Kinnon, travelling merchant, 1769". The partnership seems to have been dissolved about 1772, and in 1773 McLean printed in Edinburgh. Weir, however, remained in Paisley. McLean's daughter Elizabeth married William Kerr on February 28th, 1784, her father being then still alive. Apparently in 1761 McLean was in partnership with Joseph Galbraith, their joint imprint appearing on the 6th ed. of James Durham's *Christ Crucified.* [Metcalfe, *Hist. of Paisley,* 1909, &c.]

M‘LEAN (JAMES), bookbinder in Glasgow, 1727. Burgess and Guild Brother, as serving apprenticeship with George Laurie (*q.v.*), bookbinder, December 20th, 1727. [Scot. Rec. Soc., *Burg. and G. B. of Glasgow,* 1573–1750.]

MACLEISH (JAMES), bookbinder in Edinburgh, 1769. In Old Grayfriar's Parish. Married Margaret, daughter of John M‘Leish, minister of the Gospel at Gask, June 18th, 1769. [*Edinb. Marr. Reg.,* 1751–1800.]

MACMILLAN (JOHN), journeyman printer in Edinburgh, 1765. In New Grayfriar's Parish. Married Violet, daughter of Adam Cairns, sometime farmer in Wester Daik (? Dyke) in the parish of Drumelier, April 7th, 1765. [*Edinb. Marr. Reg.,* 1751–1800.]

MACNIVEN (JOHN), bookbinder in Edinburgh, 1773. Married Isobel, daughter of Robert Watson, mason, September 5th, 1773. [*Edinb. Marr. Reg.,* 1751–1800.] In the Marriage Register he is described as "apprentice bookbinder".

MACPHERSON (ALEXANDER), bookseller in Edinburgh, 1758. Leith Wynd. Married Anne, daughter of deceased Hector Monro, farmer in the Parish of Eterton, Ross-shire, December 16th, 1758. [*Canongate Reg. Marr.,* 1564–1800.] Possibly father of Alexander Macpherson, printer (*q.v.*).

MACPHERSON (ALEXANDER), printer in Edinburgh, 1773–4. Grass-market. Printed in partnership with Gilbert Macpherson. Married Dorothea, daughter of Duncan Stuart, January 9th, 1774. [*Edinb. Marr. Reg.,* 1751–1800.] His name and address appear in the *Edinburgh Directory* for $177\frac{3}{4}$.

MACPHERSON (GILBERT), printer in Edinburgh, 1773–4. Grass-market. In partnership with Alexander Macpherson (*q.v.*).

MARSCHAL or MARSHALL (WILLIAM), bookseller in Home, Glasgow, 1739–50 (?). Bookseller, 1739. [*N. & Q.,* 10 ser. v. 5, p. 243.] In 1741 he sold copies of the Rev. Ralph Erskine's *Sermon preached before the Associate Presbytery . . . Aug. 28, 1739, in the Parish of Kinross,* Edinburgh, printed by R. Fleming and A. Alison . . . 1741. Entered as a Burgess and Guild Brother, as serving apprentice with John Gilmour (*q.v.*), bookseller and merchant, May 25th. 1749. [Scot. Rec. Soc., *Burg. and G. B. of Glasgow,* 1573–1750.]

MARTIN (ANDREW), bookseller in Edinburgh, *c.* 1728–38. Probably succeeded his father, John Martin, in 1728. Entered in the *Edinburgh Guild Register* as a bookseller, May 12th, 1731, by right of John Martin, father. In 1738 he sold copies of the periodical called *Letters of the Critical Club.* [Couper, *Edinb. Period. Press,* II. 69.]

MARTIN (GILBERT), printer and publisher in Edinburgh, *c.* 1750–86. Advocates' Close, Luckenbooths. In partnership with John Wotherspoon (*q.v.*), as "The Apollo Press". William Russell, author of the *History of Modern Europe* (5 vols.) served his apprenticeship with this firm for the five years 1757–62. On June 28th, 1761, Martin married Margaret, daughter of John Nicolson, wright, in Moultrieshall. [*Edinb. Marr. Reg.,* 1751–1800.] He died on March 1st, 1784, according to Timperley (p. 750), but his will was not registered until July 26th, 1786. [Scot. Rec. Soc., *Edinb. Test.*] The firm printed an edition of the *British Poets* in 1765, but the exclusive copyright debarred them from including Young, Mallet, Akenside, and Gray, all of whom duly appeared in the London edition. [Knight, *Shadows of the Old Booksellers,* p. 250.] For other publications of the firm *see under* Wotherspoon.

MARTIN (JOHN), bookseller in Edinburgh, 1718–28. Little Ares. His will was registered June 14th, 1728. [Scot. Rec. Soc., *Edinb. Test.*] Father of Andrew Martin (*q.v.*), who succeeded him. *See also Dictionary,* 1668–1725.

MARTIN (WILLIAM), bookseller and auctioneer in Edinburgh, *c.* 1766–1820. Born at or near Airdrie about 1744 (he used to boast that he was "in arms" during the rebellion of 1745). He was originally bred as shoemaker, like his contemporary Lackington of London. It is uncertain when he went to Edinburgh, but for several years he resided in a small shop in the High Street, near the head of the West Bow, where he combined the two professions of bookseller and cobbler. He frequented the country towns around Edinburgh on fairs and other market days, exposing his small stock of books for sale. Eventually he did well enough to give up shoemaking and to devote his time to bookselling. His burgess ticket is dated 1786, but he must have been well established in business many years previously. In a letter of condolence written by him to the widow of his brother who died in America in 1782 he says: "My situation in business I have no cause to complain of. I have a shop in the bookselling way in the Lawnmarket of Edinburgh, to which occupation I mean to put William, my namesake, and I hope he will do very well. I will give him the best education, and he shall be as well clothed as myself . . ." The letter is dated June 2nd, 1782, and indicated unquestionably that he was then at least comfortably well off. The William he refers to was his nephew, not his son. His business continued to flourish, and in 1789 he purchased from William Brodie, cabinet maker, premises in Gourlay's Land, Old Bank Close; in one of the large rooms in which he held his auction sales. By 1792 he had become more or less famous, since his prosperity was so great as to attract the notice of a minor poet, George Galloway, who composed some verses *To Messrs Lackington and Martin, Booksellers*. About 1793 he sold his new premises to the Bank of Scotland, and removed to 94, South Bridge, where he remained for some years. He also purchased the Golf House at the east end of Bruntsfield Links, as a private residence. In 1806 he moved to 2, Lothian Street, and a year or so later retired from business. He was twice married and had several children by his first wife, but unfortunately they all died young. His second wife, whom he married in December 1788, was Katherine Robertson, daughter of a schoolmaster in Ayr. He was a member of the Society of Booksellers, and of the Merchant Company of Edinburgh. He was also a member of the Kirk Session of the Parish of St. Cuthbert's. Archibald Constable was one of his friends and prevailed upon him to sit for his portrait to Geddes, but the picture was never finished. Although rough and unfinished, it was sold at the Constable sale. He died in February 1820, nearly eighty years of age. [Timperley; *Life of Constable;* &c.]

MATHIE (PATRICK), printer and publisher in Edinburgh, 1732–60(?) Passage, next door to the Red Lion, 1740. Entered in the *Edinburgh Guild Register* as a printer, August 2nd, 1732, prentice to John Moncur (*q.v.*), printer. In 1740 he printed and published *The Patriot*, a weekly magazine, and in the same year printed John Glas's *Sermon preached in the Congregational Church of Dundee, January 9th, 1740*.

MAYNE (JOHN), printer and publisher, Dumfries, Glasgow and London, *c.* 1770–1836. Born in Dumfries and received his education at the Grammar

School there. At a very early age he became a printer and worked on a weekly newspaper called the *Dumfries Journal*, which was conducted by Professor Jackson. In 1777 he wrote the *Siller Gun*, a poem of twelve stanzas which was printed at Dumfries. About 1780 he left Dumfries and went to Glasgow, where from 1782 to 1787 he worked as apprentice to Andrew Foulis the younger. Having served his time with Foulis he went to London, where for many years he was printer, editor and joint proprietor of the *Star*. His poetical works place him high amongst Scottish poets. He died at a ripe old age on March 14th, 1836. [Timperley, p. 944; Murray, *Foulis Press*.]

MEGGAT, MEGIT, &c. (JAMES), bookbinder in Edinburgh, *c.* 1746. Married Alison, daughter of John Simpson, December 21st, 1746. [*Edinb. Marr. Reg.*, 1701–50.] Probably a relative of John Meggat (*q.v.*).

MEGGAT (JOHN), bookbinder in Edinburgh, *c.* 1742. Married Catherine Friar, daughter of John Friar, March 14th, 1742. His daughter Katherine married David Lyle, January 12th, 1777. [*Edinb. Marr. Reg.*, 1751–1800.] He died before the latter date. Probably a relative of James Meggat (*q.v.*).

MELDRUM (MRS.), bookseller in Dunfermline, 1724–8. Her name is first found in the imprint to the Rev. Ralph Erskine's *Law—Death, Gospel—Life* . . . Edinburgh, 1724. Only two more books bearing her name have been noted: both are by the same author. They are (1) *The Happy Congregation* . . . Edinb., 1726; and (2) *The Gradual Conquest* or, *Heaven Won by Little and Little* . . . Edinb., 1728. She was probably succeeded by James Beugo (*q.v.*), whose name is first met with in 1729. A William Meldrum, who may have been a descendant, printed in Dunfermline from 1813–44. [Beveridge, *Bibl. of Dunfermline*; Henderson's *Annals*; Chalmers' *History*; &c.] Omitted from *Dictionary*, 1668–1725.

MENNYE or MENZYE (J.), printer and bookseller in Aberdeen, 1770. In 1770 appeared *Seventeen select sermons . . . by Alexander Howe*. "Printed for the widow of the author by J. Mennye, Aberdeen, 1770". In the same year there appeared from his press, *Three Godly Letters*, two of which were by "That renowned martyr, Mr. James Renwicke"; the third was by Mr. John Dickson when he was a prisoner on the Bass Rock. [Information kindly supplied by Mr. G. M. Fraser of Aberdeen.]

MEUROS (JAMES), bookseller in Kilmarnock, 1750–78. Recorded in *N. & Q.*, 11 S. I, 423, as a bookseller, 1750. Sold copies of George Muir's *Synod of Jerusalem*; Glasgow, printed . . . by John Bryce . . . 1778.

MILLAR (JAMES), running stationer in Edinburgh, 1764. In Old Grayfriar's Parish. Married Jean, daughter of John Melvill, weaver in Gorgil Miln, October 14th, 1764. [*Edinb. Marr. Reg.*, 1751–1800.]

MILLAR (RICHARD), papermaker in Edinburgh, at Boag's Milne, *c.* 1760–81 (?) His daughter Mary married John Milnewright, December 28th, 1781. [*Edinb. Marr. Reg.*, 1751–1800.]

MILLAR or MILLER (WILLIAM), bookseller in Edinburgh, 1730–74(?) Opposite the guard, 1773–4. Entered in the *Edinburgh Guild Register* as a bookseller, July 1st, 1730. Prentice to James Thomson, bookseller. In 1740 he sold *The Patriot*, a magazine printed by P. Matthie (*q.v.*): he was also empowered to receive contributions to this magazine. [Couper, *Edinb. Per. Press*, v. 2. p. 83.] One of those who in 1752 sold copies of J. Orton's *Sermon on the death of the Rev. P. Doddridge*. [B.M. S. 1655 (6).] His name appears in the *Edinburgh Directory*, 177¾, whence his address is taken.

MILLER (ALEXANDER), printer in Edinburgh, 1716–50(?) In South-West Kirk Parish, 1716. Married Christian, daughter of Patrick Lindsay, smith, June 1st, 1716. [*Edinb. Marr. Reg.*, 1701–50.] He died before July 23rd, 1758, on which date his widow married Alexander Fairbairn, smith. [*Ib.* 1751–1800.] Omitted from *Dictionary*, 1668–1725.

MILLER or MILLAR, (ALEXANDER), bookseller and printer in Glasgow, 1724–45(?) In 1732 his name occurs as one of the booksellers who sold *The Fort-Royal of the Scriptures*; . . . Edinburgh; Printed by W. Cheyne, for Al. Alison . . . 1732. About 1734 in company with John, James and Mrs. Brown, he entered into partnership with the printer Alexander Carmichael (*q.v.*). By 1736 the Browns disappeared, the firm becoming Alexander Carmichael and Alexander Miller. In 1735 Miller sold the seventh (Scottish) edition of Bunyan's *Pilgrim's Progress*, [Esdaile, *Engl. Tales & Romances*, p. 175.] From 1737 Miller's name appears alone, his address in 1737–8 being "Opposite the Well in the Salt-Mercat". "In 1738 accommodation was made within the College for Alexander Miller, printer." [Murray, *R. & A Foulis*, p. 16.] In the same year he printed Brooks' *The Mute Christian under the Smarting rod*, with the imprint: "Glasgow-College". He is described as a bookseller, however, in the imprint to Isaac Ambrose's *War with devils* . . . Glasgow-College: printed for Archibald Ingram, &c., 1738. His connexion with the College appears to have been continuous until the beginning of 1741, when he printed

a reprint of Christopher Love's *Heaven's Glory; Hell's terror*. Later in that year, however, the name of Robert Foulis (*q.v.*) appears on Cicero, *De natura Deorum*, as *typis academicis*. He appears to have been also a bookbinder, for he was so described when his will was registered on September 3rd, 1742, and September 11th, 1745. [Comm. Rec. Glasgow, *Reg. Test.* 1547–1800.] As a bookbinder he was admitted Burgess and Guild Brother, gratis, March 24th, 1724. [Scot. Rec. Soc., *B. and G. B. of Glasgow*, 1573–1750.]

MILLER or MILLAR (DAVID), journeyman printer in Edinburgh, (?)1742–52. In South-West Kirk Parish. *The Edinburgh Marriage Registers*, 1701–50 and 1751–1800, contain records of three marriages under the name of David Miller, printer or journeyman printer, as below: (1) D.M. printer, married Henrietta Bain, June 6th, 1742; (2) D.M. journeyman printer, married Barbara Pittillo or Pattullo, June 30th, 1751; (3) D.M. printer, married Elizabeth Ruthven, April 12th, 1752. In each case D.M. was resident in the South-West Kirk Parish, so they may all refer to one man.

MILLER (GEORGE), bookseller and stationer at Dunbar, *c.* 1745–89. Born at Dirleton in 1725, but early went to Dunbar where he started and carried on the business of general merchant. He had a "little stock of stationery", and "sold catechisms and the Proverbs of Solomon, children's books in all the glory of richly ornamented covers and children's pictures in variety". He died on June 27th, 1789 and was survived by three sons and two daughters. His eldest son, James, succeeded him in business; his second son George, was a bookseller in Dunbar and afterwards in Haddington; his youngest son John became a bookseller and printer in Dunfermline. [Couper, *The Millers of Haddington, Dunbar and Dunfermline*, 1914.]

MILLER (THOMAS), running stationer in Edinburgh. In North Kirk Parish, 1744. Married Jane Walker, widow of Arthur Nasmyth (*q.v.*), running stationer, May 6th, 1744. He died within the succeeding twelve months, however, for on June 23rd, 1745, his widow, Jane Walker, married James Stewart (*q.v.*). [*Edinb. Marr. Reg.*, 1701–50.]

MITCHELL (JOHN), bookbinder in Edinburgh, 1744. Entered as bookbinder in the *Edinburgh Guild Register*, September 5th, 1744.

MOIR (JOHN), bookbinder in Edinburgh, 1764. Bell's Wynd. Sold copies of William Hunter's *The Black Bird, a choice collection of the most celebrated songs* . . . Edinburgh: Printed by J. Bruce & Company . . . 1764.

MONCUR (JOHN), printer in Edinburgh, 1707–35. Printer, by right of George Moncur, father, July 9th, 1707. [*Edinb. Guild Reg.*] Married (1) Geills Adam, February 20th, 1707; (2) Agnes Lethin, widow of Edward Robertson, July 6th, 1718. [*Edinb. Marr. Reg.*, 1701–50.] Burgess of Edinburgh. Prentice master of (1) Archibald Horne, July 4th, 1722; (2) Patrick Mathie (*q.v.*), August 2nd, 1732. [*Edinb. Guild. Reg.*] His will was registered June 23rd, 1735. [Scot. Rec. Soc., *Edinb. Test.*] *See also Dictionary*, 1668–1725.

MONTGOMERY (DANIEL), printer in Edinburgh, before 1746. His widow, Helen Scott, married Patrick Stephen, staymaker, October 5th, 1746. [*Edinb. Marr. Reg.*, 1701–50.] Possibly a relative of Hugh Montgomery (*see Dictionary*, 1668–1725).

MOODIE (GEORGE), bookbinder in Edinburgh, *c.* 1775–(?). Married Jean, daughter of Patrick Boyd (*q.v.*), bookbinder, November 17th, 1776. [*Edinb. Marr. Reg.*, 1751–1800.] May have succeeded Boyd, who was dead at the date of the marriage.

MOODIE (JAMES), stationer's assistant (to James Nimmo, *q.v.*) in Edinburgh, 1754. Married Agnes, daughter of John Clarke, wright in Pennycook, October 27th, 1754. [*Edinb. Marr. Reg.*, 1751–1800.]

MOODIE (THOMAS), bookbinder in Glasgow, *c.* 1720–40. Willow Acre. He, with his two brothers, owned Willow Acre, on the banks of Camlachie Burn. [Reid, *Glasgow Past & Present*, III, pp. 225, 242.] Omitted from *Dictionary*, 1668–1725.

MORE (JAMES), bookbinder in Edinburgh, 1753. In North West Kirk Parish. Married Jean, daughter of deceased John Pattullo, ships carpenter in Montrose, September 16th, 1753. [*Edinb. Marr. Reg.*, 1751–1800.] Probably a brother of John More (*q.v.*).

MORE (JOHN), bookbinder in Edinburgh, 1725–74. Brown's Close, 1773–4. Entered in the *Edinburgh Guild Register* as a bookbinder, March 10th, 1725. Probably brother of James More (*q.v.*). Married Margaret, daughter of John Pittillo [Pattullo], shipbuilder in Montrose, October 3rd, 1742. [*Edinb. Marr. Reg.*, 1701–50.] His name appears in the *Edinburgh Directory* for 177¾.

MORISON (FRANCIS), bookbinder in Perth, *c.* 1670–*c.* 1740. Freeman glazier and bookbinder. Married Elizabeth Mitchell. Deacon of the Incorporation of Wrights. Built and lived and worked in a three-storey house on the south

side of the High Street. The house has long disappeared but its site is known. It is occupied at present by the Hall of the Scone and Perth Masonic Lodge. Father of Robert Morison, senior (*q.v.*), and the first known member of the family which became famous in the history of book-production in Scotland. The exact dates of his birth, marriage and death are apparently unknown.

MORISON (JAMES), bookseller, printer and publisher, Leith and Perth, 1762–1809. Born at Perth in 1762. Commenced business as a bookseller, according to the D.N.B., at Leith. He could not, however, have been long established there, for he was early admitted a partner in his father's business at Perth. Both he and his brother Robert were exceedingly precocious, and were married very early in life, their wives being little more than girls. They then resided in Rose Terrace in flats, which were entered by a common stair. James Morison was a man of ability and under his management the business developed from a small concern to one of the most important publishing houses of the country. He was the author of many works, and to his other attainments added that of being an accomplished linguist. Amongst the most important of his writings are *Key to the Scriptures* . . . published in 2 vols. in 1806, and a *Theological Dictionary*, 1807. He was twice married; first to Margaret, daughter of Thomas Mitchell, writer, when he was only sixteen years of age. She bore him five children, and died in 1789. He then married Grace, daughter of David Lindsay, merchant and banker in Perth. By this wife he had five more children. Several of the works published by the Morison press at the end of the eighteenth century are translations of his own from the French. To this period also belong the famous editions of the Scottish poets, and an ed. of "Blind Harry's" *Wallace*, in 3 vols., which claims to be the only authentic copy from the MS. in the National Library. Besides his work as a publisher and his labours as author he was a partner, along with his brother-in-law Henry Lindsay, in the paper works of Woodend, near Huntingtower. He was an elder of the Glassite Church in Perth, and his works are chiefly of a religious nature. He died in 1809. [*D.N.B.* &c.]

MORISON (JOHN), bookseller in Perth, *c.* 1760. A member of the well-known family of printers and booksellers. His will was registered [November 25th, 1766.] September 18th, 1771. [Comm. Rec. St Andrews, *Reg. Test.* 1549–1800.]

MORISON (ROBERT), first, printer, bookseller and bookbinder, Perth and Dunkeld, 1722–91. Born at Perth in 1722. Son of Francis Morison (*q.v.*). At the age

of twenty he was "received and admitted" a member of the Incorporation of Wrights, which body protected and licensed all workmen who wrought with edged tools. The minute of his admission runs: "Perth, 31 Dec., 1742. Compeared Robert Morison, Glazier and bookbinder in Perth, son to the Deceast Francis Morison late Deacon of the Wright Calling of Perth, who was a freeman Glazier and Bookbinder, and craved to be admitted to the said two sciences, which being considered by the Calling they have received and admitted, and hereby receive and admitt the said Robert Morison to be a freeman Glazier and Bookbinder or Stationer, and to the hail liberties and privileges thereto belonging for payment of Ten Merks as his freedom Money as Bookbinder or Stationer with Eight Pounds Scots for a Dinner and Four Pounds of Officer's Fee. And he also paid Four Pounds Scots as his Foot Ball, he being married, all which was instantly paid in to the present Boxmaster, whereupon the said Robert Morison asked and took Instruments in the Clerk's hands. (Signed) Thomas Young." In 1744 or 1745 he became Postmaster at Perth, and published a *Table of Regulations of the Post Office*. A facsimile of this was published by the late David Marshall, F.S.A. Scot. The appendix gives information respecting his stock, and, in addition to innumerable items from writing-paper to cough lozenges, records that he sold "School Books; Bibles, gilt and plain; Psalm-books, ditto; and every Book (on a short Notice) at the same Price as at the place of Publication. . . ." It further states: "Books Bound in the neatest manner; just from London, a large Collection of little Books for Children, Catalogues whereof may be had gratis." In later years, about 1770 probably, he opened a branch shop at Dunkeld, but this soon passed into the hands of James Cant (*q.v.*). The *Perth Magazine* was printed by George Johnston in 1772, for Robert Morison the proprietor. This magazine came to an end on December 24th, 1773. Morison's wife was Margaret Russell, by whom he had two sons, James and Robert, and one daughter, Jacobina. He died in 1791.

MORISON (ROBERT), second, printer, publisher and bookseller, Perth and St Andrews, 1764–1853. Son of Robert Morison, 1st, and younger brother of James. Early established himself as the printer of the famous firm, and most of their publications bear the imprint "Printed by R. Morison, junior, for R. Morison & Son". He was three times married and lived to a good old age. From its inception in 1809 he printed the *Perth Courier*. In 1796 the Morisons were appointed printers to the University of St Andrews, when, with a few other works, they

issued what are usually called the "immaculate editions" of *Horace* and *Sallust*, edited by Professor John Hunter. Much of the success of this firm is without doubt due to Robert Morison the younger. He is not known to have done any literary work, like his brother, but seems to have concentrated his abilities upon the various phases of printing. He died in 1853, in his eighty-ninth year.

MORRISON or MORISON (WILLIAM), bookbinder in Edinburgh, 1757. In Old Grayfriar's Parish. Married Jean, daughter of Matthew Black, merchant in New Grayfriar's Parish, May 29th, 1757. [*Edinb. Marr. Reg.*, 1751–1800.]

MORTON (ALEXANDER), paper-maker in Edinburgh, 1726–62. In Parish of Colinton. Probably a son of James Morton (*q.v.*). Married Isobel, daughter of William Plenderleith, tailor, January 23rd, 1726. [*Edinb. Marr. Reg.*, 1701–50.] His daughter Katherine married Alexander Pennycook, wright, January 3rd, 1762. [*Ib.*, 1751–1800.]

MORTON (JAMES), papermaker in Colinton Mill, Edinburgh. *c.* 1720(?) Probably the father of Alexander Morton (*q.v.*). Died before October 27th, 1728, on which date his daughter Ann married James Smith. [*Edinb. Marr. Reg.*, 1701–50.]

MOSMAN (JOHN), printer in Edinburgh, 1717–30. At the King's Printing-house in Craig's Closs, 1727. One of His Majesty's printers, 1727. Printed Alexander Hamilton's *A new account of the East Indies* . . . Edinburgh, 1727. *See also Dictionary*, 1668–1725.

MUDIE (WALTER), papermaker in Pennycuik, 1761. Married Helen, daughter of the deceased Peter Dickson, March 19th, 1761. [*Canongate Reg. Marr.*, 1564–1800.]

MUNDELL (ROBERT), printer in Edinburgh, *c.* 1770–6. Brodie's Close, lawnmarket, 1773–4. His name is found in the *Edinburgh Directory* for 177¾. His will was registered August 30th, 1776. [Scot. Rec. Soc., *Edinb. Test.*] In 1791 Mundell & Son, possibly descendants of Robert, printed *The Bee, or Literary Intelligencer*.

MURDOCH (ROBERT), papermaker at Redhall Mill, in Parish of Hailes, 1727. Married Agnes, daughter of James White, surgeon in Bo'ness, June 30th, 1727. [*Edinb. Marr. Reg.*, 1701–50.]

MURIE ( ), printer in Glasgow, *c.* 1743. An edition of the *Westminster Confession*, printed at Glasgow in 1743, bears his name as printer.

MURRAY (ALEXANDER), printer in Edinburgh, 1734–81(?) Burnet's Close, 1739; Craig's Close, 1773. Married Margaret, daughter of James Robertson, litster in Perth, May 26th, 1734. [*Edinb. Marr. Reg.*, 1701–50.] Served his apprenticeship with Thomas Ruddiman. Entered in the *Edinburgh Guild Register* as a printer, April 11th, 1739. The imprint to the *Scots Magazine* for 1740 reads: "Printed by Sands, Brymer, Murray and Cochran." A note in the vol. describes A. Murray and J. Cochran as the printers, and W. Sands and A. Brymer as booksellers. In 1743 the *Scots Magazine* was "Printed by James Cochran and Company", but in 1744 the imprint became "Printed by W. Sands, A. Murray and J. Cochran". This partnership lasted until 1752 at least, for in that year they printed for T. Glas of Dundee an edition of Burnet's *Travels*. In 1763 a dispute arose in the office of Messrs. Murray & Cochran, about the price of composition, when William Smellie (*q.v.*), then engaged as a reader, devised a scale of prices. This seems to have been the first attempt at a regular scale in Scotland, but the first regular and acknowledged compositor's scale was not adopted until 1785. James Young worked in their office in 1755. In 1751 Murray married again, his second wife being Katherine, daughter of Thomas White, shipmaster in Anstruther. [*Edinb. Marr. Reg.*, 1751–1800.] The firm of Murray and Cochran printed in 1777 Sir Harry Moncrieff-Welwood's *Sermon, preached before the Society in Scotland for propagating Christian knowledge, on June 7, 1776*. Murray seems to have died before September 7th, 1781, on which date his daughter Katherine married James Mitchell, printer. His will was registered May 26th, 1785. [Scot. Rec. Soc., *Edinb. Test.*] He may be identical with the printer Alex. Murray who married Jean Loch of Carnbee on June 30th, 1765. The firm of Murray and Cochran existed for many years after the death of Alex. Murray. Possibly he was succeeded in the firm by a son.

MURRAY (DUNCAN), type-founder in Glasgow, *c.* 1770–(?) His daughter Mary married Alexander Watt, shoemaker, March 7th, 1791. [*Edinb. Marr. Reg.*, 1751–1800.]

MURRAY (WILLIAM), printer and publisher in Aberdeen, 1752–7. On October 3rd, 1752 *The Aberdeen Intelligencer* was started by Francis Douglas (*q.v.*) and William Murray. After running for a few years it was incorporated, after February 22nd, 1757, with its successful rival *The Aberdeen Journal*. [*Scot. N. & Q.*, v. 1, p. 4.]

MURRAY (WILLIAM), printer in Edinburgh, 1766. In Old Grayfriar's Parish. Married Elizabeth, daughter of deceased Adam Paterson, brewer, April 13th, 1766. [*Edinb. Marr. Reg.*, 1751–1800.] Possibly father of the printer of the same name who, on January 26th, 1793, married Jean, daughter of Lawrence Maclaren. [*Ib.*]

NAIRN (GEORGE), running stationer in Edinburgh, 1743. In North Kirk Parish. Married Margaret Main, widow of John Dobie (*q.v.*), running stationer, November 20th, 1743. [*Edinb. Marr. Reg.*, 1701–50.]

NAIRN (J.), of Greenyards, printer in Edinburgh, *c.* 1736. In 1736 was published *Proceedings in the submission betwixt W. R. Freebairn, his majesty's printer, and Mr. J. Blair, of Ardblair, and Mr. J. Nairn, of Greenyards, aspiring to be King's Printers*; Edinburgh, folio. [Timperley, p. 655.]

NASMYTH (ARTHUR), running stationer in Edinburgh. Before 1744. His widow, Jane Walker, married (1) Thomas Miller (*q.v.*), May 6th, 1744, and (2) James Stewart (*q.v.*), June 23rd, 1745. [*Edinb. Marr. Reg.*, 1701–50.]

NEILL (ADAM), printer in Edinburgh, 1766–1812. In the College, 1766–9; Old Fishmarket Close, 1769–1812. Entered into partnership with his brother Patrick (*q.v.*) (who had laid the foundations of the present day firm of Neill & Co.) in 1766. Robert Fleming joined him in 1769 on Patrick's retirement. Adam died in 1812 and was succeeded by two cousins, James, a son of Patrick, and Patrick, a son of Adam. In 1773 he married Helen, daughter of Andrew Douglas, glazier (May 30th). [*The Printing House of Neill*, 1918.]

NEILL (PATRICK), printer in Edinburgh, *c.* 1740–69. In the College, 1749–69, Old Fishmarket Close, 1769. Probably a son of Patrick Neill, bookbinder in Glasgow. In 1749 he entered into partnership with Gavin Hamilton (*q.v.*) and John Balfour (*q.v.*) as Hamilton, Balfour and Neill. The two first named partners retired from the firm in 1766 and the business was continued by Patrick Neill along with his brother Adam. The place of printing was then in the College buildings, but it was removed in 1769 to the Old Fishmarket Close. In the same year Patrick retired from the firm and was succeeded by Robert Fleming, who entered into partnership with Adam Neill. [*The Printing House of Neill*, 1918.]

NESTON (THOMAS), stationer in Edinburgh, 1763. Married Janet Dunbar, March 20th, 1763. [*Edinb. Marr. Reg.*, 1751–1800.]

NEWBIGGING (JOHN), running stationer in Edinburgh, 1754. In North Kirk Parish. Married Margaret, daughter of John M'Neil, gardener in Abby, October 27th, 1754. [*Edinb. Marr. Reg.*, 1751–1800.]

NEWLANDS (JOHN), bookseller and publisher in Glasgow, 1747. Head of the Gallowgate. Son-in-law of the Rev. Ralph Erskine, whose *Sermon preached immediately before the Administration of the Sacrament of the Lord's Supper, July 19, 1747*, was "Printed for J. Newlands [at Glasgow] . . . 1747".

NICOL (JAMES), printer in Aberdeen, 1710–36. *See Dictionary*, 1668–1725.

NICOLL (ROBERT), running stationer in Edinburgh. Before 1763. His daughter Christian married George Macleish, slater, June 26th, 1763. [*Edinb. Marr. Reg.*, 1751–1800.] He was then dead.

NIELL (JAMES), stationer in Edinburgh, 1764. Married Jean Melville, October 14th, 1764. [*Edinb. Marr. Reg.*, 1751–1800.]

NIMMO (JAMES), stationer in Edinburgh, 1754. In New North Kirk Parish. On October 27th, 1754 James Moodie, servant to James Nimmo, stationer, married Agnes, daughter of John Clark, wright in Pennycuik. [*Edinb. Marr. Reg.*, 1751–1800.] Probably a relative of Richard Nimmo (*q.v.*).

NIMMO (RICHARD), bookbinder and stationer in Edinburgh, 1743–4. Entered in the *Edinburgh Guild Register* as a stationer, July 20th, 1743, by right of Robert Nimmo, father. Described as a bookbinder in the list of subscribers to John Welch's *Miscellany Sermons*, 1744. Probably a relative of James Nimmo (*q.v.*).

NISBET (ALEXANDER), bookbinder in Kelso, 1744. Subscribed for a copy of John Welch's *Miscellany Sermons*, Edinburgh, 1744.

NISBET (DAVID), bookbinder in Newcastle, *c.* 1760. His daughter Anne married Patrick Mudie, gentleman's servant, June 19th, 1798. Nisbet was then dead. [*Edinb. Marr. Reg.*, 1751–1800.]

NISBET (JAMES), bookseller in Linton, 1759. His name appears in the imprint to Rev. Ralph Erskine's *Christ the People's Covenant* . . . "Edinburgh: Printed by David Gray . . . 1759".

NORRY (A.), (?) bookseller in Perth, 1747. Sold copies of Rev. Ralph Erskine's *Sermon preached immediately before the Administration of the Sacrament of the Lord's Supper, at Dunfermline, July 19, 1747*. "Glasgow: Printed for J. Newlands . . . 1747." Does not appear to have been recorded locally as a bookseller.

NOTMAN (JAMES), bookseller in Selkirk, before 1773. His will was registered March 19th, 1773. [Scot. Rec. Soc., *Edinb. Test.*]

OGILVIE (DAVID), bookbinder in Edinburgh, 1763. Married Jean Glen, May 20th, 1763. [*Canongate Reg. Marr.*, 1564–1800.]

OGSTON (MARTHA), bookseller in Edinburgh, 1688–1738 (?) *See Dictionary*, 1668–1725.

OLIPHANT (DAVID), bookseller and bookbinder in Edinburgh, 1727–44. In North-West Kirk Parish, 1727. Son of Rev. John Oliphant, Minister at Cameron. Married Jean, daughter of John Smylie, merchant in Glasgow, January 22nd, 1727. [*Edinb. Marr. Reg.*, 1701–50.] Entered as a bookbinder in the *Edinburgh Guild Register*, May 13th, 1730, and as prentice-master of James Young, junior (*q.v.*), bookbinder, August 1st, 1744. His name occurs as a bookseller in the imprint to John Currie's *A full vindication of the people's right* . . . 1733, but his main business seems to have been that of a bookbinder.

ORMISTON (WILLIAM), senior, bookbinder in Edinburgh, 1726–(?) In South West Kirk Parish, 1726. Married Isobel, daughter of John Borthwick, June 15th, 1726. [*Edinb. Marr. Reg.*, 1701–50.] Bookbinder, May 13th, 1730. [*Edinb. Guild Reg.*]. Probably succeeded by his son (see next entry).

ORMISTON (WILLIAM), junior, bookbinder in Edinburgh. In Old Grayfriar's Parish, 1757. Son of William Ormiston, senior (*q.v.*). Married Sophia, daughter of John Haigie, February 20th, 1757. [*Edinb. Marr. Reg.*, 1751–1800.]

ORR (JOHN), printer, publisher and stationer in Glasgow, *c.* 1752–66. Corner of the Salt-market. In 1752 he printed and published David Mackellar's *Hymn on Creation*, and in the same year *A Hymn of Praise and Thanks to God for all His Mercies*, in Gaelic and English. He seems to have printed and published many works in Gaelic, including, in 1755, Richard Baxter's *Call to the unconverted*; in 1756 and 1757 editions of the *Confession of Faith*, and in the latter year *The Shorter Catechism*. This last publication noted is a Gaelic ed. of Alex. Macdonald's *Poems and songs*, 1764. He died in 1766.

OSWALD (JOHN), bookbinder in Edinburgh, 1760. In Tolbooth Parish. Married Janet, daughter of James Williamson, glover in Elgin, February 3rd, 1760. [*Edinb. Marr. Reg.*, 1751–1800.]

OSWALD (WALTER), printer in Edinburgh, *c.* 1750–70. Apprentice and journeyman printer to Walter Ruddiman. In the *Scots Magazine*, 1770, p. 458, is a copy of some verses in memory of Walter Ruddiman, by W. O. (i.e. Walter Oswald).

OSWALD (WILLIAM), printer in Edinburgh, 1757. In New North Kirk Parish. Married Robina, daughter of William Christie, stabler, October 16th, 1757. [*Edinb. Marr. Reg.*, 1751–1800.]

PATERSON (DAVID), printer and bookseller, Glasgow, 1755–9; Edinburgh, 1760–*c.* 1780. Printed in partnership with John Bryce (*q.v.*) in Glasgow, from 1755 to 1759 or 1760. In 1759 their joint imprint appeared on James Durham's *Exposition of the Book of Job*. After the partnership had been dissolved Bryce continued to print in the Salt-market at Glasgow and Paterson set up in Edinburgh in the Lawn-market. In 1760 he published *The Religious Magazine, or Christian's Storehouse*, a monthly magazine, sold at 6*d*. per number. Apparently this was not a success, and it is questionable if it lived for any length of time. The B.M. has only the first two numbers. No other copies are known. His imprint appears on the title page to *Mercy and Judgment displayed in the Effects of a Gospel Ministry. A Sermon preached April 22nd, 1766.* "Edinburgh . . . 1766." His address in 1773–4 was still "Lawn-market". [*Edinb. Directory, Suppt.*] His imprint has not been found on any book of a date later than 1780, when he printed *Scotland's Opposition to the Popish Bill.*

PATERSON (ROBERT), printer in Edinburgh, 1766. In New North Kirk Parish. Married Elizabeth, daughter of John Lyall, March 23rd, 1766. [*Edinb. Marr. Reg.*, 1751–1800.]

PATERSON (WILLIAM), younger, bookbinder and stationer in Edinburgh, 1697–1732. In North Kirk Parish, 1710. In Moultrieshall, *c.* 1730. Burgess, son of Wm. Paterson, bookbinder, and by his right, October 20th, 1697. [*Edinb. Guild Reg.*] Prentice-master of George Buchanan, December 19th, 1722. [*Ib.*] His will was registered March 31st, 1732. [Scot. Rec. Soc., *Edinb. Test.*]

PATON (GEORGE), bookseller in Edinburgh, 1720–1807. Parliament Close. Son of John Paton (*q.v.*). Received a liberal education, but without any professional design, having been bred by his father to his own business. He remained in partnership with his father for some time, but apparently preferred a clerkship in the Custom-House, at £60 per annum, which left him leisure for developing his tastes as an antiquary. He became well known and several volumes of his correspondence were published between 1829 and 1835. He remained all his life a bachelor. His death took place on March 5th, 1807, at the age of eighty-seven. His valuable library was sold by auction in 1809, and his manuscripts, prints, coins, &c. in 1811. The sale of the books occupied

a month. He is not to be confused with his contemporary, George Paton, bookbinder. [Kay's *Portraits*, v. 1, pp. 244–7.]

PATON (G.), (?) bookseller in Kilmarnock, 1747. Sold copies of Rev. Ralph Erskine's *Sermon preached immediately before the Administration of the Sacrament of the Lord's Supper, at Dunfermline, July 19, 1747*; "Glasgow: Printed for J. Newlands . . . 1747".

PATON (GEORGE), printer in Glasgow, 1741–72(?) Mentioned in a list of Glasgow printers by Richard Duncan in *Notices and Documents illustrative of the literary history of Glasgow*, 1831, p. 155. A George Paton printed an ed. of Shield's *A Hind let loose* . . . Glasgow, 1797.

PATON (GEORGE), bookbinder in Edinburgh, 1753–74. Buchanan's Head, 1753; Back of Bess Wynd, 1773–4. Married Mariana, daughter of Thomas Stenhouse, smith and ferrier, August 5th, 1764. [*Edinb. Marr. Reg.*, 1751–1800.] His name appears in the *Edinburgh Directory* for 177¾.

PATON (JOHN), bookseller and bookbinder in Edinburgh, 1713–81. In the Parliament Close. Burgess of Edinburgh, 1713. [*Edin. Marr. Reg.*, 1701–50.] Sold copies of *Epistolae Jacobi Quarti* . . ., Ruddiman, 1722. A list of books then on sale by him is found at the end of Ruddiman's *Herodianus*, 1724. In 1743 he sold copies of *A Description of the Parish of Melrose*, Edinb., Ruddiman. He was one of a committee of philanthropic citizens, who, in conjunction with Provost Drummond, originated the Royal Infirmary. In the *Edinburgh Guild Register* he is mentioned as prentice-master of Thomas Paton, bookseller and binder, August 8th, 1744. He appears to have been an antiquary of some importance and at his death left his son George Paton (*q.v.*) a valuable collection of books. It is recorded that both he and his son invariably added any work of particular interest or value to their own collection, instead of placing it in the shop for sale. His will was registered May 16th, 1781. [Scot. Rec. Soc., *Edinb. Test.*] *See also Dictionary*, 1668–1725.

PATON, PATOUN, PATTON (THOMAS), bookbinder in Edinburgh, 1743–(?) In South-West Kirk Parish, 1743. Married Margaret, daughter of James Fraiter, schoolmaster in Strathmiglo, September 18th, 1743. [*Edinb. Marr. Reg.*, 1751–1800.] Prentice to John Paton (*q.v.*), bookseller and binder, August 8th, 1744. [*Edinb. Guild Reg.*] He died before June 7th, 1770, on which date his daughter Helen married John Thomson, merchant in Tolbooth Parish. [*Edinb. Marr. Reg.*, 1751–1800.]

PAUL (JOHN), bookbinder in Edinburgh, 1773–4. Foot of High School Wynd. His name is found in the *Edinburgh Directory*, 177¾ (Suppt.).

PEARSON (DAVID), chapman in Culross, 1760. Sold copies of *The Religious Magazine, or Christian's Storehouse*, 1760.

PENNINGTON (LUKE), journeyman printer in Edinburgh. In Tolbooth Parish, 1769. Married Sarah Softly, relict of Alexander Walker, upholsterer, March 5th, 1769. [*Edinb. Marr. Reg.*, 1751–1800.]

PETERS (GABRIEL), stationer in Edinburgh, 1773–4. Head of Carrubber's Close. Only known from an entry in the *Edinburgh Directory* for 177¾.

PETRIE (JOHN), printer in Edinburgh, 1768. In New North Kirk Parish. Married Janet, daughter of deceased George Allan, mason in Elgin, November 27th, 1768. [*Edinb. Marr. Reg.*, 1751–1800.]

PORTEOUS (JAMES), bookbinder in Edinburgh, 1762. In New Grayfriar's Parish. Married Janet, daughter of James Strathearn, flax-dresser in Kilsyth, October 24th, 1762. [*Edinb. Marr. Reg.*, 1751–1800.]

PORTEOUS (MATTHEW), printer in Edinburgh, *c.* 1710–30. His daughter Helen married George Miller, indweller in Stockbridgehaugh, July 31st, 1730. [*Edinb. Marr. Reg.*, 1701–50.]

PROVAN (PATRICK), bookseller in Stirling, 1734. Sold copies of Ebenezer Erskine's *The King held in the Galleries*, Edinburgh, 1734.

PURVES (GEORGE), printer in Edinburgh, 1774. In Old Kirk Parish. Married Janet, daughter of Peter M'Naughton, April 24th, 1774. [*Edinb. Marr. Reg.*, 1751–1800.] Possibly a journeyman.

PYET (JOHN), printer in Edinburgh, 1750–90(?) In South Kirk Parish. On January 28th, 1750 he married Margaret, daughter of James Leggat, merchant. [*Edinb. Marr. Reg.*, 1701–50.] His daughter Elspeth married George Buchan, June 20th, 1792. [*Ib.*, 1751–1800.] No book with his imprint has been noted.

RANDIE (DAVID), bookseller and publisher in Edinburgh, 1728–30(?) Published John Reynold's *Practical discourse of reconciliation between God and man*, 1728. His daughter Isobel married Robert Muirhead, merchant in Hamilton, September 10th, 1730. [*Edinb. Marr. Reg.*, 1701–50.]

RAMSAY (ALLAN), bookseller in Edinburgh, 1716(?)–58, *see Dictionary*, 1668–1725, *also* Creech (William) and Sibbald (James).

RAY (EBENEZER), printer in Edinburgh, 1771. In Old Kirk Parish. Married Elizabeth, daughter of Mr. Francis Morison of Hughend in the parish of Dunkeld, May 5th, 1771. [*Edinb. Marr. Reg.*, 1751–1800.]

REID (JAMES), bookseller in Leith, 1761. Subscribed to James Durham's *Christ Crucified*, 6th ed., Glasgow, M'Lean & Galbraith, 1761.

REID (JOHN), printer in Edinburgh, *c.* 1758–75(?) In the College, 1759; Castlehill, 1764; Baillie Fyfe's Close, 1773–4. On September 1st, 1759, his name first appears in the imprint to the *Edinburgh Chronicle*, together with those of Gavin Hamilton, John Balfour and Patrick Neill. In 1764 he appears as a partner of Alexander Donaldson (*q.v.*), in the printing of the *Edinburgh Advertiser*. Reid's name, however, disappeared from the imprint with No. 67, August 21st, 1764. His name occurs in the imprint to the Gaelic edition of the Rev. John Willison's *On the Shorter Catechism*, Edinburgh, 1773. The last notice of his name appears in the *Edinburgh Directory*, 177¾.

REID (WILLIAM), printer and publisher in Edinburgh, 1758–1829. Established, with others, the *Glasgow Courier*, and for a long time acted as its editor. Married Catherine, daughter of John Paterson, shoemaker, February 26th, 1788. [*Canongate Reg. Marr.*, 1564–1800.] Died in April 1829, aged 71 years. [Timperley, p. 909.]

RICHARDSON (ARCHIBALD), bookbinder in Edinburgh, 1730–50. In South Kirk Parish, 1740. Entered in the *Edinburgh Guild Register* as a bookbinder, May 13th, 1730. Married Janet Aitken (or Aikine), daughter of Thomas Aikine, tenant in Harvestoune, in Borthwick Parish, November 23rd, 1740. This Janet Aitken is not to be confused with the wife of Charles Cosh, bookbinder. His daughter Janet married Peter (?Walter) Bedfoord, sometime saddler in Edinburgh and afterwards in Dublin, November 4th, 1750. [*Edinb. Marr. Reg.*, 1701–50.]

ROBB (JAMES), stationer in Glasgow, 1748. Burgess and Guild Brother as serving apprenticeship with James Brown, stationer, August 25th, 1748. [Scot. Rec. Soc., *Burgesses and G. B. of Glasgow*, 1573–1750.] Probably a relative of John Robb (*q.v.*).

ROBB (JOHN), bookseller and bookbinder in Glasgow, 1741–78. Admitted Burgess and Guild Brother as bookbinder, gratis, May 13th, 1741. [Scot. Rec. Soc., *Burgesses and G.B. of Glasgow*, 1573–1750.] His will was registered March 5th, 1778. [Comm. Rec. Glasgow; *Reg. Test.*, 1547–1800.] His daughter Elizabeth married John Thomson, merchant, July 29th, 1783, in Edinburgh. [*Edinb. Marr. Reg.*, 1751–1800.]

ROBERTSON (ALEXANDER), printer in Edinburgh, *c.* 1750–84(?) Niddry's Wynd, 1773–4. Married Jean, daughter of deceased Dougal Campbell in (of) Balmedie in Argyleshire, April 24th, 1763. [*Edinb. Marr. Reg.*, 1751–1800.] His daughter Isobel married John Morren, printer, January 29th, 1784. Printed editions of the *Westminster Confession*, &c. between 1756 and 1778. His name appears in the *Edinburgh Directory* for 177¾, whence the above address.

ROBERTSON (FRANCIS), bookseller in Edinburgh, 1767. In Old Kirk Parish. Married Elizabeth, daughter of deceased John Young of Newhall, March 22nd, 1767. [*Edinb. Marr. Reg.*, 1751–1800.]

ROBERTSON (JAMES), printer in Glasgow, 1774–(?) Probably son of John Robertson (*q.v.*), with whom he printed about 1774. His own imprint appears on a Gaelic ed. of *The History of the feuds and conflicts among the clans in the Northern parts of Scotland*, 1780, which he printed for John Gillies, bookseller in Perth. He was printing until 1786 and probably much later.

ROBERTSON or ROBIESON (JOHN), senior, stationer in Glasgow, 1697–1728. Burgess and master, December 6th, 1697. [Scot. Rec. Soc., *Burgesses and Guild Brothers of Glasgow*, 1573–1750.] Made Guild Brother by same right, as serving apprenticeship with George Lawrie, April 6th, 1704. [*Ib.*] Father of John Robertson, junior (*q.v.*).

ROBERTSON (JOHN), printer in Edinburgh, 1719–49(?) Fish Market. Married Helen, daughter of William Cock, printer, June 12th, 1719. [*Edinb. Marr. Reg.*, 1701–50.] In partnership with Thomas Lumisden (*q.v.*). The firm of Thomas Lumisden and Company was printing as late as 1749. *See also Dictionary*, 1668–1725.

ROBERTSON (JOHN), junior, bookbinder in Glasgow, 1728–40. Son of John Robertson or Robieson, senior, stationer in Glasgow, 1697–1728. Burgess and Guild Brother, as serving apprenticeship with J. R. senior [*q.v.*], May 30th, 1728. [Scot. Rec. Soc., *Burg. and G. B. of Glasgow*, 1573–1750.] May be the same as the bookseller who is said to have been born about 1704. [Reid, *Glasgow Past and Present*, v. 3, p. 129.] He is still described as a bookbinder, prentice-master to Robert Smith, on September 4th, 1740, however. [*B. and G. B. of Glasgow.*]

ROBERTSON (JOHN), bookseller and printer in Glasgow, *c.* 1730–(?). Born about 1704. Printed in partnership with Archibald McLean (*q.v.*) in 1739, [Duncan: *Notices & Docs. Illustr. of the lit. Hist. of Glasgow*, 1831, p. 155.] By 1748 the partnership had been dissolved and Robertson alone printed several editions of the *Westminster Confession* between that date and 1770. During the latter-part of his life he took James Robertson (probably his son) into partnership. Their joint imprint occurs on books about 1774, including James Taylor's *Life of Jesus Christ.*

ROBERTSON (JOHN), printer and publisher in Edinburgh, *c.* 1760–90. Backstairs, Parliament Close, 1772–90. Married Helen, daughter of Thomas Allan, tenant in Kirkliston, December 25th, 1763. [*Edinb. Marr. Reg.*, 1751–1800.] Probably a son of John Robertson, printer, 1719–49 (*q.v.*). In 1767 he printed an edition of the *Shorter Catechism* in Gaelic. Printed and published the *Caledonian Mercury* from 1772–90. On May 31st, 1776 commenced to issue the *Caledonian Gazetteer*, which ran for only thirteen numbers. Robertson retired from the *Mercury* on July 1, 1790, disposing of the right to publish, to his friend Robert Allan. In 1780, his son, Thomas Robertson, got into serious trouble over the *Edinburgh Gazette*, of which he was editor and publisher. As he was a minor an attempt was made to fasten responsibility on his father. An account of the trial is given in Morrison's *Dict. of Decisions*, p. 13,935. [Couper, *Edinb. Period Press.*] In May 1772 John Robertson purchased from the trustees of Ruddiman's grandchildren their printing-house and materials. [Timperley, p. 722.]

ROBERTSON (PETER), bookbinder in Edinburgh, 1773. Married Ann, daughter of deceased James Forbes, lint-dresser, September 19th, 1773. [*Edinb. Marr. Reg.*, 1751–1800.]

ROBERTSON (WILLIAM), printer in Edinburgh, 1773. In the *Canongate Register of Marriages* there is an entry to the effect that on Dec. 4th, 1773, William Robertson, printer in Edinburgh, and Jean, daughter of the deceased John Mathew, farmer in Elphinston, gave up their names, &c.

ROLLAND (WILLIAM), publisher in Edinburgh, 1720–9. At the sign of the Printing Press in Parliament Close. A lawyer who, in April 1720, commenced to publish the *Caledonian Mercury*, which was printed for him by William Adams at the outset. He was fined and imprisoned in 1724 on account of duty owing on his paper. He died in 1729, when Ruddiman, who had printed the *Mercury*

since 1724, acquired the proprietorship of the paper. [Couper, *Edinburgh Period. Press.*]

ROSS (JAMES) (?) printer in Edinburgh, 1726. John Brown's *Life of Faith in Time of Trial and Affliction*, bears the imprint: "Edinburgh, James Ross, 1726."

ROSS (THOMAS), printer and bookbinder in Edinburgh, 1763–98(?) In New Grayfriar's Parish, 1763. Old Church Parish, 1798. Married Isobel, daughter of George Pratt, skinner, May 15th, 1763. His daughter Isobel married Hugh Macewen, merchant, October 12th, 1798. [*Edinb. Marr. Reg.*, 1751–1800.]

ROSS (WILLIAM), journeyman printer in Edinburgh, 1745–6. In North Kirk Parish. Married Elizabeth, daughter of James Newtone, gardener in South Leith, September 8th, 1745. [*Edinb. Marr. Reg.*, 1701–50.] He is presumably to be identified with the printer of the same name, who, on December 21st, 1746, married Isobel, daughter of David M'Cleish, writer in Inverkeithing. [*Ib.*]

ROSS (WILLIAM), stationer in Edinburgh, 1771. In Lady Yester's Parish. His daughter Margaret married William Bannerman, running stationer in Edinburgh, July 14th, 1771. [*Edinb. Marr. Reg.*, 1751–1800.]

RUDDIMAN (THOMAS) junior, printer in Edinburgh, 1739–49. Son of Thomas Ruddiman, senior, by his second wife. (*See Dictionary*, 1668–1725.) Born about 1714. On August 13th, 1739, Thomas Ruddiman, senior, resigned his share in the printing business to his son Thomas, who was then about twenty-five years of age. He had received a liberal education and had served his apprenticeship to the printing trade. His father lent him £200 on his entering the business. In 1744, on November 28th, he was entered in the *Edinburgh Guild Register* as a printer. The 1742 *Catalogue of the Advocates' Library* was "printed by Thomas, Walter and Thomas Ruddimans". The same imprint appears on books issued during the next few years, including *A Description of the Parish of Melrose* in 1743. He died on September 9th, 1747. [Chalmers, *Life of Thomas Ruddiman*, 1794; Timperley, p. 700; &c.]

RUDDIMAN (WALTER), senior, 1715–70, *see Dictionary*, 1668–1725.

RUDDIMAN (WALTER) junior, printer in Edinburgh, *c.* 1750–81. Morocco's Close, Lawn-market, 1757–62; Forrester's Wynd, Lawn-market, 1768–?. Nephew of Thomas Ruddiman, senior. In 1757 Walter Ruddiman, junior,

and Company, commenced to print and publish *The Edinburgh Magazine*. The firm was described as Wal. Ruddiman, junior, W. Auld and Company in volume 5, but reverted to the original form in volume 6 and last. Walter Ruddiman was editor. In 1768 *The Weekly Magazine or Edinburgh Amusement* made its first appearance. Walter Ruddiman, junior, was named as the printer and publisher. This was the first weekly magazine to appear in Scotland, and it was evidently intended to be a continuation of the *Edinburgh Magazine*. Ruddiman was several times in trouble with the authorities through the publication of this magazine (*see* Couper's *Edinb. Period. Press*, v. 2, pp. 118–20). In 1777 *Ruddiman's Weekly Mercury* appeared, with the imprint "printed for and by Walter and Thomas Ruddiman . . .", which became "Thomas Ruddiman and Company" on July 31st, 1782. In 1776 Walter printed Ronald Macdonald's *Collection of Poems* in Gaelic. W. & T. Ruddiman printed the 2nd ed. of the Rev. William Shaw's *Analysis of the Gaelic* in 1778. Walter Ruddiman junior, died on June 18th, 1781. [Couper, *Edinb. Period. Press*; Johnstone, *The Ruddimans in Scotland*, 1901; &c.]

RUSSELL (WILLIAM), printer in Edinburgh and London, 1741–93. Born at Windydoors, in the county of Selkirk, in 1741. Received his early education at Innerleithen. Went to Edinburgh in 1756 and about 1757 commenced to serve his apprenticeship as a printer, to Martin and Wotherspoon (*q.v.*), at the Apollo Press. He continued with them for five years, after which, until 1763, he worked in Edinburgh as a journeyman printer. In May 1767 he went to London to take up a literary career. Unsuccessful and disappointed he returned to printing, and became a press corrector in the office of William Strachan. In 1769 he obtained the position of overseer in Brown and Aldred's office. He published soon after several works, the proceeds of which enabled him to give up printing. In 1780 he went to Jamaica. His wife, to whom he was married in 1787, was a Miss Scott. After his marriage he retired to Knottyholm, near Langholm, where he spent the rest of his life. The University of St Andrews conferred the degree of LL.D. upon him in 1792. In the following year he published the first two volumes of his *History of Ancient Europe*. He died on December 25th, 1793, and was buried in the Churchyard of Westerkirk. His widow and one daughter survived him.

RUTHVEN (JAMES), printer in Edinburgh, 1773. In Tolbooth Parish. Perhaps a journeyman. Married Katherine, daughter of deceased Nicol Sime, saddler, April 18th, 1773. [*Edinb. Marr. Reg.*, 1751–1800.]

SANDILANDS (JOHN), bookbinder in Edinburgh, 1733. Entered in the *Edinburgh Guild Register* as a bookbinder, May 16th, 1733, by right of Capt. Alex. Sandilands, father.

SANDS (WILLIAM), bookseller in Edinburgh, *c.* 1736–70(?). The imprint to the *Scots Magazine* for 1739 reads: "Printed by Sands, Brymer, Murray and Cochran." Sands, however, was not a printer but a bookseller. He married, on May 2nd, 1736, Ann, daughter of the Rev. Dougall Stewart, Minister at Rothesay. In 1737 he sold copies of Ruddiman's edition of Buchanan's *Poems*. In 1743, together with Brymer, Murray and Cochran, he was concerned in the publication of *Select Transactions of . . . the Society . . . Agriculture in Scotland*. Sands, Murray and Cochran printed and published, in 1747, John Glas's *The Sabbatism of the People of God*. As late as 1760 Sands was still in business, but it is probable that he died about 1770. He was succeeded by his son-in-law, Charles Elliot (*q.v.*), who married his daughter Christian, on September 5th, 1780. Sands was then dead. [*Edinb. Marr. Reg.*, 1751–1800.]

SANGSTER (PETER), bookbinder in Edinburgh, 1765–1800(?) In Tron Parish, 1765. Peebles Wynd, 1773–4. Married (1) Jean Ramsay, April 7th, 1765. [*Edinb. Marr. Reg.*, 1751–1800.] (2) Isabella Ker, relict of Hugh Kinloch, April 9th, 1795. [*Canongate Reg. Marr.*, 1564–1800.] His name is found in the *Edinburgh Directory*, 177¾.

SCOTT (DAVID), printer in Edinburgh, *c.* 1767. In Old Grayfriar's Parish. Married Isobell, daughter of deceased John Sharp, butler to the Earl of Findlater, August 9th, 1767. May be the same as the David Scott, printer in Edinburgh, who, on December 20th, 1785, married Barbara, daughter of deceased George Cantley. [*Edinb. Marr. Reg.*, 1751–1800.]

SCOTT (JAMES), bookbinder in Edinburgh, *c.* 1770–(?). His address in 1773–4. was Gabriel's Road, Edinburgh. [*Edinb. Directory*, 177¾.]

SCOTT (WILLIAM), bookseller at Thirlestane, 1727. His name occurs in the imprint to Archibald Pitcairn's *Selecta Poemata*, Edinburgh, 1727.

SCOTT (WILLIAM), bookbinder in Edinburgh, *c.* 1750–80. One of the best known Edinburgh binders of the eighteenth century. In 1756 he bound in black morocco, inlaid with red, *The Book of Common Prayer*, printed by Adrian Watkins; in 1775 a copy of Wm. Boutcher's *Treatise on forest trees*; and in 1781 his ticket is found on a very handsomely bound copy of Mrs. Inglis's *Anna & Edgar*, 1781, in full crimson morocco. One of his most beautiful tools

shows a representation of a female figure, holding a lance and shield, underneath which is a Chippendale ornament, containing a bird, &c.

SCROGGS (JOHN), bookseller in Aberdeen. At the Broadgate, 1759. Mentioned in Brown's *Bookstalls*, vol. 1.

SELLAR (ALEXANDER), printer in Edinburgh. In South East Kirk Parish, 1753. Married Janet Milne, February 10th, 1753. [*Edinb. Marr. Reg.*, 1751–1800.] Probably a journeyman.

SHARP (WILLIAM), bookseller, stationer and bookbinder in Inverness, *c.* 1762–97. His name is first met with in the imprint to Hugh Rose's *Meditations on several subjects*, Edinburgh: "Printed for William Sharp, Bookseller in Inverness, 1762." Dr. Johnson, on his way to the Hebrides, purchased a book from a bookseller in Inverness in 1773, presumably from Sharp, as no other bookseller is known to have had a shop there so early. He was flattered by having an offer of his own *Rambler*, which was for sale in the shop. In 1774 Sharp seems to have been in partnership with the printer A. Davidson (*q.v.*). Their joint imprint occurs on a Gaelic ed. of Macfarlane's version of *The Psalms*, 1774. In 1780 he sold Duncan Lothian's *Collection of Poems* [a Gaelic ed.], Aberdeen, 1780. His will was registered August 4th, 1797. [Comm. Rec. Inverness, *Reg. Test.*, 1630–1800.]

SHAW (JAMES), printer in Edinburgh, 1756. In Old Kirk Parish. Married Mary, daughter of John Boyd, clerk in the Post office, October 31st, 1756. [*Edinb. Marr. Reg.*, 1751–1800.] Probably a journeyman.

SHIELLS or SHEILLS (ANDREW), printer in Edinburgh, 1767. In New Grayfriar's Parish. Married Katherine, daughter of Robert Forbes, December 13th, 1767. Probably father of Andrew Sheills, printer, who married Janet Brodie, relict of James Brunton, glass-grinder, June 28th, 1790, although there is a possibility that both entries refer to the same man. [*Edinb. Marr. Reg.*, 1751–1800.]

SHIELLS (JOHN), bookbinder in Edinburgh, 1769. In New North Kirk Parish. Married Ann, daughter of John Kettle, merchant, February 5th, 1769. [*Edinb. Marr. Reg.*, 1751–1800.]

SIBBALD (JAMES), bookseller and stationer in Edinburgh, 1747–1803. Parliament Square and Leith Walk. Born at Whitlaw, near Selkirk, in 1747. He was a farmer until May 1779, when he went to Edinburgh with about £100 in his

pocket, in order to commence a new career. Being acquainted with Charles Elliott (*q.v.*), bookseller, he entered his shop. In 1780 he purchased the famous circulating library which Allan Ramsay had founded, from the widow of John Yair (*q.v.*), and about the same time commenced business as a bookseller in Parliament Square. He was one of the most enterprising booksellers of his day in Edinburgh, and was the first to introduce better class engravings into that city. In 1785 he commenced the *Edinburgh Magazine or Literary Miscellany*. Early in 1791, in order to have more time to devote to literary pursuits, he made an arrangement with two young men, Messrs. Laurie and Symington, by which they were to manage the business and pay him a proportion of the profits. After conducting the *Edinburgh Herald* for a short time, he went to London. Here he produced a work entitled *Record of the Public Ministry of Jesus Christ*, which was later published in Edinburgh in 1798. In the meantime he had returned to Edinburgh, where in 1797 he brought out a musical publication, *The Vocal Magazine*. About 1800 he again took over his bookselling business and continued to conduct it until his death in April 1803. In 1802 he published his well known *Chronicle of Scottish poetry, and glossary of the Scottish language*, in 4 vols. At the time of his death he resided in Leith Walk. A caricature of him is given in Kay's *Portraits*, vol. 1, p. 411.

SIM (JOHN), corrector of the Clarendon Press, 1772. A Bachelor of Arts and a Minister. Born in Scotland. [Timperley, p. 893.]

SMELLIE (WILLIAM), printer in Edinburgh, 1752–95. Foot of Anchor-Close, 1773. Born in the Pleasance, one of the suburbs of Edinburgh, in or about the year 1740. Son of Alexander Smellie, architect or master-builder and stone-mason. Bound apprentice at about twelve years of age, on October 1st, 1752, to the firm of Hamilton, Balfour & Neill, printers, for a period of six and a half years. In 1757 Smellie, in the name of his employers, became a competitor for the prize offered by the Edinburgh Philosophical Society for the most accurate edition of a Latin classic. He produced an edition of Terence, the whole of which he set up and corrected himself, and for which the firm received the prize. At this time Smellie was still an apprentice, although about a year earlier his employers had appointed him corrector at a weekly allowance of ten shillings, or seven shillings more than he was entitled to as an apprentice. On the expiration of his apprenticeship in 1759 Smellie was appointed corrector in the office of Murray and Cochrane, with whom he remained until 1765. In 1763, according to the *Edinburgh Marriage Register*,

he married Jean Robertson. In 1765 he commenced in business as a printer in partnership with Robert and William Auld, but soon after entered into partnership with John Balfour (*q.v.*), as Smellie & Balfour. The partnership was dissolved on December 31st, 1789, and Smellie commenced to print alone. During the whole of his career he enjoyed an excellent reputation as a printer. He died on June 24th, 1795. His son Alexander succeeded him. [Kerr, *Life of Smellie*, 2 vols., 1811; &c.]

SMITH (ALEXANDER), papermaker in Aberdeen, 1771–94. A wigmaker who acquired first a half-share (from Robert Hyde, *q.v.*) in the paper mills established by Boyle and Hyde, and later, in 1773, became sole proprietor. In 1794 Smith bequeathed the lease and business to his only son, Alexander Smith, whom failing (as he did), to his grandson Alexander Pirie, the first member of the Pirie family to be connected with the papermaking industry. [Information kindly supplied by Mr. G. M. Fraser, Aberdeen.]

SMITH (ALEXANDER), running stationer in Edinburgh. Before 1772. In Old Kirk Parish. His widow, Janet Clark, married Kenneth MacInnes, January 12th, 1772. [*Edinb. Marr. Reg.*, 1751–1800.]

SMITH (BARTHOLOMEW), papermaker in Aberdeen, 1750–?. An Englishman who in 1750 erected a mill and commenced the manufacture of paper. He was succeeded by Richard Smith and Lewis Smith. For a long time the works were on a small scale. In 1820 they were acquired by Alexander Irvine and carried on as Irvine & Company until 1837, when the mills were purchased by Messrs. Arbuthnot and M'Combie. In 1856 they passed to Messrs. Pirie, and in 1865 to the Culter Mills Paper Company.

SMITH (DAVID), bookbinder in Edinburgh, 1766. In Old Grayfriar's Parish. Married Penney, daughter of James Duncan, farmer in the parish of King's Barns [Fife], June 22nd, 1766. [*Edinb. Marr. Reg.*, 1751–1800.]

SMITH (JOHN), bookseller in Glasgow, *c.* 1750(?)–81. King Street, *c.* 1760–3; No. 72, Trongate, 1763–79. A bookseller who established one of the earliest circulating libraries in Glasgow. The following advt. appeared in the *Glasgow Journal*, June 23rd, 1763: "John Smith, Bookseller, Glasgow, has removed his circulating library from the head of the New Street [King Street] to a commodious shop in Mr. Donaldson's Land in Trongate [this shop is said to have been about 16 feet by 14 feet!], opposite to the Tron Church, where he continues his circulating library as formerly, and at the usual terms: viz. ten shillings per year, five shillings and sixpence per half-year, three shillings per quarter, one shilling and sixpence per month, and one penny per night. Catalogues, consisting of near 1,500 volumes, to be had at the library, price fourpence. Every new performance on amusing or instructive subjects will be added to the library immediately on publication. N.B.—A considerable number of new books is lately come to hand." By a later advertisement in the *Glasgow Mercury* November 19th, 1778, it is evident that his son had been taken into partnership, the firm being described as John Smith & Son, booksellers and stationers. This later shop of Smith's was a once well-known dark and small shop, named by the police regulations, No. 72, Trongate, and situated directly opposite the Tron steeple. In 1779 John Smith sold a half-sheet emblematical print, representing the introduction of the Popish Bill, and priced at *6d.*; but it is not clear whether this J. S. was the father or the son. In 1776 the yearly feu-duties payable by J. S., 1st, for his part of the estate of Stobcross, came to £8 0s. 7½*d.* [Reid, *Glasgow Past and Present*, 3 vols., 1884.]

SMITH (ROBERT), bookbinder in Glasgow, 1740. Burgess and Guild Brother, as serving apprenticeship with John Robertson [junior], bookbinder, September 4th, 1740. [Scot. Rec. Soc., *Burgesses and G. B. of Glasgow*, 1573–1750.]

SMITH (ROBERT), printer and bookseller in Glasgow. At the Gilt-Bible, opposite to Gibson's Land, Salt-mercat, 1741. In the Salt-mercat, 1743. In 1741 he printed and sold Ralph Erskine's *The Main question of the Gospel catechism*; and Josiah Smith's *Character, preaching . . . of George Whitefield*. In 1743 he was printing in company with Alexander Hutcheson (*q.v.*). Their joint imprint is found upon Samuel Rutherford's *Trial and triumph of Faith*, 1743.

SMITH (W.), bookseller in Edinburgh, 1747. Sold copies of the Rev. Ralph Erskine's *A Sermon preached immediately before the Administration of the Sacrament of the Lord's Supper, July 19, 1747.* "Glasgow; Printed for J. Newlands . . . 1747."

SMITH (WILLIAM), printer in Glasgow, 1744–79. Mentioned in list of subscribers to John Welch's *Miscellany Sermons* . . . Glasgow, 1744. Printer of *The Re-Exhibition of the Testimony*, Glasgow, 1779. A bookseller of the same name sold copies of this.

SMITON or SMETON (ALEXANDER), bookbinder in Edinburgh, 1754–78. Brown's Close, Luckenbooths, 1773–4. On January 20th, 1754 the marriage arranged between Mathew Oliphant, weaver, and Agnes Carss, relict of

Alexander Weemss, barber and wigmaker, was stopped by Alexander Smeton, bookbinder. His daughter Janet, married Richard Sherriff, tenant in Prestonmains, East Lothian, November 21st, 1778. [*Edinb. Marr. Reg.*, 1751–1800.] His name appears in the *Edinburgh Directory*, 177¾.

SPALDING (CHARLES), bookseller in Edinburgh, 1771–86. Canongate. His daughter Anne married George Small, cooper, December 21st, 1771. [*Canongate Reg. Marr.*, 1564–1800.] His will was registered January 25th, 1786. [Scot. Rec. Soc., *Edinb. Test.*]

SPARKE (THOMAS), papermaker in Aberdeen, 1772–3. *See under* Hyde (Robert).

SPITTALL or SPITLE (DAVID), bookbinder in Edinburgh, 1725–*c.* 1765(?) In New North Kirk Parish, 1725. Married Jean Smibert, daughter of William Smibert, dyer, January 10th, 1725. [*Edinb. Marr. Reg.*, 1701–50.] Bookbinder July 20th, 1726, by right of spouse. [*Edinb. Guild Reg.*] He died before April 12th, 1767, on which date his daughter Mary married Michael Robb, writer. [*Edinb. Marr. Reg.*, 1751–1800.]

SPITTALL or SPITLE (HENRY), bookbinder in Edinburgh, 1717– *c.* 1750(?) In New North Kirk Parish. Entered in the *Edinburgh Guild Register* as a bookbinder, prentice to Hugh Mossman, June 24th, 1719. Married (1) Agnes, daughter of William White, farmer in the Parish of Uphall, June 13th, 1717; and (2) Mary, daughter of James Bruce, merchant, Burgess of Burntisland, July 13th, 1721. [*Edinb. Marr. Reg.*, 1701–50.] He died before August 4th, 1751, on which date his widow, Mary Bruce, married James Maxwell, shoemaker. [Ib. 1751–1800.] Omitted from *Dictionary*, 1668–1725.

SPOTTISWOODE (JAMES), paper-maker and bookseller in Edinburgh, *c.* 1773–80. Niddry's Wynd, 1776; Paper-warehouse, Milln's Square, 1773–4. Described as "of Glenfernat". Acquired the quire stock of the firm after the death of Robert Foulis on June 2nd, 1776. He also seems to have obtained their copperplates. Sold the library of Professor James Moore of Glasgow. Entered into partnership with Andrew Foulis the younger, on June 30th, 1777. His name and the address of his paper warehouse appear in the *Edinburgh Directory* for 177¾. [Murray, *Foulis Press*; &c.]

STALKER (ANDREW), bookseller and publisher in Glasgow, *c.* 1726–1771. Under the Exchange Coffee House, 1748. In or about the year 1726 he set up as a bookseller in partnership with Alexander Carmichael (*q.v.*), with whom he remained until about 1731, when he left Carmichael and established a business

of his own. In 1732, however, he employed Carmichael to print three works of Cicero. A fourth was printed at the same press in the following year for Stalker and Gavin Hamilton in Edinburgh. It is thus possible that although the partnership had been severed a business connexion may have been kept up for some years. His name is mentioned as the Glasgow agent to whom "Commissions and letters of Intelligence may be directed" in the Edinburgh periodical *The Patriot*, issued in 1740. In 1744 Robert Urie (*q.v.*) printed an edition of *The Spectator* for Andrew Stalker and John Barry (*q.v.*). In the same year he was one of a large number of Scottish printers and booksellers against whom the London booksellers took proceedings in the Court of Session. His name occurs in 1748 as publisher of *The Memoirs of Henry Guthry*, in the imprint to which his address is given as "Under the Exchange Coffee House". He was one of the first subscribers and contributors to St. Andrew's Episcopal Church at Glasgow, on March 15th, 1750. His gravestone is the oldest in date at that Church (in the south corner of the Chancel). For a time he edited the *Glasgow Journal*, living in a house which stood "across the Molendinar Burn, near the Gallowgate Bridge on the south". [Reid, *Glasgow Past and Present.*] Like most of the Glasgow booksellers of that time he held auction sales, perhaps the most important of them being one which was advertised to begin on November 23rd, 1756, from four to eight in the evening, "of curious and valuable books, consisting in part of the libraries of three worthy clergymen lately deceased". Copies of the printed catalogue of this sale are still to be met with. His will was registered on May 2nd and 16th, 1771. [Comm. Rec. Glasgow, *Reg. Test.*, 1547–1800.]

STARK (JAMES), bookseller in Dundee, 1766. Alexander Nicol's *Poems on several subjects, both comical and serious. . . .* Edinburgh, 1766, was "Printed for the Author, and James Stark, bookseller in Dundee . . .".

STEVENSON (A.), (?) bookseller in Edinburgh, 1749. The imprint to *Collection of the laws in favour of the Reformation in Scotland*, reads: "Edinburgh, Printed by W. Cheyne, for A. Stevenson, and sold by him, at his House, South-side of the Tolbooth, 1749."

STEWART (GEORGE), bookseller and bookbinder in Edinburgh, 1711–45. A little above the Cross, 1713. Parliament Close, 1730. Name occurs first as a bookbinder in the list of subscribers to Abercromby's *Martial Atchievements of the Scots Nation* . . . Edinb., 1711. Married Anna, daughter of James Edmondstoun, writer, December 7th, 1712. [*Edinb. Marr. Reg.*, 1701–50.]

Prentice-master of Alex. Davidson (*q.v.*), September 7th, 1720. [*Edinb. Guild Reg.*] Will registered August 13th, 1745. [Scot. Rec. Soc., *Edinb. Test.*] From 1713 onwards his name appears in the imprints to various books. *See also Dictionary*, 1668–1725.

STEWART (JAMES), bookseller in Edinburgh, 1713–45. Bookseller, May 20th, 1713. [*Edinb. Guild Reg.*] Married Jane Walker, widow of (1) Arthur Nasmyth (*q.v.*) and (2) Thomas Miller (*q.v.*), June 23rd, 1745. [*Edinb. Marr. Reg.*, 1701–50.] Omitted from *Dictionary*, 1668–1725.

STILTON (JOHN), printer in Edinburgh, 1736. In South Kirk Parish. Married Jean Gibb, February 15th, 1736. [*Edinb. Marr. Reg.*, 1701–50.] Possibly a journeyman.

STIRLING (JOHN), printer in Edinburgh, 1771–1807. Married Margaret, daughter of Henry Stirling in [of] Kemback, March 2nd, 1771. [*Canongate Reg. Marr.*, 1564–1800.] He died January 19th, 1807. [Nichols, *Lit. Anec.* v. 3, p. 693.]

STUART, *see* Stewart.

SYMMER (ALEXANDER), bookseller and stationer in Edinburgh, 1720–50. In the Parliament Square, 1729. Sold the *Caledonian Mercury* which was printed by the Ruddimans. Stationer (*Edinb. Guild Reg.*), July 27th, 1720. In the imprint to *History . . . of Church and State in Scotland*, Edinburgh, Ruddiman, 1734, he is described as "Undertaker". He seems to have married in 1736, but the name of his wife does not appear to be in the Register of Marriages. His daughter Jean married Alexander Learmouth on December 12th, 1762. In 1729 he sold an English translation of Pietro Giannone's *Civil History of the Kingdom of Naples*, folio, and in 1743 his name occurs in the imprint to *Select Transactions of the Society for . . . Agriculture in Scotland*, Edinburgh. His will was registered January 2nd, 1750. [Scot. Rec. Soc., *Edinb. Test.*]

SYMON (JAMES), printer in Edinburgh, 1762. In Old Kirk Parish. Married Ann, daughter of deceased John King, maltman in Crail, January 24th, 1762. [*Edinb. Marr. Reg.*, 1751–1800.] Perhaps a journeyman.

TAIT (JAMES), bookbinder in Edinburgh. In Old Kirk Parish, 1768. College Wynd, 1773–4. Married (1) Christian Man, July 3rd, 1768; (2) Margaret Alexander, June 26th, 1788. [*Edinb. Marr. Reg.*, 1751–1800.] His name is found in the *Edinburgh Directory*, 177¾.

TAIT (JOHN), papermaker in Edinburgh, 1775. Married Betty, daughter of John Gibson, weaver in Colinton, November 12th, 1775. [*Edinb. Marr. Reg.*, 1751–1800.]

TAYLOR (ANDREW), printer in Edinburgh, 1759. In Old Kirk Parish. Probably a journeyman. Married Katherine, daughter of John Donaldson, July 22nd, 1759. [*Edinb. Marr. Reg.*, 1751–1800.]

TAYLOR (PATRICK), printer in Edinburgh. Before 1764. His will was registered May 3rd, 1764. [Scot. Rec. Soc., *Edinb. Test.*] Probably a journeyman.

TAYLOR (R.), printer and bookseller in Berwick-upon-Tweed, *c.* 1752–75(?) A book published in Berwick in 1753 is stated to have been "printed for the author by R. Taylor". Other books issued in that town in 1765 are said to have been "printed for R. Taylor". In 1774 he printed a *History of the battle of Flodden.* [Hilson, *Berwick-upon-Tweed Typography*, in *Hist. Berwicks. Nat. Club.*, v. 23.] On July 18th, 1770, it was decided in the Court of Chancery that Mr. Taylor, a bookseller, of Berwick-upon-Tweed, should account to the executors of Andrew Millar, for the sale of a pirated edition of Thomson's *Seasons*, Mr. Millar being the proprietor of the *Seasons*. [Timperley, p. 722.] John Taylor, who disposed of his business as a bookseller, stationer and bookbinder to G. Walker in 1803 may have been R. Taylor's successor. The book (1753) referred to by Mr. Hilson (*see above*) was no doubt Stephen Jackson's *A Thought on Creation.*

TELFER (JOHN), printer (?journeyman) in Edinburgh, 1738. In North Kirk Parish. Married Margaret, daughter of Daniel Tweedie, printer, February 26th, 1738. [*Edinb. Marr. Reg.*, 1701–50.]

TENANT (   ), printer in Edinburgh, 1773–4. Foot of Hume's Close. In partnership with . . . Wilson (*q.v.*). Possibly to be identified with one of the printers entered under Tennent (John).

TENNENT or TENNANT (JOHN), printer in Edinburgh, 1771–8. In Tron Parish, 1771. Married Sarah, daughter of Alexander Dallas, silk dyer and deacon of the dysters, November 3rd, 1771. [*Edinb. Marr. Reg.*, 1751–1800.] His will was registered July 17th, 1778. [Scot. Rec. Soc., *Edinb. Test.*] Another John Tennent, probably his son, married Barbara, daughter of Archibald White, August 18th, 1780. [*Edinb. Marr. Reg.*, 1751–1800.]

THOMSON (ALEXANDER), bookseller in Aberdeen, 1751–55(?) At the Broadgate. His name occurs in the imprint to *The Works of . . . Benjamin Whichcote, D.D.*, 4 vols., Aberdeen, 1751. Bookseller, 1752. [*Scot. N. & Q.*, 1, p. 4.] In 1755 he published *A Sermon* by Robert Traill, Minister of Banff.

THOMSON (ALEXANDER), papermaker in Edinburgh, 1775. In Lasswade Parish. Married Betty, daughter of David Hamilton, weaver, April 23rd, 1775. [*Edinb. Marr. Reg.*, 1751–1800.]

THOMSON (JAMES), bookseller in Edinburgh. Named in the *Edinburgh Guild Register* as prentice master of William Millar (*q.v.*), July 1st, 1730.

THOMSON (JOSEPH), printer (?journeyman) in Glasgow, *c.* 1770–86(?) On December 14th, 1784, Robert Hamilton, running stationer in Edinburgh, married Elizabeth, daughter of Joseph Thomson, printer in Glasgow. [*Edinb. Marr. Reg.*, 1751–1800.]

TILLOCH (ALEXANDER), printer in Glasgow, 1759–1825. Born at Glasgow on February 28th, 1759. His father was a tobacconist and for many years a magistrate. In 1781 he conceived the idea of stereotype printing, apparently without any knowledge of the work of Ged, or Vander Mey. On January 1st, 1782 he entered into a fourteen years' partnership with Andrew Foulis the younger, Hugh Anderson, and James Harvey, printers in Glasgow, as Andrew Foulis and Company. He next went to London, and on his return to Glasgow entered into partnership with his brother and brother-in-law as tobacconists. Not satisfied with this trade, he again turned his attention to printing and either singly or in partnership carried on that profession for some time in his native city. In 1787 he again went to London, where he spent the remainder of his life in literary and scientific pursuits. He purchased, with others, *The Star*, in 1789, and became its editor. The last work which he engaged in was to superintend the *Mechanic's Oracle*, published in parts by Henry Fisher at the Caxton Press, but he is best remembered as editor of the famous *Philosophical Magazine*. He died on January 26th, 1825. [Timperley, p. 895; *D.N.B.*, &c.]

TOD (JOHN), (?)bookseller in St Andrews, before 1772. Merchant and postmaster. His will was registered May 27th, 1772. [Comm. Rec. St Andrews, *Reg. Test.*, 1549–1800.] Possibly a relative of John Tod, stationer in Arbroath, whose will was registered July 1st, 1794. [*Ib.*]

TRAILL (JOHN), bookseller and stationer in Edinburgh, 1732–74. Parliament Close. His name is first met with in the imprint to John Currie's *Overture con-*

sidered . . . Printed by T. Lumisden and J. Robertson . . . 1732. In 1734 R. Fleming & Company printed for him *Vindication of the Protestant Doctrine concerning Justification.* He was a member, in 1743, of the Soc. of Improvers in the knowledge of Agric. in Scotland. His name is found in the imprint to the Rev. J. Ortin's *Sermon on the death of the Nonconformist Divine the Rev. P. Doddridge*, 1752. He is entered in the *Edinburgh Directory* for $177\frac{3}{4}$.

TURNER (ALLAN OR ALEXANDER), printer in Edinburgh, 1766. Probably a journeyman. Married Kennedy, daughter of William Daw (or Dow), dyer in Portsburgh, October 26th, 1766. [*Edinb. Marr. Reg.*, 1751–1800.]

TWEEDIE (DANIEL), printer in Edinburgh, *c.* 1738. His daughter Margaret married John Telfer (*q.v.*), printer, February 26th, 1738. [*Edinb. Marr. Reg.*, 1701–50.] No book bearing his name in the imprint has been noted. Omitted from *Dictionary*, 1668–1725.

TWEEDIE (JAMES), proof reader in the printing office of the Foulis Press, *c.* 1750. Described as a student. [Murray, *Foulis Press*, p. 27, &c.]

TYTLER (JAMES), printer in Edinburgh, 1772–92. Born about 1747. Son of George Tytler, minister of Fearn in the Presbytery of Brechin. Became apprentice to a surgeon in Forfar and attended medical classes at Edinburgh University, defraying his expenses by voyages as a surgeon to Greenland during vacations. Having married during his medical course, he resolved to practice as a surgeon in Edinburgh, but, failing in this, opened an apothecary's shop in Leith. His first wife, a daughter of James Young, writer to the Signet, deserted him. He next married, in 1779, a Miss Cairns, by whom he had one daughter. His third wife, whom he married in 1782, was a Miss Aikenhead. An accumulation of debts in Leith caused him to remove, first to Berwick, and then to Newcastle where he opened a laboratory. This also was an unsuccessful venture, and, once more in debt, he returned to Edinburgh in 1772. Here he became a literary hack and scientific dabbler as well as journeyman printer. While in the debtor's refuge at Holyrood he constructed a printing press upon a principle different from those in general use. With this press he succeeded in printing, in 1772, a volume of *Essays on the most important subjects of Natural and Revealed Religion.* This was followed by *A Letter to Mr. John Barclay on the Doctrine of Assurance.* Next appeared the *Gentleman's and Lady's Magazine*, published monthly, but soon discontinued. He also commenced an abridgement of *Universal History*. In 1776 he was engaged to edit the 2nd edition of the *Encyclopaedia Britannica*, at the astounding salary of seventeen shillings a week, and at this rate of pay he not only edited it, but wrote about three-fourths of the whole work. He was also engaged to conduct the 3rd edition of that work. In 1780 he commenced a periodical, *The Weekly Mirror*, but this was soon discontinued. In the midst of other scientific work he constructed a fire balloon, with which, on August 27th, 1784 he made an ascent at Comely Gardens, Edinburgh, to a height of 350 feet. [*Gent. Mag.*, 1784.] He was later nicknamed "Balloon Tytler". In 1786 he published *The Observer*, and in 1788 a *System of Geography*. He started *The Historical Register* in 1792, but a warrant was issued for his apprehension in connexion with his republican views, and he fled from Edinburgh. Crossing to Ireland, he sailed from thence to America, where he conducted a newspaper in Salem, Mass., until his death in 1805, in his fifty-eighth year. [*D.N.B.*; *Life of Tytler*; &c.]

URIE (ROBERT), printer and bookseller in Glasgow, *c.* 1744–71. In 1744 he obtained type from the foundry of Alexander Wilson (*q.v.*) and printed an edition of the *Spectator* for Andrew Stalker (*q.v.*) and John Barry. Admitted Burgess and Guild Brother, as serving appr. with deceased Alex. Miller, July 28th, 1748. [Scot. Rec. Soc., *Burg. and G. B. of Glasgow*, 1573–1750]. He employed the most expert workmen, and used the best paper, and with such a combination is considered by many to have excelled the Foulis Press. His 1750 ed. of the Greek *New Testament* is superior to that of Ruddiman. He printed largely for the trade. His chief productions, other than those already mentioned, were Francis Hutcheson's *Reflections upon laughter* . . . for Daniel Baxter, bookseller, 1750; Pope's *Homer*, 1753; a translation of Count Algarotti's *Essay on painting*, 1764; *Economy of Human life*, 1769; and various eds. of Buchanan's *Psalms*, and *De Jure Regni*; Harvey's *Exercitationes anatomicae*; and translations of the works of Rousseau, Voltaire, Fénélon, and D'Alembert; between 1750 and 1769. His will was registered December 6th, 1771. [Glasgow Comm. Rec., *Reg. Test.*, 1547–1800.] [Murray, *Letters of Foulis*; &c.]

URQUHART (JAMES), bookseller in Stirling, 1730–1. In the Public Accounts of Stirling for 1730–1, occurs the payment "to James Urquhart for the *Echo* [*The Echo*, or *Edinburgh Weekly Journal*], a newspaper furnished the toun from the post office for two years and five months—£18 17*s.* 6*d.*"—*Records*, 1667–1752, p. 359. [Couper, *Edinburgh Period. Press*, 2, 65.]

VEITCH (GEORGE), running stationer in Edinburgh. Married Agnes Begg [i.e. Gregg], August 6th, 1749. [*Edinb. Marr. Reg.*, 1701–50.] She was the widow of (1) John Wilson (*q.v.*) and (2) George Weston (*q.v.*), also running stationers.

WALKER (PATRICK), printer in Edinburgh, 1727–32. An author who probably possessed a small private printing press. He printed his own work: *Some remarkable passages in the lives and deaths of Cargill, Peden, Semple, Welwood, Richard Cameron and others* . . . 3 vols., Edinburgh, Patrick Walker, 1727–32.

WALKER (ROBERT), printer in Edinburgh, *c.* 1775. In Old Grayfriar's Parish. Married Janet, daughter of deceased James Walker, day labourer at Donibristle, December 10th, 1775. [*Edinb. Marr. Reg.*, 1751–1800.]

WALKER (WILLIAM), printer in Glasgow, *c.* 1760. In Reid's *Glasgow Past and Present*, vol. 1, pp. 236, 238, it is said that Walker was originally a printer in Glasgow, afterwards a teller or accountant in the "Glasgow Arms Bank", and in the latter part of his life, for a period of about twenty or thirty years, the respected clerk of the general Session of Glasgow. He was born about ten years before the 1745 rebellion, and died in 1820.

WATKINS (ADRIAN), printer in Edinburgh, *c.* 1748–70. One of his majesty's printers for Scotland, with Richard Watkins (*q.v.*). In 1748 he printed alone *The Holy Bible, containing the Old and New Testaments: Newly translated.* . . . Another Bible followed in 1752. In 1756 *The Book of Common Prayer and Administration of the Sacraments* . . . was issued from his press. He died before May 5th, 1778, on which date his daughter Mary married David Boyd of Dalkeith. [*Edinb. Marr. Reg.*, 1751–1800.]

WATKINS (RICHARD), printer in Edinburgh, *c.* 1740–5(?) One of his majesty's printers for Scotland. Printer of the *Acts*, 1743–5, and of the *Statutes at large concerning elections of members of Parliament for Scotland*, 1744. *See* Watkins (Adrian).

WATSON (ADAM), papermaker at Pennycuik, *c.* 1760–86. He had two daughters, one of whom, Margaret, married William Croll, September 2nd, 1778. The other, Janet, married James Gibson, papermaker, December 30th, 1786. [*Edinb. Marr. Reg.*, 1751–1800.]

WATT (JOHN), corrector of press, Edinburgh, before 1778. Employed as corrector in Messrs. Ruddiman's printing house at Edinburgh, about 1760. He died before August 27th, 1778, on which date his daughter Anna married John Cumming. [*Edinb. Marr. Reg.*, 1751–1800.]

WEBSTER (   ), printer in Edinburgh, 1735. In partnership with . . . Duncan. Their joint imprint appears on Mrs. Ross's *Memoirs of Spiritual exercises written with her own hand*, Edinburgh, 1735.

WEBSTER (A.), bookseller (?) in Kirkcaldy, 1747. Sold copies of Rev. Ralph Erskine's *Sermon preached immediately before the Administration of the Sacrament of the Lord's Supper, at Dunfermline, July 19, 1747*; "Glasgow: Printed for J. Newlands . . . 1747".

WEDDERSPOON (JOHN), *see* Wotherspoon.

WEIR (ALEXANDER), printer and bookseller in Paisley, *c.* 1760–80(?) Near the Cross, 1769–(?) Originally a bookseller. In or about 1769 entered into partnership with Archibald M^c^Lean (*q.v.*), with whom he produced the first book printed in Paisley. Weir is described as a bookseller as late as 1771, but after the dissolution of the partnership in 1772 or 1773 he appears to have become a printer. In 1774 a translation of *Don Quixote* was printed and sold in the burgh by Alex. Weir.

WEIR (JAMES), bookseller in Cessford, 1740–1(?) Sold books printed by Alexander Alison (*q.v.*), in 1740. His name appears in the imprint to the Rev. Ralph Erskine's *Sermon preached before the Associate Presbytery on a Fast-Day appointed by them, viz. Tuesday, Aug. 28, 1739 in the Parish of Kinross*; Edinburgh, "printed by R. Fleming and A. Alison . . . 1741".

WELLS (JOHN), printer in Edinburgh and Florida, *c.* 1750–90. Served his apprenticeship in Donaldson's printing house in Edinburgh. Born in Charleston. Became Florida's first printer in 1784. [Black, *Scotland's mark on America*, p. 109.]

WEMYSS (WILLIAM), printer in Leith, 1772. His daughter Isobel married Dalrymple Brodie, slater in Leith, November 29th, 1772. Possibly a relative of the bookseller of the same name in Edinburgh, who, on Sept. 30th, 1789, married Anne, daughter of John Baptie, vintner. [*Edinb. Marr. Reg.*, 1751–1800.]

WESTON or WASTONE (GEORGE), running stationer in Edinburgh. In North Kirk Parish, 1744. Married Agnes Gregg, widow of John Wilson (*q.v.*), running stationer, March 25th, 1744. He died before August 6th, 1749, on which date his widow married George Veitch (*q.v.*), also a running stationer. [*Edinb. Marr. Reg.*, 1701–50.]

WESTON (THOMAS), running stationer in Edinburgh, 1763. In Old Kirk Parish. Married Janet, daughter of Alexander Dunbar (*q.v.*), running stationer, March 20th, 1763. [*Edinb. Marr. Reg.*, 1751–1800.]

WHITE (CHARLES), printer (?journeyman) in Edinburgh, 1772. In New Grayfriar's Parish. Married Katherine, daughter of Robert Briar, labourer in the parish of Douglas, May 24th, 1772. [*Edinb. Marr. Reg.*, 1751–1800.]

WHYTE (JAMES), papermaker in Edinburgh. In Tron Parish, 1764. Married Janet, daughter of deceased Alexander Mackie, April 20th, 1764. [*Edinb. Marr. Reg.*, 1751–1800.]

WILKEN (JAMES), bookseller in Paisley, 1759–61. J. Witherspoon's *Trial of Religious Truth by its moral influence* was printed in Glasgow, 1759, for James Wilken, bookseller in Paisley, as was also the sixth edition of James Durham's *Christ Crucified*, Glasgow: "Printed by Arch. M^c^Lean and Joseph Galbraith, 1761".

WILLIAMSON (ADAM), printer in Edinburgh, 1760–1832. Journeyman printer. Worked all his life in Edinburgh. A good pressman, well respected by his employers and fellow workmen, and popular as a companion. Died October 3rd, 1832, aged 72 years. [Timperley, p. 927.] Married Margaret, daughter of Henry Johnston, December 22nd, 1782. [*Canongate Reg., Marr.*, 1564–1800.]

WILLIAMSON (GEORGE), printer in Edinburgh, *c.* 1770–84. Fellow apprentice with David Ramsay. For some time employed in the *Courant* office. Gave up printing and became King's Messenger about 1784. [Kay's *Portraits*, vol. 2, p. 120.]

WILLIAMSON (PETER), printer, publisher and bookseller in Edinburgh, *c.* 1768–99. Head of Forrester's Wynd, 1772; Dunbar's Close, Lawn-market, 1773–4. Son of James Williamson, crofter. Born at Himley in the parish of Aboyne, Aberdeenshire, in 1730. When about ten years of age he was kidnapped and transported to America, where he was sold for a period of seven years to a fellow-countryman in Pennsylvania. His subsequent remarkable experiences prior to his return to Aberdeen in 1758, he recorded in his tract entitled *French and Indian cruelty exemplified in the life and various vicissitudes of Peter Williamson . . . with a curious discourse on kidnapping*. In Aberdeen he was accused of having issued a scurrilous and infamous libel on the Corporation of the city and the whole members thereof. He was convicted, fined, and banished from the city, while his tract was ordered to be publicly burnt at the

Market Cross. His appeal against the Corporation was successful, and in 1762 he was awarded £100 damages. He was also successful in a second suit against the parties engaged in the trade of kidnapping, in 1765. A little later he settled in Edinburgh, where he combined the occupations of bookseller, printer, publisher and keeper of a tavern, "Indian Peter's Coffee Room" [Fergusson, *Rising of the Session*]. In 1773 he issued the first Edinburgh Directory. He published from March 8th to August 30th, 1776, the *Scots Spy, or Critical Observer*, which is valuable for its local information. A second series, called the *New Scots Spy* ran from August 29th, to November 14th, 1777. About the same time he set on foot in Edinburgh the first penny-post, which became so profitable in his hands that when the Government took it over in 1793 it was thought necessary to allow him a pension of £25 per annum. He married, in November 1777, Jean, daughter of John Wilson, bookseller in Edinburgh, but divorced her in 1788. A portrait of him is given by Kay in his *Original Portraits*, vol. 1, p. 128, and another "in the dress of a Delaware Indian" is prefixed to various editions of his *Life*. Among the works issued from his press were editions of the *Psalms in metre* (1779), of Sir David Lindsay's *Poems* (1776), of Thomas Baillie's *Royal Charter unto Kings by God Himself* (1773), and of William Meston's *Mob contra mob*. The *Life and curious adventures of Peter Williamson* was published at Aberdeen in 1801 and has run through many editions since. He died in Edinburgh on December 19th, 1799. [*D.N.B.*; *Life*; Kay's *Portraits*; &c.]

WILLISON (DAVID), printer in Edinburgh, *c.* 1770–1813(?) Craig's Close. Baillie Willison, father-in-law of Archibald Constable. It was in a dingy back room of Willison's printing house that Jeffreys and his fellow-writers surreptitiously corrected the proofs of their *Edinburgh Review*. In 1790 Willison printed Andrew Shirreff's *Poems chiefly in the Scottish dialect*. In 1794 several sermons by the Rev. Thomas Hardy, D.D. were issued by Willison. He printed in 1808 *The Edinburgh Medical and Surgical Journal* "for Archibald Constable and Company", and in 1800 his name appears as the printer of some numbers of *The Farmer's Magazine*. He died apparently about 1813. [Constable's *Lit. Corr.*; &c.]

WILSON (   ), printer in Edinburgh, 1773–4. Foot of Hume's Close. This entry is taken from the *Edinburgh Directory* $177\frac{3}{4}$, where Wilson is given as being in partnership with Tenant, but which Wilson and which Tenant (or possibly Tennent) are indicated is not clear.

WILSON (ALBERT), bookbinder in Edinburgh, *c.* 1750. His daughter Clementina married Arthur M'Pherson, May 6th, 1750. [*Edinb. Marr. Reg.*, 1701–50.]

WILSON (ALEXANDER), type-founder in St Andrews, 1742–4; Glasgow, 1744–60. Known as the "father of Scottish letter-founders". Born at St Andrews in 1714. Intended for the medical profession and received a liberal education. Went to London in 1737, where he obtained work with a surgeon and apothecary. In or about 1738 David Gregory, Professor of Mathematics at St Andrews, being in London, introduced Wilson to Dr. Charles Stewart, physician to Lord Isla (afterwards Duke of Argyle). Stewart brought him to the notice of Lord Isla, who became interested in him. Chancing to visit a letter-foundry one day Wilson was led to believe that a certain improvement might be effected, which would reward the inventor considerably. He imparted his ideas to his friend John Bain (*q.v., at p.* 371), another native of St Andrews resident in London. The pair decided to devote themselves to the business of letter-founding, and entered into a partnership. Soon afterwards, finding themselves unable to carry on, they returned to St Andrews, where they gave up the idea of the new invention but set about pursuing the ordinary methods of making type. According to Southey's *Life of Bell*, Wilson was greatly assisted in his type-founding experiments by Alexander Bell. Curiously enough Southey makes no reference to Bain, while in no other account has any mention of Bell been found in connexion with the work. Wilson and Bell (and presumably Bain), worked in a garret over Bell's shop at the corner of Church Street and South Street. Their first letter-foundry was opened in 1742 and for two years they remained in St Andrews. A small measure of success induced them to remove in 1744 to Camlachie, Glasgow, where they hoped to extend their sales to Ireland and North America. In 1747 Bain left Glasgow and settled in Dublin to cultivate the Irish connexion. Two years later the partnership was dissolved. In 1748 Wilson commenced to supply the types for the University Press at Glasgow. Through the influence of his old patron, Lord Isla, now Duke of Argyle, Wilson was appointed to the chair of Practical Astronomy in Glasgow University, in 1760. He was succeeded in his business by his sons and their descendants.

WILSON (ALEXANDER), papermaker in Edinburgh, 1770. In Lasswade. Married Mary, daughter of William Hogg, mason, November 4th, 1770. [*Edin. Marr. Reg.*, 1751–1800.]

WILSON (EBENEZER), bookseller in Dumfries, *c.* 1760–90. Married Mary, daughter of Francis Carruthers of Whitecroft, April 10th, 1768. [*Edinb. Marr. Reg.*, 1751–1800.] He was a shareholder in the firm of Douglas, Heron & Co., bankers, which failed in 1772, Wilson thereby losing £500. He seems to have continued in business until his death, about 1790. His will was registered February 16th, 1790 and June 17th, 1791. [Comm. Rec. Dumfries, *Reg. Test.*, 1642–1800.] In 1766 *A Military History of Germany and of England . . .* was printed at Edinburgh "for Ebenezer Wilson, bookseller in Dumfries".

WILSON (HERBERT), bookbinder and bookseller in Edinburgh, 1714–55(?) In North West Kirk Parish, 1716. Entered in the *Edinb. Guild Register* as a bookbinder, December 8th, 1714, by right of Thomas Wilson, stabler. Married Christian, daughter of Colonel James Douglass, July 1st, 1716. [*Edinb. Marr. Reg.*, 1701–50.] Probably to be identified with the bookseller whose will was registered January 18th, 1755. [Scot. Rec. Soc., *Edinb. Test.*] Omitted from *Dictionary*, 1668–1725.

WILSON (JAMES), running stationer in Edinburgh, 1763. In New Kirk Parish. Married Jean, daughter of deceased Alexander Robieson, farmer in Blackford in Perthshire, May 15th, 1763. [*Edinb. Marr. Reg.*, 1751–1800.]

WILSON (JOHN), bookbinder and stationer in Glasgow, 1692–1726. Burgess and Guild Brother, September 29th, 1692. [Scot. Rec. Soc., *Burgesses and G.B. of Glasgow*, 1573–1750.] *See also Dictionary*, 1668–1725.

WILSON (JOHN), running stationer in Edinburgh. (?)–1744. Married Agnes Gregg. His will was registered June 13th, 1744 [Scot. Rec. Soc., *Edinb. Test.*], his widow having already married George Weston (*q.v.*), running stationer, on March 25th, 1744. [*Edinb. Marr. Reg.*, 1701–50.] In 1749 Agnes Gregg again married a stationer, George Veitch (*q.v.*). [*Ib.*]

WILSON (JOHN), bookseller in Edinburgh, 1768–87. Front of the Exchange, 1773–4; In New Kirk Parish, 1771. His name appears in the *Edinburgh Directory* for $177\frac{3}{4}$. Of his daughters, Ann married Charles Heriot, bookseller, September 25, 1771; Jean married Peter Williamson, vintner, November 10th, 1771; and Mary married John Macduff, bookseller, September 29th, 1787. [*Edinb. Marr. Reg.*, 1751–1800.]

WILSON (JOHN), printer and publisher in Kilmarnock, *c.* 1770–1821. Born in Kilmarnock in 1750. Famous as the publisher of the Kilmarnock edition of

Burns. Founded in 1803 the first Ayrshire newspaper, the *Ayr Advertiser*. Died in 1821.

WILSON (RICHARD), printer in Edinburgh, 1768–94(?) In Old Grayfriar's Parish. Married Martha, daughter of George Richardson, tenant in parish of Gladsmure, April 10th, 1768. [*Edinb. Marr. Reg.*, 1751–1800.] His daughter Margaret married William Anderson, shoemaker, May 29th, 1794. [*Canongate Reg. Marr.*, 1564–1800.]

WILSON (ROBERT), journeyman printer in Edinburgh, 1759–68. In Old Kirk Parish, 1759; Old Grayfriar's Parish, 1768. He was three times married; [*Edinb. Marr. Reg.*, 1751–1800; *Canongate Reg. Marr.*, 1564–1800.]

WILSON (SAMUEL), printer in Edinburgh. Before 1762. His will was registered September 28th, 1762. [Scot. Rec. Soc., *Edinb. Test.*]

WILSON (THOMAS), papermaker in Edinburgh, 1759. In Lady Yester's Parish. Married Lillias, daughter of deceased William Leggat, surgeon in Musselburgh, August 5th, 1759. [*Edinb. Marr. Reg.*, 1751–1800.]

WOOD (JOHN), bookseller and bookbinder in Edinburgh, 1744–78. In South West Kirk Parish, 1745. Luckenbooths, 1773–4. "Bookseller, April 4th, 1744. Late prentice to Lauchlan Hunter (*q.v.*), by right of Lauchlan Hunter." [*Edinb. Guild Reg.*]. Married Ann, daughter of William Galloway, June 30th, 1745. [*Edinb. Marr. Reg.*, 1701–50.] In 1774 he was named in an action brought by John Hinton of London against Alexander Donaldson (*q.v.*), John Wood, and James Menrose. The decision was published by James Boswell, one of the counsel, Edinburgh, 1774. His name has not been noticed on any book later than 1778, when it appeared, as a bookseller, in the imprint to George Muir's *Synod of Jerusalem*, Glasgow, printed and sold by John Bryce (&c.), 1778.

WOTHERSPOON, WEDDERSPOON, &c. (JOHN), printer in Edinburgh, *c.* 1760–76. Advocates' Close, Luckenbooths. In partnership with Gilbert Martin (*q.v.*) as "The Apollo Press". Married Janet, daughter of William Mitchell, accountant, September 5th, 1765. [*Canongate Reg. Marr.*, 1564–1800.] In 1763 Martin and Wotherspoon commenced printing and publishing *The Edinburgh Museum, or North British Magazine*, which lasted till December 1764. *The Edinburgh Repository of 1774*, which only lasted about three months, bears Wotherspoon's name. His will was registered May 24th, 1776.

WRIGHT (CHARLES), bookseller and stationer in Edinburgh, Parliament Close, 1750–74. His name is first met with in 1750 in the imprint to the Edinburgh ed. of *The Rambler*. In the same year he married Jean, daughter of Lieut. George Agnew of Ireland, (June 24th). [*Edinb. Marr. Reg.*, 1701–50.] On June 25th, 1758 he was married to Eupham, daughter of Henry Guthrie, writer. [*Ib.*, 1751–1800.] His name appears in the *Edinburgh Directory* for $177\frac{3}{4}$. He may have been the father of the bookseller of the same name who married Ann Turner on October 7th, 1793.

WRIGHT (ROBERT), bookbinder in Edinburgh, 1767. Married Isabella, daughter of James Forrest, smith in Stonehive, June 5th, 1767. [*Canongate Reg. Marr.*, 1564–1800.]

WYLLIE (JAMES), bookbinder in Edinburgh, 1773. In New North Kirk Parish. Married Joan, daughter of James Raeburn, indweller in Tron Parish, August 7th, 1773. [*Edinb. Marr. Reg.*, 1751–1800.]

YAIR (JOHN), bookseller in Edinburgh, 1742–64. Parliament Close. Entered in the *Edinburgh Guild Register* as a bookseller, September 8th, 1742, by right of Margaret Mitchell, spouse, daughter of William Mitchell, tailor. Purchased Allan Ramsay's circulating library in 1757. His will was registered April 20th, 1764. [Scot. Rec. Soc., *Edinb. Test.*] He was succeeded by his widow Margaret Yair (*q.v.*).

YAIR (MARGARET), Mrs., bookseller in Edinburgh, 1764–*c.* 1800. Parliament Close. Wife of John Yair (*q.v.*), whom she succeeded in business in 1764. She continued to run the circulating library founded by Allan Ramsay until 1780, when it was sold to James Sibbald (*q.v.*). Her name appears in the *Edinburgh Directory*, $177\frac{3}{4}$.

YOUNG (ADAM), printer in Edinburgh, 1773. Married Kathron, daughter of John Watson, weaver in Cyrus [?], October 13th, 1773. [*Canongate Reg. Marr.*, 1564–1800.]

YOUNG (ALEXANDER), printer in Edinburgh, 1769. In New Kirk Parish. Married Frances Hodges, relict of Charles Hodges, watchmaker in New Grayfriar's Parish, May 28th, 1769. [*Edinb. Marr. Reg.*, 1751–1800.]

YOUNG (JAMES), first, bookbinder in Edinburgh, 1737–44. Entered in the *Edinburgh Guild Register* as a bookbinder, May 25th and June 1st, 1737, by right of Andrew Young, merchant, father. Mentioned in the list of subscribers to John Welch's *Miscellany Sermons*, 1744. Probably father of James Young, second (*q.v.*).

YOUNG (JAMES), second, bookbinder in Edinburgh, 1744–53. Probably son of James Young first (*q.v.*). Entered in the *Edinburgh Guild Register* as a bookbinder, August 1st, 1744, prentice to David Oliphant, bookbinder (*q.v.*). Mentioned in the list of subscribers to John Welch's *Miscellany Sermons*, 1744, of which work he took 26 copies. Married Helen, daughter of Andrew Quarey, farmer in Sessford in the parish of Morebattle, May 6th, 1753. [*Edinb. Marr. Reg.*, 1751–1800.]

YOUNG (JAMES), printer in Edinburgh, 1755–9(?) Servant to Messrs. Murray and Cochran, printers, 1755. Married Eliot, daughter of James Ker, November 9th, 1755. Died before April 13th, 1760, on which date his widow married James Johnston, tailor. [*Edinb. Marr. Reg.*, 1751–1800.]

YOUNG (THOMAS), bookbinder in Edinburgh, 1771. His daughter Helen married James Hogg, writer, on November 10th, 1771. [*Edinb. Marr. Reg.*, 1751–1800.] No other record of this binder has been noted.

YORSTON (JAMES), printer in Edinburgh, *c.* 1770. Died before November 5th, 1782, on which date his daughter Jean married John Cumming. [*Edinb. Marr. Reg.*, 1751–1800.] Probably a journeyman.

YUILL (ROBERT), bookbinder in Greenock, *c.* 1774–6. Named in list of subscribers to the Rev. James Renwick's *Choice Collection of Sermons* . . ., Glasgow, Bryce, 1776.

ADDENDUM

BAIN (JOHN), type-founder, 1742–90(?). St. Andrews, 1742–4; Camlachie (Glasgow), 1744–7; Dublin, 1747–86(?); Philadelphia, U.S.A., 1787–90(?). Born at St. Andrews. For his early career *see under* Wilson (Alexander), his partner. After the dissolution of partnership in 1749 Bain appears to have remained in Ireland for a considerable period. About 1786, or perhaps a little earlier, emigrated to America where, in partnership with his grandson, he established the first type-foundry in Philadelphia, in 1787. Their firm cast the types for a portion of the American ed. of the *Encyclopaedia Britannica*, reprinted in Philadelphia in 1791. Bain died or retired about 1790. Archibald Binny (1763–1838), born in Portobello, near Edinburgh, and James Ronaldson (d. 1841), also born in Scotland, succeeded to and carried on the business. In 1797 they cast the first $ sign used in America.

IRISH PRINTERS, BOOKSELLERS, AND STATIONERS, 1726–1775

IRISH PRINTERS, BOOKSELLERS, AND STATIONERS, 1726–1775

By E. R. MCC. DIX.

ADAMS (JAMES), printer in Dublin, 1767. His will was proved in the Diocesan Court of Dublin this year.

AFLECK (J.), bookseller in Dublin, "At Buchanan's Head in Dame Street", 1750 (?)

ALLEN (G.), printer in Dublin, "At the Two Bibles in Dame Street", 1773. In 1773 he signed the petition to the Irish House of Commons respecting paper. [B.M. 1890. e. 5 (239).]

ANBUREY (WILLIAM-SHAW), printer in Dublin, (1) In "Abby" [*sic*] Street (1727); (2) In "Caple" (*sic*) Street (1730). 1727–30. *See* Watts (J.) & Anburey (W. S.).

ARMITAGE (J.), bookseller in Dublin, 1776. Perhaps successor to Thomas Armitage (*q.v.*)?

ARMITAGE (THOMAS), bookseller in Dublin, "In Draper's Court, near Nicholas Gate", 1759–76.

BABE (HENRY), printer in Dublin, at the "Yellow Lyon" in Thomas Street, 1738.

BACON (THOMAS), bookseller in Dublin, "At Bacon's Coffee House in Essex Street", 1742.

BAGNELL (PHINEAS), bookseller in Cork, 1754.

BAGNELL (PHINEAS), & Co., printers in Cork, "Castle Street", 1768–74. They printed an edition of King's *The State of the Protestants of Ireland*, &c.

BAGNELL (PHINEAS & GEORGE), printers in Cork, (1) "Near the Exchange" in 1756; (2) "In Castle Street" ten years later. 1755–1774. They printed the 7th Edition of Temple's *History of the Irish Rebellion* in 1756. They acquired and printed the *Cork Evening Post*.

BATE (EDWARD), printer in Dublin, "In George's Lane", 1746–50. He was the son-in-law of Stephen Powell (*q.v.*). He printed Harris's *Hibernica* in 1747.

BELL (ROBERT), bookseller in Dublin, in "Stephen Street, opposite Angier Street", 1759–67. He was one of the publishers of an edition of Sir James Ware's *Works* (1764) in 2 vols.

BENNETT (GEORGE), bookseller and printer in Cork, 1714–47. *See Dictionary*, 1668–1725. He was an Alderman, and in 1724 was Mayor of Cork. He died before September 1747.

BENSON (THOMAS), bookseller and publisher in Dublin, 1727–8. His shop sign was "Shakespeare's Head".

BINAULD (WILLIAM), printer and bookseller in Dublin, "At the Bible in Eustace Street", 1713–32. Administration (Intestate) was granted of his personal estate by the Diocesan Court at Dublin. No imprint of his is known. He is described as a bookseller in the Index of the Diocesan Court.

BIRN (T.), printer in Dublin, in "Thomas Street", 1756. *See* James Byrn of Thomas Street.

BIXOU (or TABB), printer in Limerick, 1722–3, *see* Terry (Samuel) and Bixou (or Tabb).

BLOW (DANIEL), printer in Belfast, 1759–78, &c. Probably a son or relative of James Blow. He joined with H. B. P. Grierson (*q.v.*) in publishing a 12° edition of the *Bible* in 1765.

BLOW (JAMES), printer in Belfast, 1707–58. His will was proved in 1759 in the Prerogative Court at Dublin. Brother-in-law of Geo. Grierson, printer, of Dublin (*q.v.*). *See Dictionary*, 1668–1725. He joined in some printing with John Hay (*q.v.*).

BLYTH (JAMES), printer in Londonderry, 1773–7. A partner with George Douglas (*q.v.*) in printing the *Londonderry Journal* in 1773 (from No. 62 on). He printed in 4to a pamphlet containing two sermons in 1776.

BONHAM (GEORGE), printer in Dublin, "At Horace's Head in William Street", 1774–9. He was printer to the Royal Irish Academy from 1788.

BOOKSELLERS (THE COMPANY OF), booksellers in Cork, 1768–73.

BOWES (PHILLIP), bookseller in Dublin, "In Church Street", 1772. Successor presumably to Richard Bowes (*q.v.*).

BOWES (RICHARD), bookseller and printer in Dublin, "In Church Street near the old Bridge", 1771.

BOYCE (WILLIAM), printer in Dublin, "May Lane", 1772. Administration (Intestate) was granted of his personal estate this year by the Diocesan Court, Dublin.

BRADLEY (ABRAHAM), printer in Dublin, (1) "At the Golden-Ball and Ring opposite Sycamore Alley, in Dame's Street"; (2) "At the Two Bibles in Dame Street"; (3) "At the 'King's Arms, and Two Bibles' in Dame Street" (after his appointment as King's Stationer). 1730–59. He was Stationer to the King in 1749 and printer to House of Commons in 1756.

BRADLEY (HULTON), bookseller in Dublin, 1758–68. Successor to Abraham Bradley (*q.v.*), and had the same address. He married Miss Dorothy Gerrard on April 15th, 1758. He published the Works of *Epictetus* in 1759.

BRADLEY (JOHN), bookseller in Dublin, "In Castle Lane", 1748.

BRIEN (WILLIAM), bookseller in Dublin, "In Dame Street", or with "Near Crow Street" added, 1744–53.

BROCK (STEARNE or STERNE), bookseller in Dublin, (1) In Essex Street near Essex Quay; (2) At the "Stationers Arms" in Castle Street; and (3) In Dame Street at the Corner of Crow Street. 1729–37. Administration (Intestate) was granted of his personal estate in 1737 by the Diocesan Court at Dublin.

BURKE (MARTIN), printer in Galway, Back Street, 1769–70. Printer of the *Connaught Journal*, which he called *Burke's Connaught Journal* for greater distinction, *see* O'Connor.

BURROWES (HENRY), bookseller in Dublin, "In Hendrick Street", 1775.

BUSTEED (GEO.), printer in Cork, 1765–8. He printed for the Corporation.

BUSTEED (JOHN), printer in Cork, "Paul Street", 1764–76. He printed the *Cork Chronicle*. He also did Corporation printing. He married Sara Saunders of Dublin in November 1770.

BUTLER (JOHN), printer and bookseller in Dublin, on "Cork Hill", 1751–4.

BUTLER (MICHAEL), printer in Kilkenny, 1758–79. He married Ellen Archdekin in 1758 and died on May 8th, 1779. [Authority, Canon Carrigan, P.P.] No imprint with his name is known, but he may have been included in that of

"Edward Crofton *and Company*" (*c.* 1759) (*q.v.*). He was probably uncle or brother of the wife of Edmund Finn, printer of Kilkenny (*q.v.*). Her maiden name was "Catherine Butler" and her first child was christened "Michael".

BUTLER (THOMAS), bookseller in Dublin, at "The Whip and Spur" in Ross Lane, Bridge Street, 1744.

BUTREE (JOHN), bookseller in Dublin, "Near the Barrack", 1766.

BYRN (JAMES), printer in Dublin, (1) "In Thomas Street" (1749); (2) "At the corner of Keysar's (or Kezar's) Lane in Cook Street" (1760). 1749–66. He printed some of Sir R. M. Cox's pamphlets in the "Lucas" controversy; also the first Irish edition of Henry VIII's *Defence of the Seven Sacraments*.

CALWELL (JER.), printer in Waterford, Broad Street, 1747–61. He did a good deal of printing, chiefly small books, and many of his imprints are undated.

CARPENTER (DANIEL), printer in Newry, 1761–83. The first printer in Newry as far as known. He printed a great deal. He died February 24th, 1793.

CARRICK (JOHN), printer in Dublin, "Bedford Row", 1774.

CARSON (JAMES), printer and publisher in Dublin, (1) "In Coghill's Court, opposite to the Castle Market" (1724–43); (2) "At the Bagnio Slip, Temple Bar" 1749). 1713–67. *See Dictionary*, 1668–1725. For four or five years, from 1725, he published on Saturdays the *Dublin Weekly Journal*. To this Dr. Jas. Arbuckle contributed. Carson's principal printed volume was C. O'Connor's translation of Father Geoffrey Keating's *History of Ireland*. He was called the "facetious Jimmy Carson", or "of facetious memory". He died in 1767. His *Recollections* (1745) passed through two editions. *See* Waters (Henry).

CARTER (CORNELIUS), printer in Dublin, 1696–1727. *See Dictionary*, 1668–1725. He was imprisoned in 1727 for publishing false intelligence relative to Gibraltar.

CECIL (GEORGE), printer in Dublin, 1768. He printed Jos. Sterling's *Bombarino*, &c.

CHAMBERLAIN(E) (D. or DILLON), printer and bookseller in Dublin, 1760–80. He was printing in 1760 when his address was "In Smock Alley". He was also a bookseller. *See next entry.*

CHAMBERLAINE (DILLON) and POTTS (J.), printers in Dublin, Dame Street, 1765–6. (*See* Chamberlaine (D.).)

CHANDLER (E.), bookseller in Cork, on "Fin's Quay", 1774.

CHANTREY (E.), bookseller in Dublin, 1726.

CHERRY (JOHN), printer in Limerick, 1761–9. Only two items with his imprint survive.

CLARE (B.), bookseller in Dublin, 1749.

CLIFFORD (N.), bookseller in Wexford, 1774.

COLLES (JOHN), bookseller in Dublin, "In Dame Street", the "Corner of Temple-Lane", 1774–76.

COLLES (WM.), bookseller in Dublin, (1) "In Dame Street"; (2) later, "No. 19, Dame Street". 1767–82.

COLLINS (EDWARD), printer in Clonmel, 1771–88. The first printer in Clonmel. He printed in 1771 or 1772 its earliest Journal, the *Hibernian Gazette or Universal Advertiser*, afterwards named the *Clonmel Gazette*, &c. He printed alone for several years, but in or about 1790 joined in partnership with him one George Heaslip, and they printed the *Gazette* together. Collins was described as a bookseller in 1774 and in 1777–8.

CONDY (G.), bookseller in Cork, 1760.

CONNOR (CHAS.), bookseller in Dublin, "At Pope's Head on the Blind Key near Essex Gate", 1743–4.

COOPER (T.), printer in Dublin, 1755. (Qy. a Pseudonym.)

CORCORAN (B. or BART. or BARTHOLOMEW), printer in Dublin, "At Inn's Quay near the Cloister" (1766). 1746–91. His will was proved in 1792 in the Prerogative Court at Dublin.

COTTER (JOSEPH), bookseller in Dublin, "Under Dick's Coffee House", 1747–9.

COTTER (SARAH), bookseller in Dublin, 1751–65. Successor to Joseph Cotter (*q.v.*) at the same place, "Under Dick's Coffee House in Skinner's Row"—presumably his widow or a relative. In 1751 the imprint of S. Cotter appears at the foot of a *Poem on Mrs. Woffington's performing the character of Andromache, in the "Distrest Mother"* [B.M. 1890. e. 5 (64)].

COTTON (THOS.), printer in Waterford, 1729, &c. Publisher of the Waterford *Flying Post*. No copy of it has survived. He is described as a bookseller in 1729. Perhaps the same as Thos. Cotton of Cork who, about 1715, printed, in partnership with Andrew Welsh (*q.v.*), a political broadsheet in Cork.

COTTON (THOS.), printer in Cork, *c.* 1715. *See previous entry.*

COULTER (JAMES), printer in Londonderry, 1741. A sermon survives with his imprint.

CRAMPTON (PHILLIP), bookseller and publisher in Dublin, (1) "At Addison's Head, opposite the Horse Guard in Dame Street, At the Corner of Castle Lane"; (2) "At the Angel and Bible" in Dame Street (in or about 1746). 1728–48. He retired from business in 1707 and was succeeded by Peter Wilson (*q.v.*). In *Dublin Courant* (Apl 2–5) he advertised his retirement and sale of books.

CRAWLEY (ESTHER) & Son, printers in Waterford, at "The Euclid's Head, Peter Street", 1765–73. They started the *Waterford Journal* and carried it on for many years.

CROFTON (EDWARD) & Co., printers in Kilkenny, 1759 (?) Nothing is known of this firm, whose one imprint is undated. The date is therefore conjectural. In an early number of Finn's *Leinster Journal* (1767) appears as an advertisement an appeal on behalf of "Edwd. Crofton" for 40 years a citizen of Kilkenny, who had failed in trade.

CRONIN (MR. ? TIMOTHY), bookseller in Cork, 1754.

CROOKE (ANDREW), King's printer in Dublin, "At the King's Arms in Copper Alley" (?–1732). 1681–1732. *See Dictionary*, 1668–1725 (p. 86). Much of his printing was official (*Statutes*, &c.). *See also* Crooke (Anne).

CROOKE (ANNE), printer in Dublin, "In Pembroke Court, Copper Alley", 1733. Probably the widow of Andrew Crooke (*q.v.* in *Dictionary*, 1668–1725) who died in or about 1732.

CROSS (E.), bookseller in Dublin, 1773–6. In 1773 this bookseller signed the petition to the Irish House of Commons respecting paper. B.M. 1890. e. 5 (239).]

CROSS (RICHARD), bookseller and printer in Dublin, "Bridge Street", 1772–1809. A leading Catholic bookseller, &c. His will was proved in 1809 in the Prerogative Court, Dublin.

CUMING or CUMMING (THOMAS), printer in Cork (1745 ?)–1747.

DALTON (JAMES), bookseller in Dublin, (1) "At the Corner of Bride's Alley in Patrick St."; (2) later "In Temple Bar". 1736–60.

DALTON (SAMUEL), printer, bookseller, and publisher in Dublin, "In Warburgh Street", 1730–41.

DANIELL (COMBRA), bookseller in Cork, 1729–34. His will was proved in the Cork and Ross Diocesan Court in 1734.

DAVYS (F.), bookseller in Dublin, "In Ross Lane", 1727.

DICKIE (WILLIAM), printer in Armagh, "Market Street" (1770). 1745–70. The first printer in Armagh as far as is known. He may have begun his work in 1743 or even in 1740. The printing press first used here was made by Francis Joy (*q.v.*) who, after retiring from his printing press in Belfast and giving it to his sons, took to paper-making and also invented a method for making "The Iron Screws and Brass Box" of printing presses whereby these presses were made in Belfast and set up in Armagh, &c., *vide* Joy's Petition to House of Commons (Ireland) in 1749. Dickie's address in 1770 was "Market Street". At this time he was married and had two apprentices. His imprint is not on record after this year. He died at Armagh in September 1771 (*vide Sleator's Gazette*). The chief extant output of his press are religious works, such as Sermons.

DICKSON (CHRISTOPHER), printer in Dublin, "In the Post Office Yard in Sycamore Alley", 1727–37.

DICKSON (RICHARD), printer in Dublin, (1) Dame's Street—"Opposite the Castle Market"; (2) The Globe on Essex Bridge (1730); (3) Silver Court, in Castle Street (1733). 1718–48. He appears in imprints in 1725 and 1726, with E. Needham (*q.v.*). He published a Newspaper called *The Silver Court Gazette*, &c. He was the eldest son of Francis (1708–1714) and Elizabeth Dickson (1714–22). *See Dictionary*, 1668–1725.

DIGBY (EDWARD), printer in Cork, 1770.

DILLON (LUKE), bookseller in Dublin, "At the Bible in High Street", 1740. His will was proved in 1740, in the Prerogative Court at Dublin. His imprint has not been noted. He was succeeded by John Fleming (*q.v.*).

DINNIS (GEORGE) printer in Dublin, 1737. Married Sarah Young (widow) on 2nd of March 1737 in St John's Parish Church.

DOBSON (E.), printer in Dublin, "The Stationers Arms, in Castle Street", 1719–32. Son of Eliphal Dobson (1682–1719) [*see Dictionary*, 1668–1725]. He traded at the same address. His will was proved in 1732 in the Prerogative Court, at Dublin. In the printed "Wills" Index his first name is given as "Elisshal". *See* Hyde (S.) *and* Dobson ("E.").

DOBSON (J.), *see* Hyde (S.) and Dobson ("J.").

DONNOGHUE (DENIS), printer in Cork, (1) "Near Dennis's Lane in Main Street"; (2) later, "Broad Lane", 1772–6. He printed the *Cork Gazette*.

DOUGLAS (GEORGE), printer in Londonderry, 1772–96. He founded the *Londonderry Journal and Donegal and Tyrone Advertiser* in June 1772. *See* Blyth (James). He printed a good deal.

DOWEY (JOHN), publisher in Dublin, "At the Sign of the Cock, Werburgh Street", 1745.

DOWLING (LUKE), bookseller and stationer in Dublin, in High Street, 1758. He died this year. He was an eminent Catholic bookseller. His will was proved at Dublin.

DUNBAR (ROBERT), printer in Dublin, 1758. His will was proved this year in the Prerogative Court at Dublin. His imprint is not known.

DUNNE (L.), printer in Dublin, 1754.

DYTON (T. OR TIMOTHY), printer in Dublin, 1767–75. Succeeded Alice James (*q.v.*) and had the same address, viz: "At Newton's Head, Dame Street" in 1767 and, later, simply "In Dame Street" or, "No. 11, Dame Street". He printed for the Corporation in 1775.

EDMOND (BRICE), bookseller in Dublin, "At Addison's Head in Dame Street", 1756.

EDWARDS (MARY), bookseller and stationer in Cork, Castle Street, 1775.

ENNIS (R.), printer in Dublin, "Thomas Street", 1775.

ESDALL (J. OR JAMES), printer and bookseller in Dublin, (1) "At Fishamble Street" (1744); (2) "At the Corner of Copper Alley, Cork Hill" (1745–9); (3) "On Cork Hill" only later. 1744–55. He was apprenticed to George Faulkner (*q.v.*), started *Esdall's Newsletter* in 1745, and published the *Censor or The Citizens Journal* (a Saturday paper) in 1749. Chas. Lucas was the Editor—and Esdall got into trouble with the House of Commons over some issues of it and, later, for printing Lucas's pamphlets. He died in March 1755, and his will was proved that year in the Prerogative Court, Dublin. His printing was carried on "for his children". Faulkner's *Dublin Journal* of March 22–5, 1755 has a full obituary notice of J. Esdall, who left a widow and four children.

EWING (ALEXANDER), *see* Ewing (George and Alexander).

EWING (GEORGE), bookseller in Dublin, "At the Angel & Bible in Dame Street, opposite the Castle Market" (1722–1742). 1722–48. In 1746 he took Alex. Ewing into partnership. *See next item.* Powell (S) and O'Reilly (R) both printed for Geo. Ewing.

EWING (GEORGE and ALEXANDER), printers and booksellers in Dublin, 1746–64. George took Alexander into partnership and they carried on business at the "Angel & Bible" in Dame Street. They printed Doyne's version in English of Tasso's *Delivery of Jerusalem*. George died first and his will was proved in the Prerogative Court in 1764. He is described as a bookseller. Then Alexander (alone) continued in 1764, but died that or the next year. His will is proved in 1765 in the Prerogative Court at Dublin.

EWING (THOMAS), printer and bookseller in Dublin, (1) "Dame Street"; (2) later, "Capel Street". 1767–75. His will was proved in 1776 in the Prerogative Court at Dublin. He printed some of Dr. Charles Lucas's Political Pamphlets, an edition of Shakespeare's Plays in thirteen parts with engraved title-pages, and an edition of Johnson's *Dictionary* (called the *4th*).

EXSHAW (EDWARD), bookseller in Dublin, (1) At the Bible on the Blind Key, near Cork Hill (1735–9); (2) At the Bible on Cork Hill, over against the old Exchange (1739–44, in succession to Thomas Hume). 1735–48. He took John Exshaw (*q.v.*) into partnership in 1748, but died that year. His will was proved in 1748 in the Prerogative Court at Dublin.

EXSHAW (JOHN), bookseller, printer, and publisher in Dublin, 1749–76. His address was "The Bible" in Dame Street in 1741. On Edward's death John's name appears alone "At the Bible on Cork Hill", as appears in his imprint in 1749. Sarah Exshaw joined him in partnership in 1749, and so continued till 1754. He married a Sarah Wilson in 1759. John Exshaw printed alone from 1756, and, even at earlier dates, his name only appears in imprints, viz: in 1751 and 1752. He printed the *English Registry* for some years and also *Exshaw's Magazine*. His will was proved in 1776 in the Prerogative Court at Dublin.

EXSHAW (SARAH), *see* Exshaw (John).

EYRES (N.), printer in Cork, 1752.

FACKMAN (WM.), printer in Cork, 1766. He printed for the Corporation.

FAIRBROTHER (SAMUEL), printer and stationer in Dublin, "In Skinner's Row, over against The Tholsel" at the sign of "the King's Arms", 1714–34. [*See Dictionary*, 1668–1725.] Mrs. Elizabeth Ray (widow of Joseph Ray) left him by will her printing press. He was satirized by Sheridan for pirating Faulkner's edition of Swift's *Works*.

FARRIER, (correctly FERRAR) (WM.), bookseller in Limerick, 1729–1753.

FAULKNER (GEORGE), printer in Dublin, 1724–75. Apprenticed to Thomas Hume, or Humes (*q.v.*). His address in 1730 was "Essex Street", and later (1765) "In Parliament Street". He has been called "Swift's Printer". He published the *Dublin Journal* for many years. He was an Alderman of the City of Dublin. His will was proved in 1775 in the Prerogative Court at Dublin. The output from his press was very considerable. [*See D.N.B.*] His mark was "G. F." in monogram. His nephew Thomas Todd Faulkner continued the business from 1776.

FERRAR (J. OR JOHN), printer and bookseller in Limerick, 1768–75 (? and later). A man of learning and travel, intimately connected with Limerick. His descendants are still to be found in Dublin, where he died. He was also a bookseller in 1754. He printed and published the *Limerick Chronicle*, which started in 1768 or 1769.

FINN (EDMOND), printer in Cork, 1766. One imprint only of his is known for Cork. He went to Kilkenny.

FINN (EDMUND OR EDMOND), printer and stationer in Kilkenny, 1767–77. The founder, printer, and publisher of the *Leinster Journal* which started in 1767. His earliest stated address was "St. Mary's Churchyard", i.e. in 1767, later it was "High Street". He married Catherine Butler in or about 1768. Their first child "Michael" was baptized on October 10th, 1769. [*Authority*, Canon Carrigan.] E. Finn died on Saturday, April 5th, 1777, leaving surviving him his widow, Catherine Finn, who carried on the Journal and printing business for some years. His will was proved in the Prerogative Court at Dublin in 1777 and he was then described as printer and bookseller. It is possible Finn was working in Kilkenny before 1767, or he may have come to it in 1766 from Cork (*vide*, E. Finn, Cork, 1766).

FISHER (JOHN), bookseller in Dublin, (1) Old Change on Cork Hill, (2) "In Little Ship Street", 1763.

FITZSIMONS (JAMES), bookseller in Dublin, "Chapel Alley, Bridge Street", 1772.

FITZSIMONS (RICHARD), bookseller in Dublin, "In High Street", 1765–73. In 1773 he signed the Petition to the Irish House of Commons respecting paper [B.M. 1890. e. 5 (239)].

FLEMING (JOHN), bookseller in Dublin, "At the Angel and Bible in High Street", 1740–9. He succeeded Luke Dillon (*q.v.*). Perhaps the same as John Fleming, 1764 (*q.v.*).

FLEMING (JOHN), bookseller in Dublin, "In Sycamore Alley", 1764. Perhaps the same as John Fleming, 1740–9 (*q.v.*).

FLEMING (JOHN), printer and bookseller in Drogheda, 1772–85. The first printer here whose name is known. He was also a bookseller in 1777–8. The *Drogheda Journal* was possibly started by him in 1775 or even earlier, but in 1781 this Journal was printed by Charles Evans, a rival printer. Only eight items from Fleming's press survive. Fleming died in 1785 and left a will which was proved.

FLIN, FLINN, or FLYN (LAURENCE), bookseller in Dublin, (1) "In Winetavern Street, opposite Cook Street"; (2) "The Bible in Castle Street" or "Castle Street" only. 1754–71. He published in 1759 an edition of the *New Testament* in Irish (Roman Letter) for use in Scotland, also W. Harris's *History, &c., of Dublin*, in 1766. His will was proved in 1771 in the Prerogative Court at Dublin.

FLYN or FLYNN (W. or WILLIAM), printer in Cork, (1) "At the Sign of Shakespeare" in 1768; (2) "Near the Exchange" in 1771, &c. 1767–1801 (? 1795). He printed and published the *Hibernian Chronicle* for many years, and two editions of the *Modern Monitor*. (The will of "Wm. Flyn" of Cork was proved in the Cork Diocesan Court in 1795.)

FORREST (WILLIAM), printer in Dublin, "At Hoey's Alley", 1728.

FRANCE (RICHARD), printer in Dublin, 1764. His will was proved in the Diocesan Court at Dublin this year. No imprint of his is known.

FULLER (MARY), printer in Dublin, "At the Globe in Meath Street", 1736–7. She was the widow of, and successor to, Samuel Fuller (*q.v.*). Her will was proved in 1737 in the Prerogative Court, Dublin.

FULLER (SAMUEL), printer and bookseller in Dublin, "At the Globe & Scales (or "The Globe") in Meath Street", 1720–36. His will was proved in 1736 in the Prerogative Court at Dublin.

GARDNER (R[OBERT]), printer and bookseller in Belfast, 1713–34. [*See Dictionary*, 1668–1725.]

GARLAND (HALHED), printer in Dublin, "At Walshe's Coffee House, in Essex Street", 1748. He published a paper called *The Tickler*, carried on by Paul Heffernan in opposition to Dr. Chas. Lucas, and also another called *The Patriot* (2 Nos.).

GIBSON (DAVID), publisher in Dublin, Bridge Street, 1755.

GILBERT (WILLIAM), bookseller in Dublin, "46, Sth. Gt. George's Street", 1773–1801, and later. In 1773 he signed the Petition to the House of Commons respecting paper. [B.M. 1890. e. 5 (239).]

GILLASPY (JOHN), stationer at Dublin, 1773. His will was proved in the Prerogative Court there this year.

GLYNN (HUGH), publisher in Waterford, 1740. The founder of the *Waterford Newsletter*.

GOLDING (ELIZABETH), bookseller in Dublin, 1751. (Qy. will in Prerogative Court, 1757.) Perhaps widow of George Golding, 1740 (*q.v.*).

GOLDING (GEORGE), publisher in Dublin at the "King's Head" in High Street, near Cornmarket, 1740. *See preceding entry.*

GORDON (ALEXR.), printer in Dublin, 1766. His will was proved in the Prerogative Court at Dublin. No imprint of his is known.

GORMAN (BARTHOLOMEW), printer in Dublin, "Bridge Street", 1763–71.

GOULDING (CHRISTR.), printer in Dublin, "At the Reindeer in Montrath Street", 1736–46. He printed small song books and describes himself as successor to C. Hicks. His will was proved in 1746 in the Prerogative Court, Dublin.

GOULDING (SIMON), printer in Dublin, in "Montrath Street" (1746–)1752. He was successor to Christopher Goulding (*q.v.*), and presumably a relative. His will was proved in the Diocesan Court at Dublin in 1752.

GOWAN (JONATHAN), printer in Dublin, in "Back Lane" or "At the Sign of The Spinning Wheel in Back Lane opposite to Maculla's Court", 1726–56. He was one of the lesser printers and mainly printed ephemeral productions.

GREEN (CUSACK), printer in Dublin, the "Coal Key", 1761–2.

GRIERSON (GEORGE), King's Printer in Dublin, (1) "At the two Bibles in Essex Street" (?–1733); (2) "The King's Arms and Two Bibles in Essex Street" (1733–53). 1709–53. *See Dictionary*, 1668–1725 (p. 134). The famous printer and founder of the family, members of which were, for several generations, printers in Dublin. He became King's Printer in 1727. He died in 1753, and was succeeded by his son George Abraham Grierson (*q.v.*). His will was proved in 1753 in the Prerogative Court at Dublin. The output of his press was considerable and varied, and much of great importance. He printed editions of several Classics (Virgil, Horace, &c.) and some editions of the *Bible* and *Book of Common Prayer*. He was brother-in-law of James Blow (*q.v.*).

GRIERSON (GEORGE ABRAHAM), printer in Dublin, 1753–5. He was the son of George Grierson (*q.v.*) who died in 1753 and he carried on the business in the printing office at the King's Arms and Two Bibles, in Essex Street. He only survived his father for two years. He died in September 1755, aged 27, and his will was proved in that year in the Prerogative Court in Dublin. He was King's Printer also. His Executor carried on the business from his death in 1756 to 1758, and printed two editions of the *Book of Common Prayer* and *Statutes*. There was a long obituary notice of him in Faulkner's *Dub. Jnl.* of September 23–7, 1755.

GRIERSON (HUGH BOULTER PRIMROSE), printer in Dublin, 1758–70. A son of George Grierson (I) by his 2nd wife (sister of James Blow of Belfast, printer, *q.v.*); he became King's Printer and carried on business first "At the King's Arms in Dame's Street", and afterwards "At the King's Arms in Parliament Street", i.e. in 1767. He was a stationer as well as printer, and his will was proved in 1771 in the Prerogative Court at Dublin. He printed several editions of the *Book of Common Prayer & Psalms*, also an edition of the *Bible*, *Statutes*, &c. *See* Hay (David).

GRIERSON (JANE) & Co., booksellers in Dublin, 1758–9.

GRIERSON (JANE) (alone), bookseller in Dublin, "At the Corner of Castle Lane in Dame Street", 1764. She worked as printer with the Executor of G. A. Grierson 1756–7.

HAMILTON (EDWARD), bookseller in Dublin, "At the Corner of Christ Church Lane, High Street", 1728–9. *See* Hamilton (Edward), stationer, who is perhaps the same.

HAMILTON (EDWARD), stationer in Dublin, 1743. His will was proved this year in the Prerogative Court, Dublin. Perhaps the same as E. Hamilton, above.

HARBIN (THOMAS), printer in Dublin, "Opposite Crane Lane", 1725–6. *See Dictionary*, 1668–1725. He printed alone in 1725–6.

HARDING (SARAH), printer in Dublin, (1) "Opposite the Hand and Pen on the Blind Key" near Fishamble St. (1725); (2) "Next door to the Crown in Copper Alley" (1727–?). 1725–8. Widow of John Harding [*see Dictionary*, 1668–1725]. She printed two or three pamphlets for Dean Swift. As an ornament she used the Arms of France. She printed *The Intelligencer*. She was imprisoned for printing in 1728 a satirical poem.

HARRISON (G.), printer in Dublin, (1) "In Fleet Street"; (2) "On Temple Bar". 1754–5.

HARRISON (GEORGE), printer in Cork, at "37, Meeting-House Lane", or "The Corner of Meeting-House Lane", 1732–54. He printed K'Eogh's *Botanalogia* [sic] *Universalis Hibernica*, in 1735. The will of a "George Harrison" was proved in the Cork Diocesan Court in 1762, possibly the above printer, but see Mary Harrison (1757).

HARRISON (MARY), printer in Cork, 1757. She did printing for the Corporation. Possibly the widow or daughter of Geo. Harrison (*q.v.*).

HAWKER (HENRY), bookseller in Dublin, "In Dame Street" or, "At Homer's Head in Dame Street", 1749–50.

HAY (DAVID), printer in Dublin, 1770–3. Assignee of Hugh Boulter Grierson (*q.v.*), and was the King's Printer. His will was proved in 1773 in the Prerogative Court, Dublin. His Executors continued the business "At the King's Arms, Parliament Street" from 1773–82, and printed several editions of the book of *Common Prayer*, *Statutes*, the *Bible*, &c.

HAY (JOHN), bookseller and printer in Belfast, 1747–76. He joined with James Blow (*q.v.*) and James Magee (*q.v.*) in 1747 and 1748 in some printing, and similarly with Magee in 1755, 1770, 1771, and 1772. He also joined (in 1765) H. & R. Joy, in printing an *Introduction to English Grammar*.

HAY (J. and D.), printers in Belfast, 1760.

HAY (MARY), printer in Dublin, "At the King's Arms in Parliament Street", 1773–5. She was probably the widow of David Hay (*q.v.*).

HEASLIP (GEORGE), *see* Collins (Edward).

HEATLY (WM.), bookseller in Dublin, "At the Bible & Dove in College Green", 1733–42. His will was proved in the Prerogative Court, Dublin, in 1742.

HICKS (C.), *see* Goulding (Christr.).

HOEY (JAMES), Senr. (alone), printer in Dublin, 1730–74. After being for about four years a partner of George Faulkner, he started for himself. His earliest address was "In Christchurch Yard". He is described as "Senr." in 1765. Later his address was "At the Pamphlet Shop in Skinner's Row opposite to the Tholsel", or simply "In Skinner's Row"; then "At the Sign of The Mercury, in Skinner's Row". His ornament was "The Plough". There was a large and varied output from his press. His will was proved in 1777 in the Prerogative Court at Dublin.

HOEY (JAMES), Senr. & FAULKNER (GEORGE), or FAULKNER & HOEY, printers in Dublin, (1) At Christchurch Yard (1727); (2) Skinner's Row (1729). 1727–30. This partnership only lasted three or four years.

HOEY (JAMES), Junr., bookseller and printer in Dublin, At the Mercury, in Skinner's Row (1758); In Parliament Street (1765–81). ? 1759–81. He published a newspaper called *Hoey's Mercury* which was the Government organ for a few years. It appeared thrice a week. He was the son of James Hoey, Senior (*q.v.*), Faulkner's partner. He died in 1781 or 1782, intestate, as in the latter year Administration (Intestate) of his personal estate was granted by the Diocesan Court of Dublin. He executed much printing work, including an edition of Croxall's *Collection of Novels*, &c., in six volumes.

HOEY (PETER), publisher in Dublin, at "Milton's Head, Skinner's Row", 1770. *See next entry.*

HOEY (PETER), bookseller and printer in Dublin, "At the Mercury in Skinner's Row", ? 1770. 1771–1806. He was also a bookseller. Probably a son or other relative of James Hoey, Sr., of same address (*q.v.*) and perhaps identical with Peter Hoey of the "Milton's Head" (1770), *see above*. He printed the *Public Journal* for 1771–73.

HUME or HUMES (THOMAS), printer in Dublin, "Essex Street", 1715–28. *See Dictionary*, 1668–1725. His mark in 1717 was a monogram. He printed Crossly's *Peerage of Ireland* and published the *Dublin Gazette or Weekly Courant.*

HUNTER (JAMES), bookseller and printer in Dublin, "In Sycamore Alley", 1760–88. His will was proved in 1789 in the Prerogative Court at Dublin.

HUSBAND (J[OHN] A[BBOTT]), printer and bookseller, (1) "Coghill's Court, Dame Street"; (2) "28, Abbey Street" (1776). 1765–94. His will was proved in 1795 in the Dublin Diocesan Court.

HUSSEY (NICHOLAS), printer in Dublin, "On the Blind Key", 1729–(1730?). He published in 1729 the *Weekly Post, or The Dublin Impartial News-Letter*, on Tuesdays and Wednesdays.

HUTCHINSON (THOMAS), publisher in Dublin, "At the Reindeer in Charles Street", 1753.

HUTCHINSON (THOS.), stationer in Galway, 1754. Publisher of the *Connaught Journal*, *see* O'Connor.

HYDE or HIDE (JOHN), bookseller in Dublin, "Dame Street", 1709–28. *See Dictionary*, 1668–1725, p. 326. One of the Executors of Elizabeth Ray's will (1713). His own will was proved in the Prerogative Court at Dublin in 1728. *See* Hyde (J.) and Dobson (E.) (1728); also Hyde (S.) (1730, &c.).

HYDE (J.) and DOBSON (E.), booksellers in Dublin, 1728. The first partner was no doubt John Hyde, bookseller (*q.v.*), whose will was proved this year.

HYDE (S.), printer in Dublin, "In Dame Street" (1734–46). 1730–46. He had been a partner of E. Dobson (*q.v.*) in 1730. He was probably a son or other relative of John Hyde (*q.v.*). He was perhaps a partner of one J. Dobson in 1733 (*see* Hyde (S.) and Dobson (J.)). He printed an edition of the *Book of Common Prayer* in 1730 and also an edition of Tate and Brady's *Psalms*.

HYDE (S.) and DOBSON (E.), booksellers and printers in Dublin, "In Dame Street", 1730. *See* Dobson (E.).

HYDE (S.) and DOBSON ("J."), printers in Dublin, 1733. These names are found together in one imprint. Perhaps "J." is an error for "E.". *See above.*

INGHAM (CHARLES), bookseller in Dublin, "In Skinner's Row", 1769–73. In 1773 he signed the petition to the Irish House of Commons respecting paper. [B.M. 1890. e. 5 (239).]

JACKSON (ISAAC), printer and publisher in Dublin, (1) "At (or In) Meath Street" (1739); (2) "At the Globe in Meath Street" (1758). 1739–72. He was also a bookseller in 1772; and his will was proved that year in the Prerogative Court, Dublin.

JACKSON (ROBERT), bookseller and printer in Dublin, (1) "In Meath Street"; (2) "The Globe, in Meath Street"; (3) "20, Meath Street". 1772–92. Successor to and presumably the son of Isaac Jackson (*q.v.*). His will was proved in the Diocesan Court at Dublin in 1793. He printed Quaker literature.

JAMES (ALICE), printer in Dublin, 1760. Successor to Richard James (*q.v.*) and carried on business at the same address. She printed the *Dublin Gazette Extraordinary*. She was succeeded by T. Dyton (*q.v.*).

JAMES (RICHARD), printer, &c., in Dublin, (1) "At Dame Street, opposite Sycamore Alley" (1747); (2) enlarged to "At Newton's Head in Dame Street" (1748–56). 1746–55. He was printer of the *Dublin Gazette* in 1755.

JENKIN (CALEB), bookseller in Dublin, "Dame Street", 1772–85.

JOHNSTON (RICHARD), printer and bookseller in Belfast, 1753 (?1758)—60.

JOHNSTON (WILLIAM), bookseller in Dublin, "In Crooked Staff", 1749.

JONES (E.), printer in Dublin, "Opposite Coppingers Alley in Clarendon Street", 1739–60. He published Ware's *Works* in 1739. *See* Theophilus Jones (1735) and J. Jones. Was E. Jones their successor?

JONES (J.), printer in Dublin, "In Clarendon Street", 1737. Perhaps successor to Theophilus Jones (*q.v.*). *Also see* Jones (E.).

JONES (THEO.), printer in Dublin, "In Clarendon Street, opposite to Coppinger's Lane" (1735). 1735–6. He published the *Dublin Evening Post* (Vol. IV) in 1735. *See* Jones (J.), 1737, and Jones (E.), 1739.

JONES (WOOD GIBSON), printer in Dublin, Suffolk Street, 1768–70. He went to Newry and started a newspaper there in 1770 (*vide Irish Book Lover*, vol. VI, p. 15).

JONES (WOOD GIBSON) and WYNNE (CHRISTOPHER), printers in Newry, 1770–2; afterwards JONES & Co., 1774; and JONES (WOOD GIBSON) alone, 1775. Jones and Wynne also printed the earliest newspaper here, called *The Newry Journal*, commencing probably in 1770. One issue of 1774 survives.

JOY (FRANCIS), printer in Belfast, "At the Peacock in Bridge Street", 1737–45. He founded the *Belfast Newsletter*, and printed it for some years. He gave over his business to his sons. *See also under* Dickie (William).

JOY (HENRY and ROBERT), printers in Belfast, "High Street", 1745–85 &c. Sons of Francis Joy and continued to print the *Belfast Newsletter*. Robert's will was proved in 1785, and Henry's in 1789, both in the Prerogative Court at Dublin. *See* Hay (John).

KELBURN or KILBURN (JAMES), bookseller in Dublin, "At the Three Golden Balls in Georges Lane", 1739–51. He published several of Dr. Charles Lucas's political Addresses.

KELLY (IGNATIUS), bookseller and stationer in Dublin, "In St. Mary's Lane", 1741–53. He published works of Catholic devotion. His will was proved in 1753 in the Prerogative Court at Dublin.

KIERNAN (FARRELL), printer in Dublin, "Christ Church Lane", 1770–71.

KIERNAN (MARY), printer and bookseller in "Christchurch Yard", Dublin in 1772. Probably widow of F. Kiernan (*q.v.*).

KINNIER or KENNEAR (J.), printer and paper-maker in Dublin, "At the Green Man in Fishamble Street", 1746–85.

KINNIER (J.) and LONG (A.), printers in Dublin, (1) "At the Green Man on the Blind Key" (1745); (2) "At the Corner of Fishamble Street, near the Blind Key" (1746). 1745–6. They joined in partnership during these years. *See* Long (A.).

KINNIER (W.), printer in Carlow, "Dublin Street", 1773–86. The first printer in Carlow. He is first mentioned on his marriage in 1773 with a Miss Mary Gilbert of Clones, Co. Wexford. He died in 1786. He was probably a relative or connexion of J. Kinnier (*q.v.*), printer, in Dublin in 1746. W. Kinnier was printer and publisher of the *Carlow Journal* or *Leinster Chronicle*, the first newspaper printed there—and as it is averred that the Journal began in 1770 it is probable that Kinnier came to Carlow in that year or even earlier.

KNIGHT (GEORGE and JAMES), printers in Cork, "In Castle Street", 1754. They printed and published the *Cork Evening Post*, for one year.

KNOWLES (T.), printer in Dublin, "In Essex Street", 1749–50. He printed an ephemeral periodical called the *Censor Extraordinary* which ran to twenty-three nos., also the *Church Monitor* (two issues). Printer of a broadside, *A new project for the destruction of Printing and Bookselling; for the Benefit of the Learned World*. Dublin: printed by T. Knowles in Essex Street, 1750.

LAUTIL (PIERRE), bookseller in Dublin, "In Dame's Street", 1749.

LAW (ANN), printer in Dublin, "At the Reindeer in Montrath Street", 1763. *See* C. Goulding. Query his successor? An S. Law signed the petition to the Irish House of Commons respecting paper in 1773. [B.M. 1890. e. 5 (239).]

LAWLER (T.), printer in Dublin, at "The Golden Key, Dame Street", 1730.

LAWRENCE (MARY). *See* Watson (John).

LEATHLEY (MRS. ANNE or ANN), printer and bookseller in Dublin, 1761–70. Probably the widow of Joseph Leathley (*q.v.*). In 1773 she signed the petition to the Irish House of Commons respecting paper. [B.M. 1890. e. 5 (237).] She may have lived till 1776, in which year Wm. Hallhead calls himself her successor.

LEATHLEY (JOSEPH), printer and bookseller in Dublin, Dame Street, "At the corner of Sycamore Alley", 1719–54. His will was proved in 1757 in the Prerogative Court at Dublin.

LONG (A. or AUGUSTUS (1748)), printer in Dublin, (1) "At Essex Bridge" (1746); (2) "Under Walsh's Coffee House" in Essex Street (1748–52). 1745–55. He was married to Elizabeth Phillips, a granddaughter of Phillip Limborch, an eminent Dutch divine, on May 5th, 1745. He died in June 1755. There is an obituary notice of him in Faulkner's *Dub. Jnl.* of June 24–8, 1755.

LORD (HENRY), printer in Dublin, at "The Angel & Bible, Cook Street", 1750–5. He was the first Catholic printer of the century in Dublin. *Vide* Jas. Collins's *Life in Old Dublin*, p. 156. *See* Lord (P.) below.

LORD (P.), printer in Dublin, "At the Angel & Bible in Cook Street", 1750–60. Successor to Henry Lord (*q.v.*). He printed pamphlets in defence of the Roman Catholics, for example, Charles O'Conor's *Case of the Roman Catholics of Ireland*.

LORD (T.), bookseller and printer in Cork, at "Exchange Coffee House" in Castle Street, 1770–1.

LOWIS (JOHN), stationer and printer in Londonderry, 1735, and printed there in 1745. A Sermon survives with his imprint.

LOWIS (ROBERT), printer in Londonderry, 1771. Presumably a relative of John Lowis (*q.v.*). Only one 4to pamphlet bears his imprint.

LOWRY (ISAAC), printer in Londonderry, 1764. A Sermon survives with his imprint.

LYNCH (ELIZABETH), printer and Law-bookseller in Dublin, (1) "In Skinner's Row"; (2) "In the Four Courts". 1770–91.

LYNEALL (GEORGE), printer in Dublin, "Chequer Lane", 1773. He married Mary Jane George (spinster) of St. Mary's Parish, Dublin, early this year. He went to Wexford and printed there in 1779.

MACLANE (EDWARD), printer in Dublin, 1729. Married Sarah Lester (spinster), on 18th August of this year. [*Vide* St. Michan's Parish Register.]

McCLELLAND (JOSHUA), bookseller in Dublin, at "The Sycamore Tree in Sycamore Alley", 1733.

McCULLOCH (ALEXR.), printer in Birr, 1774–5. The first printer in Birr. He started its first newspaper namely, the *Birr Weekly Journal*, of which no copy is extant, but it is known from his Crown Bond dated May 20th, 1774 (since destroyed). He was probably the "Alexr. McCulloh", printer in Dublin from 1762 to 1772, and may have settled in Birr prior to 1774, say in 1772 or 1773. One book only exists bearing his imprint in 1775—an Arithmetic.

McCULLOH (ALEXANDER), printer in Dublin, (1) "At Skinner's Row" (1762); (2) "At Henry Street" (1766–?). 1754–72. He published in 1754 the *General Advertiser* and, in 1756, the *Dublin Evening Post*. He also published the 1st vol. of the *Freeman's Journal*, 1763–4 in conjunction with William Williamson (*q.v.*).

MACKY (S.), printer in Cork, "On the Flags, near North Gate", 1773.

MAGEE (JAMES), printer in Belfast, (1) "Near the Fourcorners in Bridge Street"; (2) "At the Crown and Bible in Bridge Street". 1736–89. *See* Hay (John), Potts (John), and Wilson (Samuel).

MAHON or MEIGHANE (PATK.), bookseller in Drogheda, 1690–1700.

MAIN (ROBERT), bookseller in Dublin, (1) "In Dame Street, opposite Fownes Street"; (2) "At Homer's Head in Dame Street" (1752). 1750–4.

MANNING (WM.), stationer in Dublin, High Street, 1726. Publisher of *The Dublin Postman* in that year.

MARCHBANK (R. or ROBERT), bookseller and printer in Dublin, "At Cole's Alley, Castle Street" (1773–?). 1770–1800. He was the "University" printer from 1746 to 1773 (*see* Typographia Academiae).

MARTIN (RICHARD), printer in Wexford, 1774. He printed the *Wexford Journal* in this year, as was proved by his Crown Bond of that date (now destroyed). The Journal is said to have begun in 1769, so perhaps Martin founded it then.

MARTINEAU (Z.), bookseller, in Dublin, "Next door to the Play House on the Lower Blind Key", 1745.

MASON (J.), printer in Dublin, "Dames-Street", 1727.

MILLIKEN (J.), bookseller in Dublin, (1) "Skinner's Row"; (2) "In College Green". 1768–73. He published Walter Harris's *Hibernica* in 1770 and an edition of Mollyneux's *Case of Ireland* in 1773.

MILLS (M. or MICHAEL), printer and bookseller in Dublin, (1) "St. Audeon's Arch"; (2) "Capel Street", and "No. 135, Capel Street". 1768–98.

MITCHELL (JOHN), bookseller in Dublin, "In Sycamore Alley", 1763–8. *See next entry.*

MITCHELL (JOHN), printer in Dublin, "Skinner's Row", 1771. Perhaps the same as John Mitchell, bookseller (*q.v.*), or his son?

MONCRIEFF (RICHARD), bookseller in Dublin, "In Capel Street", 1770–90. He published an edition of Voltaire's *Works* in twenty-four 12° vols. (Qy. Alderman. ? Will Prerogative 1798.)

MOORE (A.), bookseller in Dublin, 1754. Possibly widow of T. Moore. The name occurs in the imprint to Lodge's *Peerage*, 1754.

MOORE (THOMAS), bookseller in Dublin, "At Erasmus' Head, in Dame Street", 1737–50. He left a widow, Anne. Her will was proved in 1754 at Dublin.

MORRISON (JOHN), described as a "Stationer" in Dublin, 1726. Administration (Intestate) of his personal estate was granted by the Diocesan Court at Dublin in this year. His name has not been noted in any imprint.

MURPHY (JOHN), bookseller and printer in Dublin, "In Skinner's Row", 1759–73. In 1773 he signed the petition to the Irish House of Commons, concerning paper.

MUSGRAVE (THEOPHILUS), printer in Dublin, 1729. He appears in one imprint.

NEEDHAM (E.), printer in Dublin, "Next door to the Angel and Bible in Dame Street", 1725–7. In 1725 he joined with R. Dickson (*q.v.*) in reprinting a London pamphlet, "At the Cheshire Cheese in Crane Lane". They also published the *Dublin Intelligence or Weekly Gazette* in 1726 "At the Seven Stars, opposite the Castle Market", and in 1727, the *Whitehall Gazette*.

NELSON (OLIVER), printer in Dublin, "At Milton's Head in Skinner's Row", 1738–75. He was printer to the City of Dublin from 1761–72, and published the *Dublin Courant*. His will was proved in 1775 in the Prerogative Court, Dublin, and he was there described as a "Stationer". He married Elizabeth Nelson (spinster) in 1738 in St. Michan's Church.

NORRIS (RICHARD), bookseller in Dublin, 1721–34. Latest address "At the Corner of Crane Lane, in Essex Street".

NORTH (MICHAEL), bookseller in Dublin, "At the Bible Mitre in the Blind Key", 1760.

O'CONNOR ( ), publisher of *The Galway Chronicle*, Galway, 1775. Not a single copy of any Galway Journals for the years 1754, 1769–70, and 1775 is reported as extant now. James Hardiman, the historian of *Galway*, is the sole authority for the names and dates of their printers and publishers. *See* Hutchinson (Thos.) *and* Burke (Martin).

O'CONNOR (JAMES), bookseller and publisher in Drogheda, 1728.

OWEN (MARY), bookseller in Dublin, "In Skinner's Row", 1747–53. Presumably the widow or daughter of Robert Owen (*q.v.*).

OWEN (ROBERT), bookseller and printer in Dublin, "At the Sign of the Dolphin" in Skinner's Row, 1713–47. Captain of the Lord Mayor's Regiment of Militia. He died in or about 1747. (Qy. will proved in Prerogative Court, Dublin, in 1747. Called a "Merchant" in the index.)

PARKER (JAMES) & Co., printers in Dublin, "28, Temple Bar", 1775, and later. James Parker's will was proved in 1778 in the Prerogative Court at Dublin.

PARKER (MICHAEL), printer in Sligo, "In Castle Street", 1771–91. The first printer in Sligo. He published the *Sligo Journal and Weekly Advertiser*, commencing 1771, and may have started his printing press prior to 1771. He gave his Crown Bond in June 1774. He died at Sligo in September 1791. His will was proved the following year in the Prerogative Court.

PEMBROCK (THOS.), printer in Cork, 1730. He did printing for the Corporation.

PENNELL (J.), bookseller in Dublin, (1) "At the Three Blue Bonnets, Patrick Street"; and (2) "At the Hercules" in the same street. 1730–7.

PEPYAT (MARY), printer in Dublin, 1755. Printer to the City of Dublin. She was sister of Jeremiah and Sylvanus (*see next item*).

PEPYAT (SYLVANUS or SILVANUS), bookseller in Dublin, "In Skinner's Row", 1731–8. Son or brother of Jeremiah Pepyat, for whom *see Dictionary*, 1668–1725.

PILKINGTON (M. or MARTHA), printer and bookseller in Cork, "In Castle Street", 1739–57. Besides pamphlets, she did printing for the Corporation of Cork. Perhaps the widow or daughter of Thomas Pilkington (*q.v.*).

PILKINGTON (THOMAS), bookseller in Cork, Castle Street, 1729–43.

PORTER (JAMES), bookseller in Dublin, "Skinner's Row", &c., 1769–91.

POTTS (J[AMES?]), printer and bookseller in Dublin, "At Swift's Head, in Dame Street", 1761–75. Apprenticed to George Faulkner (*q.v.*). In 1766 he published the *Dublin Courier* on Tuesdays and Saturdays, and, in 1771, he started the *Hibernian Magazine*. He was publisher at one period of *Saunder's Newsletter*. He was also a stationer. He died in 1775 and was succeeded by James Potts whose will was proved in 1796 in the Prerogative Court, Dublin. He printed with Chamberlaine (D.) and Watson (S.).

POTTS (J.) and WATSON (S.), printers in Dublin, in "Dame Street", 1762. *See previous entry and also* Watson (S.).

POTTS (JOHN), printer in Belfast, 1736. He joined with Samuel Wilson (*q.v.*) and James Magee (*q.v.*) in printing or publishing a Funeral Sermon this year.

POWELL (SAMUEL), I, printer in Dublin, Crane Lane, 1728 (or 1729)–72. Son of Stephen Powell. To him was apprenticed Thomas Gent, a native of Dublin who settled afterwards as a printer in York [*see Dictionary*, 1668–1725]. Samuel Powell built a large printing office in Dame Street opposite Fownes Street in 1762. The productions of his press were numerous and generally very creditably turned out. In 1734 he printed the posthumous sermons of Dr. Samuel Clarke in two handsome folio volumes, for a Dublin bookseller, Stearne Brock (*q.v.*), who sent them to England and sold them at £1 6*s*. in sheets, as against £2 charged (also for sheets) for the English edition in ten volumes octavo.

Knapton, the publisher of the English edition, was one of those who petitioned the House of Commons for an alteration of the Copyright Act of 8 Anne and appeared before the Committee of the House (*Journals H. of C.*, vol XXII, p. 400, &c.). Powell's principal address was Crane Lane. In 1744 he printed the Rev. J. P. Droz's *Literary Journal*, the first critical and literary journal published in Ireland. In 1750 he was printer to the "Incorporated Society for promoting English Protestant Schools". Samuel Powell took his son into partnership, but the son (also named Samuel) died in 1766 intestate and his father took out administration to his personal estate in the Diocesan Court at Dublin. The father continued the business at Dame Street alone after his son's death and died in 1772 at an advanced age. His will was proved in the Prerogative Court at Dublin in 1775. *See* Risk (George).

POWELL (SAMUEL or S.) and Son, printers in Dublin. *See* Powell (Samuel), I.

POWELL (SAMUEL), II, printer in Dublin. *See* Powell (Samuel), I.

POWELL (STEPHEN), printer in Dublin, 1697–1728. The first of a family of Dublin printers, starting in 1697. *See Dictionary*, 1668–1725, pp. 243–4. His latest (known) address (in 1717) was "At the Sign of the Printing Press in Copper Alley". He died in 1728 or 1729, leaving a widow, Deborah Powell, a son, Samuel Powell, and a daughter (wife of Edward Bate (*q.v.*), also a Dublin printer).

POWELL (WILLIAM), printer in Dublin, "At the Corner of Christchurch Lane over against the Tholsel", 1743–5. Perhaps the same as "W. Powell" (1749), *see next entry*.

POWELL (W.), bookseller in Dublin, 1749. Perhaps the same as William Powell, 1743–5 (*q.v.*).

PRICE (SAMUEL), bookseller in Dublin, (1) "In Dame Street" or, "In Dame Street over against Crane Lane"; (2) "55, Henry Street". 1752–83. His will was proved in 1783 in the Prerogative Court at Dublin.

PROCTOR (EPHRAIM), printer in Athlone, 1774–93. The first printer in Athlone and the publisher of the first Journal appearing in this town, the *Athlone Chronicle*. This is known mainly from his Crown Bond, dated 1774 (since lost in the destruction of the Public Records Office, Dublin, in June, 1922). He may have started work prior to this year, possibly in 1770. He lived and worked in Athlone for many years. One copy only of his *Athlone Chronicle*

exists, that for July 12–16, 1788. It is in Lord Iveagh's Library at Farmleigh, co. Dublin, and is No. 56 of vol. XIX. Proctor executed another Crown Bond in this year, 1788, in connexion with this Journal. Nothing else from his press is known. An "Ephraim Procter" (or Proctor) was married in 1764 to Alice Harrison.

PUE (JAMES), printer in Dublin, 1758–62. He was nephew of Richard Pue (*q.v.*) and succeeded him in the business. His will was proved in 1762 in the Prerogative Court, Dublin.

PUE (RICHARD), printer in Dublin (16--), 1726–58. Publisher of *Pue's Occurrences* from 1703 or perhaps 1700. "Dick's Coffee House" was so called from his connexion with it. Pue died in 1758 and was succeeded by his nephew James (*q.v.*).

PUE (SARAH), printer in Dublin, 1762–7. She was the widow of James Pue (*q.v.*) and continued to publish the Newspaper *Pue's Occurrences* for a year or so, after which time it was printed by John Roe (*q.v.*).

RAMSAY (   ), bookseller in Belfast, 1729.

RAMSAY (HUGH), bookseller and printer in Waterford, 1740–54 (? and later). He was a "Stationer" in 1740, in which year he was married to Mary Vaughan. He was a bookseller in 1754, and was presumably the printer who was in partnership with James Ramsay in 1765, *see next entry*.

RAMSAY (HUGH and JAS.), printers in Waterford, "The Quay" (1772). 1765–75 and later. They started the *Waterford Chronicle* in 1765 and carried it on for many years. They printed several books.

RANSOM (WILLIAM), bookseller in Dublin, 1748. The will of William Ransom, "Stationer" of Dublin was proved in 1783 in the Prerogative Court there.

REILLY (A.), printer in Dublin, (1) "At the Stationers' Hall on Cork Hill" (1741); (2) "On Cork Hill" only (1744–53). 1741–58 (–1763?). He was successor to Richard Reilly (*q.v.*), and no doubt a relative. He continued printing the *Dublin Newsletter*, previously published by Richard.

REILLY (R.), printer in Dublin, "The Stationers' Hall on Cork Hill", 1725–41. The "Dublin University" printer in 1739. He published the *Dublin Newsletter* in 1740. Administration (Intestate) of his personal estate was granted by the Prerogative Court at Dublin in 1741. *See also* Reilly (A.).

REYNOLDS (JOHN), printer in Loughrea, 1766–72. Founded the *Connaught Mercury* in 1765. Only a couple of torn nos. survived till June 1922, when these perished in the destruction of the Public Records Office.

RHAMES (AARON), printer in Dublin, (1) At the Three Keys in Nicholas Street; (2) "In Capel Street". 1709–34. *See Dictionary*, 1668–1725, where 1700 as his earliest date should be corrected to 1709. The first of a family of printers who, for two or three generations, worked in Dublin. The output of his press was considerable and varied, and some of it of much importance. He printed more than one edition of the English *Bible*, and *Book of Common Prayer* and *Psalms*. The original of his will was lodged in 1734 in the Prerogative Court at Dublin. *See also* Rhames (Margaret).

RHAMES (JOSEPH), printer and bookseller in Dublin, "At Tillotson's Head, Capel Street", 1743. He succeeded Margaret Rhames (*q.v.*), and was the third member of this family who carried on printing, &c., in Dublin.

RHAMES (M. or MARGARET), printer in Dublin, "Tillotson's Head, in Capel Street" (1743). 1735–43. Probably widow or daughter of Aaron Rhames [*see Dictionary*, 1668–1725]. (The will of "Margaret Rhames, Dublin, widow" was proved in 1756 in the Prerogative Court, Dublin.) She printed an edition of Burnet's *Life of Wm. Bedell*, and of *Siris* by Bishop Berkeley.

RICHEY (THOMAS), bookseller in Dublin, "At Euclids Head in Dame Street, opposite Crow Street", 1763.

RICHEY (THOS.), printer in Waterford, "Peter Street", 1765. One item of his press alone survives.

RIDER (EBENEZER), printer and bookseller in Dublin, "In George's Lane" (1736–40). 1734–45. He was brother of Pressick Rider [*see Dictionary*, 1668–1725].

RISK (GEORGE), bookseller in Dublin, 1716–50. He first appears in 1716 at "The Sign of the London in Dame's Street", and in 1725–6 "At the Corner of Castle Lane in Dames Street near the Horse Guard". From 1728 on, his address was "At Shakespeare's Head in Dames Street". For marks he had (1) *G. R.* in monogram in 1718, and (2) *Shakespeare's Head* in 1726. Sl. Powell, Senior, (*q.v.*) printed most of the works having Risk's name in the imprint.

ROE (JOHN), printer in Dublin (1767?)–1774. He printed *Pue's Occurrences* after the death of Sarah Pue (*q.v.*). His will was proved in 1774 in the Prerogative Court, Dublin. Sarah Roe and David Gibbal, who were subsequently in possession of *Pue's Occurrences,* sold it, in 1776, to John Hillary.

ROSS (THOMAS), bookseller in Limerick, 1729.

ROSS (WILLIAM), bookseller in Dublin, "In Grafton Street", 1763–5. He printed Philip Doyne's *Irene,* &c. Administration (Intestate) was granted by the Diocesan Court, Dublin, in 1765.

RUDD (JAMES), bookseller in Dublin, "At the Sign of Apollo in Dame Street", 1758.

RUSH (JOHN), printer in Dublin, 1772. His will was proved in the Diocesan Court, Dublin, this year.

SARGENT (W.), printer in Cork, 1775? The will of a "W. Sargent" was proved in the Cork Diocesan Court in 1778.

SAUNDERS (HENRY), printer, publisher, and bookseller in Dublin, (1) "Christ Church Lane" (1753–60); (2) "At the Salmon, in Castle Street" (1761); (3) "20 Great Ship Street" (1773). 1753–88. He was also publisher of *Saunders Newsletter,* originally appearing three times a week, and containing twelve columns.

SCOTT (JAS.), bookseller in Kilkenny, 1748–54.

SHEPPARD (JOSEPH), bookseller in Dublin, "In Ann Street", 1773 and later. In 1777 he was in partnership with G. Nugent.

SHEPPARD (JOSIAH), bookseller in Dublin, "In Skinner's Row", 1765–91. He was bookseller and stationer to the "Magdalen Asylum".

SLEATER (WILLIAM), printer, &c., in Dublin, (1) "At Pope's Head, on Cork Hill"; (2) "In Castle Street" (from 1768 on). 1756–89. He was printer at the University Press in 1758. He printed and published *The Public Gazateer* [sic] on Tuesdays and Fridays from 1758 to 1763, and many books and pamphlets. His will was proved in 1789 in the Prerogative Court, Dublin.

SMITH (F.), bookseller in Dublin, 1775–80.

SMITH (JOHN) (alone), bookseller in Dublin, "At the Philosopher's Head on the Blind Quay", or "On the Blind Quay", 1739–56. He published an edition of the *History of Tom Jones* in 1749, and an edition of Sallust's *Works* in 1744.

SMITH (JOHN) and BRUCE (WM.), booksellers in Dublin, "On the Blind Key", 1726–37. Their names appear in the imprint of the first book printed at the Dublin University Press in 1736.

SMITH (R[OBERT]), bookseller in Belfast, 1775.

SMITH (S. OR SAMUEL), bookseller in Dublin, "In Essex Street", 1758–67.

SMITH (W.), printer in Dublin, Dames Street, 1773. This was probably William Smith the younger.

SMITH (W.), Junr., bookseller in Dublin, 1759.

SMITH (W. and W.), booksellers in Dublin, 1767–9. The will of Wm. Smith, the elder, was proved in 1771, in the Prerogative Court at Dublin.

SMITH (WILLIAM), bookseller in Dublin, (1) "In Dames Street" (1727); (2) "At the Hercules near Castle Market, in Dames Street" (1728–38); (3) "In Dames Street" (1743–8). 1725–64. *See* Smith (W. and W.).

SPOTSWOOD (W. OR WILLIAM), printer in Dublin, "College Green", 1774–84. *See* Stewart and Spotswood (1772).

STEPHENSON ( ), bookseller in Newry, 1754–7⅞. *See* Stevenson (Geo.).

STEVENSON (CATHERINE), printer in Londonderry, 1772. One pamphlet bears her imprint.

STEVENSON (GEO.), bookseller in Newry, 1768–74. He died in 1774 and his will was proved the following year in the Prerogative Court at Dublin.

STEVENSON (ROBERT), printer in Newry, 1775–83, &c. Probably a relative of George Stevenson. Robert Stevenson published in 1775 the *Newry Journal and Public Advertiser.* This was probably the newspaper of Jones & Co., acquired by Stevenson from them. He died in or before 1788 when his will was proved in the Prerogative Court at Dublin.

STEWART (R.), bookseller and printer in Dublin, "200, Abbey Street", 1775?–6.

STEWART (THOMAS), bookseller and stationer in Newry, 176––71 and in Dublin, 1772–1802. He was first a bookseller in Newry but, having married a daughter of John Watson (*q.v.*) of Dublin, bookseller, he left there and came to Dublin in 1771 to take over the business of his father-in-law, upon the death of the latter. His first address in Dublin was "At the Bible & Crown, on the

Merchant's Kay, near the Old Bridge", previously occupied by John Watson (*q.v.*). He married Miss Jane Vaunce on May 21st, 1774. His will was proved in 1802, in the Prerogative Court, Dublin. He was one of the publishers of the *Gentlemen's & Citizen's Almanac* from 1776–94.

STEWART & Co., printers in Dublin, "In College Green", 1771.

STEWART and SPOTSWOOD, printers in Dublin, "In College Green", 1772. They published the *Dublin Chronicle* in 1770. *See* Spotswood (William).

STOKES (JAMES), printer in Kilkenny, 1762. Stated to have printed de Burgo's *Hibernia Dominicana* this year. (*Vide* imprint on one copy given in *Heber Sale Catalogue,* namely, Kilkenniae, ex Typographia Jacobi Stokes juxta Praetorium, 1762. This was Pope Leo the XII's copy.) [*See Heber Sale Catalogue,* Part IV, 6th Day's Sale, 1180, p. 155.]

STRINGER (SARAH), printer, "At Dick's Coffee House, In Skinner's Row" or in "Skinner's Row" only, 1768.

STUART (A. OR ALEXANDER), printer in Dublin, (1) " At the Circulating Library in Dame Street, Opposite George's lane"; (2) "In St. Audoen's Arch". 1774–89. He printed a periodical called *St. Patrick's Anti-Stamp Chronicle.*

SULLIVAN (MR.), bookseller in Cork, 1754–77.

SWINEY (EUGENE), printer in Cork, (1) "Near the Exchange"; (2) "At the Peacock in Castle Street", 1754–72. He printed a good number of small books, plays, &c., also the *Corke Journal* and a large folio edition of Caussin's *The Holy Court,* &c.

TAYLOR (THOMAS), printer in Dublin, "The Boot and Three Pigeons" in Bridge Street (1740–). 1740–7. His will was proved in 1747 in the Prerogative Court at Dublin. No imprint of his is known.

TERRY (SAMUEL) and BIXOU or TABB, printers in Limerick, 1722–3: TERRY (S.) (alone), 1725. Terry came from Cork where he was a bookseller and printer in 1721 [*see Dictionary,* 1668–1725]. Nothing is known of Bixou.

THIBOUST (ABRAHAM), printer in Dublin, 1732. Married Magdelen Brunnell (spinster) on 6 July. *Vide* St Michan's Parish Register.

TORBUCK (J.), bookseller, &c., in Dublin, (1) "In Cavan's Street near the Court House", in 1749; (2) "At the Sign of Bristol in Sycamore Alley". 1749–54. N.B. "*Cavan's*" may stand for "*Kevin's*", the modern name.

TWEEDY (THOMAS), printer in Dublin, 1747. His will was proved this year in the Prerogative Court at Dublin. No other evidence of him exists.

TYPOGRAPHIA ACADEMIAE, Dublin, 1734–47. This was the printing press of Trinity College, Dublin. The following were some of the printers who worked at this press: R. Reilly in 1739; R. Marchbank in 1746–73; W. Sleater in 1758; W. Watson in 1773. John Hawkey's editions of Virgil, Terence, Sallust, &c., were printed at this press, 1745–67.

VALANCE (J.), bookseller in Dublin, 1774–1808. His will was proved in the Prerogative Court, Dublin, in 1808.

WALKER (T. OR THOMAS), bookseller in Dublin, "At Cicero's Head, Dame Street" or "Dame Street" only (No. 79), 1770–86. He acquired and published the *Hibernian Magazine* in succession to James Potts (*q.v.*).

WALSH (THOS.), printer in Dublin, "At Dick's Coffee House in Skinner's Row", 1725–8. He published in 1727 a newspaper called "*Walsh's Dublin Weekly Impartial News Letter*" which appeared every Wednesday, and in 1729 he printed *Walsh's Dublin Post-Boy.*

WARE (JOHN), bookseller and printer in Dublin (1704–)1726. He called himself, in 1726, 'one of His Majesty's Servants".

WATERS (EDWARD), printer in Dublin, 1708–36. *See Dictionary,* 1668–1725. Address in 1728, "On the back of the Blind Quay, almost opposite to King George on Horse-back, near Essex Bridge". Later "In Dame Street". His trade-sign was "the Phoenix". He published the *Dublin Journal.* In 1720 he was prosecuted as printer of Swift's *Proposal for the use of Irish Manufacture.*

WATERS (HENRY), printer in Dublin, "At the Bagnio-Slip, on Temple Bar", 1754. N.B. This was James Carson's address in 1759.

WATSON (JOHN), bookseller and publisher in Dublin, "On the Merchant's Key, near the Old Bridge" (1729–31); "At the Bible and Crown, on the Merchant's Quay near the Old Bridge" (1752–66). 1729–69. Successor to Mary Lawrence (1709–24, or later). He published *The Gentleman & Citizen's Almanack* for many years, i.e. from 1729 to his decease in 1769. In 1767 the title of the firm was John Watson and Son. John Watson's will was proved in 1769 in the Prerogative Court of Dublin. He was succeeded by Samuel Watson (*q.v.*). Thos. Stewart of Newry (*q.v.*) was married to a daughter of John Watson. *See next entry.*

WATSON (JOHN) and Son, booksellers at Dublin, "At the Bible and Crown, on the Merchant's Quay near the Old Bridge", 1767. *See* Watson (John).

WATSON (SAMUEL), bookseller and publisher in Dublin, (1) "At Virgil's Head in Dame Street" or "In Dame Street" only; (2) "48, Dame Street". 1761–98, and later. A son (or relative) of John Watson (1729, &c.) (*q.v.*). He was the publisher of the *Gentleman's and Citizen's Almanack* for many years. See Potts (J.) and Watson (S.).

WATSON (THOMAS), bookseller in Dublin, "At the Poet's Head in Capel Street", 1755–6. The first of a family of booksellers and printers.

WATSON (THOMAS), stationer in Dublin, "Opposite Shaw's Court, Dame Street", 1774–80.

WATSON (WILLIAM), bookseller and printer in Dublin, 1757–92. Successor to Thomas Watson (of Capel St.) (*q.v.*) and carried on business at the same address. He was printer to the University in 1761, and, later, printer to the cheap Repository for Religious and Moral Tracts.

WATTS (ANNE), bookseller in Dublin, 1763. Evidently successor to Richard Watts (*q.v.*) having the same address: perhaps his widow.

WATTS (ELIZABETH), bookseller in Dublin, 1764–7. Also at Skinner's Row, and evidently successor to "Anne"; perhaps her daughter.

WATTS (J.), printer in Dublin, "Opposite the Watch-House, on the North Side of College Green" (1727). 1725–8. *See also* Watts (J.) and Anburey (W.-S.).

WATTS (J.) and ANBUREY (W.-S.), printers in Dublin, at Capel Street, 1730. *See* Anburey (W.-S.).

WATTS (R[ICHARD]), bookseller in Dublin, "In Skinner's Row", 1761–2. An apprentice of Peter Wilson (*q.v.*), in 1749. He died in or about 1762, in which year his will was proved in the Prerogative Court at Dublin.

WELSH (ANDREW), printer in Cork, "Castle Street", 1715–27. *See Dictionary*, 1668–1725. N.B. A poem to Col. Boyle on his being chosen Speaker of the House of Commons (on October 4th 1733) was printed by "Andrew Welsh", presumably the above printer, but possibly by his son (*see next entry*). *See* Cotton (Thos.).

WELSH (ANDREW), Jnr., printer in Cork, "Near the Corner of Castle Street", 1738–9. He went in 1739 to Limerick. He was probably the son of Andrew Welsh, printer in Cork from 1715 to 1727 (*q.v.*).

WELSH (ANDREW, Jr.), printer in Limerick, 1739; WELSH (ANDREW), 1740–69. Andrew Welsh, Jr., was also a printer in Cork in 1738, and presumably a son of Andrew Welsh, printer in Cork from 1722 to 1733 (?) [*see Dictionary*, 1668–1725]. If the father died in 1740, the son would then cease to call himself "Jun." He printed from the start the *Limerick Journal* in 1739 which was renamed the *Munster Journal* in 1749 and later. There was a large and varied output from his press, including an edition of Bigg's *Military History of Europe*, 1749 (500 pp., 8vo.), and Ferrar's *History of Limerick*, 1767.

WELSH (T. or THOS.), printer in Limerick, 1769–77. Almost nothing is known of this printer save the books, &c., which he printed. He was probably a son or relative of Andrew Welsh. Their names are given together in the *Limerick Directory* of 1769 with the one address John Street. Thos. Welsh printed the *Munster Journal* in 1776–7, and was then in the Irishtown. He executed a Crown Bond in 1776.

WHALLEY (MARY), printer or publisher in Dublin, 1726–1728 (?). Widow of Jno. Whalley and his successor. She continued his Almanacs in Bell Alley off Golden Lane.

WHITE (THOS.), bookseller and printer in Cork, 1774–80. He printed, in partnership with W. Flyn, a small book by Jas. Poulson, in 1775.

WHITEHOUSE (THOMAS), bookseller in Dublin, "Under the Cocoa and Coffee House", 1726.

WHITEHOUSE (T. and J.), booksellers in Dublin, "At the State Lottery Office in Nicholas Street", 1762–5.

WHITESTONE (WM.), bookseller in Dublin, (1) "Opposite Dick's Coffee House, Skinner's Row"; (2) "At Shakespeare's Head in Skinner's Row"; (3) "29, Caple Street". 1759–78.

WILCOX (J.), printer in Dublin, "In Dame Street", 1749. He printed *The Apologist*, &c., in reply to *The Censor*.

WILLIAMS (J. or JAMES), bookseller and stationer in Dublin, (1) "The Book, Paper, and Parchment Warehouse"; (2) later, "5, Skinner's Row". 1764–86.

His will was proved in 1787 in the Prerogative Court at Dublin. Many books were printed for Williams, including W. Harris's *History of Dublin* and editions of Goldsmith's *Essays* and *The Vicar of Wakefield*.

WILLIAMSON (MATTHEW), bookseller and publisher in Dublin, "In Dame Street, over against Sycamore Alley", at "The Golden Ball", 1750–2. He published the *Universal Advertiser*, which opposed Primate Stone and supported the "Boyle" Party.

WILLIAMSON (WILLIAM), bookseller in Dublin, "At Maecenas' Head in Bride Street", 1757–64. He joined A. McCulloch (*q.v.*) in publishing the first volume of the *Freemans Journal*.

WILMOT (JOHN) (of St. John's, Dublin), printer in Dublin, 1746. His will was proved in the Diocesan Court in Dublin this year.

WILMOT (WILLIAM), printer in Dublin, "On the Blind Quay", 1724–7. *See Dictionary*, 1668–1725. Administration (Intestate) was granted, in 1727, by the Diocesan Court at Dublin, of his personal estate.

WILSON (G.), printer in Waterford, 1735. He printed one very small book this year.

WILSON (G.), bookseller in Dublin, 1751.

WILSON (PETER), bookseller (and Music Publisher) in Dublin, (1) "At Gay's Head, near Fownes Street, in Dame Street" (1743–6); (2) "At the Corner of Castle Lane opposite the Old Horse Guard in Dame Street" (1748), when he succeeded P. Crampton (*q.v.*); (3) "At Addison's Head, Dame Street"; (4) "In Dame Street" only. 1743–71. His name appears in many imprints. He took into partnership William Wilson (*q.v.*) (presumably his son or a relative) in 1769, and during 1770. He probably died in 1771 or 1772 as "William Wilson" alone appears from 1772 onwards, his address being merely "Dame Street". In 1749 Peter Wilson and his apprentice R. Watts (*q.v.*) were summoned before the House of Commons for printing papers relative to the dispute with Charles Lucas, and in 1764 he was imprisoned for a month for publishing in his *Dublin Magazine* a paragraph reflecting on a Member. This magazine appeared monthly for two years, and was illustrated with engravings. He also printed the first *Dublin Directory*.

WILSON, (RICHARD), Printer in Dublin 1751. Married Ann Wild (spinster) on 6th June (*vide* St. Michan's Parish Register).

WILSON (ROBERT OR RT. W.), printer in Dublin in "Cook Street", 1753. Printed an *Elegy on Capt. Spencer* (Satire).

WILSON (SAMUEL), printer in Belfast, 1736–44. He printed in conjunction with James Magee for some years, and also once alone, and once in conjunction with J. Potts (*q.v.*) and J. Magee (*q.v.*).

WILSON (WM.), printer in Monaghan, 1770. The first printer in Monaghan as far as at present known. Only one pamphlet exists with his name in the imprint, and nothing more is known of him.

WILSON (WILLIAM) (alone), bookseller and printer in Dublin, "6 Dame Street", 1772–1801. His sign, in 1773, &c., was "Homer's Head". He published a *Directory of Dublin* in 1776, &c.

WINTER (WM.), stationer in Dublin, 1727. His will was proved in the Diocesan Court of Dublin this year. His name does not appear in any imprint. (Perhaps a relative of Wm. Winter, bookseller 1681–92, mentioned in *Dictionary*, 1668–1725.)

WOGAN (PAT), bookseller in Dublin, (1) "In Church Street"; and (2) "At Merchant's Quay" (?). 1771–95. The principal Catholic bookseller of his day in Dublin. He first appears in the *Dublin Directory* of 1775 as of 23 Old Bridge, and so continues until 1795 and perhaps later. Pat Wogan's name first appears in an imprint of 1771 as a bookseller or publisher. He is given as a *printer* of a Missal in 1777.

WORRALL (JOSIAH), bookseller in Dublin, "Opposite to The Swan Tavern, on the Blind Key", 1726–7.

WYNNE (C[ORNELIUS?]), bookseller and publisher in Dublin, "At the Parrot in *Caple* [sic] Street", 1742–57 (? 1779). (The will of "Cornelius Wynne of Dublin, Stationer", was proved in 1779 in the Prerogative Court. Perhaps the same as above.)

INDEXES

NOTE ON THE INDEXES

OWING to the arrangement of this Dictionary in separate sections dealing respectively with English, Scottish, and Irish printers, it has been thought advisable to divide the index into similar sections. The few foreign places mentioned are, however, brought together into a single list.

The names of those who worked at each place are arranged chronologically according to the dates given in the body of the work. It should, however, be noted that in many cases where a man worked at more than a single place the dates of his connexion with each cannot be accurately determined. In such cases the dates given are generally those of his *total* activity.

Many men connected with the trade varied the character of their business in the course of their career, appearing at one time as printers, at others as booksellers, bookbinders, &c. As it is generally impossible to assign precise dates to these different activities it seemed misleading to attempt in the index to distinguish the particular branches of the trade to which each person belonged.

In the English section an asterisk before the name indicates that further information will be found in the *Dictionary*, 1868–1725.

I. INDEX OF PLACES IN ENGLAND AND WALES OTHER THAN LONDON

ALNWICK: A. Graham, 1746–86.

ALTON (Hants): W. Cranston, 1740–1.

ANDOVER: A. Uwins, 1725–7.

APPLEBY: L. Wilkinson, 1766.

ARUNDEL: T. Miles, 1746–56; T. White, 1766–74.

ASHBY DE LA ZOUCH: M. Unwin, 1728.

ASHFORD: ( ) Broadfoot, 1737–50.

ASHBURTON: J. Fursman, 1770–3.

AYLESBURY: T. Dagnall, 1776.

BARNARD CASTLE: ( ) Bainbridge, 1764.

BARNSLEY: ( ) Lord, 1736–54.

BARNSTAPLE: J. Gaydon, sen., 1732; J. Gaydon, jr., 1732–5; A. Gaydon, 1734; F. Murch, 1763–95.

BATH: W. Bally, 1720–74; H. Leake (I), *c.* 1720; J. Leake (I), 1724(?)–64; B. Matthews, 1725–55; S. Leake, *c.* 1726; J. Wilson, 1726–45; J. Warrener, or Warener, 1728; B. Lyon, 1729; T. Hinton, 1730; S. Lobb, 1730–1(?); F. Farley, 1733–41; R. Goadby, 1740–5; T. Boddeley, 1740–56; W. Frederick, *c.* 1742–76; S. Martin, 1755–7; C. Pope, 1760–8; W. Taylor, 1760–73; H. Leake (II), 1764–6(?); J. Leake (II), 1765(?)–90; W. Archer, 1768; J. Basnett, 1770; T. Mills, *c.* 1770–5; S. Hazard, 1772–1806; A. Tennent, 1773; L. Bull, *c.* 1773–90; R. Crutwell, 1773–99; A. W. Hibbart, 1776.

BEDFORD: B. Hyatt, 1773; T. Woodward, 1773.

BERKHAMPSTEAD: ( ) Townson, 1735.

BERWICK-UPON-TWEED: R. Taylor, 1753–76 (cf. also Scottish section).

BEWDLEY: ( ) Radnal, 1771.

BIDEFORD: Mrs. Manning, 1763–4.

BIRMINGHAM: A. Johnson, 1725; H. Butler, 1726–58; T. Warren, 1727–42; T. Aris, 1741–61; F. Woolaston, 1750–4; J. Baskerville, 1750(?)–75; W. Hutton, 1750–1815; Esther Butler, 1758–70; R. Martin, 1763(?); J. Sketchley, 1763–76; N. Boden, 1769–70; J. Crompton, 1770; T. Holliwell, 1770; S. Sketchley, 1770; C. Earl, 1770–8; M. Swinney, 1770–1812; Sarah Baskerville, 1775–7.

BISHOP AUCKLAND: ( ) Emm, 1764.

BLANDFORD: ( ) Pitt, 1744; W. Sollers, 1775.

BOSTON: R. Worley, 1758; T. Farrar or Ferrour, 1758–9; C. Preston, 1759.

BRACKLEY: J. Payne, 1772.

BRADFORD: D. Rocket, 1737; J. Wood, 1760; J. Hartley, 1776; G. Nicholson, 1776.

BRAINTREE: Mrs. Thorn, 1773(?).

BRECON: M. Jones, 1772.

BRIDGEWATER: ( ) Codrington, 1745.

BRIDGNORTH: B. Haslewood, 1730–93.

BRISTOL: F. Farley, 1718–53; S. Farley (II), 1718(?)–54; W. Cosley, or Cossley, 1726–50; T. Sendall, 1728; Mrs. Martha Lewis, 1728–47; Mrs. Frances Wall, 1728–48; H. Greep, 1732; A. Brown, 1732–76; ( ) Penn, widow, 1733; W. Evans, 1733–45; T. Cadell, 1739–75; B. Hickey, 1742(?)–52(?); A. Hooke, 1742–53; F. Farley & Co., 1744; R. Winpenny, 1744; S. Bonner, 1746–89; J. Palmer, 1748–71; E. Ward, 1749–60; J. Crofts, 1750; W. Pine, 1753–1803; Sarah Farley, 1754; Eliz. Farley, 1754–67; S. Farley (III), 1754–74; T. Grant, 1755; E. Farley & Son, 1758–9; J. Grabham and W. Pine, 1759–60; I. Moore, 1764–8; T. Cocking, 1767–83; J. B. Beckett 1774; Hester Farley, 1774–5; M. Ward, 1774–6; W. Gant, 1775; J. Sketchley, 1775; Rouths & Nelson, 1775–6; G. Routh, 1775–8.

BUCKINGHAM: B. Seeley, 1747–76.

BUNGAY: T. Miller, 1755–1804.

BUNNY, Notts.: H. Wainwright, 1727–8.

BURY ST. EDMUNDS: ( ) Bailey or Baily, 1725; Mrs. Watson, 1729; R. Haworth, *c.* 1740; S. Watson, 1745–8; M. Watson, 1750; W. Green, 1755–69; Eliz. Rogers, 1755–74; M. Steel, 1757–75; J. W. Pasham, 1776–83.

CALNE, Wilts: ( ) Parradise, 1747.

Cambridge: F. Hopkins, *c.* 1722–58; W. Fenner, 1725–34; *T. James, 1730–8; J. Crownfield, *c.* 1730–44; Mary Fenner, 1734–8; ( ) Thurlborne, 1735–51; T. Merrill, *c.* 1736–82; Cornelius (II), and J. Crownfield, *c.* 1743–60; T. James, *c.* 1744–58; R. Walker, 1744–58(?); R. Watts, *c.* 1745–52; J. Merrill, *c.* 1750; S. and J. James, *c.* 1750–73; J. Nicholson, 1752–96; W. Woodyer, *c.* 1756–9; R. Matthews, *c.* 1758–73; T. and J. Merrill, *c.* 1758–75; J. Paris, *c.* 1759–79; J. Woodyer, 1759–82; T. Fletcher and F. Hodson, 1762–77; F. Hodson, 1762–1812; J. and J. Merrill, *c.* 1773–95.

Cambridge University: *Cornelius Crownfield (I), 1698–1743; J. Bentham, 1740–78; J. Baskerville, 1758–63; J. Archdeacon, 1766–95.

Canterbury: R. Fenner (III), 1729–41(?); W. Flacton, 1730–98; Mrs. Fenner, 1732–41; J. Flacton, 1738–90(?); T. Smith, 1753–88; J. Simmons, 1768–1807.

Carlisle: R. Cook, or Cooke, 1739; T. Harris, 1746; ( ) Railton, 1755; A. Campbell, 1776.

Carmarthen: ( ) Williams, 1772.

Chatham: S. Neale, 1754–5; ( ) Bolton, 1761.

Chelmsford: S. Lobb, 1728–31; W. Green, 1731–55; J. Buckland, 1736; R. Lobb, 1745–9; T. Toft, 1755(?)–69(?); C. Frost, 1769–76; L. Hassell, 1769–71; R. Lobb, 1771; S. Gray, 1773(?)–6; S. Jackson, 1773–5; W. Clacher, 1776–1813.

Cheltenham, T. Price, 1735–69.

Chesham: *S. Dagnall, 1720–6; S. Coe, 1740.

Chester: P. Potter, 1732–9; Elizabeth Adams, 1733(?)–56; J. Rowley, 1745; T. Ledsham, 1746–9; P. Joynson, 1747; J. Page, 1747; J. Read, 1747; J. Adams, 1748; J. Lawton, 1767–71; J. Monk, 1771–5; P. Broster, 1774–5; C. Barker, 1774; G. Bulkeley, 1774–5; E. Monk, 1775; J. Poole, 1775–8; O. Adams (?)–1797.

Chesterfield: S. Gunter, 1725; Mrs. Slater, 1731(?)–38(?).

Chichester: T. Wall, 1746; J. Lee, 1749; P. Humphrey, 1766–74; W. Andrews, 1770.

Chippenham: R. (?) Warne, 1742(?)–5(?).

Cirencester: J. Ballinger, 1726; J. Turner, 1735; G. Hill, 1741–59; S. Rudder, 1749–1801.

Colchester: Eliz. Hewers, 1726–7; H. Boad, 1735–6; J. Kendall, sen. and jun., 1736–73; J. Pilborough, 1733–71; T. Kendall, 1749–73; R. Keymer, 1750(?)–76(?); W. Keymer, 1750–1813; H. Keymer, 1764.

Congleton: S. Parsons, 1747–65; T. Pursall, 1756.

Coventry: *W. Ratten, 1716–26; J. Jopson, 1741–59; S. Bailey or Bailye, 1743; J. Ratten, 1744–76; T. Luckman, 1756(?)–76; ( ) Parker, 1767–76; J. W. Piercy, 1770–6; W. Jones, 1774.

Cranbrooke: J. Maule, 1737–56.

Dartmouth: T. Tremlett, 1756; W. Craven, 1763–78.

Daventry: J. Smith, 1739–44; J. Clay, 1744–75; T. Clay, 1775–6.

Deptford, W. Rowles, 1756.

Derby: *J. Roe, or Rowe, 1725–54; ( ) Trimer, or Trimmer, 1749–53; S. Fox, 1755–8.

Devizes: T. Sherwood, 1744; T. Burrough, or Burroughs, 1744–74; Mrs. Maynard, 1765.

Diss: ( ) Shuckforth, 1742.

Doncaster: ( ) Inman, or Ingman, 1736–63.

Dorchester: S. Gould, 1733–83.

Dorking: J. Smith, 1746.

Dover: P. Newport, 1760(?)–72; R. Brydon, 1773–6.

Drayton: ( ) Taylor, 1738–9.

Dudley: ( ) Stokes, 1730–7.

Durham: J. Waghorn, 1727–30; J. Ross, 1733–6; Mrs. Waghorn, 1733–6; I. Lane, 1740 (?); J. Richardson, 1750–63; R. Clifton, 1764; R. Manisty, 1764–6; Pat. Sanderson, 1764–75.

Eton: J. Pote, 1730–87.

Evesham: ( ) Andrew, 1749–63.

Exeter: E. Farley, 1725–9; A. Bryce, 1726; J. March, 1726; N. Thorn, 1726–42; A. Tozer, 1727–65; E. Farley (II), 1735; E. Score, jr., 1740–79; B. Thorn, 1742–91; J. Drew, 1745–8; F. Farley, 1741; J. Spencer, 1761–5; W. Andrews, 1763–4; R. Trewman, 1764–76; J. Spence, 1765; W. Grigg, 1765–89; R. Thorn, 1771–89; M. Allison, 1753; ( ) Mallison, 1753.

Faversham: S. Doorne, 1770–5.

Frome: ( ) Keeping, 1747.

Gainsborough: ( ) Carlton, 1728.

Gateshead: E. Clarke, 1772.

Gloucester: *G. Harris, sen., 1702–38; J. Palmer, 1728–53; Eliz. Palmer, 1744–51; R. Bond, 1753–71; J. Pitt, or Pytt, 1771–98.

Godmanchester: M. Catlin, 1744–8.

Gosport: J. Gover, 1735–44; M. Maberley, 1750.

Grantham: T. Wightman, 1726.

Greenwich: T. Henderson, 1748; T. Cole, 1770.

Guildford: S. Parvish, 1731; J. Russell, 1761–1804; C. Martin, 1769.

Hadleigh: R. Keymer, 1750(?)–76(?).

Halesworth: ( ) Tippell, 1751.

Halifax: J. Hodgson, 1737–8; N. Binns, 1750(?)–1801; W. Edwards, 1758–1808; P. Darby, 1760–3; A. Smith, 1763.

Harwich: W. Enefer, 1769.

Helston: I. Head, 1753.

Hempsted (Herts.): D. Turner, 1739.

Hereford: J. Wilde, or Wild, 1714–57(?); Jas. Hunt, 1726; J. Hunt, 1726; W. Smith, 1739; P. Hodges, 1740–69; C. Pugh, 1762(?)–76; C. Badham, 1769–76.

Hertford: S. Austin, 1768–76.

Hexham: J. Featherston, 1764.

Holms Chapel, Cheshire: ( ) Vernon, 1756.

Honiton: A. Brown, 1763–73.

Hull: *T. Ryles, 1707–36; *G. Ferraby, 1718–36; ( ) Munby, 1736; J. Mace, 1740(?)–58(?).

Huntingdon: M. Catlin, 1744–8; J. Ellington, 1755; J. Jenkinson, 1768–1807.

Ipswich: Eliz. Craighton, or Creighton, 1728–76; W. Craighton, 1733–65; J. Shave, 1745–98; H. Battly, 1763; T. Page, 1763; S. (and W.) Jackson, 1773–5; C. Punchard, 1774.

Isleworth: F. Hall, 1760–1.

Kelvedon: C. Ley, 1773.

Kendal: T. Ashburner, 1730–76; T. Cotton, 1731; A. Ashburner, 1763; W. Pennington, 1776.

Kidderminster: H. Moseley, 1748–9.

Kimbolton: M. Catlin, 1744–8.

King's Lynn: ( ) Harwick, 1728; W. Garratt, 1740–62; W. Whittingham, 1768–97.

Kingston-upon-Thames: T. Bellamy, 1754–7.

Knutsford: ( ) Hewit, 1738; J. Leech, 1753–6; J. Shipton, 1753.

Lancaster: ( ) Gray, 1761.

Leeds: *J. Swale, 1714–42; J. Hirst, 1730; J. Lister, 1736–53; G. Wright, 1754(?)–1818; S. Howgate, (?)–1761; G. Copperthwaite, 1763–71; J. Binns, 1766–96; J. Bowling, 1767–76.

Leicester: *S. Martin, 1705–37; ( ) Hartshorne, 1714–35; G. Brice, 1744–6; T. Martin, 1746–57; J. Gregory, 1757–89; J. Ireland, 1769–1810.

Lewes: E. Verrall, 1734–66; A. Lee, 1745; W. Lee, 1745–56.

Lichfield: *M. Johnson, 1685–1731; R. Bailey or Bayley, 1729–53; Sarah Johnson, 1737–49.

Lincoln: W. Wood, 1729(?)–87.

Liverpool: A. Sadler, 1728–41; J. Ansdell or Ansdale, 1728–77; J. Sadler, 1740–65; R. Fleetwood, 1746–62; P. Whitfield, 1748–56; R. Williamson, 1751–76; ( ) Valans, 1756; J. Gore, 1762–76; T. Cowburne, 1766; J. Sibbald, 1766–76; Nevett & Co., 1766–76; T. Johnson, 1775–7; A. Christie, 1776; S. Crane, 1776; J. Dunbabin, 1776; Margaret Eyres, 1776; W. Nevett, 1776.

Loughborough: M. Unwin. 1728.

Ludlow: ( ) Smart, 1771.

Lutterworth: J. Clay, 1744–75.

Lymington: R. Welch, 1744.

Lynn: Mrs. Hollingworth, 1742; T. Hollingworth, 1748(?)–69(?); J. Lee, 1749.

Macclesfield: *J. Rathbourne, or Rathbone, 1723–56.

Maidstone: E. Gorham, 1736 56; ( ) Johnson, 1737; J. Bishop, 1741; W. Mercer, 1765; ( ) Blake, *c.* 1775.

Maldon: S. Gray, 1773–6.

Malton: J. Nickson, 1750.

Manchester: *W. Clayton, 1700–32; John(?) Hodges, 1728; Mary Johnson, 1738; R. Lees, 1738; J. Hopps, 1740–76; W. Holmbe, 1741; W. Stuart or

Stewart, 1742(?)–62(?); S. Newton, 1748–61; T. Newton, 1749–62(?); J. Harrop, 1749–76; J. Schofield, 1754; E. Warren, 1755; J. Anderton, 1756–62; A. Clark, or Clarke, 1756–74; J. Pue, 1760; J. Haslingden, 1760–76; W. Norton, 1761; W. Newton, 1762–75; J. Bottomley, 1763; J. Prescott, 1771; M. Townson, 1772.

Mansfield (Notts.): J. Heath, 1753.

Market Drayton: E. Darby, 1756.

Market Harborough: W. Harrod, 1768–1806.

Marlborough: *J. Buckridge, 1704–45; (   ) Gillmore, 1745; E. Harold, 1774.

Middlewich: J. Schofield, 1756.

Millbrook: J. Jordaine, 1756.

Modbury, Devon: (   ) Tozer, 1770.

Monmouth: J. Crofts, 1726–8.

Mortlake: (   ) Middleton, 1761.

Nantwich: (   ) Taylor, 1738–9; (   ) Church, 1756; J. Bromley, 1774–5; E. Snelson, 1775–6.

Newbury: J. Wimpey, 1761; J. Willis, 1769(?)–71(?).

Newcastle-under-Lyme: R. Parsons, 1734–42; S. Parsons, 1747–65.

Newcastle-upon-Tyne: R. Akenhead, sen., 1722–51; (   ) Shaw, widow, 1724; S. Ross, 1732; J. Button, 1733; L. Umfreville, 1733–6; I. Lane & Co., 1734–6; J. Harrison, 1736–59; T. Umfreville, 1737–43; I. Thompson, 1737–76; J. Linn, 1739; T. Middleton, 1740–1; J. Barber, 1740–81; J. Flemming, 1741–66; J. Gooding, 1743–51; H. Reed, 1747–54; J. Fitzgerald, 1749–54; W. Charnley, 1749–1803; R. Akenhead, jun., 1750; M. Turnbull, 1755–76; T. Slack, 1755–84; D. Nisbet, *c.* 1760; R. Marchbank, 1761; T. Saint, 1761–88; J. Atkinson, 1769–88; T. Angus, 1774–6; J. Chalmers, 1775–81; E. Humble, 1775–1820; D. Akenhead, 1776; I. Robson & Co., 1776–88.

Newport (I. of Wight): J. Wise, 1768.

Northampton: (   ) Fowler, 1727–44; W. Dicey, 1730(?)–54; C. Dicey, 1736–64; M. Catlin, 1744–8; J. Pasham, 1744–9; W. Smart, 1744–9; R. Dicey, 1746–9; H. Woolley, 1746–9; T. Dicey, 1758; S. Gray, 1758; W. Tomson, 1758; R. Smith, 1770–6; T. Burnham, 1775–6; J. Lacy, *b. cf.* 1776–91(?).

Northwich: (   ) Maltus, 1756.

Norwich: *T. Goddard, 1703–46; J. Carlos, 1730–46; J. Redwood, 1735–42; J. Ferguson, 1741–74; R. Goodman, 1742; J. Gleed, 1742(?)–53(?); R. Davey, or Davy, 1746–8; C. Berry, 1751–76; L. Hansard, 1752; J. Crouse, 1761–96; W. Chase, 1765; M. Booth, 1767–83; S. White, 1769–71; R. Beatniffe, 1773–1818.

Nottingham: R. Willis, 1734; G. Ayscough, 1734–46; T. Collyer, 1734–54; Anne Ayscough [1719]–32(?); J. Murray, 1738; J. Heath, 1744–60; G. Burbage, 1747–1807; S. Cresswell, 1753(?)–86.

Ormskirk: (   ) Grice, 1738.

Oxford: Rich. Gilman, 1665(?)–1730; J. Brookland, 1693–1729; R. Green, 1700–46; S. Richardson, 1715–55; *C. Combes, sen., 1722–31; H. Lichfield, 1726; J. Rudhall, 1726–8; N. Cox, 1726–31; O. Adams, 1726–97; T. Sedgeley, 1727–34; R. Clements, 1728–56; Mary Fletcher, 1729–51; J. Fletcher, sen., 1730–95; S. Parker, 1730(?)–96; (   ) Piesley, 1735; M. Thomas, 1738; L. Wilmot, 1741; T. Baskett, 1742–61; R. Baskett, 1742–4; M. Baskett, 1742–67; J. Barrett, 1744–53; T. Richardson, 1749; D. Prince, 1750–96; W. Jackson, 1753–95; R. Walker, *c.* 1755; Z. Richardson, 1756–78; J. Fletcher, jr., 1756–96; T. Wright, 1765–98; R. Bliss, 1770–5; J. Lister, 1772–3.

Pembroke: (   ) Wilmot, 1771.

Penrith: T. Corney, *c.* 1726.

Penzance: J. Mitchell, 1753–6.

Peterborough: G. Boucher, 1714–55; G. Knapp, 1767; (   ) Horden, 1770(?); J. Jacob, 1775–95.

Pinchbeck (Lincoln): R. Worley, *c.* 1758.

Plymouth: B. Smithurst, 1739; Eliz. Smith, 1753; T. Rhodes, 1754; O. Adams, 1758–64; H. Whitfield, 1759; R. Weatherley, 1759–78; Z. Freno, *c.* 1763; J. Wallis, 1763–89; W. Andrews, 1765; (   ) Haydon, 1770; Mrs. Maurice, 1770; J. Whitfield, or Whitfeld, 1770.

Pontefract: J. Lindsey, or Lindley, 1769.

Poole: J. Brassett, 1744; J. Moore, 1765.

Portsmouth: L. Cullimore, 1702–31; *H. Grove, 1718–44; G. Everden, 1725; (   ) Wilkinson, 1744; W. Horton, 1751–5; R. Carr, 1751–77; (   ) Harding, 1767.

Preston (Lancs.): W. Prescott, or Prescot, 1709(?)–28(?); M. Prescott, 1728; W. Stuart or Stewart, 1742(?)–62(?); J. Stanley, 1745; J. Moon, 1745–62; E. Sergent, 1762; (   ) Smalley, 1762.

Ramsgate: R. Fenner, 1736–7.

Reading: W. Eyres, 1727–34; J. Newbury, 1730–44; C. Micklewright, 1742–50; D. Henry, 1745; Carnan & Co., 1765; S. Blackman, 1767.

Redruth: R. Gray, 1753;

Reigate: T. Pickstone, *c.* 1770.

Ripponden (?): (   ) Wilkinson, 1746.

Rochdale: J. Schofield, 1758–60.

Rochester: T. Fisher, 1765(?)–93.

Romsey: J. Whiting, 1768.

Ross: J. Blunt, 1741–53.

Rotherhithe: N. Whitefield, 1770.

Rugby: J. Clay, 1744–75.

Rye: (   ) Hogben, 1756.

St. Austell: J. Nankivell, 1752–3.

St. Ives (Hunts): M. Catlin, 1744–8.

St. Neots: W. Tans'ur, 1743–83; M. Catlin, 1744–8; T. Claridge, 1768–80.

Salisbury: E. Easton (I), 1725(?)–53; C. Hooton, 1729–30; B. Collins, 1729–85; W. Collins, 1730–64; E. Easton (II), 1742–95; Hodson & Johnson, 1774–6;

Sandbach: R. Hulse, 1756.

Sandwich: J. Silver, 1726(?)–39(?); S. Silver, 1751(?)–72(?).

Scarborough: A. Clark, or Clarke, 1733.

Shaftesbury: R. Woolridge, 1744–75(?).

Sheffield: Mrs. Simmons, or Symmonds, 1731; W. Ward, 1736–63; J. Garnet, 1737–53; S. Simmons, 1738; T. Gales, 1756(?)–1809.

Sherborne: *J. Cook, or Cooke, 1713–46; W. Bettinson, 1731–46; J. Cooke, *c.* 1732; G. Price, 1737; Hannah Bettinson, 1746; J. Bettinson, 1746; W. Cruttwell, 1764–1804.

Shrewsbury: T. Durston, 1714–47; T. Gittins, 1727; J. Rogers, 1729; R. Lathrop, 1739–47; J. Cotton, 1746–65; J. Eddowes, 1749–75; J. Cotton, 1761; T. Wood, 1772–1801; S. Pryse, 1775–6.

Smarden (Kent.): (   ) Hogben, 1756.

Southampton: T. Baker, 1767–76; J. Linden, 1768–76.

Southwell (Notts): W. Hutton, 1749.

Spalding: J. Albin, 1775–1800.

Stamford: T. Bailey, 1710–28; W. Thompson, 1726; F. Howgrave, 1738–51; A. Rogers, 1744–50.

Stockton: J. Pickering, 1763–6.

Stourbridge: T. Wilde, 1748; (   ) West, 1771.

Stratford-upon-Avon: T. Pasham, 1745; (   ) Keating, 1749–72.

Strawberry Hill: *see* Twickenham.

Sunderland: T. Lightfoot, 1760; J. Graham, 1767–76; H. Craighton, or Creighton, 1770–6.

Swaffham: J. Lee, 1749(?).

Taunton: *W. Norris, 1718–55; J. Dinning, 1725–6; H. Chaulkin, 1750; Miss Anderton, 1765–79.

Tavistock: Eliz. Smith, 1753; T. Smith, 1753.

Tenbury: (   ) Wilden, 1771.

Tenterden: T. Winder, 1737.

Tewkesbury: T. Price, 1735–69; (   ) Ashmead, 1753; S. Harward, 1760–1809.

Tiverton: Sam. Dyer, 1716–26; W. Shutt, or Shute, 1725–32; J. Parkhouse, 1740(?)–1819; P. Parkhouse, 1750(?)–53; M. Hodge, 1759.

Tonbridge: (   ) Baker, 1765.

Totnes: R. Legassicke, 1739; J. Trownson, 1750–73; W. Cleave, 1773.

Tring: T. Williams, 1726.

Truro: J. Painter, 1753–70; (   ) Buckland, 1776.

Tunbridge: (   ) Penn, 1731.

Twickenham: Strawberry Hill Press, 1757–89; T. Kirgate, 1765–89.

Uppingham: J. Cook, or Cooke, 1729–44.

Wakefield: T. Kellington, 1758; (   ) Meggitt, 1769.

Wallingford: B. Martin, 1776.

Waltham (Leicestershire): W. East, 1748–54.

Waltham Cross: H. Richardson, 1740.

Warminster: (   ) Goodenough, 1745.

Warrington: J. Eyres, 1731–56(?); (   ) Higginson, 1738; W. Eyres, 1756–76; T. Eyres, 1756–76(?); T. Bancks, 1761–74.

WARWICK: ( ) Hopkins, 1733; J. Hopkinson, 1735–43; J. Sharp, or Sharpe, 1769–91.

WELLS: ( ) Hawkes, 1742; J. Cass, 1753.

WHITBY: C. Plummer, 1770(?)–76.

WHITCHURCH: ( ) Gough, 1738.

WHITEHAVEN: J. Dunn, 1771–5; J. Ware & Sons, 1776.

WIGAN: ( ) Layland, 1738; W. Stuart, or Stewart, 1742(?)–62(?).

WINCANTON: ( ) Slade, 1745.

WINCHESTER: *W. Colson, 1705–41; J. Eyres, or Ayres, 1720(?)–58; W. Clarke, c. 1730; W. Eyres, or Ayres, c. 1739; W. Prior, 1743(?)–56(?); T. Burdon, 1760–5; J. Wilkes, 1762–1810; J. Meaisey, 1765(?) 68(?); W. Greenville, or Grenville, 1765–75; J. Burdon, 1773–1802.

WINDSOR: R. Westcote, 1761; J. Blakeney, 1774.

WITHAM: S. Rogers, 1769.

WOLVERHAMPTON: G. Wilson, 1744; S. (?) Unett, 1749–55; Mary Wilson, 1755.

WORCESTER: S. Mountford, 1725–48; E. Wolley, 1726–40; T. Olivers, 1746; J. Mountford, 1748; H. Berrow, 1748–77; R. Lewis, 1753–71; S. Gamidge 1758–68.

WREXHAM: T. Payne, c. 1730; E. or C. Wicksteed, 1730.

YARMOUTH: W. Eaton, 1728–76; ( ) Powell, 1757; J. Ives, 1772–6.

YEALAND (Westmoreland): J. and J. Jenkinson, 1762.

YEOVIL: R. Goadby, 1748–9.

YORK: *R. Manklin, or Mancklin, 1697–1739; T. Hammond, jr., 1730–40; J. Hildyard, 1731–57; R. Chandler, 1732–44; A. Staples, 1734–9; C. Ward, 1734(?)–45; N. Bell, 1739–78; S. Hildyard, 1740; J. Jackson, 1740–70; W. Shaw, 1741; J. Gilfillan, 1741–52; B. Barstow [partner S. Stabler], 1744–50; S. Stabler [partner Benjamin Barstow], 1744–50; J. Wilson, 1749–61; ( ) Hotham, 1752; N. Nickson, 1754 (?58)–77; ( ) Wilson, 1755; J. Hinxman, 1757–60; J. Todd, 1757–1811; T. Atkinson, 1758; Anne Ward, 1759–89; W. Tesseyman, 1763(?)–1811; H. Sotheran, 1764(?)–76(?); D. Peck, 1768–80(?); C. Etherington, 1770–5.

II. INDEX OF PLACES IN SCOTLAND OTHER THAN EDINBURGH

ABERDEEN: R. Farquhar (I), 1692–1753; J. Nicol, 1710–36; Jas. Chalmers (I), 1736–64; A. Gordon, b. 1742; A. Angus, 1744–1802; J. Leiper, 1747–8; F. Douglas, 1748–69; B. Smith, 1750–?; J. Angus, c. 1750–1828; A. Thomson, 1751–55(?); W. Murray, 1752–7; R. Farquhar (II), 1753–62(?); A. Angus, 1754–1830; J. Scroggs, 1759; J. Boyle, 1760–92(?); A. Cheyne, 1764; G. Fowler, 1764; Jas. Chalmers (II), 1764–1810; J. Fotheringham, 1769; G. Johnstone, 1769; J. Mennye or Menzye, 1770; R. Hyde, 1770–2; A. Smith, 1771–94; T. Sparke, 1772–3.

AYRE: G. Knox, c. 1760.

BERWICK-UPON-TWEED: R. Taylor, c. 1752–75(?).

BIGGAR: A. Brown, b. 1764.

BORROWSTONNESS (Bo-ness): J. Jack, 1774–6.

BRAUGHTY in the Parish of Fosway: T. Beveridge, 1729.

CATHCART (New Paper Miln): J. Hall, 1763.

CESSFORD: J. Weir, 1740–1(?).

CROSSCAUSEWAY: W. Duncan, b. 1770.

CULROSS: D. Pearson, 1760; G. Gray, 1766.

DALMUIR: E. Collins, c. 1775.

DUMFRIES, G. Fulton, 1752–1831; E. Wilson, c. 1760–90; J. Mayne, c. 1770–c. 1780; W. Boyd, c. 1773–77(?); R. Jackson, c. 1773–1811.

DUNBAR: G. Miller, c. 1745–89.

DUNDEE: T. Glass, c. 1750–63; H. Galbraith, c. 1750–75; J. Stark, 1766; J. Lundie, b. 1769; T. Colville, c. 1770–1819.

DUNFERMLINE: Mrs. Meldrum, 1724–8; R. Beveridge, 1729; J. Beugo, 1729–52; G. Beugo, 1762; J. Horn, 1764.

DUNKELD, J. Cant, c. 1770–1812; R. Morison (I), 1722–91.

FALKIRK, J. Liddel, 1734.

GLASGOW: J. Broune, or Broun, 1661–1730(?); J. Wilson, 1692–1726; J. Robertson or Robieson, sen., 1697–1728; G. Laurie, 1704–27; A. Ingram, 1704–70; J. Brown, 1715–66; J. Duncan, sen., 1717–c. 1754; W. Duncan, 1717–65; T. Moodie, c. 1720–40; J. Glassford, c. 1720–83; A. Carmichael, 1724–36; A. Miller, 1724–45(?); D. Graham, c. 1724–79; A. Stalker, c. 1726–71; J. McLean, 1727; J. Robertson, jr., 1728–40; H. Luke, b. 1729; J. Robertson, c. 1730–(?); J. Hamilton, c. 1730–80; A. Hutcheson, 1731–80(?); Mrs. Agnes Brown, 1734; J. Lang, 1734; J. Brown, 1734–99(?); M. Alexander, 1737; J. Dechman, 1738; A. McLean, c. 1738–68; J. McCoul, 1739; W. Gray, 1739; W. Marschal, 1739–50(?); R. Smith, 1740; J. Brown, 1741; P. Davie, 1741; R. Smith, 1741; G. Paton, 1741–72(?); R. Foulis, 1741–76; J. Robb, 1741–78; A. Carlile, 1742–52; D. Duncan, 1743; ( ) Murie, c. 1743; J. Barry, 1744–8; D. Baxter, 1744–50; A. Wilson, 1744–60; R. Urie, c. 1744–71; W. Smith, 1744–79; A. Foulis, c. 1746–75; J. Newlands, 1747; J. Robb, 1748; J. Brown, c. 1748; J. Gilmour, 1749–73; J. Tweedie, 1750; J. Fleming, c. 1750–70; D. Campbell, c. 1750–80; J. Smith, c. 1750(?)–81; J. Bryce, c. 1750–86; ( ) M'Callum, 1751; ( ) Knox, 1752; J. Orr, c. 1752–66; G. Fulton, 1752–1831; G. Luke, b. 1754; D. Paterson, 1755–9; J. Finlay, 1756; A. Tilloch, 1759–1825; Mrs. Eliz. Dewar (née Foulis), c. 1760; W. Walker, c. 1760; J. Barr, 1761; J. Galbraith, 1761; J. Duncan, jr., c. 1769–1802; R. Macdonald, 1770; G. Ballantyne, c. 1770; R. Farie, c. 1770; D. Murray, c. 1770–(?); J. Thomson, c. 1770–86(?); J. Robertson, 1774–(?); J. Mayne, c. 1780–87.

GREENOCK: R. Yuill, c. 1774–6; W. McAlpine, c. 1776–?.

HADDINGTON: Baillie Cadel, 1747.

HAILES (Redhall Mills): R. Murdoch, 1727.

INVERNESS: W. Sharp, c. 1762–97; A. Davidson, 1774–85(?).

JEDBURGH: T. Caverhill, 1747.

KELSO: A. Nisbet, 1744.

KILMARNOCK: G. Paton, 1747; J. Meuros, 1750–78; J. Wilson, c. 1770–1821.

KINROSS: Eliz. or Elspeth Hutchison, b. 1765.

KIRKALDY: A. Webster, 1747; D. Heggie, b. 1765.

LANARK: W. Gray, 1740.

LASSWADE: W. McLaren, c. 1770.

LEITH: J. Reid, 1761; J. Morison, 1762–1809; W. Coke, 1764–1819; W. Wemyss, 1772.

LINTON: G. Forest, 1747; J. Nisbet, 1759.

LOCHGOIN: J. Howie, c. 1774.

NEWLANDS-BORLAND: W. Johnston, 1741.

PAISLEY: J. Wilken, 1759–61; A. Weir, c. 1760–80(?); A. McLean, 1769–73; W. McArthur, 1774.

PENNYCUIK: A. Watson, c. 1760–86; W. Mudie, 1761.

PERTH: F. Morison, c. 1670–c. 1740; R. Morison (I), 1722–91; A. Beck, 1739; A. Norry, 1747; J. Morison, c. 1760; J. Bisset, 1762–94; J. Morison, 1762–1809; R. Morison (II), 1764–1853; G. Johnstone, c. 1770–?.

SAINT ANDREWS: P. Bower, 1723–1814; A. Bell, c. 1742; A. Wilson, 1742–4; R. Morison (II), 1764–1853; J. Tod, b. 1772.

SELKIRK: J. Notman, b. 1773.

STIRLING: J. Urquhart, 1730–1; P. Provan, 1734; J. Jaffrey, 1747.

THIRLESTANE: W. Scott, 1727.

WOODEND, near Huntingtower: H. Lindsay, c. 1760–1820?.

III. INDEX OF PLACES IN IRELAND

ARMAGH: W. Dickie, 1745–70.

ATHLONE: E. Proctor, 1774–93.

BELFAST: J. Blow, 1707–58; R. Gardner, 1713–34; Ramsay, 1729; J. Potts, 1736; S. Wilson, 1736–44; J. Magee, 1736–89; F. Joy, 1737–45; H. and R. Joy, 1745–85; J. Hay, 1747–76; R. Johnston, 1753 (?1758)–60; D. Blow, 1759–78; J. and D. Hay, 1760; R. Smith, 1775.

BIRR: A. McCulloch, 1774–5.

CARLOW: W. Kinnnier, 1773–86.

CLONMEL: E. Collins, 1771–88.

CORK: G. Bennett, 1714–47; A. Welsh, 1715–27; J. O'Connor, 1728; C. Daniell, 1729–34; T. Pilkington, 1729–43; T. Pembrock, 1730; G. Harrison, 1732–54; A. Welsh, jun., 1738–9; Martha Pilkington, 1739–57; T. Cuming or Cumming, 1745(?)–7; N. Eyres, 1752; P. Bagnell, 1754; T.(?) Cronin, 1754; G. and J. Knight, 1754; E. Swiney, 1754–72; Sullivan, 1754–77; P. and G. Bagnell, 1755–74; Mary Harrison, 1757; G. Condy, 1760; J. Busteed, 1764–76; G. Busteed, 1765–68; W. Fackman, 1766; E. Finn, 1766; W. Flyn, or Flynn, 1767–1801 (?1795); The Company of Booksellers, 1768–73; P. Bagnell & Co., 1768–74; E. Digby, 1770; T. Lord, 1770–1; D. Donnoghue, 1772–6; S. Macky, 1773; E. Chandler, 1774; May Edwards, 1775; T. White, 1774–80 W. Sargent, 1775.

DROGHEDA: P. Mahon or Meighane, 1690–1700; J. Fleming, 1772–85.

DUBLIN: A. Crooke, 1681–1732; C. Carter, 1696–1727; S. Powell, 1697–1728; J. Ware (1704)–26; E. Waters, 1708–36; J. Hyde or Hide, 1709–28; A. Rhames, 1709–34; G. Grierson, 1709–53; W. Binauld, 1713–32; R. Owen, 1713–47; J. Carson, 1713–67; S. Fairbrother, 1714–34; T. Hume, or Humes, 1715–28; G. Risk, 1716–50; R. Dickson, 1718–48; E. Dobson, 1719–32; J. Leathley, 1719–54; S. Fuller, 1720–36; R. Norris, 1721–34; G. Ewing, 1722–48; W. Wilmot, 1724–7; G. Faulkner, 1724–75; T. Harbin, 1725–6; E. Needham, 1725–7; Sarah Harding, 1725–8; T. Walsh, 1725–8; J. Watts,

1725–8; R. Reilly, 1725–41; W. Smith, 1725–64; E. Chantrey, 1726; W. Manning, 1726; J. Morrison, 1726; T. Whitehouse, 1726; J. Worrall, 1726–7; M. Whalley, 1726–8(?); J. Smith and W. Bruce, 1726–37; J. Gowan, 1726–56; R. Pue, 1726–58; F. Davys, 1727; J. Mason, 1727; W. Winter, 1727; T. Benson, 1727–8; W.-S. Anbury, 1727–30; J. Hoey, sen., and G. Faulkner, 1727–30; C. Dickson, 1727–37; W. Forrest, 1728; J. Hyde and E. Dobson, 1728; E. Hamilton, 1728–9; C. Phillip, 1728–47; Sam. Powell I, 1728(9)–72; E. MacLane, 1729; T. Musgrave, 1729; N. Hussey, 1729–30(?); S. Brock, 1729–37; J. Watson, 1729–69; S. Hyde and E. Dobson, 1730; T. Lawler, 1730; J. Watts and W. S. Anbury, 1730; J. Pennell, 1730–7; S. Dalton, 1730–41; S. Hyde, 1730–46; A. Bradley, 1730–59; J. Hoey, sen., 1730–74; S. Pepyat, 1731–8; A. Thiboust, 1732; Anne Crooke, 1733; S. Hyde and J. Dobson, 1733; J. McClelland, 1733; W. Heatly, 1733–42; E. Rider, 1734–45; Typographia Academiae, 1734–47; T. Jones, 1735–6; Margaret Rhames, 1735–43; E. Exshaw, 1735–48; Mary Fuller, 1736–7; C. Goulding, 1736–46; J. Dalton, 1736–60; G. Dinnis, 1737; J. Jones, 1737; T. Moore, 1737–50; H. Babe, 1738; O. Nelson, 1738–75; J. Kelburn or Kilburn, 1739–51; J. Smith, 1739–56; E. Jones, 1739–60; I. Jackson, 1739–72; L. Dillon, 1740; G. Golding, 1740; T. Taylor, 1740–7; J. Fleming, 1740–9; I. Kelly, 1741–53; A. Reilly, 1741–63(?); T. Bacon, 1742; C. Wynne, 1742–57 (?1779); E. Hamilton, 1743; J. Rhames, 1743; C. Connor, 1743–4; W. Powell, 1743–5; P. Wilson, 1743–71; T. Butler, 1744; W. Brien, 1744–53; J. Esdall, 1744–55; J. Dowey, 1745; Z. Martineau, 1745; A. Long, 1745–55; J. Kinnier and A. Long, 1745–6; J. Wilmot, 1746; E. Bate, 1746–50; S. Goulding (1746–)52; R. James, 1746–55; G. and A. Ewing, 1746–64; J. Kinnier or Kennear, 1746–85; T. Tweedy, 1747; J. Cotter, 1747–9; M. Owen, 1747–53; J. Bradley, 1748; H. Garland, 1748; W. Ransom, 1748; B. Clare, 1749; W. Johnston, 1749; P. Lautil, 1749; W. Powell, 1749; J. Wilcock, 1749; H. Hawker, 1749–50; T. Knowles, 1749–50; J. Torbuck, 1749–54; J. Byrn, 1749–66; J. Exshaw, 1749–76; J. Afleck, 1750(?); M. Williamson, 1750–2; R. Main, 1750–4; H. Lord, 1750–5; P. Lord, 1750–60; Sam. Powell (II), ?1750–66; S. Powell & Son, ?1750–66; Eliz. Golding, 1751; G. Wilson, 1751; R. Wilson, 1751; J. Butler, 1751–4; Sarah Cotter, 1751–65; S. Price, 1752–83; T. Hutchinson, 1753; R. Wilson, 1753; G. A. Grierson, 1753–5; H. Saunders, 1753–88; L. Dunne, 1754; A. Moore, 1754; H. Waters, 1754; G. Harrison, 1754–5; L. Flin, Flinn, or Flyn, 1754–71; A. McCulloh, 1754–72; T. Cooper, 1755; D. Gibson, 1755; M. Pepyat, 1755; T. Watson, 1755–6; T. Birn, 1756; B. Edmond, 1756 W. Sleater, 1756–89; W. Williamson, 1757–64; W. Watson, 1757–92; L. Dowlin, 1758; R. Dunbar, 1758; J. Rudd, 1758; Jane Grierson & Co.,

1758–9; J. Pue, 1758–62; S. Smith, 1758–67; H. Bradley, 1758–68; H. B. P. Grierson, 1758–70; W. Smith, jr., 1759; R. Bell, 1759–67; J. Murphy, 1759–73; T. Armitage, 1759–76; W. Whitestone, 1759–78; J. Hoey, jr., ?1759–81; Alice James, 1760; M. North, 1760; E. Chamberlain, 1760–80; J. Hunter, 1760–88; C. Green, 1761–2; R. Watts, 1761–2; J. Potts, 1761–75; S. Watson, 1761–98; J. Potts and S. Watson, 1762; T. and J. Whitehouse, 1762–5; Sarah Pue, 1762–7; J. Fisher, 1763; Ann Law, 1763; T. Richey, 1763; Anne Watts, 1763; W. Ross, 1763–5; J. Mitchell, 1763–8; B. Gorman, 1763–71; J. Fleming, 1764; R. France, 1764; Jane Grierson, 1764; Eliz. Watts, 1764–7; J. Williams, 1764–86; D. Chamberlaine and J. Potts, 1765–6; R. Fitzsimons, 1765–73; J. Sheppard, 1765–91; J. A. Husband, 1765–94; J. Butree, 1766; A. Gordon, 1766; B. Corcoran, 1766–91; J. Adams, 1767; J. Watson & Son, 1767; W. and W. Smith, 1767–9; Mrs. A. Leathley, 1767–73; J. Roe, (1767?)–1774; T. Dyton, 1767–75; T. Ewing, 1767–75; W. Colles, 1767–82; G. Cecil, 1768; Sarah Stringer, 1768; W. G. Jones, 1768–70; J. Milliken, 1768–73; M. Mills, 1768–98; C. Ingham, 1769–73; J. Porter, 1769–91; P. Hoey, 1770; F. Kiernan, 1770–1; D. Hay, 1770–3; T. Walker, 1770–86; R. Moncrieff, 1770–90; Eliz. Lynch, 1770–91; R. Marchbank, 1770–1800; P. Hoey, ?1770, 1776–1806; R. Bowes, 1771; J. Mitchell, 1771; Stewart & Co., 1771; P. Wogan, 1771–95; P. Bowes, 1772; W. Boyce, 1772; J. Fitzsimons, 1772; Mary Kiernan, 1772; J. Rush, 1772; Stewart and Spotswood, 1772; C. Jenkin, 1772–85; R. Jackson, 1772–92; W. Wilson, 1772–1801; T. Stewart, 1772–1802; R. Cross, 1772–1809; G. Allen, 1773; J. Gillaspy, 1773; G. Lyneall, 1773; J. Sheppard, 1773; W. Smith, 1773; Mary Hay, 1773–5; E. Cross, 1773–6; W. Gilbert, 1773–1801; J. Carrick, 1774; J. Colles, 1774–6; T. Watson, 1774–80; W. Spotswood, 1774–84; A. Stuart, 1774–89; G. Bonham, 1774–99; J. Valance, 1774–1808; H. Burrowes, 1775; R. Ennis, 1775; J. Parker & Co., 1775–?; R. Stewart, 1775–6; F. Smith, 1775–80; J. Armitage, 1776; P. Hoey, 1776–1806.

KILKENNY: J. Scot, 1748–54; M. Butler, 1758–79; E. Crofton & Co., 1759(?); J. Stokes, 1762; E. Finn, 1767–77.

LIMERICK: S. Terry and Bixou or Tabb, 1722–3; S. Terry, 1725; W. Farrier, 1729–53; T. Ross, 1729; A. Welsh, jr., 1739; A. Welsh, 1740–69; J. Cherry, 1761–9; J. Ferrar, 1768–75; T. Welsh, 1769–77.

LONDONDERRY: J. Lowis, 1735; J. Coulter, 1741; I. Lowry, 1764; Esther Crawley & Son, 1765–73; R. Lowis, 1771; Catherine Stevenson, 1772; G. Douglas, 1772–96; J. Blyth, 1773–7.

LOUGHREA: J. Reynolds, 1766–72.

MONAGHAN: W. Wilson, 1770.

GALWAY: T. Hutchinson, 1754; M. Burke, 1769–70; O'Connor, 1775.

NEWRY: Stephenson, 1754–78; D. Carpenter, 1761–83; T. Stewart, 176–-71; G. Stevenson, 1768–74; W. G. Jones and C. Wynne, 1770–2; Jones & Co., 1774; W. G. Jones, 1775; R. Stevenson, 1775–83.

SLIGO: M. Parker, 1771–91.

WATERFORD: T. Cotton, 1729; G. Wilson, 1735; H. Glynn, 1740; H. Ramsay, 1740–54; J. Calwell, 1747–61; T. Richey, 1765; H. and J. Ramsay, 1765–75;

WEXFORD: R. Martin, 1774; N. Clifford, 1774; G. Lyneall, 1779.

IV. INDEX OF PLACES ABROAD

FLORIDA: J. Wells, 1784–90 (Scottish section).
JAMAICA: J. Ged, 1748–9 (Scot. Sec.); W. Ged, 1748(?)–67 (Scot. sec.).
ROTTERDAM: T. Johnson, 1735 (Engl. sec.).

V. INDEX OF CIRCULATING LIBRARIES IN ENGLAND AND SCOTLAND

Arranged in order of date.

BATH: Benjamin Matthews, 1725–55.
EDINBURGH: Allan Ramsay, 1726–55.
BRISTOL: Thomas Sendall, 1728.
LONDON: Francis and John Noble, 1739(?)–92.
LONDON: (   ) Wright, 1740.
LONDON: Willoughby Minors, or Mynors, 1744.
CAMBRIDGE: Robert Watts, *c.* 1745–52.
BIRMINGHAM: William Hutton, 1750–1815.
CAMBRIDGE: John Nicholson, 1752–96.
LONDON: John Fuller, 1755–76.
LONDON: Thomas Lowndes, 1756–84.
EDINBURGH: John Yair, 1757–64.
EDINBURGH: William Gray, 1758–78.
DOVER: Peter Newport, 1760–72.
GLASGOW: John Smith, *c.* 1760–79.
BARNSTAPLE: Fidelio Murch, 1763–95.
EDINBURGH: Margaret Yair, 1765–80.
LONDON: A. Cooke, 1765.
SOUTHAMPTON: Thomas Baker, 1767–76.
CHELMSFORD: Charles Frost, 1769–76.
LONDON: Samuel James, *c.* 1770.
BATH: Samuel Hazard, 1772–1806.

LONDON: Thomas Hookham, 1772–5.
BATH: Lewis Bull, *c.* 1773–90.
MARGATE: Samuel Silver, 1773–6(?).
BATH: Mrs. M. Bally, 1774.
LONDON: Thomas Jordan Hookham, *c.* 1775.
LONDON: Samuel Noble, *c.* 1775.
LONDON: C. Rice, *c.* 1775.
EDINBURGH: Alexander M'Caslan or M'Aslan, 1779–93(?).
ABERDEEN: Alexander Angus & Son, 1779–1802.
CANTERBURY: James Simmons, 1780–1807.